Get started with your **Connected Casebook**

Redeem your code below to access the **e-book** with search, highlighting, and note-taking capabilities; **case briefing** and **outlining** tools to support efficient learning; and more.

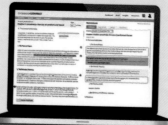

1. Go to www.casebookconnect.com
2. Enter your access code in the box and click **Register**
3. Follow the steps to complete your registration and verify your email address

If you have already registered at CasebookConnect.com, simply log into your account and redeem additional access codes from your Dashboard.

ACCESS CODE:
Scratch off with care.

STXT40926262440.

Is this a used casebook? Access code already redeemed? Purchase a digital version at **CasebookConnect.com/catalog**.

If you purchased a digital bundle with additional components, your additional access codes will appear below.

"I liked being able to search quickly while in class."

"Being able to highlight and easily create case briefs was a fantastic resource and time saver for me!"

"I loved it! I was able to study on the go and create a more effective outline."

For technical support, please visit http://support.wklegaledu.com.

_____ **CONFLICT OF LAWS**

ASPEN CASEBOOK SERIES

CONFLICT OF LAWS

Cases, Materials, and Problems

Second Edition

LAURA E. LITTLE
CHARLES B. KLEIN PROFESSOR OF LAW AND GOVERNMENT
TEMPLE UNIVERSITY'S
BEASLEY SCHOOL OF LAW

ASSOCIATE REPORTER FOR THE RESTATEMENT
(THIRD) OF CONFLICT OF LAWS

Wolters Kluwer

Printed in the United States of America.

3 4 5 6 7 8 9 0

ISBN 978-1-4548-7490-4

Library of Congress Cataloging-in-Publication Data

Names: Little, Laura E., 1957- author.
Title: Conflict of laws : cases, materials, and problems / Laura E. Little,
    Charles B. Klein Professor of Law and Government, Temple University's
    Beasley School of Law, Associate Reporter for the Restatement (Third) of
    Conflict of Laws.
Description: Second edition. | New York : Wolters Kluwer, [2018] | Series:
    Aspen casebook series | Includes bibliographical references and index.
Identifiers: LCCN 2017056958 | ISBN 9781454874904
Subjects: LCSH: Conflict of laws — United States. | LCGFT: Casebooks
Classification: LCC KF410 .L58 2018 | DDC 342.73/042 — dc23
LC record available at https://lccn.loc.gov/2017056958

About Wolters Kluwer Legal & Regulatory U.S.

Wolters Kluwer Legal & Regulatory U.S. delivers expert content and solutions in the areas of law, corporate compliance, health compliance, reimbursement, and legal education. Its practical solutions help customers successfully navigate the demands of a changing environment to drive their daily activities, enhance decision quality and inspire confident outcomes.

Serving customers worldwide, its legal and regulatory portfolio includes products under the Aspen Publishers, CCH Incorporated, Kluwer Law International, ftwilliam.com and MediRegs names. They are regarded as exceptional and trusted resources for general legal and practice-specific knowledge, compliance and risk management, dynamic workflow solutions, and expert commentary.

This book is for Rich, Cate, and Graham.

SUMMARY OF CONTENTS

CONTENTS

Acknowledgments

I am indebted for research assistance from many talented Temple Law School students and graduates: Kendahl Lester, Katherine Burke, Derek Kane, Jacob Nemon, Diane Akerman, Lana Ulrich, Theresa Hearn, Alisha Welch, Lisanne Faigen, Alice Ko, Merideth Ketterer, Matthew Quan, Ryan Healy, Sharon Ulak, Justin Alexander, Scott Pritchard, James Stinsman, Goldie Greenstein, Jonathan Long, and Laura Heacock. Shannon Markley, Elizabeth Young, Erica Maier, and Greg Green provided paralegal support and many colleagues provided me with guidance and support, particularly Jeffrey Dunoff, Theresa Glennon, Rachel Rebouché, David Kairys, and Peter Spiro. Thanks to them all.

I am also grateful to the following for allowing me to reprint all or part of their work in this book:

American Law Institute, selections from Restatement, Conflict of Laws, Copyright 1934 by The American Law Institute. Reprinted with permission. All rights reserved.

American Law Institute, selections from Restatement (Second), Conflict of Laws, Copyright 1971 by The American Law Institute. Reprinted with permission. All rights reserved.

Bella, Patricia L., Paul Berman, Brett Frischman, and David Post, Cyberlaw: Problems of Policy & Jurisprudence in the Information Age 17-24 (West 2010). Reprinted with permission. Currie, Brainerd, "Comments on Babcock v. Jackson," 63 Colum. L. Rev. 1233, 1242-1243 (1963). Reprinted with permission.

Currie, Brainerd, "Full Faith and Credit to Foreign Land Decrees," 21 U. Chi. L. Rev. 620, 672-676 (1954). Reprinted with permission.

Knop, Karen, "Citizenship, Public and Private," 71 Law & Contemp. Prob. 309 (2009). Reprinted with permission.

Laprès, Daniel Licra and UEJF v. Yahoo!, Tribunal de Grande Instance de Paris, May 22, 2000 Translation from French to English reprinted by permission of Daniel Laprès, www.lapres.net/yahen.html.

Leflar, Robert A., "Conflicts Law: More on Choice-Influencing Considerations," 54 Cal. L. Rev. 1584, 1585-1588 (1966), No. 4, reprinted by permission of California Law Review, Inc., http://www.law.berkely.edu/studnets/jrnlorgs/journals.

Mabrey, Ken, Nesting Doll Illustration for Figure 1-2. Reprinted with permission.

Noth, Paul/The New Yorker Collection/www.cartoonbank.com, reprinted from the New Yorker Magazine 10/4/2010.

If you were to tell a lay person that you are taking a course in conflict of laws, you would likely be faced with a blank stare. You might add something like "Well, it's about when laws conflict with each other and how to resolve that conflict. In that way, conflict of laws is kind of the law of laws and it regulates how laws interact with each other." That description might provoke at least a glimmer of understanding.

As a newcomer to the discipline of conflict of laws, you might be reassured to find that the best way to approach the subject is to remain mindful that—like all law—it regulates human affairs. When humans interact, they sometimes clash and sometimes defer to one another. Often they do both—either explicitly or implicitly coming up with ways to share control. And that, it turns out, is what it's all about: whether to defer or share control.

Because conflict of laws has developed in the structured realm of law, its doctrines have themselves become highly formalized. Further complications and abstractions arise because conflict of laws operates in the context of regulating clashes between artificial entities—and generally, those entities are governmental sovereigns. Those abstractions provide potential for creating invigorating puzzles for lawyers. The puzzles can be fun. But the abstractions also raise the risk that legal principles become divorced from the more accessible, easily comprehensible components of real life. For conflict of laws to retain meaning anchored in human relations, it is important to identify the consequences of the conflict of laws decisions for the lives of the litigants.

The field of conflict of laws sometimes displays an unfortunate disconnect between the theory of conflict of laws and the real-life consequences of power clashes between governmental sovereigns. A major goal of this book is to encourage enthusiasm for the elegance of conflict of laws doctrine. Perhaps as a consequence of conflict of laws' abstract character — or perhaps out of affinity with old-fashioned things — law professors have generally adhered to an approach to conflict of laws teaching that is venerable, but outdated. This book ventures a dramatic change of pace.

While celebrating the traditional qualities of the discipline, this book also tries to situate conflict of laws within contemporary problems that will confront you — with regularity no doubt — in law practice or otherwise. Accordingly, nearly every small section of the book contains at least one problem designed to show how the particular area of conflict of laws doctrine presented actually plays out in real life. Conflict of laws is crucially important to how people should plan their affairs, and thus is a key part of a lawyer's job in giving fully informed advice and in structuring transactions. In the transactional drafting process, an able lawyer will attempt to "predict" how the parties' affairs will unfold, "provide" for those occurrences though various contingencies in the transactional documents, and sometimes even "protect" the client from the results of untoward events and disintegrating relationships by specifying certain remedies.[1] For each of these steps, the drafting lawyer should consider which law would most favorably protect the client's interests and take steps to make it more likely that law will apply.

Conflict of laws also includes many concepts useful for the litigator's toolbox. A litigator who is nimble in understanding and using these tools is better able to represent her client not only in litigation itself, but also in rendering advice aimed at avoiding litigation and explaining its likely consequences.

For these reasons, conflict of laws is enormously practical and — indeed — essential to skilled lawyering. This book would be inadequate, however, if it did not also explore an altogether different side of conflict of laws. Perhaps more than any other legal discipline (except jurisprudence itself), conflict of laws provides a clear lens into the patterns of how

---

1. SCOTT J. BURNHAM, DRAFTING AND ANALYZING CONTRACTS §1.3, at 329 (3d ed.) (articulating the "predict," "provide," and "protect" components of drafting transactional documents).

governments interact with each other and into the nature of law itself. From the governmental perspective, the discipline explores the co-equal relationships between sister states in the United States and between foreign nationals — as well as the more hierarchical relationship between the United States federal government and state governments. In exploring these relationships, conflict of laws exposes and examines jurisprudential questions such as the legitimate reach of legal authority, the possible sources for a government's prerogative to control an individual's affairs, as well as the relationship between legal rules and public policy.

These governmental and jurisprudential issues make conflict of laws particularly rewarding. You will find lawyers, scholars, and lay people who ridicule the complexity of conflict of laws and its inability to give a clear bottom-line answer to most legal questions. But that view fails to appreciate how conflict of laws strikes at the heart of power itself. One would not expect such a subject matter to be clean or uncomplicated. What one can expect, however, is for the subject to be fascinating and illuminating. One hopes this book does not disappoint.

A. *COURSE THEMES*

As a starting point in defining what conflict of laws is all about, you might find it helpful to remember that — since the field is about "conflict" and about government by "laws" — the field by definition involves more than one governmental entity. Although a governmental entity can be internally conflicted, that is not what we are talking about here. Rather, conflict of laws starts from the proposition that it "takes two to make a fight" and then seeks to find a reasoned resolution for the conflict between two governmental entities. This concept helps to pin down two overarching themes of this book: (i) conflict of laws governs how governments interact with each other and (ii) conflict of laws reveals qualities that distinguish law from less formal influences on human interaction, such as social norms, policies, or brute force. Weaving in and out of these themes are five other questions:

(1) How do rules of conduct obtain authority in human society?
(2) What is the optimum structure for a federalist system?
(3) How should government operate in the global era?
(4) How does one determine whether local public policies are so important that they displace other governmental concerns such as respect for another sovereign?
(5) How does technology — such as the internet — change how governments and people interact?

In today's world, these themes are interwoven into most legal pro-blems.[2] Accordingly, this book dispenses with an approach taken in older casebooks of segregating internet problems and international issues into separate chapters. Those topics appear throughout the book, reflecting the reality that transnational and international legal issues are a staple of law practice in the United States, no longer reserved for specialists.[3] With the goal of fostering a contemporary lawyering style that is both effective in servicing clients and in providing responsible leadership on social issues, the book also contains discussion of litigation strategy, fairness, and procedural justice. In particular, you will encounter extensive discussion of procedural values such as consistency, predictability, and efficiency.

Lest the above is somehow not sufficient to hold interest, you will also find discussion in this book about unique qualities of the legal process, rea-soning, and rhetoric in conflicts case law. These unique qualities seem to result from the intractable nature of conflict of laws problems: there is simply no "right" answer to many power clashes presented in most conflict of laws cases. Some conflict of laws problems — such as the clash between state and federal law — contain a "tie breaker" that points to a ready answer, such as the supremacy clause of the United States Constitution. More commonly, however, conflicting laws come from sovereigns of equal status. When this occurs, courts must be creative to designate a rational "winner." The result-ing analysis takes many forms, but provides you with a chance to become more expert in some of the rhetorical and linguistic devices useful where human affairs requires lawyers to operate with subtlety, creativity, and some-times even stealth. For example, conflict of laws questions often require some kind of characterization. Courts must sort the facts of a dispute into

2. Laura E. Little, *Conflict of Laws Structure and Vision: Updating a Venerable Discipline*, 31 GEORGIA ST. U. L. REV. 231 (2015) (discussing how contemporary conflict of laws problems manifest these five themes).

3. *See, e.g.*, Susan L. DeJarnatt & Mark C. Rahdert, *Preparing for Globalized Law Practice: The Need to Include International and Comparative Law in the Legal Writing Curriculum*, 17 LEGAL WRITING 3 (2011) (reporting on results of survey suggesting that a substantial majority of practitioners in a United States metropolitan area handled matters requiring knowledge of international or foreign law); M.C. Minow, *Globalizing Property: Incorporating Comparative and International Law into First Year Property Courses*, 54 J. LEGAL ED. 183, 185-186 (2004) (arguing for the need to globalize law school curriculum on matters implicating both litigation and transactional practice). Moreover, the United States continuing to act as a magnet for international litigation, which requires United States lawyers with international expertise. *See, e.g.*, GARY B. BORN & PETER B. RUTLEDGE, INTERNATIONAL CIVIL LITIGATION IN U.S. COURTS 3 (outlining reasons why the United States is "a particularly attractive forum for plaintiffs) (5th ed. 2011); David J. Levy, Foreword to INTERNATIONAL LITIGATION: DEFENDING AND SUING FOREIGN PARTIES IN U.S. COURTS xi, xii (David J. Levy ed.) (noting that the increasingly globalized economy has led to more international litigation in United States courts); Anne-Marie Slaughter & David Bosco, *Plaintiff's Diplomacy*, 79.5 FOREIGN AFF. 102, 104 (2000) (noting an increasing trend of filing suit in United States courts for violations of international law); *see also* William Glaberson, *U.S. Courts Become Arbiters of Global Rights and Wrongs*, N.Y. TIMES, June 21, 2001, *available at* http://www.nytimes.com/2001/06/21/national/21LEGA.html.

various legal categories: is the issue one of contract or tort? Substantive or procedural? Is her partner a "spouse" for the purpose of both the domestic relations law *and* the probate code? Is charitable immunity a loss allocating rule or a conduct regulating rule? The type of thinking required to frame these questions is common in all forms of lawyering, whether it be counseling, brief writing, arguing, negotiating, or interacting with the press. The material in this book provides you with an opportunity to think meaningfully about rhetorical techniques and to practice using them.

B. WHAT ARE THE STAKES?

As you become acquainted with the complexities of conflict of laws doctrine, try not to become distracted away from the tremendously large stakes that often hang in the balance. Remembering the significance of the legal issues in a case is helpful to identifying what is motivating the parties and the court, and thus provides greater insight into the reasoning and bottom line of the decision.

Many ways exist for illustrating how important conflict of laws can be to people's lives, but two examples — one historical and one contemporary — are particularly apt:

(1) *The Historical*: the lawsuit that gave rise to the United States Supreme Court's decision in *Dred Scott v. Sanford*, 60 U.S. (19 How.) 393 (1856), and

(2) *The Contemporary*: political, practical, and legal struggles over consumer rights versus corporate efficiency.

Both contexts are laden with conflict of laws issues and both contexts implicate powerful social and cultural issues of their day: the institution of slavery and social attitudes toward consumers and corporations.

Dred Scott dealt with the issue of status: when enslaved persons were brought into a free state, were they free or enslaved? The answer came from choice of law principles of the time, which broke down as interstate relationships deteriorated in the mid-1800s.[4] Indeed, for many years leading up to the Civil War, conflict of laws issues arose in fugitive slave cases as well as

---

4. For further discussion of the conflict of laws implications of *Dred Scott v. Sanford*, and other slavery cases, see, e.g., Louise Weinberg, *Methodological Interventions and the Slavery Cases — or, Night Thoughts of a Legal Realist*, 56 Md. L. Rev. 1316 (1997); Jane Larson, *"A House Divided": Using Dred Scott to Teach Conflict of Laws*, 27 U. Tol. L. Rev. 577 (1996). *See also* Robert M. Cover, Justice Accused (1975) (describing how anti-slavery judges in the antebellum northern United States were able to enforce laws they found morally repugnant because their commitment to the judicial role enabled them to dedicate themselves to fidelity to legal principles, including conflict of laws principles).

cases where persons held in slavery claimed freedom upon being transported by their "owners" to free states. These cases raised state choice of
law puzzles, issues pertaining to the constitutional duty of full faith and
credit due to sister state laws governing slavery, and questions about the
extent to which federal Fugitive Slave Act preempted state law. Ultimately,
federal constitutional doctrine—in the form of the Thirteenth Amendment—provided clear guidance.

In the contemporary context, the power struggle between consumers
and corporations manifests in many conflict of laws contexts. Under what
circumstances does a "click: I agree" during hasty Internet transactions bind
consumers who later find out that they entered into a contract subject to a
highly unfavorable law? What happens when consumers' home state provides laws protecting the consumers' rights and when the manufacturer of
the consumers' car comes from a state that does not protect the consumers'
rights? Or, on another topic, what law governs the circumstances under
which same-sex spouses may lawfully adopt a child? The child's home
state? The spouses' home state? Some other place? It is matters of this profound magnitude that this book covers.

C.   TRIPARTITE STRUCTURE OF CONFLICT OF LAWS

From one perspective, conflict of laws is about power. Specifically, conflict of laws principles designate which sovereign should win when an issue
arises over which sovereignty gets to control the disposition of a lawsuit and
the scope of rights implicated in a dispute. In the United States, the power
struggle often occurs between two states. This is sometimes called a horizontal conflict, since the states are on an equal plane in terms of sovereign
power. The United States Constitution provides some guidance on how to
handle these conflicts by imposing an obligation on one state to give "full
faith and credit" to the laws of sister states. Yet—as you will see—this full
faith and credit obligation provides only partial guidance.

In the global context, two sovereign nations are also on an equal plane
and thus can also become ensnared in horizontal conflict of laws. Where one
sovereign has a claim to superiority—such as position of the federal government in relation to state governments in the United States system—a vertical
conflict of laws is presented. Finally, there is the complicated situation where
state authority conflicts with the authority of a foreign, non–United States
sovereign. This conflict has qualities of both a horizontal and a vertical clash.

Whether the conflict is vertical or horizontal, the law generally provides
three sets of legal rules for resolving the conflict: personal jurisdiction doctrine, choice of law doctrine, and judgments doctrine. Personal jurisdiction
doctrine governs the prerogative of forum courts to exercise power over
particular litigants to a controversy. (A forum court is the court where a

lawsuit is filed.) Sometimes called judicial jurisdiction, court power to resolve disputes between people has evolved over the years, switching from an emphasis on citizenship and territorial power to an emphasis on party contacts within the jurisdiction where the court sits.

By contrast to personal jurisdiction rules, choice of law doctrines designate what legal rules (or laws) govern human affairs where more than one jurisdiction could make a claim for control in a particular situation. The question of what legal rules control people's lives is sometimes called legislative jurisdiction. A forum court will apply a choice of law doctrine to determine which sovereign has power to prescribe the general legal principles that govern the parties' rights at issue in a lawsuit.

Judgments law focuses on the effect of judicial decrees that affect the rights of parties to the litigation that gave rise to the decree. Judgments law determines the power of judicial enforcement of laws, designating what effect a court judgment rendered in one jurisdiction should have in other jurisdictions. While judgments law pertains to court decrees that resolve the rights of parties to a dispute, personal jurisdiction law pertains only to whether a particular court has the power to even entertain the dispute in the first place. Moreover, court judgments resolve the rights of specific parties in specific disputes. This is different from the general legal principles that are chosen when a court applies choice of law doctrine to ascertain which sovereign has the prerogative of enunciating the general legal rules that govern a dispute.[5]

As you will see in the materials that follow, you can easily sort some legal problems into one of three doctrines. For example, the question of whether a California court may entertain a lawsuit filed against an out-of-state corporation seems plainly to present a personal jurisdiction problem. Likewise, the question of whether Illinois or Singapore principles governing the duty of care in a negligence action filed in Illinois suggests a choice of law analysis. Finally, judgments law would seem to control whether a court in Louisiana must enforce a New York court decree requiring the parties to honor a surrogate motherhood contract that is contrary to public policies of Louisiana. You will see, however, that particular legal problems do not sort so easily into one of three doctrines. The reason for this is that the three doctrines each derive from the same impetus: the law's attempt to resolve power struggles between sovereigns. If you have trouble figuring out which of the three doctrines works best, that probably means you have a deep understanding of a conflict of laws tenet: the three doctrines are merely manifestations of the

---

5. International law traditionally enunciates three categories of jurisdiction that resemble the personal jurisdiction, choice of law, and judgments components of domestic conflict of laws. These international law categories include adjudicative, prescriptive, and enforcement authority. Although the two sets of principles overlap, courts and scholars have struggled to identify precise similarities and differences.

same basic questions of power. You can think of the three doctrines as legs to a three-legged stool: the conflict of laws stool.

The American approach to conflict of laws owes its lineage in substantial part to the work of a Dutch thinker named Ulric Huber. Huber conceived of the conflict of laws power question as one of sovereign prerogative. Specifically, he argued that sovereigns have dominion over those who are present in the territory as well as those who are its "subjects." As for the effect of one sovereign's law within the jurisdiction of another sovereign, Huber maintained that one sovereign should accept the law of other sovereigns in appropriate circumstances because of comity, and not because any supremacy principle or overriding principle of justice requires the sovereign to follow the law of another sovereignty.[6] (Comity is a principle whereby one sovereign voluntarily accommodates itself to the law of another sovereign because individual fairness or governmental concerns suggest that it is appropriate to do so.) Huber's position presents the core of the power controversy: to what extent do justice principles actually require one sovereign to cede to the extraterritorial effect of another sovereign's law? It is helpful to remain mindful of this key question as you make your way through the material in this course. As you will read in Chapter 2, Huber's ideas proved enormously influential for United States Supreme Court Justice Joseph Story, who incorporated them into his 1834 treatise on the conflict of laws.

D. MORE ON VOCABULARY AND CHARACTERIZING THE POWER CLASH

"Conflict of laws" is the term used in the United States for the power struggle among sovereigns. In United States jurisprudence, we generally think of conflict of laws as pertaining to disputes in a private civil context — not in criminal cases or cases dealing with the constitutional relationship between a citizen and the state. In other parts of the world, the term "private international law" is often invoked when referring to what Americans think of as conflict of laws — and generally refers to legal principles governing choice of law, personal jurisdiction, and judgments. As the world is becoming more

---

6. In a work published in 1689, Huber asserted the following core propositions:

1. The laws of each state have force within the limits of that government and bind all subjects to it, but not beyond.
2. All persons within the limits of a government, whether they live there permanently or temporarily, are deemed to be subjects thereof.
3. Sovereigns will so act by way of comity that rights acquired within the limits of a government retain their force everywhere so far as they do not cause prejudice to the power or rights of such government or its subjects.

Ulric Huber, *De Conflictu Legaum Diversarum in Diversis Imperiis (On the Conflict of Diverse Laws of Different States)*, in ERNEST G. LORENZEN, SELECTED ARTICLES ON THE CONFLICT OF LAWS 136-137 (1947).

integrated and the distinction between what is "private" and "public" starts to erode, these distinctions may become less meaningful. In the meantime, however, they are part of the traditional lexicon of which you should be aware.

Some of terms in the discipline are terms of art, and thus have a precise definition beyond that in common parlance. For example, the term "law" refers to an exercise of sovereign authority that can come in a variety of forms, including statutes, common law principles from court decisions, court rules of procedure, court judgments, court rulings on motions, and an individual court's exercise of personal jurisdiction over parties to the law-suit. Thus, when we talk about conflict of laws, we might be referring to a conflict among laws appearing in any one of these forms. Technically speaking, "conflict of laws" is different from "choice of law." "Conflict of laws" is the umbrella term including the three subject matters described above: personal jurisdiction, choice of law, and judgment recognition questions. Thus, "choice of law" is only a subset of "conflict of laws," pertaining only to the process of selecting legal principles to govern parties' lives. Because the terms (conflict of laws and choice of law) are similar, they are sometimes used interchangeably. This book endeavors to keep the terms separate in order to avoid confusion. Finally, it is helpful to remember that—within the domestic discipline of conflict of laws — the term "state" usually refers to a state within the United States, but in the international context, the term often refers to the more generic concept of a sovereign government. This book uses the terms "country" or "foreign country" in the international context so as to avoid confusion. Likewise, many conflict of laws sources use "foreign state" to denote a different state of the United States than the forum. Accordingly, this book uses the terms "foreign country" when discussing an international matter. For similar reasons, the book will use "foreign country judgment" when discussing international matters, since conflict of laws materials often use the phrase "foreign judgment" when discussing a United States state's obligations toward the judgment of a United States sister state.

INTRODUCTORY PROBLEM: CASSANDRA AND JULIAN

Cassandra is a resident of New Jersey. She researched and wrote an article about Julian, which was published in a newspaper. A resident of Ohio, Julian is convinced that the article defames him and he files a defamation suit against Cassandra in Ohio. Cassandra has never been to Ohio and has never had anything to do with Ohio. Unbeknownst to her, however, the newspaper distributes 20 papers in the state (less than 1 percent of its total circulation). Although Cassandra never appeared before the Ohio court, Julian convinced the court to entertain his lawsuit. Applying Ohio law, the court decided that Cassandra had defamed him and entered judgment against Cassandra in the amount of $100,000. Julian wishes to turn this judgment from a piece of paper into cash in his pocket. He knows that the only way he can do so is to enforce the judgment. He hires a private investigator who finds out that Cassandra has all her assets in New Jersey. Accordingly, Julian files suit in New Jersey, asking the New Jersey court to enforce the judgment against Cassandra. Cassandra consults you to defend this action, and you recall the "three legs" of conflict of laws: personal jurisdiction, choice of law, and recognition of judgments. Framing your arguments in terms of these three legs, what type of arguments would you make?

CHAPTER 1

PERSONAL JURISDICTION AND FORUM CHOICE

The law of personal jurisdiction is important to this course for two general reasons. First, it provides a set of doctrines that controls how courts may legitimately relate to potential litigants in a world where more than one sovereign can make a claim to adjudicating a controversy. These doctrines incorporate concerns related to power and fairness, and beckon a way of thinking that proves useful in understanding both choice of law and judgment recognition problems as well. Second, personal jurisdiction law presents strategy questions that are important to litigants choosing the jurisdiction in which to file their lawsuit as they evaluate which jurisdiction would best serve their interest in prevailing in a lawsuit. A plaintiff's choice of forum can determine the outcome of a lawsuit. Accordingly, attorneys wishing to maximize their chance of ensuring the best result for their clients need to evaluate their chances of getting a case adjudicated before a court that will likely apply the most favorable laws under the most favorable conditions for their clients. Personal jurisdiction is the key concept controlling the choice of forum. Forum selection issues are also important for transactional lawyers, who structure deals and draft contracts mindful of possible litigation arising from the transaction.

Personal jurisdiction principles thus provide a portal into all of the material in this course. As you begin to understand why personal jurisdiction is so important to a state's or country's judicial system, you will start to appreciate the role of choice of law and enforcement of judgments as well. As an introduction to the integrated nature of personal jurisdiction, choice of law, and judgment recognition, consider how forum choice influences the "bottom line" of litigation:

(1) Party Convenience: Parties generally prefer to litigate in their home jurisdiction, where they are familiar with the court system and general community. This familiarity makes it more likely that they will be able to conduct effective, cost-efficient litigation.

(2) Choice of Law Approach: As will be explored in detail later in this volume, the court where a lawsuit is filed (the "forum") will apply its own choice of law principles to determine which law governs the parties' rights in a case where more than one jurisdiction may legitimately provide these governing principles. The choice of law approach used has a powerful influence on the "substantive" legal principles applied — and ultimately impacts the outcome of the suit.

(3) Procedural Law: A forum court applies its own procedures in conducting the litigation. Although received wisdom says that procedural law should not determine the outcome of litigation, the practical reality is that litigation's outcome is affected by the procedures a court follows.

(4) Enforcing a Judgment: One ultimate measure of a plaintiff's success in litigation is a fully satisfied judgment. Without the ability to enforce a judgment, a "prevailing" plaintiff has only a piece of paper representing the court's judgment. A plaintiff seeking to maximize her chances of satisfying a judgment against the defendant will find that the best place to litigate is in a jurisdiction where the defendant has substantial assets located. A jurisdiction where the defendant's substantial assets are located provides the cheapest and easiest place to obtain a meaningful judgment.

The goal of this chapter is to interweave strategic matters about choice of forum with theoretical concerns of power and fairness. The personal jurisdiction principles presented first in this chapter capture the power and fairness concerns most explicitly. The strategy questions rise to the surface in the material at the end of the chapter, which presents other material pertaining to the location of a lawsuit, including venue, the doctrine of forum non conveniens, and forum selection clauses. While personal jurisdiction presents equally, if not more important, rules that control the strategy questions, these latter doctrines operate more obviously as tools for a defendant to veto the location of a lawsuit. Navigating the world of forum choice can be even more intricate in the international context, and this chapter touches on some of the concepts related to personal jurisdiction but unique to international litigation, such as sovereign immunity and the act of state doctrine.

As you will see below, personal jurisdiction doctrine itself is largely a creature of United States Supreme Court decisions interpreting the United States Constitution. The personal jurisdiction material in this chapter will focus on these constitutional principles. It is important to remember, however, that compliance with constitutional limitations is not sufficient to permit a court to exercise personal jurisdiction. As a logistical and legal matter, one must find a statute that authorizes a court to exercise personal jurisdiction. In other words, a state legislature must make a political decision that personal jurisdiction is appropriate in given circumstances. The state legislatures are free to authorize jurisdiction to the greatest extent permitted under the United States Constitution, and

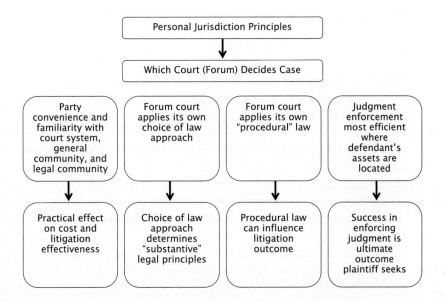

Figure 1-1: Strategic Reasons Why Personal Jurisdiction Is So Important

frequently they exercise that power to the fullest. Federal courts generally follow the lead of state legislatures, looking to state law to determine whether statutory authorization is present. Accordingly, the question of whether personal jurisdiction exists is generally answered the same way as whether the case is filed in state court or in a federal court within the state.

One final preliminary note: in contrast to the other chapters of the book, this chapter paints with a broad brush—providing an overview of the subject matter without laboring over all of the finer points of personal jurisdiction law and forum choice doctrines. This approach reflects the view that—while crucial to understanding our complex litigation systems—the personal jurisdiction and litigation practice material is analytically most important in a course on Conflict of Laws as a foil for illuminating larger questions of jurisdictional power and forum shopping. That is not an invitation to skim, however, since the material presented below contains important subtleties that bear on the power of courts to govern in a multijurisdictional world as well as the facility of lawyers to navigate adroitly in that world.

A. BACKGROUND ON PERSONAL JURISDICTION IN THE UNITED STATES

To refresh your recollection of the specific types of concern that inform personal jurisdiction issues in the United States, consider the litigation mentioned in the introduction to this book—a defamation action between Cassandra and Julian.

INTRODUCTORY PROBLEM: CASSANDRA AND JULIAN REDUX (PERSONAL JURISDICTION ISSUES)

Cassandra is a resident of New Jersey. She researched and wrote an article about Julian, which was published in a newspaper. A resident of Ohio, Julian is convinced that the article defames him and he files a defamation suit against Cassandra in Ohio. Cassandra has never been to Ohio and has never had anything to do with Ohio. Unbeknownst to her, however, the newspaper distributes 20 papers in the state (less than 1 percent of its total circulation). Although Cassandra never appeared before the Ohio court, Julian would like to convince the court to entertain the lawsuit and enter a judgment on the merits. What types of factors bear on whether or not the court should exercise jurisdiction over his lawsuit?

1. Evolution of the Doctrine

A logical starting place for reviewing the evolution of personal jurisdiction law in the United States is *Pennoyer v. Neff*, 95 U.S. 714 (1878). On one hand, *Pennoyer v. Neff* is an unremarkable decision in its analysis of a court's adjudicatory authority by reference to territorial power — specifically, *Pennoyer v. Neff* announced a presence principle, instructing that a court's jurisdiction to adjudicate depends on a physical connection between the parties and the particular geographical location where the court sits. More remarkably, the *Pennoyer* Court put this inquiry together with the Fourteenth Amendment's due process clause, establishing that the due process clause accommodates three types of adjudicatory power: in personam jurisdiction, in rem jurisdiction, and quasi in rem jurisdiction. According to *Pennoyer v. Neff*, in personam jurisdiction pertains to a court's power over the defendant's person, and properly arises when the defendant is physically served with process within the forum state. In rem and quasi in rem jurisdiction, however, depend on the presence of property within the state where the court sits. In rem jurisdiction applies to a court's power over specific property in dispute; quasi in rem jurisdiction often arises where the parties are actually disputing something other than title to the property that is located in the state. Under the quasi in rem theory, the court generally retains power over the actual dispute because of the presence of the unrelated property in the forum state.

From the time the Court announced the presence principle of *Pennoyer v. Neff*, it became riddled with exceptions. Even the *Pennoyer* Court itself suggested that a state could adjudicate a divorce involving a nonresident who is not present in the state and could condition a license grant on consent to receive service of process in the state. Subsequent developments in transportation and communication required further exceptions to the notion that valid in personam jurisdiction depended on actual in-state service of process. Modern realities challenged the doctrines of *Pennoyer v. Neff,* which ultimately proved unworkable.

The United States Supreme Court replaced the *Pennoyer v. Neff* principle in *International Shoe Co. v. Washington,* 326 U.S. 310 (1945). The *International Shoe* case was an action brought by the State of Washington to force the defendant, International Shoe Company, to pay a Washington unemployment tax. International Shoe actually manufactured shoes out of state, but employed sales personnel who resided in Washington and were paid on commission. International Shoe did not own real estate in Washington, though it occasionally rented rooms for displaying shoe samples. The company permitted its sales personnel to display only one shoe as a sample—the notion being that International Shoe was not *really* doing business in the state if it did not ship an entire pair of shoes into the state. When orders were made, they were accepted only by the company's headquarters outside of Washington (and not by the itinerant sales personnel) and the buyers were actually required to pay the freight charges to get their order shipped to Washington. In short, International Shoe had apparently tried hard to structure its business so as not to be deemed "present" in Washington for personal jurisdiction purposes.

As a lawsuit against a corporation, *International Shoe v. Washington* presented a difficult problem for *Pennoyer*'s conception of personal jurisdiction: how does one determine whether an artificial entity such as a corporation is actually present in the state for the purpose of service of process? By the structure of its affairs, the International Shoe Company seemed to have tried to avoid appearing "present" in Washington for personal jurisdiction purposes. But the Supreme Court took a different tack—thus undermining International Shoe's apparent efforts to elude jurisdiction.

Replacing *Pennoyer*'s "gotcha" approach of determining personal jurisdiction by reference to presence, the *International Shoe* Court declared that "due process requires only that in order to subject a defendant to a judgment *in personam,* if he be not present within the territory of the forum, he have certain minimum contacts with it such that maintenance of the suit does not offend 'traditional notions of fair play and substantial justice.'" *International Shoe* thus seems to have substituted *Pennoyer*'s presence principle with a more abstract notion of "fair play and substantial justice." In deciding whether the "fair play and substantial justice" principle was satisfied in the case, the Court evaluated tangible contacts that the defendant had with the forum state—the sales personnel, the room rental, and the shoe samples. Ultimately, the Court concluded that due process allowed the state court to assert personal jurisdiction because the contacts amounted to activities within the state that were "systematic and continuous."

Over the next two decades, the Supreme Court tried again and again to give substance to the broad terms used in *International Shoe:* "fair play and substantial justice," "systematic and continuous," and "minimum contacts." One line of the doctrine developed to elaborate on these terms took shape in the concepts of "general jurisdiction" and "specific jurisdiction." Another line of cases focused more on minimum contacts as well as concerns related to individual fairness and the effective operation of litigation systems. Finally, the Court also revisited the notion of presence. Each of these lines of doctrine is explored below, followed by a discussion of unique personal jurisdiction issues that arise concerning jurisdiction over matters that arise out of internet activity and matters with international overtones. Before further embarking on these various lines of doctrine relating to personal jurisdiction, a brief discussion of service of process is in order.

2. *Service of Process*

In a civil case, the plaintiff gives notice of the suit to the defendant with "service of process." The term "service" refers to the method of delivery. "Process" generally refers to two documents: a complaint drafted by the plaintiff and a summons issued by the court explaining that a response is required by a certain date. Although the rules governing service of process are largely technical, they are informed by the due process requirement that one should not be subject to a deprivation of life, liberty, or property without adequate notice. Moreover, proper service of process is a necessary condition for the court to have jurisdiction over the case.

Federal Rule of Civil Procedure 4 allows service to occur in one of three ways: by delivering process personally to the defendant; by "substitute" service, which involves delivering process at the defendant's abode; and by serving an agent authorized by appointment or by law to receive the process. Rule 4 also allows service in accordance with the rules of the state where the action is pending or where service takes place. Additionally, Rule 4 allows a defendant to waive service, by authorizing service by mail. Finally, for corporations and partnerships, Rule 4 authorizes service on "an officer, a managing or general agent, or any other agent authorized by appointment or by law to receive service of process."

Personal jurisdiction is generally assessed on a state-wide basis, and service of process is the means by which a court ensures that personal jurisdiction has been perfected. Accordingly, the rules governing the geographical boundaries of service of process generally refer to state boundaries. Service is proper anywhere within the state where the lawsuit is pending. Rule 4 authorizes service beyond state boundaries in particular circumstances. Most importantly, the Rule allows nationwide service of process (1) where authorized by federal statute and (2) where the court is exercising federal question jurisdiction and the defendant is not subject to personal jurisdiction in any one state. In this later instance, the theory is that the point of reference for evaluating the power of a federal entity exercising federal power may constitutionally be extended to the entire federal territory. Thus, the federal court's assertion of personal jurisdiction in these circumstances is constitutional where the defendant has sufficient contacts throughout the United States.

B.   THE GENERAL JURISDICTION/SPECIFIC JURISDICTION DISTINCTION

In decisions subsequent to *International Shoe Co. v. Washington*, 326 U.S. 310 (1945), the Supreme Court made clear that a defendant need not have a close affiliation with the forum to justify personal jurisdiction so long as the lawsuit arose out of the defendant's activities there. So long as a plaintiff can establish that her claim "**arises out of or relates to**" the defendant's forum activities, the plaintiff can establish the forum court's "specific jurisdiction." This is different from the situation where the defendant's contacts with the forum are so extensive that the forum court has "general jurisdiction" over all causes of action concerning the defendant.

Drawing from language in *International Shoe* itself, the Court later suggested that general jurisdiction requires "**systematic and continuous**" activity in the forum. Little guidance appears in subsequent Supreme Court cases about the quantum of contacts necessary to establish general jurisdiction. In one case, *Perkins v. Benguet Consolidated Mining Co.*, 342 U.S. 437 (1952), the Court concluded that an out-of-state corporation engaged in "continuous and systematic" activity in Ohio when its president, general manager, and primary shareholder set up an office there and used Ohio bank accounts to pay corporate salaries and other expenses.

In *Helicopteros Nacionales de Colombia, S.A. v. Hall*, 466 U.S. 408 (1984), the Supreme Court added more to our understanding of general jurisdiction and clarified how it differs from specific jurisdiction. Specifically, the Court reinforced the standards: while general jurisdiction is premised on systematic and continuous activity in the forum, specific jurisdiction exists when the plaintiff's claims arise out of or relate to the plaintiff's contacts with the forum state. Subsequent opinions helped to fill in what it takes to be systematic and continuous — as well as what facts courts deem give rise to or relate to a plaintiff's cause of action.

In a number of cases after *Helicopteros*, the U.S. Supreme Court has explored the facts necessary to satisfy the general jurisdiction and specific jurisdiction standards. Most commentators have observed a strong tendency to protect corporations in these series of cases. Do you agree?

Goodyear Dunlop Tires Operations v. Brown

180 L. Ed. 2d 796 (2011)

Justice GINSBURG delivered the opinion of the Court.

This case concerns the jurisdiction of state courts over corporations organized and operating abroad. We address, in particular, this question: Are foreign subsidiaries of a United States parent corporation amenable to suit in state court on claims unrelated to any activity of the subsidiaries in the forum State?

A bus accident outside Paris that took the lives of two 13-year-old boys from North Carolina gave rise to the litigation we here consider. Attributing the accident to a defective tire manufactured in Turkey at the plant of a foreign subsidiary of The Goodyear Tire and Rubber Company (Goodyear USA), the boys' parents commenced an action for damages in a North Carolina state court; they named as defendants Goodyear USA, an Ohio corporation, and three of its subsidiaries, organized and operating, respectively, in Turkey, France, and Luxembourg. Goodyear USA, which had plants in North Carolina and regularly engaged in commercial activity there, did not contest the North Carolina court's jurisdiction over it; Goodyear USA's foreign subsidiaries, however, maintained that North Carolina lacked adjudicatory authority over them.

. . .

Because the episode-in-suit, the bus accident, occurred in France, and the tire alleged to have caused the accident was manufactured and sold abroad, North Carolina courts lacked specific jurisdiction to adjudicate the controversy. The North Carolina Court of Appeals so acknowledged. Were the foreign subsidiaries nonetheless amenable to general jurisdiction in North Carolina courts? Confusing or blending general and specific jurisdictional inquiries, the North Carolina courts answered yes. Some of the tires made abroad by Goodyear's foreign subsidiaries, the North Carolina Court of Appeals stressed, had reached North Carolina through "the stream of commerce"; that connection, the Court of Appeals believed, gave North Carolina courts the handle needed for the exercise of general jurisdiction over the foreign corporations.

A connection so limited between the forum and the foreign corporation, we hold, is an inadequate basis for the exercise of general jurisdiction. Such a connection does not establish the "continuous and systematic" affiliation necessary to empower North Carolina courts to entertain claims unrelated to the foreign corporation's contacts with the State.

I

On April 18, 2004, a bus destined for Charles de Gaulle Airport overturned on a road outside Paris, France. Passengers on the bus were young soccer players from North Carolina. . . . Two 13-year-olds . . . sustained fatal injuries. The boys' parents . . . filed a suit for wrongful-death damages in the Superior Court of Onslow County, North Carolina, in their capacity as administrators of the boys' estates. Attributing the accident to a tire that failed when its plies separated, the parents alleged negligence in the "design, construction, testing, and inspection" of the tire.

Goodyear Luxembourg Tires, SA (Goodyear Luxembourg), Goodyear Lastikleri T. A. S. (Goodyear Turkey), and Goodyear Dunlop Tires France, SA (Goodyear France), petitioners here, were named as defendants. Incorporated in Luxembourg, Turkey, and France, respectively, petitioners are indirect subsidiaries of Goodyear USA, an Ohio corporation also named as a defendant in the suit. Petitioners manufacture tires primarily for sale in European and Asian markets. Their tires differ . . . from tires ordinarily sold in the United States. They are designed to carry significantly heavier loads, and to serve under road conditions and speed limits in the manufacturers' primary markets.

In contrast to the parent company, Goodyear USA, which does not contest the North Carolina courts' personal jurisdiction over it, petitioners are not registered to do business in North Carolina. They have no place of business, employees, or bank accounts in North Carolina. They do not design, manufacture, or advertise their products in North Carolina. And they do not solicit business in North Carolina or themselves sell or ship tires to North Carolina customers. Even so, a small percentage of petitioners' tires (tens of thousands out of tens of millions manufactured between 2004 and 2007) were distributed within North Carolina by other Goodyear USA affiliates. These tires were typically custom ordered to equip specialized vehicles such as cement mixers, waste haulers, and boat and horse trailers. Petitioners state, and respondents do not here deny, that the type of tire involved in the accident, a Goodyear Regional RHS tire manufactured by Goodyear Turkey, was never distributed in North Carolina.

Petitioners moved to dismiss the claims against them for want of personal jurisdiction. The trial court denied the motion, and [ultimately the North Carolina Court of Appeals ruled that the general jurisdiction] threshold was crossed . . . when petitioners placed their tires "in the stream of interstate commerce without any limitation on the extent to which those tires could be sold in North Carolina."

[Although the court observed that petitioners took no "affirmative action to cause tires which they had manufactured to be shipped into North Carolina," the court found that tires made by petitioners reached North Carolina by virtue of a "highly-organized distribution process" involving other Goodyear USA subsidiaries.] Petitioners, the court noted, made "no attempt to keep these tires from reaching the North Carolina market." Indeed, the very tire involved in the accident, the court observed, conformed to tire standards established by the U.S. Department of Transportation and bore markings required for sale in the United States. As further support, the court invoked North Carolina's "interest in providing a forum in which its citizens are able to seek redress for [their] injuries," and noted the hardship North Carolina plaintiffs would experience "[were they] required to litigate their claims in France," a country to which they have no ties. . . .

We . . . decide whether the general jurisdiction the North Carolina courts asserted over petitioners is consistent with the Due Process Clause of the Fourteenth Amendment.

II

. . .

B

To justify the exercise of general jurisdiction over petitioners, the North Carolina courts relied on the petitioners' placement of their tires in the "stream of commerce." The stream-of-commerce metaphor has been invoked frequently in lower court decisions.... Typically, in such cases, a nonresident defendant, acting *outside* the forum, places in the stream of commerce a product that ultimately causes harm *inside* the forum.

...

The North Carolina court's stream-of-commerce analysis elided the essential difference between case-specific and all-purpose (general) jurisdiction. Flow of a manufacturer's products into the forum, we have explained, may bolster an affiliation germane to *specific* jurisdiction. ... A corporation's "continuous activity of some sorts within a state," *International Shoe* instructed, "is not enough to support the demand that the corporation be amenable to suits unrelated to that activity." Our 1952 decision in *Perkins v. Benguet Consol. Mining Co.* remains "[t]he textbook case of general jurisdiction appropriately exercised over a foreign corporation that has not consented to suit in the forum."

Sued in Ohio, the defendant in *Perkins* was a Philippine mining corporation that had ceased activities in the Philippines during World War II. To the extent that the company was conducting any business during and immediately after the Japanese occupation of the Philippines, it was doing so in Ohio: the corporation's president maintained his office there, kept the company files in that office, and supervised from the Ohio office "the necessarily limited wartime activities of the company." Although the claim-in-suit did not arise in Ohio, this Court ruled that it would not violate due process for Ohio to adjudicate the controversy.

We next addressed the exercise of general jurisdiction over an out-of-state corporation over three decades later, in *Helicopteros*. [In *Helicopteros*, we determined that the "links to Texas" — the forum state] did not "constitute the kind of continuous and systematic general business contacts ... found to exist in *Perkins*," and were insufficient to support the exercise of jurisdiction over a claim that neither "ar[o]se out of ... no[r] related to" the defendant's activities in Texas.

Helicopteros concluded that "mere purchases [made in the forum State], even if occurring at regular intervals, are not enough to warrant a State's assertion of [general] jurisdiction over a nonresident corporation in a cause of action not related to those purchase transactions." We see no reason to differentiate from the ties to Texas held insufficient in *Helicopteros*, the sales of petitioners' tires sporadically made in North Carolina through intermediaries. Under the sprawling view of general jurisdiction urged by respondents and embraced by the North Carolina Court of Appeals, any substantial manufacturer or seller of goods would be amenable to suit, on any claim for relief, wherever its products are distributed.

Measured against *Helicopteros* and *Perkins*, North Carolina is not a forum in which it would be permissible to subject petitioners to general jurisdiction. Unlike the defendant in *Perkins*, whose sole wartime business activity was conducted in Ohio, petitioners are in no sense at home in North Carolina. Their attenuated connections to the State fall far short of the "the continuous and systematic general business contacts" necessary to empower North Carolina to entertain suit against them on claims unrelated to anything that connects them to the State.

C

Respondents belatedly assert a "single enterprise" theory, asking us to consolidate petitioners' ties to North Carolina with those of Goodyear USA and other Goodyear entities. In effect, respondents would have us pierce Goodyear corporate veils, at least for jurisdictional purposes. Neither below nor in their brief in opposition to the petition for certiorari did respondents urge disregard of petitioners' discrete status as subsidiaries and treatment of all Goodyear entities as a "unitary business," so that jurisdiction over the parent would draw in the subsidiaries as well. Respondents have therefore forfeited this contention, and we do not address it. . . .

For the reasons stated, the judgment of the North Carolina Court of Appeals is *Reversed.*

Notes on
GOODYEAR DUNLOP

1. *Goodyear Dunlop* elaborated on *International Shoe*'s emphasis on contacts as a way of measuring fairness and justice. How do contacts accomplish that?

2. All the Justices in both *Helicopteros* and *Goodyear Dunlop* agreed on the general jurisdiction standard: continuous and systematic activity in the state. Under this standard, jurisdiction is proper irrespective of whether that activity is related to the lawsuit. How can that approach comport with principles of "fair play and substantial justice"? In other words, how does the general jurisdiction standard ensure that it is fair for a court to exercise jurisdiction over a particular defendant?

3. Is there a difference between the two components of the specific jurisdiction standard: a cause of action that "arises out of" defendant's activities in the forum and a cause of action that "relates to" defendant's activities in the forum? In your view, which of the two — "arises out of" or "relates to" — is the stronger basis for jurisdiction? Why?

4. The *Goodyear* Court had no problem concluding that specific jurisdiction did not exist in the case. What types of contacts would have given rise to specific jurisdiction in that case? The *Goodyear* decision implies that systematic and continuous *purchases* from a state cannot provide the basis for general jurisdiction, while continuous and systematic *sales* in a state can provide a basis for general jurisdiction. Why the difference?

5. Is the dichotomy between specific jurisdiction and general jurisdiction artificial? Where personal jurisdiction is an issue, it seems like most corporate and individual activities fall somewhere along two continuums. On one hand, the quantity of the defendant's contacts within the forum state can easily fall between no contacts and "continuous and systematic activity." On the other hand, the relationship between the defendant's

contacts within the forum and the plaintiff's claim can also fall between a really close relationship and no relationship at all. Is there a way to develop a rule that accommodates a hybrid situation where a court has "a touch" of general jurisdiction and "a touch" of specific jurisdiction? Plenty of courts have endorsed such an approach, which is often associated with the court's decision in *Camelback Ski Corp. v. Behning*, 539 A.2d 1107, 1111 (Md. 1988). But these holdings are now dubious. Consider whether this hybrid approach is still viable after the U.S. Supreme Court's decision in *Bristol-Myers Squibb Co. v. Superior Court*, 137 S. Ct. 1773 (2017), presented below.

6. As a litigator, which of the two theories—general jurisdiction and specific jurisdiction—would you prefer as a potential basis for the court's power? Which is the stronger—i.e., least problematic—basis for jurisdiction?

7. If an individual or entity has suffered some kind of injury (in contract, tort, or otherwise) and would like to pursue legal remedies, one would expect that they usually would make inquiries to an attorney in their home state. One might assume that the attorney would first consider whether jurisdiction in the home state is possible. Which basis of jurisdiction would the attorney likely first consider? What type of considerations would make the attorney consider something other than the home state as the best state for suit?

8. Domicile is a concept that weaves throughout conflict of laws. A person's domicile is the place that she centers her life and considers her home. The home, or "central link," for a corporation is usually the principal place of business. As will be explored further in Chapter 2, both the intent to make a place one's home as well as some physical presence is required to establish a domicile. In older case law, the United States Supreme Court recognized that the Constitution allows personal jurisdiction based on domicile within the forum state. In *Milliken v. Meyer*, 311 U.S. 457 (1940), the Court explained:

> Domicile in the state is alone sufficient to bring an absent defendant within the reach of the state's jurisdiction. . . . The state which accords him privileges and affords protection to him and his property by virtue of his domicile may also exact reciprocal duties. . . . One such incident of domicile is amenability to suit within the state even during sojourns without the state, where the state has provided and employed a reasonable method for apprising such an absent party of the proceedings against him.

Id. at 462-464.

The *Milliken* holding is regarded as accurate under current case law—with domicile treated as a basis for general jurisdiction and believed constitutionally sufficient so long as notice is proper. But the law—particularly as reflected in the draft Restatement (Third) of Conflict of Laws—is evolving.

The situation for corporations is different than for individuals. Although corporations employ individuals, own property, and conduct activity, they are artificial legal constructs and thus have no physical presence in the same way as individuals. Standard definitions of corporate domicile speak both in terms of where corporations are incorporated and where they primarily conduct their business. Justice Ginsburg endorsed a related concept in *Goodyear* in connection with personal jurisdiction analysis: she suggests that general jurisdiction is present over a foreign corporation "when their affiliations with the State are so 'continuous and systematic' as to render them essentially at home in the forum State."

The problem below provides an opportunity to explore some the issues that arise as one tries to classify whether contacts amount to general or specific jurisdiction.

PROBLEM 1-1: HARRY'S, THE MOTORCYCLE DEALER, AND ARNOLD, THE ACTOR

Arnold Plaintiff (Arnold) is a movie actor with a distinctive tough guy image. He is a resident of Texas. Harry's Harleys, Inc. (Harry's) is a motorcycle dealer incorporated in New Mexico with its principal place of business there. Without Arnold's permission, Harry's used pictures of Arnold as part of its advertising campaign in a local New Mexico newspaper. The New Mexico newspaper has mostly local circulation, although a handful of Texas residents who live near the Texas/New Mexico border have it delivered to their homes. The Texas circulation amounts to about 1 percent of the total circulation of the newspaper, but is known to the newspaper and listed in the circulation statistics passed on to potential advertisers such as Harry's.

Harry's does business almost exclusively in New Mexico and the motorcycles it sells are made in neither New Mexico nor Texas. Harry's occasionally purchases motorcycles that are handled (through the stream of commerce) by Texas suppliers, although it has never bought a motorcycle directly from a Texas supplier. The only other contacts that Harry's has with Texas are the following: (1) Harry's has form sales contracts with suppliers, which the suppliers drafted, and included in the contracts is a choice of law provision specifying that Texas law governs the contract; (2) Harry's regularly retains the service of a Texas-based direct mail marketing company; and (3) Harry's has hired a sales training company that is incorporated in Texas.

Arnold has filed suit against Harry's for unauthorized appropriation of his visage. Arnold's complaint states that he is harmed by Harry's use of his image in the advertisement, which diminishes his reputation and subjects him to potential overexposure of his image. He explains that he has in the past taken pains to protect his image from "over-saturation." Arnold has filed suit in a Texas court against Harry's and Harry's has moved to dismiss the suit for lack of personal jurisdiction.

The Texas court is seeking to determine whether it can exercise general or specific jurisdiction against Harry's. Is there general jurisdiction in Texas? Is there specific jurisdiction in Texas? If the Texas court does have specific jurisdiction, is the specific jurisdiction the result of a claim that "arises out of" contacts within Texas or that is "related to" contacts within Texas? Both? If the Texas court has specific jurisdiction, can it award damages just for the over-saturation that occurred in Texas or can it award for the over-saturation that occurred in New Mexico as well?

Helicopteros, Goodyear Dunlop, and other Supreme Court decisions do little to pin down precisely what quantity of contacts amounts to general jurisdiction. The Court suggested that merely purchasing products in the forum state is insufficient to establish general jurisdiction. Nonetheless, corporations may engage in a number of other economic activities in a forum state — such as opening branches, dealing with distributors, and advertising. We have only limited information about many of these additional activities the Supreme Court deems necessary to establish general jurisdiction — that is, what it means for a corporation to be "at home." Likewise, the Supreme Court has not detailed precisely what relationship is necessary between the contact and the underlying legal theories of a case to establish specific jurisdiction. That said, the Court has provided significant further guidance on these issues. Consider the following case.

C.   MINIMUM CONTACTS AND FAIRNESS FACTORS

Daimler AG v. Bauman
134 S. Ct. 746 (2014)

Justice GINSBURG delivered the opinion of the Court.

This case concerns the authority of a court in the United States to entertain a claim brought by foreign plaintiffs against a foreign defendant based on events occurring entirely outside the United States. . . . The question presented is whether the Due Process Clause of the Fourteenth Amendment precludes the District Court from exercising jurisdiction over Daimler in this case, given the absence of any California connection to the atrocities, perpetrators, or victims described in the complaint. Plaintiffs invoked the court's general or all-purpose jurisdiction. California, they urge, is a place where Daimler may be sued on any and all claims against it, wherever in the world the claims may arise. . . . Exercises of personal jurisdiction so exorbitant, we hold, are barred by due process constraints on the assertion of adjudicatory authority. . . . Instructed by [our decision in *Goodyear v. Brown*], we conclude Daimler is not "at home" in California, and cannot be sued there for injuries plaintiffs attribute to MB Argentina's conduct in Argentina.

       I

    In 2004, plaintiffs (respondents here) filed suit in the United States District Court for the Northern District of California, alleging that MB Argentina collaborated with Argentinian state security forces to kidnap, detain, torture, and kill plaintiffs and their relatives during the military dictatorship in place there from 1976 through 1983, a period known as Argentina's "Dirty War." Based on those allegations, plaintiffs asserted claims under the Alien Tort Statute and the Torture Victim Protection Act of, as well as claims for wrongful death and intentional infliction of emotional distress under the laws of California and Argentina . . . no part of MB Argentina's alleged collaboration with Argentinian authorities took place in California or anywhere else in the United States.

    Plaintiffs' operative complaint names only one corporate defendant: Daimler, the petitioner here. Plaintiffs seek to hold Daimler vicariously liable for MB Argentina's alleged malfeasance. Daimler is a German *Aktiengesellschaft* (public stock company) that manufactures Mercedes–Benz vehicles in Germany and has its headquarters in Stuttgart. At times relevant to this case, MB Argentina was a subsidiary wholly owned by Daimler's predecessor in interest.

    Daimler moved to dismiss the action for want of personal jurisdiction. Opposing the motion, plaintiffs submitted declarations and exhibits purporting to demonstrate the presence of Daimler itself in California. Alternatively, plaintiffs maintained that jurisdiction over Daimler could be founded on the California contacts of MBUSA, a distinct corporate entity that, according to plaintiffs, should be treated as Daimler's agent for jurisdictional purposes.

    MBUSA, an indirect subsidiary of Daimler, is a Delaware limited liability corporation. MBUSA serves as Daimler's exclusive importer and distributor in the United States, purchasing Mercedes–Benz automobiles from Daimler in Germany, then importing those vehicles, and ultimately distributing them to independent dealerships located throughout the Nation. Although MBUSA's principal place of business is in New Jersey, MBUSA has multiple California-based facilities, including a regional office in Costa Mesa, a Vehicle Preparation Center in Carson, and a Classic Center in Irvine. According to the record developed below, MBUSA is the largest supplier of luxury vehicles to the California market. In particular, over 10% of all sales of new vehicles in the United States take place in California, and MBUSA's California sales account for 2.4% of Daimler's worldwide sales.

    The relationship between Daimler and MBUSA is delineated in a General Distributor Agreement, which sets forth requirements for MBUSA's distribution of Mercedes–Benz vehicles in the United States. That agreement established MBUSA as an "independent contracto[r]" that "buy[s] and sell[s] [vehicles] . . . as an independent business for [its] own account." App. 179a. The agreement "does not make [MBUSA] . . . a general or special agent, partner, joint venturer or employee of DAIMLERCHRYSLER or any DaimlerChrysler

Group Company"; MBUSA "ha[s] no authority to make binding obligations for or act on behalf of DAIMLERCHRYSLER or any DaimlerChrysler Group Company."

[The district court granted Daimler's motion to dismiss, and the Ninth Circuit ultimately reversed the district court]. We granted certiorari to decide whether, consistent with the Due Process Clause of the Fourteenth Amendment, Daimler is amenable to suit in California courts for claims involving only foreign plaintiffs and conduct occurring entirely abroad. . . .

III

. . . "The canonical opinion in this area remains *International Shoe* [*Co. v. Washington*], in which we held that a State may authorize its courts to exercise personal jurisdiction over an out-of-state defendant if the defendant has 'certain minimum contacts with [the State] such that the maintenance of the suit does not offend "traditional notions of fair play and substantial justice."'" . . . As we have since explained, "[a] court may assert general jurisdiction over foreign (sister-state or foreign-country) corporations to hear any and all claims against them when their affiliations with the State are so 'continuous and systematic' as to render them essentially at home in the forum State." . . . Since *International Shoe*, "specific jurisdiction has become the centerpiece of modern jurisdiction theory, while general jurisdiction [has played] a reduced role." *Goodyear Dunlop Tires Operations, S.A. v. Brown.*

. . . [G]eneral and specific jurisdiction have followed markedly different trajectories post-*International Shoe*. Specific jurisdiction has [expanded jurisdiction], but we have declined to stretch general jurisdiction beyond limits traditionally recognized.

IV

. . .

A

In sustaining the exercise of general jurisdiction over Daimler, the Ninth Circuit relied on an agency theory, determining that MBUSA acted as Daimler's agent for jurisdictional purposes and then attributing MBUSA's California contacts to Daimler. The Ninth Circuit's agency analysis derived from Circuit precedent considering principally whether the subsidiary "performs services that are sufficiently important to the foreign corporation that if it did not have a representative to perform them, the corporation's own officials would undertake to perform substantially similar services."

[The Supreme Court observed that this Ninth Circuit's agency reasoning failed to recognize that an agent for one purpose is not necessarily an agent for all purposes.] A subsidiary, for example, might be its parent's agent for claims arising in the place where the subsidiary operates, yet not its agent regarding claims arising elsewhere. . . .

The Ninth Circuit's agency finding rested primarily on its observation that MBUSA's services were "important" to Daimler, as gauged by Daimler's hypothetical readiness to perform those services itself if MBUSA did not exist. Formulated this way, the inquiry into importance stacks the deck, for it will always yield a pro-jurisdiction answer: "Anything a corporation does through an independent contractor, subsidiary, or distributor is presumably something that the corporation would do 'by other means' if the independent contractor, subsidiary, or distributor did not exist." The Ninth Circuit's agency theory thus appears to subject foreign corporations to general jurisdiction whenever they have an in-state subsidiary or affiliate, an outcome that would sweep beyond even the "sprawling view of general jurisdiction" we rejected in *Goodyear*.

B

Even if we were to assume that MBUSA is at home in California, and further to assume MBUSA's contacts are imputable to Daimler, there would still be no basis to subject Daimler to general jurisdiction in California, for Daimler's slim contacts with the State hardly render it at home there.

Goodyear made clear that only a limited set of affiliations with a forum will render a defendant amenable to all-purpose jurisdiction there. "For an individual, the paradigm forum for the exercise of general jurisdiction is the individual's domicile; for a corporation, it is an equivalent place, one in which the corporation is fairly regarded as at home." With respect to a corporation, the place of incorporation and principal place of business are "paradig[m] . . . bases for general jurisdiction." Those affiliations have the virtue of being unique — that is, each ordinarily indicates only one place — as well as easily ascertainable. These bases afford plaintiffs recourse to at least one clear and certain forum in which a corporate defendant may be sued on any and all claims.

Goodyear did not hold that a corporation may be subject to general jurisdiction *only* in a forum where it is incorporated or has its principal place of business; it simply typed those places paradigm all-purpose forums. Plaintiffs would have us look beyond the exemplar bases *Goodyear* identified, and approve the exercise of general jurisdiction in every State in which a corporation "engages in a substantial, continuous, and systematic course of business." That formulation, we hold, is unacceptably grasping. . . . [T]he inquiry under *Goodyear* is not whether a foreign corporation's in-forum contacts can be said to be in some sense "continuous and systematic," it is whether that corporation's "affiliations with the State are so 'continuous and systematic' as to render [it] essentially at home in the forum State."[19]

Here, neither Daimler nor MBUSA is incorporated in California, nor does either entity have its principal place of business there. If Daimler's California activities sufficed to allow adjudication of this Argentina-rooted case in California,

19. We do not foreclose the possibility that in an exceptional case, a corporation's operations in a forum other than its formal place of incorporation or principal place of business may be so substantial and of such a nature as to render the corporation at home in that State. But this case presents no occasion to explore that question, because Daimler's activities in California plainly do not approach that level.

the same global reach would presumably be available in every other State in which MBUSA's sales are sizable. Such exorbitant exercises of all-purpose jurisdiction would scarcely permit out-of-state defendants "to structure their primary conduct with some minimum assurance as to where that conduct will and will not render them liable to suit."

It was therefore error for the Ninth Circuit to conclude that Daimler, even with MBUSA's contacts attributed to it, was at home in California, and hence subject to suit there on claims by foreign plaintiffs having nothing to do with anything that occurred or had its principal impact in California.

. . . The Ninth Circuit, moreover, paid little heed to the risks to international comity its expansive view of general jurisdiction posed. Other nations do not share the uninhibited approach to personal jurisdiction advanced by the Court of Appeals in this case. In the European Union, for example, a corporation may generally be sued in the nation in which it is "domiciled," a term defined to refer only to the location of the corporation's "statutory seat," "central administration," or "principal place of business." The Solicitor General informs us, in this regard, that "foreign governments' objections to some domestic courts' expansive views of general jurisdiction have in the past impeded negotiations of international agreements on the reciprocal recognition and enforcement of judgments." Considerations of international rapport thus reinforce our determination that subjecting Daimler to the general jurisdiction of courts in California would not accord with the "fair play and substantial justice" due process demands.

* * *

For the reasons stated, the judgment of the United States Court of Appeals for the Ninth Circuit is *reversed*.

Notes on
DAIMLER

1. *Goodyear* and *Daimler* discussed when corporations are "at home" for the purpose of general jurisdiction. These opinions provide no guidance, however, on where unincorporated entities such as limited liability companies and partnerships should be deemed at home. Should the same rules apply for corporations as apply for unincorporated entities? This is not the case for subject matter jurisdiction based on diversity of citizenship. In the diversity of citizenship context, the rules differ according to what kind of business entity is a party to case.

2. In footnote 20 of its *Daimler* opinion, the majority referred to a checklist of several fairness factors that the U.S. Supreme Court has identified for assessing whether the exercise of jurisdiction comports with principles of reasonableness and citizen fairness. In the *Daimler* footnote, the Court stated that "[i]mposing such a checklist in cases of general jurisdiction would hardly promote the efficient disposition of an issue that should be resolved

expeditiously at the outset of litigation." The checklist to which the majority referred is discussed in detail below in connection with *Asahi Metal Industry Co. v. Superior Court of California*, 480 U.S. 102 (1987). *Asahi* was a specific (not a general) jurisdiction case. As you read *Asahi* and other specific jurisdiction cases, consider whether the Supreme Court is poised to disavow the fairness factor checklist for specific jurisdiction cases as well as general jurisdiction cases. Although the *Daimler* Court did not explicitly limit its criticism of the fairness checklist to general jurisdiction for corporations, one wonders whether it intended to disavow the checklist for general jurisdiction cases pertaining to natural persons.

As the U.S. Supreme Court tightens the rules on one legal theory, one observes litigants pursuing other legal theories that may equally support their goals. With the restrictions on corporate general jurisdiction emerging from *Daimler* and *Goodyear*, litigants looked to specific jurisdiction as a theory to justify a forum court's power over a corporate defendant. The next case, however, quickly dashed hopes that specific jurisdiction could provide a way around the squeeze on general jurisdiction.

Bristol-Myers Squibb Co. v. Superior Court of California

137 S. Ct. 1773 (2017)

Justice ALITO delivered the opinion of the Court.

More than 600 plaintiffs, most of whom are not California residents, filed this civil action in a California state court against Bristol-Myers Squibb Company (BMS), asserting a variety of state-law claims based on injuries allegedly caused by a BMS drug called Plavix. The California Supreme Court held that the California courts have specific jurisdiction to entertain the nonresidents' claims. We now reverse.

I

A

BMS, a large pharmaceutical company, is incorporated in Delaware and headquartered in New York, and it maintains substantial operations in both New York and New Jersey. Over 50 percent of BMS's work force in the United States is employed in those two States.

BMS also engages in business activities in other jurisdictions, including California. Five of the company's research and laboratory facilities, which employ a total of around 160 employees, are located there. BMS also employs about 250 sales representatives in California and maintains a small state-government advocacy office in Sacramento.

One of the pharmaceuticals that BMS manufactures and sells is Plavix, a prescription drug that thins the blood and inhibits blood clotting. BMS did not develop Plavix in California, did not create a marketing strategy for Plavix in California, and did not manufacture, label, package, or work on the regulatory approval of the product in California. BMS instead engaged in all of these activities in either New York or New Jersey. But BMS does sell Plavix in California. Between 2006 and 2012, it sold almost 187 million Plavix pills in the State and took in more than $900 million from those sales. This amounts to a little over one percent of the company's nationwide sales revenue.

B

A group of plaintiffs — consisting of 86 California residents and 592 residents from 33 other States — filed eight separate complaints in California Superior Court, alleging that Plavix had damaged their health. All the complaints asserted 13 claims under California law, including products liability, negligent misrepresentation, and misleading advertising claims. The nonresident plaintiffs did not allege that they obtained Plavix through California physicians or from any other California source; nor did they claim that they were injured by Plavix or were treated for their injuries in California.

[In proceedings below, the California Supreme Court held that under *Daimler v. Bauman*, general jurisdiction was clearly lacking, but that the California courts had specific jurisdiction over the nonresidents' claims against BMS. The majority of the California Supreme Court] applied a "sliding scale approach to specific jurisdiction." Under this approach, "the more wide ranging the defendant's forum contacts, the more readily is shown a connection between the forum contacts and the claim." Applying this test, the majority concluded that "BMS's extensive contacts with California" permitted the exercise of specific jurisdiction "based on a less direct connection between BMS's forum activities and plaintiffs' claims than might otherwise be required." This attenuated requirement was met, the majority found, because the claims of the nonresidents were similar in several ways to the claims of the California residents (as to which specific jurisdiction was uncontested). The court noted that "[b]oth the resident and nonresident plaintiffs' claims are based on the same allegedly defective product and the assertedly misleading marketing and promotion of that product." And while acknowledging that "there is no claim that Plavix itself was designed and developed in [BMS's California research facilities]," the court thought it significant that other research was done in the State.

We granted certiorari to decide whether the California courts' exercise of jurisdiction in this case violates the Due Process Clause of the Fourteenth Amendment.

II

B

In determining whether personal jurisdiction is present, a court must consider a variety of interests. These include "the interests of the forum State and of the plaintiff in proceeding with the cause in the plaintiff's forum of choice." But the "primary concern" is "the burden on the defendant." Assessing this burden obviously requires a court to consider the practical problems resulting from litigating in the forum, but it also encompasses the more abstract matter of submitting to the coercive power of a State that may have little legitimate interest in the claims in question. As we have put it, restrictions on personal jurisdiction "are more than a guarantee of immunity from inconvenient or distant litigation. They are a consequence of territorial limitations on the power of the respective States." "[T]he States retain many essential attributes of sovereignty, including, in particular, the sovereign power to try causes in their courts. The sovereignty of each State . . . implie[s] a limitation on the sovereignty of all its sister States." And at times, this federalism interest may be decisive. As we [have] explained, "[e]ven if the defendant would suffer minimal or no inconvenience from being forced to litigate before the tribunals of another State; even if the forum State has a strong interest in applying its law to the controversy; even if the forum State is the most convenient location for litigation, the Due Process Clause, acting as an instrument of interstate federalism, may sometimes act to divest the State of its power to render a valid judgment."

III

A

Our settled principles regarding specific jurisdiction control this case. In order for a court to exercise specific jurisdiction over a claim, there must be an "affiliation between the forum and the underlying controversy, principally, [an] activity or an occurrence that takes place in the forum State." When there is no such connection, specific jurisdiction is lacking regardless of the extent of a defendant's unconnected activities in the State.

For this reason, the California Supreme Court's "sliding scale approach" is difficult to square with our precedents. Under the California approach, the strength of the requisite connection between the forum and the specific claims at issue is relaxed if the defendant has extensive forum contacts that are unrelated to those claims. Our cases provide no support for this approach, which resembles a loose and spurious form of general jurisdiction. For specific jurisdiction, a defendant's general connections with the forum are not enough. As we have said, "[a] corporation's 'continuous activity of some sorts within a state . . . is not enough to support the demand that the corporation be amenable to suits unrelated to that activity.'"

The present case illustrates the danger of the California approach. The State Supreme Court found that specific jurisdiction was present without identifying any adequate link between the State and the nonresidents' claims. As noted, the nonresidents were not prescribed Plavix in California, did not purchase Plavix in California, did not ingest Plavix in California, and were not injured by Plavix in California. The mere fact that *other* plaintiffs were prescribed, obtained, and ingested Plavix in California — and allegedly sustained the same injuries as did the nonresidents — does not allow the State to assert specific jurisdiction over the nonresidents' claims. As we have explained, "a defendant's relationship with a . . . third party, standing alone, is an insufficient basis for jurisdiction." . . . What is needed — and what is missing here — is a connection between the forum and the specific claims at issue.

In today's case, the connection between the nonresidents' claims and the forum is [weak]. The relevant plaintiffs are not California residents and do not claim to have suffered harm in that State. In addition . . . all the conduct giving rise to the nonresidents' claims occurred elsewhere. It follows that the California courts cannot claim specific jurisdiction.

B

The nonresidents maintain that two of our cases support the decision below, but they misinterpret those precedents.

In *Keeton v. Hustler Magazine, Inc.*, 465 U.S. 770 (1984), a New York resident sued Hustler in New Hampshire, claiming that she had been libeled in five issues of the magazine, which was distributed throughout the country, including in New Hampshire, where it sold 10,000 to 15,000 copies per month. Concluding that specific jurisdiction was present, we relied principally on the connection between the circulation of the magazine in New Hampshire and damage allegedly caused within the State. We noted that "[f]alse statements of fact harm both the subject of the falsehood and the readers of the statement." This factor amply distinguishes *Keeton* from the present case, for here the nonresidents' claims involve no harm in California and no harm to California residents.

The nonresident plaintiffs in this case point to our holding in *Keeton* that there was jurisdiction in New Hampshire to entertain the plaintiff's request for damages suffered outside the State, but that holding concerned jurisdiction to determine *the scope of a claim* involving in-state injury and injury to residents of the State, not, as in this case, jurisdiction to entertain claims involving no in-state injury and no injury to residents of the forum State. *Keeton* held that there was jurisdiction in New Hampshire to consider the full measure of the plaintiff's claim, but whether she could actually recover out-of-state damages was a merits question governed by New Hampshire libel law.

The Court's decision in *Phillips Petroleum Co. v. Shutts*, 472 U.S. 797 (1985), which involved a class action filed in Kansas, is even less relevant. The Kansas court exercised personal jurisdiction over the claims of nonresident class members, and the defendant, Phillips Petroleum, argued that this violated the due process rights of these class members because they lacked minimum contacts with the State.[2] According to the defendant, the out-of-state class members should not have been

2. The Court held that the defendant had standing to argue that the Kansas court had improperly exercised personal jurisdiction over the claims of the out-of-state class members because that holding materially affected the defendant's own interests, specifically, the res judicata effect of an adverse judgment. 472 U.S., at 803-806, 105 S. Ct. 2965.

kept in the case unless they affirmatively opted in, instead of merely failing to opt out after receiving notice.

Holding that there had been no due process violation, the Court explained that the authority of a State to entertain the claims of nonresident class members is entirely different from its authority to exercise jurisdiction over an out-of-state defendant. Since *Shutts* concerned the due process rights of *plaintiffs*, it has no bearing on the question presented here. . . .

IV

Our straightforward application in this case of settled principles of personal jurisdiction will not result in the parade of horribles that respondents conjure up. Our decision does not prevent the California and out-of-state plaintiffs from joining together in a consolidated action in the States that have general jurisdiction over BMS. BMS concedes that such suits could be brought in either New York or Delaware. Alternatively, the plaintiffs who are residents of a particular State — for example, the 92 plaintiffs from Texas and the 71 from Ohio — could probably sue together in their home States.

* * *

The judgment of the California Supreme Court is reversed, and the case is remanded for further proceedings not inconsistent with this opinion.

Justice SOTOMAYOR, dissenting.

. . . The majority's rule will make it difficult to aggregate the claims of plaintiffs across the country whose claims may be worth little alone. It will make it impossible to bring a nationwide mass action in state court against defendants who are "at home" in different States. And it will result in piecemeal litigation and the bifurcation of claims. None of this is necessary. A core concern in this Court's personal jurisdiction cases is fairness. And there is nothing unfair about subjecting a massive corporation to suit in a State for a nationwide course of conduct that injures both forum residents and nonresidents alike.

. . . [O]ur decision in *Keeton v. Hustler Magazine, Inc.*, suggests that there should be no such barrier to the exercise of jurisdiction here. In *Keeton*, a New York resident brought suit against an Ohio corporation, a magazine, in New Hampshire for libel. She alleged that the magazine's nationwide course of conduct — its publication of defamatory statements — had injured her in every State, including New Hampshire. This Court unanimously rejected the defendant's argument that it should not be subject to "nationwide damages" when only a small portion of those damages arose in the forum State; exposure to such liability, the Court explained, was the consequence of having "continuously and deliberately exploited the New Hampshire market," The majority today dismisses *Keeton* on the ground that the defendant there faced one plaintiff's claim arising out of its nationwide course of conduct, whereas Bristol-Myers faces many more plaintiffs' claims. But this is a distinction without a difference: In either case, a defendant will face liability in a single State for a single course of conduct that has impact in many States. *Keeton* informs us that there is no unfairness in such a result.

B

I fear the consequences of the majority's decision today will be substantial.
Even absent a rigid requirement that a defendant's in-state conduct must actually
cause a plaintiff's claim, the upshot of today's opinion is that plaintiffs cannot join
their claims together and sue a defendant in a State in which only some of them
have been injured. That rule is likely to have consequences far beyond this case.

First, and most prominently, the Court's opinion in this case will make it
profoundly difficult for plaintiffs who are injured in different States by a defendant's nationwide course of conduct to sue that defendant in a single, consolidated action. The holding of today's opinion is that such an action cannot be
brought in a State in which only some plaintiffs were injured. Not to worry,
says the majority: The plaintiffs here could have sued Bristol-Myers in
New York or Delaware; could "probably" have subdivided their separate claims
into 34 lawsuits in the States in which they were injured; and might have been able
to bring a single suit in federal court (an "open . . . question"). . . . The effect of
the Court's opinion today is to eliminate nationwide mass actions in any State
other than those in which a defendant is "'essentially at home.'" Such a rule
hands one more tool to corporate defendants determined to prevent the aggregation of individual claims, and forces injured plaintiffs to bear the burden of
bringing suit in what will often be far flung jurisdictions.

Second, the Court's opinion today may make it impossible to bring certain
mass actions at all. After this case, it is difficult to imagine where it might be possible to bring a nationwide mass action against two or more defendants headquartered and incorporated in different States. There will be no State where both
defendants are "at home," and so no State in which the suit can proceed.
What about a nationwide mass action brought against a defendant not headquartered or incorporated in the United States? Such a defendant is not "at home" in
any State. Especially in a world in which defendants are subject to general jurisdiction in only a handful of States, the effect of today's opinion will be to curtail —
and in some cases eliminate — plaintiffs' ability to hold corporations fully
accountable for their nationwide conduct.

Notes on
BRISTOL-MYERS

1. Does *Bristol-Myers* leave any possibility for jurisdiction in the forum
state to remedy a defendant's misconduct outside the forum that is identical
to misconduct that has occurred in the forum?

2. Is Justice Sotomayor correct that *Keeton v. Hustler Magazine* provided a
basis for jurisdiction based on harm that occurred in the forum as well as
throughout the nation? Are you persuaded by the majority's argument that,
in *Keeton,* the forum court's adjudication of whether the plaintiff could

recover for damages occurring outside the forum was simply a matter governed by substantive state law, rather than personal jurisdiction rules?

3. Justice Sotomayor's dissent suggests that *Bristol-Myers* could create significant problems for nationwide or multistate class actions filed in jurisdictions where the defendant is not "at home." Presumably, the decision also casts doubt on personal jurisdiction in suits when the named plaintiff is not a resident of the state where the suit is brought. Is it possible, however, that *Bristol-Myers* might also create problems for defendants who face multiple named plaintiffs who are now forced to bring multiple suits in many states? Might *Bristol-Myers* also negatively affect litigation efficiency because the decision complicates the process of settling national class actions?

4. What should one make of the reduced role of fairness concerns in *Bristol-Myers*? The *Bristol-Myers* Court spoke of the importance of personal jurisdiction's burden on the defendant, but placed little or no weight on any other fairness factors that are emphasized in early decisions, such as the plaintiff's interest in obtaining relief, the forum state's interest in the suit, and the interest of the several states in efficiently enforcing shared policies. The fairness factors are discussed in detail below in connection with *Asahi Metal Industry Co. v. Superior Court of California*. Should we assume that these fairness factors are no longer part of the personal jurisdiction analysis? Is the true motivation behind the majority's decision the Court's attempt to reinforce a version of federalism in which each state retains as much individual sovereignty as possible?

In mapping personal jurisdiction doctrine, the United States Supreme Court has provided substantially more guidance than just the distinction between specific and general jurisdiction. Historically, the Court has shown significant interest in the constitutional underpinnings of personal jurisdiction doctrine, making clear that the *International Shoe* test consists of two parts: evaluation of contacts and evaluation of fairness. Moreover, the Court announced that in assessing adequacy of contacts in the context of specific jurisdiction, courts must find that the defendant purposely availed herself of the benefits of a state's laws and that it was foreseeable that the defendant could be sued in the forum.

The United States Supreme Court first announced major refinements of these concepts in the context of an automobile accident case, *World-Wide Volkswagen v. Woodson*, 444 U.S. 286 (1980). In *World-Wide Volkswagen*, the Court made clear that *International Shoe*'s emphasis on contacts had two purposes: protecting defendants from litigation in an unfairly burdensome locality and ensuring that states do not overreach their power and invade the prerogatives of other states. The Court explained that analysis of contacts protects against a state usurping another's power. As for the fairness to the defendant, the Court listed five factors:

(1) the burden on the defendant from litigating in the forum;

(2)   the forum state's interest in adjudicating the suit;
(3)   the plaintiff's interest in obtaining convenient and effective relief;
(4)   the interest of the interstate judicial system in obtaining the most efficient resolution of controversies; and
(5)   "the shared interest of the several states in furthering fundamental substantive social policies."

Following *World-Wide Volkswagen*, the Supreme Court decided two defamation cases that provided a vehicle for explaining both the fairness factors and the contacts requirements. In one case, *Keeton v. Hustler Magazine*, 465 U.S. 770 (1984), the plaintiff sued a magazine publisher in New Hampshire because that state had the only statute of limitations that was long enough to allow the case to proceed. The Court upheld personal jurisdiction in New Hampshire, not only allowing the action to proceed on the basis of injury incurred in New Hampshire, but for injury occurring elsewhere as well. Providing reasoning that sheds light on the fifth fairness factor from *World-Wide Volkswagen*, the Court explained that New Hampshire had a "substantial interest in cooperating with other States . . . to provide a forum for efficiently litigating all issues and damages claims arising out of a libel in a unitary proceeding." This language was ignored and *Keeton* was distinguished in the *Bristol-Myers Squibb* case.

The second defamation case was similarly favorable to a forum's exercise of personal jurisdiction. In *Calder v. Jones*, 465 U.S. 783 (1984), the Court evaluated whether courts in California had jurisdiction over the writer and editor of a *National Enquirer* story about actress Shirley Jones. Although the writer and editor worked only in Florida, the Supreme Court held that they had "aimed" their work at California where Jones lived and would suffer greatest harm. In other words, the defendants had a significant contact with California not because they had done something when they personally went there, but because they intentionally caused an effect there. As shown later in this chapter, *Calder*'s recognition that jurisdiction can arise from effects within a jurisdiction has proven important to courts trying to evaluate personal jurisdiction questions where forum effects result from an out-of-state defendant's internet activity.

The next significant case in this line was *Burger King Corp. v. Rudzewicz*, 471 U.S. 462 (1985), in which the Court shed light on the meaning of the fairness factors. As for the burden on the defendant, the *Burger King* Court explained that mere inconvenience was not enough. Instead, litigation in the forum must be "'so gravely difficult and inconvenient' that a party unfairly is at a 'severe disadvantage' in comparison to his opponent." Moreover, the Court stated, "Absent compelling considerations, a defendant who has purposely derived commercial benefit from his affiliation in a forum may not defeat jurisdiction there simply because of his adversary's greater net wealth." *Burger King* is significant for these explanations of concern with defendant's fairness, its emphasis on the defendant's purposeful activities directed toward the forum, and its application of the two-pronged contacts/fairness approach in the context of a contract case. The next case, however, provided even more explanation of the fairness factors.

Asahi Metal Industry Co. v. Superior Court of California
480 U.S. 102 (1987)

O'CONNOR, J., announced the judgment of the Court and delivered the opinion for a unanimous Court with respect to Part I, the opinion of the Court with respect to Part II-B, in which REHNQUIST, C.J., and BRENNAN, WHITE, MARSHALL, BLACKMUN, POWELL, and STEVENS, JJ., joined, and an opinion with respect to Parts II-A and III, in which REHNQUIST, C.J., and POWELL and SCALIA, JJ., joined. BRENNAN, J., filed an opinion concurring in part and concurring in the judgment, in which WHITE, MARSHALL, and BLACKMUN, JJ., joined. STEVENS, J., filed an opinion concurring in part and concurring in the judgment, in which WHITE and BLACKMUN, JJ., joined.

This case presents the question whether the mere awareness on the part of a foreign defendant that the components it manufactured, sold, and delivered outside the United States would reach the forum State in the stream of commerce constitutes "minimum contacts" between the defendant and the forum State such that the exercise of jurisdiction "does not offend 'traditional notions of fair play and substantial justice.'"

On September 23, 1978, . . . in . . . California, Gary Zurcher lost control of his Honda motorcycle and collided with a tractor. Zurcher was severely injured, and his passenger and wife, Ruth Ann Moreno, was killed. In September 1979, Zurcher filed a product liability action in the Superior Court of the State of California. . . . Zurcher alleged that the 1978 accident was caused by a sudden loss of air and an explosion in the rear tire of the motorcycle, and alleged that the motorcycle tire, tube, and sealant were defective. Zurcher's complaint named, *inter alia*, Cheng Shin Rubber Industrial Co., Ltd. (Cheng Shin), the Taiwanese manufacturer of the tube. Cheng Shin in turn filed a cross-complaint seeking indemnification from its codefendants and from petitioner, Asahi Metal Industry Co., Ltd. (Asahi), the manufacturer of the tube's valve assembly. Zurcher's claims against Cheng Shin and the other defendants were eventually settled and dismissed, leaving only Cheng Shin's indemnity action against Asahi.

. . . Asahi moved to quash Cheng Shin's service of summons, arguing the State could not exert jurisdiction over it consistent with the Due Process Clause of the Fourteenth Amendment.

In relation to the motion, the following information was submitted by Asahi and Cheng Shin. Asahi is a Japanese corporation. It manufactures tire valve assemblies in Japan and sells the assemblies to Cheng Shin, and to several other tire manufacturers, for use as components in finished tire tubes. Asahi's sales to Cheng Shin took place in Taiwan. The shipments from Asahi to Cheng Shin were sent from Japan to Taiwan. Cheng Shin bought and incorporated into its tire tubes 150,000 Asahi valve assemblies in 1978; 500,000 in 1979; 500,000 in 1980; 100,000 in 1981; and 100,000 in 1982. Sales to Cheng Shin accounted for 1.24 percent of Asahi's income in 1981 and 0.44 percent in 1982. Cheng Shin alleged that approximately 20 percent of its sales in the United States are in California. Cheng Shin purchases valve assemblies from other suppliers as well, and sells finished tubes throughout the world. . . .

An affidavit of a manager of Cheng Shin whose duties included the purchasing of component parts stated: "'In discussions with Asahi regarding the purchase of valve stem assemblies the fact that my Company sells tubes throughout the world and specifically the United States has been discussed. I am informed and believe that Asahi was fully aware that valve stem assemblies sold to my Company and to others would end up throughout the United States and in California.'" An affidavit of the president of Asahi, on the other hand, declared that Asahi "'has never contemplated that its limited sales of tire valves to Cheng Shin in Taiwan would subject it to lawsuits in California.'"

. . . [T]he Superior Court denied the motion to quash summons, stating: "Asahi obviously does business on an international scale. It is not unreasonable that they defend claims of defect in their product on an international scale." [The California Supreme Court agreed with this ruling.]

We . . . now reverse.

II

A

. . . Applying the principle that minimum contacts must be based on an act of the defendant, the Court in *World-Wide Volkswagen Corp. v. Woodson*, 444 U.S. 286 (1980), rejected the assertion that a *consumer's* unilateral act of bringing the defendant's product into the forum State was a sufficient constitutional basis for personal jurisdiction over the defendant. . . . The Court disclaimed . . . the idea that "foreseeability is wholly irrelevant" to personal jurisdiction, concluding that "[t]he forum State does not exceed its powers under the Due Process Clause if it asserts personal jurisdiction over a corporation that delivers its products into the stream of commerce with the expectation that they will be purchased by consumers in the forum State." . . .

In the present case . . . the State Court of Appeal did not read the Due Process Clause, as interpreted by *World-Wide Volkswagen*, to allow "mere foreseeability that the product will enter the forum state [to] be enough by itself to establish jurisdiction over the distributor and retailer." . . . We now find this . . . position to be consonant with the requirements of due process. The "substantial connection," between the defendant and the forum State necessary for a finding of minimum contacts must come about by *an action of the defendant purposefully directed toward the forum State*. The placement of a product into the stream of commerce, without more, is not an act of the defendant purposefully directed toward the forum State. Additional conduct of the defendant may indicate an intent or purpose to serve the market in the forum State, for example, designing the product for the market in the forum State, advertising in the forum State, establishing channels for providing regular advice to customers in the forum State, or marketing the product through a distributor who has agreed to serve as the sales agent in the forum State. But a defendant's awareness that the stream of commerce may or will sweep the product into the forum State does not convert the mere act of placing the product into the stream into an act purposefully directed toward the forum State.

Assuming, *arguendo*, that respondents have established Asahi's awareness that some of the valves sold to Cheng Shin would be incorporated into tire tubes sold in California, respondents have not demonstrated any action by Asahi to purposefully avail itself of the California market. Asahi does not do business in California. It has no office, agents, employees, or property in California. It does not advertise or otherwise solicit business in California. It did not create, control, or employ the distribution system that brought its valves to California. There is no evidence that Asahi designed its product in anticipation of sales in California. On the basis of these facts, the exertion of personal jurisdiction over Asahi by the Superior Court of California[*] exceeds the limits of due process.

B

We have previously explained that the determination of the reasonableness of the exercise of jurisdiction in each case will depend on an evaluation of several factors. A court must consider the burden on the defendant, the interests of the forum State, and the plaintiff's interest in obtaining relief. It must also weigh in its determination "the interstate judicial system's interest in obtaining the most efficient resolution of controversies; and the shared interest of the several States in furthering fundamental substantive social policies." *World-Wide Volkswagen*, 444 U.S., at 292, 100 S. Ct., at 564 (citations omitted).

A consideration of these factors in the present case clearly reveals the unreasonableness of the assertion of jurisdiction over Asahi, even apart from the question of the placement of goods in the stream of commerce.

Certainly the burden on the defendant in this case is severe. Asahi has been commanded by the Supreme Court of California not only to traverse the distance between Asahi's headquarters in Japan and the Superior Court of California in and for the County of Solano, but also to submit its dispute with Cheng Shin to a foreign nation's judicial system. The unique burdens placed upon one who must defend oneself in a foreign legal system should have significant weight in assessing the reasonableness of stretching the long arm of personal jurisdiction over national borders.

When minimum contacts have been established, often the interests of the plaintiff and the forum in the exercise of jurisdiction will justify even the serious burdens placed on the alien defendant. In the present case, however, the interests of the plaintiff and the forum in California's assertion of jurisdiction over Asahi are slight. All that remains is a claim for indemnification asserted by Cheng Shin, a Taiwanese corporation, against Asahi. The transaction on which the indemnification claim is based took place in Taiwan; Asahi's components were shipped from Japan to Taiwan. Cheng Shin has not demonstrated that it is more convenient for it to litigate its indemnification claim against Asahi in California rather than in Taiwan or Japan.

---

* We have no occasion here to determine whether Congress could, consistent with the Due Process Clause of the Fifth Amendment, authorize federal court personal jurisdiction over alien defendants based on the aggregate of national contacts, rather than on the contacts between the defendant and the State in which the federal court sits.

Because the plaintiff is not a California resident, California's legitimate interests in the dispute have considerably diminished. The Supreme Court of California argued that the State had an interest in "protecting its consumers by ensuring that foreign manufacturers comply with the state's safety standards." The State's definition of California's interest, however, was overly broad. The dispute between Cheng Shin and Asahi is primarily about indemnification rather than safety standards. Moreover, it is not at all clear at this point that California law should govern the question whether a Japanese corporation should indemnify a Taiwanese corporation on the basis of a sale made in Taiwan and a shipment of goods from Japan to Taiwan. The possibility of being haled into a California court as a result of an accident involving Asahi's components undoubtedly creates an additional deterrent to the manufacture of unsafe components; however, similar pressures will be placed on Asahi by the purchasers of its components as long as those who use Asahi components in their final products, and sell those products in California, are subject to the application of California tort law.

World-Wide Volkswagen also admonished courts to take into consideration the interests of the "several States," in addition to the forum State, in the efficient judicial resolution of the dispute and the advancement of substantive policies. In the present case, this advice calls for a court to consider the procedural and substantive policies of other *nations* whose interests are affected by the assertion of jurisdiction by the California court. The procedural and substantive interests of other nations in a state court's assertion of jurisdiction over an alien defendant will differ from case to case. In every case, however, those interests, as well as the Federal interest in Government's foreign relations policies, will be best served by a careful inquiry into the reasonableness of the assertion of jurisdiction in the particular case, and an unwillingness to find the serious burdens on an alien defendant outweighed by minimal interests on the part of the plaintiff or the forum State. "Great care and reserve should be exercised when extending our notions of personal jurisdiction into the international field."

III

Because the facts of this case do not establish minimum contacts such that the exercise of personal jurisdiction is consistent with fair play and substantial justice, the judgment of the Supreme Court of California is reversed, and the case is remanded for further proceedings not inconsistent with this opinion.

It is so ordered.

Justice BRENNAN, with whom Justice WHITE, Justice MARSHALL, and Justice BLACKMUN join, concurring in part and concurring in the judgment.

I do not agree with the interpretation in Part II-A of the stream-of-commerce theory, nor with the conclusion that Asahi did not "purposely avail itself of the California market." I do agree, however, with the Court's conclusion in Part II-B that the exercise of personal jurisdiction over Asahi in this case would not comport with "fair play and substantial justice." This is one of those rare cases in which "minimum requirements inherent in the concept of 'fair play and substantial justice' . . . defeat the reasonableness of jurisdiction even [though] the defendant has purposefully engaged in forum activities." I therefore join Parts I and II-B of the Court's opinion, and write separately to explain my disagreement with Part II-A.

Part II-A states that "a defendant's awareness that the stream of commerce may or will sweep the product into the forum State does not convert the mere act of placing the product into the stream into an act purposefully directed toward the forum State." Under this view, a plaintiff would be required to show "[a]dditional conduct" directed toward the forum before finding the exercise of jurisdiction over the defendant to be consistent with the Due Process Clause. I see no need for such a showing, however. The stream of commerce refers not to unpredictable currents or eddies, but to the regular and anticipated flow of products from manufacture to distribution to retail sale. As long as a participant in this process is aware that the final product is being marketed in the forum State, the possibility of a lawsuit there cannot come as a surprise. Nor will the litigation present a burden for which there is no corresponding benefit. A defendant who has placed goods in the stream of commerce benefits economically from the retail sale of the final product in the forum State, and indirectly benefits from the State's laws that regulate and facilitate commercial activity. These benefits accrue regardless of whether that participant directly conducts business in the forum State, or engages in additional conduct directed toward that State. Accordingly, most courts and commentators have found that jurisdiction premised on the placement of a product into the stream of commerce is consistent with the Due Process Clause, and have not required a showing of additional conduct.

. . . In this case, the facts found by the California Supreme Court support its finding of minimum contacts. The court found that "[a]lthough Asahi did not design or control the system of distribution that carried its valve assemblies into California, Asahi was aware of the distribution system's operation, and it knew that it would benefit economically from the sale in California of products incorporating its components." Accordingly, I cannot join the determination in Part II-A that Asahi's regular and extensive sales of component parts to a manufacturer it knew was making regular sales of the final product in California is insufficient to establish minimum contacts with California.

Justice STEVENS, with whom Justice WHITE and Justice BLACKMUN join, concurring in part and concurring in the judgment.

The judgment of the Supreme Court of California should be reversed for the reasons stated in Part II-B of the Court's opinion. While I join Parts I and II-B, I do not join Part II-A for two reasons. First, it is not necessary to the Court's decision. An examination of minimum contacts is not always necessary to determine whether a state court's assertion of personal jurisdiction is constitutional. Part II-B establishes, after considering the factors set forth in *World-Wide Volkswagen Corp. v. Woodson*, 444 U.S. 286, 292 (1980), that California's exercise of jurisdiction over Asahi in this case would be "unreasonable and unfair." This finding alone requires reversal; this case fits within the rule that "minimum requirements inherent in the concept of 'fair play and substantial justice' may defeat the reasonableness of jurisdiction even if the defendant has purposefully engaged in forum activities." Accordingly, I see no reason in this case for the plurality to articulate "purposeful direction" or any other test as the nexus between an act of a defendant and the forum State that is necessary to establish minimum contacts.

Second, even assuming that the test ought to be formulated here, Part II-A misapplies it to the facts of this case. The plurality seems to assume that an unwavering line can be drawn between "mere awareness" that a component will find its way into the forum State and "purposeful availment" of the forum's market. Over the course of its dealings with Cheng Shin, Asahi has arguably engaged in a higher quantum of conduct than "[t]he placement of a product into the stream of commerce, without more. . . ." Whether or not this conduct rises to the level of purposeful availment requires a constitutional determination that is affected by the volume, the value, and the hazardous character of the components. In most circumstances I would be inclined to conclude that a regular course of dealing that results in deliveries of over 100,000 units annually over a period of several years would constitute "purposeful availment" even though the item delivered to the forum State was a standard product marketed throughout the world.

Notes on
ASAHI

1. The Supreme Court in *Asahi* was badly splintered. How might one decipher a "holding" from the various opinions?

- Contacts: No opinion in *Asahi* garnered a majority of the Justices' votes on the issue of minimum contacts. In order to ascertain guidance for future cases, can one identify a "common denominator" in the minimum contacts test that would satisfy five of the Justices? First, one could observe that all of the Justices in *Asahi* would likely agree that sufficient contacts would exist in a case that satisfied the contacts test in Justice O'Connor's opinion. This, however, is more a principle of inclusion: it identifies fact patterns that the Justices agree would indisputably present minimum contacts, but does not provide a consensus test for the "grey areas." Alternatively, one might articulate a test using both Justice Brennan's opinion and Justice Stevens's opinion. To establish minimum contacts, Justice Brennan would require only purposeful activity arising from a regular and anticipated flow of products into the forum state for commercial sale and Justice Stevens seemed satisfied with a regular course of dealing that resulted in substantial deliveries in the forum state over a period of years. Couldn't one combine these two standards with relative ease?
- Fairness: What is the relationship between the fairness prong of the inquiry and the minimum contacts prong? Every Justice except Justice Scalia joined Part II-B of Justice O'Connor's opinion. Is there

an inference that one can draw from his decision not to join the rest of the Court in discussing the fairness factors?

2. The two-pronged analysis focusing on minimum contacts and fairness is more complex and pervasive than the general/specific jurisdiction analysis. The Supreme Court has never been entirely clear about the proper relationship between the two types of analyses. Recent decisions in *Daimler AG v. Bauman* and *Bristol-Myers Squibb v. Superior Court* suggest that the fairness factor checklist has no role to play, particularly for a general jurisdiction case. In a footnote of the *Daimler* opinion, the Court stated that "[i]mposing such a checklist in cases of general jurisdiction would hardly promote the efficient disposition of an issue that should be resolved expeditiously at the outset of litigation." Although the *Daimler* Court did not explicitly limit its criticism of the checklist to general jurisdiction for corporations, one wonders whether it intended to disavow the checklist for general jurisdiction cases pertaining to natural persons.

After a two-decade long hiatus from deciding personal jurisdiction cases, the Supreme Court granted review in *J. McIntyre Machinery v. Nicastro*. Expectations were high that the Court would clarify the uncertainties left in the wake of *Asahi*. Evaluate whether the Court met these expectations.

J. McIntyre Machinery, Ltd. V. Nicastro
564 U.S. 873 (2011)

Justice KENNEDY announced the judgment of the Court and delivered an opinion, in which THE CHIEF JUSTICE, Justice SCALIA, and Justice THOMAS join. BREYER, J., filed an opinion concurring in the judgment, in which ALITO, J., joined. GINSBURG, J., filed a dissenting opinion, in which SOTOMAYOR and KAGAN, JJ., joined.

Whether a person or entity is subject to the jurisdiction of a state court despite not having been present in the State either at the time of suit or at the time of the alleged injury, and despite not having consented to the exercise of jurisdiction, is a question that arises with great frequency in the routine course of litigation. The rules and standards for determining when a State does or does not have jurisdiction over an absent party have been unclear because of decades-old questions left open in *Asahi Metal Industry Co. v. Superior Court of Cal., Solano Cty.*, 480 U.S. 102 (1987).

Here, the Supreme Court of New Jersey, relying in part on *Asahi*, held that New Jersey's courts can exercise jurisdiction over a foreign manufacturer of a product so long as the manufacturer "knows or reasonably should know that its products are distributed through a nationwide distribution system that might lead to those products being sold in any of the fifty states." *Nicastro v.*

McIntyre Machinery America, Ltd., 987 A.2d 575, 591, 592 (2010). Applying that test, the court concluded that a British manufacturer of scrap metal machines was subject to jurisdiction in New Jersey, even though at no time had it advertised in, sent goods to, or in any relevant sense targeted the State.

That decision cannot be sustained. Although the New Jersey Supreme Court issued an extensive opinion with careful attention to this Court's cases and to its own precedent, the "stream of commerce" metaphor carried the decision far afield. Due process protects the defendant's right not to be coerced except by lawful judicial power. As a general rule, the exercise of judicial power is not lawful unless the defendant "purposefully avails itself of the privilege of conducting activities within the forum State, thus invoking the benefits and protections of its laws." *Hanson v. Denckla*, 357 U.S. 235, 253 (1958). There may be exceptions, say, for instance, in cases involving an intentional tort. But the general rule is applicable in this products-liability case, and the so-called "stream-of-commerce" doctrine cannot displace it.

I

This case arises from a products-liability suit filed in New Jersey state court. Robert Nicastro seriously injured his hand while using a metal-shearing machine manufactured by J. McIntyre Machinery, Ltd. (J. McIntyre). The accident occurred in New Jersey, but the machine was manufactured in England, where J. McIntyre is incorporated and operates. The question here is whether the New Jersey courts have jurisdiction over J. McIntyre, notwithstanding the fact that the company at no time either marketed goods in the State or shipped them there. Nicastro was a plaintiff in the New Jersey trial court and is the respondent here; J. McIntyre was a defendant and is now the petitioner.

At oral argument in this Court, Nicastro's counsel stressed three [facts:]

First, an independent company agreed to sell J. McIntyre's machines in the United States. J. McIntyre itself did not sell its machines to buyers in this country beyond the U.S. distributor, and there is no allegation that the distributor was under J. McIntyre's control.

Second, J. McIntyre officials attended annual conventions for the scrap recycling industry to advertise J. McIntyre's machines alongside the distributor. The conventions took place in various States, but never in New Jersey.

Third, no more than four machines (the record suggests only one), including the machine that caused the injuries that are the basis for this suit, ended up in New Jersey.

In addition to these facts emphasized by petitioner, the New Jersey Supreme Court noted that J. McIntyre held both United States and European patents on its recycling technology. It also noted that the U.S. distributor "structured [its] advertising and sales efforts in accordance with" J. McIntyre's "direction and guidance whenever possible," and that "at least some of the machines were sold on consignment to" the distributor.

In light of these facts, the New Jersey Supreme Court concluded that New Jersey courts could exercise jurisdiction over petitioner without contravention of the Due Process Clause. Jurisdiction was proper, in that court's view, because the injury occurred in New Jersey; because petitioner knew or reasonably should have known "that its products are distributed through a nationwide distribution system that might lead to those products being sold in any of the fifty states"; and because petitioner failed to "take some reasonable step to prevent the distribution of its products in this State."

Both the New Jersey Supreme Court's holding and its account of what it called "[t]he stream-of-commerce doctrine of jurisdiction," were incorrect, however. This Court's *Asahi* decision may be responsible in part for that court's error regarding the stream of commerce, and this case presents an opportunity to provide greater clarity.

II . . .

The imprecision arising from *Asahi*, for the most part, results from its statement of the relation between jurisdiction and the "stream of commerce." The stream of commerce . . . refers to the movement of goods from manufacturers through distributors to consumers, yet beyond that descriptive purpose its meaning is far from exact. This Court has stated that a defendant's placing goods into the stream of commerce "with the expectation that they will be purchased by consumers within the forum State" may indicate purposeful availment. But that statement does not amend the general rule of personal jurisdiction. It merely observes that a defendant may in an appropriate case be subject to jurisdiction without entering the forum — itself an unexceptional proposition — as where manufacturers or distributors "seek to serve" a given State's market. The principal inquiry in cases of this sort is whether the defendant's activities manifest an intention to submit to the power of a sovereign. In other words, the defendant must "purposefully avai[l] itself of the privilege of conducting activities within the forum State, thus invoking the benefits and protections of its laws." Sometimes a defendant does so by sending its goods rather than its agents. The defendant's transmission of goods permits the exercise of jurisdiction only where the defendant can be said to have targeted the forum; as a general rule, it is not enough that the defendant might have predicted that its goods will reach the forum State.

In *Asahi*, an opinion by Justice Brennan for four Justices outlined a different approach. It discarded the central concept of sovereign authority in favor of considerations of fairness and foreseeability. As that concurrence contended, "jurisdiction premised on the placement of a product into the stream of commerce [without more] is consistent with the Due Process Clause," for "[a]s long as a participant in this process is aware that the final product is being marketed in the forum State, the possibility of a lawsuit there cannot come as a surprise." It was the premise of the concurring opinion that the defendant's ability to anticipate suit renders the assertion of jurisdiction fair. In this way, the opinion made foreseeability the touchstone of jurisdiction.

The standard set forth in Justice Brennan's concurrence was rejected in an opinion written by Justice O'Connor; but the relevant part of that opinion, too, commanded the assent of only four Justices, not a majority of the Court. That opinion stated: "The 'substantial connection' between the defendant and the forum State necessary for a finding of minimum contacts must come about by an action of the defendant purposefully directed toward the forum State. The placement of a product into the stream of commerce, without more, is not an act of the defendant purposefully directed toward the forum State."

Since *Asahi* was decided, the courts have sought to reconcile the competing opinions. But Justice Brennan's concurrence, advocating a rule based on general notions of fairness and foreseeability, is inconsistent with the premises of lawful judicial power. This Court's precedents make clear that it is the defendant's actions, not his expectations, that empower a State's courts to subject him to judgment.

. . . Because the United States is a distinct sovereign, a defendant may in principle be subject to the jurisdiction of the courts of the United States but not of any particular State. This is consistent with the premises and unique genius of our Constitution. . . . For jurisdiction, a litigant may have the requisite relationship with the United States Government but not with the government of any individual State. That would be an exceptional case, however. If the defendant is a domestic domiciliary, the courts of its home State are available and can exercise general jurisdiction. And if another State were to assert jurisdiction in an inappropriate case, it would upset the federal balance, which posits that each State has a sovereignty that is not subject to unlawful intrusion by other States. Furthermore, foreign corporations will often target or concentrate on particular States, subjecting them to specific jurisdiction in those forums.

. . .

III

In this case, petitioner directed marketing and sales efforts at the United States. It may be that, assuming it were otherwise empowered to legislate on the subject, the Congress could authorize the exercise of jurisdiction in appropriate courts. That circumstance is not presented in this case, however, and it is neither necessary nor appropriate to address here any constitutional concerns that might be attendant to that exercise of power. Nor is it necessary to determine what substantive law might apply were Congress to authorize jurisdiction in a federal court in New Jersey. A sovereign's legislative authority to regulate conduct may present considerations different from those presented by its authority to subject a defendant to judgment in its courts. Here the question concerns the authority of a New Jersey state court to exercise jurisdiction, so it is petitioner's purposeful contacts with New Jersey, not with the United States, that alone are relevant.

Respondent has not established that J. McIntyre engaged in conduct purposefully directed at New Jersey. Recall that respondent's claim of jurisdiction centers on three facts: The distributor agreed to sell J. McIntyre's machines in the United States; J. McIntyre officials attended trade shows in several States but not in New Jersey; and up to four machines ended up in New Jersey. The British manufacturer had no office in New Jersey; it neither paid taxes nor owned property there; and it neither advertised in, nor sent any employees to, the State. Indeed, after discovery the trial court found that the "defendant does not have a single contact with New Jersey short of the machine in question ending up in this state." These facts may reveal an intent to serve the U.S. market, but they do not show that J. McIntyre purposefully availed itself of the New Jersey market.

. . .

Due process protects petitioner's right to be subject only to lawful authority. At no time did petitioner engage in any activities in New Jersey that reveal an intent to invoke or benefit from the protection of its laws. New Jersey is without power to adjudge the rights and liabilities of J. McIntyre, and its exercise of jurisdiction would violate due process. The contrary judgment of the New Jersey Supreme Court is *Reversed.*

Justice BREYER, with whom Justice ALITO joins, concurring in the judgment.

The Supreme Court of New Jersey adopted a broad understanding of the scope of personal jurisdiction based on its view that "[t]he increasingly fast-paced globalization of the world economy has removed national borders as barriers to trade." I do not doubt that there have been many recent changes in commerce and communication, many of which are not anticipated by our precedents. But this case does not present any of those issues. So I think it unwise to announce a rule of broad applicability without full consideration of the modern-day consequences.

In my view, the outcome of this case is determined by our precedents. Based on the facts found by the New Jersey courts, respondent Robert Nicastro failed to meet his burden to demonstrate that it was constitutionally proper to exercise jurisdiction over petitioner J. McIntyre Machinery, Ltd. (British Manufacturer), a British firm that manufactures scrap-metal machines in Great Britain and sells them through an independent distributor in the United States (American Distributor). On that basis, I agree with the plurality that the contrary judgment of the Supreme Court of New Jersey should be reversed.

I

. . . None of our precedents finds that a single isolated sale, even if accompanied by the kind of sales effort indicated here, is sufficient. Rather, this Court's previous holdings suggest the contrary. The Court has held that a single sale to a customer who takes an accident-causing product to a different State (where the accident takes place) is not a sufficient basis for asserting jurisdiction. And the Court, in separate opinions, has strongly suggested that a single sale of a product in a State does not constitute an adequate basis for asserting jurisdiction over an out-of-state defendant, even if that defendant places his goods in the stream of commerce, fully aware (and hoping) that such a sale will take place.

Here, the relevant facts found by the New Jersey Supreme Court show no "regular . . . flow" or "regular course" of sales in New Jersey; and there is no "something more," such as special state-related design, advertising, advice, marketing, or anything else. Mr. Nicastro, who here bears the burden of proving jurisdiction, has shown no specific effort by the British Manufacturer to sell in New Jersey. He has introduced no list of potential New Jersey customers who might, for example, have regularly attended trade shows. And he has not otherwise shown that the British Manufacturer "purposefully avail[ed] itself of the privilege of conducting activities" within New Jersey, or that it delivered its goods in the stream of commerce "with the expectation that they will be purchased" by New Jersey users.

There may well have been other facts that Mr. Nicastro could have demonstrated in support of jurisdiction. And the dissent considers some of those facts. But the plaintiff bears the burden of establishing jurisdiction, and here I would take the facts precisely as the New Jersey Supreme Court stated them.

Accordingly, on the record present here, resolving this case requires no more than adhering to our precedents.

II

I would not go further. Because the incident at issue in this case does not implicate modern concerns, and because the factual record leaves many open questions, this is an unsuitable vehicle for making broad pronouncements that refashion basic jurisdictional rules.

A

The plurality seems to state strict rules that limit jurisdiction where a defendant does not "inten[d] to submit to the power of a sovereign" and cannot "be said to have targeted the forum." But what do those standards mean when a company targets the world by selling products from its Web site? And does it matter if, instead of shipping the products directly, a company consigns the products through an intermediary (say, Amazon.com) who then receives and fulfills the orders? And what if the company markets its products through popup advertisements that it knows will be viewed in a forum? Those issues have serious commercial consequences but are totally absent in this case.

B

But though I do not agree with the plurality's seemingly strict no-jurisdiction rule, I am not persuaded by the absolute approach adopted by the New Jersey Supreme Court and urged by respondent and his *amici.* Under that view, a producer is subject to jurisdiction for a products-liability action so long as it "knows or reasonably should know that its products are distributed through a nationwide distribution system that *might* lead to those products being sold in any of the fifty states." In the context of this case, I cannot agree.

For one thing, to adopt this view would abandon the heretofore accepted inquiry of whether, focusing upon the relationship between "the defendant, the *forum*, and the litigation," it is fair, in light of the defendant's contacts *with that forum*, to subject the defendant to suit there. It would ordinarily rest jurisdiction instead upon no more than the occurrence of a product-based accident in

the forum State. But this Court has rejected the notion that a defendant's amenability to suit "travel[s] with the chattel."

For another, I cannot reconcile so automatic a rule with the constitutional
demand for "minimum contacts" and "purposefu[l] avail[ment]," each of which
rest upon a particular notion of defendant-focused fairness. A rule like the New
Jersey Supreme Court's would permit every State to assert jurisdiction in a products-liability suit against any domestic manufacturer who sells its products (made
anywhere in the United States) to a national distributor, no matter how large or
small the manufacturer, no matter how distant the forum, and no matter how few
the number of items that end up in the particular forum at issue. . . .

Further, the fact that the defendant is a foreign, rather than a domestic, manufacturer makes the basic fairness of an absolute rule yet more uncertain. I am
again less certain than is the New Jersey Supreme Court that the nature of
international commerce has changed so significantly as to require a new approach
to personal jurisdiction. . . . It may be that a larger firm can readily "alleviate the
risk of burdensome litigation by procuring insurance, passing the expected costs on
to customers, or, if the risks are too great, severing its connection with the State."
But manufacturers come in many shapes and sizes. It may be fundamentally unfair
to require a small Egyptian shirt maker, a Brazilian manufacturing cooperative, or a
Kenyan coffee farmer, selling its products through international distributors, to
respond to products-liability tort suits in virtually every State in the United States,
even those in respect to which the foreign firm has no connection at all but the sale
of a single (allegedly defective) good. . . .

C

At a minimum, I would not work such a change to the law in the way either
the plurality or the New Jersey Supreme Court suggests without a better
understanding of the relevant contemporary commercial circumstances. . . .

Justice GINSBURG, with whom Justice SOTOMAYOR and Justice KAGAN join,
dissenting.

A foreign industrialist seeks to develop a market in the United States for
machines it manufactures. It hopes to derive substantial revenue from sales it
makes to United States purchasers. Where in the United States buyers reside
does not matter to this manufacturer. Its goal is simply to sell as much as it
can, wherever it can. It excludes no region or State from the market it wishes
to reach. But, all things considered, it prefers to avoid products liability litigation
in the United States. To that end, it engages a U.S. distributor to ship its machines
stateside. Has it succeeded in escaping personal jurisdiction in a State where one
of its products is sold and causes injury or even death to a local user? . . .

The machine that injured Nicastro, a "McIntyre Model 640 Shear," sold in
the United States for $24,900 in 1995, and features a "massive cutting capacity,"
id., at 44a. According to McIntyre UK's product brochure, the machine is "use[d]
throughout the [w]orld." McIntyre UK represented in the brochure that, by
"incorporat[ing] off-the-shelf hydraulic parts from suppliers with international
sales outlets," the 640 Shear's design guarantees serviceability "wherever [its

customers] may be based." The instruction manual advises "owner[s] and operators of a 640 Shear [to] make themselves aware of [applicable health and safety regulations]," including "the American National Standards Institute Regulations (USA) for the use of Scrap Metal Processing Equipment."

Nicastro operated the 640 Shear in the course of his employment at Curcio Scrap Metal (CSM) in . . . New Jersey. . . . CSM's owner, Frank Curcio, "first heard of [McIntyre UK's] machine while attending an Institute of Scrap Metal Industries [(ISRI)] convention in Las Vegas in 1994 or 1995, where [McIntyre UK] was an exhibitor." ISRI "presents the world's largest scrap recycling industry trade show each year." The event attracts "owners [and] managers of scrap processing companies" and others "interested in seeing—and purchasing—new equipment." According to ISRI, more than 3,000 potential buyers of scrap processing and recycling equipment attend its annual conventions, "primarily because th[e] exposition provides them with the most comprehensive industry-related shopping experience concentrated in a single, convenient location." . . .

McIntyre UK representatives attended every ISRI convention from 1990 through 2005. These annual expositions were held in diverse venues across the United States; in addition to Las Vegas, conventions were held 1990-2005 in New Orleans, Orlando, San Antonio, and San Francisco. McIntyre UK's president, Michael Pownall, regularly attended ISRI conventions. He attended ISRI's Las Vegas convention the year CSM's owner first learned of, and saw, the 640 Shear. McIntyre UK exhibited its products at ISRI trade shows, the company acknowledged, hoping to reach "anyone interested in the machine from anywhere in the United States."

Although McIntyre UK's U.S. sales figures are not in the record, it appears that for several years in the 1990's, earnings from sales of McIntyre UK products in the United States "ha[d] been good" in comparison to "the rest of the world." . . .

In a November 23, 1999 letter to McIntyre America, McIntyre UK's president spoke plainly about the manufacturer's objective in authorizing the exclusive distributorship: "All we wish to do is sell our products in the [United] States—and get paid!" Notably, McIntyre America was concerned about U.S. litigation involving McIntyre UK products, in which the distributor had been named as a defendant. McIntyre UK counseled McIntyre America to respond personally to the litigation, but reassured its distributor that "the product was built and designed by McIntyre Machinery in the UK and the buck stops here—if there's something wrong with the machine." Answering jurisdictional interrogatories, McIntyre UK stated that it had been named as a defendant in lawsuits in Illinois, Kentucky, Massachusetts, and West Virginia. And in correspondence with McIntyre America, McIntyre UK noted that the manufacturer had products liability insurance coverage.

Over the years, McIntyre America distributed several McIntyre UK products to U.S. customers, including, in addition to the 640 Shear, McIntyre UK's "Niagara" and "Tardis" systems, wire strippers, and can machines. . . . To achieve McIntyre UK's objective, *i.e.*, "to sell [its] machines to customers throughout the United States," "the two companies [were acting] closely in concert with each other." McIntyre UK never instructed its distributor to avoid certain States or regions of the country; rather, as just noted, the manufacturer engaged McIntyre America to attract customers "from anywhere in the United States."

In sum, McIntyre UK's regular attendance and exhibitions at ISRI conventions was surely a purposeful step to reach customers for its products "anywhere in the United States." At least as purposeful was McIntyre UK's engagement of McIntyre America as the conduit for sales of McIntyre UK's machines to buyers "throughout the United States." Given McIntyre UK's endeavors to reach and profit from the United States market as a whole, Nicastro's suit, I would hold, has been brought in a forum entirely appropriate for the adjudication of his claim. He alleges that McIntyre UK's shear machine was defectively designed or manufactured and, as a result, caused injury to him at his workplace. The machine arrived in Nicastro's New Jersey workplace not randomly or fortuitously, but as a result of the U.S. connections and distribution system that McIntyre UK deliberately arranged. On what sensible view of the allocation of adjudicatory authority could the place of Nicastro's injury within the United States be deemed off limits for his products liability claim against a foreign manufacturer who targeted the United States (including all the States that constitute the Nation) as the territory it sought to develop?

II

A few points on which there should be no genuine debate bear statement at the outset. . . . [N]o issue of the fair and reasonable allocation of adjudicatory authority among States of the United States is present in this case. New Jersey's exercise of personal jurisdiction over a foreign manufacturer whose dangerous product caused a workplace injury in New Jersey does not tread on the domain, or diminish the sovereignty, of any sister State. Indeed, among States of the United States, the State in which the injury occurred would seem most suitable for litigation of a products liability tort claim. [In addition,] the constitutional limits on a state court's adjudicatory authority derive from considerations of due process, not state sovereignty. . . .

Finally, in *International Shoe* itself, and decisions thereafter, the Court has made plain that legal fictions, notably "presence" and "implied consent," should be discarded, for they conceal the actual bases on which jurisdiction rests. . . . Whatever the state of academic debate over the role of consent in modern jurisdictional doctrines, the plurality's notion that consent is the animating concept draws no support from controlling decisions of this Court. Quite the contrary, the Court has explained, a forum can exercise jurisdiction when its contacts with the controversy are sufficient; invocation of a fictitious consent, the Court has repeatedly said, is unnecessary and unhelpful.

III

This case is illustrative of marketing arrangements for sales in the United States common in today's commercial world. A foreign-country manufacturer engages a U.S. company to promote and distribute the manufacturer's products, not in any particular State, but anywhere and everywhere in the United States the distributor can attract purchasers. The product proves defective and injures a user in the State where the user lives or works. Often, as here, the manufacturer will have liability insurance covering personal injuries caused by its products.

The modern approach to jurisdiction over corporations and other legal entities, ushered in by *International Shoe*, gave prime place to reason and fairness. Is it not fair and reasonable, given the mode of trading of which this case is an example, to require the international seller to defend at the place its products cause injury? Do not litigational convenience and choice-of-law considerations point in that direction? On what measure of reason and fairness can it be considered undue to require McIntyre UK to defend in New Jersey as an incident of its efforts to develop a market for its industrial machines anywhere and everywhere in the United States? Is not the burden on McIntyre UK to defend in New Jersey fair, *i.e.*, a reasonable cost of transacting business internationally, in comparison to the burden on Nicastro to go to Nottingham, England to gain recompense for an injury he sustained using McIntyre's product at his workplace in Saddle Brook, New Jersey?

McIntyre UK dealt with the United States as a single market. Like most foreign manufacturers, it was concerned not with the prospect of suit in State X as opposed to State Y, but rather with its subjection to suit anywhere in the United States. As a McIntyre UK officer wrote in an e-mail to McIntyre America: "American law — who needs it?!" . . . If McIntyre UK is answerable in the United States at all, is it not "perfectly appropriate to permit the exercise of that jurisdiction . . . at the place of injury"?

In sum, McIntyre UK, by engaging McIntyre America to promote and sell its machines in the United States, "purposefully availed itself" of the United States market nationwide, not a market in a single State or a discrete collection of States. . . . How could McIntyre UK not have intended, by its actions targeting a national market, to sell products in the fourth largest destination for imports among all States of the United States and the largest scrap metal market? . . .

IV

A

While this Court has not considered in any prior case the now-prevalent pattern presented here — a foreign-country manufacturer enlisting a U.S. distributor to develop a market in the United States for the manufacturer's products — none of the Court's decisions tug against the judgment made by the New Jersey Supreme Court. . . . The decision [in *Asahi Metal Industry Co. v. Superior Court of California*, 480 U.S. 102 (1987)] was not a close call. The Court had before it a foreign plaintiff, the Taiwanese manufacturer, and a foreign defendant, the Japanese valve-assembly maker, and the indemnification dispute concerned a transaction between those parties that occurred abroad. All agreed on the bottom line: The Japanese valve-assembly manufacturer was not reasonably brought into the California courts to litigate a dispute with another foreign party over a transaction that took place outside the United States. . . . Asahi, unlike McIntyre UK, did not itself seek out customers in the United States, it engaged no distributor to promote its wares here, it appeared at no tradeshows in the United States, and, of course, it had no Web site advertising its products to the world. Moreover, Asahi was a component-part manufacturer with "little control over the final destination of its products once they were delivered into the stream of commerce." It was important to the Court in *Asahi* that "those who use Asahi components in their final products, and sell those products in California, [would be] subject to the application of California tort law." To hold that *Asahi* controls this case would, to put it bluntly, be dead wrong.

B

The Court's judgment also puts United States plaintiffs at a disadvantage in comparison to similarly situated complainants elsewhere in the world. Of particular note, within the European Union, in which the United Kingdom is a participant, the jurisdiction New Jersey would have exercised is not at all exceptional. The European Regulation on Jurisdiction and the Recognition and Enforcement of Judgments provides for the exercise of specific jurisdiction "in matters relating to tort . . . in the courts for the place where the harmful event occurred." Council Reg. 44/2001, Art. 5, 2001 O.J. (L. 12) 4. The European Court of Justice has interpreted this prescription to authorize jurisdiction either where the harmful act occurred or at the place of injury.

. . . For the reasons stated, I would hold McIntyre UK answerable in New Jersey for the harm Nicastro suffered at his workplace in that State using McIntyre UK's shearing machine. . . .

Notes on
McINTYRE

1. Recall that *Asahi* followed the lead of the United States Supreme Court in *World Wide Volkswagen*, by dividing the analysis into two components: contacts and fairness. None of the Justices formally followed this dichotomy in the various *Nicastro* opinions. Consider, however, whether you can discern the Justices' views in these various components:

- Contacts: Recall that no opinion in *Asahi* garnered a majority of the Justices' votes on the issue of minimum contacts. One could identify a "common denominator" among their approaches by observing that all of the *Asahi* Justices appeared to agree that sufficient contacts would exist in a case that satisfied the contacts test in Justice O'Connor's opinion. Or one could combine Justice Brennan's opinion with Justice Stevens's opinion. Justice Brennan required only purposeful activity arising from a regular and anticipated flow of products into the forum state for commercial sale and Justice Stevens seemed satisfied with a regular course of dealing that resulted in substantial deliveries in the forum state over a period of years. After *McIntyre*, may one safely assume that Justice O'Connor provides a rule of inclusion, at least providing some guidance as to what type of fact pattern does satisfy the minimum contacts standard. Is it still appropriate after *McIntyre* to follow a test that combines Justice Brennan's and Justice Stevens's approach?

- Fairness: None of the *McIntyre* Justices mentioned the fairness factors articulated first in *World Wide Volkswagen* and endorsed by eight of the Justices in *Asahi*. Should the fairness factors still be considered a discrete part of the legal doctrine? Could the omission simply result from five Justices concluding that discussion of the factor was unnecessary, since New Jersey lacked the minimum contacts — or power — to adjudicate the controversy? In their opinions, Justices Breyer and Ginsburg both discussed matters that implicate the fairness factors, such as the size of the defendant's company, distance between defendant's business and the forum, and likelihood that the plaintiff would be able to litigate if the chosen forum was unavailable. Does this suggest that the factors are relevant to the analysis, but no longer a separate component of the analysis?

2. Attempting to divorce federalism from due process concerns, Justice Ginsburg states that "the constitutional limits on a state court's adjudicatory authority derive from considerations of due process, not state sovereignty." Is this position consistent with other personal jurisdiction decisions? Consider this focus on federalism over fairness in light of the Court's decision in *Bristol-Myers Squibb v. Superior Court.* Consider also this statement as you compare the Court's decision in *Burnham v. Superior Court of California*, 495 U.S. 604 (1990), set forth below.

3. As is often the case with dissents, Justice Ginsburg provides a more detailed exposition of the facts than the plurality or concurrence. Do you think that the facts she mentions made *McIntyre* a closer case than the plurality suggested? Should a personal jurisdiction inquiry be so fact-laden? A rich literature analyzes whether subject matter jurisdiction rules should strive for simplicity and clarity. Should the same arguments govern for personal jurisdiction?

PROBLEM 1-2: INJURIES FROM STREAM OF COMMERCE PRODUCTS

Two years ago, Jerry, a six-month-old resident of Texas, was severely burned when his toy caught fire. Jerry's parents are people of modest means, but they were able to find a lawyer who agreed to file suit on Jerry's behalf in a Texas court. The named defendants are the retailer who sold the toy, the manufacturer of the toy, and the purchasing agent who purchased the toy on behalf of the retailer. Both the manufacturer and purchasing agent are Hong Kong corporations. The manufacturer has moved to dismiss the suit against it for lack of personal jurisdiction.

The manufacturer has never been physically present in Texas. Although the manufacturer makes all of the toys sold by the retailer, the two have never had a direct commercial relationship. Instead, the retailer deals only with the purchasing agent (with whom the retailer has conducted business for the last 40 years). The parties followed the same procedure for the transaction at issue here as they follow for all their transactions with each other: the manufacturer makes the toys in Hong Kong and sells them to the purchasing agent there. The purchasing agent then delivers the toys to a shipper in Hong Kong, who in turn transports the toys to the Texas retailer. The shipper is chosen by the retailer and receives a fee paid directly by the Texas retailer. The purchasing agent also receives payment for its services directly from the Texas retailer.

The manufacturer has moved to dismiss the Texas action against it on the ground that the court lacks personal jurisdiction. Should the court grant the motion?

PROBLEM 1-3: HARRY'S, THE MOTORCYCLE DEALER, AND ARNOLD, THE ACTOR (REVISITED)

Look back at Problem 1-1 concerning Harry's Harleys, which included in its advertisements the image of an actor named Arnold without his consent. The newspaper in which the advertisement ran had a very small circulation in Texas, and Harry's had a few tangential Texas contacts. How do the doctrines from *Daimler*, *Bristol-Myers*, and *Asahi* influence your analysis of whether the Texas court had personal jurisdiction over Harry's Harleys?

D.   PRESENCE IN THE JURISDICTION

1.   *Presence of Property*

One of the patterns you will discern in this course (and — in fact — in all of law) is the special status of property. Often, rules bend and exceptions emerge to accommodate personal interests in real and personal property. In the judicial jurisdiction context, courts traditionally recognized two special types of power over property actions: in rem and quasi in rem jurisdiction. These contrast with in personam jurisdiction where the forum court's power is premised on power over the defendant's person.

For in rem jurisdiction, courts exercise power over property for the purpose of adjudicating all interests in the property. Although individuals may assert a personal interest in the property, the court does not exercise power over the person of the defendant, only over the property. In an in rem action, the property is the subject matter of the lawsuit and the court determines the interests in the property of all persons in the world. A common example is foreclosure proceedings, in which the government seeks to establish its right to property used in the commission of a crime.

In quasi in rem actions, property provides the basis for the court's power, but the subject matter of the lawsuit is often not the property. As is the case for in rem jurisdiction, a court exercising quasi in rem jurisdiction does not exercise power over the person of the defendant. Unlike for in rem jurisdiction, a court exercising quasi in rem jurisdiction does not necessarily adjudicate issues relating to ownership in the property.[1] Rather, the court may adjudicate a claim against the defendant personally — on non-property-related matters — but satisfaction of the claim (through attachment, garnishment, or similar mechanism) occurs by executing on the property. The value of an adjudicated claim is by necessity limited by the value of the property, since it is the property that gives the court its power.

In both types of actions, the presence of property within the jurisdiction entitles the court to exercise dominion over the property. After *International Shoe v. Washington* dispensed with the starkly territorial view of judicial power reflected in the Supreme Court's 1878 decision in *Pennoyer v. Neff*, the question lingered whether courts could still exercise judicial jurisdiction premised on the presence of property in the state. The case *Shaffer v. Heitner*, 433 U.S. 186 (1977), concluded that the *International Shoe* standard should govern for in rem jurisdiction cases. Indeed, the *Shaffer* Court made this sweeping statement: "all assertions of state-court jurisdiction must be evaluated according to the standards set forth in *International Shoe* and its progeny." The import of this statement turns out to have significance for jurisdiction based solely on personal presence as well. The question of whether in rem jurisdiction survives after *Shaffer* may not be crucial to answer. After all, specific jurisdiction will exist in a situation when in rem jurisdiction would have justified an exercise of the court's power, no? In other words, when the subject of a dispute is the defendant's property in the forum, the property provides a contact from which the cause of action arises, thus giving rise to specific jurisdiction. As the *Shaffer* Court pointed out, "when claims to the property itself are the source of the underlying controversy between the plaintiff and

---

1. The law does recognize a form of quasi in rem jurisdiction where the subject matter of the lawsuit is the property providing the foundation for the court's power, but the plaintiff seeks only to have her interest established against the claim of a designated person or persons. In this instance, the court has power because of the presence of land within the jurisdiction, even if the court has no power over the adverse claimant. *See* Restatement (Second) of Conflict of Laws, Chap. 3, Introductory Note to Topic 2 (1971). An example is a mortgage foreclosure action, in which the lender seeks to establish its rights in the mortgaged real estate based on the borrower's failure to make required payments.

the defendant, it would be unusual for the State where the property is located not to have jurisdiction."

Advances in technology have created a new need for in rem jurisdiction in certain internet disputes. Indeed, the United States Congress authorized the use of in rem jurisdiction in the Anticybersquatting Consumer Protection Act. Cybersquatters generally register internet domain names that potentially infringe another's trademark, with the hope of either selling the domain name to the trademark owner or intercepting traffic intended for the trademark owner's business. Because cybersquatters often operate under aliases, plaintiffs find it difficult to locate them geographically. Accordingly, the Act provides an alternative to in personam jurisdiction where such jurisdiction is unavailable, allowing the trademark owner to "file an in rem civil action against the domain name in the judicial district in which the domain name registrar, domain name registry, or other domain name authority . . . is located. . . ." 15 U.S.C. §1125(d)(2). In such a case, remedies are limited to the forfeiture or cancellation of the domain name or the transfer of the domain name to the trademark owner.

The question remains, however, whether quasi in rem jurisdiction survives *Shaffer*. The *Shaffer* opinion itself contained ambiguity, but a subsequent United States Supreme Court case suggests that quasi in rem jurisdiction does not survive. Some might argue that the majority opinion somewhat mysteriously suggests that quasi in rem jurisdiction might be available when "no other forum is available to the plaintiff." Yet the remainder of the opinion makes clear that a constitutional problem arises when the property seized as the jurisdictional foundation in a quasi in rem case has nothing to do with the plaintiff's cause of action (and the defendant has no other contacts with the forum). Supporting a negative view of quasi in rem jurisdiction is the Court's subsequent decision in *Rush v. Savchuk*, 444 U.S. 320 (1980), which further highlighted the difficulties with the quasi in rem jurisdiction.

After *Shaffer*, the question remained whether the presence of a person in the territory of a state was sufficient to establish jurisdiction. The next case takes up that question.

2. *Presence of Persons*

After *International Shoe* dispensed with *Pennoyer v. Neff*'s territorial view of judicial power and *Shaffer v. Heitner* vigorously applied the *International Shoe* contacts approach to property cases, the question lingered whether transient presence of a person within a jurisdiction was sufficient to give the jurisdiction's courts power over that person. The Supreme Court finally took up that question in *Burnham v. Superior Court of California*. The tone and length of the opinions in *Burnham* reveal that the Justices had a lot more on their agenda than settling a fine point of personal jurisdiction doctrine. As you read the opinions, identify and evaluate the various opinions' views on the following themes: (1) how do the Justices define due process and relate the definition to fairness; (2) what does the opinion reveal about the Justices' general theories of jurisdictional power; and (3) what does the opinion reveal about the Justices' specific theories of federalism. The notes that follow the next case explore these themes further.

Burnham v. Superior Court of California

495 U.S. 604 (1990)

Justice SCALIA announced the judgment of the Court and delivered an opinion in which THE CHIEF JUSTICE and Justice KENNEDY join, and in which Justice WHITE joins with respect to Parts I, II-A, II-B, and II-C.

The question presented is whether the Due Process Clause of the Fourteenth Amendment denies California courts jurisdiction over a nonresident, who was personally served with process while temporarily in that State, in a suit unrelated to his activities in the State.

I

Petitioner Dennis Burnham married Francie Burnham in 1976 in West Virginia. In 1977 the couple moved to New Jersey, where their two children were born. In July 1987 the Burnhams decided to separate. They agreed that Mrs. Burnham, who intended to move to California, would take custody of the children. Shortly before Mrs. Burnham departed for California that same month, she and petitioner agreed that she would file for divorce on grounds of "irreconcilable differences."

In October 1987, petitioner filed for divorce in New Jersey state court. . . . Petitioner did not, however, obtain an issuance of summons against his wife and did not attempt to serve her with process. Mrs. Burnham . . . brought suit for divorce in California state court in early January 1988.

In late January, petitioner visited southern California on business, after which he went north to visit his children in the San Francisco Bay area, where his wife resided. He took the older child to San Francisco for the weekend. Upon returning the child to Mrs. Burnham's home on January 24, 1988, petitioner was served with a California court summons and a copy of Mrs. Burnham's divorce petition. He then returned to New Jersey.

[Mr. Burnham made a special appearance in the California Superior Court, moving to quash the service of process on the ground that the court lacked personal jurisdiction. Both the Superior Court and the California Court of Appeals denied his request for relief, and the United States Supreme Court granted certiorari.]

II

A

. . .

To determine whether the assertion of personal jurisdiction is consistent with due process, we have long relied on the principles traditionally followed by

American courts in marking out the territorial limits of each State's authority. That criterion was first announced in *Pennoyer v. Neff*, in which we stated that due process "mean[s] a course of legal proceedings according to those rules and principles which have been established in our systems of jurisprudence for the protection and enforcement of private rights," including the "well-established principles of public law respecting the jurisdiction of an independent State over persons and property." In what has become the classic expression of the criterion, we said in *International Shoe Co. v. Washington*, 326 U.S. 310 (1945), that a state court's assertion of personal jurisdiction satisfies the Due Process Clause if it does not violate "'traditional notions of fair play and substantial justice.'" Since *International Shoe*, we have only been called upon to decide whether these "traditional notions" permit States to exercise jurisdiction over absent defendants in a manner that deviates from the rules of jurisdiction applied in the 19th century. We have held such deviations permissible, but only with respect to suits arising out of the absent defendant's contacts with the State.[1] The question we must decide today is whether due process requires a similar connection between the litigation and the defendant's contacts with the State in cases where the defendant is physically present in the State at the time process is served upon him.

B

Among the most firmly established principles of personal jurisdiction in American tradition is that the courts of a State have jurisdiction over nonresidents who are physically present in the State. The view developed early that each State had the power to hale before its courts any individual who could be found within its borders, and that once having acquired jurisdiction over such a person by properly serving him with process, the State could retain jurisdiction to enter judgment against him, no matter how fleeting his visit. . . . Accurate or not, . . . judging by the evidence of contemporaneous or near-contemporaneous decisions, one must conclude that [this] understanding was shared by American courts at the crucial time for present purposes: 1868, when the Fourteenth Amendment was adopted.

Decisions in the courts of many States in the 19th and early 20th centuries held that personal service upon a physically present defendant sufficed to confer jurisdiction, without regard to whether the defendant was only briefly in the State

---

1. We have said that "[e]ven when the cause of action does not arise out of or relate to the foreign corporation's activities in the forum State, due process is not offended by a State's subjecting the corporation to its in personam jurisdiction when there are sufficient contacts between the State and the foreign corporation." *Helicopteros Nacionales de Colombia v. Hall*, 466 U.S., at 414. Our only holding supporting that statement, however, involved "regular service of summons upon [the corporation's] president while he was in [the forum State] acting in that capacity." *See Perkins v. Benguet Consolidated Mining Co.*, 342 U.S. 437, 440 (1952). It may be that whatever special rule exists permitting "continuous and systematic" contacts, to support jurisdiction with respect to matters unrelated to activity in the forum applies only to corporations, which have never fitted comfortably in a jurisdictional regime based primarily upon "de facto power over the defendant's person." *International Shoe Co. v. Washington*, 326 U.S. 310, 316, (1945). . . .

or whether the cause of action was related to his activities there. . . . Particularly striking is the fact that, as far as we have been able to determine, not one American case from the period (or, for that matter, not one American case until 1978) held, or even suggested, that in-state personal service on an individual was insufficient to confer personal jurisdiction. . . .

This American jurisdictional practice is, moreover, not merely old; it is continuing. It remains the practice of, not only a substantial number of the States, but as far as we are aware all the States and the Federal Government — if one disregards (as one must for this purpose) the few opinions since 1978 that have erroneously said, on grounds similar to those that petitioner presses here, that this Court's due process decisions render the practice unconstitutional. . . .

C

Despite this formidable body of precedent, petitioner contends, in reliance on our decisions applying the *International Shoe* standard, that in the absence of "continuous and systematic" contacts with the forum, . . . a nonresident defendant can be subjected to judgment only as to matters that arise out of or relate to his contacts with the forum. This argument rests on a thorough misunderstanding of our cases.

. . . As *International Shoe* suggests, the defendant's litigation-related "minimum contacts" may take the place of physical presence as the basis for jurisdiction:

> Historically the jurisdiction of courts to render judgment in personam is grounded on their de facto power over the defendant's person. Hence his presence within the territorial jurisdiction of a court was prerequisite to its rendition of a judgment personally binding on him. But now that the *capias ad respondendum* has given way to personal service of summons or other form of notice, due process requires only that in order to subject a defendant to a judgment in personam, if he be not present within the territory of the forum, he have certain minimum contacts with it such that the maintenance of the suit does not offend "traditional notions of fair play and substantial justice."

Nothing in *International Shoe* or the cases that have followed it, however, offers support for the very different proposition petitioner seeks to establish today: that a defendant's presence in the forum is not only unnecessary to validate novel, nontraditional assertions of jurisdiction, but is itself no longer sufficient to establish jurisdiction. That proposition is unfaithful to both elementary logic and the foundations of our due process jurisprudence.

The short of the matter is that jurisdiction based on physical presence alone constitutes due process because it is one of the continuing traditions of our legal system that define the due process standard of "traditional notions of fair play and substantial justice." That standard was developed by analogy to "physical presence," and it would be perverse to say it could now be turned against that touchstone of jurisdiction.

D

Petitioner's strongest argument, though we ultimately reject it, relies upon our decision in *Shaffer v. Heitner*, 433 U.S. 186 (1977). . . . It goes too far to say, as petitioner contends, that *Shaffer* compels the conclusion that a State lacks jurisdiction over an individual unless the litigation arises out of his activities in the State. *Shaffer*, like *International Shoe*, involved jurisdiction over an absent defendant, and it stands for nothing more than the proposition that when the "minimum contact" that is a substitute for physical presence consists of property ownership it must, like other minimum contacts, be related to the litigation. Petitioner wrenches out of its context our statement in *Shaffer* that "all assertions of state-court jurisdiction must be evaluated according to the standards set forth in *International Shoe* and its progeny." When read together with the two sentences that preceded it, the meaning of this statement becomes clear:

> "The fiction that an assertion of jurisdiction over property is anything but an assertion of jurisdiction over the owner of the property supports an ancient form without substantial modern justification. Its continued acceptance would serve only to allow state-court jurisdiction that is fundamentally unfair to the defendant.
>
> We therefore conclude that all assertions of state-court jurisdiction must be evaluated according to the standards set forth in *International Shoe* and its progeny."

Shaffer was saying, in other words, not that all bases for the assertion of in personam jurisdiction (including, presumably, in-state service) must be treated alike and subjected to the "minimum contacts" analysis of *International Shoe*, but rather that quasi in rem jurisdiction, that fictional "ancient form," and in personam jurisdiction, are really one and the same and must be treated alike — leading to the conclusion that quasi in rem jurisdiction, i.e., that form of in personam jurisdiction based upon a "property ownership" contact and by definition unaccompanied by personal, in-state service, must satisfy the litigation-relatedness requirement of *International Shoe*. The logic of *Shaffer*'s holding — which places all suits against absent nonresidents on the same constitutional footing, regardless of whether a separate Latin label is attached to one particular basis of contact — does not compel the conclusion that physically present defendants must be treated identically to absent ones. As we have demonstrated at length, our tradition has treated the two classes of defendants quite differently, and it is unreasonable to read *Shaffer* as casually obliterating that distinction. *International Shoe* confined its "minimum contacts" requirement to situations in which the defendant "be not present within the territory of the forum," and nothing in *Shaffer* expands that requirement beyond that.

It is fair to say, however, that while our holding today does not contradict *Shaffer*, our basic approach to the due process question is different. We have conducted no independent inquiry into the desirability or fairness of the prevailing in-state service rule, leaving that judgment to the legislatures that are free to amend it; for our purposes, its validation is its pedigree, as the phrase "traditional notions of fair play and substantial justice" makes clear. *Shaffer* did conduct such an independent inquiry, asserting that "'traditional notions of fair play and substantial justice' can be as readily offended by the perpetuation of ancient forms that are no longer justified as by the adoption of new procedures that are inconsistent with the basic values of our constitutional heritage." . . . While in no way receding from or casting doubt upon the holding of *Shaffer* or any other case, we reaffirm today our time-honored approach. For new procedures, hitherto unknown, the Due Process Clause requires analysis to determine whether "traditional notions of fair play and substantial justice" have been offended. But a doctrine of personal jurisdiction that dates back to the adoption of the Fourteenth Amendment and is still generally observed unquestionably meets that standard.

III

A few words in response to Justice Brennan's opinion concurring in the judgment: It insists that we apply "contemporary notions of due process" to determine the constitutionality of California's assertion of jurisdiction. But our analysis today comports with that prescription, at least if we give it the only sense allowed by our precedents. The "contemporary notions of due process" applicable to personal jurisdiction are the enduring "traditional notions of fair play and substantial justice" established as the test by *International Shoe*. By its very language, that test is satisfied if a state court adheres to jurisdictional rules that are generally applied and have always been applied in the United States.

But the concurrence's proposed standard of "contemporary notions of due process" requires more: It measures state-court jurisdiction not only against traditional doctrines in this country, including current state-court practice, but also against each Justice's subjective assessment of what is fair and just. Authority for that seductive standard is not to be found in any of our personal jurisdiction cases. It is, indeed, an outright break with the test of "traditional notions of fair play and substantial justice," which would have to be reformulated "*our* notions of fair play and substantial justice."

The subjectivity, and hence inadequacy, of this approach becomes apparent when the concurrence tries to explain why the assertion of jurisdiction in the present case meets its standard of continuing-American-tradition-plus-innate-fairness. . . .

The difference between us and Justice Brennan has . . . to do with whether changes are to be adopted as progressive by the American people or decreed as progressive by the Justices of this Court. Nothing we say today prevents individual States from limiting or entirely abandoning the in-state-service basis of jurisdiction. And nothing prevents an overwhelming majority of them from doing so, with the consequence that the "traditional notions of fairness" that this Court applies may change. But the States have overwhelmingly declined to adopt such limitation or abandonment, evidently not considering it to be progress. . . . The question is whether, armed with no authority other than individual Justices' perceptions of fairness that conflict with both past and current practice, this Court can compel the States to make such a change on the ground that "due process" requires it. We hold that it cannot.

Because the Due Process Clause does not prohibit the California courts from exercising jurisdiction over petitioner based on the fact of in-state service of process, the judgment is Affirmed.

Justice WHITE, concurring in part and concurring in the judgment.

I join Parts I, II-A, II-B, and II-C of Justice Scalia's opinion and concur in the judgment of affirmance. The rule allowing jurisdiction to be obtained over a nonresident by personal service in the forum State, without more, has been and is so widely accepted throughout this country that I could not possibly strike it down, either on its face or as applied in this case, on the ground that it denies due process of law guaranteed by the Fourteenth Amendment. Although the Court has the authority under the Amendment to examine even traditionally accepted procedures and declare them invalid, e.g., *Shaffer v. Heitner*, 433 U.S. 186 (1977), there has been no showing here or elsewhere that as a general proposition the rule is so arbitrary and lacking in common sense in so many instances that it should be held violative of due process in every case. Furthermore, until such a showing is made, which would be difficult indeed, claims in individual cases that the rule would operate unfairly as applied to the particular nonresident involved need not be entertained. At least this would be the case where presence in the forum State is intentional, which would almost always be the fact. Otherwise, there would be endless, fact-specific litigation in the trial and appellate courts, including this one. Here, personal service in California, without more, is enough, and I agree that the judgment should be affirmed.

Justice BRENNAN, with whom Justice MARSHALL, Justice BLACKMUN, and Justice O'CONNOR join, concurring in the judgment.

I

I believe that the approach adopted by Justice Scalia's opinion today — reliance solely on historical pedigree — is foreclosed by our decisions in *International Shoe Co. v. Washington*, 326 U.S. 310 (1945), and *Shaffer v. Heitner*, 433 U.S. 186 (1977). In *International Shoe*, we held that a state court's assertion of personal jurisdiction does not violate the Due Process Clause if it is consistent with "'traditional notions of fair play and substantial justice.'" In *Shaffer*, we stated that "all assertions of state-court jurisdiction must be evaluated according to the standards set forth in *International Shoe* and its progeny." The critical insight of *Shaffer* is that all rules of jurisdiction, even ancient ones, must satisfy contemporary notions of due process. No longer were we content to limit our jurisdictional analysis to pronouncements that "[t]he foundation of jurisdiction is physical power," and that "every State possesses exclusive jurisdiction and sovereignty over persons and property within its territory." While acknowledging that "history must be considered as supporting the proposition that jurisdiction based solely on the presence of property satisfie[d] the demands of due process," we found that this factor could not be "decisive." We recognized that "'[t]raditional notions of fair play and substantial justice' can be as readily offended by the perpetuation of ancient forms that are no longer justified as by the adoption of new procedures that are inconsistent with the basic values of our constitutional heritage." I agree with this approach and continue to believe that "the minimum-contacts analysis developed in *International Shoe* . . . represents a far more sensible construct for the exercise of state-court jurisdiction than the patchwork of legal and factual fictions that has been generated from the decision in *Pennoyer v. Neff.*"

While our holding in *Shaffer* may have been limited to quasi in rem jurisdiction, our mode of analysis was not. Indeed, that we were willing in *Shaffer* to examine anew the appropriateness of the quasi in rem rule — until that time dutifully accepted by American courts for at least a century — demonstrates that we did not believe that the "pedigree" of a jurisdictional practice was dispositive in deciding whether it was consistent with due process. If we could discard an "ancient form without substantial modern justification" in *Shaffer*, we can do so again.[3]

. . . Lower courts, commentators, and the American Law Institute all have interpreted *International Shoe* and *Shaffer* to mean that every assertion of state-court jurisdiction, even one pursuant to a "traditional" rule such as transient jurisdiction, must comport with contemporary notions of due process. Notwithstanding the nimble gymnastics of Justice Scalia's opinion today, it is not faithful to our decision in *Shaffer*.

. . .

II

Tradition, though alone not dispositive, is of course relevant to the question whether the rule of transient jurisdiction is consistent with due process.[7] Tradition is salient not in the sense that practices of the past are automatically reasonable today; indeed, under such a standard, the legitimacy of transient jurisdiction would be called into question because the rule's historical "pedigree" is a matter of intense debate. The rule was a stranger to the common law and was rather weakly implanted in American jurisprudence "at the crucial time for present purposes: 1868, when the Fourteenth Amendment was adopted." For much of the

3. Even Justice Scalia's opinion concedes that sometimes courts may discard "traditional" rules when they no longer comport with contemporary notions of due process. For example, although, beginning with the Romans, judicial tribunals for over a millenium [sic] permitted jurisdiction to be acquired by force, see L. Wenger, Institutes of the Roman Law of Civil Procedure 46-47 (O. Fisk trans., rev. ed. 1986), by the 19th century, as Justice Scalia acknowledges, this method had largely disappeared. I do not see why Justice Scalia's opinion assumes that there is no further progress to be made and that the evolution of our legal system, and the society in which it operates, ended 100 years ago.

7. I do not propose that the "contemporary notions of due process" to be applied are no more than "each Justice's subjective assessment of what is fair and just." Rather, the inquiry is guided by our decisions beginning with *International Shoe Co. v. Washington*, 326 U.S. 310 (1945), and the specific factors that we have developed to ascertain whether a jurisdictional rule comports with "traditional notions of fair play and substantial justice." See, e.g., *Asahi Metal Industry Co. v. Superior Court of California*, 480 U.S. 102, 113 (1987) (noting "several factors," including "the burden on the defendant, the interests of the forum State, and the plaintiff's interest in obtaining relief"). This analysis may not be "mechanical or quantitative," *International Shoe*, 326 U.S., at 319, but neither is it "freestanding," or dependent on personal whim. Our experience with this approach demonstrates that it is well within our competence to employ.

19th century, American courts did not uniformly recognize the concept of transient jurisdiction, and it appears that the transient rule did not receive wide currency until well after our decision in *Pennoyer v. Neff*, 95 U.S. 714 (1878).

Rather, I find the historical background relevant because, however murky the jurisprudential origins of transient jurisdiction, the fact that American courts have announced the rule for perhaps a century (first in dicta, more recently in holdings) provides a defendant voluntarily present in a particular State today "clear notice that [he] is subject to suit" in the forum. . . . The transient rule is consistent with reasonable expectations and is entitled to a strong presumption that it comports with due process. "If I visit another State, . . . I knowingly assume some risk that the State will exercise its power over my property or my person while there. My contact with the State, though minimal, gives rise to predictable risks." *Shaffer*, 433 U.S., at 218, 97 S. Ct., at 2587 (Stevens, J., concurring in judgment). Thus, proposed revisions to the Restatement (Second) of Conflict of Laws §28, p. 39 (1986), provide that "[a] state has power to exercise judicial jurisdiction over an individual who is present within its territory unless the individual's relationship to the state is so attenuated as to make the exercise of such jurisdiction unreasonable." [11]

By visiting the forum State, a transient defendant actually "avail[s]" himself of significant benefits provided by the State. His health and safety are guaranteed by the State's police, fire, and emergency medical services; he is free to travel on the State's roads and waterways; he likely enjoys the fruits of the State's economy as well. . . . Without transient jurisdiction, an asymmetry would arise: A transient would have the full benefit of the power of the forum State's courts as a plaintiff while retaining immunity from their authority as a defendant.

The potential burdens on a transient defendant are slight. "'[M]odern transportation and communications have made it much less burdensome for a party sued to defend himself'" in a State outside his place of residence. That the defendant has already journeyed at least once before to the forum — as evidenced by the fact that he was served with process there — is an indication that suit in the forum likely would not be prohibitively inconvenient. Finally, any burdens that do arise can be ameliorated by a variety of procedural devices. For these reasons, as a rule the exercise of personal jurisdiction over a defendant based on his voluntary presence in the forum will satisfy the requirements of due process. *See* n.11, *supra*.

In this case, it is undisputed that petitioner was served with process while voluntarily and knowingly in the State of California. I therefore concur in the judgment.

Justice STEVENS, concurring in the judgment.

As I explained in my separate writing, I did not join the Court's opinion in *Shaffer v. Heitner*, 433 U.S. 186 (1977), because I was concerned by its unnecessarily broad reach. The same concern prevents me from joining either Justice Scalia's or Justice Brennan's opinion in this case. For me, it is sufficient to note that the historical evidence and consensus identified by Justice Scalia, the considerations

---

11. As the Restatement suggests, there may be cases in which a defendant's involuntary or unknowing presence in a State does not support the exercise of personal jurisdiction over him. The facts of the instant case do not require us to determine the outer limits of the transient jurisdiction rule.

of fairness identified by Justice Brennan, and the common sense displayed by Justice White, all combine to demonstrate that this is, indeed, a very easy case.[*] Accordingly, I agree that the judgment should be affirmed.

Notes on
BURNHAM

1. What is the "bottom line" rule of *Burnham* on the constitutionality of jurisdiction based on transient presence in the forum state? Justice Scalia, Justice Brennan, and Justice White each propose an approach, but not one of these opinions garnered the votes of a majority of the Justices. How might one combine all or some of the opinions to identify a rule to guide attorneys seeking to evaluate the propriety of jurisdiction based solely on service of process in the forum?

2. In his opinion, Justice Scalia ventured the following summary of his reasoning about transient presence and due process: "The short of the matter is that jurisdiction based on physical presence alone constitutes due process because it is one of the continuing traditions of our legal system that define the due process standard of 'traditional notions of fair play and substantial justice.'" Is this a tautological statement? That is, does it simply say that due process is due process — or does it suggest something more than that? The statement seems tied to Justice Scalia's pedigree-equals-legitimacy approach to due process. From this perspective, does the statement contribute anything to our understanding of what procedures comply with constitutional due process standards?

3. Justice Scalia expresses a dim view of Justice Brennan's "reasonableness factors." Does his treatment of these factors suggest why he may not have joined that opinion of the Court respecting fairness factors in *Asahi Metal Industry Co. v. Superior Court of California?*

4. Both Justice Scalia's and Justice Brennan's opinions each garnered the votes of three other Justices. Thus, Justice Scalia's opinion is not technically a "plurality" opinion. Yet — as the first opinion in the case — the Scalia opinion has more prominence (and presumably influence) than Brennan's. Why might Justice Scalia's opinion appear in the lead position?

5. Assume that you are a plaintiff's attorney presented with facts similar to *Burnham* and that you are confident that you could establish that a particular forum has specific jurisdiction over a defendant. Is there any reason that you might go out of your way to ensure that the defendant is served with process while in the forum? In other words, would you have any strategic reason to take advantage of the *Burnham* rule, even though you think you could establish jurisdiction otherwise?

---

* Perhaps the adage about hard cases making bad law should be revised to cover easy cases.

6. From the point of view of a defense lawyer, the decision to allow personal jurisdiction based on transient presence provides an important topic for legal advice. Where providing counsel to potential defendants, a lawyer might apprise the client that travelling to a particular jurisdiction may increase the hazard of having to litigate a lawsuit there as well.

7. Since *Burnham* was decided, transient presence jurisdiction has proven quite useful in acquiring jurisdiction over foreign nationals who happen to be present in the United States. Service while the foreign defendant is in the United States allows a plaintiff to avoid the complexities of personal jurisdiction and service of process requirements of foreign nations. Even more specifically, plaintiffs have found useful transient presence jurisdiction in the area of human rights litigation, where the plaintiff seeks to sue a foreign defendant for human rights violations committed outside the United States. *See, e.g., Kadic v. Karadzic*, 70 F.3d 232 (2d Cir. 1995); *Shaolian-Tehrani v. Khatami*, 2008 U.S. Dist. LEXIS 30611 (S.D.N.Y. Mar. 17, 2008); *Doe v. Qi*, 349 F. Supp. 2d 1258 (N.D. Cal. 2004). These cases help to illustrate the potentially high stakes of personal jurisdiction doctrine: without valid personal jurisdiction, the United States lawsuit could not proceed and international human rights standards might not be enforced. Further discussion of this issue appears in the section regarding personal jurisdiction in international disputes at the end of this chapter.

8. A review of the votes in personal jurisdiction cases by the various Supreme Court Justices reveals a curious pattern. Those Justices normally associated with the liberal end of the ideological spectrum (and associated with a propensity toward expansively reading federal civil rights guarantees such as due process) often vote in favor of the forum's personal jurisdiction — thus making it more difficult in future cases to find a due process violation. By contrast, those Justices normally associated with the conservative end of the ideological spectrum (and accompanying disposition against expansively reading federal civil rights guarantees) often vote against the forum's personal jurisdiction — thus making it easier to find a due process violation. What accounts for these votes? Could the Justices be motivated by different or "larger" issues than personal jurisdiction doctrine? In *Burnham*, however, the Justices arguably deviated from this pattern — with Justice Scalia taking a broad view of personal jurisdiction, spurning doctrinal qualifications where the territorial sovereignty of a state is implicated. Does this apparent change in voting pattern help to identify larger concerns that may motivate the Justices, such as the role of territoriality and state sovereignty in our federalist system? Regardless of how one might analyze the voting pattern, is it fair to say that the Justices' conception of the appropriate balance of federal and state power in the United States influences their personal jurisdiction votes?

9. The U.S. Supreme Court in *Daimler A.G. v. Baumer* observes that the "paradigm" location where a natural person is subject to general jurisdiction is the person's domicile. The *Daimler* Court did not, however, mention that under *Burnham*, a natural person is usually subject to general jurisdiction where she is served with process. What is the effect of *Daimler* on *Burnham*? Possibly not much. *Daimler* focused primarily on general jurisdiction principles governing corporations, and nothing in the opinion suggested that the Court intended to undermine the *Burnham* holding for natural persons.

E. PERSONAL JURISDICTION AND THE INTERNET

1. Introduction to Personal Jurisdiction and the Internet

The transnational web of computer networks known as the internet is now an integral and indispensable part of modern life. When internet use first became pervasive, courts and scholars proposed that they might need to retool Conflict of Laws principles to account for the lack of territorially based boundaries in cyberspace. For example, in an influential article, Professors David Johnson and David Post argued that geographically oriented legal principles would likely prove inadequate to govern where internet disputes arise and that cyberspace requires distinct rules.[2] Given the unique qualities of the internet, courts and commentators first isolated discussion of internet issues from other legal concerns. As the internet has become more integral to personal and business interaction, however, efforts to isolate internet issues from other legal problems have proven illusory. Hardly a case emerges that does not have some element of its facts grounded in a website connection, email exchange, blog, chat room, or the like.

As the law has become more acclimated to internet issues, many have suggested that new legal principles may not be necessary to govern in cyberspace. This is particularly true in the context of personal jurisdiction, where some have suggested that courts have done no more than put "new wine" in "old bottles."[3]

2. David Johnson & David Post, *Law and Borders — The Rise of Law in Cyberspace*, 48 STAN. L. REV. 1367, 1376 (1996). Professors Johnson and Post stated as follows:

Because events on the Net occur everywhere but nowhere in particular, are engaged in by online personae who are both "real" (possessing reputations, able to perform services, and deploy intellectual assets) and "intangible" (not necessarily or traceably tied to any particular person in the physical sense), and concern "things" (messages, databases, standing relationships) that are not necessarily separated from one another by any physical boundaries, no physical jurisdiction has a more compelling claim than any other to subject these events exclusively to its laws.

3. Martin H. Redish, *Of New Wine and Old Bottles: Personal Jurisdiction, the Internet and the Nature of Constitutional Evolution*, 38 JURIMETRICS J. 575 (1998).

You will in fact note familiar concepts in the two representative cases that follow. You will also note that United States courts continue to place considerable relevance on state boundaries — analyzing what contacts occurred where. You should judge for yourself, however, whether the cross-border nature of internet communications and transactions calls for more creative or revolutionary thinking than has heretofore appeared in the cases.

In the context of personal jurisdiction in the internet, the United States District Courts and United States Courts of Appeals have contributed the vast majority of legal guidance in the United States. Many of the major personal jurisdiction cases of the United States Supreme Court were handed down before widespread internet use. State courts have been remarkably silent. In analyzing internet disputes, lower federal courts have continued to use contacts as a point of reference. Courts in several other countries, however, do not follow a similar matrix and allow jurisdiction in a forum without the defendant's purposeful contact there. Within the European Union, for example, a tort victim may bring a claim in the place where harm occurred and consumers may bring suits in their domicile.[4] Likewise, as you will see in detail in connection with choice of law, other countries have asserted jurisdiction over United States defendants whose internet activity originated in the United States. In a case that sent shock waves around the international media community — where a United States company posted information on a website in the United States — Australia upheld jurisdiction based solely on an injury to reputation suffered by an Australian plaintiff in Australia. *Dow Jones & Co. v. Gutnick* (2002) 210 C.L.R. 575 (Austrl.) Numerous other examples abound, including France's assertion of jurisdiction over United States-based Yahoo! in an attempt to ensure French residents could not access sites offering Nazi memorabilia, and legal action by Italian authorities against Google officials for allowing a website to make available a video of teenagers bullying a Down's Syndrome child.

In United States law, jurisdictional issues relating to the internet implicate many legal categories. For example, as mentioned above in connection with *Shaffer v. Heitner,* Congress has authorized in rem jurisdiction in cybersquatting cases. Anticybersquatting Consumer Protection Act, 15 U.S.C. §1125. Likewise, internet disputes often present questions relating to whether a party may properly consent to jurisdiction in a particular case. Consider, for example, the "I agree" boxes you need to check before proceeding to the meaningful part of a website, application, or transaction. Consent questions are explored immediately below in the forum selection clause material. Of particular interest here are cases where the court grappled with whether to assert personal jurisdiction over a defendant who has availed herself of the forum by virtue of internet activities. First, though, it may be helpful to look at some basics of internet architecture, provided in the perspective that follows.

---

4. The Brussels Regulation, Council Regulation 44/2001, art. 5(3), art. 16, 2001 O.J. (L12) 1 (EC).

PERSPECTIVE ON INTERNET ARCHITECTURE AND USE
---

1. An Overview of Internet Operation. As an overview of internet operation, consider the following excepts from a leading Cyberlaw casebook, PATRICIA L. BELLIA, PAUL SCHIFF BERMAN, BRETT M. FRISCHMAN & DAVID G. POST, CYBERLAW: PROBLEMS OF POLICY & JURISPRUDENCE IN THE INFORMATION AGE (2010):

The Internet, as most people know by now, is not a physical entity but rather a network of networks—an inter-network, a set of communications links and communications rules (known as "protocols") allowing computers, and computer networks, to exchange information with one another. It is only one of many thousands of such inter-networks out there; numerous businesses, for example, operate private inter-networks linking their remote office or retail locations together. The Internet had its origins in 1969. . . .

* * *

A partial list of . . ." unique design principles and features" around which the Internet has been built would include the following:

A. *Decentralized Control.* Unlike many other networks . . . , TCP/IP networks like the Internet have no central "server" responsible for managing network traffic and seeing to it that messages reach their intended destinations. Instead, messages make their way from one network host to another by traversing the network one "hop" at a time.

* * *

A message from Network A—say, in Austin, Texas—can thus take any one of a large number of alternate paths to reach its destination at Network P (Paris, France); it might travel via routers in Atlanta, Philadelphia, Newfoundland and Stockholm before reaching its destination, or, alternatively, if that path were for some reason unavailable, via Chicago, Denver, Mexico City, Mumbai, and Brussels. This feature—known to the engineers as *redundancy*—allows the Internet to continue to function notwithstanding damage to, or failure by, a portion of the network; messages can be routed around the damaged portion and through alternate paths. . . . No single entity—academic, corporate, governmental, or non-profit—administers the Internet. It exists and functions as a result of the fact that hundreds of thousands of separate operators of computers and computer networks independently decided to use common data transfer protocols to exchange communications and information with other computers (which in turn exchange communications and information with still other computers). . . . *American Civil Liberties Union v. Reno,* 929 F. Supp. 824, 832 (E.D. Pa. 1996), *aff'd,* 521 U.S. 844 (1997).

B. *Openness.* The Internet is an "open" network in several senses. First, the . . . protocols, which are required in order to send and to receive messages over the Internet, are publicly accessible and non-proprietary. . . . Second, the Internet is "open" in the sense that it is easy to join; with no central server that must be informed of a new network participant, in order to communicate with others over the Internet one need only obtain the necessary software and arrange for a connection to any one of the thousands of Internet service providers worldwide. Third, the Internet is open in the sense that it can inter-connect networks that may themselves use different operating systems and underlying technologies.

C. *Packet-switching.* The Internet is a "packet-switched" network (as contrasted with *circuit-switched* networks such as the telephone network). Packet-switching means that before being transmitted over the inter-network, a message is broken up into small, fixed-length blocks (or "packets"), and each of the packets is then routed independently of the others to the recipient machine. That recipient machine is then responsible for re-assembling all of the packets—which are likely to arrive out of order, given the different routes they have taken—back into a single message. As a consequence, the physical communication lines connecting any two users on the Internet can be performing that same task for thousands, or hundreds of thousands, of users more-or-less simultaneously, as packet follows packet follows packet across the wires. By contrast, a circuit-switched network—like the telephone network—identifies a single line between sender and recipient and keeps that line "open," dedicated exclusively to that one connection, until the communication between the two is completed. Packet-switching not only makes it more difficult to intercept and interpret messages traveling over the network (because messages have been disassembled before transmission) . . . it allows for a much more efficient use of available transmission capacity, allowing many more communications between many more users to travel over the same physical facilities, compared to circuit-switched networks.

D. *Digital Information.* The inter-network transmits information only in digital form, as on-off pulses of electrical energy representing the binary digits "1" and "0." Physical distance is thus largely irrelevant to online communications; digital information can move nearly as quickly across the globe as across town, with no significant degradation in quality. From a technical perspective, there is no music, or pornography, or message boards, or virtual worlds, or books for sale, etc. on the Internet; there are only massive strings of 1s and 0s. And because digital information can be copied instantly and (virtually) without error . . . , copying is an essential part of the architecture itself. For example, messages are reproduced each time they move from one router to another across the network. Similarly, every time one accesses a website, a copy of the requested page is produced on one's own computer.

E. *Layered Architecture.* . . .

[The internet has a layered design,] conventionally divided into four layers: an "Application Layer" at the top, a "Transport Layer" beneath that, a "Network Layer" beneath that, and a "Physical Layer" beneath that. . . . To see roughly how Internet layering operates, suppose that you are sitting in a law school classroom, connected via a fiber optic cable to your school's local area network [LAN] and, through that connection, to the Internet, and you have just sent a request for a web page located at http://www.aclu.org. The protocols used at the *Physical Layer* determine how the electrical transmissions produced by your computer are to be converted into strings of digital bits by the LAN server; most (but by no means all) LANs use the Ethernet protocol suite for this task. . . . Once the Physical Layer protocols have translated your otherwise-meaningless pulses of electricity into a meaningful series of binary digits, the message is handed over to the protocols at the *Network Layer.* The Internet's Network Layer . . . determines how the bit-strings that you have sent to your LAN server are routed over the inter-network to the correct recipient ("www.aclu.org"). On the Internet, the *Internet Protocol* suite is used for these tasks.

Finally, there is the *Application Layer.* . . . [T]he recipient of your message has to decode and interpret it—to determine whether it is a request for a copy of a particular file residing on the recipient's computer, or an e-mail message, or a voice communication, or a music file, or something else. . . .

This architecture . . . allows specialization at each layer of the protocol stack; protocols at each layer operate independently of the protocols in the other layers. The Network Layer protocols can be designed to route packets from one place to another as quickly and as efficiently as possible, without having to know anything about what the bit-strings that are being routed "mean." Similarly, applications can interpret the data they send to each other without worrying about how it got there just as plumbers, doctors, lawyers, chemists, and insurance salesmen can develop and all use their own specialized lingoes for communication, secure in the knowledge the postal service will deliver their letters correctly.

F. *End-to-End Design.* The end-to-end design principle is closely linked to the principle of layered architecture; it holds that, wherever possible, functions should be placed at the *higher* layers of the protocol stack, *i.e.*, that as much as possible should be left to software running in the *Applications* Layer—at the user "end" rather than in the network "center." The lower-level protocols are kept as simple and unobtrusive as possible, focused only on the minimal function of transmitting data. End-to-end design means that the Physical, Network, and Transport Layer protocols will deliver a network user's bits wherever directed—what happens to them after that point is of no concern to the network itself but is controlled entirely by the applications running on the user's machine.

So while the basic Internet Protocol (IP), for example, *could* do much more than just addressing and routing—checking for malicious code, for instance, or more aggressive security and authentication of sender identity, or any number of other functions—end-to-end leaves these functions for users to implement if they wish (or not).

End-to-end design has profound implications for the Internet's growth and utilization. It grants the maximum possible autonomy to applications running "on top" of the basic network protocols themselves, giving application-writers the freedom to achieve their goals in whatever manner they see fit, and to innovate whenever and however they like. Virtually all of the network's "intelligence"—the processing required to *interpret* the bit-strings delivered over the Internet by the lower level protocols—is located in the software running in the applications layer. Bits are bits; the network will move them around for you as directed no matter what they mean, or what they are intended to do when they reach their destination. Innovation comes in the form of new applications—email, or instant messaging, or the World Wide Web, or VoIP (Voice over Internet Protocol), or peer-to-peer file-sharing—developed and deployed at the edges of the network, not the center; the center need not participate in (nor even have any information about) those new applications. . . . This is, again, in stark contrast to the telephone network, which was designed to allow very simple devices at the edges—telephones—to connect to a very sophisticated central processing core. . . .

PATRICIA L. BELLIA, PAUL SCHIFF BERMAN, BRETT M. FRISCHMAN & DAVID G. POST, CYBER-LAW: PROBLEMS OF POLICY & JURISPRUDENCE IN THE INFORMATION AGE 17-24 (2010).

2. An Overview of World Wide Web Operation. Much of the initial case law attempting to regulate matters related to the internet specifically concerned the

World Wide Web. The following is a description of the World Wide Web that appeared in one of the path-breaking decisions, *American Civil Liberties Union v. Reno*, 929 F. Supp. 824, 836-838 (E.D. Pa. 1996), *aff'd*, 521 U.S. 844 (1997):

- ... The [World Wide] Web utilizes a "hypertext" formatting language called hypertext markup language (HTML), and programs that "browse" the Web can display HTML documents containing text, images, sound, animation and moving video. Any HTML document can include links to other types of information or resources, so that while viewing an HTML document that, for example, describes resources available on the Internet, one can "click" using a computer mouse on the description of the resource and be immediately connected to the resource itself.

- The World Wide Web (W3C) was created to serve as the platform for a global, online store of knowledge, containing information from a diversity of sources and accessible to Internet users around the world. Though information on the Web is contained in individual computers, the fact that each of these computers is connected to the Internet through W3C protocols allows all of the information to become part of a single body of knowledge.

- The World Wide Web is a series of documents stored in different computers all over the Internet. Documents contain information stored in a variety of formats, including text, still images, sounds, and video. An essential element of the Web is that any document has an address (rather like a telephone number). Most Web documents contain "links." These are short sections of text or image which refer to another document.

- Many organizations now have "home pages" on the Web. These are documents which provide a set of links designed to represent the organization, and through links from the home page, guide the user directly or indirectly to information about or relevant to that organization.

- The World Wide Web exists fundamentally as a platform through which people and organizations can communicate through shared information. When information is made available, it is said to be "published" on the Web. Publishing on the Web simply requires that the "publisher" has a computer connected to the Internet and that the computer is running W3C server software.

- Web publishers have a choice to make their Web sites open to the general pool of all Internet users, or close them, thus making the information accessible only to those with advance authorization. Many publishers choose to keep their sites open to all in order to give their information the widest potential audience. In the event that the publishers choose to maintain restrictions on access, this may be accomplished by assigning specific user names and passwords as a prerequisite to access to the site. Or, in the case of Web sites maintained for internal use of one organization, access will only be allowed from other computers within that organization's local network.

- Running on tens of thousands of individual computers on the Internet, the Web is what is known as a distributed system. The Web was designed so that organizations with computers containing information can become part of the Web simply by attaching their computers to the Internet and running appropriate World Wide Web software. No single organization controls any membership in the Web, nor is there any single centralized point from which individual Web sites or services can be blocked from the Web. From a user's perspective, it may appear to be a single, integrated system, but in reality it has no centralized control point.
- The Web's open, distributed, decentralized nature stands in sharp contrast to most information systems that have come before it. Private information services such as Westlaw, Lexis/Nexis, and Dialog, have contained large storehouses of knowledge, and can be accessed from the Internet with the appropriate passwords and access software. However, these databases are not linked together into a single whole, as is the World Wide Web.

2. *Personal Jurisdiction Doctrine and the Internet*

Near the beginning of its development, legal thinkers believed the internet posed a daunting challenge for courts evaluating personal jurisdiction. To begin your inquiry into whether this has in fact proved true, consider the following problem:

PROBLEM 1-4: MEAN SPIRIT HITS THE NET

An acquaintance of yours named Mean Spirit lives in State A. You've been acquainted with Mean Spirit for quite some time, and Mean Spirit knows that you live in neighboring State B, that your boss lives in State B, and that you work in State B. Somehow, Mean Spirit got your email address as well as your boss's email address. Mean Spirit sends your boss an email (with a copy to you) that asserts falsely that you have been interviewing for other jobs and suggests that you should be fired. You wish to sue Mean Spirit for interference with your contractual relationship with your employer in the courts of State B. You know that aside from the email, Mean Spirit has had some contact with State B on matters unrelated to you, but not a lot. You are sure that the State B contacts do not approach continuous and systematic activity. Given that Mean Spirit used the internet as the means for communication, should you expect to have difficulty establishing personal jurisdiction?

In Problem 1-4, Mean Spirit's internet activities were confined to sending emails. But what about claims that arise from a defendant's other internet activities, such as maintaining and interacting through a website? If the defendant knows that State B citizens will probably make use of the defendant's website, which the defendant established and maintains while in State A, is that sufficient for personal jurisdiction? Perhaps the most famous early internet case to grapple with the question was *Zippo Manufacturing Co. v. Zippo Dot Com, Inc.*, 952 F. Supp. 1119 (W.D. Pa. 1997). The district judge in *Zippo* reasoned that the type of website activity involved in a case determined whether a defendant had sufficient contacts in given case, and sorted website activity on a sliding scale:

- Passive Websites: On one end of the spectrum were passive websites, in which the defendant merely posts information that is accessible from the forum state. In such an instance, the court reasoned that the defendant does not purposefully avail herself of the forum, but merely makes "information available to those who are interested." *Zippo*, 952 F. Supp. at 1124.
- Interactive Websites: In the middle of the spectrum, a defendant maintains an interactive website, which she can use to receive or send information.
- Active Websites: On the other end of the spectrum, a defendant uses an active website to transmit files to the forum, enter contracts with forum residents, and the like.

Zippo itself involved an active website, which was supported by seven internet service providers in the forum, had 3,000 subscribers in the forum, and downloaded electronic messages from the forum. Under these circumstances, the court held that the forum had personal jurisdiction over the defendant, Zippo Dot Com, in a trademark infringement action brought by the manufacturer of Zippo lighters.

Cybersell, Inc. v. Cybersell, Inc.
130 F.3d 414 (9th Cir. 1997)

RYMER, Circuit Judge.

We are asked to hold that the allegedly infringing use of a service mark in a home page on the World Wide Web suffices for personal jurisdiction in the state where the holder of the mark has its principal place of business. [Cybersell AZ] advertises for commercial services over the Internet, [and claims that Cybersell FL], a Florida corporation that offers web page construction services over the Internet, infringed its federally registered mark and should be amenable to suit in Arizona because cyberspace is without borders and a web site which advertises a product or service is necessarily intended for use on a world wide basis. The district court disagreed, and so do we. Instead, applying our normal "minimum contacts" analysis, we conclude that it would not comport with "traditional notions of fair play and substantial justice," for Arizona to exercise personal jurisdiction over an allegedly infringing Florida web site advertiser who has no contacts with Arizona other than maintaining a home page that is accessible to Arizonans, and everyone else, over the Internet. We therefore affirm. . . .

II

[The court begins its personal jurisdiction analysis by observing that the applicable long arm statute — that of Arizona — allows personal jurisdiction over the parties to the maximum extent permitted by the United States Constitution.]

A court may assert either specific or general jurisdiction over a defendant. Cybersell AZ concedes that general jurisdiction over Cybersell FL doesn't exist in Arizona, so the only issue in this case is whether specific jurisdiction is available.

We use a three-part test to determine whether a district court may exercise specific jurisdiction over a nonresident defendant:

(1) The nonresident defendant must do some act or consummate some transaction with the forum or perform some act by which he purposefully avails himself of the privilege of conducting activities in the forum, thereby invoking the benefits and protections;

(2) the claim must be one which arises out of or results from the defendant's forum-related activities; and

(3) exercise of jurisdiction must be reasonable.

Cybersell AZ argues that the test is met because trademark infringement occurs when the passing off of the mark occurs, which in this case, it submits, happened when the name "Cybersell" was used on the Internet in connection with advertising. Cybersell FL, on the other hand, contends that a party should not be subject to nationwide, or perhaps worldwide, jurisdiction simply for using the Internet.

A

[W]e turn to the first requirement, which is the most critical. As the Supreme Court emphasized in *Hanson v. Denckla,* "it is essential in each case that there be some act by which the defendant purposefully avails itself of the privilege of conducting activities within the forum State, thus invoking the benefits and protections of its laws." We recently explained that the "purposeful availment" requirement is satisfied if the defendant has taken deliberate action within the forum state or if he has created continuing obligations to forum residents. "It is not required that a defendant be physically present within, or have physical contacts with, the forum, provided that his efforts 'are purposefully directed' toward forum residents." . . .

. . . CompuServe is a computer information service headquartered in Columbus, Ohio, that contracts with individual subscribers to provide access to computing and information services via the Internet. It also operates as an electronic conduit to provide computer software products to its subscribers. Computer software generated and distributed in this way is often referred to as "shareware." Patterson is a Texas resident who subscribed to CompuServe and placed items of "shareware" on the CompuServe system pursuant to a "Shareware Registration Agreement" with

CompuServe which provided, among other things, that it was "to be governed by and construed in accordance with" Ohio law. During the course of this relationship, Patterson electronically transmitted thirty-two master software files to CompuServe, which CompuServe stored and displayed to its subscribers. Sales were made in Ohio and elsewhere, and funds were transmitted through CompuServe in Ohio to Patterson in Texas. In effect, Patterson used CompuServe as a distribution center to market his software. When Patterson threatened litigation over allegedly infringing CompuServe software, CompuServe filed suit in Ohio seeking a declaratory judgment of noninfringement. The court found that Patterson's relationship with CompuServe as a software provider and marketer was a crucial indicator that Patterson had knowingly reached out to CompuServe's Ohio home and benefitted from CompuServe's handling of his software and fees. Because Patterson had chosen to transmit his product from Texas to CompuServe's system in Ohio, and that system provided access to his software to others to whom he advertised and sold his product, the court concluded that Patterson purposefully availed himself of the privilege of doing business in Ohio.

B

Here, Cybersell FL has conducted no commercial activity over the Internet in Arizona. All that it did was post an essentially passive home page on the web, using the name "CyberSell," which Cybersell AZ was in the process of registering as a federal service mark. While there is no question that anyone, anywhere could access that home page and thereby learn about the services offered, we cannot see how from that fact alone it can be inferred that Cybersell FL deliberately directed its merchandising efforts toward Arizona residents.

Cybersell FL did nothing to encourage people in Arizona to access its site, and there is no evidence that any part of its business (let alone a continuous part of its business) was sought or achieved in Arizona. To the contrary, it appears to be an operation where business was primarily generated by the personal contacts of one of its founders. While those contacts are not entirely local, they aren't in Arizona either. No Arizonan except for Cybersell AZ "hit" Cybersell FL's web site. There is no evidence that any Arizona resident signed up for Cybersell FL's web construction services. It entered into no contracts in Arizona, made no sales in Arizona, received no telephone calls from Arizona, earned no income from Arizona, and sent no messages over the Internet to Arizona. The only message it received over the Internet from Arizona was from Cybersell AZ. Cybersell FL did not have an "800" number, let alone a toll-free number that also used the "Cybersell" name. The interactivity of its web page is limited to receiving the browser's name and address and an indication of interest—signing up for the service is not an option, nor did anyone from Arizona do so. No money changed hands on the Internet from (or through) Arizona. In short, Cybersell FL has done no act and has consummated no transaction, nor has it performed any act by which it purposefully availed itself of the privilege of conducting activities, in Arizona, thereby invoking the benefits and protections of Arizona law.

We therefore hold that Cybersell FL's contacts are insufficient to establish "purposeful availment." Cybersell AZ has thus failed to satisfy the first prong of our three-part test for specific jurisdiction. We decline to go further solely on the footing that Cybersell AZ has alleged trademark infringement over the Internet by Cybersell FL's use of the registered name "Cybersell" on an essentially passive web page advertisement. Otherwise, every complaint arising out of alleged trademark infringement on the Internet would automatically result in personal jurisdiction wherever the plaintiff's principal place of business is located. That would not comport with traditional notions of what qualifies as purposeful activity invoking the benefits and protections of the forum state.

III

Cybersell AZ . . . invokes the "effects" test employed in *Calder v. Jones*, 465 U.S. 783 (1984), and *Core-Vent Corp. v. Nobel Industries*, 11 F.3d 1482 (9th Cir. 1993), with respect to intentional torts directed to the plaintiff, causing injury where the plaintiff lives. However, we don't see this as a *Calder* case. Because Shirley Jones was who she was (a famous entertainer who lived and worked in California) and was libeled by a story in the National Enquirer, which was published in Florida but had a nationwide circulation with a large audience in California, the Court could easily hold that California was the "focal point both of the story and of the harm suffered" and so jurisdiction in California based on the "effects" of the defendants' Florida conduct was proper. There is nothing comparable about Cybersell FL's web page. Nor does the "effects" test apply with the same force to Cybersell AZ as it would to an individual, because a corporation "does not suffer harm in a particular geographic location in the same sense that an individual does." Cybersell FL's web page simply was not aimed intentionally at Arizona knowing that harm was likely to be caused there to Cybersell AZ.

IV

We conclude that the essentially passive nature of Cybersell FL's activity in posting a home page on the World Wide Web that allegedly used the service mark of Cybersell AZ does not qualify as purposeful activity invoking the benefits and protections of Arizona. As it engaged in no commercial activity and had no other contacts via the Internet or otherwise in Arizona, Cybersell FL lacks sufficient minimum contacts with Arizona for personal jurisdiction to be asserted over it there.

Young v. New Haven Advocate

315 F.3d 256 (4th Cir. 2002)

MICHAEL, Circuit Judge.

The question in this appeal is whether two Connecticut newspapers and certain of their staff (sometimes, the "newspaper defendants") subjected themselves to personal jurisdiction in Virginia by posting on the Internet news articles that, in the context of discussing the State of Connecticut's policy of housing its prisoners in Virginia institutions, allegedly defamed the warden of a Virginia prison. . . . [W]e hold that a court in Virginia cannot constitutionally exercise jurisdiction over the Connecticut-based newspaper defendants because they did not manifest an intent to aim their websites or the posted articles at a Virginia audience. Accordingly, we reverse the district court's order denying the defendants' motion to dismiss for lack of personal jurisdiction.

I.

Sometime in the late 1990s the State of Connecticut was faced with substantial overcrowding in its maximum security prisons. To alleviate the problem, Connecticut contracted with the Commonwealth of Virginia to house Connecticut prisoners in Virginia's correctional facilities. Beginning in late 1999 Connecticut transferred about 500 prisoners, mostly African-American and Hispanic, to the Wallens Ridge State Prison, a "supermax" facility in Big Stone Gap, Virginia. The plaintiff, Stanley Young, is the warden at Wallens Ridge. Connecticut's arrangement to incarcerate a sizeable number of its offenders in Virginia prisons provoked considerable public debate in Connecticut. Several Connecticut legislators openly criticized the policy, and there were demonstrations against it at the state capitol in Hartford.

Connecticut newspapers, including defendants the New Haven Advocate (the Advocate) and the Hartford Courant (the Courant), began reporting on the controversy. On March 30, 2000, the Advocate published a news article, written by one of its reporters, defendant Camille Jackson, about the transfer of Connecticut inmates to Wallens Ridge. The article discussed the allegedly harsh conditions at the Virginia prison and pointed out that the long trip to southwestern Virginia made visits by prisoners' families difficult or impossible. In the middle of her lengthy article, Jackson mentioned a class action that inmates transferred from Connecticut had filed against Warden Young and the Connecticut Commissioner of Corrections. The inmates alleged a lack of proper hygiene and medical care and the denial of religious privileges at Wallens Ridge. Finally, a paragraph at the end of the article reported that a Connecticut state senator had expressed concern about the presence of Confederate Civil War memorabilia in Warden Young's office. At about the same time the Courant published three columns, written by defendant-reporter Amy Pagnozzi, questioning the practice of relocating Connecticut inmates to Virginia prisons. The columns reported on letters written home by inmates who alleged cruelty by prison guards. In one column Pagnozzi called Wallens Ridge a "cut-rate gulag." Warden Young was not mentioned in any of the Pagnozzi columns.

On May 12, 2000, Warden Young sued the two newspapers, their editors (Gail Thompson and Brian Toolan), and the two reporters for libel in a diversity action filed in the Western District of Virginia. He claimed that the newspapers' articles imply that he "is a racist who advocates racism" and that he "encourages abuse of inmates by the guards" at Wallens Ridge. Young alleged that the newspapers circulated the allegedly defamatory articles throughout the world by posting them on their Internet websites.

. . . The Advocate is a free newspaper published once a week in New Haven, Connecticut. It is distributed in New Haven and the surrounding area, and some of its content is published on the Internet. The Advocate has a small number of subscribers, and none of them are in Virginia. The Courant is published daily in Hartford, Connecticut. The newspaper is distributed in and around Hartford, and some of its content is published on the Internet. When the articles in question were published, the Courant had eight mail subscribers in Virginia. Neither newspaper solicits subscriptions from Virginia residents. No one from either newspaper, not even the reporters, traveled to Virginia to work on the articles about Connecticut's prisoner transfer policy. The two reporters made a few telephone calls into Virginia to gather some information for the articles. Both interviewed by telephone a spokesman for the Virginia Department of Corrections. All other interviews were done with people located in Connecticut. The two reporters wrote their articles in Connecticut. The individual defendants (the reporters and editors) do not have any traditional contacts with the Commonwealth of Virginia. They do not live in Virginia, solicit any business there, or have any assets or business relationships there. The newspapers do not have offices or employees in Virginia, and they do not regularly solicit or do business in Virginia. Finally, the newspapers do not derive any substantial revenue from goods used or services rendered in Virginia.

. . .

II.

. . .

B.

[The court noted that the plaintiff, Warden Young, had premised his personal jurisdiction claim only on the basis of specific jurisdiction, and thus confined its analysis to that issue.] We turn to whether the district court can exercise specific jurisdiction over the newspaper defendants, namely, the two newspapers, the two editors, and the two reporters. To begin with, we can put aside the few Virginia contacts that are not Internet based because Warden Young does not rely on them. Thus, Young does not claim that the reporters' few telephone calls into Virginia or the Courant's eight Virginia subscribers are sufficient to establish personal jurisdiction over those defendants. Nor did the district court rely on these traditional contacts.

Warden Young argues that the district court has specific personal jurisdiction over the newspaper defendants (hereafter, the "newspapers") because of the following contacts between them and Virginia: (1) the newspapers, knowing that Young was a Virginia resident, intentionally discussed and defamed him in their articles, (2) the newspapers posted the articles on their websites, which were accessible in Virginia, and (3) the primary effects of the defamatory statements on Young's reputation were felt in Virginia. Young emphasizes that he is not arguing that jurisdiction is proper in any location where defamatory Internet content can be accessed, which would be anywhere in the world. Rather, Young argues that personal jurisdiction is proper in Virginia because the newspapers understood that their defamatory articles, which were available to Virginia residents on the

Internet, would expose Young to public hatred, contempt, and ridicule in Virginia, where he lived and worked. As the district court put it, "[t]he defendants were all well aware of the fact that the plaintiff was employed as a warden within the Virginia correctional system and resided in Virginia," and they "also should have been aware that any harm suffered by Young from the circulation of these articles on the Internet would primarily occur in Virginia."

Young frames his argument in a way that makes one thing clear: if the newspapers' contacts with Virginia were sufficient to establish personal jurisdiction, those contacts arose solely from the newspapers' Internet-based activities. Recently . . . we discussed the challenges presented in applying traditional jurisdictional principles to decide when "an out-of-state citizen, through electronic contacts, has conceptually 'entered' the State via the Internet for jurisdictional purposes." [W]e held that "specific jurisdiction in the Internet context may be based only on an out-of-state person's Internet activity directed at [the forum state] and causing injury that gives rise to a potential claim cognizable in [that state]." We noted that this standard for determining specific jurisdiction based on Internet contacts is consistent with the one used by the Supreme Court in *Calder v. Jones*, 465 U.S. 783 (1984). . . .

Warden Young argues that *Calder* requires a finding of jurisdiction in this case simply because the newspapers posted articles on their Internet websites that discussed the warden and his Virginia prison, and he would feel the effects of any libel in Virginia, where he lives and works. *Calder* does not sweep that broadly, as we have recognized. For example, we [have] emphasized how important it is in light of *Calder* to look at whether the defendant has expressly aimed or directed its conduct toward the forum state. [We have also held] "that a State may, consistent with due process, exercise judicial power over a person outside of the State when that person (1) directs electronic activity into the State, (2) with the manifested intent of engaging in business or other interactions within the State, and (3) that activity creates, in a person within the State, a potential cause of action cognizable in the State's courts."

When the Internet activity is, as here, the posting of news articles on a website, the . . . test works more smoothly when parts one and two of the test are considered together. We thus ask whether the newspapers manifested an intent to direct their website content — which included certain articles discussing conditions in a Virginia prison — to a Virginia audience. . . . "[A] person's act of placing information on the Internet" is not sufficient by itself. Otherwise, a "person placing information on the Internet would be subject to personal jurisdiction in every State," and the traditional due process principles governing a State's jurisdiction over persons outside of its borders would be subverted. The fact that the newspapers' websites could be accessed anywhere, including Virginia, does not by itself demonstrate that the newspapers were intentionally directing their website content to a Virginia audience. Something more than posting and accessibility is needed to "indicate that the [newspapers] purposefully (albeit electronically) directed [their] activity in a substantial way to the forum state." The newspapers must, through the Internet postings, manifest an intent to target and focus on Virginia readers.

We therefore turn to the pages from the newspapers' websites that Warden Young placed in the record, and we examine their general thrust and content. The overall content of both websites is decidedly local, and neither newspaper's website contains advertisements aimed at a Virginia audience. For example, the website that distributes the Courant, ctnow.com, provides access to local (Connecticut) weather and traffic information and links to websites for the University of Connecticut and Connecticut state government. The Advocate's website features stories focusing on New Haven, such as one entitled "The Best of New Haven." In sum, it appears that these newspapers maintain their websites to serve local readers in Connecticut, to expand the reach of their papers within their local markets, and to provide their local markets with a place for classified ads. The websites are not designed to attract or serve a Virginia audience.

We also examine the specific articles Young complains about to determine whether they were posted on the Internet with the intent to target a Virginia audience. The articles included discussions about the allegedly harsh conditions at the Wallens Ridge prison, where Young was warden. One article mentioned Young by name and quoted a Connecticut state senator who reported that Young had Confederate Civil War memorabilia in his office. The focus of the articles, however, was the Connecticut prisoner transfer policy and its impact on the transferred prisoners and their families back home in Connecticut. The articles reported on and encouraged a public debate in Connecticut about whether the transfer policy was sound or practical for that state and its citizens. Connecticut, not Virginia, was the focal point of the articles. . . . In sum, the newspapers do not have sufficient Internet contacts with Virginia to permit the district court to exercise specific jurisdiction over them.[*]

REVERSED.

Notes on
PERSONAL JURISDICTION AND THE INTERNET

1. The internet is not the first technology to challenge traditional personal jurisdiction principles. Other innovations that have raised questions about personal jurisdiction doctrine's territorial focus include automobiles, telephones, facsimile machines, radio, and television. For example, wide use of automobiles stretched personal jurisdiction doctrine by making it common for individuals to be transitory (i.e., only temporarily present in a jurisdiction's territory) and by minimizing geographical distances. Yet automobile travel still takes place within a territorial framework — unlike internet communication, which is independent of geography and borders. Because facsimile and telephone communications have borderless qualities

---

[*] Because the newspapers did not intentionally direct Internet activity to Virginia, and jurisdiction fails on that ground, we have no need to explore the last part of the . . . inquiry, that is, whether the challenged conduct created a cause of action in Virginia.

now, particularly in the era of satellite communication, their analogy with email communication is close. Perhaps it is for that reason that personal jurisdiction cases based on email communication seem so easy for courts, who have become accustomed to facsimiles and telephone calls. The analogy breaks down, however, when one compares World Wide Web communications with facsimile and telephone communications because information posted on the web flows from one communicator to many recipients — rather than "one-to-one" as in most facsimiles and telephone calls. DAN JERKER B. SVANTESSON, PRIVATE INTERNATIONAL LAW AND THE INTERNET 34-35 (2007).

To be sure, radio and television also effect communication from "one-to-many." *Id* . But internet communication still has other qualities that distinguish it from radio and television. As modes of communication, radio and television generally require greater knowledge and sophistication from those who use them than is required by the internet. First, transmission capabilities are more accessible for the internet. Moreover — unlike for radio and television broadcasting — internet transmission is omnipresent in the sense that the same website can be accessed on servers throughout the world. Generally, radio and television broadcasts also more consistently possess geographic identifiers than internet communications. Although some domain names do have country codes (e.g., "cn," "au," "it," "edu," or "com"), one usually encounters difficulty identifying the dispatcher and the receiver of internet communications. *See* SVANTESSON, *supra*, at 34-39.

These analogies and distinctions all go to the question of whether personal jurisdiction cases analyzing telephone calls, radio, and television are useful in analyzing internet cases. Courts frequently proceed as though the analogies are useful, often using the case law as interchangeable. Sometimes the technological quirks of the internet, however, prove quite important. For example, the general lack of geographical markers on internet communication plays a significant role in evaluating whether a defendant who has used the internet has *purposely* made a contact with the forum.

One debate relevant to the question of whether an internet communication amounts to "purposeful availment" remains unresolved. The debate concerns whether internet communication results from a "pull" technology in contrast to a "push" technology. Some have argued that the internet is not "pushed" into any particular jurisdiction in the same way as television and radio (and thus disqualifying an internet posting from being a jurisdictional contact). Others, however, have reasoned that this argument ignores the ability of pervasive internet communications to impose considerable influence on people and events. *See, e.g.*, Webopedia, http://www.webopedia.com/TERM/p/push.html (stating that the World Wide Web is a pull technology, but email is a push technology); *Dow Jones v. Gutnick* (2002) 210 C.L.R. 575, 648 (Austrl.) (Callinan, J.) (observing that the argument that the internet is not "pushed into any particular jurisdiction . . . ignores the commercial and social realities that greater publication produces both greater profit and broader persuasion").

2. Do the facts of *Cybersell* and *Young* support the proposition that the World Wide Web is primarily a "pull" technology? What types of actions might a defendant undertake to make it more likely that the World Wide Web would be characterized as a "push" technology? Do not forget that internet applications other than email and the World Wide Web, such as chatrooms and usenet, can also provide contacts relevant to personal jurisdiction and may yield different results.

3. Both the *Cybersell* and *Young* courts reject the plaintiff's attempt to invoke *Calder v. Jones*, in which the United States Supreme Court held that the defendants had "aimed" their work at California because that was where the plaintiff lived and would suffer greatest harm. Are you persuaded that *Cybersell* and *Young* are distinguishable from *Calder v. Jones*? Note that in cases similar to *Cybersell*, see, e.g., *Inset Systems, Inc. v. Instruction Set, Inc.*, 937 F. Supp. 161 (D. Conn. 1996), the court came to an opposite conclusion about the *Calder v. Jones* effects test.

In applying *Calder v. Jones*, some lower courts have devised a three-part inquiry, concluding that jurisdiction exists if the defendant has engaged in "(1) intentional action; (2) expressly aimed at the forum state; (3) causing harm, the brunt of which is suffered, and the defendant knows is likely to be suffered in the forum state." *Panavision International L.P. v. Toeppen*, 141 F.3d 1316, 1321 (9th Cir. 1998). Through these requirements, the lower courts ensure the effects test hews close to the constitutional requirement that the defendant target activity toward the forum.

Different types of "wrongs" yield different types of injuries. For example, defamation leads to injury to reputation and trademark infringement may simply amount to theft of the value of a trademark. These different injuries might be "felt" in different places — thus leading to different conclusions about where the effect of the defendant's conduct occurred. Are patterns likely to emerge, with harm most likely occurring in particular locations depending on the precise cause of action or theory of liability? In other words, should the *Calder v. Jones* "effects test" apply differently according to differences in the cause of action? Should the effects test also apply differently where the defendant communicates the message electronically, rather than orally or in hard copy print?

4. Several countries other than the United States have used some kind of "effects" test to exercise jurisdiction over foreign defendants for online activities. Indeed, Germany, France, the United Kingdom, Italy, Canada, and Australia have all used a version of an effects test in international internet cases that is more expansive than that applied in the United States. The "purposeful availment" requirement of United States due process law requires the defendant to have targeted the jurisdiction exercising personal

jurisdiction. By contrast, the other countries listed above handed down decisions reflecting jurisdiction based on the foreseeability that a foreign defendant's conduct *may* have effect in the forum. *See, e.g.*, Developments, *The Law of Media: V. Internet Jurisdiction: A Comparative Analysis*, 120 HARV. L. REV. 1031 (2007) (discussing cases in Australia, the United Kingdom, and Canada); Yulia A. Timofeeva, *Worldwide Prescriptive Jurisdiction in Internet Content Controversies: A Comparative Analysis*, 20 CONN. J. INT'L L. 199 (2005) (discussing cases in Germany, France, Italy, Canada, and Australia).

The "effects" test is not only a creature of domestic law of the various countries, but is also reflected in general theories of judicial jurisdiction in international law. This "effects test," along with other international law theories, enables a domestic court in one country to exercise jurisdiction over extraterritorial conduct abroad. The international law theories of judicial jurisdiction are discussed in the next section of this chapter.

5. Both *Cybersell* and *Young* presented the personal jurisdiction dispute as one involving specific jurisdiction. Until recently, courts were not inclined to find general jurisdiction based on internet activity. *See, e.g., Weber v. Jolly Hotels*, 977 F. Supp. 327, 333-334 (D.N.J. 1997) (holding that maintenance of website accessible in New Jersey did not render Italian hotel subject to jurisdiction in New Jersey). The court of appeals did find general jurisdiction, however, in *Gator.com Corp. v. L.L. Bean, Inc.*, 341 F.3d 1072 (9th Cir. 2003). Focusing on L.L. Bean's web activities rather the hard copy catalogues that it sends into California, the court evaluated whether California had general jurisdiction over L.L. Bean and concluded that the website was "clearly and deliberately structured to operate as a sophisticated virtual store in California." *Id.* at 1078. Using analysis from *Zippo*, the court held that L.L. Bean's active website, which included accepting California orders and sending emails to customers in the state, was tantamount to physical presence in the state and thus qualified as continuous and systematic activity in the state. The *L.L. Bean* dispute was rendered moot by subsequent developments on appeal, but the case nonetheless stands as an important development, having provoked considerable reaction. On the basis of more unusual facts, the court in *Lakin v. Prudential Securities, Inc.*, 348 F.3d 704, 711 (8th Cir. 2003), also found allegations sufficient to make a prima facie showing of general jurisdiction. *See also Mieczkowski v. Masco Corp.*, 997 F. Supp. 782, 785-788 (E.D. Tex. 1998) (holding that the nature of manufacturer's website combined with business volume in the state and other factors provided basis for general jurisdiction in action by parents of three-year-old who was asphyxiated when entangled in a bunk bed). Consider how the decision in these cases might be affected by the United States Supreme Court's *Goodyear* and *Daimler* decisions.

6. How useful is the *Zippo* analysis, prompting courts to categorize the type of website activity among three categories: "passive," "active," and

"interactive"? How meaningful are these distinctions? Are these categories uniformly useful in all cases? Courts are in disagreement whether the *Zippo* approach applies in a general jurisdiction case. *See Lakin v. Prudential Securities, Inc.*, 348 F.3d 704, 711 (8th Cir. 2003) (outlining disagreement among courts).

7. Note that the court in *Young* stated that it did not consider non-internet activities, since the plaintiff, Warden Young, did not rely on any of these activities as the basis of jurisdiction. Likewise, *Gator.com Corp. v. L.L. Bean, Inc.*, 341 F.3d 1072 (9th Cir. 2003), discussed in Note 5 above, ignored the defendant's copious internet activities. Do these two cases reflect the appropriate approach? Should not all of the defendant's activities — internet and non-internet — be considered?

When one considers how individuals and businesses conduct their affairs, one realizes that most cases will involve mixed internet and non-internet activity, with non-internet activity — such as an in-person visit or a telephone — providing that extra effort that makes clear a defendant has targeted the state. So, for example, the defendant may have maintained a website, but also may have engaged in non-internet activity that tips the scales in favor of jurisdiction. *See, e.g., Blumenthal v. Drudge*, 992 F. Supp. 44, 54-57 (D.D.C. 1998), in which the District of Columbia court found jurisdiction over the owner of the Drudge Report (which originates on a California server) for allegedly defamatory statements dealing with Washington, D.C. politics. Although the defendant had argued that the website was "passive," the court found jurisdiction appropriate given that Drudge had used solicited information from Washington, D.C. by telephone, United States mail, and personal appearance.

8. Often absent from internet personal jurisdiction cases is examination of the fairness factors discussed in *Asahi*. Nothing in those Supreme Court decisions suggested that any particular class of case or defendant should be insulated from or excused from the protection of the fairness factors. Some courts have applied the fairness factors consistently in internet cases, at least before the U.S. Supreme Court decisions in *Goodyear* and *Daimler*.

PROBLEM 1-5: SHAKEY'S THEATRE GOES CYBER

A theatre in Virginia, Shakey's, features Shakespearean plays in an original Elizabethan setting. Shakey's is run by local residents and has largely local patrons. The theatre management hired someone to create a website, which provides information concerning its plays, including the performance schedule and ticket prices. The website instructs anyone who wants a ticket to call Shakey's and purchase the ticket over the phone.

Graham is a citizen of Pennsylvania, who accessed the website and then phoned Shakey's to purchase tickets to a play. After making the phone purchase, Graham travelled to Shakey's in Virginia, and while attending a play there, was burnt when candlewax dripped from an overhead candelabra onto on his face. Graham filed a negligence suit against Shakey's in Pennsylvania to recover for his medical bills and his loss of income resulting from the burn to his face.

Shakey's has moved to dismiss the case for lack of personal jurisdiction, accurately pointing out that the only arguable contact it has had with the state is the posting of information on the web that could be accessed from Pennsylvania. Shakey's further argues that it runs its production with a skeleton staff, and would need to cancel shows so that one of its employees could travel to Pennsylvania and represent the theatre in the litigation.

Should the court grant Shakey's motion? Would your answer change if Shakey's website allowed customers to purchase tickets through the website using their credit cards?

PROBLEM 1-6: CHRISTMAS TREES OR FIREWORKS?

A Hong Kong manufacturer of artificial Christmas trees, Sung Company Limited, exported its products to the United States, where they were sold in "big box" stores all over the country — the "big box" stores representing the largest and most recognized retailers in the United States. Most of Sung's product sales took place in the United States — and the United States sales were substantial (nearly $2 billion). Approximately 7 percent of Sung's United States sales occur in Oklahoma, and Sung has long been aware that its big box store clients have over 180 retail outlets throughout Oklahoma. Sung makes the sales of all its products in the United States through negotiations with the purchasers for the big box stores, none of whom operate out of Oklahoma. The artificial trees are shipped from Hong Kong to port cities in the United States, where the shippers route them on behalf of Sung to distribution hubs throughout the United States. The big box stores operate the distribution hubs.

Sung's only direct connection to the United States is a website providing information about the trees, including product manuals, warranty information, and answers to frequently asked questions. Warranty services are available in the United States through an agent who handles warranty requests. The agent who handles the warranty requests is located in South Carolina, and is prepared to answer requests from anywhere in the world. Finally, Sung's website is maintained in Hong Kong and does not provide any opportunity to purchase the trees from the site or to interact with the website operator.

Following a house fire in Oklahoma from a Sung Christmas tree that ignited, homeowners filed suit in Oklahoma, alleging that the tree was defective because of its propensity to burn. Sung then moved to dismiss the suit for lack of personal jurisdiction. Should the court grant the motion?

F. *INTERNATIONAL AND COMPARATIVE JURISDICTION ISSUES*

Legal issues raised by courts adjudicating international disputes are broad ranging, and include such matters as subject matter jurisdiction of domestic courts and the role of international and transnational tribunals such as the International Court of Justice, the International Criminal Court, and the European Court of Human Rights. Pertinent to the current chapter are specific issues relating to the exercise of personal jurisdiction over international litigants by federal and state courts in the United States. This section first explores United States legal principles governing personal jurisdiction over international disputes and service of process questions. Often questions arise about the authority of the United States to regulate conduct that occurs outside its borders. These matters—which are often conceived as questions of jurisdiction to prescribe rather than questions of jurisdiction to adjudicate—are reviewed in Chapter 3 in connection with extraterritorial application of United States law. This section ends with comparative materials on the European Union—providing an opportunity to compare the European Union's jurisdictional rules for disputes between citizens of Member States with jurisdictional rules followed in the United States.

1. *Personal Jurisdiction over Parties in International Disputes*

So far, our focus on personal jurisdiction has concentrated largely on horizontal conflicts among states of the United States—analyzing whether a state court may assert personal jurisdiction over a domiciliary of another state. We have seen that personal jurisdiction does arise in the vertical context, with a federal court sitting in one state exercising power over a defendant from another state. With some exceptions for nationwide jurisdiction sometimes available for federal courts, the personal jurisdiction analysis is the same for both of these domestic contexts, whether the conflict is vertical or horizontal. Although international disputes raise different concerns than wholly domestic disputes, in many ways, analysis of a state or federal court's jurisdiction over foreign parties is quite similar to the analysis deployed in wholly domestic contexts. This section introduces some of the special concerns and legal provisions unique to the international disputes.

Why might international disputes raise unique concerns? Federalism and separation of powers provide important general reasons why international cases might be different than wholly domestic disputes. Where a state court asserts jurisdiction over foreign parties, the state court is asserting itself in a matter that implicates an area generally reserved for federal authority—foreign affairs. If the international suit arises in federal court, the question of whether the federal court should assert personal jurisdiction implicates horizontal separation of powers among the branches of the federal government. The United States Constitution bestows on the Legislative and Executive branches of the federal government broad powers over foreign affairs. Although the Constitution contains only sparse language concerning the President's power, the United States Supreme Court at one time identified "the very delicate plenary, exclusive power of the President as the sole organ of the federal government in the field of international relations[.]"[5]

Despite this pronouncement, the Court has also recognized Congress's substantial powers over international matters, particularly over foreign commerce.[6] The allocation of foreign affairs authority between the President and Congress is thus indistinct and ambiguous. Nonetheless, the Supreme Court has clearly delimited judicial authority in this area. Specifically, the Court states that "the foreign relations of our Government is committed by the Constitution to the Executive and the Legislative — 'the political' — Departments of the Government."[7]

In light of "the political" branches' dominance in foreign affairs, federal courts have developed a number of doctrines designed to restrain judicial power over foreign affairs, including their power over international litigation. Many of these doctrines take the form of barriers to adjudication — such as the political question doctrine, the act of state doctrine, and sovereign immunity — and are explored at the end of this chapter in the section related to forum choice and obstacles to exercising power over foreign nations.

United States personal jurisdiction doctrine itself also reflects constraints on circumstances when courts in the United States may exercise power over foreign litigants. In particular, *Asahi Metal Industry Co. v. Superior Court*, 480 U.S. 102 (1987), reproduced earlier in this chapter, discusses the constraints. That portion of *Asahi* that garnered a majority vote (Part II-B) articulated two separate constraints on foreign litigation in the course of discussing personal jurisdiction doctrine's fairness factors. Alluding to the separation of powers implications of assertions of judicial power in cases with international elements, the *Asahi* Court first made clear its assumption that asserting personal jurisdiction over foreign defendants influences foreign policies and United States foreign relations. Indeed, the Court invoked Justice Harlan's admonition in *United States v. First National City Bank*, 379 U.S. 378, 404 (1965), that "[g]reat care and reserve should be exercised when extending out notions of personal jurisdiction into the international field." Moreover, the Court's due process analysis was solicitous to Asahi Metal Industry itself, not only proceeding on the assumption that the alien corporation was entitled to full due process protection in United States courts, but also emphasizing the need for *heightened* restraint on asserting jurisdiction over such corporations. The Court explained that "[t]he unique burdens placed upon one who must defend oneself in a foreign legal system should have significant weight in assessing the reasonableness of stretching the long arm of personal

5. *United States v. Curtiss-Wright Export Corp.*, 299 U.S. 304, 320 (1936).
6. *See, e.g., Dames & Moore v. Regan*, 453 U.S. 654, 669 (1981) (explaining that Congress enjoys control over the President's foreign affairs power, such control varying "along a spectrum running from explicit congressional authorization to explicit congressional prohibition").
7. *Oetjin v. Central Leather Co.*, 246 U.S. 297, 302 (1918).

jurisdiction over national borders." International law scholar and practitioner Gary Born describes the burdens of litigating abroad as follows:

> In many international cases one party will be required to follow procedural rules that differ markedly from those in its home jurisdiction. The most important differences involve broad discovery in the United States, greater reliance on the adversary system, trial by jury, different [attorney fee arrangements], the relatively greater size of United States damage awards, and different choice-of-law rules. In addition, one litigant will generally be a significantly greater distance from the forum than in purely domestic cases, and time differences, language barriers, mail delays, transportation difficulties, and other logistical obstacles . . . will create further hardships.

Gary Born, *Reflections on Judicial Jurisdiction in International Cases*, 17 GA. J. INT'L & COMP. L. 1, 24-25 n.102 (1987).

The *Asahi* Court did not state that each of these inconveniences was relevant to the due process fairness analysis. Nor did the Court specify whether the analysis should include the effect of personal jurisdiction on United States commercial concerns, such as attempts to facilitate international trade and to make American firms more competitive internationally. The generality of the fairness factors as well as the Court's statement that foreign relations requires courts to proceed with broad-ranging sensitivity suggest that all such matters have a legitimate role to play in personal jurisdiction analysis.

Although the relevance of the fairness factors remains open to doubt, the Court's decision in *Daimler*—as well as its earlier decision in *Helicopteros*—took note of the special sensitivity required for evaluating personal jurisdiction questions for corporations. Neither case, however provided guidance on the specific role of fairness factors necessarily reflected in the pair of 2011 general jurisdiction cases also presented above: *Goodyear Dunlop Tires Operations, S.A. v. Brown* and *J. McIntyre Machinery, Ltd. v. Nicastro*.

The final strand of personal jurisdiction doctrine that bears noting is jurisdiction based on presence in the territory where the court sits, otherwise known as "tag jurisdiction." As illustrated immediately below, service of process on a defendant present outside the geographical boundaries of the United States can raise logistical and legal challenges. These challenges can be avoided if one can establish proper jurisdiction by serving international defendants with process while they are temporarily present in the United States. Accordingly, tag jurisdiction can be particularly appealing in international cases, and has proven particularly useful in human rights cases.

Since the United States Supreme Court's decision in *Burnham v. Superior Court of California*, 495 U.S. 604 (1990), lower courts in the United States have grappled with how far tag jurisdiction extends to foreign defendants as well as whether the rule of *Burnham* applies to corporations. United States courts have generally allowed jurisdiction based on presence in international litigation, and it has proved quite useful in human rights litigation.

Tag jurisdiction, however, is not favored in international law. Indeed, in negotiations over the proposed Hague Jurisdiction and Judgments Convention (which ultimately failed to become law), European participants insisted that tag jurisdiction should be prohibited.

2. Regulation of Service of Process for Transnational Controversies

A number of mechanisms are available for serving a foreign defendant in a United States court action. United States precedent has long permitted service of the defendant within the United States, rather than in the defendant's home country. If the defendant can be served within the United States, then the complexities of transnational service of process can be avoided. Nonetheless, Federal Rule of Civil Procedure 4(f) also grants authority for service outside the United States and recognizes that a defendant in a foreign country may waive formal service as well. Moreover, Rule 4(f)(1) permits "any internationally agreed means of service that is reasonably calculated to give notice," specifically embracing the Hague Convention on the Service Abroad of Judicial and Extrajudicial Documents (the Hague Service Convention). This Convention applies only when the country where one seeks to effect service is a signatory, a status that now includes over 50 nations. *See* http://www.hcch.net/index_en.php?act=conventions.status&cid=17.

The Hague Service Convention provides that signatories must designate a "Central Authority" to which one directs requests for service. Upon receipt of proper documents, the Central Authority effects service. Federal Rule of Civil Procedure 4 makes clear that service accomplished consistent with the Hague Service Convention is sufficient under the Rule.

If service is desired in a country that has not signed the Hague Service Convention or there is another reason why an "internationally agreed means" to effect service is lacking, then other options exist under Rule 4(f)(2). First, the plaintiff can effect service in the manner specified under the local law of the country. The plaintiff can also ask the foreign country for instructions on how to serve process (using a document sometimes called a "letter rogatory" or "letter of request"). Other options include service by personal delivery to an individual (not a corporation) or by return-receipt mail dispatched by a court clerk unless prohibited by local law, and service "by other means not prohibited by international agreement, as the court orders."

Transnational litigation often includes corporate parties that may have complex corporate structures and affiliated entities. Questions arise as to whether service on one entity or representative of an entity is sufficient to effect service on a related entity. The following case reckons with that question.

Volkswagenwerk Aktiengesellschaft v. Schlunk

486 U.S. 694 (1988)

O'CONNOR, J., delivered the opinion of the Court, in which REHNQUIST, C.J., and WHITE, STEVENS, SCALIA, and KENNEDY, JJ., joined. BRENNAN, J., filed an opinion concurring in the judgment, in which MARSHALL and BLACKMUN, JJ., joined.

Justice O'CONNOR delivered the opinion of the Court.

This case involves an attempt to serve process on a foreign corporation by serving its domestic subsidiary which, under state law, is the foreign corporation's involuntary agent for service of process. We must decide whether such service is compatible with the Convention on Service Abroad of Judicial and Extrajudicial Documents in Civil and Commercial Matters, Nov. 15, 1965 (Hague Service Convention).

I

[This is a product liability action filed by Herwig Schlunk in Illinois state court against Volkswagen of America, Inc. (VWoA). Schlunk successfully served VWoA and then amended his complaint to add Volkswagen Aktiengesellschaft (VWAG), a corporation established under the laws of the Germany. VWoA is a wholly owned subsidiary of VWAG. Schlunk attempted to serve his amended complaint on VWAG by serving VWoA as VWAG's agent. In the Illinois court, VWAG asserted that it could be served only in accordance with the Hague Service Convention, and that Schlunk had not complied with the Convention's requirements. The court denied VWAG's motion, observing that VWoA is registered to do business in Illinois and has a registered agent for receipt of process in Illinois.] The court then reasoned that VWoA and VWAG are so closely related that VWoA is VWAG's agent for service of process as a matter of law, notwithstanding VWAG's failure or refusal to appoint VWoA formally as an agent. The court relied on the facts that VWoA is a wholly owned subsidiary of VWAG, that a majority of the members of the board of directors of VWoA are members of the board of VWAG, and that VWoA is by contract the exclusive importer and distributor of VWAG products sold in the United States. The court concluded that, because service was accomplished within the United States, the Hague Service Convention did not apply. [The Illinois appellate court agreed with this reasoning.]

II

The Hague Service Convention is a multilateral treaty that was formulated in 1964. . . . The primary innovation of the Convention is that it requires each state to establish a central authority to receive requests for service of documents from other countries. Once a central authority receives a request in the proper form, it must serve the documents by a method prescribed by the internal law of the receiving state or by a method designated by the requester and compatible with that law. The central authority must then provide a certificate of service that conforms to a specified model. A state also may consent to methods of service within its boundaries other than a request to its central authority. The remaining provisions of the Convention that are relevant here limit the circumstances in which a default judgment may be entered against a defendant who had to be served abroad and did not appear, and provide some means for relief from such a judgment.

Article 1 defines the scope of the Convention, which is the subject of controversy in this case. It says: "The present Convention shall apply in all cases, in civil or commercial matters, where there is occasion to transmit a judicial or extrajudicial document for service abroad." This language is mandatory. . . . By virtue of the Supremacy Clause, U.S. Const., Art. VI, the Convention pre-empts inconsistent methods of service prescribed by state law in all cases to which it applies. Schlunk does not purport to have served his complaint on VWAG in accordance with the Convention. Therefore, if service of process in this case falls within Article 1 of the Convention, the trial court should have granted VWAG's motion to quash.

When interpreting a treaty, we "begin 'with the text of the treaty and the context in which the written words are used.'" Other general rules of construction may be brought to bear on difficult or ambiguous passages. "'Treaties are construed more liberally than private agreements, and to ascertain their meaning we may look beyond the written words to the history of the treaty, the negotiations, and the practical construction adopted by the parties.'"

The Convention does not specify the circumstances in which there is "occasion to transmit" a complaint "for service abroad." But at least the term "service of process" has a well-established technical meaning. Service of process refers to a formal delivery of documents that is legally sufficient to charge the defendant with notice of a pending action. The legal sufficiency of a formal delivery of documents must be measured against some standard. The Convention does not prescribe a standard, so we almost necessarily must refer to the internal law of the forum state. If the internal law of the forum state defines the applicable method of serving process as requiring the transmittal of documents abroad, then the Hague Service Convention applies.

The negotiating history supports our view that Article 1 refers to service of process in the technical sense. . . . The negotiating history of the Convention also indicates that whether there is service abroad must be determined by reference to the law of the forum state. . . .

VWAG protests that it is inconsistent with the purpose of the Convention to interpret it as applying only when the internal law of the forum requires service abroad. One of the two stated objectives of the Convention is "to create appropriate means to ensure that judicial and extrajudicial documents to be served abroad shall be brought to the notice of the addressee in sufficient time." The Convention cannot assure adequate notice, VWAG argues, if the forum's internal law determines whether it applies. VWAG warns that countries could circumvent the Convention by defining methods of service of process that do not require transmission of documents abroad. Indeed, VWAG contends that one such method of service already exists and that it troubled the Conference: notification au parquet.

Notification au parquet permits service of process on a foreign defendant by the deposit of documents with a designated local official. Although the official generally is supposed to transmit the documents abroad to the defendant, the statute of limitations begins to run from the time that the official receives the documents, and there allegedly is no sanction for failure to transmit them.

There is no question but that the Conference wanted to eliminate notification au parquet. It included in the Convention two provisions that address the problem. Article 15 says that a judgment may not be entered unless a foreign defendant received adequate and timely notice of the lawsuit. Article 16 provides means whereby a defendant who did not receive such notice may seek relief from a judgment that has become final. Like Article 1, however, Articles 15 and 16 apply only when documents must be transmitted abroad for the purpose of service. VWAG argues that, if this determination is made according to the internal law of the forum state, the Convention will fail to eliminate variants of notification au parquet that do not expressly require transmittal of documents to foreign defendants. Yet such methods of service of process are the least likely to provide a defendant with actual notice.

. . . [N]either the language of the Convention nor the negotiating history contradicts our interpretation of the Convention, according to which the internal law of the forum is presumed to determine whether there is occasion for service abroad.

Nor are we persuaded that the general purposes of the Convention require a different conclusion. One important objective of the Convention is to provide means to facilitate service of process abroad. Thus the first stated purpose of the Convention is "to create" appropriate means for service abroad, and the second stated purpose is "to improve the organization of mutual judicial assistance for that purpose by simplifying and expediting the procedure." By requiring each state to establish a central authority to assist in the service of process, the Convention implements this enabling function. Nothing in our decision today interferes with this requirement.

VWAG correctly maintains that the Convention also aims to ensure that there will be adequate notice in cases in which there is occasion to serve process abroad. Thus compliance with the Convention is mandatory in all cases to which it applies, and Articles 15 and 16 provide an indirect sanction against those who ignore it. Our interpretation of the Convention does not necessarily advance this particular objective, inasmuch as it makes recourse to the Convention's means of service dependent on the forum's internal law. But we do not think that this country, or any other country, will draft its internal laws deliberately so as to circumvent the Convention in cases in which it would be appropriate to transmit judicial documents for service abroad. For example, there has been no question in this country of excepting foreign nationals from the protection of our Due Process Clause. Under that Clause, foreign nationals are assured of either personal service, which typically will require service abroad and trigger the Convention, or substituted service that provides "notice reasonably calculated, under all the circumstances, to apprise interested parties of the pendency of the action and afford them an opportunity to present their objections." *Mullane v. Central Hanover Bank & Trust Co.*, 339 U.S. 306, 314 (1950).

Furthermore, nothing that we say today prevents compliance with the Convention even when the internal law of the forum does not so require. The Convention provides simple and certain means by which to serve process on a foreign national. Those who eschew its procedures risk discovering that the forum's internal law required transmittal of documents for service abroad, and that the Convention therefore provided the exclusive means of valid service. In addition, parties that comply with the Convention ultimately may find it easier to enforce their judgments abroad. For these reasons, we anticipate that parties may resort to the Convention voluntarily, even in cases that fall outside the scope of its mandatory application.

III

In this case, the Illinois long-arm statute authorized Schlunk to serve VWAG by substituted service on VWoA, without sending documents to Germany. VWAG has not petitioned for review of the Illinois Appellate Court's holding that service was proper as a matter of Illinois law. VWAG contends, however, that service on VWAG was not complete until VWoA transmitted the complaint to VWAG in Germany. According to VWAG, this transmission constituted service abroad under the Hague Service Convention.

VWAG explains that, as a practical matter, VWoA was certain to transmit the complaint to Germany to notify VWAG of the litigation. Indeed, as a legal matter, the Due Process Clause requires every method of service to provide "notice reasonably calculated, under all the circumstances, to apprise interested parties of the pendency of the action and afford them an opportunity to present their objections." VWAG argues that, because of this notice requirement, every case involving service on a foreign national will present an "occasion to transmit a judicial . . . document for service abroad" within the meaning of Article 1. VWAG emphasizes that in this case, the Appellate Court upheld service only after determining that "the relationship between VWAG and VWoA is so close that it is certain that VWAG 'was fully apprised of the pendency of the action'" by delivery of the summons to VWoA.

We reject this argument. Where service on a domestic agent is valid and complete under both state law and the Due Process Clause, our inquiry ends and the Convention has no further implications. Whatever internal, private communications take place between the agent and a foreign principal are beyond the concerns of this case. The only transmittal to which the Convention applies is a transmittal abroad that is required as a necessary part of service. And, contrary to VWAG's assertion, the Due Process Clause does not require an official transmittal of documents abroad every time there is service on a foreign national. Applying this analysis, we conclude that this case does not present an occasion to transmit a judicial document for service abroad within the meaning of Article 1. Therefore the Hague Service Convention does not apply, and service was proper. The judgment of the Appellate Court is affirmed.

Notes on
SCHLUNK

1. The result in *Schlunk* effectively cedes to the lawmaking power of domestic authorities' initial control over the question of whether the Hague Service Convention applies in particular cases. Does this result respect the intention of the Convention? Justice Brennan argues in his concurrence that it is difficult to believe those that framed the Convention truly wanted to grant domestic authorities freedom to decide what circumstances, if any, the Convention would control.

2. Although *Schlunk* is a "service of process" case, it reflects reasoning common to choice of law issues. Ultimately, the case required the Court to determine what law should govern whether service was effective here. The answer was Illinois law. But the determinative factor in reaching this result was the Court's answer to a preliminary question: which law gets to determine whether international service is required? The Court determined that it was state law that governed whether in fact the Convention applied: the Convention's foreign service provisions were never implicated because state law provided a mode of domestic service. Does this give too much power to state law to control the operation of an international treaty? As it turns out, the decision to defer to the law of the forum (Illinois) on this threshold procedural issue is common in choice of law analysis. While it seems unremarkable to allow the forum to control a procedural law question, the result is to grant considerable control to the forum. Such is the nature of procedural law—and the importance of studying topics like this!

3. One can conceptualize *Schlunk*'s analytical process as three nesting dolls. The largest doll—the veneer to the analysis—suggests that international law controls the service issue. That is, the Hague Service Convention determines when it applies by stating that its terms govern when there is occasion to make "service abroad." But hidden interior dolls (representing domestic law) truly control this analysis: domestic law determines whether domestic service is available. If domestic service is available, no occasion exists to "make service abroad." To ascertain domestic law, we look to federal law: Federal Rule of Civil Procedure 4 as well as a federal law interpretation of the treaty in which the federal government is a signatory. Federal law, however, represents the middle nesting doll, since federal law points to state law to determine whether domestic service is available.

Figure 1-2: State Law Controls the Operation of Federal and International Law

4. In connection with personal jurisdiction in a domestic setting, we saw that practical considerations sometimes favor service based on presence in the jurisdiction. Practical considerations may also determine whether an attorney chooses to comply with the service requirements of the Hague Service Convention—even in cases where the requirements are not mandatory. As the *Schlunk* Court observed, parties complying with the Convention may encounter fewer problems enforcing judgments abroad, even if the Convention did not technically require the parties to comply with its terms.

PROBLEM 1-7: MOTORCYCLE MADNESS

Tamachi Japan is a Japanese company that manufactures motorcycles. It has a wholly owned subsidiary, Tamachi USA, which is a California corporation that assists with the sales of motorcycles in United States. Tamachi Japan and Tamachi USA scrupulously maintain separate corporate identities: the two corporations maintained entirely separate management teams and made clear to contracting parties that officers of neither corporation had the authority to make contracts on behalf of the other corporation.

Tamachi USA has a registered agent in Virginia and Tamachi Japan does not have registered agents anywhere in the United States. Mary, a resident of Virginia, was injured when she was riding her Tamachi motorcycle in Virginia. She filed suit in United States District Court against Tamachi Japan and Tamachi USA, invoking the federal court's diversity of citizenship jurisdiction. The United States and Japan are both signatories of the Hague Service Convention.

To serve Tamachi USA, Mary had a copy of the summons and complaint delivered to Tamachi USA's registered agent in Virginia. Mary attempted to serve Tamachi Japan under the provision of a Virginia statute that stated that a foreign corporation may be served by "substituted service." Pursuant to Virginia law, Mary served the summons and complaint intended for Tamachi Japan on the Secretary of the Commonwealth of Virginia. As directed by Virginia statute, the Secretary then mailed the papers to Tamachi Japan's main offices in Tokyo. The statute that directed the Secretary to do this states that service on the Secretary by mail "shall be sufficient so long as the Secretary promptly mails a copy of the complaint and summons to the defendant the papers are intended for." The Virginia service provisions do not, however, designate a domestic subsidiary to act as an involuntary agent for service of process on its foreign parent corporation.

Tamachi Japan has moved to dismiss the suit against it for failure to effect proper service of process. Mary responds that Tamachi Japan received adequate service in two ways: (1) she properly served Tamachi Japan's subsidiary Tamachi USA; and (2) she properly served Tamachi Japan through the substituted service provision of Virginia law. Should the district court accept either (or both) of these arguments?

3. Comparative Material: Jurisdiction Regulation Among European Union Members

As a quasi-federation of sovereignties, the European Union (EU) provides many useful points of comparison with United States law. Conflict of laws is no exception, since the EU has developed regulations governing all three aspects of conflict of laws: jurisdiction, choice of law, and judgments. This book reviews each of these aspects of EU regulation: Chapter 2 reviews the basic structure of the EU and various choice of law regulations; Chapter 4 reviews EU regulations respecting judgment recognition and enforcement. This section reviews the EU governance of jurisdiction, which appears in a regulation known as Brussels I.

The Brussels I regulation harmonizes jurisdiction rules for international disputes concerning civil and commercial matters. The EU coordinated these rules to facilitate the single European market, and to lay the foundations for establishing a single area of freedom, security, and justice.

The Brussels I regulation aims to create a set of highly predictable rules on jurisdiction, revolving around the principle that jurisdiction depends on a link between the territory of the Member State and the dispute. The general rule is that "persons domiciled in a Member State shall, whatever their nationality, be sued in the courts of that Member State." A Member State does not gain jurisdiction over a defendant simply because she was physically served process there. If a defendant is not domiciled in a Member State, the general rule is that she is not subject to the seized court's national rules of jurisdiction. A court is deemed seized "when the document instituting the proceedings or an equivalent document is lodged with the court, provided that the plaintiff has not subsequently failed to take the steps he was required to take to have service effected on the defendant," and the rules provide an alternative moment of seizure in jurisdictions where service on the defendant is required first. For an individual, domicile is defined by the national law of the court seized. The place of domicile for a company is determined by the location of its statutory seat (generally the country of registered incorporation), central administration, or principal place of business. Unlike under United States law, Brussels I provides no systematic and continuous contacts test that grants a Member State general jurisdiction over a company.

A defendant may be sued in a Member State that is not her domicile under specific circumstances, "based on a close link between the court and the action or in order to facilitate the sound administration of justice." A subject matter nexus may provide an alternative forum with jurisdiction. For example in contract disputes, the Member State where the contract is to be performed will have jurisdiction. Likewise in a tort action, the Member State where the "harmful event occurred" will have jurisdiction. For insurance contracts, consumer contracts, and employment contracts, the Brussels I regulation provides special jurisdictional rules that specifically favor the weaker party to the dispute. The subject matter of the dispute can also lead to a Member State having exclusive jurisdiction, regardless of the domicile of the defendant. A dispute over "rights *in rem* in immovable property," for instance, can only proceed in the Member State where the property is located.

Brussels I also provides rules governing forum selection clauses. Parties cannot circumvent the rules to protect weaker parties or the rules for exclusive jurisdiction, but they can bypass the general rule on jurisdiction by agreement, as long as one party is domiciled in a Member State and the chosen court is in a Member State. The chosen court, which is presumed to have exclusive jurisdiction, need not have any connection with the dispute or the parties to be valid. A defendant can also choose to accept a court's jurisdiction by entering an appearance before the court of a Member State without contesting its jurisdiction.

A common tactic to delay litigation under Brussels I is for one party to bring suit in a Member State different from that named in a valid choice of court agreement, and to take advantage of the regulations *lis pendens* or related action rules. Brussels I favors legal certainty, and in order to prevent contradictory judgments "involving the same cause of action and between the same parties," the regulation specifies that after the first court is seized, all other courts must decline jurisdiction over any parallel proceedings until the first court's jurisdiction is established. This is in contrast with American practice, which gives priority to the first judgment rendered, but generally tolerates litigation pending in more than one forum before the first judgment is rendered.[9] In the EU, if the first seized

---

9. Ralf Michaels, *Two Paradigms of Jurisdiction*, 27 MICH. J. INT'L L. 1003, 1062 (2006).

court establishes jurisdiction over the proceeding, all other courts must decline jurisdiction. Thus, a party can delay proceedings by rushing to file suit in a court contrary to that named in the choice of court agreement, because then the chosen court will not be able to exercise jurisdiction until the first seized court has established it does not have jurisdiction.[10]

European jurisdictional theory centers on predictability, as opposed to American jurisdictional theory, which focuses on fairness in individual cases, even at the expense of predictability.[11] Forum non conveniens, which allows a court to decline jurisdiction in favor of a more appropriate forum, is accepted practice in America. The doctrine is not available under Brussels I: if a court has jurisdiction under its rules, it must exercise jurisdiction. The European rules also have special rules for multiparty cases developed for the purpose of convenience and uniform judgments. Under the EU rules, a defendant that is domiciled in a Member State may be sued "where [s]he is one of a number of defendants, in the courts for the place where any one of them is domiciled." This requires no minimum contacts between the defendant and the forum, and enables an expansive jurisdictional reach in certain cases.

G. OTHER MATTERS RELATED TO FORUM CHOICE

When a plaintiff considers where she should file suit, a number of items should appear on her checklist. Preliminarily, she must identify the jurisdictions where the court has personal jurisdiction over the defendant and where she can successfully serve the defendant with process. Next she must find a court with proper subject matter jurisdiction. Subject matter jurisdiction bears on the competency to adjudicate the subject matter of the suit, and can include such matters as amount in controversy and citizenship of the parties. In the United States, she will likely consider whether a state or federal court has subject matter jurisdiction. Often, procedural differences between state and federal courts in the same location may make one court system or the other much more attractive to the plaintiff. The types of procedural differences that may matter to the plaintiff are the availability of a jury trial, the method of selecting judges (appointment versus election), the geographical area from which a jury pool is drawn, and pleading rules. These distinctions between state and federal court are discussed further in Chapter 3, in connection with the doctrine of *Erie Railroad Co. v. Tompkins*, 304 U.S. 64 (1938).

Once the plaintiff considers personal jurisdiction and subject matter jurisdiction, she should focus on other obstacles that are the subject of this section. First, she must evaluate where — within the court system that she chooses — venue is proper. Venue rules are generally codified and reflect a legislative

---

10. Michael Bogdan, Concise Introduction to EU Private International Law 71 (Europa Law Pub. 2006).

11. Ralf Michaels, *Two Paradigms of Jurisdiction*, 27 Mich. J. Int'l L. 1003, 1062 (2006).

decision about convenient places for litigation. Other matters that she might consider include whether the defendant might be able to veto her choice of forum by filing a motion asking the court to dismiss the case under the doctrine of forum non conveniens. Forum non conveniens is a discretionary doctrine, allowing a court to dismiss an action in favor of another forum. Materials explaining the doctrine appear below after the venue discussion. Sometimes, parties actually agree that any disputes between them should be litigated in a particular forum. While courts are not inclined to allow parties to actually take away court power, courts do honor these agreements in most circumstances. Materials addressing these agreements, usually in the form of "forum selection clauses," are presented after the forum non conveniens materials.

Plaintiffs in cases with international elements face additional obstacles, which are described below after the forum selection clause material. Some of these hurdles arise only where the plaintiff is complaining about activities attributable to a foreign state; other problems arise where the lawsuit implicates the foreign affairs powers of the Congress and President of the United States.

As this chapter's materials reveal, a competent attorney representing a party in litigation must make many strategic decisions bearing on the forum where a lawsuit is litigated. In fact, the system is set up so that the competent attorney has significant incentive to compare the various advantages and disadvantages of jurisdictions available for the lawsuit. The architecture of the world's civil justice system invites such shopping for a favorable forum, although courts are often heard to malign the practice of strategically evaluating the merits of one jurisdiction over another. Cases are replete with admonitions about the evils of "forum shopping," and the final section of this chapter takes up this practice.

Finally, the whole notion of strategizing about where to file a lawsuit provides a springboard for learning about choice of law rules. Indeed, one of the most important considerations for a party considering where to litigate is identifying a jurisdiction that will choose to apply substantive legal principles that make it most likely the party will prevail. The principles that the jurisdiction uses to choose those substantive legal principles are choice of law rules. The rules vary widely among jurisdictions, and are covered in detail throughout Chapter 2. Choice of law rules, however, also have a subsidiary influence on the operation of other forum choice obstacles, including venue statutes and the forum non conveniens doctrine, which are discussed immediately below.

1. Venue and Venue Transfer

Venue requirements regulate where within a court system a lawsuit may be filed. Although venue shares the concept of location with personal jurisdiction, personal jurisdiction refers to the power of a court to adjudicate, while venue is the place where the adjudicative power may be exercised. Unlike personal jurisdiction, venue is almost exclusively statutory and does not have an integral constitutional component.[12] Nonetheless, venue provisions are inspired by fairness concerns, designed to protect parties (particularly defendants) from the burden of litigating in an inconvenient forum.

State statutes generally require venue to be laid in particular counties and federal statutes require venue to be laid in particular judicial districts. Venue statutes can be relatively complex, although they usually allow a lawsuit to be filed in the place of the defendant's residence or the place where the plaintiff's claim arose. In federal court suits against alien defendants, venue is not generally a concern, since the Alien Venue Statute provides that "[a]n alien may be sued in any district." 28 U.S.C. §1391. Even in mixed suits with alien defendants and domestic defendants (i.e., defendants who are resident in the United States), courts focus only on the state residence of the domestic defendants in evaluating whether venue is proper.

Federal and state systems allow a court to transfer venue from one place to another within the specific court system. Courts may transfer litigation from an improper venue to a proper one or from one proper venue to another (usually if the transferee location is much more convenient or consistent with the efficient administration of justice). Transfer motions are generally a defendant's litigation tool, allowing the defendant to override the plaintiff's choice of forum. In federal court, one statute — 28 U.S.C. §1404(a) — governs transfers when the original federal court (the transferor court) is a proper venue and permits transfers for "the convenience of parties and witnesses, in the interest of justice." Another statute — 28 U.S.C. §1406(a) — governs transfers when the transferor court is an improper venue. The case that follows gives an example of a straightforward application of §1404(a). As you review it, consider why the parties would be fighting over the location of the litigation as well as the various political, economic, and judicial administration concerns that bear on the court of appeals decision.

In re Genentech, Inc.

566 F.3d 1338 (Fed. Cir. 2009)

LINN, Circuit Judge.

Genentech, Inc. ("Genentech") and Biogen Idec Inc. ("Biogen") petition for a writ of mandamus to direct the United States District Court for the Eastern District of Texas to vacate its March 19, 2009 order denying the petitioners' motion to transfer venue, and to direct that court to transfer the case to the United States District Court for the Northern District of California. Sanofi-Aventis Deutschland GmbH ("Sanofi") opposes. The petitioners move for leave to reply.

---

12. Although venue statutes are not initially informed by constitutional concerns, they may implicate constitutional problems. For example, a venue statute might run afoul of the due process clause if it requires suits to be filed in inaccessible or unfair locations.

I. BACKGROUND

Genentech, which is headquartered in San Francisco, California, and Biogen, which has facilities in San Diego, California, are defendants in a patent infringement suit brought by the German company, Sanofi. Sanofi brought the suit in the District Court for the Eastern District of Texas, a venue which indisputably has no connection to any of the witnesses or evidence relevant to the cause of action. On the same day, the petitioners filed a related declaratory judgment action in the Northern District of California, seeking a declaration of invalidity and noninfringement of Sanofi's patents.

The petitioners filed a motion pursuant to 28 U.S.C. §1404(a) to transfer the Texas case to the Northern District of California. The petitioners argued that at least ten potential material witnesses, including two of the patent prosecution attorneys, reside in the Northern District, and at least four additional potential witnesses are residents of California. The petitioners further argued that all of their documents relating to the development and marketing of the accused infringing products were either in the proposed transferee jurisdiction or in San Diego, California.

Sanofi opposed transfer, contending that the Eastern District of Texas was the proper venue. Sanofi argued that the Eastern District of Texas was centrally located between the parties and would be more convenient for the six inventors who reside in Europe, a prior art author who resides in Iowa who could be a potential witness, and the remaining four prosecuting patent attorneys who reside on the U.S. East Coast. Sanofi also argued that a denial of transfer could prevent a waste of judicial resources by avoiding the need for the Northern District of California to decide whether it had personal jurisdiction over Sanofi with regard to the petitioners' declaratory judgment action.

... [T]he Eastern District of Texas denied petitioners' request to transfer. ... The petitioners ask us for a writ of mandamus directing the Eastern District of Texas to vacate its order and transfer the case pursuant to 28 U.S.C. §1404(a).

II. DISCUSSION

[The court described the extraordinary nature of the writ of mandamus, which it said should be used to only "to correct a clear abuse of discretion or usurpation of judicial power." The court did note, however, that the mandamus remedy was available to redress a clearly erroneous denial of a §1404(a) transfer.]

A. TRANSFER OF VENUE PURSUANT TO 28 U.S.C. §1404(a)

The basic principles governing transfer of venue under the law of the Fifth Circuit are well settled and are not in dispute here. Pursuant to §1404(a), "[f]or the convenience of parties and witnesses, in the interest of justice, a district court may transfer any civil action to another district court or division where it might have been brought." 28 U.S.C. §1404(a). A motion to transfer venue should be granted upon a showing that the transferee venue "is clearly more convenient" than the venue chosen by the plaintiff.

In assessing whether a defendant has met its burden of demonstrating the need to transfer, the Fifth Circuit applies the "public" and "private" factors for determining forum non conveniens. As we noted in *TS Tech*, the private interest factors include "(1) the relative ease of access to sources of proof; (2) the availability of compulsory process to secure the attendance of witnesses; (3) the cost of attendance for willing witnesses; and (4) all other practical problems that make a trial easy, expeditious and inexpensive." The public interest factors include "(1) the administrative difficulties flowing from court congestion; (2) the local interest in having localized interests decided at home; (3) the familiarity of the forum with the law that will govern the case; and (4) the avoidance of unnecessary problems of conflicts of laws [or in] the application of foreign law."

B. APPLICATION OF THE FACTORS

[The court reviewed the district court findings. The court also noted that there was (1) "no dispute between the parties that this case could have been brought by Sanofi in the Northern District of California" and (2) "no dispute between the parties regarding . . . the familiarity of the forum factor and conflict of laws factor."]

i. Convenience of the Witnesses and Parties

We start with an important factor, the convenience for and cost of attendance of witnesses. [The court noted that facts to consider include additional expenses and increased time away from work for witnesses.]

The petitioners identified at least ten witnesses within the Northern District of California, including at least three non-party witnesses who had knowledge of material facts relevant to the case. Two of the identified witnesses within the transferee venue were attorneys responsible for the prosecution of some of the patents-in-suit. The other witnesses within the venue had knowledge of the development and/or manufacture of the accused infringing products. The petitioners also identified at least four additional witnesses that had knowledge of material facts relevant to the case outside of the proposed alternative venue but within California, including at least three non-party witnesses. Although no witness resides in the Eastern District of Texas, the district court stated that this factor only "slightly" favored transfer.

The court gave four reasons why the Northern District of California was not clearly more convenient for the witnesses. First, the court stated that the petitioners had failed to identify any "key witnesses" within the transferee venue. Second, the court asserted that the six inventors traveling from Europe and Switzerland would be more inconvenienced in having to testify in California than Texas. Third, the court stated that Texas was more centrally located for the European witnesses as well as a potential witness regarding prior art from Iowa and the remaining patent prosecution attorneys who reside on the East Coast. Finally, the court cited several of its recent orders for the proposition that this factor should not weigh in favor of transfer unless transfer would be convenient for all the witnesses.

Regarding the court's assessment that the petitioners failed to identify any "key witnesses" within the venue, the petitioners were held to a higher standard than required by the law. A district court should assess the relevance and materiality of the information the witness may provide. Requiring a defendant to show that the potential witness has more than relevant and material information at this point in the litigation or risk facing denial of transfer on that basis is unnecessary. It is clear from the parties' filings below that inequitable conduct, infringement, and invalidity might be issues at trial. The petitioners have identified witnesses relevant to those issues, and the identification of those witnesses weighs in favor of transfer. It was not necessary for the district court to evaluate the significance of the identified witnesses' testimony.

. . . The witnesses from Europe will be required to travel a significant distance no matter where they testify. In contrast to the foreign witnesses, there are a substantial number of witnesses residing within the transferee venue who would be unnecessarily inconvenienced by having to travel away from home to testify in the Eastern District of Texas. . . .

. . . Because a substantial number of material witnesses reside within the transferee venue and the state of California, and no witnesses reside within the Eastern District of Texas, the district court clearly erred in not determining this factor to weigh substantially in favor of transfer.

Concerning the convenience of the parties . . . , Genentech is headquartered within the Northern District of California. Biogen conducts research and development from its facilities in San Diego, California and . . . some of its employees and managers would have to travel approximately half the distance to attend trial in Northern District of California than in the Eastern District of Texas. Sanofi is a German corporation that will be traveling a great distance no matter which venue the case is tried in and will be only slightly more inconvenienced by the case being tried in California than in Texas. Thus, the parties' convenience factor favored transfer, and not only slightly.

ii. Availability of Compulsory Process

Pursuant to Rule 45(b)(2)(C) of the Federal Rules of Civil Procedure, a district court may compel attendance through the issuance of a subpoena at any place within the district of the court by which it is issued or at any place within 100 miles of where the deposition, trial, or hearing is being held. As noted above, there is a substantial number of witnesses within the subpoena power of the Northern District of California and no witness who can be compelled to appear in the Eastern District of Texas. The fact that the transferee venue is a venue with usable subpoena power here weighs in favor of transfer, and not only slightly.

iii. Access to Evidence

"In patent infringement cases, the bulk of the relevant evidence usually comes from the accused infringer. Consequently, the place where the defendant's documents are kept weighs in favor of transfer to that location." . . . Here, Genentech informed the district court that all of its corporate documents relating to the development, manufacturing, and marketing of eight of the nine accused infringing products are housed in its headquarters, which is in the transferee venue. Biogen informed the district court that all of its relevant materials relating to the ninth allegedly infringing product are housed at its facilities in San Diego, California.

The district court . . . stated that this factor was neutral. . . . We . . . conclude that the district court clearly erred. Keeping this case in Texas will impose a significant and unnecessary burden on the petitioners to transport documents that would not be incurred if the case were to proceed in the Northern District of California. Furthermore, because the documents housed in Europe and Washington, D.C. will need to be transported in any event, it is only slightly more inconvenient or costly to require the transportation of those materials to California than Texas. Thus, this factor weighs in favor of transfer.

iv. Practical Problems

In its order, the District Court for the Eastern District of Texas cited two issues regarding the practicality of trying this case in the Eastern District of Texas instead of the Northern District of California. One of the issues the court found to weigh significantly against transfer was that Genentech had previously chosen to file a different suit in the Eastern District of Texas. The court reasoned that "Genentech cannot avail itself of the Eastern District's courts when it suits them, only to complain little more than two years later that the Eastern District is an inconvenient venue in a subsequent suit."

We agree with the petitioners that the district court's consideration of the previous case was clear error. . . . The Supreme Court has long held that §1404(a) requires "individualized, case-by-case consideration of convenience and fairness." The court does not suggest that Genentech's previous lawsuit involved the same parties, witnesses, evidence, and facts. Thus, the court clearly erred in finding Genentech's prior suit weighed against transfer.

The court also stated that the possibility of the Northern District of California lacking jurisdiction over Sanofi was a "critical" problem, weighing heavily against transfer. We . . . cannot agree that this issue weighs heavily against transfer and conclude that the court . . . erred. There is no requirement under §1404(a) that a transferee court have jurisdiction over the plaintiff or that there be sufficient minimum contacts with the plaintiff; there is only a requirement that the transferee court have jurisdiction over the defendants in the transferred complaint. . . .

v. Court Congestion

In its order, the district court found that administrative difficulties caused by court congestion weighed against transfer. In explaining this factor, the court cited the parties' opposing statistics regarding the rate of disposition in the two venues. . . .

To the extent that court congestion is relevant, the speed with which a case can come to trial and be resolved may be a factor. We do not disturb the district court's suggestion that it could dispose of the case more quickly than if the case was transferred to the Northern District of California. . . . Without attempting to predict how this case would be resolved and which court might resolve it more quickly, we merely note that when, as here, several relevant factors weigh in favor of transfer and others are neutral, then the speed of the transferee district court should not alone outweigh all of those other factors.

vi. Local Interest

The petitioners also argue that the district court failed to adequately consider the Northern District of California's interest in having this case tried within the venue. We note that even if this factor only "slightly" favors transfer, as the district court indicated, it nevertheless favors transfer along with several other relevant factors.

C. RIGHT TO MANDAMUS RELIEF

A court may deny a petition for mandamus "[i]f the facts and circumstances are rationally capable of providing reasons for what the district court has done." Nevertheless, mandamus relief in §1404(a) cases is permitted when the petitioner is able to demonstrate that the denial of transfer was a "clear" abuse of discretion such that refusing transfer produced a "patently erroneous result."

. . . In denying transfer, the district court clearly abused its discretion and produced a patently erroneous result. . . . The petitioners have also demonstrated that they have no other means of obtaining their request for relief. . . . [W]e grant the petition for a writ of mandamus.

Notes on
GENENTECH

1. As illustrated in *Genentech*, the decision whether to grant a transfer motion tends to be a fact-laden inquiry. Used in *Genentech*, a writ of mandamus is the standard procedural vehicle in federal court for gaining appellate review. The extraordinary nature of this remedy reduces the chances of convincing an appellate court to overturn a district court's ruling on a transfer motion. Given that the standard for granting mandamus is high, do you think that the court of appeals was sufficiently deferential to the district court?

2. What do you think of the court of appeals' decision to reject — with little explanation and no qualification — the plaintiff's argument that the defendant who was trying to seek transfer had previously chosen to file suit in the Texas district? Given that the defendant's convenience is a relevant factor to a venue transfer motion, does it not matter that the defendant had actually *chosen* to litigate in the district that it is now complaining is inconvenient?

3. Sometimes jurisdictions make a name for themselves because of their expertise, speed, and/or litigant preferences. Where the jurisdictions render speedy and big verdicts, they provide a strong incentive for plaintiffs to file suit there — and for defendants to seek a venue transfer. What is the attraction of the Eastern District of Texas for the plaintiff in *Genentech*?

Courts for the Eastern District of Texas are present in a number of towns (at last check, these towns included Tyler, Beaumont, Lufkin, Marshall, Paris, Sherman, and Texarkana), but Marshall, Texas seems to be particularly attractive for patent litigation. Despite its relatively small size and rural location, the United States District Court in Marshall, Texas sometimes entertained more patent lawsuits than federal district courts in San Francisco, Chicago, New York City, and Washington. What's the draw of Marshall? As *Genentech* suggests, the "rocket docket" there brings cases to trial quickly, with plaintiff-friendly verdicts—described as "Texas-sized" awards. In addition, the district's local rules and reported hostility to summary judgment require defendants to invest significant resources in the front end of litigation, providing a strategic benefit to plaintiffs (particularly plaintiffs who wish to prompt a swift settlement). Interestingly, the economic boom from the patent litigation is palpable: the town experienced increased investment in real estate as well as hotel and restaurant business, even during recessionary times. *See* Julie Creswell, *So Small a Town, So Many Patent Suits,* N.Y. TIMES, Sept. 24, 2006. It is hard to gauge how factors like these— economic benefits from preserving a town's reputation as favoring a particular type of party or a particular legal position—bear on a local trial court's decision whether to grant a venue motion.

Since *Genentech* was decided, the U.S. Supreme Court handed down a decision that might substantially reduce the patent docket in the Eastern District of Texas. In *TC Heartland LLC v. Kraft Foods Group Brands LLC,* 137 S. Ct. 1514 (2007), the Supreme Court held that the patent venue statute required that infringement suits against domestic corporations be brought where the corporation is incorporated or where the corporation engaged in an infringement act and has a "regular and established place of business." Because so many domestic companies are incorporated in Delaware, one might speculate that the *TC Heartland* decision might replace the Eastern District of Texas with the District of Delaware. Delaware's practices, however, do not require the same early investment in discovery by defendants as do those in the Eastern District of Texas, thus reducing plaintiffs' strategic advantages. Delaware is also not necessarily regarded as pro-plaintiff. As a consequence, the *TC Heartland* decision may ultimately steer cases away from Texas and toward the broad variety of jurisdictions where defendants happen to commit infringing acts and have a regular and established place of business.

4. As noted earlier, there are two main statutes governing transfer of venue: 28 U.S.C. §1404(a), which governs transfers when the original federal court (the transferor court) is a proper venue, and 28 U.S.C. §1406(a), which governs transfers when the transferor court is an improper venue. Issues have arisen about the scope of these two transfer statutes where personal jurisdiction is lacking. In *Goldlawr, Inc. v. Heiman,* 369 U.S. 463 (1962), the Supreme Court held that a transferor court that lacked personal

jurisdiction over a defendant can successfully transfer a case pursuant to §1406(a). Most federal courts agree that this ruling applies in a §1404(a) situation as well (when venue is proper in the transferor court). Section 1404(a) allows transfer to a district court where a suit "might have been brought." Interpreting this language in *Hoffman v. Blaski*, 363 U.S. 335 (1960), the Supreme Court held that in order to effect a valid transfer under §1404(a), the transferee court must be a proper venue and must have personal jurisdiction over the defendants. Presumably this holding applies for §1406(a) transferee courts as well, since that section allows the transferor court to transfer only to a district where the action "might have been brought."

The forum where a lawsuit is litigated has a powerful influence over which choice of law rules apply when the laws of more than one jurisdiction might provide the rules of decision for resolution of the dispute. Rules of decision are the substantive legal principles that govern the rights and liabilities of citizens, and are applied by a court to determine the result of disputes brought before a court. (Rules of decision are sometimes contrasted with procedural rules, which govern only the conduct of litigation — the process by which rights and liabilities are determined.) As powerfully illustrated in Chapter 2, choice of law rules vary considerably from forum to forum. Thus, litigants not only need to concern themselves with possible rules of decision governing their suit, but they must also focus on the likely choice of law rules that will be used to identify which jurisdiction actually provides the rules of decision. Choice of law rules come from the forum where a lawsuit is filed. In federal court, the governing choice of law rules are those of the state where the federal court sits. Thus, a judge of the U.S. District Court for the Southern District of Ohio will apply Ohio choice of law rules if a question arises about which conflicting state laws should govern a question.

Given the connection between location and choice of law rules, the transfer options of §§1404(a) and 1406(a) provide an important tool for litigants concerned about influencing choice of law rules applied in their dispute. If changing venue could change choice of law rules, litigants would have strong incentive to use §§1404(a) and 1406(a) as a vehicle for changing the laws that apply to their disputes. The Supreme Court reckoned with this incentive in the following case.

Van Dusen v. Barrack

376 U.S. 612 (1964)

Mr. Justice GOLDBERG delivered the opinion of the Court.

This case involves the construction and application of §1404(a) . . . which allows a "change of venue" within the federal judicial system, [and] provides that: "For the convenience of parties and witnesses, in the interest of justice, a district court may transfer any civil action to any other district or division where it might have been brought." 28 U.S.C. §1404(a).

The facts, which need but brief statement here, reveal that the disputed change of venue is set against the background of an alleged mass tort. On October 4, 1960, shortly after departing from a Boston airport, a commercial airliner, scheduled to fly from Boston to Philadelphia, plunged into Boston Harbor. As a result of the crash, over 150 actions for personal injury and wrongful death have been instituted against the airline, various manufacturers, the United States, and, in some cases, the Massachusetts Port Authority. In most of these actions the plaintiffs have alleged that the crash resulted from the defendants' negligence in permitting the aircraft's engines to ingest some birds. More than 100 actions were brought in the United States District Court for the District of Massachusetts, and more than 45 actions in the United States District Court for the Eastern District of Pennsylvania.

The present case concerns 40 of the wrongful death actions brought in the Eastern District of Pennsylvania by personal representatives of victims of the crash. The defendants, petitioners in this Court, moved under §1404(a) to transfer these actions to the District of Massachusetts, where it was alleged that most of the witnesses resided and where over 100 other actions are pending. The District Court granted the motion, holding that the transfer was justified regardless of whether the transferred actions would be governed by the laws and choice-of-law rules of Pennsylvania or of Massachusetts. The District Court also specifically held that transfer was not precluded by the fact that the plaintiffs had not qualified under Massachusetts law to sue as representatives of the decedents. The plaintiffs, respondents in this Court, sought a writ of mandamus from the Court of Appeals and successfully contended that the District Court erred and should vacate its order of transfer. The Court of Appeals held that a §1404(a) transfer could be granted only if at the time the suits were brought, the plaintiffs had qualified to sue in Massachusetts, the State of the transferee District Court. . . .

We granted certiorari to review important questions concerning the construction and operation of §1404(a). For reasons to be stated below, we hold that the judgment of the Court of Appeals must be reversed, that both the Court of Appeals and the District Court erred in their fundamental assumptions regarding the state law to be applied to an action transferred under §1404(a), and that accordingly the case must be remanded to the District Court.

I. WHERE THE ACTION "MIGHT HAVE BEEN BROUGHT"

Section 1404(a) reflects an increased desire to have federal civil suits tried in the federal system at the place called for in the particular case by considerations of convenience and justice. . . . The purpose of the section is to prevent the waste "of time, energy and money" and "to protect litigants, witnesses and the public against unnecessary inconvenience and expense. . . ." To this end it empowers a district court to transfer "any civil action" to another district court if the transfer is warranted by the convenience of parties and witnesses and promotes the interest of justice. This transfer power is, however, expressly limited by the final clause of §1404(a) restricting transfer to those federal districts in which the action "might have been brought." Although in the present case the plaintiffs were qualified to bring suit as personal representatives under Pennsylvania law (the law of the State of the transferor federal court), the Court of Appeals ruled that the defendants' transfer motion must be denied because at the time the suits were brought in Pennsylvania (the transferor forum) the complainants had not obtained the appointments requisite to initiate such actions in Massachusetts (the transferee forum). . . .

[The United States Supreme Court held that the Court of Appeals had erred in this determination, noting that a §1404(a) transfer does not "effect a change of law" but essentially only authorizes "a change of courtrooms," thus allowing the Pennsylvania appointments to remain valid in the complainants' actions in the transferee forum.]

II. "The Interest of Justice": Effect of a Change of Venue upon Applicable State Law

A. The plaintiffs contend that the change of venue ordered by the District Court was necessarily precluded by the likelihood that it would be accompanied by a highly prejudicial change in the applicable state law. The prejudice alleged is not limited to that which might flow from the Massachusetts laws governing capacity to sue. Indeed, the plaintiffs emphasize the likelihood that the defendants' ultimate reason for seeking transfer is to move to a forum where recoveries for wrongful death are restricted to sharply limited punitive damages rather than compensation for the loss suffered. It is argued that Pennsylvania choice-of-law rules would result in the application of laws substantially different from those that would be applied by courts sitting in Massachusetts. The District Court held, however, that transfer could be ordered regardless of the state laws and choice-of-law rules to be applied in the transferee forum and regardless of the possibility that the laws applicable in the transferor State would significantly differ from those applicable in the transferee State. This ruling assumed that transfer to a more convenient forum may be granted on a defendant's motion even though that transfer would seriously prejudice the plaintiff's legal claim. If this assumption is valid, the plaintiffs argue, transfer is necessarily precluded — regardless of convenience and other considerations — as against the "interest of justice" in dealing with plaintiffs who have either exercised the venue privilege conferred by federal statutes, or had their cases removed from state into federal court.

If conflict of laws rules are laid aside, it is clear that Massachusetts (the State of the transferee court) and Pennsylvania (the State of the transferor court) have significantly different laws concerning recovery for wrongful death. The Massachusetts Death Act provides that one who negligently causes the death of another "shall be liable in damages in the sum of not less than two thousand nor more than twenty thousand dollars, to be assessed with reference to the degree of his culpability. . . ." By contrast, under Pennsylvania law the recovery of damages (1) is based upon the more common principle of compensation for losses rather than upon the degree of the tortfeasor's culpability and (2) is not limited to $20,000. Some of the defendants urge, however, that these differences are irrelevant to the present case because Pennsylvania state courts, applying their own choice of law rules, would require that the Massachusetts Death Act be applied in its entirety, including its culpability principle and damage limitation. It follows that a federal district court sitting in Pennsylvania, and referring, as is required by *Klaxon Co. v. Stentor Elec. Mfg. Co., Inc.*, 313 U.S. 487, to Pennsylvania choice-of-law rules, would therefore be applying the same substantive rules as would a state or federal court in Massachusetts if the actions had been commenced there. This argument highlights the fact that the most convenient forum is frequently the place where the cause of action arose and that the conflict-of-laws rules of other States may often refer to the substantive rules of the more convenient forum. . . .

The possibilities suggested by the plaintiffs' argument illustrate the difficulties that would arise if a change of venue, granted at the motion of a defendant, were to result in a change of law. Although in the present case the contentions concern rules relating to capacity to sue and damages, in other cases the transferee forum might have a shorter statute of limitations or might refuse to adjudicate a claim which would have been actionable in the transferor State. In such cases a defendant's motion to transfer could be tantamount to a motion to dismiss. In light, therefore, of this background and the facts of the present case, we need not and do not consider the merits of the contentions concerning the meaning and proper application of Pennsylvania's laws and choice of law rules. For present purposes it is enough that the potential prejudice to the plaintiffs is so substantial as to require review of the assumption that a change of state law would be a permissible result of transfer under §1404(a). . . .

There is nothing . . . in the language or policy of §1404(a) to justify its use by defendants to defeat the advantages accruing to plaintiffs who have chosen a forum which, although it was inconvenient, was a proper venue. In this regard the transfer provisions of §1404(a) may be compared with those of §1406(a). Although both sections were broadly designed to allow transfer instead of dismissal, §1406(a) provides for transfer from forums in which venue is wrongly or improperly laid, whereas, in contrast, §1404(a) operates on the premises that the plaintiff has properly exercised his venue privilege. This distinction underlines the fact that Congress, in passing §1404(a), was primarily concerned with the problems arising where, despite the propriety of the plaintiff's venue selection, the chosen forum was an inconvenient one.

In considering the Judicial Code, Congress was particularly aware of the need for provisions to mitigate abuses stemming from broad federal venue provisions. . . . This legislative background supports the view that §1404(a) was not designed to narrow the plaintiff's venue privilege or to defeat the state-law advantages that might accrue from the exercise of this venue privilege but rather the provision was simply to counteract the inconveniences that flowed from the venue statutes by permitting transfer to a convenient federal court. The legislative history of §1404(a) certainly does not justify the rather startling conclusion that one might "get a change of law as a bonus for a change of venue." Indeed, an interpretation accepting such a rule would go far to frustrate the remedial purposes of §1404(a). If a change of law were in the offing, the parties might well regard the section primarily as a forum-shopping instrument. And, more importantly, courts would at least be reluctant to grant transfers, despite considerations of convenience, if to do so might conceivably prejudice the claim of a plaintiff who had initially selected a permissible forum. We believe, therefore, that both the history and purposes of §1404(a) indicate that it should be regarded as a federal judicial housekeeping measure, dealing with the placement of litigation in the federal courts and generally intended, on the basis of convenience and fairness, simply to authorize a change of courtrooms.

[The Court further concluded that its determination that the choice of law rules from the transferor court should apply in the transferee court is consistent with the policies of *Erie R.R. Co. v. Tompkins*, 304 U.S. 64 (1934).]

We conclude, therefore, that . . . , where the defendants seek transfer, the transferee district court must be obligated to apply the state law that would have been applied if there had been no change of venue. A change of venue under §1404(a) should be, with respect to state law, but a change of courtrooms.[40] . . . We, therefore, reject . . . plaintiffs' contention that the transfer was necessarily precluded by the likelihood that a prejudicial change of law would result. In so ruling . . . we do not . . . consider whether in all cases §1404(a) would require the application of the law of the transferor, as opposed to the transferee, state. We do not attempt to determine whether, for example, the same considerations would govern if a plaintiff sought transfer under §1404(a) or if it was contended that the transferor state would simply have dismissed the action on the ground of forum non conveniens. . . .

Reversed and remanded.

Notes on
VAN DUSEN v. BARRACK

1. Should the holding of *Van Dusen v. Barrack* apply in a situation such as *Goldlawr, Inc. v. Heiman*, 369 U.S. 466 (1962), where the transferor court lacks personal jurisdiction over the defendant? In other words, where a case is transferred because the first court did not have personal jurisdiction over the defendant, should the second court apply the choice of law rules that would have applied in the first court?

2. The United States Supreme Court did extend the *Van Dusen* holding to a §1404(a) transfer initiated by a plaintiff. In *Ferens v. John Deere Co.*, 494 U.S. 516 (1990), a plaintiff injured in Pennsylvania failed to file suit within the two-year statute of limitations controlling there. The plaintiff instead

---

40. Of course the transferee District Court may apply its own rules governing the conduct and dispatch of cases in its court. We are only concerned here with those state laws of the transferor State which would significantly affect the outcome of the case.

filed suit after the two-year mark in a federal district court in Mississippi, which has a six-year statute of limitations. The plaintiff then filed a §1404(a) transfer to the more convenient Pennsylvania forum and the Supreme Court ruled that the longer statute of limitation applied. Is this holding consistent with the intent of avoiding choice of law reflected in *Van Dusen?*

PROBLEM 1-8: CHOICE OF LAW AFTER PILAR'S §1404(a) TRANSFER

Dan filed a diversity action against Pilar in the United States District Court for the District of Delaware. Although the District of Delaware was a proper venue, Pilar filed a §1404(a) motion to transfer the case to the Southern District of New York and the court granted the motion. Assume that Delaware choice of law rules make clear that the law that should provide the rules of decision governing the controversy is the law of the Philippines. New York choice of law rules, however, would designate New York law as the governing law. Which choice of law rules will govern? Which law will provide the rules of decision?

PROBLEM 1-9: CHOICE OF LAW AFTER PILAR'S §1406(a) TRANSFER

Consider the same facts as Problem 1-8, except now venue is not proper in the transferor court (the United States District Court for the District of Delaware) and Pilar's motion to transfer comes under §1406(a). So the facts are now as follows: Dan filed a diversity action against Pilar in the United States District Court for the District of Delaware. The District of Delaware was not a proper venue, and Pilar filed a §1406(a) motion to transfer the case to the Southern District of New York. The Delaware District Court granted the motion. As in Problem 1-8, assume that Delaware choice of law rules made clear that the law that should provide the rules of decision governing the controversy is the law of the Philippines. New York choice of law rules, however, would designate New York law as the governing law. Should the same result apply here as applied in Problem 1-8? Which choice of law rules should govern? Which law should provide the rules of decision?

2. *Forum Non Conveniens*

You will likely not be surprised to learn that the phrase forum non conveniens means "the forum is not convenient." Thus, like concepts of venue, the doctrine of forum non conveniens focuses on the location of a lawsuit. Moreover, like a venue transfer motion, a motion to dismiss under the doctrine of forum non conveniens allows a defendant to override a plaintiff's choice of forum. Unlike for a venue transfer motion, however, a defendant who wins a forum non conveniens motion succeeds in getting a case dismissed altogether. Why? When a court grants a forum non conveniens motion, it makes the determination that the litigation should continue in another judicial system altogether. Given the existence of venue transfer provisions for case transfers within a judicial system, the forum non conveniens document is necessary in federal court only so that a litigant may move an action to courts of a foreign nation. *See American Dredging Co. v. Miller*, 510 U.S. 443, 449 n.2 (1994) (observing that as a result of §1404(a), forum non conveniens applies in federal court "only in cases where the alternative forum is abroad"); *see also Sinochem Int'l Co. v. Malaysia Int'l Shipping Corp.*, 549 U.S. 422, 430 (2007) (stating that for cases moved within the federal court system, §1404(a) effectively codifies the doctrine of forum non conveniens). A majority of state courts follow an approach to forum non conveniens that is essentially the same as that followed in federal court.[13] A significant difference exists between state and federal court forum non conveniens determinations: while federal courts will focus on whether the proper forum is in another country, state courts also will focus on whether another state's courts are the proper forum. In addition, federal courts have the ability to transfer venue of a case to a location far across the United States, while state courts do not have the ability to transfer a case to another state. A state court's inability to transfer a case to another state may affect the state court's calculus for adjudicating forum non conveniens motions.

The case that follows sets forth the federal approach to forum non conveniens. A significant component of the doctrine is the "private and public interest factors," which had been announced in an earlier case, *Gulf Oil v. Gilbert*, 330 U.S. 501 (1947). The *Piper Aircraft Co. v. Reyno* Court restates them in footnote 6 of the opinion.

Piper Aircraft Company v. Reyno

454 U.S. 235 (1981)

Justice MARSHALL delivered the opinion of the Court. . . .

I

A

In July 1976, a small commercial aircraft crashed in the Scottish highlands during the course of a charter flight from Blackpool to Perth. The pilot and five

---

13. David W. Robertson & Paula K. Speck, *Access to State Courts in Transnational Personal Injury Cases: Forum Non Conveniens and Antisuit Injunctions*, 68 TEX. L. REV. 937 950-951 & nn.73-79 (1990) (reporting that as of 1990, 32 states followed a forum non conveniens doctrine nearly identical to the federal approach, two states reject the doctrine entirely, nine states had their own approach, and nine states did not have determinate law on the subject).

passengers were killed instantly. The decedents were all Scottish subjects and residents, as are their heirs and next of kin. There were no eyewitnesses to the accident. At the time of the crash the plane was subject to Scottish air traffic control.

The aircraft, a twin-engine Piper Aztec, was manufactured in Pennsylvania by petitioner Piper Aircraft Co. (Piper). The propellers were manufactured in Ohio by petitioner Hartzell Propeller, Inc. (Hartzell). At the time of the crash the aircraft was registered in Great Britain and was owned and maintained by Air Navigation and Trading Co., Ltd. (Air Navigation). It was operated by McDonald Aviation, Ltd. (McDonald), a Scottish air taxi service. Both Air Navigation and McDonald were organized in the United Kingdom. The wreckage of the plane is now in a hangar in Farnsborough, England. . . .

In July 1977, a California probate court appointed respondent Gaynell Reyno administratrix of the estates of the five passengers. Reyno is not related to and does not know any of the decedents or their survivors; she was a legal secretary to the attorney who filed this lawsuit. Several days after her appointment, Reyno commenced separate wrongful-death actions against Piper and Hartzell in the Superior Court of California, claiming negligence and strict liability. Air Navigation, McDonald, and the estate of the pilot are not parties to this litigation. The survivors of the five passengers whose estates are represented by Reyno filed a separate action in the United Kingdom against Air Navigation, McDonald, and the pilot's estate. Reyno candidly admits that the action against Piper and Hartzell was filed in the United States because its laws regarding liability, capacity to sue, and damages are more favorable to her position than are those of Scotland. Scottish law does not recognize strict liability in tort. Moreover, it permits wrongful-death actions only when brought by a decedent's relatives. The relatives may sue only for "loss of support and society."

On petitioners' motion, the suit was removed to the United States District Court for the Central District of California [which subsequently] transferred the case to the Middle District of Pennsylvania.

B

In May 1978, after the suit had been transferred, both Hartzell and Piper moved to dismiss the action on the ground of forum non conveniens. The District Court granted these motions in October 1979. It relied on the balancing test set forth by this Court in *Gulf Oil Corp. v. Gilbert*, 330 U.S. 501 (1947), [in which] the Court stated that a plaintiff's choice of forum should rarely be disturbed. However, when an alternative forum has jurisdiction to hear the case, and when trial in the chosen forum would "establish . . . oppressiveness and vexation to a defendant . . . out of all proportion to plaintiff's convenience," or when the "chosen forum [is] inappropriate because of considerations affecting the court's own administrative and legal problems," the court may, in the exercise of its sound discretion, dismiss the case. To guide trial court discretion, the Court provided a list of "private interest factors" affecting the convenience of the litigants, and a list of "public interest factors" affecting the convenience of the forum.[6]

...

c

On appeal, the United States Court of Appeals for the Third Circuit reversed and remanded for trial. The decision to reverse appears to be based on two alternative grounds. First, the Court held that the District Court abused its discretion in conducting the *Gilbert* analysis. Second, the Court held that dismissal is never appropriate where the law of the alternative forum is less favorable to the plaintiff. . . .

In this opinion, we begin by considering whether the Court of Appeals properly held that the possibility of an unfavorable change in law automatically bars dismissal. Since we conclude that the Court of Appeals erred, we then consider its review of the District Court's *Gilbert* analysis to determine whether dismissal was otherwise appropriate. We believe that it is necessary to discuss the *Gilbert* analysis in order to properly dispose of the cases.

II

The Court of Appeals erred in holding that plaintiffs may defeat a motion to dismiss on the ground of forum non conveniens merely by showing that the substantive law that would be applied in the alternative forum is less favorable to the plaintiffs than that of the present forum. The possibility of a change in substantive law should ordinarily not be given conclusive or even substantial weight in the forum non conveniens inquiry. . . .

Under *Gilbert*, dismissal will ordinarily be appropriate where trial in the plaintiff's chosen forum imposes a heavy burden on the defendant or the court, and where the plaintiff is unable to offer any specific reasons of convenience supporting his choice. If substantial weight were given to the possibility of an unfavorable change in law, however, dismissal might be barred even where trial in the chosen forum was plainly inconvenient. . . .

The Court of Appeals' decision is inconsistent with . . . earlier forum non conveniens decisions in another respect. Those decisions have repeatedly emphasized the need to retain flexibility. In *Gilbert*, the Court refused to identify specific

---

6. The factors pertaining to the private interests of the litigants included the "relative ease of access to sources of proof; availability of compulsory process for attendance of unwilling, and the cost of obtaining attendance of willing, witnesses; possibility of view of premises, if view would be appropriate to the action; and all other practical problems that make trial of a case easy, expeditious and inexpensive." *Gilbert*, 330 U.S., at 508. The public factors bearing on the question included the administrative difficulties flowing from court congestion; the "local interest in having localized controversies decided at home"; the interest in having the trial of a diversity case in a forum that is at home with the law that must govern the action; the avoidance of unnecessary problems in conflict of laws, or in the application of foreign law; and the unfairness of burdening citizens in an unrelated forum with jury duty. Id., at 509.

circumstances "which will justify or require either grant or denial of remedy." . . . If central emphasis were placed on any one factor, the forum non conveniens doctrine would lose much of the . . . flexibility that makes it so valuable.

In fact, if conclusive or substantial weight were given to the possibility of a change in law, the forum non conveniens doctrine would become virtually useless. Jurisdiction and venue requirements are often easily satisfied. As a result, many plaintiffs are able to choose from among several forums. Ordinarily, these plaintiffs will select that forum whose choice-of-law rules are most advantageous. Thus, if the possibility of an unfavorable change in substantive law is given substantial weight in the forum non conveniens inquiry, dismissal would rarely be proper. . . .

The Court of Appeals' approach is not only inconsistent with the purpose of the forum non conveniens doctrine, but also poses substantial practical problems. If the possibility of a change in law were given substantial weight, deciding motions to dismiss on the ground of forum non conveniens would become quite difficult. Choice-of-law analysis would become extremely important, and the courts would frequently be required to interpret the law of foreign jurisdictions. First, the trial court would have to determine what law would apply if the case were tried in the chosen forum, and what law would apply if the case were tried in the alternative forum. It would then have to compare the rights, remedies, and procedures available under the law that would be applied in each forum. Dismissal would be appropriate only if the court concluded that the law applied by the alternative forum is as favorable to the plaintiff as that of the chosen forum. The doctrine of forum non conveniens, however, is designed in part to help courts avoid conducting complex exercises in comparative law. As we stated in *Gilbert*, the public interest factors point towards dismissal where the court would be required to "untangle problems in conflict of laws, and in law foreign to itself."

Upholding the decision of the Court of Appeals would result in other practical problems. At least where the foreign plaintiff named an American manufacturer as defendant, a court could not dismiss the case on grounds of forum non conveniens where dismissal might lead to an unfavorable change in law. The American courts, which are already extremely attractive to foreign plaintiffs, would become even more attractive. The flow of litigation into the United States would increase and further congest already crowded courts.

The Court of Appeals based its decision, at least in part, on an analogy between dismissals on grounds of forum non conveniens and transfers between federal courts pursuant to §1404(a). In *Van Dusen v. Barrack*, 376 U.S. 612 (1964), this Court ruled that a §1404(a) transfer should not result in a change in the applicable law. Relying on dictum in an earlier Third Circuit opinion interpreting *Van Dusen*, the court below held that that principle is also applicable to a dismissal on forum non conveniens grounds. However, §1404(a) transfers are different than dismissals on the ground of forum non conveniens.

Congress enacted §1404(a) to permit change of venue between federal courts. Although the statute was drafted in accordance with the doctrine of forum non conveniens, it was intended to be a revision rather than a codification of the common law. District courts were given more discretion to transfer under §1404(a) than they had to dismiss on grounds of forum non conveniens.

The reasoning employed in *Van Dusen v. Barrack* is simply inapplicable to dismissals on grounds of forum non conveniens. That case did not discuss the common-law doctrine. Rather, it focused on "the construction and application" of §1404(a). Emphasizing the remedial purpose of the statute, *Barrack* concluded that Congress could not have intended a transfer to be accompanied by a change in law. The statute was designed as a "federal housekeeping measure," allowing easy change of venue within a unified federal system. The Court feared that if a change in venue were accompanied by a change in law, forum-shopping parties would take unfair advantage of the relaxed standards for transfer. The rule was necessary to ensure the just and efficient operation of the statute.

We do not hold that the possibility of an unfavorable change in law should never be a relevant consideration in a forum non conveniens inquiry. Of course, if the remedy provided by the alternative forum is so clearly inadequate or unsatisfactory that it is no remedy at all, the unfavorable change in law may be given substantial weight; the district court may conclude that dismissal would not be in the interests of justice. In these cases, however, the remedies that would be provided by the Scottish courts do not fall within this category. Although the relatives of the decedents may not be able to rely on a strict liability theory, and although their potential damages award may be smaller, there is no danger that they will be deprived of any remedy or treated unfairly.

III

The Court of Appeals also erred in rejecting the District Court's *Gilbert* analysis. . . .

A

The District Court acknowledged that there is ordinarily a strong presumption in favor of the plaintiff's choice of forum, which may be overcome only when the private and public interest factors clearly point towards trial in the alternative forum. It held, however, that the presumption applies with less force when the plaintiff or real parties in interest are foreign.

The District Court's distinction between resident or citizen plaintiffs and foreign plaintiffs is fully justified. . . . When the home forum has been chosen, it is reasonable to assume that this choice is convenient. When the plaintiff is foreign, however, this assumption is much less reasonable. Because the central purpose of any forum non conveniens inquiry is to ensure that the trial is convenient, a foreign plaintiff's choice deserves less deference.

B

The forum non conveniens determination is committed to the sound discretion of the trial court. It may be reversed only when there has been a clear abuse of discretion; where the court has considered all relevant public and private interest factors, and where its balancing of these factors is reasonable, its decision deserves substantial deference.

(1)

In analyzing the private interest factors, the District Court stated that the connections with Scotland are "overwhelming." This characterization may be somewhat exaggerated. Particularly with respect to the question of relative ease of access to sources of proof, the private interests point in both directions. As respondent emphasizes, records concerning the design, manufacture, and testing of the propeller and plane are located in the United States. She would have greater access to sources of proof relevant to her strict liability and negligence theories if trial were held here. However, the District Court did not act unreasonably in concluding that fewer evidentiary problems would be posed if the trial were held in Scotland. A large proportion of the relevant evidence is located in Great Britain.

The Court of Appeals found that the problems of proof could not be given any weight because Piper and Hartzell failed to describe with specificity the evidence they would not be able to obtain if trial were held in the United States. It suggested that defendants seeking forum non conveniens dismissal must submit affidavits identifying the witnesses they would call and the testimony these witnesses would provide if the trial were held in the alternative forum. Such detail is not necessary. Piper and Hartzell have moved for dismissal precisely because many crucial witnesses are located beyond the reach of compulsory process, and thus are difficult to identify or interview. Requiring extensive investigation would defeat the purpose of their motion. Of course, defendants must provide enough information to enable the District Court to balance the parties' interests. Our examination of the record convinces us that sufficient information was provided here. Both Piper and Hartzell submitted affidavits describing the evidentiary problems they would face if the trial were held in the United States.

The Court of Appeals apparently relied on an analogy to motions to transfer under 28 U.S.C. §1404(a). . . . As we have explained, however, dismissals on grounds of forum non conveniens and §1404(a) transfers are not directly comparable.

The District Court correctly concluded that the problems posed by the inability to implead potential third-party defendants clearly supported holding the trial in Scotland. Joinder of the pilot's estate, Air Navigation, and McDonald is crucial to the presentation of petitioners' defense. If Piper and Hartzell can show that the accident was caused not by a design defect, but rather by the negligence of the pilot, the plane's owners, or the charter company, they will be relieved of all liability. It is true, of course, that if Hartzell and Piper were found liable after a trial in the United States, they could institute an action for indemnity or contribution against these parties in Scotland. It would be far more convenient, however, to resolve all claims in one trial. . . . Forcing petitioners to rely on actions for indemnity or contributions would be "burdensome" but not "unfair." Finding that trial in the plaintiff's chosen forum would be burdensome, however, is sufficient to support dismissal on grounds of forum non conveniens.

(2)

The District Court's review of the factors relating to the public interest was also reasonable. On the basis of its choice-of-law analysis, it concluded that if the case were tried in the Middle District of Pennsylvania, Pennsylvania law would apply to Piper and Scottish law to Hartzell. It stated that a trial involving two sets of laws would be confusing to the jury. It also noted its own lack of familiarity with Scottish law. Consideration of these problems was clearly appropriate under *Gilbert*; in that case we explicitly held that the need to apply foreign law pointed towards dismissal. The Court of Appeals found that the District Court's choice-of-law analysis was incorrect, and that American law would apply to both Hartzell and Piper. Thus, lack of familiarity with foreign law would not be a problem. Even if the Court of Appeals' conclusion is correct, however, all other public interest factors favored trial in Scotland.

Scotland has a very strong interest in this litigation. The accident occurred in its airspace. All of the decedents were Scottish. Apart from Piper and Hartzell, all potential plaintiffs and defendants are either Scottish or English. As we stated in *Gilbert*, there is "a local interest in having localized controversies decided at home." Respondent argues that American citizens have an interest in ensuring that American manufacturers are deterred from producing defective products, and that additional deterrence might be obtained if Piper and Hartzell were tried in the United States, where they could be sued on the basis of both negligence and strict liability. However, the incremental deterrence that would be gained if this trial were held in an American court is likely to be insignificant. The American interest in this accident is simply not sufficient to justify the enormous commitment of judicial time and resources that would inevitably be required if the case were to be tried here.

IV

The Court of Appeals erred in holding that the possibility of an unfavorable change in law bars dismissal on the ground of forum non conveniens. It also erred in rejecting the District Court's *Gilbert* analysis. The District Court properly decided that the presumption in favor of the respondent's forum choice applied with less than maximum force because the real parties in interest are foreign. It did not act unreasonably in deciding that the private interests pointed towards trial in Scotland. Nor did it act unreasonably in deciding that the public interests favored trial in Scotland. Thus, the judgment of the Court of Appeals is reversed.

Notes on
PIPER *AND THE FORUM NON CONVENIENS DOCTRINE*

1. As a practical matter, forum non conveniens motions are often granted conditionally — with the court agreeing to dismiss the case, subject to parties agreeing to certain matters such as waiving objection to personal jurisdiction, allowing discovery according to United States rules and customs, or waiving a statute of limitations defense in an alternate forum. This conditional approach is reflected in the *Piper* Court's suggestion about providing records in footnote 25 of the opinion. The concept that a litigant might add a condition or qualification when agreeing to accept another's proposal is a common component of negotiation, and even has an important role to play (where undertaken respectfully and politely) when litigants are brokering resolutions through a judge within the litigation context.

2. Although many states fashion their forum non conveniens rules after federal rules, the states are not obligated to do so. Federal forum non conveniens law is a matter of federal court administration, which is not binding under federal supremacy principles on the law applied in state courts. Nor is a federal court dismissal on forum non conveniens grounds preclusive of a state court's decision to litigate the merits of a case, even where the state court is in the same state as the federal court. The earlier federal court dismissal is not a dismissal on the merits; it is simply a determination that the federal forum is not appropriate. *See Chick Kam Choo v. Exxon Corp.*, 486 U.S. 140 (1988).

3. Because federal forum non conveniens motions arise in cases with foreign elements, the motions often spotlight the magnetic appeal of the United States court system for foreign plaintiffs. Reasons why the United States court system may attract foreign plaintiffs include (i) high compensatory damages, (ii) the possibility of recovering punitive damages, (iii) a contingency fee system that enables a plaintiff to avoid the risk of incurring high attorneys' fees without a positive verdict, (iv) liberal discovery rules, and (v) class action apparatus. In oft-quoted language, one-time "Master of the Rolls" Lord Denning has stated: "As a moth is drawn to light, so is a litigant drawn to the United States. If he can only get his case into their courts, he stands to win a fortune." *Smith Kline & French Labs., Ltd. v. Bloch*, (1982) 1 W.L.R. 730 (C.A.) 733 (Eng.). For insight into the operation of forum non conveniens doctrines in cases with international elements, see Jeffrey A. Van Detta, *The Irony of Instrumentalism: Using Dworkin's Principle-Rule Distinction to Reconceptualize Metaphorically a Substance-Procedure Dissonance Exemplified by Forum Non Conveniens Dismissals in International Product Injury Cases*, 87 MARQUETTE L. REV. 425 (Spring 2004). 4. The United States Supreme Court has ruled that a district court may dismiss a case pursuant to the doctrine of forum non conveniens even before considering questions of personal and subject matter jurisdiction. Speaking for a unanimous Supreme Court, Justice Ginsburg reasoned that a court may undertake a

forum non conveniens motion as a threshold inquiry, since such motions do not require the court to engage its law-declaring powers. *Sinochem v. Malaysia,* 549 U.S. 422 (2007). Accordingly, the Court ruled that a "district court therefore may dispose of an action by a *forum non conveniens* dismissal, bypassing questions of subject-matter and personal jurisdiction, when considerations of convenience, fairness, and judicial economy so warrant." *Id.* at 432.

Perhaps unwittingly, the *Sinochem* Court elevated the importance of forum non conveniens law for the efficiency-minded defendant. Several foreign governments, however, implemented a countervailing force in the form of legislation that makes their local courts unavailable when a lawsuit was first filed in another country and dismissed on forum non conveniens grounds. *See generally* Winston Anderson, *Forum Non Conveniens Checkmated: The Emergence of Retaliatory Legislation,* 10 J. TRANSNAT'L L. & POL'Y 183 (2001) (discussing legislation from several Latin American countries).

5. Many lower federal courts have distilled the federal forum non conveniens doctrine to the following two-part test: (1) determine whether an alternative forum is available and adequate; and (2) if so, consider whether a forum non conveniens dismissal would serve the parties' private interests and the alternative forum's public interests.

6. In applying the first component of the two-part test mentioned in Note 5, federal courts are sometimes cast in the role of explicitly evaluating the quality of justice offered in other countries. As illustrated in *Piper* itself, courts may need to evaluate the adequacy of the legal theories as well as the damage systems available in other countries. Perhaps mindful of the delicacy of these inquiries, federal courts often use a light touch, noting, for example, that a United States court should not second-guess legislative choices of developing countries. *See, e.g., In re Union Carbide Corp. Gas Plant Disaster at Bhopal, India in December, 1984,* 634 F. Supp. 842, 867 (S.D.N.Y. 1986), *aff'd as modified,* 809 F.2d 195 (2d Cir. 1987) (stating that "to retain the litigation in this forum . . . would be yet another example of imperialism, another situation in which an established sovereign inflicted its rules, its standards and values on a developing nation"); *Gonzales v. Chrysler Corp.,* 301 F.3d 377, 382 (5th Cir. 1977) (noting that Mexican tort law resulted from balancing competing policies and seeing "no warrant" for imposing the federal court's "own view of what is a good policy for the citizens of Mexico").

One can occasionally find a court deciding that a forum is inadequate because of a corrupt judicial system. The standard applied, however, is high, with courts declining to endorse a forum non conveniens dismissal based on allegations that a foreign system suffers from delay, small damages, inefficiency, cumbersome procedural requirements, or restricted liability theories. *Compare Stroitelstvo Bulgeria Ltd. v. Bulgarian-American Enter. Fund,* 589 F.3d 417 (7th Cir.

2009) (refusing to find that Bulgaria is an inadequate forum, even in light of showing that Bulgaria offered diminished opportunities under liability and procedural law), and *Tuazon v. R.J. Reynolds Tobacco Co.*, 433 F.3d 1163 (9th Cir. 2006) (refusing to find judicial system in Philippines inadequate, even in light of showing of delay, small damage verdicts, human rights concerns, and bias in the criminal justice system), *with Bhatnagar by Bhatnagar v. Surrenda Overseas*, 52 F.3d 1220 (3d Cir. 1995) (finding India is an inadequate forum on the basis of expert affidavits stating that Indian legal system was in "virtual collapse" and suffered 15- to 20-year average delay in litigation), *and Eastman Kodak Co. v. Kavlin*, 978 F. Supp. 1078, 1084 (S.D. Fla. 1997) (relying on detailed statements by Bolivian Minister of Justice and other experts stating that Bolivian courts were riddled with extortion and corruption, and finding that corruption and delay in those courts rendered fair trial impossible). An interesting domestic counterpoint to these cases is *Radeljak v. DaimlerChrysler Corp.*, 719 N.W.2d 40 (Mich. 2006). In *Radeljak*, the court found that Michigan's connection with a Michigan-based vehicle manufacturer injected possible bias in a product liability suit. The court thus found that the Michigan connections rendered Croatia a more appropriate forum for the product liability suit than Michigan courts.

Consider the foreign legislation described in Note 4 making local courts unavailable where a lawsuit was first filed in another country and dismissed on forum non conveniens grounds. Does a country's enactment of this legislation mean that a U.S. court considering a forum non conveniens motion should evaluate whether the country is unavailable or inadequate? *See Paulownia Plantation de Panama Corp. v. Rajamannan*, 2009 Minn. LEXIS 774 (Minn. Nov. 5, 2009) (reversing court's conclusion that Panama was not an available forum because of Panama statute removing competency of Panamanian courts to adjudicate suits dismissed by a foreign judge on forum non conveniens grounds).

PROBLEM 1-10: SMOKING IN ALBINLAND

Chelsea Plaintiff was born and raised in a country outside the United States (hypothetically) known as Albinland. She started smoking when she was 13, and smoked for more than 50 years. About 10 years ago, she began to experience a chronic cough and dizziness, and was diagnosed with a pulmonary disorder. She then moved to Portland, Oregon to join her daughter who is a United States citizen. The year after she immigrated to Portland, Chelsea filed suit against a United States tobacco company, Reynolds Morris (RM), which is incorporated in New Jersey but has its principal place of business in North Carolina.

Chelsea filed her suit in the United States District Court in Portland, alleging that RM participated in a world-wide conspiracy to conceal the harmful effects of smoking. RM does extensive business in Oregon, selling, distributing, and advertising cigarettes in Oregon as well as funding research at the university there. RM was also involved in financing opposition to anti-smoking legislation in Oregon. Chelsea alleges that the conspiracy began in the United States, but moved abroad as RM started to develop markets in Albinland and elsewhere.

RM has moved to dismiss the case on the basis of forum non conveniens, proposing that the case should be re-filed in Albinland. RM filed an affidavit from a former Justice of the Albinland Court of Appeals, stating generally that the judicial system there has formal procedures for litigation, a discovery process, and provides for "tort relief." RM also noted that a few witnesses that may be important in the case reside in Albinland and will be outside the compulsory process of the federal court in Portland, Oregon.

Chelsea defends this motion, making a general statement that the Albinland judicial system is corrupt and has small damage verdicts. Chelsea attaches to her brief a United States Department of State report that analyzes the judicial systems of various countries. Albinland is mentioned in the report as a jurisdiction with an unfair criminal justice system and a record of human rights abuses. She also notes that most of the witnesses in the case reside in the United States, a substantial number of whom are in Oregon. Should the federal district court in Oregon grant RM's motion?

3.   Consent to Jurisdiction and Forum Selection Clauses

Sometimes a defendant may either consent or waive a right to object to personal jurisdiction and venue. In that event, the usual personal jurisdiction, venue, and forum non conveniens analysis will likely not apply. In commercial transactions, parties often make their consent explicit in agreements, specifying the forum where they wish to resolve potential disputes. These provisions are called forum selection clauses. Parties may choose a particular forum for a variety of reasons: convenience, neutrality, forum expertise, preference for certain laws that will govern their dispute if it is litigated in the chosen forum, or the desire to avoid litigation over jurisdiction or venue questions.

The principles governing the enforceability and construction of forum selection clauses in the United States are derived from common law, but also have roots in due process fairness concerns. Historically, courts viewed forum selection clauses as unenforceable, concerned that the clauses represented the parties' attempt to manipulate court jurisdiction — something the parties do not have the prerogative to manipulate. The United States Supreme Court, however, significantly changed direction in *M/S Bremen v. Zapata Off-Shore Co.*, 407 U.S. 1 (1972). Later, the Court decided *Carnival Cruise Lines, Inc. v. Shute*, 499 U.S. 585 (1991) — which refined basic standards governing whether to enforce forum selection clauses. *Bremen* set the stage for general acceptance of the clauses, and *Carnival Cruise Lines* provided guidance on how to handle such clauses in form contracts.

M/S Bremen v. Zapata Off-Shore Company

407 U.S. 1 (1972)

Chief Justice BURGER delivered the opinion of the Court.

We granted certiorari to review a judgment of the United States Court of Appeals for the Fifth Circuit declining to enforce a forum-selection clause governing disputes arising under an international towage contract between petitioners and respondent. For the reasons stated hereafter, we vacate the judgment of the Court of Appeals.

In November 1967, respondent Zapata, a Houston-based American corporation, contracted with petitioner Unterweser, a German corporation, to tow Zapata's ocean-going, self-elevating drilling rig Chaparral from Louisiana to a point off Ravenna, Italy, in the Adriatic Sea, where Zapata had agreed to drill certain wells.

Zapata had solicited bids for the towage, and several companies including Unterweser had responded. Unterweser was the low bidder and Zapata requested it to submit a contract, which it did. The contract submitted by Unterweser contained the following provision . . . :

Any dispute arising must be treated before the London Court of Justice.

In addition the contract contained two clauses purporting to exculpate Unterweser from liability for damages to the towed barge.

After reviewing the contract and making several changes, but without any alteration in the forum-selection or exculpatory clauses, a Zapata vice president executed the contract and forwarded it to Unterweser in Germany, where Unterweser accepted the changes, and the contract became effective.

On January 5, 1968, Unterweser's deep sea tug Bremen departed Venice, Louisiana, with the Chaparral in tow bound for Italy. On January 9, while the flotilla was in international waters in the middle of the Gulf of Mexico, a severe storm arose. The sharp roll of the Chaparral in Gulf waters caused its elevator legs, which had been raised for the voyage, to break off and fall into the sea, seriously damaging the Chaparral. In this emergency situation Zapata instructed the Bremen to tow its damaged rig to Tampa, Florida, the nearest port of refuge.

On January 12, Zapata, ignoring its contract promise to litigate "any dispute arising" in the English courts, commenced . . . suit . . . in the United States District Court at Tampa, seeking $3,500,000 damages against Unterweser . . . and the Bremen . . . , alleging negligent towage and breach of contract. . . .

We hold . . . that far too little weight and effect were given to the forum clause in resolving this controversy. For at least two decades we have witnessed an expansion of overseas commercial activities by business enterprises based in the United States. The barrier of distance that once tended to confine a business concern to a modest territory no longer does so. Here we see an American company with special expertise contracting with a foreign company to tow a complex machine thousands of miles across seas and oceans. The expansion of American business and industry will hardly be encouraged if, notwithstanding solemn contracts, we insist on a parochial concept that all disputes must be resolved under our laws and in our courts. [Insisting that suit must be filed in the United States] would be a heavy hand . . . on . . . international commercial dealings by Americans. We cannot have trade and commerce in world markets and international waters exclusively on our terms, governed by our laws, and resolved in our courts.

Forum-selection clauses have historically not been favored by American courts. Many courts, federal and state, have declined to enforce such clauses on the ground that they were "contrary to public policy," or that their effect was to "oust the jurisdiction" of the court. Although this view apparently still has considerable acceptance, other courts are tending to adopt a more hospitable attitude toward forum-selection clauses. This view . . . is that such clauses are prima facie valid and should be enforced unless enforcement is shown by the resisting party to be "unreasonable" under the circumstances. We believe this is the correct doctrine to be followed by federal district courts sitting in admiralty. It is merely the other side of the proposition recognized by this Court in *National Equipment Rental, Ltd. v. Szukhent*, 375 U.S. 311 (1964), holding that in federal courts a party may validly consent to be sued in a jurisdiction where he cannot be found for service of process through contractual designation of an "agent" for receipt of process in that jurisdiction. In so holding, the Court stated: "[I]t is settled . . . that parties to a contract may agree in advance to submit to the jurisdiction of a given court to permit notice to be served by the opposing party, or even to waive notice altogether." This approach is substantially followed in other common-law countries including England. It is the view advanced by noted scholars and that adopted by the Restatement of the Conflict of Laws. It accords with ancient concepts of freedom of contract and reflects an appreciation of the expanding horizons of American contractors who seek business in all parts of the world. Not surprisingly, foreign businessmen prefer, as do we, to have disputes resolved in their own courts, but if that choice is not available, then in a neutral forum with expertise in the subject matter. Plainly, the courts of England meet the standards of neutrality and long experience in admiralty litigation. The choice of that forum was made in an arm's-length negotiation by experienced and sophisticated businessmen, and absent some compelling and countervailing reason it should be honored by the parties and enforced by the courts.

The argument that such clauses are improper because they tend to "oust" a court of jurisdiction is hardly more than a vestigial legal fiction. It appears to rest at core on historical judicial resistance to any attempt to reduce the power and business of a particular court and has little place in an era when all courts are overloaded and when businesses once essentially local now operate in world markets. It reflects . . . a provincial attitude regarding the fairness of other tribunals. No one seriously contends in this case that the forum selection clause "ousted" the District Court of jurisdiction over Zapata's action. The threshold question is whether that court should have exercised its jurisdiction to do more than give effect to the legitimate expectations of the parties, manifested in their freely negotiated agreement, by specifically enforcing the forum clause.

There are compelling reasons why a freely negotiated private international agreement, unaffected by fraud, undue influence, or overweening bargaining power, such as that involved here, should be given full effect. In this case, for example, we are concerned with a far from routine transaction between companies of two different nations contemplating the tow of an extremely costly piece of equipment from Louisiana across the Gulf of Mexico and the Atlantic Ocean, through the Mediterranean Sea to its final destination in the Adriatic Sea. In the course of its voyage, it was to traverse the waters of many jurisdictions. The Chaparral could have been damaged at any point along the route, and there were countless possible ports of refuge. That the accident occurred in the Gulf of Mexico and the barge was towed to Tampa in an emergency were mere fortuities. It cannot be doubted for a moment that the parties sought to provide for a neutral forum for the resolution of any disputes arising during the tow. Manifestly much uncertainty and possibly great inconvenience to both parties could arise if a suit could be maintained in any jurisdiction in which an accident might occur or if jurisdiction were left to any place where the Bremen or Unterweser might happen to be found.[15] The elimination of all such uncertainties by agreeing in advance on a forum acceptable to both parties is an indispensable element in international trade, commerce, and contracting. There is strong evidence that the forum clause was a vital part of the agreement, and it would be unrealistic to think that the parties did not conduct their negotiations, including fixing the monetary terms, with the consequences of the forum clause figuring prominently in their calculations. . . .

Thus, in the light of present-day commercial realities and expanding international trade we conclude that the forum clause should control absent a strong showing that it should be set aside. Although their opinions are not altogether explicit, it seems reasonably clear that the District Court and the Court of Appeals placed the burden on Unterweser to show that London would be a more convenient forum than Tampa, although the contract expressly resolved that issue. The correct approach would have been to enforce the forum clause specifically unless Zapata could clearly show that enforcement would be unreasonable and unjust, or that the clause was invalid for such reasons as fraud or overreaching. Accordingly, the case must be remanded for reconsideration.

We note, however, that there is nothing in the record . . . that would support a refusal to enforce the forum clause. . . . A contractual choice-of-forum clause should be held unenforceable if enforcement would contravene a strong public policy of the forum in which suit is brought, whether declared by statute or by judicial decision[, but no such applicable policy reaches this case].

Courts have also suggested that a forum clause, even though it is freely bargained for and contravenes no important public policy of the forum, may nevertheless be "unreasonable" and unenforceable if the chosen forum is seriously inconvenient for the trial of the action. Of course, where it can be said with reasonable assurance that at the time they entered the contract, the parties to a freely negotiated private international commercial agreement contemplated the claimed inconvenience, it is difficult to see why any such claim of inconvenience should be heard to render the forum clause unenforceable. We are not here dealing with an agreement between two Americans to resolve their essentially local disputes in a remote alien forum. In such a case, the serious inconvenience

---

15. At the very least, the clause was an effort to eliminate all uncertainty as to the nature, location, and outlook of the forum in which these companies of differing nationalities might find themselves. Moreover, while the contract here did not specifically provide that the substantive law of England should be applied, it is the general rule in English courts that the parties are assumed, absent contrary indication, to have designated the forum with the view that it should apply its own law. It is therefore reasonable to conclude that the forum clause was also an effort to obtain certainty as to the applicable substantive law. . . .

of the contractual forum to one or both of the parties might carry greater weight in determining the reasonableness of the forum clause. The remoteness of the forum might suggest that the agreement was an adhesive one, or that the parties did not have the particular controversy in mind when they made their agreement; yet even there the party claiming should bear a heavy burden of proof. Similarly, selection of a remote forum to apply differing foreign law to an essentially American controversy might contravene an important public policy of the forum. . . .

This case, however, involves a freely negotiated international commercial transaction between a German and an American corporation for towage of a vessel from the Gulf of Mexico to the Adriatic Sea. As noted, selection of a London forum was . . . a reasonable effort to bring vital certainty to this international transaction and to provide a neutral forum experienced and capable in the resolution of admiralty litigation. Whatever "inconvenience" Zapata would suffer by being forced to litigate in the contractual forum as it agreed to do was clearly foreseeable at the time of contracting. In such circumstances it should be incumbent on the party seeking to escape his contract to show that trial in the contractual forum will be so gravely difficult and inconvenient that he will for all practical purposes be deprived of his day in court. Absent that, there is no basis for concluding that it would be unfair, unjust, or unreasonable to hold that party to his bargain. . . .

Zapata's remaining contentions do not require extended treatment. It is clear that Unterweser's action in filing its limitation complaint in the District Court in Tampa was, so far as Zapata was concerned, solely a defensive measure made necessary as a response to Zapata's breach of the forum clause of the contract. . . . The judgment of the Court of Appeals is vacated and the case is remanded for further proceedings consistent with this opinion.

Notes on
BREMEN

1. *Bremen* is an admiralty case and some confusion initially surrounded whether its approach to forum selection clauses extended beyond that context. Ultimately, however, most lower courts abandoned the prohibition of forum selection clauses. An amendment to the Restatement (Second) Conflict of Law §80 followed in 1986, which provided that forum selection clauses would be given effect unless "unfair or unreasonable." While states generally now follow this approach, some differences between state and federal law may exist. Thus, a federal court exercising diversity of citizenship jurisdiction faces a difficult decision whether to apply federal law as announced in *Bremen* and its progeny or to apply state rules. As Chapter 3 describes, federal courts exercising diversity jurisdiction apply the choice of law rules of the forum state — and forum selection clauses are often characterized as a form of choice of law rule.

2. Throughout *Bremen*, the Court references the enforceability of the contractual clauses exculpating Unterweser from liability for damages. As Justice Douglas suggests in his dissent, the enforceability of this clause might very much depend on where the matter was litigated (i.e., not enforceable in the United States and enforceable in England). This observation helps to illustrate the high stakes with choice of forum clauses: the question of whether to enforce the clause reaches beyond mere questions of efficiency, convenience, and judicial administration.

3. How do the venue rules operate when a contract has a forum selection clause that the plaintiff has not honored? In *Atlantic Marine Construction Co., Inc., v. U.S. District Court for the Western District of Texas*, 571 U.S. __(2013), the U.S. Supreme Court said that the forum selection clause may be enforced by a motion to transfer venue under §1404(a). Exhibiting deference to the power of a forum selection clause, the Supreme Court stated that a district court should transfer a case when a §1404(a) motion is filed in a forum not designated by the forum selection clause, unless extraordinary circumstances unrelated to the convenience of the parties clearly disfavor a transfer.

3. Even given the general acceptance of forum selection clauses, a party may ask a court not to enforce them. For example, a party may argue that a clause is unenforceable because it is affected by fraud or duress. Likewise, a party may argue that the essential character of the chosen forum has sufficiently changed between the time of the agreement and the litigation so as to render it unfair to require a party to litigate in the chosen forum. Finally, a party may argue that inequality of bargaining power between the contracting parties should preclude judicial enforcement of the clause. The next case, *Carnival Cruise Lines, Inc. v. Shute*, 499 U.S. 585 (1991), takes up that issue.

Carnival Cruise Lines, Inc. v. Shute

499 U.S. 585 (1991)

Justice BLACKMUN delivered the opinion of the Court.

In this admiralty case we primarily consider whether the United States Court of Appeals for the Ninth Circuit correctly refused to enforce a forum-selection clause contained in tickets issued by petitioner Carnival Cruise Lines, Inc., to respondents Eulala and Russel Shute.

I

The Shutes, through an Arlington, Wash., travel agent, purchased passage for a 7-day cruise on petitioner's ship, the Tropicale. Respondents paid the fare to the agent who forwarded the payment to petitioner's headquarters in Miami, Fla. Petitioner then prepared the tickets and sent them to respondents in the State of

Washington. The face of each ticket, at its left-hand lower corner, contained this admonition:

SUBJECT TO CONDITIONS OF
CONTRACT ON LAST PAGES
IMPORTANT! PLEASE READ CONTRACT
ON LAST PAGES 1, 2, 3

The following appeared on "contract page 1" of each ticket:

**TERMS AND CONDITIONS OF PASSAGE
CONTRACT TICKET**

. . .

3. (a) The acceptance of this ticket by the person or persons named hereon as passengers shall be deemed to be an acceptance and agreement by each of them of all of the terms and conditions of this Passage Contract Ticket.

. . .

8. It is agreed by and between the passenger and the Carrier that all disputes and matters whatsoever arising under, in connection with or incident to this Contract shall be litigated, if at all, in and before a Court located in the State of Florida, U.S.A., to the exclusion of the Courts of any other state or country.

The last quoted paragraph is the forum-selection clause at issue.

II

Respondents boarded the Tropicale in Los Angeles, Cal. The ship sailed to Puerto Vallarta, Mexico, and then returned to Los Angeles. While the ship was in international waters off the Mexican coast, respondent Eulala Shute was injured when she slipped on a deck mat during a guided tour of the ship's galley. Respondents filed suit against petitioner in the United States District Court for the Western District of Washington, claiming that Mrs. Shute's injuries had been caused by the negligence of Carnival Cruise Lines and its employees.

Petitioner moved for summary judgment, contending that the forum clause in respondents' tickets required the Shutes to bring their suit against petitioner in a court in the State of Florida. Petitioner contended, alternatively, that the District Court lacked personal jurisdiction over petitioner because petitioner's contacts with the State of Washington were insubstantial. The District Court granted the motion, holding that petitioner's contacts with Washington were constitutionally insufficient to support the exercise of personal jurisdiction.

The Court of Appeals reversed. Reasoning that "but for" petitioner's solicitation of business in Washington, respondents would not have taken the cruise and Mrs. Shute would not have been injured, the court concluded that petitioner had sufficient contacts with Washington to justify the District Court's exercise of personal jurisdiction.

Turning to the forum-selection clause, the Court of Appeals acknowledged that a court concerned with the enforceability of such a clause must begin its analysis with *The Bremen v. Zapata Off-Shore Co., 407 U.S. 1 (1972),* where this Court held that forum-selection clauses, although not "historically . . . favored," are "prima facie valid." *Id.,* at 9-10. The appellate court concluded that the forum clause should not be enforced because it "was not freely bargained for." Id., at 389. As an "independent justification" for refusing to enforce the clause, the Court of Appeals noted that there was evidence in the record to indicate that "the Shutes are physically and financially incapable of pursuing this litigation in Florida" and that the enforcement of the clause would operate to deprive them of their day in court and thereby contravene this Court's holding in *The Bremen.*

We granted certiorari to address the question whether the Court of Appeals was correct in holding that the District Court should hear respondents' tort claim against petitioner. Because we find the forum-selection clause to be dispositive of this question, we need not consider petitioner's constitutional argument as to personal jurisdiction.

III

We begin by noting the boundaries of our inquiry. First, this is a case in admiralty, and federal law governs the enforceability of the forum-selection clause we scrutinize. Second, we do not address the question whether respondents had sufficient notice of the forum clause before entering the contract for passage. Respondents essentially have conceded that they had notice of the forum-selection provision. . . .

Within this context, respondents urge that the forum clause should not be enforced because, contrary to this Court's teachings in *The Bremen,* the clause was not the product of negotiation, and enforcement effectively would deprive respondents of their day in court. Additionally, respondents contend that the clause violates the Limitation of Vessel Owner's Liability Act, 46 U.S.C. App. §183c. We consider these arguments in turn.

IV

A

Both petitioner and respondents argue vigorously that the Court's opinion in *The Bremen* governs this case, and each side purports to find ample support for its position in that opinion's broad-ranging language. This seeming paradox derives in large part from key factual differences between this case and *The Bremen,* differences that preclude an automatic and simple application of *The Bremen*'s general principles to the facts here.

In applying *The Bremen,* the Court of Appeals in the present litigation took note of the foregoing "reasonableness" factors and rather automatically decided that the forum-selection clause was unenforceable because, unlike the parties in *The Bremen,* respondents are not business persons and did not negotiate the terms of the clause with petitioner. Alternatively, the Court of Appeals ruled that the clause should not be enforced because enforcement effectively would deprive respondents of an opportunity to litigate their claim against petitioner.

The Bremen concerned a "far from routine transaction between companies of two different nations contemplating the tow of an extremely costly piece of equipment from Louisiana across the Gulf of Mexico and the Atlantic Ocean, through the Mediterranean Sea to its final destination in the Adriatic Sea." Id., at 13. These facts suggest that, even apart from the evidence of negotiation regarding the forum clause, it was entirely reasonable for the Court in The Bremen to have expected Unterweser and Zapata to have negotiated with care in selecting a forum for the resolution of disputes arising from their special towing contract.

In contrast, respondents' passage contract was purely routine and doubtless nearly identical to every commercial passage contract issued by petitioner and most other cruise lines. In this context, it would be entirely unreasonable for us to assume that respondents — or any other cruise passenger — would negotiate with petitioner the terms of a forum-selection clause in an ordinary commercial cruise ticket. Common sense dictates that a ticket of this kind will be a form contract the terms of which are not subject to negotiation, and that an individual purchasing the ticket will not have bargaining parity with the cruise line. But by ignoring the crucial differences in the business contexts in which the respective contracts were executed, the Court of Appeals' analysis seems to us to have distorted somewhat this Court's holding in The Bremen.

In evaluating the reasonableness of the forum clause at issue in this case, we must refine the analysis of The Bremen to account for the realities of form passage contracts. As an initial matter, we do not adopt the Court of Appeals' determination that a nonnegotiated forum-selection clause in a form ticket contract is never enforceable simply because it is not the subject of bargaining. Including a reasonable forum clause in a form contract . . . well may be permissible for several reasons: First, a cruise line has a special interest in limiting the fora in which it potentially could be subject to suit. Because a cruise ship typically carries passengers from many locales, it is not unlikely that a mishap on a cruise could subject the cruise line to litigation in several different fora. Additionally, a clause establishing ex ante the forum for dispute resolution has the salutary effect of dispelling any confusion about where suits arising from the contract must be brought and defended, sparing litigants the time and expense of pretrial motions to determine the correct forum and conserving judicial resources that otherwise would be devoted to deciding those motions. Finally, it stands to reason that passengers who purchase tickets containing a forum clause like that at issue in this case benefit [from] reduced fares reflecting the savings that the cruise line enjoys by limiting the fora in which it may be sued.

We also note that the Court of Appeals' "independent justification" for its conclusion that The Bremen dictates that the clause should not be enforced because "[t]here is evidence in the record to indicate that the Shutes are physically and financially incapable of pursuing this litigation in Florida." We do not defer to the Court of Appeals' findings of fact. In dismissing the case for lack of personal jurisdiction over petitioner, the District Court made no finding regarding the physical and financial impediments to the Shutes' pursuing their case in

Florida. The Court of Appeals' conclusory reference to the record provides no basis for this Court to validate the finding of inconvenience. Furthermore, the Court of Appeals did not place in proper context this Court's statement in *The Bremen* that "the serious inconvenience of the contractual forum to one or both of the parties might carry greater weight in determining the reasonableness of the forum clause." 407 U.S., at 17. The Court made this statement in evaluating a hypothetical "agreement between two Americans to resolve their essentially local disputes in a remote alien forum." In the present case, Florida is not a "remote alien forum," nor — given . . . that Mrs. Shute's accident occurred off the coast of Mexico — is this dispute an essentially local one inherently more suited to resolution in the State of Washington than in Florida. In light of these distinctions, and because respondents do not claim lack of notice of the forum clause, we conclude that they have not satisfied the "heavy burden of proof," required to set aside the clause on grounds of inconvenience.

It bears emphasis that forum-selection clauses contained in form passage contracts are subject to judicial scrutiny for fundamental fairness. In this case, there is no indication that petitioner set Florida as the forum in which disputes were to be resolved as a means of discouraging cruise passengers from pursuing legitimate claims. Any suggestion of such a bad-faith motive is belied by two facts: Petitioner has its principal place of business in Florida, and many of its cruises depart from and return to Florida ports. Similarly, there is no evidence that petitioner obtained respondents' accession to the forum clause by fraud or overreaching. Finally, respondents have conceded that they were given notice of the forum provision and, therefore, presumably retained the option of rejecting the contract with impunity. In the case before us, therefore, we conclude that the Court of Appeals erred in refusing to enforce the forum-selection clause.

[Finally, the Court rejected the contention that the forum-selection clause at issue violates the Vessel Owner's Liability Act, 46 U.S.C. App. §183c.]

The judgment of the Court of Appeals is reversed.

Justice STEVENS, with whom Justice MARSHALL joins, dissenting.

The Court prefaces its legal analysis with a factual statement that implies that a purchaser of a Carnival Cruise Lines passenger ticket is fully and fairly notified about the existence of the choice of forum clause in the fine print on the back of the ticket. Even if this implication were accurate, I would disagree with the Court's analysis. But, given the Court's preface, I begin my dissent by noting that only the most meticulous passenger is likely to become aware of the forum-selection provision. I have therefore appended to this opinion a facsimile of the relevant text, using the type size that actually appears in the ticket itself. A careful reader will find the forum-selection clause in the 8th of the 25 numbered paragraphs.

Of course, many passengers, like the respondents in this case, will not have an opportunity to read paragraph 8 until they have actually purchased their tickets. By this point, the passengers will already have accepted the condition set forth in paragraph 16(a), which provides that "[t]he Carrier shall not be liable to make any refund to passengers in respect of . . . tickets wholly or partly not used by a passenger." Not knowing whether or not that provision is legally enforceable,

I assume that the average passenger would accept the risk of having to file suit in Florida in the event of an injury, rather than canceling—without a refund—a planned vacation at the last minute. The fact that the cruise line can reduce its litigation costs, and therefore its liability insurance premiums, by forcing this choice on its passengers does not, in my opinion, suffice to render the provision reasonable. . . .

The Bremen, which the Court effectively treats as controlling this case, had nothing to say about stipulations printed on the back of passenger tickets. That case involved the enforceability of a forum-selection clause in a freely negotiated international agreement between two large corporations providing for the towage of a vessel from the Gulf of Mexico to the Adriatic Sea. The Court recognized that such towage agreements had generally been held unenforceable in American courts, but held that the doctrine of those cases did not extend to commercial arrangements between parties with equal bargaining power. . . . I respectfully dissent.

Notes on
CARNIVAL CRUISE LINES *AND FORUM SELECTION CLAUSES GENERALLY*

1. The *Carnival Cruise Lines* majority stated that it could avoid the question whether the Shutes had adequate notice of the forum selection provision because the Shutes "essentially . . . conceded" they did have notice. This leaves open a question as to whether a court should enforce a forum selection clause in those cases where consumers establish that the fine print on a form contract eluded their attention. Lower state and federal courts have taken a variety of stances on this question, with some courts placing importance on whether the consumer would have had an opportunity to reject the forum selection clause with forfeiture or penalty if they had been aware of the clause. Judge Easterbrook, whose views tend to receive national attention, provides the following explanation for why a party should be bound by a clause she never actually saw:

> . . . A contract need not be read to be effective; people who accept take the risk that the unread terms may in retrospect prove unwelcome. Terms [of a transaction] stand or fall together. If they constitute the parties' contract because [the plaintiff] had an opportunity to return the [product] after reading them, then all must be enforced. . . . [*Carnival Cruise Lines*] enforces a forum-selection clause that was included among three pages of terms attached to a cruise ship ticket. . . . *Carnival Cruise Lines* exemplif[ies] the many commercial transactions in which people pay for products with terms to follow. . . . Payment preceding the revelation of full terms is common . . . for many endeavors. Practical considerations support allowing vendors to enclose the full legal terms with their products. Cashiers cannot be expected

to read legal documents to customers before ringing up sales. If the staff at the other end of the phone for direct-sales operations . . . had to read the four-page statement of terms before taking the buyer's credit card number, the droning voice would anesthetize rather than enlighten many potential buyers. . . . Customers as a group are better off when vendors skip costly and ineffectual steps such as telephonic recitation, and use instead a simple approve-or-return device.

Hill v. Gateway 2000, Inc., 105 F.3d 1147, 1148-1149 (7th Cir. 1997).

2. The issue raised in *Carnival Cruise Lines* has crucial importance in internet cases. Transactions over the internet often include long contracts that flash on the screen, which sometimes require consumers to click a box that says "I agree" or "I consent" before completing the transaction. Although courts in the United States have sometimes followed a favorable approach toward forum selection clauses in the internet context, they have not always done so. *Compare Freedman v. America Online, Inc.*, 294 F. Supp. 2d 238 (D. Conn. 2003) (enforcing forum selection clause in internet service agreement), *vacated in part on other grounds*, 2004 WL 234661 (D. Conn. Jan. 30, 2004), *and Caspi v. Microsoft Network L.L.C.*, 323 N.J. Super. 118 (N.J. Super. Ct. App. Div. 1999) (upholding forum selection clause on MSN membership agreement, noting existence of competition in internet service industry providing consumers with choices as to which service they select), *with Scarcella v. America Online*, 11 Misc. 3d 19, 811 N.Y.S.2d 858 (2005) (refusing to enforce forum selection clause in internet service agreement in the context of consumer's small claims action against internet service provider), *and America Online, Inc. v. Superior Court of Alameda County*, 90 Cal. App. 4th 1, 108 Cal. Rptr. 699 (1st App. Cal. 2001) (refusing to enforce forum selection clause in internet service agreement, noting that the governing law of the forum designated in the forum selection clause would provide less protection than the law of the jurisdiction where the consumer actually filed the lawsuit).

3. International instruments formalize court treatment of forum selection clauses throughout the world. For example, European countries have for many years followed conventions endorsing a favorable approach toward forum selection clauses.[14] In 2005, the Hague Conference on Private International Law adopted the Hague Convention on Choice of Court Agreements. The Convention, which the United States has not yet ratified, provides for the recognition of forum selection clauses in international

---

14. *See, e.g.*, ZHENG SOPHIA TANG, ELECTRONIC CONSUMER CONTRACTS IN THE CONFLICT OF LAWS 122-147 (2009) (describing treatment of choice of court clauses under the Brussels I Regulation as well as issues surrounding such clauses in the context of internet consumer contracts); Frank Vischer, *Forum Selection and Arbitration Clauses Under the Brussels and Lugano Conventions and Under Swiss Law*, in INTERNATIONAL DISPUTE RESOLUTION: THE REGULATION OF FORUM SELECTION 74 (Jack Goldsmith ed., 1996) (describing the relevant Brussels and Lugano Conventions as reflecting concern with "predictability of result and a favorable attitude to the parties' autonomy in conflict of laws").

commercial transactions. The Convention also enables a court to validate forum selection clauses in order to establish jurisdiction to recognize and enforce foreign judgments. Finally, the Convention creates a mechanism for governments to declare their willingness to enforce nonexclusive forum selection agreements. The Convention cannot have force unless at least two countries accede to it. Mexico is the only country to have done so, although the United States and the European Union became signatories in 2009. *See generally* Walter W. Heiser, *The Hague Convention on Choice of Court Agreements*, 31 U. PA. J. INT'L L. 1013 (2010).

4. A device related to forum selection clauses is arbitration clauses. Arbitration clauses not only designate the "place" where parties resolve a dispute, but also specify a particular legal regime for resolute. Specifically, parties contract to have their disputes resolved by arbitrators and to be finally bound (or not) by the arbitration that should apply. Binding arbitration effectively prevents parties from resorting to traditional courts for resolution.

Arbitration has become much more established and popular in the United States in the last few decades — a phenomena the United States Supreme Court has encouraged in a series of decisions favoring it as a method of resolving disputes. Such clauses generally provide parties with substantial benefits: (1) the ability to designate a particular arbitrator with expertise in the subject matter of the dispute (which may improve the efficiency and accuracy of decisions); (2) the ability to control the time, place, and procedures governing dispute resolution; (3) the ability to keep the dispute resolution confidential; and (4) the ability to exercise significant control over which law and other principles govern the resolution. Questions arise, however, as to whether parties should be allowed this type of autonomy. Legal principles and official tribunals are in place for a variety of reasons. Should private parties really be able to exercise such latitude in circumventing these protections? Aren't arbitration clauses particularly problematic where the parties have unequal bargaining power?

5. Some jurisdictions, most notably Delaware, allow corporations to include forum selection provisions in their bylaws. *See, e.g., Boilermakers Local 154 Ret. Fund v. Chevron Corp.*, 73 A.3d 934 (Del. Ch. 2013) (upholding validity of forum selection bylaws that are adopted by boards of directors without shareholder approval). Delaware has traditionally been the chosen forum in these bylaw provisions, given its reputation for laws and courts that are company-friendly and sophisticated in corporate matters. The question lurks, however, about whether Delaware will continue indefinitely to serve as the most hospitable forum for corporate litigation. Developments in Delaware law—such as regulation of settlements of stockholder merger litigation — may inject uncertainty into whether Delaware litigation is truly corporate-friendly.

6. Issues concerning forum selection clauses include the question of whether they should be enforced as well as how they should be interpreted. Enforceability concerns are described in Problem 1-11 below. Courts encounter a number of issues that arise as a result of ambiguities in clause language and have articulated some rules that help in construing clauses. These matters are discussed in Problem 1-12, which gives you a chance to draft language with the intent of avoiding ambiguities and other problems.

PROBLEM 1-11: DISCOMFORT WITH FIESTA

Alice and Ben are both disabled residents of New York. Alice suffers from severe multiple sclerosis and must use a wheelchair to facilitate her movement. Because of her high medical expenses, Alice's financial means are extremely limited. Ben is a quadriplegic who is independently wealthy despite his medical costs.

Fiesta Cruises is a corporation that runs cruises throughout the United States and is incorporated and headquartered in California. After saving for two years, Alice purchased a ticket on the cheapest available Fiesta cruise. Ben, too, purchased a ticket. In telephone conversations, Fiesta assured both Alice and Ben that their ship will be accessible to disabled persons. When Alice and Ben received their tickets a week before the cruise, certain terms and conditions were listed on the back of the tickets. These terms included the following provision: "The laws and courts of California shall apply."

Upon boarding the ship, Alice and Ben discovered that neither their rooms nor the rest of the ship's facilities are disabled-accessible. As a result, they had a disappointing and uncomfortable trip, and they sued Fiesta in New York federal court under the Americans with Disabilities Act for failing to provide accessible accommodations. Fiesta moved to dismiss for lack of personal jurisdiction, citing the forum selection clause. Should the New York district court grant the motion?

Case reporters are filled with decisions settling disputes about the proper construction of choice of forum clauses. Disputes arise because clauses are ambiguously worded or the litigation raises issues that the parties could have anticipated, but did not. Obviously, these are problems to try to avoid in the contracts that you draft. That is not to say, however, that there will not be times when prudence counsels keeping a clause ambiguous or vague. It may be that you are unable to predict the future on a particular matter and therefore need to keep your options open. Or, your contract negotiations may have become contentious and you (and your client) have made a judgment that the "deal" is more important than the vague possibility of future litigation. In that event, you might want to avoid fighting over the forum selection clause or to avoid pointing out the other lawyer's sloppy drafting. Sometimes it is simply better to sacrifice future certainty for a present resolution. Although you may decide to live with an ambiguous forum selection clause, any ambiguity in the clause should be the result of a conscious decision. In order to ensure that ambiguities are purposeful, you should acquaint yourself with possible pitfalls. The following problem illustrates potential drafting difficulties to anticipate.

PROBLEM 1-12: FORUM SELECTION CLAUSE DRAFTING

Try your hand at the follow drafting exercises:

a. *Which Court*: Sometimes parties want to make clear in their forum selection clause the precise court or courts in which they want to litigate. A frequent problem is determining whether they wish to litigate in state or federal court. Draft a forum selection clause that avoids this problem.

b. *Scope of Clause*: Consider a situation where the parties have a straightforward contractual arrangement—say, where party A agrees to sell goods to party B. But life becomes complicated and it turns out that party A believes that party B has engaged in some kind of tortious interference with party A's contractual relationships with a third party (party C) in a matter peripherally related to the original contract between party A and party B. Or perhaps party A believes that party B's behavior under the contract has prompted party A to breach its fiduciary duties to others. Assume that you are drafting the forum selection clause and that you anticipate the possibility that these peripheral causes of action may arise between party A and party B. How would you draft the clause in order to encompass these and other tangentially related causes of action?

c. *Exclusive or Non-exclusive*: Parties have the option of making their chosen jurisdiction exclusive—in which case suits can be brought only in the chosen forum—or of making their choice non-exclusive. Sometimes United States courts refer to this distinction as the question of whether the clause is mandatory (requiring suits to be brought in the named forum) or permissive (allowing suits to brought in jurisdictions other than the named forum). Civil law countries often refer to exclusive or mandatory clauses as "derogation" clauses and non-exclusive or permissive clauses as "prorogation" clauses. Courts show a slight preference for exclusive clauses—which tend to be the most common in the United States today.

   What language would you use to capture the intent that your cause should be interpreted as exclusive? Non-exclusive? If you wanted to keep the matter ambiguous, what language would you use?

d. *Creating an Incentive Not to Litigate*: How might one draft a forum selection clause that designates a potential site or sites for litigation, but nonetheless sends a disincentive to the parties to file litigation?

4. *Principles Governing When Courts in the United States May Exercise Power in International Cases*

A number of doctrines bear on whether a litigant may successfully invoke the power of a forum within the United States to adjudicate matters implicating international issues concerning a foreign sovereign. For the most part, these are limitations that a litigant must consider in evaluating the forum's ability to provide meaningful relief. The limitations include general principles of subject matter jurisdiction, the political question doctrine, foreign sovereign immunity, and the act of state doctrine. All four of these doctrines are crucial to a plaintiff's forum choice in that they govern whether the plaintiff can obtain relief in *any* court of the United States. In addition, all four implicate important issues of separation of powers among the branches of the federal government. This section reviews each of the four concepts and provides more in-depth coverage of two matters: sovereign immunity and the act of state doctrine.

a. Subject Matter Jurisdiction

Subject matter jurisdiction refers to the power of a court to adjudicate specific types of cases. Because many state courts are courts of general subject matter jurisdiction, many cases implicating foreign or international matters may nominally fall within the state courts' subject matter jurisdiction. Nonetheless, other doctrines, such as the constitutional doctrines restricting state court power over foreign relations, can restrict the state courts' abilities to exercise this apparent power.

Unlike many state courts, federal courts are courts of limited jurisdiction. Federal court subject matter jurisdiction must not only derive from a power listed in Article III of the United States Constitution, but also must be founded in a specific act of Congress conferring subject matter jurisdiction on the federal courts. Statutory authorizations on matters implicating international concerns often include jurisdiction in actions (1) arising under federal law; (2) premised on diversity of citizenship of the parties; (3) arising from disputes between the United States and foreign parties ("alienage jurisdiction"); (4) arising under the Alien Tort Statute; and (5) concerning foreign states and authorized under the Foreign Sovereign Immunities Act. Later in this book, you will encounter matters related to the Alien Tort Statute in connection with Chapter 3's presentation on federal common law and the United States Supreme Court's decision in *Sosa v. Alvarez Machain (Alvarez-Machain II)*, 542 U.S. 692 (2004). *Sosa* held that that the Alien Tort Statute authorizes federal courts to hear certain claims brought by aliens and defined by "the law of nations and recognized at common law." Finally, matters related to the Foreign Sovereign Immunities Act are explored later in this chapter in connection with the sovereign immunity discussion.

b.   The Political Question Doctrine

Derived from inherent constitutional limitations on federal court power, the political question doctrine prevents federal courts from resolving issues that are more appropriately handled by other branches of government. The Supreme Court has enunciated a number of factors for courts to consider in evaluating whether the doctrine should bar judicial consideration of an issue, including "a textually demonstrable commitment of the issues to a coordinate political department; . . . the impossibility of deciding without an initial policy determination of a kind clearly for nonjudicial discretion; . . . an unusual need for unquestioning adherence to a political decision already made; or the potentiality of embarrassment from multifarious pronouncements by various departments on one question." *Baker v. Carr*, 369 U.S. 186, 217 (1962).

The question of when these factors should trigger the political question bar is not settled. On one hand, the United States Supreme Court has stated that "the very nature of executive decisions as to foreign policy is political, not judicial. Such decisions . . . are delicate, complex, and involve large elements of prophesy. . . . They are decisions of a kind for which the Judiciary has neither aptitude, facilities nor responsibility. . . ." *Chicago & Southern Air Lines v. Waterman S.S. Corp.*, 333 U.S. 103, 111 (1948). On the other hand, many have argued that the constitutional provisions governing foreign policy have no meaning without judicial enforcement. Lower courts grappling with the political question doctrine in the international context have reached contradictory results. *Compare, e.g., Gonzalez-Vera v. Kissinger*, 449 F.3d 1260 (D.C. Cir. 2006) (invoking doctrine to bar adjudication of clams against former United States officials for human rights abuses by Chilean officials), *Whiteman v. Dorotheum GmbH & Co. KG*, 431 F.3d 57 (2d Cir. 2005) (invoking doctrine to bar claims against Austria and its instrumentalities arising from the Nazi confiscation of properties), *and Joo v. Japan*, 413 F.3d 45, 52-53 (2d Cir. 2005) (invoking doctrine to bar adjudication of claims by alleged "comfort women" against Japanese army), *with Gross v. German Found. Indus. Initiative*, 456 F.3d 363 (3d Cir. 2006) (refusing to apply doctrine to bar claims in slave labor claims from World War II), *and Klinghoffer v. Achille Lauro SNC*, 937 F.2d 44 (2d Cir. 1991) (refusing to apply doctrine as a bar to suit against PLO for hijacking and murder).

c.   Foreign Sovereign Immunity

Immunity from suit arises in at least three distinct contexts in international litigation. "Diplomatic" or "consular" immunity protects certain state representatives from criminal and, to some degree, civil liability. "Head-of-state" immunity provides nearly absolute protection from liability under United States law for sitting heads of state. The immunity doctrine with the greatest practical scope, however, is "sovereign immunity" — sometimes referred to as "state immunity." As discussed in Chapter 3, sovereign immunity implicates relationships between state courts as well as relationships between state and federal courts in the United States. This section reviews concepts unique to *foreign* sovereign immunity, which governs the immunity from jurisdiction that foreign states (as well as their instrumentalities and agencies) enjoy in lawsuits filed in United States federal and state courts.

Explaining the intellectual foundations of foreign sovereign immunity in the classic case of *The Schooner Exchange v. M'Faddon,* 11 U.S. (7 Cranch.) 116 (1812), Chief Justice John Marshall explained that any exception to a nation's "exclusive and absolute" jurisdiction over its territory arises only by virtue of the nation's consent or waiver. Chief Justice Marshall reasoned that although the world's sovereignties possess "equal rights and equal independence," the sovereignties "have consented to a relaxation in practice, in cases under certain peculiar circumstances, of that absolute and complete jurisdiction within their respective territories which sovereignty confers." After *The Schooner Exchange,* the United States courts adhered to a norm of absolute sovereign immunity—particularly in actions against foreign sovereigns friendly to the United States. A change became clear, however, with the 1952 letter to the Acting Attorney General from the Acting Legal Adviser of the State Department, Jack B. Tate, articulating the Executive branch's view that sovereign immunity should not be recognized with respect to private acts of the state, such as commercial activities. Courts deferred to this Executive branch judgment reflected in the Tate letter, taking their instructions from the Department of State about what constituted private actions outside the scope of immunity.

Transferring responsibility for foreign sovereign immunity determinations from the Executive to the Judicial branch, Congress enacted a framework for foreign sovereign immunity in the Foreign Sovereign Immunities Act (FSIA), 28 U.S.C. §1602. Enacted in 1976, the Act provides "the sole and exclusive standards to be used in resolving questions of sovereign immunity raised by foreign states before state and federal courts in the United States." [15]

The FSIA provides for an integrated procedural system governing foreign state immunity, covering immunity standards, service of process, attachment of state property, and judgment enforcement. At bottom, the FSIA is a jurisdictional statute, allowing federal courts to exercise power in those instances where the foreign state does not enjoy immunity—specifically those cases where the foreign states are sued for "commercial" or "private" acts rather than "sovereign acts." [16]

The FSIA generally steers clear of enunciating substantive principles of liability.

---

15. H.R. Rep. No. 1487, 9th Cong., 2d Sess. 12, reprinted in 1976 U.S. Code Cong. & Admin. News at 6610-6611.
16. *Verlinden BV v. Central Bank of Nigeria,* 461 U.S. 480 (1983).

26 Department of State Bulletin 984 (1952)
Changed Policy Concerning the Granting of Sovereign
Immunity to Foreign Governments

[Following is the text of a letter addressed to Acting Attorney General Philip B. Perlman by the Department's Acting Legal Adviser, Jack B. Tate.]

May 19, 1952

MY DEAR MR. ATTORNEY GENERAL:

The Department of State has for some time had under consideration the question whether the practice of the Government in granting immunity from suit to foreign governments made parties defendant in the courts of the United States without their consent should not be changed. The Department has now reached the conclusion that such immunity should no longer be granted in certain types of cases. In view of the obvious interest of your Department in this matter I should like to point out briefly some of the facts which influenced the Department's decision.

A study of the law of sovereign immunity reveals the existence of two conflicting concepts of sovereign immunity, each widely held and firmly established. According to the classical or absolute theory of sovereign immunity, a sovereign cannot, without his consent, be made a respondent in the courts of another sovereign. According to the newer or restrictive theory of sovereign immunity, the immunity of the sovereign is recognized with regard to sovereign or public acts (*jure imperii*) of a state, but not with respect to private acts (*jure gestionis*). There is agreement by proponents of both theories, supported by practice, that sovereign immunity should not be claimed or granted in actions with respect to real property (diplomatic and perhaps consular property excepted) or with respect to the disposition of the property of a deceased person even though a foreign sovereign is the beneficiary.

The classical or virtually absolute theory of sovereign immunity has generally been followed by the courts of the United States, the British Commonwealth, Czechoslovakia, Estonia, and probably Poland.

The decisions of the courts of Brazil, Chile, China, Hungary, Japan, Luxembourg, Norway, and Portugal may be deemed to support the classical theory of immunity if one or at most two old decisions anterior to the development of the restrictive theory may be considered sufficient on which to base a conclusion.

The position of the Netherlands, Sweden, and Argentina is less clear since although immunity has been granted in recent cases coming before the courts of those countries, the facts were such that immunity would have been granted under either the absolute or restrictive theory. However, constant references by the courts of these three countries to the distinction between public and private acts of the state, even though the distinction was not involved in the result of the case, may indicate an intention to leave the way open for a possible application of the restrictive theory of immunity if and when "the occasion presents itself."

A trend to the restrictive theory is already evident in the Netherlands where the lower courts have started to apply that theory following a Supreme Court decision to the effect that immunity would have been applicable in the case under consideration under either theory.

The German courts, after a period of hesitation at the end of the nineteenth century have held to the classical theory, but it should be noted that the refusal of the Supreme Court in 1921 to yield to pressure by the lower courts for the newer theory was based on the view that that theory had not yet developed sufficiently to justify a change. In view of the growth of the restrictive theory since that time the German courts might take a different view today.

The newer or restrictive theory of sovereign immunity has always been supported by the courts of Belgium and Italy. It was adopted in turn by the courts of Egypt and of Switzerland. In addition, the courts of France, Austria, and Greece, which were traditionally supporters of the classical theory, reversed their position in the 20's to embrace the restrictive theory. Rumania, Peru, and possibly Denmark also appear to follow this theory.

Furthermore, it should be observed that in most of the countries still following the classical theory there is a school of influential writers favoring the restrictive theory and the views of writers, at least in civil law countries, are a major factor in the development of the law. Moreover, the leanings of the lower courts in civil law countries are more significant in shaping the law than they are in common law countries where the rule of precedent prevails and the trend in these lower courts is to the restrictive theory.

Of related interest to this question is the fact that ten of the thirteen countries which have been classified above as supporters of the classical theory have ratified the Brussels Convention of 1926 under which immunity for government owned merchant vessels is waived. In addition the United States, which is not a party to the Convention, some years ago announced and has since followed, a policy of not claiming immunity for its public owned or operated merchant vessels. Keeping in mind the importance played by cases involving public vessels in the field of sovereign immunity, it is thus noteworthy that these ten countries (Brazil, Chile, Estonia, Germany, Hungary, Netherlands, Norway, Poland, Portugal, Sweden) and the United States have already relinquished by treaty or in practice an important part of the immunity which they claim under the classical theory.

It is thus evident that with the possible exception of the United Kingdom little support has been found except on the part of the Soviet Union and its satellites for continued full acceptance of the absolute theory of sovereign immunity. There are evidences that British authorities are aware of its deficiencies and ready for a change. The reasons which obviously motivate state trading countries in adhering to the theory with perhaps increasing rigidity are most persuasive that the United States should change its policy. Furthermore, the granting of sovereign immunity to foreign governments in the courts of the United States is most inconsistent with the action of the Government of the United States in subjecting itself to suit in these same courts in both contract and tort and with its long established policy of not claiming immunity in foreign jurisdictions for its merchant vessels. Finally, the Department feels that the widespread and increasing practice on the part of governments of engaging in commercial activities makes necessary a practice which will enable persons doing business with them to have their rights determined in the courts. For these reasons it will hereafter be the Department's policy to follow the restrictive theory of sovereign immunity in the consideration of requests of foreign governments for a grant of sovereign immunity.

It is realized that a shift in policy by the executive cannot control the courts but it is felt that the courts are less likely to allow a plea of sovereign immunity where the executive has declined to do so. There have been indications that at least some Justices of the Supreme Court feel that in this matter courts should follow the branch of the Government charged with responsibility for the conduct of foreign relations.

In order that your Department, which is charged with representing the interests of the Government before the courts, may be adequately informed it will be the Department's practice to advise you of all requests by foreign governments for the grant of immunity from suit and of the Department's action thereon.

Sincerely yours,
For the Secretary of State:
Jack B. TATE
Acting Legal Adviser

The FSIA's grant of immunity for foreign states is subject to nine exceptions:

(1) commercial activity with a United States nexus;
(2) noncommercial torts in the United States;
(3) expropriation of property located in the United States in violation of international law;
(4) waiver of immunity;
(5) arbitration-related matters;
(6) rights to property in the United States acquired by gift or succession, or rights to immoveable property situated within the United States;
(7) certain admiralty matters;
(8) counterclaims against the state; and
(9) involvement in certain acts of terrorism.

Questions also arise, however, whether the FSIA applies at all to acts that occurred before its enactment in 1976. The case that follows takes up that question.

Republic of Austria v. Altmann

541 U.S. 677 (2004)

Justice STEVENS delivered the opinion of the Court.

[In 1998, an Austrian journalist discovered evidence in the Austrian Gallery archives that works in the Gallery's collection had not been donated by their rightful owners but had been seized by the Nazis or expropriated by the Austrian Republic after World War II. Based on this information, an heiress of the original owner of six Gustav Klimt paintings sued the Republic of Austria and the Austrian Gallery (Gallery), an instrumentality of the Republic. These defendants moved to dismiss, asserting a claim of sovereign immunity. They claimed that they enjoyed absolute immunity, since the alleged appropriation took place prior to the time the Tate letter was issued. The lower courts dismissed this argument, and held that the "expropriation exception" of the Foreign Sovereign Immunities Act, 28 U.S.C. §1605(a)(3) applied to the case. The expropriation exception deprives a foreign state or its agencies or instrumentalities of the sovereign immunity defense, where that entity "is engaged in a commercial activity in the United States" and the case is one "in which rights in property taken in violation of international law are in issue," §1605(a)(3).

The United States Supreme Court agreed to hear the case, but did not agree to review the expropriation exception ruling. Instead the Court granted certiorari only on "the question whether the Foreign Sovereign Immunities Act of 1976 . . . , which grants foreign states immunity from the jurisdiction of federal and state courts but expressly exempts certain cases, including 'case[s] . . . in which rights in property taken in violation of international law are in issue' . . . applies to claims that . . . are based on conduct that occurred before the Act's enactment, and even before the United States adopted the so-called 'restrictive theory' of sovereign immunity in 1952."]

. . .

III

Chief Justice Marshall's opinion in *Schooner Exchange v. McFaddon*, 7 Cranch 116 (1812), is generally viewed as the source of our foreign sovereign immunity jurisprudence. In that case, the libellants claimed to be the rightful owners of a French ship that had taken refuge in the port of Philadelphia. The Court first emphasized that the jurisdiction of the United States over persons and property within its territory "is susceptible of no limitation not imposed by itself," and thus foreign sovereigns have no right to immunity in our courts. Id., at 136. Chief Justice Marshall went on to explain, however, that as a matter of comity, members of the international community had implicitly agreed to waive the exercise of jurisdiction over other sovereigns in certain classes of cases, such as those involving foreign ministers or the person of the sovereign. Accepting a suggestion advanced by the Executive Branch, the Chief Justice concluded that the implied waiver theory also served to exempt the Schooner Exchange — "a national armed vessel . . . of the emperor of France" — from United States courts' jurisdiction. Id., at 145-146.

In accordance with Chief Justice Marshall's observation that foreign sovereign immunity is a matter of grace and comity rather than a constitutional requirement, this Court has "consistently . . . deferred to the decisions of the political branches — in particular, those of the Executive Branch — on whether

Notes on
ALTMANN

1. As Justice Kennedy's dissent argues, the *Altmann* Court's suggestion that the Executive branch can intervene in litigation against a foreign sovereign in order to argue against accepting jurisdiction raises potent separation of powers issues. Are not courts able to handle such decisions without such a formal mechanism for Executive branch input? Which of the three branches of the federal government would be most threatened by encouraging this practice of formalized Executive branch input? Is the majority's suggestion for Executive branch input significantly different from the approach suggested in the Tate letter?

2. As explained above, the United States's position on foreign sovereign immunity shifted from granting absolute immunity to granting only restrictive immunity under the position expressed in the Tate letter and later codified in the FSIA. Thus, the decision whether the restrictive immunity approach should apply to conduct that occurred before the Tate letter issued or the FSIA became law was quite significant. In holding the FSIA retroactive, the *Altmann* Court rejected the Executive branch's request to narrow the Act's retroactive application. Could this have motivated the majority to suggest a mechanism for the Executive branch to suggest immunity in particular cases?

3. Much of the debate about which branch controls foreign sovereign immunity might be avoided with a bright line rule of absolute immunity. This raises questions about the utility of the restrictive immunity approach. The expropriation exception explored in *Altmann* is neither the exclusive nor most common restriction on foreign sovereign immunity. Exceptions to immunity exist for a number of contexts, including commercial activity, waiver, torts, takings, arbitration agreements, and terrorism. Indeed, the exception for commercial activity is likely the restriction that generates the greatest amount of litigation, with foreign sovereigns fighting hard to convince a court to characterize the dispute activity as sovereign rather than commercial. The FSIA defines "commercial activity" as:

> Either a regular course of commercial conduct or a particular commercial transaction or act. The commercial character of an activity shall be determined by reference to the nature of the course of conduct or particular transaction or act, rather than by reference to its purpose.

28 U.S.C. §1603(d). What value is expressed in the decision to protect "sovereign" activity from liability, but to subject to liability a foreign state's commercial activity?

d. The Act of State Doctrine

A judicially created set of principles, the act of state doctrine instructs that United States courts should presume that a foreign government's official acts within its own territory are valid. This mandate finds its roots in international considerations as well as the United States Constitution.

Like foreign sovereign immunity, the history of the act of state doctrine details a sensitive dynamic between courts and the Executive branch of the federal government. At one point, the Executive branch followed a practice of issuing what were called "Bernstein letters,"[17] in which the United States government would communicate that it had no objection to a court adjudicating a specific dispute against a foreign government.

In the decision that follows, *Banco Nacional de Cuba v. Sabbatino*, 376 U.S. 398 (1964), the Supreme Court potentially broadened the doctrine, establishing it as a potential offensive tool for a plaintiff as well as a defensive mechanism for a defendant. As explained in the notes following *Sabbatino*, courts and Congress have limited the case's effect and broad pronouncements. As a consequence, the act of state doctrine has become complex over time, with courts developing many exceptions as they walk the line between avoiding political controversy and applying legal standards. Nonetheless, although the law in this area has been dynamic, the *Sabbatino* decision still stands as a classic enunciation of the values and concerns underlying the act of state doctrine.

Banco Nacional de Cuba v. Sabbatino

376 U.S. 398 (1964)

Mr. Justice HARLAN delivered the opinion of the Court.

[After the United Stated reduced Cuba's quota for sugar imports, the Cuban government nationalized the property of United States citizens in Cuba. One of the companies whose property was nationalized, Compania Azucarera Vertientes (C.A.V.), had contracted to sell sugar to a United States broker, Farr, Whitlock. After the nationalization, Farr, Whitlock entered into a second contract for sugar with the Cuban government, which acted as the sugar's new owner. Farr, Whitlock shipped the sugar and turned the proceeds over to the C.A.V. receiver, Peter Sabbatino, rather than to Cuba. The Cuban government had assigned the right to receive payment to Banco Nacional de Cuba, which subsequently filed suit against Farr, Whitlock. Farr, Whitlock defended by arguing that the Cuban government violated international law in seizing the sugar.]

The question which brought this case here, and is now found to be the dispositive issue, is whether the so-called act of state doctrine serves to sustain

---

17. The letters took their name from an unpopular court of appeals decision in *Bernstein v. Van Heyghen Freres Sociéte Anonyme*, 163 F.2d 246 (2d Cir. 1947), in which the court dismissed a case to recover confiscated Jewish property, ruling that the Nazi confiscation of this property in Germany was an act of state shielded by the act of state doctrine.

petitioner's claims in this litigation. Such claims are ultimately founded on a decree of the Government of Cuba expropriating certain property, the right to the proceeds of which is here in controversy. The act of state doctrine in its traditional formulation precludes the courts of this country from inquiring into the validity of the public acts a recognized foreign sovereign power committed within its own territory. . . .

IV.

The classic American statement of the act of state doctrine, which appears to have taken root in England as early as 1674, and began to emerge in the jurisprudence of this country in the late eighteenth and early nineteenth centuries, is found in *Underhill v. Hernandez*:

> Every sovereign state is bound to respect the independence of every other sovereign state, and the courts of one country will not sit in judgment on the acts of the government of another, done within its own territory. Redress of grievances by reason of such acts must be obtained through the means open to be availed of by sovereign powers as between themselves.

None of this Court's subsequent cases in which the act of state doctrine was directly or peripherally involved manifest any retreat from *Underhill*. . . .

The outcome of this case . . . turns upon whether any of the contentions urged by respondents against the application of the act of state doctrine in the premises is acceptable: (1) that the doctrine does not apply to acts of state which violate international law, as is claimed to be the case here; (2) that the doctrine is inapplicable unless the Executive specifically interposes it in a particular case; and (3) that, in any event, the doctrine may not be invoked by a foreign government plaintiff in our courts.

V.

Preliminarily, we discuss the foundations on which we deem the act of state doctrine to rest, and more particularly the question of whether state or federal law governs its application in a federal diversity case.[20]

We do not believe that this doctrine is compelled either by the inherent nature of sovereign authority, as some of the earlier decision seem to imply, or by some principle of international law. If a transaction takes place in one jurisdiction and the forum is in another, the forum does not by dismissing an action or by applying its own law purport to divest the first jurisdiction of its territorial sovereignty; it merely declines to adjudicate or makes applicable its own law to parties or property before it. The refusal of one country to enforce the penal laws

---

20. Although the complaint in this case alleged both diversity and federal question jurisdiction, the Court of Appeals reached jurisdiction only on the former ground, 307 F.2d at 852. We need not decide, for reasons appearing hereafter, whether federal question jurisdiction also existed.

of another is a typical example of an instance when a court will not entertain a cause of action arising in another jurisdiction. While historic notions of sovereign authority do bear upon the wisdom of employing the act of state doctrine, they do not dictate its existence.

That international law does not require application of the doctrine is evidenced by the practice of nations. Most of the countries rendering decisions on the subject fail to follow the rule rigidly. No international arbitral or judicial decision discovered suggests that international law prescribes recognition of sovereign acts of foreign governments, and apparently no claim has ever been raised before an international tribunal that failure to apply the act of state doctrine constitutes a breach of international obligation. If international law does not prescribe use of the doctrine, neither does it forbid application of the rule even if it is claimed that the act of state in question violated international law. The traditional view of international law is that it establishes substantive principles for determining whether one country has wronged another. Because of its peculiar nation-to-nation character the usual method for an individual to seek relief is to exhaust local remedies and then repair to the executive authorities of his own state to persuade them to champion his claim in diplomacy or before an international tribunal. Although it is, of course, true that United States courts apply international law as a part of our own in appropriate circumstances, the public law of nations can hardly dictate to a country which is in theory wronged how to treat that wrong within its domestic borders.

. . . The text of the Constitution does not require the act of state doctrine; it does not irrevocably remove from the judiciary the capacity to review the validity of foreign acts of state.

The act of state doctrine does, however, have "constitutional" underpinnings. It arises out of the basic relationships between branches of government in a system of separation of powers. It concerns the competency of dissimilar institutions to make and implement particular kinds of decisions in the area of international relations. The doctrine as formulated in past decisions expresses the strong sense of the Judicial Branch that its engagement in the task of passing on the validity of foreign acts of state may hinder rather than further this country's pursuit of goals both for itself and for the community of nations as a whole in the international sphere. . . . Whatever considerations are thought to predominate, it is plain that the problems involved are uniquely federal in nature. . . .

We could perhaps in this diversity action avoid the question of deciding whether federal or state law is applicable to this aspect of the litigation. New York has enunciated the act of state doctrine in terms that echo those of federal decisions decided during the reign of *Swift v. Tyson*, 16 Pet. 1. . . . Thus our conclusions might well be the same whether we dealt with this problem as one of state law, see *Erie R. Co. v. Tompkins*, 304 U.S. 64; *Klaxon Co. v. Stentor Elec. Mfg. Co.*, 313 U.S. 487, or federal law.

However, we are constrained to make it clear that an issue concerned with a basic choice regarding the competence and function of the Judiciary and the National Executive in ordering our relationships with other members of the international community must be treated exclusively as an aspect of federal law.[23] It seems fair to assume that the Court did not have rules like the act of state doctrine in mind when it decided *Erie R. Co. v. Tompkins.* Soon thereafter, Professor Philip C. Jessup, now a judge of the International Court of Justice, recognized the potential dangers were *Erie* extended to legal problems affecting international relations. He cautioned that rules of international law should not be left to divergent and perhaps parochial state interpretations. His basic rationale is equally applicable to the act of state doctrine.

The Court in the pre-*Erie* act of state cases, although not burdened by the problem of the source of applicable law, used language sufficiently strong and broadsweeping to suggest that state courts were not left free to develop their own doctrines . . . (as they would have been had this Court merely been interpreting common law under *Swift v. Tyson,* supra). . . . We are not without other precedent for a determination that federal law governs; there are enclaves of federal judge-made law which bind the States. . . . Principles formulated by federal judicial law have been thought by this Court to be necessary to protect uniquely federal interests. Of course the federal interest guarded in all these cases is one the ultimate statement of which is derived from a federal statute. Perhaps more directly in point are the bodies of law applied between States over boundaries and in regard to the apportionment of interstate waters. . . .

We conclude that the scope of the act of state doctrine must be determined according to federal law.

VI.

If the act of state doctrine is a principle of decision binding on federal and state courts alike but compelled by neither international law nor the Constitution, its continuing vitality depends on its capacity to reflect the proper distribution of functions between the judicial and political branches of the Government on matters bearing upon foreign affairs. It should be apparent that the greater the degree of codification or consensus concerning a particular area of international law, the more appropriate it is for the judiciary to render decisions regarding it, since the courts can then focus on the application of an agreed principle to circumstances of fact rather than on the sensitive task of establishing a principle not inconsistent with the national interest or with international justice. It is also evident that some aspects of international law touch much more sharply on national nerves than do others; the less important the implications of an issue are for our foreign relations, the weaker the justification for exclusivity in the political branches. The balance of relevant considerations may also be shifted if the government which perpetrated the challenged act of state is no longer in existence . . . for the political interest of this country may, as a result, be measurably altered. Therefore, rather than laying down or reaffirming an inflexible and all-encompassing rule in this case, we decide only that the Judicial Branch will not

23. At least this is true when the Court limits the scope of judicial inquiry. We need not now consider whether a state court might, in certain circumstances, adhere to a more restrictive view concerning the scope of examination of foreign acts than that required by this Court.

examine the validity of a taking of property within its own territory by a foreign sovereign government, extant and recognized by this country at the time of suit, in the absence of a treaty or other unambiguous agreement regarding controlling legal principles, even if the complaint alleges that the taking violates customary international law.

There are few if any issues in international law today on which opinion seems to be so divided as the limitations on a state's power to expropriate the property of aliens. There is, of course, authority, in international judicial and arbitral decisions, in the expressions of national governments, and among commentators for the view that a taking is improper under international law if it is not for a public purpose, is discriminatory, or is without provision for prompt, adequate, and effective compensation. . . . The disagreement as to relevant international law standards reflects an even more basic divergence between the national interests of capital importing and capital exporting nations and between the social ideologies of those countries that favor state control of a considerable portion of the means of production and those that adhere to a free enterprise system. It is difficult to imagine the courts of this country embarking on adjudication in an area which touches more sensitively the practical and ideological goals of the various members of the community of nations.

. . . Following an expropriation of any significance, the Executive engages in diplomacy aimed to assure that United States citizens who are harmed are compensated fairly. . . . Such decisions would, if the acts involved were declared invalid, often be likely to give offense to the expropriating country; since the concept of territorial sovereignty is so deep seated, any state may resent the refusal of the courts of another sovereign to accord validity to acts within its territorial borders. Piecemeal dispositions of this sort involving the probability of affront to another state could seriously interfere with negotiations being carried on by the Executive Branch and might prevent or render less favorable the terms of an agreement that could otherwise be reached. . . .

The dangers of such adjudication are present regardless of whether the State Department has, as it did in this case, asserted that the relevant act violated international law. If the Executive Branch has undertaken negotiations with an expropriating country, but has refrained from claims of violation of the law of nations, a determination to that effect by a court might be regarded as a serious insult, while a finding of compliance with international law would greatly strengthen the bargaining hand of the other state with consequent detriment to American interests.

Even if the State Department has proclaimed the impropriety of the expropriation, the stamp of approval of its view by a judicial tribunal, however impartial, might increase any affront and the judicial decision might occur at a time, almost always well after the taking, when such an impact would be contrary to our national interest. Considerably more serious and far-reaching consequences would flow from a judicial finding that international law standards had been met if that determination flew in the face of a State Department proclamation to the contrary. When articulating principles of international law in its relations with other states, the Executive Branch speaks not only as an interpreter of generally accepted and traditional rules, as would the courts, but also as an advocate of standards it believes desirable for the community of nations and protective of national concerns. In short, whatever way the matter is cut, the possibility of conflict between the Judicial and Executive Branches could hardly be avoided.

Respondents contend that, even if there is not agreement regarding general standards for determining the validity of expropriations, the alleged combination of retaliation, discrimination, and inadequate compensation makes it patently clear that this particular expropriation was in violation of international law. If this view is accurate, it would still be unwise for the courts so to determine. Such a decision now would require the drawing of more difficult lines in subsequent cases and these would involve the possibility of conflict with the Executive view. Even if the courts avoided this course, either by presuming the validity of an act of state whenever the international law standard was thought unclear or by following the State Department declaration in such a situation, the very expression of judicial uncertainty might provide embarrassment to the Executive Branch.

. . .

However offensive to the public policy of this country and its constituent States an expropriation of this kind may be, we conclude that both the national interest and progress toward the goal of establishing the rule of law among nations are best served by maintaining intact the act of state doctrine in this realm of its application.

VII.

Finally, we must determine whether Cuba's status as a plaintiff in this case dictates a result at variance with the conclusions reached above. If the Court were to distinguish between suits brought by sovereign states and those of assignees, the rule would have little effect unless a careful examination were made in each case to determine if the private party suing had taken property in good faith. Such an inquiry would be exceptionally difficult, since the relevant transaction would almost invariably have occurred outside our borders. If such an investigation were deemed irrelevant, a state could always assign its claim.

It is true that the problem of security of title is not directly presented in the instance of a sovereign plaintiff, although were such a plaintiff denied relief, it would ship its goods elsewhere, thereby creating an alteration in the flow of trade. The sensitivity in regard to foreign relations and the possibility of embarrassment of the Executive are, of course, heightened by the presence of a sovereign plaintiff. The rebuke to a recognized power would be more pointed were it a suitor in our courts. . . .

Respondents offer another theory for treating the case differently because of Cuba's participation. It is claimed that the forum should simply apply its own law to all the relevant transactions. An analogy is drawn to the area of sovereign immunity . . . in which, if a foreign country seeks redress in our courts, counterclaims are permissible. But immunity relates to the prerogative right not to have sovereign property subject to suit; fairness has been thought to require that when the sovereign seeks recovery, it be subject to legitimate counterclaims against it. The act of state doctrine, however, although it shares with the immunity doctrine a respect for sovereign states, concerns the limits for determining the validity of an otherwise applicable rule of law. It is plain that if a recognized government sued on a contract with a United States citizen, concededly legitimate by the locus of its making, performance, and most significant contacts, the forum would not apply its own substantive law of contracts. Since the act of state doctrine reflects the desirability of presuming the relevant transaction valid, the same result follows; the forum may not apply its local law regarding foreign expropriations. . . .

The judgment of the Court of Appeals is reversed and the case is remanded to the District Court for proceedings consistent with this opinion. It is so ordered.

Mr. Justice WHITE, dissenting.

I am dismayed that the Court has, with one broad stroke, declared the ascertainment and application of international law beyond the competence of the courts of the United States in a large and important category of cases. I am also disappointed in the Court's declaration that the acts of a sovereign state with regard to the property of aliens within its borders are beyond the reach of international law in the courts of this country. However clearly established that law may be, a sovereign may violate it with impunity, except insofar as the political branches of the government may provide a remedy. This backward-looking doctrine, never before declared in this Court, is carried a disconcerting step further: not only are the courts powerless to question acts of state proscribed by international law but they are likewise powerless to refuse to adjudicate the claim founded upon a foreign law; they must render judgment and thereby validate the lawless act. Since the Court expressly extends its ruling to all acts of state expropriating property, however clearly inconsistent with the international community, all discriminatory expropriations of the property of aliens, as for example the taking of properties of persons belonging to certain races, religions or nationalities, are entitled to automatic validation in the courts of the United States. No other civilized country has found such a rigid rule necessary for the survival of the executive branch of its government; the executive of no other government seems to require such insulation from international law adjudications in its courts; and no other judiciary is apparently so incompetent to ascertain and apply international law.

I do not believe that the act of state doctrine, as judicially fashioned in this Court, and the reasons underlying it, require American courts to decide cases in disregard of international law and of the rights of litigants to a full determination on the merits. . . .

IV.

The reasons for nonreview, based as they are on traditional concepts of territorial sovereignty, lose much of their force when the foreign act of state is shown to be a violation of international law. All legitimate exercises of sovereign power, whether territorial or otherwise, should be exercised consistently with rules of international law, including those rules which mark the bounds of lawful state action against aliens or their property located within the territorial confines of the foreign state. Although a state may reasonably expect that the validity of its laws operating on property within its jurisdiction will not be defined by local notions of public policy of numerous other states (although a different situation may well be presented when courts of another state are asked to lend their enforcement machinery to effectuate the foreign act), it cannot with impunity ignore the rules governing the conduct of all nations and expect that other nations and tribunals will view its acts as within the permissible scope of territorial sovereignty. Contrariwise, to refuse inquiry into the question of whether norms of the international community have been contravened by the act of state under review would seem to deny the existence or purport of such norms, a view that seems inconsistent with the role of international law in ordering the relations between nations. Finally, the impartial application of international law would not only be an affirmation of the existence and binding effect of international rules of order, but also a refutation of the notion that this body of law consists of no more than the divergent and parochial views of the capital importing and exporting nations, the socialist and free-enterprise nations.

Of course, there are many unsettled areas of international law, as there are of domestic law, and these areas present sensitive problems of accommodating the interests of nations that subscribe to divergent economic and political systems. It may be that certain nationalizations of property for a public purpose fall within this area. Also, it may be that domestic courts, as compared to international tribunals, or arbitral commissions, have a different and less active role to play in formulating new rules of international law or in choosing between rules not yet adhered to by any substantial group of nations. Where a clear violation of international law is not demonstrated, I would agree that principles of comity underlying the act of state doctrine warrant recognition and enforcement of the foreign act. But none of these considerations relieve a court of the obligation to make an inquiry into the validity of the foreign act, none of them warrant a flat rule of no inquiry at all. The vice of the act of state doctrine as formulated by the Court and applied in this case, where the decree is alleged not only to be confiscatory but also retaliatory and discriminatory and has been found by two courts to be a flagrant violation of international law, is that it precludes any such examination and proscribes any decision on whether Cuban Law No. 851 contravenes an accepted principle of international law.

. . .

V.

There remains for consideration the relationship between the act of state doctrine and the power of the executive over matters touching upon the foreign affairs of the Nation. It is urged that the act of state doctrine is a necessary corollary of the executive's authority to direct the foreign relations of the United States and accordingly any exception in the doctrine, even if limited to clear violations of international law, would impede or embarrass the executive in discharging his constitutional responsibilities. Thus, according to the Court, even if principles of comity do not preclude inquiry into the validity of a foreign act under international law, due regard for the executive function forbids such examination in the courts.

Without doubt political matters in the realm of foreign affairs are within the exclusive domain of the Executive Branch, as, for example, issues for which there are no available standards or which are textually committed by the Constitution to the executive. But this is far from saying that the Constitution vests in the executive exclusive absolute control of foreign affairs or that the validity of a foreign act of state is necessarily a political question. International law, as well as a treaty or executive agreement, provides an ascertainable standard for adjudicating the validity of some foreign acts, and courts are competent to apply this body of law, notwithstanding that there may be some cases where comity dictates giving effect to the foreign act because it is not clearly condemned under generally accepted principles of international law. . . .

A valid statute, treaty or executive agreement could, I assume, confine the power of federal courts to review or award relief in respect of foreign acts or otherwise displace international law as the rule of decision. I would not disregard a declaration by the Secretary of State or the President that an adjudication in the courts of the validity of a foreign expropriation would impede relations between the United States and the foreign government or the settlement of the controversy through diplomatic channels. . . .

. . . Where the courts are requested to apply the act of state doctrine at the behest of the State Department, it does not follow that the courts are to proceed to adjudicate the action without examining the validity of the foreign act under international law. The foreign relations considerations and potential of embarrassment to the executive inhere in examination of the foreign act and in the result following from such an examination, not in the matter of who wins. Thus, all the Department of State can legitimately request is nonexamination of the foreign act. It has no proper interest or authority in having courts decide a controversy upon anything less than all of the applicable law or to decide it in accordance with the executive's view of the outcome that best comports with the foreign or domestic affairs of the day. We are not dealing here with those cases where a court refuses to measure a foreign statute against public policy of the forum or against the fundamental law of the foreign state itself. In those cases the judicially created act of state doctrine is an aspect of the conflicts of law rules of the forum and renders the foreign law controlling. But where a court refuses to examine foreign law under principles of international law, which it is required to do, solely because the Executive Branch requests the court, for its own reasons, to abstain from deciding the controlling issue in the controversy, then in my view, the executive has removed the case from the realm of the law to the realm of politics, and a court must decline to proceed with the case. The proper disposition is to stay the proceedings until circumstances permit an adjudication or to dismiss the action where an adjudication within a reasonable time does not seem feasible. To do otherwise would not be in accordance with the obligation of courts to decide controversies justly and in accordance with the law applicable to the case.

It is argued that abstention in the case at bar would allow C.A.V. to retain possession of the proceeds from the sugar and would encourage wrongfully deprived owners to engage in devious conduct or "self-help" in order to compel the sovereign or one deriving title from him into the position of plaintiff. The short answer to this is that it begs the question; negotiation of the documents by Farr and retention of the proceeds by C.A.V. is unlawful if, but only if, Cuba acquired title to the shipment by virtue of the nationalization decree. This is the issue that cannot be decided in the case if deference to the State Department's recommendation is paid (assuming for the moment that such a recommendation has been made). Nor is it apparent that "self-help," if such it be deemed, in the form of refusing to recognize title derived from unlawful paramount force is disruptful of or contrary to a peaceful international order. Furthermore, a court has ample means at its disposal to prevent a party who has engaged in wrongful conduct from setting up defenses which would allow him to profit from the wrongdoing. Where the act of state doctrine becomes a rule of judicial abstention rather than a rule of decision for the courts, the proper disposition is dismissal of the complaint or staying the litigation until the bar is lifted, regardless of who has possession of the property whose title is in dispute. . . .

Notes on
SABBATINO

1. *Sabbatino* is brimming with diverse threads of legal doctrine, constitutional theory, and matters of international political concern. As a first step to sorting through these matters, consider first why *Sabbatino* belongs in *this* section of *this* chapter. Fundamentally, this chapter covers the bottom line question of whether a particular forum is available to resolve a claim, providing the plaintiff with relief. Where the act of state doctrine under *Sabbatino* applies, the doctrine disempowers a forum from reaching the merits of the plaintiff's claim, effectively eliminating the forum's ability to provide the plaintiff's requested relief. Because the act of state doctrine is triggered where a court is asked to evaluate actions of a foreign government, *Sabbatino* belongs in *this* section of the chapter, which focuses on obstacles to a forum's ability to adjudicate matters with international implications.

2. In reaching their decision, the Justices in the majority and Justice White in dissent discussed matters well beyond the bottom line question of whether a court within the United States could adjudicate the merits of the plaintiff's claim. In this way, the *Sabbatino* decision actually foreshadows several issues treated in other chapters elsewhere in this book, including the following:

- *Erie* **and Federal Common Law:** The Court decided that federal court-made law, not state law under the doctrine of *Erie Railroad v. Tompkins*, governs whether the act of state doctrine applies in a given case. Federal common law and *Erie Railroad v. Tompkins* are covered in Chapter 3, which covers the relationship between state and federal law.

- **International Law:** Justice White's opinion (and to some degree the opinion of the Court) analyzes the role and mandate of international law in the courts of the United States, another matter covered in Chapter 3.
- **Choice of Law:** At the time of *Sabbatino*, the general choice of law rule provided that the place where a commodity was located at the time of the transfer would provide the governing law on the question of ownership. Presumably this would have been the law of Cuba, since the sugar was located there at the time of appropriation. The act of state doctrine, however, eliminated the analytical step of referring to the sugar's location because it required the court to accept the validity of the Cuban government's action. In this way, the act of state doctrine operated as a mandated choice of law principle. Choice of law principles are covered in detail in Chapter 2.
- **Separation of Powers:** Both the majority opinion and Justice White's dissent focus on the role of the Executive branch over foreign relations matters — particularly those matters with political implications. Justice White highlights how this principle comes into tension with a court's obligation to decide controversies, to give meaning to general legal principles, and to ensure individualized justice for litigants. These separations of power concerns represent an overarching theme of this book, permeating each chapter.

3. Because the act of state doctrine's focus is the acts of a foreign state, one might think that the doctrine was confined to cases where a foreign government is a litigant. But that is incorrect: a private party may also successfully argue that the court's disposition of the party's case would implicate the legitimacy of a foreign government act. The party thus can benefit from the act of state doctrine's assumption that a particular government action is valid. This application to private parties broadens the scope of the doctrine in influencing available forums for the litigating the merits of disputes.

4. Despite the sweeping implications of the *Sabbatino* opinion in light of constitutional and international theory, the Court piled on qualifications to its holding as if it were appending decorations to a Christmas tree! Consider how these qualifications in Part VI of its decision actually limit the Court's ruling:

[R]ather than laying down or reaffirming an inflexible and all-encompassing rule in this case, we decide only that the Judicial Branch will not examine the validity of a taking of property within its own territory by a foreign sovereign government, extant and recognized by this country at the time of suit, in the absence of a treaty or other unambiguous agreement regarding controlling legal principles, even if the complaint alleges that the taking violates customary international law.

5. The Court's attempt to limit its holding turned out to be unnecessary, as Congress enacted a statute known as the "Second Hickenlooper Amendment," which reversed the specific result in the case.[18] Moreover, not only did Congress undermine the specific force of *Sabbatino*'s precise holding, but subsequent developments have also limited the general reach of the act of state doctrine. For example, courts have identified exceptions to the doctrine for cases challenging a foreign government's human rights abuses, and Congress confirmed this approach in 1992 with the Torture Victim Protection Act, 28 U.S.C. §1350 note. To a limited extent, courts have also tried to identify a commercial exception to the doctrine, similar to that available for foreign sovereign immunity. More firmly established than a commercial exception is a "treaty" or "international law" exception to the doctrine. Even *Sabbatino*'s holding "tips its hat" to a treaty exception when it states that the doctrine applies "in the absence of a treaty or other unambiguous agreement regarding controlling legal principles." Presumably a treaty can provide an internationally embraced principle binding on a foreign state and clearly applicable in a United States court without gravely offending the sovereign.

6. Perhaps the most sweeping limitation of *Sabbatino*'s articulation of the act of state doctrine came in *W.S. Kirkpatrick & Co. v. Envtl. Tectonics Corp.*, 493 U.S. 400 (1990). In that case, the defendant argued that a charge by one United States contractor that another used bribery to win a lucrative contract implicated the act of state doctrine. The United State Supreme Court was unconvinced, distinguishing between two situations. First are situations covered by the doctrine in which a party seeks to declare invalid "an official act

18. The amendment provides:

Notwithstanding any other provision of law, no court in the United States shall decline on the ground of the federal act of state doctrine to make a determination on the merits giving effect to the principles of international law in a case in which a claim of title or other right to property is asserted by any party including a foreign state (or a party claiming through such state) based upon (or traced through) a confiscation or other taking after January 1, 1959, by an act of that state in violation of the principles of international law, including the principles of compensation and the other standards set out in this subsection: Provided, That this subparagraph shall not be applicable (1) in any case in which an act of a foreign state is not contrary to international law or with respect to a claim of title or other right to property acquired pursuant to an irrevocable letter of credit of not more than 180 days duration issued in good faith prior to the time of the confiscation or other taking, or (2) in any case with respect to which the President determines that application of the act of state doctrine is required in that particular case by the foreign policy interests of the United States and a suggestion to this effect is filed on his behalf in that case with the court.

22 U.S.C. §2370(e)(2).

of a foreign sovereign" that takes place within the sovereign's territory. The Court distinguished these situations from cases in which a court merely imputes "unlawful motivation" to foreign officials. Reasoning that the later situation is outside the scope of the act of state doctrine, the Court stated:

> . . . Courts of the United State have the power, and ordinarily the obligation, to decide cases and controversies properly presented to them. The act of state doctrine does not establish an exception for cases and controversies that may embarrass foreign governments, but merely requires that, in the process of deciding, the acts of foreign sovereigns taken within their own jurisdictions shall be deemed valid.

493 U.S. at 409.

Courts and commentators have debated how much *Kirkpatrick* undercuts the scope of the act of state doctrine. While all agree that *Kirkpatrick* eroded the doctrine's impact, courts and litigants still treat the doctrine as a significant component of international litigation within the United States. While occasionally a plaintiff's tool, the doctrine continues to provide a significant avoidance mechanism for defendants seeking to avoid court scrutiny of particular foreign activity.

7. To test your understanding of the doctrine, consider how it compares with the other doctrines regulating the availability of United States courts to regulate international matters. How is the act of state doctrine different than foreign sovereign immunity? How is the act of state doctrine different than the political question doctrine?

PROBLEM 1-13: SUING SAMANTARO

Lauro was a resident of a Latin American nation known as L/A Country, which suffered a brutal civil war. At the time of the civil war, the military in L/A Country contained rival groups. Lauro lived in a village that was attacked by the military. Two units were present in the area around the village at the time of the attack: one unit led by Lieutenant Hurtado and another led by Lieutenant Samantaro. The unit led by Lieutenant Hurtado raided homes in the village, torturing and killing residents for two days. Lauro was tortured during that time. He alleges that Lieutenant Samantaro's unit knew that the abuse was occurring and did not notify Samantaro's superiors in the military structure, even though Samantaro possessed the communication equipment to do so.

Ultimately, the civil war settled and a democratic government took power in L/A Country. The United States has recognized the new democratic government—and both the new government and the United States have condemned the actions and inactions of Hurtado and Samantaro. In fact, the new government filed criminal charges against Hurtado and Samantaro. Hurtado, however, died soon after charges were filed. Samantaro has eluded prosecution because he is out of the country, having taken up residence in Virginia.

Lauro filed a civil action against Samantaro in the United States District Court for the Eastern District of Virginia pursuant to the Alien Tort Statute and the Torture Victim Protection Act, 28 U.S.C. §1350. Lauro seeks damages for the injuries he suffered from the torture at the hands of the L/A Country military during the civil war. The embassy of L/A Country has filed a letter with the district judge in the Eastern District of Virginia stating that Samantaro was not acting in an official capacity at the time of the raids on the village.

Samantaro raises two defenses based on foreign sovereign immunity: arguing that the Foreign Sovereign Immunities Act and the act of state doctrine shield him from liability. Samantaro maintains that both doctrines prevent the suit from succeeding against him. Should the district court accept either or both of these defenses?

PERSPECTIVE ON THE DOMESTIC AND INTERNATIONAL FORUM-SHOPPING SYSTEM

From the perspective of legal practice, modern conflict of laws cases have a dominant message: the forum where a lawsuit is filed enormously influences which party ultimately succeeds. A particular forum can provide numerous practical, logistical, and procedural advantages for one litigant and potentially serious disadvantages for others. Even matters as simple as knowing where to get documents duplicated and enjoying the comfort of sleeping in one's own bed during a protracted trial can impact litigation success. Likewise, you will see in Chapter 2 that — in the final analysis — forum courts tend to favor applying their own law governing the rights of the parties to a lawsuit. This choice of law influence on litigation's bottom line cannot be understated.

As the litigant who files the papers initiating suit, plaintiffs exert considerable control over where a lawsuit is filed. The consequences of forum choice give plaintiffs an incentive to shop far and wide for the place that delivers the optimum balance among convenience, reduced legal barriers to litigation, favorable substantive legal regulation, and helpful court procedures. Some argue that the prerogative of forum choice is an appropriate tradeoff for the burden that plaintiffs must generally bear in proving the elements of their case.

Plaintiffs do, however, encounter at least one potent check on their ability to file in an optimum forum: personal jurisdiction requirements. Indeed, defendants are unlikely to waive personal jurisdiction challenges, and the constitutional minimums required for a court to assert personal jurisdiction are meaningful and sometimes significant. Yet — in today's globally integrated world — defendants often have constitutionally sufficient contacts exposing them to suit in a number of jurisdictions. This possibility of proper personal jurisdiction within a number of forums thus makes more significant the other potential restrictions on forum choice reviewed earlier in this chapter.

Litigant incentives and strategic behavior form only part of the forum-shopping story. Forums themselves may host complicated forces that attract or repel litigation. These forces relate to such matters as (i) a desire to foster economic benefits in a particular locale or a particular population group within the locale; (ii) cultural or sociological characteristics reflected in court systems that prefer one type of litigant over another; (iii) sociological or legal preferences for greater or lesser damages; and (iv) intended or unintended byproducts of regulatory schemes. Sometimes these forces combine to empower particular jurisdictions to lure a disproportionate percentage of cases in a particular category.

Courts and scholars often invoke "forum shopping" as a pejorative. Yet an informed decision about what, if any, preventive action to take against forum shopping requires appreciation of the forces that create the practice as well as the reasons why it is generally condemned. Some circumstances present easy judgments: for example, a party's decision to litigate in a specific jurisdiction so as to benefit from the jurisdiction's widespread corruption is not a practice regulators should promote or respect. Little can be said in favor of a litigant's benefiting from or engaging in a practice that reinforces a corrupt judicial system. In most cases, however, the causes and effects of forum shopping are more subtle and complicated, and the decision whether government should seek to avert its occurrence may require fine-tuned consideration of the facts of each context.

Forum shopping may involve a number of choices: the choice between United States courts and courts of foreign countries, the choice among courts of foreign countries, the choice between federal courts in the United States and state courts in the United States, and the choice between different state courts in the United States. Chapter 3, which extensively analyzes federal/state relations in the United States and analyzes the *Erie* doctrine, discusses forum shopping between state and federal courts. As explored in that section, forces that promote forum shopping between state and federal courts are varied, and include differences among internal state law, difference among choice of law methodologies followed in states, and stare decisis policies. Consider the following cross-sample of other factors that might influence forum shopping in other contexts as well:

Attractive Forums

The United States as a "Magnet Forum" in Transnational Litigation[19] Critics have observed that the United States is an appealing place for injured foreigners to file suit and to avail themselves of generally larger damage verdicts and diminished legal barriers than are found in court systems elsewhere in the world. Plaintiffs are attracted to several features of the United States system: (i) the jury trial system; (ii) attorneys' fee practices that both allow contingency fees and disallow fee shifting to unsuccessful plaintiffs; (iii) liberal pretrial discovery rules; (iv) class action

---

19. *See generally* RUSSELL J. WEINTRAUB, COMMENTARY ON THE CONFLICT OF LAWS 294-295 (6th ed. 2010) (using the term "magnet forum" and discussing attraction of United States courts for foreign plaintiffs).

procedures; and (v) plaintiff-favoring liability rules. Even if a United States court decides that foreign law should govern the plaintiff's cause of action as well as the damages awarded, a foreign plaintiff may still benefit from the United States's procedural system, proclivity toward large damage awards, and general sympathy toward specific types of claims. Sometimes forum shopping might even include defendant shopping—with foreign plaintiffs tailoring their claims so as to seek redress for their injury in actions against a United States defendant in United States courts. For example, a victim of human rights abuses may aver that a United States company "aided and abetted" the perpetuation of human rights abuses. This allows the victim to seek potentially large damages in an amenable forum, averting such obstacles to challenging a foreign government's actions as the act of state doctrine, foreign sovereign immunity, and the political question doctrine.[20]

Exceptions to the "United States as magnet" exist. For example, some European plaintiffs may fare better in their home courts. Similarly, in the defamation area, the United States Supreme Court has erected such significant constitutional barriers to liability that plaintiffs are attracted to file suit elsewhere—particularly in the internet era where libel can be "communicated" throughout the world. This has lead to "libel tourism," with plaintiffs traveling to other magnet forums such as London or Sydney—where the defamation laws are more plaintiff-friendly—in order to sue defendants that are based in the United States.[21] Indeed, at least some scholarship has identified a possible trend away from foreign plaintiffs using United States courts.[22] Finally, one should remember that litigation often must succeed in more than one jurisdiction. For example, the debtor in a transnational bankruptcy may not succeed in consolidating the bankruptcy proceedings in one place. Multiple jurisdictions may exert power over various assets located within their borders.[23]

In considering whether the United States should institute any changes designed to discourage foreign plaintiffs, one should assess whether the doctrine of forum non conveniens (applied predominantly in lawsuits with foreign elements) provides sufficient regulatory oversight or could do so if applied more rigorously. Other mechanisms such as choice of law rules, venue requirements, justiciability restrictions (such as the standing doctrine), more stringent scrutiny of contractual choice of forum provisions, and discretionary tools might also prove useful. One need consider, however, the possibility for retaliation by other jurisdictions, which might interpret United States courts' aggressive use of tools such as forum non conveniens as a protectionist maneuver. Indeed,

20. *See, e.g.,* Georgene M. Vairo, *International Forum Shopping in Human Rights Cases,* NAT'L L.J., Feb. 21, 2008, *available at* http://www.law.com/jsp/article.jsp?id-900005560278.

21. *See, e.g.,* Laura E. Little, *Just a Joke: Defamatory Humor and Incongruity's Promise,* 21 S. CAL. INTERDISC. L.J. 99, 138 n.188 (citing Sarah Lyall, *England, Long a Libel Mecca, Reviews Laws,* N.Y. TIMES, Dec. 11, 2009, at A1, which associates the name "sue" with London). The United States has responded to libel tourism by seeking to regulate the enforceability of certain foreign libel judgments in the United States. This response is covered in Chapter 4, relating to judgments.

22. *See* Christopher A. Whytock, *The Evolving Forum Shopping System,* 96 CORNELL L. REV. 481 (2011).

23. *See* Robert K. Rasmussen, *Resolving Transnational Insolvencies Through Private Ordering,* 98 MICH. L. REV. 2252, 2253-2254 (2000).

several countries have already responded, enacting provisions such as those that
divest local courts of jurisdiction once a plaintiff has filed suit in a foreign country.
In this way, countries disqualify themselves as alternative forums in the case of a
forum non conveniens dismissal and thus discourage United States courts from
granting such dismissals in the first place.[24] Finally, considered judgments about
regulating forum shopping should focus beyond litigation behavior. For example,
scholars have documented how differences among adjudicatory results in
different jurisdictions can distort trade and investment behavior.[25]

Attractive forums within the United States: Within the United States, various
forums are attractive for certain types of cases and litigants. For example, this
chapter's discussion of venue already depicted a United States District Court in
a small Texas town that attracts a disproportionate percentage of patent cases—
reputedly because of the court's speedy case disposition and plaintiff-friendly verdicts.[26] Also within the federal court system are forces rendering some judicial
districts much more attractive to bankruptcy filings than other districts.[27]

Forum differences are pronounced and well studied for litigants choosing
among state courts. Not only are some states more attractive to plaintiffs (and less
attractive to defendants) than others, but specific locations—counties, cities, and
towns—can garner nationwide reputations among litigants. For example, the
United States Chamber of Commerce evaluated state liability systems, scrutinizing
a number of factors such as treatment of class actions, punitive and other
damages, timeliness, discovery and evidentiary policies, judges' impartiality and
competence, as well as jury predictability and fairness. Surveying corporate attorneys' opinions about these matters, the survey identified strong jurisdictional preferences, including preferences that distinguished among different counties and
cities within states.[28] Other policy groups keep lists of jurisdictions that they identify as systematically problematic. For example, the American Tort Reform Association (ATRA) maintains a list of "Judicial Hellholes," which names fora that
promote laws and procedures that ATRA believes to unfairly affect defendants in

24. *See, e.g.,* Cassandra Burke Robertson, *Transnational Litigation and Institutional Choice,* 51
B.C. L. Rev. 1081, 1116 (2010), for a discussion of this retaliatory legislation.
25. Alan O. Sykes, *Transnational Forum Shopping as a Trade and Investment Issue,* 37 J. Legal
Stud. 339 (2008).
26. Another notable example of a forum known for plaintiff-friendly verdicts is Texarkana,
Texas, which provides unique opportunities for forum shopping within the same locale.
Texarkana, Texas is described on a promotional site, http://www.discoverourtown.com/AR/
Texarkana/Attractions/172184.html, as follows: "The only federal building in the country sited in
two states and the only federal courthouse located in two circuits, the 5th and the 8th, and two
districts, the Eastern District of Texas and the Western District of Arkansas."
27. *See, e.g.,* Melissa B. Jacoby, *Fast, Cheap, and Creditor-Controlled: Is Corporate Reorganization
Failing?,* 54 Buff. L. Rev. 401, 402 (2006) (reporting on observations that "[a] high repeat filing
rate first afflicted two 'magnet' venues, the District of Delaware and the Southern District of
New York, then spread nationwide as other judges have tried to attract cases to their own courts").
28. U.S. Chamber Inst. for Legal Reform, 2007 U.S. Chamber of Commerce State Liability
Systems Ranking Study (2007). The respondents ranked Delaware, Nebraska, and New Hampshire
as "best" in their treatment of tort and contract litigation and West Virginia, Louisiana, and
Mississippi as "worst." In addition, they zeroed in on Los Angeles, California and Chicago/Cook
County, Illinois as the cities and counties with the least fair and reasonable litigation environment.
Id. at 16, 18, 21.

civil lawsuits.[29] One of the factors ATRA uses for composing the list is "judge-condoned forum shopping," referring to a practice of allowing plaintiffs to file and maintain personal injury suits with little or no connection to the jurisdiction. To remedy this forum shopping, ATRA proposes tort reform policies, such as limits on damages and abolition of joint and several liability. For a persuasive discussion of how venue reform and not tort reform more effectively regulates forum shopping, see Keith H. Beyler, *Illinois Venue Reform: Not Tort Reform Rants*, 43 Loy. U. Chi. L.J. 757 (2012).

States also develop reputations for expertise in specific subject matters. Classic examples are Delaware's expertise in corporate law and Connecticut's expertise with insurance law. Often, of course, the reputation is accompanied by formally codified or unofficially documented preferences for certain outcomes. These matters might be reflected in the explicit substantive and procedural law of the jurisdiction as well as non-law-related factors such as location, transportation, and other infrastructure within the jurisdiction. For example, Nevada's reputation for rendering easy divorces is likely the product of both the state's official legal requirements as well as the state's appeal as a tourist destination and a relatively easy locale in which to set up a temporary household. By contrast, a jurisdiction might offer substantive legal advantage for high stakes trials, but—for various reasons—does not provide the "brick and mortar" comforts that usually accompany such events. The *New York Times* reported, for example, that a Walt Disney Company shareholder trial in downstate Delaware required big city lawyers to create temporary offices in old houses and beach hotels, a task that included paying facilities to upgrade electrical systems to accommodate the high-tech photocopiers. *See* Maureen Milford, *Big-City Lawyers on the Road Scrape for Office Space*, N.Y. Times, Nov. 17, 2004.

Forum Incentives and Techniques for Attracting Litigants

A rich body of scholarship analyzes forces operating in particular locales that result in legal regulations and informal practices designed to attract certain parties to the jurisdiction. In some cases, the parties are not actually litigants, but entities that wish to benefit from the jurisdiction's status regulations—such as organizations seeking to incorporate under Delaware's corporation laws. When later confronted with litigation, however, these organizations often find themselves returning to the status-giving jurisdiction, making it more likely that the same body of legal regulations will govern the suit's disposition. Commentators, scholars, and corporate lawyers generally agree that Delaware has powerful incentives to remain in the corporate chartering business, benefitting from revenue flowing to the state from corporate charter sales and taxes as well as from the prestige and revenue enjoyed by Delaware's courts and practicing corporate bar.

In a wholly different context, scholars have also pointed out the possible economic incentive at work in jurisdictions considering whether to recognize same-sex marriage. This would seem particularly true of jurisdictions with an

---

29. American Tort Reform Found, Judicial Hellholes (2011/2012), *available at* http://www.judicialhellholes.org/wp-content/uploads/2011/12/Judicial-Hellholes-2011.pdf.

established tourism infrastructure, which would benefit from having out-of-state citizens travel to marry and then honeymoon in the same-sex marriage jurisdiction.[30]

Bankruptcy is another lightning rod in the forum shopping debate. In writings inspiring considerable controversy, Professor Lynn LoPucki has argued that United States bankruptcy courts are in fierce competition with each other, competition that has unleashed a dramatic chain of consequences stemming from forum shopping:

> [C]ourt competition is an active, deliberate response by the court to forum shopping. When courts compete, they change what they are doing to make themselves more attractive to forum shoppers. . . . The court that offers forum shoppers the most may be the only one that gets the cases in the end, but all the judges who compete are corrupted along way.[31]

Why do judges compete for bankruptcy cases? LoPucki maintains that prestige, professional satisfaction, and self-preservation are at work. Judges wish to appease powerful members of the bankruptcy bar and the business community — who act as "case placers" — so that the judges can attract big and interesting cases to their venues. Moreover, since bankruptcy judges are not appointed for life, they depend for their reappointment on the support of the local bankruptcy bar, particularly powerful members of the bar who influence where cases are filed and benefit from practicing in a forum with robust bankruptcy activity. And how do judges compete? LoPucki argues that the judges make rulings that affect such matters as professional fees, trustee appointments, conflicts of interests, and taxes — matters that are sufficiently important to the business community and bankruptcy bar to influence where bankruptcy petitions are filed.[32]

While many of LoPucki's claims are contested by other bankruptcy scholars,[33] he raises points that illuminate important considerations of self-interest and power that forum shopping can exploit and exaggerate. Forum shopping is indeed a complex phenomenon, implicating such "micro" concerns as hotel space and electrical capacity at real estate surrounding courthouses and such "macro" concerns as judicial corruption, global economic performance, and the effects of cross-border transactions on the power of national governments![34]

---

30. Jennifer Gerarda Brown, *Competitive Federalism and the Legislative Incentives to Recognize Same-Sex Marriage*, 68 S. Cal. L. Rev. 745 (1995) (analyzing economic incentives for states to recognize same-sex marriage).

31. Lynn M. LoPucki, Courting Failure: How Competition for Big Cases Is Corrupting the Bankruptcy Courts 137 (2005).

32. Lynn M. LoPucki, Response, *Where Do You Get Off? A Reply to Courting Failure's Critics*, 54 Buff. L. Rev. 511, 512-515 (2006) (reviewing arguments about why bankruptcy judges are under pressure and how they respond to the pressure).

33. *See, e.g.*, Melissa B. Jacoby, *Fast, Cheap, and Creditor-Controlled: Is Corporate Reorganization Failing?*, 54 Buff. L. Rev. 401 (2006).

34. *See, e.g.*, Fleur Johns, *Performing Party Autonomy*, 71 Law & Contemp. Probs. 243 (2008) (discussing these macro concerns in the context of contractual choice of forum and choice of law clauses).

PROBLEM 1-14: FINDING AND CRITIQUING A FORUM-SHOPPING EXAMPLE

Consider whether — in your legal training so far — you have encountered a forum characteristic that can influence whether a plaintiff does or does not want to file suit in a particular locale. Characteristics you might have noticed could derive from the substance of legal requirements in a particular jurisdiction, the composition of juries, or more subtle matters such as quirks in the court's procedural rules or the geographical location of the courthouse. Once you have identified an example, consider next whether plaintiffs (and their attorneys) who allow the characteristic to influence where they file a lawsuit are acting in a morally neutral manner. Also consider whether considerations of fairness and public policy counsel the jurisdiction to take action to eliminate the characteristic causing the forum shopping.

CHAPTER 2

HORIZONTAL CHOICE OF LAW METHODOLOGY: CHOOSING AMONG LAWS GOVERNING CONDUCT

Horizontal choice of law confronts the question of which competing legal principles should govern a controversy where sovereigns sharing equal status could make a claim for control. In tracing the roots of the various horizontal approaches used in the United States, one can meaningfully start with the work of seventeenth-century Dutch thinker Ulric Huber, who identified sovereign territorial prerogative as the key concept in choice of law. Huber argued that comity — voluntary acceptance of another sovereign's law — should be the foundation for one sovereign to accept the law of another sovereign in appropriate circumstances. Maintaining that a forum should retain discretion over whether to follow another sovereign's law, Huber rejected the notion that overriding principles of justice require one sovereign to follow the law of another.

{ Comity principle [handwritten margin note]

Huber's ideas proved enormously influential for United States Supreme Court Justice Joseph Story, who incorporated them into an 1834 treatise. Story expounded on Huber's comity principle, offering the following explanation for why one jurisdiction would even consider applying another jurisdiction's law:

> [T]he rules which are to govern [a dispute] are those which arise from mutual interest and utility; from a sense of the inconveniences which would result from a

163

contrary doctrine; and from a sort of moral necessity to do justice, in order that justice may be done to us in return.[1]

Subsequently, Professor Joseph Beale urged replacing the comity principle with the notion of parties' "vested rights," a concept explicitly embraced by Justice Holmes in 1904. The vested rights concept firmly took hold in United States law, and was further reinforced when Beale became the Reporter for the First Restatement of Conflict of Laws. Despite academic criticism, the First Restatement approach enjoyed nearly universal acceptance among courts of the United States until the early 1960s.

Change came at the hands of Professor Brainerd Currie, who articulated an approach driven by the purpose of the relevant laws rather than the parties' vested rights. This focus on a law's purpose shifted analysis to whether, in a given case, competing jurisdictions had an actual interest in having their laws govern the facts of the dispute. Currie's innovations launched a series of refinements and other new approaches, all now comprising a corpus of modern choice of law methodologies. The American Law Institute responded to these changes, finishing the Restatement (Second) of Conflict of Laws in 1971. The Second Restatement might reasonably be described as laying out a kitchen sink approach, constituting an awkward compromise between the rule-based approach of the Restatement (First) and the flexibility of the modern methodologies. Despite the criticism it has faced, the Restatement (Second) is now the most widely followed approach for resolving choice of law problems in the United States. Along with the Restatement (First), the Restatement (Second) is enormously important to foreign citizens trying to figure out precisely *what* the content of United States law might be, where they encounter a situation governed by state, not federal law.

In short, the evolution of conflict of laws method is filled with experimentation and marked by considerable change. A remarkable aspect of this history is the enormous influence of law professors in the development and dissemination of choice of law methodologies. Possible reasons for this influence are the dominance of court-made law (and accompanying scarcity of legislation) in the area, the abstract nature of the subject matter (which calls out for scholarly guidance), and the analytical kinship between choice of law inquiries and foundational questions about the nature of law.

Whatever the explanation, the pervasive influence of academic writings is both a boon and a bane. In the materials that follow you will witness the scholarly influence and observe how courts refine, adapt, and, alas, sometimes butcher the abstract theories developed in academic journals. It is important to remember as you review the following materials that, although the discipline is deeply influenced by academic writings, its impact on the lives of ordinary citizens is profound. Horizontal choice of law decisions affect whether torture victims

---

1. JOSEPH STORY, COMMENTARIES ON THE CONFLICT OF LAWS, FOREIGN AND DOMESTIC §35, at 34 (1834).

recover, whether marriages are recognized, whether individuals receive inheritances, and the like.

Another characteristic that you will soon observe in American choice of law cases is that they are largely creatures of state law. Occasionally, you will encounter cases coming from federal court, but these will largely involve instances where a federal court is exercising diversity of citizenship jurisdiction and attempting to identify and apply state law. As a consequence, the cases display wide variety and may appear more random than, for example, you would observe in reading a line of United States Supreme Court cases tracing a particular legal problem. Remember that this ad hoc quality is common in all state common law contexts—although multiplicity of approaches *may* be unique—and adds interest to the enterprise of identifying the optimal analysis in multijurisdictional conflicts.

The question of what law should govern a multijurisdictional conflict arises only because a court might entertain the possibility of applying something other than forum law. Huber suggested that this inquiry should be voluntary. But is it appropriate for a court to even make the inquiry? Should we have a rule that says courts may apply only the law of their home jurisdiction? Consider these questions in light of the following problem:

INTRODUCTORY PROBLEM: CASSANDRA AND JULIAN REDUX (HORIZONTAL CHOICE OF LAW ISSUES)

Cassandra is a resident of New Jersey. She researched and wrote an article about Julian, which was published in a newspaper. A resident of Ohio, Julian is convinced that the article defames him and he files a defamation suit against Cassandra in Ohio. Cassandra has never been to Ohio and has never had anything to do with Ohio. Unbeknownst to her, however, the newspaper distributes 20 papers in Ohio (less than 1 percent of its total circulation).

Julian filed suit against Cassandra in a state court in Ohio, and the Ohio court concluded that it had personal jurisdiction against Cassandra. Assume for the purposes of this problem that the defamation laws of New Jersey and Ohio differ in important respects, making it much easier for a plaintiff to prevail under Ohio law than under New Jersey law. What are the arguments in favor of the Ohio court simply applying forum law: that is, the law of Ohio governing defamation liability? What are the arguments in favor of the Ohio court considering the possibility of applying the defamation law of another state? If the Ohio court should consider that possibility, what types of facts, policies, or concerns should it evaluate?

The United States courts now follow a variety of choices of law approaches. Two of the approaches are governed by provisions in the American Law Institute's restatements of law: the Restatement (First) of Conflict of Laws and the Restatement (Second) of Conflict of Laws. In the forty years between these two restatements of law, several other approaches emerged: governmental interest analysis, comparative impairment, and the better rule of law approach. In addition, individual states have developed their own hybrid choice of law approaches. This chapter provides an overview of all of these approaches to solving choice of law problems. In addition to this array of alternative methods for resolving choice of law disputes, two more developments are worthy of note. First, two states (Louisiana and Oregon) as well as Puerto Rico have taken an entirely different strategy to the usual common law method of developing choice of law rules: they have enacted comprehensive choice of law statutes. Second, in 2014, the American Law Institute authorized the development of a new restatement of conflict of laws. Work is well underway on this project, although it will likely be several years before the project is completed. A brief overview of this project—the Restatement (Third) of Conflict of Laws— appears at the end of this chapter.

A. RESTATEMENT (FIRST) OF CONFLICT OF LAWS

The Restatement (First) of Conflict of Laws presents what is known as the "traditional" or "vested rights" approach to choice of law. This approach had a stranglehold on United States courts in the nineteenth century and the first half of the twentieth century. Scholars and courts have developed new rules that have become more popular than the Restatement (First), and courts now have the benefit of a Restatement (Second) of Conflict of Laws. In addition, the American Law Institute has now authorized a Third Restatement of Conflict of Laws, and work on the project is well underway. Nonetheless, the Restatement (First) merits careful study for several reasons. First, a significant number of states still follow the Restatement (First) approach. Even for those jurisdictions that have moved on to more recently developed choice of law methodologies, the Restatement (First) holds insights for understanding the new methodologies followed in the United States and elsewhere. In addition, many states have abandoned the First Restatement for contract and tort law, yet retain its traditional rules for other legal issues. Indeed, it is hard to find a jurisdiction in the United States whose law does not contain strong evidence of the Restatement (First). In some instances this may be detritis: that is, a vestige or remainder left behind when the jurisdiction moved onto another methodology. In other instances, the Restatement (First) rule or influence remains because the jurisdiction's courts deem it to provide the most just and workable solution. Finally, the Restatement (Third) of Conflict of Laws has sought to hew closer to the rule-like approach of the Restatement (First) than followed in the Restatement (Second). Although the Restatement (Third) will not embrace the same rigidity as the Restatement (First), one benefits from observing how a rule-oriented approach navigates the challenges of a choice of law determination.

The First Restatement was initially published in 1934, and, like all of the initial Restatement projects undertaken by the American Law Institute, represents an attempt to codify principles of common law appearing in court opinions. Some of the case law selections excerpted below predate the First Restatement's publication, but nonetheless provide the same legal rule that was later "restated" in the First Restatement. Other cases set forth below actually postdate the Restatement (Second) of Conflict of Laws, and are the product of jurisdictions that have chosen to retain the traditional approach of the Restatement (First).

In designating which law should govern a dispute, the Restatement (First) focuses on the geographical location where the parties' rights vested. To make this designation, the Restatement (First) identifies certain activities, events, and relationships that transform the parties' aspirations and generally applicable principles of law into enforceable legal obligations or rights. Professor Joseph Beale described this vested rights theory as follows: "Law being a general rule to govern future transactions, its method of creating rights is to provide that upon the happening of a certain event a right shall accrue. . . . The creation of a right is therefore conditioned upon the happening of an event." 1 Joseph Beale, Treatise on the Conflict of Laws §73, at 107 (1916).

To see how the vested rights logic works, take the example of a contract negotiation over the sale of a car. At the time parties are negotiating, they might have hopes and beliefs about how the transaction should unfold — including such matters as how much money will be paid and when delivery will occur. These hopes and beliefs are not legally enforceable at the time that the parties begin negotiating. Nonetheless, once the parties sign a contract that embodies details about terms such as a price and delivery, the parties' understanding about those matters become vested rights, which are entitled to legal enforcement in court. Accordingly, the location where the parties make their contract will often be the place where their contract rights vest and thus the jurisdiction that provides the legal principles that govern the parties' dispute.

For the various categories of law, the Restatement (First) seeks to pinpoint those activities, events, or relationships that transform general hopes and principles of law into legally enforceable rights. Obviously, these will vary according to which category of law the case concerns. For example, the place of making of a contract will usually not control the conflict of laws issue in a property dispute or a tort suit. Other events, activities, or relationships will likely be more significant for those types of suits. In order to provide a sense of how the First Restatement identifies which events, activities, or relationships trigger a vested right, this section will survey the Restatement (First) provisions in various important categories of law. We start first with torts, known in the old-fashioned world of the First Restatement as the law of wrongs.

1. Torts

a. Unintentional Torts

Alabama G.S.R.R. Co. v. Carroll
97 Ala. 126, 11 So. 803 (1892)

Action by W.D. Carroll against the Alabama Great Southern Railroad Company to recover damages for personal injuries received while serving as a brakeman on defendant's road. From a judgment for plaintiff, defendant appeals. Reversed.

McCLELLAN, J.

The plaintiff, W.D. Carroll, is, and was at the time of entering into the service of the defendant, the Alabama Great Southern Railroad Company, and at the time of being injured in that service, a citizen of Alabama. The defendant is an Alabama corporation, operating a railroad extending from Chattanooga, in the state of Tennessee, through Alabama to Meridian, in the state of Mississippi. At the time of the casualty complained of plaintiff was in the service of the defendant in the capacity of brakeman on freight trains running from Birmingham, Ala., to Meridian, Miss., under a contract which was made in the state of Alabama. The injury was caused by the breaking of a link between two cars in a freight train which was proceeding from Birmingham to Meridian. The point at which the link broke and the injury was suffered was in the state of Mississippi. The evidence tended to show that the link which broke was a defective link, and that it was in a defective condition when the train left Birmingham. . . . The evidence went also to show that the defect in this link consisted in or resulted from its having been bent while cold; that this tended to weaken the iron, and in this instance had cracked the link somewhat on the outer curve of the bend, and that the link broke at the point of this crack. It was shown to be the duty of certain employee of defendant stationed along its line to inspect the links attached to cars to be put in trains, or forming the couplings between cars in trains at Chattanooga, Birmingham, and some points between Birmingham and the place where this link broke, and also that it was the duty of the conductor of freight trains, and the other train men, to maintain such inspection as occasion afforded throughout the runs or trips of such trains; and the evidence affords ground for inference that there was a negligent omission on the part of such employees to perform this duty, or, if performed, the failure to discover the defect in, and to remove, this link was the result of negligence. . . .

The only negligence . . . is that of persons whose duty it was to inspect the links of the train, and remove such as were defective, and replace them with others which were not defective. This was the negligence, not of the master, the defendant, but of fellow servants of the plaintiff, for which at common law the defendant is not liable. . . . This being the common law applicable to the premises as understood and declared in Alabama, it will be presumed in our courts, as thus declared, to be the common law of Mississippi, unless the evidence shows a different rule to have been announced by the supreme court of that state as being the common law thereof. The evidence adduced here fails to show any such thing, but, to the contrary, it is made to appear, from the testimony of Judge Arnold, and by the decisions of the supreme court of Mississippi, which were introduced on the trial below, that that court is in full accord with this one in this respect. Indeed, if anything, those decisions go further than this court has ever gone in applying the doctrine of fellow servants to the exemption of railway companies from liability to one servant for injuries resulting from the negligence of another. . . .

It is, however, further contended that the plaintiff, if his evidence be believed, has made out a case for the recovery sought under the employers' liability act of Alabama, it being clearly shown that there is no such or similar law of force in the state of Mississippi. Considering this position in the abstract, — that is, dissociated from the facts of this particular case, which are supposed to exert an important influence upon it, — there cannot be two opinions as to its being unsound and untenable. So looked at, we do not understand appellee's counsel even to deny either the proposition or its application to this case, — that there can be no recovery in one state for injuries to the person sustained in another, unless the infliction of the injuries is actionable under the law of the state in which they were received. Certainly this is the well-established rule of law, subject, in some jurisdictions, to the qualification that the infliction of the injuries would also support an action in the state where the suit is brought had they been received within that state. . . .

But it is claimed that the facts of this case take it out of the general rule which the authorities cited above abundantly support, and authorize the courts of Alabama to subject the defendant to the payment of damages under section 2590 of the Code, although the injuries counted on were sustained in Mississippi under circumstances which involved no liability on the defendant by the laws of that state. This insistence is, in the first instance, based on that aspect of the evidence which goes to show that the negligence which produced the casualty transpired in Alabama, and the theory that, wherever the consequences of that negligence manifested itself, a recovery can be had in Alabama. We are referred to no authority in support of this proposition, and exhaustive investigation on our part has failed to disclose any. . . .

It is admitted, or at least cannot be denied, that negligence of duty unproductive of damnifying results will not authorize or support a recovery. Up to the time this train passed out of Alabama no injury had resulted. For all that occurred in Alabama, therefore, no cause of action whatever arose. The fact which created the right to sue, — the injury, — without which confessedly no action would lie anywhere, transpired in the state of Mississippi. It was in that state, therefore, necessarily that the cause of action, if any, arose; and whether a cause of action arose and existed at all, or not, must in all reason be determined by the law which obtained at the time and place when and where the fact which is relied on to justify a recovery transpired. Section 2590 of the Code of Alabama had no efficacy beyond the lines of Alabama. It cannot be allowed to operate

upon facts occurring in another state, so as to evolve out of them rights and
liabilities which do not exist under the law of that state, which is of course
paramount in the premises. Where the facts occur in Alabama, and a liability
becomes fixed in Alabama, it may be enforced in another state having like enactments, or whose policy is not opposed to the spirit of such enactments; but this is
quite a different matter. This is but enforcing the statute upon facts to which it is
applicable, all of which occurred within the territory for the government of
which it was enacted. Section 2590 of the Code, in other words, is to be interpreted in the light of universally recognized principles of private, international,
or interstate law, as if its operation had been expressly limited to this state, and as
if its first line read as follows: "When a personal injury is received in Alabama by a
servant or employe," etc. The negligent infliction of an injury here, under statutory circumstances, creates a right of action here, which, being transitory, may
be enforced in any other state or country the comity of which admits of it; but for
an injury inflicted elsewhere than in Alabama our statute gives no right of recovery, and the aggrieved party must look to the local law to ascertain what his rights
are. Under that law this plaintiff had no cause of action, as we have seen, and
hence he has no rights which our courts can enforce, unless it be upon a consideration to be presently adverted to. We have not been inattentive to the suggestions of counsel in this connection, which are based upon that rule of the
statutory and common criminal law under which a murderer is punishable
where the fatal blow is delivered, regardless of the place where death ensues.
This principle is patently without application here. There would be some analogy if the plaintiff had been stricken in Alabama, and suffered in Mississippi,
which is not the fact. There is however, an analogy which is afforded by the
criminal law, but which points away from the conclusion appellee's counsel
desire us to reach. This is found in that well-established doctrine of criminal
law that where the unlawful act is committed in one jurisdiction or state, and
takes effect — produces the result which it is the purpose of the law to prevent,
or, it having ensued, punish for — in another jurisdiction or state, the crime is
deemed to have been committed and is punished in that jurisdiction or state in
which the result is manifested, and not where the act was committed.

    . . .

[The court next rejected an argument that this case should be decided as a
contract case, emphasizing that it conceived of the case as presenting negligence
issues. This portion of the decision is set forth below in connection with discussion
of the characterization process in the Restatement (First).]

    . . .

The foregoing views will suffice to indicate the grounds of our opinion
that the rights of this plaintiff are determinable solely by the law of the State of
Mississippi, and of our conclusion that upon no aspect or tendency of the
evidence as to the circumstances under which the injury was sustained, and
as to the laws of Mississippi obtaining in the premises, was the plaintiff entitled to recover.

Notes on

CARROLL

1. The conflict of laws rule applied in *Carroll* is known as the <u>lex loci delicti</u> rule, requiring a court to apply the law of the jurisdiction in which the wrong occurs. In cases where the wrongful act and the injury occur in different states, the "wrong" is not deemed complete until the plaintiff suffers injury. Thus, the place of injury supplies the governing legal rules.

2. Although *Carroll* is an old case, its influence lives on — particularly in jurisdictions that officially continue to adhere to the Restatement (First). Consider the decision of the United States District Court in *Ben-Joseph v. Mt. Airy Auto Transporters, LLC*, 529 F. Supp. 2d 604 (D. Md. 2008). As a United States District Court exercising diversity of citizenship jurisdiction, the *Ben-Joseph* court evaluated the choice of law problem in the case using the choice of law methodology of the forum state, Maryland. Following Maryland's decision to adhere to the Restatement (First), the *Ben-Joseph* court refused to apply Maryland law governing punitive damages in a suit arising from negligent inspection and maintenance of brakes in Maryland. Instead, the court determined that New Jersey punitive damages law governed because the Maryland negligence had allegedly resulted in a motor vehicle accident that occurred in New Jersey.

3. Compare the reasoning of *Carroll* and *Ben-Joseph* with *Rationis Enterprises Inc. of Panama v. Hyundai Mipo Dockyard Co.*, 426 F.3d 580 (2d Cir. 2005), adjudicating a suit arising when a ship sank on the high seas as a result of defective welding that occurred in Korea. The court concluded that Korean law should apply because Korea was the "place of the wrongful act." The court reasoned that this is not the place of the sinking, but instead where the negligence took place. According to the court, "it is the state where the negligence occurs that has the greatest interest in regulating the behavior of the parties." *Id.* at 587. Are you persuaded by this reasoning from *Hyundai*? Do you think *Hyundai* articulates a better approach to answer the choice of law question in multi-jurisdictional tort cases than that provided in *Carroll*? Doesn't *Hyundai*'s emphasis on the interest of the place of negligence have particularly strong force in *Carroll*—given that the plaintiff was domiciled in the state of negligence (Alabama) and was hired by the defendant in Alabama for work that primarily occurred there as well? On the other hand, one might argue that the place where the tort occurs has "the greatest interest in striking a reasonable balance among safety, cost, and other factors pertinent to the design and administration of a system of tort law." *Spinozzi v. ITT Sheraton Corp.*, 174 F.3d 842, 845 (7th Cir. 1999) (Posner, J.). The debate about whether place of injury or place of wrongdoing is more important appears throughout choice of law issues, particularly in connection with the Restatement (First).

4. As the contrast with the *Hyundai* case reveals, the lex loci delicti rule of *Carroll* and *Ben-Joseph* is not particularly fine-tuned to the regulatory interests of

the affected jurisdictions in governing the lives of the litigants or regulating the occurrence that gave rise to the lawsuit. State regulatory goals are simply not part of the internal logic of the lex loci delecti rule. Instead, the rule is the vehicle in tort cases for identifying where the parties' rights vested. Indeed, as explained in the introduction to this section, identifying where parties' rights vest is the controlling logic for the traditional choice of law methodology reflected in *Carroll* and *Joseph*, and codified in the Restatement (First).

5. Those criticizing the vested rights approach embodied in the Restatement (First) sometimes cite its failure to account for the purposes behind laws or the regulatory interests motivating states to articulate legal principles that govern parties or their conduct. Despite this potential criticism, can you identify any arguments in favor of the lex loci delecti rule, which was reflected in *Carroll*, and later included in the Restatement (First)?

The provisions in the Restatement (First) of Conflict of Laws reflect a broad range in drafting approaches. As is true with many codifications, some provisions are truly straightforward and clear, while others are deceptively simple. Sections 377 and 378 below arguably provide examples of this latter category. Although apparently short and unqualified, §377 and §378 reflect the perennial debate regarding whether the place of injury or the place of negligence should provide governing legal principles, settling on the place of injury as the general rule in multijurisdictional tort actions. The comment to §377 reveals occasional difficulties with the rule. In contrast to the apparently simple provisions, some of the Restatement (First) rules are complicated on their face and require a tenacious approach to reading. Section 380 below is an example of one such section.

From the Restatement (First) of Conflict of Laws, on the Subject of Wrongs:

§377. The Place of Wrong

The place of wrong is in the state where the last event necessary to make an actor liable for an alleged tort takes place.

. . .

Note:

Summary of Rules in Important Situations Determining Where a Tort is Committed.

1. *Except in the case of harm from poison, when a person sustains bodily harm, the place of wrong is the place where the harmful force takes effect upon the body.*

Such a force is first set in motion by some human being. It is quite immaterial in what state he set the force in motion. It must alone or in cooperation with other forces harm the body of another. The person harmed may thereafter go into another state and die from the injury or suffer other loss therefrom. The place where this last event happens is also immaterial. The question is only where did the force impinge upon his body.

Illustration: . . . A, standing in state X, fires a gun and lodges a bullet in the body of B who is standing in state Y. The place of wrong is in Y.

2. *When a person causes another voluntarily to take a deleterious substance that takes effect within the body, the place of the wrong is where the deleterious substance takes effect and not where it is administered.*

Illustration: . . . A, in state X, mails to B in state Y a package containing poisoned candy. B eats the candy in State Y and gets on a train to go to state W. After the train has passed to state Z, he becomes ill as a result of the poison and eventually dies from the poison in state W. The place of wrong is state Z.

. . .

4. *When a person sustains loss by fraud, the place of wrong is where the loss is sustained, not where fraudulent representations are made.*

5. *Ilustrations:* A, in state X, makes false misrepresentations by letter to B in Y as a result of which B sends certain chattels from Y to A, in X. A keeps the chattels. The place of the wrong is in state Y where B parted with the chattels.

§378. Law Governing Plaintiff's Injury

The law of the place of wrong determines whether a person has sustained a legal injury.

As mentioned above, the provision that follows, §380, requires a tenacious reading strategy. The best attitude for approaching this kind of provision is to think of it as an opportunity to practice active interpretation of complicated texts—a skill required in much of law, particularly when one reads statutes or seeks to understand complicated transaction documents. Active interpretation calls for comparing various components of the provision's language and flipping one's concentration back and forth between the sections as if putting together a jigsaw puzzle. Of course, when assembling a jigsaw puzzle, one fruitfully might begin with a look at the "big picture" it depicts. One might discover this big picture from reading section headings, identifying case law interpretations, or skimming the provision or its comments and illustrations. Using this approach, one discovers from reading the comments and illustration to §380 that the provision allows for an exception to the general notion that the place of injury will provide the governing legal standards under the mandate of §§377 and 378. The case that follows, *Laboratory Corp. of America v. Hood*, 395 Md. 608, 911 A.2d 841 (2006), reinforces this big picture depiction of §380. The skill of careful reading comes in as one tries to determine which portion of the provision's language enables §380 to operate as an exception to the place of injury approach.

From the Restatement (First) of Conflict of Laws, on the Subject of Wrongs:

§380. Application of Standard of Care

(1) Except as stated in Subsection (2), where by the law of the place of wrong, the liability-creating character of the actor's conduct depends upon the

application of a standard of care, the application of such standard will be made by the forum in accordance with its own rules of evidence, inference and judgment.

(2) Where by the law of the place of wrong, the liability-creating character of the actor's conduct depends upon the application of a standard of care, and such standard has been defined in particular situations by statute or judicial decision of the law of the place of the actor's conduct, such application of the standard will be made by the forum.

. . .

Comment:

a. Finding of negligence in particular case. Under the rule stated in §379, the liability-creating character of the actor's conduct is determined by the law of the place of wrong. Where, however, the law of the place of wrong prescribes a standard of care by which the actor's conduct is to be judged, the application of such standard to the facts in a particular case must necessarily be made by a fact-finding body at the forum in accordance with local procedure. Thus, if the general standard of the conduct of a reasonable man has not been defined by statute or judicial decision of the state of acting, the question whether the actor's conduct is negligent is decided by the forum in accordance with its own rules of evidence, inference and judgment. Negligence is lack of due care under the circumstances; and what care should be given under certain circumstances is a question for adjudication in each particular case. The tribunal at the forum will decide this question and will not be influenced by the fact that another court, even the court of the state where a defendant acted, would have come to a different conclusion on the facts proved. . . .

Illustration:

. . . By the law of state X, it is settled that due care requires that every locomotive be equipped with an efficient spark arrester; by the law of state Y, there is no such requirement. By the law of both X and Y, a railway company is liable for fires only if they are negligently started. A locomotive being carefully run in state Y throws out sparks which would not have escaped if there had been a spark arrester, and thereby sets fire to a stack of wheat in state X. The company will not be held liable for the fire.

§383. Causation.

Whether an act is the legal cause of another's injury is determined by the law of the place of wrong.

Laboratory Corp. of America v. Hood

911 A.2d 841 (Md. 2006)

Argued before BELL, C.J.; RAKER, WILNER, CATHELL, HARRELL, BATTAGLIA, and GREENE, JJ. Opinion by WILNER, J.

[The Maryland Court of Appeals began by explaining that the United States District Court for the District of Maryland had certified questions to the court in a "wrongful birth" action by Karen and Scott Hood, Maryland residents, against two North Carolina corporations — Laboratory Corporation of America and Laboratory Corporation of America Holdings (collectively, LabCorp).

The Hoods argued that LabCorp negligently misread a chromatograph of
the DNA from an amniotic fluid specimen extracted from Ms. Hood, "erroneously reporting that the fetus was not likely to be affected by cystic fibrosis (CF)."
Relying on the erroneous report, Ms. Hood decided to continue her pregnancy,
which resulted in the birth of their son, Luke, who has CF. The Hoods sought to
recover damages for the cost of raising and caring for Luke.

The Maryland Court of Appeals explained that the district court had certified
three questions for the Court of Appeals to answer. One of the questions was:

> In a case where a medical laboratory receives a specimen from a Maryland
> physician and erroneously interprets the specimen in another State, causing injury
> in Maryland to Maryland residents, should this court follow the "standard of care"
> exception in the Restatement (First) of Conflicts of Law §380(2) and apply the
> substantive law of the State where the erroneous interpretation took place?]

. . .

[W]hile Maryland recognizes an action of this kind by the parents, North
Carolina apparently does not, and the District Court, which must apply Maryland
law, including the Maryland law on conflicts of law, desires to know whether, in
the situation at hand and if the action were filed in a Maryland court, we would
apply the substantive law of Maryland, where the injury occurred, or of North
Carolina, where the negligent acts or omissions took place.

. . .

The Hoods are Maryland residents. Their first child, Zachary, was born in
1997 and was diagnosed with CF when he was two. In the present state of medical
science, persons with CF are doomed to suffer from lung, gastrointestinal, pan-
creatic, heart, and other organ diseases, and rarely live beyond their mid-30s.
In order to develop CF, a child must receive a particular gene mutation from
both parents. After Zachary was diagnosed, the Hoods learned that they both
carry the recessive delta F508 gene mutation that causes one of the most severe
forms of CF. Because they are both carriers of that mutation, each of Karen's
pregnancies carries a 25% risk of the child having CF.

In 1999, Ms. Hood became pregnant again, and she and her husband were
referred by Ms. Hood's obstetrician to a genetic counselor. Genetic testing performed on the fetus revealed that it had CF, whereupon Ms. Hood terminated the
pregnancy. In August, 2001, she became pregnant the third time and again
decided to have the fetus tested. The Hoods had already made the decision to
terminate the pregnancy if the fetus tested positive for CF. On November 27,
2001, Ms. Hood had an amniocentesis performed, in Maryland, by her obstetrician, Thomas Pinkert.

LabCorp operates a nationwide network of 35 primary testing locations and
more than 1,100 patient service centers, eight of which are located in Maryland.
Although it receives specimens from physicians and from its various patient service centers throughout the country, LabCorp performs all of its genetic testing
on amniotic fluid at its Center for Molecular Biology and Pathology in North
Carolina. The company markets genetic testing services to couples such as the

Hoods. Before the specimen taken from Ms. Hood was sent to LabCorp for testing, the Hoods' genetic counselor, Amy Kimball, who worked in Dr. Pinkert's office in Maryland, informed LabCorp that both Karen and Scott Hood carried the CF gene. The sample was sent to the LabCorp facility in North Carolina, where the DNA in it was subjected to a chromatograph that was analyzed by two LabCorp employees, Marcia Eisenberg and Nicholas Brown.

In conformance with the analysis done by Eisenberg and Brown, LabCorp reported to Dr. Pinkert that, although both parents were carriers of the delta F508 mutation, the amniotic fluid was negative for 31 common CF genetic mutations, and "[t]his fetus is not expected to be a carrier of cystic fibrosis or be affected by cystic fibrosis." . . . Based on the LabCorp report, the Hoods elected to continue the pregnancy, resulting in the birth of Luke on May 3, 2002. Three months later, the child was found to be positive for CF. In September, 2002, LabCorp issued a corrected report which noted that the original chromatograph did, indeed, demonstrate that the fetus was positive for the delta F508 mutation that causes CF . . . —and stated that Eisenberg and Brown had misread the chromatograph.

The District Court . . . held that, under Maryland law, the Hoods' action was for negligence, not breach of contract, and that the Maryland law of negligence therefore applied. The court observed that, in diversity cases, such as the one at hand, it was obliged to apply Maryland's choice of law rules and determined that Maryland adheres to lex loci delicti principles for all tort claims, i.e., we apply the law of the place where the tort or wrong was committed. It concluded that, under our application of those principles, the place where the last event required to give rise to the tort occurred determines the law that should apply, that in personal injury claims the last event required to give rise to the tort is the injury, and that the injury in this action occurred in Maryland, where Luke was born.

LabCorp asserted in the District Court that, even if lex loci delicti principles apply, the court should recognize the exception to those principles enunciated in Restatement (First) of Conflict of Laws §380(2). Section 380(2) states:

> Where by the law of the place of the wrong, the liability-creating character of the actor's conduct depends upon the application of a standard of care, and such standard has been defined in particular situations by statute or judicial decision of the law of the place of the actor's conduct, such application of the standard will be made by the forum.

Labcorp's argument was that its potential liability flows from the issuance of the erroneous report by Eisenberg and Brown, that any breach of the standard of care therefore occurred in North Carolina, and that, under §380(2), North Carolina law should dictate whether those employees breached a duty owed to the Hoods. Labcorp posited, and the court acknowledged, that the U.S. Court of Appeals for the Fourth Circuit had assumed that Maryland would recognize the §380(2) exception in negligence cases. The District Court pointed out, however, that this Court had never determined whether that exception should apply, and that is what led it to certify the first question.

Whether Maryland or North Carolina law applies is critical to the Hoods' case. . . . [T]he North Carolina Supreme Court has held that the parents of a child born with even severe birth defects did not suffer any legally cognizable injury, and thus the Hoods' action could not succeed under North Carolina law. . . .

Standard of Care Exception in Restatement §380(2)

Unlike most other States, which have abandoned the lex loci delicti approach espoused in . . . the Restatement (First) of Conflict of Laws, . . . Maryland continues to adhere generally to the lex loci delicti principle in tort cases. Under that approach, where the events giving rise to a tort action occur in more than one State, we apply the law of the State where the injury — the last event required to constitute the tort — occurred.

. . .

Section 380 is part of the series of sections articulating the [lex loci delecti] doctrine. Section 377 defines the "place of wrong" as the place where the last event necessary to make an actor liable for an alleged tort takes place, which in this case, as the District Court correctly determined, is Maryland. Section 378 declares that the law of the place of wrong determines whether a person has sustained a legal injury; §379 makes that law determinative of whether a person is responsible for unintended harm; §383 applies that law in determining causation; §385 applies that law in determining whether contributory negligence precludes recovery in whole or in part; §386 applies that law with respect to the "fellow servant" rule; §387 applies it in determining vicarious liability; §388 applies it to defenses; §390 applies it to whether an action survives the death of the tortfeasor or the injured person.

In this mix is §380, which deals with standard of care. Section 380(1) states the general rule that "where by the law of the place of wrong, the liability-creating character of the actor's conduct depends upon the application of a standard of care, the application of such standard will be made by the forum in accordance with its own rules of evidence, inference and judgment." In other words, the substantive standard of care to be applied is that of the place of wrong, but its application to the facts presented to the forum court is to be determined in accordance with the rules of evidence, inference, and judgment of the forum State. Section 380(2) carves out a limited exception to that rule. If, under the law of the place of wrong, the liability-creating character of the actor's conduct depends upon the application of a standard of care *and such standard has been defined in particular situations by statute or judicial decision of the law of the place of the actor's conduct,* such application of the standard will be made by the forum." (Emphasis added).

These principles are clarified in two comments to §380. Comment a., which explains the general principle in §380(1), begins by recalling that, under the rule stated in §379, the liability-creating character of the actor's conduct is determined by the law of the place of wrong. The comment then notes the obvious proposition that, where the law of the place of wrong prescribes a standard of care by which the actor's conduct is to be judged, "the application of such standard to the facts in a particular case must necessarily be made by a fact-finding body at the forum in accordance with local procedure." Thus:

> [I]f the general standard of the conduct of a reasonable man has not been defined by statute or judicial decision of the [S]tate of acting, the question whether the actor's conduct is negligent is decided by the forum in accordance with its own rules of evidence, inference and judgment. Negligence is lack of due care under the circumstances; and what care should be given under certain circumstances is a question for adjudication in each particular case. The tribunal at the forum will decide this question and will not be influenced by the fact that another court, even the court of the [S]tate where a defendant acted, would have come to a different conclusion on the facts proved.

Comment b., captioned "Negligence per se and breach of statutory duty," explains the exception in §380(2):

> If, by the law of the place of the actor's conduct, the general standard of due care has been defined by judicial decision so as to pronounce certain conduct, as specific acts or omissions, to be or not to be negligent, the forum will apply the standard in the same manner although under the local law the case would have been for the judgment of the jury on the facts in question. So too, if by statute or other legislative enactment of the [S]tate of the actor's conduct the general standard of due care has been narrowed in a particular situation, the forum will make a similar application of the standard of care although under the local law the case would have been one for the jury because no such statute there existed.

As explicated in these comments, for a State that follows the lex loci delicti rule, both the general provision in §380(1) and the limited exception in §380(2) make perfectly good sense. If the standard of care under the law of the place of acting is simply that of reasonableness, either general reasonableness or reasonableness for a person in the defendant's position, and there is no more particular guidance under that law with respect to the application of that standard to the facts at hand, the forum court would have to determine from the facts presented to it and in accordance with its own procedures whether that standard has been met. If, on the other hand, the State where the acts were committed has determined, either by judicial decision or statute, that a person who commits those acts either has, or has not, breached the applicable standard of care and therefore either is, or is not, negligent as a matter of law, the forum court must act in conformance with that judicial decision or statute, even if its own law, or the law of the place of wrong, is different.[1]

---

1. In this case, because Maryland is both the place of wrong and the locus of the forum court, there are only two options — Maryland law or North Carolina law. In other settings, the forum court could be in a third State, in which event, assuming a lex loci delicti approach and but for §380, the law of three States could be put in play. In that situation, the forum court would generally apply Maryland law (law of the place of wrong) except that, for purposes of applying the applicable standard of care, would look to its own law unless North Carolina, by statute or judicial decision, had declared the conduct at issue to constitute or not constitute a breach, in which event it would apply that aspect of North Carolina law.

LabCorp suggests an unfairness to that approach, but we perceive no unfairness. A person who commits a tort in another State should, as a general rule, be liable in accordance with the law of that State — where the harm was done. The narrow exception, that requires looking to the law of the State where the conduct was committed, applies only where the existence and nature of the duty or its breach depends on a standard of care and that State, by statute or judicial ruling, has defined the particular conduct as either complying or not complying with the applicable standard of care. The exception gives deference to the notion that, where the law of the place of conduct is so clear and particular, persons in that place have a right to rely on that law and should not suffer adverse consequences for conforming their conduct to it.

Accordingly, our specific answer to the first certified question is that, where applicable, Maryland does recognize and would apply §380(2) of the Restatement (First). The question, as framed, is somewhat broader than that, however. It asks whether the District Court should follow the standard of care exception in §380(2) "and apply the substantive law of the state where the erroneous interpretation took place." That aspect of the question assumes that, if Maryland would adopt §380(2), the substantive law of North Carolina would apply.

That is not necessarily the case. We would apply North Carolina law only if and to the extent that such law, by statute or judicial decision, specifically determines the effect of applying the applicable North Carolina standard of care to the facts at hand. If there is a statute or judicial decision in North Carolina that would dictate whether the conduct of LabCorp, through its employees, did or did not breach the applicable standard of care, we would . . . act in conformance with that statute or judicial decision; otherwise, as both the forum State and the place of wrong, we would apply Maryland law. The submissions of counsel to us do not indicate that there is any North Carolina statute on point. . . .

[Interpreting North Carolina case law, the Maryland Court of Appeals gave the opinion that the case law also did not express an exceptional standard of care. The court noted, however, that the interpretation of the North Carolina case law in light of the facts of this case was a matter for the district court on further proceedings.]

Notes on
THE RESTATEMENT SECTIONS AND HOOD

1. One has an easy time pinpointing the place of the wrong where the defendant's negligent conduct and the resulting injury occur in the same jurisdiction. Where this is not the case, §§377, 378, 380, and 383 (together with accompanying comments and illustrations) attempt to provide courts with guidance on how to determine the place of wrong. Is this guidance satisfactory? For example, consider comment 2 to §377, which instructs that "[w]here a person causes another voluntarily to take a deleterious substance that takes effect on the body, the place of the wrong is where the

deleterious substance takes effect and not where it is administered." Does comment 2 propose the obviously correct resolution of a cross-border poisoning? Might one reasonably argue that, in many cases, harm becomes inevitable where the poison is administered, thus making administration of the poison the last event necessary to make the actor liable?

2. As you will see, the Restatement (First) of Conflict of Laws generally follows a formal approach to choice of law determinations, a formality that is not necessarily fine-tuned to the equities of each particular case. The Restatement (First) operates on the theory that a cause of action becomes complete and the parties' rights vest upon the occurrence of certain events, suggesting that vesting can occur without regard to idiosyncrasies of the law as applied to the specific case. Is §380(2) consistent with that formalism? The *Hood* court suggested that the section is designed to ensure fairness "where the law of the place of conduct is so clear and particular, persons in that place have a right to rely on that law and should not suffer adverse consequences for conforming their conduct to it." This language suggests a flexibility not often found in the First Restatement.

3. The Restatement (First) of Conflict of Laws presents another exception to the last event test for torts in §382, which provides that a person required, forbidden, or privileged to act "by the law of the place of acting will not be held liable" for the results in another state.

4. Complications with identifying the precise location of injury have multiplied with the development of information technology, commercial distribution systems, transportation, and urban populations that span more than one state. Consider airplane passengers becoming sick from bacteria-infected airplane food. In many cases, few would know where the place of acting occurred or where the place of injury occurred. Case reporters are filled with examples of situations where a tort occurs at the border between states or is split between different sides of a border.[2]

PROBLEM 2-1: THE ERRANT BASEBALL

Standing in State X, Richard threw a baseball to his daughter, who was standing in State Y. At the time, Richard failed to notice that his daughter was

---

2. *See, e.g., Bays v. Jenks*, 573 F. Supp. 306 (W.D. Va. 1983) (applying lex loci delicti rule where chase began in West Virginia and ended in Virginia); *Sacra v. Sacra*, 426 A.2d 7 (Md. Ct. Spec. App. 1981) (analyzing where the "last event" occurred where two cars collided in Delaware, but the collision sent one of the cars crashing into a Maryland utility pole); *see also Pittman v. Maldania, Inc.*, 2001 Del. Super. LEXIS 549 (applying the Restatement (Second) of Conflict of Laws in case where jet ski rental office effectively straddled the Delaware/Maryland border and the plaintiff was injured a short distance away in Maryland).

standing in front of a window. Richard's daughter failed to catch the ball, which broke the window. The window's owner sued Richard for negligence in State X, which follows the Restatement (First) of Conflict of Laws. Assume that the law governing negligence varies slightly between the two jurisdictions, X and Y. Which negligence law should govern the action between Richard and the window owner?

PROBLEM 2-2: THE DOG BITE

The State of Harsh imposes liability on the owner of a dog that bites someone if the owner did not take reasonable care in keeping the dog on a leash. The State of Propensity imposes liability on the owner only if the dog has shown a dangerous propensity by having bitten someone in the past. Sally lives in the State of Harsh. Her dog escapes from her house and wanders into the State of Propensity, where the dog bites Pam. The dog had never bitten anyone before. Pam sues Sally for damages resulting from the bite in a jurisdiction that follows the Restatement (First) of Conflict of Laws. Which law governs?

PROBLEM 2-3: THE MAGIC MOMENT OF ADDICTION

Rosa started sneaking cigarettes every month or so starting when she was 13, and living in North Carolina. She remembers that at that time, the cigarettes always made her feel sick to her stomach, and that she would avoid smoking for several weeks every time she tried a cigarette. At the age of 18, Rosa went off to college in South Carolina, where she started smoking more regularly. It was in South Carolina that — for the first time — she found herself actually craving a cigarette. She was a two-pack-a-day smoker by the time she graduated at age 21. Rosa has no recollection, however, of her two-pack-a-day habit impinging on her enjoyment of life at that time.

Rosa has always smoked a brand manufactured in Virginia by Phillip Reynolds, and recalls advertisements throughout her adolescence and young adulthood portraying cigarette smoking as outdoorsy, sophisticated, and healthy. The advertisements were pervasive in billboards, magazines, and other print media throughout the United States.

After college graduation, Rosa moved to Arkansas, where she has worked for the past 20 years. She has continued to smoke two to three packs of cigarettes a day and has found that her addiction to cigarettes severely curtails her ability to engage in a wide range of activities. She has unsuccessfully tried several times to quit the habit. Rosa filed suit against Phillip Reynolds, alleging that the company is guilty of negligent misrepresentation for failing to inform consumers that cigarettes contain an extremely addictive ingredient: nicotine. Assume that the law of negligent misrepresentation varies considerably in North Carolina, South Carolina, Virginia, and

Arkansas. Under the Restatement (First), which law should govern the negligent misrepresentation claim?

PROBLEM 2-4: THADDEUS TAPE RECORDS IN PRIVACY

The State of Privacy has a criminal statute that provides for criminal liability where someone tape records a telephone conversation without the consent of all persons to the conversation (unless the tape recording is made pursuant to a warrant issued in a criminal investigation). The Supreme Court of the State of Privacy has ruled that, even in the absence of a criminal prosecution for violating this statute, an individual who violates this provision shall be found to have engaged in a per se violation of the standard of care applicable in a civil tort action for invasion of privacy. The State of Privacy Supreme Court has also ruled that where the violator is a government official, failure to obtain consent to tape or a warrant constitutes a violation of the State of Privacy's constitutional protection of privacy rights of individuals. The State of Lax has a cause of action for invasion of privacy, which has a general standard of care. The State of Lax does not have any law that specifically prohibits tape recording another without consent.

Thaddeus is a private person who taped his phone conversation with his friend Aisha without her consent. At the time of the tape recording, Thaddeus was located in the State of Privacy, and Aisha was located in the State of Lax. Thaddeus played the tape for another person one time, while he and the other person were located in the State of Lax. Once she learned that Thaddeus had made the tape and played it for another person, Aisha filed suit against him in the State of Privacy, which applies the Restatement (First) of Conflict of Laws. She alleges that Thaddeus is liable to her for invasion of privacy. Will the law of Privacy or the law of Lax govern the standard of care applied in this invasion of privacy suit?

b. Intentional Torts

Dominican Republic v. AES Corporation

466 F. Supp. 2d 680 (E.D. Va. 2006)

Opinion by: GERALD BRUCE LEE

This matter is before the Court on Defendant AES Corporation, AES Aggregate Services, Ltd., AES Atlantis, AES Puerto Rico, L.P., Silver Spot Enterprises, and Roger Charles Fina's Motion to Dismiss. The Government of the Dominican Republic brought this suit complaining that several American companies polluted Samana Bay and Manzanillo by dumping coal ash. . . .

[The court explained that the Dominican Republic asserted several claims including nuisance, products liability, aiding and abetting the violation of laws prohibiting bribery and regulating waste disposal, and civil conspiracy to violate the laws prohibiting bribery and regulating waste disposal. The court further explained that it needed to decide several issues, including the question "whether Virginia choice of law principles require the law of the Dominican Republic to govern Plaintiff's claims and, if so, whether the law of the Dominican Republic recognizes the common law causes of action asserted."] . . .

I. Background

The . . . Dominican Republic alleges that the AES Corporation formed a civil conspiracy to carry out several illegal acts (including bribery and death threats) in order to dispose of hazardous coal ash in a manner less expensive than safe disposal. Because the Government of the Dominican Republic does not think its own courts can resolve this matter in a fair and impartial manner, it brought suit in the Eastern District of Virginia. The Dominican Republic alleges that the AES conspiracy polluted Manzanillo and Samana Bay, wrecked the beach, caused nearby residents to suffer physical injuries that required the state-run healthcare system to provide medical care, hampered tourism, and caused business in the region to suffer. In addition, some inhabitants of the Dominican Republic have suffered respiratory problems from breathing polluted air which the state-run healthcare system has addressed.

For the purposes of this motion, the Court assumes the following facts are true. AES of Arlington, Virginia, is the parent company of more than 700 subsidiaries, including AES Puerto Rico, AES Atlantis, and AES Aggregate Services ("AES Defendants"). AES Puerto Rico discovered that it could not find commercial uses for its coal ash, a byproduct of its coal burning power plant. Disposal costs for the 1000 tons of coal ash generated by the plant each day would have been substantial, approximately $100-200 U.S. per ton. AES created AES Aggregate Services, Ltd., "a Cayman Islands subsidiary, to enter into a contract with Defendant AES Puerto Rico." Plaintiff alleges that AES executive Sarah Slusser directed the formation of AES Aggregate Services while at AES headquarters in Arlington, Virginia, part of the idea being that AES could create the illusion that the Puerto Rico plant's ash would be disposed of in accord with relevant law. When the initial contract between AES Puerto Rico and AES Aggregate Services to dispose of the ash in the Bahamas failed (because the Bahamas refused to accept it), AES hired Silver Spot Enterprises.

The Government of the Dominican Republic alleges that AES hired Silver Spot Enterprises of Delray Beach, FL to transport the waste out of Puerto Rico. Silver Spot Enterprises has a Dominican Republic subsidiary, Multigestiones Valenza ("MV"). The entities negotiated the contract in Florida. The Government of the Dominican Republic alleges that a conspiracy formed among the AES Defendants; Silver Spot; MV; Trans Dominicana de Desarollo ("TDD") (a Dominican company holding the concession for the port of Manzanillo); the former Undersecretary of Environmental Management in the Ministry of the Environment, Rene Ledesma; the former Director of the National Port Authority, Rosendo Arsenio Borges; and elected and unelected officials of the government of the Dominican Republic, including the municipal government of Manzanillo and provinces of Montecristi and Samana. The object of the conspiracy involved disposal of tons of coal ash without incurring the costs of proper shipment and/or disposal. In addition, Plaintiff alleges that the conspirators are conspiring currently to prevent discovery, investigation, and prosecution of their acts. Plaintiff fears that if the courts of the Dominican Republic were to take up the issues, they would be unlawfully influenced in ways that could allow the Defendants to evade accountability for their actions.

Plaintiff alleges that from October 2003 to March 2004, Defendants transported ten (10) barge-loads of compacted coal ash from Puerto Rico to the Dominican Republic. The Dominican Academy of Sciences found that the coal ash had high levels of arsenic, cadmium, nickel, beryllium, chromium, and vanadium. Four barges (on or about October 20, November 12, December 2, 2003 and January 18, 2004) left approximately 30,000 tons of coal ash in Manzanillo, exposed to the elements. The flying unattended coal ash harmed nearby residents of the Manzanillo area; they experienced skin lesions, and several elderly residents and children had difficulty breathing. Several residents were hospitalized. The dumping contributed to, or resulted in, six (6) deaths and five (5) serious illnesses. The waste destroyed a mangrove wetland. Tourist activity declined dramatically.

Samana Bay suffered major damage from the coal ash pollution also. . . . Again, several residents were injured, suffering skin lesions and breathing difficulties. Six (6) residents were hospitalized with acute respiratory distress. Samana Bay region tourism declined dramatically and has not improved; hotel occupancy decreased by 70 percent. Local fish sales have declined. Environmentalists and marine biologists have expressed concern about the possible effects on the whale population and the reputation of the Dominican Republic for protecting whales.

The port of Manzanillo refused to allow the first barge into the Dominican Republic on October 20, 2003 because Silver Spot did not have a permit from the Environment Ministry. District Attorney Arias aided in preventing the dumping. District Attorney Arias was aware that after the country halted the attempted import of sewage from Philadelphia, Pennsylvania, the Dominican Republic passed a law forbidding the importation of biological, industrial, and residential waste. Having failed to unload the ash in the Dominican Republic, Roger Charles Fina, owner of Silver Spot, attempted to unload in Haiti; when unsuccessful, he dumped twenty-five percent into the Haitian coastal waters.

Later, the Defendants acquired a permit from the Dominican Republic to dump ash. Plaintiff alleges that the Dominican Republic issued the permit without the proper review process or the environmental impact statement required by law in the Dominican Republic. Originally, a "sham" contract between Silver Spot and TDD maintained the pretense that the coal ash would be used for commercial purposes; for example, it filled potholes. Fina attempted twice in 2003 to bribe Congressman Rafael Emilio Betances with $40,000 in order to obtain permits and licenses to bring ash to Manzanillo. Betances rejected the offers.

District Attorney Arias objected officially and publicly to Defendants' disposal of the coal ash. District Attorney Arias claims his protests of the Silver Spot actions led to "harassment, attempted physical assault, death threats, and the attempted burning of his car." He refused to accept a bribe from a TDD officer to stop opposing the ash disposal. Plaintiff alleges that unnamed corrupt or coerced Dominican Republic officials fired Arias on or about May 9, 2004.

Plaintiff alleges that AES Puerto Rico paid bribes to Dominican Republic government officials when its executives, Al Dyer and David Stone, traveled to the Dominican Republic. Plaintiff alleges that the AES Corporation knew of the actions of its subsidiaries. The Dominican Republic eventually revoked the permits.

The Dominican Republic seeks compensatory and punitive damages for environmental damages (including removing the ash, restoring local ecology, and monitoring cleanup), healthcare costs for injured residents, and economic damages for the loss of tourism.

. . .

B. ANALYSIS

[The court held that the Dominican Republic has standing to bring suit in the United States and dismissed the RICO claims because the facts alleged were "insufficient to establish a pattern of racketeering activity." The court also dismissed the product liability claim because "both parties agree that the coal ash is not a 'product.'" The court ruled that the act of state doctrine did not bar plaintiff's claims because "a public act is not at issue." As a preliminary to its choice of law reasoning, the court observed that "Virginia choice of law rules govern tort actions filed in the Eastern District of Virginia, and that Virginia applies the law of the place of the wrong," which is "the place where the injury was suffered, not where the tortious act took place."]

. . .

4. Choice of Law

. . . The Court finds, under Virginia choice of law principles, that the law of the Dominican Republic applies to Plaintiff's nuisance, civil conspiracy, and aiding and abetting claims because the place of injury occurred where the coal ash was dumped in the Dominican Republic. In [*Milton v. IIT Research Inst.*, 138 F.3d 519, 521 (4th Cir. 1998),] despite the fact that the plaintiff experienced lost income and emotional distress from his wrongful discharge while in Virginia, the law of Maryland applied because that was the location of the discharge. Although Plaintiff uses Milton to argue that the place of the wrong could be Virginia, Puerto Rico, or Florida (in addition to the Dominican Republic), the nuisance plainly occurred in the Dominican Republic.

Viewing all facts in a light most favorable to the Plaintiff, this Court finds that the law of the Dominican Republic recognizes claims for common law nuisance, civil conspiracy, and aiding and abetting. The Attorney General for Defense of the Environment and Natural Resources for the Dominican Republic, Andres M. Chalas Velazquez, stated under oath that the Dominican Civil Code allow claims for nuisance. The Dominican Republic also has a cause of action for persons harmed by the environmental releases of others.

In addition, the Attorney General stated that criminal proceedings do not need to take place before a Plaintiff can bring a civil suit for conspiracy and aiding and abetting — civil actions of this type may be pursued with penal actions, or they can be filed separately before civil courts. Also, Attorney Perez Gomez stated that [the country's environmental laws], allows the Government of the Dominican Republic itself to claim damages independent of penal actions. In addition, the Secretary of State for the Environment and Natural Resources may bring an action for damages before a civil court even if the penal action is abandoned or an administrative penalty imposed.

Therefore, viewing the facts in a light most favorable to the Plaintiff, the Plaintiff has cognizable claims for nuisance, conspiracy, and aiding and abetting under the law of the Dominican Republic, and the law of the Dominican Republic should be applied to those claims.

Notes on
DOMINICAN REPUBLIC v. AES CORPORATION

1. The court in *Dominican Republic v. AES Corporation* applied the place of wrong rule in a straightforward way, apparently undaunted by the widespread nature of the harm, the international character of the events, and the allegedly intentional nature of the wrong done. This is not uncommon for contemporary cases applying the First Restatement.

2. Should analysis differ for intentional and unintentional torts? On one hand, one might argue that in cases where the wrongful conduct and injury occur in different places, the jurisdiction where conduct occurs might have a particularly strong claim for regulating in those cases (such as in *Dominican Republic v. AES Corporation*) where the conduct was planned and intentional. A place of conduct rule can also avoid difficulties arising where there are several victims of wrongful conduct who suffer injury in various different jurisdictions. On the other hand, the notion that a cause of action is not complete — and rights do not vest — until injury occurs might be equally applicable for intentional torts as for unintentional torts. The notes to Restatement (First) §377 make clear that the section applies to intentional torts. In addition, one might argue that where, as in *Dominican Republic v. AES Corporation*, defendants are alleged to have structured their intentional behavior so as to appear law abiding in the place they are acting, a choice of law approach that focuses on the place of injury may provide a safety net against defendants' planned subterfuge. A defendant may be able to plan her own conduct to elude regulation, but might find it difficult to control where and how a plaintiff experiences harm.

3. The court in *Dominican Republic v. AES Corporation* used statements of several Dominican public officials to establish the substance of the law of the

Dominican Republic. This is not an unusual contemporary approach to ascertaining foreign law. Courts have followed different approaches, however, to this important inquiry. Various views on the appropriate approach to proof of foreign law are summarized after the problems below.

PROBLEM 2-5: FRIEDA FALSIFIES FROG CREDENTIALS

After reading a Mark Twain story about a frog race, Serena got the idea of opening a frog-racing booth at a local amusement park. Serena lives in State S and plans to operate the booth in State S. Knowing that she needs the frogs to last for at least five full years in order to make a profit, she concluded that she would only pursue the enterprise if she could acquire frogs that were likely to live at least five years in captivity. Serena heard through friends that Frieda operated a frog farm in State F. From her home in State S, Serena sent Frieda an email in State F, asking about the cost of the frogs as well as the projected life expectancy. While in State F, Frieda typed out an email to Serena falsely reporting that she handled only a special breed of a frog that performed well under the conditions in which Serena planned to keep the frogs, and that Serena could expect the frogs to live an average of eight years. Frieda was aware of several studies showing that the frogs that she breed actually lived only a year or less when handled frequently by humans and maintained under conditions such as Serena planned. Frieda shipped the frogs from State F to State S. Serena pressed them into service at the amusement park, but they died ten months later. Accordingly, Serena was unable to recoup her investment and ultimately went out of business.

Serena has sued Frieda for Fraud in State S, which follows the Restatement (First) of Conflict of Laws. The law of fraud in State S is very different than the law of fraud in State F. Which law should govern the fraud action?

PROBLEM 2-6: CASSANDRA AND JULIAN: THE PLACE OF PUBLICATION PROBLEM

Consider Cassandra and Julian again: Cassandra is a resident of New Jersey and Julian is a resident of Ohio. Cassandra researched and wrote an article about Julian, which was published in a newspaper. Julian asserts that the article blackens his reputation by asserting false facts, and that Cassandra knew the article was false when she wrote it. He maintains that the publication of the article diminished others' respect for him in all of the places where he has business dealings (primarily Ohio, New Jersey, and Pennsylvania). Cassandra has never been to Ohio and has never had anything to do with Ohio. Unbeknownst to her, however, the newspaper distributes 20 papers in Ohio (less than 1 percent of its total circulation). The newspaper also circulates in New Jersey and Pennsylvania. When the article was published, the newspaper edition containing the article hit the newsstands in Ohio, New Jersey, and Pennsylvania at the same time. Assume for the purposes of this problem that the defamation laws of Ohio, New Jersey, and Pennsylvania differ in important respects. Assume Julian has filed a defamation action in a jurisdiction that follows the Restatement (First) of Conflict of Laws. Which jurisdiction's law of defamation should govern?

PERSPECTIVE ON PROOF OF FOREIGN LAW

Courts in the United States have referred to laws of foreign countries in adjudicating disputes for well over a hundred years.[3] Yet, as late as the middle of the twentieth century, courts viewed "law" as including forum law, and deemed foreign legal principles to be facts to be proven like other facts in the case. The notion was that true "law" is only those norms that have binding force in the court's territory: that is, the legal principles of the forum. A party seeking to have the forum court rely on legal principles of other jurisdictions had to plead and prove these principles in accordance with the rules of pleading and evidence that govern other facts. This fact-based approach was later replaced in most United States jurisdictions with statutes or rules requiring courts to take judicial notice of "foreign law" — an obligation that sometimes encompassed the law of various domestic states as well as foreign countries. More recently, state and federal courts have taken the position that foreign law is indeed "law," which can be ascertained by the court with the parties' assistance.

Formal procedure regarding ascertaining foreign law is theoretically the same for both domestic law (the law of sister states) and the law of other countries. In practice, however, matters regarding foreign country laws are far more challenging. Scholars have documented a historic reluctance of many United States courts to use foreign country law to decide disputes. In many instances, courts may simply use domestic law if the litigants do not raise or fully brief issues relating to the content of foreign country law. As Louise Ellen Teitz has explained, courts confronted with insufficient proof of the substance of foreign country law will often simply "apply the forum's law, relying on the traditional conflicts of law presumption that foreign law is the same as that of the forum."[4] The court may simply assume "from the absence of sufficient proof of foreign law that the parties have consented to application of the forum's law."[5] Alternatively, courts have been known to heavily favor domestic law when undertaking a full scale choice of

---

3. *See, e.g., Nashua Sav. Bank v. Anglo-American Land,* Mortgage & Agency Co., 189 U.S. 221, 228-229 (1903) (outlining methods for proving foreign law); *Ennis v. Smith,* 55 U.S. 400, 426 (1853) (allowing French Civil Code to be admitted into evidence).

4. Louise Ellen Teitz, *From the Courthouse in Tobago to the Internet: The Increasing Need to Prove Foreign Law in U.S. Courts,* 34 J. MAR. L. & COM. 97, 101 (2003).

5. *Id.* at 101. For an illuminating history of this presumption, see Michael Steven Green, *Horizontal Erie and the Presumption of Foreign Law,* 109 MICH. L. REV. 1237, 1267-1268 (2011).

law analysis, so as to ensure that easily ascertainable and known domestic law principles ultimately govern.[6] Aside from ignoring or steering clear of potential foreign law issues, courts also have shown a tendency to grant forum non conveniens dismissals when confronting cases involving law from another country.[7]

This reluctance to discover and apply the law of other countries seems to be diminishing. Today, courts routinely require parties to provide references to foreign law, and parties sometimes fulfill that obligation by soliciting testimony (or affidavits) of actual foreign officials to establish the substance of foreign law.[8] Parties do not need to secure the cooperation of a foreign official and most commonly simply hire a foreign expert that prepares an affidavit or declaration on the substance of foreign law. Federal Rule of Civil Procedure 44.1, which applies in federal court and provided a model for some state procedural rules and statutes,[9] speaks to this process of establishing the content of foreign law. As citations to Rule 44.1 have increased dramatically since the beginning of the twenty-first century, it appears that courts are becoming more comfortable with the idea of applying foreign law and the process of ascertaining its substance.[10] Rule 44.1 provides:

> A party who intends to raise an issue about a foreign country's law must give notice by a pleading or other writing. In determining foreign law, the court may consider any relevant material or source, including testimony, whether or not submitted by a party or admissible under the Federal Rules of Evidence. The court's determination must be treated as a ruling on a question of law.

Despite the mention of foreign experts in Rule 44.1, a court need not rely on parties' submissions in determining federal law. In fact, Rule 44.1 does not provide for any special qualification for an expert, and a judge may decide that the expert opinion is not worth crediting. Indeed, a majority of the United States Court of Appeals for the Seventh Circuit has now gone on record discouraging the use of expert opinions and arguing against courts relying on party submissions when the courts identify the substance of foreign law. In a majority opinion, Judge Easterbrook wrote:

> The Committee Note in 1966, when Rule 44.1 was adopted, explains that a court "may engage in its own research and consider any relevant material thus

6. Judge Roger J. Miner, *The Reception of Foreign Law in the U.S. Federal Courts*, 43 AM. J. COM. L. 581, 583 (1995); Jacob Dolinger, *Application, Proof, and Interpretation of Foreign Law: A Comparative Study in Private International Law*, 12 ARIZ. J. INT'L & COM. LAW 223, 267-270 (1995).

7. Matthew J. Wilson, *Demystifying the Determination of Foreign Law in U.S. Courts: Opening the Door to a Greater Global Understanding*, 46 WAKE FOREST L. REV. 887, 896-897 (2011); Walter W. Heiser, *Forum Non Conveniens and Choice of Law: The Impact of Applying Foreign Law in Transnational Tort Actions*, 51 WAYNE L. REV. 1161, 1176-1177 (2005).

8. *See* PETER HAY, PATRICK J. BORCHERS & SYMEON C. SYMEONIDES, CONFLICT OF LAWS 605-606 (5th ed. 2010).

9. Many states have enacted the Uniform Judicial Notice of Foreign Law Act, which functions much like Federal Rule 44.1. *See* William Ewald, *Comparative Law and Unification of Laws: Complexity of Sources of Transnational Law: United States Report*, 58 AM. J. COMP. L. 59, 66-67 (2010).

10. Marcus S. Quintanilla & Christopher A. Whytock, *The New Multipolarity in Transnational Litigation: Foreign Courts, Foreign Judgments, and Foreign Law*, 18 SW. J. INT'L L. 31, 39-40 (2011).

found. The court may have at its disposal better foreign law materials than counsel have presented, or may wish to reexamine and amplify material that has been presented by counsel in partisan fashion or in insufficient detail."

Sometimes federal courts must interpret foreign statutes or decisions that have not been translated into English or glossed in treatises or other sources. Then experts' declarations and testimony may be essential. But French law, and the law of most other nations that engage in extensive international commerce, is widely available in English. Judges can use not only accepted (sometimes official) translations of statutes and decisions but also ample secondary literature, such as treatises and scholarly commentary. . . . Trying to establish foreign law through experts' declarations not only is expensive (experts must be located and paid) but also adds an adversary's spin, which the court then must discount. Published sources such as treatises do not have the slant that characterizes the warring declarations presented in this case. . . .

Bodum USA, Inc. v. La Cafetiere, Inc., 621 F.3d 624, 628-629 (7th Cir. 2010). Judge Posner wrote a concurring opinion in this case and echoed the disapproval of paid experts, whom he stated are "selected on the basis of the convergence of their views with the litigating position of the client, or their willingness to fall in with the views urged upon them by the client." *Id.* at 633 (Posner, J., concurring). The matter, however, is still open for debate. Indeed, in the same case, Judge Wood expressed an opposing view. Observing that Rule 44.1 does not suggest or require any hierarchy for appropriate foreign law sources, Judge Wood argued that "[e]xercises in comparative law are notoriously difficult, because the U.S. reader is likely to miss nuances in the foreign law, to fail to appreciate the way in which one branch of the other country's law interacts with another, or to assume erroneously that the foreign law mirrors U.S. law when it does not." *Id.* at 368-369. Many nuances in the operation of foreign law, such as the existence or nonexistence of a system of precedent and stare decisis, might trip up one trying to discern the substance of foreign law.[11] Because of complications of this sort, Judge Wood reasons that foreign law experts, who are often the authors of the leading treatises, can guide the court by efficiently providing both context and precision on the parameters of foreign law.

In navigating this debate, one set of scholars recommends that litigators wishing to use expert opinions encourage experts to prepare a balanced document with a scholarly tone, rather than a brief or advocacy document. Marcus Quintanilla and Christopher Whytock explain that the expert should create a document that resembles "a mini law review article precisely focused on the foreign legal issues that matter to the client . . . footnoted with the same kind of rigor one would expect in a law review article, and [with a tone that is] as

11. For a discussion of various approaches to stare decisis and precedent in the world, *see, e.g.,* Marjan Ajevski, *Preconditions for Stare Decisis — What International Law Can Learn from Comparative Constitutional Law*, MultiRights Research Paper, No. 12-06 (MultiRights: The Legitimacy of Multi-level Human Rights Judiciary 2012), available at http://ssrn.com/abstract=2083647.

neutral as possible without letting the declaration devolve into an abstract commentary."[12]

The topic of foreign law is currently covered in the draft Restatement (Third) of Conflict of Laws. The draft provides that issues of forum law are legal (not factual) and that a court may consider any relevant material in determining foreign law issues, whether or not submitted by a party or admissible under rules of evidence. The draft further allows either party or the court to raise a foreign law issue (upon reasonable notice) and instructs that when a court concludes that it has insufficient information about the content of foreign law, it may request further information from the parties and ultimately apply forum law if it does not receive sufficient information.

The process of proving foreign law is not the only litigation issue that arises in the context of conflict of law problems. Indeed, the potential for competing laws that might dispose of a dispute implicates questions throughout litigation as to the appropriate procedure for raising and preserving conflict of laws issues, a matter discussed in the following note.

PERSPECTIVE ON RAISING AND PRESERVING CONFLICT OF LAWS ISSUES IN LITIGATION

Courts now generally view a conflict of laws dispute as implicating legal (rather than factual) issues. Accordingly, a litigant may seek to raise an argument regarding what law governs as the litigant would raise any other legal issue: in a pleading, a motion to dismiss, a motion for summary judgment, in a pretrial hearing, and the like.

Some jurisdictions have formal or informal rules about the timing and manner of raising conflict of laws matters. If a litigant fails to satisfy these requirements, the presumption in favor of forum law will prevail. The requirements, however, are not always explicit and easy to ascertain. This ambiguity can be problematic, since many jurisdictions adhere closely to the default in favor of forum law governing. For example, California requires a party to raise a choice of law argument to persuade the court to apply the law of a foreign state law instead of the forum state's law; in the absence of a party raising such an argument, the court will adhere to forum law. *Hurtado v. Superior Court*, 522 P.2d 666, 670 (Cal. 1974). Furthermore, for class action claims, California maintains a strict requirement, placing the burden on the defendant to demonstrate that another state's law should apply. *Bruno v. Eckhart Corp.*, 280 F.R.D. 540, 545 (C.D. Cal. 2012) (citing *Washington Mutual Bank, FA v. Superior Court*, 15 P.3d 1071, 1081 (Cal. 2001)).

Likewise, Texas follows the principle that, in the absence of a pleading, proof of law from another jurisdiction, or a motion to take judicial notice of the laws

---

12. Marcus S. Quintanilla & Christopher A. Whytock, *The New Multipolarity in Transnational Litigation: Foreign Courts, Foreign Judgments, and Foreign Law*, 18 Sw. J. Int'l L. 31, 47 (2011).

of another jurisdiction, laws of other jurisdictions are presumed to be the same as those of Texas, and the court will apply Texas law. *In re Estates of Garcia-Chapa*, 33 S.W.3d 859, 863 (Tex. Ct. App. 2000). Wisconsin choice of law practice also presumes that forum law governs unless litigants establish that another state's law has greater significance. *State Farm Mut. Auto. Ins. Co. v. Gillette*, 641 N.W.2d 662, 676 (Wis. 2002).

Certain jurisdictions restrict some mandated choice of law procedures to specific contexts. For example, New Jersey has particular requirements for litigating conflict of laws, particularly for mass tort litigation. Courts in New Jersey retain the discretion to consider the applicability of foreign law when the issue is raised, even if not previously pled. Nonetheless, New Jersey courts have directed mass tort attorneys in New Jersey to identify "legal issues as early as possible, starting in most cases at the initial pre-trial conference." *Bailey v. Wyeth, Inc.*, 28 A.3d 856, 862 (N.J. Super. Ct. Law Div. 2008). New Jersey courts have explained that mass tort litigants bear the "obligation to call the applicability of another state's law to the court's attention in time to be properly considered." *Id.* at 863.

Where specific procedural rules govern the practice of litigating conflict of laws issues, the question may arise as to which procedural rules should govern. The answer will nearly always be the procedural rules that govern will be those of the forum court and not another jurisdiction whose laws may govern another aspect of the case. *See, e.g.*, Restatement (Second) of Conflict of Laws §§122, 127 (pointing to local law of the forum for judicial administration and pleading rules); Restatement (First) of Conflict of Laws §585 (pointing to law of forum for all matters of procedure).

The failure to raise a choice of law problem at an early time can result in a finding of waiver for the purposes of appeal. Likewise, the Alabama rule regarding preserving the choice of law issue indicates that the choice of law issue cannot be raised for the first time on appeal. *Rich v. Colonial Ins. Co. of CA*, 709 So. 2d 487, 488 (Ala. Civ. App. 1997) (*citing* Ala. R. App. P. Rule 4(a)(3)). Similarly, in Utah, parties must raise a conflict of laws issue at the trial court level in order for it to be preserved for appellate review. *O'Dea v. Olea*, 217 P.3d 704, 709 (Utah 2009) (citing Utah R. App. P. 24(a)(5)(A)-(B)).

Again, the precise rules on the proper timing for raising a conflict of laws issue are often somewhat vague. For example, United States Court of Appeals for the Seventh Circuit has stated that to preserve a choice of law issue for appeal, a party is required only to notify the court in a "timely" manner of the applicability of another state's law, but has not elaborated on what "timely" means precisely. *Jaurequi v. John Deere Co.*, 986 F.2d 170, 173 (7th Cir. 1993). In another example, the Louisiana Supreme Court noted that although a lower court should have considered a choice of law issue, the defendant did not raise the issue during the pleadings stage or any other time in the lower courts. From this inaction, the Louisiana Supreme Court concluded the defendant had conceded that application of Louisiana law was proper. *Sensebe v. Canal Indem. Co.*, 58 So. 3d 441, 443 n.1 (La. 2011).

One decision by a Texas appellate court provides some guidance on what might amount to sufficient notification to the trial court of a potential conflict of laws issue. In *Greenberg Traurig of New York, P.C. v. Moody*, 161 S.W.3d 56, 69 (Tex. Ct. App. 2004), the trial court applied Texas law to an action, but on appeal the court found that the appellant had preserved the choice of law error in the lower court by asserting in several trial contexts that New York law should apply, including a summary judgment motion; a trial brief regarding attorney disciplinary rules; in oral arguments to the trial court; at the hearing on the motion to enter judgment; and in a post-trial motion. *Id.* The *Greenberg* court found these actions sufficient to comply with Texas Rule of Appellate Procedure 33.1, which requires that a party wishing to preserve an issue for appellate review to make an objection or argument known to the trial court in a sufficiently specific and timely manner for the trial court to be aware of the matter and make a ruling.

When a conflict of laws issue is raised in the early stages of litigation, it can provide the basis for a case dismissal. This often occurs when the choice of law issue pertains to an affirmative defense such as a statute of frauds, a prior settlement agreement, or a capacity to sue issue. One particularly common affirmative defense that can present a case-dispositive choice of law issue concerns statutes of limitations. In *Kat House Productions v. Paul, Hastings, Janofsky & Walker, LLP*, 897 N.Y.S.2d 90, 91 (N.Y. App. Div. 2010), an appellate court affirmed the trial court's decision to grant the defendant's motion to dismiss on statute of limitations grounds. Applying New York's statute pertaining to sister state statutes of limitation, the court found that because the plaintiff's malpractice claims arose in California, California's one-year statute of limitations was applicable and the case should be dismissed as untimely. *See also Alvarado v. H & R Block, Inc.*, 24 S.W.3d 236, 241 (Mo. Ct. App. 2000) (granting motion to dismiss upon applying a California statute of limitations in a suit filed in Missouri). For a somewhat different case in which a statute of limitations resulted in dismissal, consider *Stivers v. Ellington*, 140 S.W.3d 599, 600 (Ky. Ct. App. 2010). In this case the Kentucky court concluded that the Kentucky statute governed limitations issues in multijurisdictional cases and granted a motion to dismiss premised on Kentucky's own statute of limitations.

Although many of the rules surrounding litigation of conflict of laws matters are vague, the message the existing rules send to attorneys is clear. Able advocacy and representation requires that an attorney anticipate and research potential conflict of laws matters before the first complaint is filed. Only then can the attorney be sure to make informed decisions about where to file suit, how to conduct the litigation, and how to preserve potential conflicts matters for appeal.

2. Contracts

Unlike torts, contracts are usually the product of knowing and intentional participation of the parties involved. This difference is reflected in the legal conception of an enforceable contract and the consequences of a breach of contract. As such, the logic of when the parties obtain a vested right to sue differs from in tort. There are at least three possible theories that might inform the contracts vested rights rules: (1) when parties contract, they generally presume that certain laws will govern their dealings and this law should govern; (2) the law of the place of performance (or failure to perform) should govern the parties' dealings; and (3) the place where the parties made the contract should govern their dealings. In his influential treatise, Professor Beale favored the place-of-making rule.[13] This presumption in favor of the place-of-making rule made its way into Restatement (First) of Conflict of Laws. As you will see in the Restatement sections and the cases that follow, however, the place-of-making rule does not always prevail. One thing is for sure, however: unlike an injury from a wrongful act in tort, the question of whether an enforceable contract exists and how its terms should operate depends on the abstract legal construction of enforceable promises, and for that reason is removed from tangible realities. This, you will see, opens up possibilities for even more metaphysical, complicated reasoning than we observed in the tort cases.

Before you read the contracts cases, however, take a look at the following Restatement (First) provisions.

From the Restatement (First) of Conflict of Laws, on the Subject of Contracts:

§311. Place of Contracting

The law of the forum decides as a preliminary question by the law of which state questions arising concerning the formation of a contract are to be determined, and this state is, in the Restatement of this Subject, called the "place of contracting." . . .

Comment:
. . .
d. Determination of "place of contracting." Under its Conflict of Laws rules, in determining the place of contracting, the forum ascertains the place in which, under the general law of Contracts, the principal event necessary to make a contract occurs. The forum at this stage of the investigation does not seek to ascertain whether there is a contract. It examines the facts of the transaction in question only so far as is necessary to determine the place of the principal event, if any, which, under the general law of Contracts, would result in a contract. Then, and not until then, does the forum refer to the law of such state to ascertain if, under that law, there is a contract, although of course there normally will be a contract unless the local law of Contracts of the state to which reference is thus made differs from the general law of Contracts as understood at the forum.

---

13. Joseph H. Beale, A Treatise on the Conflict of Laws §332.1 (1935).

§332. Law Governing Validity of Contract

The law of the place of contracting determines the validity and effect of a promise with respect to
>   (a) capacity to make the contract;
>   (b) the necessary form, if any, in which the promise must be made;
>   (c) the mutual assent or consideration, if any, required to make a promise binding;
>   (d) any other requirements for making a promise binding;
>   (e) fraud, illegality, or any other circumstances which make a promise void or voidable;
>   (f) except as stated in §358, the nature and extent of the duty for the performance of which a party becomes bound;
>   (g) the time when and the place where the promise is by its terms to be performed;
>   (h) the absolute or conditional character of the promise.

§333. Capacity to Contract

The law of the place of contracting determines the capacity to enter into a contract.

§334. Formalities for Contracting

The law of the place of contracting determines the formalities required for making a contract.

> Comment:

> *a.* The law of the place of contracting determines whether the contract must be in writing in order to be valid. It also determines the adequacy of the writing and the necessity for witnesses and acknowledgment before a notary public or other public officer.
> *b. Statutes of frauds.* The requirements of writing may be a requirement of procedure or a requirement of validity, or both. If, for instance, the statute of frauds of the place of contracting is interpreted as meaning that no evidence of an oral contract will be received by the court, it is a procedural statute, and inapplicable in the courts of any other state (see §598). If, however, the statute of frauds of the place of contracting is interpreted as making satisfaction of the statute essential to the binding character of the promise, no action can be maintained on an oral promise there made in that or any state; and if the statute of frauds of the place of contracting makes an oral promise voidable, and the promisor avoids such a promise, the same result follows. If the statute of frauds of the place of contracting is procedural only and that of the forum goes to substance only, an oral contract will be enforced though it does not conform to either statute.

§340. Contracts to Transfer or to Convey Land

The law of the place of contracting determines the validity of a promise to transfer or to convey land.

§355. Place of Performance

The place of performance is the state where, either by specific provision or by interpretation of the language of the promise, the promise is to be performed.

§358. Law Governing Performance

The duty for the performance of which a party to a contract is bound will be discharged by compliance with the law of the place of performance of the promise with respect to:
    (a) the manner of performance;
    (b) the time and locality of performance;
    (c) the person or persons by whom or to whom performance shall be made or rendered;
    (d) the sufficiency of performance;
    (e) excuse for non-performance.

    Comment:

    a. Questions of performance. The language of a contract must be interpreted to make clear the intention of the parties. The obligation of the contract is fixed by the law of the place of contracting and comes into effect at that time. After the language of the contract is made clear by interpretation and the duty imposed by the law of the place of contracting is ascertained, there may still remain problems connected with the details of performance of such duty (see §332, Comment *c*). The law of the place of performance determines the manner and method as well as the legality of the acts required for performance. Thus, when the time comes for performance, it may be that the duties of carrying out an apparently simple promise are not at all clear by reason of the development of unforeseen circumstances or by reason of the existence of legal restrictions and qualifications imposed by the law of the state of performance. The rule stated in this Section expresses the general principle that all questions concerning the manner of performance, the exact time and conditions of performance, the person or persons to whom performance shall be rendered and similar questions of detail are determined by the law of the place where performance is to be made.
    b. Practical line separating question of obligation from question of performance. While the law of the place of performance is applicable to determine the manner and sufficiency and conditions under which performance is to be made, it is not applicable to the point where the substantial obligation of the parties is materially altered. As stated in §332, Comment *c*, there is no logical line which separates questions of the obligation of the contract, which is determined by the law of the place of contracting, from questions of performance, determined by the law of the place of performance. There is, however, a practical line which is drawn in every case by the particular circumstances thereof. When the application of the law of the place of contracting would extend to the determination of the minute details of the manner, method, time and sufficiency of performance so that it would be an unreasonable regulation of acts in the place of performance, the law of the place of contracting will cease to control and the law of the place of performance will be applied. On the other hand, when the

application of the law of the place of performance would extend to a regulation of the substance of the obligation to which the parties purported to bind themselves so that it would unreasonably determine the effect of an agreement made in the place of contracting, the law of the place of performance will give way to the law of the place of contracting.

§360. Illegality of Performance

(1) If performance of a contract is illegal by the law of the place of performance at the time for performance, there is no obligation to perform so long as the illegality continues.

(2) If the illegality of performance is temporary and the obligation of the contract still continues, whether the contract must be performed within a reasonable time after its performance becomes legal depends upon the law of the place of performance.

. . .

b. Performance illegal when agreement made. If the performance of the agreement would be illegal by the law of the place of performance at the time the agreement was made, and if such fact was known to the parties at the time, there is no contract by the law of the place of contracting. . . . If the promisor knew of the illegality of performance at the time of contracting and concealed such fact from the other party, the law of the place of contracting may hold the promisor as guaranteeing the legality of performance or may impose a duty on him to pay damages for the fraudulent non-disclosure. . . .

d. Performance becomes illegal after contract is made. The fact that the performance of a contract is forbidden by the law of the place of performance does not necessarily affect its binding character as a contract although it does affect the duty of performance. Thus, if a contract is made in New York to do and act in Russia which at the time of the agreement it was lawful to do and then, before the time for the performance, the act is made illegal by Russian law, the contract is still binding upon the parties as a valid obligation although the duty to perform the act promised is suspended, at least for the time being.

§361. What Amounts to Performance

The law of the place of performance determines the details of the manner of performing the duty imposed by the contract.

Comment:

a. The interpretation of the meaning of language in a contract depends upon the law of Contracts and is not a question of Conflict of Laws (see §332, Comment *a*). The legal effect of the language so interpreted as creating an obligation depends upon the law of the place of contracting (see §332), but the law of the place of performance determines the method and manner of performance.

Illustrations:

1. A agrees to sell and B to buy goods to be inspected in state X. The law of X determines the method of inspection.

§370. Law Determining Breach in Performance

The law of the place of performance determines whether a breach has occurred.

Linn v. Employers Reinsurance Corp.

139 A.2d 638 (Pa. 1958)

Opinion by Mr. Justice COHEN.

Plaintiff insurance brokers brought this action in law to require the defendant insurance company to account and pay to them commissions on insurance premiums received since 1953 from a New Jersey company. At the close of plaintiff's evidence, the trial judge entered a nonsuit which the court *en banc* refused to remove, and this appeal followed.

From the undisputed evidence it appears that in 1926 the plaintiffs were engaged in the insurance brokerage business in Philadelphia. In that year plaintiffs offered to place with the defendant contracts for the reinsurance of certain risks undertaken by the Selected Risks Insurance Company of New Jersey for a consideration of five per cent of all premiums collected by the defendant on such policies. Plaintiff Linn went to New York City to negotiate an agreement with one William Ehmann, an agent of the defendant. Ehmann stated that he would first have to obtain authority to accept the offer from the defendant's home office in Kansas City. He promised that he would communicate with the plaintiff "as soon as he could get word from Kansas City." Linn then returned to Philadelphia, and subsequently received a telephone call from Ehmann accepting the offer.

We recognize that the formal validity of a contract is determined by the law of the state in which the contract was made. Since the provisions of the Statute of Frauds relate to formal validity, it is to the statute of the place of contracting that we must refer.[3] It is therefore necessary for us to determine in which state the contract was made.

When a principal authorizes an agent to accept an offer made by a third party, as the defendant authorized Ehmann in the present case, the place of contracting is where the agent accepts the offer.

This Court has not heretofore been required to determine the place where an acceptance spoken over the telephone is effective.

Professor Williston and the Restatement of Contracts take the position that a contract made over the telephone is no different from a contract made where the parties orally address one another in each other's presence. In the latter case the offeror does not have the risk of hearing an acceptance addressed to him, and a contract is formed only if the acceptance is heard. Consequently, the place of contracting is where the acceptance is heard and not where the acceptance is spoken.

---

3. The rules embodied in the Pennsylvania Statute of Frauds are matters of substance not procedure, and apply only to contracts made in Pennsylvania. *Bernstein v. Lipper Mfg. Co.*, 307 Pa. 36, 160 Atl. 770 (1932); GOODRICH, CONFLICT OF LAWS §88 (3rd ed. 1949); Lorenzen, *The Statute of Frauds and the Conflict of Laws*, 32 YALE L.J. 311 (1923).

While we agree that this analysis represents a sound theoretical view, the reported cases which consider this issue are uniform in holding that by analogy to the situations in which acceptance is mailed or telegraphed, an acceptance by telephone is effective, and a contract is created at the place where the acceptor speaks. . . . Restatement, Conflict of Laws, supra, §326, comment c. In fact, where the federal courts are charged with the duty of applying Pennsylvania law they have reached this conclusion.

We believe that in this day of multistate commercial transactions it is particularly desirable that the determination of the place of contracting be the same regardless of the state in which suit is brought. The absence of uniformity makes the rights and liabilities of parties to a contract dependent upon the choice of the state in which suit is instituted and thus encourages "forum-shopping." For this reason we chose to follow the established pattern of decisions and hold that acceptance by telephone of an offer takes place where the words are spoken.

Applying this principle to the facts before us, we conclude that the state where the contract was made is the state from which Ehmann telephoned the defendant's acceptance to Linn. However, contrary to the trial court's determination, there is no evidence in the record to indicate from which state Ehmann spoke. It is likely that he telephoned from his New York office, but it is also possible that he called from Kansas City or even Philadelphia; we cannot substitute speculation for evidence. The record of this case, therefore, must be remitted to the court below for determination of this question.

[The court remanded the case, which was tried and a second appeal followed. In the following excerpt from its opinion in the second appeal, published at 397 Pa. 153, 153 A.2d 638 (1959), the Pennsylvania Supreme Court further discussed the question of where the contract was made between Linn and Employers Reinsurance Corporation.]

. . .

The court below submitted the issue of where the contract was made to the jury:

> The question is simply this: Was this contract completed and made in New York? Was the acceptance made in New York? Whether that acceptance be by the spoken word over the telephone to Mr. Linn or whether it was by an act of Mr. Ehmann which was in the nature of an acceptance, could only be construed as an acceptance. If the acceptance was not in New York but was at any other place, your verdict should be for the plaintiffs. If, however, it was in New York, your verdict must be for the defendant.

The jury returned a verdict for the plaintiffs upon which the court entered an order for the accounting.

Defendant, although denying the existence of such an oral contract in its pleadings, admitted at trial the existence of an oral agreement which it contended was made in New York and hence is barred by the New York Statute of Frauds. Whether or not the defendant was entitled to have this affirmative contention submitted to the jury is now immaterial. At least the jury, by its verdict, has determined that defendant's contention as to the applicability of New York law has not been sustained by the evidence. Testimony was presented to them adequate to support their finding that a telephone call of acceptance was made and that the said telephone call was not made in the State of New York. While it is true that plaintiffs have the ultimate burden of proof in convincing the jury that a valid contract was entered into, the burden of producing evidence to show that this contract was made in New York was alleged and necessarily assumed by defendant. This burden was not met. Since it was not established that the laws of New York are applicable, the laws of the forum, Pennsylvania, are presumed to apply. Unlike the New York Statute of Frauds the various provisions in the Pennsylvania statute do not require that an agreement of this sort be in writing even if it is not to be performed within a year. It has been said that the Statute of Frauds, where applicable, is not a mere rule of evidence, but rather, is a limitation of judicial authority to afford a remedy. Our statutes do not so limit the authority of this court to grant a remedy in this case.

Defendant has also alleged that this contract had no limit as to the time it was to run and was therefore terminable at will after a reasonable time. The cases cited by defendant to support this position involve situations where the contract contemplated that performance continue on both sides, as for instance an employment contract. We agree that in such a case the employment may be terminated at will by either party. This, however, is not such a case. Here the plaintiffs did all they had contracted to do, i.e., they secured the reinsurance business for defendant under an agreement that they receive 5% of the premiums so long as the business continues. There was no requirement that the plaintiffs were to perform any other service. Defendant has thus received full performance from plaintiffs and cannot now be permitted to accept the benefits of its agreement while at the same time repudiate the obligations it assumed and has recognized for twenty-seven years. So long as the fruits of this agreement are enjoyed, the consideration agreed upon must be paid in accordance with the contract under which it was given.

In the light of the disposition we make of this case it is unnecessary for us to consider plaintiffs' contention that even if the New York Statute of Frauds does apply its effect was waived by the admission of defendant's counsel that an oral agreement had been entered into.

Notes on
LINN AND RESTATEMENT PRINCIPLES GOVERNING CONTRACT FORMATION AND VALIDITY QUESTIONS

1. In *Linn*, the court stated that the law of the jurisdiction where the contract was made governed the validity of the contract. Pennsylvania law was favorable to the plaintiff and New York law was not. The plaintiff won. Does this mean that the plaintiff established that the contract was made in

Pennsylvania? Not really. Rather, the matter concerned burdens of proof. On the second round of appeals, quoted above, the Pennsylvania Supreme Court stated,

> While it is true that plaintiffs have the ultimate burden of proof in convincing the jury that a valid contract was entered into, the burden of producing evidence to show that this contract was made in New York was alleged and necessarily assumed by defendant. This burden was not met. Since it was not established that the laws of New York are applicable, the laws of the forum, Pennsylvania, are presumed to apply.

What "burden" was not met?

2. By making the "place of making" the operative concept, the Restatement (First) puts a premium on the precise twists and turns of the contract negotiation. One can just as easily imagine a conversation in which the plaintiff accepted an offer as one in which an offer was accepted by a defendant.[14] This is a complication that would arise whenever the parties to the conversation are in different states — whether the negotiation occurred by landline, cellphone, instant messaging, email, or in person (assuming the negotiators are standing on different sides of state line!). Is it appropriate to make the result so dependent on the specifics of the discourse?

3. Note that — before the *Linn* court could grapple with the question of where the contract was made — the court needed to identify the legal rule that would govern this question. The parties' likely presence in different states at the time of contracting complicated matters. Even though some authorities suggested otherwise, the *Linn* court embraced an answer to the question provided in the Restatement (First) of Conflict of Laws §326, comment *c*, which provides: "When an acceptance is to be given by telephone, the place of contracting is where the acceptor speaks his acceptance."

The Restatement (First) of Conflict of Laws, however, does not provide an answer for every factual situation in which one needs to identify where a contract is made. In a situation where specific guidance is lacking, the Restatement (First) provides the general advice that "the forum ascertains the place in which, under the general law of Contracts, the principal event necessary to make a contract occurs." §326, comment *d*. Thus, sometimes the place-of-contracting question is treated as a conflict of laws question and sometimes it is treated as something that should be answered by the "general law of Contracts." This notion of a "general law of Contracts" had currency

---

14. *See* Lea Brilmayer, Jack Goldsmith & Erin O'Hara O'Connor, Conflict of Laws: Cases and Materials 49 (6th ed. 2002) (providing alternative, equally plausible, scripts in which either Linn or the broker's representative accepted the offer) (citing Crampton, Currie & Kay, Conflict of Laws 25 (3d ed. 1981)).

during the era when the American Law Institute finalized the Restatement (First). The problem is that under today's jurisprudential outlook—in which most legal thinkers reject the concept of natural law—the general law of Contracts does not really exist. What, then, is a court today supposed to do? One approach is for the court to identify prevailing forum contract rules. Many courts, however, have handled the issue as a conflict of laws matter, reading the Restatement (First) to enunciate a "last act" rule similar to the "last act" rule in torts. Under this approach to contract formation, a court may find the place of contracting by identifying "the place in which the last act that forms the contract" occurs. *Crellin Technologies v. Equipmentlease Corp.*, 18 F.3d 1 (1st Cir. 1994). *See, e.g., Rahmani v. Resorts International Hotel, Inc.*, 20 F. Supp. 2d 932, 934 (E.D. Va. 1998).

PROBLEM 2-7: A WORK IN PROGRESS OR A FINAL CONTRACT?

Delivery Corp. was incorporated and operated its business in State D. It had a fleet of trucks that it used to operate a delivery business. Cautious Bank had financed the purchase of the trucks and held a security interest in each of them. Delivery Corp. was in financial distress in December and its president approached Truck Corp. with a proposal to alleviate the distress. Under the proposal, Truck Corp. would purchase the entire fleet of trucks and then lease the fleet back to Delivery Corp. for it to use in its business (this would give Delivery Corp. the cash infusion that it needed). The president of Truck Corp., which operated its business and was incorporated in State T, said he was interested in the deal. Both presidents acknowledged that there were two issues pertaining to whether the arrangement would be finalized: Delivery Corp. needed to get clearance from Cautious Bank to pursue the deal and Truck Corp. needed to get its own financing.

The two presidents met in State T several times in January to discuss the details of their deal. Both agreed it would not make sense to proceed further until Cautious Bank agreed to lift its security interest. Cautious Bank finally notified Delivery Corp. it would do so on February 15 and Delivery Corp.'s president made a call from its State D office to the Truck Corp. president in State T:

Delivery Corp. president (State D):	Hey, guess what? Cautious Bank finally came through—it agreed to lift the security interests on the fleet. Looks like we have a deal.
Truck Corp. president (State T):	Yep. Sure does.

Delivery Corp. president (State D):	Yep. Let's meet and start the formalities.
Truck Corp. president (State T):	Sure. I'll make my way to State D next Wednesday, and come to your office at 1:00 P.M. In the meantime, I'll meet with my lender to request the financing.

They met in State D as planned, where they discussed details of the arrangement. Truck Corp. president told Delivery president that Truck Corp.'s bank needed to evaluate Delivery Corp.'s financial statements before releasing any money to finance the sale/leaseback. At that meeting, they executed two documents—called subordination and option agreements—both of which had been prepared by Delivery Corp. Both parties agree that the documents are meaningless unless a sale/leaseback contract had actually been created.

The next day, Truck Corp.'s president followed up with the company's lender, which informed the president that Delivery Corp.'s financial situation was too precarious for it to authorize any financing. Truck Corp.'s president then informed Delivery Corp. that it did not get the financing and that Truck Corp. would not be going forward with the deal with Delivery Corp. Delivery Corp.'s president responded that this was a breach of contract, and that Truck Corp. had a contractual duty of good faith to look elsewhere for financing.

Assume that Delivery Corp.'s president is correct in her statement of the law of State D, which would recognize a contract existed between the parties and would impose a duty of good faith to attempt alternative financing. Truck Corp. takes the position that no contract existed, since the negotiations were contingent on its securing financing from *its own* lender. Assume that this position reflects a correct understanding of the law of State T. State T law would not recognize that a contract had been formed until all potential conditions were satisfied *and* would decline to impose a duty of good faith on the parties under these circumstances.

Delivery Corp. has filed suit for breach of contract against Truck Corp. in State D, which applies the Restatement (First) of Conflict of Laws. What law will govern whether a contract exists and whether Trucking Corp. breached a duty of good faith?

PROBLEM 2-8: THE OUT-OF-STATE DOCTOR

Rinalda was a resident of State R. She filled out an application for life insurance from Longevity Life Insurance Company and sent it to its home office in State L by United States mail. While in State L, a representative of Longevity prepared and executed an insurance policy agreement for Rinalda and sent it to her along with a Statement of Good Health for her doctor to sign. The representative sent these two documents from State L to Rinalda's home in State R, with a cover letter stating that the policy would be effective upon her execution of the agreement and her doctor's execution of the Statement of Good Health. The insurance contract itself said: "This policy is contingent upon the execution of the Statement of Good Health by the personal physician of the insured." Rinalda executed the policy agreement at her home in State R and placed it in a United States mailbox in State R. Rinalda then took the Statement of Good Health to her doctor to sign in State D. The doctor signed the Statement of Good Health in State D. On her way home, Rinalda stopped at a mailbox in State D and mailed the executed Statement of Good Health to the Longevity offices in State L.

Four years later, Longevity learned that Rinalda may have misrepresented her health condition in the application and informed Rinalda that it had rescinded the life insurance policy. Under the law of States L and R, Longevity had a right to make this rescission. Under the law of State D, however, the policy became "incontestable" after it had been in force for two years, and could be rescinded or cancelled only for nonpayment of premiums. Rinalda has filed suit against Longevity in a forum that applies the Restatement (First) of Conflict of Laws. Which state's law governs the effectiveness of the rescission: State L, R, or D?

PROBLEM 2-9: THE CASINO'S LURE

A citizen of State D, Darrell, first visited the Champion Casino in State C five years ago. Noticing that Darrell appeared to be a wealthy woman with a penchant for gambling, representatives of Champion began to visit her at her home in State D in order to urge her to return. These representatives promised to provide Darrell with free hotel rooms and meals any time that she came to gamble in State D. These "junket" offers succeeded, since Darrell soon began taking regular trips to the Champion Casino and became a compulsive gambler. She lost a considerable amount of money over the next several years, and has now filed a contract suit against Champion Casino, seeking rescission of her contracts with Champion and restitutionary damages based on the money she lost at the casino. Darrell's theory is that the contracts were made in her State D home, when Champion promised the hotel rooms and meals (Champion's offers) and she promised (her acceptances) to travel to State C to gamble at Champion Casino. Champion's theory, however, is that any contracts that were created did not come into existence until Darrell actually traveled to State C and placed gambling bets at Champion's casino.

Under both State C and State D law, a contract arising from an exchange of promises must be based on absolute mutuality of obligation — where each party can hold the other to their affirmative agreement. The two states' laws differ considerably, however, on whether contracts pertaining to gambling are legal. State D has a strong policy against gambling and holds any contract pertaining to gambling void as against public policy. On the other hand, gambling is a robust legal industry in State C. Not only are gambling contracts legal in State C, but the state legislation governing the casino industry explicitly approves junket arrangements such as that offered to Darrell. Which law should govern the validity of the alleged contract between Darrell and Champion?

Moses v. Halstead & Allstate Insurance Company

581 F.3d 1248 (10th Cir. 2009)

SEYMOUR, Circuit Judge.

Shelby Moses brings this appeal, asserting that the district court erred in its choice-of-law and state-law determinations. Ms. Moses requested a garnishment order, in Kansas, against Allstate Insurance Company ("Allstate") for its alleged negligent or bad faith refusal to settle Ms. Moses' claim against Chris Halstead, Allstate's insured. The district court found for Allstate, concluding that Missouri law applies and requires an actual assignment to Ms. Moses by the insured of its claim against Allstate for its failure to settle, an assignment Ms. Moses does not have. Because we conclude that Kansas law applies to this dispute, we reverse and remand.

I.

In Missouri, on November 22, 1996, Chris Halstead wrecked a car given to Ms. Moses by her father and insured by Allstate. Allstate had issued the insurance policy in Kansas to Ms. Moses' father, a Kansas resident, covering liability for uninsured motorist benefits. Ms. Moses, a passenger in the car, was injured in the accident. Shortly thereafter her father reported the accident to Allstate, requesting coverage for his daughter's injuries. Allstate began an investigation.

A year later, Ms. Moses' counsel made an offer to Allstate to settle her claims against Mr. Halstead under the Allstate policy for the policy limit of $25,000. Allstate rejected Ms. Moses' offer. Both Ms. Moses' offer to settle and Allstate's rejection of it occurred in Kansas.

Ms. Moses then filed a tort action against Mr. Halstead in Missouri, the place of the accident. The jury awarded her $100,000 in actual damages. After the judgment was entered, Allstate paid Ms. Moses $25,000 in partial satisfaction of the judgment. Ms. Moses registered the judgment in Kansas state court and requested an Order of Garnishment against Allstate for its alleged negligent or bad faith refusal to settle with her on her claim against Mr. Halstead. Allstate removed the case to federal court. [Ultimately, the district court decided that Missouri law should govern the claim, holding (1) that Allstate had acted in bad faith in refusing to settle and entered judgment for Ms. Moses; but that (2) Missouri law required that the insured, Mr. Halstead, assign his rights to Ms. Moses *before* she could recover in an action against the insurance company for its bad faith refusal to settle. Because Mr. Halstead had not assigned his claim against Allstate (for bad faith refusal to settle) to Ms. Moses, the district court ruled in favor for Allstate and rejected Ms. Moses' argument that the court should have applied Kansas law, which would not require an assignment in these circumstances.]

II.

[The court of appeals noted that it would use a de novo (plenary) standard of review in evaluating the district court's decision "whether Missouri or Kansas law governs the negligent or bad faith refusal to settle claim."]

A. THE GOVERNING LAW

In Kansas, an insurance company can be held liable not only for acting in bad faith but also for acting negligently. In Missouri, however, to hold an insurance company liable for bad faith refusal to settle the plaintiff must provide proof that the insurer acted in bad faith. The district court, in this diversity case, was initially correct in applying Kansas law to determine whether Kansas or Missouri law should govern Ms. Moses' negligent or bad faith refusal to settle claim.

In Kansas, an insurer's duties are contractually based.[1] Breach of this contractual duty, however, is determined by a tort standard of care. *See id.* Since 1957, Kansas courts "have used 'negligence,' 'due care,' and other tort expressions to describe the substance of what is a contract duty." *Id.* This contract-tort fusion has created confusion in defining the duty of good faith, and in describing situations involving negligent or bad faith breaches of duties to settle and defend. *See id.*

This case involves two issues regarding the district court's choice-of-law determination arising out of the insurance contract. First, whether the district court erred in applying Missouri law to determine whether Allstate had a contractual obligation to act in good faith to settle. Second, whether the district court was wrong in applying Missouri law to the question of Allstate's fulfillment of such obligation.

1. Law Governing the Existence of Allstate's Contractual Obligation to Act in Good Faith to Settle

Kansas courts follow the Restatement (First) of Conflict of Laws (1934) in addressing choice-of-law issues. The Restatement contains two general rules for contracts cases. *See* Restatement (First) of Conflict of Laws §§332 and 358 (1934).

When the question raised by the contractual dispute goes to the substance of the obligation, Kansas courts apply the primary rule contained in section 332, *lex loci contractus*, which calls for the application of the law of the state where the contract is made. It is only when the question goes to the manner and method of performance that the law of the place of performance applies.

Kansas courts have struggled in determining whether questions raised in cases before them are governed by the law of the place of performance or the place where the contract was made. *See Novak v. Mutual of Omaha Ins. Co.*, 29 Kan. App. 2d 526, 28 P.3d 1033 (2001), applying *lex loci contractus* when determining validity of contract provision, and *Aselco, Inc. v. Hartford Ins. Group*, 28 Kan. App. 2d 839, 21 P.3d 1011 (2001), applying performance rule on duty to defend issue and *lex loci contractus* to contract interpretation issue). The Restatement recognizes the difficulty in drawing a line between these concepts. . . .

Allstate relied on *Aselco* in arguing that the law of the place of performance of Allstate's duty to defend should apply, asserting that the Missouri tort action was

---

1. Kansas courts "see little distinction in principle between a garnishment proceeding to establish an indebtedness within policy limits and one to establish an indebtedness outside these limits arising from a breach of the insurer's duty to exercise reasonable care and good faith in settling a claim against the insured. In either case the action sounds in contract." *Glenn v. Fleming*, 247 Kan. 296, 799 P.2d 79, 89 (1990).

where the duty to defend occurred. Ms. Moses, on the other hand, relied on *Novak*, which rejects *Aselco*'s approach, to contend the law of the place of contracting should apply. The district court agreed with Allstate.

In *Aselco*, a panel of the Kansas Court of Appeals held that where an insurance company's performance of its duty to defend takes place in Kansas, Kansas law governs the determination of the existence of such duty. But *Aselco* neither cited to any Kansas cases nor offered any analysis for its holding. Moreover, *Aselco* so held despite admitting that it was not required to reach the governing law issue because it was not raised in the trial court.

A few months later in *Novak*, another panel of the Kansas Court of Appeals, including one of the judges on *Aselco*, declined to follow *Aselco* to apply the place of performance rule. The court held that the law of the place where the contract was made governed the validity of the one-year limitations provision in the contract. The panel noted that "[a]lthough some Kansas conflicts cases have involved issues of performance, few cases have used the place of performance rule to resolve contract choice of law decisions." *Id.* at 1039.

Aselco and *Novak* each declared it was following the Restatement (First) of Conflicts of Law (1934). But neither case actually explained how its analysis comported with the Restatement. *Aselco* stated that "[b]ecause [the insurance company's] performance of its duty to defend would have taken place in Kansas, Kansas law governs the determination of the existence of the duty." *Aselco*, 21 P.3d at 1018. *Novak* relied on the fact that an overwhelming majority of Kansas Supreme Court and Court of Appeals cases have applied the law of place of contracting. In *Layne Christensen Co.*, however, a case decided a few months later by the same panel that decided *Aselco*, the court provided further guidance on what question to ask in applying the Restatement. *See Layne Christensen Co.*, 38 P.3d at 766-67 (holding that the meaning of the coverage limit is governed by the law of place of contracting because it goes to the substance of obligation). In *Layne Christensen Co.*, the court acknowledged the *Novak* and *Aselco* panels' struggles in applying the law of the place of performance versus the place of contracting. *See id.* at 766. It did not endorse either outcome. Instead, it followed Kansas Supreme Court precedent adopting the test set out in the Restatement and provided guidance based on section 358, Comment b. . . .

The Kansas Supreme Court has not directly addressed whether the law of place of contracting or performance governs the question whether an injured party may, under Kansas law, bring an action for negligent or bad faith refusal to settle against a tortfeasor's insurance company in a garnishment action. Therefore, we "must predict what the Kansas Supreme Court would do if faced with the issue."

Based on the foregoing analysis, we predict that the Kansas Supreme Court would agree with the reasoning of *Layne Christensen Co.* and hold that whether Ms. Moses has a cause of action for negligent or bad faith refusal to settle against Allstate goes to the substance of Allstate's contractual duties rather than the manner of performance under the insurance policy. Therefore, the issue is governed by the law of the place where the contract was made, in this case Kansas. Accordingly, we reverse the district court's decision applying Missouri law to this issue.

2. Law Governing Whether Allstate Fulfilled Its Contractual Obligation to Act in Good Faith in Response to Ms. Moses' Settlement Offer

Applying the *Layne Christensen Co.* test, we address the next issue before us: does determining whether Allstate fulfilled its contractual obligation to act in good faith to settle Ms. Moses' claim go to the substance of the obligation or the manner and method of performance? In general, fulfillment of a contractual obligation goes to the manner and method of performance by the party charged with the obligation. Therefore, the law of the place of performance determines whether Allstate fulfilled its contractual obligation to act in good faith to settle. The record shows that both Ms. Moses' offer to settle and Allstate's rejection of the offer took place in Kansas. Accordingly, Kansas is the place Allstate was required to perform its contractual obligation to consider Ms. Moses' settlement offer in good faith, and the district court should have applied Kansas law to determine whether Allstate fulfilled this contractual obligation.

[The court then applied Kansas law and determined that the plaintiff, Ms. Moses, did not need to obtain an assignment of rights from Mr. Halstead before she acquired the right, as his judgment creditor, to bring a claim against Allstate in excess of the policy limit for a negligent or bad faith refusal to settle. The court of appeals further noted that the district court did not have the opportunity to apply Kansas law to its findings of fact regarding whether Allstate used reasonable care and good faith in efforts to settle the claim. Thus, the court of appeals remanded the case to the district court to give it an opportunity to do so.]

Notes on
MOSES v. ALSTEAD & ALLSTATE INSURANCE CO.

1. The *Moses* case first raised a perennial question that frequently arises in Restatement (First) cases: whether a legal issue should be analyzed using the choice of law rules for contract or the choice of law rules for tort. Although the court analyzed the duty to defend issue as contractual, the court did not provide an explanation for this characterization. Do you agree that the legal issues "sound" in contract rather than tort? This chapter focuses on this characterization process in detail below.

2. The *Moses* court spent considerable analysis on the more specific characterization question of whether the contract issue implicated formation or performance. Which is the better conception of the legal issues here: place of making or place of performance? Which is most consistent with the "last event" test used for tort and often used in contract? The place-of-performance rule avoids some of the metaphysical problems of contract formation explored in *Linn*. Does the place-of-performance rule replace these formation problems with new ones?

3. Professor Beale argued that allowing the parties' intended law to govern their dealings granted them improper legal control: "It practically

makes a legislative body of any two persons who choose to get together and contract."[15] As for the place-of-performance rule, he stated that "[a]ny attempt to make the law of the place of performance govern the act of contracting is an attempt to give to that law exterritorial effect."[16] Beale believed, however, that the place-of-making rule promoted certainty, since it was easiest for the parties to ascertain and control. The parties know where they are negotiating a contract and are able to seek legal advice about governing legal principles in the place where they are negotiating.

4. The distinction between issues of validity and issues of performance is a tool for courts wishing to achieve a particular result, enabling the court to avoid the law of the place of making by characterizing a legal issue as a place-of-performance problem. Consider this as you work through the next problem.

PROBLEM 2-10: SHOULD BIRTHPLACE GOVERN?

Jose and Jill signed a contract in which they agreed that they would pay Monica for carrying their child. Monica signed the contract as well. All the parties signed the contract in State C. Although the contract says nothing about governing law, evidence suggests that all parties assumed, however, that the contract would be governed by the law of State B. The contract stated that Monica should receive prenatal care in State B, should give birth in a hospital in State B, and that Jose and Jill should make the payment in State B. This contract is invalid under the law of State C, but enforceable under the law of State B. Which law should govern?

PROBLEM 2-11: THE EMAIL EXCHANGE

Polly Plaintiff owned a small car that she wanted to sell. Dora Defendant was a citizen of State D, who wished to purchase the car. Dora is only 17 years old, has never been outside State D, and has never done other business with anyone outside State D.

Dora found out that Polly was selling the car from a "Craigslist" advertisement on the internet. The advertisement said that the car was garaged in State P. From her home in D, Dora emailed Polly in State P. Dora's initial email triggered a series of emails between the two women. The emails stated:

15. Joseph H. Beale, *What Law Governs the Validity of a Contract*, 23 HARV. L. REV. 1, 260 (1909).
16. *Id.* at 267.

Email #1 (from Dora, State D):	"I read about your car on Craigslist and am interested in buying it. Do you have maintenance records for the car?"
Email #2 (from Polly, State P):	"Nice to get your message. Yes, I have extensive maintenance records. The car is in excellent condition. Where do you live?"
Email #3 (from Dora, State D):	"I live in State D. I'm willing to pay $2,000 for car."
Email #4 (from Polly, State P):	"It's a deal."
Email #5 (from Dora, State D):	"I don't have a way to get the car, since I'm only 17 and my parents don't want me to go too far from home. Can you drive the car to my house in State D tomorrow? If so, I can pay you then and you can leave the car with me. Please bring the maintenance records with you."
Email #6 (from Polly, State P):	"I will do that. See you tomorrow."

Polly drove the car to State D the next day as promised. When she got there, Dora said she had a change of heart and would not follow through with the deal.

Polly has filed suit against Dora. Polly filed the lawsuit in a State P state court. The suit asserts a cause of action for breach of contract. Dora has made a motion to dismiss the suit, arguing that that she can fully avoid any liability for breach of contract because she was 17 at the time any contract with Polly was made. She points out that, under State D law, individuals who are under 18 are *not* capable of incurring contract liability. State P law, on the other hand, provides that individuals over the age of 16 are deemed capable of entering into contracts and incurring liability if they fail to honor their contractual promises. Aside from this difference regarding the age at which individuals are capable of contracting, both State P and D have contract law that is identical in all other relevant respects and would recognize the agreement between Dora and Polly as an enforceable contract.

Under the Restatement (First) of Conflict of Laws, should the State P court apply State D law and dismiss the lawsuit on the ground that Dora was not capable of entering into an enforceable contract?

As you can see, the Restatement (First) has been around for a while, and, in some ways, reflects an outmoded view of the law. You have no doubt also started to notice that despite its apparently straightforward, black letter rules, the Restatement (First) invites considerable complication in court analysis and party argument. On this basis, one might think that courts might become disillusioned with the approach. In addition, the Restatement (First) reflects a decidedly old-fashioned focus on territory: emphasizing the location of events above other factors that might bear on difficult horizontal choice of law questions. Many state courts have jettisoned the Restatement (First) approach in favor of a more modern "flavor" of choice of law methodology. But this has by no means been an overwhelming trend. After a number of courts decided to abandon the approach several decades ago, the number of jurisdictions deciding to stick with it has remained relatively constant. Where courts consider changing the jurisdiction's choice of law approach, they generally do so piecemeal—according to doctrinal category such as contract, tort, and property. In the case that follows, the court evaluated whether to adhere to the Restatement (First) of Conflict of Laws for contracts.

Sturiano v. Brooks

523 So. 2d 1126 (Fla. 1988)

Opinion by Justice KOGAN.

[This lawsuit began as a negligence action, but implicated an insurance contract issue. The insurance contract issue pertained to whether the contract covered claims between spouses. This in turn raised a choice of law dilemma because the law where the insurance contract was made, New York, differed from the law of Florida, which had significant contacts with the case. In the course of adjudicating the insurance contract issue, the lower court certified to the Florida Supreme Court the question of whether the First Restatement rule of lex loci contractus should govern the choice of law problem. The Florida Supreme Court had earlier abandoned the traditional choice of law rules for tort and limitations of actions.]

This action is before the Court on review of a decision by the Fourth District Court of Appeal. . . . Because the court certified two questions to this Court as being of great public importance, we have jurisdiction.

. . .

The . . . question posed by the fourth district requires us to address the doctrine of lex loci contractus. Specifically, we must examine whether the rule requiring that the laws of the jurisdiction where the contract was executed should apply. The fourth district has certified the following question:

> DOES THE LEX LOCI CONTRACTUS RULE GOVERN THE RIGHTS AND LIABILITIES OF THE PARTIES IN DETERMINING THE APPLICABLE LAW ON AN ISSUE OF INSURANCE COVERAGE, PRECLUDING CONSIDERATION BY THE FLORIDA COURTS OF OTHER RELEVANT FACTORS, SUCH AS THE SIGNIFICANT RELATIONSHIP BETWEEN FLORIDA AND THE PARTIES AND/ OR THE TRANSACTION?

We answer the certified question in the affirmative, limiting this answer to contracts for automobile insurance, and approve the decision of the district court.

The Sturianos, lifelong residents of New York, purchased automobile insurance in New York six years prior to the accident which took the life of Vito Sturiano and injured Josephine Sturiano. Subsequently, the couple moved to Florida each year for the winter months. They did not notify the insurance company of this migration, and the insurance company had no way of knowing that such a move had taken place.

Under the doctrine of lex loci contractus, it is clear that New York law must apply. That rule specifies that the law of the jurisdiction where the contract was executed should control. However, in recent years this doctrine has been criticized and, in several jurisdictions, discarded in favor of the more flexible "significant relationships" test.

[The court quotes here the significant relationship test for contracts from the modern Second Restatement of Conflict of Laws. This test lists five separate factors for a court to consider in making a choice of law determination. The place where a contract is made is only one of those five factors.]

. . .

Sturiano argues that in this modern, migratory society, choice of law rules must be flexible to allow courts to apply the laws which best accommodate the parties and the host jurisdiction. She contends that the archaic and inflexible rule of lex loci contractus does not address modern issues or problems in the area of conflict of laws. While it is true that lex loci contractus is an inflexible rule, we believe that this inflexibility is necessary to ensure stability in contract arrangements. When parties come to terms in an agreement, they do so with the implied acknowledgment that the laws of that jurisdiction will control absent some provision to the contrary. This benefits both parties, not merely an insurance company. The view espoused in the Restatement fails, in our opinion, to adequately provide security to the parties to a contract.

Although lex loci contractus is old, it is not yet outdated. The very reason Sturiano gives as support for discarding lex loci contractus, namely that we live in a migratory, transitory society, provides support for upholding that doctrine. Parties have a right to know what the agreement they have executed provides. To allow one party to modify the contract simply by moving to another state would substantially restrict the power to enter into valid, binding, and stable contracts. There can be no doubt that the parties to insurance contracts bargained and paid for the provisions in the agreement, including those provisions that apply the statutory law of that state.

We recognize that this Court has discarded the analogous doctrine of lex loci delicti with respect to tort actions[8] and limitations of actions.[9] However, we believe that the reasoning controlling those decisions does not apply in the instant case. With tort law, there is no agreement, no foreseen set of rules and statutes which the parties had recognized would control the litigation. In the case of an insurance contract, the parties enter into that contract with the acknowledgment that the laws of that jurisdiction control their actions. In essence, that jurisdiction's laws are incorporated by implication into the agreement. The parties to this contract did not bargain for Florida or any other state's laws to control. We must presume that the parties did bargain for, or at least expected, New York law to apply.

For these reasons, we answer the certified question concerning conflict of laws in the affirmative, limiting that answer to situations involving automobile insurance policies. . . .

8. *Bishop v. Florida Specialty Paint Co.*, 389 So. 2d 999 (Fla. 1980).
9. *Bates v. Cook, Inc.*, 509 So. 2d 1112 (Fla. 1987).

Concurrence by Justice GRIMES, joined by Justice OVERTON, in which Justice EHRLICH concurred in part.

The more I read of it the more I tend to agree with Dean Prosser when he said that "the realm of the conflict of laws is a dismal swamp, filled with quaking quagmires, and inhabited by learned but eccentric professors who theorize about mysterious matters in a strange and incomprehensible jargon. The ordinary court, or lawyer, is quite lost when engulfed and entangled in it."

The rule of lex loci contractus has been roundly criticized as mechanistic and unworkable in practice. It has seldom been applied to issues concerning the performance of a contract. While it is true that more states retain lex loci contractus than have abandoned it, perhaps this is so only because many of them have not addressed the issue in recent years. The emerging consensus, even in cases involving questions of contract validity, is to apply the most significant relationship test [the Second Restatement of Conflict of Laws].

In this complex area of law concerning which I claim no expertise, I am inclined toward the recommendations of the American Law Institute. Because contractual disputes arise in such a great variety of settings, rules of broad application cannot do justice to the various interests and expectations involved. While the application of the significant relationship test may be less certain, it reflects a more realistic standard by which a choice of laws may be made. Furthermore, I believe the majority's concern for predictability and the parties' right to know what the agreement provides is adequately taken into account by factors (d) (the protection of justified expectations) and (f) (certainty, predictability and uniformity of result) of section 6 of the Second Restatement which is made applicable [under the section that governs contracts].

I nevertheless agree with the result reached in the instant case because it would come out the same under the Second Restatement. . . .

Notes on

STURIANO v. BROOKS

1. The *Sturiano* majority suggested that the Restatement (First) is a more certain approach to horizontal choice of law decisions than the Restatement (Second) of Conflict of Laws, which allows consideration of such factors as the residence of the parties and the location of the subject matter of the contract. Do you agree with the suggestion that the Restatement (First) promotes predictability? As you read the other material related to the Restatement (First), consider whether the approach promotes sufficient flexibility as to render unpredictable court decisions applying the approach. Some argue that the exceptions and analytical "maneuver" techniques of the Restatement (First) make a broad range of results possible, perhaps the same range as available under other, purportedly more flexible methodologies. In evaluating the First Restatement materials, also consider whether the approach allows courts to integrate specific case equities and to avoid

insensitive, mechanical results. Is the *Sturiano* concurrence correct that a multifactor approach is a more realistic standard for modern life?

2. As the Florida Supreme Court explained in *Sturiano*, the majority believed it appropriate to have a different choice of law methodology for contract issues that arise in state courts than for tort or limitations issues. What do you think of this decision to have different choice of law methodologies in place in Florida?

3. Property

Both within and without the area of conflict of laws, courts evince a special solicitude for property. They show special concern for maintaining principles of property ownership, special concern with territorial power over property, and a willingness to make special rules to ensure the maintenance of legal order where property issues are concerned. This is particularly true where real property is concerned. Consistent with this general tendency to promote legal certainty and power over property, the Restatement (First) of Conflict of Laws reflects a not-so-subtle theme in its rules respecting property: apply the law of the state where the land is. As with other areas with the Restatement (First), however, what appears straightforward is always open for interpretation. Given the uniformity of the property rules, however, the courts tend to find room to maneuver by questioning whether the property rules apply at all. The case that follows the sample sections below illustrates this tendency.

From the Restatement (First) of Conflict of Laws, on the Subject of Property:

§214. Legal Effect and Interpretation of Words Used in an Instrument of Conveyance

(1) Words used in an instrument of conveyance of an interest in land which, by the law of the state where the land is, have a given operative effect irrespective of the intent of the conveyor, will be accorded such effect in any state.

(2) Words used in an instrument of conveyance of an interest in land which, by the law of the state where the land is, have a given operative effect unless a contrary intent is shown by admissible evidence, will be accorded such effect in any state.

(3) The meaning of words used in an instrument of conveyance of an interest in land which, by the law of the state where the land is, are accorded neither of the effects described in Subsections (1) and (2), is, in the absence of controlling circumstances to the contrary, determined in accordance with usage at the domicil of the conveyor at the time of the conveyance.

§215. Validity of Conveyance of Interest in Land

The validity of a conveyance of an interest in land is determined by the law of the state where the land is.

§216. *Capacity to Convey Interest in Land*

Capacity to make a valid conveyance of an interest in land is determined by the law of the state where the land is.

Comment:

a. If the grantor has capacity to make a valid conveyance according to the law of the state where the land is, it is immaterial that he has no capacity according to the law of the state of his domicil or of the state in which the conveyance is made.

b. If the grantor has no capacity to make a valid conveyance according to the law of the state where the land is, it is immaterial that he has capacity according to the law or the state of his domicil or of the state in which the conveyance is made.

c. If the law of the state in which the land is refers capacity to make a valid conveyance of an interest in land to the law of another state, the latter law determines capacity. The common law does not refer to another law, but the question may be presented in a civil law state or in a common law state as the result of statutes (see §8).

§217. *Formalities of Conveyance of Interest in Land*

The formalities necessary for the validity of a conveyance of an interest in land are determined by the law of the state where the land is.

§218. *Substantial Validity of Conveyance of Interest in Land*

Whether a conveyance of an interest in land, which is in due form and is made by a party who has capacity to convey it, is in other respects valid, is determined by the law of the state where the land is.

§220. *Effect of Conveyance of Interest in Land*

The effect upon interests in land of a conveyance is determined by the law of the state where the land is.

Illustrations:

1. A, domiciled in state Y, owner of Blackacre, which is situated in state X, conveys Blackacre to B. A dies. Whether A's widow is barred of dower by the conveyance is determined by the law of X.

2. Whiteacre, situated in state X, is held by A for life, remainder to the heirs of B. A is domiciled in state Y. A conveys Whiteacre to C. Whether this conveyance destroys the remainder is determined by the law of X.

§221. *Nature of Interest Created by Conveyance of Land*

The nature of the interest in land created by a conveyance is determined by the law of the state where the land is.

Comment:

a. Whether a conveyance without the use of words of inheritance passes a fee simple or a life estate or other estate depends upon the law of the state where the land is.

b. Whether a conveyance operates to pass a legal or an equitable estate depends upon the law of the state where the land is.

§225. *Mortgage on Land; By What Law Determined*

The validity and effect of a mortgage on land is determined by the law of the state where the land is.

Comment:

a. The capacity to make a valid mortgage, whether formal requirements of the instrument have been complied with, its validity in other respects and the character of the interests created in the mortgagee are determined, as in the case of conveyances in general, by the law of the state in which the land is. Thus, that law determines whether the creation of a valid mortgage requires a written document, a seal, witnesses, acknowledgment, or recording the conveyance; whether the consideration is sufficient; and whether the transaction gives the mortgagee a legal title, an equitable title or only a lien.

§235. *Power of Appointment of Land; How Exercised*

A power to appoint land by will or deed can be exercised only by a will or deed valid by the law of the state where the land is.

§237. *Effect of Marriage on Existing Interests in Land*

The effect of marriage upon interests in land owned by a spouse at the time of marriage is determined by the law of the state where the land is.

§245. *Inheritance of Land*

The law of the state where the land is determines its devolution upon the death of the owner intestate.

§247. *Claim of Adopted Child to Inherit*

Whether an adopted child is an heir and the extent to which he may inherit an interest in land is determined by the law of the state where the land is.

§249. *Will of Land*

The validity and effect of a will of an interest in land are determined by the law of the state where the land is.

§250. Revocation of Will of Land

The effectiveness of an intended revocation of a will of an interest in land is determined by the law of the state where the land is.

Hill v. Hill

262 A.2d 661 (Del. Ch. 1970)

DUFFY, Chancellor.

The action is one to enforce a pre-nuptial agreement which a surviving wife says she honored and her husband did not before he died.

A.

Plaintiff is Sara Gideon Hill, widow of Harry Murdock Hill. Defendants are the residuary legatees and devisees under Mr. Hill's will and the beneficiary of insurance policies on his life: his mother, Anna Mary Hill, his sister, Ruth M. Huhn, and his brother, Thomas Wallace Hill. All defendants have moved to dismiss the complaint on the ground that it fails to state a claim upon which relief can be granted.

Plaintiff alleges that she and Mr. Hill signed a contract on December 30, 1965 in Salisbury, Maryland, where they were married on the following day. He died domiciled in Delaware on October 20, 1967. The agreement was recorded in the Office of the Recorder of Deeds for Sussex County, Delaware, on March 12, 1968.

The agreement recites that the parties respectively own certain property: Mr. Hill owns real property in . . . Delaware, stocks, securities and insurance policies upon his life; his intended wife owns two properties in . . . Pennsylvania, one alone and another with her son as joint tenants with right of survivorship. The dispositive parts of the agreement state:

1. The intended husband will within thirty days after the marriage by proper deed convey all of his real property to him and the intended wife as tenants by the entireties.

2. The intended wife will within thirty days after the marriage takes place by proper deed convey her real estate situated on the South side of Springs Avenue in the Borough of Gettysburg, Pennsylvania, to her and the intended husband as tenants by entireties.

3. The intended husband will within thirty days after the marriage takes place transfer all of his stocks and securities, other than United States Savings Bonds, to him and the intended wife as joint tenants with right of survivorship.

4. The intended husband will, within thirty days after the marriage takes place have the intended wife named primary beneficiary on all life insurance policies owned by him at the time of the execution of this agreement insuring his life and agrees not to thereafter change the primary beneficiary on such policies during the lifetime of the intended wife. . . .

5. The intended wife agrees that if her said son, William Gideon, dies without issue during her lifetime, and if the aforesaid property situated on the West side of Baltimore Street in Gettysburg, Pennsylvania, then becomes vested in her by right of survivorship, she will within thirty days after the death of her said son by proper deed convey such real estate to her and the intended husband as tenants by entireties.

Mr. Hill's probated will directs that his residuary estate, which includes real property at Hearn's Pond (near Seaford), Delaware, be divided into equal parts and distributed to the three defendants.[1] He named his mother as the beneficiary of life insurance.

Plaintiff alleges that she performed all of the obligations required of her under the agreement and that she remained Mr. Hill's wife until his death. She says that Mr. Hill performed several of his obligations but he failed, through oversight, to: (a) execute a deed transferring the Hearn's Pond property to himself and plaintiff as tenants by the entireties, and (b) make plaintiff a beneficiary of all his life insurance.

Mrs. Hill says that she is the equitable owner of the Hearn's Pond property and she claims the proceeds of the insurance. She thus seeks an order requiring defendants to hold their respective interests in those properties in trust for her.

B.

The legal issue on which the parties are at odds is narrow and, as in so many disputes, the result turns, not on which side offers "better" law, but which of equally sound principles is applicable. The inquiry begins with a contract, which is the foundation of plaintiff's claim. That contract, say defendants, if it is enforced here, would affect title to Delaware real estate. For that reason, defendants argue, Delaware law governs and under our law the agreement is a nullity because it does not conform technically to 13 Del. C. §301, which provides:

A man and woman in contemplation of matrimony, by a marriage contract executed in the presence of two witnesses at least ten days before the solemnization of the marriage, may determine what rights each shall have in the other's estate during marriage and after its dissolution by death, and may bar each other of all rights in their respective estates not so secured to them, and any such contract duly acknowledged before any officer authorized to take acknowledgments may be recorded in the deed records in the office of the Recorder in any and all counties of the State.

Are the requirements of this statute applicable to the pre-nuptial agreement made in Maryland and relating to real property in Delaware and Pennsylvania? That is the issue forced by defendants' motion to dismiss and it is crucial because plaintiff tacitly concedes that the agreement was not executed in the presence of

---

1. Mr. Hill's will is dated August 8, 1967 and, apparently, the property at Hearn's Pond was the only real estate he owned.

two witnesses at least ten days before the date of marriage, and it was not duly acknowledged before an officer authorized to take acknowledgments.

It is well established that the law of the situs of real property determines the effect of actions involving its ownership. . . . But the agreement between the Hills can hardly be characterized as a title document or as a document designed to in some way directly affect title to Delaware real estate. It is certainly true that the agreement concerns real estate and that it commits the parties to do something about real estate in two different states. And that points up its true nature, which is this: in contemplation of marriage the Hills promised each other to take certain specified acts as to stock, securities, life insurance — and real estate. That is what the contract said, that is what the parties expected it to accomplish. I therefore find applicable the principles stated in 16 Am. Jur. 2d, Conflict of Laws §15.

> It has been broadly stated that contracts or executory contracts relating to real property are governed by the law of the jurisdiction or place where the property is located. However, a distinction is made between contracts directly affecting title to real property, which are to be so construed according to the law of the state where the property is situated, and contracts which while relating to real property, do not directly affect the title to or an interest in the property itself but are purely personal. Agreements of the latter nature are governed by the usual rules of contracts, and will not be influenced by the lex rei sitae.

The same distinction is made by the Restatement (First) Conflict of Laws §340, which provides:

> The law of the place of contracting determines the validity of a promise to transfer or to convey land.

. . .

Neither the purpose nor the effect of the agreement was to act as an instrument of conveyance. It was simply an agreement whereby two people prior to marriage decided to fix their respective interests in real property, securities and life insurance proceeds. In short, the agreement was a "personal contract" as opposed to one directly affecting real property and under Delaware choice of law rules, the law of the place of making the contract determines whether or not it is enforceable. Since the agreement was made in Maryland, the law of that State governs its validity.[2]

. . .

The Maryland Court of Appeals has recently reviewed the law as to pre-nuptial agreements and in *Hartz v. Hartz*, 248 Md. 47, 234 A.2d 865 (1967) Chief Judge Hammond wrote:

2. It should also be said that I am unaware of any Delaware policy which precludes recognition or enforcement of the agreement. 13 Del. C. §301 is permissive in language and does not purport, by its terms, to state the only cognizable procedure for creating a valid pre-nuptial agreement. The law of the State where it was made attaches obligations to what the Hills did, and Delaware public policy does not prohibit enforcement of those obligations here.

The law on the point in Maryland is clear and well established. The validity, propriety and, indeed, favor in the eyes of the law of antenuptial agreements settling or barring property rights of the parties is recognized.

Defendants not having shown any reason why the agreement is invalid under Maryland law, it follows that their motion to dismiss the complaint must be denied.

[On appeal of this ruling, the Supreme Court of Delaware affirmed the Court of Chancery, on the basis of the Chancellor's opinion. *Hill v. Hill*, 269 A.2d 212 (1970).]

Notes on
HILL v. HILL *AND THE SITUS RULE*

1. As you will note from a review of the Restatement (First) rules governing real property, the rules reflect a slavish respect for the dominance of the jurisdiction that serves as a situs of the property. Is this emphasis appropriate? While the situs rule is subject to criticism, commentators note that it is crucial to title recording systems in the United States. Since those systems are established according to the territorial location of property, land purchasers (and their title companies) are able to assume that legal questions are governed by situs law in performing title searches. *See, e.g.*, ROBERT LEFLAR, AMERICAN CONFLICTS LAW 410-411 (1968). Other arguments in favor of the situs rule are similarly territorial, noting that the situs jurisdiction has the greatest control and interest in the property. Whatever its justification, the situs rule has firm roots. In Chapter 4, you will note that the situs rule has a significant role in whether judgments respecting land are entitled to full faith and credit.

2. Given the absolute nature of the situs rule, courts wishing to avoid its force often use the contract/property sorting technique reflected in *Hill*. In fact, the court had a variety of characterizations it could have deployed to resolve the *Hill* issue. If the court characterized the case as presenting a real property or a probate issue, the court would have likely applied Delaware law, where the property was located and the will was being probated. If characterized as presenting a marriage issue, the case would have called for application of the law where the marriage was celebrated — Maryland — and the court would have thus reached the same result as it did by applying the law where the contract was made. Do you agree that the court was correct in characterizing the dispute as a contract problem, rather than one arising in property or marriage? Does it matter that the flaws that could have proven determinative to the case pertained to formalities of making the contract?

3. In choosing the contract characterization, the *Hill* Court used the distinction between a contract to convey or transfer title to real estate (for which the situs rule would apply) and executory contracts that require a

transfer of property (for which a contract choice of law rule would apply). Sometimes this distinction is framed as separating contracts pertaining to personal obligations and contracts pertaining directly to real property. Is this distinction helpful and determinate — or is it overformalistic and indeterminate? In a case dealing with a similar issue pertaining to an antenuptial contract in *Kyle v. Kyle*, 128 So. 2d 427 (Fla. 1961), the court came to an opposite conclusion from that reached in *Hill*—determining that compliance with the contract principles of the place of contracting (Canada) was not sufficient to allow a contractual clause to undermine the property rights of a woman that existed under the law of the place where the property was located. Choosing to characterize the issue as one arising under property law, the court concluded that "the agreement had a direct relationship to certain real property . . . and affects title to it." *Kyle*, 128 So. 2d at 431. Couldn't similar reasoning have supported a result contrary to the one reached in *Hill*?

4. The First Restatement rules regarding personal property (also called personalty) generally point to the law of the state where the personal property is located. Not surprisingly, courts get around this orientation through characterization and other techniques. Thus, for example, a contract for the sale of personal property may be subject to the contract rules. Moreover, a particularly troublesome aspect of personal property is its capacity to be moved. Accordingly, courts often look to the domicile of a decedent at death in adjudicating questions of succession to personalty. Similarly, domicile also tends to play a role in adjudicating the interest of one spouse in another's personalty. Even more problematic is intangible property, to which the Restatement (First) generally applies the situs rule, even though courts sometimes encounter considerable difficulty ascertaining the actual location of such intangibles as a bank account, an interest in a corporation, or intellectual property. Sometimes state law will provide a fictional presumption regarding the location of such intangibles.

PROBLEM 2-12: JESSICA'S PROPERTY TRANSACTION

Jessica was born in State J, and has lived there throughout her life. At the time of her birth, Jessica's grandmother gave her an acre of land (which is located in State L), placing Jessica's name on the deed. When Jessica turned 17 years old, she decided that she needed to raise money for her college education. Just a few days after her seventeenth birthday, she found a buyer for the acre of land, Ben, who lived in State J. While in State J, Jessica agreed to sell the property to Ben, accepted payment for the property from Ben, and signed a deed giving Ben title to the property. Under the law of State J, Jessica was old enough to convey property and to enter into a valid contract. Under the law of State L, however, Jessica had neither the capacity to enter into a valid contract nor the capacity to convey property until she reached 18. After having finished the transaction (but before she turned 18), Jessica learned that the purchase price was far below market value. She wishes to set aside the transaction, and has filed suit in a jurisdiction that applies the Restatement (First). Which law will govern whether the conveyance is effective?

PROBLEM 2-13: MRS. BARRIE'S WILL

Mrs. Barrie was a resident of Illinois, and executed a will that left her property to her church. Some of the property included 100 acres of land in Iowa. Her will was properly signed and witnessed in Illinois, but was found after her death with the word "cancelled" written on its face. Under the laws of Illinois, the will was deemed void and her property devised to her heirs under the Illinois law of intestate succession. Under the laws of Iowa, however, the will remained in effect and her property could be distributed as specified in the will. Under the Restatement (First), which law should govern the disposition of the Iowa property?

PROBLEM 2-14: A TALE OF ADOPTED GRANDCHILDREN

Victoria had two children, Austin and Alice. Alice had two children of her own, whom Victoria adored. Austin married and fathered one child, Betsy. He also adopted his wife's daughters from a prior marriage, Janet and Jane. Austin's mother, Victoria, did not like Janet and Jane.

While she was domiciled in State V, Victoria visited a lawyer, who drew up a will that stated that she left her estate to her surviving children and the "issue" of her deceased children. Most of Victoria's property was in State V, but she owned one valuable piece of land in State L. At the time she reviewed the will, she asked her lawyer whether Janet and Jane would be considered "issue." Referring to case law in State V, the lawyer said that Janet and Jane were not "issue" because they had been adopted. Victoria replied "good," and signed the will according to all of the formalities required in State V. She told several people during her life that she was not leaving any of her estate to Janet and Jane.

Victoria died and her will was filed for probate in State V, which follows the Restatement (First). Victoria was predeceased by Austin, and thus the question arose as to whether Janet and Jane would inherit anything under her will. As correctly identified by Victoria's lawyer at the time of the will signing, State V did not recognize Janet and Jane as "issue" because they were adopted. State L, however, does recognize adopted children and grandchildren as "issue." Case law in both State V and State L contains many statements regarding the importance for courts overseeing the probate of wills to give effect to the intention of the testatrix or testator. Should the court in State V allow Janet and Jane to inherit anything from Victoria's estate?

4. *Marriage*

Marriage presents a complex constellation of questions ranging from public policy concerns implicating the validity of a union to the role that the marriage status plays in determining rights to support, child custody, inheritance, and other privileges associated with marriage. The role of the Restatement (First) rules in these matters is complicated. From a solely traditional viewpoint, the Restatement (First) rules represent an uneasy compromise between the vision of marriage as contract — to be governed by the jurisdiction where the marriage is celebrated — and the vision of marriage as status — to be governed by the principles of morality and public policy of the jurisdiction where the parties are domiciled. In today's world, the complexities are magnified because the First Restatement principles continue to influence the governing standards for marriage even in those jurisdictions that no longer follow the First Restatement. Furthermore, in some instances, the First Restatement rules are outmoded and even downright unconstitutional. The First Restatement rules, nonetheless, have played a key role in setting the stage for modern choice of law problems, including those raised by same-sex marriage and assisted reproductive technology. Consider the following cross-section of the Restatement (First) rules, and pay particular attention to how the rules defer to place of celebration in establishing the "contractual" formalities of marriage and to place of domicile in governing those public policy matters that control the "status" of marriage.

From the Restatement (First) of Conflict of Laws, on the Subject of Marriage:

§121. *Law Governing Validity of Marriage*

Except as stated in §§131 and 132, a marriage is valid everywhere if the requirements of the marriage law of the state where the contract of marriage takes place are complied with.

Comment:

a. Section 131 applies to remarriage after divorce. Section 132 applies to polygamous, incestuous, and abhorrent marriages.

b. Analysis of marriage. Marriage, by the law of all Christian countries, is based upon the consent of the parties. There are, therefore, two legal steps in the creation of the status in a common law state: the mutual consent to the marriage, forming the contract of marriage; and the legal creation of the relationship predicated by some law upon the valid consent of the individuals concerned to take each other as husband and wife.

c. The marriage contract. The contract of marriage comprises any form of mutual consent from a formal ceremony to a mere exchange of written or oral promises, which may be required by the law of the place where the ceremony takes place or the promises are exchanged. For cases of marriage by proxy or by correspondence, see §§124 and 125.

   d. The marriage status. Since the domestic status of marriage is governed, like all domestic status, by the law of the domicil or domicils of the parties, it is that law which ultimately creates the marriage status. Because the domicils of the parties concerned might have different laws in this respect, this would lead to great difficulty, if it were not for the fact that all Anglo-American states agree in creating the status of marriage (except in rare cases considered in §§131 and 132) in every case where there is a contract of marriage valid in the state where the contract is made.

   . . .

§122. Requirements of State of Celebration

   A marriage is invalid everywhere if any mandatory requirement of the marriage law of the state in which the marriage is celebrated is not complied with.

§123. "Common Law" Marriage

   A marriage without any formal ceremony is valid everywhere if the acts alleged to have created it took place in a state in which such a marriage is valid.

§129. Evasion of Requirement of Domicil

   If the requirements of the law of the state of celebration are complied with, the marriage is valid everywhere, except under the circumstances stated in §§131 and 132, although the parties to the marriage went to that state in order to evade the requirements of the law of their domicil.

§131. Remarriage After Parties to Divorce Both Forbidden to Remarry

   If by statute each party to a divorce granted in the state is forbidden for a certain time or during the life of the other party, to marry again, and one party goes into another state and marries, being permitted to do so by the law of that state, the marriage is valid everywhere, even in the state where the divorce was granted, unless

   (a) the time named is a time within which an appeal to a higher court may be taken; or

   (b) the statute which forbids the parties to marry is interpreted as being applicable to the marriage of domiciliaries in another state; or

   (c) the marriage is otherwise invalid under the rule stated in §132.

§132. Marriage Declared Void by Law of Domicil

   A marriage which is against the law of the state of domicil of either party, though the requirements of the law of the state of celebration have been complied with, will be invalid everywhere in the following cases:

   (a) polygamous marriage,

(b) incestuous marriage between persons so closely related that their marriage is contrary to a strong public policy of the domicil,

(c) marriage between persons of different races where such marriages are at the domicil regarded as odious,[17]

(d) marriage of a domiciliary which a statute at the domicil makes void even though celebrated in another state.

Comment:

a. Rationale. The rule stated in this Section recognizes the paramount interest of the domiciliary state in the marital status. As stated in §121, a marriage is in most particulars governed by the law of the state where the marriage contract takes place. If the requirements of such state are complied with, the marriage will usually be valid in every state. Under the rule stated in this Section, however, if a marriage violates a particularly strong policy of the domicil of either party, it will be invalid not only in the domicil of the party in question but in the state in which the marriage contract was rendered and any other state.

b. Clauses (a), (b) and (c) state respects in which a marriage may offend a strong policy of the domiciliary state. This statement, however, is not intended to be an exclusive enumeration and if a marriage offends a strong policy of the domicil in any other respect, such marriage will be invalid everywhere.

c. By polygamous marriage is meant any marriage where one of the parties has a living undivorced spouse, even though that party in good faith believes otherwise. Whether a marriage comes within the rules stated in clauses (a) and (b) is to be determined by the law of the domicil or domicils of the parties. Whether a mixed marriage is so odious as to fall within clause (c) is to be determined in view of the social customs of the domicil or domicils of the parties. Such a marriage, to be odious as the word is used in this Section, must not only be prohibited by statute but must offend a deep-rooted sense of morality predominant in the state.

§133. Effect of Foreign Marriage

Except as stated in §134, a state will give the same effect to a marriage created by the law of another state that it gives to a marriage created by its own law.

Comment:

a. Section 134 excepts from the rule stated in this Section marriages contrary to the public policy of the forum.

b. The status of marriage having been validly created, the incidents which result from the existence of the status (see §134, Comment *a*) are determined by the law of the place where they are sought to be exercised.

Illustration:

1. A and B are married in state X and come to live in state Y. By the law of X, a man may forcibly control his wife; by the law of Y he may not. A, in Y, uses force to control B's acts. He is guilty of battery.

---

17. Is this provision valid today? *See Loving v. Virginia,* 388 U.S. 1 (1967) (finding prohibition of marriage between members of different races to violate the Fourteenth Amendment's due process and equal protection clauses).

c. Interests collateral to the marriage, as for instance marital interests in property or the legitimacy of issue, will be determined by the law under which such interests are created (see §§237, 238, 289, 290 and 137).

Illustration:

1. A and B are married in state X. A owns land in state Y. A dies. B's interests in the land are determined by the law of Y.

§134. Marriage Contrary to Public Policy

If any effect of a marriage created by the law of one state is deemed by the courts of another state sufficiently offensive to the policy of the latter state, the latter state will refuse to give that effect to the marriage.

Comment:

a. Distinction between recognition of marriage and according a particular effect. The action of the state in refusing to give effect to a marriage on the ground stated in this Section does not deny the validity of the marriage, but precludes the enjoyment within the state of some particular right or other interest incident to the marriage. Wherever a particularly strong policy of the state of the domicil at the time of the marriage is concerned, the validity of the marriage may be involved under the rule stated in §§131 and 132. If the question is that of giving effect to a marriage in a state where neither party was domiciled at the time of the marriage, the case does not fall under §§131 or 132 but is within the rule stated in this Section.

b. The mere fact that the foreign marriage would have been contrary to the statute of the forum had it occurred within the state, does not make it so offensive to local policy as to be refused enforcement.

PROBLEM 2-15: A JUSTICE OF THE PEACE CEREMONY

A is a man from State A. B is a woman from State B. A and B were married in the State of Celebration by a justice of the peace. Under the law of State of Celebration, a justice of the peace has the power to marry a man and a woman. Neither State A nor State B recognize a marriage performed by a justice of the peace as valid, but instead require the marriage to be performed by a judge of higher status than justice of the peace or by a representative of religious clergy. After the marriage in State of Celebration, the couple bought a house in State B and moved in together, intending to make the place their home. B works for an employer in State B and is trying to get A (whom she believes to be her husband) covered under B's work health care insurance. B's employer takes the position that A and B are not validly married. All jurisdictions apply the First Restatement of Conflict of Laws. Is B's employer correct that A and B should not be considered validly married in State B?

In re May's Estate

114 N.E.2d 4 (N.Y. 1953)

LEWIS, Chief Judge.

In this proceeding, involving the administration of the estate of Fannie May, deceased, we are to determine whether the marriage in 1913 between the respondent Sam May and the decedent, who was his niece by the half blood which marriage was celebrated in Rhode Island, where concededly such marriage is valid is to be given legal effect in New York where statute law declares incestuous and void a marriage between uncle and niece.

The question thus presented arises from proof of the following facts: The petitioner Alice May Greenberg, one of six children born of the Rhode Island marriage of Sam and Fannie May, petitioned in 1951 for letters of administration of the estate of her mother Fannie May, who had died in 1945. Thereupon, the respondent Sam May, who asserts the validity of his marriage to the decedent, filed an objection to the issuance to petitioner of such letters of administration upon the ground that he is the surviving husband of the decedent and accordingly, under section 118 of the Surrogate's Court Act, he has the paramount right to administer her estate. Contemporaneously with, and in support of the objection filed by Sam May, his daughter Sirel Lenrow and his sons Harry May and Morris B. May who are children of the challenged marriage filed objections to the issuance of letters of administration to their sister, the petitioner, and by such objections consented that letters of administration be issued to their father Sam May.

The petitioner, supported by her sisters Ruth Weisbrout and Evelyn May, contended throughout this proceeding that her father is not the surviving spouse of her mother because, although their marriage was valid in Rhode Island, the marriage never had validity in New York where they were then resident and where they retained their residence until the decedent's death.

The record shows that for . . . more than five years prior to his marriage to decedent the respondent Sam May had resided in . . . Wisconsin; that he came to New York in . . . 1912, and within a month thereafter he and the decedent both of whom were adherents of the Jewish faith went to . . . Rhode Island, where, on January 21, 1913, they entered into a ceremonial marriage performed by and at the home of a Jewish rabbi. The certificate issued upon that marriage gave the age of each party as twenty-six years and the residence of each as "New York, N.Y." Two weeks after their marriage in Rhode Island the respondent May and the decedent returned to . . . New York, where they lived as man and wife for thirty-two years until the decedent's death in 1945. Meantime the six children were born who are parties to this proceeding.

A further significant item of proof to which more particular reference will be made was the fact that in Rhode Island on January 21, 1913, the date of the marriage here involved, there were effective statutes which prohibited the marriage of an uncle and a niece, excluding, however, those instances of which the present case is one where the marriage solemnized is between persons of the Jewish faith within the degrees of affinity and consanguinity allowed by their religion.

In Surrogate's Court, where letters of administration were granted to the petitioner, the Surrogate ruled that although the marriage of Sam May and the decedent in Rhode Island in 1913 was valid in that State, such marriage was not only void in New York as opposed to natural law but is contrary to the provisions of subdivision 3 of §5 of the Domestic Relations Law. Accordingly the Surrogate concluded that Sam May did not qualify in this jurisdiction for letters of administration as the surviving spouse of the decedent.

At the Appellate Division the order of the Surrogate was reversed on the law and the proceeding was remitted to Surrogate's Court with direction that letters of administration upon decedent's estate be granted to Sam May who was held to be the surviving spouse of the decedent. In reaching that decision the Appellate Division concluded that the 1913 marriage of Sam May and the decedent in Rhode Island, being concededly valid in that State, is valid in New York where the degree of consanguinity of uncle and niece is not so close as to be repugnant to our concept of natural law, and that the statute, Domestic Relations Law §5, subd. 3, which declares such a marriage to be incestuous and void lacks express language which gives it extraterritorial force. The case comes to us upon appeal as of right by the petitioner and her two sisters Ruth Weisbrout and Evelyn May.

We regard the law as settled that, subject to two exceptions [cases within the prohibition of positive law; and cases involving polygamy or incest in a degree regarded generally as within the prohibition of natural law] and in the absence of a statute expressly regulating within the domiciliary State marriages solemnized abroad, the legality of a marriage between persons sui juris is to be determined by the law of the place where it is celebrated. . . .

The statute of New York upon which the appellants rely . . .

§5. Incestuous and void marriages

A marriage is incestuous and void whether the relatives are legitimate or illegitimate between either:

. . .

3. An uncle and niece or an aunt and nephew.

If a marriage prohibited by the foregoing provisions of this section be solemnized it shall be void, and the parties thereto shall each be fined not less than fifty nor more than one hundred dollars and may, in the discretion of the court in addition to said fine, be imprisoned for a term not exceeding six months. Any person who shall knowingly and wilfully solemnize such marriage, or procure or aid in the solemnization of the same, shall be deemed guilty of a misdemeanor and shall be fined or imprisoned in like manner.

Although the New York statute quoted above declares to be incestuous and void a marriage between an uncle and a niece and imposes penal measures upon the parties thereto, it is important to note that the statute does not by express terms regulate a marriage solemnized in another State where as in our present case, the marriage was concededly legal. In the case at hand, as we have seen, the parties to the challenged marriage were adherents of the Jewish faith which, according to Biblical law and Jewish tradition made the subject of proof in this case permits a marriage between an uncle and a niece; they were married by a Jewish rabbi in the State of Rhode Island where, on the date of such marriage in 1913 and ever since, a statute forbidding the marriage of an uncle and a niece was expressly qualified by the following statutory exceptions appearing in 1913 in Rhode Island General Laws:

> §4. The provisions of the preceding sections shall not extend to, or in any way affect, any marriage which shall be solemnized among the Jews, within the degrees of affinity or consanguinity allowed by their religion.
>
> §9. Any marriage which may be had and solemnized among the people called Quakers, or Friends, in the manner and form used or practised in their societies, or among persons professing the Jewish religion, according to their rites and ceremonies, shall be good and valid in law; and wherever the words "minister" and "elder" are used in this chapter, they shall be held to include all of the persons connected with the society of Friends, or Quakers, and with the Jewish religion, who perform or have charge of the marriage ceremony according to their rites and ceremonies.

As section 5 of the New York Domestic Relations Law . . . does not expressly declare void a marriage of its domiciliaries solemnized in a foreign State where such marriage is valid, the statute's scope should not be extended by judicial construction. Indeed, had the Legislature been so disposed it could have declared by appropriate enactment that marriages contracted in another State which if entered into here would be void shall have no force in this State. Although examples of such legislation are not wanting, we find none in New York which serve to give subdivision 3 of section 5 of the Domestic Relations Law extraterritorial effectiveness. Accordingly, as to the first exception to the general rule that a marriage valid where performed is valid everywhere, we conclude that, absent any New York statute expressing clearly the Legislature's intent to regulate within this State marriages of its domiciliaries solemnized abroad, there is no "positive law" in this jurisdiction which serves to interdict the 1913 marriage in Rhode Island of the respondent Sam May and the decedent.

As to the application of the second exception to the marriage here involved between persons of the Jewish faith whose kinship was not in the direct ascending or descending line of consanguinity and who were not brother and sister we conclude that such marriage, solemnized, as it was, in accord with the ritual of the Jewish faith in a State whose legislative body has declared such a marriage to be "good and valid in law," was not offensive to the public sense of morality to a degree regarded generally with abhorrence and thus was not within the inhibitions of natural law.

    . . .

DESMOND, Judge (dissenting).

It is fundamental that every State has the right to determine the marital status of its own citizens. . . . Exercising that right, New York has declared in section 5 of the Domestic Relations Law that a marriage between uncle and niece is incestuous, void and criminal. Such marriages, while not within the Levitical forbidden degrees of the Old Testament, have been condemned by public opinion for centuries . . . and are void, by statute in (it would seem) forty-seven of the States of the Union (all except Georgia, see Martindale-Hubbell, Law Digests, and except, also, that Rhode Island, one of the forty-seven, exempts from its local statute "any marriage which shall be solemnized among the Jews, within the degrees of affinity or consanguinity allowed by their religion"). It is undisputed here that this uncle and niece were both domiciled in New York in 1913, when they left New York for the sole purpose of going to Rhode Island to be married there, and that they were married in that State conformably to its laws (see above) and immediately returned to New York and ever afterwards resided in this State. That Rhode Island marriage, between two New York residents, was, in New York, absolutely void for any and all purposes, by positive New York law which declares a strong public policy of this State.

The general rule that "a marriage valid where solemnized is valid everywhere" (see Restatement, Conflict of Laws §121) does not apply. To that rule there is a proviso or exception, recognized, it would seem, by all the States, as follows: "unless contrary to the prohibitions of natural law or the express prohibitions of a statute." Section 132 of the Restatement of Conflict of Laws states the rule apparently followed throughout America: "A marriage which is against the law of the state of domicil of either party, though the requirements of the law of the state of celebration have been complied with, will be invalid everywhere in the following cases: . . . (b) incestuous marriage between persons so closely related that their marriage is contrary to a strong public policy of the domicil." . . . New York, as a sovereign State with absolute powers over the marital status of its citizens, has enacted such legislation, but we, by this decision, are denying it efficacy.

. . . Section 5 of the Domestic Relations Law, the one we are concerned with here, lists the marriages which are "incestuous and void" in New York, as being those between parent and child, brother and sister, uncle and niece, and aunt and nephew. All such misalliances are incestuous, and all, equally, are void. The policy, language, meaning and validity of the statute are beyond dispute. It should be enforced by the courts.

Catalano v. Catalano

170 A.2d 726 (Conn. 1961)

MURPHY, Justice.

The plaintiff appealed to the Superior Court from the action of the Probate Court for the district of Hartford in denying her application for a widow's allowance for support from the estate of Fred Catalano. The parties have stipulated as to the facts, and the Superior Court has reserved the matter for the advice of this court.[1]

The material facts are these: Fred Catalano, a widower and citizen of this state, was married on December 8, 1951, in Italy to the plaintiff, his niece, an Italian subject. Such a marriage was prohibited by §87 of the Italian Civil Code, but since the parties obtained a legal dispensation for the marriage from the Italian authorities, it was valid in Italy. Fred returned to this country. The plaintiff remained in Italy until 1956, when she joined Fred and they came to Hartford, where they lived as husband and wife until his death in 1958. A son was born to the couple. The plaintiff claims to be the surviving spouse of the decedent and, as such, entitled to an allowance for support under the provisions of [Connecticut law].

The determination of the question propounded depends upon the interrelation and judicial interpretation of three statutes, §§46-1, 46-6, 53-223.[2]

Legislation prohibiting the marriage of uncle and niece was originally enacted . . . in 1702 . . . [providing] that no man should marry any woman within the degrees of kindred specified, including that of uncle and niece. . . . It has been the declared public policy of this state continuously since 1702 to prohibit marriages of uncle and niece and declare them void.

It is the generally accepted rule that a marriage valid where the ceremony is performed is valid everywhere. There are, however, certain exceptions to that rule, including one which regards as invalid incestuous marriages between persons so closely related that their marriage is contrary to the strong public policy of the domicil though valid where celebrated. Restatement Conflict of Laws §132 (b). That exception may be expressed in the terms of a statute or by necessary implication. Section 46-6 only validates foreign marriages which could have been legally entered into in this state at the time they were contracted. As §46-1 created an impediment to the union of uncle and niece in this state, the plaintiff and her uncle lacked the legal capacity which §46-6 makes a prerequisite to the validity, in this state, of such a marriage as theirs. A state has the authority to declare what marriages of its citizens shall be recognized as valid, regardless of the fact that the marriages may have been entered into in foreign jurisdictions where they were valid.

---

1. The question upon which advice is desired is: "Was Maria Catalano the surviving spouse of Fred Catalano under the laws of the State of Connecticut as of the date of his death on October 11, 1958, and as such was she qualified to receive support under section 25-250 of the General Statutes, Revision of 1958?"

2. Sec. 46-1. Kindred who shall not marry. No man shall marry his mother, grandmother, daughter, granddaughter, sister, aunt, niece, stepmother or stepdaughter, and no woman shall marry her father, grandfather, son, grandson, brother, uncle, nephew, stepfather or stepson; and, if any man or woman marries within the degrees aforesaid, such marriage shall be void.

Sec. 46-6. When marriages in foreign countries are valid. All marriages where one or both parties are citizens of this state, celebrated in a foreign country in conformity with the law of that country, shall be valid, provided each party would have legal capacity to contract such marriage in this state. . . .

Sec. 53-223. Incest. Every man and woman who marry or carnally know each other, being within any of the degrees of kindred specified in section 46-1, shall be imprisoned in the State Prison not more than ten years.

To determine whether the marriage in the instant case is contrary to the public policy of this state, it is only necessary to consider that marriages between uncle and niece have been interdicted and declared void continuously since 1702 and that ever since then it has been a crime for such kindred to either marry or carnally know each other. At the time of the plaintiff's marriage in 1951, the penalty for incest was, and it has continued to be, imprisonment in the state prison for not more than ten years. This relatively high penalty clearly reflects the strong public policy of this state. We cannot completely disregard the import and intent of our statutory law and engage in judicial legislation. The marriage of the plaintiff and Fred Catalano, though valid in Italy under its laws, was not valid in Connecticut because it contravened the public policy of this state. The plaintiff therefore cannot qualify under §46-250 as the surviving spouse of Fred Catalano.

We answer the question propounded "No."

MELLITZ, Justice (dissenting).

We are dealing here with the marriage status of a woman who was validly married at the place of her domicil and who, so far as the record discloses, was entirely innocent of any intent to evade the laws of Connecticut. Mrs. Catalano was a resident and domiciliary of Italy when her uncle came from America and married her in Italy. Although he returned to America soon after the marriage, she continued to reside in Italy for almost five years before she came to America and took up her residence in Connecticut, where she gave birth to a son. There is no suggestion anywhere in the record that at the time of the marriage she intended to come to America, that the parties had any intention of coming to live in Connecticut, or that the marriage was entered into in Italy for the purpose of evading the laws of Connecticut. If a marriage status resulting from a valid marriage, such as the one here, is to be destroyed, the issue bastardized, and the relations of the parties branded as illicit, it should follow only from an explicit enactment of the legislature, giving clear expression to a public policy which compels such harsh consequences to ensue from a marriage entered into under the circumstances disclosed here.

The cases cited in the majority opinion which deal with the question we have here are all cases where the parties went to a foreign state to evade the law of the domicil and the marriage celebrated in the foreign state was refused recognition in the place of their domicil when they returned to live there after the marriage. . . .

The provisions of §46-1, prohibiting marriages within specified degrees of consanguinity, apply only to marriages celebrated in Connecticut and are not given extraterritorial operation by the provisions of §46-6. The first sentence of §46-6 . . . does not purport to invalidate or declare void in Connecticut foreign marriages celebrated in contravention of the laws of Connecticut. It is a validating statute and declares valid the marriage of a citizen of Connecticut celebrated in a foreign country in conformity with the law of that country, provided each party would have legal capacity to contract the marriage in Connecticut. Capacity, in the sense employed in the statute, is defined in 2 Beale, Conflict of Laws §121.6, as follows: "By capacity to enter into a marriage is meant a quality which legally prevents the person in question marrying anyone; it does not refer to some quality which prevents the particular marriage in question, though the person may marry someone else. A typical example of capacity is nonage, or having a living spouse. A typical example of a quality which prevents the particular marriage, though the person has capacity to marry, is consanguinity." That it is capacity in this sense which is meant in the first sentence of §46-6 finds confirmation in the fact that, under other portions of the statute, a valid foreign marriage of a Connecticut citizen requires, in addition to certain specified formalities, only that the parties have the qualities which entitle them to obtain a marriage license in Connecticut.[3]

The presentation of the license certificate to the officiating clergyman operates to give him authority to celebrate the marriage in the foreign country. Nothing in these provisions of the statute requires that the persons to be married under them have capacity to contract the particular marriage in this state. There is no requirement under §46-5, which deals with marriage licenses, that, as a prerequisite to the obtaining of a license, the relationship to each other of the parties to be married should be made known or disclosed to the registrar. If, therefore, the parties comply with the requirements of §46-5 and obtain a license pursuant thereto, a marriage celebrated in a foreign country in conformity with the provisions of §46-6 will be recognized as valid.

The majority opinion incorrectly gives to §46-6 the effect of the provisions of the Uniform Marriage Evasion Act, 9 U.L.A. 480, which was never adopted in this state. The act was approved in 1912 by the national conference of commissioners on uniform state laws. The first section provided: "If any person residing and intending to continue to reside in this state who is disabled or prohibited from contracting marriage under the laws of this state shall go into another state or country and there contract a marriage prohibited and declared void by the laws of this state, such marriage shall be null and void for all purposes in this state with the same effect as though such prohibited marriage had been entered into in this state." . . . The legislature must be presumed to have been aware, in 1913, of the provisions of the uniform act, yet it did not adopt that act. Instead, it enacted §46-6. The language of §46-6 bears no resemblance to the language of the uniform act, and . . . cannot be given effect as declaring that a marriage which was contracted in a foreign country and which would be void if entered into in Connecticut shall have no force in this state.

---

3. Sec. 46-6. . . . All marriages when one or both parties are citizens of this state, celebrated in a foreign country, in the presence of the ambassador or minister to that country from the United States or in the presence of a consular officer of the United States accredited to such country, at a place within his consular jurisdiction, by any ordained or licensed clergyman engaged in the work of the ministry in any state of the United States or in any foreign country, shall be valid, provided a license certificate, such as is required by the laws of this state, shall have been obtained from the registrar of vital statistics of the town in this state to which one or both of the parties to such marriage belong; and such registrar is authorized to act in such matter. Such license certificate presented to such clergyman shall operate as a license for the celebration by him of such marriage in such foreign country, and the provisions of the laws of this state shall apply to such a license certificate, except that the return thereof shall be made to such registrar. . . .

I do not share the view that the public policy of this state requires or warrants the result reached by the majority. . . . In whatever terms "capacity," under the provisions of §46-6, may be conceived, it relates to the capacity of the parties to enter into the contract of marriage. After the marriage, the relation between the Catalanos became a status, no longer resting merely on contract. A contract of marriage is sui generis. It is simply introductory to the creation of a *status*, and what that *status* is the law determines. A contract executed in contravention of law may yet establish a *status* which the law will recognize, and, if one of the contracting parties were innocent of any intention to violate the law, may recognize as carrying with it in his favor the same rights and duties as if the contract had been entirely unexceptionable. Mrs. Catalano was innocent of any intent to violate our laws, and she is entitled to have recognition here of her marriage status, with all of the rights flowing from that status.

The answer to the question in the reservation should be "Yes."

Notes on
IN RE MAY'S ESTATE *AND* CATALANO v. CATALANO

1. Note that outcome in *Catalano* is likely not the most common answer to the question of whether to recognize marriages between close relatives where the marriage is valid where celebrated. The result of *May* appears to be preferred by courts—whether or or not they are applying more modern methodologies. *See, e.g., Ghassemi v. Ghassemi,* 998 So. 2d. 731 (La. Ct. App. 2008) (upholding first cousin marriage in the face of forum prohibition, concluding marriage does not violate strong state policy); *Mason v. Mason,* 775 N.E.2d 706 (Ind. Ct. App. 2002) (upholding first cousin marriage in the face of forum prohibition, concluding marriage does not violate strong state policy).

2. Is *May*'s result distinguishable from *Catalano*'s result? Is there anything about the *May* marriage—or the context in which it was being challenged—that might have made the Court more favorably disposed toward finding the *May* marriage valid than the *Catalano* court may have been toward the marriage in that case?

3. One possible distinction between *May* and *Catalano* is simply that the courts were interpreting different statutes and divining different statutory intent. The *May* majority declined to give the marriage prohibition effect outside the state (which courts refer to as extraterritorial effect) and the *Catalano* majority freely gave the statutory prohibition extraterritorial effect. The dissents in both cases, however, focused on this extraterritorial question in highlighting their differences with the majority. Did the dissents have the better arguments?

4. The parties in both *May* and *Catalano* were challenging the validity of the marriages in the context of probate. Yet the statutes referred to by both courts in evaluating the validity of the marriages were not designed to handle

probate matters. In fact, both cases concerned statutes that addressed the criminal law and domestic relations ramifications of the marriages—not policies related to support and inheritance. Is it fair to conclude that the intent of the legislature declared in one context (domestic relations and criminal law) should govern in an entirely different context (probate)? Might one argue that a uniform definition for all parts of a jurisdiction's law—statutes, case law, and constitutional provisions—is particularly important in the context of marriage? Does the status of marriage have ramifications that call for a uniform rule?

The United States Congress codified a uniform definition of the words "marriage" and "spouse" for the purpose of the United States Code. Enacted as part of the Defense of Marriage Act in 1996, the statutory definition derived from a desire to disapprove same-sex marriage. The statute provided:

> In determining the meaning of any Act of Congress, or of any ruling, regulation, or interpretation of the various administrative bureaus and agencies of the United States, the word "marriage" means only a legal union between one man and one woman as husband and wife, and the word "spouse" refers only to a person of the opposite sex who is a husband or wife.

1 U.S.C. §7. This definitional statute was cited in disputes implicating a broad range of same-sex partnerships issues, including health insurance coverage, immigration status, child rearing, income tax status, and judgment liens in bankruptcy. Yet courts have also used the statute outside of the same-sex context. Indeed, one court cited the statute's use of present tense in order to distinguish between food stamp eligibility of widowed spouses and eligibility of divorced spouses. *Aleman v. Glickman*, 217 F.3d 1191 (9th Cir. 2000). How important is it that, in all probability, no federal legislator who voted in favor of this definitional provision had any inkling that it would be used in this way to interpret the rights of widowed and divorced spouses in marriages between men and women? Ultimately, however, the United States Supreme Court invalidated the definition in *United States v. Windsor*, 133 S. Ct. 2675 (2013), holding that—for federal law purposes—the U.S. Constitution prohibited limiting the definition of marriage to the union of one man and one woman. Subsequently in *Obergefell v. Hodges*, 135 S. Ct. 2584 (2015), the Supreme Court held that state law prohibitions against same-sex marriage are also unconstitutional. *Obergefell* and the Defense of Marriage Act (DOMA) are discussed further in the Perspective on Same-Sex Marriage below.

PROBLEM 2-16: ANDY EVADES THE MARRIAGE IMPEDIMENT

Andy and Celine were married and were domiciled in State D. Andy told Celine that he wanted a divorce and they completed the necessary paperwork to make that happen. On January 2, a court in State D issued a judgment of divorce. State D has a statute that provides that a party to whom divorce has been granted in State D may not remarry within two years of the date of the decree in State D or any other other state. On February 14 of the same year, Andy went to State C and married Missy, who was domiciled in State D. State C did not have an impediment on the marriage between Andy and Missy. They returned to State D to live, and within a month the question arose whether they were validly married. Are Andy and Missy validly married under the rules of the Restatement (First)?

PROBLEM 2-17: ANOTHER STATE'S REAL PROPERTY

Jun and Mareko were married in State M. Mareko owned real property in State P. Mareko died in State M. Under the Restatement (First), which law governs whether Mareko has any interest in the property?

Sometimes analysis does not end with a court's conclusion under the First Restatement that no marriage exists under the laws of the place of celebration because some aspect of those laws was not satisfied. If the parties held themselves out as members of a community that recognizes common law marriage, then they may be able to acquire the status of spouse, despite problems with the place of celebration. *See, e.g., Kelderhaus v. Kelderhaus,* 467 S.E.2d 303, 305 (Va. Ct. App. 1996). Consider this proposition in evaluating the following problem.

PROBLEM 2-18: THE UNTIMELY DIVORCE

Franco was married to Marie in Michigan. They separated and moved to France. While in France, Franco met Francine and they decided to marry. Franco arranged with a lawyer to divorce Marie, filled out the papers, and was advised by the lawyer that the divorce would be final on May 31. That same year, on June 30, Franco and Francine married in France. A month later, on July 31, Franco received papers showing that the divorce had become final on July 15. Francine never heard about these papers and did not know that the divorce was being finalized later than expected. By the law of France, Franco and Francine were never married because Franco was still married when they celebrated and solemnized their marriage. France does not recognize common law marriages.

On August 15, Franco and Francine moved to State D in the United States, where they were domiciled until Franco died. State D recognizes common law marriage, deeming the parties to be married if they hold themselves out as husband and wife for two years, and if they take actions that reflect their sincere belief that they are in fact married. Franco and Francine lived together in State D, told their relatives, neighbors, and employers that they were married, opened bank accounts in joint names, and filed federal tax documents declaring themselves a married couple.

Continuing to reside in State D for two more years, the couple bought a house together there. Franco decided that he should take out an insurance policy to ensure that Francine could cover the mortgage payments in the event of his death. He did in fact take out the life insurance policy, but neglected to name a beneficiary. Under the terms of the policy, the default beneficiary would be Franco's "spouse" and, if he had no "spouse," then his next of kin. Franco died in an accident shortly after obtaining the policy. Franco's next of kin — his brother Greedy — claims that he is entitled to the insurance proceeds, arguing that Francine was not really Franco's lawful spouse. Under the Restatement (First), is Greedy correct?

PERSPECTIVE ON SAME-SEX MARRIAGE: AN OVERVIEW OF HISTORY AND LEGAL ISSUES IN THE UNITED STATES

At the time the Restatement (First) of Conflict of Laws was written in the 1930s, the drafters likely did not anticipate how its rules might apply to same-sex marriage issues. In fact, the same-sex marriage movement did not become widespread until the 1970s. Once the movement took hold, legal principles such as the Restatement (First) rules, more modern choice of law rules, and myriad other laws needed to be interpreted, reinterpreted, challenged, and sometimes discarded as issues arose regarding the legitimacy and effect of unions between individuals of the same sex.

Whenever social, political, or technological change occurs, existing legal rules must accommodate — sometimes dramatically. The same-sex marriage movement has produced particularly far-reaching consequences because marriage has many aspects in human society. First and foremost, marriage reflects rules regarding partner selection. While many of those rules are cultural, some — such as those regarding age of consent to marry — are codified. Other aspects of marriage include (1) procedures for formalizing the partners' commitment to the marriage (including licensing as well as civil and religious wedding rituals); (2) the economic and financial rules for forming the partnership, running a household, owning property, and rearing children; and (3) the principles and procedures governing dissolution (including dissolution by reason of death and volition). Because the United States family law system treats marriage as a legal status, and not just a contractual relationship, partners do not have the prerogative to enunciate all of their own rules governing their marriage. Rather, they must accept rules prescribed by law and culture. Indeed, their decision to "marry" includes a decision to be bound by preexisting rules.

One of the first initiatives in the same-sex marriage movement advocated for local governments and private employers to recognize nonmarital relationships called "domestic partnerships." Domestic partnerships generally had a legal status that enabled partners to meet practical needs, such as coverage under a partner's health insurance, without challenging established social norms of opposite-sex marriage. Usually, domestic partnership did not require a ceremony, did not legally change the financial relationship between the partners, and did not implicate marital property law.

The marriage equality movement began to grow in the 1990s as the number of same-sex couples in committed partnerships increased. After courts in Hawaii recognized the rights of same-sex couples to marry under the state's marriage laws, Congress passed the Defense of Marriage Act (DOMA). Enacted in 1996, DOMA defines a marriage for federal law purposes as an opposite-sex union only. DOMA thus eliminated the possibility that same-sex marriages would be recognized under federal law, disqualifying the participants in those marriages from treatment as married individuals for the purposes of such federal laws as the Bankruptcy Code and the Internal Revenue Code. DOMA further provided:

> No State, territory, or possession of the United States, or Indian tribe, shall be required to give effect to any public act, record, or judicial proceeding of any other State, territory, possession, or tribe respecting a relationship between persons of the same sex that is treated as a marriage under the laws of such other State, territory, possession, or tribe, or a right or claim arising from such relationship.

28 U.S.C. §1738(c). This second component of DOMA provided federal imprimatur to a state's decision not to recognize a same-sex marriage celebrated and recognized in another jurisdiction. Thus, where the issue of the validity of a same-sex marriage celebrated in one state was raised in a court proceeding in another state, the court invoked its own public policy exception to recognition of the marriage, knowing that DOMA provided federal authority for doing so.

Since the Hawaii decision and the congressional reaction, social and legal struggle over same-sex marriage continued in the United States. Court battles raged, state legislative initiatives were passed and defeated, and state constitutions were amended. Different forms of same-sex unions proliferated, some essentially equivalent to opposite-sex marriages, and some with reduced benefits and recognition. Marriage equivalents were generally called either civil unions or domestic partnerships. States providing marriage equivalents usually required the parties to register their union and represent that the partners to the union did not belong to any other union. State law often provided that partners wishing to dissolve their union would have to use the same divorce procedures as opposite-sex couples. Other states chose not to recognize marriage equivalents, but instead instituted registration schemes that provided limited marriage rights and duties for same-sex partners.

The resulting mosaic of laws governing same-sex unions in the United States created a great deal of confusion. Adding to the uncertainty, state laws were a moving target, frequently changing as American society struggled toward equilibrium on the issue. DOMA reinforced this uncertainty, since it ensured that the rights and responsibilities extended in the state where the legal relationship was created would not necessarily be recognized in another state of the Union.

This variety of laws and uncertainty gave rise to many conflict of laws issues implicating the incidents of marriage. Many legal issues pertaining to the incidents of marriage — property ownership, rights to spousal benefits, inheritance, taxation, medical decisionmaking, parentage presumptions, child custody, adoption rights, and the like — turn on the question of whether a marriage is valid. Thus, courts confronting these issues often faced the task of deciding which set of state law rules governing validity should prevail. If, after evaluating competing laws, a court determined that the governing law validated the marriage, then the court next had to determine how that status affected the particular matter in dispute. (So, for example, a determination that two individuals were validly married could result in the court awarding inheritance rights to a putative spouse rather than a child of the deceased.) Overlaid on the choice of law issue on marriage validity was the question of marriage recognition. Even though a jurisdiction may not have deemed a marriage valid under its own laws, the jurisdiction may have choosen nonetheless to recognize another jurisdiction's view that the parties were married. Why would a jurisdiction have extended such recognition? Several important motivations could be at work: deference to a sister state, understanding of the need for uniformity of legal regulation, or respect for the individual rights of parties who claim the status of spouses.

Two decisions of the United States Supreme Court eliminated much of this uncertainty, complexity, and turmoil. First the Supreme Court decided *United States v. Windsor*, 133 S. Ct. 2675 (2013), which declared unconstitutional DOMA's federal law definition of marriage as limited to a one man and one woman. Thereafter, the Court agreed in *Obergefell v. Hodges* to review cases presenting the following two questions: (i) whether the Fourteenth Amendment requires a state to license a marriage between individuals of the same sex; and (2) whether a state must recognize such a marriage if validly entered in a sister state. As to the first question, the Court held that the Due Process and Equal Protection Clauses of the Fourteenth Amendment to the United States Consitution prohibited a state from refusing to recognize same-sex marriages under its own law. Relying principally on the Due Process Clause, the Court ruled that principles of individual dignity and the right to autonomy required same-sex partners to enjoy the right to marry. As to the second question, the Court held that "there is no lawful basis for a State to refuse to recognize a lawful same-sex marriage performed in another State on the ground of its same-sex character."

Several questions remained after *Obergefell.* First, although the decision unquestionably provided constitutional guarantee for the right of same sex couples to marry, some jurisdictions took the position that this guarantee did not necessarily extend to the incidents of marriage. The United States Supreme Court, however, appears to have undercut this position. In *Pavan v. Smith*, 582 U.S. ——— (2017), the Court held that a state rule that requires a child's birth certificate to list the non-biological father if he is married to the biological mother must be extended to same-sex spouses. In so holding, the Court emphasized that the Constitution entitles same-sex couples to civil marriage "on the same terms and conditions as opposite-sex couples."

Another question that remained after *Obergefell* concerned the status of marriage alternatives such as civil unions and domestic partnerships. The general consensus is that questions regarding these constructs will diminish over time. This is particularly true in states that repealed their laws governing marriage alternatives in the wake of *Obergefell*. Some issues may remain, however, for those who entered into a union before *Obergefell*. So, for example, some jurisdictions have shown a willingness to extend the provisions of divorce and property distribution laws to those who wish to dissolve their civil unions or domestic partnerships, while this matter is not so clear in other jurisdictions. Moreover, as concerns of transgendered individuals have recently come to the fore, additional issues arise as laws struggle to accommodate challenges raised by such matters as gender transitions, gender reassignment surgery, and gender nonconformity. *Obergefell* did not speak directly to this issue.

Further discussion of *Obergefell* appears in Chapter 3 regarding United States constitutional constraints on choice of law and in Chapter 4 regarding the role of judgments law in recognition of the validity of a marriage and its incidents.

5. *Structural Mechanics and Escape Valves*

The subject matter rules surveyed above provide most of the raw material for conflict of laws analysis under the First Restatement. Yet a number of questions arise as to how to choose and apply those subject matter rules. Those questions are answered by other parts of the Restatement (First) rules, some of which lay out guidelines for the mechanics of First Restatement reasoning. The rules address such matters as: What law governs procedural questions? How does one pick which subject matter category of Restatement rules governs a particular legal issue? When a Restatement (First) rule designates another jurisdiction's law to govern, does that mandate include the other jurisdiction's choice of law rules? What if a forum court just cannot bring itself to apply another jurisdiction's law, which the forum believes is against its public policy?

While designed to provide necessary guidance, these structural principles often "loosen the joints" of First Restatement reasoning. As such, the rules have taken the nickname "escape valves" given by several generations of conflict of laws thinkers: the notion being that the structural rules enable judges to avoid the outcome apparently dictated by the rigid subject matter rules. Some bemoan the apparent sacrifice in uniformity and predictability that the escape valves accomplish. Others point out that these rules give courts instruments for manipulation and result-oriented decision making. As you come to understand these mechanical principles, ask yourself whether these accusations are correct. Do the structural concepts reviewed below make possible a more just result in the cases?

Are the courts abusing the concepts? Would the same result-oriented decision making take place in the absence of these concepts?

a. Substance and Procedure

From the Restatement (First) of Conflict of Laws, on the Subject of Procedure:

§584. Determination of Whether Question Is One of Procedure

The court at the forum determines according to its own Conflict of Laws rule whether a given question is one of substance or procedure.

§585. What Law Governs Procedure

All matters of procedure are governed by the law of the forum.

§588. Parties

The law of the forum determines who may and who must sue and be sued.

One of the essential choices a court must make in resolving a choice of law issue under the First Restatement is categorizing the particular issue as "substantive" or "procedural." As the Restatement Rules set forth above make clear, this particular categorization can have significant consequence. The problem, however, is categorization is sometimes notoriously difficult. First is the problem of how the categories shall be defined. Next is the question whether the two categories should be mutually exclusive or whether rules might be envisioned along a continuum ranging from purely substantive to purely procedural.[18] Sometimes a particular rule can even be viewed as substantive for some purposes and procedural for another. This last problem is illustrated in the case that follows.

Sampson v. Channell

110 F.2d 754 (1st Cir. 1940)

MAGRUDER, J.

On this appeal the question presented may be stated simply, but the answer is not free from difficulty. A car driven by defendant's testator collided in Maine with a car driven by the plaintiff, injuring both the plaintiff and his wife, who was a passenger. The wife sued and recovered judgment. . . . In this, the husband's action, the jury found specially that the plaintiff's injury was caused by the

---

18. For a persuasive argument that despite the analytical appeal of viewing most rules as falling into the grey area between pure substance and pure procedure, the consequences of the characterization often require courts to stick to a "black-white" approach. Jennifer S. Hendricks, *In Defense of the Substance-Procedure Dichotomy*, 89 WASH. U. L. REV. 103 (2011).

negligence of defendant's testator, but brought in a general verdict for the defendant on the issue of contributory negligence. Judgment was entered for the defendant.

The action was brought in the federal district court for Massachusetts, there being the requisite diversity of citizenship. On the issue of contributory negligence the plaintiff requested the court to charge the jury, in accordance with the local Massachusetts rule, that "the burden of proving lack of care on the part of the plaintiff is on the defendant." This the court declined to do, but upon the contrary charged, in accordance with the Maine law, that the burden was upon the plaintiff to show affirmatively that no want of ordinary care on his part contributed to cause his injuries. The sole question raised is as to the correctness of this charge, and refusal to charge as requested.

Inquiry must first be directed to whether a federal court, in diversity of citizenship cases, must follow the applicable state rule as to incidence of burden of proof. If the answer is in the affirmative, the further point to be considered is whether the applicable state rule here is that of Massachusetts, where the action was brought, or Maine, where the accident occurred.

It would be an over-simplification to say that the case turns on whether burden of proof is a matter of substance or procedure. These are not clean-cut categories. During the reign of *Swift v. Tyson*, 1842, 16 Pet. 1, the federal courts in diversity of citizenship cases consistently held that the defendant had the burden of proving the plaintiff's contributory negligence, even though the suit arose in a state whose local rule was the contrary. They avoided having to apply the local rule . . . by saying that burden of proof was not a mere matter of procedure but concerned substantive rights, as to which the federal courts on a matter of "general law" were free to take their own view. The question of classification also arose where suit was brought in one state on an alleged tort committed in another state. But here it was generally held, in the state courts at least, that burden of proof as to contributory negligence was a matter of procedure; hence the rule of the forum would be applied despite a contrary rule of the locus delicti. In these two groups of cases the courts were talking about the same thing and labelling it differently, but in each instance the result was the same; the court was choosing the appropriate classification to enable it to apply its own familiar rule.

. . .

It is apparent, then, that burden of proof does not fall within either category of "substance" or "procedure" by virtue of any intrinsic compulsion, but the matter has been made to turn upon the purpose at hand to be served by the classification. Therefore, inasmuch as the older decisions in the federal courts, applying in diversity cases the federal rule as to burden of proof as a matter of "general law," are founded upon an assumption no longer valid since *Erie Railroad Co. v. Tompkins*, 304 U.S. 64, their classification of burden of proof as a matter of substance should be re-examined in the light of the objective and policy disclosed in the *Tompkins* case.

The opinion in that case sets forth as a moving consideration of policy that it is unfair and unseemly to have the outcome of litigation substantially affected by the fortuitous existence of diversity of citizenship. Hence, the greater likelihood there is that litigation would come out one way in the federal court and another way in the state court if the federal court failed to apply a particular local rule, the stronger the urge would be to classify the rule as not a mere matter of procedure but one of substantive law falling within the mandate of the *Tompkins* case. There will be, inescapably, a twilight zone between the two categories where a rational classification could be made either way, and where Congress directly, or the Supreme Court under authority of . . . 28 U.S.C.A. §§726b, 723c, would have power to prescribe a so-called rule of procedure for the federal courts. . . .

It seems to be said in *Francis v. Humphrey, D.C.*, 25 F. Supp. 1, 4, and was suggested by counsel in the case at bar, that the question whether in diversity of citizenship cases burden of proof is to be classified as a matter of procedure or substantive law is to be determined by following the classification made by the courts of the state. . . . But once that is determined, the rule is the same whether it is labeled substantive law or procedure. Furthermore, as already pointed out, such a classification by the state court for one purpose does not mean that the classification is valid for another purpose. Surely the question whether a particular subject-matter falls within the power of the Supreme Court to prescribe rules of procedure under the Act of 1934, or is a matter of substantive law governed by the doctrine of the *Tompkins* case, cannot be foreclosed by the label given to the subject-matter by the state courts.

The inquiry then must be: considering the policy underlying *Erie Railroad Co. v. Tompkins*, supra, would that policy best be served by classifying burden of proof as to contributory negligence as a matter of procedure or substantive law? The incidence of burden of proof may determine the outcome of the case. This is true where the evidence is conflicting and the jury is not convinced either way. It is more pointedly true where, as sometimes happens, the injured person dies and no evidence is available on the issue of contributory negligence. If, in such a case, the burden of proof is on the defendant, the plaintiff wins, assuming the other elements of the cause of action are established. If the burden is on the plaintiff, however, the defendant wins. Assuming the state rule to be one way and the federal rule the other, then the accident of citizenship becomes decisive of the litigation. The situation seems to call for the application of the rule in the *Tompkins* case. There is no important counter-consideration here, for the state rule can be easily ascertained and applied by the federal court without any administrative inconvenience. In thus concluding that for this purpose the incidence of the burden of proof as to contributory negligence is to be classified as a matter of substantive law, we are in harmony with the spirit of the *Tompkins* case, and at the same time are adhering to the classification maintained in an unbroken line of federal court decisions under *Swift v. Tyson*, supra. Federal courts in other circuits have held, since the *Tompkins* decision, that the state rule as to burden of proof must now be applied in diversity of citizenship cases.

. . .

Thus far, the case has been discussed as though suit had been brought in the federal court sitting in the state where the alleged tort occurred. But there is the complicating factor that the accident occurred in Maine and suit was brought in Massachusetts. This makes it necessary to consider three further points:

First, if the plaintiff had sued in a Massachusetts state court, would the Massachusetts Supreme Judicial Court have allowed the application of the Maine rule as to burden of proof? The answer is, no. The Court would have said that burden of proof is a matter of procedure only, and would have applied the Massachusetts rule that the burden is on the defendant to establish the plaintiff's contributory negligence. Such was the holding in *Levy v. Steiger*, 124 N.E. 477, and *Smith v. Brown, Mass.*, 19 N.E.2d 732. . . . It follows, therefore, that the unimpeachable law of Massachusetts in the case at bar is, that in a suit brought in Massachusetts the burden of proof as to contributory negligence is on the defendant, despite the contrary rule applicable in Maine where the accident occurred.

. . .

Until the point is finally ruled upon by the Supreme Court, lower courts must piece out as best they can the implications of the *Tompkins* case. The theory is that the federal court in Massachusetts sits as a court coordinate with the Massachusetts state courts to apply the Massachusetts law in diversity of citizenship cases. . . . The powerful argument by Holmes, J., dissenting, in *Black & White Taxi Co. v. Brown & Yellow Taxi Co.*, 276 U.S. 518, cited with approval by the majority opinion in the *Tompkins* case, seems to be applicable to that portion of the Massachusetts common law relating to conflict of laws quite as much as to the common law of contracts or torts. Except in the limited range of cases . . . where state court decisions on points of conflict of laws are subject to reversal by the United States Supreme Court under the federal constitution, the rules applicable to conflict of laws are not "a transcendental body of law outside of any particular state but obligatory within it." If the federal court in Massachusetts on points of conflict of laws may disregard the law of Massachusetts as formulated by the Supreme Judicial Court and take its own view as a matter of "general law," then the ghost of *Swift v. Tyson*, supra, still walks abroad, somewhat shrunken in size, yet capable of much mischief. In the case at bar, it is difficult to see that any gain in the direction of uniformity would be achieved by creating a discrepancy between the rules of law applicable in the Massachusetts state and federal courts, respectively, in order to bring the law of the Massachusetts federal court in harmony with the law that would be applied in the state courts of Maine.

Our conclusion is that the court below was bound to apply the law as to burden of proof as it would have been applied by the state courts in Massachusetts.

This result may seem to present a surface incongruity, viz., the deference owing to the substantive law of Massachusetts as pronounced by its courts requires the federal court in that state to apply a Massachusetts rule as to burden of proof which the highest state court insists is procedural only. The explanation is that reasons of policy, set forth in the *Tompkins* case, make it desirable for the federal court in diversity of citizenship cases to apply the state rule, because the incidence of burden of proof is likely to have a decisive influence on the outcome of litigation; and this is true regardless of whether the state court characterizes the rule as one of procedure or substantive law. Certainly the federal court in Massachusetts cannot treat burden of proof as a matter of procedure in order to disregard the

Massachusetts rule, and then treat it as substantive law in order to apply the Maine rule. Under the conclusion we have reached, if suit were brought in Massachusetts, the state and federal courts there would be in harmony as to burden of proof; and if suit were brought in Maine, the state and federal courts there would likewise be in harmony on this important matter. It is true that the rule applied in the Maine courts would not be the same as the rule applied in the Massachusetts courts. But this is a disparity that existed prior to *Erie Railroad v. Tompkins,* supra, and cannot be corrected by the doctrine of that case. It is a disparity that exists because Massachusetts may constitutionally maintain a rule of conflict of laws to the effect that the incidence of burden of proof is a matter of "procedure" to be governed by the law of the forum. *Levy v. Steiger,* supra.

For error in the instructions given to the jury on the burden of proof, the judgment must be reversed and the cause remanded for further proceedings not inconsistent with this opinion. . . .

Notes on
SAMPSON v. CHANNELL

1. After *Erie R.R. v. Tompkins,* the Supreme Court spent several decades clarifying the scope of the decision. *Sampson v. Channell* was decided well before this clarifying case law — much of which is reviewed in Chapter 3. Nonetheless, the *Sampson* court's reasoning remains remarkably accurate today, particularly its clear-eyed distinction between the substance/procedure characterization for the purpose of choosing between state and federal law (vertical choice of law or *Erie* purposes) and the substance/procedure characterization for the purpose of choosing between state laws (horizontal choice of law). Nonetheless, the Court's emphasis on the outcome determinative effect of the burden of proof does not reflect further refinements of the *Erie* doctrine. The outcome determination test sweeps too broadly many contexts: if the parties are litigating vigorously the question of whether a particular rule should apply or not, one can assume that it will have an important effect on outcome, regardless of which label — substance or procedure — the rule bears. At the same time, the *Sampson* court accurately projected the result in *Klaxon Co. v. Stentor Manufacturing Co.,* 313 U.S. 487 (1941), which held that a court exercising diversity of citizenship jurisdiction should apply the forum state's conflict of law rules governing horizontal choice of law. *Klaxon* is discussed further in Chapter 3.

2. In deciding that burden of proof could be substantive for *Erie,* vertical choice of law purposes, and procedural for horizontal choice of law purposes, the *Sampson* court pointed out that different values and concerns underlie the choice of law inquiry for the two situations. It is therefore important to pin down those varying values and concerns. As an initial matter, it may be helpful to consider that the vertical choice of law between state and federal law often occurs in diversity of citizenship cases, when the

federal court is acting as a neutral arbiter of claims that otherwise would be litigated in state court. In this instance, federal courts view their role as mimicking what would occur in an unbiased state forum. This concern is not crucial to the horizontal choice of law inquiry—which focuses on whether there are compelling reasons not to apply forum state law.

3. Why are courts inclined to apply their own procedural rules? Are there normative judgments attached to substantive rules that are usually absent from procedural rules? If so, perhaps a forum court can apply its procedural rules without interfering with out-of-state rights and responsibilities.

4. How might you define a procedural rule for horizontal choice of law purposes? A venerable conflict of laws scholar, Walter Wheeler Cook, ventured the following test for distinguishing between substance and procedure:

> If we admit that the "substantive" shades off by imperceptible degrees into the "procedural," and that the "line" between them does not "exist," to be discovered merely by logic and analysis, but is rather to be drawn so as best to carry out our purpose, we see that our problem resolves itself substantially into this: How far can the court of the forum go in applying the rules taken from the foreign system of law without unduly hindering or inconveniencing itself?

W.W. Cook, The Logical and Legal Basis of the Conflict of Laws 166 (1942).

5. The Restatement (First) classifies many matters as procedural, including the following: judicial jurisdiction, forms of action (e.g., whether a suit presents a tort or a contract claim), capacity to be a litigant, service of process, designation of proper parties to a lawsuit, pleading, proof of facts, presumptions, inferences, trial by judge or jury, competency and credibility of witnesses, admissibility of evidence, execution of judgments, and statutes of limitations. Restatement (First) of Conflict of Laws §§586-606. Courts and litigants have perennially encountered difficulty classifying matters as procedural or substantive. Common problem areas include matters related to: immunity, statutes of frauds, testimonial privilege, remedies questions, parol evidence, survival of actions, and direct actions.

PROBLEM 2-19: WIRETAP EVIDENCE

Lurch Lynch was a journalist who worked on an investigative story concerning Fran Fraud. Lurch phoned Fran for a comment on the story while both were located in State A. Unbeknownst to Fran, Lurch recorded the telephone conversation. After the story was published, Fran sued Lurch in a State B court for defamation. State A makes it a misdemeanor to tape record a conversation without the consent of all participants. Where this proscription is violated, State A prohibits the tape recording or a transcript of the recording from being introduced into evidence in any proceeding. State B, however, has no such proscription and allows a court to introduce evidence of tape recorded conversations so long as one of the parties to the conversation consented to the taping.

The tape recorded conversation is unquestionably relevant to the defamation action pending in State B. Lurch argues that the State B court should admit the tape recorded conversation into evidence in the defamation proceeding, pointing out that he provided the requisite consent himself by making the tape. Should the State B court admit the evidence?

PROBLEM 2-20: DAMAGES LIMITATION

Kelly was a State A resident who bought a ticket to fly from State A to State B. The plane crashed in State B, Kelly died, and her estate sued for wrongful death in a State A court. State B had a law limiting recovery to $100,000 in any wrongful death action. This law's purpose is to protect insurance companies and defendants from run-away verdicts. State A's damages law, however, had no such limitation. The State A legislature considered enacting the limitation, but concluded that it would discourage meritorious lawsuits. Should the State A court apply the limitation on damages from State B's law to the case?

b.   Characterization

Because the Restatement (First) of Conflict of Laws presents a set of rules organized according to substantive category, the Restatement (First) approach to resolving conflicts formally requires a legal analyst to engage in the process of characterization. Given that the Restatement's subject matter categories are defined in terms of legal concepts such as contract, tort, and property, the legal analyst's first step in the choice of law process is to decide *which* area of law to identify with the legal issue in dispute. This process of matching a general label with a legal issue is sometimes called "primary characterization."

Once the legal analyst has settled on a primary characterization, she must turn to secondary characterization: determining which subset of rules should govern. For example, the analyst may conclude that a prenuptial agreement issue presents a contracts problem and not a marriage problem. Having chosen the "contract" label, however, she may encounter the additional decision whether the issue pertains to contract obligation or contract performance. *See* Restatement (First) of Conflict of Laws §358 comment *b* (discussing the process of characterizing whether a contract issue is one of obligation or performance). Alternatively, the analyst may need to wrestle with an even finer distinction, such as whether the issue implicates capacity to transfer property rather than capacity to make a contract to transfer property. *See* Restatement (First) of Conflict of Laws §333 comment *a* (discussing the process of characterizing facts that may be governed by these two capacity concepts).

Some argue that the characterization process renders the Restatement (First) complicated and indeterminate. The result, the argument continues, is to render the choice of law approach unpredictable and vulnerable to disingenuous manipulation. A more upbeat perspective views characterization as an opportunity for creative lawyering. Indeed, lawyers characterize all the time, whether it be by framing a problem in a brief, pitching an offer in a negotiation, spinning a legal disposition to the media, or reorienting parties' attention from one goal to another in mediating a dispute settlement.

And the good news is that the skills required for characterization are those you brought to law school — common sense as well as the ability to strategize and to brainstorm. Matching these tools with the formal rules presented in the Restatement (First) presents endless possibilities. You will have a chance to try your hand with characterization in a relatively elaborate problem below, entitled "A Characterization Carnival in the States of Humble and Sin." First, however, are two classic cases, which present different characterizations of similar legal problems. In evaluating the cases, consider how the courts reached apparently conflicting results as well as what techniques the courts used in framing the legal issues and selecting the corresponding choice of law rules.

Alabama G.S.R.R. Co. v. Carroll

11 So. 803 (Ala. 1892)

McCLELLAN, J.

[This is an action brought by a railway worker for injuries resulting from the negligence of a fellow worker in failing to detect a defect in a link between two train cars when the train left Alabama. The link broke and injured the plaintiff in Mississippi. In the first part of the opinion, set forth earlier in this chapter, the court noted that Mississippi common law provided that the employer would not be liable for the fellow employee's liability. Alabama, however, had legislatively changed this rule in the Employer's Liability Act. Apparently eager to get around the tort choice of law principle that the place of the injury (Mississippi) governs, the plaintiff emphasized that he formed his employment relationship with the defendant in Alabama.]

. . .

Another consideration . . . it is insisted . . . entitles this plaintiff to recover here under the [Alabama] employers' liability act for an injury inflicted beyond the territorial operation of that act. This is claimed upon the fact that at the time plaintiff was injured he was in the discharge of duties which rested on him by the terms of a contract between him and the defendant, which had been entered into in Alabama, and hence was an Alabama contract, in connection with the facts that plaintiff was and is a citizen of this state, and the defendant is an Alabama corporation. These latter facts — of citizenship and domicile, respectively, of plaintiff and defendant — are of no importance in this connection, it seems to us, further than this: they may tend to show that the contract was made here, which is not controverted and, if the plaintiff has a cause of action at all, he, by reason of them, may prosecute it in our courts. They have no bearing on the primary question of the existence of a cause of action, and, as that is the question before us, we need not further advert to the fact of plaintiff's citizenship or defendant's domicile.

. . .

The theory [of the plaintiff] is that the employers' liability act became a part of [the employment] contract, that the duties and liabilities which it prescribes became contractual duties and liabilities, or duties and liabilities springing out of the contract, and that these duties attended upon the execution whenever its performance was required, in Mississippi as well as in Alabama, and that the liability prescribed for a failure to perform any of such duties attached upon such failure and consequent injury wherever it occurred, and was enforceable here, because imposed by an Alabama contract, notwithstanding the remission of duty and the resulting injury occurred in Mississippi, under whose laws no liability was incurred by such remission. The argument is that a contract for service is a condition precedent to the application of the statute, and that, "as soon as the contract is made, the rights and obligations of the parties under the employers' act became vested and fixed," so that "no subsequent repeal of the law could deprive the injured party of his rights, nor discharge the master from his liabilities," etc. If this argument is sound, and it is sound if the duties and liabilities prescribed by the act can be said to be contractual duties and obligations at all, it would lead to conclusions, the possibility of which has not hitherto been suggested by any court or law writer, and which, to say the least, would be astounding to the profession.

. . .

[We conclude that] the duties and liabilities incident to the relation between the plaintiff and the defendant, which are involved in this case, are not imposed by, and do not rest in or spring from, the contract between the parties. The only office of the contract, under section 2590 of the Code, is the establishment of a relation between them, that of master and servant; and it is upon that relation, that incident or consequence of the contract, and not upon the rights of the parties under the contract, that our statute operates. The law is not concerned with the contractual stipulations, except in so far as to determine from them that the relation upon which it is to operate exists. Finding this relation, the statute imposes certain duties and liabilities on the parties to it, wholly regardless of the stipulations of the contract as to the rights of the parties under it, and, it may be, in the teeth of such stipulations. It is the purpose of the statute, and must be the limit of its operation, to govern persons standing in the relation of master and servants to each other, in respect of their conduct in certain particulars within the state of Alabama. Mississippi has the same right to establish governmental rules for such persons within her borders as Alabama, and she has established rules which are different from those of our law; and the conduct of such persons towards each other is, when its legality is brought in question, to be adjudged by the rules of the one or the other state, as it falls territorially within the one or the other. . . .

The foregoing views will suffice to indicate the grounds of our opinion that the rights of this plaintiff are determinable solely by the law of the state of Mississippi, and of our conclusion that upon no aspect or tendency of the evidence as to the circumstances under which the injury was sustained, and as to the laws of Mississippi obtaining in the premises, was the plaintiff entitled to recover.

Levy v. Daniels' U-Drive Auto Renting Co.

143 A. 163 (Conn. 1928)

WHEELER, C.J.

The complaint alleged these facts: The defendant, Daniels' U-Drive Auto Renting Company, Incorporated, rented in Hartford to Sack an automobile, which he operated, and in which Levy, the plaintiff, was a passenger. During the time the automobile was rented and operated, the defendant renting company was subject to section 21 of chapter 195 of the Public Acts of Connecticut, 1925, which provides:

> Any person renting or leasing to another any motor vehicle owned by him shall be liable for any damage to any person or property caused by the operation of such motor vehicle while so rented or leased.

While the plaintiff was a passenger, Sack brought the car to a stop on the main highway at Longmeadow, Mass., and negligently allowed it to stand directly in the path of automobiles proceeding southerly in the same direction his automobile was headed, without giving sufficient warning to automobiles approaching from his rear, and without having a tail light in operation, and when, due to inclement weather, the visibility was reduced to an exceedingly low degree. At this time the defendant Maginn negligently ran into and upon the rear end of the car Sack was operating, and threw plaintiff forcibly forward, causing him serious injuries. The specific acts of Maginn's negligence are set up at length in the complaint; it is not essential at this time to recite them. The plaintiff suffered his severe injuries in consequence of the concurrent negligence of both defendants.

The defendant demurred to the complaint upon several grounds, upon only one of which the trial court rested its decision; namely, that the liability of the defendant must be determined by the law of Massachusetts, which did not impose upon persons renting automobiles any such obligation as the Connecticut act did. . . .

It is the defendant's contention in support of this ground of demurrer that the action set forth in the complaint is one of tort, and, since Massachusetts has no statute like, or substantially like, the Connecticut act, it must be determined by the common law of that state, under which the plaintiff must prove, to prevail, the negligence of the defendant in renting a defective motor vehicle and in failing to disclose the defect. If this were the true theory of the complaint, the conclusion thus reached must have followed. "The locus delicti determined the existence of the cause of action." Under the law of Massachusetts, the plaintiff concededly would have a cause of action against Sack and Maginn for their tortious conduct in the operation of the cars they were driving. The plaintiff concedes the correctness of this. His counsel, however, construes the complaint as one in its nature contractual. The act makes him who rents or leases any motor vehicle to another liable for any damage to any person or property caused by the operation of the motor vehicle while so rented or leased. Liability for "damage caused by the operation of such motor vehicle" means [damage] caused by its tortious operation. This was undoubtedly the legislative intent; otherwise the act would be invalid. The plaintiff concedes this to be the true construction of these words, and the defendant acquiesces in this construction.

[T]he complaint alleges a tortious operation of the automobile rented to Sack by the defendant, causing the injuries to the plaintiff as alleged, and constituting an action ex delicto. The statute gives, in terms, the injured person a right of action against the defendant which rented the automobile to Sack, though the injury occurred in Massachusetts. It was a right which the statute gave directly, not derivatively, to the injured person as a consequence of the contract of hiring. The purpose of the statute was not primarily to give the injured person a right of recovery against the tortious operator of the car, but to protect the safety of the traffic upon highways by providing an incentive to him who rented motor vehicles to rent them to competent and careful operators, by making him liable for damage resulting from the tortious operation of the rented vehicles. The common law would not hold the defendant liable upon the facts recited in the complaint for the negligence of Sack in the operation of this automobile.

The statute made the liability of the person renting motor vehicles a part of every contract of hiring a motor vehicle in Connecticut. . . . A liability arising out of a contract depends upon the law of the place of contract, "unless the contract is to be performed or to have its beneficial operation and effect elsewhere, or it is made with reference to the law of another place."

. . .

If the liability of this defendant under this statute is contractual, no question can arise as to the plaintiff's right to enforce this contract, provided the obligation imposed upon this defendant was for the "direct, sole and exclusive benefit" of the plaintiff. The contract was made in Connecticut; at the instant of its making the statute made a part of the contract of hiring the liability of the defendant which the plaintiff seeks to enforce. The law inserted in the contract this provision. The statute did not create the liability; it imposed it in case the defendant voluntarily rented the automobile. Whether the defendant entered into this contract of hiring was his own voluntary act; if he did he must accept the condition upon which the law permitted the making of the contract. The contract was for the "direct, sole, and exclusive benefit" of the plaintiff, who is alleged to have been injured through the tortious operation of the automobile rented by the defendant to Sack. . . . The contract was made for him and every other member of the public. That the beneficiary was undisturbed because each of the public was a beneficiary is of no consequence. His injury determines his identity and right of action. . . . The demurrer should have been overruled.

Notes on
CARROLL *AND* LEVY

1. Compare the decisions of the *Carroll* and *Levy* courts on the characterization issue. Why might one say they are inconsistent?

2. Does it make a difference that the plaintiff in *Carroll* was bound by a contract to the defendant, but the *Levy* plaintiff was not? If anything, shouldn't this distinction have pointed to reverse results in both cases?

3. In both cases, the courts considered whether to incorporate a statute into a contract. One might try to reconcile the two decisions by highlighting differences in the statutes. In evaluating whether to incorporate the statutes into the contracts, both courts made reference to the "purpose" behind the statutes. How might this line of reasoning lead to reconciling the cases?

4. As we will see below, consideration of the purpose behind statutes proves crucial to the modern methodologies. How appropriate is this mode of analysis in the context of the territorial approach? Is a law's goal relevant to determine where parties' rights vest?

5. Between the two cases, which one has the more just result in terms of who bears the loss from the accidents? Could you argue that the Alabama legislature intended that the employer bear liability under facts of *Carroll*? By similar reasoning, might you also argue that the Connecticut legislature intended for defendants such as Daniels' U-Drive to incur liability under the circumstances of *Levy*? If so, that could shed some light on why some decisions seem to turn on characterization technique. Might one say that characterization technique allows courts to avoid inappropriate or unjust results of the traditional choice of law rules? Is it legitimate for courts to do this?

PROBLEM 2-21: A CHARACTERIZATION CARNIVAL IN THE STATES OF HUMBLE AND SIN

While on vacation in the State of Sin, Polly was handed a flyer promising a beautiful apartment at a local residence hotel, owned by individuals who were domiciled in the State of Sin. The flyer included the statement "Full Satisfaction or Your Money Back!" The flyer persuaded Polly to go to the residence hotel and to contract to stay in an apartment for a week. At the time of checking in, Polly signed a form that explained that she must pay $100 when checking into the apartment, but could pay for the remaining $400 rental upon her return home.

Polly was pleased that the rental included exclusive use of the beach in front her apartment. Nevertheless, she was not satisfied with her stay at the apartment because the mattress was infested with bed bugs. Indeed, Polly woke up each morning with welts on her body from the bug bites. Although the welts disappeared within an hour of waking, she found that first hour quite uncomfortable.

After her last night at the hotel, Polly packed her bags and several hours later left for her home state of Humble. Once home in Humble, she sent the residence hotel a money order for the $400 balance. She then regretted paying that sum, having remembered the flyer and talked to her friends about the bed bugs. While at her home in the State of Humble, Polly phoned the manager of the residence motel and demanded her money back. While sitting in his office in the State of Sin, the manager refused Polly's demand.

Polly filed suit in a state court in the State of Humble against the residence hotel, seeking to recover the money she paid for the apartment. The parties are disputing whether Polly may use the flyer to make out her case. Under the law of the State of Humble, a court may exercise its discretion to allow one of the parties to tell the jury about the flyer in order to demonstrate the precise terms of the rental contract. In exercising its discretion, a court applying Humble state law should consider the complexity of the case as well as the other material available to establish the terms of the contract. Under the law of the State of Sin, the flyer is "mere puffery" and is deemed inherently unreliable to establish the terms of a contract. For that reason, the courts in Sin have uniformly prevented admission of such flyers under all circumstances.

The State of Humble follows the Restatement (First) of Conflict of Laws. Given this assumption, which law (Humble state law or Sin state law) should govern the question whether the jury should hear about the flyer?

Epilogue to the Characterization Carnival Problem:

Some accuse courts of manipulating the characterization process in order to reach a predetermined result or to apply a law the court favors. Cynics might also argue that the process ensnares courts in a game of battling characterizations, deployed ruthlessly until a winning "spin" ultimately emerges. But can't one also see the process simply as courts' appreciating multiple perspectives on one problem and recognizing inherent ambiguities in perception, reasoning, and decision making? A key to success in navigating all human relations is acknowledging that others may possess a valid, competing point of view. And a key to successful lawyering is accepting ambiguity and the contingent nature of "truth." As nice as it would be to identify clear, uncomplicated, and unassailable resolutions to legal problems, such easy answers rarely exist. Since we cannot change this reality, perhaps we should embrace it. Having done so, we can enjoy the creative process of generating alternative "takes" on a legal problem and perhaps in the process learn to become more tolerant of others. And, as far as the judicial process is concerned, courts are well suited to ensure justice by tailoring legal principles to equities of a particular case. Might characterization technique allow courts to account best for interests of competing states and parties as they resolve disputes?

c. Renvoi

In re Estate of Joseph Damato

206 A.2d 171 (N.J. Super. Ct. App. Div. 1965)

LABRECQUE, J.A.D.

This is an appeal from a judgment of the Probate Division awarding the balances in two out-of-state bank accounts to decedent's son Philip Damato.

The facts are not in dispute. Decedent died on November 6, 1960, a resident of Paterson, New Jersey. Although he had been engaged in the wastepaper business in the Paterson area for many years, he also had business interests in Florida, including the operation of a small stable of race horses. His will was admitted to probate by the Surrogate of Passaic County. . . . [T]he executor filed a verified complaint praying, *inter alia,* for instructions as to the disposition of the balances remaining in two savings accounts in the Bank of Hollywood, Hollywood, Florida, which are the subject of the present controversy. . . .

Both Philip and James Damato were sons of the decedent. Philip worked for his father in the Paterson business and never knew of the accounts until after the death of his father. The passbooks for both accounts remained in decedent's possession and were found among his papers in Florida.

In awarding the balance in each account to Philip, the trial judge held that the transactions were governed by the law of Florida, their *situs,* and since Florida had adopted the rule of *In re Totten,* 179 N.Y. 112, 71 N.E. 748, 70 L.R.A. 711 (Ct. App. 1904), they were effective to pass the balance in each account to Philip upon the death of the decedent. . . .

The law is well settled that the creation of an *inter vivos* trust in money or securities, as distinguished from a testamentary trust, is governed by the law of the *situs* of the money or securities. The validity of an *inter vivos* trust of choses in action is determined by the law of the place where the transaction takes place. Restatement, *supra,* §294, subsec. (2).

The savings bank trust doctrine which the trial judge found to be dispositive of the issue before him was set forth in its present form in *In re Totten, supra,* to the effect that:

A deposit by one person of his own money in his own name and as trustee for another, standing alone, does not establish an irrevocable trust during the lifetime of the depositor. It is a tentative trust merely, revocable at will, until the depositor dies or completes the gift in his lifetime by some unequivocal act or declaration, such as delivery of the passbook or notice to the beneficiary. In case the depositor dies before the beneficiary without revocation, or some decisive act or declaration of disaffirmance, the presumption arises that an absolute trust is created as to the balance on hand at the death of the depositor.

In *Cutts v. Najdrowski, supra,* the court held that where a New Jersey resident opened an account in a New York savings bank in his name in trust for another, since the transaction was effective there, it was effective here to pass title to the balance in the account at the depositor's death, to the other person named, under the Totten trust doctrine. It was so held notwithstanding that such a transaction, had it been consummated here by a New Jersey resident, would have been invalid to pass title as violative of our statute of wills or as an ineffective gift *inter vivos.* Since then, however, N.J.S.A. 17:9A-216 has been held effective to pass valid title to the balance, at death, in such an account, to the beneficiary named.

The trial judge . . . held that the law of Florida applied. Concluding that the Totten trust doctrine had been adopted in Florida, he found that title to the bank balances passed to respondent. In so doing, he applied the substantive law of Florida found in *Seymour v. Seymour,* 85 So. 2d 726 (Fla. Sup. Ct. 1956).

Appellant urges that in thus applying Florida substantive law, instead of Florida conflict of laws, the trial judge fell into error. Specifically, it is argued that in *Seymour* the court was passing upon the validity, as a trust, of an account established by a domiciliary of Florida in a Florida bank, whereas we are here concerned with an account opened in Florida by a domiciliary of New Jersey. Under Florida conflicts law, the argument continues, the doctrine of *mobilia sequuntur personam* would be applied. Turning, then, to the law of decedent's domicile, New Jersey, appellant invokes *Swetland v. Swetland,* 105 N.J. Eq. 608 (Ch. 1930), *affirmed* 107 N.J. Eq. 504 (E. & A. 1931), as holding the transaction to be ineffective as a trust of the accounts in question. Appellant thus seeks to invoke the doctrine of *renvoi* to defeat respondent's claim.

However, we find it unnecessary to determine the Florida conflicts rule which would be applicable in view of the conclusions which follow.

We are satisfied that the trial judge correctly ruled that the substantive law of Florida should be applied to the transaction in question. . . . In the Restatement, Conflict of Laws, §7, p. 11 (1934), the rule as to conflicts is set forth as follows:

> Except as stated in §8 [concerning matters involving title to land and the validity of divorce decrees], when there is a difference in the Conflict of Laws of two states whose laws are involved in a problem, the rule of Conflict of Laws of the forum is applied;
>
>> (a) in all cases where as a preliminary to determining the choice of law it is necessary to determine the quality and character of legal ideas, these are determined by the forum according to its law;
>>
>> (b) where in making the choice of law to govern a certain situation the law of another state is to be applied, since the only Conflict of Laws used in the determination of the case is the Conflict of Laws of the forum, the foreign law to be applied is the law applicable to the matter in hand and not the Conflict of Laws of the foreign state.

In comment (d) to subsection (b) the learned authors note that, under the rule stated, the court of the forum, in a matter involving a contract, applies only the contract law of the other state, and this "may result in a decision contrary to that which would be reached by a court in that state, the law of which is being applied, by reason of the fact that a different Conflict of Laws rule prevails in the latter state."

The rule set forth in the Restatement seems grounded in reason for, if appellant's view were to be upheld, the courts would be faced with a possible unending circuity. Thus, if the Florida conflicts rule would refer the matter back to New Jersey, New Jersey, applying its full body of law, including its conflict rules, would again refer to the law of Florida. . . . The circular process would then begin anew and continue *ad infinitum*. Such was the problem posed in *In re Tallmadge*, 109 Misc. 696, 181 N.Y.S. 336 (Surr. Ct. 1919), where application of the *renvoi* doctrine was denied on account of its inconsistency with common law theory of the conflict of laws, its fundamental unsoundness and the chaos which would result from its application to conflicts arising between the laws of the several states.

Accordingly, we hold that where, in a proceeding in this State, the validity of a transaction in a foreign state — except one involving title to land or the validity of a divorce, as to which we make no determination — is, by virtue of our conflict of laws principles, made to depend upon the laws of such state, the foreign law to be applied is the law applicable to the matter in hand and not the conflict of laws of the foreign state. Restatement, Conflict of Laws, *supra*, §7(b).

The judgment is accordingly affirmed.

Notes on
DAMATO

1. In discussing the doctrine of renvoi, a few definitions and observations are helpful:

- *Internal law* includes all of a jurisdiction's law MINUS the jurisdiction's *choice of law* rules.
- *Internal law* is occasionally called "substantive law," but this phrase is best reserved for the puzzling debate about the distinction between substance and procedure.
- *Internal law* is also sometimes called *local law* or *domestic law.*
- A jurisdiction's *whole law* includes its *choice of law* rules PLUS its *internal law.*
- The term "renvoi" means "to return" or "to send back unopened." Thus, when a forum court "allows renvoi," it applies a foreign jurisdiction's whole law, which might include the choice of law mandate to apply the law of the forum. In that instance, where the forum court allows one round of renvoi, it applies only the forum's internal law.

2. Would the renvoi complication arise if all jurisdictions applied the same choice of law approach? Proper consideration of this question requires thought about what constitutes a jurisdiction's choice of law approach. Is it simply a forum court's formal declaration that the jurisdiction has adopted an official choice of law approach? Or does it include the jurisdiction's

interpretation of the rules of a particular approach, its favored characterizations of particular legal issues, and its case law precedent applying choice of law rules to particular facts?

3. Consider the following cartoon by writer/artist Paul Noth. Does the screen in the cartoon accurately depict what one would see if in fact one would do an ultrasound on the belly of a Russian nesting doll? Does the cartoon provide an accurate metaphor for the process of renvoi?

4. As noted in *Damato*, the Restatement (First) rule provides that where a forum's choice of law analysis points to another state's law, the forum should apply only the internal law of the other state. Restatement (First) of Conflict of Laws §7. The First Restatement makes an exception, however, for matters involving the validity of divorce decrees and title to land. *Id.* at §8. Why make an exception for these two categories? Think about the values that should guide a choice of law inquiry. One value frequently mentioned is avoiding forum shopping. The general Restatement (First) approach to renvoi actually encourages forum shopping, since filing suit in one jurisdiction can reward a litigant who does not like the result of another possible forum's choice of law inquiry. Does the exception for divorce and land title cases therefore discourage forum shopping in those contexts?

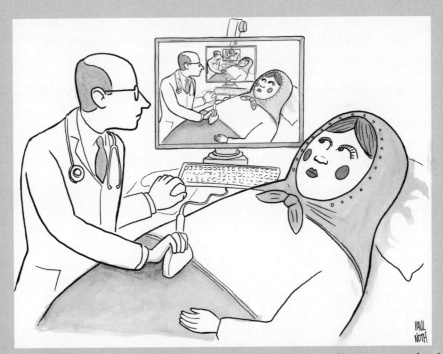

Figure 2-1: © Paul Noth/The New Yorker Collection http://www.cartoonbank.com.

5. If the forum state has a choice of law rule that points to the whole law of another jurisdiction, does it matter whether the second jurisdiction allows

renvoi? The answer is often yes. For example, jurisdiction 1 might point to jurisdiction 2, which allows renvoi. In that instance, jurisdiction 2 might point back to jurisdiction 1 or might point to jurisdiction 3. The former result is called "remission" and the second result is called "transmission." If transmission occurs, one must consider whether jurisdiction 3 would allow renvoi. If, on the other hand, jurisdiction 2 allows renvoi but nonetheless has a choice of law rule that points to its own internal law, jurisdiction 2's policy on renvoi does not affect the result. *See* Peter Hay, Patrick J. Borchers & Symeon C. Symeonides, Conflict of Laws 163-165 (5th ed. 2010).

6. In thinking about *Damato,* consider whether it actually honors the intent of Florida lawmakers to apply only Florida's internal law to the facts of the case. Would it not be more faithful to that intent to "do what Florida would do" — and apply Florida's choice of law rules as well? As illustrated later in this chapter, renvoi issues persist with modern methodologies that were developed after the Restatement (First). In many instances, however, renvoi analysis is actually helpful in implementing modern methodologies' emphasis on law's intent or goals.

7. Courts and commentators include the renvoi mechanism on the list of Restatement (First) escape devices because it can enable a forum court to avoid applying a foreign jurisidiction's law where the forum court is not comfortable doing so. Commentators have suggested that this dynamic was at work when the High Court of Australia revived the renvoi doctrine in *Neilson v. Overseas Projects Corporation of Victoria Ltd* (2005) 223 C.L.R. 331 (Austl.). In that case, the plaintiff, Mrs. Neilson, was injured when she fell down stairs in her apartment in Wuhan, China. Her husband's employer was an Australian company that had provided the apartment, and she sued the employer in Australia six years after the accident had occurred. Like the First Restatement choice of law rule, the Australian choice of law rule pointed to the law of the place of the accident, which meant that the People's Republic of China provided the governing law. Chinese law would have barred the claim under its statute of limitations. The High Court of Australia refused to apply Chinese law, reasoning that the Australian choice of law rule referred to the whole of the law of the place of the wrong. Accordingly, the court reasoned, the applicable law was referred back to Australia, the Australian statute of limitations applied, and Mrs. Neilson's claim was not time barred. If, as some have suggested, the Australia High Court was motivated by a desire to apply Australian law to Australian citizens rather than a desire to invigorate the renvoi doctrine, is there another way the court could have accomplished this result? The traditional First Restatement approach would have characterized the statute of limitations as procedural and applied forum law. Australia, however, like most jurisdictions, regards time limitations as substantive. Alternatively, perhaps the matter could have been be resolved by reference to the Australian interest in the case.

Further discussion of these matters appears in the section on statute of limitations later in this chapter.

8. Questions concerning renvoi have no doubt arisen ever since courts began to grapple with choice of law questions. One might expect, however, that the questions may become more prevalent with increasing globalism and ease of access to the law of other jurisdictions. As an example, consider the court's decision in *Iran v. Berend* [2007] EWHC 132 (Q.B.) (Eng.), a dispute over ownership of a shard from an ancient Iranian ruin. In *Berend*, the Islamic Republic of Iran filed a suit in London, claiming ownership in the face of a competing claim by a French patron of the arts. English conflict of law rules would not look to Iran, the state of origin, for governing law, but instead looked to the law of the situs of the shard at the time of transfer, which occurred in France. The legal problem, however, was whether the English court should apply French conflict of law rules and if so, whether the French courts would have applied Iranian law. The court determined not to apply French conflict of law rules (declining to introduce renvoi issues into the suit) and thus decided the case in accordance with French internal law.

PROBLEM 2-22: GUEST STATUTES MEET RENVOI

Alexandra and Genevieve are domiciled in Homestate. Alexandra decided to drive her car to Accidentstate, and invited Genevieve to ride with her. Genevieve accepted the invitation. While in Accidentstate, they have an accident. Genevieve filed suit against Alexandra, alleging Alexandra's negligence and seeking over $75,000 damages. Homestate has a rule that provides that where an invited guest is injured in an automobile driven by another, any damages the guest recovers from the host are capped at $10,000. Homestate has a choice of law rule that provides that the law of domicile should govern damages limitation of this kind. Accidentstate has no limitation on damages for a case such as this. Assume that Genevieve has filed suit in Accidentstate, which follows the Restatement (First) of Conflict of Laws. What role will renvoi play in the analysis?

PROBLEM 2-23: THE MOTEL TRENCH

In an effort to repair a water leak, the owner of a motel, Oscar, dug a deep trench behind the motel's main building. Unsure of whether he had successfully repaired the leak, Oscar did not fill in the trench for several weeks in case he needed to do more work with the subterranean plumbing. Oscar did, however, put many warning signs and a fence around the trench. One night, an intoxicated guest, Dan, decided to investigate behind the fence surrounding the trench, fell into the trench, and was severely injured. The motel is located in the State of Strict Liability, and both Oscar and Dan are residents of the nearby State of Negligence.

Before choosing a forum, Dan evaluated whether to sue Oscar in the State of Strict Liability or the State of Negligence. He discovered that the law of the State of Strict Liability provides that maintaining a deep hole near a building such as a motel is an especially dangerous activity, and subjects the individual responsible for maintaining the hole to strict liability. The law of the State of Negligence, however, does not impose liability without fault on the part of the individual responsible for maintaining the hole. These differences are significant, since Oscar has made clear that he would like to argue that Dan was contributorily negligent, an argument that might prevail under a negligence standard, but will have no weight if Oscar is held to a strict liability standard. Further complicating matters, however, is the choice of law rule in the State of Strict Liability, which would look to the domicile of the parties in determining which law would apply, and would designate Negligence law under the facts of this case. The choice of law rule in the State of Negligence, however, would point to the place where the accident occurred (Strict Liability) for the governing law. Negligence choice of law rules, however, make clear that where the rules point to another jurisidiction's law, the court should consider the whole law of that jurisdiction.

Dan filed a suit against Oscar in the State of Strict Liability to recover for damages resulting from his fall into the trench. What law will the Strict Liability court apply? Assuming that the courts of the State of Strict Liability have stated that they will follow the rule on renvoi set forth in the First Restatement, what, if anything, should the court do with the choice of law rule of the State of Negligence? Did Dan make the right decision in filing the lawsuit in Strict Liability rather than Negligence? Would the result be different if the State of Strict Liability did not follow the First Restatement policy on renvoi?

PROBLEM 2-24: THE LAND EXCEPTION

Arno, the owner of land in the State of Locus, executes conveyance papers in the State of Execution. The conveyance papers satisfy the real property laws of the State of Execution, but not the State of Locus. Locus has a rule that provides that conveyance papers concerning property located in the state will be treated as valid if the papers satisfy the real property rules of the State of Execution, even if they do not satisfy the real property rules of the State of Locus.

Arno has filed suit in Arbiter State in an attempt to settle title to the land in Locus. Arbiter State follows the First Restatement on questions of property as well as on questions pertaining renvoi. Should Arbiter State recognize Arno's title to the land as valid?[19]

---

19. *See* Restatement (First) of Conflict of Laws §8, comment b, illustration 1.

d.   Public Policy

From the Restatement (First) of Conflict of Laws, on the Subject of Procedure:

§612. Action Contrary to Public Policy

No action can be maintained upon a cause of action created in another state the enforcement of which is contrary to the strong public policy of the forum.

Comment:

a. Distinction between policy denying access to courts and policy refusing to apply foreign rule of law. The rule stated in this Section is applicable when the entire basis of the claim upon which suit is brought is so contrary to the public policy of the forum that it will withhold altogether the use of its courts to enforce the claim. A distinction is to be noted between such a policy and the policy which, while it does not require denial of access to the courts of the forum, nevertheless requires the courts to apply certain local rules in the course of the litigation to enforce the local notions concerning the manner and method in which the courts of that state should function. This latter policy may be called the procedural policy of the forum. This procedural policy differs from the policy which denies access to the local courts under the rule stated in this Section in the following respect: in the former case, the legal relations between the parties as determined by foreign law will be enforced subject to certain limitations imposed by foreign law.

b. The mere difference between the laws of the two states will not render the enforcement of a cause of action created in one state contrary to the public policy of the other.

Loucks v. Standard Oil Co. of New York

120 N.E. 198 (N.Y. 1918)

CARDOZO, J.

The action is brought to recover damages for injuries resulting in death. The plaintiffs are the administrators of the estate of Everett A. Loucks. Their intestate, while traveling on a highway in the state of Massachusetts, was run down and killed through the negligence of the defendant's servants then engaged in its business. He left a wife and two children, residents of New York. A statute of Massachusetts provides that:

If a person or corporation by his or its negligence, or by the negligence of his or its agents or servants while engaged in his or its business, causes the death of a person who is in the exercise of due care, and not in his or its employment or service, he or it shall be liable in damages in the sum of not less than $500, nor more than $10,000, to be assessed with reference to the degree of his or its culpability, or . . . that of his or its . . . servants, to be recovered in an action of tort commenced within two years after the injury which caused the death, by the executor or administrator of the deceased, one-half thereof to the use of the widow and one-half to the use of the children of the deceased, or, if there are no children, the whole to the use of the widow, or, if there is no widow, the whole to the use of the next of kin.

The question is whether a right of action under that statute may be enforced in our courts.

"The courts of no country execute the penal laws of another." *The Antelope*, 10 Wheat. 66, 6 L. Ed. 268. The defendant invokes that principle as applicable here. Penal in one sense the statute indisputably is. The damages are not limited to compensation; they are proportioned to the offender's guilt. A minimum recovery of $500 is allowed in every case. But the question is not whether the statute is penal in some sense. The question is whether it is penal within the rules of private international law. A statute penal in that sense is one that awards a penalty to the state, or to a public officer in its behalf, or to a member of the public, suing in the interest of the whole community to redress a public wrong. The purpose must be, not reparation to one aggrieved, but vindication of the public justice. The Massachusetts statute has been classified in some jurisdictions as penal, and in others as remedial. . . . The courts of Massachusetts have said that the question is still an open one. No matter how they may have characterized the act as penal, they have not meant to hold that it is penal for every purpose. . . .

We think the better reason is with those cases which hold that the statute is not penal in the international sense. On that branch of the controversy, indeed, there is no division of opinion among us. It is true that the offender is punished, but the purpose of the punishment is reparation to those aggrieved by his offense. The common law did not give a cause of action to surviving relatives. In the light of modern legislation, its rule is an anachronism. Nearly everywhere, the principle is now embodied in statute that the next of kin are wronged by the killing of their kinsman. . . . They sue to redress an outrage peculiar to themselves.

We cannot fail to see in the history of the Massachusetts statutes a developing expression of this policy and purpose. The statutes have their distant beginnings in the criminal law. To some extent the vestiges of criminal forms survive. But the old forms have been filled with a new content. The purpose which informs and vitalizes them is the protection of the survivors. . . .

Through all this legislation there runs a common purpose. It is penal in one element and one only; the damages are punitive. But the punishment of the wrongdoer is not designed as atonement for a crime; it is solace to the individual who has suffered a private wrong. This is seen in many tokens. The employer may be innocent himself. . . . The executor or administrator who sues under this statute is not the champion of the peace and order and public justice of the commonwealth of Massachusetts. He is the representative of the outraged family. He vindicates a private right.

Another question remains. Even though the statute is not penal, it differs from our own. We must determine whether the difference is a sufficient reason for declining jurisdiction. A tort committed in one state creates a right of action that may be sued upon in another unless public policy forbids. That is the generally accepted rule in the United States. . . . The question is whether the enforcement of a right of action for tort under the statutes of another state is to be conditioned upon the existence of a kindred statute here. . . . A foreign statute is not law in this state, but it gives rise to an obligation, which, if transitory, "follows the person and may be enforced wherever the person may be found." "No law can exist as such except the law of the land; but . . . it is a principle of every civilized law that vested rights shall be protected." Beale, Conflict of Laws, §51. The plaintiff owns something, and we help him to get it. We do this unless some sound reason of public policy makes it unwise for us to lend our aid. "The law of the forum is material only as setting a limit of policy beyond which such obligations will not be enforced there." . . .

Our own scheme of legislation may be different. We may even have no legislation on the subject. That is not enough to show that public policy forbids us to enforce the foreign right. A right of action is property. If a foreign statute gives the right, the mere fact that we do not give a like right is no reason for refusing to help the plaintiff in getting what belongs to him. We are not so provincial as to say that every solution of a problem is wrong because we deal with it otherwise at home. Similarity of legislation has indeed this importance; its presence shows beyond question that the foreign statute does not offend the local policy. But its absence does not prove the contrary. . . . The misleading word "comity" has been responsible for much of the trouble. It has been fertile in suggesting a discretion unregulated by general principles. Beale, Conflict of Laws, §71.

The courts are not free to refuse to enforce a foreign right at the pleasure of the judges, to suit the individual notion of expediency or fairness. They do not close their doors, unless help would violate some fundamental principle of justice, some prevalent conception of good morals, some deep-rooted tradition of the common weal.

This test applied, there is nothing in the Massachusetts statute that outrages the public policy of New York. We have a statute which gives a civil remedy where death is caused in our own state. We have thought it so important that we have now imbedded it in the Constitution. The fundamental policy is that there shall be some atonement for the wrong. Through the defendant's negligence, a resident of New York has been killed in Massachusetts. He has left a widow and children, who are also residents. The law of Massachusetts gives them a recompense for his death. It cannot be that public policy forbids our courts to help in collecting what belongs to them. We cannot give them the same judgment that our law would give if the wrong had been done here. Very likely we cannot give them as much. But that is no reason for refusing to give them what we can. We shall not make things better by sending them to another state, where the defendant may not be found, and where suit may be impossible. Nor is there anything to shock our sense of justice in the possibility of a punitive recovery. The penalty is not extravagant. It conveys no hint of arbitrary confiscation. It varies between moderate limits according to the defendant's guilt. We shall not feel the pricks of conscience, if the offender pays the survivors in proportion to the measure of his offense.

We have no public policy that prohibits exemplary damages or civil penalties. We give them for many wrongs. To exclude all penal actions would be to wipe out the distinction between the penalties of public justice and the remedies of private law. . . .

We hold, then, that public policy does not prohibit the assumption of jurisdiction by our courts and that this being so, mere differences of remedy do not count. . . . We must apply the same rules that are applicable to other torts; and the tendency of those rules to-day is toward a larger comity. . . . The fundamental public policy is perceived to be that rights lawfully vested shall be everywhere maintained. At least, that is so among the states of the Union. . . . The test of similarity has been abandoned there. If it has ever been accepted here, we think it should be abandoned now.

The judgment of the Appellate Division should be reversed. . . .

Notes on
LOUCKS

1. What would Judge Cardozo have done if he had determined that the Massachusetts wrongful death statute offended New York public policy? Would he have applied New York law to the controversy or would he have dismissed the lawsuit? If the New York court had determined that the Massachusetts wrongful death statute was against New York public policy, what would have been the most appropriate course of action? In legal systems outside of the United States, a court refusing to apply the foreign law on public policy grounds might replace the law with another from the same set of laws or with forum law.

2. *Loucks* sets forth the classic statement of public policy for the purpose of conflict of laws:

> The courts are not free to refuse to enforce a foreign right at the pleasure of the judges, to suit the individual notion of expediency or fairness. They do not close their doors, unless help would violate some fundamental principle of justice, some prevalent conception of good morals, some deep-rooted tradition of the common weal.

This sets a high bar for what might constitute a sufficiently serious public policy to merit ignoring or refusing to honor another jurisdiction's law. What matters implicate "a concept of good morals" or "a deep-rooted tradition of the common weal"? How is this standard different than a constitutional standard, such as that embodied in the Fourteenth Amendment's due process clause? Although diversity persists among the laws of the various states of the United States, are there many laws that implicate fundamentally different notions of fairness, well-being, and moral justice?

3. Is the public policy exception legitimate? Or is it the public policy exception simply a doctrinal excuse for provincialism? In a classic study of the public policy exception, Professors Paulsen and Sovern suggested that

provincialism was not the motivation for courts invoking the exception. Instead, they found that most cases rejecting another jurisdiction's law were cases "in which the forum had some important connection." They therefore concluded that the exception merely served as a handy way to justify forum law governing in "cases where the forum court perceived a strong prerogative to apply forum law, but did not identify another mechanism within existing choice of law analysis for doing so." Monrad G. Paulsen & Michael I. Sovern, *"Public Policy" in the Conflict of Laws*, 56 COLUM. L. REV. 969 (1956). Under this interpretation, the public policy exception is simply a way "to avoid the application of a choice of law rule which the forum wishes to avoid." *Id.* at 981. When invoking the exception, the forum court is, in essence, not necessarily entering a frontal assault on "the content of the foreign law" but instead on "its own choice of law rule." Is this a meaningful distinction? Is it meaningful in the context of the workings of federalism, but essentially irrelevant to the parties?

4. Is the public policy exception consistent with the goals and approach of the Restatement (First) of Conflict of Laws?

Raskin v. Allison

57 P.3d 30 (Kan. Ct. App. 2002)

PADDOCK, J.:

This is an interlocutory appeal by the plaintiffs from the partial summary judgment granted to defendants on a choice-of-law question. The trial court found the substantive law of Mexico would govern the claims in this personal injury action where the injuries occurred in Mexico although all parties were Kansas residents. We affirm.

The facts are brief and uncontroverted. Kaley Raskin and Jenna Turnbaugh, both minors, received personal injuries resulting from a collision of the water craft they occupied and a water craft operated by Chad Leathers in the ocean waters off Cabo San Lucas, Mexico.

Kaley's and Jenna's parents filed this action individually and as next friends to their minor daughters against Ken and Karen Allison individually and as guardians ad litem for their minor son and stepson, Chad Leathers. Plaintiffs' claims were framed on the theories of negligence and negligent entrustment. . . .

Kansas follows the rule that the law of the state where the tort occurred, lex loci delicti, should apply.

Here, plaintiffs do not dispute the injuries were sustained in Mexican waters and that under the rule of lex loci delicti, Mexican law would normally control. However, plaintiffs argue the rule should not apply in this case because (1) all the parties are residents of Kansas, (2) Kansas has never invoked the rule in a case where a foreign country's law would apply, and (3) the rule of comity requires that Kansas protect its own residents and apply Kansas law.

Kansas Residents

Plaintiffs argue that because all the parties are Kansas residents, Kansas has the greater interest in applying its substantive law; therefore, the case should be governed by Kansas law.

However, the Kansas Supreme Court has repeatedly applied the law of the place of the injury, even when all the parties were residents of Kansas. In each of those cases, the law of the place of injury was less favorable to the plaintiffs than Kansas law. . . .

Because the Kansas Supreme Court has consistently applied the rule of lex loci delicti in tort cases, even when all parties are Kansas residents, plaintiffs' first argument fails.

Application to Foreign Countries

Plaintiffs also contend that because Kansas courts have never applied the lex loci delicti rule to apply the law of a foreign country, the rule should be rejected in this case. Plaintiffs are correct in asserting that neither of the Kansas appellate courts have applied the law of a foreign country in a tort case. This court, however, recently applied Canadian law in a contract case where the contract was made in Canada by applying the rule of lex loci contractus.

Plaintiffs have not cited compelling authority that the rule of lex loci delicti does not apply in cases involving foreign countries. . . .

Comity v. Lex Loci Delicti

Finally, plaintiffs challenge the lex loci delicti rule by arguing principles of comity mitigate against applying Mexican law. Plaintiffs are wide of the mark by trying to distinguish comity principles from choice-of-law principles. Choice-of-law principles, essentially, are rules defining when a court will extend comity to the laws of another state. Both principles are inextricably joined.

. . . While the court is not required to apply Mexico's law under principles of comity, the lex loci delicti rule is well established under Kansas law and there is no indication that Kansas intends to abandon the rule. For example, the [Kansas] Supreme Court rejected the analytical approach which allows the forum court to apply the law of the jurisdiction most intimately concerned with the outcome of the particular litigation.

Public Policy Exception

Actually, the thread that weaves through all of the plaintiffs' arguments is that damage limitations purportedly contained in Mexico's law are contrary to Kansas public policy and should not be enforced by Kansas courts. Plaintiffs seem to argue that public policy is defined by Kansas legislative enactments and since the Kansas Legislature had not enacted statutes with damage limitations similar to those in Mexico, Mexican laws are therefore contrary to Kansas public policy. Plaintiffs cite no authority establishing what damage limitations exist in Mexico. However, a recent case cited by defendants appeared to support the conclusion that Mexico recognizes that contributory negligence is a complete defense in a tort claim. Also, Mexican law apparently limits recovery of damages in tort cases to the amount of the injured party's medical and rehabilitative expense and lost wages at the minimum wage rate. Plaintiffs assert these damage limitations in their brief.

Kansas cases consistently hold that a Kansas court will not apply the law of another state to a claim if that other state's law is contrary to Kansas public policy. . . . In *Brenner v. Oppenheimer & Co., Inc.*, 44 P.3d 364 (2002), the Supreme Court invalidated a contractual choice-of-law provision finding that its reference to New York law was contrary to "strong public policy" in Kansas and would not be enforced. In its discussion, the Supreme Court held that a "strong public policy" is one "'so thoroughly established as a state of public mind so united and so definite and fixed that its existence is not subject to any substantial doubt.'" The *Brenner* court found a strong public policy in the fact that the incorporation of New York law into the contract between a Kansas resident and a securities broker evaded Kansas' securities law prohibiting the sale of unregistered securities.

The only other Kansas cases refusing to apply the law of other states as required by traditional choice-of-law rules are *Dale v. Railroad Co.*, 57 Kan. 601, 47 Pac. 521 (1897) (refusing to apply New Mexico's penal statute); *Barbour v. Campbell*, 101 Kan. 616, 168 Pac. 879 (1917) (dismissing case seeking to enforce Idaho contract which violated Kansas' statute of frauds); *Peters v. Peters*, 177 Kan. 100, 106-07, 276 P.2d 302 (1952) (finding second wife was not a "legal widow" of decedent under Kansas law because remarriage occurred less than 6 months after Kansas divorce); and *Westerman v. Westerman*, 121 Kan. 501, 247 Pac. 863 (1926) (finding Missouri marriage contrary to Kansas public policy because marriage occurred less than 6 months after Kansas divorce).

None of these cases appear to set forth a public policy exception as broad as plaintiffs are arguing here. Kansas appears to be following the prevailing view that the public policy exception in conflict of law theory should be narrowly limited. As previously noted, the plaintiffs here appear to contend that if the law of another jurisdiction is different than Kansas law, it is contrary to Kansas public policy.

The Kansas Supreme Court has repeatedly upheld the application of the law of other states in tort cases even when those laws impose a higher burden of proof on plaintiffs before they can recover damages. . . . The Supreme Court has even upheld the application of another State's wrongful death statute even though that statute excluded some types of damages allowed under Kansas law.

Thus, Kansas cases indicate the "public policy" exception in the choice-of-law context is limited and generally not triggered because of limitations on damages or higher burdens of proof.

. . . [T]he Tenth Circuit once stated:

> . . . The mere fact that the law of the foreign state differs from the law of the state in which recognition is sought is not enough to make the foreign law inapplicable. . . . Indeed, this Court is reminded of the oft-paraphrased advice of

St. Ambrose, Catholic bishop of Milan in the fourth century, to St. Augustine. "When you are at Rome, live in the Roman style; when you are elsewhere, live as they do elsewhere."

Brennan v. University of Kansas, 451 F.2d 1287, 1289-90 (10th Cir. 1971).

The record before the court fails to establish a sound basis to refuse to apply Mexican law in this case based on the public policy exception. The limitations on damages allegedly contained in Mexican law do not appear to violate a "strong public policy" as defined by prior Kansas Supreme Court decisions. . . .

Notes on
RASKIN *AND THE PUBLIC POLICY EXCEPTION GENERALLY*

1. The *Raskin* court seemed to criticize the plaintiff for suggesting an analytical kinship between the public policy exception and the concern with applying a foreign jurisdiction's law in a case involving domestic domiciliaries. Is the *Raskin* court correct in suggesting that these two concepts are entirely distinct? Isn't the theory behind the public policy exception that a court legitimately exercising power in a particular case may articulate discomfort in applying a foreign jurisdiction's law, and may properly decline to apply the foreign law on the basis of that discomfort?

2. The First Restatement section on public policy, §612, quoted at the beginning of this section on public policy, is limited to allowing causes of action contrary to the forum's strong public policy. As described in the comments, this distinguishes between denying access to courts and refusing to apply a foreign law. Courts following the traditional public policy exception, however, tend to focus on individual principles of law and generally do not concern themselves with the question of whether the legal principles give rise to a cause of action that itself is contrary to the forum's public policy. *See, e.g., Johnson v. Occidental Fire & Casualty Co. of N. Carolina,* 954 F.2d 1581 (11th Cir. 1992) (issue regarding what constitutes an admission that no-fault insurance provisions apply or an admission of liability or bad faith); *Kilberg v. Northeast Airlines,* 9 N.Y.2d 34, 211 N.Y.S.2d 133 (N.Y. 1961) (issue regarding damages cap).

Note that the Massachusetts wrongful death statute at issue in *Loucks* governed the plaintiff's cause of action rather than some portion of the defense, as in *Raskin.* Was that fact crucial to the *Loucks* court's reasoning? Should the distinction between a cause of action and a defense make a difference for the purpose of the public policy exception?

3. On a number of occasions, legislatures within the United States have considered provisions that would ban courts from using foreign law in their deliberations. For example, a 2011 North Carolina measure would have made it unlawful for state judges to consider "foreign law," which presumably meant law from sources other than the state and federal governments of

the United States. In November 2010, Oklahoma voters adopted the "Save Our State Amendment," which catalogs legal sources that Oklahoma courts may use when deciding cases, and those the courts may not use. Forbidden sources included "the legal precepts of other nations or cultures," international law, and "Sharia Law." *See* John T. Parry, *Oklahoma's Save Our State Amendment and the Conflict of Laws*, 64 OKLA. L. REV. 161 (2012). This Oklahoma provision, however, has been struck down as unconstitutional. *Awad v. Ziria*, 670 F.3d 1111 (10th Cir. 2012). Numerous other state provisions have been proposed. Indeed, Alabama has adopted a similar provision: Ala. Cons. Art. 1, §13.50 (2016).

Even in the United States Congress, the proposed Constitution Restoration Act of 2005, H.R. 1070, 109th Cong. §201, sought to confine courts of the United States to consideration of only one non-American source: "English constitutional and [English] common law up until the time of the adoption of the Constitution of the United States." These initiatives are considered more fully in Chapter 3 in a section regarding use of international and comparative law principles in United States cases. In the meantime, consider whether the spirit behind the bills is similar to the public policy exception. Conceived as applying to principles of law (rather than causes of action), the public public policy exception represents a judgment—similar to that reflected in these bills—that certain types of laws are so inimical to what the forum stands for that forum courts should not exercise authority in connection with them.

4. The public policy exception has an unequivocal place on the list of escape devices that the courts use to avoid the result that may follow from the First Restatement's subject matter rules. Whatever one might say about the process of using this escape device, the public policy exception is certainly a candid and forthright vehicle for avoiding distasteful results. On balance, does the public policy exception add to or detract from coherent and uniform application of the Restatement (First) of Conflict of Laws? After reading *Raskin*, do you have any more thoughts on whether the exception is a legitimate part of choice of law analysis or whether it is consistent with the goals and spirit of the First Restatement?

Alexander v. General Motors Corporation

267 Ga. 339 (1996)

BENHAM, Chief Justice.

Alexander was injured while driving in Virginia when the driver's seat of his General Motors vehicle, purchased new in Georgia, failed in a collision and caused him to be ejected from the vehicle. He sued General Motors in Georgia under a strict liability theory. The trial court granted partial summary judgment to General Motors, ruling that because the injuries occurred in Virginia, that state's substantive law would be applied. Because there is no strict liability action under Virginia law, the trial court dismissed those claims and permitted Alexander to amend the complaint to state a claim based on negligence under Virginia law. The Court of Appeals affirmed that judgment, concluding that since Virginia products liability law is not radically dissimilar to Georgia law and pursues similar public policy by different methods, it does not contravene Georgia public policy, and the "public policy" exception to the rule of *lex loci delicti* does not apply. We granted Alexander's petition for certiorari to consider whether, since Virginia does not recognize recovery on the basis of strict liability, the application of the rule of *lex loci delicti* would contravene the public policy embodied in [Georgia law]. For the reasons stated below, we conclude that the rule of *lex loci delicti* should not be applied, and reverse the contrary decision of the Court of Appeals.

1.

The opinion by the Court of Appeals correctly states the choice of law principles applicable to this case, including the public policy exception to the rule of *lex loci delicti*. However, the conclusion in that opinion that "Virginia products liability law is not radically dissimilar to Georgia law but rather pursues a similar public policy by somewhat different methods," misses the crucial point that Georgia's public policy of shifting to manufacturers the burden of loss caused by defective products is effectuated by precisely those "somewhat different methods."

As is pointed out in the majority opinion of the Court of Appeals, Virginia does not recognize a claim for strict liability in tort in products liability actions. Instead, Virginia continues to rely on warranty law and negligence principles. In a claim for breach of an implied warranty of merchantability, which the majority opinion of the Court of Appeals describes as Virginia's "functional equivalent" to strict liability, Virginia law requires one injured by an allegedly defective product to notify the manufacturer of the breach of implied warranty within a reasonable time. In Georgia, however, OCGA §51-1-11 imposes strict liability in tort without requiring any similar notification. A claim in negligence in a Virginia products liability case differs from a strict liability claim in Georgia in that the latter eliminates questions of negligence and the usual defenses to negligence. This comparison demonstrates that Virginia law and Georgia law are radically dissimilar in terms of the burden placed on persons seeking recompense for injuries caused by defective products.

The present case is an excellent example of how the differences in method affect the substantive result. Applying Virginia law, the trial court not only dismissed the strict liability claim because Virginia law does not provide for it, but by relegating Alexander to an action based only on negligence, foreclosed pursuit of any warranty claim. Such a result is antithetical to the policy of which OCGA §51-1-11 is an expression:

The manufacturer is made liable for a new product that is defective when it leaves his hands and is the proximate cause of injury. Reasonable care in inspecting, designing and manufacturing a product is not a defense because the language creating the tortious misconduct is manufacturing a defective product, and this high burden of care is demanded to safeguard the life and person from injury as a matter of public policy.

Ford Motor Co. v. Carter, 141 Ga. App. 371(2), 233 S.E.2d 444 (1977).

Because Virginia law would place Alexander in exactly the position from which OCGA §51-1-11 was intended to protect those who are injured by defective products placed in the stream of commerce in this state, we conclude that it is contrary to the public policy of this state as expressed in that statute. Accordingly, Alexander is entitled to have Georgia law applied to his claims against General Motors. The decision of the Court of Appeals must, therefore, be reversed.

Note on
ALEXANDER v. GENERAL MOTORS

1. *Loucks v. Standard Oil Co.* and *Raskin v. Allison* reject the public policy exception. This case accepts it. Do you agree that the policy at issue in this case (the availability of a strict liability theory) is categorically different from the public policies at issue in *Loucks* and *Raskin*? Courts make public policy judgments in other conflict of laws contexts, such as when they must determine whether enforcing a choice of law clause would offend the public policy of a state with a materially greater interest in governing the dispute. In a case discussed later in this volume, *DeSantis v. Wackenhut,* the court confronted whether to enforce a contractual choice of law clause under the Restatement (Second) for an issue about enforcing noncompetition clauses. The court concluded that it would be against the public policy of the most interested state to enforce a noncompetition clause under the law designated in the party's contract. Is strict liability as important to public policy as a noncompetition clause? How does strict liability compare with the policies at issue in *Loucks* and *Raskin*?

2. For evaluating whether a foreign jurisdiction's law violates the forum's public policy, whose opinion matters? Not to be rude, but: does your opinion matter? You are most likely an outside observer. Does the judgment of whether something violates the public policy of a forum depend solely on the judgment of those that govern in the forum, such as the legislators and the judges who interpret statutory intent (and who may independently make common law)?

PROBLEM 2-25: THE MOTEL TRENCH REDUX

In an effort to repair a water leak, the owner of a motel, Oscar, dug a deep trench behind the motel's main building. Unsure of whether he had successfully repaired the leak, Oscar did not fill in the trench for several weeks in case he needed to do more work with the subterranean plumbing. Oscar did, however, put many warning signs and a fence around the trench. One night, an intoxicated guest, Dan, decided to investigate behind the fence surrounding the trench, fell into the trench, and was severely injured. The motel is located in the State of Strict Liability, and both Oscar and Dan are residents of the nearby State of Negligence.

Assume that Dan has decided to sue Oscar in the State of Negligence, since that is the most convenient for him. Knowing that the State of Negligence applies the Restatement (First) of Conflict of Laws, Dan assumed that the Negligence state court will apply the strict liability laws of the State of Strict Liability. In arguing that the court should not apply the State of Strict Liability's law, Oscar points to instances where members of the State of Negligence legislature have said, "In this state, we do not impose liability without fault." Oscar maintains that such statements establish that imposing liability under a strict liability theory would be contrary to the public policy of the State of Negligence. Should the court in the State of Negligence accept this argument?

PROBLEM 2-26: ANN'S ANTENUPTIAL AGREEMENT

Ann was a resident of State A and Dimitri was a resident of State D. They both were widowed and had adult children. They decided to marry and—one day before their marriage in State A—signed an antenuptial agreement (also in State A) in which they released their marital rights to inherit each other's property. At the time of their marriage, Ann and Dimitri intended to live out their days together in State A. On a vacation in State D, however, Dimitri died and his will (which contained no provision for Ann) was probated in State D. Thereafter, Ann filed a petition in State D to receive her elective share of his estate, and Dimitri's children opposed the petition.

Both States A and D approve the use of antenuptial agreements and favor their enforcement in probate and divorce proceedings. State A has no particular requirements relating to the execution of such agreements. State D, however, provides that, for such agreements to be enforceable in the probate context, the party wishing to enforce the agreement must establish certain proof requirements. In particular, State D requires that the party seeking to enforce the agreement prove that, at the time of execution, the parties to the agreement must have fully disclosed their financial holdings to the other party. Dimitri's children are not able to provide that proof.

Accordingly, if State D law applies, the antenuptial agreement will not be enforceable in the probate proceeding.

Both States A and D follow the Restatement (First) of Conflict of Laws. Which law should govern whether to enforce the antenuptial agreement?

PERSPECTIVE ON PUBLIC POLICY

One can conceive of public policy both broadly and narrowly. From a broad perspective, public policy is often an important impetus behind any type of law. It is always an important concept in conflict of laws because differences in jurisdictions' views on the public policies bearing on a particular subject matter often yield different laws on the matter.

Sometimes a jurisdiction's public policy on a matter may be so potent that it inspires the jurisdiction's courts to refuse to apply the law of another jurisdiction reflecting a contrary public policy. This is termed the "public policy exception" to choice of law analysis, and is often listed among other escape devices. One can think of the public policy exception as a recognition of a forum court's gag reflex: although reasoned analysis may point to another jurisdiction's law applying to an issue, the forum court just cannot bring itself to do that. Sometimes, the public policy reflex may be so severe and the lawsuit may be so intertwined with the offending policy that the forum may simply dismiss the case.

Courts suggest that the disagreement over public policy must be *really* severe — with the other jurisdiction's public policy appearing "truly obnoxious" — before a court will refuse to apply another jurisdiction's law. *Brink's Ltd. v. South African Airways*, 93 F.3d 1022, 1031 (2d Cir. 1996), *cert. denied*, 519 U.S. 116 (1997). The classic incantation — ritualistically invoked by courts discussing the public policy exception — includes a quote from an old Cardozo opinion: "When otherwise applicable foreign law would 'violate some fundamental principle of justice, some prevalent conception of good morals, some deep rooted tradition of the common weal' the court may refuse to enforce it." *Cooney v. Osgood Machinery, Inc.*, 81 N.Y.2d 66, 78, 612 N.E. 2d 277, 284, 595 N.Y.S.2d 919, 926 (1993) (*quoting Loucks v. Standard Oil Co.*, 224 N.Y. 99, 111, 120 N.E. 198, 202 (1918)).

Despite the nearly universal presence of the Cardozo language in opinions dealing with the public policy exception, courts apply it in different ways. In the Restatement (First) context, courts generally use it as a straightforward escape hatch, allowing them to avoid completely the application of foreign law against the forum's public policy. As illustrated in the more modern methodologies, courts sometimes require a threshold showing of forum interest or forum contacts before using the forum's public policy as a veto for the choice of law result. In other words, courts apply the public policy exception in a number of different ways.

Consider whether the public policy exception is consistent with the choice of law enterprise. If a jurisdiction is willing to apply anything other than its own law, is it not acknowledging that another jurisdiction's public policies are worthy of governing certain parts of life? And, if after reasoning through the conflict of laws concerns in a case, the jurisdiction concludes that its conflicts principles point to another jurisdiction's laws, shouldn't that be the end of the matter? Of course, matters exist that go to the core of what defines a civilized society, and where a law takes a position contrary to that definition, a court should not be expected to enforce that law. But those are matters presenting the types of values protected by the federal and state constitutions, are they not? In other words, might we say that the only legitimate basis on which courts might refuse to apply another jurisdiction's legitimate law is where that law is unconstitutional under federal or forum state law?

Or is the public policy exception an essential safety net for extreme cases? Might we say that without the public policy exception, a forum's choice of law system would never get off the ground for fear that the forum's courts would be forced to do something truly inimical to the core of the forum's legal, political, and social structures?

e. Domicile

Some sections of the First Restatement of Conflict of Laws point to an entity's domicile as a determining factor in choosing governing law. For cases governed by these sections, domicile can play a key role in choice of law decisions and can influence the ultimate outcome of a case. The law allows some "play" in identifying where an entity is domiciled, and a court can change the bottom line as to which law applies by changing its conclusion about where an entity is domiciled. Accordingly, domicile can provide yet another escape mechanism to avoid an unappealing or unjust result that would otherwise flow from First Restatement analysis. As you will see later in this chapter, domicile has even greater influence in decisions under many more modern methodologies. For that reason it provides a useful bridge concept between the traditional and contemporary choice of law approaches. But domicile is much more than a factual conclusion for courts to plug into choice of law analysis. The perspective that follows addresses some of the deeper concepts that inform domicile's role in conflict of laws, as well as qualities that distinguish it from residence and citizenship.

PERSPECTIVE ON DOMICILE, RESIDENCE, AND CITIZENSHIP

Domicile, residence, and citizenship are intertwined concepts. For conflict of laws purposes, "domicile" is the more commonly invoked term, and is key to many conflict of laws problems. Clarity of analysis benefits from distinguishing between domicile and the other two concepts, and exploring domicile's role as a portal to understanding of the connection between legal regulation and citizens subject to legal regulation. This can be difficult. First, courts and lawyers sometimes use the terms "domicile," "residence," and "citizenship" as synonyms. Where legal thinkers do distinguish the terms, each term has variant definitions. This note nonetheless ventures to nail down some uniform, foundational concepts for distinguishing the three terms.

Government generally possesses the prerogative or authority to exercise power—judicial or legislative—over entities domiciled in the territory where the government reigns, even if these persons are not actually present. The common law provides the rules for domicile, which is used to justify government power in a wide variety of contexts—to impose a tax, to extend the right to vote in democratic elections, to exercise personal jurisdiction, to grant a divorce, and the like. Under common law concepts, domicile is generally said to be where a person has a permanent home, and to which—whenever she is absent—she has the intention of returning. The Restatement (First) of Conflict of Laws §11 defines domicile as "the place with which a person has a settled connection for certain legal purposes, either because his home is there, or because that place is assigned to him by operation of law." Domicile is considered a strong justification for asserting governmental power, the notion being that someone has willingly subjected herself to the government power by intending to make a jurisdiction the center of her social and domestic life. By legal fiction or true belief, she has embraced the jurisdiction—together with its laws—as her own. One can have only one domicile, which she can establish through birth or place of origin, through choice if she is capable of choosing a domicile, or through operation of law if she lacks capacity to acquire a new domicile by choice.

An important issue concerns how the concept of domicile relates to non-natural persons such as corporations. The concept of "corporate domicile" appears throughout legal materials, and conflict of laws analysis focuses on the domicile of corporations as well as natural persons. Scholars, however, criticize the notion of corporate domicile, arguing that the domicile concept focuses on social and family factors inapplicable to corporate structure. According to this view, concepts such as "state of incorporation" and "principal place of business" are far more apt concepts for analyzing the relationship between a corporation and legal regulation. PETER HAY, PATRICK J. BORCHERS & SYMEON C. SYMEONIDES, CONFLICT OF LAWS 336-337 (5th ed. 2010). A recently endorsed approach for matching a corporation with a "home" jurisdiction is the "nerve center" test for citizenship developed in the context of the diversity jurisdiction statute governing federal courts. *Hertz Corp. v. Friend*, 130 S. Ct. 1181 (2010). A corporation's nerve center is the place where its main headquarters are situated—assuming those headquarters are situated where those who run the corporation actually coordinate and control corporate activity.[20] Corporations arguably hold greater control over their home, since those who control the corporation can choose the place of inception or birth—otherwise known as place of incorporation. Indeed, some commentators have even observed that corporate control over place of incorporation—in

---

20. The diversity jurisdiction statute, 28 U.S.C. §1332, provides the general rule that "a corporation shall be deemed a citizen of any state by which it has been incorporated and of the State where it has its principal place of business."

connection with choice of law rules that look to place of incorporation — vests in corporations considerable control over the laws regulating their affairs. ERIN A. O'HARA & LARRY E. RIBSTEIN, THE LAW MARKET 10 (2009).

Domicile differs from residence, which generally refers to where a person actually lives for a period of time. A person may have many residences, but can possess only one domicile. Moreover, one may reside in one place and be domiciled in another. Residence is a weaker basis for asserting government power than domicile because residence does not require the intention to make a permanent home. Nonetheless, if one has a residence in a particular locale, then one has presumably availed herself of the protections of that jurisdiction's laws. Under such circumstances, fairness would allow the exercise of at least some sovereign power over the resident.

The Reporters for the upcoming Restatement (Third) of Conflict of Laws sought to substitute the concept of habitual residence for the concept of domicile. The concept of habitual residence appears in international treaties as well as in much of the world's domestic law. Habitual residence — as an analytical construct — differs from domicile because a person's domicile has traditionally turned on that person's intent, whereas habitual residence focuses onobjective evidence of where a person's life is centered. The Reporters found that United States law had started to embrace the "habitual residence" concept, and that doing so would have the beneficial effect of bringing United States domestic law in line with major legal systems around the world. The consensus among the advisers and leaders of the American Law Institute, however, was that United States law is not currently positioned to embrace the habitual residence concept. The Reporters therefore changed the terminology back to "domicile," although the draft now accepted by the governing council of the American Law Institute makes clear that determinations of domicile should focus on objective evidence. The current draft of the Restatement (Third) of Conflict of Laws uses the umbrella concept "central link" to embrace both the domicile of a natural person and the central connecting factor for juridical persons — which are entities created by law, such as corporations and limited partnerships.

The relationship between citizenship and domicile (or habitual residence) is more complicated. In deciding international conflict of laws problems, many countries use the concept of citizenship in the same way that United States law uses domicile. From the perspective of states in the United States, however, the two concepts are interchangeable: a citizen of a state is generally a domiciliary of that state — and vice versa. *See* HAY ET AL., *supra*, at 398. The two concepts are not redundant, however, from the United States federal government's perspective: American citizenship is not required for domicile within the United States and domicile in the United States is not required for American citizenship. Indeed, the United States Supreme Court has determined that federal courts may exercise power over absent citizens domiciled abroad, with citizenship alone providing the basis for court power. *Blackmer v. United States*, 284 U.S. 421 (1931). The distinction between domicile and citizenship reflects the reality that domicile can change more quickly and easily than citizenship. Moreover, as is the case with residence, citizenship is sometimes not exclusive: dual citizenship has become more common in today's world.

The definitions of domicile, residence, and citizenship thus far reviewed provide a foundation for applying existing conflict of laws doctrine. Where a court is evaluating whether a jurisdiction has some claim to applying its governing principles to a particular dispute, domicile arguably provides the most fair and workable point of reference of the three. Residence can be problematic because a party can have several residences, thus failing to identify one jurisdiction with a dominant claim for governance. The same is true for citizenship where a party has citizenship in more than one nation. Moreover, because citizenship can be more difficult to change than domicile, domicile can provide a more accurate proxy for a party's *current* orientation toward community membership than citizenship. The party's current orientation provides the best measure of which community's laws the party expects to govern her affairs.

The rich scholarly literature relating to citizenship provides a basis for deeper understanding of what conflict of laws doctrines are trying to accomplish — as well as insight into conceptual issues related to world governance.[21] As compared to domicile and residence, citizenship is a far more nuanced concept, particularly in today's mobile and interconnected world. A look at citizenship concepts sheds light on various connections that may exist between an individual, her identity, and sovereign governments to which she might be subject.

As described by Professor Linda Bosniak, contemporary understandings of citizenship have elements of "status, rights, political engagement, and identity." LINDA BOSNIAK, THE CITIZEN AND THE ALIEN 18-19 (2006). To begin, citizenship includes membership in a political community, which entitles one to certain rights and privileges. This may include "civil, political, and social rights." *Id.* at 19. Citizenship can also include certain responsibilities, such as payment of taxes, compliance with rules, and participation in collective governance. Today, this latter notion includes "the process of democratic self-government, deliberative democracy, and the practice of active engagement in the life of political community." *Id.* Finally, the "identity" component of citizenship embodies the psychological connection and sense of solidarity that an individual has with a social group, usually composed of residents of a nation-state.

While historically citizenship has usually been connected to the territory (and political community) of a nation state, the concept is now sometimes expanded to supranational communities such as the European Union. Moreover, as globalization has begun to diminish the importance of territorial boundaries, humans have begun to detach their identities from physical location. For this reason, theorists such as Professor Peter Spiro argue that citizenship status is increasingly divorced from physical location and that community membership defined by reference to a nation-state has become less meaningful. PETER J. SPIRO, BEYOND CITIZENSHIP: AMERICAN IDENTITY AFTER GLOBALIZATION 4-7 (2008).

---

21. *See, e.g.*, LINDA BOSNIAK, THE CITIZEN AND THE ALIEN (2006); PETER J. SPIRO, BEYOND CITIZENSHIP: AMERICAN IDENTITY AFTER GLOBALIZATION (2008); Ralf Michaels, *Global Legal Pluralism*, 5 ANN. REV. LAW & SOC. SCI. 243 (2009); Paul Schiff Berman, *Towards a Cosmopolitan Vision of Conflict of Laws: Redefining Governmental Interests in a Global Era*, 153 U. PA. L. REV. 1819 (2005).

This process of untangling citizenship from cultural identity and group loyalty, however, is not following a smooth trajectory. The label "citizen" continues to have great consequence for matters such as immigration, entitlement to legal protections, and government services. Consider, for example, laws restricting wearing of a *burqa* and *niqab* on French territory: French authorities have suggested that *burqa* or *niqab* wearing may reflect a woman's rejection of core French values, justifying the government to refuse the woman citizenship status. This position coincides with national policy agendas implementing "integration testing" seeking to erect barriers to citizenship for immigrants. *See* Siobhán Mullally, *Civic Integration, Migrant Woman and the Veil: At the Limits of Rights?*, 74 MOD. L. REV. 27, 28-29 (2011).

Questions about personal identity and cultural affiliation may not appear to pertain directly to the choice of law inquiry concerning what law should apply in a particular lawsuit. Nonetheless, identity and affiliation bear on how readily an individual may embrace (psychologically, physically, or otherwise) a court's decision that a particular jurisdiction's law governs her dispute with another. Identity and cultural affiliation belong to the constellation of concerns for evaluating the fairness and justice of a choice of law decision.

What will be the continued relevance of conflict of laws doctrine as the world becomes more globalized and the significance of citizenship erodes? In the passage that follows, Professor Karen Knop argues that because conflict of laws aligns with the "private side" of citizenship, the discipline will continue to play an important role in world governance. To appreciate this argument, one must understand the distinction between private international law and public international law. Public international law "mostly concerns the political interactions of states" and private international law relates to "conflicts and cooperation among national legal systems." MARK WESTON JANIS, INTERNATIONAL LAW 2 (5th ed. 2008). While both private and public international law are relevant to conflict of laws method and practice, private international law is much closer to the core of conflict of laws. In fact, most scholars agree that private international law is a synonym for conflict of laws.

Generally, we think about citizenship as something very public, reflected in a social contract between the individual and the state. But citizenship matters also pertain to the more private settings generally involved in conflict of laws: settings where two individuals or other entities sue each other in a civil law suits.[22] In such settings, citizenship issues bear on whether someone can be sued or can sue and avail himself of a body of law whether or not he has even been in the territory whose government makes this law. With this background, consider Professor Knop's arguments about the private side of citizenship:

---

22. The use of private in this context takes on a slightly different aspect than the "private" in "private international law." Private in this context refers to the notion that, at least in the United States, conflict of laws doctrine is confined to civil lawsuits between private parties (with the occasional exception of lawsuits where a sovereign acts in the capacity of a private party—such as tort defendant). Thus, for example, conflict of laws doctrine in the United States does not generally encompass whether one sovereign may prosecute an individual under the sovereign's own criminal laws for crimes committed outside the sovereign's territory.

Most writers on citizenship begin with the picture of the sovereign state found in public international law, even if only to diminish or reject its significance. In this picture, each state has exclusive control over its territory, and the people of the state are joined to it by nationality. Paradigmatically, the state's laws operate within its borders, and its nationals live within its borders. From this clear-cut picture of the state, citizenship analysis may move to the blurriness caused by economic globalization, supra- and subnational institutions, mass migration, refugee flows, and other phenomena of interdependence that challenge the analysts to think differently about the boundaries of community and membership. Accordingly, we next find explorations in the direction of postnational citizenship: overlapping identities (dual nationality), a spectrum of membership (rights of noncitizens, including basic human rights and those rights specific to refugees, migrant workers, residents, and so on), and lived membership (a right to naturalization of noncitizens born and raised in the state).

In contrast, it is an obvious, but profound and underadvertised point that private international law is based on the normality of encountering the foreign. Private international law starts with a different set of assumptions about the interaction of states. It begins with the idea that there will be individual comings and goings across borders. The very raison d'etre of private international law is that the state will inevitably contain foreigners of different kinds — not only those who aspire to citizenship, but also those who are *de passage*, traders, exiles, expatriates, transmigrants — and this will necessarily draw states into a relationship with one another. Furthermore, such individuals may be regulated by the laws of more than one state and thus belong to more than one state. Private international law is tasked with where and how to work out these collisions between laws. Hence, phenomena such as globalization and mass migration do not disturb the private-international-law paradigm; they chiefly intensify what is already inherent in it. It follows that overlapping identities, different kinds of membership in the state, lived membership — virtually all of the innovative ways of theorizing identity and citizenship — correspond to traditional private-international-law techniques and their interaction with public law.

In the common law, the individual's relationship to place also differs from public to private. Short of full-fledged citizenship, the law of public membership is concerned with *residence*. At its most minimal, residence is simply some length of physical presence. As a metric of legal entitlement — perhaps ultimately to citizenship — residence tends to assume some positive contribution to or participation in the life of the state. For example, illegal immigrants are part of the economy, or foreign workers send their children to school. Residence is keyed to the individual's vertical relationship to the state.

Private international law could, of course, share public law's marker of belonging and employ nationality as the legal link. . . . [For example, access] to the English courts operates on a distinct notion of "home," found in tests for jurisdiction such as *domicile.* Jurisdiction does not rest simply on the subject's humanity and presence within the state, as it does for the purposes of many human rights, which immediately include the subject. But unlike the assumptions made about residence in certain citizenship theories, residence as an element of domicile is not concerned with participation in the life of the state or some notion of graduated interdependence that would demand inclusion. Instead, the relationship to place is quite literally to the place and not to the state. A person can be domiciled in a country without ever naturalizing and, conversely, can naturalize without necessarily being found to be domiciled in that country. In fact, the relationship to place may even be against the state. The element of intent in domicile allows for the individual's self-exclusion or inclusion, and on the individual's own terms. Domicile is formally committed to "my choice, my way," whereas nationality is a two-way relationship and a relationship based on the acceptance of common values. . . . [I]f an individual is domiciled in a state other than her state of nationality, the result is overlapping state-based identities *without* dual nationality; a set of entitlements grounded in domicile *as well as* human rights and any rights specific to her as a refugee, migrant worker, resident, or other recognized category of nonnational; and a membership capable of reflecting that individual's *lived* attachment to or disattachment from the state *in real time.*

Karen Knop, *Citizenship, Public and Private,* 71 LAW & CONTEMP. PROBS. 309, 319-321 (2008).

The following set of cases arises from inheritance tax litigation over the estate of a prominent businessman, John Dorrance, founder and majority owner of the Campbell Soup Company. For a good part of his married life, Dr. Dorrance was domiciled at an estate known as Pomona Farms in Cinnaminson, New Jersey. In 1925, he acquired a new residence, known as Woodcrest, in Radnor, Pennsylvania. You will see in reviewing these cases that the evidence suggested that his family life became centered in Pennsylvania. Yet he took pains to make several formal declarations indicating his continued intention to retain a New Jersey domicile. Following his death, both Pennsylvania and New Jersey authorities took the position that he died domiciled in their states, and that his estate therefore owed taxes to the respective states. Perhaps not surprisingly, the Pennsylvania and New Jersey courts issued contradictory rulings, concluding that Dorrance died domiciled in their respective states. Which court got it right?

In re Dorrance's Estate

309 Pa. 151 (Pa. 1932)

Opinion by Mr. Chief Justice FRAZER:
[This is an appeal from a decree bassed on the finding that John T. Dorrance was domiciled in Cinnaminson Township, Burlington County, New Jersey, and not in Pennsylvania for inheritance tax purposes. The Pennsylvania Supreme Court first noted that it would review the domicile determination as a conclusion of law and as a ultimate questions of fact. The court also noted that the deceased, John T. Dorrance, was born in Pennsylvania, became employed at the Joseph Campbell Preserve Company in Camden, New Jersey, after his education, and remained with that firm and its corporate successor, the Campbell Soup

Company, until his death. Dorrance made his residence in Camden at the start of his career, and moved to Philadelphia with his wife, living there until 1911.]

... In 1909 Dorrance purchased a country place known as Pomona Farms in Cinnaminson Township, Burlington County, New Jersey. He later conveyed the title to this property to the Campbell Preserve Company and thereafter leased the premises from that company. ... Dorrance and his family entered into possession on May 7, 1911, and ... from this date until November 14, 1925, decedent's domicile was in New Jersey.

During the years which passed from the time of his first association with the Campbell Company, Dorrance rose rapidly in the management and control of the business. The company itself grew into one of the largest canning and preserving enterprises in this country. ... Dorrance became the head of the company and from 1915 until his death was the owner of all its capital stock. In 1922 the company was reorganized as the Campbell Soup Company, a New Jersey corporation with offices in Camden. At the time of his death Dorrance had amassed an immense fortune. ...

In 1925 he purchased a large ... estate known as "Woodcrest" located in Radnor, Delaware County, Pennsylvania, in the suburbs of Philadelphia. ... Speaking of the purchase of the Radnor Estate, Mrs. Dorrance, the widow, testified as follows:

"It was purchased so that our children would be more in contact with children and where they could go to school more easily with children with their prospects in life, and where we could do some entertaining for my oldest daughter who was then coming of age and who mingled with the world; and where I ... would be nearer my associates." In 1925 the children comprised four daughters aged respectively, 18, 16, 14 and 10, and one son in his sixth year.

The house at Radnor was first occupied by the Dorrance family on November 14, 1925, at which time their entire personal effects were removed from Cinnaminson to Radnor. The Commonwealth contends that from this date until his death, almost five years later, Dorrance was domiciled in Pennsylvania. Despite an attempt on the part of the executors to demonstrate that the former home in New Jersey was maintained as the principal home and establishment of decedent, and that there was a mere occasional occupancy of the Radnor place, it is our opinion the evidence clearly indicates that from 1925 until the autumn of 1930, the Radnor Estate was the real and only home of the Dorrances, and except for occasional visits [elsewhere], "Woodcrest" was occupied continuously by decedent and his family until his death, and at present is the family home. The place at Cinnaminson was retained in substantially the same condition as before the acquisition of "Woodcrest," but with the number of servants reduced from ten to two. It was occupied after 1926 by the mother and sister of Dorrance, who remained there until their deaths in 1928 and 1929 respectively. During their occupancy, one or two rooms in the house were reserved for Dorrance and his wife and available for their temporary use at any time. The evidence is not convincing that Dorrance used the Cinnaminson residence for any extended period after removal of his family to Radnor. Undoubtedly he made occasional visits to the place, but these can be accounted for on several grounds: his mother and sister were both living there and eventually developed fatal illnesses; the Cinnaminson place was in the midst of the experimental farms of the soup company; above all, in addition to a claimed sentimental attachment to Cinnaminson, he was anxious to give color to his asserted intention to retain New Jersey as the place of his domicile.

Much of the vast amount of testimony and exhibits introduced by both appellant and appellees is immaterial to the issue, but there are a number of facts which, in our opinion, establish beyond question that continuously since 1925 the true home of Dorrance and his family was in Pennsylvania, and that the New Jersey residence was retained by him merely to lend weight to the fiction that he was domiciled there. Before 1925 Dorrance employed ten servants at Cinnaminson. After 1925 there were never more than four, and after the death of Dorrance's mother in 1929 only two. At "Woodcrest" sixteen servants were employed in the house and ten to twelve others worked on the grounds. There was a corresponding difference in the running expenses of the two properties. In 1924 the living expenses at Cinnaminson were slightly over twenty-nine thousand dollars. After 1925 the expenditures were considerably diminished and in 1929 amounted to approximately $6,500. On the other hand, the maintenance of the Radnor Estate exceeded $90,000 in 1929, and the year before amounted to approximately $95,000.

Although the comparative size of two residences is not conclusive of the fact of domicile, it is evidence of the intention to make one place the principal home. The expenditure of a very large sum of money for a residence which is not adapted to nor designed for mere seasonal occupancy is strong indication of an intention to make it the principal residence and main establishment of the family, particularly where the new residence is more elaborate and pretentious than any former abode.

. . . The sumptuous residence in Pennsylvania was consistently chosen by Dorrance himself, as well as his wife and children, for all the outstanding events of their social life. Dorrance gave a number of large dinner parties there for men, principally business associates and friends, at which more than sixty guests were usually present. He and his wife entertained smaller groups for dinner quite frequently. His children invited their friends to "Woodcrest" for parties. One of his daughters was married in 1926 at the Radnor Church and the wedding reception was held at "Woodcrest"; another, who was at the debutante age, was presented to society at an elaborate affair there in 1929.

. . .

Servants who had been in the household during the period in question testified that, except when he was absent on vacations, Dorrance spent practically every night at his home in Radnor. He traveled back and forth daily from Radnor to his office in Camden. His weekends were spent at the Radnor place. . . . The children were entered in schools from the Radnor residence and with their mother regularly attended St. Martin's Church in Radnor Township. Dorrance himself did not transfer his membership to the Radnor Church but maintained his affiliation with a church in Riverton, New Jersey. This latter was only one of many things which he did to avoid the appearance of identifying himself with the community in which he resided with his family; and that these acts, together with his declarations of residence in New Jersey, were intended to bolster his assertions that he remained domiciled in New Jersey, there can be little doubt. His real motive and the reasons which prompted this course of conduct are apparent.

With a remarkable demonstration of the same business acumen and sagacity which enabled him to accumulate his enormous personal fortune, he carefully drew his wills (all except the last one previous to 1925), with the intent of retaining for his children, after his death, his 100% interest in the Campbell Soup Company. This he would be able to do under the laws of New Jersey by the accumulation of income for the payment of inheritance and estate taxes, and with the assurance that his wife could not elect to take personalty against his will, which would not be possible under the laws of Pennsylvania. In addition, it was a matter of considerable importance for him to declare himself a resident of New Jersey in respect to the payment of annual taxes on personal property, as his stock in the soup company, as well as United States and New Jersey government securities, were exempt from the tax in that state. By claiming a residence in New Jersey, Dorrance was able to effect a large annual saving in taxation. Taxation matters were discussed by him in his conversations with leading business men and bankers in Philadelphia and emphasized by his New Jersey counsel. For that reason, Dorrance informed others he hesitated to take up residence at Radnor, and when contemplating the purchase of "Woodcrest" he consulted his attorney, who advised him that retention of his New Jersey domicile "was largely a matter of intention." Consequently, following his removal to the estate at Radnor, he scrupulously endeavored to declare in formal documents and on many occasions that he was a resident of New Jersey. Upon the advice of his attorney he executed an agreement with his wife that their residence should remain at Cinnaminson despite the occupancy of "Woodcrest" during "a portion of each year." The agreement stated that both would refrain from voting elsewhere than in Burlington County, New Jersey, and contained other clauses of a similar nature. Dorrance refused to accept a directorship in the Pennsylvania Railroad until assured by the president of the company that it was not necessary for more than a majority of the directors of that corporation to be residents of Pennsylvania. On many occasions and in various formal documents executed after 1925 he stated his residence to be at Cinnaminson, but counsel for the Commonwealth has indicated several instances in which Dr. Dorrance did give his address as Radnor. Mrs. Dorrance was not as consistent as her husband in her declarations concerning residence. . . . All the members of the family were listed in the social register with address as Woodcrest, Radnor. In 1929, for the first time, the residence at Cinnaminson was included with that of Radnor.

A circumstance of considerable importance was the fact that after 1925 many of Dorrance's friends and acquaintances assumed he had become a resident of Pennsylvania. Dorrance discussed this with his lawyer, stating he had denied to them any intention of giving up his domicile in New Jersey. . . .

We come now to an examination of the law applicable in determining the domicile of decedent. The precise question is as follows: May expressions of a man

to the effect that he desires to retain a domicile of choice in one state, prevail over
the intention to make a new home manifested by an actual removal to the new
residence in another state, and accompanied by a manner of living which can
leave no doubt that the new abode is the principal residence and establishment,
particularly where the wish to retain the old domicile is colored by the motive of
regulating his affairs after death in a manner not permitted by the laws of the state
removed to, and is also bound up with the purpose of avoiding payment of
substantial taxes on personal property? We are of opinion that such is not the
law and that John T. Dorrance was domiciled in Pennsylvania at the time of his
death.

. . . With a few scattered expressions to the contrary, the law is generally settled that, as regards the determination of domicile, a person's expression of desire
may not supersede the effect of his conduct. . . . "Every person must have a
domicile somewhere and a man cannot elect to make his home in one place
for the general purposes of life, and in another place for the purposes of taxation": *Feehan v. Tax Commissioner,* 237 Mass. 169, 171. "A declaration [as to
domicile] that is self-serving and not followed by acts in accordance with the declaration will not be regarded as conclusive, but will yield to the intent which the
acts and conduct of the person clearly indicate."

The celebrated English author, A. V. Dicey, whose statements concerning the
law of domicile are frequently quoted with approval in this country, in his book
"Conflict of Laws," . . . says: "Direct expressions, however, of intention may be
worth little as evidence. The person who uses them may not know what constitutes
a domicile. He may call a place his home, simply because he often lives there. He
may wish to be, or to appear, domiciled in one country, while in fact residing
permanently and intending so to reside, i.e., being domiciled, in another. . . ."

An attempt was made by counsel for appellees during the argument and in
the briefs to show that Dorrance at no time intended to make his Radnor Estate a
permanent home and that he contemplated returning to Cinnaminson at an
indefinite future time. Assuming such to be the case, there is no doubt that
such vague intention of resuming a former domicile will not prevent the acquisition of a new one. "If a person changes his domicile without any present intention of removing therefrom it is none the less his domicile, although he may
entertain a floating intention to return, or to move somewhere else at some future
period. . . . If there be both actual residence and intention of remaining — the
animus manendi — then a domicile is established": *Worsham v. Ligon,* 144 G.
707. "If a person has actually removed to another place, with an intention of
remaining there for an indefinite time, and as a place of fixed present domicile,
it is to be deemed his place of domicile, notwithstanding he may entertain a floating intention to return at some future period": *Gilbert v. David,* 235 U.S. 561, 569,
quoting Story's "Conflict of Laws." . . .

Having now ascertained that intention alone cannot defeat the acquisition of
a new domicile where other facts show a change of domicile has actually occurred,
it remains to consider whether the evidence in this case is sufficient to warrant a
finding that Dorrance was domiciled in Pennsylvana, as contended by appellant.
It is true the burden of showing a change from a former domicile is upon the party

asserting it, but the fact of residence in a particular place is prima facie evidence of domicile. . . . The Commonwealth having established by adequate evidence that, at the time of his death, Dorrance had an actual residence in Pennsylvania, it was incumbent upon the executors to rebut the presumption arising therefrom. . . . This, in our opinion, they have failed to do. . . .

One of the most satisfactory definitions of domicile is that stated by Story in his "Conflict of Laws": "By the term domicile in its ordinary acceptation is meant the place where a person lives or has his home. In a strict legal sense that is properly the domicile of a person where he has his true, fixed, permanent home and principal establishment, and to which, whenever he is absent, he has the intention of returning." To acquire a domicile of choice two things must concur: "(1) Physical presence in the place where domicile is alleged to have been acquired; (2) Intent to make that place the home of the party": Goodrich "Conflict of Laws."

. . . In our opinion the evidence clearly establishes the legal domicile of Dr. Dorrance to be in Pennsylvania and accordingly there is due the Commonwealth an inheritance transfer tax, based upon the agreed value of his estate at the time of his death.

[Dissenting opinions by Justices SCHAFFER and KEPHART omitted.]

In re Dorrance's Estate

170 A. 601 (N.J. Prerog. Ct. 1934), *aff'd mem.* Dorrance v. Thayer-Martin, 176 A. 902 (N.J. 1935)

In re estate of John T. Dorrance, deceased. Ethel M. Dorrance et al., executors, &c., appellants v. J. H. Thayer-Martin, tax commissioner, respondent.

BUCHANAN, Vice-Ordinary.

[The court recounted the procedural background for the case, noting that the New Jersey tax commissioner had originally assessed transfer inheritance tax amounting to nearly $17 million against the estate of John T. Dorrance. The court noted that the estate had taken the position that Dorrance was not domiciled in New Jersey at the time of his death, and that therefore the tax commissioner had erred in including the value of Dorrance's intangible personal property in computing the tax.]

The essential issue is therefore whether or not Dr. Dorrance, at the time of his death, was domiciled in New Jersey. If he was, then the tax in question is correct (at least substantially); if he was not, then no tax can be levied by New Jersey, except as to the few thousand dollars of tangible personal property located here — for almost the whole of the estate (of some $115,000,000) consisted of stocks, bonds, and other intangible personalty. . . .

[The court summarized the tax proceeding against the estate in Pennsylvania, and the parties' arguments. First, the court considered the contention that the estate should be estopped or precluded from taking the position that "Dr. Dorrance was not domiciled in New Jersey." The court found that this contention "may well be . . . sound," noting that the estate had earlier taken the position (consistent with Dorrance's wishes) that Dorrance *was* domiciled in New Jersey *before* the Pennsylvania authorities had won the inheritance tax case.

The New Jersey court next rejected the estate's assertion that it was bound by full faith and credit principles to accept the decision in Pennsylvania courts that Dorrance was domiciled in Pennsylvania. The court stated that full faith and credit principles allow it to inquire into the jurisdiction of the Pennsylvania courts. If Dorrance was not domiciled in Pennsylvania, the New Jersey court reasoned that the Pennsylvania courts lacked power to impose an inheritance tax determination. The New Jersey court therefore viewed the domicile question as integral to the Pennsylvania court's power, and therefore reached the merits of the domicile question. The New Jersey court formulated the question for decision as whether Dorrance became domiciled in Pennsylvania later in his life and stayed a domiciliary there until his death.]

The evidence shows that Dr. Dorrance after finishing his education went to work at Camden, New Jersey, in 1907, and lived in the same place; that he continued to reside in Camden after his marriage in 1906; that he and his wife finally found the kind of a home they wanted at Cinnaminson, New Jersey, and established themselves in it as their home in 1911. The evidence need not be recited in detail, but it clearly establishes that at that time that house became in fact the residence and home of Dr. Dorrance and his family; that Dr. Dorrance intended it as his fixed and permanent residence and home; that he intended it to remain such indefinitely; that he had no intention at that time that it should not always remain his home. In short, the evidence establishes beyond any doubt that in 1911 Dr. Dorrance became and was domiciled at Cinnaminson, New Jersey, and that that place continued to be both his actual residence or home and his legal domicile, at least until 1925. . . .

The evidence further shows that in 1925 he purchased a house and grounds at Radnor, Pennsylvania, and made extensive improvements, with the intent and purpose that this place should be a residence for himself and his family; and that in the latter part of 1925 he and his family moved into the Radnor house and actually occupied it as a residence; that from that time to the time of his death Dr. Dorrance actually occupied the Radnor house as a residence most of the time . . . and the instances of his occupation of the Cinnaminson residence were not particularly frequent and were of comparatively short duration, and the instances of occupation of the Cinnaminson residence by his wife and children were even less frequent and of even shorter duration than his own.

If the question of the domicile of Dr. Dorrance at the time of his death depended only upon the fact as to what residence he chiefly occupied as a home during the five years preceding his death, it would probably be conceded by the respondent that his domicile was in Pennsylvania. That fact, however, is neither the determining factor, nor a controlling factor, in this case, under the law of domicile.

There are certain fundamental principles of the law of domicile, so thoroughly established everywhere as to be frequently called "axiomatic." Among them are the following:

1. When a man has acquired a domicile in a particular place, that place remains his domicile until he acquires another domicile.

2. To effectuate such a change of domicile it is requisite that he shall in fact remove from the old domicile to the new, with the intention of abandoning the old domicile and of remaining permanently or indefinitely in the new.

3. The burden of proof to establish that a change of domicile has occurred rests upon the party so asserting.

4. A man has the right to choose his own domicile, and his motive in such choice is immaterial.

5. A man may have more than one residence (such as a summer residence and a winter residence), but he cannot have more than one domicile at any given time.

6. If a man has more than one residence during a given period, he has the right to select which one of them shall be his domicile.

. . .

The appellants (and the Pennsylvania court) rely on the facts that Dr. Dorrance purchased the Radnor house and improved it with the intention of using it as a residence or home for himself and his family; that it was far larger, more expensive and pretentious than the old home at Cinnaminson; that he thereafter — except for European trips and summer vacations — occupied it by far the greatest part of the time (and his family even more so). . . .

The evidence in the present case is overwhelming that . . . Dr. Dorrance . . . never had the intention of abandoning his home at Cinnaminson; he never had the intention of making the Radnor residence his permanent home; he always had the intention of returning to his home at Cinnaminson.

. . . His life had been spent in New Jersey; his business had been there for years and was still there; all of his own interests were there; it was there that he had his home and there he wanted to remain. . . . His children, however, were growing up. He had four daughters, the eldest was eighteen. For the purpose of completing their education and giving them social advantages deemed necessary or advisable for their benefit in approaching maturity, he yielded to his wife's arguments and solicitations and established the new residence and home in Radnor. But it is entirely clear from the proofs that he did this with no intention of abandoning the home at Cinnaminson; with no intention that the Radnor house should be his permanent home; with every intention that the Radnor house was not to be his permanent home but only a temporary home for so long only as should be requisite or advisable to complete their education and give them the proper social preparation for their start in life, and with the intent that as soon, at least, as that had been done — if not indeed earlier — he would return to his home in Cinnaminson.

That this was his intent was manifested in almost innumerable ways. It is difficult, if not impossible, to conceive of a case in which the items of evidence in this behalf could be more numerous. It appears from his conversations and his correspondence with his wife, his relatives, his lawyers, his friends, his business associates, his servants, and many others with whom he came in contact. His business remained at Camden, near the Cinnaminson house; his office remained at Camden; his securities remained in the Camden banks; his personal counsel and legal advisor continued to be Judge Lippincott whose offices were in Camden and whose home was near Cinnaminson.

He continued actively as a member of the vestry and senior warden of Christ Church, at Riverton, New Jersey, near Cinnaminson. He was interested in investments in New Jersey and not in Pennsylvania. He was assessed and taxed on his personal property in Cinnaminson and not in Radnor. He and his wife continued to vote in Cinnaminson; neither one ever voted in Radnor. He was active politically in various ways in New Jersey, but not in Pennsylvania. He was appointed to, and served for several years on, a commission of the State of New Jersey. His motor vehicle registrations and drivers licenses were from New Jersey.

His intention to retain his residence in New Jersey is evidenced by many, many written statements and declarations, many of them in legal documents or instruments of various kinds, some of them under oath, and including his will — an instrument of particular importance, not only because of the nature and solemn character of such an instrument, but because of the particular and forceful nature of the expressions therein as to his residence.

. . . The foregoing is by no means an exhaustive recital of all the evidence on the point; but enough has been mentioned to show the great weight of evidence to prove that he had no intent to abandon the Cinnaminson house as his permanent home; that it continued, as always, the "old homestead"; that he intended the Radnor house only as a temporary, not a permanent home; that he always intended to return to the permanent home at Cinnaminson.

It results therefore that he never acquired a legal domicile in Pennsylvania; that he never lost his legal domicile in New Jersey; that the Pennsylvania court was without jurisdiction to levy transfer inheritance tax on the intangible personal property of his estate; that the Pennsylvania assessment was illegal, invalid; that the decision of the Pennsylvania court is in nowise binding upon this court or the tax commissioner of this state; that New Jersey has the right — and the sole right — to levy transfer inheritance tax upon the intangible personal estate; and that to that extent, and so far as that ground of appeal is concerned, the present tax must be affirmed.

Notes on
THE DORRANCE CASES

1. Both the New Jersey and Pennsylvania courts generally agreed on the legal principles governing the domicile question, but disagreed on the significance they placed on the efforts Dorrance made to suggest his continued domicile in New Jersey after his family's life in Radnor, Pennsylvania became

more meaningful. Consider the courts' varying views on the following fact: before purchasing the residence in Radnor, Pennsylvania, John Dorrance consulted an attorney who advised Dorrance that he would not lose his New Jersey domicile if he purchased the Radnor property. Did this fact help the Dorrance estate prove that Dorrance retained his New Jersey domicile until his death? Or does it cut the other way: suggesting that Dorrance lost his New Jersey domicile and died a domiciliary of Pennsylvania?

2. The subsequent history of the *Dorrance* cases suggests that the estate tried mightily (and unsuccessfully) to avoid double taxation. The history unfolded as follows: as reflected in the decisions above, the Pennsylvania Supreme Court decision preceded the New Jersey Supreme Court decision. The estate tried to take the Pennsylvania Supreme Court decision to the United States Supreme Court, which denied review, 287 U.S. 660 (1932). The state common law concept of domicile was unreviewable in the United States Supreme Court and any full faith and credit or due process claims had not been properly preserved. Next, the Dorrance estate unsuccessfully attempted to invoke the original jurisdiction of the United States Supreme Court on the theory that the dispute presented a conflict between states. *New Jersey v. Pennsylvania*, 287 U.S. 580 (1932); *Pennsylvania v. New Jersey*, 288 U.S. 618 (1933).

The estate then paid taxes in Pennsylvania, and unsuccessfully raised a constitutional challenge in the ongoing New Jersey tax enforcement proceeding there. *In re Dorrance's Estate*, 170 A. 601 (N.J. Prerog. Ct. 1934), *aff'd*, 176 A. 902 (N.J. 1935), *aff'd*, 184 A. 743 (N.J. 1936).

Next, the estate tried a flanking maneuver: requesting a federal court to issue an injunction of the New Jersey enforcement action. Ultimately, the United States Supreme Court ruled that such an injunction would be barred by the Anti-Injunction Act, 28 U.S.C. §2283. *Hill v. Martin*, 296 U.S. 393 (1935). Apparently having exhausted all avenues for relief, the estate then paid the New Jersey probate taxes. *See generally* Kathleen Leslie Roin, *Due Process Limits on State Estate Taxation: An Analogy to the State Corporate Income Tax*, 94 YALE L.J. 1229, 1231 n.10 (1985).

According to news coverage, the Commonwealth of Pennsylvania sought to collect $31,465,200 inheritance taxes from the estate it valued at $200,000,000. New Jersey imposed taxes of $12,000,000 on an appraisal there of $114,850,733. The estate paid federal taxes in the amount of $9,500,000. *Dorrance, Death & Taxes*, TIME, Nov. 1, 1931, *available at* http://www.time.com/time/magazine/article/0,9171,753116,00.html.

3. The *Dorrance* cases as well as the procedural wrangles that occurred after they were handed down illustrate the tolerance for duplicative litigation reflected in our federalist system. As the cases demonstrate, this tolerance often yields conflicting rulings—as cases going to litigation often

involve questions over which reasonable minds might differ. Should procedural systems in the United States be changed in order to reduce this possibility for conflicting rulings? In the context of proceedings simultaneously pending in state and federal courts, judicially created abstention doctrines serve to reduce friction that might result from the duplicate litigation. For cases proceeding on separate tracks in different state court systems, the full faith and credit clause together with preclusion doctrines serve to reduce the amount of conflicting rulings. As demonstrated in Chapter 4, however, full faith and credit as well as preclusion principles trigger only when litigation has reached a final judgment. Consider, however, how you — as a lawyer for the Dorrance estate — might have sought to preserve the estate's ability to avail itself of these principles.

4. Domicile rules can have significance beyond the individuals whose domicile is at issue. Take the example of voter registration in a college town. Should students who reside in a college town be considered domiciliaries for the purpose of voter registration? Although students represent diverse political affiliations, some institutions of higher education tend to attract students with certain political preferences. Consider, for example, the composition of the student body of Reverend Falwell's Liberty University in Virginia in contrast with the composition of the student body of Oberlin College in Ohio. Here is a cross-section of some of the rulings: *People v. Osborne*, 135 N.W. 921, 923 (Mich. 1912) (finding that students cannot become electors in the areas in which their institutions are located because such an action would make them gain or lose a residence while a student, unless student had no domicile and made the college town her domicile in good faith, becoming a citizen of the town); *Chomeau v. Roth*, 72 S.W.2d 997, 999 (Mo. Ct. App. 1934) (observing that fixed intention of seminary students of not returning to their original residences after graduation but remaining in the seminary for an indefinite time was evidence that students abandoned their original domicile in favor of college town); *Lloyd v. Babb*, 251 S.E.2d 843, 864 (N.C. 1979) (holding that student is entitled to register to vote in a place where she is attending school if she (1) has abandoned her prior home, (2) has a present intent of making the place she is attending school her home, and (3) intends to remain in the college town as long as she is a student there and until she acquires a new domicile); *Wilson v. Symm*, 341 F. Supp. 8, 15 (S.D. Tex. 1972) (ruling that states may follow a rebuttable presumption that college or university students are nonresidents for the sake of voting provided states give students a reasonable opportunity to prove domicile in the college town). For an analysis of a controversy within New Hampshire regarding the effect of a narrow definition of domicile on student voting, see John B. Greabe, *A Federal Baseline for the Right to Vote*, 112 Colum. L. Rev. Sidebar 62 (2012).

PROBLEM 2-27: LUCINDA'S MOVE

Lucinda lived her entire life in Pennsylvania. In April 2012, she decided to move to Trenton, New Jersey. She made an announcement to her parents and her friends. Using her cell phone in Pennsylvania, she rented an apartment in Trenton, with the lease to begin on June 1. Lucinda quit her job in Pennsylvania effective May 30. Early on June 1, Lucinda loaded all her belongings into her car and began her journey from Pennsylvania to New Jersey. She arrived in Trenton, New Jersey and unloaded her belongings. She then decided that she would return to a friend's house in Pennsylvania for dinner. After dinner, she began her journey back to the Trenton apartment, but got involved in a car accident and died before her car passed over into New Jersey. Where was she domiciled when she died?

PROBLEM 2-28: OLLIE'S IDEA OF PERFECT: EUGENE, OREGON

Ollie has never been to Oregon, but has carefully studied the state. He believes that the cultural and political orientation of the Eugene, Oregon population closely aligns with his own beliefs and preferences. Ollie physically resides in South Carolina, is employed in South Carolina, and feels compelled to remain in South Carolina in order to care for his aging father. Nonetheless, he would like to associate himself formally and symbolically with Oregon, and has therefore signed a document that formally declares himself to be an Oregon domiciliary. Ollie would like to pay taxes as a resident of Oregon and to vote in elections there. What are the arguments in favor of allowing him to do so? What are the arguments against allowing him to do so?

B. *EARLY CRITIQUE OF THE RESTATEMENT (FIRST) AND EVOLUTION OF THE CENTER OF GRAVITY APPROACH*

The vested rights approach of the Restatement (First) of Conflict of Laws has proven durable; many jurisdictions continue to adhere to its tenets. Nonetheless, courts and commentators have long observed problems with the approach, problems that have inspired new approaches to choice of law questions. Early critique of the vested rights approach took two tracks, highlighting intellectual flaws in the approach's assumptions and results. One of the first intellectual critiques of the vested rights approach came in the work of Professor Walter Wheeler Cook, who drew on the legal realist movement in arguing that the approach embodies the faulty premise that verifiable "rights" exist independently of the court that decides whether to enforce them. According to Cook, a "right" has no existence apart from the discretion of a judicial official, and is only a predictive term "by means of which we describe to each other what prophecies we make as to the probable occurrence" that a judge will act in a certain way. WALTER WHEELER COOK, THE LOGICAL AND LEGAL BASES OF THE CONFLICT OF LAWS 30 (1942). In choice of law analysis, Cook reasoned, we cannot pin down determinate rights, but can merely predict what a judge in a particular jurisdiction might do. Realistically, then, we should not speak of "enforcing vested rights" in a choice of law case.

Cook took this analytical critique one step further in evaluating how a court should do justice in a case with multijurisdictional elements. Using the legal realist notion of predicting what a court will do, Cook argued that a forum court does not really enforce the rights of a foreign jurisdiction. Rather, a foreign right is only a prediction of what a foreign court would do if faced with the same dispute, with the same facts. To do the most accurate job of predicting, the forum court must not only apply the internal rules of the foreign jurisdiction, but must also consider how a foreign court would handle the multijurisdictional aspects of the case. (Although the forum court might attempt to accomplish this through the vehicle of the renvoi doctrine, Cook was wary of the complications caused by that doctrine and instead took this analytical wrinkle as a reason to reject the vested rights theory altogether.)

Another major strain of criticism directed at the vested rights approach focused on its methods and results. In particular, Professor David Cavers criticized the vested rights approach as "jurisdiction selecting": focusing exclusively on the appropriate place (or territory) to provide governing law. He maintained that justice and social expediency counseled making a choice of law decision by reference to the content of laws. According to Cavers, a court should identify what result would follow in a particular case through the application of competing laws, and evaluate these results "in the light of those facts . . . which, from the standpoint of justice between the litigating individuals or of those broader considerations of social policy which conflicting laws may evoke, link [the facts] to one law or the other. . . ." David Cavers, *A Critique of the Choice of Law Problem*, 47 HARV. L. REV. 173, 192-193 (1933). In other words, Cavers argued that choice of law analysis should be "law selecting," not "jurisdiction selecting."

Apparently influenced by Cook and Cavers, courts began to experiment with other methods for solving choice of law problems. One new method took the name "center of gravity" or "grouping of contacts" approach. This approach counseled against rigid determinations based on the location of events, and directed courts instead to emphasize "the law of the place 'which has the most significant contacts with the matter in dispute.'" *Auten v. Auten*, 124 N.E.2d 99, 102 (N.Y. 1954). In reading the following case, evaluate whether the center of gravity approach eliminates the practical and analytical problems of the Restatement (First) of Conflict of Laws.

Haag v. Barnes
175 N.E.2d 441 (N.Y. 1961)

FULD, J.

This appeal is concerned with the effect in New York of an agreement made in another State for the support of a child born out of wedlock.

The complainant Dorothy Haag alleges that in 1947 she moved from Minnesota and took up residence in New York City and that since then she has been a resident of this State. The defendant Norman Barnes, on the other hand, is now and was, during the period involved in this litigation, a resident of Illinois.

According to the statements contained in the complainant's affidavits, she met the defendant in the spring of 1954 in New York. She was a law secretary and had been hired by the defendant through an agency to do work for him while he was in New York on one of his business trips. The relationship between the man and the girl soon "ripened into friendship" and, on the basis of representations that he loved her and planned to divorce his wife and marry her, she was "importuned" into having sexual relations with him.

The complainant further alleges that she became pregnant as a result of having sexual relations with the defendant and that, upon being informed of this, he asked her to move to Illinois to be near him. She refused and, instead, went to live in California with her sister to await the birth of her child. Fearing that the defendant was losing interest in her, however, she returned to Chicago before the child was born and, upon attempting to communicate with the defendant, was referred to his attorney. The latter told Dorothy to choose a hospital in Chicago, which she did, and the baby was born there in December, 1955, the defendant paying the expenses.

Shortly after the birth of the child, her attempts to see the defendant in New York failed and she was advised by his attorney to return to Chicago in order that an agreement might be made for the support of her and her child. Returning to that city, she procured an attorney, recommended by a friend in New York, and signed an agreement on January 12, 1956. The agreement provides, in pertinent part, as follows:

1. It recites payment to the complainant by the defendant of $2,000 between September, 1955 and January, 1956 and a willingness on his part to support her child in the future, on condition that such payments "shall not constitute an admission" that he is the child's father;
2. The defendant promises to pay $50 a week and $75 a month, i.e., a total of $275 a month, "continuing while [the child] is alive and until she attains the age of sixteen years";
3. The complainant agrees "to properly support, maintain, educate, and care for [the child]";
4. The complainant agrees to keep the child in Illinois for at least two years, except if she marries within that period;

5. The complainant "[remises], [releases] and forever [discharges] Norman Barnes . . . from all manner of actions . . . which [she] now has against [him] or ever had or which she . . . hereafter can, shall or may have, for, upon or by reason of any matter, cause or thing whatsoever . . . including . . . the support of [the child]"; and
6. The parties agree that their agreement "shall in all respects be interpreted, construed and governed by the laws of the State of Illinois."

Shortly after the agreement was signed, the complainant received permission, pursuant to one of its provisions, to live in California where she remained for two years. She then returned to New York where she and her child have ever since been supported by the defendant in full compliance with the terms of his agreement. In fact, he has provided sums far in excess of his agreement; all told, we were informed on oral argument, the defendant has paid the complainant some $30,000.

The present proceeding was instituted in 1959 by the service of a complaint and the defendant was thereafter arrested pursuant to section 64 of the New York City Criminal Courts Act. A motion, made by the defendant, to dismiss the proceeding was granted by the Court of Special Sessions and the resulting order was affirmed by the Appellate Division.

The ground urged for dismissal was that the parties had entered into an agreement providing for the support of the child which has been fully performed; that in this agreement the complainant relinquished the right to bring any action for the support of the child; and that, in any event, the action is precluded by the laws of the State of Illinois which, the parties expressly agreed, would govern their rights under the agreement. In opposition, the complainant contended that New York, not Illinois, law applies; that the agreement in question is not a sufficient basis for a motion to dismiss under either section 63 of the New York City Criminal Courts Act or section 121 of the Domestic Relations Law, since both of these provisions provide that "An agreement or compromise made by the mother . . . shall be binding only when the court shall have determined that adequate provision has been made"; and that, even were the Illinois law to apply, it does not bar the present proceeding.

The motion to dismiss was properly granted; the complainant may not upset a support agreement which is itself perfectly consistent with the public policy of this State, which was entered into in Illinois with the understanding that it would be governed by the laws of that State and which constitutes a bar to a suit for further support under Illinois law.

The complainant is correct in her position that, since the agreement was not court approved, it may not be held to be a bar to her suit under New York internal law. On the other hand, it is clear that the agreement is a bar under the internal law of Illinois since it provides, in the language of that State's statute, for a "sum not less than eight hundred dollars." . . . The simple question before us, therefore, is whether the law of New York or of Illinois applies. . . . [T]he answer is . . . that Illinois law applies.

The agreement . . . recites that it "shall in all respects be interpreted, construed and governed by the laws of the State of Illinois" and, since it was also drawn and signed by the complainant in Illinois, the traditional conflicts rule would, without doubt, treat these factors as conclusive and result in applying Illinois law. But, even if the parties' intention and the place of the making of the contract are not given decisive effect, they are nevertheless to be given heavy weight in determining which jurisdiction "'has the most significant contacts with the matter in dispute.'" And, when these important factors are taken together with other of the "significant contacts" in the case, they likewise point to Illinois law. Among these other Illinois contacts are the following: (1) both parties are designated in the agreement as being "of Chicago, Illinois," and the defendant's place of business is and always has been in Illinois; (2) the child was born in Illinois; (3) the persons designated to act as agents for the principals (except for a third alternate) are Illinois residents, as are the attorneys for both parties who drew the agreement; and (4) all contributions for support always have been, and still are being, made from Chicago.

Contrasted with these Illinois contacts, the New York contacts are of far less weight and significance. Chief among these is the fact that child and mother presently live in New York and that part of the "liaison" took place in New York. When these contacts are measured against the parties' clearly expressed intention to have their agreement governed by Illinois law and the more numerous and more substantial Illinois contacts, it may not be gainsaid that the "center of gravity" of this agreement is Illinois and that, absent compelling public policy to the contrary, Illinois law should apply.

As to the question of public policy, we would emphasize that the issue is *not* whether the New York statute reflects a different public policy from that of the Illinois statute, but rather whether enforcement of the particular agreement before us under Illinois law represents an affront to our public policy. It is settled that the New York Paternity Law requires something more than the provision of "the bare necessities otherwise required to be supplied by the community," that, "although providing for indemnification of the community, [it] is chiefly concerned with the welfare of the child." In our judgment, enforcement of the support agreement in this case under Illinois law and the refusal to allow its provisions to be reopened in the present proceeding does not do violence to this policy.

As matter of fact, the agreement before us clearly goes beyond "indemnification of the community" and the provision of "bare necessities." Whether we read it as a whole, or look only to the financial provisions concerned . . . , we must conclude that "the welfare of the child" is fully protected. The public policy of this State having been satisfied, there is no reason why we should not enforce the provisions of the parties' support agreement under Illinois law and treat the agreement as a bar to the present action for support.

The order of the Appellate Division should be affirmed.

Notes on
HAAG v. BARNES

1. How does the center of gravity approach in *Haag v. Barnes* fare in light of Professor Cook's critique of the vested rights approach? Is it more consistent with a legal realist vision of the legal process than the First Restatement? Does the center of gravity approach take greater account of the multijurisdictional nature of disputes than is reflected in the territorial orientation of the First Restatement?

2. How does the center of gravity approach fare in light of Professor Cavers's argument that choice of law decisions should make reference to the content of the laws in conflict? Is the center of gravity approach "law selecting" or "jurisdiction selecting"?

3. Commentators have observed that in *Haag v. Barnes*, Judge Fuld does not provide extensive reasoning to explain his decision that Illinois's contacts were weightier than New York's and that Illinois was the center of gravity for the parties' dispute. One might say, in fact, that the decision has an intuitive quality — as opposed to being analytically and explicitly cerebral. Is it appropriate for judges to make decisions by reference to their intuition? Does it give their opinions an arbitrarily authoritative quality (e.g., "I'm the mommy, that's why!")? Or, by contrast, does obvious use of intuition provide humanity, and hence legitimacy and accessibility, to exercises of judicial power? Whether or not intuition has a legitimate role to play in adjudication, do you suspect it provides an important influence in many court rulings?

On one hand, case law is filled with derogatory references to "judicial intuition." *See, e.g., Lane v. Williams*, 455 U.S. 624, 636-637 (1982) (Marshall, J., dissenting) (arguing that reasoning lacks a basis in law and "appears to derive from nothing more than judicial intuition"); *United States v. Johnson*, 316 F.3d 818, 820 (8th Cir. 2003) (Riley, J., dissenting) ("The district court's reliance on 'you know it when you see it' either presumes materiality, willfulness and falseness or relies on judicial intuition. Judicial intuition is helpful, but intuition alone is not enough to increase punishment. Proof is.").

On the other hand, judges occasionally acknowledge and embrace the key role of intuition in the common law process. Justice Holmes is famous for his assertion that matters such as "intuitions of public policy . . . have had a good deal more to do than the syllogism in determining the rules by which men should be governed." OLIVER WENDELL HOLMES, JR., THE COMMON LAW 1 (1881). Another well-known illustration comes from Justice Stewart's concurrence in *Jacobellis v. Ohio*, 378 U.S. 184, 197 (1964), in which he described the process of identifying hard-core pornography: "I shall not today attempt further to define the kinds of material I understand to be embraced within that shorthand description; and perhaps I could never succeed in intelligibly doing so. But I know it when I see it, and the motion picture involved in this case is not that."

While legal thinkers may be startled by an admission such as Justice Stewart's appearing in a judicial opinion, they have nonetheless been intrigued with the connection between intuition and judicial decision making. A rich scholarly literature has developed, exploring such questions as whether intuition is "non-rational" or illogical, whether judicial reasoning merely masks intuitive judgments, and whether intuition enhances the moral component of decision making. *See, e.g.,* Larry Alexander, *The Banality of Legal Reasoning,* 73 NOTRE DAME L. REV. 517, 524 (1998) (contrasting the process of reasoning with intuition); Paul Gewirtz, *On "I Know It When I See It,"* 105 YALE L.J. 1023, 1024-1031 (1996) (discussing limits of articulating standards and expectations about opinions reflecting a "conscious process of deduction"); Joseph C. Hutcheson, Jr., *The Judgment Intuitive: The Function of the "Hunch" in Judicial Decision,* 14 CORNELL L.Q. 274, 278, 285-287 (1929) (exploring the tension between accommodating intuition and the need to make a judicial opinion appear reasonable); Douglas Lind, *Logic, Intuition, and the Positivist Legacy of H.L.A. Hart,* 52 SMU L. REV. 135, 148-165 (1999) (exploring connections among logic, intuition, and legal formalism); R. George Wright, *The Role of Intuition in Judicial Decisionmaking,* 42 HOUS. L. REV. 1381, 1398-1420 (2006) (describing various forms of judicial reasoning and its dependence on intuition).

4. One contemporary scholar argues that conflict of laws confronts human problems that extend beyond analytical puzzles that pertain to political power, sources of formal authority, and individual rights. Professor Annalise Riles argues that conflict of laws must grapple with issues relating to cultural clashes. A forum court confronting a conflicts case must evaluate and understand a foreign value system, a value system responsible for a legal rule at variance with domestic law. Riles notes that cultural value clashes appear in "seemingly exotic disputes," such as fights about enforcing "agreements stemming from Islamic banking practices," as well as in "more mundane" state tort litigation. Annalise Riles, *Cultural Conflicts,* 71 LAW & CONTEMP. PROBS. 273, 275 (2008). Indeed, in *Haag v. Barnes,* the question whether to enforce a child support agreement or whether to treat a support issue as a criminal matter no doubt represents conflicting cultural attitudes about paternalism toward unwed mothers, freedom of contract, and the gravity of parental support obligations.

Riles observes that cultural conflicts are not always apparent to judges and litigants, and are generally "submerged" in standard choice of law doctrine. *Id.* Does intuition have a role to play in helping to identify the contours and consequences of these cultural differences? Do Riles's observations make the case for *more* routinized, cerebral, and formal legal analysis or less? What is the best way for judges to decide "'fair' in a case of cultural conflict"? *Id.*

> 5. One common complaint about the center of gravity approach is that a court applying the approach does not need to explain the significance of the contacts it weighs and thus does not provide future guidance on how to segregate contacts that matter from those that do not. In addition, the approach does not provide a formal analytical vehicle for articulating and evaluating principles of justice and policy such as freedom of contract or providing a financial safety net for unwed mothers and their children. Despite these limitations, the center of gravity approach has proven enormously influential; it is still followed under the nomenclature "significant contacts" approach in a handful of states and is incorporated into the Restatement (Second) of Conflict of Laws. Many cite the next case, *Babcock v. Jackson,* as an improvement on the free-flowing analysis of *Haag v. Barnes.* Evaluate whether you agree.

Babcock v. Jackson

191 N.E.2d 279 (N.Y. 1963)

Fuld, J.

On Friday, September 16, 1960, Miss Georgia Babcock and her friends, Mr. and Mrs. William Jackson, all residents of Rochester, left that city in Mr. Jackson's automobile, Miss Babcock as guest, for a week-end trip to Canada. Some hours later, as Mr. Jackson was driving in the Province of Ontario, he apparently lost control of the car; it went off the highway into an adjacent stone wall, and Miss Babcock was seriously injured. Upon her return to this State, she brought the present action against William Jackson, alleging negligence on his part in operating his automobile.

At the time of the accident, there was in force in Ontario a statute providing that "the owner or driver of a motor vehicle, other than a vehicle operated in the business of carrying passengers for compensation, is not liable for any loss or damage resulting from bodily injury to, or the death of any person being carried in . . . the motor vehicle." Even though no such bar is recognized under this State's substantive law of torts, the defendant moved to dismiss the complaint on the ground that the law of the place where the accident occurred governs and that Ontario's guest statute bars recovery. [The court below affirmed the judgment of dismissal.]

The question presented is simply drawn. Shall the law of the place of the tort *invariably* govern the availability of relief for the tort or shall the applicable choice of law rule also reflect a consideration of other factors which are relevant to the purposes served by the enforcement or denial of the remedy?

The traditional choice of law rule, embodied in the original Restatement of Conflict of Laws (§384), and until recently unquestioningly followed in this court has been that the substantive rights and liabilities arising out of a tortious occurrence are determinable by the law of the place of the tort. It had its conceptual foundation in the vested rights doctrine, namely, that a right to recover for a foreign tort owes its creation to the law of the jurisdiction where the injury occurred and depends for its existence and extent solely on such law. Although espoused by such great figures as Justice Holmes, the vested rights doctrine has long since been discredited because it fails to take account of underlying policy considerations in evaluating the significance to be ascribed to the circumstance that an act had a foreign situs in determining the rights and liabilities which arise out of that act. . . . More particularly, as applied to torts, the theory ignores the interest which jurisdictions other than that where the tort occurred may have in the resolution of particular issues. It is for this very reason that, despite the advantages of certainty, ease of application and predictability which it affords, there has in recent years been increasing criticism of the traditional rule by commentators and a judicial trend towards its abandonment or modification. . . .

In *Auten v. Auten* (308 N.Y. 155), . . . this court abandoned [traditional rules for contract choice of law questions] and applied what has been termed the "center of gravity" or "grouping of contacts" theory of the conflict of laws. "Under this theory," we declared in the *Auten* case, "the courts, instead of regarding as conclusive the parties' intention or the place of making or performance, lay emphasis rather upon the law of the place 'which has the most significant contacts with the matter in dispute'" (308 N.Y., at p. 160). The "center of gravity" rule . . . has not only been applied in other cases in this State, as well as in other jurisdictions, but has supplanted the prior rigid and set contract rules in the most current draft of the Restatement of Conflict of Laws. (See Restatement, Second, Conflict of Laws, §332b [Tentative Draft No. 6, 1960].)

Realization of the unjust and anomalous results which may ensue from application of the traditional rule in tort cases has also prompted judicial search for a more satisfactory alternative in that area. . . . The same judicial disposition is also reflected in a variety of other decisions. . . . These numerous cases differ in many ways but they are all similar in two important respects. First, by one rationale or another, they rejected the inexorable application of the law of the place of the tort where that place has no reasonable or relevant interest in the particular issue involved. And, second, in each of these cases the courts, after examining the particular circumstances presented, applied the law of some jurisdiction other than the place of the tort because it had a more compelling interest in the application of its law to the legal issue involved.

The "center of gravity" or "grouping of contacts" doctrine adopted by this court in conflicts cases involving contracts impresses us as likewise affording the appropriate approach for accommodating the competing interests in tort cases with multi-State contacts. Justice, fairness and "the best practical result" . . . may best be achieved by giving controlling effect to the law of the jurisdiction which, because of its relationship or contact with the occurrence or the parties, has the greatest concern with the specific issue raised in the litigation. The merit of such a rule is that "it gives to the place 'having the most interest in the problem' paramount control over the legal issues arising out of a particular factual context" and thereby allows the forum to apply "the policy of the jurisdiction 'most intimately concerned with the outcome of [the] particular litigation.'" (*Auten v. Auten*, 308 N.Y. 155, 161) Comparison of the relative "contacts" and "interests" of New York and Ontario in this litigation, vis-a-vis the issue here presented, makes it clear that the concern of New York is unquestionably the greater and more direct and that the interest of Ontario is at best minimal. The present action involves injuries sustained by a New York guest as the result of the negligence of a New York host in the operation of an automobile, garaged, licensed and undoubtedly insured in New York, in the course of a week-end journey which began and was to end there. In sharp contrast, Ontario's sole relationship with the occurrence is the purely adventitious circumstance that the accident occurred there.

New York's policy of requiring a tort-feasor to compensate his guest for injuries caused by his negligence cannot be doubted — as attested by the fact that the Legislature of this State has repeatedly refused to enact a statute denying or limiting recovery in such cases and our courts have neither reason nor warrant for departing from that policy simply because the accident, solely affecting New York residents and arising out of the operation of a New York based automobile, happened beyond its borders. Per contra, Ontario has no conceivable interest in denying a remedy to a New York guest against his New York host for injuries suffered in Ontario by reason of conduct which was tortious under Ontario law. The object of Ontario's guest statute, it has been said, is "to prevent the fraudulent assertion of claims by passengers, in collusion with the drivers, against insurance companies" . . . and, quite obviously, the fraudulent claims intended to be prevented by the statute are those asserted against Ontario defendants and their insurance carriers, not New York defendants and their insurance carriers. Whether New York defendants are imposed upon or their insurers defrauded by a New York plaintiff is scarcely a valid legislative concern of Ontario simply because the accident occurred there, any more so than if the accident had happened in some other jurisdiction.

It is hardly necessary to say that Ontario's interest is quite different from what it would have been had the issue related to the manner in which the defendant had been driving his car at the time of the accident. Where the defendant's exercise of due care in the operation of his automobile is in issue, the jurisdiction in which the allegedly wrongful conduct occurred will usually have a predominant, if not exclusive, concern. In such a case, it is appropriate to look to the law of the place of the tort so as to give effect to that jurisdiction's interest in regulating conduct within its borders, and it would be almost unthinkable to seek the applicable rule in the law of some other place.

The issue here, however, is not whether the defendant offended against a rule of the road prescribed by Ontario for motorists generally or whether he violated some standard of conduct imposed by that jurisdiction, but rather whether the plaintiff, because she was a guest in the defendant's automobile, is barred from recovering damages for a wrong concededly committed. As to that issue, it is New York, the place where the parties resided, where their guest-host relationship arose and where the trip began and was to end, rather than Ontario, the place of the fortuitous occurrence of the accident, which has the dominant contacts and the superior claim for application of its law. Although the rightness or wrongness of defendant's conduct may depend upon the law of the particular jurisdiction through which the automobile passes, the rights and liabilities of the parties which stem from their guest-host relationship should remain constant and not vary and shift as the automobile proceeds from place to place. Indeed, such a result, we note, accords with "the interests of the host in procuring liability insurance adequate under the applicable law, and the interests of his insurer in reasonable calculability of the premium."

Although the traditional rule has in the past been applied by this court in giving controlling effect to the guest statute of the foreign jurisdiction in which the accident occurred it is not amiss to point out that the question here posed was neither raised nor considered in those cases and that the question has never been presented in so stark a manner as in the case before us with a statute so unique as Ontario's.[13] Be that as it may, however, reconsideration of the inflexible traditional rule persuades us, as already indicated, that, in failing to take into account essential policy considerations and objectives, its application may lead to unjust and anomalous results. This being so, the rule, formulated as it was by the courts, should be discarded.[14]

In conclusion, then, there is no reason why all issues arising out of a tort claim must be resolved by reference to the law of the same jurisdiction. Where the issue involves standards of conduct, it is more than likely that it is the law of the place of the tort which will be controlling but the disposition of other issues must turn, as does the issue of the standard of conduct itself, on the law of the jurisdiction which has the strongest interest in the resolution of the particular issue presented.

The judgment appealed from should be reversed, with costs, and the motion to dismiss the complaint denied.

Notes on
BABCOCK v. JACKSON

1. Did Judge Fuld do a better job in *Babcock* than he did in *Haag v. Barnes* with providing reasons why certain contacts were more weighty or meaningful than other contacts? If so, what were those reasons? Try to determine whether *Babcock* articulated a discernible analysis, which another court might use as a guide in resolving a factually distinct choice of law dispute.

2. *Babcock* is considered an early example of governmental interest analysis, which directs a court to identify policies behind laws and then to evaluate whether it would effectuate those policies to apply them to the

---

13. We note that the Supreme Court of Canada has upheld the refusal of the Quebec courts to apply the Ontario guest statute to an accident affecting Quebec residents which occurred in Ontario. (*See McLean v. Pettigrew*, [1945] 2 D.L.R. 65.) This decision was dictated by the court's resort to the English choice of law rule, whereby the foreign tort is deemed actionable if actionable by the law of the forum and not justifiable by the law of the place of the tort. (*See Phillips v. Eyre*, [1870] L.R. 6 Q.B. 1, 28-29; *see, also*, DICEY, CONFLICT OF LAWS [7th ed. 1958], p. 940.) However that may be, it would seem incongruous for this court to apply Ontario's unique statute in circumstances under which its own sister Provinces would not.

14. It of course follows from our decision herein that, given the facts of the present case, the result would be the same and the law of New York applied where the foreign guest statute requires a showing of gross negligence.

particular case. Can you pinpoint where the *Babcock* court engages this type of analysis in the opinion? As you read through the various categories of conflicts outlined in the governmental interest analysis section below, try to identify which category describes *Babcock*: true conflict, false conflict, unprovided-for case, or disinterested forum.

3. Note the statement in the second to last paragraph of the *Babcock* opinion: "[t]here is no reason why all issues arising out of a tort claim must be resolved by reference to the law of the same jurisdiction." The *Babcock* court is suggesting here that a different law could govern the guest statute question than would govern another issue in the case, such as the standard of conduct (i.e., strict liability, gross negligence, reasonable care) or contributory negligence. This suggestion refers to the practice of depeçage, which allows splicing the issues in a case and engaging in a separate choice of law analysis for each. A note later in this chapter reviews the rationales for and consequences of depeçage.

4. What do you make of the *Babcock* court's reference — in footnote 13 near the end of the opinion — to what the Quebec courts would have done in this case? This seems to be a reference to the choice of law analysis that the Quebec courts might have done had they adjudicated the controversy. Why is that a relevant consideration? How does that kind of analysis relate to the doctrine of renvoi?

PROBLEM 2-29: INSURANCE FOR PUNITIVES?

The State of No-Insurance has a law that precludes insurance companies from insuring against the risk that the insured will have to pay punitive damages. Although this law arguably protects insurance companies from runaway verdicts that could bankrupt them, the law also ensures that a party does not avoid the regulatory purpose and effect of punitive damages: to deter outrageous conduct. The law of the State of Yes-Insurance allows parties to enter a contract of insurance in which the insurer agrees to indemnify the insured if the insured is subject to a punitive damages award. The rationale of the law is to honor parties' intent and to foster freedom of contract.

Frieda Fraud was a securities broker who was licensed to do business in the State of No-Insurance and the State of Yes-Insurance. She is domiciled in the State of Yes-Insurance, and does most of her business there. In the State of Yes-Insurance, she entered into an insurance contract with Indemnity Corp., in which Indemnity Corp. agreed that it would pay "all sums" that Frieda might become legally obligated to pay in a personal injury action. Indemnity Corp. is licensed to do business in both the State of Yes-Insurance and the State of No-Insurance, but is incorporated and has its principal place of business in the State of Yes-Insurance.

While sitting in her office in Yes-Insurance, Frieda called Dave Defrauded on the phone to sell him securities. At the time of the call, Dave was at his home in No-Insurance. Based on Frieda's fraudulent representations during that call, Dave agreed to purchase the securities. Dave spoke the acceptance of Frieda's offer while he was seated on his living room couch in No-Insurance. As a consequence of this transaction, Dave lost all his savings and had to apply for welfare assistance from the State of No-Insurance.

After he discovered the fraud, Dave filed suit against Frieda in the State of Yes-Insurance to recover for the fraud. The Yes-Insurance court issued a judgment for compensatory and punitive damages against Frieda. Indemnity Corp. agreed to cover the compensatory portion of the verdict, but not punitive portion. Frieda then sued Indemnity Corp. in a State of No-Insurance court. Assuming that the State of No-Insurance court applies the approach of *Haag v. Barnes*, which law will govern the question of whether Indemnity Corp. should cover the punitive damages award under the contract with Frieda? Would the result be different under the approach of *Babcock*?

C.   GOVERNMENTAL INTEREST ANALYSIS

As illustrated above, courts and scholars that moved away from the vested rights approach of the Restatement (First) of Conflict of Laws cast a broader eye in identifying relevant contacts than the First Restatement's focus on the territorial occurrence of events. Next, as illustrated in *Babcock v. Jackson*, courts began to evaluate the significance of this newly expanded universe of relevant contacts in light of the purpose behind laws.

Perhaps the most powerful intellectual force behind this transition was Professor Brainerd Currie, whose scholarship has influenced scores of academics and judges. For Currie, choice of law rules should seek to accommodate political interests of the jurisdictions with a claim to regulating parties' disputes. A key tenet of Currie's approach is that courts undertaking a choice of law analysis must primarily interpret and construe conflicting state laws so as to gauge whether the case actually implicated the political interests of relevant jurisdictions. Currie believed that courts may not inappropriately weigh and value policies or interests motivating laws, but nonetheless believed courts fully competent to evaluate whether the legislative purpose behind the laws suggested that the court should apply the laws in cases with multijurisdictional elements. Currie advocated that in undertaking this evaluation in a particular case, courts should exercise restraint in determining what state policies exist and where state interests lie.

As you will see below, a discrepancy exists between governmental interest analysis in Currie's theory and governmental interest analysis in practice. Although courts say they are applying governmental interest analysis, their reasoning does not necessarily mirror that which Currie propounded. (Similarly, courts may say they are applying something other than interest analysis — such as a "significant contacts" approach or the Restatement (Second) of Conflict of

Laws approach — yet engage in an analysis that tracks Currie's thinking.) In order to understand what courts may be trying to do, however, we will benefit from taking a look at Currie's theoretical formulations. He described his proposed methodology in the following restatement-like format:

> If I were asked to restate the law of conflict of laws I would decline the honor. A descriptive restatement with any sort of internal consistency is impossible. Much of the existing law, or pseudo law, of the subject is irrational; profound changes destructive of the fundamental tenets of the traditional system are gathering momentum. On the assumption that the project admits of a statement of what is reasonable in existing law and what may reasonably be desired for the future, however, I volunteer the following as a substitute for all that part of the Restatement dealing with choice of law (for the purpose of finding the rule of decision):
>
> §1. When a court is asked to apply the law of a foreign state different from the law of the forum, it should inquire into the policies expressed in the respective laws, and into the circumstances in which it is reasonable for the respective states to assert an interest in the application of those policies. In making these determinations the court should employ the ordinary processes of construction and interpretation.
>
> §2. If the court finds that one state has an interest in the application of its policy in the circumstances of the case and the other has none, it should apply the law of the only interested state.
>
> §3. If the court finds an apparent conflict between the interests of the two states it should reconsider. A more moderate and restrained interpretation of the policy or interest of one state or the other may avoid conflict.
>
> §4. If, upon reconsideration, the court finds that a conflict between the legitimate interests of the two states is unavoidable, it should apply the law of the forum.
>
> §5. If the forum is disinterested, but an unavoidable conflict exists between the laws of the two other states, and the court cannot with justice decline to adjudicate the case, it should apply the law of the forum — until someone comes along with a better idea.
>
> §6. The conflict of interest between states will result in different dispositions of the same problem, depending on where the action is brought. If with respect to a particular problem this appears seriously to infringe a strong national interest in uniformity of decision, the court should not attempt to improvise a solution sacrificing the legitimate interest of its own state, but should leave to Congress, exercising its powers under the full faith and credit clause, the determination of which interest shall be required to yield.
>
> The explanatory note might run a little longer.

Brainerd Currie, *Comments on* Babcock v. Jackson, *A Recent Development in Conflict of Laws*, 63 Colum. L. Rev. 1233, 1242-1243 (1963) (footnotes omitted).

Currie's proposal spawned a new vocabulary for describing the various components of interest analysis. First is the idea that, even though a jurisdiction might espouse a *policy* behind its laws, the jurisdiction does not have an *interest* in applying its law unless some contact or factor in the case implicates the policy motivating the law. For example, the policy of compensating tort victims may not give rise to a jurisdiction's interest in applying its law unless the jurisdiction has a connection with the case that makes it interested in compensating the particular tort victim involved in the lawsuit (such as the victim's domicile in the jurisdiction). This distinction between an interest and a policy gives rise to a number of possible configurations, as described in Currie's restatement:

- If upon analysis, the court determines that one jurisdiction has an interest and another does not, this is called a *false conflict*, calling for the application of the law of the interested state as described in §2 of Currie's restatement.
- If — in considering forum law and the law of another jurisdiction — the court thinks that both jurisdictions might have an interest, it confronts this *apparent conflict* by taking another look at laws with a *restrained and moderate interpretation*, as described in §3 of Currie's restatement.
- If the conflict persists after the *restrained and moderate interpretation*, then §4 of Currie's restatement instructs that the court must handle this *true conflict* by applying forum law.
- If a *true conflict* exists and the court determines that the forum actually has no claim to applying its own law, this is a case of a *disinterested forum*. Section 5 of Currie's restatement suggests that the court should apply forum law if it cannot justify dismissing the case under the doctrine of forum non conveniens.
- An *unprovided-for case* occurs when no state has an interest in application of its law. Currie suggested four different approaches for handling unprovided-for cases: (1) apply the law of the forum; (2) apply the law that appears most "enlightened and humane"; (3) apply the law that aids the litigant who is a forum resident; and (4) apply the law that treats foreign litigants in the same way that their home state would treat them.

BRAINERD CURRIE, SELECTED ESSAYS ON THE CONFLICT OF LAWS 153-156 (1963). Note that even though the fourth approach appears less discriminatory than the third approach, the results would usually be the same under either approach.

1. *False Conflicts*

Schultz v. Boy Scouts of America, Inc.

480 N.E.2d 679 (N.Y. 1985)

SIMONS, J.

Plaintiffs, Richard E. and Margaret Schultz, instituted this action to recover damages for personal injuries they and their sons, Richard and Christopher, suffered because the boys were sexually abused by defendant Edmund Coakeley and for damages sustained as a result of Christopher's wrongful death after he committed suicide. Coakeley, a brother in the Franciscan order, was the boys' school teacher and leader of their scout troop. Plaintiffs allege that the sexual abuse occurred while Coakeley was acting in those capacities and the causes of action before us on this appeal charge defendants Boy Scouts of America, Inc., and the Brothers of the Poor of St. Francis, Inc. (sued as Franciscan Brothers of the Poor, Inc.), with negligently hiring and supervising him.

Plaintiffs are domiciled in New Jersey and some of the injuries were sustained there. Thus, a choice-of-law issue is presented because New Jersey recognizes the doctrine of charitable immunity and New York does not. Defendants contend New Jersey law governs this litigation. . . . Following the rationale of *Babcock v. Jackson* (12 N.Y.2d 473) and similar cases, we hold that New Jersey law applies and that plaintiffs are precluded from relitigating its effect on the claims they assert.

I

[Plaintiffs' two sons, Richard (age 13) and Christopher (age 11), attended Assumption School in New Jersey, which had an agreement with defendant Brothers of the Poor of St. Francis, Inc., which supplied teachers for the school. Brother Edmund Coakeley taught both sons and also served as the scoutmaster of Boy Scout Troop 337, a locally chartered Boy Scout troop sponsored and approved by defendant Boy Scouts of America. In July 1978, Coakeley took Christopher Schultz to a Boy Scout camp located in upstate New York. The complaint alleged Coakeley sexually abused Christopher and Richard at the camp and continued to abuse Christopher upon his return to New Jersey. The plaintiffs claimed that Coakeley's acts caused both boys to suffer severe psychological, emotional, and mental pain and suffering and that this distress caused Christopher to commit suicide. The plaintiffs charged both defendants "with negligence in assigning Coakeley to positions of trust where he could molest young boys and in failing to dismiss him despite actual or constructive notice that Coakeley had previously been dismissed from another Boy Scout camp for similar improper conduct." Defendants argued that plaintiffs' claims were barred by New Jersey's charitable immunity statute.]

II

A

The choice-of-law question presented in the action against defendant Boy Scouts of America is whether New York should apply its law in an action involving codomiciliaries of New Jersey when tortious acts were committed in New York. This is the posture of the appeal although defendant is a Federally chartered corporation created exclusively for educational and charitable purposes pursuant to an act of Congress that originally maintained its national headquarters in New Brunswick, New Jersey, but moved to Dallas, Texas, in 1979. New Jersey is considered defendant's domicile because its national headquarters was in that State. . . . Its change of domicile after the commission of the wrongs from New

Jersey to Texas, which no longer recognizes the doctrine of charitable immunity provides New York with no greater interest in this action than it would have without the change. . . .

The question presented in the action against defendant Franciscan Brothers is what law should apply when the parties' different domiciles have conflicting charitable immunity rules. The Franciscan order is incorporated in Ohio and it is a domiciliary of that State. At the time these causes of action arose Ohio, like New Jersey, recognized charitable immunity. The Ohio rule denied immunity in actions based on negligent hiring and supervision, however, whereas New Jersey does not. For this reason, no doubt, defendant Franciscan Brothers does not claim Ohio law governs and the choice is between the law of New York and the law of New Jersey.

. . .

The first and fourth causes of action, the wrongful death of Christopher and plaintiffs' own psychological and other injuries respectively, allege injuries inflicted in New Jersey. New York's only interests in these claims are as the forum State and as the jurisdiction where the tortious conduct underlying plaintiffs' claims against defendants, i.e., the negligent assignment and failure to dismiss Coakeley, occurred. Standing alone, these interests are insufficient to warrant application of New York law, at least when the relevant issue is a loss-distribution rule, like charitable immunity, rather than one regulating conduct. The second and third causes of action seek damages for the psychological, emotional and physical injuries suffered by Christopher and Richard Schultz, injuries which occurred in both New York and New Jersey, because a fair reading of the complaint indicates that both boys suffered injuries when Coakeley molested them and also after they returned home. These two causes of action sufficiently implicate New York's interests to require a resolution of the choice-of-law problem in the case.

B

Historically, choice-of-law conflicts in tort actions have been resolved by applying the law of the place of the wrong. In *Babcock v. Jackson* (12 N.Y.2d 473, *supra*), we departed from traditional doctrine, however, and refused to invariably apply the rule of *lex loci delicti* to determine the availability of relief for commission of a tort. . . . The [*Babcock*] analysis was flexible and to the extent that it may have placed too much emphasis on contact-counting without specifying the relative significance of those contacts, the necessary refinements were added in later decisions of this court. In four of the five subsequent tort cases presenting the same *Babcock*-style fact pattern of common New York domiciliaries and a foreign locus having loss-distribution rules in conflict with those of New York we reached results consistent with *Babcock* and applied New York law. . . . In each of the five cases, however, the court rejected the indiscriminate grouping of contacts, which in *Babcock* had been a consideration coequal to interest analysis, because it bore no reasonable relation to the underlying policies of conflicting rules of recovery in tort actions. Interest analysis became the relevant analytical approach to choice of law in tort actions in New York. "[The] law of the jurisdiction having the greatest interest in the litigation will be applied and . . . the [only] facts or contacts which obtain significance in defining State interests are those which relate to the purpose of the particular law in conflict." Under this formulation, the significant contacts are, almost exclusively, the parties' domiciles and the locus of the tort.

. . . These decisions also establish that the relative interests of the domicile and locus jurisdictions in having their laws apply will depend on the particular tort issue in conflict in the case. Thus, when the conflicting rules involve the appropriate standards of conduct, rules of the road, for example, the law of the place of the tort "will usually have a predominant, if not exclusive, concern" . . . because the locus jurisdiction's interests in protecting the reasonable expectations of the parties who relied on it to govern their primary conduct and in the admonitory effect that applying its law will have on similar conduct in the future assume critical importance and outweigh any interests of the common-domicile jurisdiction. Conversely, when the jurisdictions' conflicting rules relate to allocating losses that result from admittedly tortious conduct, as they do here, rules such as those limiting damages in wrongful death actions, vicarious liability rules, or immunities from suit, considerations of the State's admonitory interest and party reliance are less important. Under those circumstances, the locus jurisdiction has at best a minimal interest in determining the right of recovery or the extent of the remedy in an action by a foreign domiciliary for injuries resulting from the conduct of a codomiciliary that was tortious under the laws of both jurisdictions. Analysis then favors the jurisdiction of common domicile because of its interest in enforcing the decisions of both parties to accept both the benefits and the burdens of identifying with that jurisdiction and to submit themselves to its authority.[2]

These considerations made the need for change in the *lex loci delicti* rule obvious in *Babcock*, but the validity of this interest analysis is more clearly demonstrated in the split domicile case of *Neumeier v. Kuehner* (31 N.Y.2d 121, *supra*). In *Neumeier* we applied Ontario's guest statute in an action on behalf of an Ontario decedent against a New York defendant at least in part because the Ontario statute, which contained reciprocal benefits and burdens depending on one's status as either host or guest, was "obviously addressed" to Ontario domiciliaries such as plaintiff's decedent. In *Babcock* New York had an important interest in protecting its own residents injured in a foreign State against unfair or anachronistic statutes of that State but it had no similar interest in *Neumeier* in protecting a guest domiciled in Ontario and injured there.

C

As to defendant Boy Scouts, this case is but a slight variation of our *Babcock* line of decisions and differs from them on only two grounds: (1) the issue involved is charitable immunity rather than a guest statute, and (2) it presents a fact pattern which one commentator has characterized as a "reverse" *Babcock* case

---

2. New York's rule holding charities liable for their tortious acts, or its rule of nonimmunity as the dissent characterizes it, is also a loss-allocating rule, just as New Jersey's charitable immunity statute is.

because New York is the place of the tort rather than the jurisdiction of the parties' common domicile.

Although most of our major choice-of-law decisions after *Babcock* involved foreign guest statutes in actions for personal injuries, we have not so limited them, but have applied the *Babcock* reasoning to other tort issues as well. Nor is there any logical basis for distinguishing guest statutes from other loss-distributing rules because they all share the characteristic of being postevent remedial rules designed to allocate the burden of losses resulting from tortious conduct in which the jurisdiction of the parties' common domicile has a paramount interest. There is even less reason for distinguishing *Babcock* here where the conflicting rules involve the defense of charitable immunity. . . . Both plaintiffs and defendant Boy Scouts in this case have chosen to identify themselves in the most concrete form possible, domicile, with a jurisdiction that has weighed the interests of charitable tort-feasors and their victims and decided to retain the defense of charitable immunity. Significantly, the New Jersey statute excepts from its protection actions by nonbeneficiaries of the charity who suffer injuries as a result of the negligence of its employees or agents. Plaintiffs and their sons, however, were beneficiaries of the Boy Scouts' charitable activities in New Jersey and should be bound by the benefits and burdens of that choice. Additionally, the State of New Jersey is intimately interested in seeing that the parties' associational interests are respected and its own loss-distributing rules are enforced so that the underlying policy, which is undoubtedly to encourage the growth of charitable work within its borders, is effectuated.

Thus, if this were a straight *Babcock* fact pattern, rather than the reverse, we . . . would apply the law of the parties' common domicile. Because this case presents the first case for our review in which New York is the forum-locus rather than the parties' common domicile, however, we consider the reasons most often advanced for applying the law of the forum-locus and those supporting application of the law of the common domicile.

The three reasons most often urged in support of applying the law of the forum-locus in cases such as this are: (1) to protect medical creditors who provided services to injured parties in the locus State, (2) to prevent injured tort victims from becoming public wards in the locus State and (3) the deterrent effect application of locus law has on future tort-feasors in the locus State. The first two reasons share common weaknesses. First, in the abstract, neither reason necessarily requires application of the locus jurisdiction's law, but rather invariably mandates application of the law of the jurisdiction that would either allow recovery or allow the greater recovery. They are subject to criticism, therefore, as being biased in favor of recovery. Second, on the facts of this case neither reason is relevant since the record contains no evidence that there are New York medical creditors or that plaintiffs are or will likely become wards of this State. Finally, although it is conceivable that application of New York's law in this case would have some deterrent effect on future tortious conduct in this State, New York's deterrent interest is considerably less because none of the parties is a resident and the rule in conflict is loss-allocating rather than conduct-regulating.

Conversely, there are persuasive reasons for consistently applying the law of the parties' common domicile. First, it significantly reduces forum-shopping opportunities, because the same law will be applied by the common-domicile and locus jurisdictions, the two most likely forums. Second, it rebuts charges that the forum-locus is biased in favor of its own laws and in favor of rules permitting recovery. Third, the concepts of mutuality and reciprocity support consistent application of the common-domicile law. In any given case, one person could be either plaintiff or defendant and one State could be either the parties' common domicile or the locus, and yet the applicable law would not change depending on their status. Finally, it produces a rule that is easy to apply and brings a modicum of predictability and certainty to an area of the law needing both.

As to defendant Franciscan Brothers . . . [it is important that] the parties are domiciled in different jurisdictions with conflicting loss-distribution rules and the locus of the tort is New York, a separate jurisdiction. In that situation the law of the place of the tort will normally apply, unless displacing it "'will advance' the relevant substantive law purposes without impairing the smooth working of the multi-state system or producing great uncertainty for litigant." For the same reasons stated in our analysis of the action against defendant Boy Scouts, application of the law of New Jersey in plaintiffs' action against defendant Franciscan Brothers would further that State's interest in enforcing the decision of its domiciliaries to accept the burdens as well as the benefits of that State's loss-distribution tort rules and its interest in promoting the continuation and expansion of defendant's charitable activities in that State. Conversely, although application of New Jersey's law may not affirmatively advance the substantive law purposes of New York, it will not frustrate those interests because New York has no significant interest in applying its own law to this dispute. Finally, application of New Jersey law will enhance "the smooth working of the multi-state system" by actually reducing the incentive for forum shopping and it will provide certainty for the litigants whose only reasonable expectation surely would have been that the law of the jurisdiction where plaintiffs are domiciled and defendant sends its teachers would apply, not the law of New York where the parties had only isolated and infrequent contacts as a result of Coakeley's position as Boy Scout leader. Thus, we conclude that defendant Franciscan Brothers has met its burden of demonstrating that the law of New Jersey, rather than the law of New York, should govern plaintiffs' action against it.

III

Plaintiffs contend that even if the New Jersey charitable immunity statute is applicable to this action, it should not be enforced because it is contrary to the public policy of New York.

The public policy doctrine is an exception to implementing an otherwise applicable choice of law in which the forum refuses to apply a portion of foreign law because it is contrary or repugnant to its State's own public policy. The doctrine is considered only after the court has determined that the applicable substantive law under relevant choice-of-law principles is not the forum's law. Having found that, the court must enforce the foreign law "unless some sound reason of public policy makes it unwise for us to lend our aid."

The party seeking to invoke the doctrine has the burden of proving that the foreign law is contrary to New York public policy. It is a heavy burden for public policy is not measured by individual notions of expediency and fairness or by a showing that the foreign law is unreasonable or unwise. Public policy is found in the State's Constitution, statutes and judicial decisions and the proponent of the exception must establish that to enforce the foreign law "would violate some fundamental principle of justice, some prevalent conception of good morals, some deep-rooted tradition of the common weal" expressed in them. In addition, the proponent must establish that there are enough important contacts between the parties, the occurrence and the New York forum to implicate our public policy and thus preclude enforcement of the foreign law. . . .[3]

When we have employed the exception in the past and refused to enforce otherwise applicable foreign law, the contacts between the New York forum, the parties and the transaction involved were substantial enough to threaten our public policy. Thus, in *Kilberg v. Northeast Airlines* (9 N.Y.2d 34), we found the law of the place of tort, Massachusetts, appropriate to a wrongful death action but refused to apply its statutory limit on damages because it was contrary to New York public policy, expressed in our State Constitution, prohibiting limitations on such damages. Insofar as the decedent was a resident, who had purchased his ticket and boarded his flight in New York and the defendant carried on extensive operations here, New York's interest in providing its residents with full compensation for wrongful death was jeopardized and led us to reject the Massachusetts limitation. . . .

Thus, although New York discarded the doctrine of charitable immunity long ago and enforcement of New Jersey's statute might well run counter to our fundamental public policy, we need not decide that issue because there are not sufficient contacts between New York, the parties and the transactions involved to implicate our public policy and call for its enforcement. . . . Accordingly, the order of the Appellate Division should be affirmed, with costs.

JASEN, J. (dissenting).

I respectfully dissent. In my view, the majority overstates the significance of New Jersey's interests in having its law apply in this case and understates the interests of New York. . . .

New Jersey's interests, denominated by the majority as loss-distribution, are hardly pressing under the circumstances. While it is true that laws providing for charitable immunity typically are intended to serve the purpose of protecting and promoting the charities incorporated within a state's jurisdiction, that function is virtually irrelevant in this case. Presently, neither corporate defendant is a resident

3. The United States Supreme Court has recently reaffirmed that "the Full Faith and Credit Clause does not require a State to apply another State's law in violation of its own legitimate public policy" (*Nevada v. Hall*, 440 U.S. 410, 422). It has also stated unequivocally that for a State to either choose its substantive law or refuse to apply a sister State's law "in a constitutionally permissible manner, that State must have a significant contact or significant aggregation of contacts, creating state interests, such that choice of its law is neither arbitrary nor fundamentally unfair." (*Allstate Ins. Co. v. Hague*, 449 U.S. 302, 313; *see, id.*, at p. 308, and n.10.) There thus is some doubt whether we could constitutionally choose to apply New York law in this case although in view of our disposition we need not decide the question.

of New Jersey. . . . The Brothers of the Poor of St. Francis (the Franciscan Brothers) has at all relevant times been a resident of the State of Ohio, a jurisdiction which recognizes only a limited charitable immunity that does not extend to negligence in the selection and retention of personnel The Boy Scouts of America, although originally incorporated in New Jersey at the time of its alleged tortious conduct, has since relocated in Texas, a State which has wholly rejected charitable immunity. While ordinarily a change in residence subsequent to the events upon which a lawsuit is predicated ought not to affect the rights and liabilities of the parties in order to avoid forum-shopping, there is no such reason to deny giving effect to the change in residence here. Rather, a defendant's post-tort change in residence — as opposed to that of a plaintiff — is often critical insofar as it affects state interest analysis.

It simply cannot be disputed that New Jersey presently has a much diminished interest, if any at all, in shielding the Boy Scouts of America from liability — let alone the Franciscan Brothers which has never been a New Jersey resident. The majority does not question that conclusion, but merely states that the change in residence does not enhance New York's interest. While the latter may be true in the abstract, the point, of course, is that New Jersey's interest in the application of its charitable immunity law has been substantially reduced.

Consequently, because the majority cannot in actuality rely upon New Jersey's interest in protecting resident charities — into which category neither corporate defendant now falls — the decision today is, in effect, predicated almost exclusively upon the plaintiffs' New Jersey domicile. What emerges from the majority's holding is an entirely untoward rule that nonresident plaintiffs are somehow less entitled to the protections of this State's law while they are within our borders. Besides smacking of arbitrary and injudicious discrimination against guests in this State and before our courts, such a position, without more, has severely limited, if any, validity in resolving conflicts questions. This is especially so where, as here, the defendants' contacts with the foreign State are insignificant for the purposes of interest analysis while, at the same time, the parties' contacts with New York are so clear and direct, and the resulting interests of this State so strong.

There can be no question that this State has a paramount interest in preventing and protecting against injurious misconduct within its borders. This interest is particularly vital and compelling where, as here, the tortious misconduct involves sexual abuse and exploitation of children, regardless of the residency of the victims and the tort-feasors.

As the majority stresses, a charitable immunity law such as New Jersey's typically serves a loss-distribution purpose reflecting a legislative paternalism toward resident charities. But that is obviously not true with regard to a rule, such as New York's, which denies charitable immunity. Consequently, it is mistaken to adjudge the propriety of applying the latter law by giving weight only to the interests served by the former. A closer attention to the specific policy purposes of New York's charitable nonimmunity rule is essential to a more appropriate resolution of the conflict.

[T]here can be little doubt that New York has an interest in insuring that justice be done to nonresidents who have come to this State and suffered serious injuries herein. There is no cogent reason to deem that interest any weaker whether such guests are here for the purpose of conducting business or personal affairs, or, as in this case, have chosen to spend their vacation in New York. Likewise, it cannot be denied that this State has a strong legitimate interest in deterring serious tortious misconduct, including the kind of reprehensible malfeasance that has victimized the nonresident infant plaintiffs in this case. Indeed, this deterrence function of tort law, whether it be in the form of imposing liability or denying immunity, is a substantial interest of the locus state which is almost universally acknowledged by both commentators and the courts to be a prominent factor deserving significant consideration in the resolution of conflicts problems. While the majority mentions New York's interest in deterrence, it dismisses that interest in short fashion by referring to the "rule in conflict" as being "loss-allocating rather than conduct-regulating." Of course, there is not one but two rules at issue, and the majority's characterization is accurate only with regard to New Jersey's law granting immunity, not with regard to New York's rule denying the same.

. . .

Additionally, apart from the foregoing, I believe that this court ought not to apply New Jersey's law of charitable immunity by reason of its incompatibility with this State's settled public policy. Almost 30 years ago, when this court abolished charitable immunity for this State, we explained that the rule was inherently incongruous, contrary to both good morals and sound law, out of tune with modern day needs, unfair and confused. Surely, a rule deemed so archaic and anachronistic by this court ought not now to be given effect and, thereby, insulate defendants from whatever responsibility they should bear for the heinous acts of misconduct performed in this State. . . .

. . . For all these reasons, I would reverse the order of the Appellate Division, apply the law of New York denying immunity to defendant charities, and permit plaintiffs to proceed on their complaint.

Notes on
SCHULTZ v. BOY SCOUTS OF AMERICA

1. Compare *Schultz* to the case immediately before it, *Babcock v. Jackson*. Why is *Schultz* described as a reverse *Babcock* situation? Which case has the most defensible reasoning and result, *Schultz* or *Babcock*?

2. The facts of *Schultz* are indisputably tragic, and the result of the decision harsh, denying the plaintiffs an opportunity to proceed against the "deep pocket" charities. This raises the question why the court worked so hard to conclude that the forum state, New York, had no interest in applying its law. In the language of interest analysis, the *Schultz* court found that the case presented a false conflict, and thus applied the law of the interested state. Of all of the possible permutations of interested and disinterested states, a false conflict yields perhaps the most intellectually and morally desirable result. Fairness and common sense easily justify applying a jurisdiction's law where that jurisdiction is the only one actually "interested" in

having its law applied. One wonders if, in its desire for a clear answer, the court overlooked possible arguments that might suggest that New York or Ohio had an interest in having their law applied. Can you think of any such arguments that the court might have overlooked?

3. Currie acknowledged that the central component of governmental interest analysis is construction and interpretation of potentially conflicting laws. Sometimes this is an easy task, with the plain language of a statute supported by legislative history exposing a clear purpose. Sometimes the legal analyst must struggle to ascertain a law's purpose — searching through precedent, legislative history, expert witness opinions, imagination, and the like. Scholars have frequently observed problems with this process. Professor Lea Brilmayer argues that judges often make arbitrary decisions or reflect personal preferences in determining the purpose behind laws. Lea Brilmayer, *Interest Analysis and the Myth of Legislative Intent*, 78 MICH. L. REV. 392, 405 (1980). Likewise, Professor Joseph William Singer observes that judges ignore multiple purposes behind laws so as to make it more likely to resolve the case as a false conflict. Joseph William Singer, *Facing Real Conflicts*, 24 CORNELL INT'L L.J. 197, 219-220 (1991).

Professor Larry Kramer observes that the process of interpretation actually has two steps: not only must a court evaluate the reason why a jurisdiction adopted a law for the purpose of a domestic case, but a court must also determine which contacts implicate that purpose in a multijurisdictional case. Larry Kramer, *Rethinking Choice of Law*, 90 COLUM. L. REV. 277, 299 (1990). This complication not only makes the interpretation more intellectually challenging, it also provides more opportunities for states to make protectionist and self-serving decisions. *See, e.g.*, John Hart Ely, *Choice of Law and the State's Interest in Protecting Its Own*, 23 WM. & MARY L. REV. 173, 192-199 (1981). As you read other governmental interest analysis cases, note how often courts extend the protections and benefits of laws to forum domiciliaries only.

4. A form of characterization drove the analysis in *Schultz*: the decision whether charitable immunity was loss-allocating or conduct-regulating. Once the court characterized the rule as loss-allocating, it placed significant emphasis on the "common domicile" of the parties. Why is it that the parties' common domicile was so important to a loss-allocating rule?

Evaluate whether tort rules can be meaningfully sorted into these two categories. Scholars differ over whether these categories are useful and accurate, and many scholars point out that tort principles are often capable of classification as both conduct-regulating and loss-allocating. *See, e.g.*, Erin O'Hara & Larry Ribstein, *From Politics to Efficiency in Choice of Law*, 67 U. CHI. L. REV. 1151, 1168 (2000) (pointing out that the distinction "breaks down in practice"); Wendy Collins Perdue, *A Reexamination of the Distinction Between "Loss-Allocating" and "Conduct-Regulating Rules,"* 60 LA. L. REV. 1251, 1252 (2000) (observing that most tort rules are both conduct-regulating and loss-allocating, since the rules often have both compensation and deterrence goals); Symeon Symeonides, *The Need for a Third Conflicts Restatement (and a Proposal for Tort Conflicts)*, 75 IND. L.J. 437, 452-453 (2000) (finding the distinction useful since it enables courts to consider two competing conflict of laws principles, "territoriality and personality of laws"). Despite scholarly disagreement, courts continue to find the distinction helpful. *See, e.g., Padula v. Lilarn Properties Corp.*, 644 N.E.2d 1001 (N.Y. App. 1994).

As currently drafted and approved, the Torts Chapter of the Restatement (Third) of Conflict of Laws relies heavily on the distinction between loss-allocating and conduct-regulating rules. The draft embraces the notion that states have a strong interest in applying loss-allocating rules when doing so would benefit a domiciliary to the detriment of an out-of-state party or another domiciliary, but a weaker interest in applying loss-allocating rules to conduct that occurs outside state borders. Do you think that the distinction between loss allocating and conduct regulating is sufficiently clear to provide a useful choice of law standard?

5. How does the public policy analysis in *Schultz* compare with public policy analysis in cases such as *Loucks v. Standard Oil* and *Raskin v. Allison*, set forth earlier in this chapter?

6. *Schultz* is not the last word on choice of law methodology in New York. Although New York courts continue to rely on the loss distribution/conduct regulation distinction, choice of law has continued to evolve in the state. Critics observe, however, that contemporary cases do not reflect the clarity and leadership of cases such as *Babcock* and *Schulz*. A more current case applying New York choice of law principles, *Bakalar v. Fischer*, 619 F.3d 136 (2d Cir. 2010), appears later in this chapter in a section on hybrid methodology, and is followed by a brief explication of more current New York choice of law jurisprudence.

7. Compare *Schultz* with *P.V. ex rel. T.V. v. Camp Jaycee*, 962 A.2d 453 (N.J. 2008), set forth later in this chapter. In *Camp Jaycee*, the New Jersey Supreme Court declined to apply New Jersey's charitable immunity protections in another sexual abuse case.

PROBLEM 2-30: A PICNIC IN GUEST STATUTE STATE

Damien Driver and Gayla Guests are residents of Liability State. Damien picked up Gayla in Liability State for a picnic in Guest Statute State. They travelled to Guest Statute State where they had an automobile accident, and Gayla sustained injuries. Gayla sues Damien in a jurisdiction that follows Currie's governmental interest analysis and seeks damages for the injuries she received from the accident. Guest Statute State has a guest statute providing that a guest in an automobile that is involved in an accident cannot recover in an action brought against the host driver of the automobile. The purpose of this statute is to protect insurance companies by preventing collusive suits against insurers by hosts and guests. Liability State recently repealed its guest statute. The legislative history supporting the repeal states that the legislature concluded that the paramount interest in a host/guest accident is to ensure that an injured guest receives full compensation. Damien's car is insured by a Liability State insurance company and the insurance contract was executed in Liability State. Which law is likely to govern the question of whether Damien is shielded from liability?

PROBLEM 2-31: PADDY'S STRICT AND VICARIOUS LIABILITY SUIT

Paddy is a New York resident who was injured in Massachusetts while working at a construction site. The site was owned by Lilly's Properties, a New York corporation. Paddy sued Lilly's, claiming that Lilly's was liable under a theory of strict liability and vicarious liability. Assume that New York recognizes strict liability and vicarious liability under these circumstances and that Massachusetts does not. Under Massachusetts law, liability would attach only upon showing actual negligence on the part of the employer in failing to properly train or to properly supervise the employee whose actions actually caused an unsafe condition at the construction site. Paddy filed suit in a jurisdiction that follows governmental interest analysis. Which law is likely to govern: New York or Massachusetts?

2. *Apparent or True Conflicts*

Lilienthal v. Kaufman

395 P.2d 543 (Or. 1964)

DENECKE, J.

This is an action to collect two promissory notes. The defense is that the defendant maker has previously been declared a spendthrift by an Oregon court and placed under a guardianship and that the guardian has declared the obligations void. The plaintiff's counter is that the notes were executed and delivered in California, that the law of California does not recognize the disability of a spendthrift, and that the Oregon court is bound to apply the law of the place of the making of the contract. The trial court rejected plaintiff's argument and held for the defendant.

This same defendant spendthrift was the prevailing party in our recent decision in *Olshen v. Kaufman,* 235 Or. 423, 385 P.2d 161 (1963). In that case the spendthrift and the plaintiff, an Oregon resident, had gone into a joint venture to purchase binoculars for resale. For this purpose plaintiff had advanced moneys to the spendthrift. The spendthrift had repaid plaintiff by his personal check for the amount advanced and for plaintiff's share of the profits of such venture. The check had not been paid because the spendthrift had had insufficient funds in his account. The action was for the unpaid balance of the check.

The evidence in that case showed that the plaintiff had been unaware that Kaufman was under a spendthrift guardianship. The guardian testified that he knew Kaufman was engaging in some business and had bank accounts and that he had admonished him to cease these practices; but he could not control the spendthrift.

The statute applicable in that case and in this one is ORS 126.335:

> After the appointment of a guardian for the spendthrift, all contracts, except for necessaries, and all gifts, sales and transfers of real or personal estate made by such spendthrift thereafter and before the termination of the guardianship are voidable. (Repealed 1961, ch 344, §109, now ORS 126.280).

We held in that case that the voiding of the contract by the guardian precluded recovery by the plaintiff and that the spendthrift and the guardian were not estopped to deny the validity of plaintiff's claim. Plaintiff does not seek to overturn the principle of that decision but contends it has no application because the law of California governs, and under California law the plaintiff's claim is valid.

The facts here are identical to those in *Olshen v. Kaufman*, supra, except for the California locale for portions of the transaction. The notes were for the repayment of advances to finance another joint venture to sell binoculars. The plaintiff was unaware that defendant had been declared a spendthrift and placed under guardianship. The guardian, upon demand for payment by the plaintiff, declared the notes void. The issue is solely one involving the principles of conflict of laws. . . .

Before entering the choice-of-law area of the general field of conflict of laws, we must determine whether the laws of the states having a connection with the controversy are in conflict. Defendant did not expressly concede that under the law of California the defendant's obligation would be enforceable, but his counsel did state that if this proceeding were in the courts of California, the plaintiff probably would recover. We agree.

. . . Incapacity of a spendthrift to contract is a disability created by the legislature. California has no such legislation. In addition, the Civil Code of California provides that all persons are capable of contracting except minors, persons judicially determined to be of unsound mind, and persons deprived of civil rights. §1556. Furthermore, §1913 of the California Code of Civil Procedure provides: ". . . that the authority of a guardian . . . does not extend beyond the jurisdiction of the Government under which he was invested with his authority."

Plaintiff contends that the substantive issue of whether or not an obligation is valid and binding is governed by the law of the place of making, California. This court has repeated stated that the law of the place of contract "must govern as to the validity, interpretation, and construction of the contract. . . ."

. . . There is no need to decide that our previous statements that the law of the place of contract governs were in error. Our purpose is to state that this portion of our decision is not founded upon that principle because of our doubt that it is correct if the *only* connection of the state whose law would govern is that it was the place of making.

In this case California had more connection with the transaction than being merely the place where the contract was executed. The defendant went to San

Francisco to ask the plaintiff, a California resident, for money for the defendant's venture. The money was loaned to defendant in San Francisco, and by the terms of the note, it was to be repaid to plaintiff in San Francisco.

On these facts, apart from *lex loci contractus*, other accepted principles of conflict of laws lead to the conclusion that the law of California should be applied. *Sterrett v. Stoddard Lbr. Co.*, 150 Or. 491, 504, 46 P.2d 1023 (1935), rests, at least in part, on the proposition that the validity of a note is determined by the law of the place of payment. . . .

There is another conflict principle calling for the application of California law. . . . The "rule" is that, if the contract is valid under the law of any jurisdiction having significant connection with the contract, i.e., place of making place of performance, etc., the law of that jurisdiction validating the contract will be applied. This would also agree with the intention of the parties, if they had had any intentions in this regard. They must have intended their agreement to be valid. . . .

. . . The "rule of validation" is appealing because it is founded upon the same reasoning that is followed in other aspects of the law of contracts. This court and all other courts reiterate that contracts are "sacred and shall be enforced by the courts of justice unless some other over-powering rule of public policy intervenes which renders such agreement illegal or unenforceable. . . . Without such a rule the commerce of the world would soon lapse into a chaotic state." . . .

Thus far all signs have pointed to applying the law of California and holding the contract enforceable. There is, however, an obstacle to cross before this end can be logically reached. In *Olshen v. Kaufman*, supra, we decided that the law of Oregon, at least as applied to persons domiciled in Oregon contracting in Oregon for performance in Oregon, is that spendthrifts' contracts are voidable. Are the choice-of-law principles of conflict of laws so superior that they overcome this principle of Oregon law?

To answer this question we must determine, upon some basis, whether the interests of Oregon are so basic and important that we should not apply California law despite its several intimate connections with the transaction. The traditional method used by this court and most others is framed in the terminology of "public policy." The court decides whether or not the public policy of the forum is so strong that the law of the forum must prevail although another jurisdiction, with different laws, has more and closer contacts with the transaction. Included in "public policy" we must consider the economic and social interests of Oregon. When these factors are included in a consideration of whether the law of the forum should be applied this traditional approach is very similar to that advocated by many legal scholars. This latter theory is "that choice-of-law rules should rationally advance the policies or interests of the several states (or of the nations in the world community)."

The traditional test this court and many others have used in determining whether the public policy of the forum prevents the application of otherwise applicable conflict of laws principles is stated in the oft-quoted opinion of Mr. Justice Cardozo in *Loucks v. Standard Oil Co. of N.Y.*, 224 N.Y. 99, 120 N.E. 198 (1918). . . .

How "deep rooted [the] tradition of the common weal," particularly regarding spendthrifts, is illustrated by our decisions on foreign marriages. This court has decided that Oregon's policy voiding spendthrifts' contracts is not so strong as to void an Oregon spendthrift's marriage contract made in Washington. *Sturgis v. Sturgis*, 51 Or. 10, 93 P. 696, (1908). . . .

However, as previously stated, if we include in our search for the public policy of the forum a consideration of the various interests that the forum has in this litigation, we are guided by more definite criteria. In addition to the interests of the forum, we should consider the interests of the other jurisdictions which have some connection with the transaction.

Some of the interests of Oregon in this litigation are set forth in *Olshen v. Kaufman*, supra. The spendthrift's family which is to be protected by the establishment of the guardianship is presumably an Oregon family. The public authority which may be charged with the expense of supporting the spendthrift or his family, if he is permitted to go unrestrained upon his wasteful way, will probably be an Oregon public authority. These, obviously, are interests of some substance.

Oregon has other interests and policies regarding this matter which were not necessary to discuss in *Olshen*. As previously stated, Oregon, as well as all other states, has a strong policy favoring the validity and enforceability of contracts. This policy applies whether the contract is made and to be performed in Oregon or elsewhere.

The defendant's conduct, — borrowing money with the belief that the repayment of such loan could be avoided — is a species of fraud. Oregon and all other states have a strong policy of protecting innocent persons from fraud. "The law . . . is intended as a protection to even the foolishly credulous, as against the machinations of the designedly wicked."

It is in Oregon's commercial interest to encourage citizens of other states to conduct business with Oregonians. If Oregonians acquire a reputation for not honoring their agreements, commercial intercourse with Oregonians will be discouraged. If there are Oregon laws, somewhat unique to Oregon, which permit an Oregonian to escape his otherwise binding obligations, persons may well avoid commercial dealings with Oregonians.

The substance of these commercial considerations, however, is deflated by the recollection that the Oregon Legislature has determined, despite the weight of these considerations, that a spendthrift's contracts are voidable.

California's most direct interest in this transaction is having its citizen creditor paid. As previously noted, California's policy is that any creditor, in California or otherwise, should be paid even though the debtor is a spendthrift. California probably has another, although more intangible, interest involved. It is presumably to every state's benefit to have the reputation of being a jurisdiction in which contracts can be made and performance be promised with the certain knowledge that such contracts will be enforced. Both of these interests, particularly the former, are also of substance.

We have, then, two jurisdictions, each with several close connections with the transaction, and each with a substantial interest, which will be served or thwarted, depending upon which law is applied. The interests of neither jurisdiction are clearly more important than those of the other. We are of the opinion that in such a case the public policy of Oregon should prevail and the law of Oregon should be applied; we should apply that choice-of-law rule which will "advance the policies or interests of" Oregon.

Courts are instruments of state policy. The Oregon Legislature has adopted a policy to avoid possible hardship to an Oregon family of a spendthrift and to avoid possible expenditure of Oregon public funds which might occur if the spendthrift is required to pay his obligations. In litigation Oregon courts are the appropriate instrument to enforce this policy. The mechanical application of choice-of-law rules would be the only apparent reason for an Oregon court advancing the interests of California over the equally valid interests of Oregon. The present principles of conflict of laws are not favorable to such mechanical application.

We hold that the spendthrift law of Oregon is applicable and the plaintiff cannot recover.

Notes on
LILIENTHAL

1. As noted earlier, the process of interpreting a law's purpose can be fraught with challenges. Consider whether the Oregon court successfully navigated these challenges in *Lilienthal.* The court recognized that promoting commercial transactions with Oregon residents was an important state interest. Nonetheless, the court also pointed out that the legislature had not chosen to give dominance to this purpose, but rather had decided to protect a spendthrift and his family from ill-advised financial transactions. In giving dominance to the latter purpose, the court provided no role for the apparent balance of interests that underlies the Oregon law. The court might have instead used this balance to justify applying California law, thereby accommodating California's interest in enforcing the spendthrift's contract. Would that approach be true to Currie's approach? The next case, *Bernkrant v. Fowler,* suggests that it might be. One argument is that Currie wanted courts to consider the multijurisdictional context of the case before them, and to ask whether a restrained and moderate interpretation of laws suggests that the legislature did not intend the same balance of competing policies in that multijurisdictional context as in a purely domestic case. In light of this reasoning, one might argue that the Oregon legislature did not mean to strike the same balance of policies in a case with all Oregon elements as it would for a contract made outside the state with a nonresident. Perhaps, then, the legislature did not intend the spendthrift trust law to apply extraterritorially.

In evaluating this argument, consider also the choice of law approach that governed at the time that the *Lilienthal* parties made the contract for the binoculars deal. As the *Lilienthal* court pointed out at the beginning of the opinion, the place-of-making rule had been the prevailing choice of law rule in Oregon for some time, presumably in place when the Oregon legislature enacted the spendthrift trust statute and when parties made the contract. If we are to charge the Oregon legislators with knowledge of the place-of-making rule, what does that suggest about the legislators' intent? Does the rule make it less likely or more likely that the Oregon legislature would have intended the spendthrift trust law to apply in a situation where a spendthrift made an out-of-state contract?

2. The court defended its decision to apply forum law, stating that courts are the "appropriate instrument" of forum state policy in litigation. One can certainly make an argument that — in a democracy — a jurisdiction's courts ultimately get their authority from the people, and should therefore implement the people's preference as expressed in legislatively enacted laws. Brainerd Currie agreed with the *Lilienthal* court's thinking:

> The sensible and clearly constitutional thing for any court to do, confronted with a true conflict of interests, is to apply its own law. . . . It should apply its own law . . . simply because a court should never apply any other law except when there is a good reason for doing so.

BRAINERD CURRIE, SELECTED ESSAYS ON THE CONFLICT OF LAWS 119 (1963). Are there any reasons why a presumption in favor of forum law is not a good idea in a true conflict situation?

3. Scholars debate whether a court that applies forum law to resolve true conflicts unfairly discriminates against noncitizens. *Compare* John Hart Ely, *Choice of Law and the State's Interest in Protecting Its Own*, 23 WM. & MARY L. REV. 173, 192-199 (1981) (arguing that the approach discriminates unconstitutionally), *and* Douglas Laycock, *Equal Citizens of Equal and Territorial States: The Constitutional Foundations of Choice of Law*, 92 COLUM. L. REV. 249, 276 (1992) (arguing that the approach discriminates inappropriately), *with* Louise Weinberg, *On Departing from Forum Law*, 35 MERCER L. REV. 595, 596-597 & n.4 (1981) (arguing that the approach is appropriate, since states may legitimately confine the reach of their laws to residents). Professor Ely argued that significant problems emerged from the tendency for governmental interest analysis to emphasize domicile over other possible connecting factors. Moreover, as Professor Lea Brilmayer has pointed out, the approach encourages the presumption that a state's law is intended to protect domiciliaries of the state, and thus discourages thoughtful investigation of other policies. Lea Brilmayer, *Rights, Fairness, and Choice of Law*, 98 YALE L.J. 1277, 1315 (1989).

Although the due process, equal protection, and full faith and credit protections of the United States Constitution all provide fodder for constitutional attacks on the governmental interest analysis, the privileges and immunities clauses have most often inspired criticism. Anticipating potential constitutional objections to his approach, Professor Currie maintained that the approach avoided constitutional problems by its rational moderation, and its admonition for states to "subordinate . . . [self-interest] freely, even gladly, to the constitutional restraints required and made possible by the federal union." CURRIE, *supra*, at 525. Further discussion of potential constitutional critiques of governmental interest analysis appears in Chapter 3.

PROBLEM 2-32: A DAMAGES LIMITATION QUESTION

Kahn, a resident of Full Damages State, traveled to Limited Damages State to be treated by a physician there. The physician treated Kahn at a famous, world-class research hospital in Limited Damages State, but the treatment of Kahn was unsuccessful. Kahn died at the hospital. His wife filed suit in Full Damages State against the hospital, arguing that Full Damages State's wrongful death law applied. Assume that Full Damages State's wrongful death statute does not limit recovery, but that Limited Damages State's wrongful death statute limits damages to between $5,000 and $50,000. Limited Damages State's statute requires that damages falling in this range should "be assessed with reference to the degree of the tortfeasor's culpability." Assume that the forum — Full Damages State — follows Currie's governmental interest analysis. Which state's damages provision will likely govern?

PROBLEM 2-33: DRAFTING A CAPACITY STATUTE

Assume that you are a legislator in the State of Oregon trying to draft a statute that validates the result in *Lilienthal*. In particular, you would like to draft a statute that makes clear that the state's law depriving individuals of capacity to contract should apply to contracts made out of state by an out-of-state party who should have known that another party to the contract lacked legal capacity to independently enter into the contract. Try your hand at drafting the statute.

Bernkrant v. Fowler

360 P.2d 906 (Cal. 1961)

TRAYNOR, Justice.

. . . Some time before 1954 plaintiffs purchased the Granrud Garden Apartments in Las Vegas, Nevada. In 1954 the property was encumbered by a . . . second deed of trust given to secure an installment note payable to Granrud at $200 per month plus interest. Granrud's note and deed of trust provided for subordination to a deed of trust plaintiffs might execute to secure a construction loan. In July 1954, there remained unpaid approximately $24,000 on the note payable to Granrud. At that time Granrud wished to buy a trailer park and asked plaintiffs to refinance their obligations and pay a substantial part of their indebtedness to him. At a meeting in Las Vegas he stated that if plaintiffs would do so, he would provide by will that any debt that remained on the purchase price at the time of his death would be cancelled and forgiven. Plaintiffs then arranged for a new loan [using] the proceeds to pay the balance of the loan secured by the existing first deed of trust and $13,114.20 of their indebtedness to Granrud. They executed a new note for the balance of $9,227 owing Granrud, payable in installments. . . .

Granrud died testate on March 4, 1956, a resident of Los Angeles County. His will, dated January 23, 1956 . . . made no provision for cancelling the balance of $6,425 due on the note at the time of his death. Plaintiffs have continued to make regular payments of principal and interest to defendant under protest.

Plaintiffs brought this action to have the note cancelled and discharged and the property reconveyed to them and to recover the amounts paid defendant after Granrud's death. [Although the trial court concluded that both the Nevada and the California statutes of frauds barred the action, the California Supreme Court concluded that the contract was valid under Nevada law.]

We are therefore confronted with a contract that is valid under the law of Nevada but invalid under the California statute of frauds if that statute is applicable. We have no doubt that California's interest in protecting estates being probated here from false claims based on alleged oral contracts to make wills is constitutionally sufficient to justify the Legislature's making our statute of frauds applicable to all such contracts sought to be enforced against such estates. . . . Legislature, however, is ordinarily concerned with enacting laws to govern purely local transactions, and it has not spelled out the extent to which the statute of frauds is to apply to contract having substantial contacts with another state. Accordingly, we must determine its scope in the light of applicable principles of the law of conflict of laws.

In the present case plaintiffs were residents of Nevada, the contract was made in Nevada, and plaintiffs performed it there. If Granrud was a resident of Nevada at the time the contract was made, the California statute of frauds, in the absence of a plain legislative direction to the contrary, could not reasonably be interpreted as applying to the contract even though Granrud subsequently moved to California and died here. The basic policy of upholding the expectations of the parties by enforcing contracts valid under the only law apparently applicable would preclude an interpretation of our statute of frauds that would make it apply to and thus invalidate the contract because Granrud moved to California and died here. . . . Just as parties to local transactions cannot be expected to take cognizance of the law of other jurisdictions, they cannot be expected to anticipate a change in the local statute of frauds. Protection of rights growing out of valid contracts precludes interpreting the general language of the statute of frauds to destroy such rights whether the possible applicability of the statute arises from the movement of one or more of the parties across state lines or subsequent enactment of the statute.

In the present case, however, there is no finding as to where Granrud was domiciled at the time the contract was made. Since he had a bank account in California at that time and died a resident here less than two years later it may be that he was domiciled here when the contract was made. Even if he was, the result should be the same. The contract was made in Nevada and performed by plaintiffs there, and it involved the refinancing of obligations arising from the sale of Nevada land and secured by interests therein. Nevada has a substantial interest in the contract and in protecting the rights of its residents who are parties thereto, and its policy is that the contract is valid and enforcible. California's policy is also to enforce lawful contracts. That policy, however, must be subordinated in the case of any contract that does not meet the requirements of an applicable statute of frauds. In determining whether the contract herein is subject to the California statute of frauds, we must consider both the policy to protect the reasonable expectations of the parties and the policy of the statute of frauds. It is true that if Granrud was domiciled here at the time the contract was made, plaintiffs may have been alerted to the possibility that the California statute of frauds might apply. Since California, however, would have no interest in applying its own statute of frauds unless Granrud remained here until his death, plaintiffs were not bound to know that California's statute might ultimately be invoked against them. Unless they could rely on their own law, they would have to look to the laws of all of the jurisdictions to which Granrud might move regardless of where he was domiciled when the contract was made. We conclude, therefore, that the contract herein does not fall within our statute of frauds. Since there is thus no conflict between the law of California and the law of Nevada, we can give effect to the common policy of both states to enforce lawful contracts and sustain Nevada's interest in protecting its residents and their reasonable expectations growing out of a transaction substantially related to that state without subordinating any legitimate interest of this state.

The judgment is reversed.

Notes on
BERNKRANT

1. The *Bernkrant* court was somewhat ambiguous when it stated that Nevada law and California law did not conflict. That is, it was not completely clear whether the court meant that the two laws never had the same field of operation or whether it simply meant that there was no conflict in this multi-jurisdictional context (in other words a "false conflict" for the purpose of Currie's governmental interest analysis). Most interpret the opinion as finding a "false conflict." Indeed, Professor Currie regarded *Bernkrant* as a "brilliant" specimen of restrained and moderate interpretation. According to Currie, the mere appearance of a true conflict "is a sound reason why the conception should be re-examined, with a view to a more moderate and restrained interpretation both of the policy and of the circumstances in which it must be applied to effectuate the forum's legitimate purpose." Brainerd Currie, *The Disinterested Third State*, 28 LAW & CONTEMP. PROBS. 754, 757 (1963). Do you agree that *Bernkrant* court acted in a restrained manner—or might one say that it strained to avoid a true conflict?

2. In *Bernkrant*, the real estate and the contract were situated in Nevada. Consider how you would use the following in supporting the court's restrained and moderate interpretation if the following were true: at the time the deal was made, Nevada's choice of law principles would apply Nevada law and California's choice of law principles would apply Nevada law to the question whether the oral contract was valid. Aren't both of these choice of law results suggestive of a legislative intent not to have

California's statute of frauds principles apply to this Nevada contract? This "renvoi-type analysis" can be useful in trying to undertake a restrained and moderate interpretation.

3. Many analytical techniques are available for avoiding a true conflict of laws with a restrained and moderate interpretation. In addition to the renvoi-type analysis described immediately above, examples include:

- a conclusion that a state statute has no extraterritorial reach and does not bind activities outside the jurisdiction;
- a conclusion that a state statute results from a balance of purposes that does not apply in a case with multijurisdictional elements;
- a conclusion that the legislature intended a law's protection to extend only to domiciliaries; and
- a conclusion that the legislature intended a law's restrictions or burdens to apply only to domiciliaries.

4. Although governmental interest analysis has proven intellectually attractive to many courts, they struggle with the proper way to handle true conflicts. Reflexively applying forum law in a true conflict strikes many thinkers as unfair to the parties, inadequately deferential to the other interested state, or simply lazy and intellectually dishonest. Courts and scholars have therefore developed alternatives to Currie's forum law resolution of true conflicts. Some courts follow a balancing solution, which is described at the end of this section on governmental interest analysis. Other courts follow a refinement of governmental interest analysis known as comparative impairment. Several others have developed unique approaches, portrayed later in this chapter in the section on hybrid approaches.

PROBLEM 2-34: ZIPPY'S FORFEITURE WORRIES

Sam purchased a car from a dealer in Texas. He executed a promissory note and gave the dealer a security interest in the car. On the same day, the dealer assigned the note and security interest to a Texas corporation, Zippy Loan, which is in the business of financing car sales. The security agreement prohibited Sam from taking the car out of state without permission of the dealer or its assigns. In violation of this agreement and without Zippy's (or the dealer's) knowledge, Sam drove the car to Oklahoma. In Oklahoma, Sam was arrested while using the car to transport marijuana.

Assume that in connection with the criminal proceedings against Sam, the Oklahoma Attorney General seized the car and began a forfeiture action. Zippy has intervened in the matter in order to ensure that the car is forfeited only subject to

Zippy's lien. Specifically, Zippy seeks to require that, should the court enter a forfeiture judgment, the Attorney General must pay Zippy the remaining part of the purchase price Sam owes under the promissory note. Under Oklahoma law, Zippy cannot claim this right unless it investigated Sam's moral responsibility and character before taking an interest in the car. Zippy performed no such investigation, but nonetheless wishes to maintain a priority position in getting paid under the note.

Assume that Texas has no forfeiture law comparable to Oklahoma's. Texas commercial law, however, makes clear that a security interest in a vehicle is valid where, as here, the entity taking the interest had no knowledge that the vehicle will be used illegally. To have a valid security interest in Texas, a lender need not investigate the debtor's character. Would a court applying governmental interest analysis choose Texas or Oklahoma law to govern the extent of Zippy's interest in the car?

3. No Interest or Unprovided-for Cases

Erwin v. Thomas

506 P.2d 494 (Or. 1973)

HOLMAN, Justice.

This is an action for damages for loss of consortium alleged to have been suffered when plaintiff's husband was injured in an accident. Plaintiff appealed from a judgment for defendant which was entered after a demurrer was sustained to plaintiff's complaint and plaintiff refused to plead further.

Defendant Thomas, while operating a truck in the state of Washington in the course of his employment for defendant Shepler, is alleged to have negligently injured plaintiff's husband. Defendant Thomas is an Oregon resident and his employer, defendant Shepler, is an Oregon corporation. Plaintiff and her injured husband are residents of Washington. Washington, by court decision, has followed the common law rule that no cause of action exists by a wife for loss of consortium. Oregon allows such an action, ORS 108.010.

The issue is whether Oregon law or Washington law is applicable. It is with some trepidation that a court enters the maze of choice of law in tort cases. No two authorities agree. Until recently, this court was committed to the traditional, arbitrary, and much criticized rule that in tort cases the law of the place of the wrong, Lex loci delicti commissi, governs. However, in the case of *Casey v. Manson Constr. Co.*, 247 Or. 274, 428 P.2d 898 (1967), this court adopted the equally maligned and almost universally criticized "most significant relationship" approach of Restatement (Second) Conflict of Laws.

. . .

Where, in the particular factual context, the interests and policies of one state are involved and those of the other are not (or, if they are, they are involved in only a minor way), reason would seem to dictate that the law of the state whose policies and interests are vitally involved should apply; or, if those of neither state are vitally involved, that the law of the forum should apply. It may well be that determining what interests or policies are behind the law of a particular state is far from an exact science and is something about which there can be legitimate disagreement; but, on the other hand, it is the kind of an exercise, for better or for worse, which courts do every day and, therefore, feel secure in doing. If such a claimed conflict can be so disposed of, whether it is called false or not, the disposition certainly seems preferable to wandering off into the jungle with a compass which everyone but its maker says is defective.

Let us examine the interests involved in the present case. Washington has decided that the rights of a married woman whose husband is injured are not sufficiently important to cause the negligent defendant who is responsible for the injury to pay the wife for her loss. It has weighed the matter in favor of protection of defendants. No Washington defendant is going to have to respond for damages in the present case, since the defendant is an Oregonian. Washington has little concern whether other states require non-Washingtonians to respond to such claims. Washington policy cannot be offended if the court of another state affords rights to a Washington woman which Washington does not afford, so long as a Washington defendant is not required to respond. The state of Washington appears to have no material or urgent policy or interest which would be offended by applying Oregon law.

On the other hand, what is Oregon's interest? Oregon, obviously, is protective of the rights of married women and believes that they should be allowed to recover for negligently inflicted loss of consortium. However, it is stretching the imagination more than a trifle to conceive that the Oregon Legislature was concerned about the rights of all the nonresident married women in the nation whose husbands would be injured outside of the state of Oregon. Even if Oregon were so concerned, it would offend no substantial Washington interest.

It is apparent, therefore, that neither state has a vital interest in the outcome of this litigation and there can be no conceivable material conflict of policies or interests if an Oregon court does what comes naturally and applies Oregon law. Professor Currie expresses it thusly:

> . . . The closest approximation to the renvoi problem that will be encountered under the suggested method is the case in which neither state has an interest in the application of its law and policy; in that event, the forum would apply its own law simply on the ground that that is the more convenient disposition. . . . B. Currie, Notes on Methods and Objectives in the Conflict of Laws, Selected Essays on the Conflict of Laws 184 (1963).

An examination of the writings of those scholars who believe that an actual controversy exists in a situation similar to the present indicates, without an exception, they would reach the same result as we do, by either different or partially different reasoning.

. . . Where policies and interests can be identified with a fair degree of assurance and there appears to be no substantial conflict, we do not believe it is necessary to have recourse in the "contacts" of Section 145(2) of Restatement (Second) Conflict of Laws.

The judgment of the trial court is reversed and the case is remanded for further proceedings.

BRYSON, J., dissenting

... I do not believe we can or should bestow Oregon statutory rights for women on women of the state of Washington.

Obviously the plaintiff could not bring this action in her state, Washington, but the majority opinion holds that by merely stepping over the state boundary into Oregon she is then bestowed with the right given wives who are residents of the state of Oregon, which includes the right of action for loss of consortium of her husband.

There is definitely a conflict in the policy of the states of Washington and Oregon regarding the right to bring an action for loss of consortium.

Notes on
ERWIN

1. The *Erwin* court noted that at that time, Oregon followed the Restatement (Second) of Conflict of Laws, which was written after governmental interest analysis took hold in the courts. As you will see, the Restatement (Second) integrates governmental interest analysis, but also invites alternative reasoning. As courts often do, the *Erwin* court declines to engage in the alternative reasoning and thus produced an opinion that appears to present pure governmental interest analysis.

2. Brainerd Currie advocated for applying forum law in conflict cases, including unprovided-for cases where no jurisdiction had an interest in applying its law. He also advocated in favor of applying forum law where the forum was disinterested, but only if forum law overlapped with the law of an interested jurisdiction. In that context, he nonetheless expressed "equanimity" toward the possibility that the forum court apply the law it believes to be "the more enlightened and humane," in accordance with the "needs of our society." Brainerd Currie, *The Disinterested Third State*, 28 LAW & CONTEMP. PROBS. 754, 778-780 (1963).

3. Currie took the position that multistate disputes should be resolved in the same manner as single-state disputes. Is Currie's suggestion that forum law apply in an unprovided-for case consistent with this position? In a single-state situation, a forum court might simply dismiss a claim for which no legal consequences attach. Shouldn't the forum court in a multistate unprovided-for case situation also simply enter judgment against the plaintiff and dismiss the suit? For insightful discussion of these and other arguments pertaining to unprovided-for cases, see Larry Kramer, *The Myth of the Unprovided-for Case*, 75 VA. L. REV. 1045 (1989); Larry Kramer, *Rethinking Choice of Law*, 90 COLUM.

L. REV. 277, 293-307 (1990); Kermit Roosevelt III, *The Myth of Choice of Law: Rethinking Conflicts*, 97 MICH. L. REV. 2448 (1999).

4. When the various configurations are tallied, one sees that governmental interest analysis invites courts to apply forum law in nearly every situation. Recall the arguments against this result: does the dominance of forum law cast a shadow on the efficacy and validity of governmental interest analysis?

PROBLEM 2-35: MORRIS JAMES'S CIGARETTE FRAUD

Cary Cigarette smoked cigarettes produced by Morris James Company for the ten years that she lived in the State of Dakota. She quit smoking and thereafter moved to the State of Jersey. While living in the State of Jersey, Cary first developed lung cancer. She then moved to Forum State where she died a year later. Cary's estate is being administered in Forum State. The representatives of her estate, who are all domiciled in Forum State, have filed a wrongful death suit in Forum State Court against Morris James Company, which is incorporated and has its principal place of business in Old Carolina. In their complaint, the representatives allege that Morris James Company is responsible for Cary's death. To support this allegation, they aver — in conclusory terms — that Morris James Company defrauded Cary in the company's advertising by glamorizing cigarette smoking and by concealing smoking's deleterious health effects. According to the complaint, this fraud induced Cary to smoke. Morris James Company has moved to dismiss the complaint for failure to state a claim. Specifically, the Company argues that the complaint's failure to give sufficient facts of the alleged fraud makes it impossible to answer the complaint meaningfully and makes plain the estate's inability to establish the strenuous requirements for a fraud-in-advertising claim.

The relevant jurisdictions have the following laws pertinent to Morris James Company's arguments:

Forum State, State of Jersey, and State of Dakota: (1) A fraud plaintiff has a special burden of alleging fraud with specificity; and (2) In order to succeed, fraud-in-advertising claims must establish a strong and direct relationship between the advertising and the injury suffered.

State of Old Carolina: (1) The pleading requirements for fraud are the same as the requirements governing any other cause of action; and (2) In order to establish fraud in advertising, a plaintiff need show only that there is a reasonable possibility that the advertising caused the injury suffered.

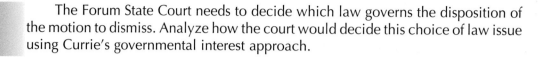

The Forum State Court needs to decide which law governs the disposition of the motion to dismiss. Analyze how the court would decide this choice of law issue using Currie's governmental interest approach.

4. *Experimenting with Balancing Interests*

One of the strongest incentives for courts following some form of governmental interest analysis is to find only one state with an interest, and thus to handle the case as a false conflict, applying the law of the only interested state. Sometimes, however, courts simply are unable to justify this path and then must confront how to dispose of a true conflict. Courts have looked for alternatives to Currie's lockstep "apply forum law" solution to true conflicts, experimenting with various resolutions. New Jersey is one of several jurisdictions to experiment. Although New Jersey has now officially abandoned governmental interest analysis, the following two cases provide thoughtful and instructive lessons on how to deal with this thorny problem.

D'Agostino v. Johnson & Johnson, Inc.

628 A.2d 305 (N.J. 1993)

O'HERN, J.

[D'Agostino was a United States citizen, resident of Switzerland, and employee of Cilag, a Swiss subsidiary of Johnson & Johnson Corporation (J & J). He had an at-will employment contract, with a Swiss choice of law clause. When D'Agostino registered a new pharmaceutical with Swiss regulators, his supervisor directed him to pay "consulting fees" to the authorities. D'Agostino believed the fees were a bribe, refused to pay them, and was fired. D'Agostino then filed a New Jersey wrongful termination suit, arguing that J & J arranged the alleged bribe and retaliatory firing — all violations of the federal Foreign Corrupt Practices Act (FCPA), which was incorporated through case law into New Jersey law. By contrast, Swiss law would have regarded the payments as legal "consulting fees" and the firing as lawful.

Applying New Jersey law, the trial court granted partial summary judgment for plaintiff. The New Jersey Appellate Division reversed, and applied Swiss law.]

In this appeal we must consider . . . whether Swiss or domestic law governs the claims asserted in the New Jersey forum against a New Jersey corporation and its officers. We hold that because the underlying controversy 1) involves an alleged violation in New Jersey of the Foreign Corrupt Practices Act, 15 U.S.C.A. §§78dd-1 to -2 (hereinafter FCPA), which sets forth a domestic policy against bribery of a foreign regulatory official; 2) involves the participation of a United States citizen who might have been exposed to criminal prosecution had the conduct violated the FCPA and was an alleged violation of a New Jersey corporation's internal policy against such overseas commercial bribery; and 3) because violation of the governmental policies could have an indirect effect on the domestic market for pharmaceutical products and the health and welfare of this forum's citizens, New Jersey's interests in resolving this dispute under its laws outweigh the Swiss interest in the at-will employment relationship that would not seek to deter such conduct through its civil law. . . .

II

. . .

For determining choice-of-law, New Jersey no longer follows the rule that the place where the wrong occurred controls. *Veazey v. Doremus*, 103 N.J. 244, 247, 510 A.2d 1187 (1986). Today, New Jersey uses "the more flexible governmental-interest analysis in choice-of-law decisions." *Ibid.* "Under that analysis, the determinative law is that of the state with the greatest interest in governing the particular issue." *Id.* at 248, 510 A.2d 1187. Once a conflict is determined

> the next step is to identify the governmental policies underlying the law of each state and how those policies are affected by each state's contacts to the litigation and to the parties. If a state's contacts are not related to the policies underlying its law, then that state does not possess an interest in having its law apply. Consequently, the qualitative, not the quantitative, nature of a state's contacts ultimately determines whether its law should apply.

. . . New Jersey has no interest in regulating Swiss employment relationships. But this case is not about regulating just Swiss employment relationships. It is as much about regulating the conduct of parent companies in New Jersey that engage in corrupt practices through a subsidiary's employees. For the "particular issue" here is the tort liability of a domestic corporation for ordering and directing the discharge of a subsidiary's employee for the refusal to participate in corrupt practices. That issue is not encapsulated within a Swiss employment doctrine but embraces as well the conduct here of a New Jersey parent company that has assertedly engaged in conduct that would violate a clear mandate of public policy. . . . The question is: does the FCPA constitute a state policy and does the FCPA have an intended extraterritorial effect?

A

We will consider first whether a clear mandate of public policy relates to a domestic company's overseas activities, and then examine New Jersey's contacts with that mandate, if it exists, in the circumstances of this case.

In New Jersey, in the absence of a contract, an employee may be fired for any reason, be it good cause, no cause, or even morally-wrong cause, but not when the discharge is contrary to a clear mandate of public policy. . . . Federal law and policy can constitute New Jersey's clear mandate of public policy. [The court embraced "cases specifically adopting the FCPA as a state policy."]

. . .

The mere existence of a policy does not mean that it will be invoked. "A 'clear mandate of public policy' must be one that on balance is beneficial to the public."

That requires a weighing of the competing interests. . . . The FCPA makes unlawful the giving of a gift to a foreign official in order to influence a decision of a foreign government.

> The FCPA was intended to stop bribery of foreign officials and political parties by domestic corporations. Bribery abroad was considered a "severe" United States foreign policy problem; it embarrasses friendly governments, causes a decline of foreign esteem for the United States and casts suspicion on the activities of our enterprises, giving credence to our foreign opponents. H.R. Rep. No. 640, 95th Cong., 1st Sess. 5 (1977). The FCPA thus represents a legislative judgment that our foreign relations will be bettered by a strict anti-bribery statute.

The FCPA expresses a strong public interest against the bribing of foreign officials by domestic companies. . . . Congress, through the FCPA, has expressed a need to protect the public against the bribing of foreign officials by domestic companies. That federal policy represents a clear mandate of state policy, especially when a violation of the federal policy has an impact on the health and welfare of the forum state. The record contains evidence that members of the College of Experts participated in institutional review boards analyzing clinical results for drugs Cilag was attempting to register in Switzerland. Those boards were necessary not for registration in Switzerland but for the Swiss documents to be used in the United States for the registration of the drug by the Food and Drug Administration. New Jersey is a worldwide leader in the pharmaceutical markets. The effect of commercial bribery abroad has a potential effect on New Jersey and the health and welfare of its citizens.

On the other side of our balancing analysis is the interest of comity that is implicated by the extraterritorial application of the FCPA in a wrongful-discharge case. The FCPA expressly applies extraterritorially to United States citizens working for foreign subsidiaries of domestic companies. 15 U.S.C.A. §78dd-2(a)(2)(B) (subjecting United States citizen working overseas to five-years imprisonment for violating FCPA). "[A]pplication of United States law to *United States nationals* abroad ordinarily raises considerably less serious questions of international comity than does the application of United States law to *foreign nationals* abroad." *EEOC v. Arabian Am. Oil Co.*, 499 U.S. 244, 274 (1991) (Marshall, J., dissenting). . . . We also note that the Conscientious Employee Protection Act, N.J.S.A. 34:19-1 to -8, has codified much of the common-law retaliatory-discharge claim and includes an activity that is a violation of law or a crime. We do not suggest that the "whistle blower" act itself has an extraterritorial effect; rather it reflects our common-law employment law, which will apply extraterritorially only when the underlying clear mandate of public policy is intended to have an extraterritorial effect.

Not only can federal policy constitute state policy, it can also apply extraterritorially when Congress intends that the policy have overseas applications. The FCPA is intended to govern United States citizens abroad, and applying the policies of the FCPA to D'Agostino's claim is an intended and permissible extraterritorial effect. In declining to assert jurisdiction over foreign subsidiaries the

FCPA focuses liability on the parent and the United States national acting as its overseas operative. . . . Not only could D'Agostino be liable under the FCPA, but more likely J & J could be held liable as a parent of a subsidiary whose agent bribed a foreign official.

. . . The FCPA's policy of preventing the bribery of foreign officials by domestic companies, combined with the alleged reason for the bribe — to influence the registration of drugs in Switzerland and the United States — suggests a strong public interest in this case. Any opposing interest involving extraterritoriality does not outweigh this forum's interests in preventing bribery, which could have a negative impact on public health and safety in New Jersey. Having determined that the mandate of public policy is beneficial to the public, we must consider New Jersey's and Switzerland's "contacts" with the potential tort liability of a domestic corporation for ordering and directing the discharge of a foreign subsidiary's employee for the refusal to participate in corrupt practices.

B

. . . We recognize that Switzerland has an interest in governing the employment relationships between a Swiss company and a Swiss resident. Switzerland does have an undoubted interest in preventing bribery, although that interest is not a policy effectuated through such Swiss employment law; rather, it is a policy underlying Swiss criminal law. And Switzerland does have a strong interest in maintaining a uniform approach to employee/employer relations (as with any state), especially when one considers its small size, location, tradition of neutrality, and openness to trade, foreign business, and foreign employees. Thus, Switzerland has an interest in having its law apply to an employment relationship involving a Swiss resident and a Swiss company. . . . But it does not have an interest in condoning corporate bribery orchestrated beyond its boundaries. . . .

In addition, D'Agostino was hired through the efforts of an employment agency chosen by J & J and was interviewed by the J & J organization in Germany, not in Switzerland. D'Agostino thought he was entering into a long-term career with J & J that would eventually involve a United States-based position with the company. Both D'Agostino's hiring and termination announcements were issued by J & J's international subsidiary in New Jersey and distributed to J & J's managers and Executive Committee in New Jersey. Plaintiff's firing followed shortly after a meeting at J & J's corporate headquarters in New Jersey at which the unsuccessful registration of a drug was discussed.

Those alleged facts and inferences reveal J & J's extensive supervisory role and involvement in Cilag and D'Agostino's employment situation. As noted, the thesis of plaintiff's case is that J & J orchestrated in New Jersey the bribing of a foreign official, allegedly in violation of the FCPA and potentially subjecting a United States citizen to criminal prosecution, and plaintiff's subsequent dismissal for failing to pay the bribe. If proven, the extensive New Jersey contacts and the qualitative nature of the underlying controversy lead us to conclude that New Jersey law should govern this dispute.

C

. . . Switzerland has a strong interest in at-will employment. . . . However, New Jersey has a qualitatively different interest in protecting employees against wrongful discharges ordered by New Jersey corporations. . . . Allowing New Jersey law to apply provides . . . the fairness and certainty for the parties involved that we were concerned. . . . J & J, as a New Jersey company, is well aware of the FCPA and its dictates. In fact, it has its own Policy Statement against the use of corporate funds for unlawful purposes, including bribes or payoffs.

Incorporating the FCPA as a clear mandate of New Jersey policy does not undermine any valid expectation of J & J. Hence, we are not exporting New Jersey employment law so much as applying New Jersey domestic policy, drawn from federal sources, to a domestic company. . . . New Jersey law does not regulate conduct outside the state. Rather, New Jersey law regulates conduct in New Jersey, such as J & J's alleged orchestration of the bribing of a foreign official and firing of plaintiff. To use an extreme example, we would not doubt that New Jersey law could interdict a criminal conspiracy, orchestrated in New Jersey, to harm interests elsewhere.

. . .

V

This is an unusual case. It has aspects of both tort and contract law. In addition, the case involves both domestic and international concerns. As such, it does not fit easily within any of the conventional rubrics for choice of law. . . . In considering all of the other factors and the quality of New Jersey's interest in the underlying controversy as well as this State's contacts with the controversy, we believe that as between Switzerland and this forum New Jersey has the greatest interest. In particular, we do not see how a domestic corporation could have any "justified expectations," that it was free to put at jeopardy overseas employees who refuse to participate in commercial bribery. In making such a ruling, we do not export New Jersey employment law to the overseas subsidiaries of domestic corporations. We incorporate a domestic policy intended to affect, at most here, conduct in New Jersey that has a forbidden extraterritorial effect. The allegations in this case present a distinct New Jersey involvement both in the hiring and firing of D'Agostino.

And if the domestic officers had nothing to do with D'Agostino's firing for failure to go along with the bribe, the case is truly closed. This is not a case in which the mandate of policy directly controls the employment relationship of a subsidiary, as it might be in the case of discriminatory domestic-hiring practice. . . . Rather, this is a case in which the violation of public policy arises from the parent's direct, not vicarious, interference with the forum policy.

The premise of plaintiff's case is that the J & J officials ordered and directed the plan to dismiss him; his case cannot hereafter be converted into one of *respondeat superior* or vicarious liability for the unplanned acts of Swiss managers. If the facts are as J & J asserts, the discharge will implicate only Swiss interests, and the case will be dismissed under applicable principles of Swiss law. If the facts are as plaintiff asserts, that the payments that he refused to make were intended to influence Swiss regulatory officials, an asserted violation of the FCPA, and if J & J ordered D'Agostino's discharge and employment quarantine for refusal to go along with the arrangement and its coverup, the case implicates important New Jersey interests that are qualitatively greater than the Swiss interest in employment relationships and therefore calls for the application of domestic law. We repeat, however, what we said at the outset of the opinion: these are but D'Agostino's allegations that remain to be proven.

The judgment of the Appellate Division is reversed and the matter remanded for further proceedings consistent with this opinion.

Notes on
D'AGOSTINO

1. As the *D'Agostino* court suggested, the case's challenges arose from its many hybrid qualities: contract/tort theories of liability, domestic/international contexts, as well as federal law incorporated into state law. Within increasingly globalized legal environments, this type of blurring among the lines of legal authority has proliferated. Does globalism itself enhance the inadequacy of Currie's "apply forum law" approach to true conflicts? Which is better suited to the challenges of handling complex issues of extraterritoriality and overlapping authority: Currie's solution or the qualitative weighing of interests illustrated in *D'Agostino*?

2. The *D'Agostino* court's discussion of extraterritoriality was informed in part by a line of cases pertaining to the extraterritorial reach of United States federal statutes, cases which Chapter 3 explores in greater detail. The court did not, however, end its analysis with an observation that the federal statute at issue in the case, the FCPA, expressly applied outside the boundaries of the United States. Why? Might the answer come from how the court focused the conflict of laws issue on New Jersey employment law (which incorporated the FCPA), rather than on the FCPA itself? Perhaps because of this approach, the court's treatment of extraterritoriality focused on the choice of law concern of where the defendant's conduct occurred. Are you convinced by the court's conclusion that the critical conduct occurred in New Jersey? Was the injury confined to Switzerland?

Rowe v. Hoffmann-La Roche
917 A.2d 767 (N.J. 2007)

Judge LEFELT (temporarily assigned) delivered the opinion of the Court.

[Plaintiff Robert Rowe, a Michigan resident, sued two New Jersey pharmaceutical manufacturers, Hoffmann-La Roche, Inc. and Roche Laboratories, Inc. Rowe alleged that the manufacturers failed to warn adequately about the health risks of an acne drug (Accutane) approved by the federal *failed to warn about Accutane*

Food and Drug Administration (FDA). Rowe had become depressed and attempted suicide after he discontinued Accutane, ultimately crashing a car into a house in an apparent suicide attempt.

[Under Michigan law, the FDA approval results in a conclusive determination that the health risk warnings issued by defendants regarding the drug were adequate. New Jersey law, however, considers the FDA approval to have created only a rebuttable presumption of adequacy. As a consequence of this difference, the court observed that "plaintiff's suit is viable in New Jersey but precluded in Michigan."]

. . .

Gov't int!

[W]e currently subscribe to . . . flexible governmental-interests analysis. . . . If there is an actual conflict of laws, . . . [t]he Court must "identify the governmental policies underlying the law of each state" and determine whether "those policies are affected by each state's contacts to the litigation and to the parties." We must apply the law of "the state with the greatest interest in governing the particular issue."

All parties agree that this case presents an actual conflict. . . . Because an actual conflict exists between New Jersey and Michigan on the very issue in dispute — Rowe's failure-to-warn claim against Hoffmann — we must advance to the next step of the governmental interest analysis. . . .

π arg

The legislative history of the [New Jersey statute (NJPLA)] does not specifically address why the Legislature created only a rebuttable presumption of adequacy for FDA approval of prescription drug warnings. Rowe argues, however, that New Jersey has an interest in applying its rebuttable presumption of adequacy here because Hoffmann is a New Jersey company that has manufactured Accutane in New Jersey. . . . [We point out that New Jersey law] does create a presumption of adequacy rather than simply recognizing FDA approval as one factor to be considered in determining the adequacy of the warnings. . . . The NJPLA impliedly accepts that the presumption of adequacy will not be rebutted in all cases. It accepts FDA regulation as sufficient, at least in part, to deter New Jersey pharmaceutical companies from manufacturing unsafe prescription drugs. The FDA requires that the labeling accompanying a prescription drug "describe serious adverse reactions and potential safety hazards" and that the labeling "be revised to include a warning as soon as there is reasonable evidence of an association of a serious hazard with a drug." 21 C.F.R. §201.100(e). If any labeling "is false or misleading in any particular and was not corrected within a reasonable time," among other enforcement options, the FDA may withdraw approval for the drug. 21 U.S.C.A. §355(e). As this Court has stated, "absent deliberate concealment or nondisclosure of after-acquired knowledge of harmful effects, compliance with FDA standards should be virtually dispositive" of a failure-to-warn claim. *Perez v. Wyeth Labs., Inc.*, 161 N.J. 1, 25, 734 A.2d 1245 (1999).

The Legislature also provides in the NJPLA that FDA approval of prescription drugs conclusively prohibits an award of punitive damages in products liability actions. This provision, along with the rebuttable-presumption[,] . . . cede[s] to FDA regulation some of this State's interest in policing local pharmaceutical manufacturers, thereby reducing New Jersey's interest in applying its law to this case.

interests are congruent

The predominant object of the law is not to encourage tort recoveries by plaintiffs, whether New Jersey citizens or not, in order to deter this State's drug manufacturers. On the contrary, the law limits the liability of manufacturers of FDA-approved products by reducing the burden placed on them by product liability litigation. The Legislature carefully balanced the need to protect individuals against the need to protect an industry with a significant relationship to our economy and public health. New Jersey's interest in applying its law to Rowe's failure-to-warn issue, when properly discerned, is not antithetical to Michigan's interest but substantially congruent.

The relevant Michigan statute . . . was enacted by the Michigan Legislature in 1996 as part of a comprehensive reform of Michigan's tort law. The Michigan Legislature's express purpose was to immunize pharmaceutical companies that market FDA-approved prescription drugs from liability in a products liability suit. . . . Michigan's interest in making prescription drugs more available to its residents is supported by the legislative history of the law. . . . Supporters in the Michigan State Senate recognized that "[c]onsumers . . . suffer when they are denied new products that would increase public safety or improve their quality of life. . . . [P]roduct liability litigation . . . has added substantially to the cost and unavailability of many goods and services." Senate Fiscal Agency Bill Analysis to S.B. 344 & H.B. 4508, at 10 (Jan. 1, 1996). . . . Michigan "was concerned that unlimited liability for drug manufacturers would threaten the financial viability of many enterprises and could add substantially to the cost and unavailability of many drugs." . . .

A want make drug more avail.

This case presents a true conflict of laws because both New Jersey and Michigan have interests that would be furthered by applying their respective statutes to Rowe's failure-to-warn claim against Hoffmann. . . . In this instance, New Jersey's interest is limited and outweighed by Michigan's interest in making more prescription drugs generally available to its citizens.

MI > NJ

Furthermore, comity precludes closing our eyes to Michigan's interest. Even if we were to question the effectiveness of the Michigan statute in accomplishing its goal, "it is the forum state's duty to disregard its own substantive preference." . The question is not whether Michigan or New Jersey passed the better law; that is a normative judgment best suited for the legislative process. Our inquiry is limited to which state has the greatest interest in applying its law to Rowe's failure-to-warn claim.

To allow a life-long Michigan resident who received an FDA-approved drug in Michigan and alleges injuries sustained in Michigan to by-pass his own state's law and obtain compensation for his injuries in this State's courts completely undercuts Michigan's interests, while overvaluing our true interest in this litigation.

In this instance, where the challenged drug was approved by the FDA and suit was brought by an out-of-state plaintiff who has no cause of action in his home state, this State's interest in ensuring that our corporations are deterred from producing unsafe products . . . is not paramount. Our interest in deterring local manufacturing corporations from providing inadequate product warnings, within the context of an FDA approved drug, must yield to Michigan's interest.

. . .

The judgment of the Appellate Division is reversed and the case is remanded to the Law Division for reinstatement of the trial court's order dismissing the lawsuit.

. . .

Judge STERN (temporarily assigned), dissenting.

I travel the same path as the majority but reach a different destination. . . . Certainly, as the majority develops, Michigan has significant interests in furthering its legislative design. However, those interests in protecting consumers with respect to prescription costs and availability (and even more broadly with respect to tort reform) are remote and outweighed in a New Jersey forum when the Michigan resident brings his or her suit in New Jersey against a New Jersey manufacturer, particularly because he or she is subject to the "rebuttable" presumption of the warning or label's adequacy.

Notes on
ROWE

1. Soon after *Rowe*, the New Jersey Supreme Court changed course and adopted yet another approach to resolving choice of law questions. This case, *P.V. ex rel. T.V. v. Camp Jaycee*, 962 A.2d 453 (N.J. 2008), appears later in this chapter. When you read the *Camp Jaycee* case, evaluate whether the two cases reflect substantially different approaches. New Jersey's decision to move on to another approach, however, does not render its balancing decisions irrelevant. Indeed, other jurisdictions have experimented with a balancing approach for resolving true conflicts, see, e.g., *Cipolla v. Shaposka*, 267 A.2d 854 (Pa. 1970),[23] and evidence of balancing reasoning appears in decisions purporting to follow other approaches such as the Restatement (Second) of Conflict of Law.

2. Consider the results in *Rowe* and *D'Agostino* in light of the criticism that governmental interest analysis overvalues forum law and promotes forum protectionism. Do these cases refute that criticism or support it? Although the New Jersey court in *D'Agostino* applied forum law, it did so to the detriment of Johnson & Johnson, a New Jersey company. In *Rowe*, by contrast, the court declined to apply forum law, but the result in the case protected New Jersey manufacturers. What is more relevant to concerns about protectionism and discrimination against nonresidents: a court's decision to apply forum law or to reach a result that favors the interest of a forum domiciliary at the expense of a nondomiciliary?

3. Compare the *Rowe* court's analysis with the court's analysis in *Bernkrant*. In *Rowe*, the court reasoned that the law was the result of a legislative

23. Professor Symeonides identifies the District of Columbia as another jurisdiction that weighs state interest as part of governmental interest analysis. Symeon C. Symeonides, *Choice of Law in the American Courts in 2010: Twenty-Fourth Annual Survey*, 59 AM. J. COMP. L. 303 n.150 (2011).

compromise, and that the terms of the compromise brought the New Jersey law partially in line with the Michigan law: "The [New Jersey] Legislature carefully balanced the need to protect individuals against the need to protect an industry with a significant relationship to our economy and public health. New Jersey's interest in applying its law to Rowe's failure-to-warn issue, when properly discerned, is not antithetical to Michigan's interest but substantially congruent." The *Rowe* court then used this reasoning to perform a qualitative weighing analysis that led to applying Michigan law. Isn't this reasoning similar to, if not identical to, the restrained and moderate interpretation step that Professor Currie described for governmental interest analysis, and that he praised the *Bernkrant* court for using?

4. As explored elsewhere in this chapter, choice of law decisions in products liability cases can create powerful economic incentives that influence corporate decisions and allocation of society's resources. If, for example, the New Jersey court in *Rowe* had decided to apply New Jersey law to the case, the court would have allowed the plaintiff to receive more favorable treatment than he would have received under his home state (Michigan) law. What type of incentive would such a decision give to plaintiffs from states with laws like Michigan who must choose a forum for suing New Jersey manufacturers? What type of incentive would such a decision give to manufacturers deciding whether to situate their operations in New Jersey?

An argument that often emerges in products liability cases is whether huge damages verdicts will have the unwelcome effect of making products too expensive for consumers to afford or even too expensive for manufacturers to make. Isn't this an argument that can be integrated into every case that deals with a suit related to a defective product? Does it add to meaningful analysis of a choice of law issue?

PROBLEM 2-36: SWEAR OR AFFIRM?

Alyssa is from Carolina and Dara is from West Georgia. Their cars collided on a highway in Carolina. Alyssa brought suit against Dara in Carolina. Dara wishes to testify in her own defense. Under Carolina law, a witness must take an oath by swearing to tell the truth by placing her hand on the Bible (New and Old Testaments) before testifying. The history of this law explains that accurate testimony is necessary to justice and an oath on the Bible sends a signal to the witness of the gravity of the act of lying while under oath. Despite religious objections that a witness may have, Carolina made the judgment that truthful testimony was more important. Under West Georgia law, a witness need only "affirm" the truth of her testimony and attest to knowledge of the penalties of perjury. The history of this West Georgia law explains that the law seeks to accommodate those who are offended by being required to "swear" to tell the truth while at the same time signaling to the witness the importance of truthful testimony. Assume that Carolina applies governmental interest analysis and that West Georgia applies the Restatement (First) of Conflict of Laws.

Dara does not want to swear to tell the truth by placing her hand on a Bible before testifying. What is likely to be the result in the case if the court applied the flexible approach to governmental interest analysis reflected in *D'Agostino*? Would this be any different than the formal approach proposed by Professor Currie?

D. COMPARATIVE IMPAIRMENT

Professor William Baxter developed the comparative impairment approach as a refinement to governmental interest analysis. He agreed with the central tenet of governmental interest analysis: courts should be instruments of state policy. Accepting the notion that the law of the only interested state should apply where a false conflict occurs, Baxter nonetheless devised a new resolution for true conflicts. For true conflicts, Baxter proposed that courts should apply the law of the state whose interest would be most impaired if its law did not apply to a particular controversy. William Baxter, *Choice of Law and the Federal System*, 16 STAN. L. REV. 1, 12-13 (1963). The negative formulation of this test is no accident: Baxter's approach focuses on avoiding negative consequences. Specifically, he instructs a court to evaluate the harm that would result if the court did not enforce a state's interests in a particular case. In comparing the interests of two states, the court should seek to minimize harm to state interests by favoring the law of the jurisdiction that would be most damaged if its law did not apply. The theory is that, over time and in the aggregate, all jurisdictions would be better off with this approach, since each jurisdiction would have its interest satisfied in cases where it really matters to them.

Comparative impairment provides a vehicle for assessing the wisdom of other choice of law methodologies, and has proved a catalyst for developing theoretical support and critique of modern choice of law. California courts follow the approach with regularity, and the Louisiana choice of law codification resembles the approach, although the codification ultimately does not "emulate" comparative impairment. Symeon C. Symeonides, *The Conflicts Book of the Louisiana Civil Code: Civilian, American, or Original?*, 83 TUL. L. REV. 1041, 1052 (2009).

Offshore Rental Company v. Continental Oil Company
583 P.2d 721 (Cal. 1978)

TOBRINER, J.

This case presents a problem of conflict of laws. Plaintiff, a California corporation, sues for the loss of services of a "key" employee, whom defendant negligently injured on defendant's premises in Louisiana. The trial court, applying

Louisiana law, concluded that plaintiff could not maintain a cause of action against defendant, and accordingly dismissed the complaint. Plaintiff appeals from the judgment, contending that under California law an employer has a cause of action for negligent injury to a key employee and that the trial court should therefore have applied California law. As we explain, we have concluded that the trial court correctly applied Louisiana law in this case, and thus we affirm the judgment.

Plaintiff Offshore Rental Company, a California corporation, maintains its principal place of business in California, but derives its revenues in large part from leasing oil drilling equipment in Louisiana's Gulf Coast area. Headquartered in New York, defendant Continental Oil Company, a Delaware corporation, does business in California, Louisiana, and other states.

In November 1967, plaintiff opened an office in Houston, Texas, for the purpose of establishing a base closer to the Gulf Coast. In June 1968 plaintiff's vice-president, Howard C. Kaylor, went from that office to Louisiana to confer with defendant's representatives. During the course of that trip defendant negligently caused injury to Kaylor on defendant's premises in Louisiana.

At the time of his injury, Kaylor was responsible for obtaining contracts for plaintiff's increased business in Louisiana. Although defendant compensated Kaylor for his injuries, plaintiff subsequently filed the underlying action in California to recover $5 million in damages occasioned by the loss of Kaylor's services. . . .

The matter presently before us involves two states: California, the forum, a place of business for defendant, as well as plaintiff's state of incorporation and principal place of business; and Louisiana, the locus of the business of both plaintiff and defendant out of which the injury arose, and the place of the injury. . . . [The court pointed out that Louisiana law did not allow a cause of action by a corporate plaintiff for the loss of its officer, but that some California cases supported plaintiff's assertion that a corporation may pursue an action against a third party for loss caused by an injury to a key employee due to the negligence of the third party. The court noted that §49 of the California Civil Code provides that "[t]he rights of personal relations forbid: . . . (c) Any injury to a servant which affects his ability to serve his master. . . ."]

If we assume, for purposes of analysis, that section 49 does provide an employer with a cause of action for negligent injury to a key employee, the laws of California and Louisiana are directly in conflict. . . .

Turning first to Louisiana, we note that Louisiana's refusal to permit recovery for loss of a key employee's services is predicated on the view that allowing recovery would lead to "undesirable social and legal consequences." We interpret this conclusion as indicating Louisiana's policy to protect negligent resident tortfeasors acting within Louisiana's borders from the financial hardships caused by the assessment of excessive legal liability or exaggerated claims resulting from the loss of services of a key employee. Clearly the present defendant is a member of the class which Louisiana law seeks to protect, since defendant is a Louisiana "resident" whose negligence on its own premises has caused the injury in question. Thus Louisiana's interest in the application of its law to the present case is evident: negation of plaintiff's cause of action serves Louisiana's policy of avoidance of extended financial hardship to the negligent defendant.

Nevertheless, we recognize as equally clear the fact that application of California law to the present case will further California's interest. California, through section 49, expresses an interest in protecting California employers from economic harm because of negligent injury to a key employee inflicted by a third party. Moreover, California's policy of protection extends beyond such an injury inflicted within California, since California's economy and tax revenues are affected regardless of the situs of physical injury. Thus, California is interested in applying its law in the present case to plaintiff Offshore, a California corporate employer that suffered injury in Louisiana by the loss of the services of its key employee.

Hence this case involves a true conflict between the law of Louisiana and the law of California. In *Bernhard v. Harrah's Club*, 546 P.2d 719 (1976), we described the proper resolution of such a case. We rejected the notion that in a situation of true conflict the law of the forum should always be applied. Instead, as we stated, "Once [a] preliminary analysis has identified a true conflict of the governmental interests involved as applied to the parties under the particular circumstances of the case, the 'comparative impairment' approach to the resolution of such conflict seeks to determine which state's interest would be more impaired if its policy were subordinated to the policy of the other state. This analysis proceeds on the principle that true conflicts should be resolved by applying the law of the state whose interest would be the more impaired if its law were not applied."

As Professor Horowitz has explained, this analysis does not involve the court in "weighing" the conflicting governmental interests "in the sense of determining which conflicting law manifest[s] the 'better' or the 'worthier' social policy on the specific issue. An attempted balancing of conflicting state policies in that sense . . . is difficult to justify in the context of a federal system in which, within constitutional limits, states are empowered to mold their policies as they wish." (Horowitz, *The Law of Choice of Law in California—A Restatement* (1974) 21 UCLA L. Rev. 719, 753.)

Rather, the resolution of true conflict cases may be described as "essentially a process of allocating respective spheres of lawmaking influence." (Baxter, *Choice of Law and the Federal System* (1963) 16 Stan. L. Rev. 1, 11-12.) The process of allocation demands several inquiries. First, while "[it] is not always possible to say fairly whether [the] policy [underlying a state's law] is one that was much more *strongly held* in the past than it is now, . . . this ground of analysis should not be ignored." (Italics added.) (Von Mehren & Trautman, The Law of Multistate Problems (1965) p. 377.)

Professor Freund has pointed out that "Statutes [in a domestic case], by reason of their pattern or their prevalence, may evidence a legal climate of opinion which makes less oppressive the responsibility of the judge in choosing between two inferences from a statute or between two possible rules of law. [Footnote omitted.] A similar resort may be made in multistate cases. *If one of the competing laws is archaic and isolated in the context of the laws of the federal union, it may not unreasonably have to yield to the more prevalent and progressive law, other factors of choice being roughly equal.* . . . Perhaps one of the functions of conflict-of-laws decisions is to serve as growing pains for the law of a state, at all events in a federation such as our own." (Italics added.) (Freund, *Chief Justice Stone and the Conflict of Laws* (1946) 59 Harv. L. Rev. 1210, 1216.)

Thus the current status of a statute is an important factor to be considered in a determination of comparative impairment: the policy underlying a jurisdiction's law may be deemed "attenuated and anachronistic and properly . . . be limited to domestic occurrences in the event of [a multistate] clash of interests." (Freund, *Chief Justice Stone, supra,* 59 Harv. L. Rev. 1210, 1224.) Moreover, a particular statute may be an antique not only in comparison to the laws of the federal union, but also as compared with other laws of the state of its enactment. Such a statute may be infrequently enforced or interpreted even within its own jurisdiction, and, as an anachronism in that sense, should have a limited application in a conflicts case.

Another chief criterion in the comparative impairment analysis is the "maximum attainment of underlying purpose by all governmental entities. This necessitates identifying the focal point of concern of the contending lawmaking groups and ascertaining the *comparative pertinence* of that concern to the immediate case." (Italics added.) (Baxter, *Choice of Law, supra,* 16 Stan. L. Rev. 1, 12.) The policy underlying a statute may be less "comparatively pertinent" if the original object of the statute is no longer of pressing importance: a statute which was once intended to remedy a matter of grave public concern may since have fallen in significance to the periphery of the state's laws. . . . Moreover, the policy underlying a statute may also be less "comparatively pertinent" if the same policy may easily be satisfied by some means other than enforcement of the statute itself. Insurance, for example, may satisfy the underlying purpose of a statute originally intended to provide compensation to tort victims. The fact that parties may reasonably be expected to plan their transactions with insurance in mind may therefore constitute a relevant element in the resolution of a true conflict.

In sum, the comparative impairment approach to the resolution of true conflicts attempts to determine the relative commitment of the respective states to the laws involved. The approach incorporates several factors for consideration: the history and current status of the states' laws; the function and purpose of those laws.

Applying the comparative impairment analysis to the present case, we first probe the history and current status of the laws before us. The majority of common law states that have considered the matter do not sanction actions for harm to business employees, recognizing that even if injury to the master-servant relationship were at one time the basis for an action at common law, the radical change in the nature of that relationship since medieval times nullifies any right by a modern corporate employer to recover for negligent injury to his employees. [By] discarding the obsolete concept of recovery for loss of a servant's services, the Louisiana courts have thus joined the "main stream" of American jurisdictions. . . .

Indeed California has itself exhibited little concern in applying section 49 to the employer-employee relationship: despite the provisions of the antique statute, no California court has heretofore squarely held that California law provides an action for harm to business employees, and no California court has recently considered the issue at all. If, as we have assumed, section 49 does provide an action for harm to key corporate employees, in Professor Freund's words the section constitutes a law "archaic and isolated in the context of the laws of the federal union." We therefore conclude that the trial judge in the present case correctly applied Louisiana, rather than California, law, since California's interest in the application of its unusual and outmoded statute is comparatively less strong than Louisiana's corollary interest, so lately expressed, in its "prevalent and progressive" law.

An examination of the function and purpose of the respective laws before us provides additional support for our limitation of the reach of California law in the present case. The accident in question occurred within Louisiana's borders; although the law of the place of the wrong is not necessarily the applicable law for all tort actions, the situs of the injury remains a relevant consideration. At the heart of Louisiana's denial of liability lies the vital interest in promoting freedom of investment and enterprise *within Louisiana's borders*, among investors incorporated both in Louisiana and elsewhere. The imposition of liability on defendant, therefore, would strike at the essence of a compelling Louisiana law.

Furthermore, in connection with our search for the proper law to apply based on the "maximum attainment of underlying purpose by all governmental entities," we note the realistic fact that insurance is available to guard against the exigencies of the present case. As one commentator has remarked, "[The] fact that the potential [tort] victim does not usually calculate his risk and plan his insurance program accordingly, hardly detracts from the consideration that he can fairly be made to bear the consequences of not doing so." (Ehrenzweig, A Treatise on the Conflict of Laws (1962) pp. 575-576.) The present plaintiff, a business corporation, is a potential "victim" peculiarly able to calculate such risks and to plan accordingly. Plaintiff could have obtained protection against the occurrence of injury to its corporate vice-president by purchasing key employee insurance, certainly a reasonable and foreseeable business expense. By entering Louisiana, plaintiff "exposed [it]self to the risks of the territory," and should not expect to subject defendant to a financial hazard that Louisiana law had not created. . . .

Although it is equally true that defendant is a business corporation able to calculate the risks of potential tort liability and to plan accordingly, because defendant's operations in Louisiana presumably involved dealing with key employees of companies incorporated in diverse states defendant would most reasonably have anticipated a need for the protection of premises' liability insurance based on Louisiana law. Accordingly, under these circumstances, we conclude that the burden of obtaining insurance for the loss at issue here is most properly borne by the plaintiff corporation.

. . . Upon examination of the nature and purpose of the states' respective laws, . . . we have determined that the California statute has historically been of minimal importance in the fabric of California law, and that the Louisiana courts have recently interpreted their analogous Louisiana statute narrowly in light of that statute's obsolescence. We do not believe that California's interests in the application of its law to the present case are so compelling as to prevent an accommodation to the stronger, more current interest of Louisiana. We conclude therefore that Louisiana's interests would be the more impaired if its law were not applied, and consequently that Louisiana law governs the present case. Since the law of Louisiana provides no cause of action for the present plaintiff, we hold that the trial court correctly dismissed plaintiff's cause of action. The judgment is affirmed.

Notes on
OFFSHORE

1. By focusing solely on the consequences of applying one law versus another, Professor Baxter's solution to apparent conflicts reflects a different theoretical orientation than Currie's governmental interest analysis and the balancing solution pursued in some jurisdictions. Comparative impairment differs from governmental interest analysis because comparative impairment directs courts to evaluate impaired state interests rather than simply applying forum law. How is comparative impairment different than the balancing solution? At least part of the answer can be seen in how a court might treat a less important, yet more impaired, interest. Comparative impairment directs the court to apply the law of jurisdiction with the most impaired interest, even if that interest is less important or not as "weighty." In other words, a court should not apply a jurisdiction's law simply because the law serves a more important interest than the other jurisdiction's law. Only by focusing on the actual impairments can the comparative impairment approach succeed, when applied over a series of cases, in maximizing regulatory satisfaction of state policies.

2. Despite the theoretical difference between comparative impairment and governmental interest analysis or balancing, one wonders whether comparative impairment really does yield different results than these other approaches. Even if the *Offshore* court did not explicitly balance the interests of Louisiana and California, didn't the court likely reach the same result that balancing would have produced? Indeed, how can a court evaluate whether one state's interest is more impaired than another without first evaluating the extent of each state's interest? Moreover, couldn't the *Offshore* court have avoided the true conflict analysis altogether by using a more restrained and moderate interpretation? In that event, the *Offshore* court would have reached the same result, but instead would have decided that California would not have intended for an out-of-state third party to bear liability. Indeed, one could even argue that the *Offshore* court actually

"forced" a conflict: the court only *assumed* for the purpose of discussion that California's section 49 actually authorized a cause of action against the defendant.

3. Professor Baxter explained that a court undertaking comparative impairment must understand that two "distinct types of governmental objectives" exist: "internal and external." Internal objectives are those underlying each "state's resolution of conflicting private interests," while external objectives are implicated "when a transaction affects persons identified with different states." In choosing which external objective must yield to another external objective in a conflicts case, the court should "subordinate . . . the external objective of the state whose internal objective will be least impaired in general scope and impact" by a decision not to apply the state's law in the case. William Baxter, *Choice of Law and the Federal System*, 16 STAN. L. REV. 1, 17-18 (1963). Beyond the "internal" and "external" distinction, Baxter gave only sketchy details about precisely what type of objectives mattered. However, he did establish that courts should consider objectives intrinsic to the law — such as specific goals that a law is designed to achieve. Thus, for example, Baxter would want courts to consider that an objective underlying civil negligence law is to encourage people to act more safely, and to ask whether this objective would be impaired if the jurisdiction's law did not apply in a particular case. He made clear that in making this determination, courts could consider whether other laws at work in the jurisdiction helped to satisfy that objective. So, for example, if criminal laws in the jurisdiction also provided incentives for people to act more safely in the circumstance of the particular case, that would provide one reason to subordinate the civil negligence law in the case.

What was not clear, however, is whether Baxter intended courts to consider practical objectives. Take, for example, a state that follows a defendant-protecting products liability law for the purpose of protecting what happens to be the most important industry to the state's economy — say, car manufacturing. Should the importance of that industry to the state's economy matter for the purpose of evaluating impairments? Also — Baxter did not specify how courts should evaluate objectives. How might we determine whether an objective really means something to a state? Is it appropriate for the analysis to be both qualitative and quantitative?

In application, courts tend to look to an array of factors, including those that are theoretical and intrinsic to the law as well as those that are practical and extrinsic. Did the court take this broad view in *Offshore*? As you read the more recent *McCann* opinion below, evaluate whether the court in that case took a broader or narrower view of state objectives than in *Offshore*. Also look to whether the courts evaluated these objectives qualitatively (e.g., how much does the objective mean to the overall state scheme of regulation?), quantitatively (e.g., how many objectives are there?), or both.

4. What do you make of the court's conclusion that the California law was "arcane and isolated in the context of the laws of the federal union"? Is that an appropriate concern to weigh in determining impairments? Apparently, Professor Baxter hadn't thought so, because he had earlier expressed disapproval of that type of assessment. *See* William Baxter, *Choice of Law and the Federal System*, 16 STAN. L. REV. 1, 18 & n.39 (1963) (describing assessment of whether a law is arcane or outdated as a "super-value-judgment approach"). This type of reasoning may be controversial in that it places the court in a position of evaluating which law it actually "likes" better. Even though Baxter may not have intended this reasoning to inform a comparative impairment analysis, you will note, below, that a court's evaluation of "the better rule of law" is a formal component of a choice of law approach that bears that name.

PROBLEM 2-37: ZIPPY'S FORFEITURE WORRIES REDUX

This problem presents the same facts as Zippy Loan from Problem 2-34, except this time the forum resolves true conflicts using the comparative impairment approach. Here are the facts again:

Sam purchased a car from a dealer in Texas. He executed a promissory note and gave the dealer a security interest in the car. On the same day, the dealer assigned the note and security interest to a Texas corporation, Zippy Loan, which is in the business of financing car sales. The security agreement prohibited Sam from taking the car out of state without permission of the dealer or its assigns. In violation of this agreement and without Zippy's (or the dealer's) knowledge, Sam drove the car to Oklahoma. In Oklahoma, Sam was arrested while using the car to transport marijuana.

Assume that in connection with the criminal proceedings against Sam, the Oklahoma Attorney General seized the car and began a forfeiture action. Zippy has intervened in the matter in order to ensure that the car is forfeited only subject to Zippy's lien. Specifically, Zippy seeks to require that, should the court enter a forfeiture judgment, the Attorney General must pay Zippy the remaining part of the purchase price Sam owes under the promissory note. Under Oklahoma law, Zippy cannot claim this right unless it investigated Sam's moral responsibility and character *before* taking an interest in the car. Zippy performed no such investigation, but nonetheless wishes to maintain a priority position in getting paid under the note.

Assume that Texas has no forfeiture law comparable to Oklahoma's. Texas commercial law, however, makes clear that a security interest in a vehicle is valid where, as here, the entity taking the interest had no knowledge that the vehicle would be used illegally. To have a valid security interest in Texas, a lender need not investigate the debtor's character. Assuming that the Oklahoma forfeiture court will apply comparative impairment, which law will govern whether Zippy will maintain its priority?

McCann v. Foster Wheeler LLC
225 P.3d 516 (Cal. 2010)

GEORGE, C.J.

This case presents a choice-of-law issue arising in a lawsuit filed by plaintiff Terry McCann (plaintiff) to recover damages for an illness, mesothelioma, allegedly caused by his exposure to asbestos. Although the complaint seeks recovery from numerous defendants, the issue before us relates solely to the potential liability of a single defendant, Foster Wheeler LLC (Foster Wheeler), a company that specially designed, manufactured, and provided advice regarding the installation of a very large boiler at an oil refinery in Oklahoma in 1957. At the time the boiler was being installed at the Oklahoma refinery, plaintiff, then an Oklahoma resident and a newly hired engineering sales trainee employed by the construction company that was installing the boiler, allegedly was exposed to asbestos at various times over a two-week period while he observed the application of asbestos insulation to the boiler by an independent insulation contractor.

[After working at various jobs in Minnesota and Illinois, plaintiff moved to California in 1975, retired in 2001 and, continuing to reside in California, plaintiff was diagnosed with mesothelioma in 2005. Plaintiff then filed this action, naming numerous defendants, including Foster Wheeler.]

Prior to trial, Foster Wheeler moved for summary judgment [arguing] that plaintiff's action against it was governed by, and barred under, an Oklahoma statute of repose that required any cause of action against a designer or constructor of an improvement to real property to be filed within 10 years of the substantial completion of the improvement. In opposing the motion, plaintiff contended . . . that his cause of action for an injury or illness caused by exposure to asbestos should be governed by the relevant California statute of limitations (under which the action would have been timely filed), rather than by Oklahoma law. . . .

[The trial court determined that Oklahoma law governed the timeliness issue, that Foster Wheeler fell within the terms of the Oklahoma statute, and dismissed Foster Wheeler as a defendant in plaintiff's underlying action. The Court of Appeal, however, reversed, holding that California law should govern and reasoning that Oklahoma's interest in its statute of repose "is substantially . . . an interest in protecting Oklahoma defendants from liability for conduct occurring in Oklahoma." Since New York was the location of Foster Wheeler's corporate headquarters, the Court of Appeal found that Foster Wheeler was not "among the defendants in whose favor Oklahoma's statute of repose is primarily directed" and consequently that "any significant interest of Oklahoma in the application of its statute of repose . . . is difficult to discern." The Court of Appeal further concluded that the case presented a true conflict, and that "the interests of

California would be more impaired by the application of Oklahoma law than would be the interests of Oklahoma by the failure to apply its law."]

... [W]e granted review primarily to consider whether the Court of Appeal was correct in determining (1) that Oklahoma's interest in the application of its statute of repose is substantially limited to application of the statute to companies headquartered in Oklahoma and does not equally encompass out-of-state companies who design or construct improvements to real property located in Oklahoma, and (2) that California's interests, rather than Oklahoma's interests, would be more impaired by the failure to apply the respective state's law on the facts presented here.

For the reasons discussed more fully below, we conclude that the decision of the Court of Appeal should be reversed.

I

[The court explained that the alleged liability is based on a two-week asbestos exposure in Oklahoma in 1957, nearly 50 years before plaintiff's mesothelioma diagnosis. The exposure came from a steam generator designed and manufactured in New York by Foster Wheeler, which had its corporate headquarters in New York. The generator was installed by plaintiff's employer TRECO, which was engaged by an Oklahoma company, Sunray, to construct the expansion of Sunray's Oklahoma oil refinery. As specified in the Sunray and Foster Wheeler contract, the generator came to Sunray without insulation. Sunray hired a company other than TRECO to install the insulation around the boiler. Plaintiff argued that "Foster Wheeler specified the need for insulation and knew or should have known the insulation was likely to contain asbestos."

When plaintiff began work with TRECO, he observed construction, but did not assist in installation of the insulation. Plaintiff "recalled observing the sawing of block insulation, the preparation and installation of insulating cement on the boiler, and the rising of dust clouds created by the mixing of the cement." As to the amount of time he spent around the boiler, plaintiff testified that a "wild guess" would be "two or three days in total." After the installation, plaintiff moved to Minnesota and then Illinois. He later moved to California, where he served for 21 years as the executive director of Toastmasters International, an organization dedicated to helping people become better public speakers. After his retirement in 2001, plaintiff continued to reside in California and was diagnosed with mesothelioma in 2005, when he filed the lawsuit, naming numerous defendants, including Foster Wheeler.]

. . .

[Foster Wheeler asserts that] under Oklahoma law plaintiff's cause of action against Foster Wheeler was barred by an Oklahoma statute of repose[2] providing that any tort action for injury arising from "the design, planning, supervision or

---

2. In *Giest v. Sequoia Ventures, Inc.* (2000) 83 Cal. App. 4th 300, 305[, 99 Cal. Rptr. 2d 476], the court explained the general difference between a statute of limitations and a statute of repose: "[W]hile a statute of limitations normally sets the time within which proceedings must be

observation of construction or construction of an improvement to real property" must be brought within 10 years of the "substantial completion" of the improvement. (Okla. Stat. tit. 12, §109 (hereafter section 109).) Because plaintiff's lawsuit was filed long after the 10-year period specified in the Oklahoma statute of repose had expired, Foster Wheeler maintained that the action against it must be dismissed.

II

Traditionally, a state's general choice-of-law rules have been formulated by courts through judicial decisions rendered under the common law, rather than by the legislature through statutory enactments. In California, over the past four decades this court's decisions have adopted and consistently applied the so-called "governmental interest" analysis as the appropriate general methodology for resolving choice-of-law questions in this state.

With respect to the category of statutes of limitation and statutes of repose, however, many jurisdictions have enacted specific statutory provisions that address the subject of choice of law. [The court explained that California had a statutory provision, known as a borrowing statute, which under some circumstances directs California courts to apply statutes of limitation and repose of another jurisdiction. The court concluded, however, that the borrowing statute was likely not applicable to the facts of this case and in any event did not absolutely control the choice of law issue. For that reason, the court concluded that it must analyze the case using common law choice of law principles.] [W]e now turn to the task of applying the general governmental interest analysis to the circumstances before us in the present case.

III

Recently . . . we summarized the mode of analysis called for by the governmental interest approach. "In brief outline, the governmental interest approach generally involves three steps. First, the court determines whether the relevant law of each of the potentially affected jurisdictions with regard to the particular issue in question is the same or different. Second, if there is a difference, the court examines each jurisdiction's interest in the application of its own law under the circumstances of the particular case to determine whether a true conflict exists. Third, if the court finds that there is a true conflict, it carefully evaluates and compares the nature and strength of the interest of each jurisdiction in the

---

commenced once a cause of action accrues, [a] statute of repose limits the time within which an action may be brought and is not related to accrual. Indeed, 'the injury need not have occurred, much less have been discovered. Unlike an ordinary statute of limitations which begins running upon accrual of the claim, [the] period contained in a statute of repose begins when a special event occurs, regardless of whether a cause of action has accrued or whether any injury has resulted.' [Citation.] A statute of repose thus is harsher than a statute of limitations in that it cuts off a right of action after a specified period of time, irrespective of accrual or even notice that a legal right has been invaded. [Citation.]"

application of its own law 'to determine which state's interest would be more impaired if its policy were subordinated to the policy of the other state,' and then ultimately applies 'the law of the state whose interest would be more impaired if its law were not applied.'"

A

With regard to the first of these steps, we agree with the Court of Appeal that "[t]he laws of Oklahoma and California clearly differ."

1

Under section 109 (the Oklahoma statute of repose), plaintiff's cause of action would be barred by the lapse of time, because that statute "bars any tort action which arises more than ten years after the substantial completion of the improvement to real property."[3]

Although the Oklahoma statute in question has been interpreted not to bar products liability actions against the manufacturers and sellers of mass-produced products—and thus would not preclude plaintiff from suing companies that manufactured or sold the asbestos insulation to which he was exposed—the Oklahoma Supreme Court has interpreted the statute of repose to protect a manufacturer/designer of a specially designed improvement to real property.

. . . [W]e . . . shall assume for purposes of determining the choice-of-law issue that Foster Wheeler's conduct brought it within the reach of the relevant Oklahoma statute of repose. Under this premise, plaintiff's action against Foster Wheeler plainly would be untimely under Oklahoma law, because this action was filed more than 10 years after substantial completion of the improvement.

2

By contrast, plaintiff's action against Foster Wheeler clearly would be timely if California law were applied. Although this state has enacted a statute of repose applicable to causes of action arising out of a latent deficiency in the design or construction of an improvement to real property that is somewhat similar to the relevant Oklahoma statute of repose, the California statute, unlike its Oklahoma counterpart, applies only to actions for injury to property, not to personal injury actions. Furthermore, California has enacted a special statute of limitations explicitly governing the time for bringing an action "for injury or illness based upon exposure to asbestos," which permits such an action to be brought up to

3. Section 109 provides in full:

No action in tort to recover damages

(i) for any deficiency in the design, planning, supervision or observation of construction or construction of an improvement to real property,
(ii) for injury to property, real or personal, arising out of any such deficiency, or
(iii) for injury to the person or for wrongful death arising out of any such deficiency, shall be brought against any person owning, leasing, or in possession of such an improvement or performing or furnishing the design, planning, supervision or observation of construction or construction of such an improvement more than ten (10) years after substantial completion of such an improvement.
. . .

one year after the plaintiff both (1) first suffered disability *and* (2) knew or reasonably should have known that the disability was caused or contributed to by exposure to asbestos. (Code Civ. Proc., §340.2.[10]) Here, plaintiff, who previously had retired for reasons unconnected to his asbestos-related illness, filed this action within a few months after he first was diagnosed with mesothelioma, and thus the action clearly would be timely under the provisions of section 340.2.

Accordingly, the law of Oklahoma clearly differs from the law of California with respect to the timeliness of plaintiff's cause of action.

B

The second step of the governmental interest analysis requires us to examine "each jurisdiction's interest in the application of its own law under the circumstances of the particular case to determine whether a true conflict exists."

Oklahoma decisions indicate that by establishing a relatively lengthy (10-year) period in which a cause of action for a deficiency in design of an improvement to real property may be brought, but at the same time terminating all liability after that deadline regardless of whether the plaintiff's injury had yet occurred or become manifest, the relevant statute of repose was intended to balance the interest of injured persons in having a remedy available for such injuries against the interest of builders, architects, and designers of real property improvements in being subject to a specified time limit during which they would remain potentially liable for their actions in connection with such improvements. The Oklahoma high court [has] held . . . that the statute of repose, by establishing this type of fixed time limit in which any cause of action must be brought, serves "the legitimate government objectives of providing a measure of security for building professionals whose liability could otherwise extend indefinitely." The court further noted that the statute "also serves the legitimate objective of avoiding the difficulties in proof which arise from the passage of time."

. . . [T]he Court of Appeal in the present case expressed the view that "Oklahoma's interest is substantially a local one, that is, an interest in protecting Oklahoma defendants from liability for conduct occurring in Oklahoma." The appellate court indicated that Oklahoma's interest in the application of this statute does not extend to, or at least does not apply as strongly to, a non-Oklahoma business that designs or constructs an improvement to real property located in Oklahoma. Because Foster Wheeler is a non-Oklahoma corporation (incorporated in Delaware, with its headquarters in New York), and because the design and

---

10. Code of Civil Procedure, section 340.2 provides in relevant part:

   (a) In any civil action for injury or illness based upon exposure to asbestos, the time for the commencement of the action shall be the later of the following:
       (1) Within one year after the date the plaintiff first suffered disability.
       (2) Within one year after the date the plaintiff either knew, or through the exercise of reasonable diligence should have known, that such disability was caused or contributed to by such exposure.
   (b) "Disability" as used in subdivision (a) means the loss of time from work as a result of such exposure which precludes the performance of the employee's regular occupation.

manufacture of the boiler occurred in New York, the Court of Appeal expressed the view that "any significant interest of Oklahoma in the application of its statute of repose . . . is difficult to discern."

We conclude that the Court of Appeal did not accurately assess the interest of Oklahoma embodied in the statute of repose here at issue. When a state adopts a rule of law limiting liability for commercial activity conducted within the state in order to provide what the state perceives is fair treatment to, and an appropriate incentive for, business enterprises, we believe that the state ordinarily has an interest in having that policy of limited liability applied to out-of-state companies that conduct business in the state, as well as to businesses incorporated or head-quartered within the state. A state has a legitimate interest in attracting out-of-state companies to do business within the state, both to obtain tax and other revenue that such businesses may generate for the state, and to advance the opportunity of state residents to obtain employment and the products and services offered by out-of-state companies. In the absence of any explicit indication that a jurisdiction's "business friendly" statute or rule of law is intended to apply only to businesses incorporated or headquartered in that jurisdiction (or that have some other designated relationship with the state — for example, to those entities licensed by the state), as a practical and realistic matter the state's interest in having that law applied to the activities of out-of-state companies within the jurisdiction is equal to its interest in the application of the law to comparable activities engaged in by local businesses situated within the jurisdiction.

This court's decision in *Offshore Rental, supra*, 22 Cal. 3d 157, supports the foregoing conclusion. In *Offshore Rental*, the plaintiff was a California company that brought suit to recover economic damages it had suffered when one of its key employees had been injured in Louisiana, allegedly as a result of the negligence of one of the defendant company's employees in Louisiana. The case presented a choice-of-law issue because California law permits a company to maintain a cause of action for the economic damage suffered by the company as a result of an injury to a key employee (an action separate from, and independent of, the employee's own personal injury action), whereas Louisiana law does not permit an employer to maintain such a cause of action (permitting only the employee's personal injury action). The defendant company in *Offshore Rental* was a Delaware corporation, headquartered in New York, that did business in Louisiana, California, and other states.

In examining the question whether Louisiana had an interest in having its law (denying the plaintiff company's cause of action for injury to a key employee) applied in the circumstances of that case, the court in *Offshore Rental, supra*, 22 Cal. 3d 157, explained: "The accident in question occurred within Louisiana's borders; although the law of the place of the wrong is not necessarily the applicable law for all tort actions, the situs of the injury remains a relevant consideration. At the heart of Louisiana's denial of liability lies the vital interest in promoting freedom of investment and enterprise within Louisiana's borders, *among investors incorporated both in Louisiana and elsewhere*. The imposition of liability on defendant, therefore, would strike at the essence of a compelling Louisiana law." Thus, although the defendant in that case was an out-of-state company doing business in Louisiana, the California court in *Offshore Rental* recognized that the interest of Louisiana in protecting companies from what the latter state viewed as excessive liability extended to such a company.

. . .

[J]ust as the Court of Appeal erred in relying on the non-Oklahoma location of Foster Wheeler's incorporation or headquarters as a basis for determining that Oklahoma lacked an interest in having its statute of repose applied here, the appellate court similarly erred in suggesting that Oklahoma's interest in having its statute applied was negated by the circumstance that the design and manufacture of the boiler in question occurred in New York rather than in Oklahoma. The statute of repose here at issue protects not only construction-related businesses that engage in their activities at the Oklahoma site of the improvement, but also commercial entities, such as establishments performing architectural and other design-improvement work, that conduct their activities away from the location of the improvement but whose potential liability flows from a plaintiff's interaction with, or exposure to, the real property improvement in Oklahoma. Under the premise that the activities of Foster Wheeler in this case bring it within the reach of the Oklahoma statute of repose, we conclude that, for purposes of the governmental interest analysis, Oklahoma clearly possesses an interest in having the statute applied in the present case and that its interest is not diminished by the circumstance that some of Foster Wheeler's activities occurred outside of Oklahoma.[12]

Accordingly, contrary to the view expressed by the Court of Appeal, we conclude that Oklahoma has a real and legitimate interest in having its statute of repose applied under the circumstances presented here.

2

At the same time, we also recognize that California has an interest in having California law applied in this case.

[T]he applicable California statute — Code of Civil Procedure section 340.2 — permits an action for injury or illness based upon exposure to asbestos to be brought up to one year after the plaintiff first suffered disability (as defined by the statute) *and* knew or reasonably should have known that the disability was caused or contributed to by such exposure. This statute, enacted in 1979 to lengthen the period of time in which an asbestos-related claim may be brought, reflects a state interest in providing persons who suffer injury or illness as a result of their exposure to asbestos a fair and reasonable opportunity to seek recovery for their injury or illness, taking into account not only the typically lengthy period

---

12. Furthermore, although the Court of Appeal appears to have assumed that plaintiff's claim against Foster Wheeler rested solely upon that entity's conduct in New York, plaintiff asserted in his opposition to the summary judgment motion that, because Foster Wheeler "knew or should have known that the normal and intended operation of its boilers would include the use and application of asbestos containing insulation, and that end users, like [plaintiff], would be exposed to asbestos during the installation of that insulation[,] Foster Wheeler . . . had a duty to warn of this foreseeable hazard." To be effective, of course, such a warning would have to have been communicated to plaintiff in Oklahoma.

between exposure to asbestos and the development of disease but also the often substantial period between the initial discovery or diagnosis of a disease and the time when the disease becomes disabling. The language of section 340.2 does not specify the class of persons to whom the statute was intended to apply, but by its terms the provision is not limited only to persons who were exposed to asbestos in California. In view of the legislation's clear recognition of the unusual nature of asbestos-related injury and illness, and the statute's objective to provide injured or ill persons a fair and adequate opportunity to seek recovery for such asbestos-related harm, we conclude that California has an interest in having this statute applied to a person, like plaintiff, who is a California resident at the time the person discovers that he or she is suffering from an asbestos-related injury or illness, even when the person's exposure to asbestos occurred outside California.

A number of prior California cases support the conclusion that California has a legitimate interest in having a statutory provision that affords a remedy for or a benefit to an injured person or business applied when, as here, the injured person or business is a California resident or business, even when the injury-producing conduct occurs outside California. In *Offshore Rental, supra,* 22 Cal. 3d 157, for example, although ultimately concluding that the Louisiana rule of law denying a cause of action for injury to a company's "key employee" should be applied, this court, in discussing the second step of the governmental interest analysis, determined that California had a real and legitimate interest in having its rule of law — permitting such a cause of action — applied in favor of a California company that had suffered such an injury, even though the injury to the company's key employee had occurred in another state. . . .

. . . Application of the California statute of limitations to a current California resident who suffers an injury or illness as a result of his or her prior exposure to asbestos in another jurisdiction would assist such residents in obtaining compensation for their injuries and in not becoming dependent on the resources of California for necessary medical, disability, and unemployment benefits.

. . . California, as well as Oklahoma, has an interest in having its own law applied in this case.

Because the applicable laws of Oklahoma and California differ and each state has an interest in having its law applied under the circumstances of the present case, we are faced with a "true conflict." . . . [I]n such instances we apply the so-called "comparative impairment" approach.

c

Under the comparative impairment analysis, we must "carefully evaluate[] and compare[] the nature and strength of the interest of each jurisdiction in the application of its own law 'to determine which state's interest would be more impaired if its policy were subordinated to the policy of the other state.'" In conducting this evaluation, our prior decisions emphasize that it is important to keep in mind that "[t]he court does not '"weigh" the conflicting governmental interests in the sense of determining which conflicting law manifested the "better" or the "worthier" social policy on the specific issue. An attempted balancing of conflicting state policies in that sense . . . is difficult to justify in the context of a federal system in which, within constitutional limits, states are empowered to mold their policies as they wish. . . . [Instead, the process] can accurately be described as . . . a problem of allocating domains of law-making power in multi-state contexts — [by determining the appropriate] limitations on the reach of state policies — as distinguished from evaluating the wisdom of those policies. . . . [E]mphasis is placed on the appropriate scope of conflicting state policies rather than on the "quality" of those policies. . . .'"

. . .

1

In light of the relevant facts of this case, we conclude that a failure to apply Oklahoma law would significantly impair Oklahoma's interest. The conduct for which plaintiff contends Foster Wheeler should be held liable — plaintiff's alleged exposure to asbestos during the application of insulation to a boiler designed and manufactured by Foster Wheeler — occurred in Oklahoma in 1957, at a time when plaintiff was present in Oklahoma and was an Oklahoma resident. . . . Oklahoma's interest in the application of its statute of repose applies equally to out-of-state businesses that design improvements to real property located in Oklahoma and to Oklahoma businesses that design such improvements situated within that state.

Although California no longer follows the old choice-of-law rule that generally called for application of the law of the jurisdiction in which a defendant's allegedly tortious conduct occurred *without regard to the nature of the issue that was before the court,* California choice-of-law cases nonetheless continue to recognize that a jurisdiction ordinarily has "the predominant interest" in regulating conduct that occurs within its borders, and in being able to assure individuals and commercial entities operating within its territory that applicable limitations on liability set forth in the jurisdiction's law will be available to those individuals and businesses in the event they are faced with litigation in the future.

In the present case, in the event Foster Wheeler were to be denied the protection afforded by the Oklahoma statute of repose and be subjected to the extended timeliness rule embodied in California law, the subordination of Oklahoma's interest in the application of its law would rest solely upon the circumstance that *after* defendant engaged in the allegedly tortious conduct in Oklahoma, plaintiff happened to move to a jurisdiction whose law provides more favorable treatment to plaintiff than that available under Oklahoma law.

Although here it is clear that plaintiff's move to California was not motivated by a desire to take advantage of the opportunities afforded by California law and cannot reasonably be characterized as an instance of forum shopping, the displacement of Oklahoma law limiting liability for conduct engaged in within Oklahoma, in favor of the law of a jurisdiction to which a plaintiff subsequently moved, would — notwithstanding the innocent motivation of the move — nonetheless significantly impair the interest of Oklahoma served by the statute of repose. If Oklahoma's statute were not to be applied because plaintiff had moved to a state with a different and less "business-friendly" law, Oklahoma could not provide any reasonable assurance — either to out-of-state companies or to Oklahoma businesses — that the time limitation embodied in its statute would operate to protect such businesses in the future. Because a commercial entity protected by the Oklahoma statute of repose has no way of knowing or controlling where a potential plaintiff may move in the future, subjecting such a defendant to a different rule of law based upon the law of a state to which a potential plaintiff ultimately may move would significantly undermine Oklahoma's interest in establishing a reliable rule of law governing a business's potential liability for conduct undertaken in Oklahoma.

2

By contrast, a failure to apply California law on the facts of the present case will effect a far less significant impairment of California's interest. Certainly, if the law of this state is not applied here, California will not be able to extend its liberal statute of limitations for asbestos-related injuries or illnesses to some potential plaintiffs whose exposure to asbestos occurred wholly outside of California. Nonetheless, our past choice-of-law decisions teach that California's interest in applying its laws providing a remedy to, or facilitating recovery by, a potential plaintiff in a case in which the defendant's allegedly tortious conduct occurred in another state is less than its interest when the defendant's conduct occurred in California. . . . [I]n a number of choice-of-law settings, California decisions have adopted a restrained view of the scope or reach of California law with regard to the imposition of liability for conduct that occurs in another jurisdiction and that would not subject the defendant to liability under the law of the other jurisdiction. Our view is that a similar restrained view of California's interest in facilitating recovery by a current California resident is warranted in evaluating the relative impairment of California's interest that would result from the failure to apply California law in the present setting.

[I]n allocating the "'respective spheres of lawmaking influence'" in cases in which a California resident is injured by a defendant's conduct occurring in another state, past California choice-of-law decisions generally hold that when the law of the other state limits or denies liability for the conduct engaged in by the defendant in its territory, that state's interest is predominant, and California's legitimate interest in providing a remedy for, or in facilitating recovery by, a current California resident properly must be subordinated because of this state's diminished authority over activity that occurs in another state. Although under the circumstances of the present case this allocation of "lawmaking influence" results in the subordination of California's interest to the interest of Oklahoma, in other instances in which a defendant is responsible for exposing persons to the risks associated with asbestos or another toxic substance through its conduct *in California*, this general principle would allocate to *California* the predominant interest in regulating the conduct.

. . .

3

For the reasons discussed above, we conclude that Oklahoma's interest (as embodied in its statute of repose) would be more impaired if its law were not applied under the circumstances of this case than would be California's interest if its statute of limitations is not applied. Accordingly, we conclude that the Court of Appeal erred in holding that California law rather than Oklahoma law should apply to the issue before us.

IV

The judgment of the Court of Appeal is reversed and the matter is remanded to that court with directions to address plaintiff's additional contention that the trial court erred in finding that the boiler in question constituted an improvement to real property within the meaning of the relevant Oklahoma statute of repose.

Notes on
MCCANN *AND CRITIQUES OF COMPARATIVE IMPAIRMENT*

1. Before embarking on a comparative impairment analysis, the *McCann* court concluded that it was not bound by California's borrowing statute relating to statutes of limitation and repose. Borrowing statutes are considered later in this chapter in connection with statutory choice of law provisions.

2. *McCann* illustrates the orientation that Baxter sought with comparative impairment: a focus on comparing the negative results of a choice of law decision. Significantly, the decision contrasts with *Offshore Rental* in that the court did not evaluate whether one law or the other was more archaic or worthier than the other.

3. Scholars give mixed reviews of comparative impairment. Focusing on its analytical kinship with game theory, some scholars have observed that comparative impairment is the choice of law approach that "arguably" best reflects economic theory, since comparative impairment "attempts to maximize the affected states' joint utility." Erin A. O'Hara & Larry E. Ribstein, *From Politics to Efficiency in Choice of Law*, 67 U. CHI. L. REV. 1151, 1173 (2000). On a critical note, Professor Larry Kramer finds comparative impairment impractical because it requires courts to treat disparate regulatory goals as though they are comparable. Specifically, he maintains that the approach calls for comparing "apples and oranges" — such as a "regulatory policy of deterrence" that animates one state's law and a "qualitatively different . . . distributive policy for allocating losses" that animates another state's law. Larry Kramer, *Rethinking Choice of Law*, 90 COLUM. L. REV. 277, 317 (1990). According to Kramer, "[t]here is no metric for making [such] a comparison." *Id.* at 317. Nor, in Kramer's view, can comparative impairment meaningfully measure "differences in the intensity of state interests." *Id.* at 317.

Another problem that Kramer has identified relates to Baxter's suggestion regarding the interest-maximizing benefits of comparative impairment:

the notion that, over time and in the aggregate, a state's impairments are avoided where it really matters to the state and suffered where the cost to the state is less significant. This reasoning requires at least some degree of reciprocity among states. Yet, as Kramer points out, "This works only if other states apply the same [choice of law] rule, for only then is a state's forbearance repaid by the reciprocal forbearance of others." Larry Kramer, *Return of the Renvoi,* 66 N.Y.U. L. Rev. 979, 1022 (1991). In a related criticism, Professors O'Hara and Allen argue that the approach is unpredictable and therefore inefficient because parties cannot foresee the results courts will reach using the approach and cannot plan their behavior accordingly. William A. Allen & Erin A. O'Hara, *Second Generation Law and Economics of Conflict of Laws: Baxter's Comparative Impairment and Beyond,* 51 Stan. L. Rev. 1011, 1014, 1031-1033 (1999).

4. Is it appropriate to ask a forum court to evaluate the forum's interests and then choose to subordinate those interests to another state? Can we expect that a forum court will be able to do this task impartially when forum law is implicated? At the least, one might argue that comparative impairment often casts courts in conflicting roles: on one hand, a court must fulfill its duty as an agent of the forum government and people who give it power; on the other hand, the court should independently compare forum impairments against those of another state. Do *McCann* and *Offshore Rental* demonstrate that these conflicting roles are not necessarily difficult to navigate, and any concern about the roles is unfounded? Would you expect all courts to show the same degree of altruism as the California courts in applying comparative impairment? California's altruism is perhaps even more impressive given that comparative impairment actually challenges a forum court's role as an impartial adjudicator more than governmental interest analysis. After all, with governmental interest analysis, the forum court does not need to worry about forsaking forum interest, and is instead allowed to indulge forum interest by applying forum law when a true conflict emerges.

CRS Recovery, Inc. v. Laxton

600 F.3d 1138 (9th Cir. 2010)

Hawkins, Circuit Judge:
This case requires application of traditional choice-of-law, tort, and property principles to an increasingly common factual setting, a dispute over the ownership of an Internet domain name. John Laxton and his assignee North Bay Real Estate, Inc. appeal the adverse summary judgment for Dale Mayberry and his assignee CRS Recovery, Inc. ("CRS"). The district court was correct to apply California law, but we find disputed issues of material fact and remand.

I. Background

A. BACKGROUND FACTS

[Mayberry, a citizen of Virginia, registered the domain name "rl.com" by contract with the domain name registrar Network Solutions, Inc., a Delaware corporation headquartered in Herndon, Virginia. . . . Mayberry's contract with Network Solutions identified the administrator of the website as Micro Access Technologies, Inc. ("MAT"), a company owned by Mayberry. Specifically, Mayberry made MAT, through "mat.net," the administrative contact for both domain names, mat.net and rl.com. He thus exercised administrative control over both websites through the e-mail address "dale@mat.net." In 2001 mat.net ceased operation. Mayberry failed to notify Network Solutions that mat.net was no longer operative.]

The parties dispute the precise circumstances of Mayberry's loss of mat.net and, therefore, the loss of rl.com. Laxton asserts that Mayberry let the registration expire by its terms, but Mayberry contends he attempted to renew the domain name. Laxton's expert claimed that Mayberry is "incorrect" in insisting the registration still belonged to Mayberry on December 19, 2003, and that Mayberry "abandoned Mat.net by letting it expire on its own terms on October 2." At his deposition, Mayberry stated that he was still the registrant of mat.net on December 19, 2003, a claim Laxton vigorously contested both at the district court and on appeal. The district court concluded that "[t]he circumstances surrounding the transfer of mat.net are not entirely clear."

Despite these unresolved factual issues, we can establish the following from the record. On December 19, 2003, a new registration of mat.net was made by a man named Li Qiang ("Qiang"). . . . Qiang's control of mat.net permitted him to designate his e-mail address as dale@mat.net and to receive e-mail at this address in place of Mayberry. Using this e-mail address, Qiang transferred ownership of the domain name rl.com to himself. Network Solutions accepted the transfer, acting in the belief that it was being made by Mayberry, who in fact was unaware of Qiang's actions. Qiang later transferred the domain name [and ultimately it was purchased by] Laxton, a citizen of California, for $15,000. Prior to the purchase, Laxton contends he checked rl.com with the World Intellectual Property Organization ("WIPO") to ensure there were no disputes involving the domain name. Determining there were none, Laxton consummated the purchase. . . .

Mayberry, meanwhile, discovered that he had lost control of both domain names. He assigned his interest in rl.com to CRS, a Virginia corporation, in exchange for an undisclosed sum of cash and the company's promise to help him recover the lost names. Contact was made with Laxton, who, having just spent thousands of dollars successfully defending rl.com from a WIPO action brought by Ralph Lauren, declined to surrender his control over the domain name. This lawsuit followed.

B. PROCEDURAL HISTORY

On October 30, 2007, Mayberry and CRS filed their second amended complaint against Laxton, Qiang, and others, charging them with theft of the two domain names. [The district court granted summary judgment for the plaintiffs on some of the counts and the plaintiffs dismissed their other causes of action.] The district court saw the primary question before it as a choice of law: Virginia's or California's. Laxton, a California defendant, urged application of Virginia law. Mayberry, a Virginia plaintiff, wanted California law to govern. Under Virginia law, the defendants claimed, the plaintiffs had only a contract. Under California law, all parties agree, the plaintiffs' domain names were intangible personal property. The court conducted a government interest analysis, concluding California had the "greater interest" and giving judgment for the plaintiffs. On appeal, Laxton alleges this choice of California law was error.

II. ANALYSIS

... CHOICE OF LAW

The parties dispute whether California or Virginia law applies in this case. When a federal court sits in diversity to hear state law claims, the conflicts laws of the forum state — here California — are used to determine which state's substantive law applies. California applies the "governmental interest" analysis. . . . The government interest analysis consists of three steps. . . .

First, the court examines the substantive law of each jurisdiction to determine whether the laws differ as applied to the relevant transaction. Second, if the laws do differ, the court must determine whether a "true conflict" exists in that each of the relevant jurisdictions has an interest in having its law applied. If only one jurisdiction has a legitimate interest in the application of its rule of decision, there is a "false conflict" and the law of the interested jurisdiction is applied. On the other hand, if more than one jurisdiction has a legitimate interest, the court must move to the third stage of the analysis, which focuses on the "comparative impairment" of the interested jurisdictions. At this stage, the court seeks to identify and apply the law of the state whose interest would be the more impaired if its law were not applied.

. . . Thus, our first inquiry is to examine whether Virginia and California provide for different treatment of domain names. Like the majority of states to have addressed the issue, California law recognizes a property interest in domain names, [and views domain names as] intangible property subject to conversion claims. . . . We have previously explained the logic of California understanding domain names as intangible property because domain names are well-defined interests, exclusive to the owner, and are bought and sold, often for high values. Domain names are thus subject to conversion under California law, notwithstanding the common law tort law distinction between tangible and intangible property for conversion claims.

Laxton argues that a garnishment case from the Supreme Court of Virginia, *Network Solutions, Inc. v. Umbro International, Inc.* ("*Umbro*"), 259 Va. 759, 529 S.E.2d 80 (Va. 2000), holds that domain names are contract rights under Virginia law. We find the case more equivocal. *Umbro* did treat domain names as contract rights, but at the same time, the opinion observed that the registrar of the name, Network Solutions, took the position that the name was "personal property." The court stated that it did "not believe that it is essential to the outcome of this case to decide whether the circuit court correctly characterized a domain name as a 'form of intellectual property.'" *Id.* at 86. The court, thus, did not disapprove of the characterization of domain names as property rights, but treated it as immaterial to the garnishment determination. *See id.* at 86-87.

. . . *Umbro* tells us only about how Virginia law treats domain names in *garnishment* actions. Particularly given the majority of states' justifiable coalescence around understanding domain names as intangible property, we decline Laxton's invitation to read *Umbro* more broadly than its text requires. . . .

[B]ecause *Umbro* does not compel the conclusion that Virginia considers domain names to be contract rights for purposes of *conversion* suits, we are not compelled to find that California law (under which domain names are property rights) and Virginia law are in conflict in this case.

On our narrow understanding of *Umbro*, California law applies. Under California choice-of-law rules, the party seeking application of foreign law bears the burden to show that the law of a foreign state should apply. At the point Laxton fails to make this showing, we default to forum (California) law.

Even if Laxton was correct in asserting Virginia treats domain names as contract rights for all purposes, however, at best his claim presents only a classic "false conflict." The district court accepted Laxton's reading of *Umbro*, concluding Virginia's treatment of domain names as contract rights in all instances reflected a policy of providing domain name purchasers "with a predictable limitation for their liability."

On appeal, Laxton argues this characterization of Virginia's interest was incorrect, again returning to the claim that *Umbro* demonstrates "Virginia's policy to control the characterizations of domain names that are acquired in that state" by Virginia citizens. Thus, whether under the district court's or Laxton's understanding of Virginia's interest, neither of which we are persuaded necessarily follows from *Umbro*, Virginia is concerned with protecting Virginia residents who purchase domain names *from* property claims, not *from asserting* property claims. Yet the defendant-purchaser, Laxton, is from California, not Virginia.[2]

Likewise, California's policy of treating domain names as intangible property rights offers no help to Laxton. In understanding domain names as intangible property subject to conversion, California seeks to protect the intangible property rights of the owners of domain names, recognizing that control of a domain name "provide[s] a sense of identity and an exclusive vehicle to market products and

2. Laxton also argues rl.com is located in Virginia and thus any alleged tort occurred in Virginia as well. However, we decline to find the location of rl.com dispositive for the California choice-of-law analysis in this case, which is based on the government interests, not the place of the wrong.

ideas." Many domain name registrants "invest substantial time and money to develop and promote websites that depend on their domain names. Ensuring that they reap the benefits of their investments reduces uncertainty and thus encourages investment in the first place, promoting the growth of the Internet overall."

California's policy in treating domain names as property is thus accurately characterized as protecting the rightful holders of domain names, encouraging investment in and development of that property. Such a policy would protect plaintiffs in suits alleging conversion of a domain name, not a defendant who allegedly converts a domain name. Further, "when the defendant is a resident of California and the tortious conduct . . . occurs [in California], California's deterrent policy of full compensation is clearly advanced by application of its own law." *Hurtado,* 522 P.2d at 672. California, therefore, has an interest in its law applying here, and Virginia does not.

Thus, even if we accept Laxton's characterization of *Umbro,* which we do not, California law would apply because this would be a case of a false conflict, since Virginia does not have an interest in its law applying given how the parties are situated with Laxton as a defendant and Mayberry as a plaintiff. Holding otherwise would encourage a race to the bottom, allowing purchasers of potentially disputed domain names, as well as cybersquatters, to reside or operate in states where intangible property is provided little or no protection from potentially tortious conversion. Such a situation could vitiate the intangible property rights of the true holders of such property notwithstanding states' well-intentioned efforts to protect these intellectual property interests.

. . .

[Applying Calfornia law, the court held that Laxton raised contested issues of material fact, reversed the grant of summary judgment, and remanded for further proceedings.]

Notes on
CRS RECOVERY

1. *CRS* Recovery is instructive in how the court distinguishes between two separate issues: (1) whether, given the uncertain content of Virginia law, any conflict exists at all between Virginia and California law; and (2) whether, assuming there is conflict in terms between Virginia and California law, there is a false conflict within the meaning of governmental interest analysis. In engaging the second question, the court employs a form of restrained and moderate interpretation, limiting the reach of Virginia law according to the domicile of the parties.

2. Consider part of the final reasoning of the *CRS Recovery* court:

Holding otherwise would encourage a race to the bottom, allowing purchasers of potentially disputed domain names, as well as cybersquatters, to reside or operate in states where intangible property is provided little or no protection from potentially tortious conversion. Such a situation could vitiate the intangible property rights of the true holders of such property notwithstanding states' well-intentioned efforts to protect these intellectual property interests.

The concept of a "race to the bottom," as it relates to choice of law, is discussed in detail in the Perspective on Race to the Bottom and Coordinated Choice of Law Rules that appears later in this chapter. For present purposes, the court's reasoning is significant in what it reveals about the court's sense of its own mission. In particular, the court's passage reveals that it is concerned about reaching a result that provides persons with the proper incentives concerning a particular public policy: protection of intangible property interests. In other words, the court was not only concerned about resolving the conflict of laws decision correctly or about reaching the just result for the particular litigants, but was also concerned about calibrating its decision on a general level, so as to send a proper message to other potential domain name holders. Is this an appropriate concern for the court? For further discussion of different orientations that a court can have in making a choice of law decision, see the Perspective on Jurisdiction-Selecting and Law-Selecting Orientations in Choice of Law, which appears in the next section of this chapter.

PROBLEM 2-38: CROSS-BORDER PHONE CALLS

Polly is an Old California resident who made and received many telephone calls with Danielle, who lives and works in the State of New Dakota. Both Polly and Danielle are businesswomen, involved in the buying and selling of medical equipment.

While Danielle was in New Dakota (and Polly was in Old California), Danielle recorded the phone calls without Polly's knowledge. Old California law makes it a crime to record telephone conversations without the consent of both parties and recognizes that the practice gives rise to a tort of invasion of privacy. New Dakota law provides that recording a phone call is lawful if at least one of the parties consents to the recording, and thus would not grant Polly an invasion of privacy cause of action.

Polly has sued Danielle for invasion of privacy based on the phone conversations that Danielle recorded without Polly's knowledge or consent. You may assume that Old California follows comparative impairment and that New Dakota follows governmental interest analysis as created by Professor Currie.

Assume that Polly filed the invasion of privacy suit in Old California. Discuss whether Old California or New Dakota law is likely to govern the issue whether the invasion of privacy cause of action can go forward.

PROBLEM 2-39: AMY'S MALPRACTICE

States A and B are states of the United States of America. Sonia Stockholder was a stockholder in Candy, Inc., a company incorporated in State A. Sonia is domiciled in State A. Candy, Inc. has its headquarters in State B and does most of its business in State B. Amy Attorney, a lawyer licensed to practice only in State B, represented Candy, Inc. Amy Attorney is domiciled in State B. At a Candy, Inc. board meeting held in State B, Amy Attorney negligently provided legal advice to the board that caused Candy, Inc. to incur substantial liability. The liability arose because Amy Attorney counseled Candy, Inc. to engage in a securities transaction that turned out to be unlawful. The securities transaction was consummated in State B.

Even though Amy is not Sonia's lawyer, Sonia has filed a malpractice action against Amy in State A, claiming that Amy's malpractice caused Sonia's stock to diminish in value. Amy has filed a motion to dismiss, arguing that she cannot be liable to Sonia because they did not have an attorney-client relationship. In support of her motion, Amy cites a rule of civil procedure in State A providing that "the only plaintiff who has standing to bring a legal malpractice action against an attorney is a plaintiff who held an attorney-client relationship with the attorney." The advisory committee notes to that Rule of Civil Procedure state that the rule has two purposes: (1) to control the number of malpractice actions flooding State A's courts and (2) to allow attorneys to be free to advise their clients without fear of personal liability to third parties.

Sonia has responded to the motion to dismiss by pointing to a legal malpractice decision written by the Supreme Court of State B, in which the court allowed non-clients to pursue a malpractice action against an attorney where the attorney should have foreseen that nonclients may be harmed by the attorney's negligent advice.

You may assume that State A follows the comparative impairment approach to choice of law and that State B follows the Restatement (First) of Conflict of Laws. Discuss which state's law is likely to govern the question whether Sonia may bring this malpractice action against Amy.

E. BETTER RULE OF LAW

Professor Robert Leflar developed an approach popularly known as the better rule of law approach, for which he proposed several choice-influencing considerations for choice of law decisions. Identifying and applying the better rule of law was only one of the considerations mentioned, but this consideration soon overshadowed the others as the most controversial and dominant of the group.

Leflar's writings at first seemed to suggest he was simply providing a *positive* representation of the considerations — meaning that he was simply describing the types of concerns that actually motivate choice of law decisions. Courts and scholars, however, quickly began to use the considerations in a *normative* manner, presenting the considerations as matters that should guide a court's decision.

At various times, five states have followed the approach: Arkansas, Minnesota, New Hampshire, Rhode Island, and Wisconsin. Most of these states, however, have retracted their embrace of the approach, usually combining it with other approaches — particularly in the context of tort issues. The better rule of law approach, however, has had a palpable and continuing influence on American choice of law thinking and practice. For this reason, the approach deserves consideration in its own right (as illustrated in the *Drinkwater* case that follows), and as an influence on the Restatement (Second) of Conflict of Laws, discussed below.

First, consider Leflar's description of the five major choice-influencing considerations:

A short restatement of the five summarized considerations is given here. . . .

A. *Predictability of Results*

Uniformity of results, regardless of forum, has always been a major goal in choice-of-law theory. Achievement of this goal would enable parties entering into a consensual transaction to plan it with reference to a body of law that would give them the results they desired. As a result, their transactions would normally be validated and their justified expectations thus protected. This would further the broad social policies of most forum states by sustaining legal arrangements in which parties have in good faith engaged themselves. At the same time it would discourage "forum shopping."

B. *Maintenance of Interstate and International Order*

Both nations and states within a nation are interested in facilitating the orderly legal control of transactions that in any fashion cross their boundary lines. Smooth conduct of affairs between the peoples of different nations is essential to modern civilization; the easy movement of persons and things — free social and economic commerce — between states in a federal nation is essential to the very existence of the federation. There must be a minimum of mutual interference with claims or aspirations to sovereignty. No forum whose concern with a set of facts is negligible should claim priority for its law over the law of a state which has a clearly superior concern with the facts; nor should any state's choice-of-law system be based upon deliberate across-the-board "forum preference." Encouragement of that measure of interstate and international intercourse which is in keeping with the interests of the forum state and its people has always been a prime function of conflicts law.

C. *Simplification of the Judicial Task*

Courts do not like to do things the hard way if an easier way serves the ends of justice substantially as well. It would be utterly impractical for a court hearing a case brought on extrastate facts to apply the whole body of procedural law of the place where the facts occurred, and not much would be gained by doing so. Courts therefore use their own procedural rules. There are, however, some outcome-determinative rules, at times classified as procedural, which are so simple that one state's rule can be used as easily as another's, so that the substance-procedure dichotomy is not sensibly applicable to them. Purely mechanical rules for choice of substantive law are also easy for courts to apply, but other considerations may outweigh simplification of the judicial task where such rules are involved. Ease in judicial performance is ordinarily not of first importance among the choice-influencing considerations, but it is important in some choices.

D. Advancement of the Forum's Governmental Interests

If a forum state has a genuine concern with the facts in a given case, a concern discoverable from its strongly felt social or legal policy, it is reasonable to expect the state's courts to act in accordance with that concern. This refers to legitimate concerns, not just to the local occurrence of some facts, or to the local existence of some rule of law that could constitutionally be applied to the facts. A state's governmental interests in the choice-of-law sense need not coincide with its rules of local law, especially if the local rules, whether statutory or judge-made, are old or out of tune with the times. A state's total governmental interest in a case is to be discovered from all the considerations that properly motivate the state in its law-making and law-administering tasks, viewed as of the time when the question is presented. So viewed, the circumstances may show that the forum is truly interested in applying its own law to a set of facts. If they do show this that conclusion becomes a major choice-influencing consideration.

E. Application of the Better Rule of Law

The better rule of law is the most controversial of the considerations, yet a potent one. If choice of law were purely a jurisdiction-selecting process, with courts first deciding which state's law should govern and checking afterward to see what that state's law was, this consideration would not be present. Everyone knows that this is not what courts do, nor what they should do. Judges know from the beginning between which rules of law, and not just which states, they are choosing. A state's "governmental interest" in a set of facts can be analyzed only by reference to the content of the competing rules of law. Choice of law is not wholly a choice between laws as distinguished from a choice between jurisdictions, but partly it is.

A judge's natural feeling that his own state's law is better than that of other states to some extent explains forum preference. Of course the local law is sometimes not better, and most judges are perfectly capable of realizing this. The inclination of any reasonable court will be to prefer rules of law which make good socio-economic sense for the time when the court speaks, whether they be its own or another state's rules. The law's legitimate concerns with "justice in the individual case," sometimes spoken of as a choice-of-law objective, and with that "protection of justified expectations of the parties" which often corresponds with Ehrenzweig's "basic rule of validation," are furthered by deliberate preference for the better rule of law. The preference is objective, not subjective. It has to do with preferred law, not preferred parties. It is "result selective" only in the same sense that in any non-conflicts case a determination of what the law is (presumably the "better law," if there was argument about the law) controls the results of litigation. In conflicts cases, just as in other cases, courts have always taken the content of competing rules into account, but they have too often used characterization, renvoi, multiple-choice rules or the like as manipulative devices to cover up what they were really doing, when there was no need at all for any cover-up.

Robert A. Leflar, *Conflicts Law: More on Choice-Influencing Considerations*, 54 CAL. L. REV. 1584, 1585-1588 (1966). © 1966 by California Law Review, Inc. Reprinted from California Law Review No. 54, No. 4, by permission of California Law Review, Inc. http://www.law.berkely.edu/studnets/jrnlorgs/journals.

Drinkwater v. American Family Mutual Insurance Company

714 N.W.2d 642 (Wis. 2006)

ANN WALSH BRADLEY, J.

. . . Medical Associates Health Plan, Inc. ("the Plan"), an Iowa corporation, appeals a circuit court judgment that applied Wisconsin law and determined that Shane Drinkwater must be made whole before the Plan was entitled to subrogation against his recovery for personal injuries. Drinkwater . . . was injured in a motor vehicle accident in Wisconsin, and the Plan paid medical expenses on his behalf through his employer's health insurance plan.

The issue is whether Iowa law or Wisconsin law applies to the Plan's subrogation claim against Drinkwater. Applying choice-of-law principles, we determine that Wisconsin law applies. Accordingly, Drinkwater must be made whole under Wisconsin law before the Plan may recover for any of Drinkwater's medical expenses. We conclude that the Plan is not entitled to subrogation against Drinkwater's recovery because he was not made whole under Wisconsin law. Therefore, we affirm the circuit court judgment.

I

The background facts relevant to this appeal are undisputed. Drinkwater is a Wisconsin resident who works at a company located in Iowa. He sustained injuries that included a severe leg fracture when another motor vehicle struck his motorcycle in September 2002 in Wisconsin. The driver of the other vehicle was also a Wisconsin resident who was covered under an insurance policy issued by a Wisconsin insurance company. Both vehicles were registered in Wisconsin.

The Plan paid health care expenses on Drinkwater's behalf pursuant to a group health insurance contract it issued to Drinkwater's employer. The Plan is an Iowa non-profit corporation and its principal offices and place of business are located in Iowa, although it has clinics in Iowa, Illinois, and Wisconsin. The contract was issued to Drinkwater's employer in Iowa.

Drinkwater commenced an action for personal injuries, naming the other driver and the driver's insurer as defendants, and naming the Plan as a potentially subrogated party. The Plan counterclaimed and cross-claimed, alleging a subrogated interest in the damages Drinkwater sought.

More specifically, the Plan alleged that pursuant to Iowa law, it was entitled to "first dollar" reimbursement and payment in full for all of its subrogated expenses without deduction or offset. It alleged that its subrogation interest was not subject to the Wisconsin "made-whole" doctrine, but rather that it was entitled to full reimbursement from any of Drinkwater's recovery based upon the terms of the Plan contract and Iowa law.

The Plan contract contained a clause providing that the contract "shall be governed by and interpreted in accordance with the laws of the State of Iowa." It also contained a subrogation clause, which provided as follows:

> If a Member suffers an injury or condition, for which benefits are provided by [the Plan], through acts or omissions of a third party for which said third party (or any person or organization liable for such third party's conduct) is or may be legally liable, or if the Member recovers benefits from any person or organization by reason of such injury or condition, [the Plan] shall be subrogated, to the extent of the reasonable cash value of benefits, supplies, and services provided by [the Plan], to all the Member's rights of recovery against any person or organization. . . .

The other driver's negligence was conceded, as was the lack of any contributory negligence on Drinkwater's part. The insurer for the other driver paid its policy limit of $250,000. . . . [T]he circuit court concluded that Drinkwater would not be made whole by receipt of the $250,000 in proceeds from the tortfeasor's insurance. Applying Wisconsin's made-whole doctrine, it determined that Drinkwater [did not need to pay out any of those funds to the Plan under a subrogation theory].

II

The parties agree that under Wisconsin subrogation law . . . the Plan would not be entitled to subrogation against Drinkwater. . . . The Plan admits that if Wisconsin's made-whole doctrine applies, then Drinkwater prevails. Conversely . . . [t]he parties agree that under Iowa law the Plan would be entitled to invade Drinkwater's recovery of $250,000 to obtain reimbursement of medical expenses it paid on his behalf. Consequently, the question of whether Wisconsin law or Iowa law applies will determine the outcome of this case. . . .

A

We begin with a review of the development and status of the made-whole doctrine in Wisconsin. The made-whole doctrine in Wisconsin has deep and firm roots. It traces back at least 75 years . . . and is based largely on the equitable nature of subrogation. . . . [Recently,] this court again reinforced the centrality of the equitable nature of subrogation, concluding that "only where an injured party has received an award . . . which pays all of his elements of damages . . . is there any occasion for subrogation." [This court explained] that "one who claims subrogation rights, whether under the aegis of either legal or conventional [contractual] subrogation, is barred from any recovery unless the insured is made whole." It said that the purpose of subrogation is to prevent a double recovery. Thus, only when an insured has received full damages from the tortfeasor and has been paid for a portion of those damages by the insurer is the insurer, under principles of equity, entitled to subrogation. When either the insurer or insured must to some extent go unpaid, the loss should be borne by the insurer because that is a risk that the insured has paid the insurer to assume. This court again reaffirmed Wisconsin's commitment to the made-whole doctrine in *Ruckel v. Gassner*, 2002 WI 67, 253 Wis. 2d 280, 646 N.W.2d 11. In a unanimous decision, it held that . . . an insured must be made whole before an insurer may exercise subrogation rights against its insured, even when unambiguous language in an insurance contract states otherwise. *Ruckel*, 2002 WI 67, 253 Wis. 2d 280, PP4, 40, 43.

Ruckel, much like the case at bar, involved medical expenses paid under a group benefit plan. The insurance contract included a subrogation clause entitling the insurer to full repayment of the expenses. It stated that the insurer's right to repayment was "prior and superior" to the right of any other person, including the beneficiary. . . .

[O]ur case law . . . establishes that in Wisconsin the made-whole doctrine can trump express language in an insurance contract. . . .

B

The Plan asserts that this is a contract case and that its Iowa choice-of-law clause is controlling. Furthermore, the Plan argues that even if the clause is not controlling, Iowa is the state with the most significant relationship to the question at hand. Thus, the Plan contends, Iowa law should control under a choice-of-law analysis. We disagree.

This court [has] recognized . . . that there is a qualification on the freedom to contract for choice of law. . . . Although parties may seek to promote "certainty and predictability in contractual relations," they will not be "permitted to do so at the expense of important public policies of a state whose law would be applicable if the parties' choice of law provision were disregarded." . . . [This] qualification on the freedom to contract for choice of law is apt here. First, this court's jurisprudence . . . establishes that in Wisconsin the made-whole doctrine trumps an express contract provision to the contrary. Second, the contractual bargaining in this case occurred between the Plan and Drinkwater's employer, not between the Plan and Drinkwater. He had no choice or opportunity to bargain as to the terms of the Plan contract. If a party who actually bargained for a choice-of-law clause may seek to set it aside based on an overriding state public policy, certainly a party who had no choice or opportunity to bargain for such a clause may do likewise, at least when it dictates his or her right to recover damages.

Moreover, the issue before us is not simply one of contract, as the Plan asserts. To treat it as such, without recognizing the tort aspects that this issue implicates, is to ignore the true nature of the question before the court. To rest the analysis of this case only on contract contravenes this court's analysis in *Ruckel*, which applied equity, not contract, to a tort recovery. In *Ruckel* we held that an insurer is not entitled to subrogation until the insured is made whole "regardless of contractual language to the contrary."

For all of these reasons, we determine that the express choice-of-law provision for Iowa law in the Plan contract does not necessarily control the Plan's subrogation right against Drinkwater's recovery for personal injuries.

Rather, we must apply a choice-of-law analysis to determine if, absent the clause, Wisconsin law would apply.

C

[For choice of law analysis, this court recently] decided *State Farm Mutual Automobile Insurance Co. v. Gillette*, 641 N.W.2d 662 (Wisc. 2002), and *Beloit Liquidating Trust v. Grade*, 677 N.W.2d 298 (Wisc. 2004). Both cases . . . supply the choice-of-law framework for our analysis here. . . .

The "first rule" in the choice-of-law analysis under *Gillette* is "that the law of the forum should presumptively apply unless it becomes clear that nonforum contacts are of the greater significance." Under *Gillette*, if it is not clear that the nonforum contacts are of greater significance, then the court applies five choice-influencing factors:

(1)   Predictability of results;
(2)   Maintenance of interstate and international order;
(3)   Simplification of the judicial task;
(4)   Advancement of the forum's governmental interests; and
(5)   Application of the better rule of law.

Gillette, 2002 WI 31, 251 Wis. 2d 561, P53, 641 N.W.2d 662. . . .[1]

The court in *Beloit Liquidating* referred to two tests to apply in a choice-of-law analysis. The first test is "whether the contacts of one state to the facts of the case are so obviously limited and minimal that application of that state's law constitutes officious intermeddling." *Beloit Liquidating*, 2004 WI 39, 270 Wis. 2d 356, P24, 677 N.W.2d 298. The second test involves an examination of the five choice-influencing factors. *Beloit Liquidating*, 2004 WI 39, 270 Wis. 2d 356, P25, 677 N.W.2d 298.

The "first rule" of *Gillette* and the first test of *Beloit Liquidating* are related. It could not "become[] clear that nonforum contacts are of the greater significance" (*Gillette*) if the nonforum state's contacts are "so obviously limited and minimal that application of that state's law constitutes officious intermeddling" (*Beloit Liquidating*).

That said, we need not address further the relationship of the "first rule" of *Gillette* and the first test of *Beloit Liquidating*. The application of either *Gillette*'s "first rule" or *Beloit Liquidating*'s first test to the facts here necessitates that we apply the five choice-influencing factors. It is not "clear" whether Iowa's contacts are of the "greater significance" (*Gillette*), yet Iowa's contacts are not "so obviously limited and minimal" that application of Iowa law would constitute officious intermeddling (*Beloit Liquidating*).

Specifically, the relevant contacts of Iowa and Wisconsin include the following:

---

1. The factors were suggested by Robert A. Leflar in his article, *Choice-Influencing Considerations in Conflicts Law*, 31 N.Y.U. L. Rev. 267 (1966).

- The accident and Drinkwater's injuries occurred in Wisconsin.
- Drinkwater is a Wisconsin resident who works at an Iowa company.
- The Plan is an Iowa corporation with its principal offices and place of business located in Iowa, although it has clinics in Iowa, Illinois, and Wisconsin.
- The Plan contract was issued in Iowa to Drinkwater's employer.
- The tortfeasor is a resident of Wisconsin and was covered under an insurance policy issued by a Wisconsin insurance company.
- Both Drinkwater and the other driver were operating vehicles registered in Wisconsin at the time of the accident.

Both Wisconsin's and Iowa's contacts are significant. It is not clear that Iowa's contacts are of greater significance. At the same time, however, Iowa's contacts are more than minimal and limited. We therefore turn to apply the five choice-influencing factors.

Predictability of results. This factor deals with the parties' expectations; put another way, what legal consequences comport with the predictions or expectations of the parties? Whether the application of Iowa law or Wisconsin law is more likely to lead to predictable and expected results under the facts of this case depends on which party's perspective on predictability and expectations is considered.

On the one hand, the application of Iowa law is consistent with the Plan's ability to predict and expect that Iowa law will apply to all its insureds or members. On the other hand, Wisconsin citizens are entitled to some assurance that when they suffer injuries within their own state, they can generally predict and expect that Wisconsin law will dictate their rights to recovery.

It may be true that the Plan reaps some benefit from the ability to know with complete predictability that Iowa law will apply. Yet, the application of Wisconsin law in this case does not completely undermine predictability for the Plan. A company such as the Plan is in a relatively good position to calculate the risks associated with decreased predictability whether Iowa law will apply. In contrast, we would not expect reasonable Wisconsin insureds to foresee that they should routinely over-insure themselves for injuries resulting from Wisconsin accidents on the off chance they might become subject to another state's law that effectively limits their recovery.

Thus, although the application of Iowa law might modestly increase predictability for the Plan, the application of Wisconsin law would facilitate predictability for Wisconsin citizens such as Drinkwater. The Plan, and those similarly situated, are in a better position to calculate the risk of a modest amount of unpredictability and adjust accordingly. The first factor therefore points at least somewhat to the application of Wisconsin law.

Maintenance of interstate order. This factor requires that a jurisdiction which is minimally concerned defer to a jurisdiction that is substantially concerned. Under the facts of this case both jurisdictions are more than minimally concerned.

We cannot say that the application of Wisconsin law would appreciably impede state-to-state commercial intercourse as compared to the application of Iowa law. Although it might be said that the application of Wisconsin law would discourage Iowa companies from hiring Wisconsin residents, it might just as easily be said that the application of Iowa law would discourage Wisconsin citizens from working for Iowa corporations. Thus, somewhat paradoxically, both Iowa and Wisconsin have at least some interest in the application of either jurisdiction's laws.

In addition, we note that this case does not appear to involve the risk of forum shopping. The accident occurred in Wisconsin, and both Drinkwater and the tortfeasor who caused his injuries are Wisconsin residents. Similarly, any fear that a prospective plaintiff would move to this state merely to take advantage of its made-whole doctrine is unfounded. All in all, the second factor does not appreciably favor Iowa law or Wisconsin law.

Simplification of the judicial task. This court has stated a general rule that the judicial task is rarely simplified when lawyers and judges must apply themselves to foreign law. . . . *Finch v. Southside Lincoln-Mercury, Inc.*, 685 N.W.2d 154 ("application of our own law, as opposed to the law of a foreign jurisdiction, will always simplify our judicial task, except where Wisconsin law is complex or uncertain as compared to that of the other jurisdiction").

The judicial task would not be simplified by the application of Iowa law. . . . [The court analyzed Iowa law, which might require it to hold a special hearing in this case.] Moreover, the . . . application of Iowa law might inject additional opportunities for litigants to game the system, thereby increasing the potential complexity of the judicial task. This factor points to the application of Wisconsin law.

Advancement of the forum's governmental interests. "The question in private litigation, such as in an automobile-accident case, is whether the proposed nonforum rule comports with the standards of fairness and justice that are embodied in the policies of the forum law." *Gillette*, 641 N.W.2d 662. "If it appears that the application of forum law will advance the governmental interest of the forum state, this fact becomes a major, though not in itself a determining, factor in the ultimate choice of law." *Gillette*, 641 N.W.2d 662.

Wisconsin has a strong interest in compensating its residents who are victims of torts. . . . Our state's made-whole doctrine, with its deep and firm roots, is a central means by which Wisconsin's interest in compensating its resident tort victims is effectuated. The court has repeatedly reaffirmed the strength and reach of the doctrine. . . .

In order for this factor to weigh in favor of the application of Wisconsin law, we need not determine that Iowa's law is a "bad law" or that it "serves no legitimate purpose." *Gillette*, 641 N.W.2d 662. We can, and do, however, determine that limiting Drinkwater's net recovery to less than the damages he would recover under Wisconsin law undermines Wisconsin's significant interest in fully compensating its citizens who are tort victims. This factor points strongly to the application of Wisconsin law.

Application of the better rule of law. As previously suggested, we need not and do not necessarily conclude that Iowa law is bad law or serves no legitimate purpose. Yet, this court's repeated affirmations of Wisconsin's made-whole doctrine must to some extent be taken as an indication of Wisconsin's view that our made-whole doctrine constitutes the better rule. This court has rejected the Iowa approach.

We cannot help but observe that the application of Iowa law would seem to work inequitable results, at least from the viewpoint of a tort system such as that in Wisconsin. At oral argument, counsel for the Plan conceded that if Drinkwater's medical expenses had been $251,000, a sum that is $1,000 more than the limits of the tortfeasor's liability insurance, under Iowa law the Plan would have been subrogated to all of Drinkwater's recovery. In other words, according to the Plan's counsel, the most severe cases of injury are those in which the injured party would be most likely to end up with a net recovery of zero. This is the type of result that, as we declared in *Ruckel*, "turn[s] the entire doctrine of subrogation on its head." *Ruckel*, 646 N.W.2d 11. The final factor thus points to . . . Wisconsin law.

Considering the five choice-influencing factors together, we conclude that Wisconsin law should apply. All of the factors either point to the application of Wisconsin law or are neutral. The parties agree, as do we, that under Wisconsin's made-whole doctrine, the Plan is not entitled to any subrogation against Drinkwater's recovery. Accordingly, we need go no further to conclude that the circuit court judgment must be affirmed.

III

In sum, we conclude that Wisconsin law applies to require that Drinkwater must be made whole before the Plan is entitled to subrogation against Drinkwater's recovery for his personal injuries. The Plan is not entitled to subrogation because Drinkwater was not made whole under Wisconsin law. Accordingly, we affirm the circuit court judgment.

DAVID T. PROSSER, J. (dissenting).

The made-whole doctrine is a well-established feature of Wisconsin tort and insurance law. I support this doctrine and wish it were the law in all jurisdictions. Unfortunately, it is not. We must recognize that fact in considering this case.

. . . Wisconsin residents will receive enhanced protection because of this court's decision if they are involved in an accident in Wisconsin. They will receive more protection than their co-workers and consequently may become more expensive to insure than their co-workers who live in Illinois or Iowa. This may have an effect on health care costs for their employers. It may have an effect on Wisconsin resident employment.

In resolving the choice of law issue presented here, the court skillfully marshals the facts and policy in a manner that supports its decision. But some of the facts carry no weight. For instance, the fact that "[t]he tortfeasor is a resident of Wisconsin and was covered under an insurance policy issued by a Wisconsin insurance company," P44, is really not relevant. The law would not be different if the tortfeasor lived in Illinois and was covered under a policy issued by an Illinois insurance company. What is important is that the tortfeasor's insurer provided liability coverage.

The fact that "[b]oth Drinkwater and the other driver were operating vehicles registered in Wisconsin at the time of the accident," id., also is not significant. It merely supplements the fact that the two drivers were Wisconsin residents.

There are three important Wisconsin-related facts: (1) Mr. Drinkwater was and is a Wisconsin resident; (2) his accident occurred in Wisconsin; and (3) his suit was filed in Wisconsin.

The rule of this case is that Wisconsin law will trump Illinois or Iowa subrogation law on a Wisconsin injury to a Wisconsin resident when the case is tried in a Wisconsin court.

What is not clear is what the result would be if there were a Wisconsin injury to an Illinois or Iowa resident and the case were tried in a Wisconsin court against the insured's home state insurer (like Medical Associates Health Plan) claiming subrogation rights. Because Wisconsin is visited by hundreds of thousands of out-of-state tourists, this sort of scenario must be anticipated.

We also do not know what the result would be if a Wisconsin resident like Mr. Drinkwater were to be injured in an Illinois or Iowa accident but able to sue in Wisconsin and bring in the out-of-state insurer claiming subrogation.

This uncertainty undermines the predictability of results. . . .

The result in this case is certainly fair to Mr. Drinkwater. The nagging concern is whether our decision will have collateral consequences to other people or the law.

Notes on
DRINKWATER *AND THE BETTER RULE OF LAW APPROACH*

1. Note that the *Drinkwater* court applied the five choice-influencing considerations only after engaging in a threshold inquiry on whether one state's law should clearly and unequivocally apply. Other courts have also embossed twists and modifications on Leflar's factors. For example, the Arkansas Supreme Court has said that the five choice-influencing considerations do not supplant the court's previous use of the place-of-the-wrong rule for torts, but are adopted in order "to soften the formulaic application of *lex loci delicti*." *Schubert v. Target Stores Inc.*, 201 S.W.3d 917, 922 (Ark. 2005). Other cases have combined the approach with the Restatement (Second) of Conflict of Laws and/or interest analysis. *See, e.g., Cribb v. Augustyn*, 696 A.2d 285, 288 (R.I. 1997) (combining choice-influencing considerations with Restatement (Second) and interest analysis); *Schlemmer v. Fireman's Fund Ins. Co.*, 730 S.W.2d 217, 218-219 (Ark. 1987) (combining choice-influencing considerations with the Restatement (Second)).

2. The *Drinkwater* majority concludes that all five choice-influencing considerations are either neutral or favor application of Wisconsin law. Do you agree with that conclusion? Or do you get the impression that the court tailored its analysis of the factors in order to support its decision to apply Wisconsin law? Does Justice Prosser make any persuasive arguments that some of the considerations might actually point toward Iowa law? If so, which considerations?

3. Suppose that in the *Drinkwater* dispute, the Plan had sued Drinkwater in Iowa, asking for a declaratory judgment that Iowa law determines the Plan's subrogation rights on Drinkwater's tort recovery. Suppose further, as is quite possible, that the Iowa courts agreed and entered the requested judgment. The full faith and credit clause would compel a Wisconsin court to recognize and enforce the Iowa judgment if the Iowa court had entered judgment first. Wasn't it therefore a tactical blunder for the Plan's lawyers to sue in Wisconsin and not Iowa? Would the Iowa court defer to the Wisconsin courts simply because the Wisconsin suit was filed first?

4. Professor Robert Leflar was a strong proponent of judicial candor as a general principle. He brought this orientation to conflict of laws, having observed that courts making choice of law decisions tacitly evaluate the merits of the laws in conflict, seeking to avoid those laws that are "anachronistic." Robert A. Leflar, *Choice-Influencing Considerations in Conflicts Law*, 41 N.Y.U. L. REV. 267, 295-304 (1966). Leflar regretted that courts often found it necessary to obfuscate their intention to avoid certain laws on the basis of content, believing justice is better served by freeing courts to openly consider which law is better. Do you agree? Why might one argue that courts should be candid in their opinions? Surely it matters to litigants trying to understand the reasons for a ruling or other courts trying to understand the scope of a ruling and its effect in subsequent cases.

Are there any occasions where a court might serve justice by *not* being fully candid about the reasons for decision? Assuming that one holds impartial and balanced decision making out as an ideal, might one worry that encouraging courts to expose their result-oriented thinking fully would actually encourage subjective thinking rather than detached impartiality? One might argue that virtue begins with hypocrisy: that is, a little disingenuousness, or the pretense of virtue, can have the salutary effect of actually moving an individual closer to the feigned ideal.

5. Professors Friedrich Juenger and Luther McDougal also proposed that courts in conflict of laws cases seek optimum justice. In fact, their suggestions are even more provocative than Professor Leflar's. Juenger proposed that a judge confronting conflicting laws should combine the laws of interested states to create a new substantive rule that best accords

with "modern standards" of justice. FRIEDRICH JUENGER, CHOICE OF LAW AND MULTISTATE JUSTICE 196-197, 236 (1993). McDougal did not think that courts should confine themselves to the laws of states involved in the dispute. Rather, he argued, courts should not be "so limited in their choice," but should instead develop the best rule that "promotes net aggregate long-term common interests." Luther L. McDougal III, *Toward Application of the Best Rule of Law in Choice of Law Cases*, 35 MERCER L. REV. 483, 483-484 (1984). Neither Juenger's nor McDougal's suggestions have taken hold in the courts.

6. Criticisms of the better rule approach abound. As suggested above, some have questioned whether it is legitimate for courts, rather than legislatures, to decide that one legal principle is superior to another—condemning the better rule approach as encouraging decision making premised on the subjective preferences of judges. And others have suggested that identifying a "better law" is sometimes not even a meaningful inquiry. *See Jepson v. General Casualty Co. of Wisconsin*, 513 N.W.2d 467, 473 (Minn. 1994) ("Sometimes different laws are neither better nor worse in an objective way, just different."). In related criticism, Professor Larry Kramer has argued that the real problem is that putting state courts in the position of evaluating which state law is more just is simply "contrary to a fundamental premise" of American federalism. Larry Kramer, *Return of the Renvoi*, 66 N.Y.U. L. REV. 979, 1019 (1991). Some argue that courts take into account the respective merits of contending laws all the time, and that no reason exists for suggesting that this practice is inappropriate when courts adjudicate in a multijurisdictional context. Moreover, Professor Leflar urged that judges are fully capable of appreciating that foreign law can be superior to forum law, and others have agreed, so long as the judge is willing to invest the "human capital" necessary to becoming "well versed" in foreign law. Nita Ghei & Francesco Parisi, *Adverse Selection and Moral Hazard in Forum Shopping: Conflicts Law as Spontaneous Order*, 25 CARDOZO L. REV. 1367, 1373 (2004).

Raising contrary concerns, Professor Symeon Symeonides has documented that the better rule of law approach yields a significant tendency for courts to apply forum law, which in turn tends to include a plaintiff-oriented bias. SYMEON C. SYMEONIDES, AMERICAN PRIVATE INTERNATIONAL LAW 125-126 (2008). *Drinkwater* is certainly an example of that tendency. *But cf.* Patrick J. Borchers, *The Choice-of-Law Revolution: An Empirical Study*, 49 WASH. & LEE L. REV. 357, 377-378 (1992) (concluding that courts applying modern methodologies prefer forum law more than those using the Restatement (First), but that courts applying interest analysis and the better rule of law approach have shown no more "propensity to favor forum law" than the Second Restatement); Michael Solimine, *An Economic and Empirical Analysis of Choice of Law*, 24 GA. L. REV. 49, 55-59 (1989) (concluding that, for all of the "modern theories," courts prefer forum law more than under the Restatement (First)). Professor Symeonides has also concluded that the better rule of law approach enables forum courts to prefer forum-domiciled litigants over foreign-domiciled ones. SYMEO-NIDES, *supra*, at 126.

PROBLEM 2-40: FLYING CARDBOARD

Trish Truckdriver drove a truck for a company that transported cardboard. She lives in State T and was injured in an accident in State A when cardboard flew out of her truck after she opened the back door of the trailer her truck pulled. Her employer, Employer Corporation, is a State T corporation. It turns out that employees of a State T corporation known as Contracting Corporation had negligently loaded the cardboard onto the truck in State T. The contract between Employer Corporation and Contracting Corporation established that Employer Corporation was required to obtain workers' compensation insurance for Employer Corporation's employees. Employer Corporation had complied with the provision.

Trish filed a workers' compensation claim against Employer Corporation in her home state, State T, and received a workers' compensation award. She then sued Contracting Corporation in State T, seeking to recover damages for the negligence of Contracting Corporation's workers. Under the law of State T, a court could award tort damages against Contracting Corporation under the circumstances of this case. Under the law of State A, however, Contracting Corporation is immune from tort liability. The law of State A provides this immunity because of the contractual provision requiring Employer Corporation to obtain workers' compensation coverage and because Trish had, in fact, received such compensation for the accident. The law of State T takes the position that, in many instances, workers' compensation does not wholly compensate an employee for her loss and that supplemental tort awards should be allowed.

State A applies the First Restatement of Conflict of Laws and State T applies the better rule of law approach. What law is the forum, State T, likely to apply to resolve the tort liability issue?

PERSPECTIVE ON JURISDICTION-SELECTING AND
LAW-SELECTING ORIENTATIONS IN CHOICE OF LAW

In discussing choice of law approaches, commentators often distinguish between "jurisdiction-selecting" and "law-selecting" orientations. The Restatement (First) of Conflict of Laws provides the prototype for a jurisdiction-selecting approach because of its focus on the jurisdictional location of persons and events in determining what law governs. One of the first scholars to criticize this slavish adherence to "what happens where" was Professor David Cavers. Cavers argued against allocating "legal problems among territorial jurisdictions," instead advocating for courts to focus on the "proper result," so that they might "decide specific cases justly." David F. Cavers, *A Critique of the Choice-of-Law Problem*, 47 HARV. L. REV. 173, 189-194 (1933). The first judicial exploration away from the Restatement (First) — in cases that adhered to the center of gravity approach — did not necessarily reflect Cavers's advice. Rather, the center of gravity approach continued a jurisdiction-selecting focus by evaluating which, among competing jurisdictions, hosted the nucleus or gravity center of relevant contacts.

The next innovation, governmental interest analysis, does reflect respect for Cavers's admonition for courts to emphasis just disposition of cases in evaluating conflicts issues. Governmental interest analysis accomplishes this by requiring courts to evaluate the content of law — identifying a law's goals and determining whether the dispute implicates those goals. For this reason, one can fairly characterize governmental interest analysis as law-selecting. Because of its kinship with governmental interest analysis, comparative impairment might be similarly labeled. Interestingly, though, comparative impairment has a jurisdiction-selecting quality in its focus on which jurisdiction would suffer most if its law did not apply. While the approach does not have the same fixation on territorial power as the Restatement (First), comparative impairment's concern with jurisdictional impairment privileges the welfare and regulatory goals of particular government units over justice concerns for litigants.

As popularized, the better rule of law approach is among the most "law-selecting" of the dominant choice of law approaches in the United States. While some of Professor Leflar's choice-influencing considerations center on generalized concern with territorial sovereignty, the most infamous consideration, application of the better rule of law, clearly focuses on the content of conflicting legal rules. Because the Restatement (Second) of Conflict of Laws embodies many of Leflar's choice-influencing considerations, it too has significant law-selecting qualities. Yet, as explored below, the Restatement (Second) contains provisions that point to one jurisdiction that presumptively provides governing legal principles in a case with multistate elements — a quality reminiscent of the jurisdiction-selecting orientation of the Restatement (First).

A review of modern methodologies thus reveals them to reflect substantial law-selecting qualities. Yet merely observing that a court follows a modern "law-selecting" choice of law approach does not tell the whole story. Other important premises and goals implicitly or explicitly guide courts in their quest to reach what Cavers would call a "just result."

The term "just result," it turns out, contains many possible analyses in a conflict of laws dispute. On one hand, the court may proceed from the perspective that it must do what scholars call "conflicts justice." When "conflicts justice" guides a court, the court seeks to ensure that it applies the law from the proper state. To reach this conclusion, the court may be guided by such factors as the needs of judicial systems, uniformity of results, avoiding forum shopping, predictability, the court's ease of determining the applicable law, and even concern with whether the parties have gained sufficient benefits from a jurisdiction's laws to fairly ask them to bear its burdens as well. *See, e.g.*, Arthur Taylor von Mehren, *Special Substantive Rules for Multistate Problems: Their Role and Significance in Contemporary Choice of Law Methodology*, 88 HARV. L. REV. 347, 348-350 (1974); Harold L. Korn, *The Choice-of-Law Revolution: A Critique*, 83 COLUM. L. REV. 772, 959-960 (1983).

Scholars contrast "conflicts justice" with "material" or "substantive" justice. "Material justice" and "substantive justice" serve as approximate synonyms, and refer to the results a court seeks in a wholly domestic case — without regard to any concern with conflicting jurisdictions or multijurisdictional elements. Gerhard Kegel explains that "conflicts law aims at the *spacially* best solution . . . [but] substantive law aims at the *materially* best solution." Gerhard Kegel, *Paternal Home and Dream Home, Traditional Conflict of Laws and the American Reformers*, 27 AM. J. COMP. L. 615, 616 (1979). Some scholars argue that courts have the same duties of fairness and justice when adjudicating multijurisdictional cases justly as they do in wholly domestic cases, and that resolving disputes in a "manner substantively fair and equitable to litigants should be an objective of conflicts law as much as internal law." Symeon Symeonides, *Result-Selectivism in Conflicts Law*, 46 WILLAMETTE L. REV. 1, 3 (2009). In the context of a choice of law determination, "substantive" or "material" justice authorizes a court to scrutinize the competing laws to evaluate which produces the most just result in the case.

A court's decision to pursue "material" or "substantive" justice does not settle all matters related to the court's orientation in making a decision. Note that in rejecting the Restatement (First) approach, Cavers admonished courts "to decide specific cases justly." Note that Cavers used the word "specific"; perhaps he sought to capture the notion that a court should focus on individualized justice for the parties to a particular case. The question arises whether it is legitimate, and beneficial, for courts to look beyond the fairness concerns unique to the parties so as to consider possible aggregate consequences of their choice of law decisions. Such broader aggregate consequences might include matters such as whether one law or another best promotes the efficient allocation of societal resources or sends improper incentives for other individuals or organizations to "game" the legal system.

So we see that a court's decision to embrace a "law-selecting" orientation involves subsidiary questions that inform which law to select. The court might consider whether a law promotes conflicts justice and/or material or substantive justice, as well as whether a law promotes both individualized justice and aggregate, societal justice.

F. RESTATEMENT (SECOND) OF CONFLICT OF LAWS

1. Introduction

The Restatement (Second) of Conflict of Laws is currently the most important choice of law approach in the United States. Close to half of the states in the United States follow the approach, and the rest of the world regards the approach as the key indicator of United States law. In addition, federal courts have declared that the Restatement (Second) of Conflict of Laws comprises the "federal" choice of law principles for cases where such principles are needed. And, finally, even courts that do not officially follow the Restatement (Second) fall into the habit of occasionally relying on it. *See, e.g., Craig v. Carrigo,* 121 S.W.3d 154 (Ark. 2003) (Arkansas Supreme Court relied on Restatement (Second) even though the jurisdiction generally uses the better rule or significant contacts approach); *American Motorists Insurance Co. v. Artra Group, Inc.,* 659 A.2d 1295, 1301 (Md. 1995) (noting that although Maryland does not generally follow the Restatement (Second), Maryland courts have cited its sections "with approval").

To appreciate how important the Restatement (Second) of Conflict of Laws is to those who do not reside in the United States, imagine the following: you are resident in a country outside of the United States trying to pin down the substance of United States law on a particular tort issue. With research, you have determined that the tort issue is governed by state law, and you could discern no applicable federal law governing the issue. Given the plethora of laws among the many states, you reckon that a Restatement is the best place to start to understand United States law on this tort issue. Let's say, however, that you understand that the ten states that are implicated in your legal problem do not follow Restatement principles on the issues of tort law. You need to figure out which state's tort law is likely to govern your tort issue. You have heard that the state where a lawsuit is filed will apply its own choice of law principles to determine which state's tort law governs. Your head is dizzy with the complexity, and you find great comfort when you discover that not only is there a Restatement (Second) of Conflict of Laws, but that a majority of the states follow it. Sure, you could research the choice of law approaches of all ten states to try to identify all potential areas of legal exposure, but that's a *really* arduous task. So long as you are satisfied that at least some of the ten states follow the Restatement (Second) of Conflicts, you believe it is rational to end your conflict of laws inquiry by ascertaining which state law would govern under that Restatement. After all, once you figure out the conflict of laws result, you still need to figure out the array of laws relating to the merits of the torts issue. To include all of the choice of law approaches would expand your analysis exponentially.

That said, the Restatement (Second) may need to yield to the Restatement (Third) of Conflict of Laws. Although far from completion, work on the Restatement (Third) is well underway. For now, however, the Restatement (Second) still reigns. This narrative helps make the case for a uniform choice of law approach in the United States, a matter explored later in this chapter in connection with

statutory choice of law rules. For present purposes, we deal with the practical observation that the Restatement (Second) of Conflict of Laws is the closest the United
States gets to having a uniform choice of law approach. Now for the bad news: the
approach is not a particularly easy one to pin down. The Restatement (First) of
Conflict of Laws has at least a fighting chance of yielding the same choice of law
result regardless of where the lawsuit was filed. As expressed in the core Restatement (Second) section, §6, the Restatement (Second) also aspires to predictability
and uniformity. But most agree that the Restatement (Second) does not achieve
that aspiration. Conceived to integrate the salutary qualities of the earlier methodologies, the Restatement (Second) gives us the "kitchen sink" of choice of law tools.
The result is an approach making possible a huge variety of analyses: one can have a
difficult time predicting what result will follow when courts get their hands on its
octopus-like methodology. In the end, the Restatement (Second)'s tests and concerns often vary according to where a lawsuit is filed.

The Restatement (Second) sections pertaining to choice of law are structured
largely according to subject matter category, such as Wrongs, Contracts, and Property. The sections offer "three levels of analysis, ranging from the very general to
the very specific." Lea Brilmayer & Raechel Anglin, *Choice of Law Theory and the
Metaphysics of the Stand-alone Trigger*, 95 Iowa L. Rev. 1125, 1161 (2010). *See* Symeon
C. Symeonides, *A New Conflicts Restatement: Why Not?*, 5 J. Priv. Int'l L. 383, 390
(2009) (explaining that the Restatement (Second) "consists of . . . provisions
that can only be described, in descending order of definiteness, as 'near rules,'
'pointers,' and 'non-rules'"). The most general analysis is delineated in §6,
which lists basic principles for courts to consider in making choice of law decisions.
This very abstract section does not guide courts or attorneys in how to use the
principles, although the comments following the section offer a few insights.
The middle level of specificity appears in sections listing basic principles for the
broad subject matter categories of Wrongs, Contracts, Property, and the like. These
sections list the likely universe of relevant contacts for cases in that subject area, and
tell courts to evaluate the contacts in light of §6 and according to the contacts'
"relative importance to the particular issue." *See, e.g.*, Restatement (Second) of
Conflict of Laws §§145, 188. Like §6, the sections contain no guidance on how
to evaluate the relative importance of the contacts. Finally, the most specific
level of guidance appears in sections that state precisely which state's law presumptively applies to certain specified issues. Examples of this level of specificity are
sprinkled throughout the subject matter categories of the Restatement (Second).

A quick review of the different aspects of the Restatement (Second) reveals its
homage to earlier approaches. The organization by legal subject matter and occasional rule-like specificity of presumptively applicable law derives from the
Restatement (First) of Conflict of Laws. The reference to policies of the forum
and other interested states invites courts to engage in governmental interest analysis. Many other considerations of §6 are reminiscent of Leflar's choice-
influencing considerations, although consideration of the better rule of law is
notably absent. Finally, the generalized lists of contacts evoke the center of gravity
approach, which encouraged courts to group contacts in order to identify the
state with the greatest claim for applying its law. But the whole collection—

making possible a huge range of analyses (and results!) — is uniquely Restatement (Second). To its details, warts and all, we now turn.

We start first with the heart of the Restatement (Second) as reflected in the section with its greatest level of generality: §6. Because of the section's importance to the whole of the Second Restatement and the vague generality of its terms, the explanatory comments to the section are largely reproduced below:

From the Restatement (Second) of Conflicts of Law:

§6. Choice-of-Law Principles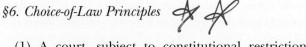

(1) A court, subject to constitutional restrictions, will follow a statutory directive of its own state on choice of law.

(2) When there is no such directive, the factors relevant to the choice of the applicable rule of law include

(a) the needs of the interstate and international systems,

(b) the relevant policies of the forum,

(c) the relevant policies of other interested states and the relative interests of those states in the determination of the particular issue,

(d) the protection of justified expectations,

(e) the basic policies underlying the particular field of law,

(f) certainty, predictability and uniformity of result, and

(g) ease in the determination and application of the law to be applied.

Comment on Subsection (1):

a. Statutes directed to choice of law. A court, subject to constitutional limitations, must follow the directions of its legislature. The court must apply a local statutory provision directed to choice of law provided that it would be constitutional to do so. . . .

b. Intended range of application of statute. A court will rarely find that a question of choice of law is explicitly covered by statute. That is to say, a court will rarely be directed by statute to apply the local law of one state, rather than the local law of another state, in the decision of a particular issue. On the other hand, the court will constantly be faced with the question whether the issue before it falls within the intended range of application of a particular statute. The court should give a local statute the range of application intended by the legislature when these intentions can be ascertained and can constitutionally be given effect. If the legislature intended that the statute should be applied to the out-of-state facts involved, the court should so apply it unless constitutional considerations forbid. On the other hand, if the legislature intended that the statute should be applied only to acts taking place within the state, the statute should not be given a wider range of application. Sometimes a statute's intended range of application will be apparent on its face, as when it expressly applies to all citizens of a state including those who are living abroad. When the statute is silent as to its range of application, the intentions of the legislature on the subject can sometimes be ascertained by a process of interpretation and construction. Provided that it is constitutional to do so, the court will apply a local statute in the manner intended by the legislature even when the local law of another state would be applicable under usual choice-of-law principles.

Comment on Subsection (2):

c. Rationale. Legislatures usually legislate, and courts usually adjudicate, only with the local situation in mind. They rarely give thought to the extent to which the laws they enact, and the common law rules they enunciate, should apply to out-of-state facts. When there are no adequate directives in the statute or in the case law, the court will take account of the factors listed in this Subsection in determining the state whose local law will be applied to determine the issue at hand. It is not suggested that this list of factors is exclusive. Undoubtedly, a court will on occasion give consideration to other factors in deciding a question of choice of law. Also it is not suggested that the factors mentioned are listed in the order of their relative importance. Varying weight will be given to a particular factor, or to a group of factors, in different areas of choice of law. So, for example, the policy in favor of effectuating the relevant policies of the state of dominant interest is given predominant weight in the rule that transfers of interests in land are governed by the law that would be applied by the courts of the situs. . . . On the other hand, the policies in favor of protecting the justified expectations of the parties and of effectuating the basic policy underlying the particular field of law come to the fore in the rule that, subject to certain limitations, the parties can choose the law to govern their contract and in the rules which provide, subject to certain limitations, for the application of a law which will uphold the validity of a trust of movables . . . or the validity of a contract against the charge of commercial usury. Similarly, the policy favoring uniformity of result comes to the fore in the rule that succession to interests in movables is governed by the law that would be applied by the courts of the state where the decedent was domiciled at the time of his death. . . .

At least some of the factors mentioned in this Subsection will point in different directions in all but the simplest case. Hence any rule of choice of law, like any other common law rule, represents an accommodation of conflicting values.

d. Needs of the interstate and international systems. Probably the most important function of choice-of-law rules is to make the interstate and international systems work well. Choice-of-law rules, among other things, should seek to further harmonious relations between states and to facilitate commercial intercourse between them. In formulating rules of choice of law, a state should have regard for the needs and policies of other states and of the community of states. . . .

e. Relevant policies of the state of the forum. Two situations should be distinguished. One is where the state of the forum has no interest in the case apart from the fact that it is the place of the trial of the action. Here the only relevant policies of the state of the forum will be embodied in its rules relating to trial administration. . . . The second situation is where the state of the forum has an interest in the case apart from the fact that it is the place of trial. In this latter situation, relevant policies of the state of the forum may be embodied in rules that do not relate to trial administration. . . .

Every rule of law, whether embodied in a statute or in a common law rule, was designed to achieve one or more purposes. A court should have regard for these purposes in determining whether to apply its own rule or the rule of another state in the decision of a particular issue. If the purposes sought to be achieved by a local statute or common law rule would be furthered by its application to out-of-state facts, this is a weighty reason why such application should be made. On the other hand, the court is under no compulsion to apply the statute or rule to such out-of-state facts since the originating legislature or court had no ascertainable intentions on the subject. The court must decide for itself whether the purposes sought to be achieved by a local statute or rule should be furthered at the expense of the other choice-of-law factors mentioned in this Subsection.

f. Relevant policies of other interested states. In determining a question of choice of law, the forum should give consideration not only to its own relevant policies . . . but also to the relevant policies of all other interested states. The forum should seek to reach a result that will achieve the best possible accommodation of these policies. The forum should also appraise the relative interests of the states involved in the determination of the particular issue. In general, it is fitting that the state whose interests are most deeply affected should have its local law applied. Which is the state of dominant interest may depend upon the issue involved. . . . The content of the relevant local law rule of a state may be significant in determining whether this state is the state with the dominant interest. So, for example, application of a state's statute or common law rule which would absolve the defendant from liability could hardly be justified on the basis of this state's interest in the welfare of the injured plaintiff.

g. Protection of justified expectations. This is an important value in all fields of the law, including choice of law. Generally speaking, it would be unfair and improper to hold a person liable under the local law of one state when he had justifiably molded his conduct to conform to the requirements of another state. Also, it is in part because of this factor that the parties are free within broad limits to choose the law to govern the validity of their contract and that the courts seek to apply a law that will sustain the validity of a trust of movables.

There are occasions, particularly in the area of negligence, when the parties act without giving thought to the legal consequences of their conduct or to the law that may be applied. In such situations, the parties have no justified expectations to protect, and this factor can play no part in the decision of a choice-of-law question.

h. Basic policies underlying particular field of law. This factor is of particular importance in situations where the policies of the interested states are largely the same but where there are nevertheless minor differences between their relevant local law rules. In such instances, there is good reason for the court to apply the local law of that state which will best achieve the basic policy, or policies, underlying the particular field of law involved. . . .

i. Predictability and uniformity of result. These are important values in all areas of the law. To the extent that they are attained in choice of law, forum shopping will be discouraged. These values can, however, be purchased at too great a price. In a rapidly developing area, such as choice of law, it is often more important that good rules be developed than that predictability and uniformity of result should be assured through continued adherence to existing rules. Predictability and uniformity of result are of particular importance in areas where the parties are likely to give advance thought to the legal consequences of their transactions. . . .

j. Ease in the determination and application of the law to be applied. Ideally, choice-of-law rules should be simple and easy to apply. This policy should not be overemphasized, since it is obviously of greater importance that choice-of-law rules lead to desirable results. . . .

k. Reciprocity. In formulating common law rules of choice of law, the courts are rarely guided by considerations of reciprocity. Private parties, it is felt, should not be made to suffer for the fact that the courts of the state from which they come give insufficient consideration to the interests of the state of the forum. It is also felt that satisfactory development of choice-of-law rules can best be attained if each court gives fair consideration to the interests of other states without regard to the question whether the courts of one or more of these other states would do the same. . . . A principle of reciprocity is also sometimes employed in statutes to permit reciprocating states to obtain by cooperative efforts what a single state could not obtain through the force of its own law. See, e.g., Uniform Reciprocal Enforcement of Support Act. . . .

PROBLEM 2-41: SHOULD THE RESTATEMENT (SECOND) §6 CONTAIN A "BETTER LAW" PROVISION?

Assume that you have been called upon to express an opinion about whether the American Law Institute should amend §6 so that it includes language inviting courts to consider the better rule of law. Assume further that you are generally uncomfortable with the idea of courts expressing and acting on their subjective preferences about which legal principles they think are best. You find this practice particularly inappropriate where a forum court is asked to evaluate whether its own law is better than that of a sister state. On the other hand, in researching this question, you have come across a compelling article by Professor Louise Weinberg: *Methodological Interventions and the Slavery Cases: Or, Night-Thoughts of a Legal Realist*, 56 MD. L. REV. 1319 (1997). Professor Weinberg points out that the history of United States slave cases—concerning return of run-away slaves and other issues related to the lawfulness of slavery—suggest that one would be mistaken in suggesting that courts can decide choice of law cases simply on the basis of mechanical concepts such as whether a forum state has an interest in applying its law. If that were the only type of concern that matters, a court would often be controlled by the principle that the slave state has an "interest" in having its enslavement laws govern. Drawing on clashes between slave states and free states, Professor Weinberg argues that the Restatement (Second) should account for and give "pride of place" to the "the requirements of justice in the individual case." *Id.* at 1366. Does this persuade you to recommend amending §6?

2. Torts → contacts determinative

As with the other substantive categories, the Restatement (Second) of Conflict of Laws provides two levels of specificity for torts cases. First, is a general provision, §145, laying out the general approach for torts and listing the contacts that are likely to be determinative in a torts case. Then, more specific rules point to a presumptive jurisdiction. Some of these rules, illustrated below in the sections pertaining to defamation, actually name the presumptive jurisdiction for a specifically identified tort.

From the Restatement (Second) of Conflicts of Law, on the Subject of Wrongs:

§145. The General Principle

(1) The rights and liabilities of the parties with respect to an issue in tort are determined by the local law of the state which, with respect to that issue, has the most significant relationship to the occurrence and the parties under the principles stated in §6.

(2) Contacts to be taken into account in applying the principles of §6 to determine the law applicable to an issue include:

(a) the place where the injury occurred,

(b) the place where the conduct causing the injury occurred,

(c) the domicil, residence, nationality, place of incorporation and place of business of the parties, and

(d) the place where the relationship, if any, between the parties is centered.

These contacts are to be evaluated according to their relative importance with respect to the particular issue.

§146. Personal Injuries

In an action for a personal injury, the local law of the state where the injury occurred determines the rights and liabilities of the parties, unless, with respect to the particular issue, some other state has a more significant relationship under the principles stated in section 6 to the occurrence and the parties, in which event the local law of the other state will be applied.

§149. Defamation

In an action for defamation, the local law of the state where the publication occurs determines the rights and liabilities of the parties, except as stated in §150, unless, with respect to the particular issue, some other state has a more significant relationship under the principles stated in §6 to the occurrence and the parties, in which event the local law of the other state will be applied.

§150. Multistate Defamation

(1) The rights and liabilities that arise from defamatory matter in any one edition of a book or newspaper, or any one broadcast over radio or television, exhibition of a motion picture, or similar aggregate communication are determined by the local law of the state which, with respect to the particular issue, has the most significant relationship to the occurrence and the parties under the principles stated in §6.

(2) When a natural person claims that he has been defamed by an aggregate communication, the state of most significant relationship will usually be the state where the person was domiciled at the time, if the matter complained of was published in that state.

(3) When a corporation, or other legal person, claims that it has been defamed by an aggregate communication, the state of most significant relationship

will usually be the state where the corporation, or other legal person, had its principal place of business at the time, if the matter complained of was published in that state.

Townsend v. Sears, Roebuck and Company
879 N.E.2d 893 (Ill. 2007)

Justice FREEMAN delivered the judgment of the court, with opinion.

Plaintiffs, Michelle Townsend, individually and on behalf of her minor son, Jacob, brought a personal injury action in the circuit court of Cook County against defendant, Sears, Roebuck and Company (Sears). A question arose as to whether Illinois or Michigan law would govern the liability and damages issues presented in the case. The circuit court ruled that Illinois law governs these substantive issues, but certified the following question of law. . . .

Whether Illinois or Michigan law applies to a products liability and negligence action where the plaintiff is a resident of Michigan and the injury occurs in Michigan, the product was manufactured in South Carolina, the defendant is a New York corporation domiciled in Illinois, and the conduct complained of, including certain design decisions, investigations of prior similar occurrences, product testing and the decision to distribute nationally in its retail stores occurred in Illinois[.]

In its answer, the appellate court reached the same conclusion as did the circuit court. . . . We disagree with the appellate and circuit courts, and hold that Michigan law governs the liability and damages issues presented in this case.

I. BACKGROUND

[The court summarized the facts of the case, explaining that James Townsend put the tractor purchased at Sears in reverse to avoid an obstacle and accidently ran over his 3½-year-old son Jacob. The accident resulted in the amputation of Jacob's right foot and severe injury to his lower right leg. His wife Michelle, individually and on behalf of Jacob, filed a complaint against Sears pleading strict product liability and negligence, premised on defective design and failure to warn.] [The complaint] alleged that Sears "designed, marketed, manufactured, inspected, tested, and sold a Sears Craftsman Lawn Tractor"; that the tractor "was defectively designed, defectively marketed and unreasonably dangerous"; and that the design created such a risk of injury to small children that a reasonably prudent designer and marketer of riding lawn tractors, being fully aware of the risk, would not have put the lawn tractor on the market. Plaintiffs specifically alleged that the tractor lacked a "no-mow-in-reverse" (NMIR) safety feature to prevent back-over injuries. Plaintiff further alleged that Sears had actual knowledge of this specific unreasonably dangerous condition.

[The trial court used the Restatement (Second) of Conflict of Laws to conclude that Illinois law should govern. The appellate court agreed Illinois has a superior interest in having its policies applied.]

Subject to constitutional limitations, the forum court applies the choice-of-law rules of its own state. . . . In the present case, the parties agree that three conflicts exist between Illinois and Michigan law. The first conflict involves liability. Illinois has adopted a rule of strict liability in tort for product design defects. In contrast, Michigan has refused to adopt the doctrine of strict liability, instead imposing a pure negligence standard for product liability actions based on defective design. The difference between the two theories lies in the concept of fault. A real conflict exists because, in a strict liability action, the inability of the defendant to know or prevent the risk is not a defense. However, such a finding would preclude a finding of negligence because the standard of care is established by other manufacturers in the industry.

The second conflict concerns compensatory damages. Illinois currently does not have a statutory cap on compensatory damages for noneconomic injuries. In contrast, Michigan currently imposes caps on noneconomic damages in product liability actions. The third conflict concerns punitive damages. Illinois does not prohibit the recovery of punitive damages in product liability cases when appropriate. Subject to specific statutory exceptions, "it is well established that generally only compensatory damages are available in Michigan and that punitive damages may not be imposed."

C. OVERVIEW: THE SECOND RESTATEMENT OF CONFLICT OF LAWS

. . . [The] multiple and diverse principles [§6 of the Restatement Second] are not listed in any order of priority, and some of them point in different directions. Thus, in tort cases, for example, these principles, by themselves, do not enable courts to formulate precise choice-of-law rules. "In some ways, §6 was a logical response to the perceived flaws of the traditional rules. Critics had identified a variety of concerns that these rules failed to take into account, and §6 offers a kind of 'laundry list' response that enables the court to consider all of them when appropriate." R. Crampton, D. Currie & H. Kay, Conflict of Laws: Cases — Comments — Questions, at 117 (5th ed. 1993).

Another fundamental concept of the Second Restatement's methodology is the concept of the "most significant relationship." "While section 6 enunciates the guiding principles of the choice-of-law process, the most-significant-relationship formula describes the *objective* of that process: to apply the law of the state that, with regard to the particular issue, has the most significant relationship with the parties and the dispute." Scoles, Conflict of Laws §2.14, at 61. Lastly, the Second Restatement provides a list of the factual contacts or connecting factors that the forum court should consider in choosing the applicable law [such as those listed for a tort case in §145(2)]. . . .

In applying the principles of section 6 to these contacts to determine the state with the most significant relationship, the forum court should consider the relevant policies of all potentially interested states and the relevant interests of those states in the decision of the particular issue. Restatement (Second) of Conflict of

Laws §145, Comment *e*, at 419 (1971). "Thus, section 145 is no more definite than section 6, and perhaps even less so. On top of the 'factors' listed in section 6, section 145 adds a generous dollop of territorial and personal contacts." Patrick Borchers, *Courts and the Second Conflicts Restatement: Some Observations and an Empirical Note*, 56 Md. L. Rev. 1232, 1239 (1997).

Also, section 145 explicitly refers to a selective, issue-oriented approach to determining choice-of-law for a particular issue presented in a tort case. . . . By prescribing this analytical approach, the Second Restatement authorizes the process of *dépeçage*, which refers to the process of cutting up a case into individual issues, each subject to a separate choice-of-law analysis. Thus, the choice-of-law principles outlined in section 6 are effectively applied only to the facts of an individual case.

D. PRESUMPTION: THE LAW OF THE STATE WHERE THE INJURY OCCURRED

The parties disagree as to the nature and effect of a choice-of-law presumptive rule applicable in this case. The Second Restatement of Conflict of Laws does not abandon rules entirely. "Separate rules are stated for different torts and for different issues in tort. In other words, the identity of the state of the most significant relationship is said to depend upon the nature of the tort and upon the particular issue." Restatement (Second) of Conflict of Laws, ch. 7, Topic 1, Introductory Note 2, at 413 (1971). . . . The Second Restatement's introduction is an understatement.

> "Once one ventures past section 145, however, the chapter dramatically changes character. Instead of infinitely open-ended sections, the Second Restatement, for the most part, articulates reasonably definite rules. To be sure, these succeeding sections contain escape valves that refer to section 6. Many of the rules echo the First Restatement's preference for choosing the law of the injury state. Others do not refer to the injury state directly, but choose connecting factors very likely, if not certain, to lead to the application of the law of the injury state. . . . Only a relatively few sections refer solely to the general formula of section 145 without providing some presumptive choice." 56 Md. L. Rev. at 1239-40.

Thus, the Second Restatement of Conflict of Laws has been described as "schizophrenic," in that one portion of its split personality consists of general sections such as sections 6 and 145, while the other portion is a set of reasonably definite rules and a preference for territorial solutions, including the injury-state rule for tort cases, endorsed by its predecessor. The general sections embody a free-form approach to choice of law, while the specific sections are quite close to the territorial system embodied by the First Restatement. 56 Md. L. Rev. at 1240.

We agree with the concern that the bench and bar have overemphasized the general sections of the Second Restatement of Conflict of Laws and have undervalued the specific presumptive rules.

> "The opponents of mechanical rules of conflict of laws may have given too little weight to the virtues of simplicity. The new, flexible standards, such as 'interest

analysis,' have caused pervasive uncertainty, higher cost of litigation, more forum shopping (a court has a natural inclination to apply the law it is most familiar with—the forum's law—and will find it easier to go with this inclination if the conflict of law rules are uncertain), and an uncritical drift in favor of plaintiffs." *Kaczmarek*, 836 F.2d at 1057 (*dictum*).

For example, plaintiffs, in support of the appellate court's judgment, actually contend that this court has never expressly authorized use of legal presumptions in choice-of-law determinations in personal injury actions. . . . Alternatively, according to plaintiffs: "Even if this court meant to utilize a legal presumption in favor of the state of injury, presumptions in Illinois are governed by the 'bursting bubble hypothesis.'" Therefore, according to plaintiffs, if the presumption exists, it is "evanescent" and "easily overcome" by any contact with another state.

We emphatically reject this contention. In *Ingersoll v. Klein*, adopting the proposed draft of what would become section 145 of the Second Restatement of Conflict of Laws, this court held that "the local law of the State where the injury occurred should determine the rights and liabilities of the parties, unless Illinois has a *more* significant relationship with the occurrence and with the parties." (Emphasis added.) *Ingersoll v. Klein*, 46 Ill. 2d 42, 45 (1970). Thus, a presumption exists, which may be overcome only by showing a *more* or *greater* significant relationship to another state. Further, subsequent to *Ingersoll*, this court has repeatedly declared that we have adopted the choice-of-law analysis of the Second Restatement of Conflict of Laws. As we have explained, this analysis includes the application of presumptive rules.

"Generally speaking, then, the Second Restatement contemplates a two-step **TEST!** process in which the court (1) chooses a presumptively applicable law under the appropriate jurisdiction-selecting rule, and (2) tests this choice against the principles of §6 in light of relevant contacts identified by general provisions like §145 (torts) and §188 (contracts)." Crampton, Conflict of Laws: Cases—Comments—Questions, at 120. "[M]aking a serious effort to consider the entire Second Restatement would improve the quality of judicial decisionmaking. Courts that are willing to follow the narrow rules of the Second Restatement would derive vastly more guidance than that which can be gleaned from sections 6, 145 [torts], and 188 [contracts]." 56 Md. L. Rev. at 1247.

In this personal injury action, the appellate court was correct to cite section 146 of the Second Restatement of Conflict of Laws in holding that, "under Illinois choice-of-law rules, the law of the place of injury controls unless another state has a more significant relationship with the occurrence and with the parties with respect to the particular issue." . . . Section 146 received insufficient consideration in the appellate court.

One court has explained this presumption as follows:

"Often, however, the simple old rules can be glimpsed through modernity's fog, though spectrally thinned to presumptions—in the latest lingo, "default rules." For in the absence of unusual circumstances, the highest scorer on the "most significant relationship" test is—the place where the tort occurred. . . . For that is the place that has the greatest interest in striking a reasonable balance among safety, cost, and other factors pertinent to the design and administration of a system of tort law. Most people affected whether as victims or as injurers by accidents and other injury-causing events are residents of the jurisdiction in which the event takes place. So if law can be assumed to be generally responsive to the values and preferences of the people who live in the community that formulated the law, the law of the place of the accident can be expected to reflect the values and preferences of the people most likely to be involved in accidents — can be expected, in other words, to be responsive and responsible law, law that internalizes the costs and benefits of the people affected by it." *Spinozzi*, 174 F.3d at 844-45.

We now apply section 146 to the record before us.

Plaintiffs are domiciled and reside in Michigan, and James works in Michigan. Plaintiffs allege that Sears' tortious conduct occurred in Illinois. Comment *e* of section 146, entitled "When conduct and injury occur in different states," addresses this specific situation. "The local law of the state where the personal injury occurred is most likely to be applied when the injured person has a settled relationship to that state, either because he is domiciled or resides there or because he does business there." Restatement (Second) of Conflict of Laws §146, Comment *e*, at 432 (1971). In contrast:

> "The state where the *conduct* occurred is even more likely to be the state of most significant relationship . . . when, in addition to the injured person's being domiciled or residing or doing business in the state, the injury occurred in the course of an activity or of a relationship which was centered there." (Emphasis added.) Restatement (Second) of Conflict of Laws §146, Comment *e*, at 432 (1971).

If this guidance were not enough, the comments to section 146 further advise: "The likelihood that some state other than that where the injury occurred is the state of most significant relationship is greater in those *relatively rare* situations where, with respect to the particular issue, the state of injury bears little relation to the occurrence and the parties." (Emphasis added.) Restatement (Second) of Conflict of Laws §146, Comment *c*, at 430-31 (1971).

In this case, Jacob was injured while James was operating the tractor mower in the front yard of their home in Michigan. This activity was centered in plaintiffs' Michigan community. Based on the record before us, a *strong* presumption exists that the law of the place of injury, Michigan, governs the substantive issues herein, unless plaintiffs can demonstrate that Michigan bears little relation to the occurrence and the parties, or put another way, that Illinois has a more significant relationship to the occurrence and the parties with respect to a particular issue.

E. ANOTHER STATE WITH A MORE SIGNIFICANT RELATIONSHIP

We now test this presumptive choice against the principles of section 6 in light of the contacts identified in section 145(2). At the outset, we observe that courts describe this analysis differently. This court has essentially first identified the four contacts listed in section 145(2) and then applied the general principles of section 6 to those contacts. Other courts have similarly described this analysis.

However, beginning in 1981, our appellate court has construed sections 6 and 145 of the Second Restatement of Conflict of Laws together to describe a three-step process for determining whether a particular contact is significant for choice-of-law purposes: (1) isolate the issue and define the conflict; (2) identify the policies embraced in the conflicting laws; and (3) examine the contacts of the respective states to determine which has a superior connection with the occurrence and thus would have a superior interest in having its policy or law applied. This description, essentially first identifying the relevant section 6 general principles and then applying the four section 145(2) contacts to the general principles, likewise accords with decisions from other courts.

. . . Our section 145 analysis confirms our presumptive choice of Michigan law as governing the substantive issues in the present case. In any event, we agree with Sears that, from a practical standpoint in most cases, it should not make a difference whether a court first looks to the section 145(2) contacts or to the section 6 general principles. In either case the Second Restatement's goal is the same — to ensure that a court is not merely "counting contacts," and that each contact is meaningful in light of the policies sought to be vindicated by the conflicting laws.

We now consider the section 145 contacts presented in this case. First, the injury occurred in Michigan. . . . In the context of a most-significant-relationship analysis, section 145 cautions that situations exist where the place of the injury will not be an important contact, for example, where the place of the injury is fortuitous. In this case, however, Michigan has a strong relationship to the occurrence and the parties. Michigan is the place where James purchased the lawn tractor, the place where he used the lawn tractor, and the place where he and the named plaintiffs, his wife Michelle and his son Jacob, are domiciled and reside.

The second contact in section 145 is the place where the conduct causing the injury occurred. According to plaintiffs' theories of the case, Sears committed the allegedly culpable acts in Illinois. The appellate court excluded from its analysis James' alleged conduct contributing to the injury, reasoning that he was not a party. 368 Ill. App. 3d at 909-10. However, Sears pled affirmative defenses alleging contributory negligence on the part of James *and Michelle*. A court's consideration of injury-causing conduct in a section 145 analysis includes all conduct from any source contributing to the injury. We view this contact as a wash.

The third contact is the domicile, residence, place of incorporation, and place of business of the parties. Here, plaintiffs reside in Michigan and Sears is headquartered in Illinois. We view this contact as a wash. The fourth contact is the place where the relationship, if any, between the parties is centered. In this case, the relationship between plaintiffs and Sears arose from James' purchase of the lawn tractor at a local Sears store doing business in Michigan.

In sum, the first contact favors Michigan; we consider the second and third contacts each a wash; and the fourth contact favors Michigan. Considered alone, these contacts certainly do not override our presumption that Michigan law governs the substantive issues presented in this case. However, we must not merely "count contacts" but, rather, consider them in light of the general principles embodied in section 6.

A detailed analysis of all seven of the section 6 general principles is unnecessary. The commentary to section 145 explains that, in a personal injury action, section 6(2)(d), the protection of justified expectations, and section 6(2)(f), certainty, predictability, and uniformity of result, are implicated only minimally in a personal injury action arising from an accident. Restatement (Second) of Conflict of Laws §145, Comment *b*, at 415-16 (1971). Similarly, section 6(2)(a), the needs of the interstate system, is only minimally implicated in personal injury actions. It cannot be said that harmonious relations between states will be advanced by applying either Michigan or Illinois law. Further, section 6(2)(g), the ease in the determination and application of the law to be applied, yields no discernible advantage to Illinois law over Michigan law in this case.

Thus, we are left to consider the following general principles embodied in section 6(2) with respect to each of the three identified conflicts: (b) the relevant policies of the forum; (c) the relevant policies of other interested states and the relative interests of those states in the determination of the particular issue; and (e) the basic policies underlying the particular field of law. In our analysis, we are mindful:

> "States do refuse to enforce foreign law that is particularly obnoxious to them. . . . But obviously the mere fact that foreign and domestic law differ on some point is not enough to invoke the exception. Otherwise in every case of an actual conflict the court of the forum state would choose its own law; there would be no law of conflict of laws." *Spinozzi*, 174 F.3d at 846-47.

Considering the policies and interests of Michigan and Illinois, and of the field of tort law, we are unable to conclude that Illinois' relationship to this case is so pivotal as to overcome the presumption that Michigan, as the state where the injury occurred, is the state with the most significant relationship.

1. Liability

The first conflict is between Illinois' strict liability standard and Michigan's negligence standard for product liability actions based on defective design. The appellate court characterized the underlying policy of Illinois' law as essentially pro-consumer and pro-corporate regulation, and characterized the underlying policy of Michigan's law as essentially producer protective. The appellate court concluded: "Illinois has a strong interest in applying its products liability law to regulate culpable conduct occurring within its borders, induce the design of safer products, and deter future misconduct." 368 Ill. App. 3d at 910. Reasonable minds may disagree as to the accuracy of the appellate court's characterization of the underlying policy of Michigan's negligence standard — the Supreme Court of Michigan might. In adopting a negligence standard for product liability actions based on defective design, that court viewed a negligence standard as being pro-consumer. First, a negligence standard would reward the careful manufacturer and punish the careless manufacturer. A fault system would produce a greater incentive to design safer products, where the careful and safe design will be rewarded with fewer claims and lower insurance premiums. Second, a verdict for a plaintiff in a design defect case is the equivalent of a determination that an entire product line is defective. *Prentis*, 421 Mich. at 689-90, 365 N.W.2d at 185. . . . "Every state has an interest in compensating its domiciliaries for their injuries. But tort rules which limit liability are entitled to the same consideration when determining choice-of-law issues as rules that impose liability." *Malena*, 264 Neb. at 769, 651 N.W.2d at 858. We trust that characterizations such as "pro-consumer" or "pro-business" will not often appear in future choice-of-law cases.

2. *Compensatory Damages for Noneconomic Injuries*   MI : √$ cap

The next conflict is between the absence of a statutory cap on compensatory damages for noneconomic injuries in Illinois, and the existence of such a cap in Michigan. The appellate court, observing that this court declared a statutory cap unconstitutional in *Best*, 179 Ill. 2d at 384-416, reasoned as follows:

> "We recognize that plaintiffs, as Michigan residents, are not subject to Illinois's constitutional protections and, therefore, Illinois would have little or no interest in protecting plaintiffs from caps on noneconomic damages. Nevertheless, we must also consider that Illinois, as the forum state where the case will be tried, has a very strong interest in its constitutional protection of separation of powers within its borders and, therefore, has a strong interest in protecting against another state's legislative encroachment on the inherent power of its judiciary to determine whether a jury verdict is excessive. Thus, Illinois has a compelling public policy interest in applying Illinois law with respect to caps on noneconomic damages." 368 Ill. App. 3d at 912.

We cannot accept this reasoning. We agree with Sears that enforcement by an Illinois court of the Michigan cap on noneconomic damages does not constitute an encroachment of separation of powers in Illinois. Rather, such enforcement simply applies a Michigan statute against a Michigan resident that has been upheld as constitutional in Michigan.

3. *Punitive Damages*   MI : q pun $ (presumps)

The last conflict is between the availability of punitive damages in product liability cases when appropriate, in Illinois, and the general unavailability of punitive damages in Michigan. The appellate court observed that the purposes of punitive damages are to punish the defendant and deter future wrongdoing. Based on this unremarkable premise, the appellate court again posited that punitive damages reflect "a corporate regulatory policy," while the disallowance of punitive damages "reflects a corporate protection policy." 368 Ill. App. 3d at 911. The appellate court then determined that "Illinois, where the alleged design defects and corporate knowledge of previous accidents occurred, has a definite interest in punishment, deterrence of future wrongdoing, and corporate accountability." The appellate court concluded:

"Michigan, the place of plaintiffs' residence and the place of injury, has an interest in assuring that plaintiffs are compensated for their injuries. Nevertheless, where the purpose of disallowing punitive damages is not related to redressing the plaintiffs' injury, once the plaintiffs are made whole by recovery of the compensatory damages to which they are entitled, the interests of Michigan law are satisfied. Accordingly, Illinois, as Sears' principal place of business and the place where the alleged corporate misconduct occurred, has the most significant relationship to the issue of punitive damages." 368 Ill. App. 3d at 911.

We disagree.

Again, the purpose of the section 145 analysis is to test our strong presumption that the law of Michigan, where plaintiffs reside and the place of injury, should govern the substantive issues in this case. The appellate court characterization that Michigan "has an interest" in this conflict is an understatement that fails to recognize the strong presumption in favor of applying Michigan law.

Also, although the appellate court cited to comments *c* and *e* of section 146, the court misapprehended their *full* meaning. Certainly, comment *c* instructs: "The extent of the interest of each of the potentially interested states should be determined on the basis, among other things, of the purpose sought to be achieved by their relevant local law rules and of the particular issue." Restatement (Second) of Conflict of Laws §146, Comment *c*, at 430 (1971). However, the comment continues on the same page to advise: "The likelihood that some state other than that where the injury occurred is the state of most significant relationship is greater in those *relatively rare* situations where, with respect to the particular issue, the state of injury bears little relation to the occurrence and the parties." (Emphasis added.) Restatement (Second) of Conflict of Laws §146, Comment *c*, at 430-31 (1971).

Likewise, the passage in comment *e*, to which the appellate court cited, actually states in full:

"[A]n important factor in determining which is the state of most significant relationship is the purpose sought to be achieved by the rule of tort law involved. If this purpose is to punish the tortfeasor and thus to deter others from following his example, there is better reason to say that the state where the conduct occurred is the state of dominant interest and that its local law should control than if the tort rule is designed primarily to compensate the victim for his injuries. . . . In the latter situation, the state where the injury occurred would seem to have a greater interest than the state of conduct. *This factor must not be over-emphasized.* To some extent, at least, *every* tort rule is designed *both* to deter other wrongdoers *and* to compensate the injured person. Undoubtedly, the relative weight of these two objectives varies somewhat from rule to rule, but in the case of a given rule it will frequently be difficult to determine which of these objectives is the more important." (Emphases added.) Restatement (Second) of Conflict of Laws §146, Comment *e*, at 432-33 (1971).

Despite this explicit caution, the appellate court not only undervalued the strong presumption in favor of Michigan law, but overemphasized its perception of the interests Illinois and Michigan have in their different concepts of tort damages.

Illinois certainly has a legitimate interest in the liability to be imposed on Illinois-based defendants under strict liability or negligence principles. However, Michigan has an equally legitimate interest in the remedies to be afforded its residents who suffer such tort injuries. And if the substantive law of these two states looks in different directions, each state would seem to have an equal interest in having its tort rule applied in the determination of the conflicting issues presented in this case. We conclude that a section 145 analysis does not override our strong presumption that the law of Michigan, as the state where plaintiffs reside and where the injury occurred, governs the conflicting issues presented in this case.

In sum, a court begins a choice-of-law analysis in a tort case by ascertaining whether a specific presumptive rule, such as section 146 in a personal injury action, applies to the disputed conflict. Next, if the presumptive rule points to a specific jurisdiction, then the court must test this presumptive choice against the principles embodied in section 6 in light of the relevant contacts identified by the general tort principle in section 145. The presumptive choice controls unless overridden by the section 145 analysis.

III. Conclusion

For the foregoing reasons, the judgment of the appellate court and the order of the circuit court of Cook County are vacated, and this cause is remanded to the circuit court for further proceedings consistent with this opinion.

Notes on

TOWNSEND v. SEARS

1. Compare the court's analysis in *Townsend v. Sears* with *Rowe v. Hoffman-Roche, Inc.*, which appears in the Governmental Interest section of this chapter. Both were products liability cases decided in the same year; both contained a configuration of facts common in products liability conflicts cases: plaintiffs bought and used a product in their home state and were subsequently injured by the product there. You'll recall that in *Rowe*, the New Jersey court chose not to apply its states' pro-plaintiff product liability law to an out-of-state plaintiff. *Townsend* reached an essentially similar result. Did the choice of law approaches followed in the two cases make a difference in the result reached? Or were the results preordained?

The result in *Rowe* and *Townsend* is quite common in products liability cases. Even cases that have used a wide variety of choice of law approaches and have resisted arguments that forum law should be applied to the exclusion of defendant-friendly non-forum law. *See, e.g., Heindel v. Pfizer, Inc.*, 381

F. Supp. 2d 364 (D.N.J. 2004); *Henderson v. Merck & Co.*, 2005 WL 2600220 (E.D. Pa. Oct. 11, 2005); *Devore v. Pfizer Inc.*, 867 N.Y.S.2d 425 (N.Y. App. Div 2008); *Cowley v. Abbott Lab. Inc.*, 476 F. Supp. 2d 1053 (W.D. Wis. 2007). The constant factors in all these cases were the following: the court applied the law of the jurisdiction where the plaintiff was domiciled, used the product, and got injured. Does this suggest that the place-of-injury presumption championed by the *Townsend* court reflects a shared intuition or sense of justice about what law should govern? If so, isn't that similar to the idea of a "vested right"? To the extent that other courts follow *Townsend*'s advocacy for presumptive rules, one wonders whether the Restatement (Second) approach will largely mirror the Restatement (First).

2. The *Townsend* court had harsh words for the lower court's characterization of the laws at issue as "pro-consumer" or "pro-business." The *Townsend* court's tone suggests that it was reacting negatively to the particular characterizations chosen, rather than to the general practice of characterization — which the Restatement (Second) retains by its use of subject matter categories for the choice of law rules. But the *Townsend* court's reaction may disclose important mischief that characterization often achieves: the process requires reducing a law or concept to its essentials in order to place the law in a legal category. But so much of life and law is so complicated (and often so filled with contradictions) that this "essentializing" can be misleading or downright wrong.

What did the *Townsend* court find so inaccurate about the "pro-business" and "pro-consumer" characterizations? Can a rule that provides for less liability in a products liability case ever be "pro-consumer"?

3. The *Townsend* court purported to engage in the process of dépeçage, a form of analysis discussed in greater detail in the Note immediately below. Arguably, the court did not engage in classic or complete dépeçage, since the bulk of its choice of law analysis approached the case as a whole. The court's separate discussion focused primarily on criticizing what the lower court had done. Shouldn't the *Townsend* court have analyzed separately the two state's punitive damages rules? For punitive damage issues, isn't the relative interest of states different than in liability rules? If punitive damages have primarily a deterrent purpose, which state has the greater claim for regulation: the state where the product was designed or the state where the product was sold?

4. Law and economics theorists have devoted considerable attention to identifying the incentives that choice of law decisions such as *Townsend* send to manufacturers of consumer products and to analyzing the interplay between such decisions and state products liability laws. Frequently, analysis starts with the proposition that each state has an interest in adopting pro-plaintiff substantive laws to provide protection to its resident consumers. However, each state also has an interest in attracting new businesses and industries, which prefer reduced liability levels through more pro-defendant

laws. Accordingly, states also have an incentive to lower their liability levels to attract more businesses that do not wish to internalize increased liability costs. State products liability laws usually represent a compromise between these opposing incentives. How does a decision like *Townsend* affect this process? Did the court in *Townsend* effectively honor this balance of incentives in deciding to apply the law where the plaintiff resided as well as purchased and used the product? Or is the *Townsend* court's decision disruptive of the balance? These — and related matters — are covered in the Perspective on the Race to the Bottom and Coordinated Choice of Law Rules, which appears later in this chapter in connection with discussion of the wisdom of having a federal choice of law code.

PERSPECTIVE ON DÉPEÇAGE

As you may have observed occasionally throughout this chapter, choice of law analysis can proceed by legal issue rather than by case, claim, or cause of action. The French word used to describe this analytical structure is "dépeçage," meaning "cutting up, dismembering, carving up." *Kelly v. Ford Motor Co.*, 942 F. Supp. 1044, 1045 n.2 (E.D. Pa. 1996). Courts that engage in dépeçage split a case into individual issues and sometimes apply laws from different jurisdictions to different aspects of a single case.

Courts only occasionally invoked dépeçage under the traditional First Restatement approach to choice of law, choosing instead to focus on identifying the overarching character of a lawsuit. A notable exception is *Haumschild v. Continental Casualty Company*, 95 N.W.2d 814 (Wis. 1959), in which the court analyzed liability questions according to the law of the place of the accident and an interspousal immunity question according to the law of the marital domicile. In other instances, courts applying the First Restatement also splice the legal issues within a particular subject matter category, so that, for example, a court might determine that the law where a contract was made governs an issue related to validity and the law where the contract was to be performed governs adequacy of performance. The process of characterizing one issue in a case as procedural and another as substantive also presents an opportunity for dépeçage under the First Restatement.

Courts began to use dépeçage in earnest, however, under modern approaches, which are more sensitive to variations in what different laws are trying to achieve. Dépeçage accounts for the reality that a state can have an interest in its law governing one legal issue in a case, but not other legal issues in the case. Moreover, using dépeçage, a court can calibrate analysis to differentials in various state concerns that may vary over legal issues within the case. This type of calibration is characteristic of modern, not traditional, approaches to choice of law.

One problem that dépeçage immediately presents is that legal issues are interdependent, do not exist in a vacuum, and do not always lend themselves to separate handling. Indeed, dépeçage can distort the effect of legal rules and can lead to unintended or inconsistent results. For example, a court could apply part of a Mexican law on wrongful death liability, but refuse to apply the part of the same statute requiring periodic payments for damages. Willis L. M. Reese, *Dépeçage: A Common Phenomenon in Choice of Law,* 73 COLUM. L. REV. 58, 65 (1973) (*citing Slater v. Mexican Nat'l R.R. Co.,* 194 U.S. 120 (1904)). Yet if the court followed the Texas practice of giving damages in a lump sum, the court would distort the Mexican law's approach to limiting damages. To account for this type of problem, some thinkers maintain that dépeçage is intended only to ensure faithfulness to the purposes of the rules applied, and courts should therefore limit the dépeçage to circumstances where the various rules' purposes are consistent with each other and will remain intact.

Supporters of a less restricted dépeçage analysis argue that the process of "issue splitting" has other goals than merely advancing the purposes of the rules. Dépeçage encourages courts to be sensitive to the factual context in which legal issues arise, inviting them to compare the effect of conflicting laws in light of case facts. Notably, the Restatement (Second) of Conflict of Laws specifically invites courts to use dépeçage not only through §6's reference to policies of the forum and other interested states, but also through other sections that direct courts to evaluate the relative significance of contacts "with respect to a particular issue." Restatement (Second) of Conflict of Laws §§145(2), 188(2).

Other critics point out additional consequences and negative implications if courts broadly apply dépeçage. First, the approach clearly complicates the choice of law analysis, multiplying the necessary reasoning, and sometimes creating results that appear to lack common sense. *See, e.g.,* Laura E. Little, *Hairsplitting and Complexity in Conflict of Laws: The Paradox of Formalism,* 37 U.C. DAVIS L. REV. 925, 934 (2004); *see also Simon v. United States,* 805 N.E.2d 798, 803-805 (Ind. 2004) (noting that Indiana does not allow dépeçage, choosing to avoid the complications it creates). In addition, a particular court's approach to splicing the various issues in a case is difficult to anticipate, thus making dépeçage problematic from the point of view of party expectations and general predictability in the law. In a related critique, Professor Christian Wilde argues that dépeçage poses the additional danger of appearing to be an independent creation of primary law rather than what it truly is: "choice of law." Christian L. Wilde, *Dépeçage in the Choice of Tort Law,* 41 S. CAL. L. REV. 329, 330 (1968). In applying laws from different jurisdictions to various issues, a court may reach a different result than if it applied the law of one jurisdiction to the entire case. While supporters of dépeçage believe this allows courts to be more flexible, Wilde argues that allowing a party to enjoy favorable results the party would not have received if a single jurisdiction's law applied permits the courts to "create" a law more favorable to a certain party. *Id.* Wilde's concerns uncover a final consequence of dépeçage: dépeçage analysis provides yet another tool for courts to engineer case outcomes. Rather than choosing the appropriate law by holistically evaluating the interests and stakes of the jurisdictions involved or the expectations of parties, a court can identify what it considers the "best law" to achieve a certain outcome and — without disclosing this discovery — use the reasoning of dépeçage to justify its result.

Despite criticism of dépeçage from the bench, bar, and academy, it remains a popular frame of analysis for modern choice of law problems. Courts in the United States continue to find dépeçage useful and appropriate — although other countries do not share the same enthusiasm.

P.V. v. Camp Jaycee
962 A.2d 453 (N.J. 2008)

Justice LONG delivered the opinion of the Court.

This choice-of-law case involves the question of whether New Jersey's charitable immunity statute, N.J.S.A. 2A:53A-7 to -11, applies to a tort committed in Pennsylvania. In 2003, a mentally disabled New Jersey resident was sexually abused at a summer camp located in Pennsylvania but operated by a New Jersey charity. Her parents sued the camp individually and on her behalf for negligent supervision at the campsite. The trial judge granted the camp's motion for summary judgment based on the doctrine of charitable immunity to which New Jersey adheres by statute. The Appellate Division reversed, declaring that Pennsylvania law governs the action because the commonwealth, which has abrogated charitable immunity and is the state in which the tortious conduct and injury occurred, has the greater governmental interest in the case. The camp filed a petition for certification that we granted.

Although we have traditionally denominated our conflicts approach as a flexible "governmental interest" analysis, we have continuously resorted to the Restatement (Second) of Conflict of Laws (1971) in resolving conflict disputes arising out of tort. That approach is the "most significant relationship" test. Under that standard, the analysis in a personal injury case begins with the section 146 presumption that the local law of the state of the injury will apply. Once the presumptively applicable law is identified, that choice is tested against the contacts detailed in section 145 and the general principles outlined in section 6 of the Second Restatement. If another state has a more significant relationship to the parties or issues, the presumption will be overcome. If not, it will govern.

Examining the facts of this case as they relate to the contacts and principles articulated in the Second Restatement, we conclude that Pennsylvania, the state in which the charity chose to operate and which is the locus of the tortious conduct and injury, has at least as significant a relationship to the issues as New Jersey, and that the presumptive choice of Pennsylvania law therefore has not been overcome.

I.

Over thirty years ago, New Jersey Camp Jaycee, Inc. (Camp Jaycee) was organized as a not-for-profit corporation to operate a summer program for mentally challenged individuals. Although Camp Jaycee was incorporated in New Jersey and maintains an administrative office here, it has chosen to carry out its primary charitable mission in the Commonwealth of Pennsylvania at a campsite in the town of Effort.

In 2003, one of Camp Jaycee's campers was P.V., a twenty-one-year-old female from New Jersey with Down syndrome and mental and emotional handicaps. P.V. had attended the camp for at least three consecutive summers. According to the complaint, in August 2003, P.V. was sexually assaulted by another camper, as a result of which she sustained injuries requiring medical treatment.

P.V.'s parents, T.V. and L.V., as guardians *ad litem* and individually, instituted a personal injury action in New Jersey against Camp Jaycee and several fictitious defendants. They alleged that Camp Jaycee and its agents, servants, and employees were careless and negligent in the supervision of P.V. "at the camp" in Pennsylvania. Camp Jaycee filed a motion to dismiss, asserting immunity from suit under the New Jersey Charitable Immunity Act (CIA). N.J.S.A. 2A:53A-7 to -11.

[The trial court held that the camp is immune from suit by a beneficiary, but the intermediate appellate court reversed, applying Pennsylvania's law abrogating charitable immunity.]

II.

Camp Jaycee argues that New Jersey has a transcendent interest in the application of its charitable immunity law because the camp was organized under the laws of New Jersey; both parties are domiciled in New Jersey; Pennsylvania has no interest in the post-event rights and liabilities of two New Jersey domiciliaries; Pennsylvania is merely "the happenstance of the situs of the accident" and no Pennsylvania citizen was injured.

P.V. counters that Pennsylvania, the state in which Camp Jaycee chose to operate; in which the tortious conduct and injury occurred; and in which the relationship of the parties was centered, has at least as great if not a greater interest than New Jersey in the resolution of this matter because of its concerns over conduct-regulation and redress to tort victims.

III.

. . . In 1967, we joined with other jurisdictions in abandoning the First Restatement approach to tort cases, embracing the modern governmental interest analysis. . . . Four years after our adoption of the governmental interest analysis, and seventeen years after the reform effort had been undertaken, the Second Restatement was finalized. To a great extent, it embraced the "reasoned elaboration" school of judicial analysis that requires a thorough explanation of every judicial decision, tied closely to the facts of the case, and an articulation of why the decision is just. . . .

As is evident, a pure governmental interest analysis is distinct from the Second Restatement approach. In the former, the strength of the countervailing governmental interests is dispositive. The latter does not focus solely on the state interests; instead, it directs courts to apply the law of the jurisdiction with "the most significant relationship" to the issue before the court. In making this determination, the court is required to consider all of the contacts that each jurisdiction has with the issue.

In other words, "rather than the Second Restatement being intended to provide a metric for determining the strength of state interests, the respective strength of the states' interests is a factor to be considered in measuring the significance of the contacts of the relevant states." *Id.* at 546.[4]

Following the promulgation of the Second Restatement, we again modified our analysis, using the Second Restatement frame-work as our methodology. . . . Although continuing to denominate our standard as a kind of governmental interest test, we now apply the Second Restatement's most significant relationship standard in tort cases. Under that standard, the law of the state of the injury is applicable unless another state has a more significant relationship to the parties and issues.

The Second Restatement assessment takes place on an issue-by-issue basis. It is qualitative, not quantitative. In other words, the inquiry does not focus solely on the number of contacts with each state, although that can be persuasive. We also look to the principles in section 6 to measure the significance of the contacts in order to determine whether the presumption has been overcome. Viewed through the section 6 prism, the state with the strongest section 145 contacts will have the most significant relationship to the parties or issues, and thus its law will be applied.

IV. *Actual Conflict*

Procedurally, the first step is to determine whether an actual conflict exists. That is done by examining the substance of the potentially applicable laws to determine whether "'there is a distinction'" between them. . . . Here, it is clear, as the parties have conceded, that an actual conflict exists between the laws of Pennsylvania and New Jersey. By enacting the CIA, the New Jersey Legislature has carved charitable corporations out of its tort law system and declared them to be free from most tort liability. That statute provides:

---

4. Our dissenting colleagues lament the loss of the "more nuanced" governmental interest approach. Post at 157-58, 962 A.2d at 468-69. The question is, more nuanced than what? It is certainly fair to suggest that the governmental interest analysis is more nuanced than its predecessor, the bright line lex loci test. However, as the Second Restatement itself underscores, the most significant relationship test embodies all of the elements of the governmental interest test plus a series of other factors deemed worthy of consideration. Restatement, supra, §6(2)(b)-(c). As a matter of simple logic, the new end point — the most significant relationship test — is more and not less nuanced than its predecessor.

No nonprofit corporation, society or association organized exclusively for religious, charitable or educational purposes or its trustees, directors, officers, employees, agents, servants, or volunteers shall, except as is hereinafter set forth, be liable to respond in damages to any person who shall suffer damage from the negligence of any agent or servant of such corporation, society or association, where such person is a beneficiary, to whatever degree, of the works of such nonprofit corporation, society or association. . . .

[N.J.S.A. 2A:53A-7(a).]

Contrary to New Jersey's policy of immunization, Pennsylvania has definitively abrogated its charitable immunity laws and has chosen to subject charitable corporations to the same tort liability as all others. Essentially then, the conflicting laws of New Jersey and Pennsylvania are two sides of the same coin — basically comprehending polar opposite positions regarding immunity from tort liability. If New Jersey law applies, the case will be dismissed. If Pennsylvania law applies, it will proceed. Because there is an evident conflict, we turn to the Restatement analysis.

V.

Once a conflict is established, our point of departure is section 146, which, in this matter, presumes that Pennsylvania law (the local law of the state where the injury occurred) will govern the rights and liabilities of the parties. In that respect, Camp Jaycee makes a fundamental misstep in its analysis by misconceiving our turn away from the black letter law of *lex loci* as rendering the place of injury of little importance. Nothing could be further from the truth, as the presumption in section 146 underscores. Indeed, "the simple old rules can be glimpsed through modernity's fog, though spectrally thinned to presumptions."

Section 146 recognizes the intuitively correct principle that the state in which the injury occurs is likely to have the predominant, if not exclusive, relationship to the parties and issues in the litigation. Restatement, *supra*, §146 comment d. It is from that vantage point that we turn to the remaining contacts set forth in sections 145 and the cornerstone principles of section 6 to determine whether New Jersey has "a more significant relationship . . . [with] the occurrence and the parties" than Pennsylvania. Restatement, *supra*, §146. Only such a finding would overcome the presumptive rule of section 146.

VI.

Under section 145, the first contact is the place where the injury occurred — Pennsylvania. Although Camp Jaycee characterizes the place of injury as Pennsylvania's only contact with the case, nothing could be further from the truth. Indeed, the second section 145 contact is the place where the conduct causing the injury occurred — that also is Pennsylvania. Despite our dissenting colleagues' contrary suggestion, the only allegation of negligence in the complaint is negligent supervision *at the Pennsylvania campsite.* . . .

The place of the injury is fortuitous when "it bears little relation to the occurrence and the parties with respect to the particular issue." Restatement, *supra*, §145 comment e (citing Restatement, *supra*, §146 comments d-e). Here, the happening of the tortious conduct and injury in Pennsylvania was not a fortuity, as Camp Jaycee contends — Pennsylvania was the *only* location in which Camp Jaycee operated its camp for mentally disabled persons. It was a permanent fixture in that location. P.V. resided in Pennsylvania for at least three summers under the control of the camp. From that standpoint, Pennsylvania was not an unanticipated detour on the way to another location; it was the final destination. *why PA matters*

The third contact is "the domicil, residence, nationality, place of incorporation and place of business of the parties." Restatement, *supra*, §145(2)(c). To be sure, P.V. is a New Jersey domiciliary, and Camp Jaycee is a New Jersey not-for-profit corporation. However, P.V. chose to attend the camp in Pennsylvania. Moreover, as the Second Restatement underscores, the use of the term "domiciliary" when referring to corporations is imprecise. Courts should focus not only on an entity's place of incorporation but also on its principal place of business. *Ibid.* Indeed, in balancing those two epicenters, "[a]t least with respect to most issues, a corporation's principal place of business is a more important contact than the place of incorporation, and this is particularly true in situations where the corporation does little, or no, business in the latter place." *Ibid.*

In this case, Camp Jaycee was incorporated for the primary purpose of running a camp for mentally disabled children and adults. As far as this record reveals, Camp Jaycee has chosen to perform that function solely in Effort, Pennsylvania, and, although it does maintain an administrative office in New Jersey, the principal place of the business *for which it was incorporated* is Pennsylvania.

The final section 145 contact is the place where the relationship between the parties is centered. Even if P.V. signed on as a camper through Camp Jaycee's administrative office in New Jersey (and the record is silent on that issue), it is of little consequence because this is not a contracts case. Rather, it is a tort action and, from that perspective, there is no question that P.V.'s relationship with Camp Jaycee was centered on her camp experience in Effort, Pennsylvania.

In sum, on one side of the contacts ledger, P.V. and Camp Jaycee are co-domiciliaries of New Jersey. On the other side of the ledger, Camp Jaycee chose to perform the sole charitable function for which it was organized in Pennsylvania; P.V. chose to attend a camp in Pennsylvania; the relationship between P.V. and Camp Jaycee was centered on the camp experience in Pennsylvania; the tortious conduct (negligent supervision) took place solely in Pennsylvania; and P.V. was injured in Pennsylvania. *why PA wins!*

Standing alone, New Jersey's contacts are certainly no greater than those of Pennsylvania. However, because our analysis is not merely quantitative, we also look to the principles of section 6 to measure the significance of those contacts.

In other words, do the section 6 considerations gin up or diminish the values to be ascribed to the contacts relative to the issue presented?

VII.

Reduced to their essence, the section 6 principles are: "(1) the interests of interstate comity; (2) the interests of the parties; (3) the interests underlying the field of tort law; (4) the interests of judicial administration; and (5) the competing interests of the states." *Erny v. State of Merola*, 171 N.J. 86, 792 A.2d 1208 (1999).

A

The competing interests of the states and relevant tort law principles overlap in this case. Both Pennsylvania and New Jersey have established tort law systems intended to compensate tort victims and deter wrong-doing. However, from that scheme, New Jersey has carved out charitable corporations and declared them to be free from most tort liability. The Legislature has determined that the proper way to encourage charity in New Jersey and to guarantee continuance of the good works charities provide is to insure they will not have to expend their resources on litigation. "[T]he essence of the public policy favoring charitable immunity is the preservation of private charitable contributions for their designated purposes." *Bieker v. Cmty. House of Moorestown*, 169 N.J. 167, 178 (2001).

. . . New Jersey's public policy in enacting the CIA is "strong" and is to be "considered remedial and be liberally construed." Although there are exceptions to the immunity provided, those exceptions do not, in any measure, water down the importance of the policy to our state, and to the extent that the Appellate Division suggested otherwise, it was wide of the mark. In any event, our focus is not on the importance of the policy to the state but on the relationship between the policy and the contacts.

Pennsylvania, on the other hand, has explicitly rejected the policy of charitable immunity. It is the characterization of Pennsylvania's policy that is at issue in this case. Camp Jaycee denominates Pennsylvania's abrogation of charitable immunity as nothing more than a post-event loss-allocation construct, which it argues renders the conduct-related contacts in Pennsylvania essentially irrelevant. In framing the issue that way, Camp Jaycee suggests that Pennsylvania's interest will not be impaired if we apply New Jersey law to bar the suit of a New Jersey citizen.

It is not surprising that, in support of that view, Camp Jaycee has relied on the decision in *Schultz v. Boy Scouts of America, Inc.*, 65 N.Y.2d 189, 480 N.E.2d 679, 491 N.Y.S.2d 90 (1985). [In *Schultz*, the court applied New Jersey charitable immunity law to a suit concerning members of a New Jersey Boy Scout troop who were sexually abused by their scoutmaster on an outing in New York. We agree with the dissenting justice in that case.]

The proper characterization of Pennsylvania's policy is that it is a measure limned for the purpose of "prevent[ion], protect[ion] and compensat[ion]." *Id.* 491 N.Y.S.2d 90, 480 N.E.2d at 691. Indeed, when a state decides to abrogate its charitable immunity law, it typically does so with the intention of insuring due care: "[I]t both assures payment of an obligation to the person injured and gives warning that justice and the law demand the exercise of care." *Bing v. Thunig*, 2 N.Y.2d 656, 143 N.E.2d 3, 8, 163 N.Y.S.2d 3 (1957). In *Flagiello v. Pennsylvania Hospital*, 417 Pa. 486, 208 A.2d 193 (1965), the Pennsylvania Supreme Court used strong language to describe its conduct-regulating interest in abolishing charitable immunity:

> Human nature being what it is, administrators of a hospital, cognizant that the hospital is insulated from tort liability, may be less likely to exercise maximum scrutiny in selecting personnel than if the hospital were held monetarily liable for slipshod, indifferent, and neglectful conduct of employees.

Our dissenting colleagues' suggestion that the heart of *Flagiello* was the transformation of hospitals into "big business" and the protection of Pennsylvania residents says too little. *Post* at 173-74, 962 A.2d at 478-79. *Flagiello* devoted equal, if not more, attention to the notion that every wrong has a remedy and the paradoxical and unjust results generally produced by the charitable immunity doctrine. *Id.* at 195, 197, 203, 204-05.

Moreover, the Pennsylvania Supreme Court has since extended *Flagiello* to include torts occurring to non-paying patients in hospitals, and torts on property owned by religious organizations. . . . Additionally, in its ruling, the court in *Flagiello* never referred specifically to Pennsylvania residents but to patients generally. . . .

Essentially then, there are two conflicting policies at issue here—New Jersey's post-event loss-allocation policy and Pennsylvania's conduct-regulation and redress policy. The question is how those policies relate to the relevant contacts.

We conclude that, in the main, the policies are aligned with Pennsylvania's contacts. As we previously stated, the fact that the conduct and injury occurred in Pennsylvania was not fortuitous. Camp Jaycee has a continuous and deliberate presence in Pennsylvania. The camp is tasked with the responsibility of supervising and caring for mentally disabled campers for extended periods of time within the commonwealth. It is that perennial presence and activity in Pennsylvania that is inextricably intertwined with Pennsylvania's interest in conduct-regulation. If Pennsylvania's tort law is to have any deterrent impact and protect other campers from the type of harm inflicted upon P.V., it must be applied in situations where tort-feasors repeatedly perform their tasks within the state, regardless of the home state of the campers. Indeed, there is no way for a state to "make its territory safe for residents without making it safe for visitors too. If it is unsafe for visitors it is unsafe for residents." Louise Weinberg, *Against Comity*, 80 Geo. L.J. 53, 89 (1991).

Concededly, New Jersey's interest in protecting its charitable corporations is aligned with the parties' co-domiciliary status in this state. However, where, as here, the plaintiff chooses to attend camp and the corporation opts to perform its primary charitable acts outside the state, the strength of that contact is diluted. Indeed, immunity laws are designed to encourage persons to engage in the particular conduct within the state. Where defendant's conduct takes place in another state, the immunity goals are diminished. Restatement, *supra*, §146 comment e.

B

The interest of interstate comity seeks to "further harmonious relations between the states and to facilitate commercial intercourse between them." Restatement, *supra*, §6 comment d. It considers "whether application of a competing state's law would frustrate the policies of other interested states." Affording immunity for the negligence committed by Camp Jaycee in Pennsylvania would significantly frustrate Pennsylvania's purpose in deterring tortious conduct within the commonwealth. . . . Although we have departed from the rigid application of the *lexi loci* approach, we have continuously deferred to the rights of other jurisdictions to regulate conduct within their borders. That is particularly so when the conduct is ongoing and directed towards residents and non-residents alike.

New Jersey can continue to protect charities operating in this state even if the law of Pennsylvania is applied to the Pennsylvania activities in this case. The converse is not true. If New Jersey's immunity law is applied, Pennsylvania's ability to regulate the conduct of those who chose to operate within its borders will be substantially impaired.

C

In respect of the parties' expectations, Camp Jaycee argues that the parties' co-domiciliary status in New Jersey gave it a reasonable belief that it would be immune under the CIA and that P.V. should have been aware of that immunity. In other words, it organized in New Jersey so it would not have to respond in tort for its wrongful actions toward beneficiaries, and P.V. understood that protection. That view overlooks the reality of this case: Camp Jaycee operates its camp in Pennsylvania; P.V. chose to attend the camp in Pennsylvania; there is nothing in the camp's certificate of incorporation to suggest that it is limited to New Jersey residents; P.V. was sexually assaulted at the camp in Pennsylvania; and this lawsuit alleges carelessness and negligence *at the camp*. . . . Thus, although the parties legitimately might have expected that Camp Jaycee's activities *in New Jersey* were immune under the CIA, they should not have expected it to carry that immunity into another state.

D

The interests of judicial administration require courts to consider issues such as practicality and ease of application, factors that in turn further the values of uniformity and predictability. As the Second Restatement points out, the section 146 presumption in favor of the law of the state of the injury, in itself, "furthers the choice-of-law values of certainty, predictability and uniformity of result and, since the state where the injury occurred will usually be readily ascertainable, of ease in the determination and application of the applicable law." Restatement, *supra*, §146 comment c. Moreover, where, as here, the contacts and principles of the Second Restatement lead inexorably to the conclusion that a particular state's relationship to the parties and issues is predominant, judicial administration considerations necessarily yield.

VIII.

... On a purely quantitative level, Pennsylvania's contacts substantially outweigh those of New Jersey, suggesting that it is the state with the most significant relationship to the parties and issue. Nevertheless, we have looked to section 6 to determine whether more or less weight should be ascribed to those contacts, thus altering the balance and warranting an override of the section 146 presumption.

Our conclusion is that the presumption has not been overcome. Although both states have strong countervailing policies regarding immunity, Pennsylvania's policy of conduct-regulation and recompense is deeply intertwined with the various Pennsylvania contacts in the case. On the contrary, New Jersey's loss-allocation policy does not warrant the assignment of priority to the parties' domicile in New Jersey in connection with activities outside the state's borders. ... In short, neither the contacts themselves nor the section 6 considerations support the conclusion that New Jersey has a more significant relationship to the case than Pennsylvania. In fact, the converse is true. Although we recognize the vitality of our own policy of immunizing charities, in this case, it must yield to the presumption favoring application of Pennsylvania law, which has not been overcome.

IX.

The judgment of the Appellate Division is affirmed. The case is remanded to the trial judge for further proceedings consistent with the principles to which we have adverted.

Justice HOENS, dissenting.

gov't int vs. signif Rel?

Today, a majority of this Court has chosen to adopt a new framework for deciding conflict of law disputes. Although stating that there is nothing novel in its approach, and although supporting that assertion with citations to parts of this Court's prior opinions (both majorities and dissents) as proof that this Court has long used the analytical model embodied in the Restatement (Second) of Conflict of Laws (1971), in reality, the majority has substituted that test for our traditional one. At the same time, the majority has tossed aside our far more nuanced "governmental interest" approach, in which the factors identified by the Restatement (Second) were but an occasionally useful guide, and embraced in its place the Restatement (Second)'s "most-significant-relationship" test. ... In adopting a new test, and in applying a test that provides a mechanism for relief, however, the majority creates consequences here in our State which our Legislature has repeatedly sought to prevent.

Because I cannot join in what I see as a majority of the Court substituting its view of an appropriate public policy for the public policy choice explicitly announced by our Legislature, I respectfully dissent. ...

Notes on

P.V. v. CAMP JAYCEE

1. Compare the *Camp Jaycee* court's approach to the Restatement (Second) with that of the *Townsend* court. One fruitful way to compare the two opinions is to evaluate the courts' use of the three levels of analysis in the Restatement (Second): (1) the general considerations of §6; (2) the specific contacts relevant to torts of §145; and (3) the highly specific presumption in favor of place of injury of §146. Both courts made much of the §146 presumption. In *Camp Jaycee*, however, the court placed greater emphasis on the competing policies behind the laws (and corresponding state interests) than the court in *Townsend*. In other words, the *Camp Jaycee* majority injected a good measure of governmental interest reasoning into its opinion (although obviously not enough to mollify the *Camp Jaycee* dissent!). Which of the three levels of Restatement (Second) analysis invites a court to engage in governmental interest analysis?

2. Now compare *Camp Jaycee* with *Schultz v. Boys Scouts of America*, reproduced above in the governmental interest analysis section of this chapter. Both decisions evaluated whether New Jersey domiciliaries were subject to New Jersey's charitable immunity statute in a situation where sexual abuse occurred outside of New Jersey. What accounts for the different results in the two cases? Is the *Camp Jaycee* dissent correct in suggesting that the majority's switch to a freewheeling Restatement (Second) approach provides the main reason for majority's ruling that the immunity statute did not apply? Could you also argue that the analytical approach of the two cases was similar, but that the characterization of the charitable immunity law varied in the two cases? In other words: *Schultz* concluded that the immunity law was intended to allocate losses among citizens and should therefore apply in an instance where both parties were citizens of the same state. *Camp Jaycee*, on the other hand, concluded that the law was conduct-regulating and that it should not apply where the relevant conduct occurred in another jurisdiction, even if that jurisdiction was not the parties' domicile.

Alternatively, could you argue that *Schultz* and *Camp Jaycee* reflect important factual differences? Although some abuse in *Schultz* occurred outside New Jersey, the victims primarily participated in charitable activities that centered in New Jersey. The *Camp Jaycee* victim, however, did not participate in New Jersey charitable activity.

3. As yet another alternative, one could account for the result in *Camp Jaycee* by focusing on *what* the majority characterized as the pertinent misconduct. Could it be that the relevant misconduct included decisions (made in New Jersey) regarding who could attend the Pennsylvania camp? The majority opinion overlooked this, focusing instead on the acts of sexual abuse (which occurred in Pennsylvania). This difference in focus obviously could impact reasoning, but could it also significantly affect the ultimate conclusion?

PROBLEM 2-42: A GUEST STATUTE IN A SECOND RESTATEMENT STATE

Nip and Tuck are both domiciled in Domicile State. Nip accepts Tuck's invitation to be Tuck's guest on an automobile trip from Domicile State through Accident State and back to Domicile State. Tuck is insured against liability by an insurance company that is incorporated with its principal place of business in Domicile State. While driving through Accident State, Tuck negligently hits a pole, which results in Nip breaking her hip. Nip brings suit to recover damages for this break in Forum State.

Under Accident State law, Tuck would not be liable to Nip. An Accident State statute provides that a guest passenger shall have no right of action against his host for negligently caused injuries. The purpose of this statute is to protect insurance companies from collusive lawsuits, trumped up between hosts and guests. Domicile State law would hold Tuck liable to Nip. The Domicile State legislature has concluded that it is more important to compensate injured tort victims than to protect against the small possibility of collusive lawsuits. Forum State applies the Restatement (Second) of Conflict of Laws. Which law is Forum State court likely to apply?

prostitute

PROBLEM 2-43: LORDON GIDDY'S CALL-GIRL DEFAMATION

A powerful politician, Lordon Giddy, was implicated in the break-in of the offices of an opponent in Virginia. In order to provide an explanation for the break-in, the politician told an audience in Maryland that the purpose of the break-in was to check the desk of the politician's secretary, Ida Max, for evidence that she was engaged in running a call-girl operation and evidence that she planned to release information suggesting that Giddy was a regular client. Lordon Giddy repeated the story in a blog post he wrote and uploaded that night in a Maryland hotel. Several days later, Giddy appeared on a live national television show broadcast from New York City. The television show is broadcast live in nearly every state of the United States. During the show, he repeated the story about Ida Max and the call-girl operation. Lordon Giddy and Ida Max are both domiciliaries of Virginia.

Ida Max has filed a defamation suit against Giddy in a jurisdiction that follows the Restatement (Second) of Conflict of Laws. Research reveals that under the laws of New York and Maryland, Giddy's statements are not capable of defamatory meaning and Max's lawsuit should be dismissed. Under Virginia law, however, the statements are capable of defamatory meaning and a trial court should submit the decision to a jury for ultimate decision. Which law should govern this question relating to defamatory meaning?

π: VA
A: VA

TORT: MD
TORT2: NY

NY/MD: dismiss
VA: φ dismiss

3.   Contracts

Refreshingly, the orientation of the Restatement (Second)'s analysis changes for contract choice of law questions. This change in orientation arises largely from the character of the contract itself: when parties contract, they enter a volitional relationship that the law promotes and respects. Unlike a car accident, a contract usually results from careful planning and interaction. Inspired by this attitude of planned autonomy, parties often include choice of law clauses in their contracts, which designate which law they wish to govern their relationship. The Restatement (Second) shows respect and deference to such clauses, distinguishing between two types of contracts: those without a chosen law and those with a choice of law clause. For the former, the Restatement (Second) contains a general provision (§188) similar to §145 for torts for designating governing law for multi-jurisdictional contracts; for contracts with choice of law clauses, the Restatement (Second) contains a nuanced provision (§187) designed to balance the policy of respecting party autonomy with the need to honor a jurisdiction's legitimate claim to govern its citizens. Several Restatement (Second) sections provide a presumptive law for specific types of contracts (such as land and insurance contracts) and for specific contract issues (such as capacity and interest rates). These provisions, however, have receded in importance as practitioners rely more and more on choice of law clauses. Given the current prevalence of such clauses, §187 is important to the deal maker's, and commercial lawyer's, toolbox.

From the Restatement (Second) of Conflict of Laws, on the Subject of Contracts:

§186. Applicable Law

Issues in contract are determined by the law chosen by the parties in accordance with the rule of §187 and otherwise by the law selected in accordance with the rule of §188.

a.   Contracts Without a Choice of Law Clause

From the Restatement (Second) of Conflict of Laws, on the Subject of Contracts:

§188. Law Governing in Absence of Effective Choice by the Parties

(1) The rights and duties of the parties with respect to an issue in contract are determined by the local law of the state which, with respect to that issue, has the most significant relationship to the transaction and the parties under the principles stated in §6.

(2) In the absence of an effective choice of law by the parties (see §187), the contacts to be taken into account in applying the principles of §6 to determine the law applicable to an issue include:
    (a) the place of contracting,
    (b) the place of negotiation of the contract,
    (c) the place of performance,

(d) the location of the subject matter of the contract, and

(e) the domicil, residence, nationality, place of incorporation and place of business of the parties.

These contacts are to be evaluated according to their relative importance with respect to the particular issue.

(3) If the place of negotiating the contract and the place of performance are in the same state, the local law of this state will usually be applied, except as otherwise provided in §§189-199 and 203.

. . .

Comment on Subsection (1):

b. Rationale. . . . The factors listed in Subsection (2) of the rule of §6 vary somewhat in importance from field to field and from issue to issue. Thus, the protection of the justified expectations of the parties is of considerable importance in contracts whereas it is of relatively little importance in torts (see §145, Comment *b*). In the torts area, it is the rare case where the parties give advance thought to the law that may be applied to determine the legal consequences of their actions. On the other hand, parties enter into contracts with forethought and are likely to consult a lawyer before doing so. . . . The need for protecting the expectations of the parties gives importance in turn to the values of certainty, predictability and uniformity of result. For unless these values are attained, the expectations of the parties are likely to be disappointed.

Protection of the justified expectations of the parties by choice-of-law rules in the field of contracts is supported both by those factors in Subsection (2) of §6 which are directed to the furtherance of the needs of the parties and by those factors which are directed to implementation of the basic policy underlying the particular field of law. Protection of the justified expectations of the parties is the basic policy underlying the field of contracts.

Protection of the justified expectations of the parties is a factor which varies somewhat in importance from issue to issue. As indicated above, this factor is of considerable importance with respect to issues involving the validity of a contract, such as capacity, formalities and substantial validity. Parties entering a contract will expect at the very least, subject perhaps to rare exceptions, that the provisions of the contract will be binding upon them. Their expectations should not be disappointed by application of the local law rule of a state which would strike down the contract or a provision thereof unless the value of protecting the expectations of the parties is substantially outweighed in the particular case by the interest of the state with the invalidating rule in having this rule applied. The extent of the interest of a state in having its rule applied should be determined in the light of the purpose sought to be achieved by the rule and by the relation of the transaction and the parties to that state (see Comment *c*).

Protection of justified expectations plays a less significant role in the choice-of-law process with respect to issues that involve the nature of the obligations imposed by a contract upon the parties rather than the validity of the contract or of some provision thereof. By and large, it is for the parties themselves to determine the nature of their contractual obligations. They can spell out these obligations in the contract or, as a short-hand device, they can provide that these obligations shall be determined by the local law of a given state (see §187, Comment *c*). If the parties do neither of these two things with respect to an issue involving the nature of their obligations, as, for example, the time of performance, the resulting gap in their contract must be filled by application of the relevant rule of contract law of a particular state. All states have gap-filling rules of this sort, and indeed such rules comprise the major content of contract law. What is important for present purposes is that a gap in a contract usually results from the fact that the parties never gave thought to the issue involved. In such a situation, the expectations of the parties with respect to that issue are unlikely to be disappointed by application of the gap-filling rule of one state rather than of the rule of another state. Hence with respect to issues of this sort, protection of the justified expectations of the parties is unlikely to play so significant a role in the choice-of-law process. As a result, greater emphasis in fashioning choice-of-law rules in this area must be given to the other choice-of-law principles mentioned in the rule of §6.

c. Purpose of contract rule. The purpose sought to be achieved by the contract rules of the potentially interested states, and the relation of these states to the transaction and the parties, are important factors to be considered in determining the state of most significant relationship. This is because the interest of a state in having its contract rule applied in the determination of a particular issue will depend upon the purpose sought to be achieved by that rule and upon the relation of the state to the transaction and the parties. So the state where a party to the contract is domiciled has an obvious interest in the application of its contract rule designed to protect that party against the unfair use of superior bargaining power. And a state where a contract provides that a given business practice is to be pursued has an obvious interest in the application of its rule designed to regulate or to deter that business practice. . . .

Comment on Subsection (2):

e. Important contacts in determining state of most significant relationship. In the absence of an effective choice of law by the parties (see §187), the forum, in applying the principles of §6 to determine the state of most significant relationship, should give consideration to the relevant policies of all potentially interested states and the relative interests of those states in the decision of the particular issue. The states which are most likely to be interested are those which have one or more of the following contacts with the transaction or the parties. Some of these contacts also figure prominently in the formulation of the applicable rules of choice of law.

The place of contracting. As used in the Restatement of this Subject, the place of contracting is the place where occurred the last act necessary, under the forum's rules of offer and acceptance, to give the contract binding effect, assuming, hypothetically, that the local law of the state where the act occurred rendered the contract binding.

Standing alone, the place of contracting is a relatively insignificant contact. . . .

The place of negotiation. The place where the parties negotiate and agree on the terms of their contract is a significant contact. Such a state has an obvious interest in the conduct of the negotiations and in the agreement reached. This contact is of less importance when there is no one single place of negotiation and agreement, as, for example, when the parties do not meet but rather conduct their negotiations from separate states by mail or telephone.

The place of performance. The state where performance is to occur under a contract has an obvious interest in the nature of the performance and in the party who is to perform. So the state where performance is to occur has an obvious interest in the question whether this performance would be illegal (see §202). When both parties are to perform in the state, this state will have so close a relationship to the transaction and the parties that it will often be the state of the applicable law even with respect to issues that do not relate strictly to performance. And this is even more likely to be so if, in addition, both parties are domiciled in the state. . . .

Situs of the subject matter of the contract. When the contract deals with a specific physical thing, such as land or a chattel, or affords protection against a localized risk, such as the dishonesty of an employee in a fixed place of employment, the location of the thing or of the risk is significant (see §§189-193). The state where the thing or the risk is located will have a natural interest in transactions affecting it. Also the parties will regard the location of the thing or of the risk as important. Indeed, when the thing or the risk is the principal subject of the contract, it can often be assumed that the parties, to the extent that they thought about the matter at all, would expect that the local law of the state where the thing or risk was located would be applied to determine many of the issues arising under the contract.

Domicil, residence, nationality, place of incorporation, and place of business of the parties. These are all places of enduring relationship to the parties. Their significance depends largely upon the issue involved and upon the extent to which they are grouped with other contacts. . . .

Comment on Subsection (3):

f. When place of negotiation and place of performance are in the same state. When the place of negotiation and the place of performance are in the same state, the local law of this state will usually be applied to govern issues arising under the contract, except as stated in §§189-199 and 203. A state having these contacts will usually be the state that has the greatest interest in the determination of issues arising under the contract. . . .

Hoiles v. Alioto

461 F.3d 1224 (10th Cir. 2006)

MURPHY, Circuit Judge.

I. INTRODUCTION

This appeal arises out of a contingent fee agreement (the "Fee Agreement") entered into by Plaintiff-Appellee Timothy Hoiles, a resident of Colorado, and Defendant-Appellant Joseph Alioto, an attorney licensed to practice law in California. Hoiles hired Alioto to assist him in selling stock he owned in a private, family-owned media company, Freedom Communications, Inc. ("Freedom"). Approximately two years after the parties entered into the Fee Agreement, Freedom was recapitalized, enabling Hoiles to exchange his shares in the company for cash. Hoiles subsequently filed suit seeking a declaratory judgment that Alioto was not entitled to a contingent fee based on the selling price of the stock. Alioto counterclaimed, asserting breach of contract, unjust enrichment, fraud, and negligent misrepresentation. The United States District Court for the District of Colorado determined Colorado law governed all issues in the case and that the Fee Agreement was unenforceable under Colorado law. The district court also dismissed Alioto's fraud and negligent misrepresentation claims. The case proceeded to trial, and the jury found in favor of Alioto on his unjust enrichment claim. Alioto challenges several of the district court's rulings on appeal. We assert jurisdiction pursuant to 28 U.S.C. 1291. Because the district court erred in applying Colorado law to determine the validity of the Fee Agreement, we reverse the district court's dismissal of Alioto's breach of contract claim. We remand with instructions for the district court to determine whether the Fee Agreement is enforceable under California law. . . .

II. BACKGROUND

[Hoiles hired a consultant, Barletta, who contacted a lawyer about representing Hoiles (on a contingency fee basis) in his attempt to sell his shares in a family-held media company, Freedom Communications. Hoiles traveled from his Colorado home to meet with Alioto in California. According to Hoiles, the parties discussed pursuing a lawsuit against Freedom shareholders to force the purchase of Hoiles's stock. Alioto claims Hoiles wanted him to take any action that was necessary to force the purchase of Hoiles's interest, and his relative's interest in Freedom. At the end of the meeting, the parties reached an oral agreement whereby Alioto would represent Hoiles on a contingent fee basis. Hoiles paid a $500,000 retainer and advanced Alioto $100,000 for expenses and costs.]

Several weeks after the meeting, Alioto faxed a letter to Hoiles in Colorado, memorializing the terms of the legal representation. The letter indicated Alioto's firm would represent Hoiles in the "Freedom Communications matter." It provided Alioto was to receive "[f]ifteen percent (15%) of anything recovered before the filing of a complaint; 20% of anything recovered after the filing of a complaint but before the commencement of the trial; and 25% of anything recovered after the commencement of the trial." If Hoiles withdrew from or dismissed the case, or refused to settle against Alioto's recommendation, he was obligated to pay a reasonable hourly rate of $1000 for Alioto's time and $500 for co-counsel's time. The Fee Agreement also required Hoiles to pay all out-of-pocket and litigation expenses. Hoiles signed the Fee Agreement in Colorado approximately six months after receiving it.

[Two years later, Freedom entered into a recapitalization agreement with another company. The cause of the recapitalization is disputed. Although Alioto contended the recapitalization resulted from his own efforts, Hoiles claims that Alioto's contribution to the recapitalization was minimal. Whatever its cause, the recapitalization enabled all Freedom shareholders, including Hoiles and other family members, to sell their shares for a total of $141,869,380.67.]

After the recapitalization, Hoiles asked Alioto to submit a billing statement for his services at $1000 per hour in accordance with the Fee Agreement. Alioto responded by demanding a $28.4 million contingent fee. Hoiles subsequently filed suit in Colorado state court seeking, *inter alia*, a declaration that Alioto was not entitled to a contingent fee. Alioto removed the case to federal district court in Colorado based on diversity, and then filed his own suit against Hoiles and [his family] in California state court. Alioto's complaint asserted claims for breach of contract, unjust enrichment, fraud, and negligent misrepresentation. Hoiles removed Alioto's California state court action to federal district court in California. The parties then filed dueling motions to dismiss for lack of personal jurisdiction, Alioto in the Colorado case and Hoiles in the California case. Each motion alternatively asked that the venue be transferred to the other federal district court. The Colorado federal district court denied Alioto's motion, and the California federal district court transferred Alioto's suit to Colorado. The two cases were consolidated in the United States District Court for the District of Colorado.

Alioto subsequently filed counterclaims in Colorado federal district court that mirrored his claims in his original California state court action. Specifically, he alleged Hoiles and [his family members] breached the Fee Agreement by failing to pay him fifteen percent of the amount they received from the sale of their Freedom shares. . . .

The district court also dismissed Alioto's breach of contract, fraud, and negligent misrepresentation claims against Hoiles. Applying Colorado's conflict of law rules, the district court determined Colorado law governed all issues in the case. The district court further determined, as a matter of law, that the Fee Agreement did not substantially comply with Colorado's rules governing contingent fee agreements. . . . The case proceeded to trial on the issue of whether Alioto was entitled to quantum meruit. The jury returned a verdict in favor of Alioto for $1,150,000, which the district court reduced by the $500,000 retainer Hoiles had previously paid.

III. DISCUSSION

A. CHOICE OF LAW FOR DETERMINING THE VALIDITY OF THE FEE AGREEMENT

. . . Because the Fee Agreement does not contain a choice of law provision, the district court was required to apply the choice of law principles of the state in which it sits, i.e., Colorado. Colorado has adopted the "most significant relationship" approach of the Restatement (Second) of Conflict of Laws ("Restatement") for resolving conflict of laws questions in contract cases. This approach requires courts to apply the law of the state which, with respect to the particular issue in dispute, has the most significant relationship to the transaction and the parties. Restatement (Second) of Conflict of Laws 188(1) (1971).

The first factor — the needs of the interstate and international systems — seeks "to further harmonious relations between states and to facilitate commercial intercourse between them." *Id.* 6 cmt. d. This factor favors the application of California law in this case. Alioto did not solicit business in Colorado. Instead, Hoiles traveled to California to retain a lawyer licensed to practice law in California. The majority of the legal services rendered pursuant to the Fee Agreement were performed in California. Strategy meetings and telephone conferences took place or were arranged from California. Part of Alioto's representation entailed consideration of a possible lawsuit against Freedom shareholders. Although suit was never filed, Alioto drafted a complaint to be filed in California state court that alleged violations of a California antitrust statute. The majority of shareholders named in the complaint were California residents.

Hoiles nevertheless contends a significant portion of services were also performed in Colorado. He argues Alioto's representation strategy required everything to come out of Hoiles' office in Colorado to ensure the interface was between Hoiles and Freedom, not Hoiles' attorneys and Freedom. To this end, Alioto regularly dictated letters to Hoiles' staff in Colorado for them to prepare and mail. Hoiles notes he also performed substantial background research and gathered documents in Colorado. Although Hoiles and his staff did substantial work in Colorado, the Fee Agreement at issue here was a contract for the rendition of Alioto's legal services. Therefore, performance of the Fee Agreement occurred largely in California where Alioto dictated the letters to Hoiles' staff and provided other legal advice. Legal services were rendered in Colorado on only one occasion: a member of Alioto's legal team traveled to Hoiles' office in Colorado for one day to review documents. Alioto himself never went to Colorado. Thus, significant services were not performed in Colorado.[3]

Applying Colorado law under these circumstances would likely impede the interstate practice of law thereby creating discordant relations between states. An attorney who is licensed to practice law only in California, does not travel outside California to solicit business, and performs legal services mainly in California is not likely to enter into attorney-client relationships with citizens from other states if he is required to conform to each state's unique contingent fee agreement requirements merely because his client is a resident of another state. The needs of the interstate system therefore favor the application of California law here.

The second and third factors consider and compare the policies of states having an interest in the dispute. Here, both Colorado and California have some interest in the validity of the Fee Agreement because the agreement was

3. Although the majority of services were performed in California, the Fee Agreement did not explicitly require services to be performed in California. We therefore decline to rely on 196 of the Restatement to resolve this dispute. Section 196 applies to contracts for the rendition of services; it creates a rebuttable presumption requiring application of the law of the state where the contract requires the services to be rendered unless some other state has a more significant relationship to the transaction and the parties. Restatement (Second) of Conflict of Laws 196 (1971). The presumption only applies, however, when the contract expressly states where services are to be performed or the place of performance can be inferred from the contract's terms, the nature of the services involved, or other circumstances. *Id.* 196 cmt. a. The Fee Agreement does not indicate where Alioto's services were to be rendered. Moreover, the district court did not determine whether the anticipated place of performance could be inferred from the contract's terms or other circumstances. Because it is not necessary for us to decide this question of fact in the first instance to resolve this case, we decline to do so.

negotiated in California and executed in Colorado by citizens of each state.[4] Hoiles contends Colorado's interest is more compelling than California's because of Colorado's need to protect its citizens who enter into contingent fee agreements. Colorado's interest in protecting its citizens is attenuated in this case, however, because Hoiles traveled outside of Colorado to solicit representation by an attorney who resides in, and is licensed to practice law in, California. Colorado's interest is further diluted because California also has enacted statutes to protect clients, regardless of their state of residence, who enter into contingent fee agreements with attorneys licensed to practice law in California. Moreover, California has an interest in enforcing these rules against attorneys licensed to practice law in California. California's interest is especially compelling where, as here, the attorney does not leave the state to solicit business and performs the majority of the services required by the agreement in California. Colorado, on the other hand, has no significant interest in enforcing its rules regulating contingent fee agreements against attorneys who are not licensed to practice law in Colorado, do not solicit business in Colorado, and do not perform legal services in Colorado. Because California's interests are more deeply affected by this dispute, factors two and three also favor the application of California law.

The fourth factor seeks to protect the parties' justified expectations. Although the parties here contest the meaning of the Fee Agreement, neither party disputes that they intended to enter into a contingent fee agreement. Hoiles traveled to California specifically to locate an attorney willing to represent him on a contingent fee basis. The parties subsequently entered into an agreement that explicitly provided for a fee based on a percentage of "anything recovered." Protecting the parties' expectations therefore requires application of whichever state's law will uphold the validity of the Fee Agreement. Alioto concedes the Fee Agreement is not enforceable under Colorado law. The parties contest the agreement's validity under California law. Therefore, only the application of California law will preserve the possibility of protecting the parties' justified expectation that they executed a valid contingent fee agreement.

The fifth factor requires consideration of which state's law "will best achieve the basic policy, or policies, underlying the particular field of law involved" in the dispute. The parties disagree as to the particular field of law at issue here. Hoiles claims the appropriate field of law is attorney-client contingent fee agreements. He contends the policies underlying this field of law include protection of the client by full, written disclosure; assumption by the attorney of the risk of no recovery; and compensation for the attorney only upon the occurrence of an agreed-upon contingency. Alioto contends the appropriate field of law is contracts. He urges us to achieve the fundamental goal of contract law — giving effect

---

4. The terms of the Fee Agreement were negotiated in California during Hoiles' and Alioto's initial meeting. At this meeting, the parties reached an oral agreement that Alioto subsequently reduced to writing. Because the written agreement was executed by Hoiles in Colorado, the place of contracting for purposes of applying the Restatement is Colorado. *See* Restatement (Second) of Conflict of Laws 188 cmt. e (indicating the place of contracting is the place where, under the forum's rules of offer and acceptance, the last act necessary to give the contract binding effect occurred).

to the intent of the parties—by applying California law to uphold the validity of the Fee Agreement. The law of contingent fee agreements is merely a subset of contract law. The Fee Agreement is both a contract and, more specifically, a contingent fee agreement. Therefore, the policies underlying both fields of law are relevant in determining the validity of the Fee Agreement.

The law governing contingent fee agreements in Colorado and California is similar. Both states require contingent fee agreements to be in writing and contain specific information to ensure full disclosure to the client. Once a contingent fee agreement is deemed valid, both states interpret the agreement by looking to its express language to ascertain the intent of the parties. Both Colorado and California also construe any ambiguous language in the agreement in favor of the client. Nevertheless, the description of information that must be disclosed in a contingent fee agreement under Colorado law is more exacting than that which must be disclosed under California law. Colorado law therefore arguably better ensures full disclosure of all pertinent information to the client. As a result, the policies underlying the law of contingent fee agreements arguably favor the application of Colorado law. We need not definitively decide this issue, however, because the policies underlying the law of contracts favor the application of California law in this case. Contract law strives to "[protect] the justified expectations of the parties." As discussed above, the application of California law might fulfill the parties' expectation that they executed a valid contingent fee agreement whereas the application of Colorado law will clearly defeat the parties' expectation. Thus, even if the policies underlying the law of contingent fee agreements favor the application of Colorado law, this fifth factor does not favor the application of Colorado law because the policies underlying the law of contracts, which are equally relevant, favor California law. At most, this factor is neutral.

The sixth factor—certainty, predictability, and uniformity of result—favors the application of California law. In this case, a citizen traveled from his residence in Colorado to California to solicit representation from an attorney licensed to practice law only in California. The majority of legal services performed pursuant to the contingent fee agreement the parties subsequently entered into were performed in California. Under these circumstances, it is predictable that California law would govern the Fee Agreement. Application of Colorado law . . . is less predictable. The relevant contacts with Colorado are limited. Although Hoiles is a Colorado resident and the Fee Agreement was signed by Hoiles in Colorado, these two contacts do not make the application of Colorado law predictable when compared to the numerous contacts with California present in this case.[5]

5. Hoiles contends other relevant contacts with Colorado include the following: Hoiles paid all expenses incurred by Alioto under the Fee Agreement from Colorado; if Hoiles breached the Fee Agreement by not paying the contingent fee, the breach occurred in Colorado; and the subject matter of the Fee Agreement, Hoiles' Freedom shares, were located in Colorado. These contacts are not persuasive. First, the origin of payments under a contract and the location of the breach are not relevant contacts under 188 of the Restatement. Second, although the location of the subject matter of the contract is relevant, it does not carry great weight in this case. See Restatement (Second) of Conflict of Laws 188(2) (noting "contacts are to be evaluated according to their relative importance with respect to the particular issue" in dispute). Alioto and Hoiles entered into a contingent fee agreement whereby Alioto would perform legal services with the aim

The application of California law in this case would also create certainty and uniformity of result. Alioto is licensed to practice law only in California. He did not leave California to solicit business in another state. The legal services he rendered pursuant to the Fee Agreement were performed largely in California. In particular, he drafted a complaint asserting claims under a California antitrust statute for filing in California state court. Alioto is entitled, under these circumstances, to anticipate that California law will govern and draft his contingent fee agreement accordingly. Requiring an attorney to conform to the law of whichever state a client happens to reside in when the attorney is not licensed to practice in that state, does not solicit business in that state, and does not perform legal services in that state would create unnecessary uncertainty.

The seventh and final factor does not favor the application of either Colorado or California law. This factor evaluates the ease in determining and applying each interested state's law. Restatement (Second) of Conflict of Laws 6(2)(g). Both Colorado and California have statutes . . . enumerating the requirements for a valid and enforceable contingent fee agreement. . . . Therefore, neither state's law would be difficult to determine or apply in assessing the validity of the Fee Agreement.

Five of the seven factors for ascertaining the state with the most significant relationship under 6 of the Restatement weigh in favor of applying California law in this case. The remaining two factors are neutral. Accordingly, California has the most significant relationship to the transaction and the parties, and its law should have been applied in determining the validity of the Fee Agreement.

. . . The district court has not assessed whether the Fee Agreement is enforceable under California law or evaluated the parties' competing interpretations of the agreement. Because these are issues best resolved in district court in the first instance, we decline to address them here. We therefore reverse the district court's determination that the Fee Agreement is unenforceable, and remand for further proceedings consistent with this opinion. . . .

Notes on
HOILES

1. The Restatement (Second) offers courts an analytical choice: they can emphasize presumptive rules, emphasize the general considerations of §6, or integrate both the presumptive rules and the §6 considerations. Critics say that some courts place too much emphasis on presumptive rules, thereby transforming the Restatement (Second) into no more than an update of the Restatement (First). This is not, however, a fair critique of *Hoiles*,

---

of enabling Hoiles to sell his Freedom shares. The majority of the legal services rendered pursuant to the Fee Agreement were performed in California. Freedom, the company whose stock Hoiles owned, is incorporated in California and has its principle place of business in California. Under these circumstances, the fact that Hoiles' stock certificates were located in Colorado is of limited relevance.

which made §6 the centerpiece of its analysis. Did the court put too much emphasis on the §6 considerations? Might one argue that the *Hoiles* court put too little emphasis on other sections? For example, the court's reasoning strongly suggests that both the place of negotiation and place of performance were in California. If this were the case, the court could have pointed to §188(3), which provides that where "the place of negotiating the contract and the place of performance are in the same state, the local law of this state will usually be applied." In addition, the court relegated much of the reasoning about the §188(2) contacts to its footnotes, presumably concluding that the §6 considerations should get top billing.

Recall the New Jersey tort opinion in *P.V. v. Camp Jaycee* (set forth immediately above), in which the court began its analysis with the Restatement (Second)'s presumptively applicable law and then used the §6 considerations to test whether the presumptive jurisdiction was indeed the place with the most significant relationship to the parties and the dispute. Would the *Hoiles* opinion have had more clarity and impact if the court had followed the rhetorical and analytical orientation of *Camp Jaycee* court? Or, on the other hand, was the *Hoiles* opinion strengthened by avoiding an upfront declaration that the Restatement (Second) presumptively designated California law? By avoiding this declaration, the court was able to carefully deliberate on each §6 factor.

2. The *Hoiles* court's reliance on upholding the validity of the contract and the parties' expectation that they entered into a valid contract is typical reasoning in contract cases under the Restatement (Second). Don't these factors stack the deck in favor of the law that upholds the contract? In instances where these factors are useful as tie-breakers, won't the court usually encounter one law that tries to restrict the circumstances under which parties can contract and one law that is less regulatory? Reasoning such as that used by the *Hoiles* court will nearly always prefer the latter law. Is this appropriate?

Naghiu v. Inter-Continental Hotels Group, Inc.

165 F.R.D. 413 (D. Del. 1996)

MURRAY M. SCHWARTZ, Senior District Judge.

Plaintiffs Leslie and Laverne Naghiu, citizens of Virginia, have filed suit in this diversity action against the Inter-Continental Hotels Group, Inc. ("Inter-Continental" or "defendant"), a Delaware corporation. Plaintiffs aver that during Leslie Naghiu's ("Naghiu" or "plaintiff") stay as a guest of defendant's hotel in Zaire, Africa in March, 1993, he was attacked in his room, causing him to suffer personal bodily injury and a loss of $146,000 in property. Laverne Naghiu claims a loss of consortium flowing from her husband's injuries.

Inter-Continental has moved for dismissal under Rule 12(b)(6) of the Federal Rules of Civil Procedure, arguing that plaintiff is not the real party in interest in this case as to the loss of personal property. In addition, Inter-Continental has moved for summary judgment under Rule 56 on the issue of whether it is liable in tort for the events that allegedly occurred on its premises.

Jurisdiction is invoked pursuant to 28 U.S.C. §1332. For the reasons stated below, the Court will grant defendant's motions as to both issues.

II. FACTUAL BACKGROUND

The Court views the facts in this case, which are rich with intrigue, in the light most favorable to the plaintiffs. Naghiu, an employee of the Christian Broadcast Network, Inc. ("CBN"), serves as the director of executive protection for Dr. Pat Robertson ("Robertson").[1] In this capacity, Naghiu coordinates security arrangements for Robertson on his trips abroad. Id. Naghiu is an employee of CBN but is not an officer or director of CBN; he has no ownership or voting control in the affairs of CBN. Naghiu's employment with CBN is based out of Virginia Beach, Virginia.

In March 1993, on behalf of Robertson, Naghiu traveled to Zaire to purchase diamonds and render humanitarian aid. To that end, Naghiu estimates that he carried on his person approximately $100,000 in cash, kept in an attaché case. . . .

As of the March, 1993 CBN expedition to Zaire, Robertson's corporation had rendered approximately two million dollars in humanitarian aid to that country. With this legacy of prior aid, CBN's March, 1993 return to Zaire was covered by the Zaire media, including television. During all of this, Naghiu was charged with the security of the attaché case containing the money. The Robertson entourage booked its stay at defendant's Inter-Continental Hotel Kinshasa ("hotel"), the only suitable lodging for business travelers in Kinshasa, Zaire. Inter-Continental admits that it routinely advised all paying guests to give their valuables, including cash, to the hotel staff for safe-keeping.

[Upon arrival at the Inter-Continental Kinshasa, Naghiu asked to procure a safe deposit box for the cash, but at least twice was told to come back later. As a result of a diamond sale, $46,000 was added to the attaché case.]

On the evening of March 23, 1993, Naghiu supped at a private residence that was ". . . 45 minutes outside of Kinshasa in an area where soldiers and military types have stopped vehicles, accosted foreigners and even Zaireans, manhandled them. Shot them." Consequently, as Naghiu has testified, he left the attaché case and its contents in his hotel room while he left the premises. He did not consider making another effort at obtaining a hotel safe deposit box. Naghiu hid the attaché case behind a couch and set of heavy drapes in his hotel room on the 19th floor.

[When Naghiu returned from dinner his hotel door appeared to be unlocked. Upon entering the room he was attacked by two men and knocked unconscious. The attaché case was apparently stolen.]

---

1. Dr. Robertson is an internationally-known televangelist, humanitarian, and former United States presidential candidate.

Naghiu subsequently filed criminal charges with the Zairean authorities. When he returned stateside, Naghiu claims that Robertson expected reimbursement of the stolen money. Robertson later told Naghiu, however, not "to worry about [the money], that [Naghiu] was bonded."

III. DISCUSSION

. . . Inter-Continental has filed a Rule 12(b)(6) motion to dismiss plaintiff's claim for recovery of the $146,000 for failure to state a claim upon which relief can be granted. . . . [Because the parties included extraneous material in litigating the motion, the court treated the matter as a summary judgment motion under Fed. R. Civ. P. 56.] . . .

C. REAL PARTY IN INTEREST — LOSS OF PERSONAL PROPERTY

Defendants first argue that plaintiff may not recover for the alleged loss of the $146,000 because plaintiff is not the real party in interest as required by the Federal Rules of Civil Procedure. Fed. R. Civ. P. 17(a) requires that "every action shall be prosecuted in the name of the real party in interest." Unless a party is "an executor, administrator, guardian, bailee, trustee of an express trust, a party with whom or in whose name a contract has been made for the benefit of another, or a party authorized by statute," a litigant cannot sue in his "own name without joining the party for whose benefit the action is brought." Fed. R. Civ. P. 17(a). The underlying aim of the rule is to ensure fairness to the defendant by protecting the defendant against a subsequent action by the party actually entitled to relief, and by ensuring that the judgment will have proper res judicata effect.

1. Choice of Law

Naghiu argues that he was a bailee of the money and as such, is a real party in interest as explicitly enumerated by Fed. R. Civ. P. 17. In analyzing plaintiff's status as bailee *vel non,* the Court looks to the substantive law creating the right being sued upon to ascertain whether plaintiff possesses a substantive right to relief. As a threshold matter, the Court must decide which jurisdiction's law controls the issue of whether plaintiff is to be considered a bailee of the $146,000.

Where, as here, the jurisdiction of a federal court is founded upon the diversity statute, 28 U.S.C. §1332, the Court applies the substantive law, including the choice of law provisions of the state in which the federal court sits. This Court therefore will look to Delaware choice of law rules to determine the substantive law that governs the dispute between Naghiu and Inter-Continental.

For choice of law questions sounding in contract,[2] Delaware courts follow the "most significant relationship" approach of the Restatement (Second) of Conflict

---

2. Delaware courts have determined that a bailment arrangement is by nature a contractual relation. *See Sports Complex, Inc. v. Golt,* 647 A.2d 382, 1994 WL 267697 (Del. 1994) (Table — Unpublished Disposition) ("a bailment exists where there is a delivery of personalty for some particular purpose . . . upon a contract. . . .") (n.b. Unpublished orders of the Supreme Court of Delaware have precedential effect in Delaware. *See* Del. Sup. Ct. R. 17(a) Commentary; *New Castle County v. Goodman,* 461 A.2d 1012, 1013 (Del. 1983)).

of Laws. Under Restatement section 188, the rights and duties of the parties with respect to an issue in contract are determined by the local law of the state with the most significant relationship to the transaction and the parties by reference to the following principles: a) the place of contracting, b) the place of negotiation of the contract, c) the place of performance, d) the location of the subject matter of the contract, and e) the domicile, residence, or place of incorporation and place of business of the parties. Restatement (Second) of Conflicts §188 (1971). Considering plaintiff as a putative bailee of CBN based in Virginia, the Court finds that factors a, b, c, d and part of e of the Restatement approach point to Virginia. Accordingly, the Court holds that Virginia has the most significant relationship to the occurrence and the parties with respect to whether plaintiff was a bailee of the cash and thus satisfies Rule 17's real party in interest requirement. Thus, Virginia law shall control as to whether plaintiff was in fact a bailee.

[The court then held that under Virginia law Naghiu could not be considered a bailee because he did not have a legal interest in the cash stolen from his hotel room. Because he never claimed to be suing on Pat Robertson's or anyone else's behalf, he is not a real party in interest. In addition, the court held that Naghiu had reasonable opportunity to locate and formally join, substitute, or seek ratification from Robertson or CBN, the real parties in interest. Because this has not occurred, the Court held "that Rule 17's real party in interest requirement has not been satisfied as to the loss of personal property in this case. As to this first issue, the Court will grant summary judgment in favor of defendant."]

D. NAGHIU'S PERSONAL INJURIES—PREMISES LIABILITY

The Court sitting in diversity must also determine what substantive law governs the tort claims in this case. Again, the Court first looks to the forum state's choice of law rules for guidance. Similar to its approach for analyzing choice of law questions for contract issues, Delaware adheres to the "most significant relationship" approach of the Restatement (Second) of Conflict of Laws for tort issues. . . . If the tort case involves personal injury, as this one does, the Court is directed by Restatement section 146 "to apply the law of the state where the injury occurred in a 'personal injury case' unless the forum state has a 'more significant relationship' under section Six principles to the 'occurrence and the parties.'" *Travelers Indem. Co. v. Lake*, 594 A.2d 38, 47 (Del. 1978).

With these principles in mind, the Court concludes that the Supreme Court of Delaware would apply Zairean law to Naghiu's claims for personal injury against Inter-Continental. As the forum wherein his alleged personal injury occurred, under section 146, Zaire has the most significant relationship to the occurrence and to the issues raised by Naghiu. Zaire is also at the heart of the parties' relationship to one another, as the Inter-Continental Hotel Kinshasa is located in that forum and it is the hotel's conduct that is at issue in this case. Thus, the majority of the Restatement factors point to Zairean law as the source of the substantive rule of decision in this case.[3]

---

3. The Supreme Court of Delaware has held that different choice of law rules under the Restatement (Second) of Conflicts apply to different causes of action, differentiating between

1. The Zairean Civil Code

Under the Federal Rules of Civil Procedure, "the court, in determining foreign law, may consider any relevant material or source." Fed. R. Civ. P. 44.1. Here, the Court accepts the parties' proffer of opinion letters expounding Zairean law authored by individuals with expertise in the relevant provisions of the Zairean Civil Code. See id. Advisory Committee Note (the Court may rely on presentation by counsel in applying foreign law). Each side has argued for application of the same provisions of Zairean law.

Zaire Civil Code Articles 258 and 259 speak to general tort liability of those who commit injury to others:

> Article 258. Any act of a man which causes damages to another obliges him by whose fault it occurred to make reparation.
> Article 259. Each person is liable for the damages he causes not only by his act but by his negligence or imprudence.

D.I. 37 at 4; D.I. 45. Citing these provisions, defendant argues that if any reparations are due plaintiff, they are owed by his assailants. However, in direct contrast to defendant's argument, its Zairean attorney "expert" opined in his letter that these provisions of Zairean code allow Naghiu, as a hotel guest who has sustained injury, to file suit against the hotel for negligence. One of plaintiff's opinion letters also paraphrased Zairean Civil Code Article 19 as "providing that no persons foreign to the hotel can get access to the premises and rooms assigned to the guests except if they were duly authorized by the innkeeper or his agent."

Naghiu argues that Inter-Continental failed to take the necessary measures in order to maintain the premises free from hazards and dangerous conditions and was thus negligent in allowing the criminals to victimize plaintiff. Although the Court accepts the general principle that under Zairean law, Inter-Continental could be liable under a negligence theory, neither party has supplied the Court with the necessary provisions of Zairean law for the Court to make an informed decision. For example, the Court is uninformed as to the standard of care to which the Inter-Continental hotel is held under circumstances such as these, and whether defendant is held to be an absolute insurer of its guests' safety. Defendant has argued that the "incident involving Naghiu was the first and only incident of a burglary or assault" on record. However, the Court does not know whether the lack of prior notice of such attacks to the hotel is significant under Zairean law.

The Court recognizes that the Zairean Civil Code may not explicitly address every aspect of innkeeper liability. In that instance, Article 1 of the Zairean Code directs that where the Zairean law is silent, other sources of law may be

---

actions in contract and tort. *Travelers Indem. Co. v. Lake*, 594 A.2d 38, 41, 47 (Del. 1991). Because the choice of law analysis is issue-specific, this Court's determination that Virginia law controlled the bailment issue is considered separately from the question of what law controls the negligence issue in this case. This process of applying the rules of different states to discrete issues within the same case is known as "dépeçage." . . .

considered, especially provisions of French or Belgian law. However, the parties have not supplied the Court with any Belgian or French law to fill in the analytical chasm left gaping in this case.

Fed. R. Civ. P. 44.1 does not address the effect of the parties' failure to supply foreign law. When such a failure has occurred, "the party who has the affirmative on an issue of foreign law loses if he fails to prove that law." 9 Wright & Miller at §2447 (collecting cases). To avoid this harsh result, other courts, including the Court of Appeals for the Third Circuit, have looked to their own forum's substantive law to fill in any gaps. The Court will therefore look to Delaware tort law.

2. Delaware Law

The rule in Delaware, similar to the analogous Zairean Civil Code provision, is that a proprietor of a public place, such as a hotel, may be subject to liability to its invitee for the harm sustained while the invitee is on the land within the scope of his invitation. *DiOssi v. Maroney*, 548 A.2d 1361, 1366 (Del. 1988) (quoting Restatement (Second) of Torts §332 comment e (1965)). However, such a proprietor is not an insurer against all personal injuries inflicted on its premises. Possessors of land are under a "residual obligation of reasonable care to protect business invitees from the acts of third persons." Id. If prior incidents of criminal conduct have occurred on the premises, Delaware courts have held a proprietor to a duty to foresee specific criminal conduct and take reasonable measures for security protection. Id. [Applying these standards, the court concluded that the plaintiff had not submitted sufficient evidence to survive summary judgment.]

IV. CONCLUSION

For the above reasons, the Court holds that plaintiff is not a real party in interest for purposes of his claim for loss of $146,000, property in which he had no legal interest. The Court also holds that plaintiff Leslie Naghiu has failed to establish the existence of the essential elements of his case with respect to his claim for negligence; it follows that plaintiff-spouse Laverne Naghiu's loss of consortium claim fails as well. The Court will therefore grant summary judgment in favor of defendant. An appropriate order will follow.

Notes on
NAGHIU

1. Note that in addressing which law governs the contract issue in the case, the *Naghiu* court did not bother discussing §6, but instead merely mentioned a few of the factors from §188. Although this a common approach for courts applying the Restatement (Second), most agree that it is not the approach directed by those who drafted the Restatement (Second). The

Hoiles court's approach is much closer to the §6-centered analysis that drafters envisioned.

2. Note that in analyzing the question whether Naghiu was a bailee under Federal Rule of Civil Procedure 17, the court did not attempt to define that term by reference to federal law principles. The court looked to state law instead. This approach is consistent with other areas of federal practice in which federal courts look to state law to give content to federal law terms, and also appears consistent with the Restatement (Second), which states that "in areas governed by national law, questions of characterization are determined by national law except where State law is referred to by national law as the rule of decision." Restatement (Second) of Conflict of Laws §7, comment *f*.

Having concluded (or assumed) that state law governs the definition of a bailee, the court then needed to categorize the term according to legal subject matter. For this characterization question, the court looked immediately to Delaware law. Because Delaware courts had characterized "a bailment arrangement in the nature of a contractual relation," the *Naghiu* court then looked to Delaware's conflict of law rules for contracts questions. The court presumably used Delaware law for this characterization question because United States District Court was exercising diversity of citizenship jurisdiction and was situated in Delaware. As the forum state, Delaware therefore provided the governing choice of law approach the district court was required to follow. This decision to treat the characterization of the operative legal term as a choice of law matter also appears consistent with the Restatement (Second), which states that "the classification and interpretation of Conflict of Laws concepts and terms are determined in accordance with the law of the forum." Restatement (Second) of Conflict of Laws §7(2). It is true that Restatement (Second) §7(3) does say that "the classification and interpretation of local law concepts and terms are determined in accordance with the law that governs the issue involved." But that latter provision could not govern the initial bailment characterization question, since it was not yet clear *which* local law would govern at that point in the analysis. In other words, the characterization of a bailment *had* to be viewed as a conflict of laws question, so that the choice of law analysis could proceed. This is all yet another example of the law-within-a-law phenomenon illustrated by the aforementioned Russian nesting dolls.

3. Note the *Naghiu* court's ease in using dépeçage to differentiate between the contract and tort issues in the case. As explained in the Perspective on Dépeçage, this is consistent with the Restatement (Second)'s direction to use issue-specific analysis.

4. What do you think of the court's approach to the proof of foreign law? Is it appropriate that the court felt moved to fill the gaps in proof on the substance of Zaire law by looking to forum law?

PROBLEM 2-44: DRINKING FOR A COTTAGE

Liz lived in the State of Sisterly Love. She was worried about her brother, James, who drank too much alcohol. One day while visiting her brother in the State of Domicile, she broached the subject with him. He scoffed at her suggestion to quit drinking. She then promised James that she would give him her family's beach cottage if he successfully stopped drinking for six months. He said he would take her up on this.

Although Liz's main residence and domicile was in Sisterly Love, her beach cottage was in the State of Domicile. James lived in the State of Domicile, was an inveterate homebody, and never left the state. Liz went back to the State of Sisterly Love and called James intermittently over the next six months to see if he was sober. James ultimately met the challenge, succeeding in forbearing from alcohol consumption for six months. After Liz refused to give him the cottage (saying the promise was in jest), James filed suit against her in Domicile State, which follows the Restatement (Second) of Conflict of Laws. Under the laws of the State of Sisterly Love, Liz's "promise" is non-enforceable. The purpose of this law is to foster humor in society: legislators in the State of Sisterly Love reasoned that individuals will shy away from jests if the law does not protect jokes from legal liability. Under the laws of the State of Domicile, Liz's "promise" is enforceable. Which law governs?

PROBLEM 2-45: SPENDY TAKES OUT A LOAN

Spendy is domiciled in State S and has been adjudicated a spendthrift there. She traveled to State U and borrowed money from Usury, who lends the money without knowledge of Spendy's spendthrift status. Under the terms of the loan, the money was to be repaid in State S. State U does not have a spendthrift law, and takes the position that lenders should be able to recover all loans.

Not surprisingly, Spendy did not repay the loan and Usury sued in a State U court. Spendy is not liable under State S law because she has been adjudicated a spendthrift there, but she would be liable under State U law. State U follows the Restatement (Second) of Conflict of Laws. Which law will govern Spendy's liability?

b.   Contracts with a Choice of Law Clause

(1)   Section 187

Section 187 is perhaps one of the greatest successes of the Second Restatement of Conflict of Laws. Even those jurisdictions that do not follow the

Restatement (Second) as a general matter tend to follow §187 for evaluating contractual choice of law clauses other than those governed by the Uniform Commercial Code. To appreciate why the section has been so successful, consider the following problem:

PROBLEM 2-46: CHOICE OF LAW CLAUSES: WHY SUCH A BIG DEAL?

In a contractual choice of law clause, the parties come to an agreement about which law will govern their contractual relationship. A common clause that parties would put in their contract would say:

The parties agree that all disputes relating to their rights under this contract shall be governed by the internal law of the state of California.

Consider first the following questions:

- Courts tend to favor choice of law clauses. Why?
- Are there any reasons why courts might not be willing to provide parties with complete control over the laws that govern their relationship?
- Are principles of federalism served by honoring choice of law clauses?

The Restatement (Second) §187 distinguishes between default and mandatory rules. Default rules are also known as presumptive or gap-filling rules; they are rules the parties could have resolved by using explicit language in their contract. For example, a law might provide, "Unless the parties agree otherwise, the service provider in a service contract will pay all transportation costs." This is a default rule, since the law allows parties to put a provision in their contract that says the service consumer will pay transportation costs. Mandatory rules are also known as prescriptive rules; they are those rules that the parties could not have contradicted in their contract. A law that provides, "Surrogate parentage contracts are forbidden in this state" is an example of a mandatory rule.

Sometimes you can tell the difference between mandatory and default rules by evaluating the topic of the rule. For example, contract interpretation rules are likely to be default rules. But a rule concerning the same topic can be a default rule in some circumstances and a mandatory rule in other circumstances. In order to appreciate and understand the difference between default and mandatory rules, consider the following examples from the comments to Restatement (Second) §187.

PROBLEM 2-47: THE MANDATORY/DEFAULT DISTINCTION IN THE RESTATEMENT (SECOND) OF CONFLICT OF LAWS §187

Consider the two scenarios below. Scenario #1 presents a default rule and scenario #2 presents a mandatory rule. See if you can explain why.

> Scenario #1: "In State X, A establishes a trust and provides that B, the trustee, shall be paid commissions at the highest rate permissible under the local law of state Y. A and B are both domiciled in X, and the trust has no relation to any state but X. In X, the highest permissible rate of commissions for trustees is 5 percent. In Y, the highest permissible rate is 4 percent." A court would have no difficulty giving effect to the choice-of-law provision as a default rule, and allowing B to receive commissions at the rate of 4 percent.
>
> Scenario #2: Same facts as above: "In State X, A establishes a trust and provides that B, the trustee, shall be paid commissions at the highest rate permissible under the local law of state Y. A and B are both domiciled in X, and the trust has no relation to any state but X." Now, however, assume "that the highest permissible rate of commissions in X is 4 percent and in Y is 5 percent." A court will not give effect to the choice-of-law provision, which now implicated a mandatory rule.

Restatement (Second) of Conflict of Laws §187, illustrations 4, 5.

Section 187 has many different working parts, and requires active reading. Not to worry, though—if you did Problem 2-47, you already have an understanding about the difference between §187(1) and §187(2) and thus appreciate the most important theory behind the section's organization. Section 187(1) governs default rules and §187(2) governs mandatory rules. As for the operation of the various parts of §187(2), it is a good idea to take a look at the section that is reprinted immediately below and then try your hand at Problem 2-48. You might want to skip over the comments after §187 for now, and come back to them after you have completed Problem 2-48.

From the Restatement (Second) of Conflict of Laws, on the Subject of Contracts:

§187. Law of the State Chosen by the Parties

(1) The law of the state chosen by the parties to govern their contractual rights and duties will be applied if the particular issue is one which the parties could have resolved by an explicit provision in their agreement directed to that issue.

(2) The law of the state chosen by the parties to govern their contractual rights and duties will be applied, even if the particular issue is one which the parties could not have resolved by an explicit provision in their agreement directed to that issue, unless either

[handwritten margin note: w/in zone of your states rules]

(a) the chosen state has no substantial relationship to the parties or the transaction and there is no other reasonable basis for the parties' choice, or

(b) application of the law of the chosen state would be contrary to a fundamental policy of a state which has a materially greater interest than the chosen state in the determination of the particular issue and which, under the rule of §188, would be the state of the applicable law in the absence of an effective choice of law by the parties.

(3) In the absence of a contrary indication of intention, the reference is to the local law of the state of the chosen law.

Comment:

b. Impropriety or mistake. A choice-of-law provision, like any other contractual provision, will not be given effect if the consent of one of the parties to its inclusion in the contract was obtained by improper means, such as by misrepresentation, duress, or undue influence, or by mistake. Whether such consent was in fact obtained by improper means or by mistake will be determined by the forum in accordance with its own legal principles. A factor which the forum may consider is whether the choice-of-law provision is contained in an "adhesion" contract, namely one that is drafted unilaterally by the dominant party and then presented on a "take-it-or-leave-it" basis to the weaker party who has no real opportunity to bargain about its terms. Such contracts are usually prepared in printed form, and frequently at least some of their provisions are in extremely small print. . . .

Comment on Subsection (1):

c. Issues the parties could have determined by explicit agreement directed to particular issue. The rule of this Subsection is a rule providing for incorporation by reference and is not a rule of choice of law. The parties, generally speaking, have power to determine the terms of their contractual engagements. They may spell out these terms in the contract. In the alternative, they may incorporate into the contract by reference extrinsic material which may, among other things, be the provisions of some foreign law. In such instances, the forum will apply the applicable provisions of the law of the designated state in order to effectuate the intentions of the parties. So much has never been doubted. The point deserves emphasis nevertheless because most rules of contract law are designed to fill gaps in a contract which the parties could themselves have filled with express provisions. This is generally true, for example, of rules relating to construction, to conditions precedent and subsequent, to sufficiency of performance and to excuse for nonperformance, including questions of frustration and impossibility. As to all such matters, the forum will apply the provisions of the chosen law.

Whether the parties could have determined a particular issue by explicit agreement directed to that issue is a question to be determined by the local law of the state selected by application of the rule of §188. Usually, however, this will be a question that would be decided the same way by the relevant local law rules of all the potentially interested states. On such occasions, there is no need for the forum to determine the state of the applicable law.

Comment on Subsection (2):

d. Issues the parties could not have determined by explicit agreement directed to particular issue. The rule of this Subsection applies only when two or more states have an interest in the determination of the particular issue. The rule does not apply when all contacts are located in a single state and when, as a consequence, there is only one interested state. Subject to this qualification, the rule of this Subsection applies when it is sought to have the chosen law determine issues which the parties could not have determined by explicit agreement directed to the particular issue. Examples of such questions are those involving capacity, formalities and substantial validity. A person cannot vest himself with contractual capacity by stating in the contract that he has such capacity. He cannot dispense with formal requirements, such as that of a writing, by agreeing with the other party that the contract shall be binding without them. Nor can he by a similar device avoid issues of substantial validity, such as whether the contract is illegal. Usually, however, the local law of the state chosen by the parties will be applied to regulate matters of this sort. And it will usually be applied even when to do so would require disregard of some local provision of the state which would otherwise be the state of the applicable law.

Permitting the parties in the usual case to choose the applicable law is not, of course, tantamount to giving them complete freedom to contract as they will. Their power to choose the applicable law is subject to the two qualifications set forth in this Subsection (see Comments *f-g*).

. . .

Comment:

f. Requirement of reasonable basis for parties' choice
. . . When the state of the chosen law has some substantial relationship to the parties or the contract, the parties will be held to have had a reasonable basis for their choice. This will be the case, for example, when this state is that where performance by one of the parties is to take place or where one of the parties is domiciled or has his principal place of business. The same will also be the case when this state is the place of contracting except, perhaps, in the unusual situation where this place is wholly fortuitous and bears no real relation either to the contract or to the parties. . . .

The parties to a multistate contract may have a reasonable basis for choosing a state with which the contract has no substantial relationship. For example, when contracting in countries whose legal systems are strange to them as well as relatively immature, the parties should be able to choose a law on the ground that they know it well and that it is sufficiently developed. For only in this way can they be sure of knowing accurately the extent of their rights and duties under the contract. So parties to a contract for the transportation of goods by sea between two countries with relatively undeveloped legal systems should be permitted to submit their contract to some well-known and highly elaborated commercial law.

g. When application of chosen law would be contrary to fundamental policy of state of otherwise applicable law. Fulfillment of the parties' expectations is not the only value in contract law; regard must also be had for state interest and for state regulation. The chosen law should not be applied without regard for the interests of the state which would be the state of the applicable law with respect to the particular issue involved in the absence of an effective choice by the parties. The forum will not refrain from applying the chosen law merely because this would lead to a different result than would be obtained under the local law of the state of the otherwise applicable law. . . .

Comment on Subsection (3):

h. Reference is to "local law" of chosen state. The reference, in the absence of a contrary indication of intention, is to the "local law" of the chosen state and not to that state's "law," which means the totality of its law including its choice-of-law rules. When they choose the state which is to furnish the law governing the validity of their contract, the parties almost certainly have the "local law," rather than the "law," of that state in mind (compare §186, Comment *b*). To apply the "law" of the chosen state would introduce the uncertainties of choice of law into the proceedings and would serve to defeat the basic objectives, namely those of certainty and predictability, which the choice-of-law provision was designed to achieve.

PROBLEM 2-48: POSITIVE AND NEGATIVE MIRROR IMAGES OF §187(2)

Circle the correct word (in bold) for completing the following two formulations of Restatement (Second) §187(2):

Negative Formulation

The parties' choice of law governs *unless*

a. the chosen state has no substantial relation to the parties or the transaction

> **AND**   **OR**

> there is no other reasonable basis for the parties' choice

> **AND**   **OR**

b. application of the chosen state's law would be contrary to a fundamental policy of the state that would be designated under §188.

Positive Formulation

The parties' choice of law governs if

a. the chosen state has a substantial relation to the parties or the transaction

> **AND**   **OR**

> there is another reasonable basis for the parties' choice

> **AND**   **OR**

b. application of the chosen state's law would not be contrary to a fundamental policy of the state that would be designated under §188.

Nedlloyd Lines B.V. v. Superior Court of San Mateo County
834 P.2d 1148 (Cal. 1992)

BAXTER, J.

We granted review to consider the effect of a choice-of-law clause in a contract between commercial entities to finance and operate an international shipping business. In our order granting review, we limited our consideration to the question whether and to what extent the law of Hong Kong, chosen in the parties' agreement, should be applied in ruling on defendant's demurrer to plaintiff's complaint.

We conclude the choice-of-law clause, which requires that the contract be "governed by" the law of Hong Kong, a jurisdiction having a substantial connection with the parties, is fully enforceable and applicable to claims for breach of the implied covenant of good faith and fair dealing and for breach of fiduciary duties allegedly arising out of the contract. Our conclusion rests on the choice-of-law rules derived from California decisions and the Restatement Second of Conflict of Laws, which reflect strong policy considerations favoring the enforcement of freely negotiated choice-of-law clauses. Based on our conclusion, we will reverse the judgments of the Court of Appeal and remand for further proceedings.

Plaintiff and real party in interest Seawinds Limited (Seawinds) is a shipping company. . . . Seawinds was incorporated in Hong Kong in late 1982 and has its principal place of business in Redwood City, California. Defendants and petitioners Nedlloyd Lines B.V., Royal Nedlloyd Group N.V., and KNSM Lines B.V. (collectively referred to as Nedlloyd) are interrelated shipping companies incorporated in the Netherlands with their principal place of business in Rotterdam.

In March 1983, Nedlloyd and other parties (including an Oregon corporation, a Hong Kong corporation, a British corporation, three individual residents of California, and a resident of Singapore) entered into a contract with Seawinds to purchase shares of Seawinds's stock. The contract, which was entitled "Shareholders' Agreement in Respect of Seawinds Limited," stated that its purpose was "to establish [Seawinds] as a joint venture company to carry on a transportation operation." The agreement also provided that Seawinds would carry on the business of the transportation company and that the parties to the agreement would use "means reasonably available" to ensure the business was a success.

The shareholders' agreement between the parties contained the following choice-of-law and forum selection provision: "This agreement shall be governed by and construed in accordance with Hong Kong law and each party hereby irrevocably submits to the non-exclusive jurisdiction and service of process of the Hong Kong courts."

In January 1989, Seawinds sued Nedlloyd, alleging in essence that Nedlloyd breached express and implied obligations under the shareholders' agreement by: "(1) engaging in activities that led to the cancellation of charter hires that were essential to Seawinds' business; (2) attempting to interfere with a proposed joint service agreement between Seawinds and the East Asiatic Company, and delaying its implementation; (3) making and then reneging on commitments to contribute additional capital, thereby dissuading others from dealing with Seawinds, and (4) making false and disparaging statements about Seawinds' business operations and financial condition." Seawinds's original and first amended complaint included causes of action for breach of contract, breach of the implied covenant of good faith and fair dealing (in both contract and tort), and breach of fiduciary duty. This matter comes before us after trial court rulings on demurrers to Seawinds's complaints.

Nedlloyd demurred to Seawinds's original complaint on the grounds that it failed to state causes of action for breach of the implied covenant of good faith and fair dealing (either in contract or in tort) and breach of fiduciary duty. In support of its demurrer, Nedlloyd contended the shareholders' agreement required the application of Hong Kong law to Seawinds's claims. In opposition to the demurrer, Seawinds argued that California law should be applied to its causes of action. . . .

I. THE PROPER TEST

We reaffirm th[e Restatement Second] approach. In determining the enforceability of arm's-length contractual choice-of-law provisions, California courts shall apply the principles set forth in Restatement section 187, which reflects a strong policy favoring enforcement of such provisions.[4] . . .

Briefly restated, the proper approach under Restatement section 187, subdivision (2) is for the court first to determine either: (1) whether the chosen state has a substantial relationship to the parties or their transaction, or (2) whether there is any other reasonable basis for the parties' choice of law. If neither of these tests is met, that is the end of the inquiry, and the court need not enforce the parties' choice of law. If, however, either test is met, the court must next determine whether the chosen state's law is contrary to a *fundamental* policy of California.[5] If there is no such conflict, the court shall enforce the parties' choice of law. If, however, there is a fundamental conflict with California law, the court must then determine whether California has a "materially greater interest than the chosen state in the determination of the particular issue. . . ." (Rest., §187, subd. (2).) If California has a materially greater interest than the chosen state, the choice of law shall not be enforced, for the obvious reason that in such circumstance we will decline to enforce a law contrary to this state's fundamental policy.[6] We now apply the Restatement test to the facts of this case.

4. There may be an exception to application of the Restatement approach. Choice-of-law issues arising from contracts subject to the Uniform Commercial Code are governed by California Commercial Code section 1105, subdivision (1), which provides that, subject to specified exceptions, the parties may choose the law of a state having a "reasonable relation" to the transaction. This "reasonable relation" test appears to be similar to the "substantial relationship" test we adopt from the Restatement. (*See* official code com. to U. Com. Code §1-105 [Cal. Code§1105 (Deering 1986) p. 10; 23A Cal. Code §1105 (West 1964) p. 37].) Neither party to this action, however, contends that California Uniform Commercial Code section 1105 applies to their contract. We therefore need not and do not determine whether and to what extent, if any, the Commercial Code and Restatement approaches are different.

5. To be more precise, we note that Restatement section 187, subdivision (2) refers not merely to the forum state — for example, California in the present case — but rather to the state ". . . which, under the rule of §188, would be the state of the applicable law in the absence of an effective choice of law by the parties." For example, there may be an occasional case in which California is the forum, and the parties have chosen the law of another state, but the law of yet a third state, rather than California's, would apply absent the parties' choice. In that situation, a California court will look to the fundamental policy of the third state in determining whether to enforce the parties' choice of law. The present case is not such a situation.

6. There may also be instances when the chosen state has a materially greater interest in the matter than does California, but enforcement of the law of the chosen state would lead to a result

II. APPLICATION OF THE TEST IN THIS CASE

. . .

B. IMPLIED COVENANT OF GOOD FAITH AND FAIR DEALING

1. Substantial Relationship or Reasonable Basis

As to the first required determination, Hong Kong — "the chosen state" — clearly has a "substantial relationship to the parties." (Rest., §187, subd. (2)(a).) The shareholders' agreement, which is incorporated by reference in Seawinds' first amended complaint, shows that Seawinds is incorporated under the laws of Hong Kong and has a registered office there. The same is true of one of the shareholder parties to the agreement — Red Coconut Trading Co. The incorporation of these parties in Hong Kong provides the required "substantial relationship." (*Id.*,) com. f [substantial relationship present when "one of the parties is domiciled" in the chosen state].

Moreover, the presence of two Hong Kong corporations as parties also provides a "reasonable basis" for a contractual provision requiring application of Hong Kong law. "If one of the parties resides in the chosen state, the parties have a reasonable basis for their choice." The reasonableness of choosing Hong Kong becomes manifest when the nature of the agreement before us is considered. A state of incorporation is certainly at least one government entity with a keen and intimate interest in internal corporate affairs, including the purchase and sale of its shares, as well as corporate management and operations. (See Corp. Code, §102 [applying California's general corporation law to domestic corporations].)

2. Existence of Fundamental Public Policy

We next consider whether application of the law chosen by the parties would be contrary to "a fundamental policy" of California. We perceive no fundamental policy of California requiring the application of California law to Seawinds's claims based on the implied covenant of good faith and fair dealing. The covenant is not a government regulatory policy designed to restrict freedom of contract, but an implied promise inserted in an agreement to carry out the presumed intentions of contracting parties.

Seawinds directs us to no authority exalting the *implied* covenant of good faith and fair dealing over the *express* covenant of these parties that Hong Kong law shall govern their agreement. We have located none. Because Seawinds has identified no fundamental policy of our state at issue in its essentially contractual dispute with Nedlloyd, the second exception to the rule of section 187 of the Restatement does not apply.

---

contrary to a fundamental policy of California. In some such cases, enforcement of the law of the chosen state may be appropriate despite California's policy to the contrary. Careful consideration, however, of California's policy and the other state's interest would be required. No such question is present in this case, and we thus need not and do not decide how Restatement section 187 would apply in such circumstances.

C. FIDUCIARY DUTY CAUSE OF ACTION

1. Scope of the Choice-of-Law Clause

Seawinds contends that, whether or not the choice-of-law clause governs Sea-winds's implied covenant claim, Seawinds's fiduciary duty claim is somehow independent of the shareholders' agreement and therefore outside the intended scope of the clause. Seawinds thus concludes California law must be applied to this claim. We disagree.

When two sophisticated, commercial entities agree to a choice-of-law clause like the one in this case, the most reasonable interpretation of their actions is that they intended for the clause to apply to all causes of action arising from or related to their contract. Initially, such an interpretation is supported by the plain meaning of the language used by the parties. The choice-of-law clause in the share-holders' agreement provides: "This agreement shall be *governed by* and construed in accordance with Hong Kong law and each party hereby irrevocably submits to the non-exclusive jurisdiction and service of process of the Hong Kong courts."[7]

The phrase "governed by" is a broad one signifying a relationship of absolute direction, control, and restraint. Thus, the clause reflects the parties' clear contemplation that "the agreement" is to be completely and absolutely controlled by Hong Kong law. No exceptions are provided. In the context of this case, the agreement to be controlled by Hong Kong law is a shareholders' agreement that expressly provides for the purchase of shares in Seawinds by Nedlloyd and creates the relationship between shareholder and corporation that gives rise to Sea-winds's cause of action. Nedlloyd's fiduciary duties, if any, arise from — and can exist only because of — the shareholders' agreement pursuant to which Sea-winds's stock was purchased by Nedlloyd.

In order to control completely the agreement of the parties, Hong Kong law must also govern the stock purchase portion of that agreement and the legal duties created by or emanating from the stock purchase, including any fiduciary duties. If Hong Kong law were not applied to these duties, it would effectively control only part of the agreement, not all of it. Such an interpretation would be inconsistent with the unrestricted character of the choice-of-law clause.

Our conclusion in this regard comports with common sense and commercial reality. When a rational businessperson enters into an agreement establishing a transaction or relationship and provides that disputes arising from the agreement shall be governed by the law of an identified jurisdiction, the logical conclusion is that he or she intended that law to apply to *all* disputes arising out of the

7. As we have noted, the choice-of-law clause states: "This agreement shall be governed by and *construed in accordance with Hong Kong law. . . .*" (Italics added.) The agreement, of course, includes the choice-of-law clause itself. Thus the question of whether that clause is ambiguous as to its scope (i.e., whether it includes the fiduciary duty claim) is a question of contract interpretation that in the normal course should be determined pursuant to Hong Kong law. The parties in this case, however, did not request judicial notice of Hong Kong law on this question of interpretation (Evid. Code, §452, subd. (f)) or supply us with evidence of the relevant aspects of that law (Evid. Code, §453, subd. (b)). The question therefore becomes one of California law.

transaction or relationship. We seriously doubt that any rational businessperson, attempting to provide by contract for an efficient and business-like resolution of possible future disputes, would intend that the laws of multiple jurisdictions would apply to a single controversy having its origin in a single, contract-based relationship. Nor do we believe such a person would reasonably desire a protracted litigation battle concerning only the threshold question of what law was to be applied to which asserted claims or issues. Indeed, the manifest purpose of a choice-of-law clause is precisely to avoid such a battle.

Seawinds's view of the problem — which would require extensive litigation of the parties' supposed intentions regarding the choice-of-law clause to the end that the laws of multiple states might be applied to their dispute — is more likely the product of postdispute litigation strategy, not predispute contractual intent. If commercially sophisticated parties (such as those now before us) truly intend the result advocated by Seawinds, they should, in fairness to one another and in the interest of economy in dispute resolution, negotiate and obtain the assent of their fellow parties to explicit contract language specifying what jurisdiction's law applies to what issues.

For the reasons stated above, we hold a valid choice-of-law clause, which provides that a specified body of law "governs" the "agreement" between the parties, encompasses all causes of action arising from or related to that agreement, regardless of how they are characterized, including tortious breaches of duties emanating from the agreement or the legal relationships it creates.

2. Enforceability of Chosen Law as to Fiduciary Duty Claim

Applying the test we have adopted, we find no reason not to apply the parties' choice of law to Seawinds's cause of action for breach of fiduciary duty. As we have explained, Hong Kong, the chosen state, has a "substantial relationship to the parties" because two of those parties are incorporated there. Moreover, their incorporation in that state affords a "reasonable basis" for choosing Hong Kong law.

Seawinds identifies no fundamental public policy of this state that would be offended by application of Hong Kong law to a claim by a Hong Kong corporation against its allegedly controlling shareholder. We are directed to no California statute or constitutional provision designed to preclude freedom of contract in this context. Indeed, even in the absence of a choice-of-law clause, Hong Kong's overriding interest in the internal affairs of corporations domiciled there would in most cases require application of its law.

For strategic reasons related to its current dispute with Nedlloyd, Seawinds seeks to create a fiduciary relationship by disregarding the law Seawinds voluntarily agreed to accept as binding — the law of a state that also happens to be Seawinds's own corporate domicile. To allow Seawinds to use California law in this fashion would further no ascertainable fundamental policy of California; indeed, it would undermine California's policy of respecting the choices made by parties to voluntarily negotiated agreements.

Notes on

NEDLLOYD

1. As efficient and appealing as they seem, choice of law clauses spawn quite a lot of litigation. Indeed, the *Nedlloyd* case and the cases that came after it provide an accurate portrayal of the litigation, which focuses both on the issues arising from §187 requirements as well as from the drafting of the clauses themselves.

2. Courts applying §187 must first determine whether the issue in dispute is a mandatory rule or a default rule. This characterization can be determinative, since parties need not worry about any justification for the selected law if the issue concerns a default rule. If, however, the rule is a mandatory rule, then several questions arise. Is the chosen jurisdiction one with a substantial relationship to the parties or the transaction? If not, the chosen law might still apply if there's a reasonable basis for the choice. When might the parties have a reasonable basis for choosing a jurisdiction that does not have a substantial relationship to the parties or the transaction? The decision in *1-800-Got Junk? v. Superior Court*—which immediately follows—illustrates such a circumstance.

But, alas, even if those two factors do not provide obstacles for the parties' chosen law, the analysis isn't ended yet: the state that would have its law applied in the absence of the parties' choice (known as the §188 state) can still have an effective veto. The veto occurs where the chosen law is contrary to a fundamental policy of the §188 state and the §188 state has a materially greater interest in applying its law than the chosen state. This, it turns out, is a particularly cumbersome step of the analysis because it requires figuring out what law would govern without the clause. (The importance of this step is illustrated below in connection with *Hodas v. Morin*, 814 N.E.2d 320 (Mass. 2004).) Does all this complexity give you any reason to question whether §187 is well designed to promote the efficiency and predictability that choice of law clauses are designed to avoid?

3. Which *Nedlloyd* opinion has the better argument on whether the choice of law clause's scope extends to the breach of fiduciary duty cause of action? The particular scope dispute in *Nedlloyd* is common: does a choice of law clause in a contract pertain to non-contract causes of action? This is not the only problem surrounding inquiry into the scope of a choice of law clause. It turns out that scope inquiry embodies many subtleties, some of which *Nedlloyd* illustrates:

- Both the majority and the dissent agree that—in the ordinary course—Hong Kong law should govern the process of answering this scope question. (It was only because the parties had not established Hong Kong law that the justices looked to California law.) Do you agree that Hong Kong law should have governed this question? The court reasoned that the scope dispute raised a contract interpretation question, and that the court should follow the clause's mandate to "construe" the clause in accordance with Hong Kong law. That analysis works only if the court has already judged the clause to be valid under §187. Also, is the court correct in charactering the question as one of contract interpretation? Couldn't you also characterize the question of the clause's scope as a choice of law issue? In that event, would it be Hong Kong law or forum law that should govern?

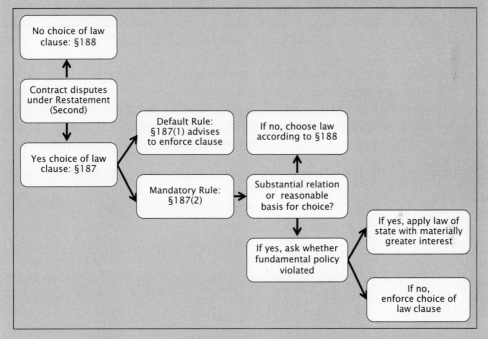

Figure 2-2: Choice of Law Clauses Under the Restatement (Second)

- Other interpretation questions regarding scope can lurk in apparently clear language. For example: when the parties agree that "State X law shall govern all disputes," did they mean both procedural and substantive law? Also, does the reference to State X law include both the internal law of State X *and* the conflict of law rules of that jurisdiction? Look back at the language of §187: does it provide any guidance on how to handle this latter question?
- The *Nedlloyd* court treated the scope issue as purely an issue of party intent. In other words, the court evaluated the scope of the clause only by asking: what did the parties intend when they chose the words they did? Yet scope disputes also implicate another, more fundamental, issue: did the parties even have the power to agree that a certain law would govern matters beyond those directly related to contract rights and contract interpretation? Courts often overlook

> this question. Should courts take a more restrictive view of choice of law clauses in the context of non-contract causes of action? After all, the law tends to be more paternalistic and intent-defeating for such causes of action than in the area of breach of contract, where legal principles tend to favor freedom of contract and party autonomy.

PROBLEM 2-49: MANDATORY OR DEFAULT DOLLARS

Henri and Hank entered into a contract whereby Hank agreed to write a poem for Henri's parents' anniversary. Henri is domiciled in Sydney, Australia and Hank is domiciled in Philadelphia, Pennsylvania, USA. They entered into the contract through emails sent over the internet. Each of the parties was in their respective domicile at the time of the email correspondence, which stated as follows:

Hank: I will be happy to write the poem for a fee of $1,000 to be sent by wire transfer to my bank account.

Henri: That's fine. I will pay you that amount by wire transfer upon receiving a poem befitting of the occasion. I need the poem in two weeks. In addition, and I know this sounds awfully formal, I've heard it is a good idea to state in writing that our agreement will be governed by the law of Australia. Please let me know if these terms are acceptable.

Hank: The terms are fine. I will get you the poem in two weeks and you will pay the agreed amount. The agreement is governed by Australian law.

Hank wrote the poem and Henri sent him an email saying how much he and his parents liked it. The parties now dispute whether the fee should be paid in Australian dollars or United States dollars. Assume that Australian law provides no legal restriction on the sum mentioned and that the amount should be assumed to be stated in Australian dollars. Assume that United States law provides no legal restriction on the sum mentioned and that the amount should be assumed to be stated in United States dollars. Which law governs the currency question?

PROBLEM 2-50: DRAFTING CHOICE OF LAW CLAUSES

The following exercises are designed to provide insight into the strategies and pitfalls of drafting a choice of law clause:

(1) Assume that you want to draft a clause that unambiguously covers contract and non-contract claims that may arise between the parties to the contract. What language might you use? Do you see any problem with using such broad language?

(2) Assume that you want to draft a clause that unambiguously covers only contract claims that may arise between the parties to the contract. What language might you use?

(3) Assume that you are negotiating a contract and the lawyer for the other party included the following in a draft: "This contract is subject to the laws of the state of Iowa." Do you foresee any ambiguities with that clause or any potential difficulties with using that language as a choice of law clause?

(4) Assume that you are negotiating a contract on behalf of a client. You are uncomfortable designating all of the law of a jurisdiction to govern the parties' rights arising from a contract, since most of the most obvious jurisdictions have laws that are both favorable and unfavorable for your client. For that reason, you do not want to include a general choice of law clause in a contract. You are, however, worried that the law of State R might govern a dispute between the parties, and would like to avoid the restitutionary remedies available in State R. Your client is domiciled in State C and the contract is being negotiated and signed in State C. State C does not have any restitutionary remedies, so you are much more comfortable with State C's remedy law. The other party to the contract is from State R and the contract will be performed there. How would you draft a clause that avoids State R's restitutionary remedies without agreeing to all of State R's law?

(5) Consider the following facts: Plaintiff was a customer and "member" of defendant's "big box" food store. The membership agreement stated that "any dispute arising out of or relating in any way" to plaintiff's relationship to defendant shall be controlled by Oregon law for all purposes. Defendant had plaintiff arrested for allegedly stealing merchandise. Plaintiff was innocent and sued defendant for false imprisonment. Should plaintiff prevail in convincing the court that the lawsuit is governed by the choice of law clause?

1-800-Got Junk? LLC v. Superior Court of Los Angeles County

116 Cal. Rptr. 3d 923 (Cal. App. 2d 2010)

Opinion by KLEIN, P.J.

Millennium Asset Recovery, Inc. (Millennium), a franchisee, is suing petitioner 1-800-Got Junk? LLC (Got Junk), the franchisor, for wrongfully terminating Millennium's franchise.[1] The franchise agreement specifies the application of the law of Washington State. Millennium seeks to enforce the choice of law provision in the franchise agreement. Got Junk contends the choice of law provision in its franchise agreement is unenforceable because there is no reasonable basis for the application of Washington law; Got Junk seeks the application of California law. Following a bifurcated choice of law trial, the trial court held Washington law applies to this action.

In the instant petition, Got Junk seeks a writ of mandate directing respondent superior court to vacate its order that the law of Washington State applies to this action and to enter a new order that California law applies. We

---

1. A "franchisee" is a person to whom a franchise is granted. (Bus. & Prof. Code, §20002.) A "franchisor" is a person who grants or has granted a franchise. (Bus. & Prof. Code, §20003.)

conclude the trial court properly gave credence to the choice of law provision in the franchise agreement and therefore we deny Got Junk's petition for writ of mandate.

The essential issues are (1) whether a reasonable basis existed for the inclusion of the Washington choice of law provision in the franchise agreement; and (2), if so, whether California public policy precludes application of the parties' chosen law.

Because a multistate franchisor has an interest in having its franchise agreements governed by a uniform body of law, Got Junk had a reasonable basis for inserting a choice of law provision in the franchise agreement. As for the designation of Washington law in particular, given that state's proximity to Got Junk's headquarters in Vancouver, Canada, there was a reasonable basis for the parties' choice of law.

The remaining issue is whether enforcement of the Washington choice of law provision is barred by section 20010 (California Franchise Relations Act (CFRA) (§20000 et seq.)). In order to protect franchisees domiciled or operating in California (§20015), section 20010 declares: "Any condition, stipulation or provision purporting to bind any person to *waive compliance* with any provision of this law is contrary to public policy and void." (Italics added.)

In this instance, Washington State is more protective of franchisees than California, in that Washington's Franchise Investment Protection Act (WFIPA) restricts the franchisor to *four situations* in which a franchisor can summarily terminate a franchise without providing notice and an opportunity to cure (Wn. Rev. Code §19.100.180), while the California statutory scheme provides for immediate termination without opportunity to cure *in the same four situations as well as numerous others.* (§20021, subds. (a)-(k).) Thus, the instant franchise agreement, by giving the franchisee superior protection under Washington law, does not require a franchisee to "waive compliance" with any provision of the CFRA. (§20010.) Therefore, enforcement of the instant choice of law provision does not contravene California public policy and is not barred by section 20010.

. . . Defendant and petitioner Got Junk, a Delaware limited liability company, the franchisor, is a junk removal franchise business headquartered in Vancouver, British Columbia, Canada.

On December 26, 2003, plaintiff and real party in interest Millennium, the franchisee, entered into an agreement with Got Junk to operate a Got Junk franchise in various territories in the Los Angeles area, including Century City, Beverly Hills and Westwood. . . .

The franchise agreement at paragraph 21.12 contains the following choice of law provision: "*Governing Law.* This agreement shall be construed and interpreted according to the laws of the state of Washington." . . . [5]

5. In addition to the choice of law provision, paragraph 21.12 contains a forum selection clause, to wit: "The King County Superior Court in Seattle or the U.S. District Court in Seattle, as appropriate, shall have *exclusive jurisdiction* to entertain any proceeding in respect of this Agreement, and Franchisee and Franchisor each attorn to the jurisdiction of such Courts in all matters related to this Agreement; provided that Franchisor may obtain relief in such other

[The parties' dispute arose when Got Junk terminated Millennium's franchise on the grounds that Millennium failed to report and pay a percentage of revenue on certain jobs. The trial court held proceedings on the issue of whether the choice of law clause should be enforced to govern this dispute.]

[At those proceedings,] Brian Scudamore, founder and chief executive of Got Junk, filed a declaration disclaiming any knowledge as to why Got Junk's franchise agreement contains a choice of law provision. Scudamore stated: "I have reviewed the wording of Section 21.12 of the Agreement . . . which states in part that the Agreement shall be 'construed and interpreted according to Washington law.' *I do not have an understanding as[to] why the Agreement states that it shall be construed and interpreted according to Washington law.* [Got Junk] has never determined that Washington law provides better protections or is more beneficial to [Got Junk] or to any of its franchisees than the laws of any other state in which [Got Junk] operates." (Italics added.)

[The trial court ruled:]

"There was a reasonable basis for [Got Junk] to designate Washington law as the law governing the agreement. Therefore, the test set forth in the Restatement (Second) of Conflicts of Law 187(2) is satisfied. [¶] Reasonableness is an objective standard. Therefore, Mr. Scudamore's declaration about what actually happened at some point and his subjective intent is really not much help. It does not contravene the objective reasonableness of the decision to designate Washington law. It's also puzzling that he does not say why Washington law was selected as he appears to be in a position to know. Therefore, as [Millennium] puts it, if it [were] selected by random use of a dart board, Mr. Scudamore appears to have had it in his power to say so and he failed to do so. . . .

"The objective facts are that it is reasonable for a company doing business in many states to designate the laws of one state in a contract that will be used in many states. If the company's lawyers are already familiar with the laws of that one state and find them favorable, they will not have to expend as much time and energy learning the laws of the remaining states. . . . [¶] . . . So [the] approach of choosing one state['s] specific scheme or franchise law is reasonable. It's also reasonable because it increases predictability and has potential to create greater uniformity, and through that uniformity, possibly cost savings."

. . . [Thereafter] Got Junk filed the instant petition for writ of mandate, seeking to overturn the trial court's ruling Washington law applies to the breach of contract action. We issued an order to show cause.

. . .

---

jurisdictions as may be necessary or desirable to obtain declaratory, injunctive or other relief to enforce the provisions of this Agreement." (Italics added.) However, the forum selection clause is not in issue in this proceeding. Neither party seeks enforcement of the forum selection clause. Millennium brought this action in the Superior Court of the State of California for the County of Los Angeles, without objection by Got Junk. We note section 20040.5 states: "A provision in a franchise agreement restricting venue to a forum outside this state is void with respect to any claim arising under or relating to a franchise agreement involving a franchise business operating within this state."

In 1980, California adopted the CFRA to protect individuals from the loss of their investments in franchises. The CFRA governs, inter alia, the termination of franchises (§20020 et seq.) and the nonrenewal of franchises (§20025 et seq.).

Section 20010 provides: "Any condition, stipulation or provision purporting to bind any person to waive compliance with any provision of this law is contrary to public policy and void." Therefore, the parties herein could not agree to "waive compliance" with any provision of the CFRA.

In this choice of law dispute, Millennium, the franchisee, has sought enforcement of the Washington choice of law provision in the franchise agreement. Got Junk, the franchisor, has resisted that position and insists on the application of California law. When the choice of law issue was tried in the court below, the parties focused on whether there was a reasonable basis for the application of Washington law. Millennium argued that in the interest of franchise uniformity, the franchise agreement properly designated Washington law to apply to the franchise agreement. Got Junk, in turn, disclaimed any knowledge of why its form franchise agreement included the choice of law provision.

Remarkably, the bifurcated choice of law trial proceeded without any consideration of the CFRA, the California statutory scheme governing franchise relations. The parties and trial court overlooked the critical issue herein, namely, the impact of the CFRA, specifically, section 20010, on the enforceability of the choice of law provision in the franchise agreement.

In order to obtain enforcement of the Washington choice of law provision, Millennium was required to show a reasonable basis for its inclusion in the franchise agreement. . . . To avoid enforcement of the choice of law provision, Got Junk then was required to show the chosen law is contrary to a fundamental public policy of this state. (*Ibid.*)

As explained below, we conclude a reasonable basis existed for the inclusion of the Washington choice of law provision in the franchise agreement. Further, California public policy is not offended by the franchise agreement's granting the franchisee greater protection than what is mandated by the CFRA. Therefore, the trial court properly gave credence to the franchise agreement's designation of Washington law. . . . We begin with the basic premise that choice of law provisions are enforceable, unless grounds exist for not enforcing them. . . . In *Washington Mutual Bank v. Superior Court*, 15 P.3d 1071 (2001), the California Supreme Court set forth the parties' respective burdens on a choice of law question as follows: "if the proponent of the clause [(here, Millennium)] demonstrates that the chosen state has a substantial relationship to the parties or their transaction, or that a reasonable basis otherwise exists for the choice of law, the parties' choice generally will be enforced *unless the other side can establish* both that the chosen law is contrary to a fundamental policy of California and that California has a materially greater interest in the determination of the particular issue."

. . . Millennium admitted in its papers below "there is no substantial relationship between [Millennium] or the transaction . . . and the State of Washington."[Nonetheless, Millennium has shown a reasonable basis exists for the franchise agreement's selection of Washington law.]

. . . [Millennium's attorney] Napell, an experienced franchise lawyer, stated there is a benefit to a franchisor and a franchise system in having a single set of rules apply to all franchisees, and because Washington State is the closest United States jurisdiction to Got Junk's headquarters in Vancouver, Canada, it was reasonable for Got Junk to have designated the law of that state in the choice of law provision. . . .

[C]ase law has recognized it is reasonable for a franchisor to designate a single state's law to apply to all of its franchise agreements. . . . [T]he trial court's determination a reasonable basis existed for the Washington choice of law provision is supported by Napell's declaration on behalf of Millennium, and is consistent with case law recognizing the interest of uniformity in franchise operations. Because a multistate franchisor has an interest in having its franchise agreements governed by one body of law, Got Junk had a reasonable basis for inserting a choice of law provision in the franchise agreement. Further, given Washington State's proximity to Got Junk's headquarters in Vancouver, Canada, there was a reasonable basis for the designation of that state's law in particular.

However, this discussion does not end our inquiry.

. . . Even if the proponent of the choice of law provision establishes a reasonable basis for the parties' choice of law, enforcement of their choice of law provision will be denied if "the other side can establish *both* that the chosen law is contrary to a fundamental policy of California *and* that California has a materially greater interest in the determination of the particular issue." As explained below, Got Junk has failed to establish the chosen law of Washington contravenes the fundamental public policy embodied in the CFRA. Therefore, Millennium is entitled to enforcement of the instant choice of law provision.

. . . The CFRA serves to protect California franchisees, typically small business owners and entrepreneurs, from abuses by franchisors in connection with the nonrenewal and termination of franchises. Courts are required to construe "the CFRA *broadly to carry out legislative intent,* that intent . . . is to protect franchise *investors*—i.e., those who 'pay for the right to enter into a business.'" . . . The provisions of the CFRA "apply to any franchise where either the franchisee is domiciled in this state or the franchised business is or has been operated in this state." (§20015.)

The statutory scheme generally prohibits termination of a franchise prior to the expiration of its term, except for good cause. "Good cause shall include, but not be limited to, the failure of the franchisee to comply with any lawful requirement of the franchise agreement after being given notice thereof and a reasonable opportunity, which in no event need be more than 30 days, to cure the failure." The statutory scheme also specifies certain grounds for immediate notice of termination without the opportunity to cure.

. . . The pivotal section of the CFRA for our purposes is section 20010, an antiwaiver provision. It states: "Any condition, stipulation or provision purporting to bind any person to waive compliance with any provision of this law is contrary to public policy and void."

The essential issue presented is whether section 20010 invalidates the Washington choice of law provision in the instant franchise agreement. . . . [Under our interpretation,] section 20010 only voids a choice of law provision which requires a franchisee to "waive compliance" with the protections of the CFRA. *Therefore, the critical inquiry is whether enforcement of the Washington choice of law provision would diminish Millennium's rights under the CFRA.*

A comparison of the CFRA and the WFIPA shows that Washington affords a franchisee far greater protection from summary termination of a franchise. The CFRA at section 20021, subdivisions (a) through (k), sets forth 11 grounds for immediate notice of termination, without giving the franchisee an opportunity to cure. In contrast, the WFIPA, which is the parties' chosen law, severely restricts the ability of a franchisor to summarily terminate a franchise. . . . Washington Revised Code section 19.100.180(2)(j) authorizes a franchisor to terminate a franchise *without notice or an opportunity to cure* in only four situations. . . . The instant franchise agreement, giving the franchisee superior protection from summary termination pursuant to Washington law, is not a waiver of compliance with the CFRA. California public policy is not offended if the franchisor contractually obligates itself to give notice and an opportunity to cure in situations where the CFRA would permit immediate termination of a franchise. *In other words, the public policy of this state is not offended by a franchise agreement giving a franchisee superior protection from summary termination under the chosen law of another state.* Therefore, enforcement of the instant choice of law provision is not barred by section 20010.

We further note that had the Legislature intended the restriction in section 20010 to have the absolute effect suggested by Got Junk, it could have so specified. By way of comparison, the CFRA, at section 20040.5, categorically prohibits *forum selection clauses* in franchise agreements, stating: "A provision in a franchise agreement restricting venue to a forum outside this state is void with respect to any claim arising under or relating to a franchise agreement involving a franchise business operating within this state."

The Legislature could have written section 20010 to categorically prohibit *choice of law provisions* in franchise agreements. Instead, section 20010 only voids a choice of law provision if the provision would subvert a franchisee's protections under the CFRA. In the instant case, the choice of law provision enhances the franchisee's protections. Therefore, the choice of law provision is valid.[11]

. . .

Finally, Got Junk contends the choice of law provision, calling for the application of Washington law, is unenforceable because "[n]owhere in WFIPA does the Washington legislature expressly declare any intent for WFIPA to apply to disputes occurring outside of Washington."

The argument is an irrelevancy. Irrespective of whether the WFIPA otherwise contains territorial restrictions on its application, the parties were free to agree that their franchise relations would be governed by Washington substantive law and they did precisely that, by way of a valid choice of law clause. Therefore, this

---

11. . . . *Taylor v. 1-800-Got-Junk?, LLC* (W.D. Wn. 2009) 632 F. Supp. 2d 1048, 1051-1052, which held the Washington choice of law clause in an Oregon Got Junk franchise's agreement was enforceable, is not on point because it does not involve the California statutory scheme. Our decision is controlled by the CFRA and specifically by section 20010 thereof.

state's superior court will adjudicate the matter pursuant to the parties' chosen law.

. . .

Notes on
GOT JUNK

1. *Got Junk* is an unusual case because the franchisee was the entity seeking to enforce the choice of law clause in the agreement. As explained in the *Got Junk* opinion, the franchisor is generally a multistate actor that has the greater incentive to seek a uniform legal standard governing its affairs. As the entity with the greatest bargaining power, the franchisor is generally the party who insists that the clause be inserted into the agreement and argues for enforcement when a dispute arises. One would think that in contrast to the statement of the Got Junk founder and chief executive, most franchisors choose the jurisdiction designated in the choice of law clause with care.

2. The *Got Junk* court essentially interpreted the governing California franchise statute as a floor that could be enhanced by greater franchisee protections, which the parties incorporated by designating Washington law. This type of analysis is akin to preemption analysis that governs the relationship between state and federal law. As discussed further in Chapter 3, so long as federal legal protections do not take the form of an absolute standard, state law may provide greater protections, so long as those greater protections do not interfere with the operation of federal law.

This, however, is not always the conclusion reached by courts interpreting the relationship between state franchise protections and choice of law provisions. For example, in *American Express Financial Advisors v. Yantis, Inc.*, 358 F. Supp. 2d 818, 827 (N.D. Iowa 2005), the court found a Minnesota choice of law provision void in light of the Iowa franchise statute, concluding the following about the Iowa statute:

> The Act "was created to protect franchisees operating in Iowa from abuses by franchisors and to equalize the bargaining power between franchisees and franchisors. . . . [T]he Act voids any choice of law provision in a franchise agreement regardless of whether the Act provides a cause of action for the injuries alleged by a plaintiff. *Id.* at §523H.14 ('*A condition, stipulation, or provision requiring the application of the law of another state in lieu of this chapter is void.*')"

3. Do you agree with the *Got Junk* court's conclusion that the parties had a reasonable basis for choosing Washington law? Certainly it seemed more convenient to the franchisor, but one wonders whether the court might have reached a different conclusion had the law been highly detrimental to the franchisee. Compare *Got Junk* with *Prows v. Pinpoint Retail Systems, Inc.*, 868 P.2d 809 (Utah 1993), in which the court refused to uphold a choice of law clause designating a state unrelated to the parties and the transaction.

The *Prows* court rejected the argument of a Canadian party to the contract that the choice was "reasonable" because the party was doing business in several American states and wanted to designate one state's law for the purpose of litigation convenience.

Other "reasonable" bases for choosing a particular law tend to be more neutral, not tending to clearly benefit one party. These include such bases as the well-developed nature of the chosen law or the parties' familiarity with it.

4. Millennium's concession in *Got Junk* that Washington had no substantial relationship to the parties and the transaction is also somewhat unusual. Although the requirement of §187(2) that the relationship be "substantial" suggests rigor, courts have been generally liberal in finding the requirement satisfied. PETER HAY, PATRICK J. BORCHERS & SYMEON C. SYMEO-NIDES, CONFLICT OF LAWS 1093 (5th ed. 2010). Most problems arise when all the relevant contacts coincide in one jurisdiction (all the parties' domiciles, the place of contract formation, the place of negotiation, and the place of performance) yet the parties nonetheless choose another jurisdiction. Place of negotiation alone also does not tend to provide a sufficiently substantial connection. Courts are more open-minded, however, when connections are dispersed among several states. *Id.* at 1093-1094.

5. Note how the court dismissed Got Junk's argument that the Washington statute could not be applied extraterritorially, holding that the parties could incorporate the protections of Washington law into their agreement irrespective of any territorial restrictions on the Washington statute. Got Junk was more successful pressing this argument in *Taylor v. 1-800-Got-Junk?, LLC*, 632 F. Supp. 2d 1048, 1051-1052 (W.D. Wash. 2009), *aff'd*, 387 Fed. Appx. 727 (9th Cir. 2010). In that case, the district court agreed with Got Junk and the Ninth Circuit affirmed, pointing out that the Washington statute applied by its terms "only to misrepresentations 'in connection with the offer, sale, or purchase'" of a franchise in Washington, citing the rule that "[w]hen a law contains geographical limitations on its application . . . courts will not apply it to parties falling outside those limitations, even if the parties stipulate that the law should apply." *Id.* at 729. Do you agree with this argument by the Ninth Circuit? Or do you think that the *Got Junk* court got it right?

PROBLEM 2-51: DIGITAL DYNAMICS MEETS INTELLECTUAL PROPERTY CLAIMS

Digital Dynamics, Inc. is in the business of editing digital images. It is incorporated in New York and has its principal place of business there. Its president and sole employee is domiciled in New York. Digital Dynamics rents a small office in California, but has no employees who are there on a regular basis.

Susan recorded several hours of an outdoor concert in Woodstock, New York with various performers. She brought the recording to Digital Dynamics for editing. She signed a contract with Digital Dynamics in which she represented that the recording did not violate any intellectual property rights of others. The contract, which was drafted by Digital Dynamics' lawyer, also had a choice of law clause that provided that "any dispute relating to or any way relevant to the obligations under the contract shall be governed by the internal law of the state of California." Susan is domiciled in New York.

Digital Dynamics completed the editing job and provided the finished product to Susan. One of the performers featured on the recording has taken the position that the edited recording violates her intellectual property rights and has threatened to sue Digital Dynamics. Digital Dynamics has filed a suit against Susan in New York, seeking to have Susan indemnify the corporation for any liability that Digital Dynamics might incur as a consequence of this alleged violation. You may assume that the law of indemnification on this intellectual property matter is similar under both New York law and California law, but that California law is more favorable to Digital Dynamics. Digital Dynamics has requested that the court enforce the choice of law clause under §187. Among other arguments, Digital Dynamics points out that, as home to the entertainment industry, California has numerous court cases and well-developed law pertaining to that industry. Should the court enforce the choice of law clause?

Hodas v. Morin

814 N.E.2d 320 (Mass. 2004)

MARSHALL, C.J.

Does a Probate and Family Court judge have authority pursuant to G. L. c. 215, §6, to issue prebirth judgments of parentage and to order the issuance of a prebirth record of birth, where neither the genetic parents nor the gestational carrier with whom they contracted to bear a child reside in Massachusetts, but where the contract specifies that the birth occur at a Massachusetts hospital? A judge in the Probate and Family Court answered that question in the negative, and dismissed the genetic parents' (plaintiffs) uncontested equity action for a declaration of paternity and maternity and for a prebirth order. She then reported her decision to the Appeals Court. On June 22, 2004, a single justice of the Appeals Court enjoined the defendant Berkshire Health Systems, Inc., corporate owner of Berkshire Medical Center in Pittsfield (hospital), from issuing any birth certificate for a child born of the gestational carrier, or filing the same with the Commissioner of Public Health. On June 25, 2004, we transferred the matter here on our own motion. We conclude that, in the circumstances here, the plaintiffs are entitled to the relief they seek: judgments of paternity and maternity and a prebirth order establishing their legal parentage.

1. *Facts.* The plaintiffs, who are married, reside in Connecticut. The gestational carrier and her husband, both nominal defendants, reside in New York. The hospital, the other nominal defendant, is a licensed Massachusetts hospital

whose statutory duties include, among others, reporting information concerning births at the hospital to the city or town clerk where the birth occurred.

In April, 2003, the plaintiffs, the gestational carrier, and the gestational carrier's husband entered into a fifteen-page "Contract Between a Genetic Father, a Genetic Mother, a Gestational Carrier and Her Husband" (gestational carrier agreement). The parties represented that each had been advised by counsel of their choice prior to entering into the agreement. Among other things, the gestational carrier agreement provided that any child resulting from the agreement would be delivered at the hospital, if at all possible, and that in any event the gestational carrier would "take all reasonable steps to give birth to any child carried pursuant to this Agreement at a Hospital located in the State of Massachusetts." It is undisputed that the parties chose Massachusetts as the site of the birth in part to facilitate obtaining a prebirth order.[5]

The parties' preference for Massachusetts was further expressed in the following choice of law provision:

> The Gestational Carrier and [her] husband agree that they are entering into this Agreement with the intention that in accordance with the laws of the State of Massachusetts, they will take whatever steps are necessary to have the Genetic Father and the Genetic Mother named as the natural, legal and genetic parents, to have the Genetic Father and the Genetic Mother named as the father and mother, respectively, of [the] child on the child's birth certificate, and to permit the Genetic Father and the Genetic Mother to obtain physical custody of any child born as the result of this Agreement. . . . The parties further agree that this Agreement shall be governed by Massachusetts law.

Approximately six months after the parties entered into the gestational carrier agreement, the gestational carrier was successfully implanted with an embryo produced from the male plaintiff's sperm and the female plaintiff's egg. The implantation took place in Connecticut. The gestational carrier received at least some prenatal care at the hospital. At oral argument on June 30, 2004, counsel informed the court that an induced delivery was planned at the hospital the following week.

. . .

3. *Choice of law.* The driving issue in this case, rather, concerns choice of law. The interested couples come from different States; the chosen hospital from yet a third. None of the individual parties resides in the Commonwealth, yet they have

---

5. In their brief to this court, the plaintiffs represented:

The hospital was chosen because it was a good hospital and was located half way between both parties. This half way point made it convenient for all parties and allowed the plaintiffs to attend prenatal appointments, view ultrasounds and experience the joy of pregnancy, although vicariously. The plaintiffs also believed that they would be able to obtain a pre-birth order in Massachusetts and that they would not have to adopt their own genetic child or go through other costly and lengthy procedures.

contracted that Massachusetts law govern the gestational carrier agreement and, by extension, the petition for judgments of parentage and for a prebirth order. We must consider whether to respect their choice.[7]

The gestational carrier agreement implicates the policies of multiple States in important questions of individual safety, health, and general welfare. Complicating matters is the fact that the laws of Connecticut, New York, and Massachusetts, the three States that potentially could govern the agreement, are not in accord. In Connecticut, where the genetic parents reside, gestational carrier agreements are not expressly prohibited by, and perhaps may be contemplated by, the recently amended statute governing the issuance of birth certificates. See Conn. Gen. Stat. c. 93, §7-48a, 2004 Conn. Legis. Serv. P.A. 04-255 (West 2004) ("On and after January 1, 2002, each birth certificate shall contain the name of the birth mother, except by the order of a court of competent jurisdiction . . ."). The gestational carrier resides in New York, a State that has expressed a strong public policy against all gestational carrier agreements. See N.Y. Dom. Rel. Law §122 (McKinney 1999) ("Surrogate parenting contracts are hereby declared contrary to the public policy of this state, and are void and unenforceable"). Massachusetts, as we have noted, recognizes gestational carrier agreements in some circumstances.

In light of these differing State policies and the parties' declared intent to follow Massachusetts law, we look to our established "functional" choice of law principles and to the Restatement (Second) of Conflict of Laws, with which those principles generally are in accord. As a rule, "where the parties have expressed a specific intent as to the governing law, Massachusetts courts will uphold the parties' choice as long as the result is not contrary to public policy." *Steranko v. Inforex, Inc.*, 5 Mass. App. Ct. 253, 260, 362 N.E.2d 222 (1977), citing Restatement (Second) of Conflict of Laws §187 (1971).[10] . . . Under the two-tiered analysis of §187(2), we readily conclude that Massachusetts has a "substantial relationship" to the transaction. See §187(2)(a). That substantial relationship is anchored in the parties' negotiated agreement for the birth to occur at a Massachusetts hospital and for a Massachusetts birth certificate to issue, and bolstered by the gestational carrier's receipt of prenatal care at a Massachusetts hospital in anticipation of delivery at that hospital. See §187 comment f, *supra* at 566-567 (place of partial performance considered to be sufficient to establish a reasonable basis for the parties' choice of law).

---

7. We are concerned here only with those portions of the gestational carrier agreement that pertain to the choice of Massachusetts law and the complaint to establish parentage and for a prebirth order. We have not been asked to express an opinion — nor do we do so — on the validity, construction, or enforceability of any other provision of the gestational carrier agreement.

10. *R.R. v. M.H.*, 426 Mass. 501, 689 N.E.2d 790 (1998), is not to the contrary. That case concerned a surrogacy agreement where the genetic mother (not married to the father) carried the child, was required to consent to the father's custody of the child prior to birth, and was to be paid $10,000 for being a gestational carrier. *Id.* at 503-504. The gestational carrier was a Massachusetts resident, the child was born in Massachusetts, and the genetic father and his wife were residents of Rhode Island. *Id.* at 503, 508. Although the gestational carrier contract provided that "Rhode Island Law shall govern the interpretation of this agreement," *id.* at 508, we applied Massachusetts law to invalidate the contract as contrary to Massachusetts public policy. . . .

Turning to the second prong of §187(2), it is a close question whether apply-ing the parties' choice of law would be "contrary to a fundamental policy" of another State with a "materially greater interest." See §187(2)(b). Certainly the interests of New York and Connecticut are material and significant, for the contracting parties reside in these States. Nevertheless, the interests of New York and Connecticut may be at cross purposes here. New York, the home of the ges-tational carrier and her husband, expressly prohibits gestational carrier agree-ments in order to protect women against exploitation as gestational carriers and to protect the gestational carrier's potential parental rights.[11] New York has thus expressed a "fundamental policy" on a matter in which it has a great interest. Connecticut, the plaintiffs' home State, is silent on the question of ges-tational carrier agreements, but in any event does not expressly prohibit the plain-tiffs from entering into such an arrangement. Massachusetts also has interests here, including interests in "establishing the rights and responsibilities of parents [of children born in Massachusetts] as soon as is practically possible" and "fur-nishing a measure of stability and protection to children born through such ges-tational surrogacy arrangements."

However, even if we were to decide that New York had a "materially greater interest" than both Connecticut and Massachusetts, New York's policy would not operate to overrule the parties' choice of law unless New York would have been the applicable law in the absence of any articulated choice by the parties. The Restatement (Second) of Conflict of Laws §187(2)(b) directs us to a list of factors enumerated in §188, to determine what law would have applied if the contract itself were silent on the issue. Again, consideration of the factors listed in §188 leads to inconclusive results. For example, the "place of contracting" and the "place of negotiation," see §188(2)(a)-(b), are both unknown, although presum-ably these activities took place in New York or Connecticut, or both. The "place of performance," see §188(2)(c), arguably is the intended place of birth (Massachu-setts), or the place of prenatal care (at least partly in Massachusetts), or the place where the pregnancy evolved (New York), or the place where the genetic carrier was inseminated (Connecticut), or any combination of these. The location of the "subject matter of the contract," see §188(2)(d), is equally difficult to determine, and the final consideration, the "domicil" of the parties, §188(2)(e) (New York or Connecticut) in this case is not helpful. Thus, whatever New York's interest in protecting the gestational carrier and her husband, it is doubtful that the prin-ciples of §188 would result in application of New York law to this particular contact.

"Where the significant contacts are so widely dispersed that determination of the state of the applicable law without regard to the parties' choice would present real difficulties," the Restatement instructs that the parties' choice of law will be honored. §187 comment g. This conclusion comports with our functional conflict of laws analysis, which requires consideration of factors such as "uniformity of

11. Massachusetts also seeks to prevent the exploitation of women by prohibiting gestational carrier agreements that compensate the gestational carrier beyond pregnancy-related expenses. Such agreements "raise the concern that, under financial pressure, a woman will permit her body to be used and her child to be given away."

result, maintenance of interstate order, and simplification of the judicial task" and "the justified expectations of the parties."

We conclude, then, that the judge should have applied the parties' choice of law, the law of Massachusetts, to resolve the plaintiffs' complaint. Although the judge in her decision prudently raised the issue of forum shopping in declining to consider the complaint, we are satisfied that, in the circumstances of this case, the parties' choice of law is one we should respect. We are also satisfied that our established conflict of laws analysis will work to prevent misuse of our courts and our laws.

4. *Conclusion.* For the foregoing reasons, on July 1, 2004 we ordered that the judgment of the Probate Court dismissing the plaintiffs' complaint be vacated, and the injunction pending appeal ordered by the single justice of the Appeals Court be dissolved. We remanded the case to the Probate and Family Court where a judgment was to enter declaring the plaintiffs to be the legal parents of the unborn child and ordering the hospital, Berkshire Health Systems, Inc., through its reporters, on the birth of the child, to place the plaintiffs' names on the record of birth created pursuant to G. L. c. 46, §§1, 3, and 3A, listing the plaintiffs as the father and mother, respectively, of the child.

Notes on
HODAS *AND ASSISTED REPRODUCTION TECHNOLOGY REGULATION*

1. The entire area of assisted reproduction technology (known as "ART") is fraught with disharmony among laws in the United States and elsewhere. ART provides an example of the federalist system's challenges — evoking images of legal struggles relating to slavery, which earlier in United States history also reflected the intersection between divisive social views and conflict of laws methodology. Because United States federalism generally reserves domestic relations law to the state realm, ART regulation varies considerably according to which state law governs (unless parties successfully frame challenges to the regulation under the United States Constitution). Serious attempts to harmonize laws have come in the form of restatements and uniform acts. *See, e.g.,* Charles P. Kindregan, Jr. & Steven H. Snyder, *Clarifying the Law of ART: The New American Bar Association Model Act Governing Assisted Reproductive Technology,* 42 FAM. L.Q. 203, 218 (2008) (describing model legislation); Helene S. Shapo, *Assisted Reproduction and the Law: Disharmony on a Divisive Social Issue,* 100 NW. L. REV. 465, 466 n.3 (2006) (summarizing initiatives to unify regulation of ART). Of particular note are two uniform statutes: the Uniform Parentage Act (UPA, first proposed in 1973) and the Uniform Status of Children of Assisted Conception Act (USCACA, first proposed in 1988). While several states adopted the UPA, the USCACA has proved more controversial and far less popular among state

legislature. The USCACA was designed to expand coverage of the UPA to cover children born of in vitro fertilization, artificial insemination with donor sperm, and surrogacy arrangements.

Suggestive of the particularly fractious reactions to surrogacy, the USCACA actually has alternative options for states to choose in regulating surrogacy contracts. One version declares such contracts void, while the other recognizes and regulates them. The culture clash among states over the surrogacy issues highlights the importance of parties using a choice of law clause to ensure predictability about parentage. Choice of law clauses are particularly well suited to surrogacy, which by nature is the product of a consensual agreement among parties. Such clauses, however, may be less useful for other types of ART arrangements, which are the subject of forms used in connection with doctor-patient relationships and other health care settings, such as informed consent forms regarding embryo storage and destruction. Sonia Bychkov Green, *Interstate Intercourse: How Modern Assisted Reproductive Technologies Challenge the Traditional Realm of Conflict of Laws*, 2009 Wis. J.L. Gender & Soc'y 25, 110 (2009).

2. Note that the Massachusetts court in *Hodas* distinguished its earlier decision in *R.R. v. M.H.*, 689 N.E.2d 790, 792 (Mass. 1998), which concerned a surrogacy contract that designated Rhode Island law as the governing law. In *R.R.*, the surrogate was from Massachusetts and the child was born there, but the contracting wife and husband were from Rhode Island. Disregarding the parties' choice of law, the *R.R.* court determined that the contract violated Massachusetts's public policy because it provided payment to the surrogate and omitted a waiting period after the child's birth.

R.R. does in fact have distinguishable facts that include both a strong connection with Massachusetts and lack of clarity in Rhode Island law on the validity of the surrogacy arrangement. Nonetheless, *R.R.* highlights how the public policy exception grants importance to forum choice. Consider New York's across-the-board condemnation of surrogacy contracts. Isn't it quite likely that, had a New York court adjudicated the *Hodas* case, the New York court would not have enforced the contract? Doesn't the existence of the fundamental policy exception promote forum shopping? With high emotional stakes, parentage is an area where uniformity and predictability are particularly crucial. To the extent that forum shopping exists, the practice has the potential to undermine those values in this context.

3. Forum shopping aside, might one argue that enforcing choice of law clauses promotes "law shopping"? One might read the *Hodas* facts as suggesting that the parties quite possibly arranged for "performance" of the contract (birth and some prenatal care) in Massachusetts in order to establish some connection with Massachusetts that might support and validate the choice of law clause. If the *Hodas* parties did that, did the court's decision inappropriately enable the parties to manipulate legal governance?

In other circumstances, courts are loath to empower parties to manipulate choice of law by their actions, such as when a party changes her domicile after an accident in order to avoid certain tort laws. Is a surrogate arrangement different from a tort suit because the surrogate arrangement results from an exercise of the parties' mutual free will? In other contract contexts, courts can be skeptical of party actions that appear designed to influence choice of law, such as where a corporate party tries to buttress a particular choice of governing law by maintaining a sham office in the jurisdiction of the chosen law. Perhaps it is not the contract context that makes a situation such as *Hodas* different, but the special circumstance of surrogacy itself.

4. The *Hodas* court concluded that the contacts among various states were too diffuse to identify a jurisdiction other than Massachusetts with a materially greater interest in applying its law under Restatement (Second) §188. While the court reached this conclusion with dispatch, the analysis illustrates the cumbersome inquiry required under §187(2). In order to complete the §187(2) analysis, a court must often dispose of the §188 inquiry embedded within that analysis. This complexity highlights yet another cost of the fundamental policy exception. Given the forum shopping and complexity costs, one wonders whether §187 should be redesigned to promote more closely its underlying goals of efficiency and predictability.

5. The fundamental policy provision of §187(2) is designed to provide a safety net for circumstances where application of a chosen law would deeply offend a state's sovereign interest in regulating affairs. If the state's sovereign interest is so important, however, why is it indulged only where that state has a materially greater interest than other states?

The word "fundamental" expresses a high threshold, suggesting that a policy must be profoundly important in order to justify rejecting the parties' chosen law. The Restatement Second declines to list policies that qualify as fundamental, but does state that the fundamental policies are "substantial." Restatement (Second) §187, comment *g*. The types of laws that tend to satisfy this test evince a purpose either to protect a group with weaker bargaining power (such as consumers, employees, and borrowers) or to regulate morality. Even some laws in those areas, however, may not be held to implicate a fundamental policy if they contain many nuances and exceptions.

PROBLEM 2-52: OLLIE'S ONLINE GAMBLING DEBTS

Ollie is a citizen of Condemnation State. He began to gamble online for personal pleasure, frequently visiting a gambling website operated by Rollie's, a corporation incorporated in Tolerant State. Rollie's operates all of its business out of

Tolerant State as well. Ollie made the initial connection with Rollie's website after an online search. Thereafter, Rollie's would send daily emails to Ollie, soliciting him to make bets. Ollie responded consistently by placing the solicited bet. Before opening an account with Rollie's, Ollie clicked "AGREED" on the terms of a usage agreement, accepting a clause that stated that all matters related to his online gambling with Rollie's would be governed by the law of Tolerant State. Tolerant State allows online gambling operations such as Rollie's. Condemnation State not only deems online gambling unlawful, but also provides for criminal penalties for those who run any gambling operation in the state. Also, the federal statute regulating online gambling does not apply to Rollie's and Ollie's activities here.

Ollie owes Rollie's a considerable sum as a result of his bets. Rollie's has filed a breach of contract action against Ollie in Tolerant State, seeking to recover the amount owed. Tolerant State follows the Restatement (Second) §187. Ollie argues that the court should not enforce the choice of law clause. What is the court likely to do?

PROBLEM 2-53: POLLY'S CAR SALE TO DORA

Polly Plaintiff, a citizen of State P, owned a small car that she wanted to sell. Dora Defendant, a citizen of State D, wished to purchase the car. Dora is only 17 years old, has never been outside State D, and has never done other business with anyone outside State D. Dora found out that Polly was selling the car from an advertisement that Polly had placed in a national newspaper circulated in State D. The advertisement said that the car was garaged in State P. From her home in State D, Dora called Polly in State P, saying she would like to buy Polly's car.

Dora and Polly agreed to make a firm contract once Polly drove to State D with the car. Once in State D (in the driveway of Dora's home), the parties finished negotiating the contact, drafted it, and signed it. The contract said that Polly would sell Dora the car for $2,000. The contract further stated: "Any dispute arising under this contract shall be governed by the internal laws of the state of State P."

Dora, however, breached the contract, having never taken custody of the car and never paying the $2,000. Polly has filed suit against Dora in a State P state court. The suit asserts a cause of action for breach of contract. Dora has filed a motion, arguing that she can fully avoid any liability for breach of contract because she was 17 at the time any contract with Polly was made. She points out that under State D law, individuals who are under 18 are *not* capable of incurring contract liability. State P law, on the other hand, provides that individuals over the age of 16 are deemed capable of entering into contracts and incurring liability if they fail to honor their contractual promises.

Assume that State P follows the Restatement (Second) of Conflict of Laws for the question whether to honor choice of law clauses in parties' contracts. Should State P grant the motion to dismiss on the ground that Dora was not legally capable of entering into a binding contract?

[handwritten: π: TX / A : ?   K : F̶4̶5̶9̶ /TX]

[handwritten: 459]

Edward DeSantis v. Wackenhut Corporation

793 S.W.2d 670 (Tex. 1990)

[handwritten: TX : antitrust / FL : ∅ anti]

HECHT, Justice.

[In this case involving a noncompetition agreement between an employer and employee, the court evaluated whether the law of the state chosen by the parties to govern their agreement should be applied].

[handwritten: TX sig rel.]

I

A

Edward DeSantis has been providing international and corporate security services, both in the CIA and the private sector for his entire career. In June 1981, while employed by R.J. Reynolds Industries in North Carolina, DeSantis interviewed for a position with Wackenhut Corporation. At that time, Wackenhut, which was chartered and headquartered in Florida, was the third largest company in the nation specializing in furnishing security guards for businesses throughout the country. DeSantis met with Wackenhut's president, founder, and majority stockholder, George Wackenhut, at the company's offices in Florida, and the two agreed that DeSantis would immediately assume the position of Wackenhut's Houston area manager. According to DeSantis, George Wackenhut promised him that the area manager's position was only temporary, and that he would soon be moved into a top executive position. George Wackenhut denies that he made any such promises to DeSantis, admitting only that he mentioned advancement to an executive position as a possible opportunity.

At Wackenhut's request, DeSantis signed a noncompetition agreement at the inception of his employment. The agreement recites that it was "made and entered into" on August 13, 1981, in Florida, although DeSantis signed it in Texas. It also recites consideration "including but not limited to the Employee's employment by the Employer." In the agreement DeSantis covenanted that as long as he was employed by Wackenhut and for two years thereafter, he would not compete in any way with Wackenhut in a forty-county area in south Texas. DeSantis expressly acknowledged that Wackenhut's client list "is a valuable, special and unique asset of [Wackenhut's] business" and agreed never to disclose it to anyone. DeSantis also agreed never to divulge any confidential or proprietary information acquired through his employment with Wackenhut. Finally, DeSantis and Wackenhut agreed "that any questions concerning interpretation or enforcement of this contract shall be governed by Florida law."

DeSantis remained manager of Wackenhut's Houston office for nearly three years, until March 1984, when he resigned under threat of termination. DeSantis contends that he was forced to quit because of disagreements with Wackehut's senior management over the profitability of the Houston office. Wackenhut contends that DeSantis was asked to resign because of his unethical solicitation of business.

Following his resignation, DeSantis invested in a company which marketed security electronics. He also formed a new company, Risk Deterrence, Inc. ("RDI"), to provide security consulting services and security guards to a limited clientele. The month following termination of his employment with Wackenhut, DeSantis sent out letters announcing his new ventures to twenty or thirty businesses, about half of which were Wackenhut clients. He added a postscript to letters to Wackenhut clients in which he disclaimed any intent to interfere with their existing contracts with Wackenhut. Within six months, however, one of Wackenhut's clients, Marathon Oil Company, had terminated its contract with Wackenhut and signed a five-year contract with RDI, and a second Wackenhut client, TRW-Mission Drilling Products, was considering doing the same. Wackenhut claims that DeSantis was acquiring its clients in violation of the noncompetition agreement. DeSantis claims that these clients began considering other security service providers only after the quality of Wackenhut's services declined, following DeSantis' departure.

B

Wackenhut sued DeSantis and RDI in October 1984 to enjoin them from violating the noncompetition agreement, and to recover damages for breach of the agreement and for tortious interference with business relations. Wackenhut alleged that DeSantis and RDI were soliciting its clients' business using confidential client and pricing information which DeSantis obtained through his employment with Wackenhut. . . . [The trial court granted relief to Wackenhut and the court of appeals affirmed].

II

We . . . consider what law is to be applied in determining whether the noncompetition agreement in this case is enforceable. Wackenhut contends that Florida law applies, as expressly agreed by the parties. DeSantis argues that Texas law applies, despite the parties' agreement.

A

This Court has not previously addressed what effect should be given to contractual choice of law provisions. We begin with what Chief Justice Marshall referred to as a principle of "universal law . . . that, in every forum, a contract is governed by the law with a view to which it was made." *Wayman v. Southard*, 23 U.S. (10 Wheat.) 1, 48, 6 L. Ed. 253 (1825). This principle derives from the most basic policy of contract law, which is the protection of the justified expectations of the parties. The parties' understanding of their respective contractual rights and obligations depends in part upon the certainty with which they may predict how the law will interpret and enforce their agreement.

When parties to a contract reside or expect to perform their respective obligations in multiple jurisdictions, they may be uncertain as to what jurisdiction's law will govern construction and enforcement of the contract. To avoid this uncertainty, they may express in their agreement their own choice that the law of a specified jurisdiction apply to their agreement. Judicial respect for their choice advances the policy of protecting their expectations. This conflict of laws concept has come to be referred to as party autonomy. However, the parties' freedom to choose what jurisdiction's law will apply to their agreement cannot be unlimited. They cannot require that their contract be governed by the law of a jurisdiction which has no relation whatever to them or their agreement. And they cannot by agreement thwart or offend the public policy of the state the law of which ought otherwise to apply. So limited, party autonomy furthers the basic policy of contract law. . . . We believe the rule is best formulated in section 187 of the Restatement and will therefore look to its provisions in our analysis of this case.

B

. . . The issue before us — whether the noncompetition agreement in this case is enforceable — is not "one which the parties could have resolved by an explicit provision in their agreement." *See* Restatement (Second) Conflict of Law §187 comment d (1971). We therefore apply section 187(2).

The parties in this case chose the law of Florida to govern their contract. Florida has a substantial relationship to the parties and the transaction because Wackenhut's corporate offices are there, and some of the negotiations between DeSantis and George Wackenhut occurred there. Thus, under section 187(2) Florida law should apply in this case unless it falls within the exception stated in section 187(2)(b). Whether that exception applies depends upon three determinations: first, whether there is a state the law of which would apply under section 188 of the Restatement absent an effective choice of law by the parties, or in other words, whether a state has a more significant relationship with the parties and their transaction than the state they chose; second, whether that state has a materially greater interest than the chosen state in deciding whether this noncompetition agreement should be enforced; and third, whether that state's fundamental policy would be contravened by the application of the law of the chosen state in this case. More particularly, we must determine: first, whether Texas has a more significant relationship to these parties and their transaction than Florida; second, whether Texas has a materially greater interest than Florida in deciding the enforceability of the noncompetition agreement in this case; and third, whether the application of Florida law in this case would be contrary to fundamental policy of Texas.

1

Section 188 of the Restatement provides that a contract is to be governed by the law of the state that "has the most significant relationship to the transaction and the parties," taking into account various contacts in light of the basic conflict of laws principles of section 6 of the Restatement. In this case, that state is Texas. Wackenhut hired DeSantis to manage its business in the Houston area. Although some of the negotiations between DeSantis and Wackenhut occurred in Florida, the noncompetition agreement was finally executed by DeSantis in Houston.[3] The place of performance for both parties was Texas, where the subject matter of the contract was located. Wackenhut may also be considered to have performed its obligations in part in Florida, from where it supervised its various operations, including its Houston office. Still, the gist of the agreement in this case was the performance of personal services in Texas. As a rule, that factor alone is conclusive in determining what state's law is to apply. *See* Restatement §196 (1971). In this case, the relationship of the transaction and parties to Texas was clearly more significant than their relationship to Florida.

2

Texas has a materially greater interest than does Florida in determining whether the noncompetition agreement in this case is enforceable. At stake here is whether a Texas resident can leave one Texas job to start a competing Texas business. Thus, Texas is directly interested in DeSantis as an employee in this state, in Wackenhut as a national employer doing business in this state, in RDI as a new competitive business being formed in the state, and in consumers of the services furnished in Texas by Wackenhut and RDI and performed by DeSantis. Texas also shares with Florida a general interest in protecting the justifiable expectations of entities doing business in several states. Florida's direct interest in the enforcement of the noncompetition agreement in this case is limited to protecting a national business headquartered in that state. Although it is always problematic for one state to balance its own interests fairly against those of another state, the circumstances of this case leave little doubt, if any, that Texas has a materially greater interest than Florida in deciding whether the noncompetition agreement in this case should be enforced.

3

Having concluded that Texas law would control the issue of enforceability of the noncompetition agreement in this case but for the parties' choice of Florida law, and that Texas' interest in deciding this issue in this case is materially greater than Florida's, we must finally determine under section 187(2)(b) whether application of Florida law to decide this issue would be contrary to fundamental policy of Texas. The Restatement offers little guidance in making this determination. Comment *g* states only that a "fundamental" policy is a "substantial" one, and that "[t]he forum will apply its own legal principles in determining whether a given policy is a fundamental one within the meaning of the present rule. . . ."

Comment *g* to section 187 does suggest that application of the law of another state is not contrary to the fundamental policy of the forum merely because it leads to a different result than would obtain under the forum's law. We agree that the result in one case cannot determine whether the issue is a matter of fundamental state policy for purposes of resolving a conflict of laws. Moreover,

---

3. The covenant itself states that it was executed in Florida, but testimony for both parties established that DeSantis signed it last in Houston.

the fact that the law of another state is materially different from the law of this state does not itself establish that application of the other state's law would offend the fundamental policy of Texas. In analyzing whether fundamental policy is offended under section 187(2)(b), the focus is on whether the law in question is a part of state policy so fundamental that the courts of the state will refuse to enforce an agreement contrary to that law, despite the parties' original intentions, and even though the agreement would be enforceable in another state connected with the transaction.[5]

Neither the Restatement nor the cases which have followed section 187 have undertaken a general definition of "fundamental policy," and we need not make the attempt in this case; for whatever its parameters, enforcement of noncompetition agreements falls well within them. This Court has held that "[a]n agreement not to compete is in restraint of trade and will not be enforced unless it is reasonable." As a general rule, unreasonable restraints of trade, including unreasonable covenants not to compete, contravene public policy. . . . What noncompetition agreements are reasonable restraints upon employees in this state, therefore, is a matter of public policy. Moreover, that policy is fundamental in that it ensures a uniform rule for enforcement of noncompetition agreements in this state. *See* Restatement §187 comment g (1971) ("a fundamental policy may be embodied in a statute which makes one or more kinds of contracts illegal or which is designed to protect a person against the oppressive use of superior bargaining power"). Absent such a policy, agreements involving residents of other states would be controlled by the law and policy of those states. An employee of one out-of-state employer might take a competing job and escape enforcement of a covenant not to compete because of the law of another state, while a neighbor suffered enforcement of an identical covenant because of the law of a third state. The resulting disruption of orderly employer-employee relations, as well as competition in the marketplace, would be unacceptable. Employers would be encouraged to attempt to invoke the most favorable state law available to govern their relationship with their employees in Texas or other states.

These same considerations and others have led virtually every court that has addressed the question of whether enforcement of noncompetition agreements is a matter of fundamental or important state policy to answer affirmatively. Not many of these courts have considered the matter specifically in the context of section 187 of the Restatement, and yet, rather remarkably, many have nevertheless expressed similar conclusions. . . . We likewise conclude that the law governing enforcement of noncompetition agreements is fundamental policy in Texas, and that to apply the law of another state to determine the enforceability of such an agreement in the circumstances of a case like this would be contrary to that policy. We therefore hold that the enforceability of the agreement in this case must be judged by Texas law, not Florida law.

5. The trial court apparently concluded that this noncompetition agreement is enforceable under both Texas and Florida law. The court of appeals concluded that the agreement is enforceable under Florida law and did not consider whether it is enforceable under Texas law. DeSantis appears to concede that the agreement is enforceable under Florida law. Wackenhut strongly argues that the agreement is enforceable under Texas law.

Notes on

DESANTIS v. WACKENHUT

1. The *DeSantis* opinion follows standard §187 analysis, although the court's determinations require an exercise in judgment. Do you agree with the court's decision that Texas has a materially greater interest in the controversy than Florida? Would a Florida court agree with that conclusion? If you were an employer such as Wackenhut, would you take any action — or pursue any particular litigation strategy — to try to avoid the possibility that the noncompetition clause would not be honored?

2. What do you think of the *DeSantis* court's conclusion that noncompetition clauses implicate fundamental policies of states? Does it influence your thinking that some legal thinkers connect the policies of noncompetition clauses with the involuntary servitude component of the Thirteenth Amendment of the United States Constitution?

PERSPECTIVE ON THEORIES OF PARTY AUTONOMY AND CHOICE OF LAW

The currently dominant approach to contractual choice of law clauses in the United States, embodied in the Restatement (Second) §187, has a long lineage. At this approach's core is the concept that entities have control over their own obligations to others, often referred to as "party autonomy." Party autonomy was arguably reflected in the earliest known conflicts rule: a Hellenistic Egyptian decree from 120-118 B.C. provided that contracts written in Egyptian were subject to the jurisdiction of Egyptian courts applying Egyptian law, while contracts written in Greek were subject to Greek courts applying Greek law. Parties could therefore designate forum and governing law by using one language or the other.[24] Bringing the concept of party autonomy to United States law, Chief John Marshall stated that "in every forum a contract is governed by the law with a view to which it was made."[25] Over half a century later, the Supreme Court was more explicit about approving party autonomy, explaining its preference for applying the law "which the parties have, either expressly or presumptively, incorporated into their contract as constituting its obligation."[26] Among choice of law scholars, party autonomy has encountered a mixed reception. Perhaps the loudest chorus comes from contemporary scholars who herald the concept as a beacon of light for clear thinking about choice of law. While these scholars celebrate choice of law

---

24. Peter Hay, Patrick J. Borchers & Symeon C. Symeonides, Conflict of Laws 1089 (5th ed. 2010).

25. *Wayman v. Southard,* 23 U.S. (10 Wheat.) 1, 48 (1825). Scholars often identify the Anglo-American roots of party autonomy with the 1760 opinion of Lord Mansfield in *Robinson v. Bland,* 2 Burr. 1077.

26. *Pritchard v. Norton,* 106 U.S. 124, 136 (1882).

clauses as key to party autonomy, they have also begun to theorize about the benefits of allowing party choice over governing legal rules outside of the contract context.

Within the United States, Professor Joseph Beale offered an early scholarly critique of party autonomy. He argued that allowing parties to choose the law that governed their relationship illegitimately empowered them to "do a legislative act."[27] Indeed, many adherents to the territorial approach to choice of law were uneasy with party autonomy, presumably assuming that allowing parties to stipulate to governing law is incompatible with the notion that parties' legal rights vest only upon the territorial occurrence of certain events. The idea that parties could contract around these vested rights seemed against the natural order of things. Areas of the world that continue to adhere to a traditional, territorial perspective on choice of law, such as Latin America, are also reluctant to embrace party autonomy.

More modern approaches to choice of law have, of course, taken a different tack to choice of law clauses. On one hand, modern approaches are solicitous of government sovereignty. By way of illustration, consider how governmental interest analysis seeks to give effect to the goals of sovereign governments. On the other hand, modern approaches have also shown considerable sensitivity to party expectations and judicial efficiencies. This orientation is illustrated in many of Professor Leflar's choice-influencing considerations as well as in the Restatement (Second) §6 factors. As incorporated into modern choice of law methodologies, these two sets of values can clash in the context of party autonomy. The approach in Restatement (Second) §187 represents a compromise between these two sets of values. Section 187 reflects a favorable orientation toward the consistency and predictability resulting from allowing party choice, but also provides a safety net in §187(2) that protects state sovereignty through its substantial connection and reasonable basis requirements as well as its fundamental policy exception.

Some lawmakers and scholars have pushed for an even greater role for party autonomy. In particular, law and economics thinkers have given voice to this point of view. Professors Erin O'Hara and Larry Ribstein argue, for example, that a choice of law system can best maximize social welfare through the vehicle of individual action, rather than promoting state interest. At the center of such a system, they maintain, is a presumption in favor of enforcing contractual choice of law clauses.[28] Although law and economics theorists recognize instances where party autonomy should not necessarily prevail, they do not identify those instances solely by reference to state power and interest — as would a governmental interest analyst or proponent of the approach in the Restatement (Second) §187. Rather, they focus instead on circumstances where one or more contracting parties may not have truly consented to the chosen law (because of duress, fraud, grossly unequal bargaining power, and the like) or circumstances where a third

---

27. 2 JOSEPH BEALE, CONFLICT OF LAWS 1079-1080 (1935).
28. Erin A. O'Hara & Larry E. Ribstein, *From Politics to Efficiency in Choice of Law*, 67 U. CHI. L. REV. 1151, 1152 (2000).

party who did not participate in the contract negotiations is affected by the choice of law.[29] In circumstances such as these, law and economics theorists reason, the mechanism of individual choice does not necessarily work efficiently, thus failing to deliver the optimum result for society.

Proponents of party autonomy in choice of law do not necessarily confine their arguments to the contract setting. They argue that room exists for giving effect to party preferences even where parties did not explicitly contract for applicable law before their dispute arises. For example, they point to torts that occur within a contractual relationship, such as product liability and professional malpractice, where a contractual designation of governing law or default rules can be triggered by party behavior.[30] Both law and theory in this area are still developing. Under United States case law, courts are generally open to parties stipulating to the law governing a tort claim arising out of a contract with a choice of law clause. United States law is unsettled, however, on the question of whether parties can stipulate to the legal principles governing torts and other disputes wholly outside the contract setting. By contrast, the Regulation of the European Union on the Law Applicable to the Non-Contractual Obligations explicitly allows parties to agree to submit non-contractual obligations to the law of their choice under certain circumstance *after* an event giving rise to damage.

A sometimes overlooked area where party choice has become increasingly important is in the context of procedural law. Parties not only contract generally about choice of law and choice of forum, but also about more specific procedural matters such as jury trial waivers, submission to arbitration, the availability of class actions, and evidentiary concerns. Contemporary courts have shown considerable tolerance for these private agreements on procedure.[31] Scholars, on the other hand, have reacted with concern. As one scholar has put it, these agreements can put an end to civil procedure as a "mandatory guarantee of procedural justice," replacing it with "market forces" that can "reshape not only the role of the private right of action between contracting parties but the broad swath of statutory, constitutional, and common law obligations" that rely on traditional procedural for enforcement.[32] Scholars continue to evaluate appropriate

---

29. Andrew T. Guzman, *Choice of Law: New Foundations*, 90 GEO. L.J. 883 (2002); Erin A. O'Hara, *Economics, Public Choice, and the Perennial Conflict of Laws*, 90 GEO. L.J. 941, 943-944 (2002). *See also* Fleur Johns, *Performing Party Autonomy*, 71 LAW & CONTEMP. PROBS. 243, 245 (2008) (discussing the importance of true consent, absent "duress, mala fides, or fraud").

30. Erin A. O'Hara & Larry E. Ribstein, *From Politics to Efficiency in Choice of Law*, 67 U. CHI. L. REV. 1151, 1208-1220 (2000).

31. *See, e.g., AT&T Mobility LLC. v. Concepcion*, 131 S. Ct. 1740, 1753 (2011) (holding that federal law preempted a California law that would render unlawful contract provision banning class actions and requiring individual arbitration in consumer disputes); *Stolt-Nielson S.A. v. AnimalFeeds Int'l Corp.*, 130 S. Ct. 1758, 1776 (2010) (ruling that parties must contract specifically to create a class action mechanism in arbitration); *Rent-a-Center v. Jackson*, 130 S. Ct. 2772, 2779 (2010) (allowing parties to agree by contract that an arbitrator may determine unconscionability even in the face of a default procedure providing for courts to decide unconscionability).

32. Jaime Dodge, *The Limits of Procedural Private Ordering*, 97 VA. L. REV. 724, 729 (2011). *See also* Daphna Kapeliuk & Alon Klement, *Contractualizing Procedure* (2009) (unpublished manuscript, available at http://ssrn.com/abstract=1323056) (suggesting guidelines for enforcing

responses that capture benefits of privatization, yet adequately protect the public values that state mandated procedures seek to promote.[33]

(2)   Other Approaches to Choice of Law Clauses: The UCC, Specific State Statutes, and Rome I

(i)   *The Uniform Commercial Code*

The Uniform Commercial Code has proven to be a lightning rod for debates about party autonomy. The Code has allowed party autonomy since 1952, but that provision has changed numerous times since then. In 2001, the provision was amended drastically to provide for nearly unfettered party autonomy for business-to-business contacts, differentiating such contracts from consumer contracts and also differentiating international contracts from solely domestic United States contracts. These amendments were a huge failure, rejected by all state legislatures and adopted only by the Virgin Islands. On one hand were fears that expanded autonomy would deprive states of their ability to govern effectively, and on the other hand was commercial opposition to the section's special solicitude for consumers and state laws designed to protect them.

The provision in place now, U.C.C. §1-301, provides that "when a transaction bears a reasonable relation to [the forum] state and also to another state or nation the parties may agree that the other state or nation shall govern their rights and duties." This "reasonable relation" standard essentially conflates the two-prong "substantial relationship" or "other reasonable basis" test of the Restatement (Second) §187. Unlike Restatement (Second) §187, the UCC provision does not include a public policy exception. This is not as dramatic as first appears, however, given the relative uniformity in commercial laws within the United States and resulting dearth of disparities in public policy judgments. U.C.C. §1-301 does limit party autonomy, listing other UCC sections and stating that any law designated in those sections governs and "a contrary agreement is effective only to the extent permitted by the law so specified." U.C.C. §1-301(c). Finally, U.C.C. §1-301 provides that for matters not covered by a choice of law agreement or other UCC sections, the forum's version of the UCC applies to transactions bearing an "appropriate" relation to the forum state. Most courts have equated the "appropriate" relation standard with the Restatement (Second) of Conflict of Laws "most significant relationship" standard.

"contractualized procedures" and arguing that jurisdictions gain competitive advantage in the interstate contract market if they recognize procedures that the parties set by contractual agreement).

33. *See, e.g.,* Kevin E. Davis & Helen Hershkoff, *Contracting for Procedure,* 53 Wm. & Mary L. Rev. 507 (2011), in which the scholars propose reforms designed to promote the private procedure's benefits while ensuring that the judicial process protects public values, produces accurate information, and remains transparent.

(ii) Specific State Statutes

Specific state statutes allow for parties to choose the law of the state for transactions above a certain dollar threshold. For example, New York courts have successfully enforced legislation that grants broad party autonomy, where the parties choose New York law. Section 5-1401 of the New York General Obligations Law provides:

> 1. The parties to any contract, agreement or undertaking, contingent or otherwise, in consideration of, or relating to any obligation arising out of a transaction covering in the aggregate not less than two hundred fifty thousand dollars, including a transaction otherwise covered by subsection one of section 1-105 of the uniform commercial code, may agree that the law of this state shall govern their rights and duties in whole or in part, whether or not such contract, agreement or undertaking bears a reasonable relation to this state. This section shall not apply to any contract, agreement or undertaking (a) for labor or personal services, (b) relating to any transaction for personal, family or household services, or (c) to the extent provided to the contrary in subsection two of section 1-105 of the uniform commercial code.
>
> 2. Nothing contained in this section shall be construed to limit or deny the enforcement of any provision respecting choice of law in any other contract, agreement or undertaking.

Other states have similar provisions. *See, e.g.,* 735 ILL. COMP. STAT. 105 §5-5 (2003); CAL. CIV. CODE §1646.5 (West 2012); DEL. CODE ANN. tit. 6, §2708 (West 2012); TEX. BUS. & COM. CODE ANN. §271 (West 2012). As discussed in Chapter 3, the United States Constitution provides constraints on a state's attempt to discriminate against the laws of another state. Consider whether these statutes — which tend to give nearly automatic credence to clauses designating one state's law, but not the law of other states — violates the spirit, if not the letter, of these constraints. One would expect that in many cases a home state court would generally enforce these provisions, while a foreign state would characterize the provisions as choice of law principles not binding on the foreign state. Does this observation aggravate or diminish the discrimination problem?

(iii) The European Union: Rome I

As elsewhere in the world, the European Union (EU) embraces the party autonomy principle. The specific European Union regulation regarding choice of law clauses, known as Rome I on the Law Applicable to Contractual Obligations, harmonizes choice of law rules regarding choice of law clauses and other contract issues in civil and commercial law in the European Union. Freedom of parties' choice to designate law governing their relationship is a central tenet of Rome I. Under this provision, the circumstances in which the parties' choice can be disregarded or circumvented are rare. Nonetheless, the parties' choice will not prevent a court from applying specific laws that cannot be avoided by contract. In some ways, however, the party autonomy principle is more potent in the EU than in the United States. Rome I contains no umbrella "reasonable relation" or similar test that must be met in order for the parties' choice to be accepted, although — as in the United States — a forum's public policy can override parties' chosen law in exceptional circumstances.

In the absence of a choice of law clause, Rome I provides rules organized by the type of contract and based on specific connecting factors. These rules are meant to provide predictability in the choice of law, but retain some discretion for courts to apply the law of the country "most closely connected to the situation."

Rome I contains specific provisions that benefit consumers, employees, and weaker contracting parties. A contract entered into by a consumer is governed by the law of the consumer's habitual residence as long certain connecting factors are present: the other contracting party is a professional who is either pursuing her commercial activity in the consumer's country of habitual residence or is directing her activity toward this country, and the contract is within the scope of these activities. If these connecting factors are present, the contract can still designate the applicable law, but may not deprive the consumer of protections offered by her home country that could not have been avoided by contract. Thus, the consumer is protected and professional parties can reasonably foresee when they cannot circumvent the consumer protections by a choice of law clause. In the absence of these specific connecting factors, Rome I's general rules for freedom of choice and absence of choice apply to consumer contracts. A similar protection extends to employees. In individual employee contracts, the parties can choose applicable law, but the employee still enjoys protection of certain laws of the country that cannot be avoided by contractual agreement and would have applied to the contract in the absence of the parties' attempted choice. As for weaker parties in general, Rome I's preamble stipulates that these parties "should be protected by conflict of law rules that are more favourable to their interests than the general rules."

In sum, the EU calibrates the balance between promoting legal regulation and honoring party autonomy differently than §187 of the Restatement (Second) of Conflict of Law or the Uniform Commercial Code. Rome I's omission of a connection requirement or a reasonableness factor renders the regulation more open to complete party autonomy than §187. Yet Rome I's explicit reference to laws that cannot be avoided by contract and special provisions for weaker parties gives more deference to legal regulation for specific circumstances. Other interesting comparisons between choice of law approaches in the United States and the European Union are reflected at the end of this chapter in a section generally describing the EU approach to choice of law generally, and to non-contract issues in particular.

4. Property   *Situs Rule!*

The situs rule lives on! One of the most rigid and broad-ranging principles in the Restatement (First) of Conflict of Laws, the situs rule remains strong in the Restatement (Second) as well. The rule governs Restatement (Second) matters ranging from marital property to inheritance, and thus touches fields of law outside of property itself, such as legitimacy, adoption, intestate succession, and construction of wills. As such, the situs rule displaces crucial state interests reflected in laws governing domestic relations, trusts, and estates, thereby arguably disregarding some of the values expressed in the heart of the Restatement (Second) — §6. Consider the following cross-section of rules from the Restatement (Second):

From the Restatement (Second) of Conflict of Laws, on the Subject of Property:

§223 Validity and Effect of Conveyance of Interest in Land

(1) Whether a conveyance transfers an interest in land and the nature of the interest transferred are determined by the law that would be applied by the courts of the situs.
(2) These courts would usually apply their own local law in determining such questions.

§233. Effect of Marriage on Existing Interests in Land

(1) The effect of marriage upon an interest in land owned by a spouse at the time of marriage is determined by the law that would be applied by the courts of the situs.
(2) These courts would usually apply their own local law in determining such questions.

§237. Legitimacy As Affecting Succession

(1) Whether a person must be legitimate in order to inherit an interest in land upon intestacy or to receive a forced share therein is determined by the law that would be applied by the courts of the situs. These courts would usually apply their own local law in determining this question.
(2) The courts of the situs would usually determine a person's legitimacy in accordance with the law selected by application of the rule of §287 [Section 287 governs the status of legitimacy — Ed.].

Farmers Exchange Bank v. Metro Contracting Services, Inc.

107 S.W.3d 381 (Mo. Ct. App. 2003)

SMITH, J.

Harlan R. Russell, the appellant, in his capacity as the president of Metro Contracting Services, Inc. (Metro), a Missouri corporation, whose sole shareholders were the appellant and his then and now former wife, Rose Mary Russell (Ms. Russell), executed two promissory notes in favor of Farmers Exchange Bank (Farmers notes), the respondent. As security for the notes, the appellant executed a personal guaranty in not only his name, but in the name of Ms. Russell, by forging her signature. Metro subsequently defaulted on the notes, prompting suit by the respondent against not only Metro, but against the Russells, under the personal guaranties, to collect the total balances then due on the notes. The suit against Ms. Russell was later dismissed due to her signature being forged. The case against the appellant proceeded to a summary judgment for the respondent in the amount of $372,791.47, plus interest and attorney's fees. The instant case arises out of the appellant's attempts to prevent the respondent from partially satisfying that judgment by attaching and executing upon the note proceeds owed to the Russells as payees of a promissory note executed by Eaton Investments, L.L.C. (Eaton note), in the principal amount of $293,000.

The appellant raises seven points on appeal, raising the question of whether the trial court erred in failing to quash the prejudgment attachment of the appellant's interest in the Eaton note and the subsequent execution thereon in satisfaction of the respondent's judgment against the appellant. The implicated and overarching issue raised with respect to these claims is whether, under the applicable and controlling law, the appellant's interest in the Eaton note was subject to attachment and execution to satisfy the judgment against him. The resolution of that issue depends on whether the Russells held the note as tenants by the entirety or as tenants in common. The parties agree that if we determine that the trial court correctly found that they held the Eaton note as tenants in common, then the court did not err in finding that the Eaton note proceeds were subject to attachment and execution and in not quashing the prejudgment attachment. The parties, however, not only disagree on the proper classification of the appellant's interest in the Eaton note, but whether Missouri or Kansas law applies in deciding that issue.

Because we find that the issue of the proper classification of the appellant's interest in the Eaton note is governed by Kansas law; that pursuant thereto his interest was as a tenant in common and, therefore, was subject, under Missouri law, to attachment and execution to satisfy the respondent's judgment against the appellant; and that the prejudgment attachment was not facially deficient, we affirm.

I.

... In resolving the appellant's claims in Points II-VI, the issue is whether Missouri or Kansas law applies in determining whether the Eaton note was held by the Russells as tenants by the entirety or as tenants in common.

The appellant's claims in Points II-VI are founded on two basic propositions, namely that the trial court should have applied Missouri law in determining the appellant's interest in the Eaton note because: (1) the law of the forum state, Missouri, governs questions of procedure, and the issue of attachment, as a remedy in this case, is an issue of procedure; and (2) §188 of the Restatement (Second) of Conflict of Laws (1971), which is followed by Missouri courts and governs issues concerning the validity of contracts, including promissory notes and the rights created thereby, mandates applying Missouri law. The respondent, on the other hand, contends that Kansas law should apply, relying on §258 of the

Restatement (Second) of Conflict of Laws (1971), dealing with property acquired during marriage.

As in every case of a conflict of laws, a court first:

> must determine at the outset whether the problem presented to it for solution relates to torts, contracts, property, or some other field, or to a matter of substance or procedure, in order to refer to the appropriate law. In other words, the court must initially, whether consciously or not, go through the process of determining the nature of the problem; otherwise, the court will not know which choice-of-law rule to apply to the case. This process is generally called "characterization," and sometimes "classification," "qualification," or "interpretation."

16 Am. Jur. 2d Conflict of Laws §3 (1998). In that vein, we initially must determine whether the issue presented in this case is one of substance or procedure in that if it is a matter of procedure, as the appellant contends, there is no dispute that the law of the forum state, Missouri, would apply.

In answering the initial conflict of laws question of substance versus procedure, we first note that Missouri law recognizes that the local law of the forum determines the method of securing obedience to court orders, as provided in §130 of the Restatement (Second) of Conflict of Laws (1971). With respect to securing obedience to court orders, Comment a of §130 includes the remedy of attachments. This fact then would be persuasive as to the appellant's position in this point if the question posed was what classifications of personal property are subject to attachment in this state. In that instance, it would be a question of remedies that would be controlled by the forum state, Missouri. However, the question posed here is not what classifications of property are subject to attachment, but whether the Eaton note was properly classified as being held by the Russells as tenants by the entirety or tenants in common, the former, unlike the latter, not being subject to attachment in this state. In other words, the conflict of laws question presented is not a question of what classifications of personal property are subject to attachment and execution, which would be governed by the laws of the forum state as a matter of procedure, but a question of how the appellant's interest in the Eaton note is classified. And, thus, because issues of one's rights and duties are substantive issues, as opposed to procedural issues which relate to enforcement of those rights and duties, the issue in our case as to whether the Eaton note proceeds were subject to attachment and execution is not a procedural issue controlled by the laws of the forum state, as the appellant contends, but a substantive issue.

Conflict of laws questions are to be answered by applying our own state's conflict of laws doctrines. In resolving a conflict of laws question as a matter of substantive law, Missouri courts have historically relied on the Restatement (Second) of Conflict of Laws. In that respect, the appellant contends that the conflicts issue presented, as a matter of substantive law, is properly classified as one of contracts governed by §188 of the Restatement (Second) of Conflict of Laws, while the respondent contends that it is one of property governed by §258. Given the nature of the dispute, we find merit in the respondent's position.

Although the underlying lawsuit between the parties was contractual in nature in that it involved a default by the appellant on the Farmers notes, the dispute on appeal is not. Rather, it concerns what property of the appellant is subject to attachment and execution, specifically whether the Eaton note proceeds were subject to attachment and execution to satisfy the respondent's judgment against the appellant, which judgment arose out of the underlying lawsuit. The dispute as to the appellant's interest in the Eaton note played no part in resolving the underlying contractual dispute between the parties. Its only significance to the underlying lawsuit is postjudgment, after the rights and duties of the parties were established under the Farmers notes.

As noted, *supra*, in determining whether the Eaton note proceeds were subject to attachment and execution by the respondent to satisfy its judgment against the appellant, we must decide the nature of the appellant's interest in those proceeds. In that regard, it is undisputed that under Missouri law if he owned them with Ms. Russell by the entireties, they were not subject to attachment and execution. The "legal relationship between a person and a thing" is a matter of property law. Thus, the conflicts issue concerning the appellant's interest in the Eaton note proceeds is properly classified as one of property. The question then is which law applies in deciding that issue, the law of Missouri or Kansas. As noted, *supra*, that question is answered by applying the law as to our own state's conflict of laws doctrines.

Section 258 of the Restatement (Second) of Conflict of Laws (1971), provides:

Interests in Movables Acquired During Marriage

> (1) The interest of a spouse in a movable acquired by the other spouse during the marriage is determined by the local law of the state which, with respect to the particular issue, has the most significant relationship to the spouses and the movable under the principles stated in §6.
> (2) In the absence of an effective choice of law by the spouses, greater weight will usually be given to the state [where] the spouses were domiciled at the time the movable was acquired than to any other contact in determining the state of the applicable law.

As to the relationship between §6 and §258, Comment b to §258 reads, in pertinent part:

> Of the factors listed in Subsection (2) of §6, that which is of particular importance in the present context is the one which calls for implementation of the relevant policies of the state with the dominant interest in the determination of the particular issue. Except in rare circumstances, this state will be the state where the spouses were domiciled at the time the movable was acquired.

Failing to find any rare circumstances, the general rule of §258 would apply here in determining whether Kansas or Missouri law applies in deciding whether the Eaton note proceeds are subject to attachment and execution. . . .

In addition to contending that §258 would not apply here because the conflict of laws issue presented is properly classified as one of contract, the appellant also contends that §258 would not apply because it only "applies to the interest of one spouse when the other spouse acquires an interest in a movable during the marriage . . . [and] . . . in the case at bar, we are dealing with an interest (payments under the Eaton Note) acquired by both spouses during the marriage and payable to them jointly." We do not read §258 in the same manner as the appellant. Giving the language used its plain and ordinary meaning, we read §258 as providing a means to determine *each* spouse's interest in a movable when acquired during the marriage by one spouse or both spouses. Logically, the language relied on by the appellant was not meant to limit the section's application to acquisitions by one spouse only, but simply reflects a means of determining each spouse's interest in property acquired during the marriage. . . .

The appellant also contends that §258 does not apply because it only applies "in the absence of an effective choice of laws," and here the "parties expressly chose to apply Missouri law to their agreement." In support of that contention, the appellant points to the choice of law provision in the notes executed by Metro in favor of the respondent, which reads: "The law of the state of Missouri will govern this agreement." While that provision would govern in the underlying contractual dispute between the parties as to the breach of the Farmers notes, it does not extend to the postjudgment dispute here over whether the Eaton note proceeds were subject to attachment and execution to satisfy the judgment for the respondent and against the appellant in the underlying lawsuit.

Having determined that the law of the state where the appellant and his former wife were domiciled when the appellant acquired an interest in the Eaton note controls in determining whether the appellant's interest in the Eaton note was as a tenant by the entirety or as a tenant in common, we turn to the issue of whether Kansas or Missouri was the domiciliary state of the Russells at the time of their acquisition of their interests in the Eaton note.

It goes without saying that the appellant acquired his interest in the Eaton note at the time of its execution by Eaton. As to the date of the note's execution, the note indicates that it was executed on October 4, 2000. As to where the Russells were domiciled at that time, the note recites the fact that the note payments were to be made to the appellant at 8909 Mohawk Road, Leawood, Kansas 66206. That address was the one designated in the 1996, 1997, and 1998 individual tax returns of the Russells, and a personal financial statement, dated January 14, 2000, as their residence address. In addition, the Russells both admitted in their answers to the respondent's petition that on November 7, 2000, their residence was 8909 Mohawk Road, Leawood, Kansas 66206. Although the appellant testified at the writ of attachment hearing on March 1, 2001, that he ceased to reside at the Leawood address *sometime* in October of 2000, the trial court was free to disbelieve him. And, even if the court chose to believe the appellant's testimony, it does not directly contradict the evidence that he resided in Kansas on October 4, 2000, when the Eaton note was executed. Thus, applying the conflict of laws doctrine of this state that the domicile state at the time that movable personal property is acquired is controlling, we find that Kansas law would apply in determining the appellant's interest in the Eaton note.

In Missouri, a conveyance to husband and wife jointly is presumed to create a tenancy by the entirety. Kansas, however, does not recognize tenancy by the entirety as to real or personal property. Rather, Kansas law, specifically §58-501 Kan. Stat. Ann. (1994), provides:

> Real or personal property granted or devised to two or more persons including a grant or devise to a husband and wife shall create in them a tenancy in common with respect to such property unless the language used in such grant or devise makes it clear that a joint tenancy was intended to be created.

. . .

After reading the Eaton note, it is abundantly clear that it is totally void of any language indicating that a joint tenancy was intended. In identifying the appellant and his wife as "the Lender," it simply reads that "the Lender is: HARLAN R. RUSSELL and ROSE M. RUSSELL." Thus, pursuant to Kansas law, the appellant's interest in the Eaton note, at the time of attachment and execution in satisfaction of the respondent's judgment, was as a tenant in common.

As we discussed, *supra*, the forum state, in this case Missouri, as a matter of procedure, controls which classifications of property are subject to attachment and execution. In that regard, it is well settled in this state that a judgment creditor, in satisfaction of the judgment debt, can attach the interest of a judgment debtor in personal property that the debtor holds as a tenant in common with a spouse, but not property held as a tenant by the entirety. Thus, because the trial court properly determined here, under Kansas law, that the appellant's interest in the Eaton note was as a tenant in common, the court did not err in failing to sustain the appellant's motion to dissolve the respondent's writ of attachment as to the proceeds.

Points II-VI are denied.

Notes on
FARMERS EXCHANGE BANK

1. Critics often observed that the rigidity of the Restatement (First) rules triggered complexity in courts' analyses as the courts sought to work around the rules in order to do justice for the parties before them. If *Farmers Exchange Bank* is any indication, the same holds true for Restatement (Second) sections pertaining to property. Although *Farmers Exchange Bank* did not concern the most rigid of all property rules — the situs rule for real property — the court treated the presumptive rule of §258 as a mandate, noting that it found no "rare circumstances" justifying application of anything other than the state of the spouse's domicile at the time a movable was acquired. In working with §258, the court engaged in many complicated forms of analysis: characterization, dépeçage, presumptions, and issues related to domicile.

2. The *Farmers Exchange Bank* court's use of characterization is particularly dizzying. Depending on how one counts, one can identify at least four times when characterization controlled the court's analysis: (1) to determine whether to apply forum procedural law concerning which property classifications are subject to attachment; (2) to determine whether to apply substantive law to determine whether the spouses held the property interest in the Eaton note proceeds as tenancy by the entirety or tenancy in common; (3) to determine whether to characterize the dispute as a contract dispute (rather than a property dispute) because the underlying lawsuit on the Farmers notes was a contract suit; and (4) to determine whether to apply the contractual choice of law clause for the Farmers notes. One might add one more characterization to this list, since at the end of the opinion, the court returns to the substance/procedure characterization. At this point in the opinion, the court splices the property interest issue, determining that the question of whether a court can attach tenancy in common property was a procedural issue within the authority of the Missouri forum court, while continuing to hold the view that the question of whether the property interest was indeed tenancy in common was a substantive issue within the authority of the spouses' earlier domicile, Kansas. Is justice served by using these kinds of twists and turns in court reasoning?

PROBLEM 2-54: ANN AND ANDY'S ANTENUPTIAL AGREEMENT

When Ann was 21, her aunt gave her a piece of real property located in State S. Ten years later, when she was domiciled in State A, Ann entered into an antenuptial agreement with Andy. Andy was also domiciled in State A and they signed the agreement there. Two weeks later they were married in State A. The agreement provided that Andy would hold one-half interest in the State S real property, and that if they divorced, Ann would pay him one-half the value of the property. They are now divorcing in State A, which applies the Restatement (Second). Under both the domestic relations and contract laws of State A, the antenuptial agreement is valid and Andy would have been deemed to have a one-half interest in the property even if the parties had not created the agreement. Under State S contract law, the antenuptial agreement is not enforceable. In addition, State S is a community property state that would not grant Andy any interest in the property Ann owned at the time of the marriage. Should the State A court enforce the antenuptial agreement?

5.   *Marriage*

From the Restatement (Second) of Conflict of Laws, on the Subject of Status:

§283. Validity of Marriage

(1) The validity of a marriage will be determined by the local law of the state which, with respect to the particular issue, has the most significant relationship to the spouses and the marriage under the principles stated in §6.

(2) A marriage which satisfies the requirements of the state where the marriage was contracted will everywhere be recognized as valid unless it violates the strong public policy of another state which had the most significant relationship to the spouses and the marriage at the time of the marriage. . . .

Comment on Subsection (2):

e. By "state where the marriage was contracted" is meant the state where the marriage was celebrated or where some other act was done that is claimed to have resulted in the creation of a marriage status. In some states, the status can be created by an act other than a formal ceremony, such as in the case of a common law marriage (see Comment *g*).

f. Formalities. The state where the marriage was celebrated, or, in the case of a common law marriage, the state where the parties cohabited while holding themselves out to be man and wife, is the state which will usually be primarily concerned with the question of formalities. These include such matters as:

1. the necessity of a license;
2. the necessity of a formal ceremony;
3. the person to perform the ceremony;
4. the manner of the performance of the ceremony.

If the requirements of this state have been complied with, the marriage will not be held invalid in other states for lack of the necessary formalities except in the unusual situation where such a result is required by the strong policy of another state which had the most significant relationship to the spouses and the marriage at the time of the marriage.

g. "Common law" marriage. Whether a marriage can be created without formal ceremony is a question relating to formalities. If the acts relied upon to create the marriage meet the requirements of the state where the acts took place, the marriage will not be held invalid for lack of the necessary formalities except in the unusual circumstances stated in Comment *f.* A marriage without ceremony is commonly called a common law marriage.

. . .

k. Marriage contrary to strong policy of state of most significant relationship. . . . [A] marriage which satisfies the requirements of the state where it was contracted will be held valid everywhere except when its invalidation is required by the strong policy of another state which had the most significant relationship to the spouses and the marriage at the time of the marriage. To date, as stated in Comment *j*, a marriage has only been invalidated when it violated a strong policy of a state where at least one of the spouses was domiciled at the time of the marriage and where both made their home immediately thereafter. The forum will apply its own legal principles in determining whether a given policy is a strong one within the meaning of the present rule.

        . . .

    m. Choice-of-law rules of state of most significant relationship. As stated above (see Comment *k*), the forum will look to the choice-of-law rules of the state of most significant relationship for whatever light these rules may shed on whether invalidation of the marriage is required by a strong policy of that state. The fact that these courts would not have applied their rule to invalidate the marriage provides conclusive evidence that no sufficiently strong policy of this state is involved. On the other hand, the fact that these courts would have invalidated the marriage by application of their rule provides persuasive evidence that the rule does embody a policy of the required sort. . . .

    On the other hand, this is not a situation where the forum applies the choice-of-law rules of the state of most significant relationship. The fact that the courts of that state would have applied their rule to invalidate the marriage does not mean that the forum should necessarily do so. The forum should only apply this rule to invalidate the marriage if it is its own judgment that the rule embodies a sufficiently strong policy to warrant doing so. . . .

In re Farraj

72 A.D.3d 1082 (N.Y. App. Div. 2010)

In May 2003 the petitioner, Rabaa M. Hanash, and Daoud Farraj, a/k/a David I. Farraj (hereinafter the decedent), participated in a formal marriage ceremony in accordance with Islamic law, at the home of the petitioner's brother in Clifton, New Jersey. Prior to the marriage ceremony, the decedent was a resident of New York and the petitioner lived at her brother's residence in New Jersey. An Imam (Islamic clergyman) came from New York to New Jersey to solemnize the marriage. However, a marriage license was not obtained. Immediately after the marriage ceremony, the petitioner and the decedent returned to Brooklyn, where they had a wedding celebration. The decedent and the petitioner lived together in New York until the decedent's death in July 2007.

    The decedent died intestate and Letters of Administration were issued to the appellant, the decedent's son from a prior marriage. Subsequently, the petitioner filed a petition to compel an accounting of the decedent's estate. The appellant moved to dismiss the petition . . . on the ground that the petitioner lacked standing as a surviving spouse, since her marriage to the decedent was invalid under New Jersey Law.

    Under the law of the State of New Jersey, the failure to obtain a marriage license renders a purported marriage absolutely void. In New York, while the Domestic Relations Law deems it necessary for all persons intending to be married to obtain a marriage license, a marriage is not void for the failure to obtain a marriage license if the marriage is solemnized. A marriage is solemnized where the parties "solemnly declare in the presence of a clergyman or magistrate and the attending witness or witnesses that they take each other as husband and wife."

Therefore, if New Jersey law is applied to determine the validity of the marriage between the petitioner and the decedent, the marriage is void. If New York law is applied, the marriage is valid. The Surrogate's Court applied New York law and denied the appellant's motion. We affirm.

The general rule is that the legality of a marriage "is to be determined by the law of the place where it is celebrated." The Restatement (Second) of Conflict of Laws §283, however, provides a more flexible approach. . . . We look to the Restatement (Second) of Conflict of Laws §283 for guidance in determining which law should govern the validity of the marriage at issue here.

The petitioner and the decedent had a justified expectation that they were married, since they participated in a formal marriage ceremony in accordance with Islamic law (*see* Restatement [Second] of Conflict of Laws §6). The only reason the petitioner and the decedent had their marriage ceremony in New Jersey was because, under Islamic law, the marriage ceremony was to be conducted in the residence of the bride's eldest male relative, which was the petitioner's brother. In addition, the intended and actual matrimonial domicile was New York, and the petitioner and the decedent held themselves out as a married couple in New York. Therefore, New York has a significant interest in the marriage between the petitioner and the decedent. While New Jersey has an interest in enforcing its marriage requirements, this interest is not particularly strong here, since the petitioner and the decedent left New Jersey immediately after the marriage ceremony, and lived in New York for the entirety of their marriage.

Therefore, the Surrogate's Court properly determined that New York had the "most significant relationship to the spouses and the marriage" and that New York law should apply to determine the validity of the marriage. Under New York law, the marriage between the petitioner and the decedent was valid, even without a marriage license, since it was solemnized. Accordingly, the appellant's motion to dismiss the proceeding was properly denied.

McPeek v. McCardle

888 N.E.2d 171 (Ind. 2008)

RUCKER, Justice.

SUMMARY

The question raised in this opinion is whether a marriage solemnized in another state in violation of that state's law may be recognized as valid in this state if the marriage complies with this state's law. The answer is yes.

FACTS AND PROCEDURAL HISTORY

As a result of her first husband's death, Edwina VanTyle became the sole owner of the family farm located in Ohio County and Switzerland County, Indiana. On June 30, 1994, armed with a marriage license obtained from the clerk of the circuit court in Ohio County, Indiana, Edwina and Charles McCardle, both residents of Indiana, traveled across state lines and were ostensibly married in the state of Ohio. The Reverend Donald S. Campbell performed the wedding ceremony and filled out the marriage certificate. Although Rev. Campbell was apparently authorized by his church to solemnize marriages in the state of Ohio, no marriage license was issued by the state of Ohio. Further, no ceremony took place in the state of Indiana. On July 1, 1994, the clerk of the circuit court in Ohio County, Indiana filed and recorded the marriage license and certificate. Shortly thereafter, in August 1994, Edwina executed a warranty deed transferring ownership of the farm to Charles McCardle and herself as husband and wife.

On July 26, 2004, Edwina died intestate. In December 2004, Edwina's two daughters and one son from her first marriage—Emma McPeek, Brenda Allen, and Caroll VanTyle (referred to collectively as "McPeek")—filed a complaint for declaratory judgment. In the complaint McPeek contended that the marriage between her mother and McCardle was void, and therefore she and her siblings were the proper owners of one-half the farm, which had been in the family for three generations. McPeek also filed a motion for summary judgment.

McCardle responded with a motion to dismiss the declaratory judgment action, contending McPeek was not a party to the marriage and therefore lacked standing to challenge its validity. . . . [T]he trial court granted the motion to dismiss, [and] agreed that McPeek lacked standing. However, the trial court concluded that the marriage was voidable under Indiana law and the weight of legal authority indicated that such marriages may not be attacked after the death of one of the parties. . . .

McPeek appealed the dismissal of her complaint. . . . The Court of Appeals affirmed the judgment of the trial court. Having previously granted McPeek's petition to transfer, we also affirm the judgment of the trial court.

. . .

DISCUSSION

McPeek argues that her mother's marriage to McCardle is void because it was solemnized in the state of Ohio without the benefit of an Ohio marriage license. McCardle does not respond to this argument head on. Instead he makes the same argument made before the trial court, namely, "once a party to a marriage is dead, her marriage may not be challenged by anyone other than the other party to the marriage."

Unless strong public policy exceptions require otherwise,[2] the law of the place where a marriage occurs generally determines the validity of a marriage. As a corollary, the general rule of law is that a marriage valid where it is performed is valid everywhere. The converse of this proposition is equally well settled: a marriage void where it is performed is void everywhere.

McPeek insists that her mother's Ohio marriage to McCardle is void. More specifically, according to McPeek, "[b]ecause the McCardle union which took

---

2. *See e.g.*, Ind. Code §31-11-1-1(b) ("A marriage between persons of the same gender is void in Indiana even if the marriage is lawful in the place where it is solemnized.").

place in Ohio did not meet the legal requirements for a lawful marriage to exist under Ohio law, Indiana must give Full Faith and Credit to the Ohio law and recognize that a lawful marriage did not occur and that their relationship was nothing more than a void common law marriage." However, our research reveals no authority declaring that a marriage solemnized in the state of Ohio without the benefit of a marriage license obtained from that state is considered a void marriage. Instead Ohio, like Indiana, draws a distinction between marriages that are void in contrast to those that are merely voidable. According to Ohio law, "There are major conceptual differences between void and voidable marriages. A voidable marriage is one which is valid when entered and which remains valid until either party secures a lawful court order dissolving the marital relationship." Conversely, "a void marriage is invalid from its inception, and the parties thereto may simply separate without benefit of a court order of divorce or annulment." The policy of Ohio is to sustain marriages "where they are not incestuous, polygamous, shocking to good morals, unalterably opposed to a well defined public policy, or prohibited." Thus, Ohio appears to label a defective marriage voidable rather than void, unless such a label is against policy considerations. "A marriage contract is a nullity ab initio *only* where expressly so declared by statute. In such a case it is absolutely void, requiring no judicial decree for its dissolution." This jurisdiction has embraced a similar view.

Our review of Ohio case and statutory authority has not revealed that a marriage solemnized in that state without the benefit of an Ohio marriage license is void as against public policy. It therefore appears that the Ohio marriage, although defective, was nonetheless valid from its inception under the laws of Ohio and remained so at least until Edwina's death because the parties did not seek dissolution. As indicated earlier, unless strong public policy exceptions require otherwise, the law of the place where a marriage occurs generally determines the validity of a marriage.

. . . We advance an alternative ground as well. Not all jurisdictions adhere to the general rule that the law of the place where the marriage occurs determines the validity of the marriage. The Restatement (Second) Conflict of Laws §283(1) (1971) advises, "The validity of a marriage will be determined by the local law of the state which, with respect to the particular issue, has the most significant relationship to the spouses and the marriage. . . ." And following the Restatement's guidance several jurisdictions have determined that even if invalid where solemnized, a marriage can be recognized as valid under the law of the forum state.

. . . Before and after their marriage, Indiana was the domiciliary of both McCardle and Edwina, and both owned real and personal property in the state of Indiana. It appears that the only contact the parties had with Ohio is that the ceremony was conducted in that state. In essence any interest Ohio may have in the McCardles' marriage is overcome by the more substantial interest this state has in recognizing the marriage of the parties who, after all, obviously anticipated that their marriage would be valid.

Accordingly, we measure the McCardles' marriage against Indiana's solemnization provisions. Before two people may marry in Indiana they must negotiate a multi-step process. The parties must first obtain a marriage license from the clerk of the circuit court of either person's county of residence. The marriage license issued by the circuit court is the legal authority for an authorized person to marry the betrothed couple. The parties must then present the marriage license to a person who is authorized to solemnize marriages. Marriages may be solemnized by, among others, a member of the clergy of a religious organization. The person solemnizing the marriage must complete a marriage certificate and file the certificate and license with the clerk of the circuit court that issued the license; the clerk must then record the certificate and license.

It is undisputed that Edwina and McCardle complied with the requisite statutes in obtaining and filing their Indiana marriage license and certificate of marriage with the clerk of the Ohio County Circuit Court. And there was no evidence presented to the trial court, and no argument made on appeal, that the couple were married in Ohio with the intent of evading the laws of this state.[3]

We conclude that where, as here, a couple has complied with Indiana's statutory requirements regarding marriage licenses, certificates, and solemnization, such that the marriage would have been valid if solemnized in this state, we will recognize the marriage as valid even if the marriage ceremony took place in another state and did not comply with that state's law or public policy.

It is worth emphasizing however that a couple intending to use or, as occurred here, has already used an Indiana marriage license for an out-of-state marriage should take the additional step of re-solemnizing their marriage in Indiana in order to avoid future questions about its validity.

Notes on
FARRAJ AND McPEEK

1. The Restatement (First) rule regarding the validity of marriage provides a categorical "place of celebration" rule. Both *Farraj* and *McPeek* illustrate how much more flexible the Restatement (Second) approach to marriage validity can be. What values and concerns guided the courts in *Farraj* and *McPeek* as they applied the Restatement (Second) and sought to identify the jurisdiction with the most significant relationship to the spouses and the marriage? Do you believe the courts' decisions might have come out differently if the marriages in question were less than six months in duration? What if the defect in the marriages had concerned a

3. Indiana Code section 31-11-8-6 provides:

A marriage is void if the parties to the marriage:
 (1) are residents of Indiana;
 (2) had their marriage solemnized in another state with the intent to
  (A) evade IC 31-11-4-4 or IC 31-11-4-11 (or IC 31-7-3-3 or IC 31-7-3-10 before their repeal); and
  (B) subsequently return to Indiana and reside in Indiana; and
 (3) without having established residence in another state in good faith, return to Indiana and reside in Indiana after the marriage is solemnized.

matter that went to the public policy of the place of celebration, such as incest?

2. The presumption in favor of validating a marriage is reflected in §210 of the Uniform Marriage and Divorce Act, which is in effect in a handful of states. That act provides:

> All marriages contracted within this State prior to the effective date of this Act, or outside this State, that were valid at the time of the contract or subsequently validated by the laws of the place in which they were contracted or by the domicile of the parties, are valid in this State.

3. The Uniform Marriage and Divorce Act (UMDA), however, is not the end of the matter. In footnote 3 to the *McPeek* opinion, the court points out an Indiana statute that reflects a different attitude to diversity in marriage laws than expressed in the UMDA. The Indiana statute declares void marriages of Indiana residents celebrated outside of the state where the residents sought to evade Indiana marriage regulations, such as the Indiana requirement for a marriage license and receipt of information regarding sexually transmitted diseases. In instances where a state does not have a statute such as Indiana's, would it be appropriate for a court applying the Restatement (Second) §283 to evaluate whether parties who married out of state were seeking to evade a requirement or prohibition of their domicile? Is evasion of a domicile law relevant to the determination of which state has the most significant relationship to the spouses and the marriage? Should evasion be determinative of that question?

There are many important ramifications to the question of what should be the effect of evading the legal requirements of one's domicile. The question implicates overarching questions about the role of regulation in citizens' lives and more specific questions bearing on choice of law rules. On a more practical level, the question is enormously important for counseling clients seeking to navigate the mosaic of laws in the United States. Few would argue with the power of a domiciliary state to enforce its laws against individuals who go out of the domiciliary state to obtain something lawful in the other state — say fireworks — and then come back to the home state to use the item, which is deemed illegal to sell or use in the home state. Does the decision to make a state one's home include the decision to submit to the state's laws for all purposes? Does the status granted (or withheld) by a couple's home state travel with the couple when they leave the state? Or does a couple's decision to migrate to another state include the decision to forfeit their former status?

Professors F. H. Buckley and Larry Ribstein suggest that the decision to move should not hold such stark consequences. Instead, they point out the benefits of allowing parties to contract for different laws that govern different aspects of their affairs: "One might like the climate and job opportunities of Virginia, but prefer to contract under New York law, incorporate in Delaware, and marry under Louisiana or Hawaii law." F.H. Buckely & Larry E. Ribstein, *Calling a Truce in the Marriage Wars*, 2001 U. ILL. L. REV. 561, 565 (2001). They observe efficiencies and other positive effects that would result if "parties can specify by contract the law that governs their contracts, corporations, or marriage without having to visit, reside, or contract in the chosen state." *Id.* at 565. The arguments of Professors Buckley and Ribstein are particularly pertinent to covenant marriage, which is available in a small number of states for individuals who voluntarily choose to enter an alternative to standard marriage. Under covenant marriage, the parties to a marriage agree to make all reasonable efforts to preserve their marriage and to restrict the availability of unilateral divorce by agreeing to obstacles to quick divorce, such as longer waiting periods.

The precise effect of these marriages for couples who migrate to states that do not have covenant marriages is not fully settled. In one case, however, an Alabama court granted a divorce under Alabama law, dissolving a covenant marriage celebrated in Louisiana. The Alabama court ruled that the law of the state where the spouse petitioning for divorce is domiciled shall determine the right to divorce. Both the petitioning spouse and his wife had moved from Louisiana and were domiciled in Alabama. *Blackburn v. Blackburn*, 180 So. 3d 16 (2015).

4. In evaluating whether the marriage in *McPeek* was valid, the court first looked to how the state that celebrated the marriage would treat the parties' status, even though the parties did not obtain a marriage certificate in that state. This type of analysis—looking to what the "issuing" state would do—is similar to the approach used with judgments. A court that is asked to honor the judgment rendered in another jurisdiction will evaluate what effect the rendering court would give to the judgment.

PROBLEM 2-55: ANGELA AND RICARDO

Angela and Ricardo were Arizona residents who traveled to visit family in Mexico. While they were visiting Mexico, they obtained necessary blood tests, a marriage certificate, and celebrated their marriage before an individual that they believed had power to perform marriages in Mexico. They returned to their Arizona domicile and lived as a married couple. Ten years later, Angela filed a request for dissolution of the marriage in an Arizona court. At that time, Ricardo discovered that the individual who married the couple did not have the power to perform the marriage under Mexican law. Ricardo therefore argued to the court that the marriage was invalid (and thus no dissolution, with resulting support obligations, should follow). While Ricardo is correct that the marriage is void under Mexican law, the marriage would have been valid if performed in Arizona. Should the Arizona court recognize the marriage as valid?

PROBLEM 2-56: FIRST COUSINS

Peggy and Aloysius are first cousins. They married in New Virginia 20 years ago, and are now 60 years old. The marriage was (and is) valid under New Virginia law. Aloysius got a job about six years ago with the state government in New State and the couple moved there. After the couple lived in New State for five years, they petitioned the court in New State for Peggy to receive spousal benefits under Aloysius's employment arrangement with the state.

New State has a statute that says that marriages between first cousins are void as incestuous. It is clear that the incest statute is motivated by a concern regarding inheritable birth defects, as it contains an exception that allows couples to marry if they can prove that they are past reproducing age. (The statute focuses on reproduction ability at the time of marriage; thus, first cousins who marry when they are presumed fertile cannot have their marriage declared valid after they can longer reproduce.)

New State follows the Restatement (Second) on issues of marriage validity, and at the time that Peggy and Aloysius moved there it followed the general rule (even for incestuous marriages) that the state with the most significant relationship to the spouses and marriage should govern. Case law prevailing at the time the couple moved to New State not only applied this rule for incestuous marriages, but also evinced a strong preference for applying the place of celebration for issues pertaining to validity. Aloysius and Peggy had been advised of this case law at the time they moved to New State. Five years after the couple moved to New State, however, the legislature changed the law, passing a statute that says: "Incestuous marriages celebrated out of state will not be recognized as valid in New State as of this date." Should the New State court grant the couple's petition to have Peggy recognized as a spouse for state employment benefit purposes?

6.   Structural Mechanics and Escape Valves

Like the Restatement (First), the Restatement (Second) approach requires characterization of issues as an initial step to applying its rules. Because the Restatement (Second) rules themselves are far more flexible than those in the Restatement (First), one would think that courts would find less need for escape valves that enable them to avoid the results that the standard rules would yield. But—true to the nature of conflict of laws itself—complications abound in Second Restatement cases, including forays into escape mechanisms such as the renvoi doctrine and public policy analysis. In fairness to the Restatement (Second), however, these are issues that are equally discernible in states following choice of law approaches that—unlike the Restatements—do not include a long set of rules organized by subject matter. The conclusion one might reach from this observation is that there's something organic or intrinsic to the conflict of laws itself that spawns this type of complexity. For further thinking on this matter, see the Perspective on Rules, Standards, and Complexity in Choice of Law, set forth later in this chapter. In the meantime, consider how the complications and escape valves manifest in the Restatement (Second) itself.

a. Substance and Procedure

From the Restatement (Second) of Conflict of Laws, on the Subject of Procedure:

§122. Issues Relating to Judicial Administration

A court usually applies its own local law rules prescribing how litigation shall be conducted even when it applies the local law rules of another state to resolve other issues in the case.

§127. Pleading and Conduct of Proceedings

The local law of the forum governs rules of pleading and the conduct of proceedings in court.

Boyd Rosene and Assoc., Inc. v. Kansas Mun. Gas Agency
174 F.3d 1115 (10th Cir. 1999)

MURPHY, Circuit Judge.

Boyd Rosene and Associates, Inc., appeals an award of attorney's fees granted to Kansas Municipal Gas Agency and the City of Winfield, Kansas. Rosene argues on appeal that under Oklahoma choice-of-law principles, Kansas law applies and the grant of attorney's fees to the defendants pursuant to Oklahoma Statute §936 was inappropriate. . . . [T]his court concludes that Oklahoma choice-of-law principles would compel the application of Kansas law on attorney's fees. Because Kansas disallows recovery of attorney's fees in the absence of a contractual or statutory provision to the contrary, the district court's award of attorney's fees is Reversed.

I. BACKGROUND

Boyd Rosene and Associates, Inc. ("Rosene") sued Kansas Municipal Gas Agency ("KMGA") and the City of Winfield, Kansas ("Winfield") in a breach of contract and tort action. Rosene filed its diversity action in federal court in the Northern District of Oklahoma. In a paragraph entitled "Choice of Law," the underlying contract provided that it was to be governed and construed in accordance with Kansas law but was silent on the issue of attorney's fees. The district court entered summary judgment in favor of the defendants, KMGA and Winfield, and ordered all parties to pay their own attorney's fees. The district court's decision was initially affirmed on appeal. KMGA and Winfield, however, successfully petitioned for rehearing *en banc* on the issue of their entitlement to attorney's fees.

Upon rehearing *en banc*, this court . . . held that in a contract suit, "rather than automatically applying the law of the state providing the substantive contract law, a district court must first apply the forum state's choice-of-law rules in resolving attorney's fees issues." The en banc court remanded the case to the district court for the application of Oklahoma's choice-of-law rules in resolving defendant's claims for attorney's fees.

In applying Oklahoma's choice-of-law rules, the district court noted that matters of procedure, in contrast to matters of substantive law, are governed by the law of the forum. The district court then held that Oklahoma's attorney's fee statutes are procedural, not substantive, and proceeded to apply Oklahoma statute §936, which provides for the imposition of attorney's fees in a breach-of-contract claim.[1]

The court concluded that KMGA and Winfield were entitled to reasonable attorney's fees on Rosene's breach-of-contract claim. . . .

A. CHOICE OF LAW: GENERAL PRINCIPLES

A federal court sitting in diversity must engage in a two-step inquiry. First, the court must determine whether a particular matter is procedural or substantive for *Erie Railroad Co. v. Tompkins* purposes. 304 U.S. 64 (1938). If the matter is procedural, then federal law applies; if the matter is substantive, then the court follows the law of the forum state. Second, if the court has determined that the matter is substantive, then it looks to the substantive law of the forum state, including its choice of law principles, to determine the applicable substantive law. These two steps are distinct inquiries; thus, what is substantive or procedural for *Erie* purposes is not necessarily substantive or procedural for choice-of-law purposes. *See Sun Oil Co. v. Wortman*, 486 U.S. 717, 726, 100 L. Ed. 2d 743, 108 S. Ct. 2117 (1988) (rejecting notion that "there is an equivalence between what is substantive under the *Erie* doctrine and what is substantive for purposes of conflict of laws"). Consequently, even though attorney's fees are substantive for diversity purposes, they are not thereby necessarily substantive under Oklahoma choice-of-law rules.

B. OKLAHOMA CHOICE OF LAW

Oklahoma choice-of-law principles require a court to apply Oklahoma rules to procedural matters even when those principles require the application of the substantive law of another jurisdiction. Unfortunately, Oklahoma law is silent on the classification of attorney's fees as substantive or procedural for choice-of-law purposes. Nonetheless, it is this court's responsibility to ascertain how the Oklahoma Supreme Court would decide the choice-of-law issue.

---

1. Section 936 provides:

> In any civil action to recover on an open account, a statement of account, account stated, note, bill, negotiable instrument, or contract relating to the purchase or sale of goods, wares, or merchandise, or for labor or services, unless otherwise provided by law or the contract which is the subject [of] the action, the prevailing party shall be allowed a reasonable attorney fee to be set by the court, to be taxed and collected as costs.

Okla. St. Ann. tit. 12, §936 (West 1988).

Oklahoma courts have classified attorney's fees as procedural, but did so in the context of determining a statute's retroactive application. KMGA argues that these cases resolve the issue here.

The characterization of an issue as procedural for retroactivity purposes cannot be so easily transplanted into a choice-of-law context. Recalling the admonition that the substantive/procedural dichotomy for *Erie* purposes is not the same for choice-of-law purposes, the Restatement (Second) of Conflict of Laws cautions generally that "[substantive/procedural] characterizations, while harmless in themselves, have led some courts into unthinking adherence to precedents that have classified a given issue as 'procedural' or 'substantive,' regardless of what purposes were involved in the earlier classifications." §122 cmt. b. The Restatement then provides the example of a decision classifying an issue as procedural for retroactivity purposes which "might mistakenly be held controlling on the question whether [the issue] is 'procedural' for choice-of-law purposes." *Id.* The Supreme Court has iterated this principle: "The line between 'substance' and 'procedure' shifts as the legal context changes. 'Each implies different variables depending upon the particular problem for which it is used.'"

The purposes underlying the substantive/procedural dichotomies employed in retroactivity and choice-of-law cases are completely different. In the choice-of-law context, most matters are treated as substantive. Only in particular instances should a court consider a matter to be procedural. If a case "has foreign contacts and . . . many issues in the case will be decided by reference to the local law of another state," a state should label an issue "procedural" and thus apply its own law only when to do so would serve the purpose of efficient judicial administration. Restatement §122 cmt. a. The range of issues relating to efficient judicial administration is narrow and includes such items as "the proper form of action, service of process, pleading, rules of discovery, mode of trial and execution and costs." *Id.* These are matters in which it would be especially disruptive or difficult for the forum to apply the local rules of another state, and in which failure to employ another state's law will not undermine interstate comity.

. . . [T]he considerations entertained by a court in classifying a particular matter as procedural or substantive are quite different depending upon whether the context is choice of law or retroactive application of a statute. Choice of law analysis concerns judicial efficiency, while retroactivity analysis primarily concerns legislative intent and only secondarily considers fairness with regard to party expectations.

While the divergent purposes of retroactivity and choice-of-law analyses render the Oklahoma retroactivity precedents inapposite in this case, this court acknowledges that both inquiries share a concern about disrupting the parties' expectations. Nonetheless, the roles of party expectations in each inquiry are meaningfully different.

. . . Absent special circumstances, courts usually honor the parties' choice of law because two "prime objectives" of contract law are "to protect the justified expectations of the parties and to make it possible for them to foretell with accuracy what will be their rights and liabilities under the contract." Restatement §187 cmt. e.

Consistent with the primacy of party expectations in determining contractual obligations, party choice of law is a significant consideration in determining whether an attorney's fees statute is substantive or procedural for state choice-of-law purposes. . . . In contrast, the parties' expectations are not given the same elevated status in retroactivity cases. Only if legislative intent is unclear are the parties' expectations considered by the court. Because parties' expectations are not critical in retroactivity cases, they were not even considered in the Oklahoma cases holding that Oklahoma's attorney's fees statute may be applied retroactively. In contrast, when determining choice-of-law issues, Oklahoma courts prioritize party expectations.

Finally, this court is not convinced that what counts as procedural for choice-of-law purposes is the same as what counts as procedural for retroactivity purposes. For support we look to the Restatement, to which Oklahoma courts routinely refer on issues relating to choice of law. Chapter six of the Restatement is dedicated to the general rule that a forum should apply its own local rules "prescribing how litigation shall be conducted even when it applies the local law rules of another state to resolve other issues in the case." §122. Oklahoma follows this general rule. Though not purporting to be exhaustive, chapter six of the Restatement surveys the matters normally considered procedural for choice-of-law purposes. The section "Rules for Management of Litigation" appears to be where a loser-pays attorney's fees provision would be listed, if at all. . . . This court is unable to discern any relationship between a loser-pays attorney's fees provision and the Restatement's classification of procedural issues for choice-of-law purposes. Moreover, KMGA fails to explain why Oklahoma's retroactivity cases compel this court to conclude that attorney's fees are also procedural in a choice-of-law context. Consequently, the retroactivity cases are not controlling in the determination of the status of attorney's fees for choice-of-law purposes.

. . . Despite the parties' arguments to the contrary, Oklahoma law provides no guidance for the classification of attorney's fees for choice-of-law purposes. . . .

The particular factual circumstances of this case lead this court to conclude that the Oklahoma Supreme Court would classify §936 attorney's fees as substantive. This conclusion is compelled by the nature of the attorney's fees statute at issue and the nature of the underlying contractual dispute.

. . .

This court recognizes a distinction, as do other courts and commentators, between loser-pays attorney's fees, that is, attorney's fees awarded to a party simply because it prevailed, and attorney's fees assessed for a willful violation of a court order or against a losing party who acted in bad faith, vexatiously, wantonly, or for oppressive reasons [hereinafter, "bad-faith attorney's fees"].

Loser-pays attorney's fees are normally not within a court's inherent power. Instead, they reflect a conscious policy choice by a legislature to depart from the American rule and codify the English rule. The authority to award bad-faith attorney's fees, though frequently codified, is usually within a court's inherent powers, which it has discretion to exercise in the interest of justice and efficient judicial administration. For example, the Oklahoma Supreme Court noted that a court's inherent power to make "an award of attorney's fees against an opponent under the 'bad faith' exception to the American Rule" was based upon its need "to manage its own affairs so as to achieve the orderly and timely disposition of cases."

The attorney's fees provided by §936 are not assessed for bad-faith litigation; they are instead simply granted to the prevailing party. While courts award bad-faith attorney's fees for reasons related to judicial administration, §936 attorney's fees do not seem to fit the same rubric.

Because parties are empowered to make contractual choice-of-law provisions, their expectations about the applicability of those choice-of-law provisions are a significant factor in the determination of whether an issue is substantive or procedural for choice-of-law purposes. In determining whether an issue is substantive or procedural, the Restatement considers whether the parties shaped their actions with reference to the local law of a certain jurisdiction.[11]

. . . In this case, the parties expressed in their choice-of-law provision that Kansas law would govern their agreement. They said nothing, however, about the allocation of attorney's fees. While Kansas law does not statutorily permit recovery of attorney's fees, it does not prohibit the parties from contracting to shift or allocate attorney's fees. The parties' failure to provide for attorney's fees, in the face of their adoption of Kansas law, indicates their expectation that each party would bear its own costs. . . . [I]f the parties contracted with an eye toward the applicable law, their expectation would have been that Kansas law would govern the recovery of attorney's fees. This court therefore concludes that, consistent with the parties' expectations, Oklahoma choice-of-law principles would apply Kansas law which does not allow recovery of attorney's fees absent a contractual provision to the contrary.

. . . A court is not permitted to slavishly adhere to the law of the state providing the substantive law. Neither, however, is a court prohibited from weighing heavily the expectations of the contracting parties when, as here, such parties' reliance is a consideration in the forum state's choice-of-law principles. . . .

. . . This court concludes that §936 attorney's fees are a substantive issue in the litigation arising from the contract between Rosene and KMGA. Accordingly, Oklahoma choice-of-law principles would compel the application of Kansas law to this issue.

---

11. The Restatement also considers whether: (1) the issue is one whose resolution would be likely to affect the ultimate result of the case; (2) the precedents have tended consistently to classify the issue as procedural or substantive for conflict-of-laws purposes; and (3) applying another jurisdiction's rules of judicial administration would unduly burden the forum. *See id.* §122, cmt. a. We note that these remaining factors leave the decision in this case in equipoise. The attorney's fees issue will not affect the ultimate disposition of this case, which weighs in favor of KMGA. On the other hand, applying the Kansas law of attorney's fees would not unduly burden the court, which weighs in favor of Rosene. Finally, as already noted, there is no consistent classification of attorney's fees to be found in either Oklahoma or Tenth Circuit law.

Notes on
ROSENE

1. Note how comfortable the *Rosene* court was with the proposition that, where the substance/procedure characterization is concerned, a court can characterize a rule one way for vertical (state/federal) choice of law purposes and adopt a different characterization for horizontal (state/state) choice of law purposes. This book confronted the same notion earlier in connection with the Restatement (First) of Conflict of Laws and the court's decision in *Sampson v. Channel. Rosene* suggests that the characterization may further vary according to context, such as whether the issue arises in cases with choice of law clauses or not. Is it appropriate for courts to be so fluid in interpreting terms of art such as "substantive" and "procedure"? Was the *Rosene* court too facile with its flexibility, suggesting that the law was mere putty in a judge's hands?

2. Do you agree with the *Rosene* court's conclusion that retroactivity and choice of law analyses have different purposes? Although it found the overlap unpersuasive, the *Rosene* court did acknowledge that party expectations are important for both contexts. Was the court correct in suggesting that legislative intent is not pertinent to choice of law purposes? Isn't the intent or purpose behind a law such as an attorneys' fees statute an integral part of choice of law analysis under the Restatement (Second)? Certainly Restatement (Second) §6 establishes that this is the case. Moreover, the *Rosene* court itself relied on the policy underpinnings of "loser pays" attorneys' fees statutes in conducting its own choice of law analysis toward the end of the opinion.

As a contrast to *Rosene*, consider the court's reasoning in the unpublished opinion in *Jefferson Wells Int'l, Inc. v. American Reprographics Co.*, No. 8213777, 2010 WL 190427 (Cal. Dist. Ct. App. 2010). In that case, the parties' contract designated Wisconsin law, which would not have allowed an attorneys' fees award. The court, however, awarded attorneys' fees to the California defendant under California law, explaining that the "interest of California in seeing its residents receive fair play with respect to attorney fees, when resort is made to the California courts, is a fundamental equitable policy of this state." *Id.* at 11 (*quoting ABF Capital Corp. v. Grove Properties Co.*, 126 Cal. App. 4th 204, 220 (2005)).

3. How might you avoid the problem presented in *Rosene* if you were an attorney representing a party entering into a transaction?

PROBLEM 2-57: AN ELEVATOR ACCIDENT

Oliver Elevator, a State O corporation, designed and manufactured elevators. A child from State E was injured by an elevator in a State E department store. The child's father, Reginald, sued Oliver Elevator in State E under the theory that the elevator was negligently designed. The State E court concluded that, under Restatement (Second) §145, State E had the most significant connection with the suit for the purpose of choosing the governing liability law and accompanying remedies. After trial, the court instructed the jury on State E law governing liability and damages, and Reginald received a large verdict. The question arose thereafter, however, whether to award prejudgment interest on this verdict. State E law provides for automatic 12 percent prejudgment interest on any verdict, and State O law provides no prejudgment interest. The State O legislature determined that prejudgment interest would provide too great of a burden on courts to calculate and impose. The State E legislature determined that prejudgment interest is actually a component of damages, with a compensatory purpose, and should be imposed as a matter of course. Which law of prejudgment interest should govern under the Restatement (Second)?

Ford Motor Company v. Leggat

904 S.W.2d 643 (Tex. 1995)

Justice CORYN delivered the opinion of the Court, in which all Justices join.

In this mandamus proceeding Ford Motor Company complains of having to produce certain documents and information concerning litigation involving its Bronco II vehicles. Because we conclude that the trial court abused its discretion by ordering the matters produced and that Ford lacks an adequate remedy by appeal, we conditionally grant the writ.

Reynauld White was killed when the Bronco II he was driving flipped and rolled over. . . . In the underlying products liability suit, his estate and survivors (the Whites) seek discovery of: (1) a 1982 report by Ford's general counsel to Ford's Policy and Strategy Committee. . . . After hearing argument but without inspecting the documents, the trial court ordered Ford to produce the documents . . . are protected by the attorney-client privilege and work-product doctrine. . . .

According to Ford, the 1982 report to the Policy and Strategy Committee contains legal advice from its principal in-house attorney to a committee of Ford's senior officers and members of its board of directors. The report was presented and discussed at a meeting that took place in Dearborn, Michigan. Ford supported its claim of privilege with the affidavit of William Burmeister, a Ford employee who has been Secretary to the Policy and Strategy Committee since 1989, and in that capacity is the custodian of the document in question. In his affidavit Burmeister described, based on personal knowledge, the usual procedures taken by Ford to assure confidentiality at the Committee's meetings, reviewed the report and the minutes of the meeting, and concluded that the report contained legal advice and that the minutes summarized the discussion of that advice. Although Ford believes the affidavit provides sufficient proof of the applicability of the corporate attorney-client privilege under Texas law, it urges the Court to apply Michigan's law of privilege because that is the state with the most significant relationship to the communication at issue.

Ford argues simply that privileges are substantive and therefore the law of the state with the most significant relationship to the particular issue applies; the Whites argue just as simply that privileges, like rules of evidence, are procedural, and therefore the law of the forum applies. The reality is more complicated. . . .

We begin with the conflict-of-law principles established by the Restatement (Second) of Conflict of Laws (1988). . . . Conflict-of-law analysis has changed in large part from the territorial approach of the Restatement (First) of Conflict of Laws in 1934 to the "significant relationship" analysis of the second Restatement. In keeping with a more functional approach, although section 138 of the Restatement provides that the law of the forum governs the general admissibility of evidence, the section governing privileged communications directs a court to identify the state of most significant relationship with a communication when determining whose law of privilege should apply. Section 139 provides:

> (1) Evidence that is not privileged under the local law of the state which has the most significant relationship with the communication will be admitted, even though it would be privileged under the local law of the forum, unless the admission of such evidence would be contrary to the strong public policy of the forum.
>
> (2) Evidence that is privileged under the local law of the state which has the most significant relationship with the communication but which is not privileged under the local law of the forum will be admitted unless there is some special reason why the forum policy favoring admission should not be given effect.

As the state where the communication took place, Michigan is the state of most significant relationship. *See* Restatement (Second) §139 cmt. e. Our analysis therefore proceeds under subsection (2).

The Restatement favors admission of the evidence unless "some special reason" not to admit it exists, and identifies four factors to consider when determining admissibility: number and nature of contacts of the forum with the parties or transaction, materiality of the evidence, kind of privilege, and fairness to the parties. *See id.* §139 cmt. d. It goes on to explain that "the forum will be more inclined to give effect to a foreign privilege that is well established and recognized in many states," and if the privilege "was probably relied upon by the parties." *Id.* The purpose of the attorney-client privilege and the reliance placed by the client on the confidential nature of the communications create special reasons why Texas should defer to the broader attorney-client privilege of Michigan in this case.

The attorney-client privilege has been recognized as "the oldest of the privileges for confidential communications known to the common law." Among communications privileges, it is the only one recognized by every state, even though its scope, as this case demonstrates, may vary. The purpose of the privilege is to ensure the free flow of information between attorney and client, ultimately serving the broader societal interest of effective administration of justice. Although we may reach a different result when confronted with other privileges, in view of the nature and purpose of the attorney-client privilege, we hold that it will be governed by the law of the state with the most significant relationship to the communication. *See* Sterk, *supra*, at 491 n. 95 ("In the case of a privilege designed to encourage open communication, C's [the state with the most significant relationship to the communication] great interest in seeing its privilege recognized should always outweigh F's [the forum state] desire to admit the testimony").

As the Michigan Court of Appeals has interpreted [the governing law], the attorney-client privilege extends to confidential communications between the employees and corporate counsel given within the scope of the employees' duties to enable the corporation to obtain legal advice. In this case, Burmeister explains in his affidavit how the committee conducts its business and what the nature of its business is, based on his personal knowledge as secretary. He avers that the committee "considers major issues affecting Ford and is the advisory committee to Ford's Office of the Chief Executive," and that the members of the committee are "Ford's officers who are members of the Board of Directors and certain other officers of Ford":

> . . . [A]ccess [to material relating to meetings of the Committee] is strictly limited. Only those within the Company or lawyers and legal assistants retained by Ford who have need to review the documents are allowed access to them.

These averments indicate that anyone who was not a member of the committee was providing information to the committee so that it could act on legal advice. The report itself contains discussion and recommendations concerning specific legal strategy. Although one can argue that Burmeister's affidavit is sufficient to establish corporate privilege even under Texas' control group test, we conclude that Michigan's law of privilege applies, and that under that law, the affidavit is sufficient and the report is privileged.

. . . Accordingly, we conditionally grant the writ and direct the trial court to vacate its order of July 29, 1994, to the extent it compels Ford to produce [certain] documents itemized on page two of the order (except for documents numbered 32529M through 37523M) and to the extent the order compels Ford to answer interrogatories 2, 3, and 4 of Plaintiffs' First Set of Interrogatories. Writ will issue only if the trial court fails to do so.

Note on
FORD MOTOR CO. v. LEGGAT

1. As reflected in Comment *a* of the Restatement Second §138, the Restatement's privilege rule rests on the efficiency and convenience of allowing a court to rely on forum law in deciding whether to admit evidence. This approach allows a court to make evidentiary rulings without the burden of studying unfamiliar laws. The Comment lists exceptions to this rule, including privileges against the disclosure of confidential information and the statute of frauds. Why must a court consider unfamiliar law on these issues, but

not other evidentiary matters? The decision to privilege certain types of communications generally rests on policy considerations other than accuracy and reliability. Indeed, the accuracy of the evidence in privileged communications is rarely subject to challenge. Circumstances exist when a forum would find no privilege protecting disclosure of information, but another jurisdiction would privilege the information from disclosure. When the foreign jurisdiction has a greater interest in having its law applied, the Restatement would require the forum court to suppress potentially accurate and probative evidence. Does the Restatement make the correct judgment on this?

b. Characterization

From the Restatement (Second) of Conflict of Laws:

§7. Characterization

(1) The classification and interpretation of legal concepts and terms involve questions of characterization, as the term is used in the Restatement of this Subject.

(2) The classification and interpretation of Conflict of Law concepts and terms are determined in accordance with the law of the forum, except as stated in §8.

(3) The classification and interpretation of local law concepts and terms are determined in accordance with the law that governs the issue involved.

The rigidity of the Restatement (First) places a greater premium on characterization than one generally observes in the Restatement (Second). Yet the subject matter organization of the Restatement (Second) maintains the importance of characterization as a threshold inquiry. The reality is that one must determine which set of conflict of rules apply in analyzing a dispute under the Restatement (Second), and thus must use characterization to make that determination. As you read the case below, consider whether the process of characterization contributes to a sense that the court is dispensing fairness and justice as it is evaluating conflicting multistate elements in the dispute.

Waddoups v. The Amalgamated Sugar Company

54 P.3d 1054 (Utah 2002)

WILKINS, Justice:

. . .

Defendant Amalgamated Sugar Company ("Amalgamated") operates a sugar processing plant near Twin Falls, Idaho. Amalgamated is headquartered in Ogden, Utah. Plaintiffs Blake Waddoups and James Sparrow worked at the Twin Falls plant as "bulk loaders," operating the system that loaded sugar into rail cars. Waddoups was hired in 1985, and Sparrow was hired in 1989. While plaintiffs were employed with Amalgamated, another employee, Michael Davis, died as a result of an accident at the Twin Falls plant. On February 16, 1995, Davis's arm was caught in the bulk-loading system's conveyor belt and was torn from his body, causing him to bleed to death.

During the accident, blood and flesh from Davis's arm contaminated the sugar present in the system. Plaintiffs insist contaminated sugar mixed with uncontaminated sugar when contaminated sugar moved through the production system and mixed with the sugar in Amalgamated's storage silos. Plaintiffs base this contention on their involvement in the cleanup process, and they state that they informed Amalgamated of this problem.

Following the February 16 accident, Waddoups placed "Quarantined" signs on both rail cars that contained the contaminated sugar. One week later, on February 23, Amalgamated officials told employees that the contaminated sugar would be destroyed. Around this time, Waddoups, accompanied by Sparrow, informed Amalgamated that he thought the sugar stored in the silos was also contaminated. Amalgamated claims the contaminated sugar loaded on the day of the accident was shipped to an animal feed producer; plaintiffs allege Amalgamated shipped contaminated sugar for human consumption, a criminal violation of the Federal Food, Drug, and Cosmetic Act. . . .

In March 1995, plaintiffs informed Amalgamated of their fear of being implicated in criminal sales of contaminated sugar by virtue of their approval of sugar shipments. They told Amalgamated that they did not want to sign documentation that accompanied shipments of sugar until Amalgamated investigated the extent of the contamination. Amalgamated allegedly threatened plaintiffs with termination.

In May 1995, plaintiffs reported to Amalgamated that they believed the rail cars that delivered the contaminated sugar had not been adequately cleaned upon return to the factory, thereby contaminating other sugar. On May 18, Waddoups threatened to reveal his knowledge to food safety agencies or the media. Waddoups was suspended for two days and warned to stop discussing the matter. Sparrow was fired on May 22, 1995, and Waddoups was fired on May 28, 1995.

Sparrow and Waddoups were members of The American Federation of Grain Millers Union. The Union and Amalgamated had entered into a collective bargaining agreement. Under the collective bargaining agreement employees could be fired only for "just cause," and any discharged employee could file a grievance which could lead to binding arbitration. Plaintiffs argue, in essence, that they were fired for threatening to "blow the whistle" on Amalgamated for selling contaminated sugar. Amalgamated insists plaintiffs were fired for excessive absenteeism, which plaintiffs claim is pretextual. . . .

[Waddoups and Sparrow filed a complaint in state court, requesting compensatory and punitive damages for the following: (1) wrongful termination of employment in violation of public policy; (2) negligent or intentional infliction of emotional distress; (3) negligent or intentional interference with a prospective economic advantage; and (4) conspiracy. After procedural wrangling in the trial court, the trial court ruled in favor of Amalgamated, determining, among other things, that (1) Idaho, not Utah, law governed plaintiffs' claims; (2) the claim for wrongful discharge in violation of Utah public policy would not succeed under Idaho law; and (3) the federal Labor Management Relations Act preempted the claim for intentional and/or negligent infliction of emotional distress. The plaintiffs had amended their complaint, which the trial court had dismissed. Plaintiffs appealed and the case reached the Utah Supreme Court, which began its analysis with the choice of law question.]

We must first consider whether Idaho or Utah law applies.[3] Once we determine whether Utah or Idaho law applies, we can determine whether the trial court erred in concluding that plaintiffs' claims were preempted by federal labor law. . . .

Plaintiffs allege that Utah law applies because, among other things, their alleged injuries — the main injury being the wrongful discharge claim in violation of Utah public policy — occurred in Utah. Amalgamated, to the contrary, insists that Idaho law governs plaintiffs' claims under the test adopted by Utah, Restatement (Second) Conflict of Laws §145 (1971).

"Since Utah is the forum state, Utah's choice of law rules determine the outcome of the conflict." In Utah we apply the "most significant relationship" approach as described in the Restatement (Second) of Conflict of Laws in determining which state's laws should apply to a given circumstance.

1. CHARACTERIZATION OF THE ACTIONS

To apply the "most significant relationship" approach, we first characterize the nature of the claim. We determine at the outset whether the problem presented relates to torts, contracts, property, or some other field, in order to identify an appropriate set of factors to determine which forum has the "most significant relationship" to the cause of action. This is essential because the particular factors considered in determining the "most significant relationship" vary according to the type of action brought. One set of factors will often be more applicable than another set depending on the area of law implicated.

Plaintiffs brought four cognizable causes of action in their initial complaint on which summary judgment was granted: (1) wrongful termination of employment in violation of public policy; (2) negligent or intentional infliction of emotional distress; (3) negligent or intentional interference with a prospective economic advantage; and (4) conspiracy. Interesting to this case is that under the current law, the claim for wrongful discharge in violation of public policy is a tort in Utah, but a contract matter in Idaho. Nevertheless, the characterization

---

3. Notably, there is a difference between Utah law and Idaho law regarding the claim of wrongful termination of employment in violation of public policy. Under Idaho law, wrongful termination in violation of public policy is a contract-based cause of action, *Hummer v. Evans*, 129 Idaho 274, 923 P.2d 981, 987 (Idaho 1996), and under Utah law, the same claim is a tort-based cause of action, *Peterson v. Browning*, 832 P.2d 1280, 1284-85 (Utah 1992).

of an action is made in accordance with the law of the forum. As a result, because plaintiffs chose Utah as their forum, we characterize their claims, *for purposes of the choice of law analysis*, in accordance with Utah law.

Plaintiffs' claims, under Utah law, are tort claims. In Utah, wrongful termination in violation of public policy is a tort. Likewise, negligent and intentional infliction of emotional distress are torts, and we recognize the tort of intentional interference with a prospective economic advantage. Civil conspiracy is also a tort. We therefore conclude that plaintiffs' claims lie entirely in tort.

2. "Most Significant Relationship" Analysis

Having concluded, for purposes of the choice of law analysis, that plaintiffs' claims sound in tort, we next determine which state "has the most significant relationship to the occurrence and the parties." Restatement (Second) Conflict of Laws §145(1) (1971). We have previously applied Section 145 of the Restatement (Second) of Conflict of Laws, accompanied by an applicable set of factors for a particular tort, as the Utah test for determining which state has the most significant relationship to a tort case. . . . With respect to the torts pled in this case, we do not find another set of factors in the Restatement to be any more helpful or applicable than those in section 145.

First, the alleged injuries to plaintiffs — wrongful discharge, infliction of emotional distress, interference with plaintiffs' employment, and conspiracy — occurred in Idaho. While Amalgamated's headquarters are located in Utah, plaintiffs were terminated from the Twin Falls plant, plaintiffs' place of employment. Second, any actions taken by factory supervisors to influence plaintiffs' termination took place in Idaho. The alleged harassment and humiliation occurred in Idaho. Therefore, the conduct causing the alleged injuries also occurred in Idaho. Third, the domicile, residence, nationality, place of incorporation, and place of business of the parties all weigh in favor of application of Idaho law. The plaintiffs lived and worked in Idaho. They also threatened to reveal the alleged wrongdoings of Amalgamated to Idaho, not Utah, food safety agencies. Again, even though Amalgamated's corporate headquarters are in Utah, the factory where plaintiffs were employed is in Idaho. Finally, the relationship between the parties was centered in Idaho. In this case, we give more weight to the location of the factory where plaintiffs worked than to the location of Amalgamated's headquarters, and the fact that the parties' relationship was centered in Twin Falls is particularly compelling. Consequently, Idaho has the most significant relationship with the parties and their employment relationship, and we therefore apply the substantive law of Idaho.

. . .

[The court then concluded — among other things — that (1) the plaintiffs' infliction of emotional distress claim was preempted by federal labor law; and (2) the plaintiffs failed to provide adequate support for interference with a prospective economic advantage and conspiracy claims. The court then evaluated whether federal law preempted the wrongful termination claim.]

Amalgamated contends that plaintiffs' wrongful termination in violation of public policy claim is preempted by federal labor law because the claim relates to the collective bargaining agreement, and the collective bargaining agreement governs the employment relationship between plaintiffs and Amalgamated. Plaintiffs disagree, insisting that the collective bargaining agreement would not be implicated in considering the wrongful discharge claim.

For the reasons explained previously, the substantive law of Idaho applies. Under Idaho law, wrongful termination in violation of public policy is a contract-based cause of action. To prove this claim, plaintiffs must demonstrate that the employer's motivation for their termination contravenes Idaho public policy. The United States Supreme Court has held that when a collective bargaining agreement is in place, a state law claim between the parties that is "substantially dependent upon analysis of the terms of an agreement made between the parties in a labor contract, that claim must either be treated as a §301 claim [under the Labor Management Relations Act] or dismissed as pre-empted by federal labor-contract law."

Resolution of plaintiffs' contract claim for wrongful discharge would substantially depend upon analysis of the terms of the collective bargaining agreement. The collective bargaining agreement governs the contractual employment relationship between plaintiffs and Amalgamated, and it dictates the circumstances under which plaintiffs could be terminated. Under Article 14 of the collective bargaining agreement, "The Company [Amalgamated] has the right to discipline or discharge employees for just cause." To determine whether plaintiffs were wrongfully discharged would inevitably require a determination of what "just cause" means in the context of the collective bargaining agreement. The meaning of just cause is subject to various interpretations, and to permit suit for this Idaho breach of employment contract claim separate from the collective bargaining agreement would undermine the goal of a unified body of federal labor law that necessarily preempts the field.

As a result, we hold that the trial court was correct to dismiss plaintiffs' claim for wrongful termination in violation of Idaho public policy as preempted. . . .

The district court order granting summary judgment on plaintiffs' initial complaint is affirmed. The district court order granting defendant's motion to dismiss plaintiffs' amended complaint is also affirmed.

Notes on
WADDOUPS

1. The *Waddoups* court presented an interesting, albeit classic, turn to its characterization analysis: the court used forum (Utah) law to determine that the causes of action should be characterized as tort claims for the purpose of a choice of law analysis. This analysis pointed to Idaho law as the source of liability rules. Then, the court analyzed the key cause of action — wrongful discharge — under the applicable Idaho law, emphasizing that the cause of

action was "contract-based" for the purpose of determining its relationship
to federal law. Look back at the Restatement (Second) §7, quoted above
(right before the *Waddoups* opinion). Is the court's analysis consistent
with that section's instructions?

2. The "tort for one purpose/contract for another purpose" conclusion
evinces the same problems observed in other conflict of laws contexts: the
conclusion requires a complex analysis, divorced from the type of common
sense that can make the law accessible to the majority of citizens who are
actually controlled by legal rules. But this complexity may be the best solution to the diversity and riches arising from and protected by our federalist
system, which includes conflicting sister state regulation and as well as
federal rules that occasionally shunt aside state regulation. Cases like
Waddoups arguably create a form of hybrid regulation that accommodates
different approaches to regulating an issue, while still providing a final adjudication of parties' rights in a multijurisdictional dispute. Although the
apparently contradictory conclusions may at first appear nonsensical
because courts avoid a uniform characterization of the cause of action,
the analysis gives each interested governmental entity a significant role in
reaching the ultimate disposition. Isn't this the most we can ask of a
federalist system?

For a thoughtful discussion of this problem in the context of a bankruptcy case, see *In re: Cyrus II Partnership*, 413 B.R. 609 (Bankr. S.D. Tex.
2009). *Cyrus* concerned the characterization of a "fraudulent conveyance"
under the Restatement (Second), taking into account the concerns of the
interested states as well as the federal bankruptcy code. This enterprise is
particularly tricky because bankruptcy embosses a uniform federal policy
on the distinct identity of various state laws. For guidance, *Cyrus* looked to
the words of Justice Frankfurter, who celebrated the diversity among state
commercial laws — even under the auspices of federal bankruptcy jurisdiction: "The Constitution did not intend that transactions that have different
legal consequences because they took place in different states shall come out
with the same result because they passed through a bankruptcy court." *Id.* at
617 (*quoting Vanston Bondholders Protective Comm. v. Green*, 329 U.S. 156, 172-
173 (1946)). For discussion of how accommodating diversity creates hybrid
legal principles, see Laura E. Little, *Empowerment Through Restraint: Reverse
Preemption or Hybrid Lawmaking?*, 59 Case W. Res. L. Rev. 955, 964-966
(2009) (describing the process of hybrid decision making in bankruptcy
choice of law analysis).

3. How does characterization under the Restatement (Second) differ
from characterization under the Restatement (First)? In *Silica Tech,
L.L.C. v. J-Fiber*, 2009 U.S. Dist. LEXIS 73700 (D. Mass. 2009), the court
opined that characterization is not as important under the Restatement
(Second) because its core section, §6, provides general considerations

that apply to all components of the Restatement (Second). *Silica* reasons that §6 is a common denominator spanning all subject matters — thus reducing the significance of the particular subject matter a court chooses to attach to a legal issue. Does the court's approach (and result) in *Waddoups* support this view of characterization under the Restatement (Second)?

PROBLEM 2-58: JUDITH'S BROKEN BIKE PEDAL

Judith bought a bicycle from BikeJoy, Inc. Judith is a citizen of state A. BikeJoy is incorporated in State A and operates one retail store, which is also in State A. While Judith was riding the bike in State B a few months after the purchase, one of the pedals snapped off and she was severely injured. In fact, Judith was hospitalized in State B for several months after the accident.

Judith has filed suit against BikeJoy in State A, alleging that BikeJoy should pay her damages under a theory of strict liability. Under State A law, strict liability should be treated as a contract cause of action. Under State B law, strict liability should be considered a tort cause of action. State A law is far more favorable to injured parties such as Judith than State B law. The court in State A is trying to determine whether it should apply Restatement (Second) §188 (the general contract section) or Restatement (Second) §145 (the general tort section) to determine whether State A or State B law should govern the cause of action. Which section of the Restatement (Second) should the court use?

c. Renvoi

The renvoi doctrine refers to the practice of a forum looking to the choice of law rules of a foreign state to determine how the foreign state would have handled choice of law if it had been the place where the action was filed. Assume that the forum decides that its choice of law principles designate the governing law of a foreign state. The foreign state might have applied the forum's internal law, it might have applied its own law, or it might have applied the law of a third jurisdiction. If the forum considers whether it should actually follow the mandate of the foreign state's choice of law rule, that consideration implicates traditional renvoi analysis. You may recall that the Restatement (First) generally rejects the notion that the forum should follow a foreign state's choice of law mandate. You may also recall, from studying the more modern choice of law approaches, that consideration of a foreign state's choice of law rule can help identify the interest of the foreign state in having its law applied. In this context, the forum court does not use renvoi in a traditional way, but instead as a tool of interpretation.

The Second Restatement instructs that courts use the traditional process of renvoi in only two circumstances. Here is the specific section:

§8. Applicability of Choice-of-Law Rules of Another State (Renvoi)

other state

(1) When directed by its own choice-of-law rule to apply "the law" of another state, the forum applies the <u>local law of the other state,</u> except as stated in Subsections (2) and (3).

(2) When the objective of the particular choice-of-law rule is that the forum reach the same result on the very facts involved as would the courts of another state, the forum will apply the choice-of-law rules of the other state, subject to considerations of practicability and feasibility.

(3) When the state of the forum has no substantial relationship to the particular issue or the parties and the courts of all interested states would concur in selecting the local law rule applicable to this issue, the forum will usually apply this rule.

According to the comments to this section, uniformity concerns motivated §8(2) and (3). Presumably, the thinking behind these provisions is that a forum's policies may overshadow "the objective of uniformity of decision" if the forum does indeed have a substantial relationship to the issue or the parties.[38] In application, however, this subtlety has not proven particularly crucial. Courts tend to consider foreign law under the Second Restatement in the same manner as under governmental interest analysis: as a tool for interpreting a foreign state's policies and interests. *See, e.g., Hamilton v. Accu-tek*, 47 F. Supp. 2d 330, 338 (E.D.N.Y. 1999) (declining to apply §8(2) and (3) in a torts case, stating that "[t]he more modern use of foreign conflicts rules is as an aid in assessing the foreign state's interest in the application of substantive law"). This reasoning comports with the spirit of the Second Restatement, which emphasizes that a court may examine a state's choice of law rules in assessing both the "existence" and "intensity" of the state's interests in having its law applied. Restatement (Second) of Conflict of Laws §8, comment k.

d. Public Policy

most of p.nif

General principles governing the role of public policy in choice of law are reviewed earlier in this chapter in the Perspective on Public Policy. How these general principles apply in the specific context of the Restatement (Second) is somewhat uncertain. One widely held view is that an actual public policy exception is unnecessary, since a court may consider its own policy under Restatement (Second) §6(2)(b) and thus can rely solely on that section in concluding that the public policy reflected in a foreign law is inimical to its own. This view was expressed by the court in *Phillips v. General Motors Corp.*, 995 P.2d 1002, 1015 (Mont. 2000), which, after announcing its intention to adopt the Restatement (Second), stated:

38. Peter Hay, Patrick J. Borchers & Symeon C. Symeonides, Conflict of Laws 1089 (5th ed. 2010).

For choice of law purposes, the public policy of a state is simply the rules, as expressed in its legislative enactments and judicial decisions, that it uses to decide controversies. . . . The purpose of a choice of law rule is to resolve conflicts between competing policies. Considerations of public policy are expressly subsumed within the most significant relationship approach. *See* Restatement (Second) §6(2)(b) and (c) (mandating consideration of the relevant policies of the forum state and other interested states). In order to determine which state has the more significant relationship, the public policies of all interested states must be considered. A "public policy" exception to the most significant relationship test would be redundant.

The Restatement (Second) itself mentions public policy in the context of entertaining a cause of action only:

§90. Action Contrary to Public Policy

No action will be entertained on a foreign cause of action the enforcement of which is contrary to the strong public policy of the forum.

In explaining the scope of this section, the official comments explain:

[The section] applies only to situations where the forum refuses to entertain the suit on the ground that the cause of action is contrary to a strong local public policy. The rule does not apply to situations where the forum does decide the controversy between the parties and, on the stated ground of public policy, applies its own local law, rather than the otherwise applicable law, in determining one or more of the issues involved.

Restatement (Second) of Conflict of Laws §90, comment a. Thus, the Restatement (Second) itself seems to open a narrow circumstance for officially invoking public policy outside of §6(2)(b) and (c). The model then seems to follow: where a forum has an interest in the case, it will simply impose its own law. If the forum does not have an interest, it will apply the law of a jurisdiction that does have an interest in the case so long as that law is not obnoxious to the forum's public policy. If the only jurisdiction with an interest in the case has a law that is contrary to the forum's public policy, the forum can dismiss the case under the doctrine of forum non conveniens. While this seems a logical framework under the Restatement (Second), it is not clear that the public policy exception will die so easily. One commentator observed that "irrespective of the choice of law system employed, there will be an irreducible number of cases in which courts will be inclined to employ public policy doctrine." John Bernard Corr, *Modern Choice of Law and Public Policy: The Emperor Has the Same Old Clothes*, 39 U. Miami L. Rev. 647, 695 (1985).

e. Domicile

Earlier in this chapter, the Perspective on Domicile, Residence, and Citizenship surveys general principles of domicile. Both the Restatement (First) and the Restatement (Second) embody these general principles, with only slight variation between the two. Perhaps the most significant difference between the Restatement (First) and the Restatement (Second) is not in the definition of the concept but in its importance and complexity. As with other modern methodologies, the Restatement (Second) puts greater emphasis on domicile in determining state interest than the Restatement (First), which is more event focused. In addition, the Restatement (Second) is more explicit in reckoning with modern regulation's intricacies, stating that the "core of domicile is everywhere the same. But in close cases, decision of a question of domicile may sometimes depend upon the purpose for which the domicile concept is used in the particular case." Restatement (Second) §11, comment o. This is aggravated for corporations, as the law varies on how to determine which states have interests in protecting corporate interests.

From the Restatement (Second) of Conflict of Laws, on the Subject of Domicil:

§11. Domicil

(1) Domicil is a place, usually a person's home, to which the rules of Conflict of Laws sometimes accord determinative significance because of the person's identification with that place.

(2) Every person has a domicil at all times and, at least for the same purpose, no person has more than one domicil at a time.

§12. Home Defined

Home is the place where a person dwells and which is the center of his domestic, social and civil life.

§13. Domicil — By What Law Determined

In applying its rules of Conflict of Laws, the forum determines domicil according to its own standards.

§16. Requisite of Physical Presence

To acquire a domicil of choice in a place, a person must be physically present there; but the establishment of a home in a particular dwelling is not necessary for the acquisition of such a domicil.

§18. Requisite Intention

To acquire a domicil of choice in a place, a person must intend to make that place his home for the time at least.

Mzamane v. Winfrey

693 F. Supp. 2d 442 (E.D. Pa. 2010)

ROBRENO, J.

Plaintiff Lerato Nomvuyo Mzamane ("Plaintiff") brings this action for defamation, and related causes of action, stemming from comments made by Oprah Winfrey ("Winfrey") regarding Plaintiff's performance as headmistress of the Oprah Winfrey Leadership Academy for Girls ("OWLAG"). Plaintiff claims that she suffered significant damage to her professional reputation as a result of Winfrey's comments.

. . .

[Plaintiff was born in Teyateyaneng, Lesotho[1] in 1969. After attending University in Nigeria, plaintiff received advance degrees in the United States. From 2000 through 2006, Plaintiff worked as an administrator at at Germantown Friends Lower School in Philadelphia ("Germantown").] In Deccember 2006, she accepted a position as a Consultant for Learner Education and Development at OWLAG.

Winfrey is the founder of co-defendants Harpo Productions, Inc. and Harpo, Inc. (collectively, "Harpo"). She is the creator and host of The Oprah Winfrey Show, which is a syndicated television program that is produced by Harpo and appears on local television stations throughout the United States and the world.

OWLAG is a private academy opened by Winfrey in South Africa, and run by the Oprah Winfrey Leadership Academy Foundation (the "Foundation"). OWLAG provides education for children from impoverished families. OWLAG began as a partnership between the Foundation and the government of South Africa. OWLAG has 28 buildings on a 52-acre campus in a small town called Henley-on-Klip near Johannesburg, South Africa. [OWLAG's costs] are funded by the Foundation. Winfrey herself was involved with multiple aspects of the planning at OWLAG, such as the architecture and construction of the school.

At OWLAG, students live in dormitories on the school's campus and are supervised by employees present in the dorms (the "Dorm Parents") at the conclusion of the students' academic day. At the time OWLAG opened it did not have Dorm Parents in place. . . .

The school opened on January 2, 2007, with an approximate enrollment of 150 seventh and eighth grade female students. The opening of OWLAG attracted media attention, including coverage by the Philadelphia Inquirer and CNN.

According to Plaintiff, at the time she accepted the consultancy position at OWLAG in December 2006, her understanding was that she would be mentored by the Interim Head of Academy, Joan Countryman, and would ascend to the position of the Head of Academy at some point in 2008. Plaintiff entered into her employment agreement for the consultancy position on December 28, 2006, however, within several days of her arrival in South Africa, she was appointed to the position of the Head of Academy ("Headmistress") in place of Ms. Countryman. Plaintiff entered into a written employment contract with the Foundation,

---

1. Lesotho is a country located in the southern portion of Africa.

which provided a fixed term of employment from January 11, 2007 to December 31, 2007.

As Headmistress, Plaintiff's "charge was to be responsible for the girls and the curriculum and the residential life of the girls at the school." Plaintiff was responsible, along with another OWLAG employee (Sonya Anderson), for hiring the Dorm Parents. Plaintiff's duties did not include media or public relations obligations related to the administration of OWLAG.

Plaintiff asserts that throughout her tenure as Headmistress she was in constant contact with Winfrey, as well as representatives of Harpo and members of the Foundation. Plaintiff contends that the substance of these communications included general administration of OWLAG, planning for OWLAG events, the progress of individual OWLAG students, and interactions with parents of OWLAG students.

As Headmistress, Plaintiff was also responsible for dealing with complaints from OWLAG students, specifically complaints about their interaction with the Dorm Parents. Plaintiff contends that she would often hear grievances from students about their treatment by Dorm Parents. After considering the merits of the complaints, Plaintiff would often instruct the respective Dorm Parent to apologize to the students and discuss the substance of the complaints with the students.

[The defamation dispute between the Plaintiff and Winfrey had its seeds in complaints about the conduct of Dorm Parents toward students. These complaints lead to unfavorable media coverage and tension between Plaintiff and Winfrey about Plaintiff's response to the complaints. During this period, Plaintiff left South Africa for the United States to participate in meetings related to OWLAG, including a meeting with Winfrey to discuss applicants for the incoming classes at OWLAG. As a result of the complaints concerning the Dorm Parents, Plaintiff was placed on administrative leave during a meeting with Winfrey in Chicago in October 2007, and later told that her employment contract would not be renewed upon its expiration on December 31, 2007.

Winfrey had a private meeting with parents in October 2007 in which she allegedly made defamatory comments about the Plaintiff. Thereafter a representative of Winfrey released the following public statement, which declared, "[W]ith respect to Plaintiff's involvement in the internal investigation: [i]n order to ensure an impartial investigation, the Head of Academy and the Academy Administration mutually agreed she would take a paid leave of absence. The Head of Academy is not the subject of the allegation of misconduct." This statement and the dismissal of Plaintiff generated significant attention from the international media. Winfrey subsequently held a press conference in Chicago, a recording of which was available electronically at Harpo's website until May 2009. Plaintiff asserts that several defamatory statements were made by Winfrey at the November Press Conference.]

. . .

Plaintiff alleges that as a result of the highly publicized statements by Winfrey regarding the alleged abuse, she was precluded from finding employment in the educational field until August 2008, at which time she obtained a temporary consultancy position with Bridge International Academy in South Africa. As of

November 2008, Plaintiff's position at Bridge International Academy became permanent.

[Plaintiff filed a complaint in state court, which was removed to federal court on the basis of diversity of citizenship. In her amended complaint, plaintiff alleged claims for defamation, false light, and intentional infliction of emotional distress. Defendants filed a motion for summary judgment.] . . . Plaintiff's claims for defamation, false light, and intentional infliction of emotional distress are based on a series of allegedly defamatory statements made by Winfrey at the October Meeting and the November Press Conference.

. . . As this Court sits in Pennsylvania, it will apply Pennsylvania's choice of law rules.

Pennsylvania employs a two-step hybrid framework to choice of law questions. Under the first step of this analysis, the Court must determine whether a real conflict exists between the respective laws. A real conflict exists only where the application of each state's substantive law produces a contrary result. Where a conflict exists, a court must proceed to the second step of the conflict inquiry . . . [, an analysis that combines] "the approaches of both [the] Restatement II (contacts establishing significant relationships) and 'interest analysis' (qualitative appraisal of the relevant States' policies with respect to the controversy)." Turning to the choice of law question before the Court, there are three potential forums whose law could control the instant dispute: South Africa, Pennsylvania, and Illinois.[9] As the law of South Africa implicates considerations of international law unique to a separate sovereign, Federal Rule of Civil Procedure 44.1 must be addressed before proceeding to the conflict analysis.

Rule 44.1 controls the application of foreign law in federal court. It provides:

> A party who intends to raise an issue about a foreign country's law must give notice by a pleading or other writing. In determining foreign law, the court may consider any relevant material or source, including testimony, whether or not submitted by a party or admissible under the Federal Rules of Evidence. The court's determination must be treated as a ruling on a question of law.

Fed. R. Civ. P. 44.1. While this rule empowers a district court with the authority to determine applicable foreign law, it imposes no obligation on the court to inquire into foreign law *sua sponte*.

Under Rule 44.1, it is incumbent upon the parties to "carry both the burden of raising the issue that foreign law may apply in an action, and the burden of adequately proving foreign law to enable the court to apply it in a particular case." Therefore, where the parties do not satisfy both of these burdens, the law of the forum will apply.

___

9. In short, South African law potentially applies because the allegedly defamatory communications were published in South Africa. Illinois law potentially applies because several of the allegedly defamatory statements emanated from Illinois and all Defendants are citizens of Illinois. Pennsylvania law potentially applies because Plaintiff was domiciled in Pennsylvania and allegedly suffered harm to her reputation in Pennsylvania.

Here, initially, neither party raised the issue of the applicability of South African law to Plaintiff's claims. Rather, both parties argued vigorously against application of South African law to the instant dispute. The Court, however, raised the issue to the parties at the hearing on summary judgment and ordered additional briefing on the topic. The Court will accept these submissions as adequate in order to address the conflict of laws issue.[10] Thus, the Court proceeds to apply Pennsylvania's conflict of laws framework, which requires examination of the applicable law of the three forums.[11]

1. PENNSYLVANIA VERSUS ILLINOIS

As a preliminary matter, the Court rejects Defendants' argument that Illinois law controls due to the choice of law provision contained in Plaintiff's employment contract with the Foundation for two reasons.[12] One, the employment contract at issue was between the Foundation and Plaintiff, and neither Winfrey nor any other Defendant is a signatory to that agreement. Two, and more importantly, the tort claims alleged do not depend upon the existence of the employment agreement. In other words, these claims are not intertwined with the performance of the employment agreement itself, rather the claims rely upon extra-contractual events beyond the scope of the forum selection provision.

I. DEFAMATION

With respect to the first step of the conflict of laws analysis, the Court finds that an actual conflict exists between the law of defamation in Pennsylvania and Illinois in light of the existence of the "innocent construction rule" recognized under Illinois law. The "innocent construction rule" provides that "even if a statement falls into one of the categories of words that are defamatory *per se*, it will not be actionable *per se* if it is reasonably capable of an innocent construction." "Stated differently, 'a statement reasonably capable of a nondefamatory interpretation, given its verbal or literary context, should be so interpreted. There is no balancing of reasonable constructions. . . .'"

In contrast [to Illinois law], under Pennsylvania law, no such innocent construction rule exists.

The Court further concludes that this difference represents an "actual" conflict in that both Illinois and Pennsylvania have an interest in applying their

10. Although it is questionable whether either party has satisfied the burden of conclusively establishing the contours of South African defamation law, as discussed in more detail below, the parties failed to address the issue of the applicability of South African law with respect to Plaintiff's claims for false light invasion of privacy and intentional infliction of emotional distress. Rather, the parties limited their briefing to a conflict analysis of South African law as to defamation only.

11. Technically the Court is required to compare the law of the three forums concurrently in resolving the choice of law issue. For purposes of clarity, however, the Court will first perform a conflict analysis for Pennsylvania and Illinois law, and then repeat this analysis with respect to South African law.

12. The text of the relevant provision provides that "[t]his Agreement and all matters or issues collateral thereto shall be governed by the laws of the State of Illinois." (Defs.' Mot. Summ. J. Ex. D-15, ¶ 9.9.)

respective laws. Illinois adopted the "innocent construction rule" in order to afford a certain degree of protection for its speakers in areas of potentially defamatory communications. Pennsylvania, on the other hand, maintains an interest in safeguarding a person's reputation from unjust harm.

Due to the existence of this actual conflict, the Court must determine which state has a materially greater interest in application of its law. This requires an examination of the relevant contacts of the respective forums and how those contacts relate to the States' policies underlying the applicable laws. The Court looks to the Restatement (Second) of Conflicts for guidance in resolving this issue.

Defendants contend that Illinois has a greater interest in having its law apply because all Defendants are citizens of Illinois and the allegedly defamatory statements made during the November Press Conference were made by Winfrey in Chicago, and that these contacts are in keeping with Illinois' asserted interest in protecting the free speech rights of its speakers. In contrast, Plaintiff posits that Pennsylvania law should apply because Plaintiff was domiciled in Pennsylvania at the time of the defamatory communications and had a bona fide interest in her reputation in Pennsylvania, and that these contacts are consistent with Pennsylvania's interest in affording the highest protection to the reputational interest of its citizens.

An individual's interest in her reputation has been described as a "valuable asset in one's business or profession." The purpose underlying defamation law is to compensate an individual for pecuniary harm to one's reputation inflicted by a defamatory statement. Therefore, the majority of courts confronted with this choice of law question have found that the plaintiff's domicile should control since this is the forum with the greater interest.

This approach is consistent with the Restatement. Under §150(2) of the Restatement (Second) of Conflicts, "[w]hen a natural person claims that he has been defamed by an aggregate communication, the state of the most significant relationship will usually be the state where the person was domiciled at the time, if the matter complained of was published in that state." Restatement (Second) of Conflicts of Law §150(2).

The parties dispute whether statements from the October Meeting were republished outside of South Africa. Defendants concede, however, that the statements from the November Press Conference were available on the internet, and therefore, were published throughout the United States, including Pennsylvania. Thus, if Plaintiff is found to have been domiciled in Pennsylvania during the operative time period, then the Restatement militates in favor of applying Pennsylvania law.

The Court finds that Plaintiff was domiciled in Pennsylvania at the time the allegedly defamatory communications were published. Plaintiff lived in Pennsylvania from 2000 through 2006 while working at Germantown. The Restatement provides that a person's domicil is usually a person's home. *Id.* §11. The Restatement further defines one's home as "the place where a person dwells and which is the center of his domestic, social and civic life." *Id.* §12. Moreover, the Restatement provides that in order "[t]o acquire a domicil of choice in a place, a person must intend to make that place his home for the time at least." *Id.* §18. The evidence presented indicates that during Plaintiff's time working at Germantown she treated Pennsylvania as her home (as defined by the Restatement) and intended to remain in Pennsylvania until the opportunity at OWLAG materialized in 2006. Moreover, as of October 8, 2007, when Plaintiff was placed on administrative leave, she remained in the United States and resumed living in Pennsylvania prior to the time that the October Meeting and the November Press Conference occurred.[13]

Furthermore, the fact that Plaintiff maintained a residence in South Africa while working at OWLAG does not undermine the conclusion that Plaintiff's domicile is Pennsylvania. According to the Restatement, a person has no more than one domicil at a time, *id.* §11, and a person retains the same domicil until it is superseded by a new domicil. *Id.* §19. While Plaintiff's employment agreement with OWLAG provided that she would maintain a residence on the OWLAG campus during the school year, the agreement clearly contemplates that Plaintiff would remain domiciled in Pennsylvania and would travel to OWLAG in connection with her position as Headmistress. For instance, the employment agreement provides that Plaintiff would receive paid accommodations for air travel "for four (4) trips per year to South Africa, one trip per calendar per quarter." Furthermore, the employment agreement provides that "[t]he Head of Academy will be based in Philadelphia, Pennsylvania with extensive travel anticipated to the Academy's location at Henley on Klip, South Africa." Thus, it is clear that by accepting the position at OWLAG, Plaintiff was in no sense renouncing her domicile in Pennsylvania.

Defendants argue that Plaintiff was not domiciled in Pennsylvania because domicil requires an intent to permanently reside in a particular forum, and since Plaintiff traveled to the United States on a visa, her domicil never changed from Kenya, her country of origin. This argument is not persuasive. It is true that courts have recognized that a visa prevents an immigrant from establishing a legal domicil in the United States under certain circumstances. *See Graham v. I.N.S.*, 998 F.2d 194, 196 (3d Cir. 1993) (finding that an alien could not establish domicil for purposes of a deportation statute because the legal definition of the term "domicil" necessitates an intent to remain in a forum indefinitely, which conflicted with a temporary worker visa's requirement that the holder have a foreign residence that he does not intend to abandon). As explained above, however, domicil for purposes of conducting a choice of law analysis under the Restatement requires only that an individual intend to reside in a particular forum for the foreseeable future. *See* Restatement 2d §18.

The Court concludes that because Plaintiff was domiciled in Pennsylvania at the time the allegedly defamatory statements were published, Pennsylvania has a

---

13. Defendants emphasize that beginning on October 9, 2007, Plaintiff stayed in Baltimore, Maryland for approximately 1 to 2 weeks, and then traveled throughout the United States to visit colleges with her daughter. (Mzamane Dep. 23:8-24:21.) Defendants posit that Plaintiff's connection to Pennsylvania is lessened by the fact that she was not physically located there at the time the allegedly defamatory communications were made. Plaintiff's physical presence on the exact dates that the statements were made is of no moment to the Court's analysis as the Plaintiff's temporarily traveling outside of Pennsylvania does not dictate that she revoked her domicile there. *See id.* §19.

greater interest than Illinois in the instant dispute. Therefore, the substantive law of Pennsylvania shall apply with respect to Plaintiff's defamation claim.

II. FALSE LIGHT

In response to the Court's directive that the parties brief the conflict of laws issue, neither party addressed any conflict with respect to Pennsylvania or Illinois law on the tort of false light invasion of privacy. As neither party has cited to a potential conflict between these two forums, and the Court *sua sponte* has determined that the basic elements required under both Pennsylvania law and Illinois law are identical, the Court finds that no conflict exists and the law of the forum controls.

III. INTENTIONAL INFLICTION OF EMOTIONAL DISTRESS

As is the case with Plaintiff's false light claim, the parties have not addressed any conflict issue between the laws of Pennsylvania and Illinois with respect to Plaintiff's claim for intentional infliction of emotional distress. Therefore, the Court will proceed on the basis that no conflict exists and apply the law of the forum to this claim. *See id.*

2. PENNSYLVANIA VERSUS SOUTH AFRICA

In order to complete the choice of law analysis, the Court must compare the laws of South Africa and Pennsylvania to determine whether any actual conflict exists, and if so, whether South Africa has a more significant interest in having its law apply to these proceedings.

I. DEFAMATION

With respect to the first step of the choice of law analysis, Pennsylvania and South Africa law conflict as to the burden of proving the falsity of a defamatory statement. Under South African law, "a defendant [must] establish, once a plaintiff has proved the publication of a defamatory statement affecting the plaintiff, that the publication was lawful because the contents of the statement were true and in the public benefit." *Khumalo & Others v. Holomisa*, 2002(1) SA 401(CC) at 29 (S.Afr.). In other words, "[t]he burden of proving truth thus falls on the defendant." *Id.* at 29-30. This is incompatible with the controlling law in Pennsylvania that a plaintiff must prove falsity with respect to matters of public concern.[14]

The Court concludes that this difference represents a true conflict. . . . Proceeding to the next step in the conflict analysis, the Court finds that Pennsylvania exhibits a more significant interest in having its law on defamation apply to the instant dispute. As explained above, Pennsylvania obviously has a substantial interest in this litigation as Plaintiff was domiciled in Pennsylvania at the time the allegedly defamatory communications were published and had a reputational interest to protect in that forum. South Africa, in contrast, does not have a

---

14. Although technically this burden-shifting requirement emanates from a federal constitutional principle, for purposes of this conflict of laws analysis, this requirement has been incorporated into Pennsylvania defamation law.

material interest in having its law apply to Plaintiff's defamation claims. It is true that the allegedly defamatory statements made at the October Meeting were published only in South Africa and that the events giving rise to the allegedly defamatory statements occurred in South Africa. Under Pennsylvania's choice of law analysis, however, these contacts must be examined in light of the underlying purpose of defamation law, which is to compensate an individual for injury to her reputation. Viewed in this context, it is clear that Plaintiff maintained a much stronger reputational interest in Pennsylvania than South Africa, and therefore, Pennsylvania has a stronger interest in having its law apply on this issue.

II. FALSE LIGHT

As explained above, Rule 44.1 of the Federal Rules of Civil Procedure directs that the litigants bear the burdens of establishing foreign law and demonstrating that it differs from United States law. *See* Fed. R. Civ. P. 44.1. Where the parties fail to carry these burdens, the Court is empowered to presume that the foreign law is the same as that of the United States, and need not engage in a choice of law analysis. As neither party provided any authority as to the tort of false light invasion of privacy under South African law, the Court concludes that Rule 44.1 has not been satisfied. Therefore a choice of law analysis is unnecessary and Pennsylvania law will apply.

III. INTENTIONAL INFLICTION OF EMOTIONAL DISTRESS

As with the tort of false light, the parties have failed to satisfy their burden of conclusively establishing South African law under Rule 44.1 with respect to the cause of action for intentional infliction of emotional distress. Therefore, the Court declines to address the choice of law question and Pennsylvania law will control.

3. PENNSYLVANIA LAW IS CONSISTENT WITH DUE PROCESS

After resolving the choice of law issue and selecting the appropriate forum's law to be applied, the Court is required to ensure that application of this law passes constitutional muster. "[F]or a State's substantive law to be selected in a constitutionally permissible manner, that State must have a significant contact or significant aggregation of contacts, creating state interests, such that choice of its law is neither arbitrary nor fundamentally unfair." *Allstate Ins. Co. v. Hague,* 449 U.S. 302, 312-13, 101 S. Ct. 633, 66 L. Ed. 2d 521 (1981).

Defendants contend that application of Pennsylvania law is constitutionally impermissible under *Hague* because the only connection to Pennsylvania is Plaintiff's "nominal residence" there.[17]

17. An individual's "residence" is distinguishable from his "domicil." The Third Circuit has recognized that "the term 'resident' has no precise meaning." *Bodin v. Brathwaite,* 459 F.2d 543, 544 (3d Cir. 1972) (citing *Willenbrock v. Rogers,* 255 F.2d 236, 237 (3d Cir. 1958)); *see also United States v. Stabler,* 169 F.2d 995, 998 (3d Cir. 1948). As explained in the Restatement:

   Domicil differs from such other places both in the nature of the connection and in the legal purposes for which such connection is important. Thus a person may be a "resident" or an "inhabitant" or a "citizen" of a place without being domiciled therein, although such "residence," "inhabitancy" or

This argument is unavailing. As explained above, Plaintiff was domiciled in Pennsylvania for the relevant period of time for purposes of this lawsuit, and Plaintiff's domicil is not an insignificant contact for purposes of applying Pennsylvania law. In contrast, Plaintiff being domiciled in Pennsylvania creates a significant state interest for Pennsylvania in providing redress for injury to Plaintiff's reputational interest.

Furthermore, as Defendants were plainly aware that Plaintiff was domiciled in Pennsylvania, and would remain so throughout the course of her employment with OWLAG (as demonstrated by the provisions of her employment contract cited above), Defendants cannot establish that application of Pennsylvania law is somehow "arbitrary or fundamentally unfair" under *Hague*. Therefore, the Court concludes that application of Pennsylvania law comports with the constitutional requirements of due process.

. . .

[In light of its finding regarding domicile and choice of law, the court analyzed each of Plaintiff's claims under Pennsylvania law. After also considering the effect of federal constitutional principles on the case, the court granted Winfrey's motion for summary judgment in part, dismissing the intentional infliction of emotional distress claim, and denied the motion in part, allowing the Plaintiff to proceed with the false light claim and the defamation claim.]

Notes on
MZAMANE

1. As the *Mzamane* court pointed out, the Restatement (Second) designates domicile as presumptively the most important contact in choosing the governing law for a defamation claim. Having made that observation, the court elevated domicile to the controlling influence in the choice of law determination. While this may not occur for all causes of action under the Restatement (Second), domicile often has a significant, if not controlling, effect on the choice of law. Pennsylvania does not follow a pure Restatement (Second) approach, but rather combines it with governmental interest analysis. Courts like the one in *Mzamane* often look to the Restatement (Second) for basic matters such as domicile, even where they apply a different choice of law approach to other aspects of the case.

Note how the contractual provisions in the *Mzamane* employment agreement impacted the choice of law analysis. The provision for four paid plane trips per year to South Africa and the statement that "[t]he Head of

---

"citizenship," may be significant for some legal purposes. Many legal questions depend upon domicil irrespective of residence, inhabitancy or citizenship.

Restatement 2d §9, cmt. a.

Academy will be based in Philadelphia, Pennsylvania" helped convince the court that the plaintiff maintained her Pennsylvania domicile. The influence of these provisions points out the importance of foresight to the consequence of language choice in contract drafting. A turn of phrase in drafting a contract can indeed affect your client's fortunes in future litigation!

2. One possibility that the *Mzamane* court did not consider is that the plaintiff changed her domicile to South Africa, and then changed it back to Pennsylvania after she was put on administrative leave. In today's mobile world, plaintiffs can easily move their domicile in the middle of events giving rise to litigation. An even more common scenario, which dogs modern courts, is the occurrence of "after acquired domicile": where a party acquires a new domicile after the incident giving rise to liability. Should such a late-breaking change in domicile make a difference in the choice of law analysis? The Restatement (Second) raises this query in the context of an accident hypothetical, but does not provide a definitive answer: "Presumably this change in domicil should have no effect upon the law governing most of the issues involving the accident. But is this true of all issues?" Restatement (Second) of Conflicts of Law, ch. 7, topic 1. intro. note 2 (1971). On one hand, courts might worry about parties trying to manipulate matters by moving their domicile, and are therefore inclined to ignore the change. On the other hand, a state's welfare interest may become implicated if an injured party moves into the state after an occurrence takes place, but before the party experiences the personal consequences of inflicted harm. In that event, courts have trouble ignoring the interest of the new domicile.

3. The proposed Restatement (Third) of Conflict of Laws has developed a new approach to domicile that emphasizes objective evidence of where persons seek to make places their homes. It remains to be seen whether this approach avoids some of the difficult factual issues presented in *Mzamane*.

G. *LEX FORI*

Few, if any, would doubt that the modern approaches to choice of law bear significant problems. Yet the prospect of courts reflexively applying forum law in the face of conflicting laws (lex fori) is often met with criticism. Despite this criticism, at least three states in contemporary times have been formally associated with a lex fori approach, at least for tort cases: Kentucky, Michigan, and Nevada. Nevada, however, has changed its allegiance to the Restatement (Second) for torts cases. Although the number of states associated with lex fori is small, the approach nonetheless bears consideration, if for no other reason than its efficient orientation to the complicated world of conflict of laws. Consider the ruminations of the Michigan Supreme Court below. Are you persuaded that the court adopted an approach meriting the moniker "lex fori" and that the court's approach is workable and wise?

Sutherland v. Kennington Truck Service, Ltd.

562 N.W.2d 466 (Mich. 1997)

MALLETT, C.J.

In this choice of law case, an Ontario driver and an Ohio driver collided while on a Michigan highway. Plaintiffs filed suit in Michigan two years and twenty-two days after the accident. Both Ohio and Ontario have two-year statutes of limitations, while Michigan has a three-year statute of limitations. The trial court applied Ontario's statute of limitations, holding that Michigan had no interest in the litigation. We reverse and hold that because neither Ohio nor Ontario have an interest in having its law applied, Michigan law will apply.

The facts in this case are fit for a law school choice of law examination. On August 14, 1989, two trucks collided on Interstate 75 in . . . Michigan. The driver of one truck, Larry G. Sutherland, is a resident of Ohio and was operating a truck licensed in Ohio. The driver of the other truck, Gregory Zavitz, is a citizen of Ontario, Canada. He was employed by Kennington Truck Service, an Ontario corporation. Zavitz's truck was owned by Elgin Leasing, which had leased the truck to Canadian Timkin. Both Elgin Leasing and Canadian Timkin are Ontario corporations.

On September 5, 1991, two years and twenty-two days after the accident, Mr. Sutherland and his wife sued defendants. . . . Defendants moved for summary disposition . . . , arguing that the court should apply either Ohio's or Ontario's statute of limitations. Both of these jurisdictions bar negligence actions filed more than two years after the cause of action arose. In response, plaintiffs argued that the case should be governed by Michigan's three-year statute of limitations.[2]

The trial court granted the motion for summary disposition. Applying "interest analysis," the court found that Michigan had no interest in the outcome of this litigation because none of the parties are Michigan citizens. The court further found that Ontario had an interest in protecting its citizens from stale claims. On this basis, the court held that Ontario's two-year statute of limitations would apply.

In an unpublished opinion per curiam, the Court of Appeals affirmed. The Court stated:

> The trial court did not err in applying the Ontario statute. . . . Although Michigan law once favored application of the law of the forum to procedural matters, such is no longer the case. Recent decisions have criticized the distinction between

2. MCL 600.5805(8); MSA 27A.5805(8). Because of the action accrued within the State of Michigan, Michigan's borrowing statute, MCL 600.5861; MSA 27A.5861, does not apply. MCL 600.5861; MSA 27A.5861 states:

> An action based upon a cause of action accruing without this state shall not be commenced after the expiration of the statute of limitations of either this state or the place without this state where the cause of action accrued, except that where the cause of action accrued in favor of a resident of this state the statute of limitations of this state shall apply. This amendatory act shall be effective as to all actions hereinafter commenced and all actions heretofor [sic] commenced now pending in the trial or appellate courts.

procedure and substance for conflict of law analysis. . . . Neither party in this action is a citizen of this state, both parties are residents of states that have a two-year statute of limitations, and the statute of limitation issue is not an issue involving conduct. . . .

We granted leave to appeal. . . .

[The court reviewed the history of the conflict of laws methodologies in the United States.]

. . . [I]n practice, all the modern approaches to conflicts of law are relatively uniform in the results they produce. Professor Borchers has surveyed cases that purport to apply the various modern approaches and concluded that none of the modern approaches differ significantly from the others in three important respects: the percentage of times that courts apply forum law, the percentage of times that plaintiffs recover, or the percentage of times that local parties prevail. . . .[15] This has led one commentator to note:

> On reading a substantial number of these cases over the years, one has a feeling that the courts may not be doing what they purport to do, that is, employing the modern choice-of-law theories in a neutral way to determine what law applies. Rather, one suspects that courts employing the new theories have a very strong preference for forum law that frequently causes them to manipulate the theories so that they end up applying forum law.[16]

This preference for forum law is hardly surprising. The tendency toward forum law promotes judicial economy: judges and attorneys are experts in their state's law, but have to expend considerable time and resources to learn another state's law.

Thus, on surveying current conflicts of law jurisprudence, one can reasonably conclude that only two distinct conflicts of law theories actually exist. One, followed by a distinct minority of states, mandates adherence to the lex loci delicti rule. The other, which bears different labels in different states, calls for courts to apply the law of the forum unless [there are] important policy considerations.

. . .

The evolution of Michigan's choice of law jurisprudence has paralleled national trends. . . . In *Abendschein v. Farrell*, 382 Mich. 510; 170 N.W.2d 137 (1969), this Court declined to join the emerging conflicts of law movement.

---

15. According to Professor Borchers' research, the Second Restatement's approach results in the application of forum law fifty-five percent of the time, with a margin of error of five percent. Interest analysis results in forum law sixty-three percent of the time, with a margin of error of ten percent. Leflar's approach yields forum law in sixty-five percent of cases, with a margin of error of eleven percent. The lex fori rule yields lex fori in seventy-seven percent of cases, with a twenty-three percent margin of error. When one considers the margins of error, one can conclude that there is no statistically significant difference between the modern approaches in terms of the application of forum law. Borchers, *The choice-of-law revolution: An empirical study*, 49 WASH. & LEE L. REV. 357, 374-375 (1992).

16. McDougal, *The real legacy of Babcock v. Jackson: Lex fori instead of lex loci delicti and now it's time for a real choice-of-law revolution*, 56 ALB. L. REV. 795, 797 (1993).

. . . Despite adherence to the traditional rule, Michigan courts continued to employ various "escape devices" in order to mitigate harsh consequences. In these cases, courts readily found public policy reasons to displace the lex loci delicti with forum law. . . .

A majority of this Court finally abandoned the lex loci delicti rule . . . [but this] did not produce a consensus on the appropriate choice of law methodology to be applied. This Court clarified much of the confusion . . . in *Olmstead v. Anderson*, 428 Mich. 1 (1987). . . . *Olmstead* provides the analytical framework for deciding this case. That is, we will apply Michigan law unless a "rational reason" to do otherwise exists. In determining whether a rational reason to displace Michigan law exists, we undertake a two-step analysis. First, we must determine if any foreign state has an interest in having its law applied. If no state has such an interest, the presumption that Michigan law will apply cannot be overcome. If a foreign state does have an interest in having its law applied, we must then determine if Michigan's interests mandate that Michigan law be applied, despite the foreign interests.

Ohio and Ontario are the only two foreign jurisdictions that potentially have an interest in having their law applied in this case. Ohio, where the plaintiffs reside, has a two-year statute of limitations for these types of actions.

However, a court could not apply Ohio law to this case without violating the defendants' due process rights. As Justice Brennan stated in *Allstate Ins v. Hague*, 449 U.S. 302, 313; 101 S. Ct. 633; 66 L. Ed. 2d 521 (1981), in order for a court to choose a state's law, "[the] State must have a significant contact or significant aggregation of contacts, creating state interests, such that choice of its law is neither arbitrary nor fundamentally unfair." In this case, the only contact that Ohio has with this litigation is that plaintiffs are Ohio residents. The United States Supreme Court has stated that the plaintiff's residence, with nothing more, is insufficient to support the choice of a state's law. *Home Ins Co v. Dick*, 281 U.S. 397, 408 (1930).

Because Ohio does not have an interest in seeing the court apply its law, Ontario is the only remaining candidate. Ontario, like Ohio, has a two-year statute of limitations. Defendants claim that because Ontario law would benefit the Ontario defendants by barring the claim, Ontario has an interest in having its statute of limitations applied. Certainly, one purpose of a statute of limitations is to protect defendants from stale claims. We do not agree, however, that Ontario has an interest in protecting the defendants from stale claims in this situation. In fact, according to Canadian and Ontario law, Ontario has an interest in having Michigan's statute of limitations applied in this case.

In the companion cases of *Tolofson v. Jensen* and *Lucas v. Gagnon*, 120 D.L.R. 4th 289 (1994), the Supreme Court of Canada adopted the lex loci delicti rule and held that Canadian courts must apply the substantive law of the jurisdiction where the tort occurred. The court also stated that statutes of limitation are substantive, not procedural, for choice of law purposes. Thus, under *Tolofson*, Canadian courts must apply the statute of limitations of the jurisdiction in which the tort occurred.

Tolofson involves residents of British Columbia who were injured in an automobile accident in Saskatchewan, and thus does not present an international choice of law problem. Justice La Forest, speaking for the court, noted that an exception to the lex loci delicti rule may exist in international tort litigation if application of the law of a foreign country "could give rise to [an] injustice." 449 U.S. at 308. . . .

We seriously doubt that an Ontario court would find that the application of Michigan's three-year statute of limitations in this case would "give rise to injustice." Certainly, no Ontario court has expressed qualms about applying American law. . . .

Thus, had plaintiffs filed this suit in Ontario, Ontario's courts would have applied Michigan's three-year statute of limitations. Because even Ontario courts would not allow the defendants to escape this claim through application of Ontario law, we do not see how Ontario can have an interest in having Michigan courts apply Ontario law.

Therefore, no foreign state has an interest in having its law applied to this case. The lex fori presumption is not overcome, and we need not evaluate Michigan's interests. Michigan's three-year statute of limitations will apply to this case.
    . . .

BRICKLEY, J. (concurring in part and dissenting in part).

I concur in the result reached by the majority. However, I write separately to express my view that the time has come for this state to abandon the interest-analysis-based approach detailed by the majority. Rather, I would adopt a lex fori approach to choice of law questions.

I am troubled by the choice of law analysis defined by the majority. . . . The majority's second factor [in its proposed analysis — evaluating whether Michigan's interests mandate that Michigan law be applied] demonstrates how its concern with the interests of other jurisdictions will result in confusion. To ascertain the interest of Ontario, the majority examines the choice of law rules of Ontario, and determines that an Ontario court would apply Michigan law if this case were before it. Therefore, the majority concludes that Ontario has no interest in this litigation. Thus, the majority requires the courts of this state to decipher and apply the choice of law rules of potentially every jurisdiction in the country, and possibly the world, before it can determine which law to apply. This is simply too great a burden. The potential for confusion and error is clear. The bench and bar of this state are experts in Michigan law. . . .

The most fundamental flaw in [the majority's] approach to choice of law is that it requires the courts of this state to choose between the laws of Michigan and those of foreign jurisdictions. As a matter of policy, the courts of this state should apply Michigan law. The application of foreign law requires a Michigan court to interpret and apply that law as if the court was sitting in that foreign jurisdiction. State courts should not presume to speak for other jurisdictions in this manner. Further, the majority's analysis requires Michigan courts to apply the law of another jurisdiction in certain cases. However, before a court can do this, it must first expressly refuse to apply the laws of this state. This refusal ignores and defeats the express will of the Legislature. Clearly, the courts of this state should avoid this outcome. . . . Moreover, there is an increased likelihood of error when Michigan courts attempt to rule on foreign laws. . . .

A second flaw with this state's choice of law methodology is that it is unpredictable. . . . [T]he majority . . . fails to define a systematic approach for determining the interests of other jurisdictions. . . . Moreover, the second part of the majority's test requires a court to weigh any foreign interests against those of Michigan. However, by finding that no other state has an interest, the majority avoids explaining how competing interests are to be weighed. . . .

The third flaw in this choice of law approach is that it allows hidden, pro-forum manipulation. The majority recognizes that courts manipulate apparently neutral choice of law rules in order to justify the application of forum law. This defeats the parties' expectation that choice of law rules will be neutrally applied. I agree with the majority's comment that this preference is not surprising. However, the majority fails to take steps to eliminate this problem. Indeed, the analysis that the majority uses to determine that Ohio and Ontario have no interest in this litigation is an example of that approach.

. . . The lex fori approach would eliminate the need for a court to employ one of the two primary techniques that courts have used to avoid the application of a foreign jurisdiction's law. The court would not have to invoke a public policy exception to a rule requiring the application of another jurisdiction's law and would not have to resort to recharacterizing an issue as procedural, rather than substantive, to allow the application of the forum's law. . . .

I am aware that the lex fori approach has been criticized for encouraging forum shopping. This supposed evil is greatly exaggerated and should not deter this state's adoption of the lex fori approach. Forum shopping is thought to be an evil because it allows a plaintiff to expose a defendant to the laws of a forum that has little involvement in the litigation, assuming that the forum has jurisdiction over the defendant. Under the approach I propose, an entity may be subjected to Michigan law concerning a cause of action that may have arisen elsewhere, if all constitutional requirements are satisfied. However, this should not prevent the adoption of the lex fori approach in this state.

Initially, it is important to recognize that a forum shopping party who chooses Michigan is asking the courts of this state to effectuate the laws and policies of Michigan. There is no reason why Michigan courts should summarily refuse this request. Rather, it is the duty of Michigan courts to effectuate these laws and policies. Assume that a plaintiff chooses to file suit in Michigan because Michigan law recognizes his claim. The application of Michigan law to this plaintiff's claim will fulfill the policy expressed by the Michigan Legislature, which recognizes the claim. Thus, forum shopping is not necessarily problematic to the extent that it leads to the fulfillment of the laws and policies of this state.

Forum shopping is also commonly assumed to be unfair to defendants. This view is based on the premise that the plaintiff has selected an unfair forum. However, the law that the defendant would have the court apply is likely to be just as unfair. Indeed, the defendant will likely urge the court to apply the law of the jurisdiction that is most certain to lead to a dismissal. Thus, while the plaintiff may "shop" for a forum whose law is beneficial to its case, the defendant is just as likely to "shop" for law favorable to it. Thus, there is really no innocent party in these situations. The fairest way to resolve this is to rely on the traditional notion that the plaintiff is the master of his lawsuit, and, as such, is entitled to choose the forum. Also, in the vast majority of cases, an entity that has sufficiently connected itself to Michigan so that a Michigan court has jurisdiction over it will not be unfairly burdened by the application of Michigan's laws.

Finally, it should be pointed out that choice of law rules that focus on interests do not automatically discourage forum shopping. Indeed, choice of law methodologies that focus on abstract interests are also vulnerable to manipulation. Thus, no choice of law system is entirely free from forum shopping. However, I feel that any negative effects that would result from forum shopping as a result of the adoption of a lex fori approach would be outweighed by the benefits of maintaining a clear, predictable choice of law system that would require Michigan courts to give effect to Michigan law.

The only limits placed on a lex fori system should be those required by the United States Constitution. . . . [Nonetheless, in] this case, . . . no constitutional limitations on lex fori are applicable. The United States Supreme Court has found that forum states have complete authority to apply their own procedural rules, including statutes of limitation. . . .

Notes on
SUTHERLAND *AND LEX FORI*

1. How would you describe the approach that the majority announced and applied in *Sutherland?* One might say that the majority instructed Michigan courts to apply Michigan law, unless the court thinks of a "rational reason" not to do so. This is not an automatic use of forum law, as the name "lex fori" would suggest. One way of describing the approach is that the majority combines a strong presumption in favor of forum law with governmental interest analysis, a combination that Professor Ralph Whitten calls a "hybrid lex fori system." Ralph U. Whitten, *U.S. Conflict-of-Laws Doctrine and Forum Shopping, International and Domestic (Revisited)*, 37 TEX. INT'L L.J. 559, 571 (2002). The concurring and dissenting opinion certainly did not think that the majority got close enough to proposing and applying the type of pure lex fori approach that the opinion would have liked.

Whatever label one might use for the majority opinion, the opinion leaves several concepts unclear. First, the court did not explain what constitutes a sufficient foreign interest to provide "a rational reason" not to apply Michigan law. Nor did the court specify when Michigan's interests mandate that Michigan law should apply even in the face of a foreign state's interest in having its own law applied.

2. Both the majority and dissent/concurrence point out that the United States Constitution provides a safety net to ensure that state choice of law determinations are not so unfair to parties or detrimental to our federal system as to violate the due process and full faith and credit clauses of the

United States Constitution. Chapter 3 covers the constitutional constraints on choice of law in greater detail.

3. The majority opinion also points out that Michigan provides some statutory supervision for multistate statute of limitations issues. Nothing in that opinion suggests the court would advocate ignoring this statutory mandate. As explained in footnote 2 of its opinion, the majority simply concluded that the mandate — in the form of a "borrowing statute" — was inapplicable in this circumstance.

4. The *Sutherland* majority's approach has many critics. For example, Professor Ralph Whitten described the majority's suggested analysis as follows: "The escape device of allowing non-forum law to apply when another state has an 'interest' assures that litigants will make, and Michigan courts will grapple with, complex choice-of-law arguments. Similarly, the fluid nature of the state-interest inquiry left open by the court virtually ensures that judicial manipulation will occur." Whitten, *supra*, at 571. Further indicting the approach, Professor Symeon C. Symeonides has observed that "experience in Michigan's lower courts" suggests that these courts now easily find a "rational reason for displacing Michigan law" where that "law is unfavorable to a Michigan litigant, especially one of Michigan's big auto manufacturers." Symeon C. Symeonides, *Choice of Law in the American Courts in 1997*, 46 Am. J. Comp. L. 233, 423 (1998).

Others have focused on the forum shopping that might result from undue emphasis on lex fori. Does the dissent dissipate all nagging concerns about the downsides of forum shopping? Is forum shopping an unequivocal evil that should be eradicated? As to the notion that forum shopping allows plaintiffs to pick a jurisdiction with the most favorable law, Professor Larry Kramer asks the provocative question: "Why are defendants entitled to anything other than the most unfavorable of the laws that can constitutionally be applied?" Larry Kramer, *Rethinking Choice of Law*, 90 Colum. L. Rev. 277, 313 n.117 (1990).

One concern about forum shopping is the notion that fairness and justice are offended where results vary according to the fortuity of where a lawsuit is filed. One must assume that treating similarly situated persons similarly is important in the United States federalist system. Does the United States really want results to vary dramatically according to which state is the forum for a lawsuit? Doesn't it strike a blow to government by rule of law to allow factors bearing on available forums to have such an impact on the fortunes of litigants? Professor Perry Dane argues that applying the law of the forum undermines the rule of law because it insufficiently respects law's embodiment of norms that exist separate from their enforcement. Perry Dane, *Vested Rights, "Vestedness," and Choice of Law*, 96 Yale L.J. 1191 (1984). On the other end of spectrum from Professor Dane is an observation by Professor Louise Weinberg. Professor Weinberg writes that the real source of concern and discrimination is the unequal treatment of similarly situated forum state residents if the forum court fails to apply forum law. Louise Weinberg, *On Departing from Forum Law*, 35 MERCER L. REV. 595, 596-597 (1981).

A related concern about forum shopping arises from the observation that, where courts rely exclusively on lex fori, doctrines of personal jurisdiction play a key role in regulating the available fora and thus the law that governs. Are doctrines governing personal jurisdiction sufficient to regulate whether it is unfair to ask someone to litigate in a jurisdiction *and* submit to its governing laws?

5. Lex fori has received similar treatment in the hands of the courts from the two other states associated with the approach, Nevada and Kentucky. While Nevada now follows the Restatement (Second) for resolving tort issues, the Nevada Supreme Court had said that forum law should apply unless another state has an overwhelming interest, meaning that it is the locus of at least two out of the following four factors: (a) where the conduct causing the injury occurred; (b) where the injury is suffered; (c) where the parties have the same domicile, residence, nationality, place of incorporation, or place of business; and (d) where the relationship, if any, between the parties is centered. *See Motenko v. MGM Dist., Inc.*, 921 P.2d 933, 935 (1996) (forum law should apply unless another state has an overwhelming interest). Kentucky's approach essentially boils down to this: "[I]f there are significant contacts—not necessarily the most significant contacts—with Kentucky, then Kentucky law should be applied." *Foster v. Leggett*, 484 S.W.2d 827, 829 (Ky. 1972). Are these approaches more likely to promote candor, predictability, and efficiency than the Michigan approach?

6. A pure lex fori approach is simple and clear. On an individual case level, the approach yields highly predictable results. As the *Sutherland* concurrence/dissent pointed out, lex fori is also efficient because forum law is likely the law known best by courts and local attorneys. This even includes an efficiency feedback loop: any time local law is applied and explained, useful precedent is likely created, thus enhancing the clarity of a forum's legal principles. Lex fori also eliminates an incentive for subterfuge, and therefore may foster judicial honesty as well. One scholar takes the position that lex fori avoids the legitimacy problems that arise because courts lack the authority to interpret the intentions of foreign state legislatures. Stanley E. Cox, *Razing Conflicts Façades to Build Better Jurisdiction Theory: The Foundation—There Is No Law But Forum Law*, 28 VAL. U. L. REV. 1, 3 (1993). Professor Cox's position is unqualified: "In reality, a state can only create and apply its own law."

In another exposition on a choice of law approach where courts simply apply their own law, two law and economics theorists have pointed out the following consequence: "Predictability about the use of forum law reduces uncertainty for parties structuring transactions. As long as parties can exit the system, the lex fori approach forces a state to internalize the external costs of bad laws, promoting competition among jurisdictions to improve substantive law." Nita Ghei & Francesco Parisi, *Adverse Selection and Moral Hazard in Forum Shopping: Conflicts Law as Spontaneous Order*, 25 CARDOZO L. REV. 1367, 1373 (2004).

While individual litigants and single jurisdiction actors may find lex fori predictable, multijurisdictional actors do not because lex fori creates different results depending on where the lawsuit is filed. Under lex fori, plaintiffs are likely to file in jurisdictions with the most favorable legal principles and reputation for larger verdicts. Plaintiff-friendly jurisdictions can expect to receive a disproportionate number of filings. Scholars Nita Ghei and Francesco Parisi foresee cascading consequences of this response to incentive. They suggest that lex fori likely fuels trial lawyers and other interest groups in their quest for plaintiff-friendly laws, and the law can become even more "skewed in their favor." *Id.* at 1374. They further argue that the "resulting legislation is 'made' law . . . giving rise to a 'made order,'" which has a "tendency toward inefficiency" as a result of the "imperfect information and the influence of interest groups." *Id.* at 1374.

H. HYBRID APPROACHES IN THE COURTS

States have become harder to pigeonhole according to which choice of law approach they faithfully follow. They not only apply different choice of law approaches for different types of legal issues, but also create their own methodologies, concocted by combining existing approaches. Scholars have described this as a tendency toward "increased eclecticism and independence" exhibited by courts grappling with choice of law in modern contexts. PETER HAY, PATRICK J. BORCHERS & SYMEON C. SYMEONIDES, CONFLICT OF LAWS 60 (5th ed. 2010). Formal characterization is often difficult, but recent attempts to categorize the various choice of law approaches in the United States have set the number of states embracing a home-grown hybrid methodology somewhere around 10 or 20 percent of the states. A thorough understanding of choice of law in the United States therefore calls for a look at some of the ways in which states combine existing methodologies. Moreover, the results of this alchemy illuminate different analytical angles on choice of law problems.

At least two of the methodologies presented earlier in this chapter might be characterized as hybrid approaches. The first is comparative impairment, which is essentially a twist on governmental interest analysis in the context of true conflicts. The second is lex fori, which one might describe as governmental interest analysis with a strong presumption in favor of forum law. Several individual states have created unique approaches not followed or replicated in sister states. The three states featured below—Hawaii, New York, and Pennsylvania—are representative of the range of individual hybrid approaches. The New York and Pennsylvania examples come from federal courts sitting in those states. As also illustrated elsewhere in this chapter, these courts are following the mandate of the *Klaxon Co. v. Stentor Elec. Mfg. Co.*, 313 U.S. 487, 496 (1941), attempting to mimic their forum state's approach to choice of law as they exercise diversity or supplemental jurisdiction. While a federal court's decision in this context does not bind state courts in subsequent cases, the federal court's attempt to discern the state's choice of law approach in what is often a complex context is a common feature of modern law practice.

In many ways, one can understand each of the hybrid approaches set forth below in terms of how it refines governmental interest analysis. As you review the cases, evaluate how the court's approach relates to governmental interest analysis, in particular focusing on how the court suggests that true conflicts should be resolved.

1. Pennsylvania

Budget Rent-a-Car System, Inc. v. Chappell

407 F.3d 166 (3d Cir. 2005)

AMBRO, Circuit Judge

We apply Pennsylvania's choice-of-law rules to determine which state's substantive law (New York's, Michigan's or Pennsylvania's) governs the extent of vicarious liability of Budget Rent-a-Car System, Inc. ("Budget"), the owner of a vehicle involved in an accident that rendered Nicole Chappell, a New York resident, permanently paralyzed. The accident occurred in Pennsylvania as Chappell and her boyfriend, Joseph Powell, III, a Michigan resident, were driving from New York to Michigan in a car Powell had rented from Budget in Michigan (and previously driven to New York).

Because the State of New York has the greatest interest in the application of its law to this dispute, we conclude that its law should apply. The contrary judgment of the District Court is reversed. . . .

On the morning of February 12, 2002, Powell rented a Nissan Xterra from Budget in Michigan. Later that day, he drove eight hours to New York to visit Chappell. Powell stayed with Chappell in New York for the rest of that week. On the evening of February 15, after Chappell completed her work week, she and Powell left New York in the Xterra, planning to drive to Michigan to spend the weekend together there.

While driving through Pennsylvania early the next morning, Powell fell asleep at the wheel. The car drifted from the left lane of Interstate 80 across the right lane and into the right guardrail, causing it to flip over. Powell escaped the crash without substantial physical injury. However, the force of the impact ejected Chappell from the Xterra, causing severe injuries. Shortly after the accident, a helicopter transported her to Mercy Hospital in Pittsburgh, where doctors diagnosed . . . spinal trauma that has rendered Chappell permanently paraplegic.

Budget initiated this action in the United States District Court for the Eastern District of Pennsylvania, seeking a declaratory judgment against Powell and Chappell and asking the Court to determine which state's substantive law governed its vicarious liability as the owner of the vehicle.[1] Budget argued that Michigan law should apply, capping its liability at $20,000. Chappell brought two counterclaims against Budget . . . and a cross-claim against Powell. She argued that Budget faced unlimited vicarious liability under New York law. . . . The District Court granted summary judgment to Budget, holding that Pennsylvania law applied. . . .

A. Legal Framework

To determine which state's substantive law governs, we must refer to the choice-of-law rules of the jurisdiction in which the District Court sits, here Pennsylvania. Under Pennsylvania law, we begin with an "interest analysis" of the policies of all interested states and then — based on the result of that analysis — characterize the case as a true conflict, false conflict, or unprovided-for case. . . . A true conflict exists "when the governmental interests of [multiple] jurisdictions would be impaired if their law were not applied." If a case presents a true conflict, Pennsylvania choice-of-law rules "call for the application of the law of the state having the most significant contacts or relationships with the particular issue." This calls for an application of the Second Restatement of Conflict of Laws §6 (1971) factors.

"A false conflict exists if only one jurisdiction's governmental interests would be impaired by the application of the other jurisdiction's law." If there is a false conflict, we must apply the law of the only interested jurisdiction. Finally, an unprovided-for case arises when no jurisdiction's interests would be impaired if its laws were not applied. *Lex loci delicti* (the law of the place of the wrong — here Pennsylvania) continues to govern unprovided-for cases.

With this background, we turn to the competing state laws we consider applying.

B. Relevant State Law Provisions on Vicarious Liability

1. new york

New York law imposes unlimited vicarious liability on the owners of vehicles. It provides that "every owner of a vehicle used or operated in [that] state shall be liable and responsible for . . . injuries to person[s] . . . resulting from negligence

---

1. The District Court exercised diversity jurisdiction pursuant to 28 U.S.C. §1332. As noted, Chappell is a New York resident and Powell is a Michigan resident. Budget Systems, Inc. was a Delaware corporation that maintained its principal place of business in Illinois. Subsequent to the accident, it was acquired by Budget, which was and remains a Delaware corporation with its principal place of business in New Jersey.

in the use or operation of such vehicle. . . ." N.Y. Veh. & Traf. Law §388(1) (McKinney 2002). By passing §388(1), the New York "legislature intended that the injured party be afforded a financially responsible insured person against whom to recover for injuries."

It is beyond dispute that §388(1) has extraterritorial scope, that is, it can apply to accidents occurring beyond New York's borders. This dispute requires us to assess the *extent* of the extraterritorial scope of §388(1). The New York Court of Appeals has held that "vicarious liability imposed by section 388(1) does not extend to owners of *vehicles that have never been registered, used, operated or intended for use within [New York].*" We later address whether (under New York law) the Xterra in our case falls within that exclusion.

2. MICHIGAN

Michigan also imposes vicarious liability on the owners of vehicles. Its law provides that "the owner of a motor vehicle is liable for an injury caused by the negligent operation of the motor vehicle . . . [if] the motor vehicle is being driven with his or her express or implied consent or knowledge." Mich. Comp. Laws §257.401(1) (2003) ("Subsection 1"). Liability is capped, however, in certain circumstances: "[The liability of] a person engaged in the business of leasing motor vehicles who is the lessor of a motor vehicle under a lease providing for the use of the motor vehicle by the lessee for a period of 30 days or less . . . is limited to $20,000.00 because of bodily injury to or death of 1 person in any 1 accident. . . ." Mich. Comp. Laws §257.401(3) (2003) ("Subsection 3"). In effect, vicarious liability is imposed on an owner when the driver's negligence causes an accident in another state so long as the owner-driver relationship was entered into in Michigan.

At the time of Chappell's accident, Michigan law provided that it was a misdemeanor for "an owner knowingly [to] permit to be operated, upon any highway, a vehicle required to be registered . . . unless there is attached to and displayed on the vehicle . . . a valid registration plate issued for the vehicle. . . ." Mich. Comp. Laws §§257.255(1), (2) (2001).

3. PENNSYLVANIA

Pennsylvania follows the common law rule that, absent an employer-employee relationship, an automobile's owner is not vicariously liable for the negligence of its driver.

. . .

B. DOES NEW YORK'S §388(1) APPLY TO THIS DISPUTE?

The District Court predicted that the State of New York would not construe §388(1) to apply to this case. . . . We disagree with the District Court's analysis and conclude that this case falls within the scope of §388(1) as that statute has been construed by New York's courts. . . . [T]he provision applies unless the accident vehicle "has *never* been registered, used, operated or intended for use within [New York]." *Fried*, 599 N.E.2d at 654 (emphasis added). Thus, the provision applies to our case. . . . [In addition,] we see no constitutional problem with the choice of New York's substantive law to govern this dispute. . . .

C. Does Michigan's Subsection 3 Apply to This Dispute?

. . . [T]he District Court concluded that Budget could not invoke Michigan's limitation of liability for short-term lessors of cars in subsection 3 because "the lease between Budget Systems and Powell was 'founded on' a misdemeanor — Budget Systems's grant of permission to operate the Xterra without a valid license plate — " and was therefore a "nullity" under Michigan law. The parties vigorously dispute the propriety of this holding. Because we conclude below that New York's interest in applying its law far outweighs any interest Michigan might have in applying subsection 3 (that is, assuming subsection 3 *would* apply), we find it unnecessary to address the competing, complex statutory interpretation arguments presented by the parties.[8] Instead, we . . . assume without holding that Michigan's subsection 3 would apply and limit Budget's liability in this case. Under this assumption, we turn to New York and Michigan's competing interests.

D. Identification and Weighing of State Interests

In choosing between Michigan and New York law,[9] we consider, *inter alia*, "the relevant policies of [the] interested states and the relative interests of those states in the determination of the particular issue." Restatement (Second) of Conflict of Laws §6 (1971). New York's §388(1) "was enacted to ensure access by injured persons to a financially responsible [party] against whom to recover for injuries and to change the common-law rule and to impose liability upon the owner of a vehicle for the negligence of a person legally operating the car with the permission, express or implied, of the owner." . . . "Another . . . interest is in assuring that New York vendors who furnish medical and hospital care to injured parties are compensated. . . . Finally, New York has a public fiscal interest in assuring that . . . New York State can recoup its welfare expense[s] from [victims'] recoveries."

Describing Michigan's subsection 3, the District Court explained that "in response to car rental companies' complaints that Subsection 1 [which provides

---

8. If Michigan's subsection 3 does not apply to this case, then only New York has an interest in applying its law and this case would be a "false conflict." New York law would clearly apply. If subsection 3 does apply, Michigan has an interest in applying its law and we must weigh the "true conflict" between its interest and that of New York. Because we conclude that New York's interest trumps in any event, we need not settle the construction of Michigan law because we reach the same result under either construction.

9. It is clear that Pennsylvania does not have an interest in applying its law to this dispute. But for the chance occurrence of the accident in Pennsylvania, there is no connection between the Commonwealth and the parties. Pennsylvania has no interest in securing a recovery for Chappell nor in limiting Budget's liability. The District Court held that Pennsylvania law applied by default under the rule of lex loci delicti because neither New York nor Michigan had an interest in applying its law. We have already stated our disagreement with those predicate determinations.

for unlimited vicarious liability] was 'inhibiting the growth of the [rental car] industry and threatening to drive some companies out of the state,' the Michigan legislature amended the law in June of 1995 [to add subsection 3]." . . . That is, subsection 3 was codified to advance Michigan's interest in preventing rental car companies from deciding not to do business (or to do less business) in the State of Michigan for fear of unlimited vicarious liability.

. . . [W]e turn to the states' relative interests in those policies. New York's interest is clear, direct and compelling. Chappell is a New York resident receiving treatment and care from medical providers in New York with the aid of New York–administered welfare programs. Each of New York's policy justifications for enacting §388(1) is directly implicated by this case, and New York's interest runs to the full extent of Chappell's recovery, dollar for dollar. It has an interest in (1) Chappell's full recovery from a financially responsible party, (2) the compensation of New York vendors who furnish medical and hospital care to Chappell, and (3) recouping the State's welfare expenses.

Michigan, unlike New York, does not have an interest in securing a recovery for an injured citizen in this case (or associated state medical expenses). Its only interest lies in the extent of Budget's liability (or, put another way, in the potential application of subsection 3's liability cap). We doubt that Michigan's interest in the application of subsection 3 is implicated at all in this case. Is it plausible that Budget will decide not to do business in the State of Michigan if it is held liable under New York law for an accident that occurred in Pennsylvania involving a car rented in Michigan? In fact, the application of New York's more stringent law in this case likely *advances* Michigan's interest in making it a relatively attractive place for rental car companies to do business by highlighting the value of Michigan's liability cap. And if potential liability in other fora would undermine Budget's decision to do business in Michigan, there are steps it can take to preserve the value of Michigan's liability cap short of pulling out of the State. For example, Budget is free to limit to intrastate travel the permissible use of vehicles it rents in Michigan. It is similarly free contractually to bar its customers from operating its vehicles in the State of New York. (We note that, far from restricting the use of vehicles in New York, Budget actually rents vehicles in that State, calling into question the necessity of a liability cap to induce rental car companies to do business in a state.) In short, Michigan's interest in this particular dispute is uncertain and tenuous at best.

We thus conclude that New York's interest in the application of its law to this dispute clearly trumps that of Michigan. Thus, under Pennsylvania's choice-of-law rules, New York law is to be applied.

Notes on
BUDGET AND *THE PENNSYLVANIA HYBRID APPROACH*

1. How is the Pennsylvania hybrid approach different from governmental interest analysis? One clue can be found in the climax of the *Budget* court's opinion: after effectively identifying a true conflict between

New York and Michigan law, the court declared that "New York's interest in the application of its law to this dispute clearly trumps that of Michigan." Governmental interest analysis provides for the forum default to apply once a true conflict is found. Under governmental interest analysis, a court would not evaluate which state's interests should "trump" another. The Pennsylvania approach, however, requires a court confronting a true conflict to ascertain the jurisdiction with the greatest interest in having its law applied to the legal issue in conflict.

2. Was the result in *Budget* different than the result that governmental interest analysis would have yielded? For the purpose of governmental interest analysis, *Budget* effectively presents a true conflict between Michigan and New York, which the parties presented for adjudication in the forum of a disinterested third state. In his summary of governmental interest analysis principles, Brainerd Currie said that "[i]f the forum is disinterested, but an unavoidable conflict exists between the laws of two other states, and the court cannot with justice decline to adjudicate the case, it should apply the law of the forum — until someone comes along with a better idea." Brainerd Currie, *Comments on* Babcock v. Jackson, *A Recent Development in Conflict of Laws*, 63 COLUM. L. REV. 1233, 1243 (1963). Other writings have suggested that if the disinterested forum does not dismiss the true conflict case under forum non conveniens, it should evaluate the laws of the interested states and apply the law that looks most like forum law or the law that the court believes is best. Regardless of which of these approaches the *Budget* court might have been chosen, none describe what the *Budget* court actually did.

3. Interestingly, the same year as *Budget*, the United States Court of Appeals for the Third Circuit confronted the same New York car-owner liability statute in another case involving a Pennsylvania accident. *Garcia v. Plaza Oldsmobile Ltd.*, 421 F.3d 216 (3d Cir. 2005). This time, however, the victim was from Pennsylvania and the car rental company was from New York. As in *Budget*, the court determined that Pennsylvania had no interest, and that New York did. The court used a different reading of the New York statute, however, to get to its conclusion. Under the reading in *Budget*, there may have been difficulty finding a New York interest since the victim was not from New York. But the court expanded its reading of New York's policies, reasoning that New York was interested in protecting the Pennsylvania victim because it had a "commendable concern" not only for the residents of New York, but "for residents of other states injured as a result of the activities of New York residents." *Garcia*, 421 F.3d at 222. Does the court seem to be stretching New York's policy here? Note that the reasoning conveniently enabled the *Garcia* court to find a false conflict and apply the law of the only interested state — an easy result to justify. As in *Budget*, the *Garcia* court applied Pennsylvania's hybrid approach. Does it appear that Pennsylvania's "spin" on governmental interest analysis eliminates or reduces the problems with governmental interest analysis?

2. *New York*

Bakalar v. Vavra

619 F.3d 136 (2d Cir. 2010)

EDWARD R. KORMAN, Judge:

This case involves a dispute over the ownership of a drawing by Egon Schiele (the "Drawing") between plaintiff David Bakalar, the current possessor of the Drawing, and defendants Milos Vavra and Leon Fischer, heirs to the estate of Franz Friedrich Grunbaum. Although the Drawing was untitled by the artist, one of the descriptive titles by which it is known is "Seated Woman with Bent Left Leg (Torso)."

Vavra and Fischer allege the following facts in their complaint. The Drawing was one of eighty-one Schieles that were included in a collection of 449 artworks owned by Grunbaum, an Austrian cabaret artist, and kept in his apartment in Vienna. Grunbaum was deprived of his possession and *dominium* over the Drawing after being arrested by the Nazis and signing a power of attorney while imprisoned at Dachau. The power of attorney, dated July 16, 1938 (four months after his imprisonment), authorized his wife Elisabeth "to file for me the legally required statement of assets and to provide on my behalf all declarations and signatures required for their legal effect according to the statutory provisions, and to represent me in general in all my affairs."

The statement of assets, to which the power of attorney referred, required Jews to list all of their property. The information was then used by the Nazis to impose confiscatory taxes and penalties of various kinds. The power to represent Grunbaum "in all [his] affairs" enabled the Nazis to compel Elisabeth to dispose of Grunbaum's assets for the purpose of paying the imposed taxes and penalties.[2] Indeed, in a report dated four days after the execution of the power of attorney, Franz Kieslinger, an appraiser for the Nazis with the Viennese auction house Dorotheum — which was "a prime selling point of loot[ed] art in Austria" — conducted an appraisal of the 449 artworks that Grunbaum kept in his apartment, including the eighty-one Schieles. On August 1, 1938, Mrs. Grunbaum signed a List of Assets "for Franz Freidr. Grunbaum, according to Power of Attorney dated

---

2. While the Nazis could simply have confiscated all of Grunbaum's possessions without a power of attorney, the manner in which they proceeded here reflected their practice of camouflaging theft with a veneer of legality. Raul Hilberg, the preeminent historian of the Nazi war against the Jews, has written: "Lawyers were everywhere and their influence was pervasive. Again and again, there was a need for legal justifications." RAUL HILBERG, PERPETRATORS VICTIMS BYSTANDERS: THE JEWISH CATASTROPHE, 1933-1945, at 71 (1992). Indeed, the U.S. Consul General in Vienna at the time observed that "[t]here is a curious respect for legalistic formalities. The signature of the person despoiled is always obtained, even if the person in question has to be sent to Dachau in order to break down his resistance." *See* LYNN H. NICHOLAS, THE RAPE OF EUROPA: THE FATE OF EUROPE'S TREASURES IN THE THIRD REICH AND THE SECOND WORLD WAR 39, Chapter 2 n.30 (First Vintage Books ed., 1994). Scholars have explained that respect for legalistic formalities was not a curious eccentricity. . . . In sum, the law "removed the question of the morality or legitimacy of the process." Peter Hayes, *Summary and Conclusions*, in CONFISCATION OF JEWISH PROPERTY IN EUROPE, 1933-1945: NEW SOURCES AND PERSPECTIVES: SYMPOSIUM 143, 147 (2003).

July 16, 1938." The valuation she placed on it was identical to that which Kieslinger had assigned it.

The manner in which the Drawing made its way from Vienna to Galerie St. Etienne, the New York art gallery from which Bakalar purchased it, is unclear. Grunbaum died in Dachau in 1941. The Registration of Death, a document filed in the district court of Vienna in which Mrs. Grunbaum reported the death of her husband, states that "[a]ccording to the deceased's widow, Elisabeth Sara Grunbaum, there is no estate." Mrs. Grunbaum was arrested by the Nazis on October 5, 1942, and died shortly thereafter in a concentration camp in Minsk. The Drawing was purchased along with forty-five other Schieles by Galerie Gutekunst, a Swiss art gallery, in February and May of 1956. The district judge found that the seller was Mathilde Lukacs-Herzl, the sister of Mrs. Grunbaum. Later the same year, on September 18, 1956, the Drawing was purchased by the Galerie St. Etienne and was shipped to it in New York. On November 12, 1963, the latter sold the drawing to David Bakalar for $4,300.

Bakalar, a resident of Massachusetts, filed this action seeking a declaratory judgment that he is the rightful owner of the Drawing. The complaint was filed after a winning bid of approximately $675,000 for the Drawing at a Sotheby's auction was withdrawn, apparently because of a letter written on behalf of Milos Vavra and Leon Fischer, which challenged Bakalar's title. Vavra and Fischer, who have been formally designated by an Austrian court as the legal heirs to the estate of Grunbaum, are the two named defendants in this case. In response to Bakalar's complaint, Vavra and Fischer, who are residents of the Czech Republic and New York, respectively, filed counterclaims for declaratory judgment, replevin, and damages. After a bench trial, a judgment was entered in the Southern District of New York, based on findings of fact and conclusions of law, which sustained the claim of David Bakalar that he was the rightful owner.

In his post-trial findings of fact and conclusion of law, the district judge reaffirmed his pretrial ruling that Swiss law applied. Under Swiss law, "a person who acquires and takes possession of an object in good faith becomes the owner, even if the seller was not entitled or authorized to transfer ownership." One "relevant exception to this rule is that if the object had been lost or stolen, the owner who previously lost the object retains the right to reclaim the object for five years." . . .

Because jurisdiction in this case is predicated on diversity of citizenship, New York's choice-of-law rules apply. Before engaging in a choice-of-law analysis, we turn to the threshold question whether there is a difference between the laws of Switzerland and New York upon which the outcome of the case is dependent. We conclude that there is a significant difference that is reflected in the laws and policies of these two jurisdictions.

Under Article 934 of the Swiss Civil Code, as summarized by Bakalar's expert, "a buyer acting in good faith will *acquire valid title to stolen property* after a period of *five years*. After the five year period, a previous owner of a stolen object is no longer entitled to request the return of the stolen object from a good-faith possessor." Moreover, as Bakalar's expert explained, Swiss law also presumes that a purchaser acts in good faith, and a plaintiff seeking to reclaim stolen property has the burden of establishing that a purchaser did not act in good faith. Significantly, according to Bakalar's expert,

> [t]here has never been a legal presumption that art works with a potential relationship to Germany during World War II (i.e. emanating from a German collection or created by artists deemed "degenerate" by the Nazis) would in general and *per se* be tainted, and that a dealer accepting such art works would automatically be subject to a heightened standard of diligence in the 1950s. Such a presumption did not in the 1950s and does not today exist in Swiss law.

B. NEW YORK LAW   → *Bakalar* ✗

Unlike Switzerland, in New York, a thief cannot pass good title. This means that, under New York law, "absent other considerations an artwork stolen during World War II still belongs to the original owner, even if there have been several subsequent buyers and even if each of those buyers was completely unaware that she was buying stolen goods." The manner in which the New York rule is applied reflects an overarching concern that New York not become a marketplace for stolen goods and, in particular, for stolen artwork.

The leading New York case in this area is *Solomon R. Guggenheim Found. v. Lubell*, 77 N.Y.2d 311, 569 N.E.2d 426, 567 N.Y.S.2d 623 (1991), which principally addresses the issue of when a cause of action for replevin accrues, thus triggering the three-year statute of limitations.... [T]he opening paragraph of [*Lubell*] begins with the observation that "[t]he backdrop for this replevin action is the New York City art market, where masterpieces command extraordinary prices at auction and illicit dealing in stolen merchandise is an industry all its own." *Lubell* then observed that "New York case law has long protected the right of the owner whose property has been stolen to recover that property, even if it is in the possession of a good-faith purchaser for value." One aspect of that protection is the rule that a cause of action for replevin against the good-faith purchaser of stolen property "accrues when the true owner makes demand for return of the chattel and the person in possession of the chattel refuses to return it. Until demand is made and refused, possession of the stolen property by the good-faith purchaser for value is not considered wrongful" and the statute of limitations does not begin to run.

While the Court of Appeals acknowledged that "the demand and refusal rule is not the only possible method of measuring the accrual of replevin claims, it does appear to be the rule that affords the most protection to true owners of stolen property," and it rejected any suggestion that less protective measures should be adopted. Thus, it declined to adopt a discovery rule "with the Statute of Limitations running from the time that the owner discovered or reasonably should have discovered the whereabouts of the work of art that had been stolen." ... In justifying this holding, the Court of Appeals observed that its decision was

NY law → must demand and be refused!

... in part influenced by [its] recognition that New York enjoys a worldwide reputation as a preeminent cultural center. To place the burden of locating stolen artwork on the true owner and to foreclose the rights of that owner to recover its property if the burden is not met would, we believe, encourage illicit trafficking in stolen art. Three years after the theft, any purchaser, good faith or not, would be able to hold onto stolen art work unless the true owner was able to establish that it had undertaken a reasonable search for the missing art. This shifting of the burden onto the wronged owner is inappropriate. In our opinion, the better rule gives the owner relatively greater protection and places the burden of investigating the provenance of a work of art on the potential purchaser.

This is not all the Court of Appeals held in *Lubell*. In the course of its opinion, it went on to agree "that the burden of proving that the painting was not stolen properly rests with [the possessor]." . . .

Against this backdrop, we turn to the issue of the appropriate choice of law and the issue of whether the Drawing was stolen. We address first the choice of law issue, because if Swiss law applies, it is immaterial whether the Drawing was stolen. . . . The interest analysis, which [now] generally applies in all choice-of-law contexts [in New York] begins with an examination of the contacts each jurisdiction has with the event giving rise to the cause of action. "Once these contacts are discovered and analyzed they will indicate (1) that there exists no true conflict of laws, . . . as in most choice of law cases, or (2) that a true conflict exists, i.e., both jurisdictions have an interest in the application of their law." *In re Crichton's Estate*, 20 N.Y.2d at 135 n.8. "In property disputes, if a conflict is identified, New York choice of law rules require the application of an 'interests analysis,' in which 'the law of the jurisdiction having the greatest interest in the litigation [is] applied and . . . the facts or contacts which obtain significance in defining State interests are those which relate to the purpose of the particular law in conflict.'"

. . . However the Drawing came into the possession of the Swiss art gallery, New York has a compelling interest in the application of its law. Indeed, it has applied its own law in a case comparable to this one without pausing to engage in a choice-of-law analysis. Simply stated, if the claim of Vavra and Fischer is credited, a stolen piece of artwork was delivered in New York to a New York art gallery, which sold it in New York to Bakalar. Indeed, Bakalar concedes that "a substantial part of the events or omissions giving rise to the claims herein" occurred in New York. These "events and omissions" made New York a "marketplace for stolen goods" and, more particularly, for stolen artwork, which was of special concern in *Lubell*.

By contrast, the resolution of an ownership dispute in the Drawing between parties who otherwise have no connection to Switzerland does not implicate any Swiss interest simply because the Drawing passed through there. While the Drawing was purchased in Switzerland by a Swiss art gallery, which resold it within five months to a New York art gallery, the application of New York law here would not have any adverse effect on the Swiss art gallery. Nor would it affect any other Swiss citizen or Swiss interest. The application of New York law may cause New York purchasers of artwork to take greater care in assuring themselves of the legitimate provenance of their purchase. This, in turn, may adversely affect the extra-territorial sale of artwork by Swiss galleries. The tenuous interest of Switzerland created by these circumstances, however, must yield to the significantly greater interest of New York . . . in preventing the state from becoming a marketplace for stolen goods. Thus, the Restatement (Second) of Conflict of Laws, which strongly tilts toward the situs rule, acknowledges that "[t]here will also be occasions when the local law of some state other than that where the chattel was situated at the time of the conveyance should be applied because of the intensity of the interest of that state in having its local law applied to determine the particular issue." Restatement (Second) of Conflict of Laws §244 cmt. g (1971). . . .

While we have focused on the laws of Switzerland and New York, there is a third jurisdiction, the laws of which are arguably relevant. The Drawing began its journey in Austria, and Austrian courts have recognized that Vavra and Fischer are the heirs to Grunbaum's estate. Certainly, Austria has no interest in defeating the claim by these heirs against a United States citizen. Nevertheless, it is relevant that after World War II, Austria enacted a statute known as the Austrian Nullification Act, which provided that "[a]ny paid and unpaid legal transactions and other legal business which occurred during the German occupation of Austria will be considered null and void if they were contracted as a consequence of any political or economic influence exercised by the German Reich in order to deprive individuals or entities of property assets or interests owned by or due them as of March 13, 1938." NichtigkeitsG [Austrian Nullification Act] No. 106/1946, §1 (Austria). The claims made on the basis of the Austrian Nullification Act were to be determined by subsequent legislation. While Austria enacted legislation relating to restitution of property from private parties — the Third Restitution Law BGB No. 54/1947, which the district judge observed imposed "a lesser burden for proving an illegitimate transfer of the Drawing in Austria," — the statute expired on July 31, 1956. Nevertheless, an opinion of the Supreme Court of Austria, a translation of which is before us, declared that the Austrian Nullification Act is "in accordance with the immutable principles of our General Civil Code that nobody is obligated to adhere to a contract that was concluded on the basis of unfair and well-founded fear." Oberster Gerichtshof [OGH] [Supreme Court] Apr. 1, 2008, Docket No. 5 Ob 272/07x (citing Austrian Civil Code §870). Moreover, the Supreme Court of Austria observed that "[e]ven though claims for expropriation of property within the meaning of the [Third Restitution Law] can no longer be asserted due to expiration of the time limit (July 31, 1956), [these principles] continue[] to be an integral part of Austrian law."

Although it is unclear whether a cause of action comparable to the counter-claims of Vavra and Fischer against Bakalar could be successfully brought in Austria, allowing the claims to go forward under New York law is consistent with the principles underlying the decision of the Supreme Court of Austria. While Austria may have allowed its restitution-enabling act to elapse eleven years after the end of WWII in order to protect Austrian citizens, the present

NY !!

case does not involve a claim against any citizen of Austria.[4] Accordingly, we conclude that Austria has no competing interest in the circumstances presented here.

In sum, we conclude that the district judge erred in holding that Swiss law, rather than New York law, applied here. Consequently, if, contrary to the holding of the district judge, the Drawing was stolen or otherwise unlawfully taken from Grunbaum, that circumstance would affect the validity of Bakalar's title.

Notwithstanding its conclusion that the manner in which the Drawing was acquired from Grunbaum would not have affected the outcome of the case, the district judge found that the Grunbaum heirs had failed to produce "any concrete evidence that the Nazis looted the Drawing or that it was otherwise taken from Grunbaum." Our reading of the record suggests that there may be such evidence, and that the district judge, by applying Swiss Law, erred in placing the burden of proof on the Grunbaum heirs in this regard. Indeed, as discussed earlier, if the district judge determines that Vavra and Fischer have made a threshold showing that they have an arguable claim to the Drawing, New York law places the burden on Bakalar, the current possessor, to prove that the Drawing was not stolen. Moreover, should the district judge conclude that the Grunbaum heirs are entitled to prevail on the issue of the validity of Bakalar's title to the Drawing, the district judge should also address the issue of laches. This defense, which Bakalar raised in response to the counterclaim of the Grunbaum heirs, is one that New York law makes available to him.

Accordingly, for the reasons stated above, we vacate the judgment of the district court and remand the case for further proceedings, including, if necessary, a new trial. . . .

Notes on
BAKALAR *AND THE NEW YORK APPROACH*

1. Bakalar is part of a larger picture. First, it was one of three choice of law cases decided in the same year (2010) regarding art lost during the Nazi era by Austrian Jewish families. Like the *Bakalar* court, the other two courts conducted a choice of law analysis, but ultimately applied forum state law. Unlike in *Bakalar*, however, the claimants lost in both of those other cases, which were litigated in the domicile of the current "owner" of the art and in the jurisdiction that was the final situs of the art. *See Museum of Fine Arts, Boston v. Seger-Thomschitz*, 623 F.3d 1 (1st Cir. 2010) (applying Massachusetts conflicts law, court ruled against claimant on the basis of Massachusetts statute of limitations); *Dunbar v. Seger-Thomschitz*, 615 F.3d 574 (5th Cir. 2010)

4. Significantly, the Republic of Austria continues to investigate all works of art acquired between 1938-1945, which are now owned by it. Indeed, as the Austrian Embassy in the United States observed, "[w]orks of art not properly obtained will be returned to their original owners or their heirs." Austrian Press and Information Service, Austrian Holocaust Restitution, http://www.austria.org/content/view/414/1. . . .

(applying Louisiana conflicts law, court ruled against claimant under Louisiana acquisitive prescription law).

State choice of law is only one of the many battlefronts in which politicians and lawyers have looked for solutions to the problem of Nazi-confiscated art. (Indeed, Chapter 1 features such a dispute in the context of federal litigation over the Foreign Sovereign Immunity Act: *Republic of Austria v. Altmann*, 541 U.S. 677 (2004).) Moreover, state choice of law doctrine has also been implicated in other theft of stolen art, much of which constitutes antiquities that some laws designate as outside of commerce and not available for acquisition by a private person. *See, e.g.*, Jennifer Anglim Kreder, *The New Battleground of Museum Ethics and Holocaust-Era Claims: Technicalities Trumping Justice or Responsible Stewardship for the Public Trust*, 88 OR. L. REV. 37 (2009); Symeon C. Symeonides, *A Choice-of-Law Rule for Conflicts Involving Stolen Cultural Property*, 38 VAND. J. TRANSNAT'L L. 1177 (2005).

2. Are you persuaded by the court's reasoning about jurisdictional interest in *Bakalar*? The court seemed to conclude that New York cared most about the issue because the state's law and policies were unequivocally protective of the rights of original owner. Such reasoning is not uncommon where courts apply some strand of governmental interest analysis. A skeptical view might denominate this as the "which state shouts the loudest?" approach to choice of law. But couldn't one conclude that a jurisdiction's decision to remain ambivalent on an issue (such as Austria) represents a strong commitment to the importance of a fine-tuned nuanced treatment of individual cases? Likewise, couldn't one conclude that a jurisdiction's decision to cut off claims of ownership at a certain point in the chain of ownership (such as under Swiss law) represents a strident interest in upholding the integrity of transactions consummated in the jurisdiction?

3. How does the choice of law methodology applied in *Bakalar* compare with Currie's "pure" governmental interest analysis? How does *Bakalar* compare with the Pennsylvania approach? Both have a similar "ring" to them — the goal being to apply the jurisdiction with the greatest or strongest interest in the case. Note, however, that — unlike Pennsylvania courts — the New York court in *Bakalar* did not solicit the help of the Restatement (Second). Had the *Bakalar* court done so, it would have been less likely to spurn the situs rule (pointing to application of Swiss law).

4. The current choice of law methodology followed in New York courts is not as determinate as *Bakalar* might suggest. Although New York courts showed impressive innovation in *Babcock v. Jackson*, 191 N.E.2d 279 (N.Y. 1963), their recent forays into choice of law doctrine have not maintained the clarity and leadership reflected in *Babcock* and its progeny. In a series of cases following *Babcock*, New York's highest court adopted a set of rules for guest statute tort cases, most thoroughly articulated in *Neumeier v. Kuehner*, 286 N.E.2d 454 (N.Y. 1972). The *Neumeier* rules turned on factual

configurations that focused largely on domicile, with a default of applying the law where the accident occurred. The rules provided as follows:

> 1. When the guest-passenger and the host-driver are domiciled in the same state, and the car is there registered, the law of that state should control and determine the standard of care which the host owes to his guest.
>
> 2. When the driver's conduct occurred in the state of his domicile and that state does not cast him in liability for that conduct, he should not be held liable by reason of the fact that liability would be imposed upon him under the tort law of the state of the victim's domicile. Conversely, when the guest was injured in the state of his own domicile and its law permits recovery, the driver who has come into that state should not — in the absence of special circumstances — be permitted to interpose the law of his state as a defense.
>
> 3. In other situations, when the passenger and the driver are domiciled in different states, the rule is necessarily less categorical. Normally, the applicable rule of decision will be that of the state where the accident occurred but not if it can be shown that displacing that normally applicable rule will advance the relevant substantive law purposes without impairing the smooth working of the multi-state system or producing great uncertainty for litigants.

Id. at 128.

Schultz v. Boys Scouts of America, 480 N.E.2d 679 (N.Y. 1985), set forth above in the section of this chapter on governmental interest analysis, suggested that these rules might apply outside guest statute situations. For example, *Schultz* formulated the choice of law decision according to the place of common domicile. Courts in New York and elsewhere also used the *Neumeier* rules outside the guest statute context. More recent cases, however, are less likely to reflect the rules. Rather, the distinction between conduct-regulating rules and loss-allocating rules has proven to be the more lasting legacy from *Schultz*, and is often used by New York courts seeking to identify the state with strongest or greatest interest in tort cases. How do the *Neumeier* rules compare with pure governmental interest analysis?

5. New York courts have been less clear on how choice of law analysis should unfold in contract cases. After the earlier "center of gravity" reasoning in cases such as *Haag v. Barnes*, 175 N.E.2d 441 (N.Y. 1961), the highest court of New York hesitated to fully abandon the reasoning in favor of interest analysis to all contract cases. In *Allstate Ins. Co. v. Stolarz*, 613 N.E.2d 936 (N.Y. 1993), the court explained that the law of the state with the strongest interest approach is not necessarily best suited for contract cases. The court reasoned that contracts involve only "private economic interests" and that public policy analysis may sometimes be difficult or inappropriate. *Id.* at 939. The court added that circumstances exist "where policies underlying conflicting laws in a contract dispute are readily

identifiable and reflect strong governmental interests, and therefore should be considered." *Id.* at 939.

The federal court in *Bakalar* characterized the dispute as a property case, not a contract case. The highest court in New York has applied the "jurisdiction-with-the-greatest-interest approach" in property cases, stating that such an approach is the general methodology for all types of cases in New York, even though the situs rule continued to "hold some sway" in property cases. *Istim, Inc. v. Chemical Bank*, 581 N.E.2d 1042, 1044 (N.Y. 1991); *see also Schoeps v. Museum of Modern Art*, 594 F. Supp. 2d 461 (S.D.N.Y. 2009) (applying general New York approach in a property dispute); *In re Thomas*, 901 N.Y.S.2d 493, 497 (N.Y. Surr. Ct. 2010), *aff'd*, 910 N.Y.S.2d 252 (2010) (ruling that the "the law that applies is the law of the state where the tangible property is located").

3. Hawaii

Mikelson v. United Services Automobile Ass'n

111 P.3d 601 (Haw. 2005)

ACOBA, J.

Defendant-Appellant United Services Automobile Association appeals from the June 19, 2002 judgment of the circuit court of the first circuit in favor of Plaintiff-Appellee Mathew S. Mikelson relating to underinsured motorist benefits. By this appeal, Defendant challenges the court's order denying Defendant's motion for order or declaration regarding choice of law, filed on April 30, 2001, and the court's findings of fact, conclusions of law, and order, filed on July 16, 2001.

For the reasons discussed herein, we hold that the court correctly (1) applied Hawai'i law on the choice of law question, (2) determined that Plaintiff was a resident of the named insured's household and, therefore, a covered person under the subject insurance policy for underinsured motorist benefits purposes, and (3) decided that the insurance policy exclusions were inapplicable. Accordingly, the June 19, 2002 judgment is affirmed.

I.

Larry D. Mikelson, father of Plaintiff, entered into an automobile insurance plan (the Policy) in California with Defendant. The Policy was effective from October 23, 1998 to April 23, 1999. Listed as "*operators*" under the Policy were Father, Ian A. Mikelson, and Plaintiff. It is not disputed that Father is identified as a named insured under the Policy. Three vehicles are listed in the Policy as being "garaged" in Redondo Beach, California.

On January 17, 1999, Plaintiff was riding a motorcycle on Kamehameha Highway. He was carrying a passenger on the motorcycle and had no license or permit to operate the vehicle at the time of the accident. As Plaintiff was approaching the intersection of Waimea Beach Park, a motor vehicle operated by a Ms. Larissa Madison made a left turn into the Park, in front of Plaintiff. This caused Plaintiff to collide with Madison's vehicle and Plaintiff fell onto the roadway, suffering injuries. The motorcycle was not insured under any policy Plaintiff had with Defendant. As a result of the accident, Plaintiff required surgery on his right knee. Within less than thirty days, Plaintiff incurred more than $17,500 in medical and ambulance expenses.

At the time of the accident, Plaintiff was a full-time student at the University of Hawai'i — West Oahu (West Oahu), and lived in the City and County of Honolulu. Plaintiff's first semester at West Oahu commenced in January 1999. The majority of Plaintiff's personal belongings remained at Father's home in California. The only personal belongings Plaintiff brought with him to Hawai'i were clothing and his surfboard. Plaintiff possessed a California driver's license at the time of the accident. The permanent address listed on the license was his Father's address in Redondo Beach, California. Plaintiff lived in California during his recovery from his surgery, but he intended to return to Hawai'i in order to continue his education in the fall semester of 1999.

Plaintiff was not employed before or at the time of the accident and, as a result, relied completely on Father for financial support. This support included payment of Plaintiff's educational and travel expenses. Plaintiff was named as a dependent on Father's Internal Revenue Service income tax returns for the years 1998 and 1999.

II.

On April 20, 1999, Plaintiff filed a civil suit against Madison for the injuries he sustained. Plaintiff obtained $20,000 pursuant to a settlement, release, and indemnity agreement that was executed on June 6, 1999. This $20,000 amount was the limit of liability under all applicable liability bonds or policies covering Madison. The $20,000 was not sufficient to cover Plaintiff's medical expenses.

As a result, Father attempted to obtain benefits under Defendant's Policy. [Defendant took the position that the Policy denied uninsured motorist coverage in this instance and argued in favor of the application of California law, which would have supported this result. Plaintiff argued that he was entitled to coverage if Hawaii's uninsured motorist statute should apply. The trial court agreed that Hawaii law should govern and judgment was entered in Plaintiff's favor. The Defendant appealed the choice of law decision, among other issues.]

. . .

As to the conflict of law issue, Plaintiff relies on *Peters v. Peters*, 63 Haw. 653, 660, 634 P.2d 586, 591 (1981), and asserts that "there is a presumption that Hawaii law applies unless another state's law 'would best serve the interests of the states and persons involved.'" This court has "moved away from the traditional and rigid conflict-of-laws rules in favor of the modern trend towards a more flexible approach looking to the state with the most significant relationship to the parties and subject matter." This flexible approach places "primary emphasis . . . on deciding which state would have the strongest interest in seeing its laws applied to the particular case." *Id.* Hence, this court has said that the interests of the states and applicable public policy reasons should determine whether Hawai'i law or another state's law should apply. "The preferred analysis, [then] in our opinion, would be an assessment of the interests and policy factors involved with a purpose of arriving at a desirable result in each situation."

In this regard, Plaintiff's reliance on *Abramson v. Aetna Cas. & Sur. Co.*, 76 F.3d 304 (9th Cir. 1996), and *Lemen v. Allstate Ins. Co.*, 938 F. Supp. 640, 643 (D. Haw. 1995), is persuasive. In *Abramson*, plaintiff, a New Jersey resident, was riding a bicycle in Hawai'i when he was fatally injured by a car driven by an underinsured motorist. Plaintiff's estate sought underinsured motorist benefits from an insurance policy that contained an anti-stacking provision. Applying Hawai'i law, the Hawai'i federal district court found the anti-stacking provision invalid.

Relying on *Peters*, the Ninth Circuit Court of Appeals affirmed the district court's ruling and stated that "Hawaii's choice-of-law approach creates a presumption that Hawaii law applies unless another state's law would best serve the interests of the states and persons involved." In balancing the interests of Hawai'i and New Jersey, the Ninth Circuit noted that "*Hawaii's interest in the application of Hawaii law to insurance policies* governing automobile accidents — which *is especially strong given the number of non-resident drivers in the state*— is not outweighed by any other state's interests." *Id.* The Ninth Circuit also approved the district court's finding that "New Jersey's interests in the insurance contract did not control the choice-of-law analysis because of the lack of any negotiation over the terms of the contract and the parties' expectations that the contract would cover the insured as he travelled throughout the United States and Canada." *Id.* Applying this same balancing of interests to the instant case, there is a strong interest in applying Hawai'i law to protect non-resident college students attending institutions within this state buttressed by the adhesionary nature of the Policy and the Policy's applicability throughout the United States.

Insofar as *Lemen* is factually similar to the case at bar, it is persuasive. In *Lemen*, the plaintiff sustained injuries in an automobile accident in Hilo, Hawai'i which led to her claim of underinsured motorist benefits under her father's policy. . . . Pursuant to *Peters*, the United States District Court for the District of Hawai'i in *Lemen* determined that Hawai'i had "a stronger interest in seeing its laws applied" for several reasons. First, according to the district court, the plaintiff's accident occurred in Hawai'i. Second, notwithstanding the fact that the plaintiff was a resident of Alaska at the time of the accident, she was living in Hawai'i while attending the University of Hawai'i as a full-time student. Third, the fact that the plaintiff's truck was uninsured at the time of the accident was irrelevant because under Hawaii law underinsured motorist coverage "follows the insured person and not the insured vehicle." Fourth, the district court determined that this court "has articulated a strong interest in protecting the rights of persons within the state to recover benefits pursuant to automobile insurance policies." *Id.* at 644. . . .

Similarly in the case at bar, the accident occurred in Hawai'i. At the time of the accident, Plaintiff was living in Hawa'i and was attending West Oahu as a full-time student. The district court's determination that Hawai'i has a strong interest in protecting those injured within its borders is consistent with this court's interpretation of Hawai'i's underinsured motorist statutes. Hawai'i's underinsured motorist statute, HRS §431:10C-301(b)(4) (1993 & Supp. 1998), is intended "to provide protection, through voluntary insurance, for persons who are injured by underinsured motorists whose liability policies are inadequate to pay for personal injuries caused by motor vehicle accidents." *Taylor v. Gov't Employees Ins. Co.*, 90 Haw. 302, 307-08, 978 P.2d 740, 745-46 (1999) (quoting the legislative history of HRS §431:10C-301). Because the purpose of Hawai'i's underinsured motorist statute is to protect persons, this court has held that under Hawai'i law, insurance "follows the insured's person." California's law, denying coverage when "the vehicle involved in a given accident" is not "as described in the policy for which the claim is made," would thus "frustrate Hawaii's state policy to protect persons injured within its boundaries."

Finally, while the Policy lacks a choice of law provision, the Policy does contain a geographical area provision that is substantially similar to the geographical area provision in the defendant's policy in *Lemen*.[2] Because the Policy affirmatively acknowledges that the terms and conditions therein apply "to accidents and losses" which occur anywhere within the United States, it is foreseeable "an insured family member . . . temporarily living out of state [may] . . . suffer a car accident," and thereby may be subjected to the laws of other states—including those of Hawai'i.

. . . [Citing *California Fed. Sav. & Loan v. Bell*, 965 P.2d 802 (Haw. App. 1998)], Defendant contends that Restatement (Second) of Conflict of Laws §188 (1971) is controlling. While the Intermediate Court of Appeals (ICA) made reference to the Restatement in *Bell*, 6 Haw. App. at 604-05, 735 P.2d at 504-05, the ICA decided the underlying choice of law issue utilizing Professor Leflar's "choice-influencing considerations" approach referred to in *Peters*.

It should be noted, however, that Professor Leflar's "choice-influencing considerations" approach was not adopted by this court in *Peters*. *Peters* indicated there are three generally accepted approaches to modern conflict of laws analysis: (1) the "governmental interests" approach advanced by Professor Currie;[3] (2) "the most significant relationship" test embodied in the Restatement (Second) of Conflict of Laws (1971); and (3) the "choice-influencing considerations" approach articulated by Professor Leflar. *Peters* did not

2. As previously mentioned, Defendant's Policy states that "this policy applies only to accidents and losses which occur: (1) during the policy period as shown in the Declarations; and (2) within the policy territory." The "policy territory" is defined as encompasing "the United States of America, its territories or possessions[.]"

3. The "governmental interests" approach considered "the governmental interests of the states whose laws might be applicable, but with a basic preference of the forum's own law." *Peters*, 63 Haw. at 662, 634 P.2d at 592.

expressly adopt one approach over another. Rather, this court concluded as said before that "the preferred analysis . . . would be an assessment of the interests and policy factors involved with a purpose of arriving at a desirable result in each situation."

In light of the foregoing, we conclude that the court was correct in applying Hawai'i law to the case at bar.

Notes on
MIKELSON *AND THE HAWAII APPROACH*

1. As the *Mikelson* court explained, Hawaii clarified its choice of law approach in *Peters v. Peters*, 634 P.2d 586, 591 (Haw. 1981), when the Hawaii Supreme Court advised that Hawaii law should apply unless another state's law "would best serve the interests of the states and persons involved." In so holding, the *Peters* court eschewed the option of adopting one of the major methodologies, deciding instead that courts should assess "interests and policy factors involved with a purpose of arriving at a desirable result in each situation." *Id.* at 593. In a later opinion, the Hawaii Supreme Court explained that Hawaii's choice of law approach is "flexible" and emphasizes determining "which state would have the strongest interest" in seeing its laws applied. *Lewis v. Lewis*, 748 P.2d 1362, 1365 (Haw. 1988).

In two cases decided before *Peters*, the United States Court of Appeals for the Ninth Circuit confronted the task of applying the choice of law rules of Hawaii as the forum state, but concluded that Hawaiian law did not provide an "appropriate conflicts rule," thus requiring the federal court of appeals to apply the general approach in the United States (the Restatement (Second)). *Commercial Ins. Co. v. Pacific-Peru Const. Corp.*, 558 F.2d 948, 952 (9th Cir. 1977); *Dashiell v. Keauhou-Kona Co.*, 487 F.2d 957, 960 (9th Cir. 1973). Do *Peters*, *Lewis*, and *Mikelson* provide an improvement on this state of affairs? After *Peters*, two U.S. District Courts relied heavily on Professor Leflar's better rule of law approach in trying to apply Hawaii's approach. *DeRoburt v. Gannett Co.*, 558 F. Supp. 1223, 1226 (D. Haw. 1983); *Jenkins v. Whittaker Corp.*, 545 F. Supp. 1117, 1118 (D. Haw. 1982). *Mikelson*, however, has now made clear that that is not the governing approach in Hawaii. One commentator has described Hawaii's approach as "esoteric." Gregory E. Smith, *Choice of Law in the United States*, 38 HASTINGS L.J. 1041, 1067-1068 (1987). Do you agree?

2. How does Hawaii's choice of law approach compare to Currie's "pure" governmental interest analysis? How does it compare with the approach followed in New York and Pennsylvania? Language from the Hawaii Supreme Court's opinions suggests theoretical similarity, particularly Hawaii's instruction to apply the law of the state with the "strongest interest"

in having its law applied. Are the Hawaii, New York, and Pennsylvania approaches similar in application as well?

3. Is it fair to say that the Hawaii approach shares kinship with the center of gravity approach in that they both rely on judicial intuition? How does the Hawaii approach compare with the better rule of law approach? Is it understandable that courts trying to discern Hawaii's approach invoked Professor Leflar and his choice-influencing considerations? Do the two approaches share analytical similarity?

4. Would it be accurate to analogize the Hawaii approach to the flexible traditions of equity jurisprudence, in which a court sitting in equity emphasizes doing justice in the individual case being adjudicated? Is such a tradition appropriate in the conflict of laws context?

PROBLEM 2-59: THE RISKY ENTREPRENEUR

Predatory Lender is incorporated in Forum State and does most of its business there. Ella Entrepreneur lives in Paternalistic State and needed money to expand her business enterprise. She travelled to Forum State and obtained a loan from Predatory Lender at a very high interest rate. The loan stated that it was made and payable in Forum State. The interest rate on Ella's loan violates the usury laws of Paternalistic State. These usury laws included a special protection for borrowers, providing that any lender that makes a loan with an excessive interest rate lacks "capacity to sue" for recovery of either the loan's interest or principal.

Consumer groups lobbied for this same legislation in Forum State, but failed. Banks and other members of the finance industry convinced Forum State lawmakers that such legislation would not only put them out of business, but would render Forum State an undesirable location for commercial transactions. The interest rate on Ella's loan from Predatory Lender complies with the usury limits in place in Forum State.

After Ella defaulted on her loan, Predatory Lender sued Ella in Forum State for interest and principal due under the note. Ella moved to dismiss the suit, arguing that, under the law of Paternalistic State, Predatory Lender lacked capacity to sue. Predatory Lender argues for the application of Forum State law, which regards the interest rate as valid and would allow the court to reach the merits of its claim.

Evaluate how the Forum State court might resolve the conflict of laws question under the following methodologies: (1) Restatement (First) of Conflict of Laws; (2) governmental interest analysis; (3) Restatement (Second) of Conflict of Laws; (4) the Hawaii approach; (5) the New York approach; and (6) the Pennsylvania approach.

545 - Lele include
Davis

I. CRITIQUES OF EXISTING CHOICE OF LAW APPROACHES

Imagine yourself in the position of choosing or creating a choice of law approach in the United States. You could choose an existing approach, guided by the field testing that has occurred in other states that have used the approach over a period of years. Or you could create your own approach, with bits and pieces of existing methodology, as at least ten states have done.

Obviously, you would want to acquaint yourself with an inventory of known problems or "ticks" in the operation of the approaches. Be careful: a review of all the problems could leave one at a loss for the best course of action. As you have seen, choice of law is bursting with analytical complexity and potential minefields. There are several reasons to take heart, however. First, inaction is always an option. This — in large part — is the solution embraced in the opinion below by the Georgia Supreme Court in *Dowis v. Mud Slingers, Inc.*, 621 S.E.2d 413 (Ga. 2005): after canvassing the modern approaches and inventorying their problems, the court retained the tried-and-true Restatement (First). One might also take additional comfort by examining the rich scholarly literature on choice of law. Although unabashedly critical of existing methodologies, this literature provides extraordinary guidance in navigating the complicated and often difficult conflict of laws terrain. A cross-section of this literature has appeared in various notes above, and is also discussed at the end of this section. While some case law and scholarly criticism takes on a scolding and disillusioning tone, much celebrates the opportunities that conflict of laws provides. As Professor Perry Dane explains, conflict of laws "forces the law to reveal its deepest assumptions, and to rub raw its contradictions and demons." Perry Dane, *Conflict of Laws*, in BLACKWELL COMPANION TO PHILOSOPHY OF LAW AND LEGAL THEORY 197 (Dennis Patterson ed., 2010). Equally important, conflict of laws presents an opportunity for lawyers to deploy their rhetorical skills and capacity for abstract analysis to negotiate the real world challenges of citizens living in a federalist nation.

As you start to think deeply about these challenges and to grapple with the variety and complexity of choice of law approaches, you may want to consider why it is that choice of law doctrine tends so dramatically toward complexity. The Note that follows takes up this question. Thereafter, consider whether — in facing this complex world of choice of law methodologies — the Georgia Supreme Court made the most rationale decision in *Dowis* in sticking with Restatement (First) of choice of law.

PERSPECTIVE ON COMPLEXITY IN CHOICE OF LAW[39]

Simplicity in law is a sound goal. Indeed, law that is acceptable governs more effectively: straightforward legal principles are more likely to appeal to the

---

39. For an expanded version of the arguments in this Perspective, *see* Laura E. Little, *Hairsplitting and Complexity in Conflict of Laws: The Paradox of Formalism*, 37 U.C. DAVIS L. REV. 925 (2004).

governed and to garner respect and emotional attachment, thus making citizens more likely to obey the law. Simplicity in the law is particularly important for threshold doctrines such as jurisdiction and choice of law: it makes little sense to require courts and litigants to expend energy on such matters when they could focus instead on the actual merits of a suit. In light of this wisdom, why is conflict of laws so prone to fine distinctions, multiple meanings, and filigreed structures of analysis? Why do courts in the United States not only tolerate these qualities, but sometimes even celebrate them as essential to fair, thoughtful, and accurate resolution of conflict of laws disputes? Several answers suggest themselves: the multi-jurisdictional context of federalism, the common law system, reluctance to disclose exercises of power, and American legal culture.

Multijurisdictional context is perhaps the most obvious explanation for conflict of laws doctrine's complexity. By definition, in every conflict of laws case, more than one jurisdiction is making a claim for regulation. By reason of this multijurisdictional nature, the cases include facts that extend across state boundaries, litigants from different jurisdictions, competing regulatory environments, and multiple litigation pending in different court systems. The presence of more than one source of law creates the perfect medium for fostering dual meaning: each jurisdiction provides an independent environment for generating the terms used in governance. No surprise, then, that the same terms are sometimes attached to different meanings by diverse law-administering bodies.

For conflict of laws within the United States, matters become even more complicated because the multiple sovereigns are overlapping, concurrent jurisdictional authorities in an overarching federalist system. Complications abound where federal law clashes with state law or municipal sovereignty runs up against state or federal authority. State-to-state conflicts, however, breed the most tangled legal rules. Because state sovereigns are coequal, no easy response or default solution to choice of law problems presents itself. Where a court decides to elevate one state's law over another's, the court is acting at odds with the premise of equality that undergirds our federalist system. As shown in Chapter 3, under present jurisprudence, the United States Constitution provides no ready answer for resolving state law conflicts. State and lower federal courts are thus left to their own devices to explain why one state rather than another is the superior lawmaker in a particular case.

The dominance of courts in the conflicts arena likely also adds to the complexity. Although there are a few areas where statutory rules govern, conflict of laws doctrine derives largely from common law discipline. Harlan Fiske Stone once stated that common law rules are "forged between the hammer and anvil of opposing counsel" and are "wrought to fit the very facts which call for [their] application."[40] Given the common law's impulse to reach the fairest judgment in light of the particulars of the case, common law rules tend to be ad hoc and fact driven.

Within the conflict of laws context, this common law tradition creates special challenges. Professor Stewart Sterk has argued that the law-centered nature of the choice of law process is in tension with mainstream views of judicial decision

---

40. Harlan F. Stone, *Some Aspect of the Problem of Law Simplification*, 23 COLUM. L. REV. 319, 321 (1923).

making.[41] Sterk observes that courts now usually resolve choice of law questions by analyzing the law's content (such as in interest analysis), while they resolve lawsuits primarily by referring to facts. As a result, courts emboss a deductive choice of law analysis on an inductive common law analysis. This, according to Sterk, creates chaos in the discipline of conflict of laws. One can argue that the battling methodologies and hybrid conflicts approaches adopted by courts around the country translate into analytical complexity.

And then there's the very sensitive fact that conflict of laws is about power struggles. This puts courts in a difficult position. On one hand, courts are the primary agents of choosing, refining, and applying conflict of laws doctrine. On the other hand, the same courts are "interested" in the resolution of the conflict of laws issue. That is, the court's own law — forum law — is usually one source of the competing laws scrutinized under conflict of laws analysis. As representatives of the sovereignty that creates forum law, forum judges therefore have a stake in the outcome. Their stake increases in the frequent cases where the law to be chosen is court-made, not statutory.

While the judge's stake is not really personal, even an official stake in the bottom line can affect decision making — if only to prompt compensating steps to eliminate the appearance of partiality. Moreover, the fact that her jurisdiction's power hangs in the outcome may inspire the judge to pursue particularly deliberate and seemingly fair analysis — analysis that can adopt a complex structure, filled with the types of exceptions and twists that characterize conflict of laws doctrine.

The adjudicator's special interest in the outcome exacerbates a trait common in communications dealing with power, a tendency to cloud meaning and avoid direct statements. Multiple motivations may underlie this tendency, including concern for the entity losing the power struggle, an intent to avoid angering the loser or an interested third party, the desire to avoid the attention of the press, and an intent to hide the resolution's true effect so as to allow the winner to reinforce her power further. Of related concern is the state's desire not to appear to be imposing negative effects on other states. Whichever of these motivations are at play in a conflict of laws decision, the judge may wish to avoid the appearance of partiality and the embarrassment of possibly enhancing her own authority. Possible manifestations of these motivations include lack of candor, dual meaning, and greater complexity in analysis.

A related factor that may increase a court's desire to obscure the true dynamics in a conflict of laws decision derives from the deeply confrontational context in which the conflicts doctrine is developed and enforced. Conflict of laws doctrine flourishes in the context of litigation. If one starts with the premise, admittedly more common in Eastern culture than Western, that law as a general matter and lawsuits in particular are evidence of a citizenry's failure to act decently of their own volition, then the discipline of conflict of laws exists as a double-barreled symbol of contentiousness. In a lawsuit, the first unwelcome message emerges because humans require law — rather than merely mutual good will and social

---

41. Stewart E. Sterk, *The Marginal Relevance of Choice of Law Theory*, 142 U. Pa. L. Rev. 949 (1994).

structure — to resolve an issue that arose in their interactions. Conflict of laws exacerbates this because the potentially relevant laws are themselves not in accord. Thus, the mere existence of conflict of laws doctrine demonstrates not only that the innate goodness of humans is too weak to control their affairs, but also that the laws created to govern in place of human benevolence are themselves in competition. Making matters even worse are the clashes among conflict doctrines themselves. What a state of disharmony!

The litigation context in which conflict of laws flourishes creates yet another source of complexity: conflicts doctrine is abstract and removed from the work-a-day world outside legal institutions. Conflict of laws rules, like much procedural law, do not regulate primary activity. As such, conflict of laws systems generally do not need to take account of unchangeables such as weather, physics, or medical fact. This untethered-to-the physical-world quality gives conflict of laws thinkers wide range in choosing starting assumptions and manufacturing complicated pathways for analytical solution.

A potentially aggravating factor is the limited universe of professionals for which the decisions are written. Conflict of laws doctrine is law for lawyers and judges — individuals who make their living navigating court systems. The necessity of providing coherent principles for lay people does not constrain or discipline those who create conflicts doctrine. All professions have an inclination to create jargon and specialized concepts; lawyers and judges are certainly not exempt.

Finally, American legal culture is a considerable cause of complicating choice of law doctrine. American legal culture tends to prefer explicit rules and specific authority for proposed action. Before rendering legal advice, the American lawyer prefers to find a legal source that specifically authorizes a transaction or course of action. This contrasts with something like Italian legal culture, where lawyers presume that a course of action is lawful unless prohibited in the civil code.[42]

This quality of America legal culture is at its height in the field of conflict of laws. One sign of the discipline's attraction to rule-based complexity is the ridicule that surrounds two of the most freewheeling of choice of law approaches, Professor Leflar's better rule of law approach and the center of gravity approach. Although reviled for their lack of structure and unpredictability, these approaches trade on intuition and common sense appeal, thereby avoiding some of the confusion arising from the analytical maze of other methodologies.

Further evidence of the inclination toward complexity in choice of law comes from the unusually strong influence of legal academics. Possibly reacting to conflict of laws' difficult qualities, or unconsciously seeking to ensure that the discipline remains in the common law realm, courts have opened their decision making to academic input on developing choice of law approaches. Indeed, Professors Currie, Baxter, and Leflar can all boast mainstream methodologies bearing their name and appearing in state court opinions throughout the United

---

42. Guido Calabresi, *Two Functions of Formalism: In Memory of Guido Tedeschi*, 67 U. Chi. L. Rev. 479, 481 (2000) (noting that "[t]he Italian's casual contempt for legal rules in practice baffles the, by contrast, extraordinary law abiding American"). Calabresi hastens to add that Italian society does tend to hold the theoretical system of law itself in "high respect," a matter that Americans regard with irony. *Id.*

States. The result imports academic culture into judicial decision making, a culture that values thorough investigation, full exposition of competing arguments, and, alas, seemingly endless documentation and footnotes.

Π:TN
A:MO

mj: GA
ins: MD

Dowis v. Mud Slingers, Inc.

621 S.E.2d 413 (Ga. 2005)

GA:A
MD:Π

HINES, Justice.

This Court granted certiorari to the Court of Appeals in *Dowis v. Mud Slinger Concrete*, 269 Ga. App. 805 (605 S.E.2d 615) (2004), to consider whether the conflict of laws rule lex loci delicti should be retained in Georgia. For the reasons which follow, this Court will not abandon the traditional rule.

Johnny Edwin Dowis, a Tennessee resident, was hired by a Missouri corporation, Mud Slingers, Inc. ("Mud Slingers"), whose president is Michael Clement Graves, to hang large sheets of precast plaster molding at a national chain hotel in Roswell, Georgia. Dowis was injured at the Roswell project when he fell four stories from the basket of a telescopic boom forklift operated by Graves.

Mud Slingers had workers' compensation insurance in Missouri, where Dowis filed his claim and received benefits. Dowis later filed this tort action in Georgia seeking damages against Mud Slingers and Graves. Dowis argued that, under Missouri's workers' compensation law, he could collect benefits and bring a tort action against Mud Slingers and/or Graves. Applying the exclusive remedy provision of the Georgia Workers' Compensation Act, and the lex loci delicti rule regarding the applicable substantive law, the trial court granted summary judgment to the defendants. The Court of Appeals affirmed . . . holding that lex loci delicti and the consequent application of Georgia's exclusive remedy provision precluded Dowis from maintaining his tort action in Georgia. In so doing, the Court of Appeals correctly noted that this Court has addressed the issue of the viability of the rule of lex loci delicti. . . .

There are several . . . approaches to the resolution of conflict of laws issues in tort cases. . . . [The court next reviewed the Restatement (First) of Conflict of Laws, Brainerd Currie's governmental interest approach, Robert Leflar's "choice-influencing considerations," and the doctrine of lex fori.]

Finally, a majority of the states that have abandoned the rule of lex loci delicti have embraced the formulation expressed in the Restatement (Second) of Conflict of Laws, which calls for an assessment of which jurisdiction has the "most significant relationship" to the dispute, based upon several sets of factors. The appellants Dowis urge that Georgia join this group of states and adopt the "most significant relationship" test of the Restatement (Second) of Conflict of Laws, and thus, allow them under Missouri law to proceed with their Georgia lawsuit against Mud Slingers and Graves. . . . So the initial question becomes whether the approach of the Restatement (Second) of Conflict of Laws is superior to the traditional rule utilized in Georgia.

The doctrine of lex loci delicti has served the resolution of conflict of laws issues in tort actions in this State for nearly 100 years. It is desirable to have stability and certainty in the law; therefore, stare decisis is a valid and compelling argument for maintaining the doctrine. Moreover, as appellants acknowledge, lex loci delicti has the virtues of consistency, predictability, and relative ease of application.

Appellants and other opponents of the rule criticize its perceived rigidness and argue that its strict application is insufficient to address the complexities of modern litigation and can lead to unjust results, in that the results may be "unrelated to the contemporary interests of the states involved or the realistic expectations of the parties." But such criticism ignores several salient facts. As appellees point out, some courts in other jurisdictions have been motivated to depart from the traditional rule in order to redress perceived unjust results by applying their own law. In fact, the first departure by a sister state from the use of lex loci delicti accomplished the application of the law of that state. See *Babcock v. Jackson*, 12 N.Y.2d 473, 191 N.E.2d 279, 240 N.Y.S.2d 743 (N.Y. Ct. App. 1963). By contrast, appellants are asking this Court to abrogate its long-used conflict of laws rule in order to bypass Georgia law. Furthermore, the criticism glosses over the fact that the courts of this State have the power to ameliorate the sometimes seeming harshness of the rule when public policy considerations dictate that they do so.

Appellants also go so far as to assert that the rule of lex loci delicti is premised upon "absolute fortuity," in that the place of the incident giving rise to the litigation is an entirely fortuitous factor. But this ignores the reality that the place of an allegedly tortious act is not irrelevant to the conflict issue, in that a state has an interest in wrongs committed within its boundaries. The crux of the matter in regard to criticism of the traditional rule is the common underlying misconception that the resolution of a conflict of laws in complex litigation requires an equally complicated mechanism to do so.

The approach taken by the Restatement (Second) of Conflict of Laws (1971) certainly fits a description of complexity. It is expansive; it provides a multi-step procedure for making the determination of which state's law should prevail. This layered analysis has been described as "eclectic" because it represents a combination of several choice-of-law methodologies. It has been said to function like a code — that is, for any given problem, several Second Restatement sections are likely to apply. This is in contrast to Restatements in other areas of law which tend to pronounce fairly discrete rules. The approach of the Restatement (Second) of Conflict of Laws has been described as working through three related functions, "in the reverse order of their best use."

. . . The very flexibility of the approach of the Restatement (Second) has proved to be problematic. There are those who have criticized it as a tool for courts to simply engage in "contact counting" without consideration of what is espoused in the Restatement (Second), that is, the interests and policies of the states in question. It has been said to have "indeterminate language and lack of concrete guidelines." Others find it:

> has the irony of dominating the field while bewildering its users. The result is a set
> of choice-of-law decisions so lacking in uniformity that the Second Restatement's

balancing test has become chimeric, taking on vastly different forms in different courts. Erratic applications may be partly due to its code-like function, which can require the application of two or more black letter sections, each with multiple analytical steps. . . . Second Restatement adoptions necessarily assume different forms in different states, even without aberrational applications.

James P. George, False Conflicts and Faulty Analyses: Judicial Misuse of Governmental Interests in the Second Restatement of Conflict of Laws, 23 Rev. of Litig. 489, 491-492 (Summer 2004).

The adoption of the Restatement (Second) approach has not brought certainty or uniformity to the law. Quite the contrary. As the Supreme Court of Alabama noted,

Some state courts routinely list [the Restatement's] relevant sections in their opinions and try to follow them; this task is easiest when the case is controlled by one of the Restatement Second's specific narrow rules. Other state courts have not been consistent in their terminology about what approach they are following, and others have retained primary emphasis on the place of the wrong in tort cases, even while abandoning the lex loci delicti for the Restatement Second. . . .

A review of cases shows that while the rule of lex loci delicti of the original Restatement is attacked because of its seeming rigidity and its insistence on the application of a few specific rules, the approach of the Restatement (Second) fails to provide enough guidance to the courts to produce even a semblance of uniformity among the states following its method.

The methodology is not only complex, but it provides no underlying principle other than applying the law of the state that has the "most significant relationship" to the issue. . . . As a result, it has become difficult to predict what a court will do when faced with choice of law issues, and each case seems to demand an ad hoc determination. For attorneys, this lack of predictability may discourage settlement; it certainly inhibits an accurate case valuation. For judges, choice of law issues take an inordinate amount of time and require a fairly complex analysis.

Shirley A. Wiegand, Fifty Conflict of Laws "Restatements": Merging Judicial Discretion and Legislative Endorsement, 65 La. L. Rev. 1, 4 (2004).

The inescapable conclusion is that the approach of the Restatement (Second) of Conflict of Laws is not superior to the traditional rule of lex loci delicti currently used in Georgia. Nor have the other major approaches mentioned earlier proven to be a panacea for the resolution of conflict of laws issues.[7] In fact, the array of "modern" conflict approaches and their seemingly unending

7. Currie's "governmental interest" approach fails to adequately deal with true conflicts and is easily manipulated by identifying alternative governmental interests of a forum law, thereby leading to forum favoritism. Leflar's "choice-influencing considerations" almost always leads the forum to select its own law; it has been described as "plagued by excessive forum favoritism." The concept of lex fori, by definition, requires that the law of the forum governs the rights and liabilities of the parties.

variations have been described as creating "a veritable playpen for judicial policy-makers."[8] Shirley A. Wiegand, Fifty Conflict of Laws "Restatements": Merging Judicial Discretion and Legislative Endorsement, 65 La. L. Rev. 1, 4 (2004). This Court declines to engage in such a policymaking exercise.[9]

Utilizing a rule in the area of conflict of laws can serve the ends of justice because it furnishes the judicial machinery by which like situations are adjudged equally. Such a rule of law can fulfill an essential function of concrete justice. This Court will retain its long-held conflict of laws rule not out of blind adherence but rather, out of the candid recognition that the subsequently-developed theories have significant problems. The relative certainty, predictability, and ease of the application of lex loci delicti, even though sometimes leading to results which may appear harsh, are preferable to the inconsistency and capriciousness that the replacement choice-of-law approaches have wrought.

The rule of lex loci delicti remains the law of Georgia, and the judgment of the Court of Appeals is affirmed.

Notes on
DOWIS *AND CHOOSING THE OPTIMAL METHODOLOGY*

1. What was the major reason that the *Dowis* court chose to stay with the Restatement (First)? Was the court convinced that it was by far the best approach? Or, to the contrary, perhaps the court was just being risk averse, inclined, like a famous Prince of Denmark, to "bear those ills we have [t]han fly to others that we know not of. . . ."[43]

2. As mentioned earlier in this chapter, courts and scholars have launched several criticisms of the Restatement (First). Many rejected the whole concept of a vested right as artificial and based on the faulty premise that rights exist independently of the courts that recognize them. Others focused on the First Restatement's failure to account for the content of laws. Still another group of critics have pointed out that the Restatement (First) requirement of identifying one jurisdiction where rights vest often produces arbitrary results that judges are then tempted to avoid through manipulative escape devices. *See, e.g., Montenko v. MGM Distributing,* 921 P.2d 933, 934 (Nev. 1996) (observing the Restatement (First) "can produce harsh results because the approach demands a blind application of the law of the place of the accident"). Recently, Professors Lea Brilmayer and Raechel

---

8. The current situation in the area of conflict theories has also been unfavorably described as "a total disaster," "chaos," "gibberish," and "a conflicts mine field in a maze constructed by professors drunk on theories." Shirley A. Wiegand, *Fifty Conflict of Laws "Restatements": Merging Judicial Discretion and Legislative Endorsement,* 65 LA. L. REV. 1, 4 (2004).

9. In the context of examining the traditional conflict of laws rule lex loci contractus, it has been suggested that any adoption of the approach of the Restatement (Second) of Conflict of Laws is a matter properly for the General Assembly.

43. William Shakespeare, *Hamlet, Prince of Denmark,* act 3, sc.1.

Anglin have argued the Restatement (First) is most problematic in those circumstances when the contact (such as the place of injury) that triggers the First Restatement choice of law rule "stands alone." Lea Brilmayer & Raechel Anglin, *Choice of Law Theory and the Metaphysics of the Stand-Alone Trigger*, 95 Iowa L. Rev. 1125, 1125 (2010). In this instance, they observe, the First Restatement appears particularly irrational and unjust because many other factors often cluster around another jurisdiction. Does *Dowis* reckon with any of these criticisms?

In fairness to the *Dowis* court, it joins several other courts and scholars who have chosen allegiance to the First Restatement, as the most time-tested of the approaches. A particularly favorable report comes from Professor Patrick Borchers, who performed an empirical study seeking to detect whether various choice of law methodologies inspired bias toward plaintiffs, toward application of forum law, and toward local parties. Borchers concluded that First Restatement courts exhibited less bias and were more sincere in earnestly following the methodology than judges applying the more modern methodologies. Patrick Borchers, *The Choice-of-Law Revolution: An Empirical Study*, 49 Wash. & Lee L. Rev. 357, 379 (1992). Likewise, empirical work by Professor Michael Solimine suggested that courts applying modern approaches tend to produce more "pro-forum and pro-tort recovery" results than those following the First Restatement. Michael E. Solimine, *An Economic and Empirical Analysis of Choice of Law*, 24 Ga. L. Rev. 49, 81-89 (1989). In addition, a later econometric study by Professor Stuart Thiel found that First Restatement courts use forum law less than courts applying modern methodologies and that interest analysis states more likely favor forum residents than states applying other approaches. Stuart Thiel, *Choice of Law and the Home-Court Advantage: Evidence*, 2 Am. L. & Econ. Rev. 291 (2000).

3. *Dowis* also has plenty of company in its criticism of the Second Restatement approach. In fact, the Second Restatement's success is remarkable given the deluge of damaging commentary among courts and scholars. While not unanimous on this point, most scholarly commentary on the Restatement (Second) is negative. For largely negative assessment of the Restatement (Second), see, e.g., Frederich K. Juenger, *A Third Conflicts Restatement?*, 75 Ind. L.J. 403, 403-406 (2000); Larry Kramer, *Choice of Law in American Courts in 1990: Trends and Developments*, 39 Am. J. Comp. L. 465, 466, 486-489 (1991); Douglas Layock, *Equal Citizens of Equal and Territorial States: The Constitutional Foundations of Choice of Law*, 92 Colum. L. Rev. 249, 253 (1992); Bruce Posnak, *The Restatement (Second): Some Not So Fine Tuning for Restatement (Third): A Very Well-Curried Leflar over Reese with Korn on the Side (Or Is It Cob?)*, 75 Ind L.J. 561 (2000); Symeon C. Symeonides, *A New Conflicts Restatement: Why Not?*, 5 J. Private Int'l L. 1 (Aug. 5, 2009); Symeon C. Symeonides, *The Need for a Third Conflicts Restatement (and a Proposal for Torts Conflicts)*, 75 Ind. L.J. 437, 439-446 (2000); Louise Weinberg, *A Structural Revision*

of the Conflicts Restatement, 75 IND. L.J. 475, 477-480 (2009). For a more positive assessment, see, e.g., Harold P. Southerland, *A Plea for the Proper Use of the Second Restatement of Conflict of Laws,* 27 VT. L. REV. 1 (2002); Gary J. Simson, *Leave Bad Enough Alone,* 75 IND. L.J. 649 (2000); Kevin Tuininga, *Forty-Plus Years of Iowa Choice-of-Law Precedent: The Aftermath of the Restatement (Second) of Conflict of Laws,* 43 CREIGHTON L. REV. 205 (2009).

4. Note the suggestion in footnote 9 of the *Dowis* opinion that the Second Restatement is so policy-based that it would be more appropriate for a legislative body to authorize its adoption than for a court to do so. Do you agree with this assessment?

5. One of the arguments that *Dowis* cited in favor of the Restatement (First) is that it provides rules of law "by which like situations are adjudged equally," thereby implementing "concrete justice." The Supreme Court of West Virginia made similar statements in rejecting the suggestion that it should no longer follow the Restatement (First):

> [Despite "pretty intellectual" arguments to the contrary], we still prefer a rule. The lesson of history is that methods of analysis that permit dissection of the jural bundle constituting a tort and its environment produce protracted litigation and voluminous, inscrutable appellate opinions, while rules get cases settled quickly and cheaply.

Paul v. National Life, 352 S.E.2d 550 (W. Va. 1986). This statement implicates the debate about which type of analytical governing instrument works best in choice of law, rules or standards. The Perspective on Rules and Standards, immediately below, takes up this question.

6. What do law and economics theorists have to say about conflict of law methodology? For the most part, theorists have used economic theory as a tool for judging the effectiveness of existing choice of law methodology, rather than as a source of choice of law doctrine itself. Professor Ralf Michaels concludes that economics "does not and probably cannot fulfill [the] function of creating doctrine itself." Ralf Michaels, *Economics of Law as Choice of Law,* 71 LAW & CONTEMP. PROBS. 73, 76 (2008).

Yet in the realm of evaluating the merits and demerits of existing approaches, law and economics yields nuanced insights. Overall, the First Restatement fares well. For example, Judge Richard Posner suggests an economic justification for the First Restatement lex loci deliciti rule for tort cases. He starts with the proposition that in tort cases involving two states, both states will have an interest in its own resident's success. RICHARD A. POSNER, ECONOMIC ANALYSIS OF LAW 806 (8th ed. 2011). Posner calls this type of interest *distributive,* and explains that each state's distributive interests offset each other and can therefore be ignored. However, he points out, each state also has allocative interests. For instance, if a resident of State A is driving in State B and injures a resident of State B, State A will have an interest in its residents being able to drive in State B without undue restrictions. *Id.* at 807. State B, on the other hand, has an interest in protecting its residents from being injured by a negligent driver. As result of these *allocative* interests, it becomes important that the accident occurred in State B. One can reasonably assume that State B's rules are tailored to the relevant conditions in that state, such as driving conditions. This may implicate details about the state's weather, geography, common recreational activities, and the like. As a consequence, State B — the place of the accident — enjoys a "comparative regulatory advantage in regard to accidents which occur in B." *Id.* Posner is not a fan of governmental interest analysis, opining that "the issue should not be" whether a state has an interest in applying its law, "but which state's law makes the best fit with circumstances of the dispute." *Id.*

For law and economics theorists, an important factor in evaluating conflict of laws methodology is transaction costs, whether these costs arise by reason of complexity, the possibility of judicial error, or a similar problem. Posner maintains that the lex loci rule fares well in light of this concern, since the other choice of law approaches tend to be more case-specific, to inject multifactor balancing into the analysis, and to otherwise foster greater uncertainty. *Id.* at 806; Richard A. Posner, *The Decline of Law as an Autonomous Discipline 1962-1987*, 100 HARV. L. REV. 761, 770 (1987). Professors Ribstein and O'Hara agree, concluding that the Restatement (First)'s clear rules "promote predictability and enable individual choice." Erin A. O'Hara & Larry E. Ribstein, *From Politics to Efficiency in Choice of Law*, 67 U. CHI. L. REV. 1151 (2000). *See also* Erin A. O'Hara & Larry E. Ribstein, *Conflict of Laws and Choice of Law*, ELGAR'S ENCYCLOPEDIA OF LAW AND ECONOMICS, Part IX, Section 9600 (Boudewijn Bouckaert et al. eds., 2000) (concluding that the First Restatement "likely provides much greater predictability despite its escape devices").

PERSPECTIVE ON RULES AND STANDARDS

Discussion of which choice of law approach is superior implicates a recurrent debate among legal thinkers: what is the most appropriate form for a law to take? Two contrasting forms that often frame this debate are rules and standards. Reaching an understanding on the question of whether rules or standards govern more effectively is helpful in assessing the merits of the various choice of law approaches.

Scholars define a "rule" as a "legal directive" requiring a decision maker to reach a certain result upon finding the presence of certain triggering facts.[44]

---

44. Kathleen Sullivan, *The Supreme Court, 1991 Term: The Justices of Rules and Standards*, 106 HARV. L. REV. 22, 58 (1992) (describing a rule as binding "a decisionmaker to respond in a determinate way to the presence of delimited triggering facts"). *See, e.g.*, Pierre Schlag, *Rules and*

Some emphasize that rules "entail an advance determination of what conduct is permissible."[45] Rules enable formalistic decision making, associated with categories defined by bright-line specifics. The First Restatement of Conflict of Laws is a rule-based approach.

By contrast to rules, standards require that the decision maker apply a "background principle or policy" to a set of facts before rendering a binding decision about the facts.[46] Standards allow the decision maker to decide whether certain conduct should be allowed *after* the conduct has occurred and the court has evaluated the conduct's effect. Standards implement functional decision making, often associated with balancing tests, and promote reasoning by reference to the purposes underlying legal directives. Modern choice of law methodologies tend to promote standards-based decision making, as reflected in the Restatement (Second) of Conflict of Laws, governmental interest analysis, comparative impairment, and the better rule of law approach.

Although out of favor for a time, the rule-based approach to decision making has experienced a resurgence of support. Proponents argue that rules reduce complex reasoning and constrain discretion, thereby promoting uniformity, efficiency, predictability, and even-handed justice. Justice Antonin Scalia is an outspoken proponent of rule-based decision making, arguing that rules of law should be pre-announced so as to limit arbitrary authority and to minimize legal administration costs.[47] Not surprisingly, rules-based decision making is popular among law and economics thinkers. Indeed, the rule-like quality of the Restatement (First) accounts for its popularity among some law and economics thinkers.[48] One scholar has argued that the standard-based thinking reflected in governmental interest analysis creates high transaction costs, which leads to "frequent forum preference and thus globally suboptimal outcomes."[49] Law and economics thinkers, however, have not reached consensus on the subject, and some celebrate the benefits of ad hoc adaptation made possible by standards.[50]

Although rule-based decision making has gained in popularity, many are dubious of its merits — particularly in the conflict of laws realm. In particular, courts and scholars observe that its simplicity is illusory, since the rigidity of rules can spawn

---

Standards, 33 UCLA L. Rev. 379, 381 (1985) (conceptualizing legal rules as "a series of directives," where each directive has "a 'trigger' . . . and a 'response' that requires or authorizes a legal consequence when that [trigger] is present").

45. Louis Kaplow, *Rules versus Standards: An Economic Analysis*, 42 Duke L.J. 557, 560 (1992). Kaplow's analysis is cited widely within legal scholarship.

46. Kathleen Sullivan, *The Justices of Rules and Standards*, 106 Harv. L. Rev., *supra* n.10 at 58. *See also* Mark D. Rosen, *Nonformalistic Law in Time and Space*, 66 U. Chi. L. Rev. 622, 623 (1999) (using the term "nonformalistic law" as synonymous with standards and defining standards as abstract concepts that "refer to the ultimate goal or policy animating the law").

47. Antonin Scalia, *The Rule of Law as a Law of Rules*, 56 U. Chi. L. Rev. 1175 (1989).

48. Richard A. Posner, Economic Analysis of Law 806 (8th ed. 2011) (arguing that the Restatement (First) avoids multifactor balancing); Erin A. O'Hara & Larry E. Ribstein, *Conflict of Laws and Choice of Law*, Elgar's Encyclopedia of Law and Economics, Part IX, Section 9600 (Boudewijn Bouckaert et al. eds., 2000) (praising the rule-like quality of the First Restatement, although advising that it be modified "to avoid frequent arbitrary results").

49. Ralf Michaels, *Economics of Law as Choice of Law*, 71 Law & Contemp. Probs. 73, 94 (2008).

50. Joel P. Trachtman, *Conflict of Laws and Accuracy in the Allocation of Government Responsibility*, 26 Vand. J. Transnat'l L. 975 (1994).

exceptions and complexity. The escape valves associated with the First Restatement provide evidence of this. Moreover, once a judge decides to make an end run around a rule, judicial candor can suffer and complications multiply. Take, for example, a court's decision to re-characterize a prenuptial agreement problem as a marriage issue, rather than a contract issue. The court making the re-characterization may seek to trigger the place of celebration's law so as to avoid an inequity that would arise if it applied the law of the place of making the contract to the specific case. What does this mean for the proper characterization for future prenuptial agreements where the inequity is not an issue? Should the court use a marriage characterization on the basis of precedent, or should the court distinguish the precedent and use a contract characterization?

In addition to pointing out deficiencies in rule-based decision making, some proponents of standards-based decision making affirmatively celebrate how the ad hoc nature of standards can make them effective regulatory instruments. These thinkers argue that standards allow courts to do what courts do best: tailor the law to the specifics of a case in order to do justice. From this point of view, the flexibility of the methodologies such as Restatement (Second) or the better rule of law approach makes it more likely that these approaches are better able to respond to the challenges of dueling jurisdictional claims and to governing in the ever-changing world.

Two choice of law scholars argue that one component of standards-based decision making, balancing, is particularly well suited to the choice of law context. They maintain that choice of law disputes require consideration of so many variables that a single "trigger factor," such as under the First Restatement, is simply not up to the task.[51] Balancing, they suggest, allows a court to take into account the number of contacts supporting a particular state's law, and results in minimizing the circumstances when laws are applied extraterritorially.

The debate about rules versus standards may likely never resolve. Understanding the two poles, however, can provide an important factor in evaluating the overall merits of competing choice of law approaches.

J. STATUTORY CHOICE OF LAW RULES

States have statutory choice of law rules on a number of specific subjects. Consider this example from the Mississippi Trusts and Estates Code stating that

> [a]ll personal property situated in this state shall descend and be distributed according to the laws of this state regulating the descent and distribution of such property, regardless of all marital right which may have accrued in other states,

51. Lea Brilmayer & Raechel Anglin, *Choice of Law Theory and the Metaphysics of the Stand-Alone Trigger*, 95 Iowa L. Rev. 1125, 1173 (2010).

and notwithstanding the domicile of the deceased may have been in another state, and whether the heirs or persons entitled to distribution be in this state or not. . . .

Miss. Code Ann. §91-1-1. Myriad other examples exist.[52] Sometimes courts interpret what might be designated as a substantive internal law provision in a state statute as a choice of law directive. For example, the Texas Supreme Court interpreted the Texas securities statute's prohibition on offering or selling unregistered securities "in this state" as a choice of law directive. *See Citizens Ins. Co. of America v. Daccach*, 217 S.W.3d 430 (Tex. 2007) (interpreting Tex. Rev. Civ. Stat. art. 581-12A, which provides that "no person, firm, corporation or dealer shall, directly or through agents, offer for sale, sell or make a sale of any securities in this state without first being registered as in this Act provided").

Where statutory choice of law rules exist, state courts nearly always defer to those laws, regardless of the choice of law approach generally followed in the jurisdiction. Some common law methodologies make explicit this deference to statutory rules. For example, the Restatement (Second) §6(1) directs that "[a] court, subject to constitutional restrictions, will follow a statutory directive of its own state on choice of law."

The first section below focuses on a particularly significant type of statutory choice of law rule enacted throughout the United States: borrowing statutes governing statutes of limitation. Another important issue pertaining to statutory choice of law rules concerns the role of comprehensive choice of law rules to replace state common law. The second section below takes up this issue.

1. Statutes of Limitation

Statutes of limitation can have an enormous influence on the fortunes of litigants (and by extension — their lawyers!). Technically speaking, most statutes of limitation limit only the time for bringing suit and do not extinguish the right to sue. Thus, if the statute of limitation has expired under forum law, one might still be able to pursue a successful lawsuit if one can convince the court to apply a non-forum statute of limitation or find a different forum in which to sue.

---

52. Examples from trusts and estates law tend to be common. Consider also this choice of law provision from the Delaware statute governing execution of wills:

A written will signed by the testator, or by some person subscribing the testator's name in the testator's presence and at the testator's express direction, is valid if executed in compliance with [Delaware statutes] or if its execution complies with the law at the time of execution of the place where the will is executed, or of the place where at the time of the execution or at the time of death the testator is domiciled, as a place of abode or is a national.

12 Del. Code §1306. Another, far different sort of statutory or constitutional directive that narrows the range of laws that can be considered are provisions such as the "Save Our State Amendment," which catalogs legal sources that Oklahoma courts may use when deciding cases, and those the courts may not use. Forbidden sources included "the legal precepts of other nations or cultures," international law, and "Sharia Law." Further discussion of such provisions appears earlier in this chapter in connection with the First Restatement and the public policy exception.

A plaintiff may have difficulty finding another forum that has personal jurisdiction over the defendant. In addition, the plaintiff may find an alternative forum that does have personal jurisdiction over the defendant, but determine this forum is inconvenient or strategically unattractive. Accordingly, the plaintiff's ability to navigate choice of law rules governing statutes of limitation regularly affects whether she will successfully pursue litigation.

The traditional approach to statutes of limitation characterized them as procedural and, accordingly, as governed by forum law. The Restatement (First) reflected this approach, recognizing exceptions for adverse possession claims and claims based on a statute that imposes a statute of limitation as a condition on the enjoyment of a right. Amid criticism that the First Restatement approach encourages forum shopping, legislatures began changing this rule through "borrowing statutes," which instruct forum courts to borrow the statute of another state under certain circumstances. The first decision below, *Duke v. Housen*, illustrates a borrowing statute framed and applied in a traditional choice of law context.

The original version of the Second Restatement of Conflict of Laws provided an approach similar to the First Restatement. The American Law Institute revised this Second Restatement provision in 1988 to provide for stronger exceptions to the presumption that forum law should apply. The second case set forth below, *DeLoach v. Alfred*, illustrates the revised Second Restatement approach to statutes of limitation. As you might imagine, courts that do not follow the Restatement (Second) but that follow some version of interest analysis will often deploy interest analysis to choose among competing statutes of limitations. Because statutes of limitations are generally designed, at least in part, to protect forum courts from being forced to adjudicate stale claims, the forum will always have a weighty interest for the purpose of interest analysis. Accordingly, interest analysis jurisdictions tend to apply forum statutes of limitation.

Another modern approach similar to the Restatement (Second) is reflected in the Uniform Conflict of Laws Limitations Act. This uniform act treats statutes of limitation as substantive and generally directs courts to apply another state's statute of limitation to claims that are "substantively based . . . upon the law" of that other state. Uniform Conflict of Laws — Limitations Act §2.

These various approaches to statutes of limitation can create a hodge-podge, with courts sometimes mixing components of each approach. Adding to the complexity is a related legislative enactment, the statute of repose, which might be described as a statute of limitation on steroids. Statutes of repose fill the gaps where statutes of limitation do not operate, such as when an injury manifests only after significant delay or when tolling rules prevent a limitations period from running. Statutes of repose now often operate in medical malpractice and products liability suits. The last case in this section, *Chang v. Baxter Healthcare Corporation*, illustrates a statute of repose in the context of a multidistrict products liability suit.

Duke v. Housen

589 P.2d 334 (Wyo. 1979)

RAPER, J.

In the appeal now before the court, appellant-defendant challenges the jury verdict and district court judgment entered against him awarding to appellee-plaintiff, based upon defendant's alleged grossly negligent infection of plaintiff with venereal disease, compensatory and punitive damages in the sum of $1,300,000. Through this appellate challenge, defendant raises the following questions:

1. Is the action barred by a statute of limitations?

. . .

For the reasons stated in detail herein, we shall reverse on the ground that the action is barred by the statute of limitations. . . .

In early April, 1970, plaintiff was living, working, and going to college part-time in the Washington, D.C. area. On April 4 of that year she was introduced by her brother to defendant; and on the same night and early morning of April 5, following dinner and dancing plus moderate drinking, engaged in sexual intercourse with defendant in the front seat of his pickup truck. On April 8th, at least partially in response to defendant's sudden and convincing professions of love and desire to marry, plaintiff met defendant at the LaGuardia airport in New York and subsequently traveled by truck with him from New York to Denver, Colorado, engaging on and off in acts of sexual intercourse with defendant along the way. Upon reaching Denver, defendant, having lost interest in plaintiff, lodged her in a local hotel and left for his home in Meeteetse, Wyoming. Plaintiff, after contacting her brother and waiting for him to arrive, subsequently traveled to Meeteetse and confronted defendant concerning his behavior. As a result, it was agreed that defendant would accompany plaintiff and her brother back to Washington, D.C. and apologize to the family; yet after arriving in Washington and discussing the situation with her family, plaintiff for some reason which is neither totally clear nor probably capable of elucidation, accompanied the defendant to New York, there occupying a hotel room together and engaged once more in sexual intercourse with him. Finally, on the morning of April 21, 1970, defendant broke off his relationship with the plaintiff and informed her for the first time that he had venereal disease, gonorrhea, and that now she probably had it too.

At trial, through the presentation of voluminous testimony by both parties, it was established that at some time prior to March 22, 1970, defendant had become aware that he was probably infected with venereal disease for on that day he visited a doctor in Dallas, Texas, complaining of pain and a urethral discharge. In response, the examining physician took a sample of the discharge for testing and administered a large dosage of fast-acting penicillin, telling defendant to return the next day for the test results. When defendant returned on March 23, 1970, the test results for gonorrhea having been found positive, a larger dose of a longer-acting penicillin was administered and defendant was advised to see his own doctor for further treatment. Defendant then left by plane for

New York, arriving the same day, March 23, where immediately upon arrival he contacted his own physician, who after an external examination, stated that he could find no "clinical evidence of gonorrhea" — defendant had no current urethral discharge. On the basis of the previous treatment and this current information, defendant asserted at trial that it was his belief that as of his first sexual contact with the plaintiff on the night of April 4-5, 1970, his infection with gonorrhea had been cured.

Plaintiff, after being told by defendant on April 21, 1970, that she had probably contracted gonorrhea from him and should see a doctor, left New York for Washington, D.C. and, the following day, April 22, 1970, visited her personal physician who through a smear test confirmed that gonorrhea was present. In response to medication, plaintiff's infection with what her physician described as a "classic case of asymptomatic gonorrhea" was arrested by May 14, 1970, but more serious problems were to develop. Beginning in January, 1973, plaintiff noticed a pain in her lower right side which by March, 1973, had become so severe and constant as to require medical attention. After various external medical tests provided negative results and antibiotic medication proved ineffective, major exploratory surgery was performed in July, 1973. As a result, plaintiff's physician found that because of the gonorrhea infection, and possibly other related secondary infections as well, scar tissue adhesions had formed within a number of areas of appellee's lower abdomen. He testified that although he had lysed (loosened or detached by surgical procedures) the adhesions, thus somewhat relieving temporarily the severe pain, because of the nature of the scar tissue involved, new adhesions would eventually form and the pain would very probably return again and continue in this cyclical manner for the remainder of plaintiff's life. He further advised that because of the scarring involved, plaintiff's ability to bear children had been greatly reduced. . . .

Plaintiff filed this action on April 19, 1974, seeking hospital expenses, doctor's expenses, wage loss, future medical expense, as well as damages for pain and suffering, present and future. In addition, based on an allegation that defendant was guilty of gross negligence when he infected her with gonorrhea, plaintiff requested $1 million in exemplary damages. By interrogatory, the jury found that defendant had been infected with gonorrhea at the time of his relations with plaintiff between April 4 and April 21, 1970; and by verdict awarded plaintiff $300,000.00 in compensatory damages, and $1,000,000.00 in exemplary or punitive damages. Following denial of various post-trial motions, the appeal herein was filed.

By way of both the answer filed in response to plaintiff's complaint as well as by motions prior, during and after trial, defendant alleged and strongly argued that based upon applicable statutes and case law, plaintiff's cause of action had been barred by the passage of time and her complaint should therefore be dismissed. Rule 8(c), W.R.C.P. requires that the statute of limitations be specifically set forth as an affirmative defense. In response, the trial judge ruled that inasmuch as plaintiff's scar adhesions had not been discovered until a date much later than when the infection itself had occurred, the applicable time period for limitation of action purposes was to be computed only from discovery of the adhesions; and defendant's assertion was thus denied.

Statutes of limitation have long been a part of the jurisprudence of the United States, all its states and the State of Wyoming. They are pragmatic devices to save courts from stale claim litigation and sparse citizens from having to defend when memories have faded, witnesses are unavailable by death or disappearance and evidence is lost. Statutes of limitation are arbitrary by their very nature and do not discriminate between the just and unjust claim. They are not judicially made but represent legislative and public policy controlling the right to litigate. The statutes operate against even the most meritorious of claims and courts have no right to deny their application. When considering the statute of limitations, the nature of injury, its extent, the amount of money damages involved, social considerations, and the emotional appeal the facts may have must pass to the background. The circumstances are only significant in the bearing they may have on where the cause of action arose, when it arose and when the time expired for pursuing the applicable judicial remedy.

At the very foundation of plaintiff's claim against defendant lie the principles of the law of tort. One who negligently exposes another to an infectious or contagious disease, which such other person thereby contracts, can be held liable in damages for his actions. Yet while the basic claim raised by plaintiff, albeit an unusual one, sounds in tort, the circumstance of its pursuance in Wyoming is somewhat unique. Since, as the evidence points up, there was no sexual contact between plaintiff and defendant in Wyoming, nor any tortious injury in this state, simple logic reveals that there could be no tortious conduct, no negligent exposure of plaintiff's body to disease by defendant in this, the forum state. There can be no question that plaintiff's cause of action could only be found as having arisen elsewhere.

. . .

The heavy weight of authority in interstate tort cases such as here with elements in different jurisdictions, is that the law of the place where the plaintiff sustains injury to her person controls. Restatement of Conflict of Laws, §377. At common law, the limitation period of the forum jurisdiction, the lex fori, generally controlled the time within which causes of action had to be pursued, regardless of the fact that the cause itself in all its elements may have accrued outside the forum jurisdiction. Only when the limitation of action statute of the foreign jurisdiction in which the cause arose could be deemed substantive law rather than procedural would the foreign statute be applied by the forum court. In order to avoid the confusion and problems associated with attempting to determine when a foreign limitation of action statute was substantive or procedural, a majority of states, including Wyoming, enacted what are referred to as "borrowing" statutes. Section 1-3-117, which we find to be controlling in this regard, is simple and clear:

If by the laws of the state or country where the cause of action arose the action is barred, it is also barred in this state.

The plaintiff takes an unusual position that since the case is tried in Wyoming, it must be tried under Wyoming law as a whole, including §1-3-105, prescribing a period of limitation of four years "after the cause of action accrues," pertaining to causes of action arising in Wyoming. She then asserts that under the statutory section, since she discovered she was infected with gonorrhea "around April 22, 1970," her action was timely brought within the Wyoming four year period by filing her complaint on April 19, 1974. She elects to ignore the borrowing statute, §1-3-117, supra.

[We are constrained] by the legislative policy of the state announced in its limitations "borrowing" statute . . . to require its courts to bar suits if the right to sue had already expired in another jurisdiction where the crucial combination of circumstances giving the right to sue had taken place, the existence of which affords a party a right to judicial interference in his behalf.

Plaintiff also argues, and the trial judge so held, that the statute of limitations did not commence to run until October, 1973, when adhesions resulting from the infection were discovered because it is the injury therefrom for which the damages are sought. That position is not the accepted rule. . . .

The jury found as a fact that the defendant was the bearer of gonorrhea during the period April 4, 1970 to April 21, 1970. The plaintiff's testimony, admitted by the defendant, is that sexual intercourse between the plaintiff and defendant took place on the dates and in other state jurisdictions in accordance with an itinerary as follows:

April 4-5, 1970. State of Virginia.
April 7-8, 1970. Tuxedo, New York.
April 8-9, 1970. Erie, Pennsylvania.
April 9-10, 1970. State of Iowa.
April 10-11, 1970. Ogallala, Nebraska.
April 20-21, 1970. New York City, New York.

There is no evidence of sexual intercourse taking place in the State of Wyoming. We must therefore look elsewhere for a jurisdiction in which the cause arose. While it is perhaps unusual that the defendant perpetrated his negligent acts and caused injury to plaintiff's body in several different states and which may give an appearance of complexity, an application of settled rules of tort law in the jurisdictions involved clears away any suggestion of obscurity.

The limitation of action statute of the foreign jurisdiction in which the cause in question arose is applied by the forum court irregardless [sic] of whether or not the foreign limitation could be characterized as substantive or procedural. Thus, in almost all instances, if a plaintiff's cause of action is time-barred in the jurisdiction in which the cause of action arose, it would be barred by the passage of time in the forum court as well. Such a rule not only clears up any substantive procedural conflict problem, but eliminates as well the possibility of the plaintiff shopping for a favorable forum in which to revive a dead claim. It thus becomes of acute importance in the situation at bar to specifically determine, for limitation of actions purposes, where and when plaintiff's cause of action arose. In making such a determination based upon a borrowed limitational period, in all jurisdictions having a borrowing statute, with the exception of Ohio, not only is the specific prescriptive period utilized, but all of its accouterments as well whether in the form of additional statutory provisions or interpretive judicial decisions:

> But when such [limitational] statute is so borrowed, it is not wrenched bodily out of its own setting, but taken along with it are the court decisions of its own state which interpret and apply it, and the companion statutes which limit and restrict its operation. This we think is the general law.

Thus, in applying a "borrowed" statute, we must consider not only the borrowed limitation of action statute itself, but also any applicable tolling or other statutes as well as pertinent court cases. In effect, plaintiff's cause must be viewed as if filed in the state where under the laws of that state a cause of action accrued.

We find and hold that a cause of action arose in the state of New York on April 8, 1970 and April 21, 1970. New York City, New York was the place where the defendant committed his second and last acts of negligence in communicating disease to the plaintiff. In New York it has long been the rule that in classic actions of negligence, damage is the gist and essence of a plaintiff's cause, *Schwartz v. Heyden Newport Chemical Corporation*, 1963, 12 N.Y.2d 212, 237 N.Y.S.2d 714, 188 N.E.2d 142, and the statute of limitations commences to run at the time injury is produced (in personal injury cases) and there is damage to the structure of the body. *Schwartz* holds that the cause of action is complete when the invasion of the body by injury takes place "independently of any actual pecuniary damage." The injury is considered a trespass upon the person of the injured plaintiff.

The court in *Schwartz* strongly relied on *Schmidt v. Merchants Despatch Transportation Company*, supra, the court in the latter case stating at 200 N.E. at 827 . . . , "That does not mean that the cause of action accrues only when the injured person knows or should know that the injury has occurred. The injury occurs when there is a wrongful invasion of personal or property rights and then the cause of action accrues. . . ."

The *Schmidt* doctrine as applied to this case means that a cause of action arose in New York when the defendant had sexual intercourse with the plaintiff at the Motel in the Mountains in Tuxedo, New York on the morning of April 8, 1970. At that time he introduced into the body of the plaintiff infectious pus producing bacteria known as gonococci, which causes the disease of gonorrhea. There is no question but that under the law of New York the defendant was guilty of a tortious act of negligence and the plaintiff was injured by the placement in her body of deleterious matter. Then on the morning of April 21, 1970, the defendant once again at a hotel in New York City, New York repeated the tortious act and once again in the same fashion introduced into the body of plaintiff the bacteria of gonococci. . . .

. . . Having concluded a cause of action accrued in the State of New York, the "borrowing" statute of Wyoming controls the determination of whether or not plaintiff's action has been barred. Under New York law, an action to recover damages for personal injury, unless involving certain specific causes of action not relevant here, must be commenced within three years.

Plaintiff's cause of action accrued in New York at the latest on April 21, 1970, the date of last sexual contact between the parties. Disregarding for the moment any other possibly applicable statute, plaintiff's action not having been filed until April 19, 1974, it appears to be barred, and defendant has so asserted.

. . .

In other jurisdictions in which defendant committed his acts of negligence, the cause of action is likewise either barred by a statute of limitations or no cause of action there arose. The defendant's first installment of negligence, April 4-5, 1970, was in the State of Virginia. Arguably, under the law of that state, the cause of action could have arisen there; if indeed it did, it is likewise barred by that state's limitations. In Virginia, the appropriate limitational period for personal injuries of the kind sustained herein is two years, and even though the defendant did not then and does not now reside in Virginia, he was still subject to the personal jurisdiction of its courts through its long arm statutes because of his allegedly tortious conduct within the state.

. . . [Virginia case law instructs that the Virginia statute of limitations] begins to run upon the date of last exposure, then the cause of action arose in New York City, New York, on April 22, 1970 where the last act of sexual intercourse took place. In the first instance, the plaintiff is barred in Virginia by its two year statute of limitations. In the other no cause of action arose in Virginia. . . .

Even if it could be considered that a cause of action arose in Pennsylvania, its statute of limitations bars any action there. The Pennsylvania statute of limitations, 12 P.S. §34, provides that a personal injury action "must be brought within two years from the time when the injury was done and not afterwards." The tolling statute of Pennsylvania, 12 P.S. §40, applies only to residents. . . . The presence of plaintiff and defendant in Pennsylvania was only transient.

We must also conclude that no cause of action arose in Iowa. Iowa follows the Restatement, Conflict of Laws, §377 rule that: "The place of wrong is in the state where the last event necessary to make an actor liable for an alleged tort takes place." Since Iowa follows the discovery rule, as noted, it would appear that it was in Washington, D.C. that the cause of action accrued as far as that state is concerned because it was in the District of Columbia that plaintiff discovered that she had in fact suffered injury by virtue of the negligent conduct of the defendant.

Nebraska also follows the majority rule that a cause of action accrues when injury actually occurs and there is a basis for a cause of action. [On the basis of Nebraska law and the occurrences in Nebraska, we concluded that the Nebraska statute of limitations does not apply.]

We foreclose Washington, D.C. as the place where a cause of action arose because no tortious act was committed there, nor was that a place where the plaintiff was injured by the implanting of infection by the defendant. It is true that Washington, D.C. was the place where plaintiff incurred medical expense for diagnosis and treatment of the injury inflicted upon her but has no controlling force as to where the cause arose. While she had money damages in the District of Columbia, her physical injury of contracting gonorrhea took place elsewhere. . . . We therefore must conclude after extensive research that by virtue of Wyoming's borrowing statute, the filing of plaintiff's complaint on April 19, 1974 was untimely.

Reversed with directions to vacate the judgment for plaintiff and enter judgment for the defendant.

Notes on
DUKE v. HOUSEN

1. Although *Duke* concerned a borrowing statute that had modified the traditional view that forum law should govern statute of limitation questions, the reasoning in the case nonetheless has a traditional quality. The borrowing statute in Wyoming is framed in terms of First Restatement thinking: finding the jurisdiction where the "cause of action arose" reflects a territorial emphasis on the occurrence of events. It is no surprise that the Wyoming legislature expressed the borrowing statute in this way, since Wyoming has long been a First Restatement state. The type of borrowing statute applied in *Duke* is common among borrowing statutes. How might one draft a borrowing statute to incorporate more modern thinking on choice of law?

2. Did the *Duke* court apply the borrowing statute appropriately? When one parses the analysis needed for applying borrowing statutes of this kind, one finds that the analysis reflects three separate questions:

- **Question 1:** Where did the cause of action arise?
- **Question 2:** What is the "chunk of time" (the "limitations period") that can pass between when the cause of action arises and when the lawsuit is commenced?
- **Question 3:** How does one calculate the limitations period, including starting point, ending point, and any gaps in between?

Before even answering these questions, one must grapple with a threshold issue: what law should govern resolution of the questions? For example: is the question of where a cause of action arose a conflict of laws question to be determined by forum conflict of laws principles? How did the *Duke* court handle this? In determining that the cause of action arose in New York, the *Duke* court looked to a New York decision, *Schwartz,* which reflected a doctrine known as the *Schmidt* doctrine (derived from another New York case). Should the *Duke* court have relied on New York law to answer where the cause of action arose? What are the arguments that Wyoming law should apply instead?

Having determined that the cause of action arose in New York, the *Duke* court applied the New York limitations period, three years. Is this the correct approach to the second question?

3. Of the three questions listed in Note 2, question 3 includes the issue of when a claim accrues, which is synonymous with the question of when one

starts counting the limitations period. Question 3 also includes the question of when a statute of limitations is "tolled," which is synonymous with whether some action or inaction has stopped the limitations period from running.

What is the best way to approach question 3? What law should govern how one answers the question? One approach is reflected in the Uniform Conflict of Laws Limitations §3: "If the statute of limitations of another state applies to the assertion of a claim in this State, the other state's relevant statutes and other rules of law governing tolling and accrual apply in computing the limitations period, but its statutes and other rules governing conflict of laws do not apply." Is this what the *Duke* court did?

4. The judges in *Duke* were unanimous that the borrowing statute applied, and did not discuss how the statute of limitation issue would be handled in the absence of the borrowing statute. Sometimes borrowing statutes have a more limited scope than the Wyoming statute in *Duke,* and other choice of law analysis must resolve the conflicting statutes of limitation. The next case, *DeLoach v. Alfred,* illustrates such a circumstance. In other instances, a court may simply decide that it will not follow the forum's borrowing statute and will instead apply the forum's general choice of law methodology. Although unusual, the following excerpt from *McCann v. Foster Wheeler LLC,* 225 P.3d 516 (Cal. 2010), presents such an instance. Most of the *McCann v. Foster Wheeler LLC* opinion is set forth above in connection with comparative impairment analysis. The excerpt that follows provides a useful description of the history and impetus behind borrowing statutes. As you review the excerpt, evaluate whether you approve of how the courts accommodated the legislative intent behind the borrowing statute with changes in the choice of law methodology that the state experienced after the borrowing statute became law.

Here is the excerpt:

... Traditionally, a state's general choice-of-law rules have been formulated by courts through judicial decisions rendered under the common law, rather than by the legislature through statutory enactments. In California, over the past four decades this court's decisions have adopted and consistently applied the so-called "governmental interest" analysis as the appropriate general methodology for resolving choice-of-law questions in this state.

With respect to the category of statutes of limitation and statutes of repose, however, many jurisdictions have enacted specific statutory provisions that address the subject of choice of law. As discussed in a leading treatise and a number of law review articles, a majority of American states have adopted so-called "borrowing statutes" that direct the courts of a state, in lawsuits filed within that state, to apply or "borrow" the relevant statute of limitations or statute of repose *of a foreign jurisdiction* under the particular circumstances specified in the statute, rather than to apply the statute of limitations of the forum jurisdiction.

The general popularity of borrowing statutes is explained by the common law background against which such statutes were enacted. Under early common law conflict-of-law principles, rules of law ordinarily were characterized as either "substantive" or "procedural," and procedural matters universally were held to be governed by the local or forum law. Because early common law decisions characterized statutes of limitations as procedural rather than substantive, the general rule at that time was that the local statute of limitations of the forum state — rather than another state's statute of limitations — applied to an action filed in the forum state, regardless of the location of the most significant events and circumstances underlying the cause of action or relating to the parties. Thus, even when a cause of action arose out of an accident in one state and all the parties were residents of that state, if a lawsuit was filed in a different state, the court in which the action was filed generally would apply its own state's statute of limitations, rather than the statute of limitations of the other state.

When the period specified in the forum state's statute of limitations was *shorter* than that in the other state's statute of limitations, application of the early common law rule would not necessarily create a serious problem or result in an unfair result, because if the forum's statute of limitations had expired, the plaintiff, at least as a theoretical matter, still could bring the action in the other state. A more problematic situation was presented, however, when the period provided in the applicable statute of limitations of the forum state was *longer* than that in the applicable statute of limitations in the state where the cause of action arose. In that setting, a plaintiff who failed to timely file an action in the state in which the action arose would be provided the opportunity to search out another jurisdiction in which the applicable period under the relevant statute of limitations for the cause of action at issue was longer and in which the action could be maintained — a classic example of questionable forum shopping.

This is the principal problem to which borrowing statutes were generally addressed. Although the provisions of the various states' borrowing statutes differ in a variety of respects, these enactments typically "borrow" the statute of another state when the cause of action in question "arose," "originated," or "accrued" in the other state and would be barred as untimely in that state. Many borrowing statutes, however, also include exceptions that exempt from the reach of the borrowing statute lawsuits that are filed in the courts of the enacting state by residents or citizens of that state. . . .

[California's borrowing statute, §361,] provides in full: "When a cause of action has arisen in another State, or in a foreign country, and by the laws thereof an action thereon cannot there be maintained against a person by reason of the lapse of time, an action thereon shall not be maintained against him in this State, except in favor of one who has been a citizen of this State, and who has held the cause of action from the time it accrued."

Section 361 thus creates a general rule that when a cause of action has arisen in another jurisdiction but cannot be maintained against a particular defendant in that jurisdiction because of the lapse of time, the action cannot be maintained against that defendant in a California court. The statute contains an exception, however, for a plaintiff "who has been a citizen of this

State, and who has held the cause of action from the time it accrued." Past cases establish that this exception applies only where the plaintiff was a California citizen at the time the cause of action accrued, and does not extend to a plaintiff who became a citizen of California after the cause of action accrued but before the lawsuit in question was filed.

Although application of section 361 generally is straightforward in a case involving, for example, a typical automobile accident — in which the allegedly tortious conduct, the resulting injury, and compensable damage all occur at the same time and in the same place — proper application of the statute is more problematic in a case, like the present one, in which the defendant's allegedly injury-producing conduct occurred in another state at a much earlier date but the plaintiff's resulting illness or injury does not become apparent and reasonably is not discovered until many decades later, at a time when the plaintiff has established residence in California. In the factual setting here at issue, it may be reasonably debatable whether plaintiff's cause of action against Foster Wheeler "arose" in Oklahoma or instead in California for purposes of section 361, and whether plaintiff was a citizen of California or of Oklahoma at the time the cause of action "accrued" within the meaning of the term as used in this borrowing statute.

Even if we assume either that the cause of action at issue "arose" in California for purposes of section 361 or that plaintiff was a citizen of California from the time the cause of action "accrued" within the meaning of this statute — and thus that section 361 does not *require* application of Oklahoma law rather than California law on the facts of this case — we agree . . . that this statute cannot properly be interpreted *to compel* application of the California statute of limitations without consideration of California's generally applicable choice-of-law principles. Although at the time section 361 was adopted, the then prevailing choice-of-law doctrine generally would have called for the application of the relevant California statute of limitations in a case in which section 361 did not mandate application of another jurisdiction's law nothing in section 361 indicates that this statute was intended to freeze the then prevailing general choice-of-law rules into a statutory command, so as to curtail the judiciary's long-standing authority to adopt and modify choice-of-law principles pursuant to its traditional common law role. Accordingly, now that the earlier methodology for resolving choice-of-law issues has been replaced in this state by the governmental interest mode of analysis, in those instances in which section 361 does not mandate application of another jurisdiction's statute of limitations or statute of repose the question whether the relevant California statute of limitations (or statute of repose) or, instead, another jurisdiction's statute of limitations (or statute of repose) should be applied in a particular case must be determined through application of the governmental interest analysis that governs choice-of-law issues generally.

McCann v. Foster Wheeler LLC, 225 P.3d 516, 524-527 (Cal. 2010).

DeLoach v. Alfred

960 P.2d 628 (Ariz. 1998)

FELDMAN, Justice

We granted review to determine which state's statute of limitations applies to an Arizona case arising out of a Tennessee automobile accident. The plaintiff is a California resident; one defendant is an Arizona resident, and the other a Tennessee resident. . . .

The facts are undisputed. Kevin Hamblin ("Plaintiff"), a California resident, was injured in a June 19, 1994, automobile accident in Tennessee. He was a passenger in a car operated by Kevin DeLoach that collided with a car owned by Budget Rent-A-Car and driven by William Moore. On June 19, 1996, Plaintiff filed the tort action in Arizona against Budget Rent-A-Car of Memphis, Moore and his wife, both Tennessee residents, and DeLoach and his wife ("Petitioners"), both Arizona residents. Budget has been dismissed from the action. The Moores have neither answered nor otherwise appeared.

Petitioners filed a motion for summary judgment based on Tennessee's one-year statute of limitations for tort actions. They argued that the locus of the accident, rather than the forum, determines which statute of limitations applies. Plaintiff opposed the motion, urging the trial judge to apply this state's two-year statute of limitations to his claim against Petitioners. He argued that Arizona applies its own law to procedural matters such as limitations provisions. The judge agreed and denied the motion for summary judgment.

The threshold question concerned the proper analysis for deciding which statute of limitations applied. There are at least three approaches to deciding choice of law questions involving conflicting statutes of limitations. Under the traditional approach, statutes of limitations are viewed as presumptively procedural, in which case the law of the forum applies. Arizona has historically applied this approach. This approach was adopted in Restatement (Second) of Conflicts of Laws §§142 and 143 (1971) (hereafter Restatement). The Restatement was revised in 1988, however, to employ a type of interest analysis approach recognized by the drafters as the "emerging trend" among courts. Under that approach, a court must analyze conflicts between statutes of limitations, emphasizing the significance of the relationship between the forum and the claims. *See* Restatement §142 (1988). A third approach exists under Uniform Conflict of Laws-Limitations Act §2. Under that act, not adopted in Arizona, if a claim is substantively based on the law of another state, the limitations period of that state applies. The court of appeals followed the interest analysis approach of revised Restatement §142. The parties do not challenge the use of that section.

Applying revised section 142 to the facts in this case, the court of appeals concluded that Arizona has no substantial interest in the case, Tennessee's relationship to the accident is more significant, and application of Arizona's statute of limitations would frustrate Tennessee's policy. Plaintiff advanced three issues in his petition for review, but we granted review on the third issue only: whether "the court of appeals erred in its [application] of the Restatement."

DISCUSSION

We note as a very important preliminary matter that the Tennessee defendants are not involved in this litigation. The Moores were named as defendants and were served with process in Tennessee but have neither answered nor otherwise appeared in the action. Although this action was pending in the trial court for seven months or more, the Moores did nothing to manifest consent to Arizona jurisdiction. On the record before us, the Moores have either settled or are most certainly not subject to personal jurisdiction in Arizona. They did not object to and have not challenged the trial court's application of the Arizona statute of limitations. The Moores were not parties to the special action brought by Petitioners in the court of appeals; nor are they parties to this petition for review. Given their nonappearance and the apparent lack of personal jurisdiction over them, we believe the Moores' interests are not affected by and are not relevant to our decision on choice of law. The persons affected are Plaintiff, the California resident who chose this forum, and Petitioners, Arizona residents.

Revised Restatement §142 provides:

> Whether a claim will be maintained against the defense of the statute of limitations is determined under the principles stated in §6. *In general*, unless the exceptional circumstances of the case make such a result unreasonable:
>   (1) *The forum will apply its own statute of limitations barring the claim.*
>   (2) *The forum will apply its own statute of limitations permitting the claim unless:*
>   (a) maintenance of the claim would serve no substantial interest of the forum; *and*
>   (b) the claim would be barred under the statute of limitations of a state having a more significant relationship to the parties and the occurrence.

. . . As the court of appeals explained, the revised Restatement displaced the traditional substantive/procedural analysis concerning statutes of limitations with the choice of law interest factor analysis stated in section 6. *DeLoach*, 191 Ariz., 952 P.2d at 324. However, the court failed to recognize that section 142 does not simply import the pure interest analysis of section 6. Rather, revised section 142 begins with the *general rule* that the limitations period of the forum will apply, unless exceptional circumstances make such a result unreasonable and, in cases in which the claim will not be barred under the forum's statute, either of the conjunctive factors stated in section 142(2) is not satisfied. . . .

With this understanding, we turn to applying the current Restatement rule to the facts in this case. We must determine whether the general rule applying the forum's statute of limitations obtains, whether there exist exceptional circumstances, or whether the two factors mentioned in section 142(2) would require application of Tennessee's shorter statute. Comment g to revised section 142 is instructive:

> The forum will entertain a claim that is not barred by its statute of limitations, but is barred by the statute of limitations of one or more other states, in situations where allowing the claim would advance a substantial forum interest and would

not seriously impinge upon the interests of other states. . . . There are also situations where the forum will entertain an action that is not barred by its statute of limitations even though the forum is not the state of most significant relationship to other issues. Suppose, for example, that two domiciliaries of state X are involved in an automobile accident in state Y. In this case, the local law of state Y may govern substantive issues in the case under the rule stated in §146. Yet it would be appropriate for an X court to entertain the claim if it was not barred by the X statute of limitations even though it would be barred by the Y statute. Entertainment of the claim under such circumstances would not violate any Y policy and might further the policy of X. *The same would be true if the accident in state Y* [Tennessee] *had involved domiciliaries of states X and Z* [California and Arizona] *and, although the statute of limitations had run in Y, it had not done so in either X or Z. In such a case, it would be appropriate for a court of either X or Z to entertain the claim.*

(Emphasis added.)

The operative facts of our case are nearly indistinguishable from the empha-sized example provided in the comment. The court of appeals, however, believed that naming the Moores as defendants was determinative. Applying Restatement §142(2)(b), the court held:

> We can see no substantial interest of this state that would be served by allowing a case involving a foreign plaintiff and a foreign defendant to proceed here against a state resident. The accident occurred in Tennessee, the plaintiff is a California resident, and the remaining defendants, other than the DeLoaches, are residents of Tennessee. On these facts alone, Arizona's relationship to the parties and the occurrence is not nearly as significant as Tennessee's. That state's one-year statute of limitations reflects its policy decision that personal injury claims can quickly become stale and should, therefore, be asserted within one year. Application of a two-year limitation period would frustrate the policy of the state with a more significant relationship to the action and the parties.

But we have recognized, to the contrary, that the state of injury does *not* have a significant interest in the question of compensation when the injured party is a non-resident. In this case, Tennessee's only interest arises from its policy of bar-ring what it considers to be stale claims in actions against Tennessee residents. But the action against the Tennessee residents is barred if brought in Tennessee and cannot be maintained in Arizona for lack of in personam jurisdiction. We do not believe the mere fact that the Moores were named in the action is determinative.

We also disagree with the court of appeals' conclusion that Arizona has no significant interest in this case. Arizona's two-year statute reflects the substantial interest underlying its policy requiring its citizens to answer for the harm they cause. Arizona courts have long recognized that, in addition to making injured plaintiffs whole, holding tortfeasors accountable also advances the important interest in deterring wrongful conduct. Further, we have long recognized that the state where the injury occurred "has less interest in deterrence and less ability to control behavior by deterrence . . . than the state where the tortfeasor is domiciled." Thus the policy of deterrence extends to providing a forum for redress against Arizona defendants for their negligent conduct outside the state.

The court of appeals held that it would frustrate Tennessee policy to apply the lengthier Arizona limitations period. We fail to see how applying Arizona's limitations period will frustrate Tennessee's policy. A state's limitations period reflects that state's choice of when claims become stale and the time when defendants should no longer fear being sued. As noted, the Tennessee defendants can no longer be sued in Tennessee and on this record are not subject to personal jurisdiction in Arizona. . . .

Finally, our general approach to limitations defenses is pertinent. We note that the "defense of statute of limitations is never favored by the courts. . . ." In addition, we observe that the legislature has expressed only limited interests in importing foreign statutes of limitations, demonstrated by the very narrow scope of our borrowing statute. *See* A.R.S. §12-506 (barring claims against immigrants if claims were barred by foreign statute of limitations or released from payment by the bankruptcy or insolvency laws of the state or country from which they migrated).

Because Arizona's interest in the case is at least as substantial and as significant as Tennessee's, neither of the exceptions in section 142(2) is applicable. Under the revised Restatement formula, therefore, the general rule applying the forum's statute of limitations will apply absent exceptional circumstances making that result unreasonable. *See* Restatement §142.

. . .

Finally, applying the Arizona statute of limitations is entirely consistent with the choice of law factors enumerated in Restatement §6. We have addressed factors (b) and (c) of section 6 (the relevant policies of the forum and the relevant policies and interests of Arizona and Tennessee) in our discussion of section 142. Applying Arizona's limitations period also protects the justified expectations of the parties. *See* Restatement §6(2)(d). Petitioners' expectation of being subject to legal action for their tortious conduct for two years under the Arizona statute and the Moores' expectation of repose after one year are satisfied. We also find that the basic policies underlying tort law — to deter wrongful conduct and compensate victims for their loss — are satisfied by permitting the action to go forward in Arizona. *See* Restatement §6(2)(e). Finally, we observe that in this case the general rule of revised Restatement §142 applying the statute of the forum produces certainty, predictability, and uniformity of result. *See* Restatement §6(2)(f). . . .

Conclusion

Under the facts of this case, the Arizona limitations period applies to an Arizona defendant sued in Arizona by a California plaintiff for damages resulting from tortious conduct in Tennessee. The court of appeals' opinion is vacated, the trial judge's denial of summary judgment on the statute of limitations issue is approved, and the matter is remanded to the trial court for further proceedings consistent with this opinion.

Notes on
DELOACH v. ALFRED

1. In *DeLoach*, the Arizona court confronted a borrowing statute with limited scope. The court looked the Restatement (Second)'s guidance on the statute of limitations questions only after finding the borrowing statute inapplicable. This is the most common approach to handling borrowing statutes, and contrasts with the California Supreme Court's approach in *McCann v. Foster Wheeler LLC*, 225 P.3d 516 (Cal. 2010), excerpted above.

2. Professor Symeon Symeonides has admired the *DeLoach* case, describing it as a "faithful and intelligent application of §142" of the Restatement (Second) with a "credible articulation of the forum's interest in applying its longer statute of limitation." Symeon C. Symeonides, *Choice of Law in the American Courts in 1998: Twelfth Annual Survey*, 47 AM. J. COMP. L. 327, 383 (1999). He reasoned: "[T]he fact that the forum has a longer limitation period means that the claim is not considered stale enough. This means that the interests implicated in the cases of this pattern are substantive and depend on the forum's relationship with the parties and the case." *Id.*

To be sure, the *DeLoach* court provided a lot of reasoning about the forum and non-forum interests in the case. Should statute of limitations inquiries require such complex analysis? Are the arguments in favor of bright-line, simple rules stronger for statute of limitations questions than for other choice of law questions?

3. The Arizona Supreme Court's reasoning turned on its assumption that no personal jurisdiction existed over the Tennessee defendants, the Moores. While it is true that the Moores had not participated in the proceedings, the record was spare on whether there was personal jurisdiction or not. Should the court have simply handled the matter as an assumption that no personal jurisdiction existed? If it did not handle the issue in this way, what other options were available to the court?

4. The *DeLoach* court concluded that the Arizona defendants must live with the forum's longer statute of limitations, even though the plaintiff was from out of state, the accident occurred out of state, and the other out-of-state defendants were unavailable. Does this seem like unnecessarily harsh treatment of a home-state defendant? Or does the court's decision reflect evidence of fair and evenhanded justice? For a decision concluding that the plaintiff's out-of-state domicile should nullify the forum's interest in holding defendants accountable in a statute of limitations dispute, see *Hall v. General Motors Corp.*, 582 N.W.2d 866 (Mich. Ct. App. 1998).

5. The *DeLoach* court said that applying forum law in the case served the policy of uniformity of result reflected in Restatement (Second) §6. Do you agree?

Chang v. Baxter Healthcare Corporation

599 F.3d 728 (7th Cir. 2010)

POSNER, Circuit Judge.

. . . The present case [was] filed originally in California by residents of Taiwan but transferred by the multidistrict panel to the district court in Chicago [and joined with other products liability cases in which plaintiffs claim to have been infected with HIV from defendant's blood-clotting factor]. The main tort claim is that the defendants acquired blood from high-risk donors, processed it improperly in California where they manufactured clotting factors, and after discovering that the factors were contaminated by HIV nevertheless continued to distribute the product in foreign countries while withdrawing them from distribution in the United States. Thus, the . . . plaintiffs in this case, or the decedents whom they represent, reside, and obtained and injected the clotting factor, in a foreign country. The plaintiffs also charge that the defendants fraudulently induced them to enter into a settlement agreement that released the defendants from liability in exchange for paying $60,000 to each plaintiff. The breach of contract claim alleges violation of a term of the settlement.

The district judge dismissed some of the plaintiffs' claims as untimely and the others on the ground of *forum non conveniens*. . . .

The critical issue so far as the dismissals on the merits are concerned is choice of law. When a diversity case is transferred by the multidistrict litigation panel, the law applied is that of the jurisdiction from which the case was transferred, in this case California. The plaintiffs' claims that the district judge dismissed on the merits he dismissed as untimely under California law.

California statutes of limitations don't begin to run until the plaintiff discovers, or should in the exercise of reasonable diligence have discovered, that he has a claim against the defendant. But the discovery rule would not save the plaintiffs' tort claims from dismissal for untimeliness. True, the plaintiffs argue that they didn't have enough information on which to base a suit until a *New York Times* article about the contamination of clotting factors with HIV was published on May 22, 2003, and therefore that their suit, filed in 2004, was timely, since the California statute of limitations for personal-injury claims is two years. But as the district court found, the plaintiffs had had a reasonable basis to suspect that they had a cause of action more than five years before the article appeared, when their counsel had begun negotiations with two of the defendants to settle negligence claims arising from the contamination of the defendants' clotting factors with HIV. These negotiations culminated in the settlement in 1998 on which the plaintiffs' breach of contract claim is based.

The plaintiffs argue that the limitations period should have been tolled by defendants' "fraudulent concealment" because when entering into the settlement agreement they said they had done nothing wrong and that they were offering financial aid purely as a humanitarian gesture. The plaintiffs are mistaken. Denial of liability when negotiating a settlement agreement is the norm; it is not evidence of fraudulent concealment of anything.

The district court was also correct in ruling in the alternative that a California court would apply ("borrow" is the technical legal term) the Taiwanese 10-year statute of repose, because the plaintiffs' tort claims arose under Taiwanese law. The hemophiliacs whom the plaintiffs represent were infected in the 1980s, more than a decade before these suits were brought.

A statute of repose, which is designed specifically for products-liability suits, cuts off liability after a fixed number of years, whether or not the plaintiff should have discovered within that period that he had a claim. A statute of repose thus overrides the discovery rule. It does this because of the long latency of many product defects, which can under a discovery rule impose vast and unpredictable products liability on manufacturers.

If the plaintiffs' tort claims arose in Taiwan, California law makes the Taiwanese statute of repose applicable to those claims. The reason is California's "borrowing" statute, which—sensibly designed to discourage forum shopping—provides that "when a cause of action has arisen in another State, or in a foreign country, and by the laws thereof an action thereon cannot there be maintained against a person by reason of the lapse of time, an action thereon shall not be maintained against him in this State, except in favor of one who has been a citizen of this State, and who has held the cause of action from the time it accrued." Cal. Civ. P. Code §361. The plaintiffs argue that their claims arose in California, not Taiwan, because it was in California that the defendants failed to process their clotting factors in a way that would prevent contamination by HIV. But with immaterial exceptions such as trespass, where purely nominal damages can be awarded even if there is no tangible harm, because "a continuing trespass may ripen into a prescriptive right and deprive a property owner of title to his or her land," there is no tort without an injury. That is the rule in California, as elsewhere. The tort of which the plaintiffs complain thus occurred in Taiwan. . . . The case on which the plaintiffs principally rely, *McKee v. Dodd*, 152 Cal. 637, 93 P. 854 (1908), was a breach of contract case rather than a tort case. The breach had been committed in New York, the place where payment was due, and the suit was held to have arisen there. A claim of breach of contract is complete when the breach is committed, and indeed one can obtain a judgment in a breach of contract action without proving any loss at all. Anyway the plaintiff was in New York when the breach occurred, so the injury also occurred there, just as it occurred in Taiwan in the present case.

The plaintiffs concede that the suit "accrued" in Taiwan but deny that it "arose" there. They misunderstand those terms. A claim "accrues" when the statute of limitations begins to run; a claim that could not have been discovered by the date on which it arose will not (in a jurisdiction with a discovery rule) accrue then. The terms "arose" and "accrued" often are conflated, because, other than in cases in which the discovery rule is invoked, usually the date on which the cause of action "accrues" is also the date on which it "arises." The plaintiffs' claims arose in Taiwan, and that's all that matters.

California courts would apply the Taiwanese statute of repose in this case even if there were no borrowing statute. Applying the "balancing of interests approach" that California courts use to resolve conflict of laws issues, a California court would reason that if Taiwan will not provide a remedy to its own citizens, there is no reason for California to do so. What interest has California in treating Taiwanese plaintiffs more generously than Taiwan treats them?

. . .

Affirmed.

Notes on
CHANG

1. Note that the forum court in *Chang* case is a United States District Court in Illinois. The choice of law analysis, however, concerns California law and Taiwan law. California law is in the picture because the case transferred from California as part of the multidistrict litigation procedure in federal courts. This is the appropriate analysis for multidistrict litigation, which is described in detail further below in connection with multiparty actions.

2. In addressing an argument about where the claim accrued, the *Chang* court made clear that the terms "accrue" and "arose" should not be confused: "A claim 'accrues' when the statute of limitations begins to run; a claim that could not have been discovered by the date on which it arose will not (in a jurisdiction with a discovery rule) accrue then. The terms 'accrued' and 'arose' often are conflated, because, other than in cases in which the discovery rule is invoked, usually the date on which the cause of action 'accrues' is also the date on which it 'arises.'" Recall discussion of the three questions embedded in borrowing statutes presented in the notes after the *Duke* case above. How would you frame the distinction between "accrues" and "arose" in terms of those questions? Which question does the "accrual" discussion trigger? The term "arose" obviously goes to question 1: "Where did the cause of action arise?"

3. Is there anything anomalous about how the borrowing statute at issue in *Chang* used the traditional concept of where a cause of action arose? As the *Chang* court observed, this concept is resolved by reference to where the injury occurred, a classically First Restatement concept. But the First Restatement will likely not resolve any other conflict of laws questions that arise in the case. Rather, the court would press into service California's usual comparative impairment principles. Do you see anything wrong with using more than one choice of law approach in a case? Could mixing old and new choice of law analyses create inappropriate incongruity? Couldn't a court end up applying the statute of limitations from a state that does not provide the governing rules for the rest of the case because the state lacks any cognizable "interest" in the dispute? What type of reform or analytical approach might eliminate this possibility?

4. In the final part of the *Chang* opinion, the court uses "even if" reasoning: the court asserts that, even if the borrowing statute did not apply, California would come to same conclusion using its usual, general

choice of law analysis: "a California court would reason that if Taiwan will not provide a remedy to its own citizens, there is no reason for California to do so. What interest has California in treating Taiwanese plaintiffs more generously than Taiwan treats them?" Is this the type of thinking that the court used in the *DeLoach* opinion: determining whether a court would grant a litigant the opportunity to pursue litigation or to avoid liability according to whether the litigant is a citizen of the forum state?

5. The effects of a liberal decision regarding a statute of limitations may be complex. Many agree that a decision that effectively extends the limitations period for cases with multi-state elements may promote litigation tourism, with litigants attracted to states with a liberal approach to applying the state's generous statute of limitations to out-of-state plaintiffs. Yet other parts of the forum's choice of law rules may allow these out-of-state plaintiffs to avoid the forum's defendant-friendly liability rules. As a result, plaintiffs can get the benefit of the forum's generous statute of limitations, while enjoying the more plaintiff-friendly substantive provisions of another state. Some argue that the New Jersey Supreme Court's statute of limitations decision in *McCarrell v. Hoffmann-La Roche, Inc.*, 227 N.J. 569 (2017), has produced this result, particularly for pharmaceutical litigation. *Will New Jersey Attract More Litigants?*, 85 U.S. LAW WEEK 1025 (Feb. 2, 2017).

PROBLEM 2-60: WANDA'S WEBSITE

Wanda, a State W resident, created her own private website, which she operates from her home in State W. On the website, Wanda negligently posted a defamatory statement about Veronica Victim, stating that Veronica had poor personal hygiene. The posting occurred in 2003. Veronica lives in State V and runs a baby-sitting service there. Wanda's website is a passive website, with no opportunity for those who read the content of the site to interact with the site. Some of Veronica's clients in State V read the defamatory statement about her and decided to stop using her baby-sitting services. By 2005, Veronica lost half of her clients, but after that, her baby-sitting business stabilized. Wanda removed the defamatory posting from the site in 2014.

In 2017, Veronica filed a negligence action against Wanda in State V court, alleging damages from the defamatory website posting. For the purposes of lawsuits of this kind, the laws of State W and State V differ in two significant ways:

1. State W law allows damages for economic harm only, but State V law allows damages for both economic and emotional harm.

2. State W has a six-year statute of limitations on suits of this kind and State V has a one-year statute of limitations.

You may assume that both State V and State W generally follow the Restatement (First) of Conflict of Laws, and that both states have a borrowing statute that provides:

> Where a cause of action arises in another state, that state's internal law should govern the parties' rights and responsibilities. If, however, the action is barred by the law of the state where the cause of action arose, it is also barred in this state.

Neither state follows the discovery rule for statute of limitation questions (instead each calculates the statute of limitation as running from the time that the injury begins to occur). Wanda has moved to dismiss on the ground that the suit is time barred under State V's statute. Is she right?

PROBLEM 2-61: PURITA'S INJURY AWAY FROM HOME

Purita is a resident of State P and was driving in a nearby state, State N. Paul is also from State P and was driving a separate car in State N. While in State N, Paul negligently collided with Purita's car. She was badly injured and rushed to a hospital in State P. Purita had worked in State P, but had to quit her job because of her injuries. She also owes a considerable amount of money in medical bills in State P and is unable to support her children, who reside with her in State P. At the time of the accident, Paul was insured by a State P insurer. Since so much time has passed since the accident, Paul has thrown out all his relevant paperwork concerning his insurance and bills immediately after the accidents.

Purita is now suing Paul in State N. The action is barred by State P's statute of limitations, but not State N's statute of limitations. State N does not have a pertinent borrowing statute and follows the Restatement (Second) for all choice of law questions. Which state's statute of limitations is likely to govern?

PROBLEM 2-62: A CHOICE OF LAW CLAUSE AND A PERSONAL LIMITATIONS PERIOD

Polly Plaintiff was a New Arkansas resident who, through a New Arkansas travel agent, purchased a four-day trip on a river boat that traveled on a portion of the Mississippi River running through the State of New Mississippi. A company called Rivertours, Inc. owned the river boat and operated the tour. Rivertours, Inc. is headquartered and incorporated in New Ohio. The contract that Polly signed when she purchased the trip had a clause that stated:

> This agreement shall be governed by and construed in accordance with the internal laws of New Ohio. All issues involved in disputes arising under this agreement shall be governed by the internal laws of New Ohio, except that any claimant

asserting a cause of action for personal injury incurred during a river boat tour must file suit within six months of the date of the accident.

While on the New Mississippi river boat trip, Polly Plaintiff slipped on the deck and hurt her left elbow. The doctor on the boat treated the injury and her left elbow appeared to heal. Nevertheless, four months after the accident, Polly woke up one morning and had no feeling in her left hand. She visited a doctor that morning who informed her that she had permanent nerve damage from the river boat accident and would never recover use of her left hand. Three months after that—a total of seven months after the accident on the river boat—Polly filed a personal injury action against Rivertours, Inc. in New Arkansas state court. Rivertours, Inc. has moved to dismiss the case, arguing that it was not timely filed.

Seeking to have the court reject this argument by Rivertours, Polly points out that New Mississippi and New Ohio each have a one-year statute of limitations on personal injury actions, and that both New Mississippi and New Ohio follow the discovery rule for calculating the limitations period. Further research discloses that New Arkansas has a six-month statute of limitations, which runs from the date of accident, whether or not the injured party is aware of the full scope of the injury at that time. Research also reveals that the legislatures of New Mississippi, New Ohio, and New Arkansas have enacted the following statute:

> If another state's law governs the substantive elements of a cause of action, that state's law also provides the relevant statute of limitations. If the statute of limitations of another state applies to the claim or cause of action, the other state's relevant statutes and other rules of law governing tolling and accrual apply in computing the limitations period.

New Mississippi, New Ohio, and New Arkansas each use the Restatement (Second) of Conflict of Laws to resolve choice of law questions relating to contract, tort, and statutes of limitations. Should the court grant the motion to dismiss by Rivertours, Inc.?

2. Comprehensive Choice of Law Rules

a. State Codes

Two states, Louisiana and Oregon, are on the forefront of developing comprehensive choice of law codes. Consistent with its civil law traditions and rich history of codifications, Louisiana enacted a comprehensive codification effective in 1992. The Louisiana codification reflects learning from choice of law approaches followed in the United States and from Louisiana's civil law tradition. The goal of Louisiana's codified approach is to apply the law of the state whose policies would be "most serious seriously impaired if its law were not applied to the particular issue." La. Civ. Code art. 3515. While the approach owes some lineage to the approaches developed by Professors Currie and Baxter, the approach does not adopt either. Symeon C. Symeonides, *The Conflicts Book of the Louisiana Civil Code: Civilian, American, or Original?*, 83 TUL. L. REV. 1041, 1053 (2009). Rather, the code seeks to identify the law of the state that, "in light of its relationship to the parties and the dispute and its policies rendered pertinent by that relationship, would bear the most serious legal, social, economic, and other consequences if its law were not applied to that issue." La. Civ. Code art. 3515 cmt. (b). Seeking a balance between certainty and flexibility, the Louisiana Civil Code employs actual choice of law rules that provide flexible as well as alternative connecting factors, escape devices that allow courts to avoid the rule's result in many instances, as well as endorsement of dépeçage (issue-by-issue choice of law analysis). Arguably like the Restatement (Second) approach, the codification seeks to provide judges with a methodology or approach while at the same time enunciating specific rules.

Effective in 2010, Oregon's codification provides more of a methodology than a set of rules. The statute has a number of unique qualities, including provisions that designate special rules for cases calling for application of forum law and cases arising in the products liability area. One particularly interesting provision, Oregon Revised Statute §31.885, honors party autonomy. This section states that where — after the parties gain knowledge of the events surrounding the dispute — parties agree to the application of law other than Oregon's, the court should enforce the agreement so long as it meets the requirements governing contractual choice of law clauses. A similar approach to party autonomy appears in Oregon Revised Statute §31.870, which provides that where the parties have "expressly or tacitly agreed to the application" forum law or where the forum has certain contacts with the case, the law of the forum should govern without exception Symeon C. Symeonides, *Choice of Law in the American Courts in 2009: Twenty-Third Annual Survey*, 58 AM. J. COMP. L. 227, 232-235 (2010).

Another key section, Oregon Revised Statute §31.875, identifies four contacts that govern choice of law determinations in tort cases: (1) place of the injurious conduct; (2) the place of the resulting injury; (3) the domicile of the injured person; and (4) the domicile of the person whose conduct caused the injury. The Act then divides the possible case permutations into the following three categories: (1) common domicile cases; (2) intrastate-conduct, split-domicile cases; and (3) cross-border-conduct, split-domicile cases. Also in the same part, Oregon Revised Statute §31.878 sets forth a general approach for cases not covered by specific rules, designating the governing law as that which is "most appropriate" in light of contacts and policies underlying disputed issues. Section 9 designates three steps for identifying the most appropriate law: (1) locating the states with relevant contacts; (2) identifying the pertinent policies of the located states; and (3) analyzing the "strength and persistence of those policies." *Id.*

A significant benefit of a comprehensive legislative scheme is the opportunity for those who create the scheme to consider competing philosophies that may animate a particular field of law. For example, the framing of the Oregon and

Louisiana codes represented an effort to accommodate both "conflicts justice" and "material" or "substantive" justice. James A.R. Nafziger, *The Louisiana and Oregon Codifications of Choice-of-Law Rules in Context*, 58 Am. J. Comp. L. 165, 179 (2010). Conflicts justice focuses on values that inform the effective operation of a conflict of laws system, such as uniformity and predictability. Material or substantive justice integrates into the choice of law analysis consideration of what law produces the optimum result in a particular case. While these concepts implicitly inform common law development of choice of law principles, one rarely observes explicit consideration of them within court decisions. As with most efforts at an integrated statutory scheme, the Oregon and Louisiana codifications therefore provide a vehicle to integrate into legal regulation carefully considered philosophical decisions and structural planning.

b. A Federal Choice of Law Code

The federal courts have stated that the Restatement (Second) of Conflict of Laws provides the federal choice of law approach. As explained further in Chapter 3, the circumstances in which federal courts adopt and follow the Restatement (Second) — as a form of *federal* law — are generally limited to bankruptcy, admiralty, maritime, and other cases with a particularly significant federal interest. This contrasts to instances such as diversity cases where a federal court might follow the Restatement (Second) as the conflict of laws approach embraced by the forum state.

As we have seen, the Restatement (Second) has many problems. If Congress were to choose to embrace the Restatement (Second) as "the federal choice of law approach," should Congress try its hand at improving it? Or should Congress develop an entirely new choice of law approach or embrace a codification that is "road tested," such as the Oregon or Louisiana approaches? Irrespective of which form a comprehensive federal code might take, Congress would need to settle a threshold issue: should federal choice of law be confined to areas of significant federal interest or should the federal code displace state legislative and common law rules as well?

In evaluating whether Congress should develop an expansive choice of law approach, one must be mindful of several questions. As a threshold matter, one must, of course, consider the scope of Congress's power to do so. Certainly, Congress has power to designate an approach to governing law on matters related to the specifically enumerated powers of Article I, section 8 of the United States Constitution. Thus, even the staunchest supporter of state sovereignty would likely agree that Congress has the power to designate the law that governs matters that concern interstate commerce. Moreover, Congress's power over the practice and procedure of federal courts includes the power to delineate the choice of law approach applied in federal court. Perhaps more controversial, but nonetheless likely recognized by the majority of authorities, is Congress's power to designate a general choice of law approach governing in the state courts. That power likely derives from the full faith and credit clause of Article IV, section 1 of the United

States Constitution, which provides that "Full Faith and Credit shall be given in each State to the public Acts, Records, and judicial Proceedings of every other State. And the Congress may by general Laws prescribe the Manner in which such Acts, Records and Proceedings shall be proved, and the Effect thereof." The scope of the full faith and credit power is explored in more detail in Chapter 3.[53]

This final congressional power issue raises a crucial distinction: although one might argue in favor of Congress's creating a choice of law code for federal courts, what are the factors bearing on whether Congress should also impose a choice of law code on state courts? If Congress were to develop a choice of law code for state courts, should it confine the code to specific areas (such as class actions or mass torts) or should it create a comprehensive statute? The latter approach would result in significant federalization of state law, and would likely meet resistance from those who champion state sovereignty and limited federal power. Finally, it is noteworthy that Congress has already had plenty of incentive and opportunity to create a uniform code and has avoided the opportunity to do so. Even if the Constitution and good judgment would counsel Congress to take on a comprehensive code, the political will to do so seems lacking. Thus, although the concepts bearing on the wisdom and ability of Congress to create a comprehensive code are important to understanding choice of law in the United States, the matter is hypothetical at least for the present time.

Notes on
A FEDERAL CHOICE OF LAW CODE

1. What is the optimum level of involvement of Congress in the business of choice of law? Often proponents of congressional restraint in any area point to the advantages of allowing states to experiment with various approaches to regulation. Has state experimentation historically yielded workable results? Or has experience yielded chaos crying out for uniform congressional guidance? Should the answer be influenced by the current state of the globalized world in which entities in the United States and other countries regularly interact? Doesn't that change make more important the development a uniform choice of law approach in the United States? (Isn't it hard enough that those in foreign countries must grapple with differences among the internal laws of the various states?)

2. For a helpful discussion of the experience of the European Union with centralized choice of law rules and the lessons that this experience

53. *See* Michael H. Gottesman, *Draining the Dismal Swamp: The Case for Federal Choice of Law Statutes*, 80 Geo. L.J. 1 (1991), for further discussion of Congress's power to enact a federal choice of law code.

holds for the United States, see Alex Mills, *Federalism in the European Union and the United States: Subsidarity, Private Law, and the Conflict of Laws*, 32 U. PA. J. INT'L L. 369 (2010).

3. Aside from the lessons of other countries, where might Congress look for guidance in developing a choice of law code? Two possible organizations are the American Law Institute (ALI) and the National Conference of Commissioners on Uniform State Laws (NCCUSL).

The ALI developed the Restatement (First) and the Restatement (Second) of Conflict of Laws. Scholars have observed that these works often do not actually "restate" existing law, but instead designate preferred rules for the future, broadly reading precedents so as to reform the law. If the ALI contributes to the uniform choice of law enterprise, the argument continues, the organization should not do so under the rubric of a Restatement (Third), which would then be available for states to adopt in an ad hoc manner. Rather, the ALI could conduct a study of the current "conflicts anarchy" in the United States and make proposals to Congress for uniform change. Ralph U. Whitten, *Curing the Deficiencies of the Conflicts Revolution: A Proposal for National Legislation on Choice of Law, Jurisdiction, and Judgments*, 37 WILLAMETTE L. REV. 259, 280-284 (2001). As an organization, the ALI is well suited to this task, since it has a national membership and lacks specific representational ties to states. Scholars, practitioners, and judges generally perceive the organization as neutral, or at least free from significant regional bias. Moreover, the ALI has already completed a major project designed to provide a mechanism for dealing with multiparty, multi forum complex litigation, Complex Litigation: Statutory Recommendations and Analysis (1994). As an attempt to create a uniform federal choice of law code for complex cases, the project arguably shows that the ALI has both the inclination and ability to develop a more comprehensive code. This expertise is also reflected in a more recent ALI project dedicated to enunciating Principles of the Law of Aggregated Litigation (2009).

The NCCUSL has not spent much effort on choice of law over the years, adopting only a handful of measures, such as the uniform law governing limitations issues. Nonetheless, the entity's great success with the Uniform Commercial Code suggests that it possesses the authority, expertise, and resources for a comprehensive undertaking such as an integrated choice of law code. As presently constituted, however, the NCCUSL is an unlikely candidate as an extensive advisor to Congress. As Professor Larry Kramer has explained, the NCCUSL is comprised of officials who are appointed from each state and negotiate uniform laws that are intended to be "positively enacted by state legislatures." Larry Kramer, *On the Need for a Uniform Choice of Law Code*, 89 MICH. L. REV. 2134, 2148 (1991). For this reason, the NCCUSL would be well suited to develop a national choice of law code to be enacted as part of state law, but not to develop a federal choice of law code to be enacted by Congress.

4. Those resisting use of federal power to regulate in areas traditionally regulated by states sometimes recognize that a federal choice of law code might provide a way to inject efficiency into the legal system. In what ways would a federal choice of law code be efficient? Operating under a variety of state laws that govern day-to-day affairs creates inefficiencies in the form of uncertainties, difficulties in planning, and complexities required by overlapping regulations. One way to avoid these inefficiencies might be to eradicate state laws altogether—creating a federal rule that regulates day-to-day affairs. Is a federal choice of law code a beneficial alternative to total preemption of state law by a federal law? Law and economics theorists suggest that a federal choice of law code might enhance United States competitiveness internationally, while allowing for state diversity and experimentation. ERIN O'HARA & LARRY RIBSTEIN, THE LAW MARKET 202-203 (2009).

PROBLEM 2-63: A FEDERAL CHOICE OF LAW CODE

Try your hand at planning how you would draft a federal law code. Would the code be long or short? That is, should it speak in general terms or in specific terms? Should the code attempt to cover every potential legal topic or should it target just a few topics? If it covers just a few topics, which ones should it cover? Which topics are most in need of uniform treatment? Which topics are most appropriate for regulation by the federal government?

PERSPECTIVE ON RACE TO THE BOTTOM AND COORDINATED CHOICE OF LAW RULES

Conflict of laws would not exist were it not for regulatory competition among governmental entities. The cumulative effects of this competition can be both beneficial and detrimental to the governmental system as a whole. Understanding these effects is key to making a considered judgment about which conflict of laws system is best, and about whether to replace the variety of choice of law approaches with a unified national (or federalized) choice of law approach.

A particularly important dynamic that results from regulatory competition is known as the "race to the bottom." This phrase refers to the tendency of states, influenced by interstate competition, to decrease regulation in order to attract businesses. This deregulation in turn threatens a reduction in social welfare. The phrase appears to derive from a dissent by Justice Brandeis, describing the trend in weaker states to create less restrictive laws to attract corporations as a "race . . . not of diligence but of laxity."[54]

The theoretical foundation for the race to the bottom is the "Prisoner's Dilemma." In the Prisoner's Dilemma paradigm, two suspects are separately inter-rogated by a prosecutor who tries to get them to confess. If neither suspect con-fesses, the prosecutor can obtain only misdemeanor convictions with intermediate length sentences for both (say, ten months). If only one suspect confesses, the prosecutor is willing to offer that suspect a plea deal with a shorter sentence (say, three months). The other non-confessing suspect would likely receive a felony conviction and a very long sentence (say, ten years). If both sus-pects confess, they will both likely be convicted of a felony and receive a shorter, but still long, sentence (say, five years).[55] Under the paradigm, each suspect will confess to the crime because each suspect mistrusts the other and believes that confessing will lead to the safest outcome. For example, if a suspect refuses to confess, the suspect risks that the other suspect confesses and leave the first sus-pect with the highest sentence of ten years. Though the outcome of confessing (either five years if both parties confess or three months if the other suspect does not) is better than the outcome of being the only party not to confess (ten-year sentence), the best outcome for both suspects is to not confess at all (ten months). The suspects' sole focus on the best outcome for themselves, as individuals, keeps them from cooperating so as to achieve the best possible outcome.

Like the suspects in the Prisoner's Dilemma, states participating in a race to the bottom dynamic operate in a self-serving manner to the detriment of the overall regulatory scheme. Each state's desire to attract business (and avoid losing current industry) leads all states to deregulate. This deregulation can harm social welfare through lax measures such as permissive environmental laws that allow increased pollution and cause health problems for residents of deregulated states. As with the confessing prisoners, deregulation may benefit a state with increased revenue from new businesses and industries, but can also cause harmful conse-quences to the state's residents. Each state acts with tunnel vision: concerned that a failure to deregulate would lead to high costs, like losing economic activity, the state does nothing to discourage other states from also deregulating themselves. If the states considered their actions in the aggregate, they might recognize that the optimum outcome for all states would be to adopt a stringent standard of regulations.

Scholars have observed a particularly clear race to the bottom dynamic in the evolution of products liability laws. States have an interest in adopting pro-plain-tiff products liability laws to provide protection to their resident consumers. However, as with environmental regulation, states also want to attract new busi-nesses and industries, and businesses prefer reduced liability levels so they do not need to increase prices to offset the cost of liability. (The cost of products liability suits is incorporated into the price of products.) Thus, states have an incentive to

---

54. *Louis K. Ligget Co. v. Lee*, 288 U.S. 517, 559 (1933).
55. *See, e.g.*, Richard L. Revesez, *Rehabilitating Interstate Competition: Rethinking the "Race-to-the-Bottom" Rationale for Federal Environmental Regulation*, 67 N.Y.U. L. Rev. 1210, 1217 (1992).

enact pro-defendant laws to attract more businesses. After the first state enacts laws that are more favorable to defendants, the next state may also lower its liability levels to also attract businesses. This leads to a race toward the lowest liability levels that consumers and regulators are willing to tolerate. As in the Prisoner's Dilemma paradigm, interstate competition prevents government from reaching the welfare-maximizing outcome for all states: a liability level in product regulation that is preferred by the collective and reflects the optimal balance between safety and cost.[56]

Scholars have also observed that in addition to competition over substantive laws regulating products, competition over choice of law principles fuels a race to the bottom in products liability regulation.[57] In today's mobile world, products do not remain within the areas in which they are made, but can be sold in or shipped to any state. This means that a consumer injured by a product likely has a choice to bring suit in the state in which she purchased the product, where the product was made, or where any of the parties reside. Each of those states could have laws with differing levels of liability for the defendant business. Assuming that plaintiffs do not encounter obstacles limiting where they can sue, they can take advantage of a forum that has the most pro-plaintiff laws. For example, a resident of State A, who purchases a product made in State B, could bring suit in either A or B. If State B has a more pro-plaintiff law, a State A resident could try to sue in State B or get State B's liability laws applied. The resident could take advantage of State B's pro-plaintiff law without suffering the costs of the law that would be incorporated into a higher product price.

As in the Prisoner's Dilemma, the greatest outcome for all those subject to products liability regulation can be achieved by cooperation. However, like the confessing prisoners, each state is likely to act in a self-serving manner with nothing binding them to act cooperatively. Professor Michael Gottesman has argued that for states, a "binding agreement" can be achieved through a uniform choice of law via federal directive. Such a directive would make efficient and optimal legal regulation more possible.[58] Professor Michael Krauss makes a similar argument, advocating for a federal choice of law statute for products liability suits.[59] He starts from the observation that for jurisdictions with plaintiff-friendly products liability laws, one would expect higher prices that internalize the cost of lawsuits. Given modern transportation, however, consumers in plaintiff-friendly states, where products are higher in price, can have access to cheaper products in defendant-friendly states. Moreover, these same consumers can avail themselves of more plaintiff-friendly (and expensive) products liability laws when suing for injuries in their home state without internalizing the costs of the more expensive

---

56. *See* Bruce L. Hay, *Conflicts of Law and State Competition in the Product Liability System*, 80 GEO. L.J. 617, 629-630 (1992); Joel P. Trachtman, *Conflict of Laws and Accuracy in the Allocation of Government Responsibility*, 26 VAND. J. TRANSNAT'L L. REV. 975, 1028-1030 (1994).

57. *See, e.g.*, Michael I. Krauss, Product *Liability and Game Theory: One More Trip to the Choice of Law Well*, 2002 B.Y.U. L. REV. 759, 776-784.

58. *See* Michael H. Gottesman, *Draining the Dismal Swamp: The Case for Federal Choice of Law Statutes*, 80 GEO. L.J. 1, 2-16 (1991).

59. Krauss, *Product Liability and Game Theory*, 2002 B.Y.U. L. REV. at 759, 807.

products of the state. Krauss argues that a uniform federal choice of law rule could solve this imbalance by requiring that the governing law in products liability suits come from the state where the retail sale of the product occurred. Under this rule, a consumer who wishes to avoid a high price occasioned by more protective products liability rules in her home state is free to purchase in another state. But when she purchases the cheaper item, she must accept the more defendant-protective products liability laws of the place where she purchased the product. Under such a choice of law rule, products liability law will start to more accurately reflect the preferences of states and consumers about the appropriate risks to incur when using a product.[60]

Professor Bruce Hay also advocates for a federal law that controls the laws governing products liability suits. Unlike Professor Krauss, however, Hay focuses primarily on predictability and planning, arguing that federal law should limit governing products liability laws to those coming from "first party" states. Under this approach, the law that governs a suit can only be of the state where the product was sold or where the producing company resides. Hay reasons that by limiting the governing law to these two states, a business can better predict which laws will apply to disputes and can plan accordingly. A business can assume that it will be liable under the laws of the state in which it is located and where it sold the product. Hay distinguishes these "first party" states from states in which products travel or are resold without the company's knowledge. Like Krauss's approach, Hay's approach tends to prevent consumers from circumventing less protective laws of defendant-friendly states without bearing the cost of the more protective regulation.[61]

The concept of "race to the top" complements "race to the bottom" theories. The term "race to the top" describes a tendency for states to make laws more efficient and beneficial. Relevant literature analyzes the possibility that state regulators seek to regulate corporate managers' incentives to attract shareholders and to attract more revenue-generating corporate charters by enacting efficient corporate laws that are favorable to managers and shareholders. At least one commentator has suggested that some movement toward more efficient laws occurs if a jurisdiction's choice of law approach allows application of something other than forum law.[62] This observation is consistent with a unified federal choice of law approach, so long as that approach would allow for application of non-forum (foreign) law.

The underlying message of all of these theories is that differences among laws affects the decision making and behavior of market participants, all of whom are potential participants in litigation and many of whom plan their activities in light of that reality. Where this difference among laws can be eliminated, such as through a uniform choice of law code, the uniform law can be designed to

60. Krauss, *Product Liability and Game Theory*, 2002 B.Y.U. L. Rev. at 759; *see also* Trachtman, *Government Responsibility*, 26 Vand. J. Transnat'l L. at 1027-1028.

61. Hay, *State Competition*, 80 Geo. L.J. at 644-646.

62. Giesela Rühl, *Methods and Approaches in Choice of Law: An Economic Perspective*, 24 Berkeley J. Int'l L. 801, 813-814 (2006).

account for and remediate possible deleterious consequences of regulatory differences and competition.

K.   MULTIPARTY ACTIONS

1.   Overview

Complex choice of law issues can arise whenever a lawsuit contains more than one plaintiff and one defendant. When does such complex litigation arise? One common context is a single incident tort, such as an airplane crash or an environmental disaster. In another context, courts must adjudicate claims by individuals exposed over a period of time to a harmful substance, such as Agent Orange, Vioxx, Bendectin, breast implants, fen-phen, and tobacco. Outside the tort area, complex litigation can also arise where consumers or others enter a contract with a business entity. Each of these multiparty actions present considerable challenges for litigation systems, and the choice of law problems inherent in the actions exacerbate the strain.

Multiparty actions can arise where a number of individuals simply join forces to file suit in one forum. More complexity arises, however, where parties request that the court certify a case as a class action and where courts consolidate actions from different locales, such as multidistrict litigation in federal courts. Often issues related to both class action status suits and multidistrict litigation converge in one case. Class actions and multidistrict litigation raise some of the most pressing challenges for choice of law theory and practice.

Class action lawsuits are procedural mechanisms that allow multiple plaintiffs to bring a cause of action as one collective group, and this group of plaintiffs is called a class. Suing as a class is a powerful tool for enforcing state and federal rights because it lowers plaintiffs' costs and increases their bargaining power, and in some situations, such as when the damage to any one plaintiff is too minimal to justify an individual lawsuit, class actions are necessary to make available a civil remedy for wrongs done. Both state and federal courts have strict rules for allowing class actions to proceed, and choice of law determinations play a key role in whether a proposed class is certified.

Rule 23 of the Federal Rules of Civil Procedure prescribes the requirements for class certification in federal court. Many states have enacted class certification rules that closely follow this federal standard. Rule 23(a) has four prerequisites any class must meet, summarized as numerosity, typicality, commonality, and adequacy of representation. Rule 23(b) lists three types of class actions; a potential class action must fall into one of these categories. The last category, Rule 23(b)(3), is where plaintiffs seek monetary damages and individual lawsuits would not prevent the plaintiffs from individually obtaining relief. The majority of certified class actions fall into this category.[63] Certification under Rule 23(b)(3) requires predominance and superiority. Under Rule 23(b)(3), predominance means that the court finds that "questions of law or fact common to class members predominate over any questions affecting only individual members." Superiority requires the court to conclude that "a class action is superior to other available methods for fairly and efficiently adjudicating the controversy." An important factor informing the superiority question is "the likely difficulties in managing a class action." These Rule 23(b)(3) factors generally require consistency in the law governing the class members. For this reason, choice of law issues often obstruct the process of convincing a court to certify nationwide class actions.

The existence of a common question of law often depends on which law applies, thus requiring a court to perform a choice of law analysis. Since class actions are often comprised of litigants from multiple states, courts may often conclude that different laws apply to different litigants. In that event, courts often refuse to certify the class.[64] Applying multiple state laws to the class can defeat predominance, as questions of law applicable only to individuals will outnumber questions common to the class. Of course, if a law is substantially similar across different states, these concerns about predominance lessen. Superiority is also tied to the choice of law determination, because applying the law of multiple states to a class action can render the class action device an inefficient method of resolving the controversy. Applying a multitude of laws in one case creates analytical difficulties for judge and jury, and complicates class administration tasks, such as notice as well as remedy calculation.

Choice of law is an important and often case-decisive battleground in class action litigation. One common strategy is for plaintiffs in nationwide class actions to argue that choice of law problems do not really exist, and that potentially applicable state laws are substantially similar, if not the same. Another approach is for plaintiffs to argue that the choice of law rules point to only one state law to govern the controversy. Indeed, to facilitate this strategy, plaintiffs may choose a forum that minimizes the possibility that choice of law will obstruct certification. In furtherance of this goal, plaintiffs may limit theories of recovery to those that will likely be governed by a uniform law, thus effectively preempting the court's concerns over predominance and manageability by creating subclasses of similar plaintiffs. Indeed, one common approach is to avoid state law claims altogether, so as to side step the choice of law stumbling block. Where state law provides the basis for a claim, defendants seeking to prevent class certification will argue that choice of law rules point toward numerous state laws, which vary greatly in their substance.

As explored further in Chapter 3, the Supreme Court has established broad constitutional constraints on class action choice of law, which may influence litigant choices. In *Phillips Petroleum Co. v. Shutts*, 472 U.S. 797, 821 (1985), the Court established that "[a court] may not take a transaction with little or no relationship to the forum and apply the law of the forum in order to satisfy the procedural

---

63. Principles of the Law of Aggregate Litigation §1.02 (2010).
64. Genevieve G. York-Erwin, *The Choice-of-Law Problem(s) in the Class Action Context*, 84 N.Y.U. L. Rev. 1793, 1794 (2009).

requirement that there be a 'common question of law.'" The Court then expounded the constitutional limit on a state applying its own law to every member of a plaintiff class: a state must have "significant contact or significant aggregation of contacts" to the claims of each plaintiff, establishing a sufficient state interest to ensure that application of the state's law is fair and reasonable. *Id.* at 821.

The certification inquiry for class actions is streamlined where the dispute implicates a uniform contract containing a choice of law provision. Often, standard form contracts provide that the state of a defendant's headquarters governs, thus seeking to eliminate the possibility that one of 49 other states (or other countries) where consumer plaintiffs reside will provide the governing law. Sometimes, however, even a form contract does not designate one uniform law. For example, a mortgage contract may designate the law of the state where the mortgaged property is located as that which governs. Accordingly, a class action against a multistate mortgagor challenging such matters as excessive fees may require more than one governing law, even if the case involves a standard contract with a choice of law clause. *See, e.g., Washington Mutual Bank v. Superior Court of Orange County,* 15 P.3d 1071 (Cal. 2001). In a decision that may significantly affect the future of class actions, the Supreme Court has cleared the way for form contracts in which parties agree to waive their ability to pursue a class action. Specifically, the Supreme Court ruled that federal preemption principles preclude courts from determining that such class action waivers in consumer contracts are unconscionable under state law. *AT&T Mobility LLC v. Concepcion,* 131 S. Ct. 1740 (2011).

Despite occasional input by the Supreme Court, barriers to class certification have continued to spawn forum shopping and gamesmanship. In response to such abuses, Congress enacted the Class Action Fairness Act (CAFA) in 2005. CAFA expanded federal jurisdiction over class action suits and other mass actions. Subject to exceptions, CAFA granted federal courts jurisdiction over class actions based on state law where the aggregate amount in controversy exceeds $5 million and minimal diversity exists. Federal courts follow Rule 23 when exercising diversity jurisdiction,[65] but they apply the choice of law rules of their forum state.[66] For this reason, CAFA does not completely prevent forum shopping, even though it effectively prevents state courts from adjudicating multistate and national class actions. Importantly, Congress declined the opportunity to include a choice of law provision in CAFA, and did not purport to change the operation of the *Erie* doctrine's mandate for application of state law as dictated by choice of law rules of the forum state. Thus, as explained by Professor Linda Silberman, "[i]n entrusting class action litigation to the federal courts without accompanying federal substantive law or federal choice of law principles, Congress has allowed the choice of law consequences to fall where they may."[67]

The other procedural mechanism for multiparty suits, multidistrict litigation (MDL), also creates a unique set of choice of law issues. For actions pending in

---

65. *See, e.g., Shady Grove Orthopedic Assoc., P.A. v. Allstate Ins. Co.,* 130 S. Ct. 1431 (2010).
66. *See Klaxon Co. v. Stentor Elec. Mfg. Co.,* 313 U.S. 487 (1941).
67. Linda Silberman, *The Role of Choice of Law in National Class Actions,* 156 U. Pa. L. Rev. 2001, 2031 (2008).

federal court, a statute, 28 U.S.C. §1407, allows a judicial panel on multidistrict litigation (MDL) to transfer actions to one district for "coordinated or consolidated pretrial proceedings" if the panel concludes that doing so will promote the "just and efficient conduct of such actions." The consolidation of cases does not create a class action; the cases remain separate individual suits. These cases are consolidated only for pretrial proceedings; efficiency and cost-saving gains of these proceedings often decrease where the cases reflect legal differences.[68] Strong arguments support the use of the MDL structure to overcome conflict of laws problems, since the MDL mechanism promotes aggregation without creating unavoidable pressure to designate a substantive law that would not otherwise govern in individual cases.[69] MDL consolidation does not formally affect the choice of law process, but complications nonetheless arise. The first source of complication derives from sheer numbers: MDL makes adjudication of thousands of claims possible. Moreover, as part of the multidistrict litigation process, plaintiffs sometimes file a master complaint in the district where the actions are transferred. Where such consolidation occurs, an issue arises as to where the "forum" state is deemed situated for the purpose of beginning choice of law analysis. The court's decision in *In re Vioxx Products Liability Litigation*, 239 F.R.D. 450 (E.D. La. 2006), set forth below, grapples with this issue.

When parties do not use class actions to remedy mass torts, the litigation strategy of both plaintiffs and defendants no longer focuses on questions such as predominance and manageability. Removing the cumbersome requirements of class certification does not mean, however, that the parties will not fight over choice of law issues. In a multidistrict litigation case emanating from a plane crash in New York, for example, the plaintiffs argued that New York law governed both their negligence and punitive damage claims.[70] The defendants replied that federal law preempted the plaintiffs' state law claims and that Virginia law governed the punitive damage claims. These arguments were typical of mass tort cases, where the question of which law governs punitive damages is often contentious.[71]

The American Law Institute has approved and published an extensive proposal that develops a method for handling multiple party, multiple forum litigation, Complex Litigation: Statutory Recommendations and Analysis (1994). The thrust of the proposal is to provide mechanisms for consolidating related litigation in one forum, whether state or federal court. Noting that the most effective method of handling complex litigation is for courts to follow national standards, the proposal sets forth six extensive rules for mass tort and contract actions designed to serve as a uniform federal choice of law code. The proposal received

68. Principles of the Law of Aggregate Litigation §1.02 (2010).
69. Andrew D. Bradt, *The Shortest Distance: Direct Filing and Choice of Law in Multidistrict Litigation*, 88 Notre Dame L. Rev.759 (2012).
70. In re Air Crash Near Clarence Ctr., New York, on February 12, 2009, 09-MD-2085, 2011 WL 2848812 (W.D.N.Y. 2011).
71. Meng v. Novartis Pharm. Corp., 2009 WL 4623715 (N.J. Super. Ct. Law. Div. 2009) (parties accepted that plaintiffs in the products liability mass action would have their claims governed by the laws of the state where they were injured, but disagreed over the law governing punitive damages).

significant, although not unanimous, scholarly praise, but has not markedly influenced case law or legislative initiatives. More recently, the ALI took up the problem of choice of law in complex litigation in its 2010 project on the Principles of the Law of Aggregate Litigation (Principles). The Principles described the goal of the project as to "identify good procedures for handling aggregate lawsuits [and the] ways of governing them that promote their efficiency and efficacy as tools for enforcing valid laws." Unlike the earlier ALI project, the Principles contain no suggestion of incorporating a national choice of law approach for aggregate cases. Focused instead on maintaining the status quo, §2.05 of the Principles "seeks largely to incorporate existing choice of law through approval of aggregate treatment in three current situations: when one law applies to all claims; when different laws are 'the same in functional content'; or when there are a limited number of patterns." Louise Ellen Teitz, *Complexity and Aggregation in Choice of Law: An Introduction to the Landscape*, 14 ROGER WILLIAMS U. L. REV. 1 (2009).

2. *Multidistrict Litigation and Class Action Cases*

In the Matter of Bridgestone/Firestone, Inc.

288 F.3d 1012 (7th Cir. 2002)

EASTERBROOK, Circuit Judge.

Firestone tires on Ford Explorer SUVs experienced an abnormally high failure rate during the late 1990s. In August 2000, while the National Highway Transportation Safety Administration was investigating, Firestone recalled and replaced some of those tires. Ford and Firestone replaced additional tires during 2001. Many suits have been filed as a result of injuries and deaths related to the tire failures. Other suits were filed by persons who own (or owned) Ford Explorers or Firestone tires that have so far performed properly; these persons seek compensation for the risk of failure, which may be reflected in diminished resale value of the vehicles and perhaps in mental stress. The Judicial Panel on Multidistrict Litigation transferred suits filed in, or removed to, federal court to the Southern District of Indiana for consolidated pretrial proceedings under 28 U.S.C. §1407(a). Once these have been completed, the cases must be returned to the originating districts for decision on the merits. In an effort to prevent retransfer, counsel representing many of the plaintiffs filed a new consolidated suit in Indianapolis and asked the judge to certify it as a nationwide class action, which would make all other suits redundant. The district court obliged and certified two nationwide classes: the first includes everyone who owns, owned, leases, or leased a Ford Explorer of model year 1991 through 2001 anytime before the first recall, and the second includes all owners and lessees from 1990 until today of [various tire types]. . . .

(handwritten: ② same legal Rules)

No class action is proper unless all litigants are governed by the same legal rules. Otherwise the class cannot satisfy the commonality and superiority requirements of Fed. R. Civ. P. 23(a), (b)(3). Yet state laws about theories such as those presented by our plaintiffs differ, and such differences have led us to hold that other warranty, fraud, or products-liability suits may not proceed as nationwide classes. The district judge, well aware of this principle, recognized that uniform law would be essential to class certification. Because plaintiffs' claims rest on state law, the choice-of-law rules come from the state in which the federal court sits. The district judge concluded that Indiana law points to the headquarters of the defendants, because that is where the products are designed and the important decisions about disclosures and sales are made. Ford and Firestone engaged in conduct that was uniform across the nation, which the district court took to imply the appropriateness of uniform law. This ruling means that all claims by the Explorer class will be resolved under Michigan law and all claims by the tire class will be resolved under Tennessee law. According to the district court, other obstacles . . . are worth overcoming in light of the efficiency of class treatment. Nor did the district court deem it important that Firestone's tires were designed in Ohio, and many were manufactured outside Tennessee, as many of Ford's vehicles are manufactured outside Michigan.

Both Ford and Firestone petitioned for interlocutory review under Fed. R. Civ. P. 23(f). We granted these requests because the suit is exceedingly unlikely to be tried. Aggregating millions of claims on account of multiple products manufactured and sold across more than ten years makes the case so unwieldy, and the stakes so large, that settlement becomes almost inevitable—and at a price that reflects the risk of a catastrophic judgment as much as, if not more than, the actual merit of the claims. Permitting appellate review before class certification can precipitate such a settlement is a principal function of Rule 23(f). Another function is permitting appellate review of important legal issues that otherwise might prove elusive. The district court's conclusion that one state's law would apply to claims by consumers throughout the country . . . is a novelty, and, if followed, would be of considerable import to other suits. Our review of this choice-of-law question is plenary, so we start there.

Indiana is a lex loci delicti state: in all but exceptional cases it applies the law of the place where harm occurred. Those class members who suffered injury or death as a result of defects were harmed in the states where the tires failed. As a practical matter, these class members can be ignored; they are sure to opt out and litigate independently. These classes therefore effectively include only those consumers whose loss (if any) is financial rather than physical: it is the class of persons whose tires did *not* fail, whose vehicles did not roll over. Many class members face no future threat of failure either, because about 30 million tires were recalled and replaced, while other tires have been used up and discarded. Financial loss (if any, a qualification we will not repeat) was suffered in the places where the vehicles and tires were purchased at excessive prices or resold at depressed prices. Those injuries occurred in all 50 states, the District of Columbia, Puerto Rico, and U.S. territories such as Guam. The *lex loci delicti* principle points to the places of these injuries, not the defendants' corporate headquarters, as the source of law.

Plaintiffs concede that until 1987 this would have been Indiana's approach. They contend, however, that *Hubbard Manufacturing Co. v. Greeson*, 515 N.E.2d 1071 (Ind. 1987), changed everything by holding that when the place of the injury "bears little connection to the legal action" a court may consider other factors, such as the place of the conduct causing the injury and the residence of the parties. It is conceivable, we suppose, that Indiana might think that a financial (or physical) injury to one of its residents, occurring within the state's borders, "bears little connection to the legal action," but the proof of that pudding is in the eating. Has Indiana since 1987 applied the law of a state where a product was designed, or promotional materials drafted, to a suit arising out of an injury in Indiana? As far as we can tell, the answer is no — not even once, and the state has had plenty of opportunities. Yet since 1987 both Indiana and this court have routinely applied Indiana law when injury caused by a defective product occurred in Indiana to Indiana residents. Neither Indiana nor any other state has applied a uniform place-of-the-defendant's-headquarters rule to products-liability cases. It is not hard to devise an argument that such a uniform rule would be good on many dimensions, but that argument has not carried the day with state judges, and it is state law rather than a quest for efficiency in litigation (or in product design decisions) that controls.

"Ah, but this is not a products-liability case!" So plaintiffs respond to the conspicuous lack of support from state decisions. And indeed it is not a products-liability suit, since all who suffered physical injury are bound to opt out. No injury, no tort, is an ingredient of every state's law. Plaintiffs describe the injury as financial rather than physical and seek to move the suit out of the tort domain and into that of contract (the vehicle was not the flawless one described and thus is not merchantable, a warranty theory) and consumer fraud (on the theory that selling products with undisclosed attributes, and thus worth less than represented, is fraudulent). It is not clear that this maneuver actually moves the locus from tort to contract. If tort law fully compensates those who are physically injured, then any recoveries by those whose products function properly mean excess compensation. As a result, most states would not entertain the sort of theory that plaintiffs press.

Obviously plaintiffs believe that Michigan and Tennessee are in the favorable minority; we need not decide. If recovery for breach of warranty or consumer fraud is possible, the injury is decidedly where the consumer is located, rather than where the seller maintains its headquarters. A contract for the sale of a car in Indiana is governed by Indiana law unless it contains a choice-of-law clause, and plaintiffs do not want to enforce any choice-of-law clause. Plaintiffs have not cited, and we could not find, any Indiana case applying any law other than Indiana's to warranty or fraud claims arising from consumer products designed (or contract terms written) out of state, unless a choice-of-law clause was involved. State consumer-protection laws vary considerably, and courts must respect these differences rather than apply one state's law to sales in other states with different rules. We do not for a second suppose that Indiana would apply Michigan law to an auto sale if Michigan permitted auto companies to conceal defects from customers; nor do we think it likely that Indiana would apply Korean law (no matter *what* Korean law on the subject may provide) to claims of deceit in the sale of Hyundai automobiles, in Indiana, to residents of Indiana, or French law to the sale of cars equipped with Michelin tires. Indiana has consistently said that sales of products in Indiana must conform to Indiana's consumer-protection laws and its rules of contract law. It follows that Indiana's choice-of-law rule selects the 50 states and multiple territories where the buyers live, and not the place of the sellers' headquarters, for these suits.

Because these claims must be adjudicated under the law of so many jurisdictions, a single nationwide class is not manageable. Lest we soon see a Rule 23(f) petition to review the certification of 50 state classes, we add that this litigation is not manageable as a class action even on a statewide basis. . . .

The district judge did not doubt that differences within the class would lead to difficulties in managing the litigation. But the judge thought it better to cope with these differences than to scatter the suits to the winds and require hundreds of judges to resolve thousands of claims under 50 or more bodies of law. Efficiency is a vital goal in any legal system — but the vision of "efficiency" underlying this class certification is the model of the central planner. Plaintiffs share the premise of the ALI's Complex Litigation Project (1993), which devotes more than 700 pages to an analysis of means to consolidate litigation as quickly as possible, by which the authors mean, before multiple trials break out. The authors take as given the benefits of that step. Yet the benefits are elusive. The central planning model — one case, one court, one set of rules, one settlement price for all involved — suppresses information that is vital to accurate resolution. What is the law of Michigan, or Arkansas, or Guam, as applied to this problem? Judges and lawyers will have to guess, because the central planning model keeps the litigation far away from state courts. . . . And if the law were clear, how would the facts (and thus the damages per plaintiff) be ascertained? One suit is an all-or-none affair, with high risk even if the parties supply all the information at their disposal. . . . [I]t is worth reiterating: only "a decentralized process of multiple trials, involving different juries, and different standards of liability, in different jurisdictions" will yield the information needed for accurate evaluation of mass tort claims. Once a series of decisions or settlements has produced an accurate evaluation of a subset of the claims (say, 1995 Explorers in Arizona equipped with a particular tire specification) the others in that subset can be settled or resolved at an established price.

No matter what one makes of the decentralized approach as an original matter, it is hard to adopt the central-planner model without violence not only to Rule 23 but also to principles of federalism. Differences across states may be costly for courts and litigants alike, but they are a fundamental aspect of our federal republic and must not be overridden in a quest to clear the queue in court. . . . The motion to certify questions of law to the Supreme Court of Michigan is denied as unnecessary in light of this opinion. The district court's order certifying two nationwide classes is reversed.

In re Vioxx Products Liability Litigation

239 F.R.D. 450 (E.D. La. 2006)

FALLON, J.

ORDER AND REASONS

Before the Court is the Plaintiffs' Steering Committee's ("PSC") Motion for Certification of a Nation-Wide Class Action for Personal Injury and Wrongful Death (Rec. Doc. 2171). The Court heard oral argument and took this motion under submission. For the following reasons, the PSC's motion is DENIED.

I. BACKGROUND

This multidistrict products liability litigation involves the prescription drug Vioxx. Merck & Co., Inc. ("Merck"), a New Jersey corporation, researched, designed, manufactured, marketed, and distributed Vioxx to relieve pain and inflammation resulting from osteoarthritis, rheumatoid arthritis, menstrual pain, and migraine headaches. On May 20, 1999, the Food and Drug Administration approved Vioxx for sale in the United States. Vioxx remained on the market until September 30, 2004, at which time Merck withdrew it from the market when data from a clinical trial known as APPROVe indicated that the use of Vioxx increased the risk of cardiovascular thrombotic events such as myocardial infarctions (heart attacks) and ischemic strokes. Thereafter, thousands of individual suits and numerous class actions were filed against Merck . . . throughout the country. . . . It is estimated that 105 million prescriptions for Vioxx were written in the United States between May 20, 1999 and September 30, 2004.

On February 16, 2005, the Judicial Panel on Multidistrict Litigation ("JPML") conferred multidistrict litigation status on Vioxx lawsuits filed in federal court and transferred all such cases to this Court to coordinate discovery and to consolidate pretrial matters. . . .

In addition to thousands of individual claims, this [Multidistrict Litigation (MDL)] currently includes over 160 class actions emanating from nearly every state. . . . [T]his opinion deals only with the personal injury and wrongful death class actions.

Master complaints help the Court and the parties focus on common issues in an efficient and effective manner and they apply to all pending class actions and to those subsequently filed, removed, or transferred to this Court as part of MDL 1657. In the Master Class Action Complaint for Cases Involving Personal Injury and Wrongful Death ("Master Complaint"), the PSC alleges that Vioxx was a defective product; that Merck misrepresented the safety of Vioxx and negligently manufactured, marketed, advertised, and sold Vioxx as a safe prescription medication, when in fact Merck knew or should have known that Vioxx was not safe for its intended purpose; and that Vioxx caused serious medical problems, and in certain patients, catastrophic injuries, and death.

On December 8, 2005, the PSC filed the instant motion to certify a nationwide class action under Rule 23(b)(3) of the Federal Rules of Civil Procedure consisting of:

> All persons residing in the United States who took Vioxx in any dose at any time between May 20, 1999 when Vioxx was first approved by the United States Food & Drug Administration ("FDA"), and September 30, 2004, when Vioxx was withdrawn from the market, and who claim personal injuries or assert wrongful death claims arising from ingestion of Vioxx.

The PSC presents Rosemary Lawrence and Raymond Gibney, both New Jersey residents, as class representatives on behalf of themselves and all others similarly situated in the United States. Ms. Lawrence is a 59-year-old woman who took Vioxx for at least eight months and suffered a pulmonary embolism on July 30, 2002. Mr. Gibney is a 76-year-old man who took Vioxx for approximately one year and suffered a heart attack on December 29, 2002. Both Ms. Lawrence and Mr. Gibney allege that their injuries were caused by Vioxx.

The PSC contends that New Jersey substantive law can and should be applied to all personal injury and wrongful death claims made by United States residents. The basic thrust of the PSC's argument in favor of applying New Jersey products liability law is that (1) Merck is headquartered in New Jersey and, thus, all of its decisions regarding the manufacturing, testing, labeling, marketing, and advertising of Vioxx originated in and emanated from New Jersey and (2) New Jersey has a unique and strong interest in regulating the conduct of its corporate citizens and specifically in deterring wrongful conduct by New Jersey pharmaceutical companies.

Merck opposes certification of a nationwide class action on two grounds. First, Merck argues that the proposed class members' claims must be adjudicated under the substantive laws of the states in which they resided, ingested, and were allegedly injured by Vioxx and, thus, there is no commonality of law. Second, Merck contends that certification is inappropriate because each plaintiff's claim involves separate and distinct factual issues.

II. LAW AND ANALYSIS

Before determining whether a nationwide class action may be certified under Rule 23 of the Federal Rules of Civil Procedure, the Court must first determine which state's or states' substantive law will govern the class. To make this determination, the Court must conduct a choice-of-law analysis. Each state has its own choice-of-law rules that its courts use to select the applicable law. Therefore, the Court must first decide which state's choice-of-law rules to apply. The Court will then apply these rules to determine which state's or states' substantive law will govern the class. Only then can the Court determine whether or not the putative nationwide class of Vioxx users satisfies the requirements of Rule 23.

A. CHOICE OF LAW

i. *Selecting the Applicable Choice-of-Law Rules*

Federal courts sitting in diversity must apply the choice-of-law rules of the forum state. In MDL cases, the forum state is typically the state in which the action was initially filed before being transferred to the MDL court. In the present case, the proposed class representatives originally filed their class action complaint in the United States District Court for the District of New Jersey; however, the PSC also subsequently filed a Master Complaint in this Court. Therefore, the Court could conceivably apply the choice-of-law rules of either New Jersey or Louisiana.

In *In re Propulsid Products Liability Litigation*, 208 F.R.D. 133, 140-41 (E.D. La. 2002), this Court was faced with the similar decision of whether to apply Indiana or Louisiana choice-of-law rules in an MDL class certification proceeding. In *Propulsid*, the Court determined that a master complaint is only an administrative device used to aid efficiency and economy and, thus, should not be given the status of an ordinary complaint. Accordingly, the Court looked to the underlying Indiana complaint and applied Indiana's choice-of-law rules.

The Court finds no reason to depart from its prior holding, especially given that the parties in this case have not urged the Court to reconsider its view and apparently agree that New Jersey choice-of-law rules should be applied. Therefore, the Court will once again look to the specific action brought before it for class certification — the New Jersey complaint — and will apply New Jersey's choice-of-law rules to determine which state's or states' substantive law would govern the proposed nationwide class.

ii. *Selecting the Applicable Substantive Law*

New Jersey applies a flexible "governmental interests" choice-of-law test to determine which state has the greatest interest in governing the specific issue in the underlying litigation. New Jersey's governmental interests test is a two-step inquiry. The first step is to determine whether an actual conflict exists between the laws of New Jersey and any other state with an interest in the litigation. In the present case, both the PSC and Merck acknowledge that there are conflicts between the law of New Jersey and the laws of the other fifty jurisdictions in regard to negligence, strict liability, failure to warn, learned intermediary, and defective design. The Court agrees, and therefore will advance to the second step.

The second step of New Jersey's governmental interests test is to determine which state has the most significant relationship to the occurrence and to the parties. In reaching this decision, the Court must identify the governmental policies of each state and how those policies are affected by the states' contacts to the litigation and to the parties. There are five factors that the Court must use to guide its decision: (1) the interests of interstate comity; (2) the interests underlying the field of tort law; (3) the interests of the parties; (4) the interests of judicial administration; and (5) the competing interests of the states. The third and fourth factors are the least significant. The fifth factor is the most important factor. The Court will now consider these five factors to determine which state has the most significant relationship to the occurrence and to the parties and, therefore, which state's or states' substantive law will govern the class.[7]

a. Interests of Interstate Comity and Tort Law

In this case, the interests of interstate comity and tort law, the first two factors, merge and will be considered together. The interests of interstate comity, the first factor, require the Court to consider whether the application of one state's law will frustrate the policies of other interested states. In the present case, the issue before the Court is not whether a specific aspect of a state's law, such as the learned intermediary doctrine or punitive damages, should be applied, but whether the entire scope of one state's products liability law, and all aspects arising thereunder, should be applied to the class. Thus, this situation requires the Court to consider the purpose of products liability laws in general, rather than just the purpose behind a specific state law.

The interests underlying the field of tort law, the second factor, require the Court to consider the degree to which deterrence and compensation, the two fundamental goals of tort law, would be furthered by the application of one state's law versus the application of every state's law. Not surprisingly, products liability laws are motivated by the same underlying purposes as the field of tort law in general, and therefore the interests of interstate comity and the interests underlying the field of tort law align in this case.

With regard to these two factors, the Court finds that each plaintiff's home jurisdiction has a stronger interest in deterring foreign corporations from personally injuring its citizens and ensuring that its citizens are compensated than New Jersey does in deterring its corporate citizens' wrongdoing. These interests arise by virtue of each state being the place where the plaintiffs reside and, therefore, the states in which the plaintiffs were prescribed Vioxx, where the plaintiffs ingested Vioxx, and where the alleged injuries occurred. Therefore, the Court finds that the first and second factors weigh in favor of applying the law of each plaintiff's home jurisdiction to his or her respective claims.

b. Interests of the Parties

The interests of the parties, the third factor, require the Court to consider each party's justified expectations and the need for predictability of result. This factor often plays a small role in the field of tort law because a party who causes an unintentional injury is generally not cognizant of the law that may be applied. Nevertheless, the Court finds that this factor supports Merck's argument.

The PSC contends that Merck's choice to operate in New Jersey means that it should reasonably expect to abide by New Jersey's laws. While this is true, it is just as true that Merck, an international corporation providing its drugs to every state

---

7. Before beginning its analysis, the Court notes that the PSC has failed to satisfy its duty of evaluating the strengths, weaknesses, and policies of all fifty-one interested jurisdictions. Parties seeking to have the law of a single jurisdiction applied to a nationwide class must assess the laws of all interested jurisdictions, not just the one of their choosing. *Id.* Without this appraisal, not only is the Court's choice-of-law analysis weakened, but the PSC's ability to satisfy its burden on class certification suffers.

in the nation, should expect to abide by every jurisdiction's laws. To the extent that problems developed with respect to Vioxx, Merck could have reasonably expected to be sued in every jurisdiction and be subject to every jurisdiction's laws. As to the individual plaintiffs, it is highly unlikely that a plaintiff residing outside of New Jersey could have reasonably expected that his or her personal injury claims would be governed by New Jersey law. As such, the Court finds that the third factor weighs in favor of applying the laws of each plaintiff's home jurisdiction to his or her respective claims.

c. Interests of Judicial Administration

The interests of judicial administration, the fourth factor, require the Court to consider the practicality of applying one jurisdiction's law in a specific instance. This factor weighs heavily in favor of applying New Jersey law. From the Court's perspective, the application of a single jurisdiction's law is more practical than the application of fifty-one different jurisdictions' laws. Therefore, the Court finds that the fourth factor weighs in favor of applying New Jersey law to the entire class. Ease of administration, however, is of minimal importance and must give way to the other factors.

d. Competing Interests of the States β

The competing interests of the states, the fifth factor, is the most important factor under New Jersey's choice-of-law scheme. In deciding the competing interests factor, the Court must consider four separate sub-elements: (1) the place where the injury occurred; (2) the place where the conduct causing the injury occurred; (3) the domicile, residence, nationality, place of incorporation, and place of business of the parties; and (4) the place where the relationship between the parties is centered. Furthermore, in personal injury litigation, the place of injury is especially important, and when the conduct and injury occur in the same state, that jurisdiction's laws will generally apply except when another jurisdiction has a demonstrably dominant interest and no policy of the situs state would be frustrated. Throughout this analysis, the Court must focus on what a given legislature intended to protect by enacting the law at issue and how that legislature's concerns will be furthered by applying its law to the multistate situation.

Regarding the place of injury, the Court finds that the jurisdiction where each plaintiff resides qualifies as the place of injury. There is no evidence indicating otherwise and such a conclusion is based on common sense. Each plaintiff most likely was prescribed Vioxx, ingested Vioxx, and allegedly suffered personal injury in his or her state of residence. As such, in the present case, the injuries occurred in fifty-one jurisdictions, fifty of which are not New Jersey.

Regarding the conduct causing the injury, the Court finds that the jurisdiction where each plaintiff resided also qualifies as the place where the injury-causing conduct occurred. The PSC, however, would have the Court conclude that New Jersey was the place where the injury-causing conduct occurred because New Jersey is where the majority, if not all, of the relevant corporate decisions occurred. However, Vioxx was advertised in, marketed in, shipped into, prescribed in, sold in, ingested in, and allegedly caused harm in fifty-one jurisdictions. Merck's conduct may have originated in New Jersey, but it was effectuated and felt by every plaintiff in their own home jurisdiction. Accordingly, the conduct causing the plaintiffs' injuries occurred, and the plaintiffs' claims arose, in fifty-one jurisdictions, fifty of which are not New Jersey.

Regarding the residence, domicile, nationality, place of incorporation, and place of business of the parties, Merck is a New Jersey corporation that predominantly operates its business in New Jersey. On the other hand, the plaintiffs reside in fifty-one jurisdictions, fifty of which are not New Jersey.

Regarding the place where the relationship is centered, the Court finds that the relationship between each plaintiff and Merck is centered in the state where each plaintiff resides. This is where each plaintiff most likely was prescribed, purchased, ingested, and allegedly harmed by Vioxx. . . . Merck consciously choose to advertise and market Vioxx throughout the United States, which ultimately led to the writing of Vioxx prescriptions, the sale of Vioxx, and the ingestion of Vioxx across the country. As such, the parties' relationships are centered in fifty-one jurisdictions, fifty of which are not New Jersey.

Accordingly, the Court finds that the competing interests of the states, the fifth and most important factor, weighs in favor of applying the law of each plaintiff's home jurisdiction to his or her respective claims.

iii. Choice-of-Law Conclusion

. . . The relevant choice-of-law factors confirm that New Jersey substantive law should not be applied to the entire class, but instead, that the substantive law of each plaintiff's home jurisdiction must be applied to his or her respective claims. With this in mind, the Court now turns to Rule 23 of the Federal Rules of Civil Procedure to determine whether the putative class should be certified.

B. CLASS CERTIFICATION

Rule 23(a) sets forth four prerequisites to any class action: (1) a class "so numerous that joinder of all members is impracticable"; (2) the existence of "questions of law or fact common to the class"; (3) class representatives with claims or defenses "typical . . . of the class"; and (4) class representatives that "will fairly and adequately protect the interests of the class." Fed. R. Civ. P. 23(a). In addition to these prerequisites, a party seeking class certification under Rule 23(b)(3) must also demonstrate that "questions of law or fact common to the members of the class predominate over any questions affecting only individual members" and that the class action is "superior to other available methods for the fair and efficient adjudication of the controversy." Fed. R. Civ. P. 23(b)(3). As the party seeking class certification, the PSC bears the burden of showing that all of these criteria are satisfied.

At the outset, the Court notes that its choice-of-law analysis presents significant hurdles to certification of a nationwide class of Vioxx users because the application of the laws of fifty-one jurisdictions to the claims of the proposed class creates problems for the typicality, adequacy, predominance, and superiority requirements of Rule 23. Moreover, even if New Jersey law could be applied to the entire class, individualized factual issues concerning specific causation and damages dominate this litigation and create independent hurdles to certification. Nevertheless, the Court will carefully analyze the requirements of Rule 23 to determine whether these apparent hurdles can be overcome.

i. Numerosity

. . . With approximately 20 million Vioxx users in the United States, the numerosity requirement is clearly satisfied.

ii. Commonality

Rule 23(a)(2) requires that there be issues of law or fact common to the class. The commonality requirement is satisfied if at least one issue's resolution will affect all or a significant number of class members. . . . The Master Complaint identifies several common questions of fact. Specifically, common questions of fact exist regarding the development, manufacturing, and testing of Vioxx. Moreover, common questions of fact exist regarding Vioxx's effects on the human body. These common questions relate to "general causation," that is, whether or not Vioxx is capable of causing adverse cardiovascular events. . . .

iii. Typicality

Rule 23(a)(3) requires that the claims of the class representatives be typical of the claims of the class. Typicality does not require that these claims be identical, but rather that they share the same essential characteristics — a similar course of conduct, or the same legal theory. In this case, both the proposed class representatives and the putative class members assert various products liability claims against Merck under theories of negligence, strict liability, failure to warn, and defective design. [One factor weighing against typicality is choice of law.] [T]he Court's choice-of-law analysis suggests that while the proposed class representatives' claims will be governed by New Jersey law, the putative class members' claims will be governed by the substantive laws of their respective jurisdictions. The applicability of multiple substantive laws also precludes a finding of typicality.

iv. Adequacy of Representation

. . . The Court has no doubts about the zeal and competence of the representatives' counsel in this case. However, the "adequate representation requirement overlaps with the typicality requirement because in the absence of typical claims, the class *representative* has no incentive to pursue the claims of the other class members." Thus, despite Herculean efforts by the PSC, the Court finds that because of the factual and legal differences among class members' claims, the proposed class representatives cannot satisfy the adequacy requirement.

v. Predominance

Rule 23(b)(3) requires that common questions of law or fact "predominate over any questions affecting only individual [class] members." To predominate, common issues must form a significant part of individual cases. The predominance requirement of Rule 23(b)(3) is "far more demanding" than the commonality requirement of Rule 23(a), because it "tests whether proposed classes are sufficiently cohesive to warrant adjudication by representation." Lastly, the cause of action as a whole must satisfy Rule 23(b)(3)'s predominance requirement.

It has been said that "[n]o class action is proper unless all litigants are governed by the same legal rules." This is because "variations in state law may swamp any common issues and defeat predominance." The PSC bears the burden of demonstrating that variations among the fifty-one applicable state laws do not "pose 'insuperable obstacles' to certification." Notwithstanding valiant efforts, the PSC has not carried its burden in this respect and, therefore, the Court finds that common questions of law do not predominate. Furthermore, courts have almost invariably found that common questions of fact do not predominate in pharmaceutical drug cases. This case is no different. . . .

. . . The PSC relies on mass accident cases to support its argument that certification is appropriate here. Despite early skepticism, mass accident, or single-situs torts, have generally been susceptible to class certification. . . . Regardless, the PSC's reliance on mass accident class actions is misplaced in this pharmaceutical litigation. The number, uniqueness, singularity, and complexity of the factual scenarios surrounding each case swamp any predominating issues.

vi. Superiority

Under Rule 23(b)(3), a district court must evaluate four factors to determine whether the class action format is superior to other methods of adjudication: the class members' interest in individually controlling their separate actions; the extent and nature of existing litigation by class members concerning the same claims; the desirability of concentrating the litigation in the particular forum; and the likely difficulties in class management. In this case, the difficulties in class management overwhelm any efficiencies that could be secured through classwide adjudication.

. . .

III. CONCLUSION

For the foregoing reasons, the PSC's Motion for Certification of a Nation-Wide Class Action for Personal Injury and Wrongful Death (Rec. Doc. 2171) is DENIED.

Notes on
BRIDGESTONE/FIRESTONE *AND* VIOXX

1. *Vioxx* and *Bridgestone/Firestone* present the class certification issue in the context of multidistrict litigation and therefore present double-barreled complications for the choice of law analysis: not only must the cases clear the class certification hurdle, but the initial analysis must reckon with the facts of transfer, master complaints, and other procedures attendant to multidistrict

litigation. Both cases follow the common practice in multidistrict litigation of treating the state where the complaint was originally filed as the "forum" jurisdiction for the purposes of choice of law purposes. Moreover, as *Vioxx* explains, any master complaint filed as part of the multidistrict litigation procedure is simply an administrative device that does not possess the status of a true complaint. The approach in both cases is consistent with the rulings of the United States Supreme Court in *Van Dusen v. Barrack*, 376 U.S. 612 (1964), and *Ferens v. John Deere Co.*, 494 U.S. 516 (1989), holding that a district court that receives a case with state law claims from another district court must apply the choice of law rules of the state where the transferor court sits.

2. The court in *Bridgestone/Firestone* applied the place of the harm rule, while the *Vioxx* court followed New Jersey's more "flexible governmental interests analysis." *Bridgestone/Firestone* described the governing choice of law approach as follows: "Indiana is a lex loci delicti state: in all but exceptional cases it applies the law of the place where harm occurred." How did this difference in the choice of law approach between Indiana and New Jersey influence the courts' reasoning? Did the difference affect the likelihood that one defendant-centered contact would control the choice of law determination?

3. When compared with *Bridgestone/Firestone*, the *Vioxx* court may have appeared less dogmatic in attitude and more methodical in discussing the various factors of Rule 23. The *Vioxx* court nonetheless reached the same conclusion as *Bridgestone/Firestone* on defendant-based contacts: they should play in the choice of law decision. In the end, wasn't this one of the most important elements of the choice of law decision? As explained above, *Phillips Petroleum Co. v. Shutts*, 472 U.S. 797, 821 (1985), requires that the law that governs in a class action must come from a state with "significant contact or significant aggregation of contacts" to the claims of each plaintiff. *Id.* at 821. In *Vioxx*, the only state that could have occurred in would have been in a jurisdiction where the defendant had a significant contact or aggregation of contacts, since factors related to the defendant were the only connection that the plaintiffs had in common. While the *Vioxx* plaintiffs all were administered the same pharmaceutical, the court reasonably concluded that the plaintiffs each received their doses (and suffered injury) in the myriad jurisdictions where they resided. Similarly, in *Bridgestone/Firestone*, the court concluded that the plaintiffs suffered their loss where "the vehicles and tires were purchased at excessive prices or resold at depressed prices," an event that would have occurred in all 50 states, the District of Columbia, and United States territories. In what type of case would you expect it is likely for plaintiffs to have the type of connection sufficient to satisfy the *Shutts* standard?

4. Although *Bridgestone/Firestone* and *Vioxx* are common in their refusal to use a defendant-based contact to guide the choice of law decision in a

products liability case, other courts come to a different conclusion. Consider, for example, the court's decision in *Ysbrand v. DaimlerChrysler*, 81 P.3d 618 (Okla. 2003), affirming a nationwide class certification on car buyers' Uniform Commercial Code warranty claims. The court held that the law of Michigan, defendant's principal place of business, applied to the claims of all the plaintiffs, reasoning as follows:

> . . . The UCC warranties are not something which is negotiated in the purchase of a new car. Thus, the relative interest of each buyer's home state in applying its version of the UCC is more or less equal. By contrast, Michigan's interest in having its regulatory scheme applied to the conduct of a Michigan manufacturer is most significant. Michigan is where the decisions concerning the design, manufacture, and distribution of the minivans were made. Michigan is the only state where conduct relevant to all class members occurred. The principal place of DaimlerChrysler's business is the most important contact with respect to the UCC warranty claims.
>
> The selection of Michigan law furthers the relevant factors stated in section 6 of the [Second] Restatement. The needs of the interstate system and the basic policies of predictability and uniformity of result require that the issue of product defect be determined in one forum with one result rather than in 51 jurisdictions with the very real possibility of conflicting decisions. While the interest of each home state in applying its local law is significant, Michigan's interest in the conduct of its manufacturer, and thus its connection to the warranty issues, is greater.

Id. at 626.

Do you think the case might have come out differently if the *Daimler-Chrysler* court had applied the Restatement (First) of Conflict of Laws, rather than the Restatement (Second) of Conflict of Laws?

5. What kind of incentives would courts send if they showed generous willingness to look to the defendant's principal place of business or incorporation for the purpose of choice of law in class actions? Wouldn't potential defendants consider which jurisdictions have favorable laws in choosing these locations?

6. Both *Vioxx* and *Bridgestone/Firestone* said, "No class action is proper unless all litigants are governed by the same legal rules." That statement does not acknowledge, however, that flexibility exists on how to define a class action. Although unusual in class actions, courts are sometimes willing to divide claims depending on the law that governs. *See, e.g., In re Telectronics Pacing Sys., Inc.*, 172 F.R.D. 271 (S.D. Ohio 1997) (certifying class for many claims, even though at least ten subclasses were necessary). Federal Rule of Civil Procedure 23(c)(5) appears to endorse this strategy: "When appropriate, a class may be divided into subclasses that are each treated as a class under this rule." Courts are also sometimes willing to certify a class on a statewide basis, rather than a nationwide basis. *Schnall v. AT&T Wireless Serv., Inc.*, 225 P.3d 929 (Wash. 2010) (en banc). As Professor Linda Silberman explains, the

certification issue is not entirely controlled by the specter of applying different laws to class actions: "It may be possible in some case to use subclasses and accommodate variations in state laws. Applicable state laws may be grouped in manageable patterns. . . ." Linda Silberman, *The Role of Choice of Law in National Class Actions*, 156 U. PA. L. REV. 2001, 2032-2033 (2008).

PROBLEM 2-64: A CIGARETTE CLASS ACTION IN LOCI STATE

Three individuals filed a complaint against three national cigarette companies and their distributors in Loci State. They asserted claims on behalf of themselves and all similarly situated Loci State residents who have suffered from physical injuries or disease from smoking cigarettes. All named individuals were born in Loci State, were raised there, and have lived most of their adult lives there. Two of the individuals started smoking cigarettes when they were quite young—in their early teens. The third individual started smoking cigarettes when he was in his early thirties. All three cigarette company defendants are incorporated in North Tobacco State and have their principal place of business there.

The complaint pleads common law causes of action for fraud and deceit and negligent misrepresentation. The plaintiffs seek compensatory and punitive damages.

The named individuals filed a motion for class certification, describing the class as (1) all current residents of Loci State who have regularly smoked cigarettes and have suffered or died from cigarette-related disease; and (2) the estates and representatives of these persons. Assume that—under the forum law of Loci State—a class should be certified only if the class action device is deemed superior to individual actions and the standard four requirements are satisfied: (1) numerosity; (2) commonality; (3) typicality; and (4) adequacy of representation. You may assume that the parties have stipulated that the numerosity and the adequacy of representation requirements are satisfied. The number of individuals in the class is approximately 5,000.

Loci State follows the Restatement (First) of Conflict of Laws. Recall that §377 of the First Restatement mandates that the "place of wrong is the state where the last event necessary to make the actor liable" takes place and that the comments to the section provide:

1. Except in the case of harm from poison, when a person sustains bodily harm, the place of the harm is the place where the harmful force takes effect upon the body.

. . .

2. When a person causes another voluntarily to take a deleterious substance which takes effect within the body, the place of the wrong is where the deleterious substance takes effect and not where it is administered.

Consider how the court will handle the choice of law determination. How is the court's choice of law determination likely to affect its disposition of the class certification request?

PROBLEM 2-65: A CIGARETTE CLASS ACTION IN FLEXIBLE STATE

Assume the same facts as Problem 2-64, except that the location of the lawsuit and the residence of putative class representatives are changed. Rather than a suit in Loci State, the suit is filed in Flexible State, which follows the Restatement (Second) of Conflict of Laws. How do these changes affect the choice of law determination? Do they make class certification less likely or more likely?

L.   INTERNET CHOICE OF LAW ISSUES

Internet activity has challenged traditional notions of governance, which historically have focused on physical, territorial boundaries. In the context of choice of law, a debate has raged about whether existing legal principles will prove adequate to govern internet disputes or, alternatively, whether cyberspace is so unique that it demands new rules. The debate has not resolved. As the internet has become more integral to modern life, existing doctrines have largely accommodated to govern most internet disputes that arise. In addition, many problems have been avoided by the pervasive use of choice of law clauses, with internet users "agreeing," with the click of a mouse, to submit their disputes to particular dispute resolution systems, to particular tribunals, and to governance by particular substantive laws.

Yet courts have continued to struggle as out-of-jurisdiction actors make their way so easily into the lives of a sovereign's citizens, injecting foreign rules and norms into daily life. A frequently cited point of clash is defamation, a cause of action regulated differently around the world. While the United States dramatically curtails defamation liability using First Amendment principles, other nations, such as Australia and the United Kingdom, are not nearly as protective of potentially defamatory expression, choosing instead to protect reputation. The result is a case such as *Dow Jones & Co. v. Gutnick*, [2002] HCA 56 (High Court of Australia 2002), in which an Australian businessman sued Dow Jones for damage to his reputation in Australia arising from an article uploaded in New Jersey, using New Jersey servers. Applying Australia law, the Australian High Court held that "publication" occurred where the article was downloaded and imposed damages for injury suffered in Australia. Courts in other countries have followed this example. *See e.g., Lewis v. King* [2004] EWCA Civ. 1329, 31, 34 (Eng.) (holding that allegedly defamatory materials uploaded on a United States-based website were "published" in the jurisdiction where they were downloaded and reasoning that the defendant effectively "targeted every jurisdiction where his text may be downloaded"); *Bangoura v. Washington Post*, [2004], 235 D.L.R.4th 564, 571 (Can. Ont. Sup. Ct. 2004) (exercising power over defamation suits based on materials uploaded onto a United States-based website and made available in Canada); *In re Moshe D.* (Court of Cassation, Italy, Dec. 27, 2000), (http://www.cdt.org/speech/ international/001227italiandecision.pdf) (holding that Italian courts have power to adjudicate a defamation case arising from a statement placed on the internet by a foreign defendant while outside of Italy) (discussed in Yulia A. Timfeeva, *Worldwide Prescriptive Jurisdiction in Internet Content Controversies: A Comparative Analysis*, 20 CONN. J. INT'L L. 199, 210-210 (2004-2005)).

Internet gambling presents another context where jurisdictions have been forced to grapple with differences in laws and norms among different countries. In *People v. World Interactive Gaming Corp.*, 714 N.Y.S.2d 844 (N.Y. Sup. Ct. 1999), the New York Attorney General had brought an enforcement action to enjoin a corporation from running a gambling operation. The corporation owned an Antiguan subsidiary, which offered internet gambling to users who transferred money to an Antiguan bank account. Within the jurisdiction of Antigua, the defendant's activities were lawful. Moreover, the gambling site required users to post an address and closed site access to users from states that prohibited gambling. Noting that the defendant had not implemented any measures to verify the accuracy of the addresses posted by users, the New York court granted the injunction, and held that the act of placing the bet in New York constituted gambling in New York. Notably, the court made this decision *without* considering whether Antigua law should govern or conducting any other choice of law analysis.

The United States Congress grappled with the challenges of online gambling in the Internet Gambling Enforcement Act of 2006. This Act does not regulate gambling head on. Instead, the Act focuses on payment providers, such as banks and credit card companies, making it unlawful for these institutions to process payments and fund transfers in connection with internet gambling. Congress's approach here is typical of other regulatory strategy in the internet context. Since traditional enforcement mechanisms and choice of law rules may not operate within the internet as they operate in the "territorial" world, analysis often focuses on *local effects* of out-of-jurisdiction internet activity.

This emphasis on local effects goes to the heart of the scholarly controversy about internet regulation. On one end of the controversy are Professors David Johnson and David Post, who argue that territorial regulation of internet activity is often both impossible (because internet actors can relocate their activities outside the reach of a regulating sovereign) and undesirable (because sovereigns should not regulate outside their borders and human civilization suffers when internet content providers are subject to multiple regulation from multiple sovereigns). *See, e.g.*, David R. Johnson & David G. Post, *Law and Borders — The Rise of Law in Cyberspace*, 48 STAN. L. REV. 1367 (1996). Professor Jack Goldsmith takes a contrary position, maintaining that a sovereign may legitimately regulate local effects of an extraterritorial act, where damage occurs within the local jurisdiction as a result of internet activity. Goldsmith also points out that fears of extraterritorial regulation are overblown, since a remote government has little means to enforce judgments it might issue against an internet actor. *See, e.g.*, Jack L. Goldsmith, *Against*

Cyberanarchy, 65 U. Cʜɪ. L. Rᴇᴠ. 1199 (1998). (This latter matter is explored in more detail in Chapter 4, concerning recognition and enforcement of judgments.)

As you review the material below, consider these different perspectives on the feasibility, legitimacy, and wisdom of internet regulation. Consider also a curious tendency in internet cases: even though cases have multijurisdictional elements, courts often do not bother with traditional choice of law analysis. Instead, they frequently focus only on whether local law can regulate. If the answer is yes, local law can regulate, then they do not engage the question whether another jurisdiction's law has a greater claim to regulation. The New York court's internet gambling decision in *World Interactive Gaming Corp.* is an example of this unilateral approach. That's not to say that the courts do not conduct a multilateral analysis in many instances — evaluating competing claims to regulation. It is nonetheless ironic that, in an era of rapid progress in technology, courts tend to indulge what could be called a regressive impulse to ignore competing regulatory claims. Significantly, the result of this impulse is that personal jurisdiction doctrine plays a pivotal role in restraining sovereign attempts to regulate. Under a unilateral orientation, courts apply their own law once they are satisfied that they possess jurisdiction to adjudicate the dispute. Thus, in these circumstances, personal jurisdiction analysis ends up being determinative of what law governs the merits of the controversy. *See, e.g.*, Paul Berman, *Towards a Cosmopolitan Vision of Conflict of Laws: Redefining Governmental Interests in a Global Era*, 153 U. Pᴀ. L. Rᴇᴠ. 1819, 1823 (2005) (observing tendency of courts to apply local law in transnational cyberspace disputes); Andrea Slane, *Tales, Techs, and Territories: Private International law, Globalization, and the Legal Construction of Borderlessness on the Internet*, 71 Lᴀᴡ & Cᴏɴᴛᴇᴍᴘ. Pʀᴏʙs. 129, 130 (2008) (stating that "courts in Internet cases almost always confine conflicts issues to the exercise of . . . personal jurisdiction . . . [and] virtually never engage in a full conflicts analysis").

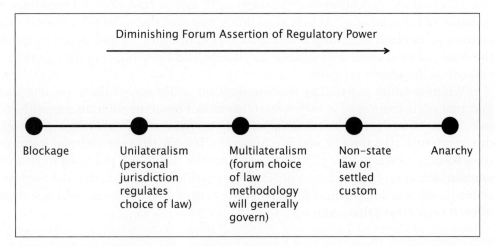

Figure 2-3: Internet Choice of Law Regulation

1. Unilateral Decisions

LICRA and UEJF v. Yahoo! Inc.
Tribunal de Grande Instance de Paris, May 22, 2000*

[Opinion by the Chief Justice.]

[Yahoo! Inc. owns Yahoo.com, which has an auction site that offered Nazi relics, insignia, flags, and other memorabilia for sale. Yahoo.com offers links to other webpages where Nazi texts are sold, webpages that also include "Holocaust revisionist" materials. The Jewish Students' Union of France (UEJF) and the League Against Racism and Antisemitism (LICRA) sued Yahoo! alleging violations of Article R. 645-2 of the French penal code, which criminalizes exhibition or sale of racist materials. The plaintiffs sought damages and an injunction, requiring Yahoo! to block access to this material in France.]

Yahoo! Inc. has argued that our court is not territorially competent over the matter, because the alleged fault is committed on the territory of the United States. . . . [Yahoo! also argues that] the duties of vigilance and prior censure which the petitioners would seek to impose upon it are impossible obligations, . . . in terms of the American Constitution, in particular the First Amendment . . . which institutes the liberty of expression and then in view of the technical impossibility of identifying surfers who visit the auction service. [Yahoo! notes that] in its charter it warns all surfers against using the service for purposes worthy of reprobation for whatsoever motive (incitement to hatred, racial or ethnic discrimination . . .).

. . . Whereas it is not challenged that surfers who call up Yahoo.com from French territory may, directly or via the link offered by Yahoo.fr, see on their screens the pages, services and sites to which Yahoo.com gives access, . . . in particular in its declension relating to Nazi objects;

Whereas the exposition for the purpose of sale of Nazi objects constitutes a violation of French law . . . as well as an offence against the collective memory of a country profoundly wounded by the atrocities committed by and in the name of the Nazi criminal enterprise against its citizens and most importantly against its citizens of the Jewish religion;

Whereas while permitting the visualization in France of these objects and eventual participation of a surfer established in France in such an exposition/sale, Yahoo! Inc. thus has committed a wrong on the territory of France, a wrong, the unintentional nature of which is apparent, but which is the cause of harm to the LICRA as well as the UEJF which both have the mission of pursuing in France any and all forms of banalization of Nazism, regardless of the fact that the litigious activity is marginal in relation with the entire business of the auction sales service offered on its site Yahoo.com . . . ;

---

* Daniel Laprès, *LICRA and UEJF v. Yahoo!*, Tribunal de Grande Instance de Paris, May 22, 2000. Translation from French to English reprinted by permission of Daniel Laprès, www.lapres.net/yahen.html.

Whereas the harm is suffered in France, our jurisdiction is therefore competent over this matter pursuant to article 46 of the New Code of Civil Procedure;

Whereas Yahoo! Inc. claims that it is technically impossible to control access to its auction service or any other service, and that therefore it cannot prohibit any surfer from France from visualizing [these services] on his screen;

Whereas it wishes nevertheless to emphasize that it warns all visitors against any uses of its services for purposes that are "worthy of reprobation for whatsoever reason," such as for purposes of racial or ethnic discrimination (cf. its user's charter);

But whereas Yahoo! Inc. is in a position to identify the geographical origin of the site which is [visited], based on the IP address of the caller, which should therefore enable it to prohibit surfers from France, by whatever means are appropriate, from accessing the services and sites the visualization of which on a screen set up in France . . . would be likely to be qualified in France as a crime and/or constitute a manifestly illegal nuisance within the meaning of articles 808 and 809 of New Code of Civil Procedure, 6 which is manifestly the case of the exhibition of uniforms, insignia, emblems reminiscent of those worn or exhibited by the Nazis;

Whereas [regarding] surfers who navigate through sites which guarantee them anonymity, Yahoo! Inc. has fewer means of control except for example through refusing systematically access to such sites to all visitors who [do] not disclose their geographical origin;

Whereas the real difficulties encountered by Yahoo do not constitute insurmountable obstacles;

That [Yahoo!] will therefore be ordered to take any and all measures of such kind as to dissuade and make impossible any consultations by surfers calling from France to its sites and services in dispute the title and/or contents of which infringe upon the internal public order of France, especially the site selling Nazi objects;

Whereas there may usefully be a debate about the nature of such measures within the confines of these proceedings;

That Yahoo will be given two months to enable it to formulate proposals of technical measures likely to lead to a settlement of this dispute;

Whereas, [regarding] Yahoo France, it bears mentioning that its site Yahoo.fr does not itself offer surfers calling from France access to the sites or [services] the title and/or the contents of which constitute infractions of French law; that therefore, it does not provide access to the site or services for auction sales of Nazi objects;

But whereas it offers surfers a link . . . entitled "further research on Yahoo. com," without any particular warning;

Or whereas, knowing what are the contents of the services offered by Yahoo. com, and in this case the service of auction sales including in one of its declensions the sale of Nazi objects, it behooves it to warn surfers, by a banner, prior to the surfer's entry into the Yahoo.com site, that should the result of his search on Yahoo.com . . . lead[] him [toward] sites, pages or forums the title and or contents of which constitute a violation of French law, such as is the case of sites which, whether directly or indirectly, intentionally or unintentionally, make the apology of Nazism, it must interrupt the consultation of the site in question lest it incur the sanctions stipulated by French law or answer to legal actions which might be initiated against it; . . .

NOW THEREFORE

[T]he Court . . .

Orders Yahoo! Inc. to take such measures as will dissuade and render impossible any and all consultation on Yahoo.com of the auction service for Nazi objects as well as any other site or service which makes apologies of Nazism or questions of the existence of Nazi crimes;

Orders Yahoo France to warn any and all surfers consulting Yahoo.fr, [that they might encounter illegal Nazi memorabilia, and in that event must] interrupt the consultation of the relevant site lest it incur the sanctions stipulated by French law or answer to actions initiated against it;

Orders [a future hearing] during which Yahoo! Inc. shall submit the measures which it intends to implement to end the harm and the nuisance suffered by the plaintiffs and to prevent any new incidents of nuisance;

Finds Yahoo! Inc. liable to pay to the LICRA an amount of 10,000 Francs on the basis of article 700 of the New Code of Civil Procedure;

Finds Yahoo! Inc. and Yahoo France liable to pay to UEJF an amount of 10,000 Francs on the basis of article 700 of the New Code of Civil Procedure;

Awards the costs of LICRA's action to be borne by Yahoo! Inc. and those of the UEJF by Yahoo! Inc. and Yahoo France.

Notes on
YAHOO!

1. Following this decision, the court issued another ruling in which it concluded it was unable to evaluate Yahoo!'s claim that it lacked the technology to block French users' access to prohibited sites and therefore appointed a panel of experts. The experts subsequently issued a report concluding that Yahoo! could use a combined process enabling it to block such access 90 percent of the time. The court then reaffirmed its ruling. Yahoo! filed suit in federal district court, seeking a declaratory judgment that the French order could not be enforced in the United States. The district court granted the request, but the en banc court of appeals reversed on procedural grounds. *Yahoo!, Inc. v. LICRA*, 169 F. Supp. 2d 1181 (N.D. Cal. 2001), *rev'd by* 379 F.3d 1120 (9th Cir. 2004), and 433 F.3d 1199 (9th Cir. 2006). The district court decision nonetheless presents an important analysis of United States law and is excerpted in Chapter 4. Significantly, Yahoo! ultimately decided on its own to ban all Nazi memorabilia from its United States auction sites. *See* Lisa Guernsey, *Yahoo to Try Harder to Rid Postings of Hateful Material*, N.Y. TIMES, Jan. 3, 2001, at section 5.

2. The question of judgment enforcement (and the possibility that the defendant might elude the judgment's enforcement) has enhanced

significance for the *Yahoo!* case because the legal clash involved entities in two separate countries, and not just two separate states. As illustrated in Chapter 4, judgment enforcement is more cumbersome across national borders than across state borders within the United States.

The international context is further heightened by the First Amendment aspects of the *Yahoo!* case. Note that the French court in *Yahoo!* unilaterally considered whether it could apply its law, and did not weigh the strength of United States constitutional values. Where two nations have competing views on fundamental matters, should there be a considered mechanism or set of principles for accommodating those differences? In the United States, we often say that the First Amendment is essential for a number of matters: (1) to promote self-governance, enlightenment, and tolerance, (2) to enhance debate, as well as (3) to increase the development and dissemination of knowledge. Are these values as important within the internet context as outside of the internet?

It is important to remember that the motivation behind the French laws was not suppression of expression, but rather promotion of human dignity and discouragement of group hatred. The French laws reflected a balance between these competing values, just as United States constitutional principles do (albeit with different weights assigned to the values). Indeed, some may argue that the prevalence of prohibitions against advocating ethnic and racial hatred in the laws of other democracies, as well as in human rights instruments, suggests that the United States might be characterized as an outlier on these issues. This observation, however, goes to the normative debate about hate speech regulation. From the point of view of speech regulation on the internet, the more salient point is that freedom of expression rules from the *most restrictive nation* may dominate if all nations follow the regulatory approach in the *Yahoo!* case. (From another point of view, of course, one might also argue that obstacles to enforcement of international judgments enable speakers in *less restrictive nations* to successfully impose their own standards of protected communication on the rest of the world.)

3. Should the standard be different for regulating a sophisticated global company such as Yahoo! than for an individual speaker or small website operator? Professor Joel Reidenberg argues that Yahoo! boasted a "global footprint" and aimed for a worldwide market. He further points out that Yahoo! maintained considerable control over its French subsidiary, which had worked hard to target French customers with French-language advertisements. Joel R. Reidenberg, *Yahoo and Democracy on the Internet*, 42 JURIMETRICS J. 261, 267-268 (2002). Do these observations put the French court's decision in a different light?

4. What does *Yahoo!* contribute to the debate discussed in the introduction of this section among internet scholars such as Professors Post, Johnson, and Goldsmith? Does the decision support Professor Goldsmith's claim that

the internet poses no problems that usual local enforcement mechanisms cannot handle?

5. *Yahoo!* presents one of many clashes between freedom of expression and regulation of other values on the internet. For example, in the celebrated *Toben* case, a German court ruled that Germany could prosecute and jail an Australian man for running a website in Australia that questioned the extent of the Holocaust (speech that was illegal in Germany, but not in Australia at the time). *See* Yulia A. Timfeeva, *Worldwide Prescriptive Jurisdiction in Internet Content Controversies: A Comparative Analysis*, 20 CONN. J. INT'L L. 199, 206-207 (2004-2005) (describing the *Toben* case).

Italy took a similar position to Germany and France in prosecuting Google executives for a third-party post of a YouTube video of teenagers from Turin, Italy teasing a disabled boy. Although Google promptly took down the three-minute video after receiving complaints, Italian authorities nonetheless took the position that Google violated privacy laws by failing to prevent the video from being uploaded in the first place. The Google officials received a six-month suspended sentence. *See, e.g.*, Adam Liptak, *When Free Worlds Collide*, N.Y. TIMES, Feb. 28, 2010, at WK.

Yet another clash has arisen between the approaches to personal privacy in the United States and those in Europe. In the United States, the law generally reflects the position that living with embarrassing Internet content is a worthwhile tradeoff for the benefits of free exchange of information. In Europe, however, the opposite is true — personal privacy trumps freedom of information. The "right to be forgotten," a common law concept that became codified in the European Union, allows European Union citizens to petition search engines to remove reputation-damaging links. *See generally*, Michael L. Rustad & Sanna Kulevska, *Reconceptualizing the Right to be Forgotten to Enable Transatlantic Data Flow*, 28 HARV. J.L. & TECH. 349, 353 (2015).

6. Might technology solve the problem of accommodating differences in speech regulation among nations? As ultimately concluded by the panel of experts in the *Yahoo!* case, geolocating software may enable tracking of internet users so that content providers might negotiate varying requirements among different jurisdictions. If in fact technology proves both effective and appropriate for this task, then the next question is who shall bear the cost of the technology? *See* Gregory S. Cooper, *A Tangled Web We Weave: Enforcing International Speech Restrictions in an Online World*, 8 PITTSBURGH J. TECH. L. & POL'Y 2, 15-18 (2007) (arguing that government, not private internet service providers or content providers, should bear the cost of geolocation technology); Horatia Muir Watt, *Yahoo! Cyber-Collision of Cultures: Who Regulates?*, 24 MICH. J. INT'L L. 673, 692-692 (2003) (advocating that cost burden of filters, electronic borders, and geolocation technologies should be borne by regulating jurisdiction).

Where maintained by content providers, the technology might provide sufficient evidence of reasonable care to avoid liability, even if the technology does not work perfectly. Understanding the necessity of settling for less than perfection in monitoring animates the court's reasoning in the next case, *Jeri-Jo v. Club Italia.*

Jeri-Jo Knitwear, Inc. v. Club Italia, Inc.
94 F. Supp. 2d 457 (S.D.N.Y. 2000)

OWEN, J.

Jeri-Jo requests this Court issue a contempt citation against the defendants for violating the Court's orders. On July 15, 1999, this Court granted Jeri-Jo's motion for summary judgment on its Lanham Act claims. The order specifically states, "Plaintiffs are entitled to injunctive relief based on my finding that defendant's have infringed plaintiffs' ENERGIE trademark." A judgment on consent was entered by the Court on December 3, 1999. That judgment permanently enjoined defendants, in the United States, from "advertising or promoting" apparel bearing Jeri-Jo's registered trademark ENERGIE or any colorable variation thereof or any confusingly similar trademark.

Defendants, Sixty S.p.A. ("Sixty") and Sixty U.S.A. (formerly known as Club Italia, Inc.), design, manufacture, sell, and distribute high price denim apparel under several labels, including the ENERGIE clothing label at issue in this case. All the clothing is designed in Italy and is sold worldwide. Sixty is the holder of valid trademarks for the ENERGIE mark in Italy, France, and Germany and has the right to sell ENERGIE apparel in numerous other countries, including Albania, Algeria, Armenia, Austria, Belgium, Bulgaria, Canada, China, Denmark, Finland, Ireland, Hong Kong, Israel, the Netherlands, North Korea, Portugal, Spain and the United Kingdom, among others.

Defendants are presently operating three Web sites at issue here, *www.miss sixty.com*, *www.sixty.net*, and *www.energie.it*. Although the servers for all three sites are located in Italy, defendants had used a United States-based company to register its *www.misssixty.com* and *www.sixty.net* sites[1] one year before the consent judgment was entered for a substantial number of products (which are legitimately sold even today in the United States) including the ENERGIE line. The third site, *www.energie.it*, is registered in Italy[2] and permits the user to view defendants' 1999/2000 collection of ENERGIE apparel. The first two sites, *www.miss sixty.com* and *www.sixty.net*, contain a hyperlink to defendants' ENERGIE apparel, but do not themselves display defendants' infringing apparel. A hyperlink is

---

1. The end portion of a domain name, for example ".com," is called the top level domain. Internet addresses that end in ".com," ".net," ".org," and ".edu" are administered by a United States company, Network Solutions, Inc.

2. Addresses administered in other countries may have different top level domain names. The ".it" indicates an Italian Web site.

highlighted text or images that when selected by the user, permits him to view another related Web document. With regard to these two sites, the highlighted text that constitutes the hyperlink is the term "ENERGIE," and by selecting this linking term, the user is transported to defendants' *www.energie.it* Web site to view defendants' 1999/2000 collection of ENERGIE apparel.

Plaintiffs contend that this constitutes "advertisement [and] promotion" within the United States, putting defendants in contempt of the consent judgment. A court has the power to hold a party in contempt where there is (1) a clear and unambiguous order, (2) clear and convincing proof of a party's non-compliance with that order, and (3) a failure to reasonably and diligently comply with the order. With the foregoing as the law, plaintiffs argue that the Court's order clearly prohibits all advertisements and promotion of defendants' ENERGIE apparel in the United States. Plaintiffs contend defendants are in violation of the order because they continue to use *www.misssixty.com* and *www.sixty.net* sites to advertise and promote their entire line which includes the infringing ENERGIE apparel to United States consumers, and have not been reasonably diligent in complying with the Court's orders because they have taken no steps at all to restrict access or the likelihood of access to these sites by United States consumers for the ENERGIE line. Plaintiff asserts defendants could have taken several steps to reduce the likelihood that a user in the United States would view their (U.S.) infringing ENERGIE collection. First, defendants could have changed the top level domain names from ".com" and ".net," which United States users are accustomed to using, to ".it," which United States users are unaccustomed to using. Second, defendant could have removed the hypertext links from the *www.misssixty.com* and *www.sixty.net* Web sites to the *www.energie.it* Web site, which displays defendants' infringing ENERGIE collection. Third, defendant could restrict access to their Italian Web site by requiring a password, which would not be issued to United States users. Thus, plaintiffs argue that defendants cannot assert that they have been reasonably and diligently complying with the Court's orders.

... Plaintiffs argue that ... defendants are flouting the Court's orders by continuing to offer information about the infringing ENERGIE apparel, i.e. promoting or advertising, through its Internet Web site which is accessible by United States consumers. Defendants argue that the elements of contempt have not been satisfied. First, defendants argue that the Court's order is not "clear and unambiguous" since it does not expressly prohibit the operation of Sixty's internationally accessible Web sites. Second, defendants contend that they are in compliance with the consent judgment and that a Web site owner does not advertise or promote products simply by posting a Web site. ... Third, defendants argue that they have diligently complied [with] the Court's orders because they investigated whether United States consumers could be blocked from their Web sites but found it was not possible to do so "conclusively." After so finding, defendants proposed to add a disclaimer to their sites indicating that the ENERGIE brand clothing from Sixty as presented on the Web sites is not available for sale or distribution in the United States and is not available for purchase by persons in the United States, and that plaintiffs own the ENERGIE trademark in the United

States and sell and distribute their own ENERGIE brand clothing in the United States. However, plaintiffs rejected this proposal.

While I agree . . . that defendant could be viewed as "advertising" in the United States in violation of the consent judgment, I cannot, however, conclude on the total record before me that defendants' conduct is of that flouting willfulness to have earned the denomination "contemnor." Defendants, one must keep in mind, *do* have world-wide rights in the mark outside the United States. Accordingly, while I direct the defendants to immediately de-link its *www.energie.it* site from its *www.misssixty.com* and *www.sixty.net* sites, I do not conclude defendants should be required to delist its *www.energie.it* site from various search engines because I do not believe an adequate evidentiary foundation has been laid to require such broad relief where even plaintiff concedes 100% perfection is not possible, and, I repeat, defendants may legitimately advertise their mark over much of the rest of the globe, and there is no showing of damage to plaintiff from the failure to act with more dispatch. Plaintiffs did observe at oral argument that perfection is not possible, the Internet being what it is. . . .

De link

Notes on
JERI-JO

1. Like the French court in the *Yahoo!* case, the *Jeri-Jo* court applied a unilateral approach. Do you have a sense of why the court did this? Do you think that the international contexts are relevant to the courts' decision to apply forum law in both *Yahoo!* and *Jeri-Jo*? How do the two decisions compare with those in which the courts applied a lex fori approach to choice of law?

2. What do you think of the *Jeri-Jo* court's suggestion that "perfect" regulation of the internet is not possible? Keeping in mind that screening and geolocation technologies are not free, do you think that the legal regulation should insist on something close to perfection?

3. The *Jeri-Jo* decision arose in a specific legal context—the plaintiff's request for the court to issue a contempt citation. Contempt is a strong remedy, bringing with it substantial penalties as well as the suggestion that the contemptuous defendant is prone to flout court orders. How did the contempt context influence the *Jeri-Jo* court's reasoning?

Barcelona.com, Inc. v. Excelentisimo Ayuntamiento de Barcelona

330 F.3d 617 (4th Cir. 2003)

NIEMEYER, Circuit Judge:

Barcelona.com, Inc. ("Bcom, Inc."), a Delaware corporation, commenced this action under the Anticybersquatting Consumer Protection Act against

Excelentisimo Ayuntamiento de Barcelona (the City Council of Barcelona, Spain) for a declaratory judgment that Bcom, Inc.'s registration and use of the domain name barcelona.com is not unlawful under the Lanham Act. The district court concluded that Bcom, Inc.'s use of barcelona.com was confusingly similar to Spanish trademarks owned by the City Council that include the word "Barcelona." Also finding bad faith on the basis that Bcom, Inc. had attempted to sell the barcelona.com domain name to the City Council for a profit, the court ordered the transfer of the domain name to the City Council.

Because the district court applied Spanish law rather than United States law . . . , we reverse the judgment of the district court denying Bcom, Inc. relief under the Anticybersquatting Consumer Protection Act, vacate its memorandum opinion and its order to transfer the domain name barcelona.com to the City Council, and remand for further proceedings consistent with this opinion.

In 1996, Mr. Joan Nogueras Cobo ("Nogueras"), a Spanish citizen, registered the domain name barcelona.com in the name of his wife, also a Spanish citizen, with the domain registrar, Network Solutions, Inc., in Herndon, Virginia. In the application for registration of the domain name, Nogueras listed himself as the administrative contact. When Nogueras met Mr. Shahab Hanif, a British citizen, in June 1999, they developed a business plan to turn barcelona.com into a tourist portal for the Barcelona, Spain, region. A few months later they formed Bcom, Inc. under Delaware law to own barcelona.com and to run the website, and Nogueras, his wife, and Hanif became Bcom, Inc.'s officers. Bcom, Inc. was formed as an American company in part because Nogueras believed that doing so would facilitate obtaining financing for the development of the website. Although Bcom, Inc. maintains a New York mailing address, it has no employees in the United States, does not own or lease office space in the United States, and does not have a telephone listing in the United States. Its computer server is in Spain.

Shortly after Nogueras registered the domain name barcelona.com in 1996, he placed some Barcelona-related information on the site. The site offered commercial services such as domain registry and web hosting, but did not offer much due to the lack of financing. Before developing the business plan with Hanif, Nogueras used a web-form on the City Council's official website to e-mail the mayor of Barcelona, Spain, proposing to "negotiate" with the City Council for its acquisition of the domain name barcelona.com, but Nogueras received no response. And even after the development of a business plan and after speaking with potential investors, Nogueras was unable to secure financing to develop the website.

In March 2000, about a year after Nogueras had e-mailed the Mayor, the City Council contacted Nogueras to learn more about Bcom, Inc. and its plans for the domain name barcelona.com. Nogueras and his marketing director met with City Council representatives, and after the meeting, sent them the business plan that was developed for Bcom, Inc.

On May 3, 2000, a lawyer for the City Council sent a letter to Nogueras demanding that Nogueras transfer the domain name barcelona.com to the City Council. The City Council owned about 150 trademarks issued in Spain, the majority of which included the word Barcelona, such as "Teatre Barcelona," "Barcelona Informacio I Grafic," and "Barcelona Informacio 010 El Tlefon Que Ho Contesta Tot." Its earlier effort in 1995 to register the domain name barcelona.es, however, was unsuccessful. The City Council's representative explained, "It was denied to Barcelona and to all place names in Spain." This representative also explained that the City Council did not try also to register barcelona.com in 1995 even though that domain name was available because "at that time . . . the world Internet that we know now was just beginning and it was not seen as a priority by the City Council." The City Council now took the position with Bcom, Inc. that its domain name barcelona.com was confusingly similar to numerous trademarks that the City Council owned.

A couple of days after the City Council sent its letter, Nogueras had the domain name barcelona.com transferred from his wife's name to Bcom, Inc., which he had neglected to do in 1999 when Bcom, Inc. was formed.

Upon Bcom, Inc.'s refusal to transfer barcelona.com to the City Council, the City Council invoked the Uniform Domain Name Dispute Resolution Policy ("UDRP") promulgated by the Internet Corporation for Assigned Names and Numbers ("ICANN") to resolve the dispute. Every domain name issued by Network Solutions, Inc. is issued under a contract, the terms of which include a provision requiring resolution of disputes through the UDRP. In accordance with that policy, the City Council filed an administrative complaint with the World Intellectual Property Organization ("WIPO"), an ICANN authorized dispute-resolution provider located in Switzerland. . . .

The WIPO [decision] concluded that barcelona.com was confusingly similar to the City Council's Spanish trademarks, that Bcom, Inc. had no legitimate interest in barcelona.com, and that Bcom, Inc.'s registration and use of barcelona.com was in bad faith. To support his conclusion that Bcom, Inc. acted in bad faith, the WIPO panelist observed that the only purpose of the business plan was "to commercially exploit information about the City of Barcelona . . . particularly . . . the information prepared and provided by [the City Council] as part of its public service." The WIPO panelist ordered that Bcom, Inc. transfer the domain name barcelona.com to the City Council.

In accordance with the UDRP's provision that required a party aggrieved by the dispute resolution process to file any court challenge within ten business days, Bcom, Inc. commenced this action . . . under the provision of the Anticybersquatting Consumer Protection Act (the "ACPA") that authorizes a domain name owner to seek recovery or restoration of its domain name when a trademark owner has overstepped its authority in causing the domain name to be suspended, disabled, or transferred. *See* 15 U.S.C. §1114(2)(D)(v). Bcom, Inc.'s complaint sought a declaratory judgment that its use of the name barcelona.com "does not infringe upon any trademark of defendant or cause confusion as to the origin, sponsorship, or approval of the website barcelona.com; . . . [and] that [the City Council] is barred from instituting any action against [Bcom, Inc.] for trademark infringement." . . .

Following a bench trial, the district court entered an . . . opinion . . . denying Bcom, Inc.'s request for declaratory judgment and directing Bcom, Inc. to "transfer the domain name barcelona.com to the [City Council] forth-with." [T]he district court proceeded in essence to apply the WIPO panelist opin-ion as well as Spanish law. The court explained that even though the City Council did not own a trademark in the name "Barcelona" alone, it owned numerous Spanish trademarks that included the word Barcelona, which could, under Spanish law as understood by the district court, be enforced against an infringing use such as barcelona.com. [T]he court stated that "the WIPO decision was correct in its determination that [Bcom, Inc.] took 'advantage of the normal con-fusion' of an Internet user by using the 'Barcelona route' because an Internet user would 'normally expect to reach some official body . . . for . . . the information.'" Referring to the facts that Bcom, Inc. engaged in little activity and attempted to sell the domain name to the City Council, the court concluded that "these factors clearly demonstrate a bad faith intent on the part of the Plaintiff and its sole shareholders to improperly profit from their registration of the domain name barcelona.com." At bottom, the court concluded that Bcom, Inc. failed to dem-onstrate, as required by 15 U.S.C. §1114(2)(D)(v), that its use of barcelona.com was "not unlawful." . . .

II

Bcom, Inc. contends that when it "sought a declaration under 15 U.S.C. §1114(2)(D)(v), it was entitled to have its conduct judged by U.S. trademark law, not Spanish trademark law." It argues that even if Spanish law applies, however, a party cannot, under Spanish law, "get a registration for a term that is only geographically descriptive, such as the word 'Barcelona.'" . . .

The City Council contends that the WIPO panelist's decision, including its reference to Spanish law, must be considered to decide this case. . . .

[W]e agree with the City Council that the WIPO proceeding is relevant to a claim under §1114(2)(D)(v), [but note that] the WIPO panelist's decision is not even entitled to deference on the merits. A brief review of the scheme established by ICANN in adopting the UDRP and by Congress in enacting the ACPA informs our resolution of this issue.

A domain name is "any alphanumeric designation which is registered with or assigned by any domain name registrar, domain name registry, or other domain name registration authority as part of an electronic address on the Internet." 15 U.S.C. §1127. To obtain a domain name, a would-be registrant simply makes appli-cation to a registrar (there are currently over 160), submits a fee, and agrees to the terms of the domain name registration agreement. Domain names are assigned on a first-come, first-served basis.

The agreement that accompanies the registration of a domain name specifies terms and conditions of the registration and the policies governing the regis-trant's continued control over the domain name, including conditions for sus-pension or transfer of the domain name.

It also provides a contractually mandated process, the UDRP, for resolution of disputes that might arise between domain name registrants and trademark owners. The UDRP is intended to provide a quick process for resolving domain name disputes by submitting them to authorized panels or panel members operating under rules of procedure established by ICANN and under "any rules and principles of law that [the panel] deems applicable." ICANN, Rules for Uniform Domain Name Dispute Resolution Policy, P 15(a), *at* http:// www. icann.org/dndr/udrp/uniform-rules.htm (Oct. 24, 1999).

Because the administrative process prescribed by the UDRP is "adjudication lite" as a result of its streamlined nature and its loose rules regarding applicable law, the UDRP itself contemplates judicial intervention, which can occur before, during, or after the UDRP's dispute resolution process is invoked. . . . Thus, when a person obtains a domain name, the person agrees, in the registration contract with the registrar, to follow the UDRP as established by ICANN.

In 1999, Congress amended the Trademark Act of 1946 (the Lanham Act) with the Anticybersquatting Consumer Protection Act (ACPA) principally for the purpose of protecting trademark owners against cyberpiracy:

> The purpose of the bill is to protect consumers and American businesses, to promote the growth of online commerce, and to provide clarity in the law for trademark owners by prohibiting the bad-faith and abusive registration of distinctive marks as Internet domain names with the intent to profit from the goodwill associated with such marks—a practice commonly referred to as "cybersquatting."

S. Rep. No. 106-140, at 4 (1999). Although the ACPA was enacted primarily to redress cyberpiracy or "cybersquatting," it also provides limited liability for trademark infringement by registrars who participate in the administration of the registration, transfer, and cancellation of domain names pursuant to a "reasonable policy" that is consistent with the purposes of the trademark laws. And to balance the rights given to trademark owners against cybersquatters, the ACPA also provides some protection to domain name registrants against "overreaching trademark owners."

In sum, domain names are issued pursuant to contractual arrangements under which the registrant agrees to a dispute resolution process, the UDRP, which is designed to resolve a large number of disputes involving domain names, but this process is not intended to interfere with or modify any "independent resolution" by a court of competent jurisdiction. Moreover, the UDRP makes no effort at unifying the law of trademarks among the nations served by the Internet. Rather, it forms part of a contractual policy developed by ICANN for use by registrars in administering the issuance and transfer of domain names. Indeed, it explicitly anticipates that judicial proceedings will continue under various nations' laws applicable to the parties.

The ACPA recognizes the UDRP only insofar as it constitutes a part of a policy followed by registrars in administering domain names. . . . [A]ny decision made by a panel under the UDRP is no more than an agreed-upon administration that is *not* given any deference under the ACPA. To the contrary, because a UDRP decision is susceptible of being grounded on principles foreign or hostile to

American law, the ACPA authorizes reversing a panel decision if such a result is called for by application of the Lanham Act. . . .

III

Now we turn to the principal issue raised in this appeal. Bcom, Inc. contends that in deciding its claim under §1114(2)(D)(v), the district court erred in applying the law of Spain rather than the law of the United States. Because the ACPA explicitly requires application of the Lanham Act, not foreign law, we agree.

Section 1114(2)(D)(v), the reverse domain name hijacking provision, states:

> A domain name registrant whose domain name has been suspended, disabled, or transferred under a policy described under clause (ii)(II) may, upon notice to the mark owner, file a civil action to establish that the registration or use of the domain name by such registrant is not unlawful under this chapter. The court may grant injunctive relief to the domain name registrant, including the reactivation of the domain name or transfer of the domain name to the domain name registrant.

15 U.S.C. §1114(2)(D)(v). Thus, to establish a right to relief against an "overreaching trademark owner" under this reverse hijacking provision, a plaintiff must establish (1) that it is a domain name registrant; (2) that its domain name was suspended, disabled, or transferred under a policy implemented by a registrar as described in 15 U.S.C. §1114(2)(D)(ii)(II); (3) that the owner of the mark that prompted the domain name to be suspended, disabled, or transferred has notice of the action by service or otherwise; and (4) that the plaintiff's registration or use of the domain name is not unlawful under the Lanham Act, as amended.

[The court concluded the first three elements were satisfied.] It is the last element that raises the principal issue on appeal. Bcom, Inc. argues that the district court erred in deciding whether Bcom, Inc. satisfied this element by applying Spanish law and then by concluding that Bcom, Inc.'s use of the domain name violated Spanish law.

It appears from the district court's memorandum opinion that it indeed did resolve the last element by applying Spanish law. Although the district court recognized that the City Council did not have a registered trademark in the name "Barcelona" alone, either in Spain or in the United States, it observed that "under Spanish law, when trademarks consisting of two or more words contain one word that stands out in a predominant manner, that dominant word must be given decisive relevance." . . . Applying Spanish trademark law in this manner, the court resolved that Bcom, Inc.'s registration and use of barcelona.com were unlawful.

It requires little discussion to demonstrate that this use of Spanish law by the district court was erroneous under the plain terms of the statute. The text of the ACPA explicitly requires application of the Lanham Act, not foreign law, to resolve an action brought under 15 U.S.C. §1114(2)(D)(v). Specifically, it authorizes an aggrieved domain name registrant to "file a civil action to establish that the registration or use of the domain name by such registrant is *not unlawful under this chapter.*" 15 U.S.C. §1114(2)(D)(v) (emphasis added). It is thus readily apparent that the cause of action created by Congress in this portion of the ACPA requires the court adjudicating such an action to determine whether the registration or use of the domain name violates the Lanham Act. Because the statutory language has a plain and unambiguous meaning that is consistent with the statutory context and application of this language in accordance with its plain meaning provides a component of a coherent statutory scheme, our statutory analysis need proceed no further.

By requiring application of United States trademark law to this action brought in a United States court by a United States corporation involving a domain name administered by a United States registrar, 15 U.S.C. §1114(2)(D)(v) is consistent with the fundamental doctrine of territoriality upon which our trademark law is presently based. . . .

It follows from incorporation of the doctrine of territoriality into United States law through Section 44 of the Lanham Act that United States courts do not entertain actions seeking to enforce trademark rights that exist only under foreign law. Yet the district court's application of foreign law in this declaratory judgment action did precisely this and thereby neglected to apply United States law as required by the statute.

When we apply the Lanham Act, not Spanish law, in determining whether Bcom, Inc.'s registration and use of barcelona.com is unlawful, the ineluctable conclusion follows that Bcom, Inc.'s registration and use of the name "Barcelona" is not unlawful. Under the Lanham Act, and apparently even under Spanish law, the City Council could not obtain a trademark interest in a purely descriptive geographical designation that refers only to the City of Barcelona. Under United States trademark law, a geographic designation can obtain trademark protection if that designation acquires secondary meaning. On the record in this case, however, there was no evidence that the public—in the United States or elsewhere—associates "Barcelona" with anything other than the City itself. Indeed, the Chief Director of the City Council submitted an affidavit stating that "the City does not own and is not using any trademarks in the United States, to identify any goods or services." Therefore, under United States trademark law, "Barcelona" should have been treated as a purely descriptive geographical term entitled to no trademark protection. It follows then that there was nothing unlawful about Nogueras' registration of barcelona.com, nor is there anything unlawful under United States trademark law about Bcom, Inc.'s continued use of that domain name.

For these reasons, we conclude that Bcom, Inc. established entitlement to relief under 15 U.S.C. §1114(2)(D)(v) with respect to the domain name <barcelona. com>, and accordingly we reverse the district court's ruling in this regard. . . .

REVERSED, VACATED, AND REMANDED.

Notes on

BARCELONA.COM

1. Unlike the *Yahoo!* and *Jeri-Jo* courts, the *Barcelona.com* court explicitly considered whether the law of Spain or the United States applied. The *Barcelona.com* court did not, however, give the choice of law issue extensive consideration. Instead, the court invoked a principle of territoriality, which it concluded mandated United States law to apply. How is the territoriality principle invoked in *Barcelona.com* different than the notions of territoriality applied under the Restatement (First) of Conflict of Laws?

2. In the process of applying the concept of United States territoriality, did the *Barcelona.com* court give any extraterritorial effect to United States law? Professor Paul Berman critiques the *Barcelona.com* decision as parochial and notes the decision's extraterritorial impact on "a Spanish trademark holder, various Spanish parties, and a web portal for tourists to Spain." Paul Schiff Berman, *Towards a Cosmopolitan Vision of Conflict of Laws: Redefining Governmental Interests in a Global Era*, 153 U. PA. L. REV. 1819, 1875 (2005). Berman argues that the court should have applied a cosmopolitan approach, taking account of the community affiliations of the various parties and the internet as a "globally connected" communication system. *Id.* at 1876. He also notes that, in addition to community norms from the United States and Spain, the court could have considered a third set of norms articulated through the World Intellectual Property Organization (WIPO) arbitrator and coming from an internet governing body—the Internet Corporation for Assigned Names and Numbers (ICANN). Berman points out that since ICANN lacks democratic accountability and is contractually imposed on website operators, it does not possess a community affiliation. He argues, however, that "nonstate entities may be an important set of norms and must at least be considered in any conflicts analysis." *Id.* at 1877.

2. Multilateral Choice of Law

Evelyn Clark v. Experian Information Solutions, Inc.

2005 U.S. Dist. LEXIS 8243 (N.D. Ill. 2005)

HOLDERMAN, J.

. . . The following are the relevant undisputed facts gleaned from the parties' submissions. [Plaintiff Evelyn] Clark is a resident of Illinois. Defendant Consumerinfo.com ("Consumerinfo") is a California corporation with its primary place of business in California. Defendant Experian Information Solutions ("Experian") is an Ohio corporation with its primary place of business in

California. Both defendants' headquarters have been located in California throughout the period of time relevant to this litigation.

At some point, the complaint alleges March of 2003, Clark accessed Consumerinfo's website ("website") from her workplace computer in . . . Illinois. Clark proceeded to engage in a transaction with defendants while on that website. That transaction forms the basis of the dispute between the parties. This court assumes, for purposes of this motion, that the defendants are equally responsible for the website Clark accessed. All of the pages Clark visited on the website are stored on Consumerinfo's servers, which have always been located in California.

During the transaction, Clark purchased a "Three Bureau Credit Report" for $24.95. Clark used her computer in Illinois to submit information to defendants in order to effectuate the transaction, which included information regarding her credit card information. That information was received by defendants in California. According to Clark, she was not only charged for the "Three Bureau Credit Report," which she was allegedly never able to view and print from her computer screen as she expected to do, but she was also charged $79.95 for defendants' CreditCheck monitoring service, which she did not know she purchased.

. . . "Under Illinois choice-of-law rules, this court will apply Illinois substantive law unless a conflict of law exists and makes a difference in the outcome of the litigation." *Nicholson v. Marine Corps W. Fed. Credit Union*, 953 F. Supp. 1012, 1015 (N.D. Ill. 1997).

Two other judges in this district have previously held that a conflict exists between the California and Illinois consumer-protection statutes, because the California Code, unlike the Illinois Code, allows a plaintiff to file suit as a "'private attorney general' acting on behalf of the 'general public.'" . . .

"Under Illinois choice-of-law principles, the 'most significant contacts' must be examined." *Jones v. State Farm Mutual Auto. Ins. Co.*, 289 Ill. App. 3d 903, 682 N.E.2d 238, 249, 224 Ill. Dec. 677 (Ill. App. Ct. 1997). In assessing the most "significant contacts," both parties rely primarily on section 145 of the Restatement (Second) of Conflict of Laws ("Restatement"). . . . Both parties also rely on section 148 of the Restatement, which exists for situations of fraud and misrepresentation when "there may be little reason in logic or persuasion to say that one state rather than another is the place of injury." Restatement §145, cmt. e. Under either test, Illinois courts do not simply tally contacts, but instead favor an "interest analysis," which "is based on the conclusion that 'contacts obtain significance only to the extent that they relate to the policies and purposes sought to be vindicated by the conflicting laws.'"

The parties dispute whether or not the place of injury in this case can be determined. This is significant because "Illinois law presumes that the law of the state where the injury occurred will govern 'unless another state has a more significant relationship to the occurrence or to the parties involved.'" Defendants argue that Clark's alleged injury occurred in Illinois. Clark does not argue that California is the place of injury, but does argue that the place of injury cannot be determined. If Clark is right, then this court should not focus on section 145 of the Restatement, which places heavy emphasis on the place of injury, but should instead focus on section 148(2). As explained below, this court rules that the place of injury in this case is Illinois, which is also the state with the greatest interest in this case. But even if this court accepted the argument that section 148 should apply because Clark's place of injury cannot be determined, this court still would hold that Illinois is the state with the most significant contacts to this case.

This court does not believe that this is a case where the place of injury cannot be determined. The Seventh Circuit has unequivocally held that in a consumer fraud case, "the injury is decidedly where the *consumer* is located." *In re Bridgestone/ Firestone Inc.*, 288 F.3d at 1017. The defendants argue that this holding by the Seventh Circuit is controlling here, but they may come to that conclusion too quickly because in *Bridgestone/Firestone* the Seventh Circuit was analyzing Indiana law. This court need not linger on the issue though, because even if not controlling, the conclusion reached by the Seventh Circuit in *Bridgestone/Firestone*—that in a consumer fraud case injury is where the consumer is located—is consistent with the law of Illinois.

. . . Furthermore, as Clark points out, Illinois courts evaluate the significance of a contact "only to the extent that [it] relates to the policies and purposes sought to be vindicated" by the underlying law. This "interest analysis" leads to the conclusion that Clark's injury in this case occurred in Illinois. Determining where the injury occurred requires an examination of the policies and purposes sought to be vindicated by the consumer-protection statutes. The primary purpose of consumer-protection statutes is to protect consumers from fraudulent sales. The focus of the statutes is protecting the consumer. The harm the statutes are designed to protect against occurs when a consumer is defrauded. It follows then from an "interest analysis," which Clark urges this court to employ, that the injury in a consumer fraud case occurs where the consumer is located. In this case, the place of Clark's injury, the first and most important contact to which section 145 points, is Illinois.

The remaining factors under section 145 are likely neutral, but in any event do not override Illinois's interest. The parties' domiciles are split between California and Illinois, and no real relationship exists between them except for the single transaction giving rise to this suit. The place of the conduct giving rise to the injury may favor California, but not so strongly as to override Illinois's interest as the state where the injury occurred. Furthermore, in regard to the conduct giving rise to her injury, Clark also admits, for purposes of venue, that a "substantial part of the events and conduct giving rise to the violations of law complained of herein occurred in or emanated" in the Northern District of Illinois.

The factors set forth in section 148(2) also point toward Illinois as having the most significant relationship to the facts underlying this litigation. [This section of] the Restatement states:

> (2) When the plaintiff's action in reliance took place in whole or in part in a state other than that where the false representations were made, the forum will consider such of the following contacts, among others, as may be present in the

particular case in determining the state which, with respect to the particular issue, has the most significant relationship to the occurrence and the parties:

  (a) the place, or places, where the plaintiff acted in reliance upon the defendant's representations,

  (b) the place where the plaintiff received the representations,

  (c) the place where the defendant made the representations,

  (d) the domicile, residence, nationality, place of incorporation and place of business of the parties,

  (e) the place where a tangible thing which is the subject of the transaction between the parties was situated at the time, and

  (f) the place where the plaintiff is to render performance under a contract which he has been induced to enter by the false representations of the defendant.

Restatement §148(2). Defendants are correct that the first factor, the place where the plaintiff acted in reliance upon the defendants' representations, is very significant in making a choice-of-law determination under this section. The comments to section 148(2) make clear that while the place where the plaintiff received the representations, and the place where the defendant made the representations are equally important, neither of those contacts are as important "as is the place where the plaintiff acted in reliance on the defendant's representations." This important contact clearly points to Illinois, where Clark encountered defendants' allegedly deceptive website. The domicile of the plaintiff, which the comments make clear is more important than the domicile of the defendants, also clearly points to Illinois.[6] Thus, Clark received and relied upon the representation all in the state of her residence, which is Illinois.

In regard to the last two contacts highlighted by section 148(2), Clark has established that the credit report she allegedly did not receive was saved on defendant Consumer info's computer servers in California, but even assuming that a saved credit report can be the tangible subject of a transaction, that contact does not tip the balance of factors in favor of applying California law. The last factor also does not strongly point toward California as Clark argues, because even if her action can be properly described as "rendering performance under a contract," Illinois is where Clark acted. Restatement §148(2)(f). Illinois is where Clark resides, where she received and relied upon the allegedly deceptive representations of defendants, and Illinois therefore is the state with the most significant contact to Clark's claim. Under section 145 or 148 of the Restatement, Illinois is the state with the most significant contacts to this case.

---

6. The comment states:

> Other contacts. The plaintiff's domicil or residence, if he is a natural person, or the principal place of business, if plaintiff is a corporation, are contacts of substantial significance when the loss is pecuniary in its nature, as is true of the situations covered by this Section. This is so because a financial loss will usually be of greatest concern to the state with which the person suffering the loss has the closest relationship.

Restatement §148(2), cmt. i.

Finally, this court comes to Clark's primary argument, which is that the policies of both States' laws favor applying the California consumer-protection statute. In short, Clark argues that from a policy standpoint, there is no harm to Illinois in applying California law. Therefore, according to Clark, this court should just apply California law because it is presumably more beneficial to Clark. This argument has been foreclosed by the Seventh Circuit and the Supreme Court. *In re Bridgestone/Firestone Inc.*, 288 F.3d at 1018 (citing *BMW of North America Inc. v. Gore*, 517 U.S. 559, 568-73, 116 S. Ct. 1589, 134 L. Ed. 2d 809 (1996)) ("State consumer-protection laws vary considerably, and courts must respect these differences rather than apply one state's law to sales in other states with different rules."). That case law also makes it clear that California's stated interest in applying its laws outside of its borders does not override Illinois's more significant contacts to this case. . . .

Notes on
CLARK

1. The court's decision in *Clark* is typical of internet disputes, particularly domestic cases. The interaction occurred between "strangers" who "met" over the internet, but the court nonetheless saw its way clear to apply a multilateral choice of law approach under the Restatement (Second) of Conflict of Laws. Do you see any explanation for the difference in approach in *Clark* as compared to largely unilateral approaches in *Yahoo!*, *Jeri-Jo*, and *Barcelona.com*? Is it the international context of these latter three decisions that makes a difference? If so, does the unilateral approach reflected in the three international decisions simply represent "growing pains"? Because the internet is inherently global, one can expect to see plenty of international internet disputes coming into the courts.

2. Do you see any difference between the court's analysis in *Clark* and other cases where the court applied the Restatement (Second) outside the internet context?

PROBLEM 2-66: AMERICA LOVES ONLINE DEALS WITH SPAM

America Loves Online is a New York company with its principal place of business in Virginia. It provides internet access and email accounts to its customers. America Loves Online (ALO) has its main office in Virginia and all of its services are located there. Get Rich Quick (GRQ) is an investment services company incorporated in New Jersey, with offices in New Jersey, Georgia, Missouri, Arizona, Colorado, and Texas. Using the services of several email companies operated out of Georgia, Missouri, and Texas, GRQ sent mass email advertisements to customers of

ALO. This caused ALO great expense and technological problems, and ALO sued GRQ for the tort of trespass. ALO's theory was that the mass spam effectively "hijacked" ALO's services for a period of time and thus amounted to an unauthorized invasion of ALO's property rights.

ALO filed this suit against GRQ in New Jersey, which follows the Restatement (Second) of Conflict of Laws. Assume that in New York, Georgia, and Texas, the tort law of trespass is limited to instances where the defendant intended to inflict injury. Under the trespass law of Virginia, New Jersey, Missouri, and Colorado, the plaintiff need only show that the defendant acted negligently. What law is likely to govern?

PROBLEM 2-67: REGULATING CHILD PORNOGRAPHY

The legislature of Protective State resolved to regulate the availability of child pornography on the internet. The legislature was motivated by a concern that child pornography not only victimized the children who were forced to participate in its creation, but also encouraged potential pedophiles, thus threatening more children with sexual assault. Finally, the legislature believed the prevalence of child pornography generally undermined the moral fabric of society. Mindful that Protective State had limited power to regulate out-of-state activity, the legislators focused their regulation on in-state internet service providers. Specifically, the Protective State legislature passed a statute that required internet service providers operating within the state to disable access to "child pornography items" that were "accessible through" the service by persons located in Protective State. The obligations under the statute applied only with respect to material accessible by subscribers in Protective State. According to the statute, anytime an internet service provider concluded it was appropriate to disable access to items under the statute, the service provider must notify the Protective State Attorney General. Under the statute, the Attorney General possesses the power to approve or reject the proposed action to disable access.

Is this statute appropriate as a matter of law and policy? Does the statute avoid the type of extraterritorial regulation at issue in disputes such as the *Yahoo!* decision? Can you anticipate any problems that might arise in implementing the statute?

M.   RESTATEMENT (THIRD) OF CONFLICT OF LAWS

In 2014, the American Law Institute authorized the development of a new restatement of conflict of laws. The Reporters have already drafted many sections (with accompanying Comments and Reporters' Notes), covering domicile, choice-of-law methodology, proving foreign law, as well as various issues relating to contracts, property, and tort. The project will take several more years to complete. Not only are there many more sections to draft, but the restatement review process is time-consuming, requiring multiple layers of rigorous review by judges, senior lawyers, and academics before final approval of each draft section.

As envisioned by the Reporters, the Restatement (Third) will be more rule-oriented than the Restatement (Second). As a consequence, the Restatement (Third) has no counterpart to section 6 of the Restatement (Second) — which the Restatement (Third) Reporters regard as a "grab bag" of concepts that have fostered inconsistent and unpredictable results. The Restatement (Third) sections that have been drafted do authorize an "escape hatch" allowing deviation from the rules set forth in the Restatement in cases where a manifestly more appropriate result emerges. The intent, however, is for courts to use this escape hatch infrequently so that the overall choice of law system can benefit from the predictability that adherence to fixed rules can generate.

N. INTERNATIONAL AND COMPARATIVE CHOICE OF LAW ISSUES

PERSPECTIVE ON THE RELATIONSHIP BETWEEN INTERNATIONAL LAW AND CONFLICT OF LAW DOCTRINES

Internet communication, nuclear energy, human migration, climate change, and water use: these are just a few parts of our shared existence on the globe calling for a coordinated system of governance. Both conflict of law doctrines and international law contribute to that system. What, then, is the relationship between these two? Perhaps impossible to answer, the question nonetheless provides deep insight into both areas of law.

International law is elusive and octopus-like because it comprises at least three sets of principles and rules: (1) those that operate among nations;[72] (2) those that govern entities interacting across national borders; and (3) those that sometimes govern some relationships between a nation and entities within its borders. Conflict of laws is not nearly so broad. In fact, when conflict of law doctrines regulate entities' interactions in different nation states, conflict of laws is usually regarded as a subset of international law. As you may have noticed in other parts of the volume, conflict of law doctrines often take on the label "private international law" where they operate across national borders. Within a federalist system, the relationship among the component sovereigns — for example, "states" in the United States, "provinces" in Canada — is regulated by domestic

---

72. International law thinkers often use the more general term "states," rather than "nations" — nomenclature that potentially raises confusion for those working primarily with choice of law in the United States.

conflict of law principles that do not usually have much "international" about them. Nonetheless, conflict of law rules are derived at least partially from international law principles, whether they regulate the relationship between nations or the component sovereigns of one nation.[73]

So, we generally regard private international law as a synonym for conflict of law doctrines operating in a transnational setting. The reference to "private" in "private international law" evokes a distinction between public and private spheres of international law, a distinction now thought inaccurate and outmoded by many scholars. The label remains in current use, however, in many places in the world outside the United States.

This is not the only way in which conflict of laws is less sweeping than general international law principles. Conflict of law doctrines generally embrace the premise that domestic law principles are central sources of authority for dispute resolution.[74] The task of conflict of law doctrines is to figure out which of those sources of authority should prevail where their terms cannot be reconciled. International law sometimes takes this as its mission. But international law also has greater aspirations, such as identifying universal norms of human governance and establishing supranational institutions. In some instances, these institutions and norms are intended to have a vertical relationship with the domestic laws of nation states. Many advocate that international law may have the effect of harmonizing domestic laws or creating hybrid principles. Where this does not occur, the vertical relationship between international and domestic laws may result in international law dominating and suppressing domestic law in the name of a superior international norm, and not, as in the usual conflict of law context, in the name of peaceful horizontal relationships among nation states.

International law's broader orientation highlights a useful observation about differences in the sources of authority for international law and conflict of law doctrines. As demonstrated earlier in this chapter, conflict of law principles are most often creatures of common law. By contrast, international law has a variety of sources. One view confines international law to principles identified by consent between sovereigns, consent memorialized in treaties or other formal instruments. Most, however, agree that custom also gives rise to international legal principles. How does one determine the content of customary international law? Means for determining the meaning of customary international law include judicial decisions and highly respected writings of international law scholars. Even today, debates about the source of international law are likely to mention the concept of "natural law,"[75] a term largely absent from current writings on conflict of laws.

73. Alex Mills, *The Private History of International Law*, 55 Int'l & Comp. L.Q. 1 (2006); Ralf Michaels, *Public and Private International Law: German Views on Global Issues*, 4 J. Private Int'l L. 121 (2008).

74. Sometimes domestic law may point to international law as the source of authority, although this occurs less in the United States than in the European Union and elsewhere.

75. *See, e.g.*, Jasper Doomen, *The Meaning of "International Law,"* 45 Int'l Law. 881, 882-883 (2011) (evaluating the meaning of international law by reference to natural law principles). *See generally* Mary Ellen O'Connell, The Power and Purpose of International Law: Insights from the Theory and Practice of Enforcement (2008).

Within the United States, state law is the major source of conflict of law doctrines, even where the choice of law dispute involves the law of a foreign nation, rather than two sister states of the United States. United States constitutional principles embodied in the full faith and credit clause and the supremacy clause provide some supervision of these state choice of law doctrines. The presence of these United States constitutional principles leads to another important point about the relationship between international law and choice of law doctrines: circumstances exist when international law displaces choice of law doctrines. The supremacy clause establishes that, where applicable, United States treaty provisions direct states to resolve conflict of law questions in a particular way. Thus, state conflict of law principles can be "trumped" by an international law instrument, such as a treaty. Examples of this are illustrated and discussed later in this chapter in connection with the United Nations Convention on Contracts for the International Sale of Goods, in Chapter 1 in connection with the Hague Service Convention, in Chapter 3 in connection with the relationship between the United States federal law and international law, and in Chapter 4 in connection with international recognition and enforcement of judgments. Finally, certain types of international law principles, know as jus cogens or preemptory norms, are a form of "super law" (more technically "nonderogable" norms), which can override other sources of international law. The international community recognizes a limited set of jus cogens rules as fundamental, encompassing such matters as prohibitions against war crimes, genocide, slavery, and torture. Where the result of a domestic conflict of law analysis might implicate a jus cogens prohibition, one would expect the conflict of law analysis to yield to the prohibition.

Despite differences between conflict of law doctrine and international law, some scholars not only highlight their similarities, but also argue that international law might benefit from greater use of conflict of laws. Starting from the premise that both conflict of law doctrine and international law "concern relations between laws," Professors Karen Knop, Ralf Michaels, and Annelise Riles see significant opportunity for overlap. They observe that both areas have "rules that determine whether a case with links to more than one jurisdiction is governed by the law of the forum or the law of one of those jurisdictions."[76] As for the benefits that conflicts doctrine offers international law, they focus on how international law operates in domestic courts. In this context, they argue that a conflict of law orientation provides a way for domestic courts to respect international law, regarding it as law (without "simplifying" international law "by characterizing it as domestic law").[77] They observe that conflict of laws brings a "wealth of experience" to inform debates about the role of international law in domestic courts, including the "technique" of conflict of laws as an "intellectual style."[78] Calling the technical nature of conflict of law doctrine "a

76. Karen Knop, Ralf Michaels & Annelise Riles, *International Law in Domestic Courts: A Conflict of Laws Approach*, 103 Am. Soc'y Int'l L. Proc. 269, 271 (2010), available at http://ssrn.com/abstract=1413189 (2009).

77. *Id.* at 270.

78. Karen Knop, Ralf Michaels & Annelise Riles, *From Multiculturalism to Technique: Feminism, Culture and the Conflict of Laws Style*, 64 Stan. L. Rev. 589, 589 (2012).

strength," and not a "shortcoming," these scholars maintain that it provides a structured technique for "thinking through problems of legal, political and cultural relativism."[79] Pointing out yet another potential use for conflict of law doctrines, international law scholars note that conflict of law principles may ameliorate fragmentation and inconsistencies in international law principles, qualities that derive from the plethora of international institutions and instruments that currently exist.[80] This array of international law scholarship thus tallies many virtues and potential contributions of conflict of laws: wisdom, technique, intellectual style, and potential for promoting tolerance and harmonization among laws, institutions, and people of the world. Consider whether you agree that conflict of law doctrines hold such promise!

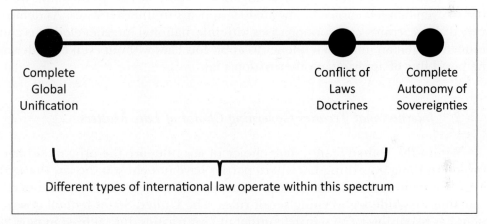

Figure 2-4: Autonomy Spectrum: The Relationship Between International Law and Conflict of Laws

1. Routine Choice of Law in International Cases

Throughout this chapter, cases illustrate how domestic courts considering cases with international elements generally follow the same, standard choice of law analysis used in wholly domestic cases. Examples include *Catalano v. Catalano*

79. *Id.* at 271. Other scholars are not so sanguine about how useful currently constituted conflict of law doctrine can be in world governance. For example, Professor Horatia Muir-Watt argues the choice of law, personal jurisdiction, and judgment recognition doctrines within international criminal law need to be reconstituted in order to avoid manipulation by private actors and to provide meaningful global governance. *See, e.g.,* Horatia Muir-Watt, *Reshaping Private International Law in a Changing World* (Apr. 28, 2008), http://conflictoflaws.net/2008/guest-editorial-muir-watt-on-reshaping-private-international-law-in-a-changing-world.

80. Ralf Michaels & Joost Pauwelyn, *Conflict of Norms or Conflict of Laws*, 22 DUKE J. COMP. & INT'L L. 349, 349-351 (2012).

(First Restatement), *D'Agostino v. Johnson & Johnson* (governmental interest analysis), *Naghiu v. Intercontinental Hotel Group* (Second Restatement), *Nedlloyd Lines B.V. v. Superior Court* (choice of law clauses), *Bakalar v. Vavra* (hybrid approaches), and *Chang v. Baxter Healthcare* (statute of limitations). Occasionally, one might see foreign cases treated differently because of the difficulty of proving the content of foreign law, a matter covered earlier in this chapter in the Perspective on Proof of Foreign Law.

One might predict that analysis might be more complicated or biased in favor of forum law and domestic litigants in cases with international elements, but the cases do not really bear this out. Indeed, an empirical study of international choice of law decisions in tort cases by United States district court judges shows that the choice of law analysis is predictable and not biased in favor forum law, plaintiffs, or local litigants.[81] A notable exception to this trend toward even-handed choice of law analysis appears in internet cases. As demonstrated above, courts confronting cases with international internet elements continue to exhibit an unusual tendency to apply local law without even considering the possibility of applying another nation's law.

2. *International Treaties Governing Choice of Law Matters*

Within the United States, state choice of law rules are the primary vehicles for determining governing law where parties have not chosen the law that governs their contract relationship. In transnational disputes, however, treaties can sometimes provide a governing set of rules. The United States federal government has been slow to recognize conflict of laws treaties due, at least in part, to the dominance of state law on the choice of law matters.

The federal government has nonetheless ratified a few of choice of law treaties, most notably the United Nations Convention on the International Sales of Goods, which took effect in 1988. In the absence of exclusion by parties to a contract, the "Convention applies to contracts of sales of goods between parties whose places of business are in different" jurisdictions, provided those jurisdictions have ratified the Convention. U.N. Convention on the International Sales of Goods, Art. 1. The Convention — which is often referred to as the CISG — generally applies if the forum's conflicts rules lead to the application of a ratifying country's law, although the United States has declared that it will not be bound by this provision.

The Convention's scope is limited, leaving many matters to the laws of signatory jurisdictions. For example, Article 96 of the Convention allows a signatory state to require that contracts must be in writing, although the Convention does not contain its own writing requirement. Questions arise where, for example, contracting parties from signatory jurisdictions enter oral sales

81. Christopher A. Whytock, *Myth or Mess? International Choice of Law in Action*, 84 N.Y.U. L. REV. 719, 723 (2009) (concluding that as a consequence of these qualities in their choice of law decisions, district judges contribute considerably to effective global governance).

contracts. One of the parties is from a jurisdiction that requires a writing; the other party is not. The following case grapples with this scenario.

Forestal Guarani S. A. v. Daros International, Inc.

613 F.3d 395 (3d Cir. 2010)

FISHER, Circuit Judge.

At issue in this appeal is the interpretation of the United Nations Convention on Contracts for the International Sale of Goods as it relates to a contract dispute between two corporations, one based in the United States and the other in Argentina. The Convention contains a provision allowing a contract to be proved even if it is not in writing but also authorizes a signatory state to make a declaration opting out of that and related provisions. The United States has not made such a declaration; Argentina has. The District Court concluded that Argentina's declaration imposed a writing requirement and that the absence of a written contract in this case precluded the plaintiff's claim. We disagree with that approach. We conclude that where, as here, one party's country of incorporation has made a declaration while the other's has not, a court must first decide, based on the forum state's choice-of-law rules, which forum's law applies, and then apply the law of the forum designated by the choice-of-law analysis.

We cannot decide on this record whether New Jersey or Argentine law applies here. Furthermore, because the parties have not briefed the issue and the District Court did not address it, we are reluctant to determine whether the claim asserted here would survive under either jurisdiction's laws. Accordingly, we will vacate the District Court's grant of summary judgment . . . and remand. . . .

I.

Forestal Guarani S.A. is an Argentina-based manufacturer of various lumber products, including wooden finger-joints. Daros International, Inc., is a New Jersey-based import-export corporation. In 1999, Forestal and Daros entered into an oral agreement whereby Daros agreed to sell Forestal's wooden finger-joints to third parties in the United States. Pursuant to that agreement, Forestal sent Daros finger-joints worth $1,857,766.06. Daros paid Forestal a total of $1,458,212.35. Forestal demanded the balance due but Daros declined to pay. In April 2002, Forestal sued Daros in the Superior Court of New Jersey, asserting a breach-of-contract claim based on Daros' refusal to pay. Daros thereafter removed the case to the United States District Court for the District of New Jersey. In its answer, Daros admitted that it had paid Forestal $1,458,212.35 in exchange for the finger-joints but denied that it owed Forestal any additional money. . . .

In June 2005, Daros moved for summary judgment, arguing that the parties lacked a written agreement in violation of the United Nations Convention on Contracts for the International Sale of Goods . . . , and that Forestal could not otherwise substantiate its damages claim with credible evidence. The District Court summarily denied the motion. . . . The Court later ordered briefing on several specific questions regarding the applicability of the CISG. Both parties . . . agreed that the CISG governed Forestal's claim. In October 2008, the District Court granted Daros' summary judgment motion, concluding that the CISG governed the parties' dispute and barred Forestal's claim because the parties' agreement was not in writing. The Court also found that Forestal had not adduced any other evidence of its alleged agreement with Daros. Forestal . . . appealed. . . .

The parties do not dispute that the CISG governs their dispute. While Daros does not deny that it had a contract with Forestal, the thrust of Daros' argument is that the parties do not have a written contract and that, under the CISG, the absence of a writing precludes Forestal's claim. While conceding that the CISG applies generally, Forestal contests the District Court's ruling on the ground that the lack of a writing, in its view, is inconsequential in light of the parties' course of dealing, as evidenced by Forestal's delivery of finger-joints to Daros and Daros' remittance of payments to Forestal, as well as an accountant's report and invoices Forestal claims show that Daros owes it money.

The CISG "applies to contracts of sale of goods between parties whose places of business are in different States . . . when the States are Contracting States[.]" 15 U.S.C. App., Art. 1(1)(a). . . . Because both the United States, where Daros is based, and Argentina, where Forestal is based, are signatories to the CISG and the alleged contract at issue involves the sale of goods, we agree with the parties that the CISG governs Forestal's claim. . . .

"The CISG strives to promote certainty among contracting parties and simplicity in judicial understanding by (1) reducing forum shopping, (2) reducing the need to resort to rules of private international law, and (3) establishing a law of sales appropriate for international transactions." These goals are explicitly enshrined in the CISG. Article 7 directs a court, in interpreting the CISG, to be mindful of "its international character and . . . the need to promote uniformity in its application and the observance of good faith in international trade." . . . [T]he CISG dispenses with certain formalities associated with proving the existence of a contract. Specifically, Article 11 instructs that "[a] contract of sale need not be concluded in or evidenced by writing and is not subject to any other requirement as to form. It may be proved by any means, including witnesses." Similarly, Article 29 permits a contract modification to be proved even if it is not in writing. And Part II of the CISG, titled "Formation of the Contract," outlines requirements governing offer and acceptance but does not impose a writing requirement.

Article 11's elimination of formal writing requirements does not apply in all instances in which the CISG governs. Article 96 of the CISG carves out an exception to Article 11, Article 29 and Part II. It says that

> [a] Contracting State whose legislation requires contracts of sale to be concluded in or evidenced by writing may at any time make a declaration in accordance with article 12 that any provision of article 11, article 29, or Part II of this Convention, that allows a contract of sale or its modification or termination by agreement or any

offer, acceptance, or other indication of intention to be made in any form other than in writing, does not apply where any party has his place of business in that State.

Article 12, to which Article 96 refers, states that

[a]ny provision of article 11, article 29 or Part II of this Convention that allows a contract of sale . . . to be made in any form other than in writing does not apply where any party has his place of business in a Contracting State which has made a declaration under article 96 of this Convention. The parties may not derogate from or vary the effect of this article.

The United States has not made an Article 96 declaration, so Article 11 governs contract formation in cases involving a United States-based litigant and a litigant based in another non-declaring signatory state. Argentina, however, has made a declaration under Article 96, thereby opting out of Article 11, Article 29 and Part II.

Our research has turned up almost no case law from courts in the United States informing how to address a case, such as this one, in which one state has made an Article 96 declaration and the other has not. Courts in foreign jurisdictions and commentators alike are divided. . . . According to one school of thought, a court must at the outset conduct a choice-of-law analysis based on private international law principles to determine which state's law governs contract formation, and then apply that law to a party's claim. In contrast, under what appears to be the minority view, a court should simply require the existence of a writing without reference to either state's law, though it is unclear what form such a writing would have to take to be considered sufficient.

. . . [W]e conclude that the majority has it right. Our conclusion is compelled by the CISG's plain language. The CISG says that "[q]uestions concerning matters governed by this Convention which are not expressly settled in it are to be settled in conformity with the general principles on which it is based or, in the absence of such principles, in conformity with the law applicable by virtue of the rules of private international law [i.e. choice of law]." 15 U.S.C. App., Art. 7(2). Because Argentina has opted out of Articles 11 and 29 as well as Part II of the CISG, the CISG does not "expressly settle" the question whether a breach-of-contract claim is sustainable in the absence of a written contract. So Article 7(2) tells us to consider the CISG's "general principles" to fill in the gap. We have already outlined some of the general principles undergirding the CISG, but we fail to see how they inform the question whether Forestal's contract claim may proceed. Indeed, given the inapplicability in this case of any of the CISG's provisions relaxing or eliminating writing requirements, we do not believe that we can answer the question presented here based on a pure application of those principles alone. Given that neither the CISG nor its founding principles explicitly or implicitly settle our inquiry, Article 7(2)'s reference to "the rules of private international law" is triggered. In other words, we have to consider the choice-of-law rules of the forum state, in this case New Jersey, to determine whether New Jersey or Argentine form requirements govern Forestal's claim.[10]

[The court then described New Jersey's most significant relationship approach, but pointed out that the parties had not briefed and the district court had not adjudicated several matters bearing on that choice of law inquiry.]

... It is true that we can affirm a district court's ruling on any ground supported by the record. There is no dispute here that Forestal's contract with Daros was verbal at best, so we could feasibly skip a choice-of-law analysis and apply both New Jersey and Argentine law to Forestal's claim to test its viability. New Jersey's statute of frauds provides that "a contract for the sale of goods for the price of $500 or more is not enforceable by way of action or defense unless there is some writing sufficient to indicate that a contract for sale has been made between the parties and signed by the party against whom enforcement is sought. . . ." N.J. Stat. Ann. §12A:2-201(1). While Forestal's claim might fail under that provision, the statute also makes several exceptions to the general rule. The parties have not briefed, and the record in this case prevents us from concluding definitively, whether any such exception is applicable here. As for Argentine law, we may safely assume that it requires some sort of writing, as Article 96 of the CISG permits a country to opt out of Article 11 only if its domestic law "requires contracts of sale to be concluded in or evidenced by writing. . . ." 15 U.S.C. App., Art. 96. We have looked at the Argentine Civil Code; it contains several provisions governing contract formation and ways of proving a contract. Forestal's offer of proof may or may not suffice under those provisions. In the end, we think it unwise either to venture into this choice-of-law thicket — the outcome of which is determinative of this case — or to engage in a largely speculative exercise about the viability of Forestal's claim under either jurisdiction's law without the benefit of either any briefing whatsoever by the parties or any analysis by the District Court on this point. Because these issues deserve a full airing, we conclude that remand is a better course of action. . . .

Notes on
FORESTAL

1. As noted by the *Forestal* court, the CISG strives to promote certainty and simplicity in judicial understanding by "(1) reducing forum shopping, (2) reducing the need to resort to rules of private international law, and (3) establishing a law of sales appropriate for international transactions." In addition,

---

10. Although the CISG's plain language obviates the need for resort to its drafting history, we note nonetheless that that history buttresses our conclusion. As one commentator has written,

the sole fact that one party has its place of business in a State that made an Article 96 reservation does not necessarily make applicable the form requirements of that State. . . . Rather, the rules of private international [law] of the forum should dictate whether any form requirements have to be met. The legislative history of the Convention appears to corroborate this view, since at the 1980 Vienna Diplomatic Conference a proposal was rejected pursuant to which the form requirements of a State that had made an Article 96 reservation had to be applied.

Article 7 of the Convention specifically directs courts interpreting its provisions to be mindful of "its international character and . . . the need to promote uniformity in its application and the observance of good faith in international trade." Did the court's decision to require the district court to engage in a choice of law analysis under New Jersey's choice of law approach serve this objective of creating a body of uniform international sales law?

2. In the United States, treaties governing choice of law matters create a complication implicating the interplay between state and federal power: the federal government holds the power to enter such treaties, but the treaties generally operate to displace state law. In other words, when the federal government ratifies a choice of law treaty, it effectively federalizes an area of law that had not previously been federalized for the purpose of internal disputes within the United States. *See* Hannah L. Buxbaum, *Conflict of Laws Conventions and Their Reception in National Legal Systems: Report for the United States*, in THE IMPACT OF THE UNIFORM LAW ON NATIONAL LAW: LIMITS AND POSSIBILITIES (J. Sanchez Cordero ed., 2010), *available at* http://ssrn.com/abstract=1745113. Does this observation support the federal court's decision in *Forestal* to apply state choice of law rules to resolve the dispute?

3. According to the district court opinion in *Forestal*, Daros removed the case from state to federal court under 28 U.S.C. §1331(a), which grants federal district courts subject matter jurisdiction for civil actions arising under a treaty of the United States. The federal court's jurisdiction was premised at least in part on the existence of federal question jurisdiction. *Forestal Guarani S.A. v. Daros Int'l Inc.*, No. 03-4821, 2008 WL 4560701, at *1. Accordingly, once the *Forestal* court decided to look to "rules of private international law" (i.e., conflict of laws principles) to resolve the dispute, the court could have looked to federal choice of law methodology, not New Jersey's choice of law methodology. The circumstances under which federal courts should apply federal choice of law methodology are discussed further in the next chapter in connection with *Klaxon v. Stentor*, 313 U.S. 487 (1941). Nonetheless, because the Restatement (Second) of Conflict of Laws is generally believed to embody the federal choice of law methodology, the result in *Forestal* would not likely be different given that New Jersey's most significant relationship approach essentially tracks the Second Restatement.

PROBLEM 2-68: WIDGET BATTLE

Widget Buyer is incorporated in the State of New Alabama, does business in that state only, and purchased widgets from Widget Seller during a phone conversation in which Widget Buyer was in New Alabama and Widget Seller was in New China. During this phone conversation, Widget Seller offered the widgets for a given price and Widget buyer declared, "Sold!" The transaction was not reduced to writing. Widget Seller is a New Chinese company and does business throughout the world.

Widget Buyer is unsatisfied with the widgets purchased and has sued Widget Seller for breach of contract in state court in New Alabama. New Alabama follows the Restatement (First) of Conflict of Laws and considers statute of frauds questions to be procedural. New Alabama has a statute of frauds, but does not require a contract such as this to be in writing. New China requires contracts such as this to be in writing, treats statute of frauds questions as procedural, and has opted out of Article 11 of the CISG by making a reservation under Article 96.

Widget Seller has moved to dismiss the complaint, claiming that the action is barred under the statute of frauds. Should the court accept this argument?

3. Comparative Material: The European Union

The European Union (EU) is a partnership, politically and economically, of a growing number of Member States, now in excess of 25 countries. As a quasi-federation of states, the EU offers many analogs to the United States, and thus provides an opportunity for enlightening comparison. As with the founding of the United States, economic cooperation served as an important impetus for the establishment of the EU as well. EU founders acted on the principle that economically interdependent countries will have an incentive to avoid conflict with each other. One of the EU's most important goals is developing a single European market, a goal fostered by coherent legal rules. To the extent that legal rules are consistent or at least harmonious and predictable, citizens of countries within the EU can plan deals, coordinate joint enterprises, and freely move among different markets.

Because EU countries maintain sovereignty and political autonomy, each country has its own unique laws. For that reason, choice of law rules are key to maintaining predictability for parties both within and outside the EU who are seeking to anticipate the legal consequences of their economic activity. To the extent that choice of law rules vary among EU Member States, clarity, uniformity, and predictability of laws becomes more difficult. The history of the EU's approach to conflict of laws reveals an evolving effort to develop a uniform scheme. Both the process of creating uniform rules and the rules themselves hold lessons for the United States.

Although disharmony in national choice of law rules impedes development of a single European market, EU authorities did not turn an early focus to harmonizing these rules. Efforts to harmonize conflict of laws[82] rules gained momentum after the Treaty of Amsterdam came into force in 1999, as that treaty promoted adopting uniform conflict of laws rules "as necessary for the proper functioning of the internal market."[83] More recently, the EU passed regulations harmonizing choice of law rules for contractual obligations and non-contractual

82. Conflict of laws outside of the United States is often transnational, and so this area of law is often referred to as private international law.

83. Treaty of Amsterdam Art. 73m, November 10, 1997, 1997 O.J. (C340).

obligations, sparking what some commentators have described as a European conflict of laws revolution. Even before these EU choice of law initiatives, many EU Member States had entered into successful conventions that governed specific matters. *See, e.g.,* Hague Convention on the Law Applicable to Traffic Accidents (May 4, 1971); Hague Convention on the Law Applicable to Products Liability (October 2, 1973). Earlier efforts to create consensus among EU states were preserved with the EU initiatives, which provide that they do not "prejudice application of international conventions to which one or more Member States" were parties.

The Brussels Convention of 1968 laid the groundwork for harmonizing choice of law in the EU by creating a system of rules governing the jurisdiction of courts and the recognition and enforcement of judgments in civil and commercial matters. The Brussels Convention, superseded by Brussels I, was the first step in unifying conflict of laws in the EU. A potential downside of Brussels I soon became apparent, since it facilitates forum shopping by allowing a claimant access to different national courts. Without an EU regulation or multilateral treaty harmonizing choice of law rules, each EU country will apply its own national choice of law rules, which can vary greatly. Some uniformity in these laws exist without EU action, through bilateral treaties or through multilateral treaties like the Hague Conventions, but none of these efforts create uniformity in choice of law rules that reciprocally match the effect of Brussels I on jurisdiction. Interestingly, then, facilitating personal jurisdiction without accompanying choice of law reform may undermine legal coordination by increasing forum shopping and thereby decreasing uniformity and predictability.

The first step in implementing a coordinated choice of law system in Europe was the Rome Convention, a multilateral treaty superseded in 2008 when the European Union adopted a regulation called "Rome I." The EU adopted the Rome I regulation in order to ensure the proper functioning of the single European market, to improve the predictability of litigation outcomes, and to reduce forum shopping. Rome I harmonizes the choice of law rules applicable to contractual obligations in civil and commercial matters. It applies universally, which means it can authorize a court to apply the law of any country, including a non-EU country.

Rome I instructs courts not to allow renvoi, and distinguishes choice of law problems where parties have chosen the governing law from those with no chosen law. Rome I encourages parties to choose the law that governs their contracts, and to specify that law in a choice of law clause inserted in the contract. A court may override the parties' choice only in rare circumstances: one instance occurs when the chosen law is manifestly incompatible with the forum country's public policy. In the absence of choice by the parties, Rome I provides specific rules to determine the applicable law. These rules use connecting factors to determine the applicable law, which vary depending on type of contract, and also include an "escape clause," stipulating that the laws of another country should be applied if it is manifestly more closely connected to the contract.

The EU regards Rome II as a necessary complement to Rome I in facilitating the ambitious aims of creating a single market and a single area of justice. Rome II harmonizes the conflict of laws rules applicable to non-contractual obligations. Unlike Rome I, which had a predecessor treaty, Rome II has no precursor. Before Rome II, conflict of laws rules for non-contractual obligations were the almost exclusive domain of national law; thus, observers regard Rome II as a "dramatic step in the federalization" of conflict of laws in Europe.[84]

Rome II's choice of law guidance is organized according to the type of non-contractual legal obligation. The concept of non-contractual obligations is amorphous, and is broad enough to cover both traditional tort liability theories as well as restitutionary concepts like unjust enrichment. In keeping with Rome I, Rome II applies universally and instructs courts not to allow renvoi.

Rome II also emphasizes freedom of choice, which is an innovative approach since party autonomy in choice of law is usually linked only to contractual obligations.[85] Parties can agree to the law governing them after the damage has occurred, and commercial parties can freely negotiate the applicable law even before the damage has occurred. Party choice is limited however, and some breaches of non-contractual obligations can trigger a mandatory provision of law from a country the parties did not choose. These mandatory laws can come from both the country where the damage occurred and the forum country. In addition, a court can refuse party choice if the law chosen proves "manifestly incompatible with the public policy of the forum."

In the absence of the parties' predetermined choice, Rome II directs courts to rules, which — like the Restatements of the Law in the United States — are organized according to the type of non-contractual obligation. For example, the rule for torts is similar to the United States' Restatement (First) of Conflict of Laws: the country where the damage occurred will supply the applicable law. This rule does not consider "where the event giving rise to the damage occurred" or where "the indirect consequences of that event occur." When the damage occurs, if both parties to the suit were habitually resident in the same country, the law of that country will apply. This exception exists in order to meet the "legitimate expectations of the two parties." An "escape clause" exists, which commands that if the tort is "manifestly more connected with a country other than that indicated" by the general rule and its exception, the law of that country will apply. This "escape clause" allows courts to apply the law of a country they deem to be the "centre of gravity" of the case.[86] One might read this to track the approach of non-Restatement (First) approaches in the United States: allowing courts to inject an intuitive sense of justice that can veto the result of mechanical rules.

Product liability rules show how Rome II regulates a specific tort. For product liability, Rome II balances the interests of the liable party and the damaged party, with the aim of "fairly spreading the risks inherent in a modern high-technology

---

84. Symeon C. Symeonides, *Rome II and Tort Conflicts: A Missed Opportunity*, 56 Am. J. Comp. L. 173, 174 (2008).

85. Mo Zhang, *Party Autonomy in Non-Contractual Obligations: Rome II and Its Impact on Choice of Law*, 39 Seton Hall L. Rev. 861, 864 (2009).

86. Rome II Regulation (EC) on the law applicable to non-contractual obligations, July 11, 1997, O.J. 2007 (L199/40).

society." To serve this balance, Rome II breaks from the general rule for torts in order to avoid the unfair outcomes that might result if the country where the damage occurred always supplied the applicable law. Indeed, the liable party may have been unable to foresee damage occurring in that country, and that country's laws may be completely unrelated to the circumstances of the case for the damaged party. Thus, Rome II uses an alternative choice of law mechanism for products liability disputes. Under this mechanism, each choice of law decision uses a common factor: whether the liable party marketed the product in the country. Accordingly, the rules require that — before a country's law applies — the liable party must have foreseen that its product will be put to use in the country. This principle is omnipresent in products liability choice of law decisions, unless the "escape clause" from the general tort rules appears appropriate. Rome II's treatment of product liability thus illustrates how the EU has sought to harmonize choice of law while promoting both justice and the functioning of its single market.

Despite these several apparently successful innovations, the EU has not been able to harmonize the choice of law rules for all torts and other non-contractual obligations. A look at some of the issues suggests considerable ideological differences among the countries of the EU, differences that manifest in the breakdown of consensus over choice of laws rules. Some struggles are reminiscent of the United States experience with hotly contested choice of law problems such as slavery, consumer protection, and same-sex marriage.

In the EU, defamation provides an important example of ideological divergence. Rome II excludes defamation, although the tort appeared in the proposed draft of the regulation. This omission is significant because conflict of laws issues are likely to arise in defamation cases, given the frequency of cross-border communications. In fact, many jurisdictions have the ability to exercise power over a single defamation claim in Europe, since the European Court of Justice[87] has held in a defamation action gainst a newspaper that the jurisdiction where a newspaper is established has power to adjudicate the claim, as well as any jurisdiction where both the newspaper was distributed and the victim claims to have been injured.[88] Despite the range of forums with jurisdiction over a defamation claim, this theory of liability was excluded from the final draft of Rome II because participants failed to reach political consensus on how to balance the interests of publishers and the victims of defamation. The proposed Rome II draft applied its general tort provisions to defamation, which would have resulted in the governing law coming from the jurisdiction where damage arises. The draft also provided an escape clause, stipulating that a court did not have to apply this law if it was "contrary to the fundamental principles of the forum as regards freedom of expression and information." This approach was thought to be fair to the victims of defamation, who expect to be able to use the law of the forum where they were injured, and also fair

---

87. The European Court of Justice is the judicial authority charged with ensuring the uniform application of EU law and reviewing the legality of EU law.

88. Case C-68/93, *Fiona Shevill, Ixora Trading Inc., Chequepoint SARL and Chequepoint International Ltd. v. Presse Alliance S.A.*, 1995 E.C.R. I-415.

to publishers, who expect to enjoy the constitutional press freedoms of the country where they are principally based when they are sued.

When the European Parliament rejected the proposed Rome II's provision on defamation, the Parliament attempted to make the applicable law in a defamation action the law of the country where "the most significant element or elements of the loss or damage occur or are likely to occur."[89] The Parliament further sought to provide that a "manifestly closer connection" with a country would justify that country's laws being applied. In proposing this amendment, the Parliament believed that publishers needed more certainty. The European Council, however, could not accept these changes, explaining that the amendment was "too generous to press editors rather than the victim of alleged defamation in the press."[90] The disagreement over how to balance these disparate interests proved insurmountable, with the only solution being to delete all defamation provisions from the final draft of Rome II and to accept the uncertainty resulting from each state applying its own national choice of law rules.

Difficulty in harmonizing choice of law rules appears in cultural differences between EU countries. This is especially reflected in Rome III, which marks a turn of Europe's attention in its harmonization process toward family law. The migration of peoples across the EU and the increasing rate of international marriages sparked efforts to develop uniform the choice of law rules for divorce.[91] Without uniform rules, a divorcing couple could not be certain of what law would apply to their case, might encounter results at odds with their expectations and might compete with each other to see who might first rush to court in order to ensure that a certain forum's law applied. Diversity exists in how EU member states resolve international divorce cases. Rome III on the law applicable to divorce stumbled during negotiations, and was tabled as an EU-wide regulation due to "insurmountable difficulties that made unanimity impossible."

Family law is closely connected with a country's culture, often reflecting its social values and religious views. This is starkly reflected in Ireland's immediate rejection of Rome III because the regulation would enable married couples to obtain divorces far more easily than allowed under Irish law, which requires that separating spouses live at least four years apart before the start of any divorce proceeding. Irish citizens can obtain divorces far more easily by travelling to other jurisdictions, but allowing Irish courts to use less arduous divorce laws proved unacceptable. By contrast, Sweden, which has much more liberal divorce laws than Ireland, also rejected Rome III due to fears that they would be required to apply Sharia law in Swedish courts. Cultural differences in divorce law, however, did not provide a barrier for all countries seeking to harmonize choice of law

89. Report on the proposal for a regulation of the European Parliament and of the Council on the law applicable to non-contractual obligations (Rome II), at 46, Eur. Parl. Com. (2003) 427 (June 27, 2005).
90. Amended proposal for a European Parliament and Council Regulation on the law applicable to non-contractual obligations (Rome II), at 6, COM (2006) 83 final (Feb. 21, 2006).
91. The Brussels II regulation established common rules on jurisdiction for matrimonial matters.

rules, and several EU Member States have already accepted Rome III, including Malta, whose national law did not even allow divorce at the time when it accepted the regulation.

Rome III took effect in 2012 and follows its predecessors by applying universally, excluding renvoi, and encouraging spouses to choose the applicable law. Spouses can choose the law applicable to their divorce, subject to certain restrictions that seek to ensure the chosen law has a connection with where the couple has lived, their nationality, or the forum where the divorce was instituted. These restrictions prevent the application of arbitrary law to the divorce proceeding. In the absence of choice, Rome III determines the applicable law through a decision tree, which looks for a country to which both spouses are connected. The laws of the country where both spouses are "habitually resident" is the preferred option, but if there is no country to which the divorcing couple is mutually connected by either residency or nationality, the law of the seized forum will apply. Thus, forum shopping is not completely eliminated under Rome III. Like the previous Rome treaties, Rome III has a public policy exception, allowing a court to opt out of applying laws that are "manifestly incompatible" with forum public policy. The intent of the public policy exception is not to ignore the cultural values of other countries, however: Rome III's preamble makes clear that courts must respect the Charter of Fundamental Rights of the European Union, which prohibits discrimination based on religion and political beliefs.

The EU regulations pertaining to choice of law are an impressive accomplishment of coordination of diverse interests in service of a common goal: an integrated market. The EU community's success with developing consensus on choice of law regulation itself holds an important lesson for the United States, whether in the context of debating a national choice of law code or the need for a Third Restatement of Conflict of Laws. More specific guidance may await further experience under the Rome I, II, and III regimes. One particular area to watch is party autonomy outside of contractual relationships.

PROBLEM 2-69: CORPORATE COUNSEL'S SUBMISSION TO THE EUROPEAN COMMISSION ON ROME II

Assume that you are corporate counsel for a client involved in producing or selling media-related products, such as books, films, home video material, computer games, and the like. Assume further that your client has asked you to prepare a letter briefly outlining your concerns about Rome II, including the consideration of provisions regulating defamation actions that appeared in drafts of Rome II. You should address the letter to the European Commission responsible for drafting and revising the Rome II regulation. Outline the concerns that you would express on behalf of your client.

PERSPECTIVE ON TAKING STOCK — A RETROSPECTIVE ON THE TECHNIQUES FOR RECKONING WITH DIVERSITY AMONG LAWS

As illustrated throughout this chapter, the main technique for handling diversity among laws that potentially govern a slice of human existence is for courts and lawyers to use choice of law rules to determine which jurisdiction's laws govern. (The prospect of a non-legally trained person engaging in complex choice of law analysis is possible, but probably relatively rare.) Scholars and courts have called the laws that govern the various slices of human existence (outside of law or litigation) "primary laws," or — in the language of the renvoi doctrine — "internal laws," in an effort to distinguish these primary or internal laws from choice of law rules. The process of using choice of law rules to designate those primary laws that govern a particular situation is made complicated not only by often comparable claims of regulatory power by two or more competing jurisdictions, but also by the diversity of conflict of laws principles themselves. In many cases, the standard default of applying the forum's choice of law rules avoids this latter complication arising from differences among choice of law approaches. But the default doesn't eliminate all complexity in this regard. Take, for example, difficulties raised by renvoi or — as discussed in Chapter 3 — questions about what choice of law rules should govern a court hosting a suit arising under another sovereign's laws (such as a federal district court exercising diversity of citizenship jurisdiction or a federal bankruptcy court adjudicating a state law contract claim). The United States Congress possesses the power to eliminate at least part of these complexities, but, as we have seen, has declined to step into the fray in a systemized manner. In a parallel federalism context, we have seen that the European Union has taken a more proactive approach. And, of course, international law provides both a complication and a source of potential clarification.

Aside from using choice of law rules to handle diversity in legal regulation, legal thinkers have identified other options. In the United States and elsewhere in the world, forward looking legal thinkers and other innovators have sometimes inspired the development of uniform laws, such as the Uniform Commercial Code. Initiatives such as the Uniform Commercial Code are ground-up endeavors in the sense that the uniformity results from cooperation among co-equal sovereigns that choose to enact the uniform law. Other times, this uniformity is accomplished by fiat from a superior sovereign, such as explored in Chapter 3 in connection with federal preemption. Chapter 3 illustrates that the "superior" law is sometimes wholly a creature of the superior sovereign, but often the result of hybrid alchemy, combining elements of the laws of the superior sovereign as well as other jurisdictions.

International law can operate in a related manner. Although international law is not the product of a superior sovereign, certain international norms may attain sufficiently universal acceptance to operate to the exclusion of a particular sovereign's law. Where formally embodied in instruments such as treaties or in the form of jus cogens rules,[92] international law readily takes on the status of a superior law that can displace domestic sovereign authority and can thereby eliminate complexities arising from diversity among domestic laws. Chapter 3 explores further the relationship between international law and the federal and state laws of the United States. In related fashion, international law can operate in such a way as to leave in place domestic laws, but develop a set of primary rules to govern "transjurisdictional" interactions among entities.[93] The United Nations Convention for the International Sale of Goods is an example of such an international device.

Finally, with initiative coming from an entirely different source than international and domestic law, private parties sometimes take matters into their own hands. Indeed, those wishing to develop their own private rules for interaction attempt to eliminate choice of law uncertainties and complexities by designating which legal principles will govern their relationship. As explored in this chapter in connection with choice of law clauses in contracts, government has yet to provide private parties with full latitude to govern their own affairs.

92. Jus cogens rules are described above in the Perspective on the Relationship Between International Law and Conflict of Law Doctrines.

93. *See* RUSSELL J. WEINTRAUB, COMMENTARY ON THE CONFLICT OF LAWS 568-572 (6th ed. 2010), in which Professor Weintraub, employing the term "transjurisdictional," explains how the United Nations Convention for the International Sale of Goods eliminates conflict of laws problems.

CHAPTER 3

THE ROLE OF THE FEDERAL GOVERNMENT

This chapter explores the relationship between the United States federal government and laws derived from other sources, including state governments of the United States, governments of other countries, and international law. This chapter's material differs widely from that in Chapter 2, in large part because federal law has only one source: the federal government. As Chapter 2 illustrated, where state law governs a particular problem, we often encounter a circumstance where many different states' laws legitimately vie for control. Questions of federal control, by contrast, often turn on identifying the proper scope of federal law, since the supremacy clause of the United States leaves no doubt that federal law can displace conflicting state law. While determining the proper scope of federal law is sometimes no small task (particularly given the many sources for federal law), the task is nonetheless more manageable than juggling conflicting laws of numerous, disparate, and co-equal sovereigns such as the states of the United States.

Complications may arise where one must grapple with whether international law or the law of another nation displaces United States federal law. The latter clash (federal law versus the law of another nation) resembles the issues explored in Chapter 2 more closely than the other conflicts, and is partially covered in this chapter in connection with extraterritorial application of United States federal law. The end of this chapter directly grapples with the relationship between federal law and international law. First, however, this chapter reckons with the role of federal constitutional law in constraining the process explored in Chapter 2: choosing among competing and potentially applicable state law.

To begin the process of expanding your thoughts on the relationship of United States federal law to other laws, consider the following permutation of the problem that introduces Chapters 1, 2, and 4:

INTRODUCTORY PROBLEM: CASSANDRA AND JULIAN REDUX (VERTICAL ISSUES OF LEGAL REGULATION)

Cassandra is a resident of New Jersey. She researched and wrote an article about Julian, which was published in a newspaper. A resident of Ohio, Julian is convinced that the article defames him and he files a defamation suit against Cassandra in Ohio. At the time of the publication, Cassandra had never been to Ohio and had never had anything to do with Ohio. Unbeknownst to her, however, the newspaper distributes 20 papers in the state (less than 1 percent of its total circulation).

Julian filed suit against Cassandra in Ohio state court, and managed to serve Cassandra with process while Cassandra was knowingly and voluntarily traveling on Ohio's highways on her way to Indiana. Thus, no one contests that the Ohio court has personal jurisdiction over Cassandra. Cassandra researched Ohio law governing defamation, which she believes is extremely unfavorable to her. She would like to convince the court that it may not apply Ohio law to the lawsuit. Cassandra's instincts are that federal law may be the most sympathetic source of law for her. In what ways might federal law conceivably bear on the lawsuit? Does federal law have a role to play in supervising the decision to apply Ohio law? If so, how is this supervisory role different than the role federal law plays in determining whether Ohio can properly assert personal jurisdiction over Cassandra?

A. UMPIRING PRINCIPLES IN THE UNITED STATES CONSTITUTION

Before analyzing circumstances when federal law displaces state law in providing a rule for deciding the controversy, we first consider the role that federal law plays in supervising the state choice of law process. As noted elsewhere in this volume, the full faith and credit clause (and, to a lesser extent, the due process clause of the Fourteenth Amendment) vests the federal government with authority to create choice of law rules that govern in state and federal courts. The federal government has declined to do that on a general scale, choosing only to embrace the Restatement (Second) of Conflict of Laws on a limited basis for certain federal court actions.

The regulation of the relationships among states is a central purpose of the United States Constitution. Indeed, as Professor Kermit Roosevelt has explained, a "great aim of the Constitution is to knit the discrete sovereignties of the states into a federal union, and this purpose obviously requires rules governing the treatment of the laws, and the citizens, of sister states."[1] For this reason, one might expect robust constitutional regulation of all aspects of conflict of laws.

---

1. Kermit Roosevelt, *The Myth of Choice of Law: Rethinking Conflicts*, 97 MICH. L. REV. 2448, 2504 (1999).

That, however, has not occurred. On rare occasions, federal constitutional principles have aggressively resolved state law conflicts by displacing state regulation altogether: a primary example being the Thirteenth, Fourteenth, and Fifteen Amendments, which nullified the institution of slavery. In a more light-handed manner, the United States Supreme Court has also exercised constitutional power over state regulation by identifying general, but limited, constraints on the state law choice of law process as well as on the ability of state courts to decline to provide a forum for cases with out-of-forum elements. These two categories of federal constitutional oversight are analyzed immediately below.

1. Constitutional Constraints on Horizontal Choice of Law

The Due Process Clause of the Fourteenth Amendment Provides:

[N]o State shall . . . deprive any person of life, liberty, or property, without due process of law. . . .

The Full Faith and Credit Clause, Art. IV, §1, provides:

Full Faith and Credit shall be given in each State to the public Acts, Records, and judicial Proceedings of every other State. And the Congress may by general Laws prescribe the Manner in which such Acts, Records, and Proceedings shall be proved, and the Effect thereof.

The United States Supreme Court's early conflicts cases suggested that territorial principles such as those found in the First Restatement of Conflict of Laws possessed constitutional force by virtue of the full faith and credit clause. Indeed, the Court's early decisions suggested that the full faith and credit clause imposed an *affirmative* duty to apply a certain law in a given case, where — for example — a foreign state's interest in having its law govern outweighed the forum state's interest in applying forum law.

In subsequent legal developments, the Supreme Court not only backed off from transforming conflict of laws principles into affirmative constitutional requirements, but also incorporated the due process clause into its armory of conflicts regulation tools. The leading older case invoking the due process clause as a *negative* limitation on the state choice of law process, *Home Insurance Company v. Dick*, 281 U.S. 397 (1930), is still cited with approval in United States Supreme Court cases.

In *Dick*, the Supreme Court determined that due process prohibited a Texas state court from applying Texas law to enlarge parties' obligations under a Mexican contract lacking any Texas connections. *Dick* arose from a Mexican insurance company's policy covering a Mexican tugboat used in Mexican waters. The claim being litigated concerned a boat destroyed by fire in Mexico and owned by an individual (Dick) who was living in Mexico. Although the contract provided that no lawsuit could be brought more than one year after the date of loss, the plaintiff filed suit in Texas more than one year after the loss. Defendants defended by pointing to the one-year limitation clause, but the Texas courts invoked a Texas statute invalidating any attempt by parties to limit the time for suit to less than two years.

The Supreme Court reversed the Texas courts, holding that application of the Texas statute deprived defendants of property without due process.

Consider the following excerpts of its reasoning:

> The Texas statute as here construed and applied deprives the garnishees of property without due process of law. A state may, of course, prohibit and declare invalid the making of certain contracts within its borders. Ordinarily, it may prohibit performance within its borders, even of contracts validly made elsewhere, if they are required to be performed within the state and their performance would violate its laws. But, in the case at bar, nothing in any way relating to the policy sued on, or to the contracts of reinsurance, was ever done or required to be done in Texas. All acts relating to the making of the policy were done in Mexico. All in relation to the making of the contracts of reinsurance were done there or in New York. And, likewise, all things in regard to performance were to be done outside of Texas. Neither the Texas laws nor the Texas courts were invoked for any purpose, except by Dick in the bringing of this suit. The fact that Dick's permanent residence was in Texas is without significance. At all times here material he was physically present and acting in Mexico. Texas was therefore without power to affect the terms of contracts so made. Its attempt to impose a greater obligation than that agreed upon and to seize property in payment of the imposed obligation violates the guaranty against deprivation of property without due process of law.

Id. at 407-408.

As for the international character of the litigation and the operation of the full faith and credit clause, the *Dick* Court had the following to say:

> [I]t is urged that the Federal Constitution does not require the states to recognize and protect rights derived from the laws of foreign countries — that as to them the full faith and credit clause has no application. They rest upon the Fourteenth Amendment. Its protection extends to aliens. Moreover, the parties in interest here are American companies. The defense asserted is based on the provision of the policy and on their contracts of reinsurance. The courts of the state confused this defense with that based on the Mexican Code. They held that, even if the effect of the foreign statute was to extinguish the right, *Dick's* removal to Texas prior to the bar of the foreign statute removed the cause of action from Mexico, and subjected it to the Texas statute of limitation. And they applied the same rule to the provision in the policy. Whether or not that is a sufficient answer to the defense based on the foreign law we may not consider; for no issue under the full faith and credit clause was raised. But in Texas, as elsewhere, the contract was subject to its own limitations.

Id. at 410.

As you will note from its approach in *Dick*, the Court was concerned with establishing the outer limits for a court legitimately to apply forum law. The Court was not concerned with using the Constitution to create solutions to choice of law problems. Because *Dick* had international elements, the case did not provide the Court with an opportunity to elucidate the role of the full faith and credit clause. In subsequent cases, however, the Court has often used both the full faith and credit clause and the due process clause, essentially conflating the two clauses for the purpose of conflict of laws regulation.

After *Dick*, the Supreme Court's constitutional decisions began to demonstrate analytical kinship with modern choice of law methodologies. Indeed, two workers' compensation cases from the New Deal era defined constitutional limitations on choice of law by focusing on governmental interests behind conflicting laws. The first case, *Alaska Packers Ass'n v. Industrial Accident Comm'n*, 294 U.S. 532 (1935), concerned California workers' compensation award to a nonresident alien, who had been hired in California and injured in Alaska. Upholding the award, the Supreme Court determined that both California and Alaska had a "legitimate public interest" in resolving the dispute. The Court then purported to balance the interests of the states and concluded that California's interest was "greater than" Alaska's. For this reason, the Court found the California award consistent with the due process and full faith and credit clauses.

The second New Deal case, *Pacific Employers Ins. Co. v. Industrial Accident Comm'n*, 294 U.S. 532 (1935), concerned a Massachusetts employee injured while working in California at the direction of his Massachusetts employer. The employer challenged the California workers' compensation board's award, arguing that more stringent Massachusetts workers' compensation law should govern. Recognizing that California and Massachusetts both had interests in the dispute, the Supreme Court declined to balance those interests (as the *Alaska Packers* decision had suggested). Instead, the Court simply asked whether the forum, California, had a substantial interest in the dispute. Concluding that California did have such an interest, the Court determined that the full faith and credit clause neither required California to apply Massachusetts law nor permitted Massachusetts "to legislate across state lines" in order to prevent California "from prescribing . . . the legal consequences of acts" within its boundaries.

Consider how the case that follows, *Allstate Ins. Co. v. Hague*, continues the trend of integrating modern choice of law thinking into constitutional regulation of state choice of law decisions. Consider how the plurality and dissenting opinions apply the concept of "legitimate state interest" differently, and evaluate which approach is more appropriate. Note also that both the plurality and dissenting opinions treat the due process and full faith and credit clauses as coextensive. In reviewing the case, consider whether you agree with this decision to conflate the clauses.

Allstate Ins. Co. v. Hague

449 U.S. 302 (1981)

Justice BRENNAN announced the judgment of the Court and delivered an opinion, in which Justice WHITE, Justice MARSHALL, and Justice BLACKMUN joined.

This Court granted certiorari to determine whether the Due Process Clause of the Fourteenth Amendment or the Full Faith and Credit Clause of Art. IV, §1, of the United States Constitution bars the Minnesota Supreme Court's choice of substantive Minnesota law to govern the effect of a provision in an insurance policy issued to respondent's decedent.

I

Respondent's late husband, Ralph Hague, died of injuries suffered when a motorcycle on which he was a passenger was struck from behind by an automobile. The accident occurred in Pierce County, Wis., which is immediately across the Minnesota border from Red Wing, Minn. The operators of both vehicles were Wisconsin residents, as was the decedent, who, at the time of the accident, resided with respondent in Hager City, Wis., which is one and one-half miles from Red Wing. Mr. Hague had been employed in Red Wing for the 15 years immediately preceding his death and had commuted daily from Wisconsin to his place of employment.

Neither the operator of the motorcycle nor the operator of the automobile carried valid insurance. However, the decedent held a policy issued by petitioner Allstate Insurance Co. covering three automobiles owned by him and containing an uninsured motorist clause insuring him against loss incurred from accidents with uninsured motorists. The uninsured motorist coverage was limited to $15,000 for each automobile.[3]

After the accident, but prior to the initiation of this lawsuit, respondent moved to Red Wing. Subsequently, she married a Minnesota resident and established residence with her new husband in Savage, Minn. At approximately the same time, a Minnesota Registrar of Probate appointed respondent personal representative of her deceased husband's estate. Following her appointment, she brought this action in Minnesota District Court seeking a declaration under Minnesota law that the $15,000 uninsured motorist coverage on each of her late husband's three automobiles could be "stacked" to provide total coverage of $45,000. Petitioner defended on the ground that whether the three uninsured motorist coverages could be stacked should be determined by Wisconsin law, since the insurance policy was delivered in Wisconsin, the accident occurred in Wisconsin, and all persons involved were Wisconsin residents at the time of the accident.

The Minnesota District Court disagreed. Interpreting Wisconsin law to disallow stacking, the court concluded that Minnesota's choice-of-law rules required the application of Minnesota law permitting stacking. The court refused to apply Wisconsin law as "inimical to the public policy of Minnesota" and granted summary judgment for respondent.

The Minnesota Supreme Court . . . affirmed the District Court. The court, also interpreting Wisconsin law to prohibit stacking, applied Minnesota law

3. Ralph Hague paid a separate premium for each automobile including an additional separate premium for each uninsured motorist coverage.

after analyzing the relevant Minnesota contacts and interests within the analytical framework developed by Professor Leflar. . . . Although stating that the Minnesota contacts might not be, "in themselves, sufficient to mandate application of [Minnesota] law,"[8] under the first four factors, the court concluded that the fifth factor — application of the better rule of law — favored selection of Minnesota law. . . .

II

. . . Our sole function is to determine whether the Minnesota Supreme Court's choice of its own substantive law in this case exceeded federal constitutional limitations. Implicit in this inquiry is the recognition, long accepted by this Court, that a set of facts giving rise to a lawsuit, or a particular issue within a lawsuit, may justify, in constitutional terms, application of the law of more than one jurisdiction. As a result, the forum State may have to select one law from among the laws of several jurisdictions having some contact with the controversy.

In deciding constitutional choice-of-law questions, whether under the Due Process Clause or the Full Faith and Credit Clause,[10] this Court has traditionally examined the contacts of the State, whose law was applied, with the parties and with the occurrence or transaction giving rise to the litigation. In order to ensure that the choice of law is neither arbitrary nor fundamentally unfair, the Court has invalidated the choice of law of a State which has had no significant contact or significant aggregation of contacts, creating state interests, with the parties and the occurrence or transaction. . . .

The lesson from [earlier decisions of this Court] is that for a State's substantive law to be selected in a constitutionally permissible manner, that State must have a significant contact or significant aggregation of contacts, creating state interests, such that choice of its law is neither arbitrary nor fundamentally unfair. Application of this principle to the facts of this case persuades us that the Minnesota Supreme Court's choice of its own law did not offend the Federal Constitution.

III

Minnesota has three contacts with the parties and the occurrence giving rise to the litigation. In the aggregate, these contacts permit selection by the

8. The court apparently was referring to sufficiency as a matter of choice of law and not as a matter of constitutional limitation on its choice-of-law decision.

10. This Court has taken a similar approach in deciding choice-of-law cases under both the Due Process Clause and the Full Faith and Credit Clause. In each instance, the Court has examined the relevant contacts and resulting interests of the State whose law was applied. Although at one time the Court required a more exacting standard under the Full Faith and Credit Clause than under the Due Process Clause for evaluating the constitutionality of choice-of-law decisions, the Court has since abandoned the weighing-of-interests requirement. Different considerations are of course at issue when full faith and credit is to be accorded to acts, records, and proceedings outside the choice-of-law area, such as in the case of sister state-court judgments.

Minnesota Supreme Court of Minnesota law allowing the stacking of Mr. Hague's uninsured motorist coverages.

First, and for our purposes a very important contact, Mr. Hague was a member of Minnesota's work force, having been employed by a Red Wing, Minn., enterprise for the 15 years preceding his death. While employment status may implicate a state interest less substantial than does resident status, that interest is nevertheless important. The State of employment has police power responsibilities towards the nonresident employee that are analogous, if somewhat less profound, than towards residents. Thus, such employees use state services and amenities and may call upon state facilities in appropriate circumstances.

In addition, Mr. Hague commuted to work in Minnesota . . . and was presumably covered by his uninsured motorist coverage during the commute. The State's interest in its commuting nonresident employees reflects a state concern for the safety and well-being of its work force and the concomitant effect on Minnesota employers.

That Mr. Hague was not killed while commuting to work or while in Minnesota does not dictate a different result. To hold that the Minnesota Supreme Court's choice of Minnesota law violated the Constitution for that reason would require too narrow a view of Minnesota's relationship with the parties and the occurrence giving rise to the litigation. An automobile accident need not occur within a particular jurisdiction for that jurisdiction to be connected to the occurrence. Similarly, the occurrence of a crash fatal to a Minnesota employee in another State is a Minnesota contact. If Mr. Hague had only been injured and missed work for a few weeks the effect on the Minnesota employer would have been palpable and Minnesota's interest in having its employee made whole would be evident. Mr. Hague's death affects Minnesota's interest still more acutely, even though Mr. Hague will not return to the Minnesota work force. Minnesota's work force is surely affected by the level of protection the State extends to it, either directly or indirectly. Vindication of the rights of the estate of a Minnesota employee, therefore, is an important state concern.

Mr. Hague's residence in Wisconsin does not — as Allstate seems to argue — constitutionally mandate application of Wisconsin law to the exclusion of forum law. If, in the instant case, the accident had occurred in Minnesota between Mr. Hague and an uninsured Minnesota motorist, if the insurance contract had been executed in Minnesota covering a Minnesota registered company automobile which Mr. Hague was permitted to drive, and if a Wisconsin court sought to apply Wisconsin law, certainly Mr. Hague's residence in Wisconsin, his commute between Wisconsin and Minnesota, and the insurer's presence in Wisconsin should be adequate to apply Wisconsin's law.[22] Employment status is

22. Of course Allstate could not be certain that Wisconsin law would necessarily govern any accident which occurred in Wisconsin, whether brought in the Wisconsin courts or elsewhere. Such an expectation would give controlling significance to the wooden *lex loci delicti* doctrine. While the place of the accident is a factor to be considered in choice-of-law analysis, to apply blindly the traditional, but now largely abandoned, doctrine would fail to distinguish between the relative importance of various legal issues involved in a lawsuit as well as the relationship of other jurisdictions to the parties and the occurrence or transaction. If, for example, Mr. Hague had

not a sufficiently less important status than residence . . . when combined with Mr. Hague's daily commute across state lines and the other Minnesota contacts present, to prohibit the choice-of-law result in this case on constitutional grounds.

Second, Allstate was at all times present and doing business in Minnesota. By virtue of its presence, Allstate can hardly claim unfamiliarity with the laws of the host jurisdiction and surprise that the state courts might apply forum law to litigation in which the company is involved. "Particularly since the company was licensed to do business in [the forum], it must have known it might be sued there, and that [the forum] courts would feel bound by [forum] law." Moreover, Allstate's presence in Minnesota gave Minnesota an interest in regulating the company's insurance obligations insofar as they affected both a Minnesota resident and court-appointed representative — respondent — and a longstanding member of Minnesota's work force — Mr. Hague.

Third, respondent became a Minnesota resident prior to institution of this litigation. The stipulated facts reveal that she first settled in Red Wing, Minn., the town in which her late husband had worked. She subsequently moved to Savage, Minn., after marrying a Minnesota resident who operated an automobile service station in Bloomington, Minn. Her move to Savage occurred "almost concurrently," with the initiation of the instant case. There is no suggestion that Mrs. Hague moved to Minnesota in anticipation of this litigation or for the purpose of finding a legal climate especially hospitable to her claim.[28] The stipulated facts, sparse as they are, negate any such inference. . . .

[R]espondent's bona fide residence in Minnesota was not the sole contact Minnesota had with this litigation. And in connection with her residence in Minnesota, respondent was appointed personal representative of Mr. Hague's estate by the Registrar of Probate for the County of Goodhue, Minn. Respondent's residence and subsequent appointment in Minnesota as personal representative of her late husband's estate constitute a Minnesota contact which gives Minnesota an interest in respondent's recovery, an interest which the court below identified as full compensation for "resident accident victims" to keep them "off welfare rolls" and able "to meet financial obligations."

---

been a Wisconsin resident and employee who was injured in Wisconsin and was then taken by ambulance to a hospital in Red Wing, Minn., where he languished for several weeks before dying, Minnesota's interest in ensuring that its medical creditors were paid would be obvious. Moreover, under such circumstances, the accident itself might be reasonably characterized as a bistate occurrence beginning in Wisconsin and ending in Minnesota. Thus, reliance by the insurer that Wisconsin law would necessarily govern any accident that occurred in Wisconsin, or that the law of another jurisdiction would necessarily govern any accident that did not occur in Wisconsin, would be unwarranted.

If the law of a jurisdiction other than Wisconsin did govern, there was a substantial likelihood, with respect to uninsured motorist coverage, that stacking would be allowed. Stacking was the rule in most States at the time the policy was issued. Indeed, the Wisconsin Supreme Court identified 29 States, including Minnesota, whose law it interpreted to allow stacking, and only 9 States whose law it interpreted to prohibit stacking. Clearly then, Allstate could not have expected that an antistacking rule would govern any particular accident in which the insured might be involved and thus cannot claim unfair surprise from the Minnesota Supreme Court's choice of forum law.

28. The dissent suggests that considering respondent's postoccurrence change of residence as one of the Minnesota contacts will encourage forum shopping. *Post*, at 653. This overlooks the fact that her change of residence was bona fide and not motivated by litigation considerations.

In sum, Minnesota had a significant aggregation of contacts with the parties and the occurrence, creating state interests, such that application of its law was neither arbitrary nor fundamentally unfair. Accordingly, the choice of Minnesota law by the Minnesota Supreme Court did not violate the Due Process Clause or the Full Faith and Credit Clause.

Affirmed.

Justice STEWART took no part in the consideration or decision of this case.

Justice STEVENS, concurring in the judgment.

As I view this unusual case — in which neither precedent nor constitutional language provides sure guidance — two separate questions must be answered. First, does the Full Faith and Credit Clause *require* Minnesota, the forum State, to apply Wisconsin law? Second, does the Due Process Clause of the Fourteenth Amendment *prevent* Minnesota from applying its own law? The first inquiry implicates the federal interest in ensuring that Minnesota respect the sovereignty of the State of Wisconsin; the second implicates the litigants' interests in a fair adjudication of their rights.[3]

I realize that both this Court's analysis of choice-of-law questions[4] and scholarly criticism of those decisions have treated these two inquiries as though they were indistinguishable. Nevertheless, I am persuaded that the two constitutional provisions protect different interests and that proper analysis requires separate consideration of each.

I

The Full Faith and Credit Clause is one of several provisions in the Federal Constitution designed to transform the several States from independent sovereignties into a single, unified Nation. The Full Faith and Credit Clause implements this design by directing that a State, when acting as the forum for litigation having multistate aspects or implications, respect the legitimate interests of other States and avoid infringement upon their sovereignty. The Clause does not, however,

---

3. The two questions presented by the choice-of-law issue arise only after it is assumed or established that the defendant's contacts with the forum State are sufficient to support personal jurisdiction. Although the choice-of-law concerns — respect for another sovereign and fairness to the litigants — are similar to the two functions performed by the jurisdictional inquiry, they are not identical. In *World-Wide Volkswagen Corp. v. Woodson,* 444 U.S. 286, 291-292 (1980), we stated:

> The concept of minimum contacts, in turn, can be seen to perform two related, but distinguishable, functions. It protects the defendant against the burdens of litigating in a distant or inconvenient forum. And it acts to ensure that the States, through their courts, do not reach out beyond the limits imposed on them by their status as coequal sovereigns in a federal system.

While it has been suggested that this same minimum-contacts analysis be used to define the constitutional limitations on choice of law, the Court has made it clear over the years that the personal jurisdiction and choice-of-law inquiries are not the same.

4. Although the Court has struck down a state court's choice of forum law on both due process, and full faith and credit grounds, no clear analytical distinction between the two constitutional provisions has emerged. . . .

rigidly require the forum State to apply foreign law whenever another State has a valid interest in the litigation. On the contrary, in view of the fact that the forum State is also a sovereign in its own right, in appropriate cases it may attach paramount importance to its own legitimate interests. Accordingly, the fact that a choice-of-law decision may be unsound as a matter of conflicts law does not necessarily implicate the federal concerns embodied in the Full Faith and Credit Clause. Rather in my opinion, the Clause should not invalidate a state court's choice of forum law unless that choice threatens the federal interest in national unity by unjustifiably infringing upon the legitimate interests of another State.

In this case, I think the Minnesota courts' decision to apply Minnesota law was plainly unsound as a matter of normal conflicts law. Both the execution of the insurance contract and the accident giving rise to the litigation took place in Wisconsin. Moreover, when both of those events occurred the plaintiff, the decedent, and the operators of both vehicles were all residents of Wisconsin. Nevertheless, I do not believe that any threat to national unity or Wisconsin's sovereignty ensues from allowing the substantive question presented by this case to be determined by the law of another State.

The question on the merits is one of interpreting the meaning of the insurance contract. Neither the contract itself, nor anything else in the record, reflects any express understanding of the parties with respect to what law would be applied or with respect to whether the separate uninsured motorist coverage for each of the decedent's three cars could be "stacked." Since the policy provided coverage for accidents that might occur in other States, it was obvious to the parties at the time of contracting that it might give rise to the application of the law of States other than Wisconsin. Therefore, while Wisconsin may have an interest in ensuring that contracts formed in Wisconsin in reliance upon Wisconsin law are interpreted in accordance with that law, that interest is not implicated in this case.

Petitioner has failed to establish that Minnesota's refusal to apply Wisconsin law poses any direct or indirect threat to Wisconsin's sovereignty.[13] In the absence of any such threat, I find it unnecessary to evaluate the forum State's interest in the litigation in order to reach the conclusion that the Full Faith and Credit Clause does not require the Minnesota courts to apply Wisconsin law to the question of contract interpretation presented in this case.

II

It may be assumed that a choice-of-law decision would violate the Due Process Clause if it were totally arbitrary or if it were fundamentally unfair to either litigant. I question whether a judge's decision to apply the law of his own State could ever be described as wholly irrational. For judges are presumably familiar

13. It is clear that a litigant challenging the forum's application of its own law to a lawsuit properly brought in its courts bears the burden of establishing that this choice of law infringes upon interests protected by the Full Faith and Credit Clause. . . . It is equally clear that a state court's decision to apply its own law cannot violate the Full Faith and Credit Clause where the application of forum law does not impinge at all upon the interests of other States.

with their own state law and may find it difficult and time consuming to discover and apply correctly the law of another State. The forum State's interest in the fair and efficient administration of justice is therefore sufficient, in my judgment, to attach a presumption of validity to a forum State's decision to apply its own law to a dispute over which it has jurisdiction.

The forum State's interest in the efficient operation of its judicial system is clearly not sufficient, however, to justify the application of a rule of law that is fundamentally unfair to one of the litigants. Arguably, a litigant could demonstrate such unfairness in a variety of ways. Concern about the fairness of the forum's choice of its own rule might arise if that rule favored residents over non-residents, if it represented a dramatic departure from the rule that obtains in most American jurisdictions, or if the rule itself was unfair on its face or as applied.[15]

The application of an otherwise acceptable rule of law may result in unfairness to the litigants if, in engaging in the activity which is the subject of the litigation, they could not reasonably have anticipated that their actions would later be judged by this rule of law. A choice-of-law decision that frustrates the justifiable expectations of the parties can be fundamentally unfair. This desire to prevent unfair surprise to a litigant has been the central concern in this Court's review of choice-of-law decisions under the Due Process Clause.[16]

Neither the "stacking" rule itself, nor Minnesota's application of that rule to these litigants, raises any serious question of fairness. As the plurality observes, "[s]tacking was the rule in most States at the time the policy was issued." Moreover, the rule is consistent with the economics of a contractual relationship in which the policyholder paid three separate premiums for insurance coverage for three automobiles, including a separate premium for each uninsured motorist coverage. Nor am I persuaded that the decision of the Minnesota courts to apply the "stacking" rule in this case can be said to violate due process because that decision frustrates the reasonable expectations of the contracting parties. . . .

In this case, no express indication of the parties' expectations is available. The insurance policy provided coverage for accidents throughout the United States; thus, at the time of contracting, the parties certainly could have anticipated that the law of States other than Wisconsin would govern particular claims arising under the policy. By virtue of doing business in Minnesota, Allstate was aware that it could be sued in the Minnesota courts; Allstate also presumably was aware that Minnesota law, as well as the law of most States, permitted "stacking." . . . Therefore, the decision of the Minnesota courts to apply the law of the forum in this case does not frustrate the reasonable expectations

15. Discrimination against nonresidents would be constitutionally suspect even if the Due Process Clause were not a check upon a State's choice-of-law decisions. Moreover, both discriminatory and substantively unfair rules of law may be detected and remedied without any special choice-of-law analysis; familiar constitutional principles are available to deal with both varieties of unfairness.

16. Upon careful analysis most of the decisions of this Court that struck down on due process grounds a state court's choice of forum law can be explained as attempts to prevent a State with a minimal contact with the litigation from materially enlarging the contractual obligations of one of the parties where that party had no reason to anticipate the possibility of such enlargement.

of the contracting parties, and I can find no fundamental unfairness in that decision requiring the attention of this Court.[23]

In terms of fundamental fairness, it seems to me that two factors relied upon by the plurality—the plaintiff's postaccident move to Minnesota and the decedent's Minnesota employment—are either irrelevant to or possibly even tend to undermine the plurality's conclusion. When the expectations of the parties at the time of contracting are the central due process concern, as they are in this case, an unanticipated post–accident occurrence is clearly irrelevant for due process purposes. The fact that the plaintiff became a resident of the forum State after the accident surely cannot justify a ruling in her favor that would not be made if the plaintiff were a nonresident. Similarly, while the fact that the decedent regularly drove into Minnesota might be relevant to the expectations of the contracting parties, the fact that he did so because he was employed in Minnesota adds nothing to the due process analysis. The choice-of-law decision of the Minnesota courts is consistent with due process because it does not result in unfairness to either litigant, not because Minnesota now has an interest in the plaintiff as resident or formerly had an interest in the decedent as employee.

III

Although I regard the Minnesota courts' decision to apply forum law as unsound as a matter of conflicts law, and there is little in this record other than the presumption in favor of the forum's own law to support that decision, I concur in the plurality's judgment. It is not this Court's function to establish and impose upon state courts a federal choice-of-law rule, nor is it our function to ensure that state courts correctly apply whatever choice-of-law rules they have themselves adopted. Our authority may be exercised in the choice-of-law area only to prevent a violation of the Full Faith and Credit or the Due Process Clause. For the reasons stated above, I find no such violation in this case.

Justice POWELL, with whom THE CHIEF JUSTICE and Justice REHNQUIST join, dissenting.

My disagreement with the plurality is narrow. I accept with few reservations Part II of the plurality opinion, which sets forth the basic principles that guide us in reviewing state choice-of-law decisions under the Constitution. The Court should invalidate a forum State's decision to apply its own law only when there are no significant contacts between the State and the litigation. This modest check on state power is mandated by the Due Process Clause of the Fourteenth

---

23. Comparison of this case with *Home Ins. Co. v. Dick*, 281 U.S. 397 (1930), confirms my conclusion that the application of Minnesota law in this case does not offend the Due Process Clause. In *Home Ins. Co.*, the contract expressly provided that a particular limitations period would govern claims arising under the insurance contract and that Mexican law was to be applied in interpreting the contract; in addition, the contract was limited in effect to certain Mexican waters. The parties could hardly have made their expectations with respect to the applicable law more plain. In this case, by way of contrast, nothing in the contract suggests that Wisconsin law should be applied or that Minnesota's "stacking" rule should not be applied. In this case, unlike *Home Ins. Co.*, the court's choice of forum law results in no unfair surprise to the insurer.

Amendment and the Full Faith and Credit Clause of Art. IV, §1. I do not believe, however, that the plurality adequately analyzes the policies such review must serve. In consequence, it has found significant what appear to me to be trivial contacts between the forum State and the litigation.

I

. . . The significance of asserted contacts must be evaluated in light of the constitutional policies that oversight by this Court should serve. Two enduring policies emerge from our cases.

First, the contacts between the forum State and the litigation should not be so "slight and casual" that it would be fundamentally unfair to a litigant for the forum to apply its own State's law. The touchstone here is the reasonable expectation of the parties.

Second, the forum State must have a legitimate interest in the outcome of the litigation before it. The Full Faith and Credit Clause addresses the accommodation of sovereign power among the various States. Under limited circumstances, it requires one State to give effect to the statutory law of another State. To be sure, a forum State need not give effect to another State's law if that law is in "violation of its own legitimate public policy." Nonetheless, for a forum State to further its legitimate public policy by applying its own law to a controversy, there must be some connection between the facts giving rise to the litigation and the scope of the State's lawmaking jurisdiction.

Both the Due Process and Full Faith and Credit Clauses ensure that the States do not "reach out beyond the limits imposed on them by their status as coequal sovereigns in a federal system." As the Court [has] stated: "[T]he full faith and credit clause does not require one state to substitute for its own statute, *applicable to persons and events within it*, the conflicting statute of another state." The State has a legitimate interest in applying a rule of decision to the litigation only if the facts to which the rule will be applied have created effects within the State, toward which the State's public policy is directed. To assess the sufficiency of asserted contacts between the forum and the litigation, the court must determine if the contacts form a reasonable link between the litigation and a state policy. In short, examination of contacts addresses whether "the state has an interest in the application of its policy in this instance." If it does, the Constitution is satisfied.

In summary, the significance of the contacts between a forum State and the litigation must be assessed in light of these two important constitutional policies.[3] A contact, or a pattern of contacts, satisfies the Constitution when it protects the litigants from being unfairly surprised if the forum State applies its own law, and

---

3. The plurality today apparently recognizes that the significance of the contacts must be evaluated in light of the policies our review serves. It acknowledges that the sufficiency of the same contacts sometimes will differ in jurisdiction and choice-of-law questions. The plurality, however, pursues the rationale for the requirement of sufficient contacts in choice-of-law cases no further than to observe that the forum's application of its own law must be "neither arbitrary nor fundamentally unfair." But this general prohibition does not distinguish questions of choice of law from those of jurisdiction, or from much of the jurisprudence of the Fourteenth Amendment.

when the application of the forum's law reasonably can be understood to further a legitimate public policy of the forum State.

II

Recognition of the complexity of the constitutional inquiry requires that this Court apply these principles with restraint. Applying these principles to the facts of this case, I do not believe, however, that Minnesota had sufficient contacts with the "persons and events" in this litigation to apply its rule permitting stacking. I would agree that no reasonable expectations of the parties were frustrated. The risk insured by petitioner was not geographically limited. The close proximity of Hager City, Wis., to Minnesota, and the fact that Hague commuted daily to Red Wing, Minn., for many years should have led the insurer to realize that there was a reasonable probability that the risk would materialize in Minnesota. Under our precedents, it is plain that Minnesota could have applied its own law to an accident occurring within its borders. The fact that the accident did not, in fact, occur in Minnesota is not controlling because the expectations of the litigants *before* the cause of action accrues provide the pertinent perspective.

The more doubtful question in this case is whether application of Minnesota's substantive law reasonably furthers a legitimate state interest. The plurality attempts to give substance to the tenuous contacts between Minnesota and this litigation. Upon examination, however, these contacts are either trivial or irrelevant to the furthering of any public policy in Minnesota.

First, the postaccident residence of the plaintiff-beneficiary is constitutionally irrelevant to the choice-of-law question. The plurality today insists that *Yates* only held that a postoccurrence move to the forum State could not "in and of itself" confer power on the forum to apply its own law, but did not establish that such a change of residence was irrelevant. What the *Yates* Court held, however, was that "there was no occurrence, *nothing* done, to which the law of Georgia could apply." . . . This rule is sound. If a plaintiff could choose the substantive rules to be applied to an action by moving to a hospitable forum, the invitation to forum shopping would be irresistible. Moreover, it would permit the defendant's reasonable expectations at the time the cause of action accrues to be frustrated, because it would permit the choice-of-law question to turn on a post accrual circumstance. Finally, post accrual residence has nothing to do with facts to which the forum State proposes to apply its rule; it is unrelated to the substantive legal issues presented by the litigation.

Second, the plurality finds it significant that the insurer does business in the forum State. The State does have a legitimate interest in regulating the practices of such an insurer. But this argument proves too much. The insurer here does business in all 50 States. The forum State has no interest in regulating that conduct of the insurer unrelated to property, persons, or contracts executed within the forum State. The plurality recognizes this flaw and attempts to bolster the significance of the local presence of the insurer by combining it with the other factors deemed significant: the presence of the plaintiff and the fact that the deceased worked in the forum State. This merely restates the basic question in the case.

Third, the plurality emphasizes particularly that the insured worked in the forum State. The fact that the insured was a nonresident employee in the forum State provides a significant contact for the furtherance of some local policies. The insured's place of employment is not, however, significant in this case. Neither the nature of the insurance policy, the events related to the accident, nor the immediate question of stacking coverage is in any way affected or implicated by the insured's employment status. The plurality's opinion is understandably vague in explaining how trebling the benefits to be paid to the estate of a nonresident employee furthers any substantial state interest relating to employment. Minnesota does not wish its workers to die in automobile accidents, but permitting stacking will not further this interest. The substantive issue here is solely one of compensation, and whether the compensation provided by this policy is increased or not will have no relation to the State's employment policies or police power.

Neither taken separately nor in the aggregate do the contacts asserted by the plurality today indicate that Minnesota's application of its substantive rule in this case will further any legitimate state interest. . . . Therefore, I dissent.

Notes on
ALLSTATE

1. *Allstate* and the cases from which it derives present many complex problems, but their lesson for the process of resolving a conflicts problem is straightforward: every conflicts case has a two-part analysis: (1) the analyst must first apply the forum state's choice of law approach and determine which state law should govern the case; and (2) the analyst must then evaluate whether the result of this choice of law analysis is consistent with the United States Constitution. If the first part is done correctly, how significant is the second, constitutional part of the analysis? Should the answer differ according to the choice of law approach used? Consider the various choice of law approaches reviewed in Chapter 2: First Restatement, center of gravity, governmental interest analysis, comparative impairment, better rule of law, Second Restatement, lex fori, and the hybrid approaches. Are any of these approaches more likely to yield unconstitutional results than others would?

2. In his dissenting opinion, Justice Powell states that his disagreement with the plurality is "narrow," and that he accepts "with few reservations" that portion of the plurality opinion that sets forth the following nexus test: "[F]or a State's substantive law to be selected in a constitutionally permissible manner, that state must have a significant contact or significant aggregation of contacts, creating state interests, such that choice of its law is neither arbitrary or fundamentally unfair." It thus seems that a majority of the Justices agreed that this nexus test provides the appropriate constitutional standard. This means, does it not, that the difference between Justice Powell's orientation and the plurality's is in the application of the standard. Can you articulate that difference in application? Consider one

of the contacts that Justice Brennan found significant in the plurality opinion, such as the decedent's membership in the workforce of the state providing the governing law. Why is it that Justice Brennan found this significant, while Justice Powell did not?

3. Could one say that the nexus test articulated in the plurality opinion and apparently endorsed in Justice Powell's dissent resembles any of the choice of law methodologies you have studied? Because the test refers to contacts, two approaches in particular come to mind: governmental interest analysis and the center of gravity approach. Consider the plurality's handling of the three contacts — Mr. Hague's employment, Allstate's presence in Minnesota, and the plaintiff's post-accident move to Minnesota. Does the plurality's analysis of the three contacts most resemble governmental interest analysis or the center of gravity approach? Which of the two approaches most resembles Justice Powell's treatment of the two approaches?

4. The majority and dissenting opinions both seem to treat due process and full faith and credit analysis as unequivocally the same for due process and choice of law purposes. Do you agree with Justice Stevens's argument that the two clauses are so different and protect such different interests that it is proper only to consider the two clauses separately?

Certainly Justice Stevens is correct in observing that the due process clause regulates the rights of individuals and the full faith and credit clause regulates interstate relationships. In addition, the two clauses evince a different regulatory approach: the due process clause sets a minimum standard of fairness for how government treats individuals and the full faith and credit clause imposes an obligation of cooperation and respect on one state in its treatment of another state's laws.

Does the plurality opinion fail to give effect to the nuances and varying purposes reflected in the two laws? Could one reasonably say the nexus test incorporates the various constitutional concerns and goals of both clauses? If so, is it a grave problem that the Court did not segregate its analysis into two categories with two different constitutional labels? Look at the language of the full faith and credit clause set forth at the beginning of this section. Can you identify which words in the clause refer to a forum court's obligation, while adjudicating a controversy, to consider the possible application of the legal principles of another jurisdiction? Scholars generally regard the words "Public Acts" to refer to statutes and "judicial Proceedings" to refer to judgments. A judgment is generally regarded as a judicial resolution of specific rights of specific parties to a dispute. Where in the full faith and credit clause can one find a forum court's obligation to consider the common law, that is, legal principles set forth in court decisions concerning parties not currently before the forum court? Scholars have identified several options, and there is little consensus on this matter. Professor Michael Gottesman outlines the scholarly debate on this, and suggests that the concept of judicially created law or common law can be found in any of the three: public acts, records, and judicial proceedings. Gottesman has no trouble finding the obligation to honor the common law of another jurisdiction within any of these words: "Nothing in the proceedings of the Constitutional Convention indicates that the framers purposefully intended to empower Congress to compel one state to apply the common law rulings of another. . . . [Nonetheless if], the Constitution lives and breathes at all, it requires but the smallest inhalation to bring the common law under Full Faith and Credit." Michael Gottesman, *Draining the Dismal Swamp: The Case for Federal Choice of Law Statutes*, 80 Geo. L. J. 1, 25-26 (1991).

5. Courts and scholars often conceive of federalism as a compromise between respecting individual state autonomy on one hand and requiring states to cooperate with the federalist system on the other hand. Where does the *Allstate* nexus test fall in this spectrum?

6. Consider the plurality's test in *Allstate* and compare it to the constitutional test for personal jurisdiction. Are there circumstances in which the choice of law test would permit a state to apply its law, but the personal jurisdiction test denies it the opportunity to do so? By contrast, do circumstances exist in which the personal jurisdiction test permits a state to adjudicate the case (and apply substantive law to the claims), but forbids the court from applying its own law?

PROBLEM 3-1: AVOIDING STRICT REMEDIES LAW

Dan was a resident of Old Indiana. He drove a car owned by his father, who was also a resident of Old Indiana. The car was purchased and insured in Old Indiana. Dan was killed in the State of Old Indiana when the car he was driving collided with a train operated by the New Montana Railroad. Although the railroad was incorporated in New Montana, its principal place of business as well as almost all of its service is in Old Indiana.

As executrix of the estate, Dan's mother filed a negligence suit against the railroad in New Montana. Dan's mother is a resident of Old Indiana. As owner of the car, Dan's father was impleaded. There is a significant difference between the law of Old Indiana and New Montana on an important remedies issue. New Montana has a liberal approach to proving intangible remedies such as pain and suffering. Under the law of Old Indiana, however, one must have specific, direct evidence of such damages, in a form such as doctor's bills. No such direct evidence exists in this case.

The New Montana Railroad argues that it would be unconstitutional to apply New Montana law on the issue of proving pain and suffering. Are they correct? Would your answer differ depending on whether you applied the plurality approach in *Allstate* or the approach in Justice Powell's dissenting opinion?

PROBLEM 3-2: PARENTAL RIGHTS OF THE SPERM DONOR

A resident of South Delaware, Jaycee, decided to donate sperm at a clinic in South Delaware. The sperm was then retained in a laboratory in South Delaware. Another resident of South Delaware, Aislinn, wanted to become a mother. She went to a clinic in Missouri (where she worked) and requested artificial insemination. At the request of the physician at the Missouri clinic, Jaycee's sperm was transported to the clinic and the physician artificially inseminated Aislinn with Jaycee's sperm in Missouri. Aislinn became pregnant and gave birth to twins in South Delaware. Aislinn is bringing up the children in South Delaware, and filed a petition in South Delaware to terminate any parental rights that Jaycee may claim. Jaycee counterclaimed for recognition of his parental rights in the children. South Delaware law provides that a sperm donor such as Jaycee is presumed to lack parental rights and Missouri law provides that a sperm donor such as Jaycee is presumed to have parental rights.

Would it be constitutional for the South Delaware court to apply Missouri law in resolving Aislinn's petition?

Phillips Petroleum Co. v. Shutts

472 U.S. 797 (1985)

Justice REHNQUIST delivered the opinion of the Court.

Petitioner is a Delaware corporation which has its principal place of business in Oklahoma. During the 1970's it produced or purchased natural gas from leased land located in 11 different States, and sold most of the gas in interstate commerce. Respondents are some 28,000 of the royalty owners possessing rights to the leases from which petitioner produced the gas; they reside in all 50 States, the District of Columbia, and several foreign countries. Respondents brought a class action against petitioner in the Kansas state court, seeking to recover interest on royalty payments which had been delayed by petitioner. They recovered judgment in the trial court, and the Supreme Court of Kansas affirmed the judgment over petitioner's contentions that the Due Process Clause of the Fourteenth Amendment prevented Kansas from adjudicating the claims of all the respondents, and that the Due Process Clause and the Full Faith and Credit Clause of Article IV of the Constitution prohibited the application of Kansas law to all of the transactions between petitioner and respondents. . . . We reject petitioner's jurisdictional claim, but sustain its claim regarding the choice of law.

[Petitioner Phillips Petroleum had leased mineral rights from the respondents, agreeing to pay royalties from its oil and gas sales. When Phillips wished to raise gas prices it needed to secure approval for price increases from what was then the Federal Power Commission and is now the Federal Energy Regulatory Commission. The agency would tentatively approve the increase, subject to further research. During the interim, Phillips could raise prices, but had to refund the difference if the rates were not approved. Unsure where it might have to make this refund, Phillips did not pay increased royalties until after it received final agency approval. When it finally paid the increased royalties, it did not pay any interest on the increase to most of the royalty holders.]

Respondents Irl Shutts, Robert Anderson, and Betty Anderson filed suit against petitioner in Kansas state court, seeking interest payments on their suspended royalties which petitioner had possessed pending the Commission's approval of the price increases. Shutts is a resident of Kansas, and the Andersons live in Oklahoma. Shutts and the Andersons own gas leases in Oklahoma and Texas. Over petitioner's objection the Kansas trial court granted respondents' motion to certify the suit as a class action under Kansas law. The class as certified was comprised of 33,000 royalty owners who had royalties suspended by petitioner. The average claim of each royalty owner for interest on the suspended royalties was $100.

After the class was certified respondents provided each class member with notice through first-class mail. The notice described the action and informed each class member that he could appear in person or by counsel; otherwise each member would be represented by Shutts and the Andersons, the named plaintiffs. The notices also stated that class members would be included in the class and bound by the judgment unless they "opted out" of the lawsuit by executing and returning a "request for exclusion" that was included with the notice. The final class as certified contained 28,100 members; 3,400 had "opted out" of the class by returning the request for exclusion, and notice could not be delivered to another 1,500 members, who were also excluded. Less than 1,000 of the class members resided in Kansas. Only a minuscule amount, approximately one quarter of one percent, of the gas leases involved in the lawsuit were on Kansas land.

After petitioner's mandamus petition to decertify the class was denied, the case was tried to the court. The court found petitioner liable under Kansas law for interest on the suspended royalties to all class members. The trial court relied heavily on an earlier, unrelated class action involving the same nominal plaintiff and the same defendant. The Kansas Supreme Court had held in [this earlier case] that a gas company owed interest to royalty owners for royalties suspended pending final Commission approval of a price increase. No federal statutes touched on the liability for suspended royalties, and the court in [the earlier case] held as a matter of Kansas equity law that the applicable interest rates for computation of interest on suspended royalties were the interest rates at which the gas company would have had to reimburse its customers had its interim price increase been rejected by the Commission. The court in [the earlier case] viewed these as the fairest interest rates because they were also the rates that petitioner required the royalty owners to meet in their indemnity agreements in order to avoid suspended royalties.

The trial court in the present case applied the rule from [the earlier case], and held petitioner liable for prejudgment and postjudgment interest on the suspended royalties, computed at the Commission rates governing petitioner's three price increases. . . .

[Petitioner raised personal jurisdiction and choice of law challenges in the Supreme Court of Kansas. For the choice of law claim, Phillips claimed that

Kansas courts could not apply Kansas law to every claim in the lawsuit. The Supreme Court of Kansas rejected both claims.] First, it held that the absent class members were plaintiffs, not defendants, and thus the traditional minimum contacts test of *International Shoe* did not apply. The court held that nonresident class-action plaintiffs were only entitled to adequate notice, an opportunity to be heard, an opportunity to opt out of the case, and adequate representation by the named plaintiffs. [Since these procedural due process requirements were satisfied, the court held that] Kansas could assert jurisdiction over the plaintiff class. . . . The court also rejected petitioner's contention that Kansas law could not be applied to plaintiffs and royalty arrangements having no connection with Kansas. The court stated that generally the law of the forum controlled all claims unless "compelling reasons" existed to apply a different law. . . .

II

Reduced to its essentials, petitioner's argument is that unless out-of-state plaintiffs affirmatively consent, the Kansas courts may not exert jurisdiction over their claims. Petitioner claims that failure to execute and return the "request for exclusion" provided with the class notice cannot constitute consent of the out-of-state plaintiffs; thus Kansas courts may exercise jurisdiction over these plaintiffs only if the plaintiffs possess the sufficient "minimum contacts" with Kansas as that term is used in cases involving personal jurisdiction over out-of-state defendants. Since Kansas had no prelitigation contact with many of the plaintiffs and leases involved, petitioner claims that Kansas has exceeded its jurisdictional reach and thereby violated the due process rights of the absent plaintiffs.

. . . We think petitioner's premise is in error. The burdens placed by a State upon an absent class-action plaintiff are not of the same order or magnitude as those it places upon an absent defendant. An out-of-state defendant summoned by a plaintiff is faced with the full powers of the forum State to render judgment *against* it. The defendant must generally hire counsel and travel to the forum to defend itself from the plaintiff's claim, or suffer a default judgment. The defendant may be forced to participate in extended and often costly discovery, and will be forced to respond in damages or to comply with some other form of remedy imposed by the court should it lose the suit. The defendant may also face liability for court costs and attorney's fees. These burdens are substantial, and the minimum contacts requirement of the Due Process Clause prevents the forum State from unfairly imposing them upon the defendant.

A class-action plaintiff, however, is in quite a different posture. . . . [A] "class" or "representative" suit [is] an exception to the rule that one could not be bound by judgment *in personam* unless one was made fully a party in the traditional sense. As the Court pointed out in *Hansberry*, the class action was an invention of equity to enable it to proceed to a decree in suits where the number of those interested in the litigation was too great to permit joinder. The absent parties would be bound by the decree so long as the named parties adequately represented the absent class and the prosecution of the litigation was within the common interest.

Modern plaintiff class actions follow the same goals, permitting litigation of a suit involving common questions when there are too many plaintiffs for proper joinder. Class actions also may permit the plaintiffs to pool claims which would be uneconomical to litigate individually. For example, this lawsuit involves claims averaging about $100 per plaintiff; most of the plaintiffs would have no realistic day in court if a class action were not available.

In sharp contrast to the predicament of a defendant haled into an out-of-state forum, the plaintiffs in this suit were not haled anywhere to defend themselves upon pain of a default judgment.

A plaintiff class in Kansas and numerous other jurisdictions cannot first be certified unless the judge, with the aid of the named plaintiffs and defendant, conducts an inquiry into the common nature of the named plaintiffs' and the absent plaintiffs' claims, the adequacy of representation, the jurisdiction possessed over the class, and any other matters that will bear upon proper representation of the absent plaintiffs' interest. Unlike a defendant in a civil suit, a class-action plaintiff is not required to fend for himself. The court and named plaintiffs protect his interests. Indeed, the class-action defendant itself has a great interest in ensuring that the absent plaintiff's claims are properly before the forum. In this case, for example, the defendant sought to avoid class certification by alleging that the absent plaintiffs would not be adequately represented and were not amenable to jurisdiction.

The concern of the typical class-action rules for the absent plaintiffs is manifested in other ways. Most jurisdictions, including Kansas, require that a class action, once certified, may not be dismissed or compromised without the approval of the court. In many jurisdictions such as Kansas the court may amend the pleadings to ensure that all sections of the class are represented adequately.

Besides this continuing solicitude for their rights, absent plaintiff class members are not subject to other burdens imposed upon defendants. They need not hire counsel or appear. They are almost never subject to counterclaims or cross-claims, or liability for fees or costs. Absent plaintiff class members are not subject to coercive or punitive remedies. Nor will an adverse judgment typically bind an absent plaintiff for any damages, although a valid adverse judgment may extinguish any of the plaintiff's claims which were litigated.

Unlike a defendant in a normal civil suit, an absent class-action plaintiff is not required to do anything. He may sit back and allow the litigation to run its course, content in knowing that there are safeguards provided for his protection. In most class actions an absent plaintiff is provided at least with an opportunity to "opt out" of the class, and if he takes advantage of that opportunity he is removed from the litigation entirely. This was true of the Kansas proceedings in this case. The Kansas procedure provided for the mailing of a notice to each class member by first-class mail. The notice . . . described the action and informed the class member that he could appear in person or by counsel, in default of which he would be represented by the named plaintiffs and their attorneys. The notice further stated that class members would be included in the class and bound by the judgment unless they "opted out" by executing and returning a "request for exclusion" that was included in the notice.

. . . We reject petitioner's contention that the Due Process Clause of the Fourteenth Amendment requires that absent plaintiffs affirmatively "opt in" to the class, rather than be deemed members of the class if they do not "opt out." We think that such a contention is supported by little, if any precedent, and that it ignores the differences between class-action plaintiffs, on the one hand, and defendants in nonclass civil suits on the other. Any plaintiff may consent to jurisdiction. The essential question, then, is how stringent the requirement for a showing of consent will be.

We think that the procedure followed by Kansas, where a fully descriptive notice is sent first-class mail to each class member, with an explanation of the right to "opt out," satisfies due process. Requiring a plaintiff to affirmatively request inclusion would probably impede the prosecution of those class actions involving an aggregation of small individual claims, where a large number of claims are required to make it economical to bring suit. The plaintiff's claim may be so small, or the plaintiff so unfamiliar with the law, that he would not file suit individually, nor would he affirmatively request inclusion in the class if such a request were required by the Constitution. If, on the other hand, the plaintiff's claim is sufficiently large or important that he wishes to litigate it on his own, he will likely have retained an attorney or have thought about filing suit, and should be fully capable of exercising his right to "opt out."

In this case over 3,400 members of the potential class did "opt out," which belies the contention that "opt out" procedures result in guaranteed jurisdiction by inertia. Another 1,500 were excluded because the notice and "opt out" form was undeliverable. We think that such results show that the "opt out" procedure provided by Kansas is by no means *pro forma*, and that the Constitution does not require more to protect what must be the somewhat rare species of class member who is unwilling to execute an "opt out" form, but whose claim is nonetheless so important that he cannot be presumed to consent to being a member of the class by his failure to do so. Petitioner's "opt in" requirement would require the invalidation of scores of state statutes and of the class-action provision of the Federal Rules of Civil Procedure, 65 and for the reasons stated we do not think that the Constitution requires the State to sacrifice the obvious advantages in judicial efficiency resulting from the "opt out" approach for the protection of the *rara avis* portrayed by petitioner.

We therefore hold that the protection afforded the plaintiff class members by the Kansas statute satisfies the Due Process Clause. The interests of the absent plaintiffs are sufficiently protected by the forum State when those plaintiffs are provided with a request for exclusion that can be returned within a reasonable time to the court. . . . We conclude that the Kansas court properly asserted personal jurisdiction over the absent plaintiffs and their claims against petitioner.

III

The Kansas courts applied Kansas contract and Kansas equity law to every claim in this case, notwithstanding that over 99% of the gas leases and some 97% of the plaintiffs in the case had no apparent connection to the State of Kansas except for this lawsuit. Petitioner protested that the Kansas courts should apply the laws of the States where the leases were located, or at least apply Texas and Oklahoma law because so many of the leases came from those States. The Kansas courts disregarded this contention and found petitioner liable for interest on the suspended royalties as a matter of Kansas law, and set the interest rates under Kansas equity principles.

Petitioner contends that total application of Kansas substantive law violated the constitutional limitations on choice of law mandated by the Due Process Clause of the Fourteenth Amendment and the Full Faith and Credit Clause of Article IV, §1. We must first determine whether Kansas law conflicts in any material way with any other law which could apply. [The Court explained the differences between Kansas law and the law of other states on the issue of interest rates.]

The conflicts on the applicable interest rates, alone — which we do not think can be labeled "false conflicts" without a more thoroughgoing treatment than was accorded them by the Supreme Court of Kansas — certainly amounted to millions of dollars in liability. [T]he Supreme Court of Kansas erred in deciding on the basis that it did that the application of its laws to all claims would be constitutional.

Four Terms ago we addressed a similar situation in *Allstate Ins. Co. v. Hague*, 449 U.S. 302 (1981). . . . The plurality in *Allstate* . . . recognized . . . that the Due Process Clause and the Full Faith and Credit Clause provided modest restrictions on the application of forum law. These restrictions required "that for a State's substantive law to be selected in a constitutionally permissible manner, that State must have a significant contact or significant aggregation of contacts, creating state interests, such that choice of its law is neither arbitrary nor fundamentally unfair." The dissenting Justices were in substantial agreement with this principle. . . .

Petitioner owns property and conducts substantial business in the State, so Kansas . . . has an interest in regulating petitioner's conduct in Kansas. Moreover, oil and gas extraction is an important business to Kansas, and although only a few leases . . . are located in Kansas, hundreds of Kansas plaintiffs were affected by petitioner's suspension of royalties; thus the court held that the State has a real interest in protecting "the rights of these royalty owners both as individual residents of [Kansas] and as members of this particular class of plaintiffs." The Kansas Supreme Court pointed out that Kansas courts are . . . familiar with this type of lawsuit, and "[t]he plaintiff class members have indicated their desire to have this action determined under the laws of Kansas." Finally, the Kansas court buttressed its use of Kansas law by stating that this lawsuit was analogous to a suit against a "common fund" located in Kansas.

We do not lightly discount this description of Kansas' contacts with this litigation and its interest in applying its law. There is, however, no "common fund" located in Kansas that would require or support the application of only Kansas law to all these claims. As the Kansas court noted, petitioner commingled the suspended royalties with its general corporate accounts. There is no specific identifiable res in Kansas, nor is there any limited amount which may be depleted before every plaintiff is compensated. Only by somehow aggregating all the separate claims in this case could a "common fund" in any sense be created, and the term becomes all but meaningless when used in such an expansive sense.

We also give little credence to the idea that Kansas law should apply to all claims because the plaintiffs, by failing to opt out, evinced their desire to be bound by Kansas law. Even if one could say that the plaintiffs "consented" to the application of Kansas law by not opting out, plaintiff's desire for forum law is rarely, if ever controlling. In most cases the plaintiff shows his obvious wish for forum law by filing there. . . .

The Supreme Court of Kansas in its opinion in this case expressed the view that by reason of the fact that it was adjudicating a nationwide class action, it had much greater latitude in applying its own law to the transactions in question than might otherwise be the case:

> The general rule is that the law of the forum applies unless it is expressly shown that a different law governs, and in case of doubt, the law of the forum is preferred. . . . Where a state court determines it has jurisdiction over a nationwide class action and procedural due process guarantees of notice and adequate representation are present, we believe the law of the forum should be applied unless compelling reasons exist for applying a different law. . . . Compelling reasons do not exist to require this court to look to other state laws to determine the rights of the parties involved in this lawsuit.

We think that this is something of a "bootstrap" argument. The Kansas class-action statute, like those of most other jurisdictions, requires that there be "common issues of law or fact." But while a State may, for the reasons we have previously stated, assume jurisdiction over the claims of plaintiffs whose principal contacts are with other States, it may not use this assumption of jurisdiction as an added weight in the scale when considering the permissible constitutional limits on choice of substantive law. It may not take a transaction with little or no relationship to the forum and apply the law of the forum in order to satisfy the procedural requirement that there be a "common question of law." The issue of personal jurisdiction over plaintiffs in a class action is entirely distinct from the question of the constitutional limitations on choice of law; the latter calculus is not altered by the fact that it may be more difficult or more burdensome to comply with the constitutional limitations because of the large number of transactions which the State proposes to adjudicate and which have little connection with the forum.

Kansas must have a "significant contact or significant aggregation of contacts" to the claims asserted by each member of the plaintiff class, contacts "creating state interests," in order to ensure that the choice of Kansas law is not arbitrary or unfair. Given Kansas' lack of "interest" in claims unrelated to that State, and the substantive conflict with jurisdictions such as Texas, we conclude that application of Kansas law to every claim in this case is sufficiently arbitrary and unfair as to exceed constitutional limits.

When considering fairness in this context, an important element is the expectation of the parties. There is no indication that when the leases involving land and royalty owners outside of Kansas were executed, the parties had any idea that Kansas law would control. Neither the Due Process Clause nor the Full Faith and Credit Clause requires Kansas "to substitute for its own [laws], applicable to persons and events within it, the conflicting statute of another state," but Kansas "may not abrogate the rights of parties beyond its borders having no relation to anything done or to be done within them."

Here the Supreme Court of Kansas took the view that in a nationwide class action where procedural due process guarantees of notice and adequate representation were met, "the law of the forum should be applied unless compelling reasons exist for applying a different law." Whatever practical reasons may have commended this rule to the Supreme Court of Kansas, for the reasons already stated we do not believe that it is consistent with the decisions of this Court. We make no effort to determine for ourselves which law must apply to the various transactions involved in this lawsuit, and we reaffirm our observation in *Allstate* that in many situations a state court may be free to apply one of several choices of law. But the constitutional limitations laid down . . . must be respected even in a nationwide class action. . . .

Justice POWELL took no part in the decision of this case.

Justice STEVENS, concurring in part and dissenting in part.

. . . As the Court recognizes, there "can be no [constitutional] injury in applying Kansas law if it is not in conflict with that of any other jurisdiction connected to this suit." A fair reading of the Kansas Supreme Court's opinion in light of its earlier opinion reveals that the Kansas court has examined the laws of connected jurisdictions and has correctly concluded that there is no "direct" or "substantive" conflict between the law applied by Kansas and the laws of those other States. Kansas has merely developed general common-law principles to accommodate the novel facts of this litigation — other state courts either agree with Kansas or have not yet addressed precisely similar claims. Consequently, I conclude that the Full Faith and Credit Clause of the Constitution did not require Kansas to apply the law of any other State, and the Fourteenth Amendment's Due Process Clause did not prevent Kansas from applying its own law in this case. . . .

Notes on
PHILLIPS PETROLEUM CO. v. SHUTTS

1. The Court in *Shutts* stated that, for constitutional purposes, the propriety of a court's decision to exercise personal jurisdiction is categorically different than its decision to apply forum law. Do you agree? In *Shutts*, the Court decided that the exercise of personal jurisdiction over non-Kansas residents was constitutional, while the application of Kansas law to these same individuals was not. The two inquiries are hard to compare in this case because the personal jurisdiction challenge was made by the defendant on behalf of *plaintiffs* who had failed to opt out of the class action, but were

not necessarily embracing the litigation. If, however, you were a defendant being hauled into a forum for litigation and having your rights adjudicated by forum law, which would you find more onerous: the exercise of personal jurisdiction or the choice of forum law to govern your rights?

2. Chapter 2 explored choice of law in class actions. As noted in that chapter, the failure to identify one governing law can be the death knell of class action certification. This gives even greater significance to the Court's decision in *Shutts*. Class action certification might be much easier if the *Shutts* Court had determined that the constitutional concerns were satisfied by the forum's procedural interest in applying forum law in order to administer and adjudicate a large class action efficiently. Do you agree that this was not a sufficiently significant interest? Would you say that the Court minimized the forum's procedural interest in favor of stronger concern for the parties' expectations? Since the out-of-state plaintiffs did not seem to object to the application of Kansas law, isn't it fair to observe that the Court was most concerned that the defendant could not have anticipated Kansas law governing its non-Kansas leases? Do you think the Court should have come out differently had the particular legal issue in dispute pertained less to the amount of the defendant's financial exposure and more to the forum's adjudicatory concerns?

3. What does *Shutts* tell you about the status of the *Allstate* nexus test? Did the *Shutts* Court apply the test with more vigor than the *Allstate* plurality?

4. In a subsequent case with almost identical facts to *Shutts*, *Sun Oil v. Wortman*, 486 U.S. 717 (1988), the Kansas courts applied the Kansas statute of limitations to all class members' claims (including the claims of the majority of class members from outside Kansas). The Kansas courts reasoned that statutes of limitation were procedural. The United States Supreme Court upheld this decision, reasoning that the Constitution did not prevent a state from applying its own statute of limitations, even when it mandates that the substantive laws of another state govern. Writing for the Court in *Sun Oil*, Justice Scalia explained that statutes of limitation were treated as procedural when the Constitution was adopted and that characterization continues to be constitutional:

> [T]o address petitioner's broader point . . . that we should update our notion of what is sufficiently "substantive" to require full faith and credit: We cannot imagine what would be the basis for such an updating. As we have just observed, the words "substantive" and "procedural" themselves (besides not appearing in the Full Faith and Credit Clause) do not have a precise content, even (indeed especially) as their usage has evolved. And if one consults the purpose of their usage in the full-faith-and-credit context, that purpose is quite simply to give both the forum State and other interested States the legislative jurisdiction to which they are entitled. If we abandon the currently applied,

traditional notions of such entitlement we would embark upon the enterprise of constitutionalizing choice-of-law rules, with no compass to guide us beyond our own perceptions of what seems desirable. There is no more reason to consider recharacterizing statutes of limitation as substantive under the Full Faith and Credit Clause than there is to consider recharacterizing a host of other matters generally treated as procedural under conflicts law, and hence generally regarded as within the forum State's legislative jurisdiction. See, e.g., Restatement (Second) of Conflict of Laws §131 (remedies available), §133 (placement of burden of proof), §134 (burden of production), §135 (sufficiency of the evidence), §139 (privileges) (1971).

Id. at 727-728. Since the full faith and credit and due process tests are the same in this context, the *Sun Oil* Court concluded that the same reasoning undermined the due process challenge to applying the forum statute of limitations.

Are you persuaded by the wisdom of this reasoning? Justice Scalia warns against "constitutionalizing choice of law rules." Is "enshrining" traditional choice of law characterizations as constitutional really more justifiable than constitutionalizing choice of law rules that have evolved? Is this decision consistent with the *Allstate* approach, particularly as applied in *Shutts*? Does a forum have more of an interest in applying a statute of limitations to out-of-state claimants than it has in identifying a uniform "substantive" law to those claims as disapproved in *Shutts*?

PROBLEM 3-3: DECEPTIVE COMPUTER MARKETING

Macrohard Corporation designs and manufactures computer hardware and software. Its main offices are in the State of New Washington, and it is here that the corporation makes all of its major decisions, including marketing decisions. Around the holiday season one year, Macrohard developed an advertisement campaign trumpeting its current computers and declaring the current computers compatible with an upcoming new operating system that would debut in June of next year. Macrohard ran this advertisement campaign in newspapers and magazines distributed throughout the United States and sold these computers to consumers in every state of the United States.

A class action was filed in New Washington against Macrohard claiming that the marketing scheme was fraudulent and that the computers were not compatible with the new operating system. The law of fraud in New Washington is more plaintiff-friendly than the fraud laws in most other states. Members of the class forming the class action are residents of every state in the United States. Would it be constitutional to apply New Washington law to all claimants—including those who are not New Washington residents?

In deciding whether to apply the law of a sister state, a state may constitutionally consider both its own independent concerns as well as its duties to accommodate and cooperate with the goals of the sister state. As demonstrated in *Allstate v. Hague* and *Sun Oil* above, states have considerable latitude to indulge their own interest. Consider how the Constitution governs how courts balance independence and cooperation in the related context explored immediately below: the obligation of one state to open its court system to litigation arising in another state.

2. Constitutional Principles Imposing an Obligation to Provide a Forum

Hughes v. Fetter

341 U.S. 609 (1951)

Justice BLACK delivered the opinion of the Court.

Basing his complaint on the Illinois wrongful death statute, appellant administrator brought this action in the Wisconsin state court to recover damages for the death of Harold Hughes, who was fatally injured in an automobile accident in Illinois. The allegedly negligent driver and an insurance company were named as defendants. On their motion the trial court entered summary judgment "dismissing the complaint on the merits." It held that a Wisconsin statute, which creates a right of action only for deaths caused in that state, establishes a local public policy against Wisconsin's entertaining suits brought under the wrongful death acts of other states. The Wisconsin Supreme Court affirmed, notwithstanding the contention that the local statute so construed violated the Full Faith and Credit Clause. . . .

We are called upon to decide the narrow question whether Wisconsin, over the objection raised, can close the doors of its courts to the cause of action created by the Illinois wrongful death act.[4] Prior decisions have established that the Illinois statute is a "public act" within the provision of Art. IV that "Full Faith and Credit shall be given in each State to the public Acts . . . of every other State." It is also settled that Wisconsin cannot escape this constitutional obligation to enforce the rights and duties validly created under the laws of other states by the simple device of removing jurisdiction from courts otherwise competent. We have recognized, however, that full faith and credit does not automatically compel a forum state to subordinate its own statutory policy to a conflicting public act of another state; rather, it is for this Court to choose in each case between the

---

4. The parties concede, as they must, that if the same cause of action had previously been reduced to judgment, the Full Faith and Credit Clause would compel the courts of Wisconsin to entertain an action to enforce it. *Kenney v. Supreme Lodge*, 252 U.S. 411.

competing public policies involved. The clash of interests in cases of this type has usually been described as a conflict between the public policies of two or more states. The more basic conflict involved in the present appeal, however, is as follows: On the one hand is the strong unifying principle embodied in the Full Faith and Credit Clause looking toward maximum enforcement in each state of the obligations or rights created or recognized by the statutes of sister states;[9] on the other hand is the policy of Wisconsin, as interpreted by its highest court, against permitting Wisconsin courts to entertain this wrongful death action.[10]

We hold that Wisconsin's policy must give way. That state has no real feeling of antagonism against wrongful death suits in general. To the contrary, a forum is regularly provided for cases of this nature, the exclusionary rule extending only so far as to bar actions for death not caused locally. The Wisconsin policy, moreover, cannot be considered as an application of the forum non conveniens doctrine, whatever effect that doctrine might be given if its use resulted in denying enforcement to public acts of other states. Even if we assume that Wisconsin could refuse, by reason of particular circumstances, to hear foreign controversies to which nonresidents were parties, the present case is not one lacking a close relationship with the state. For not only were appellant, the decedent and the individual defendant all residents of Wisconsin, but also appellant was appointed administrator and the corporate defendant was created under Wisconsin laws. We also think it relevant, although not crucial here, that Wisconsin may well be the only jurisdiction in which service could be had as an original matter on the insurance company defendant. And while in the present case jurisdiction over the individual defendant apparently could be had in Illinois by substituted service, in other cases Wisconsin's exclusionary statute might amount to a deprivation of all opportunity to enforce valid death claims created by another state.

Under these circumstances, we conclude that Wisconsin's statutory policy which excludes this Illinois cause of action is forbidden by the national policy of the Full Faith and Credit Clause.[16] The judgment is reversed and the cause

9. This clause "altered the status of the several states as independent foreign sovereignties, each free to ignore rights and obligations created under the laws or established by the judicial proceedings of the others, by making each an integral part of a single nation. . . ."

10. The present case is not one where Wisconsin, having entertained appellant's lawsuit, chose to apply its own instead of Illinois' statute to measure the substantive rights involved. This distinguishes the present case from those where we have said that "Prima facie every state is entitled to enforce in its own courts its own statutes, lawfully enacted." *Alaska Packers Ass'n v. Industrial Acc. Commission*, 294 U.S. 532.

16. In certain previous cases, e.g., *Pacific Employers Ins. Co. v. Industrial Acc. Commission*, 306 U.S. 493, 502; *Alaska Packers Ass'n v. Industrial Accident Commission*, 294 U.S. 532, 547, this Court suggested that under the Full Faith and Credit Clause a forum state might make a distinction between statutes and judgments of sister states because of Congress' failure to prescribe the extra-state effect to be accorded public acts. Subsequent to these decisions the Judicial Code was revised so as to provide: "Such Acts (of the legislature of any state) . . . and judicial proceedings . . . shall have the same full faith and credit in every court within the United States . . . as they have . . . in the courts of such State . . . from which they are taken." 28 U.S.C. §1738. In deciding the present appeal, however, we have found it unnecessary to rely on any changes accomplished by the Judicial Code revision.

is remanded to the Supreme Court of Wisconsin for proceedings not inconsistent with this opinion.

Justice FRANKFURTER, whom Justice REED, Justice JACKSON, and Justice MINTON, join, dissenting.

. . . This Court has, with good reason, gone far in requiring that the courts of a State respect judgments entered by courts of other States. But the extent to which a State must recognize and enforce the rights of action created by other States is not so clear. . . . In the tort action before us, there is little reason to impose a "state of vassalage" on the forum. The liability here imposed does not rest on a pre-existing relationship between the plaintiff and defendant. There is consequently no need for fixed rules which would enable parties, at the time they enter into a transaction, to predict its consequences. . . .

This Court should certainly not require that the forum deny its own law and follow the tort law of another State where there is a reasonable basis for the forum to close its courts to the foreign cause of action. The decision of Wisconsin to open its courts to actions for wrongful deaths within the State but close them to actions for deaths outside the State may not satisfy everyone's notion of wise policy. But it is neither novel nor without reason. . . . Wisconsin may be willing to grant a right of action where witnesses will be available in Wisconsin and the courts are acquainted with a detailed local statute and cases construing it. It may not wish to subject residents to suit where out-of-state witnesses will be difficult to bring before the court, and where the court will be faced with the alternative of applying a complex foreign statute—perhaps inconsistent with that of Wisconsin on important issues—or fitting the statute to the Wisconsin pattern. The legislature may well feel that it is better to allow the courts of the State where the accident occurred to construe and apply its own statute, and that the exceptional case where the defendant cannot be served in the State where the accident occurred does not warrant a general statute allowing suit in the Wisconsin courts. The various wrongful death statutes are inconsistent on such issues as beneficiaries, the party who may bring suit, limitations on liability, comparative negligence, and the measure of damages. The measure of damages and the relation of wrongful death actions to actions for injury surviving death have raised extremely complicated problems, even for a court applying the familiar statute of its own State. These diversities reasonably suggest application by local judges versed in them.

No claim is made that Wisconsin has discriminated against the citizens of other States and thus violated Art. IV, §2 of the Constitution. Nor is a claim made that the lack of a forum in Wisconsin deprives the plaintiff of due process. Nor is it argued that Wisconsin is flouting a federal statute. The only question before us is how far the Full Faith and Credit Clause undercuts the purpose of the Constitution, made explicit by the Tenth Amendment, to leave the conduct of domestic affairs to the States. Few interests are of more dominant local concern than matters governing the administration of law. This vital interest of the States should not be sacrificed in the interest of a merely literal reading of the Full Faith and Credit Clause.

There is no support, either in reason or in the cases, for holding that this Court is to make a de novo choice between the policies underlying the laws of Wisconsin and Illinois. I cannot believe that the Full Faith and Credit Clause provided a "writer's inkhorn" so that this Court might separate right from wrong. "Prima facie every state is entitled to enforce in its own courts its own statutes, lawfully enacted. One who challenges that right, because of the force given to a conflicting statute of another state by the full faith and credit clause, assumes the burden of showing, upon some rational basis, that of the conflicting interests involved those of the foreign state are superior to those of the forum." In the present case, the decedent, the plaintiff, and the individual defendant were residents of Wisconsin. The corporate defendant was created under Wisconsin law. The suit was brought in the Wisconsin courts. No reason is apparent—and none is vouchsafed in the opinion of the Court—why the interest of Illinois is so great that it can force the courts of Wisconsin to grant relief in defiance of their own law.

Finally, it may be noted that there is no conflict here in the policies underlying the statute of Wisconsin and that of Illinois. The Illinois wrongful death statute has a proviso that "no action shall be brought or prosecuted in this State to recover damages for a death occurring outside of this State where a right of action for such death exists under the laws of the place where such death occurred and service of process in such suit may be had upon the defendant in such place." The opinion of the Court concedes that "jurisdiction over the individual defendant apparently could be had in Illinois by substituted service." Thus, in the converse of the case at bar—if Hughes had been killed in Wisconsin and suit had been brought in Illinois—the Illinois courts would apparently have dismissed the suit. There is no need to be "more Roman than the Romans."

Wells v. Simonds Abrasive Co.

345 U.S. 514 (1953)

Chief Justice VINSON delivered the opinion of the Court.

Cheek Wells was killed in Alabama when a grinding wheel with which he was working burst. The wheel had been manufactured by the respondent, a corporation with its principal place of business in Pennsylvania. The administratrix of the estate of Cheek Wells brought an action for damages in the federal court for the Eastern District of Pennsylvania after one year, but within two years, after the death. Jurisdiction was based upon diversity of citizenship.

[Petitioner had relied on a section of the Alabama Code allowing that a wrongful death action may be brought within two years from the death. The district court determined that the forum state's choice of law rule called for application of the forum state's statute of limitations.]

Long ago, we held that applying the statute of limitations of the forum to a foreign substantive right did not deny full faith and credit. Recently we referred to ". . . the well established principle of conflict of laws that 'If action is barred by the statute of limitations of the forum, no action can be maintained though action is not barred in the state where the cause of action arose.' Restatement, Conflict of Laws, §603 (1934)."

The rule that the limitations of the forum apply (which this Court has said meets the requirements of full faith and credit) is the usual conflicts rule of the states. However, there have been divergent views when a foreign statutory right unknown to the common law has a period of limitation included in the section creating the right. The Alabama statute here involved creates such a right and contains a built-in limitation. The view is held in some jurisdictions that such a limitation is so intimately connected with the right that it must be enforced in the forum state along with the substantive right.

We are not concerned with the reasons which have led some states for their own purposes to adopt the foreign limitation, instead of their own, in such a situation. The question here is whether the Full Faith and Credit Clause compels them to do so. Our prevailing rule is that the Full Faith and Credit Clause does not compel the forum state to use the period of limitation of a foreign state. We see no reason in the present situation to graft an exception onto it. Differences based upon whether the foreign right was known to the common law or upon the arrangement of the code of the foreign state are too unsubstantial to form the basis for constitutional distinctions under the Full Faith and Credit Clause.

. . . Our decision[] in *Hughes v. Fetter*, [does not change] the well-established rule that the forum state is permitted to apply its own period of limitation. The crucial factor . . . was that the forum laid an uneven hand on causes of action arising within and without the forum state. Causes of action arising in sister states were discriminated against. Here Pennsylvania applies her one-year limitation to all wrongful death actions wherever they may arise. The judgment is affirmed.

Justice JACKSON, with whom Justice BLACK and Justice MINTON join, dissenting.

We are unable to accept the results or follow the reasoning of the Court. Petitioner's decedent, a resident of Alabama, was killed in that State by a bursting emery wheel alleged to have been defective. It was manufactured by respondent, a Pennsylvania corporation. Finding it impossible to serve process on the defendant in Alabama, petitioner brought an action in the United States Court for the Eastern District of Pennsylvania. Her action was based on a statute of Alabama which conferred a right of action for wrongfully causing death and required that the action be brought within two years from the death. This she did, but her complaint was dismissed on the ground that, since the federal court was sitting in Pennsylvania, it was bound by the Pennsylvania statute of limitations of one year and, hence, that her action was barred. I believe the United States District Court, though sitting in Pennsylvania, should apply the law of Alabama, both as to liability and as to limitation. . . . We think that the better view of the case before us would be that it is Alabama law which giveth and only Alabama law that taketh away.

Notes on
HUGHES *AND* WELLS

1. The *Hughes* Court stated in note 10 that the case did not present a choice of law problem. Is that true? Couldn't one argue that the case presented the question whether the Constitution controlled the ability of Wisconsin courts to apply the Wisconsin statute closing the state's courts to the cause of action being litigated? Is there an analytical difference between analyzing whether the Wisconsin law is constitutionally valid and analyzing whether it can be constitutionally applied?

2. What did Justice Frankfurter mean in his *Hughes* dissent when he suggested that prohibiting the Wisconsin courts from applying their door-closing statute imposed on the courts a "state of vassalage"? Had the Wisconsin courts adjudicated the suit, what law would have governed the wrongful death cause of action?

3. Why is the Wisconsin door-closing statute from *Hughes* at all relevant to the Pennsylvania statute of limitation in *Wells*? What is the joint rule of the two cases?

4. Does *Hughes* shed constitutional doubt on the doctrine of forum non conveniens? In other words, does a constitutional difference exist between dismissing a suit under the doctrine of forum non conveniens and dismissing a suit under a door-closing statute?

5. Couldn't the *Wells* case easily be characterized as a choice of law decision rather than a decision pertaining to the obligation of a forum to open its courts? In fact, haven't we seen courts treat competing statutes of limitations as presenting choice of law problems? Take, for example, the decision in *Sun Oil Co. v. Wortman*, 486 U.S. 717 (1988), discussed in the notes after *Shutts* immediately above. Aside from the portion of *Sun Oil* dealing with its class action status, *Sun Oil* presented an issue of whether a forum's application of its own valid statute of limitations might be applied to govern claims of out-of-state claimants, and the Court handled the issue by relying on the traditional procedural characterization for statutes of limitation. What is to be gained from analyzing a competing statute of limitations problem as an obligation to provide a forum issue?

6. In an influential article, Professor Larry Kramer uses *Hughes* and an earlier decision — *Broderick v. Rosner*, 294 U.S. 629 (1935) — to make a claim about the full faith and credit implications of the public policy exception to choice of law. (In *Broderick*, the United States Supreme Court held New Jersey violated the full faith and credit clause when it imposed unreasonably cumbersome procedures for a New York regulator to enforce New York law against New Jersey shareholders of a New York Bank.) According to Kramer, *Hughes* and *Broderick* establish that "[a] State may adopt such system of courts and form of remedy as it sees fit. . . . But it may not, under the guise of merely affecting the remedy, deny the enforcement of claims otherwise within the

protection of the full faith and credit clause, when its courts have general jurisdiction of the subject matter and the parties." Larry Kramer, *Same Sex-Marriage, Conflict of Laws, and the Unconstitutional Public Policy Exception,* 106 YALE L.J. 1965, 1985 (1997). From this "antidiscrimination principle," Kramer reasons that "the public policy doctrine must be unconstitutional," since "'offensiveness' cannot be an appropriate reason under the Full Faith and Credit Clause for refusing to entertain a claim based on another state's law." *Id.* at 1985-1986. Kramer situates this argument in the broad purpose of the "Full Faith and Credit Clause . . . to bind states more closely together." *Id.* at 1986. He submits that the "whole point" of full faith and credit is "that states should not be free to dismiss or ignore the laws of sister states" since they are part of a "community, with mutual obligations to respect each other's laws and judgments." *Id.* Indeed, Kramer submits that, "the central object of the Clause was, in fact, to eliminate a state's prideful unwillingness to recognize other states' laws or judgments on the ground that these are inferior or unacceptable." *Id.*

As you read other cases pertaining to full faith and credit — both in this section and as it pertains to judgments — evaluate whether Kramer's arguments bear up under the language of other decisions.

7. Compare *Hughes* to an earlier case, *Tennessee Coal, Iron & R. Co. v. George,* 233 U.S. 354 (1914). *George* addressed a statute that was in some sense the inverse of the door-closing statute in *Tennessee Coal.* The *George* statute was a localizing rule that purported to require the parties to litigate a cause of action in local, not out-of-state, courts. Specifically, *George* presented the question

> whether the full faith and credit clause of the Constitution prohibited the courts of Georgia from enforcing a cause of action given by the Alabama Code, to the servant against the master, for injuries occasioned by defective machinery, when another section of the same Code provided that suits to enforce such liability "must be brought in a court of competent jurisdiction within the state of Alabama, and not elsewhere."

Id. at 358-359. Although recognizing that sometimes "right and remedy" are so intertwined that the "right cannot be enforced except in the manner and before the tribunal designated by the act," the *George* Court nonetheless held that

> the place of bringing the suit is not part of the cause of action, — the right and the remedy are not so inseparably united as to make the right dependent upon its being enforced in a particular tribunal. The cause of action is transitory, and like any other transitory action can be enforced "in any court of competent jurisdiction within the state of Alabama. . . ."

The courts of the sister state, trying the case, would be bound to give full faith and credit to all those substantial provisions of the statute which inhered in the cause of action, or which name conditions on which the right to sue depend. But venue is no part of the right; and a state cannot create a transitory cause of action and at the same time destroy the right to sue on that transitory cause of action in any court having jurisdiction. That jurisdiction is to be determined by the law of the court's creation, and cannot be defeated by the extraterritorial operation of a statute of another state, even though it created the right of action.

Id. at 359-360.

The Supreme Court reaffirmed its distaste for localizing rules in *Crider v. Zurich Ins. Co.*, 380 U.S. 39 (1965). The Georgia workers' compensation act at issue in *Crider* vested exclusive authority to adjudicate remedies under the act in a Georgia state tribunal. The Supreme Court ruled, however, that an Alabama court could entertain the petitioner's suit for remedies under the Georgia act.

Which statute is more of an assault to the workings of the federalist system: a localizing rule such as in *George* or *Crider*, or a door-closing rule such as in *Hughes*?

8. For an extensive argument that *Hughes v. Fetter* is justified by neither history, precedent, nor policy, see Ann Woolhandler & Michael G. Collins, *Faith, Credit, and Jurisdictional Obligations* (2012), available at http://ssrn.com/abstract=2054645.

PROBLEM 3-4: FOREIGN CORPORATION REGISTRATION REQUIREMENTS

State A has a law requiring all corporations doing business in the state to register with the Secretary of State in State A. This is an easy requirement to enforce for corporations that are incorporated in the state, given the extensive paperwork that a corporation must file with the state for incorporation purposes. The registration requirement is harder to enforce for out-of-state corporations (those corporations incorporated in states other than State A), since they might elude the attention of regulatory authorities when they do business in State A.

As an inducement for out-of-state corporations to register with the State A Secretary of State, State A's legislature is considering enacting a statute that provides that an out-of-state corporation that does business in the state without registering with the Secretary of State may not use the courts of the state to file lawsuits. Drawing on *Hughes* and *Wells*, please advise the State A legislature as to whether this statute would survive constitutional challenge.

Hughes and *Wells* present a state's obligation to provide a forum in the context of a cause of action clearly arising out of state. The following case puts a twist on this obligation in a case where an accident giving rise to a tort action occurs within the forum state. The issue in the case concerns whether the forum has an obligation *not* to provide a forum for the suit because the defendant would have enjoyed a form of sovereign immunity in its home state.

Consider how the Supreme Court accommodates the forum state's prerogative to satisfy its independent interests in applying its own law and its duty to cooperate with a state's limitations on its own liability.

Nevada v. Hall

440 U.S. 410 (1979)

Justice STEVENS delivered the opinion of the Court.

In this tort action arising out of an automobile collision in California, a California court has entered a judgment against the State of Nevada that Nevada's own courts could not have entered. We granted certiorari to decide whether federal law prohibits the California courts from entering such a judgment or, indeed, from asserting any jurisdiction over another sovereign State.

The respondents are California residents. They suffered severe injuries in an automobile collision on a California highway on May 13, 1968. The driver of the other vehicle, an employee of the University of Nevada, was killed in the collision. It is conceded that he was driving a car owned by the State, that he was engaged in official business, and that the University is an instrumentality of the State itself.

. . . A Nevada statute places a limit of $25,000 on any award in a tort action against the State pursuant to its statutory waiver of sovereign immunity. [After respondents filed a suit in California,] Nevada argued that the Full Faith and Credit Clause of the United States Constitution required the California courts to enforce that statute. Nevada's motion was denied and the case went to trial.

The jury concluded that the Nevada driver was negligent and awarded damages of $1,150,000 [and this was affirmed on appeal].

Despite its importance, the question whether a State may claim immunity from suit in the courts of another State has never been addressed by this Court. The question is not expressly answered by any provision of the Constitution; Nevada argues that it is implicitly answered by reference to the common understanding that no sovereign is amenable to suit without its consent—an understanding prevalent when the Constitution was framed and repeatedly reflected in this Court's opinions. In order to determine whether that understanding is embodied in the Constitution, as Nevada claims, it is necessary to consider (1) the source and scope of the traditional doctrine of sovereign immunity; (2) the impact of the doctrine on the framing of the Constitution; (3) the Full Faith and Credit Clause; and (4) other aspects of the Constitution that qualify the sovereignty of the several States.

I

The doctrine of sovereign immunity is an amalgam of two quite different concepts, one applicable to suits in the sovereign's own courts and the other to suits in the courts of another sovereign.

The immunity of a truly independent sovereign from suit in its own courts has been enjoyed as a matter of absolute right for centuries. Only the sovereign's own consent could qualify the absolute character of that immunity.

The doctrine, as it developed at common law, had its origins in the feudal system. Describing those origins, Pollock and Maitland noted that no lord could be sued by a vassal in his own court, but each petty lord was subject to suit in the courts of a higher lord. Since the King was at the apex of the feudal pyramid, there was no higher court in which he could be sued. The King's immunity rested primarily on the structure of the feudal system and secondarily on a fiction that the King could do no wrong.

We must, of course, reject the fiction. It was rejected by the colonists when they declared their independence from the Crown, and the record in this case discloses an actual wrong committed by Nevada. But the notion that immunity from suit is an attribute of sovereignty is reflected in our cases.

Mr. Chief Justice Jay described sovereignty as the "right to govern";[9] that kind of right would necessarily encompass the right to determine what suits may be brought in the sovereign's own courts. Thus, Mr. Justice Holmes explained sovereign immunity as based "on the logical and practical ground that there can be no legal right as against the authority that makes the law on which the right depends."

This explanation adequately supports the conclusion that no sovereign may be sued in its own courts without its consent, but it affords no support for a claim of immunity in another sovereign's courts. Such a claim necessarily implicates the power and authority of a second sovereign; its source must be found either in an agreement, express or implied, between the two sovereigns, or in the voluntary decision of the second to respect the dignity of the first as a matter of comity. . . . Nevada quite rightly does not ask us to review the California courts' interpretation of California law. Rather, it argues that California is not free, as a sovereign, to apply its own law, but is bound instead by a federal rule of law implicit in the Constitution that requires all of the States to adhere to the sovereign-immunity doctrine as it prevailed when the Constitution was adopted. . . .

II

Unquestionably the doctrine of sovereign immunity was a matter of importance in the early days of independence. . . . But the question whether one State might be subject to suit in the courts of another State was apparently not a matter of concern when the new Constitution was being drafted and ratified. Regardless of whether the Framers were correct in assuming, as presumably they did, that

_____

9. See *Chisholm v. Georgia*, 2 Dall. 419, 472, 1 L. Ed. 440.

prevailing notions of comity would provide adequate protection against the unlikely prospect of an attempt by the courts of one State to assert jurisdiction over another, the need for constitutional protection against that contingency was not discussed.

The debate about the suability of the States focused on the scope of the judicial power of the United States authorized by Art. III. In The Federalist, Hamilton took the position that this authorization did not extend to suits brought by an individual against a nonconsenting State. The contrary position was also advocated and actually prevailed in this Court's decision in *Chisholm v. Georgia*, 2 Dall. 419, 1 L. Ed. 440.

The *Chisholm* decision led to the prompt adoption of the Eleventh Amendment. That Amendment places explicit limits on the powers of federal courts to entertain suits against a State.[19]

The language used by the Court in cases construing these limits, like the language used during the debates on ratification of the Constitution, emphasized the widespread acceptance of the view that a sovereign State is never amenable to suit without its consent. But all of these cases, and all of the relevant debate, concerned questions of federal-court jurisdiction and the extent to which the States, by ratifying the Constitution and creating federal courts, had authorized suits against themselves in those courts. These decisions do not answer the question whether the Constitution places any limit on the exercise of one's State's power to authorize its courts to assert jurisdiction over another State. Nor does anything in Art. III authorizing the judicial power of the United States, or in the Eleventh Amendment limitation on that power, provide any basis, explicit or implicit, for this Court to impose limits on the powers of California exercised in this case. A mandate for federal-court enforcement of interstate comity must find its basis elsewhere in the Constitution.

III

Nevada claims that the Full Faith and Credit Clause of the Constitution requires California to respect the limitations on Nevada's statutory waiver of its immunity from suit. That waiver only gives Nevada's consent to suits in its own courts. Moreover, even if the waiver is treated as a consent to be sued in California, California must honor the condition attached to that consent and limit respondents' recovery to $25,000, the maximum allowable in an action in Nevada's courts.

The Full Faith and Credit Clause does require each State to give effect to official acts of other States. A judgment entered in one State must be respected

---

19. The Eleventh Amendment provides: "The Judicial power of the United States shall not be construed to extend to any suit in law or equity, commenced or prosecuted against one of the United States by Citizens of another State, or by Citizens or Subjects of any Foreign State." Even as so limited, however, the Eleventh Amendment has not accorded the States absolute sovereign immunity in federal-court actions. The States are subject to suit by both their sister States and the United States. Further, prospective injunctive and declaratory relief is available against States in suits in federal court in which state officials are the nominal defendants.

in another provided that the first State had jurisdiction over the parties and the subject matter. . . . But this Court's decision in *Pacific Insurance Co. v. Industrial Accident Comm'n*, 306 U.S. 493, clearly establishes that the Full Faith and Credit Clause does not require a State to apply another State's law in violation of its own legitimate public policy. . . . The interest of California afforded such respect in the *Pacific Insurance* case was in providing for "the bodily safety and economic protection of employees injured within it." In this case, California's interest is the closely related and equally substantial one of providing "full protection to those who are injured on its highways through the negligence of both residents and nonresidents." To effectuate this interest, California has provided by statute for jurisdiction in its courts over residents and nonresidents alike to allow those injured on its highways through the negligence of others to secure full compensation for their injuries in the California courts.

In further implementation of that policy, California has unequivocally waived its own immunity from liability for the torts committed by its own agents and authorized full recovery even against the sovereign. As the California courts have found, to require California either to surrender jurisdiction or to limit respondents' recovery to the $25,000 maximum of the Nevada statute would be obnoxious to its statutorily based policies of jurisdiction over nonresident motorists and full recovery. The Full Faith and Credit Clause does not require this result.[24]

IV

Even apart from the Full Faith and Credit Clause, Nevada argues that the Constitution implicitly establishes a Union in which the States are not free to treat each other as unfriendly sovereigns, but must respect the sovereignty of one another. While sovereign nations are free to levy discriminatory taxes on the goods of other nations or to bar their entry altogether, the States of the Union are not. Nor are the States free to deny extradition of a fugitive when a proper demand is made by the executive of another State. And the citizens in each State are entitled to all privileges and immunities of citizens in the several States.

Each of these provisions places a specific limitation on the sovereignty of the several States. Collectively they demonstrate that ours is not a union of 50 wholly independent sovereigns. But these provisions do not imply that any one State's immunity from suit in the courts of another State is anything other than a matter of comity. Indeed, in view of the Tenth Amendment's reminder that powers not delegated to the Federal Government nor prohibited to the States are reserved to the States or to the people, the existence of express limitations on state sovereignty may equally imply that caution should be exercised before concluding that unstated limitations on state power were intended by the Framers.

---

24. California's exercise of jurisdiction in this case poses no substantial threat to our constitutional system of cooperative federalism. Suits involving traffic accidents occurring outside of Nevada could hardly interfere with Nevada's capacity to fulfill its own sovereign responsibilities. We have no occasion, in this case, to consider whether different state policies, either of California or of Nevada, might require a different analysis or a different result.

In the past, this Court has presumed that the States intended to adopt policies of broad comity toward one another. But this presumption reflected an understanding of state policy, rather than a constitutional command. . . . In this case, California has "declared its will"; it has adopted as its policy full compensation in its courts for injuries on its highways resulting from the negligence of others, whether those others be residents or nonresidents, agents of the State, or private citizens. Nothing in the Federal Constitution authorizes or obligates this Court to frustrate that policy out of enforced respect for the sovereignty of Nevada.

In this Nation each sovereign governs only with the consent of the governed. The people of Nevada have consented to a system in which their State is subject only to limited liability in tort. But the people of California, who have had no voice in Nevada's decision, have adopted a different system. Each of these decisions is equally entitled to our respect.

It may be wise policy, as a matter of harmonious interstate relations, for States to accord each other immunity or to respect any established limits on liability. They are free to do so. But if a federal court were to hold, by inference from the structure of our Constitution and nothing else, that California is not free in this case to enforce its policy of full compensation, that holding would constitute the real intrusion on the sovereignty of the States — and the power of the people — in our Union.

The judgment of the California Court of Appeal is *Affirmed*.

Justice BLACKMUN, with whom THE CHIEF JUSTICE and Justice REHNQUIST join, dissenting.

. . . [T]he Court paints with a very broad brush, and I am troubled by the implications of its holding. Despite a fragile footnote disclaimer, the Court's basic and undeniable ruling is that what we have always thought of as a "sovereign State" is now to be treated in the courts of a sister State, once jurisdiction is obtained, just as any other litigant. I fear the ultimate consequences of that holding, and I suspect that the Court has opened the door to avenues of liability and interstate retaliation that will prove unsettling and upsetting for our federal system. Accordingly, I dissent.

. . . The Court, by its footnote 24, purports to confine its holding to traffic-accident torts committed outside the defendant State, and perhaps even to traffic "policies." Such facts, however, play absolutely no part in the reasoning by which the Court reaches its conclusion. The Court says merely that "California has 'declared its will'; it had adopted as its policy full compensation in its courts for injuries on its highways. . . . Nothing in the Federal Constitution authorizes or obligates this Court to frustrate that policy." There is no suggestion in this language that, if California had adopted some other policy in some other area of the law, the result would be any different. If, indeed, there is "[n]othing in the Federal Constitution" that allows frustration of California's policy, it is hard to see just how the Court could use a different analysis or reach a different result in a different case.

. . . The Court's acknowledgment, referred to above, that the Framers must have assumed that States were immune from suit in the courts of their sister States lends substantial support. The only reason why this immunity did not receive specific mention is that it was too obvious to deserve mention. The prompt passage of the Eleventh Amendment nullifying the decision in *Chisholm v. Georgia,* is surely significant. If the Framers were indeed concerned lest the States be haled before the federal courts — as the courts of a "'higher' sovereign," — how much more must they have reprehended the notion of a State's being haled before the courts of a sister State. The concept of sovereign immunity prevailed at the time of the Constitutional Convention. It is, for me, sufficiently fundamental to our federal structure to have implicit constitutional dimension. Indeed, if the Court means what it implies in its footnote 24 — that *some* state policies might require a different result — it must be suggesting that there are some federalism constraints on a State's amenability to suit in the courts of another State. If that is so, the only question is whether the facts of this case are sufficient to call the implicit constitutional right of sovereign immunity into play here. I would answer that question in the affirmative. . . .

Justice REHNQUIST, with whom THE CHIEF JUSTICE joins, dissenting.
. . . I join my Brother BLACKMUN's doubts about footnote 24 of the majority opinion. Where will the Court find its principles of "cooperative federalism"? Despite the historical justification of federal courts as neutral forums, despite an understanding shared by the Framers and, for close to 200 years, expounded by some of the most respected Members of this Court, and despite the fact that it is the operative postulate that makes sense of the Eleventh Amendment, the Court concludes that the rule that an unconsenting State is not subject to the jurisdiction of the courts of a different State finds no support "explicit or implicit" in the Constitution. If this clear guidance is not enough, I do not see how the Court's suggestion that limits on state-court jurisdiction may be found in principles of "cooperative federalism" can be taken seriously. Yet given the ingenuity of our profession, pressure for such limits will inevitably increase. Having shunned the obvious, the Court is truly adrift on uncharted waters; the ultimate balance struck in the name of "cooperative federalism" can be only a series of unsatisfactory bailing operations in fact.

I am also concerned about the practical implications of this decision. The federal system as expressed in the Constitution — with the exception of representation in the House — is built on notions of state parity. No system is truly federal otherwise. This decision cannot help but induce some "Balkanization" in state relationships as States try to isolate assets from foreign judgments and generally reduce their contacts with other jurisdictions. That will work to the detriment of smaller States — like Nevada — who are more dependent on the facilities of a dominant neighbor — in this case, California.

The problem of enforcement of a judgment against a State creates a host of additional difficulties. Assuming Nevada has no seizable assets in California, can the plaintiff obtain enforcement of California's judgment in Nevada courts? Can Nevada refuse to give the California judgment "full faith and credit" because it is against state policy? Can Nevada challenge the seizure of its assets by California in this Court? If not, are the States relegated to the choice between the gamesmanship and tests of strength that characterize international disputes, on the one hand, and the midnight seizure of assets associated with private debt collection on the other? . . .

Notes on
NEVADA v. HALL

1. What are the precise conditions under which *Nevada v. Hall* would allow one state to decline to enforce another state's sovereign immunity? Would the *Hall* Court have upheld California's decision not to enforce Nevada's sovereign immunity if California had not waived its own immunity under similar circumstances?

2. Note footnote 24 in the majority opinion. As noted in Justices Blackmun's and Rehnquist's dissent, the precise scope of footnote 24 is unclear. What would be a "substantial threat to our constitutional system of cooperative federalism" or a sufficient interference with a state's capacity "to fulfill its own sovereign responsibilities" that might justify an exception to the rule of *Nevada v. Hall*? For understanding the Justices' concern with the "sovereign responsibilities" of the states, it might be helpful to recall modern justifications for sovereign immunity, such as (1) protecting state treasuries from being exhausted through judgments in civil lawsuits; and (2) ensuring that decisions about how precious state resources are used rest with the entity that states choose (such as legislatures) rather than the civil litigation system.

3. How is *Nevada v. Hall* related to other cases dealing with the obligation to provide a forum? Of the cases discussed immediately above, which has legal issues that most resemble *Nevada v. Hall*: *Hughes v. Fetter*? *Wells v. Simonds Abrasive Co.*? *Tennessee Coal v. George*?

4. About 25 years after *Nevada v. Hall*, the Supreme Court decided another case illustrating the proposition to California that "sauce for the goose" can be "sauce for the gander." In *Franchise Tax Board of California v. Hyatt*, 538 U.S. 488 (2003) ("*Hyatt I*"), the Supreme Court confronted the inverse of *Nevada v. Hall*: that is, the Court grappled with the question whether Nevada could subject a California state entity to full liability in Nevada courts under circumstances where Nevada had waived its own immunity, but California retained for itself absolute immunity. The *Hyatt* Court found that the case was controlled by *Nevada v. Hall*.

Among the lessons of *Hyatt I* is the Court's discussion of footnote 24 from *Nevada v. Hall*, and the suggestion that it was disinclined to embark on an attempt to explain its state sovereignty concepts further:

> Our past experience with appraising and balancing state interests under the Full Faith and Credit Clause counsels against adopting [California's proposed reading of "sovereign responsibilities"]. . . . [T]he question of

which sovereign interest should be deemed more weighty is not one that can be easily answered. Yet [California's proposal] would elevate California's sovereignty interests above those of Nevada, were we to deem this lawsuit an interference with California's "core sovereign responsibilities." We rejected as "unsound in principle and unworkable in practice" a rule of state immunity from federal regulation under the Tenth Amendment that turned on whether a particular state government function was "integral" or "traditional." [California] has convinced us of neither the relative soundness nor the relative practicality of adopting a similar distinction here.

Id. at 498.

5. Recall the discussion of Professor Larry Kramer's critique of the public policy exception to choice of law using *Hughes v. Fetter* (above). Consider whether the following language from *Nevada v. Hall* casts significant doubt on the argument: "But this Court's decision in *Pacific Insurance Co. v. Industrial Accident Comm'n* clearly establishes that the Full Faith and Credit Clause does not require a State to apply another State's law in violation of its own legitimate public policy." 440 U.S. at 421-422. Before concluding definitively that the language undermines Kramer's reasoning, consider that in *Hyatt* I, the "mirror image" case decided after *Nevada v. Hall,* the Court justified its conclusion that Nevada had complied with the full faith and credit clause by stating:

> States' sovereignty interests are not foreign to the full faith and credit command, but we are not presented here with a case in which a State has exhibited a "policy of hostility to the public Acts" of a sister State. The Nevada Supreme Court sensitively applied principles of comity with a healthy regard for California's sovereign status, relying on the contours of Nevada's own sovereign immunity from suit as a benchmark for its analysis.

538 U.S. at 489. This language certainly suggests that one state's determination that another state's statute is inimical to its public policy runs into problems under the full faith and credit clause.

The question to consider, however, is how this public policy issue plays out in the case presented below — in which the United States Supreme Court revisited the same dispute addressed in *Hyatt I,* discussing the full faith and credit obligations borne by Nevada in evaluating the deference due to California's full sovereign immunity for matters relating to California tax collection. After the Supreme Court decided *Hyatt I,* the case was remanded to Nevada proceedings in which the Nevada jury awarded Hyatt nearly $400 million in damages. The Nevada Supreme Court reduced the award — though not, as California had requested, to the amount that would apply to a Nevada agency.

Franchise Tax Board of California v. Hyatt ("Hyatt II")

136 S. Ct. 1277 (2015)

Justice Breyer delivered the opinion of the Court.

In *Nevada v. Hall*, 440 U.S. 410 (1979), this Court held that one State (here, Nevada) can open the doors of its courts to a private citizen's lawsuit against another State (here, California) without the other State's consent. In this case, a private citizen, a resident of Nevada, has brought a suit in Nevada's courts against the Franchise Tax Board of California, an agency of the State of California. The board has asked us to overrule *Hall* and hold that the Nevada courts lack jurisdiction to hear this lawsuit. The Court is equally divided on this question, and we consequently affirm the Nevada courts' exercise of jurisdiction over California.

California also asks us to reverse the Nevada court's decision insofar as it awards the private citizen greater damages than Nevada law would permit a private citizen to obtain in a similar suit against Nevada's own agencies. We agree that Nevada's application of its damages law in this case reflects a special, and constitutionally forbidden, "'policy of hostility to the public Acts' of a sister State," namely, California. U.S. Const., Art. IV, §1 (Full Faith and Credit Clause). We set aside the Nevada Supreme Court's decision accordingly.

I

Gilbert P. Hyatt, the respondent here, moved from California to Nevada in the early 1990's. He says that he moved to Nevada in September 1991. California's Franchise Tax Board, however, after an investigation and tax audit, claimed that Hyatt moved to Nevada later, in April 1992, and that he consequently owed California more than $10 million in taxes, associated penalties, and interest.

Hyatt filed this lawsuit in Nevada state court against California's Franchise Tax Board, a California state agency. Hyatt sought damages for what he considered the board's abusive audit and investigation practices, including rifling through his private mail, combing through his garbage, and examining private activities at his place of worship.

California recognized that, under *Hall*, the Constitution permits Nevada's courts to assert jurisdiction over California despite California's lack of consent. California nonetheless asked the Nevada courts to dismiss the case on other constitutional grounds. California law, it pointed out, provided state agencies with immunity from lawsuits based upon actions taken during the course of collecting taxes. It argued that the Constitution's Full Faith and Credit Clause required Nevada to apply California's sovereign immunity law to Hyatt's case. Nevada's Supreme Court, however, rejected California's claim. It held that Nevada's courts, as a matter of comity, would immunize California where Nevada law would similarly immunize its own agencies and officials (*e.g.*, for actions taken in the performance of a "discretionary" function), but they would not immunize California where Nevada law permitted actions against Nevada agencies, say, for acts taken in bad faith or for intentional torts. We reviewed that decision, and we affirmed.

On remand, the case went to trial. A jury found in Hyatt's favor and awarded him close to $500 million in damages (both compensatory and punitive) and fees (including attorney's fees). California appealed. It argued that the trial court had not properly followed the Nevada Supreme Court's earlier decision. California explained that in a similar suit against similar Nevada officials, Nevada statutory law would limit damages to $50,000, and it argued that the Constitution's Full Faith and Credit Clause required Nevada to limit damages similarly here.

The Nevada Supreme Court accepted the premise that Nevada statutes would impose a $50,000 limit in a similar suit against its own officials. But the court rejected California's conclusion. Instead, while setting aside much of the damages award, it nonetheless affirmed $1 million of the award (earmarked as compensation for fraud), and it remanded for a retrial on the question of damages for intentional infliction of emotional distress. In doing so, it stated that "damages awarded on remand . . . are not subject to any statutory cap." The Nevada Supreme Court explained its holding by stating that California's efforts to control the actions of its own agencies were inadequate as applied to Nevada's own citizens. Hence, Nevada's "policy interest in providing adequate redress to Nevada's citizens [wa]s paramount to providing [California] a statutory cap on damages under comity."

California petitioned for certiorari. We agreed to decide two questions. First, whether to overrule *Hall*. And, second, if we did not do so, whether the Constitution permits Nevada to award Hyatt damages against a California state agency that are greater than those that Nevada would award in a similar suit against its own state agencies.

II

In light of our 4-to-4 affirmance of Nevada's exercise of jurisdiction over California's state agency, we must consider the second question: Whether the Constitution permits Nevada to award damages against California agencies under Nevada law that are greater than it could award against Nevada agencies in similar circumstances. We conclude that it does not. The Nevada Supreme Court has ignored both Nevada's typical rules of immunity and California's immunity-related statutes (insofar as California's statutes would prohibit a monetary recovery that is greater in amount than the maximum recovery that Nevada law would permit in similar circumstances). Instead, it has applied a special rule of law that evinces a "'policy of hostility'" toward California. Doing so violates the Constitution's requirement that "Full Faith and Credit shall be given in each State to the public Acts, Records and judicial Proceedings of every other State." Art. IV, §1.

The Court's precedents strongly support this conclusion . . . [and we] followed this same approach when we considered the litigation now before us for the first time. Nevada had permitted Hyatt to sue California in Nevada courts. Nevada's courts recognized that California's law of complete immunity would prevent any recovery in this case. The Nevada Supreme Court consequently did not apply California law. It applied Nevada law instead. We upheld that decision as consistent with the Full Faith and Credit Clause. But in doing so, we emphasized both that (1) the Clause does not require one State to apply another State's law that violates its "own legitimate public policy," and (2) Nevada's choice of law did not "exhibi[t] a 'policy of hostility to the public Acts' of a sister State." Rather, Nevada had evinced "a healthy regard for California's sovereign status," we said, by "relying on the contours of Nevada's own sovereign immunity from suit as a benchmark for its analysis."

The Nevada decision before us embodies a critical departure from its earlier approach. Nevada has not applied the principles of Nevada law ordinarily applicable to suits against Nevada's own agencies. Rather, it has applied a special rule of law applicable only in lawsuits against its sister States, such as California. With respect to damages awards greater than $50,000, the ordinary principles of Nevada law do not "conflic[t]" with California law, for both laws would grant immunity. Similarly, in respect to such amounts, the "polic[ies]" underlying California law and Nevada's usual approach are not "opposed"; they are consistent.

But that is not so in respect to Nevada's special rule. That rule, allowing damages awards greater than $50,000, is not only "opposed" to California law; it is also inconsistent with the general principles of Nevada immunity law. The Nevada Supreme Court explained its departure from those general principles by describing California's system of controlling its own agencies as failing to provide "adequate" recourse to Nevada's citizens. It expressed concerns about the fact that California's agencies "'operat[e] outside'" the systems of "'legislative control, administrative oversight, and public accountability'" that Nevada applies to its own agencies. Such an explanation, which amounts to little more than a conclusory statement disparaging California's own legislative, judicial, and administrative controls, cannot justify the application of a special and discriminatory rule. Rather, viewed through a full faith and credit lens, a State that disregards its own ordinary legal principles on this ground *is* hostile to another State. A constitutional rule that would permit this kind of discriminatory hostility is likely to cause chaotic interference by some States into the internal, legislative affairs of others. Imagine, for example, that many or all States enacted such discriminatory, special laws, and justified them on the sole basis that (in their view) a sister State's law provided inadequate protection to their citizens. Would each affected sister State have to change its own laws? Entirely? Piece-by-piece, in order to respond to the new special laws enacted by every other State? It is difficult to reconcile such a system of special and discriminatory rules with the Constitution's vision of 50 individual and equally dignified States. In light of the "constitutional equality" among the States, Nevada has not offered "sufficient policy considerations" to justify the application of a special rule of Nevada law that discriminates against its sister States. In our view, Nevada's rule lacks the "healthy regard for California's sovereign status" that was the hallmark of its earlier decision, and it reflects a constitutionally impermissible "'policy of hostility to the public Acts' of a sister State."

For these reasons, insofar as the Nevada Supreme Court has declined to apply California law in favor of a special rule of Nevada law that is hostile to its sister States, we find its decision unconstitutional. We vacate its judgment and remand the case for further proceedings not inconsistent with this opinion.

Justice ALITO concurs in the judgment.

Chief Justice ROBERTS, with whom Justice THOMAS joins, dissenting.

Petitioner Franchise Tax Board is the California agency that collects California's state income tax. Respondent Gilbert Hyatt, a resident of Nevada, filed suit in Nevada state court against the Board, alleging that it had committed numerous torts in the course of auditing his California tax returns. The Board is immune from such a suit in California courts. The last time this case was before us, we held that the Nevada Supreme Court could apply Nevada law to resolve the Board's claim that it was immune from suit in Nevada as well. Following our decision, the Nevada Supreme Court upheld a $1 million jury award against the Board after concluding that the Board did not enjoy immunity under Nevada law.

Today the Court shifts course. It now holds that the Full Faith and Credit Clause requires the Nevada Supreme Court to afford the Board immunity to the extent Nevada agencies are entitled to immunity under Nevada law. Because damages in a similar suit against Nevada agencies are capped at $50,000 by Nevada law, the Court concludes that damages against the Board must be capped at that level as well.

That seems fair. But, for better or worse, the word "fair" does not appear in the Full Faith and Credit Clause. The Court's decision is contrary to our precedent holding that the Clause does not block a State from applying its own law to redress an injury within its own borders. The opinion also departs from the text of the Clause, which — when it applies — requires a State to give *full* faith and credit to another State's laws. The Court instead permits partial credit: To comply with the Full Faith and Credit Clause, the Nevada Supreme Court need only afford the Board the same limited immunity that Nevada agencies enjoy. . . .

. . . The majority's approach is nowhere to be found in the Full Faith and Credit Clause. Where the Clause applies, it expressly requires a State to give *full* faith and credit to another State's laws. If the majority is correct that Nevada has no sufficient policy justification for applying Nevada immunity law, then California law applies. And under California law, the Board is entitled to *full* immunity. Or, if Nevada has a sufficient policy reason to apply its own law, then Nevada law applies, and the Board is subject to *full* liability.

I respectfully dissent.

Notes on
FRANCHISE TAX BOARD v. HYATT (HYATT II)

1. Note precisely what the United States Supreme Court affirmed "by an equally divided court" when it chose not to overrule *Nevada v. Hall.* The Court's holding in this regard was narrow: the Court simply determined that Nevada need not honor California's absolute immunity from suit and thus could allow the litigation to proceed. The remaining question for decision was whether Nevada could deviate from its own standard of liability and immunity when disposing of the suit. Do you agree that the Nevada

court displayed unconstitutional hostility to its sister state in its disposition of the case? More specifically: did Nevada impermissibly inject its own judgment about the adequacy of California's administrative mechanisms when deciding to deviate from its own approach to sovereign immunity in a tax setting such as presented in this case? Did the Nevada court exhibit an impermissible use of Nevada's own public policy standards in developing its compromise approach?

2. What do you think of the dissent's all-or-nothing approach to the full faith and credit clause? Chief Justice Roberts's dissent seems to suggest that if the full faith and credit clause applies to the situation, the honoring jurisdiction must simply act in an identical manner as the jurisdiction whose law is at issue. According to Chief Justice Roberts, "full" credit means absolutely "full" credit. He has a point, right? "Full" certainly does not mean comprised, augmented, or partial. But given the circumstances of this case, could it be that the Chief Justice's constitutional approach was too rigid and insufficiently nuanced?

3. One wonders whether California second-guessed the position that it had taken in *Nevada v. Hall* when litigating the *Hyatt I* and *Hyatt II* cases. After all, the logical extension of California's *Nevada v. Hall* position was that Nevada should be able to disregard California's sovereign immunity rules when California is sued in Nevada courts. During oral argument before the United States Supreme Court, the attorney for California acknowledged that California did in fact experience "some buyer's remorse" for its *Nevada v. Hall* position. *State Sovereignty Center Stage as SCOTUS Takes Up Interstate Tax Spat*, 84 U.S. Law Week 3309, 3310 (Dec. 8, 2015). The history of this sovereign immunity issue thus provides a concrete parable for the expression "be careful what you wish for. . . ." The moral might be that in developing litigation strategy and policy for an entity such as the State of California, wisdom might counsel taking the long view and asking whether a reasonable position taken today may not be desirable tomorrow!

PROBLEM 3-5: THE CHASE ACROSS THE POTOMAC

Michael Owen is a police officer employed by the police department of Arlington County, Virginia. While on late duty one night, Owen spotted a green car matching the description of a car that was used in a bank robbery earlier that day. Owen turned on his lights and siren to signal the car to pull over; in response, the car accelerated and a high-speed chase followed.

During the chase, Owen pursued the green car over the Potomac River into the District of Columbia. Once inside the District, the green car ran a traffic light at a busy intersection, striking and killing several pedestrians.

The pedestrians' survivors have sued Arlington County for damages in a "municipal" court in the District of Columbia. They assert that the deaths were caused by Owen's negligent conduct in pursuing the high-speed chase. According to the survivors, the deaths were a direct result of the County's negligent failure to train and supervise Owen properly. Arlington County has defended by claiming that the District of Columbia court should accord Arlington County immunity from suit, which the County would enjoy had the case been filed in Virginia state court. Arlington County maintains that failure to accord it sovereign immunity would frustrate its capacity to fulfill its law enforcement responsibilities.

Under District of Columbia law, the District of Columbia itself would not enjoy sovereign immunity under the circumstances here. District of Columbia case law establishes that the training and supervision of a police officer is a nondiscretionary act, for which the District of Columbia may be held liable if the act is performed negligently.

You may assume that the District of Columbia court should be treated as though it is a state court. Should the court accord Arlington County sovereign immunity in this case?

3. *Other Roles for Constitutional Regulation*

The Equal Protection Clause of the Fourteenth Amendment Provides:

[N]o State shall . . . deny any person within its jurisdiction the equal protection of the laws. . . .

The Privileges and Immunities Clause of Article IV, §2:

The Citizens of each State shall be entitled to all Privileges and Immunities of Citizens in the several States.

The Commerce Clause of Article 1, §8:

The Congress shall have power . . . To regulate Commerce with foreign Nations, and among the several States and with the Indian Tribes.

The due process and full faith and credit clauses are by far the most important sources of constitutional regulation. Nonetheless, the equal protection, privileges and immunities, and commerce clauses provide other potential theories for federal regulation of the state choice of law process. All three clauses (equal protection, privileges and immunities, and commerce) contribute to the overall goal of the Constitution to form a unified nation and to limit state power to distinguish among citizens according to their state of citizenship. Potential choice of law implications derive from these goals. More specifically, the privileges and immunities and equal protection clauses pertain to the extent to which states can use their choice of law rules to reserve the benefits of local law for local residents or for local activities. As for the commerce clause, one strand of jurisprudence — expressed in dormant commerce clause cases — provides a means for assessing the validity of state regulation as it affects multijurisdictional activities. Although the United States Supreme Court has not framed these three clauses as direct restraints on the choice of law process, their relevance to the state choice of law field is clear and thus merits serious consideration.

a. The Privilege and Immunities Clause of Article IV, §2 and the Equal Protection Clause of the Fourteenth Amendment

Through the lens of choice of law, the spirit of both the Article IV privileges and immunities and equal protection clauses is quite similar: both clauses protect against discrimination targeted at out-of-state residents and infringement on the right to travel. The two clauses nonetheless differ in at least two significant respects in this context: (1) the privileges and immunities clause does not protect corporations, while the equal protection clause does; and (2) the standard of scrutiny varies between the clauses, becoming arguably stricter for fundamental right infringements under the equal protection clause, yet more rigorous in other contexts under the privileges and immunities clause.

Classic examples of privileges and immunities clause cases include *Supreme Court of New Hampshire v. Piper*, 470 U.S. 274 (1985), and *Austin v. New Hampshire*, 420 U.S. 656 (1975). In *Piper*, a Vermont resident qualified for the New Hampshire bar, applied for admission, and was refused because she had not established a New Hampshire domicile. The United States Supreme Court held that this restriction on the Vermonter's ability to practice her trade was a privileges and immunities clause violation. In *Austin v. New Hampshire*, the Supreme Court held unconstitutional a New Hampshire state tax imposed only on nonresidents. New Hampshire justified the tax because nonresidents were not taxed at a rate higher than the rate their home state would have imposed on them. Rejecting this rationale, the *Austin* Court concluded that the taxing scheme clashed with the "policy of comity" underlying the privileges and immunities clause. In so holding, the Court explained that the clause "by making noncitizenship or nonresidence an improper basis for locating a special burden, implicates not only the individual's right to nondiscriminatory treatment but also, perhaps more so, the structural balance essential to the concept of federalism." 420 U.S. at 662.

Consider the ramifications of these constitutional rules for choice of law methodologies. In particular, recall that governmental interest analysis and other modern approaches that incorporate interest analysis proceed on the assumption that the forum has an interest in its own residents' welfare, but not necessarily the welfare of the residents of other jurisdictions. As a result, forum law generally governs where forum law promotes the interests of a resident (either because the case presents a true conflict or because the forum is the only interested state). Does this not run afoul of the prohibition against citizenship discrimination embodied in the equal protection and privileges and immunities clauses?

Brainerd Currie reckoned with the argument that the privileges and immunities clause might shed doubt on the constitutionality of governmental interest analysis. He reasoned that the privileges and immunities clause forbids extending different treatment to nonresidents than to residents only when "no substantial reason" for the discrimination exists. Such a substantial reason exists, Currie argued, where a state has an interest in applying its law to a resident party and lacks such an interest where the party is a nonresident. Currie made similar arguments for the purposes of the equal protection clause and developed further justifications based on the notion that "discrimination" can be acceptable (i.e., serve a substantial reason) if it results merely in subjecting a nonresident to law of his own state. But isn't that precisely what New Hampshire argued in favor of its tax in *Austin v. New Hampshire?* Some commentators believe so and therefore believe that Currie's reasoning does not save governmental interest analysis from constitutional infirmity.[2] Nonetheless, it is important to note that courts have shown no interest in declaring governmental interest analysis or related choice of law approaches unconstitutional under either the privileges and immunities clause or the equal protection clause.[3]

b. Dormant Commerce Clause

The commerce clause of Article I, §8 provides the foundation for many congressional acts. Even where Congress has not acted, however, the commerce clause has regulatory power over the states. In this posture, the regulatory power is called the dormant commerce clause (although the clause is not technically dormant, Congress is!). The dormant commerce clause can protect out-of-state businesses against local laws that favor local businesses or unreasonably burden the ability of out-of-state businesses to do business in the state. The dormant commerce clause also invalidates pricing laws that have the effect of regulating prices out of state.[4]

The United States Supreme Court has articulated a stringent test for state laws that discriminate against out-of-staters, subjecting such laws to the "strictest scrutiny of any purported legitimate local purpose and of the absence of nondiscriminatory alternatives." *Hughes v. Oklahoma,* 441 U.S. 322, 337 (1979). For those state laws that create an extraterritorial burden, the test is not so harsh. The Court has explained that if a statute regulates evenhandedly "to effectuate a legitimate local public interest," and has only "incidental effects on interstate commerce," the statute is constitutional "unless the burden imposed on such commerce is clearly excessive in relation to the putative local benefits." *Pike v. Bruce Church,*

---

2. *See, e.g.,* John Hart Ely, *Choice of Law and the State's Interest in Protecting Its Own,* 23 Wм. & Mary L. Rev. 173, 186-187 (1981) (arguing that *Austin* renders "the dominant contemporary choice-of-law theory unconstitutional").

3. For further discussion of the choice of law constraints provided by the privileges and immunities clause and the equal protection clause, see Michael H. Hoffheimer, Conflict of Laws 347-359 (2010).

4. *See, e.g., Healy v. The Beer Institute,* 491 U.S. 324 (1989) (invalidating statute requiring beer seller in Connecticut to certify that the price was no higher than the sale price in border states).

Inc., 397 U.S. 137, 142 (1970). The precise scope of these tests is muddled, but they have provided the basis for invalidation of laws in contexts that strongly resemble choice of law scenarios. *See, e.g., Bendix Autolite Corp. v. Midwesco Enterprises, Inc.*, 486 U.S. 888 (1988) (holding that statute of limitations may not be extended under a state tolling statute in lawsuit against out-of-state corporation served under long arm statute); *CTS Corp v. Dynamics Corp. of America*, 481 U.S. 69 (1987); *Edgar v. MITE Corp.*, 457 U.S. 624 (1982) (invalidating Illinois anti-take-over statute that applied to corporations with substantial assets in Illinois); *Midwest Title Loans, Inc. v. Mills*, 593 F.3d 660 (7th Cir. 2010) (invalidating Indiana law providing that consumer loan between an Indiana borrower and an out-of state lender is deemed to have been made in Indiana, even if entered into in another state, if the lender has advertised or solicited loans in Indiana, and subject lender to restrictions in Indiana law). In addition, the dormant commerce clause has also proven a frequently invoked theory in litigation implicating state regulation of internet activity, which by its nature usually evokes conflict of laws concerns.

PERSPECTIVE ON SAME-SEX MARRIAGE — CONSTITUTIONAL RESTRICTIONS ON ANTI-SAME-SEX MARRIAGE LAWS

Same-sex marriage provides a powerful illustration of the possible effect of United States constitutional principles on issues over which states sharply disagree. For several years, states developed a mosaic of laws governing same-sex unions in the United States: some states recognized same-sex marriage, some states refused to recognize such marriages under any circumstances, and yet another group of states refused to allow same-sex marriage to be celebrated in the state, but nevertheless recognized the validity of such marriages when celebrated elsewhere. In addition, several states recognized alternative forms of same-sex unions such as domestic partnerships and civil unions.

Conflict of laws issues proliferated, fueled by several factors. First was a federal statute, the Defense of Marriage Act (DOMA), which defined marriage for federal law purposes as the union of one man and one woman and relieved states of the obligation to recognize a same-sex marriage celebrated in a sister state. In addition, choice of law problems arose from the many legal issues pertaining to the incidents of marriage — property ownership, rights to spousal benefits, inheritance, taxation, medical decision making, parentage presumptions, child custody, adoption rights, and the like — which often turn on the question of whether a marriage is valid.

In large part, the United States Supreme Court eliminated this confusion using United States constitutional principles. First the Supreme Court decided *United States v. Windsor*, 133 S. Ct. 2675 (2013), which declared DOMA's federal law definition as unconstitutional under the Fifth Amendment. Thereafter, the Court agreed in *Obergefell v. Hodges* to review cases presenting the following two questions: (i) whether the Fourteenth Amendment requires a state to license a marriage between individuals of the same sex; and (2) whether a state must recognize such a marriage if validly entered in a sister state. As to the first question, the Court held that the Due Process and Equal Protection Clauses of the Fourteenth Amendment prohibited a state from refusing to recognize same-sex marriages under its own law. Relying principally on the Due Process Clause, the *Obergefell* Court ruled that principles of individual dignity and the right to autonomy required same-sex partners to enjoy the right to marry. As to the second question, the Court held that "there is no lawful basis for a State to refuse to recognize a lawful same-sex marriage performed in another State on the ground of its same-sex character."

After the case was decided, some jurisdictions took the position that *Obergefell*'s constitutional holding did not extend to the incidents of marriage. The United States Supreme Court now appears to have rejected this position in *Pavan v. Smith*, 582 U.S. ___ (2017). In *Pavan*, the Court held that a presumption of parentage in the form of a state rule that requires a child's birth certificate to list a non-biological father if he is married to the biological mother must be extended to same-sex spouses. The *Pavan* Court emphasized that the Constitution entitles same-sex couples to civil marriage "on the same terms and conditions as opposite-sex couples."

Some open questions still linger after *Obergefell*, such as the current status of marriage alternatives, including civil unions and domestic partnerships, which were created before constitutional recognition of same-sex marriage. These issues, however, are expected to dissipate quickly. The U.S. Supreme Court's decision to recognize constitutional protections in this area thus effectively eliminated one of the most complex choice of law puzzles in modern times.

B. THE FEDERAL GOVERNMENT AS A SOURCE OF LAW

1. Federal Supremacy and Preemption

A significant role for federal authority in the area of choice of law, both as a constitutional constraint and as a source of law, is federal preemption of state law. The supremacy clause of Article IV of the United States Constitution provides the constitutional foundation for preemption, establishing federal law as "the supreme Law of the Land" and providing that "the Judges in every State shall be bound thereby." While the supremacy clause's mandate rings clear, preemption issues are not always obvious or easily resolved. Challenges often emerge in the process of comparing federal and state law to determine whether they are capable of co-regulating or whether in fact federal law displaces state law under preemption principles.

Federal law may preempt state law expressly or implicitly. Thus, preemption occurs where federal law explicitly says that it preempts state law or where one can imply a clear congressional intent to preempt state or local law. Two types of implied preemption exist: field preemption and conflict preemption. With field preemption, the federal regulatory scheme is so pervasive that it supports the reasonable inference that Congress intended that the states could not supplement it. Conflict preemption occurs where a regulated entity cannot physically comply with both federal and state regulations or "where state law stands as an obstacle to the accomplishment and execution of the full purposes and objective of Congress." *Gade v. National Solid Waste Management*, 505 U.S. 88, 98 (1992).

Preemption doctrines are "[u]ltimately . . . about allocating governing authority between the federal and state governments." ERWIN CHEMERINSKY, CONSTITUTIONAL LAW 404 (4th ed. 2011). In making these authority-allocating decisions in the context of preemption, courts start with a presumption *against* preemption — in recognition of the limited power of the federal government and the primary authority of the states. Given this presumption, one would expect that preemption cases might be scarce. To the contrary, they are not: successful preemption claims arise in a variety of contexts and are remarkably unpredictable. Litigants in the United States Supreme Court have pressed successful claims in myriad cases under a variety of theories: express preemption (e.g., cigarette, airline regulation, medical equipment, and employee benefits cases), field preemption (e.g., immigration, airline, and labor cases), and conflict preemption (e.g., tort, bankruptcy, and occupational health cases).

One common preemption context concerns foreign relations. Because the foreign relations area by necessity implicates the interplay between United States laws, laws of foreign countries, and international law, as well as the interplay between state and federal law within the United States, the area is particularly apt for a conflict of laws course. For that reason, foreign relations cases provide the context for illustrating preemption concepts in this section.

Zschernig v. Miller

389 U.S 429 (1968)

Justice DOUGLAS delivered the opinion of the Court.

[An American citizen died intestate in Oregon. The sole heirs of his property were residents of East Germany. An Oregon statute, §111.070 (1957), allowed a nonresident alien to inherit such property only upon the existence of three conditions: (1) a reciprocal right existed for American citizens to inherit on the same terms as citizens of the alien's country; (2) American citizens possessed the right to receive payment in the United States from the estates in the alien's country; and (3) the foreign heirs could receive the proceeds of the Oregon estate without confiscation. No evidence existed that a reciprocal right existed in East Germany for American citizens. Nonetheless, the Oregon Supreme Court found that — under Article IV of the 1923 Treaty of Friendship, Commerce and Consular

Rights still effective with respect to East Germany as determined in the case of *Clark v. Allen*, 331 U.S. 503 (1947) — the East German heirs had to be permitted to take the real property despite the Oregon statute. They were not, however, permitted to take the personal property.]

[W]e held in *Clark v. Allen*, that the 1923 Treaty of Friendship, Commerce and Consular Rights "does not cover personalty located in this country and which an American citizen undertakes to leave to German nationals." . . . We do not accept the invitation to re-examine our ruling in *Clark v. Allen*. For we conclude that the history and operation of this Oregon statute make clear that §111.070 is an intrusion by the State into the field of foreign affairs which the Constitution entrusts to the President and the Congress.

. . . State courts, of course, must frequently read, construe, and apply laws of foreign nations. It has never been seriously suggested that state courts are precluded from performing that function, albeit there is a remote possibility that any holding may disturb a foreign nation — whether the matter involves commercial cases, tort cases, or some other type of controversy. . . . It now appears that in this reciprocity area under inheritance statutes, the probate courts of various States have launched inquiries into the type of governments that obtain in particular foreign nations — whether aliens under their law have enforceable rights, whether the so-called "rights" are merely dispensations turning upon the whim or caprice of government officials, whether the representation of consuls, ambassadors, and other representatives of foreign nations is credible or made in good faith, whether there is in the actual administration in the particular foreign system of law any element of confiscation. . . . As we read the decisions that followed in the wake of *Clark v. Allen*, we find that they radiate some of the attitudes of the "cold war," where the search is for the "democracy quotient" of a foreign regime as opposed to the Marxist theory. The Oregon statute introduces the concept of "confiscation," which is of course opposed to the Just Compensation Clause of the Fifth Amendment. And this has led into minute inquiries concerning the actual administration of foreign law, into the credibility of foreign diplomatic statements, and into speculation whether the fact that some received delivery of funds should "not preclude wonderment as to how many may have been denied 'the right to receive.'" . . .

That kind of state involvement in foreign affairs and international relations — matters which the Constitution entrusts solely to the Federal Government — is not sanctioned by *Clark v. Allen*. Yet such forbidden state activity has infected each of the three provisions of §111.070, as applied by Oregon.

. . . It seems inescapable that the type of probate law that Oregon enforces affects international relations in a persistent and subtle way. The practice of state courts in withholding remittances to legatees residing in Communist countries or in preventing them from assigning them is notorious. The several States, of course, have traditionally regulated the descent and distribution of estates. But those regulations must give way if they impair the effective exercise of the Nation's foreign policy. Where those laws conflict with a treaty, they must bow to the superior federal policy. Yet, even in absence of a treaty, a State's policy may disturb foreign relations. As we stated in *Hines v. Davidowitz* . . . "Experience has shown that international controversies of the gravest moment, sometimes even leading to war, may arise from real or imagined wrongs to another's subjects inflicted, or permitted, by a government." Certainly a State could not deny admission to a traveler from East Germany nor bar its citizens from going there. If there are to be such restraints, they must be provided by the Federal Government. The present Oregon law is not as gross an intrusion in the federal domain as those others might be. Yet, as we have said, it has a direct impact upon foreign relations and may well adversely affect the power of the central government to deal with those problems.

The Oregon law does, indeed, illustrate the dangers which are involved if each State, speaking through its probate courts, is permitted to establish its own foreign policy.

Reversed.

Justice MARSHALL took no part in the consideration or decision of this case.

Justice STEWART, with whom Justice BRENNAN joins, concurring.

While joining the opinion of the Court, I would go further. Under the Oregon law involved in this case, a foreigner cannot receive property from an Oregon decedent's estate unless he first meets the burden of proving, to the satisfaction of an Oregon court, that his country (1) grants to United States citizens a "reciprocal right" to take property on the same terms as its own citizens; (2) assures Americans the right "to receive payment" here of funds originating from estates in that country; and (3) gives its own citizens the "benefit, use or control" of property received from an Oregon estate "without confiscation, in whole or in part." The East German claimants in this case did not show in the Oregon courts that their country could meet any one of these criteria. I believe that all three of the statutory requirements on their face are contrary to the Constitution of the United States.

In my view, each of the three provisions of the Oregon law suffers from the same fatal infirmity. All three launch the State upon a prohibited voyage into a domain of exclusively federal competence. Any realistic attempt to apply any of the three criteria would necessarily involve the Oregon courts in an evaluation, either expressed or implied, of the administration of foreign law, the credibility of foreign diplomatic statements, and the policies of foreign governments. Of course state courts must routinely construe foreign law in the resolution of controversies properly before them, but here the courts of Oregon are thrust into these inquiries only because the Oregon Legislature has framed its inheritance laws to the prejudice of nations whose policies it disapproves and thus has trespassed upon an area where the Constitution contemplates that only the National Government shall operate. . . .

Justice HARLAN, concurring in the result.

Although I agree with the result reached in this case, I am unable to subscribe to the Court's opinion, for three reasons. First, by resting its decision on the constitutional ground that this Oregon inheritance statute infringes the federal foreign relations power, without pausing to consider whether the 1923 Treaty of

Friendship, Commerce and Consular Rights with Germany itself vitiates this application of the state statute, the Court has deliberately turned its back on a cardinal principle of judicial review. Second, correctly construed the 1923 treaty, in my opinion, renders Oregon's application of its statute in this instance impermissible, thus requiring reversal of the state judgment. Third, the Court's constitutional holding, which I reach only because the majority has done so, is in my view untenable. The impact of today's holding on state power in this field, and perhaps in other areas of the law as well, justifies a full statement of my views upon the case. . . .

. . . Essentially, the Court's basis for decision appears to be that alien inheritance laws afford state court judges an opportunity to criticize in dictum the policies of foreign governments, and that these dicta may adversely affect our foreign relations. . . . If the flaw in the statute is said to be that it requires state courts to inquire into the administration of foreign law, I would suggest that that characteristic is shared by other legal rules which I cannot believe the Court wishes to invalidate. For example, the Uniform Foreign Money-Judgments Recognition Act provides that a foreign-country money judgment shall not be recognized if it "was rendered under a system which does not provide impartial tribunals or procedures compatible with the requirements of due process of law." When there is a dispute as to the content of foreign law, the court is required under the common law to treat the question as one of fact and to consider any evidence presented as to the actual administration of the foreign legal system. And in the field of choice of law there is a nonstatutory rule that the tort law of a foreign country will not be applied if that country is shown to be "uncivilized." Surely, all of these rules possess the same "defect" as the statute now before us. Yet I assume that the Court would not find them unconstitutional.

I therefore concur in the judgment of the Court upon the sole ground that the application of the Oregon statute . . . with the 1923 Treaty of Friendship, Commerce and Consular Rights with Germany.

Notes on
ZSCHERNIG

1. As mentioned above, two types of implied preemption theories exist: field preemption or preemption based on conflict between state law and federal interests. In conflict preemption cases, the Court relies on specific expressions of federal interests threatened by state regulation. Does the *Zschernig* majority identify foreign policy interests that the Oregon statute undermined? Or, was the case one where the Court simply assumed that federal foreign policy is so important and sensitive that federal authority preempts the entire field of regulation, displacing any applicable state law?

Commentators have criticized *Zschernig* on a number of grounds, including the Court's failure to pinpoint the constitutional language that mandates preemption. One might argue that respect for state sovereignty and the limited nature of the federal government's powers counsel against finding a foreign relations preemption doctrine (sometimes referred to as the dormant foreign relations power). One could further argue that preemption should be tied to the supremacy clause operating in connection with the Constitution's specific prohibitions and affirmative grants of power. *See, e.g.,* Michael D. Ramsey, *The Power of the States in Foreign Affairs: The Original Understanding of Foreign Policy Federalism,* 75 NOTRE DAME L. REV. 341 (1999).

2. Why is it unconstitutional for a state to act on its obligation to protect the welfare of its citizens by ensuring that other jurisdictions provide them with reciprocal treatment? As Justice Harlan pointed out in his opinion, state courts consider aspects of foreign law in deciding to enforce judgments against state citizens. Don't forum state courts also enjoy wide latitude to consider international concerns when they decide other aspects of litigation involving international elements? Can you think of other examples?

How does one distinguish between what invades federal prerogative and what does not? Perhaps one might argue that the distinguishing characteristic of Oregon's law is that it yoked its own inheritance provisions to the laws of other countries, thereby improperly interfering with the foreign countries' internal prerogatives.

3. Does the act of state doctrine, discussed in Chapter 1, provide guidance on why the Oregon statute in *Zschernig* was improper?

4. Compare the *Zschernig* preemption approach to the choice of law approaches described in Chapter 2. Which choice of law approach is the most analogous? Might it be the territorial approach to choice of law? In the First Restatement context, courts did not usually inquire into the purposes of behind laws or evaluate whether those purposes clash. Rather, courts focused on categorizing the types of law involved, and matching those characterizations to the case facts in order to identify which of competing sovereigns has superior authority. The *Zschernig* Court likewise did not evaluate the purposes behind the state and federal laws to identify a clash or evaluate competing claims to authority.

Crosby v. National Foreign Trade Council

530 U.S. 363 (2000)

Justice SOUTER delivered the opinion of the Court.

The issue is whether the Burma law of the Commonwealth of Massachusetts, restricting the authority of its agencies to purchase goods or services from companies doing business with Burma, is invalid under the Supremacy Clause of the National Constitution owing to its threat of frustrating federal statutory objectives. We hold that it is.

I

In June 1996, Massachusetts adopted "An Act Regulating State Contracts with Companies Doing Business with or in Burma (Myanmar)," [which] generally bars state entities from buying goods or services from any person (defined to include a business organization) identified on a "restricted purchase list" of those doing business with Burma. Although the statute has no general provision for waiver or termination of its ban, it does exempt from boycott any entities present in Burma solely to report the news, or to provide international telecommunication goods or services, or medical supplies.

"'Doing business with Burma'" is defined broadly to cover any person

"(a) having a principal place of business, place of incorporation or its corporate headquarters in Burma (Myanmar) or having any operations, leases, franchises, majority-owned subsidiaries, distribution agreements, or any other similar agreements in Burma (Myanmar), or being the majority-owned subsidiary, licensee or franchise of such a person;

"(b) providing financial services to the government of Burma (Myanmar), including providing direct loans, underwriting government securities, providing any consulting advice or assistance, providing brokerage services, acting as a trustee or escrow agent, or otherwise acting as an agent pursuant to a contractual agreement;

"(c) promoting the importation or sale of gems, timber, oil, gas or other related products, commerce in which is largely controlled by the government of Burma (Myanmar), from Burma (Myanmar);

"(d) providing any goods or services to the government of Burma (Myanmar)." §7:22G.

There are three exceptions to the ban: (1) if the procurement is essential, and without the restricted bid, there would be no bids or insufficient competition; (2) if the procurement is of medical supplies; and (3) if the procurement efforts elicit no "comparable low bid or offer" by a person not doing business with Burma, meaning an offer that is no more than 10 percent greater than the restricted bid. To enforce the ban, the Act requires petitioner Secretary of Administration and Finance to maintain a "restricted purchase list" of all firms "doing business with Burma."

In September 1996, three months after the Massachusetts law was enacted, Congress passed a statute imposing a set of mandatory and conditional sanctions on Burma. See Foreign Operations, Export Financing, and Related Programs Appropriations Act. The federal Act has five basic parts, three substantive and two procedural.

First, it imposes three sanctions directly on Burma. It bans all aid to the Burmese Government except for humanitarian assistance, counternarcotics efforts, and promotion of human rights and democracy. The statute instructs United States representatives to international financial institutions to vote against loans or other assistance to or for Burma, and it provides that no entry visa shall be issued to any Burmese Government official unless required by treaty or to staff the

Burmese mission to the United Nations. These restrictions are to remain in effect "[u]ntil such time as the President determines and certifies to Congress that Burma has made measurable and substantial progress in improving human rights practices and implementing democratic government."

Second, the federal Act authorizes the President to impose further sanctions subject to certain conditions. He may prohibit "United States persons" from "new investment" in Burma, and shall do so if he determines and certifies to Congress that the Burmese Government has physically harmed, rearrested, or exiled Daw Aung San Suu Kyi (the opposition leader selected to receive the Nobel Peace Prize), or has committed "large-scale repression of or violence against the Democratic opposition."

Third, the statute directs the President to work to develop "a comprehensive, multilateral strategy to bring democracy to and improve human rights practices and the quality of life in Burma." He is instructed to cooperate with members of the Association of Southeast Asian Nations (ASEAN) and with other countries having major trade and investment interests in Burma to devise such an approach, and to pursue the additional objective of fostering dialogue between the ruling State Law and Order Restoration Council (SLORC) and democratic opposition groups.

As for the procedural provisions of the federal statute, the fourth section requires the President to report periodically to certain congressional committee chairmen on the progress toward democratization and better living conditions in Burma as well as on the development of the required strategy. And the fifth part of the federal Act authorizes the President "to waive, temporarily or permanently, any sanction [under the federal Act] . . . if he determines and certifies to Congress that the application of such sanction would be contrary to the national security interests of the United States."

On May 20, 1997, the President issued the Burma Executive Order, Exec. Order No. 13047, 3 CFR 202 (1997 Comp.). He certified . . . that the Government of Burma had "committed large-scale repression of the democratic opposition in Burma" and found that the Burmese Government's actions and policies constituted "an unusual and extraordinary threat to the national security and foreign policy of the United States," a threat characterized as a national emergency. The President then prohibited new investment in Burma "by United States persons," any approval or facilitation by a United States person of such new investment by foreign persons, and any transaction meant to evade or avoid the ban. The order generally incorporated the exceptions and exemptions addressed in the statute. Finally, the President delegated to the Secretary of State the tasks of working with ASEAN and other countries to develop a strategy for democracy, human rights, and the quality of life in Burma, and of making the required congressional reports.

II

Respondent National Foreign Trade Council (Council) is a nonprofit corporation representing companies engaged in foreign commerce; 34 of its members were on the Massachusetts restricted purchase list in 1998. . . . The Council [sought] declaratory and injunctive relief against the petitioner state officials

charged with administering and enforcing the state Act. . . . The Council argued
that the state law unconstitutionally infringed on the federal foreign affairs
power, violated the Foreign Commerce Clause, and was preempted by the federal
Act. . . . [T]he District Court permanently enjoined enforcement of the state Act,
holding that it "unconstitutionally impinge[d] on the federal government's
exclusive authority to regulate foreign affairs."

The United States Court of Appeals for the First Circuit affirmed,
[finding] . . . the state Act unconstitutionally interfered with the foreign affairs
power of the National Government under *Zschernig v. Miller*, . . . violated the
dormant Foreign Commerce Clause, U.S. Const., Art. I, §8, cl. 3, and was preempted by the congressional Burma Act.

III

A fundamental principle of the Constitution is that Congress has the power
to preempt state law. . . . We will find preemption where . . . "under the circumstances of [a] particular case, [the challenged state law] stands as an obstacle to
the accomplishment and execution of the full purposes and objectives of Congress." What is a sufficient obstacle is a matter of judgment, to be informed by
examining the federal statute as a whole and identifying its purpose and intended
effects.

Applying this standard, we see the state Burma law as an obstacle to the
accomplishment of Congress's full objectives under the federal Act. We find
that the state law undermines the intended purpose and "natural effect" of at
least three provisions of the federal Act, that is, its delegation of effective discretion to the President to control economic sanctions against Burma, its limitation
of sanctions solely to United States persons and new investment, and its directive
to the President to proceed diplomatically in developing a comprehensive, multilateral strategy toward Burma.[8]

A

First, Congress clearly intended the federal Act to provide the President with
flexible and effective authority over economic sanctions against Burma. Although
Congress immediately put in place a set of initial sanctions (prohibiting bilateral
aid, §570(a)(1), support for international financial assistance, §570(a)(2), and
entry by Burmese officials into the United States, §570(a)(3)), it authorized
the President to terminate any and all of those measures upon determining
and certifying that there had been progress in human rights and democracy in

---

8. We leave for another day a consideration in this context of a presumption against
preemption. Assuming, *arguendo*, that some presumption against preemption is appropriate, we
conclude, based on our analysis below, that the state Act presents a sufficient obstacle to the full
accomplishment of Congress's objectives under the federal Act to find it preempted.

Because our conclusion that the state Act conflicts with federal law is sufficient to affirm the
judgment below, we decline to speak to field preemption as a separate issue, or to pass on the First
Circuit's rulings addressing the foreign affairs power or the dormant Foreign Commerce Clause.

Burma. §570(a). It invested the President with the further power to ban new investment by United States persons, dependent only on specific Presidential findings of repression in Burma. §570(b). And, most significantly, Congress empowered the President "to waive, temporarily or permanently, any sanction [under the federal Act] . . . if he determines and certifies to Congress that the application of such sanction would be contrary to the national security interests of the United States." §570(e).

This express investiture of the President with statutory authority to act for the United States in imposing sanctions with respect to the Government of Burma, augmented by the flexibility to respond to change by suspending sanctions in the interest of national security. . . . Within the sphere defined by Congress, then, the statute has placed the President in a position with as much discretion to exercise economic leverage against Burma, with an eye toward national security, as our law will admit. And it is just this plenitude of Executive authority that we think controls the issue of preemption here. The President has been given this authority not merely to make a political statement but to achieve a political result, and the fullness of his authority shows the importance in the congressional mind of reaching that result. It is simply implausible that Congress would have gone to such lengths to empower the President if it had been willing to compromise his effectiveness by deference to every provision of state statute or local ordinance that might, if enforced, blunt the consequences of discretionary Presidential action.

And that is just what the Massachusetts Burma law would do in imposing a different, state system of economic pressure against the Burmese political regime. As will be seen, the state statute penalizes some private action that the federal Act (as administered by the President) may allow, and pulls levers of influence that the federal Act does not reach. But the point here is that the state sanctions are immediate. . . . This unyielding application undermines the President's intended statutory authority by making it impossible for him to restrain fully the coercive power of the national economy when he may choose to take the discretionary action open to him, whether he believes that the national interest requires sanctions to be lifted, or believes that the promise of lifting sanctions would move the Burmese regime in the democratic direction. Quite simply, if the Massachusetts law is enforceable the President has less to offer and less economic and diplomatic leverage as a consequence. . . .

Congress manifestly intended to limit economic pressure against the Burmese Government to a specific range. The federal Act confines its reach to United States persons, imposes limited immediate sanctions, places only a conditional ban on a carefully defined area of "new investment," and pointedly exempts contracts to sell or purchase goods, services, or technology. These detailed provisions show that Congress's calibrated Burma policy is a deliberate effort "to steer a middle path." . . .

The State has set a different course, and its statute conflicts with federal law at a number of points by penalizing individuals and conduct that Congress has explicitly exempted or excluded from sanctions. While the state Act differs from the federal in relying entirely on indirect economic leverage through third parties with Burmese connections, it otherwise stands in clear contrast to the congressional scheme in the scope of subject matter addressed. It restricts all contracts between the State and companies doing business in Burma, except when purchasing medical supplies and other essentials (or when short of comparable bids). It is specific in targeting contracts to provide financial services, and general goods and services, to the Government of Burma, and thus prohibits contracts between the State and United States persons for goods, services, or technology, even though those transactions are explicitly exempted from the ambit of new investment prohibition when the President exercises his discretionary authority to impose sanctions under the federal Act.

As with the subject of business meant to be affected, so with the class of companies doing it: the state Act's generality stands at odds with the federal discreteness. The Massachusetts law directly and indirectly imposes costs on all companies that do any business in Burma, save for those reporting news or providing international telecommunications goods or services, or medical supplies. It sanctions companies promoting the importation of natural resources controlled by the Government of Burma, or having any operations or affiliates in Burma. The state Act thus penalizes companies with pre-existing affiliates or investments, all of which lie beyond the reach of the federal Act's restrictions on "new investment" in Burmese economic development. §§570(b), 570(f)(2). The state Act, moreover, imposes restrictions on foreign companies as well as domestic, whereas the federal Act limits its reach to United States persons.

The conflicts are not rendered irrelevant by the State's argument that there is no real conflict between the statutes because they share the same goals and because some companies may comply with both sets of restrictions. The fact of a common end hardly neutralizes conflicting means. . . .

Finally, the state Act is at odds with the President's intended authority to speak for the United States among the world's nations in developing a "comprehensive, multilateral strategy to bring democracy to and improve human rights practices and the quality of life in Burma." . . . As with Congress's explicit delegation to the President of power over economic sanctions, Congress's express command to the President to take the initiative for the United States among the international community invested him with the maximum authority of the National Government.

Again, the state Act undermines the President's capacity, in this instance for effective diplomacy. It is not merely that the differences between the state and federal Acts in scope and type of sanctions threaten to complicate discussions; they compromise the very capacity of the President to speak for the Nation with one voice in dealing with other governments. . . . Because the state Act's provisions conflict with Congress's specific delegation to the President of flexible discretion, with limitation of sanctions to a limited scope of actions and actors, and with direction to develop a comprehensive, multilateral strategy under the federal Act, it is preempted, and its application is unconstitutional, under the Supremacy Clause.

The judgment of the Court of Appeals for the First Circuit is affirmed.

Notes on
CROSBY

1. Sometimes one encounters difficulty characterizing whether a pre-emption decision falls into field preemption or conflict preemption. The *Crosby* Court acknowledges this in footnote 6 of its opinion. Perhaps comparison of the different preemption decisions promotes deeper understanding. For example, consider the majority opinion in *Crosby* and the opinions in *Zschernig*. Which opinion in *Zschernig* does *Crosby* most resemble: the majority opinion or Justice Harlan's?

2. From the point of view of federalism (state/federal relations), is there a qualitative difference between preemption by the specific terms of a statute and preemption by the federal foreign relations power?

3. Is *Crosby* correctly decided? In the United States federalist system, isn't it a significant component of retained sovereignty for states to control how they spend their taxpayer dollars? Likewise, don't states have discretion over what entities with whom they do and do not engage in business with?

4. Compare the *Crosby* Court's preemption analysis to the choice of law approaches covered in Chapter 2. Which approaches does the *Crosby* analysis most resemble? The *Crosby* Court evaluates purposes behind the state and federal laws, but considers systemic factors as well. What choice of law approaches does that multipronged inquiry evoke?

5. Would you regard *Crosby* as a benefit or a set-back for those interested in human rights activism using boycott strategies to improve conditions around the world?

6. At the time that *Crosby* was decided, considerable uncertainty existed about the scope of an implicit constitutional power of the federal government akin to the dormant commerce clause: the dormant foreign relations power. *See* Peter J. Spiro, *U.S. Supreme Court Knocks Down State Burma Law,* ASIL INSIGHTS (June 2000), *available at* www.asil.org/insigh46.cfm. Justice Souter's opinion gave some support for those wishing to entrench the dormant foreign relations power because the opinion looked beyond potential state and federal law conflicts, and emphasized the federal government's need to preserve a unified federal message to the world: "It is not merely the differences between the state and federal Acts in scope and type of sanctions that threaten to complicate discussions; they compromised the very capacity of the President to speak for the Nation with one voice in dealing with other governments." Adding to this rhetoric, the Court's reliance on separation of powers principles (particularly, the strength of presidential prerogative) suggests that the Court gave only limited concern to state sovereignty in assessing federal and state power. The Court's reliance on preserving the President's discretion is also notable given the possibility that the *Crosby* majority could have relied more heavily on Congress's preferences as specifically expressed in the federal statute.

American Insurance Association v. Garamendi

539 U.S. 396 (2003)

Justice SOUTER delivered the opinion of the Court.

[The facts and procedural history of this case are complicated: the following provides the essential background. This case arises from life insurance policies issued to German Jews during World War II. In some instances, the Nazi government confiscated several life insurance policies, and in other instances, the policies were not confiscated, but insurers refused to honor them after the war on various grounds, including failure to pay premiums. The West German government paid reparations to victims of the war, but not all claimants received their payments.

Jewish survivors and descendants brought class action suits against insurance companies that did business during the Nazi era. The German and United States governments as well as German companies negotiated agreements in response. In one agreement, Germany agreed to enact legislation establishing a foundation funded with several billion deutsch marks contributed equally by the German government and German companies, for compensation to those "who suffered at the hands of German companies during the National Socialist era." Agreement Concerning the Foundation "Remembrance, Responsibility and the Future," 39 Int'l Legal Materials 1298 (2000).

The German willingness to create this fund depended on an expectation of protection suits in United States courts. To that end, President Clinton committed to a "mechanism to provide the legal peace desired by the German government and German companies" (letter from President Clinton to Chancellor Schröder). In an executive agreement, the United States government agreed that whenever a German company was sued on a Holocaust-era claim in an American court, the United States would submit a statement that "it would be in the foreign policy interests of the United States for the Foundation to be the exclusive forum and remedy for the resolution of all asserted claims against German companies arising from their involvement in the National Socialist era and World War II." 39 Int'l Legal Materials, at 1303. Although the United States government did not believe it could bind courts by guaranteeing that its foreign policy interests would "in themselves provide an independent legal basis for dismissal," the United States nonetheless agreed to tell United States courts "that U.S. policy interests favor dismissal on any valid legal ground." *Id.* at 1304. In addition, the United States promised to use its "best efforts, in a manner it considers appropriate," to get state and local governments to respect the Foundation as the exclusive mechanism. *Id.* at 1300. As for insurance claims, both the United States and Germany agreed that the German Foundation would work with an existing organization of several European insurance companies, the International Commission on Holocaust Era Insurance Claims (ICHEIC).

California later passed the Holocaust Victim Insurance Relief Act of 1999 (HVIRA), which requires any insurer doing business in that State to disclose information about policies sold in Europe between 1920 and 1945 by the company or a related company. The HVIRA penalty for failure to comply with this duty is suspension of the company's license to do business in California. In addition, HVIRA provides misdemeanor criminal sanctions for falsehood in certain required representations about whether and to whom the proceeds of each policy have been distributed.

After the California insurance officials issued subpoenas to insurance companies that had worked with the ICHEIC, the companies file a request to enjoin HVIRA on the ground that it infringed the federal foreign relations power. The district court issued a preliminary injunction and the court of appeals reversed.]

... The issue is whether HVIRA interferes with the National Government's conduct of foreign relations. We hold that it does, with the consequence that the state statute is preempted. . . .

III

The principal argument for preemption made by petitioners and the United States as *amicus curiae* is that HVIRA interferes with foreign policy of the Executive Branch, as expressed principally in the executive agreements with Germany, Austria, and France. . . . Nor is there any question generally that there is executive authority to decide what that policy should be. Although the source of the President's power to act in foreign affairs does not enjoy any textual detail, the historical gloss on the "executive Power" vested in Article II of the Constitution has recognized the President's "vast share of responsibility for the conduct of our foreign relations." While Congress holds express authority to regulate public and private dealings with other nations in its war and foreign commerce powers, in foreign affairs the President has a degree of independent authority to act.

At a more specific level, our cases have recognized that the President has authority to make "executive agreements" with other countries, requiring no ratification by the Senate or approval by Congress, this power having been exercised since the early years of the Republic. Making executive agreements to settle claims of American nationals against foreign governments is a particularly longstanding practice. . . . Given the fact that the practice goes back over 200 years and has received congressional acquiescence throughout its history, the conclusion "[t]hat the President's control of foreign relations includes the settlement of claims is indisputable."

The executive agreements at issue here do differ in one respect from those just mentioned insofar as they address claims associated with formerly belligerent states, but against corporations, not the foreign governments. But the distinction does not matter. Historically, wartime claims against even nominally private entities have become issues in international diplomacy, and three of the postwar settlements dealing with reparations implicating private parties were made by the Executive alone. . . . [U]ntangling government policy from private initiative during wartime is often so hard that diplomatic action settling claims against private parties may well be just as essential in the aftermath of hostilities as diplomacy to settle claims against foreign governments. While a sharp line between public and private acts works for many purposes in the domestic law, insisting on the same line in defining the legitimate scope of the Executive's international negotiations would hamstring the President in settling international controversies. . . . [V]alid executive agreements are fit to preempt state law. But . . . the agreements [here] include no preemption clause, and so leave their claim of preemption to rest on asserted interference with the foreign policy those agreements embody. Reliance is placed on our decision in *Zschernig v. Miller*, 389 U.S. 429 (1968). . . . The *Zschernig* majority relied on statements in a number of previous cases open to the reading that state action with more than incidental effect on foreign affairs is preempted, even absent any affirmative federal activity in the subject area of the state law, and hence without any showing of conflict. . . . Justice Harlan . . . disagreed with the *Zschernig* majority on this point, arguing that its implication of preemption of the entire field of foreign affairs was at odds with some other cases suggesting that in the absence of positive federal action "the States may legislate in areas of their traditional competence even though their statutes may have an incidental effect on foreign relations." . . . Thus, for Justice Harlan it was crucial that the challenge to the Oregon statute presented no evidence of a "specific interest of the Federal Government which might be interfered with" by the law. He would, however, have found preemption in a case of "conflicting federal policy," and on this point the majority and [Justice Harlan] . . . basically agreed: state laws "must give way if they impair the effective exercise of the Nation's foreign policy."

It is a fair question whether respect for the executive foreign relations power requires a categorical choice between the contrasting theories of field and conflict preemption evident in the *Zschernig* opinions,[11] but the question requires no answer here. For even on Justice Harlan's view, the likelihood that state legislation will produce something more than incidental effect in conflict with express foreign policy of the National Government would require preemption of the state law. And since on his view it is legislation within "areas of . . . traditional competence" that gives a State any claim to prevail, it would be reasonable to consider the strength of the state interest, judged by standards of traditional practice, when deciding how serious a conflict must be shown before declaring the state law preempted. Judged by these standards, we think petitioners and the Government have demonstrated a sufficiently clear conflict to require finding preemption here.

11. The two positions can be seen as complementary. If a State were simply to take a position on a matter of foreign policy with no serious claim to be addressing a traditional state responsibility, field preemption might be the appropriate doctrine, whether the National Government had acted and, if it had, without reference to the degree of any conflict, the principle having been established that the Constitution entrusts foreign policy exclusively to the National Government. Where, however, a State has acted within what Justice Harlan called its "traditional competence," but in a way that affects foreign relations, it might make good sense to require a conflict, of a clarity or substantiality that would vary with the strength or the traditional importance of the state concern asserted. Whether the strength of the federal foreign policy interest should itself be weighed is, of course, a further question.

IV

A

To begin with, resolving Holocaust-era insurance claims that may be held by residents of this country is a matter well within the Executive's responsibility for foreign affairs. Since claims remaining in the aftermath of hostilities may be "sources of friction" acting as an "impediment to resumption of friendly relations" between the countries involved, there is a "longstanding practice" of the national Executive to settle them in discharging its responsibility to maintain the Nation's relationships with other countries, The issue of restitution for Nazi crimes has in fact been addressed in Executive Branch diplomacy and formalized in treaties and executive agreements over the last half century, and although resolution of private claims was postponed by the Cold War, securing private interests is an express object of diplomacy today, just as it was addressed in agreements soon after the Second World War. Vindicating victims injured by acts and omissions of enemy corporations in wartime is thus within the traditional subject matter of foreign policy in which national, not state, interests are overriding, and which the National Government has addressed.

The exercise of the federal executive authority means that state law must give way where, as here, there is evidence of clear conflict between the policies adopted by the two. . . . [T]he national position, expressed unmistakably in the executive agreements signed by the President with Germany and Austria, has been to encourage European insurers to work with the ICHEIC to develop acceptable claim procedures, including procedures governing disclosure of policy information. This position . . . has also been consistently supported in the high levels of the Executive Branch, as mentioned already. The approach taken serves to resolve the several competing matters of national concern apparent in the German Foundation Agreement: the national interest in maintaining amicable relationships with current European allies; survivors' interests in a "fair and prompt" but nonadversarial resolution of their claims so as to "bring some measure of justice . . . in their lifetimes"; and the companies' interest in securing "legal peace" when they settle claims in this fashion. 39 Int'l Legal Materials, at 1304. As a way for dealing with insurance claims, moreover, the voluntary scheme protects the companies' ability to abide by their own countries' domestic privacy laws limiting disclosure of policy information.

California has taken a different tack of providing regulatory sanctions to compel disclosure and payment, supplemented by a new cause of action for Holocaust survivors if the other sanctions should fail. The situation created by the California legislation calls to mind the impact of the Massachusetts Burma law on the effective exercise of the President's power, as recounted in the statutory preemption case, *Crosby v. National Foreign Trade Council*, 530 U.S. 363 (2000). HVIRA's economic compulsion to make public disclosure, of far more information about far more policies than ICHEIC rules require, employs "a different, state system of economic pressure," and in doing so undercuts the President's diplomatic discretion and the choice he has made exercising it. Whereas the President's authority to provide for settling claims in winding up international hostilities requires flexibility in wielding "the coercive power of the national economy" as a tool of diplomacy, HVIRA denies this, by making exclusion from a large sector of the American insurance market the automatic sanction for noncompliance with the State's own policies on disclosure. "Quite simply, if the [California] law is enforceable the President has less to offer and less economic and diplomatic leverage as a consequence." The law thus "compromise[s] the very capacity of the President to speak for the Nation with one voice in dealing with other governments" to resolve claims against European companies arising out of World War II.

Crosby's facts are replicated again in the way HVIRA threatens to frustrate the operation of the particular mechanism the President has chosen. The letters from Deputy Secretary Eizenstat to California officials show well enough how the portent of further litigation and sanctions has in fact placed the Government at a disadvantage in obtaining practical results from persuading "foreign governments and foreign companies to participate voluntarily in organizations such as ICHEIC." In addition to thwarting the Government's policy of repose for companies that pay through the ICHEIC, California's indiscriminate disclosure provisions place a handicap on the ICHEIC's effectiveness (and raise a further irritant to the European allies) by undercutting European privacy protections. . . .

. . . The commissioner would justify HVIRA's ambitious disclosure requirement as protecting "legitimate consumer protection interests" in knowing which insurers have failed to pay insurance claims. . . . [T]here is no serious doubt that the state interest actually underlying HVIRA is concern for the several thousand Holocaust survivors said to be living in the State. But this fact does not displace general standards for evaluating a State's claim to apply its forum law to a particular controversy or transaction, under which the State's claim is not a strong one. "Even if a plaintiff evidences his desire for forum law by moving to the forum, we have generally accorded such a move little or no significance." *Phillips Petroleum Co. v. Shutts*, 472 U.S. 797, 820, (1985).

But should the general standard not be displaced, and the State's interest recognized as a powerful one, by virtue of the fact that California seeks to vindicate the claims of Holocaust survivors? The answer lies in recalling that the very same objective dignifies the interest of the National Government in devising its chosen mechanism for voluntary settlements, there being about 100,000 survivors in the country, only a small fraction of them in California. As against the responsibility of the United States of America, the humanity underlying the state statute could not give the State the benefit of any doubt in resolving the conflict with national policy.

C

The basic fact is that California seeks to use an iron fist where the President has consistently chosen kid gloves. We have heard powerful arguments that the iron fist would work better, and it may be that if the matter of compensation were considered in isolation from all other issues involving the European Allies, the iron fist would be the preferable policy. But our thoughts on the efficacy of the one approach versus the other are beside the point, since our business is not to judge the wisdom of the National Government's policy; dissatisfaction should be addressed to the President or, perhaps, Congress. The question relevant to preemption in this case is conflict, and the evidence here is "more than sufficient to demonstrate that the state Act stands in the way of [the President's] diplomatic objectives." *Crosby, supra*, at 386. . . .

Notes on
GARAMENDI

1. Did the majority rely on field preemption or conflict preemption in *Garamendi?* Consider the executive agreements at issue in the case: the original agreement established the German Foundation and bound the German insurance companies, the German government, and the United States government, and the other agreement specified representations the United States promised to make in United States courts in insurance litigation. Did either of these prohibit the matters covered by the state law, HVIRA?

Was there room for both the state law and executive agreements to operate in *Garamendi?* Do you agree with Justice Ginsburg that the Court was too quick to nullify the state law? Was Justice Ginsburg correct that the state and federal laws had entirely different focus, with the federal executive agreements pertaining to remedial matters (reparations) and HVIRA covering disclosure matters?

Perhaps one might argue that the *Garamendi* majority might have applied an analytical technique analogous to the restrained and moderate interpretation in governmental interest analysis to ensure that there was a "true conflict" and not merely an "apparent conflict" between state and federal law? In some preemption contexts, the Supreme Court speaks in terms of a presumption against federal preemption (which arguably operates as a presumption against a true conflict between state and federal law). The Court is less committed to such a presumption in the foreign affairs area.

2. In a decision reproduced later in this chapter, *Medellín v. Texas*, 552 U.S. 491 (2008), the Supreme Court arguably restricted *Garamendi* and foreign affairs preemption. Although *Medellín* presented a clear conflict between federal policy and state law, the *Medellín* Court rejected the United States government's argument that the President's foreign affairs power allowed him to displace state procedural law principles. Highlighting that *Garamendi* concerned disputes between "an American and foreign governments or foreign citizens," the Court distinguished *Garamendi* from the case at hand. 552 U.S. at 530. While courts and scholars have recognized a tension between *Medellín* and *Garamendi*, lower courts continue to use the decision to champion broad federal foreign relations power.

3. *Garamendi* is different than *Zschernig* and *Crosby* for a number of reasons. One significant distinction concerns the type of federal law at issue in *Garamendi*. While *Crosby* involved a federal statutory scheme and *Zschernig* relied on the Constitution's foreign relations power (with a treaty in the

background as well), *Garamendi* explicitly relied on executive agreements. Executive agreements, unlike treaties, are not subject to approval by two-thirds of the Senate. In fact, Congress need not approve executive agreements at all. Does this suggest that executive agreements should not have the same preemptive effect as laws that have been "passed on" by Congress? When confronting the issue of executive agreements in the case that followed *Garamendi*, *Medellín*, the Supreme Court suggested that Congress had long approved the tradition of using executive agreements under the circumstance of *Garamendi* (disputes between American citizens against foreign countries or foreign citizens).

4. Preemption does not occur solely by operation of a constitutional provision such as the foreign relations power or a statutory provision. Federal common law can also bar state law on matters related to foreign affairs. An example of federal common law in this area is the act of state doctrine, described in detail in Chapter 1 and illustrated in *Banco Nacional de Cuba v. Sabbatino*, 376 U.S. 398 (1964). The act of state doctrine is an interesting case study because, as shown in Chapter 1, the *Sabbatino* Court broadened the preemptive effect of the act of state doctrine, but subsequent developments in courts and Congress limited the case's effect.

In a related area, courts also make federal common law where United States military issues hang in the balance. This federal common law context is described below in *Boyle v. United Technologies Corp.*, 487 U.S. 500 (1988). Although the effect of making federal common law is to preempt applicable state law, the actual federal common law process differs from standard preemption analysis where, for example, a federal statute directly conflicts with state law. Compare the two situations when you read *Boyle v. United Technologies Corp.*

PROBLEM 3-6: NAZI CONFISCATED ART

Claude Segen, the sole surviving heir of Austrian–Jewish art collector Oskar Eiche, sought to recover a painting formerly owned by Eiche and now held by Major Metropolitan Museum. Segen filed a replevin action, averring that Eiche lost possession of the painting under duress during the Nazi era and that the Museum does not have proper title to the painting. The Museum argues that the suit is time barred under the applicable statute of limitations.

Both Segen and the Museum are United States residents, but their state residence differs. Thus, the suit was filed in federal court under diversity jurisdiction. Ordinarily, a state statute of limitations from the forum state would govern the suit. The forum state statute of limitations provides that a suit for replevin, such as here, must be brought within 3 years of the plaintiff learning of the claim. Although the actual cause of action arose over 50 years ago, Segen did not discover the painting and the nature of her rights in it until 4 years ago. She did not, however, bring suit in time to satisfy the 3-year discovery rule.

Segen argues that the state statute of limitations is preempted by two federal laws, the Holocaust Victims Redress Act of 1998 and the Terezín Declaration on Holocaust Era Assets and Related Issues. The Holocaust Victims Redress Act is a federal statute, written in broad language. The statute expresses the "sense of the Congress" that "all governments should undertake good faith efforts to facilitate the return" of Nazi-confiscated property. The Terezín Declaration is an executive agreement, written in more specific terms. The Declaration states that Nazi-era art disputes should be resolved "based on the facts and the merits" rather than on legal technicalities. The Terezín Declaration acknowledges that "various legal provisions that may impede the restitution of art and cultural property may need to be applied by courts," but urges governments to "consider all relevant issues . . . in order to achieve just and fair solutions."

How should the court resolve this dispute? Consider how your answer would change if you were to focus separately on the three decisions in this section: *Zschernig v. Miller, Crosby v. National Foreign Trade Council,* and *American Insurance Association v. Garamendi.*

PROBLEM 3-7: EXPRESS OR IMPLIED PREEMPTION FOR AIRLINE SAFETY

Frank Flight Attendant was fired for failing a drug detection urine test. But the test was negligently prepared and the result had no validity. The airline rehired him, but Frank still suffered damages from the firing. He has therefore filed a state law negligence action against the lab that negligently performed the test, Laverne's Lab. He seeks compensatory damages against Laverne's. Citing the applicable state law of negligence, Frank argues that Laverne's actions in testing his urine deviated from standards of reasonable care prevailing in the laboratory industry.

Laverne's has moved to dismiss the complaint, arguing that this state law action is preempted by federal law. Laverne's cites the Transportation Employee Testing Act (TETA). The federal statute, TETA, requires airlines to test the urine of those employees in a position to ensure the safety of passengers.

TETA contains a provision stating that "[a] state or local government may not regulate in a manner that is inconsistent with TETA or any regulations prescribed under this federal statutory scheme." TETA further provides that urine testing shall be conducted pursuant to reasonable standards commonly followed in professional laboratories. In the preamble to the statute, TETA provides that the statute is intended to ensure safety in airlines by preventing those under the influence of drugs to act in positions of authority or responsibility in the conduct of air travel. TETA also provides that an air carrier that fails to provide drug testing shall be fined according to a fine schedule provided in the statute. TETA contains no other relevant provisions and no relevant administrative regulations have been promulgated.

Discuss whether the court should grant Laverne's motion to dismiss on preemption grounds.

2. *The* Erie *Doctrine*

Principles of federal supremacy and preemption answer many issues that arise concerning the relationship between state and federal law. Yet what of those circumstances where no federal statute, treaty, or constitutional provision exists? Those circumstances also yield questions about where federal or state law should regulate. One of the most famous cases in United States law purports to guide courts grappling with such a circumstance: *Erie R. Co. v. Tompkins. Erie* has inspired a rich universe of jurisprudential thought, including deep analysis of law. Scholars still debate its ramifications for federalism and separation of powers. At bottom, however, *Erie* provides an outline for the basic approach for courts choosing between state or federal law to resolve a particular legal issue. In this way, *Erie* supplements the preemption jurisprudence and its reading of the supremacy clause. Indeed, in deciding which law governs a particular question pertaining to the United States, a court should start with the choice between state and federal law. If preemption principles or the *Erie* doctrine point to federal law, the choice of law inquiry is complete. If, on the other hand, the analysis points to state law, we know from Chapter 2 and from further concepts discussed below that the court must continue to inquire as to which state law should govern.

In presenting the *Erie* doctrine, this section will first present the constitutional and statutory underpinning of the decision. Next, the chapter will analyze how *Erie* analysis is performed differently according to the type of federal law involved. Finally, the section will present some contemporary twists on *Erie* and its implications for forum shopping.

Erie R. Co. v. Tompkins

304 U.S. 64 (1938)

Justice BRANDEIS delivered the opinion of the Court.

The question for decision is whether the oft-challenged doctrine of *Swift v. Tyson* shall now be disapproved.

Tompkins, a citizen of Pennsylvania, was injured on a dark night by a passing freight train of the Erie Railroad Company while walking along its right of way at Hughestown in that state. He claimed that the accident occurred through negligence in the operation, or maintenance, of the train; that he was rightfully on the premises as licensee because on a commonly used beaten footpath which ran for a short distance alongside the tracks; and that he was struck by something which looked like a door projecting from one of the moving cars. To enforce that claim he brought an action in the federal court for Southern New York, which had jurisdiction because the company is a corporation of that state. It denied liability; and the case was tried by a jury.

The Erie insisted that its duty to Tompkins was no greater than that owed to a trespasser. It contended, among other things, that its duty to Tompkins, and hence its liability, should be determined in accordance with the Pennsylvania law; that under the law of Pennsylvania, as declared by its highest court, persons who use pathways along the railroad right of way — that is, a longitudinal pathway as distinguished from a crossing — are to be deemed trespassers; and that the railroad is not liable for injuries to undiscovered trespassers resulting from its negligence, unless it be wanton or willful. Tompkins denied that any such rule had been established by the decisions of the Pennsylvania courts; and contended that, since there was no statute of the state on the subject, the railroad's duty and liability is to be determined in federal courts as a matter of general law.

The trial judge refused to rule that the applicable law precluded recovery. The jury brought in a verdict of $30,000; and the judgment entered thereon was affirmed by the Circuit Court of Appeals, which held that it was unnecessary to consider whether the law of Pennsylvania was as contended, because the question was one not of local, but of general, law, and that "upon questions of general law the federal courts are free, in absence of a local statute, to exercise their independent judgment as to what the law is.

The Erie had contended that application of the Pennsylvania rule was required, among other things, by section 34 of the Federal Judiciary Act of September 24, 1789, which provides: "The laws of the several States, except where the Constitution, treaties, or statutes of the United States otherwise require or provide, shall be regarded as rules of decision in trials at common law, in the courts of the United States, in cases where they apply."

Because of the importance of the question whether the federal court was free to disregard the alleged rule of the Pennsylvania common law, we granted certiorari.

First. Swift v. Tyson held that federal courts exercising jurisdiction on the ground of diversity of citizenship need not, in matters of general jurisprudence, apply the unwritten law of the state as declared by its highest court; that they are free to exercise an independent judgment as to what the common law of the state is — or should be; and that, as there stated by Mr. Justice Story:

> the true interpretation of the 34th section limited its application to state laws, strictly local, that is to say, to the positive statutes of the state, and the construction thereof adopted by the local tribunals, and to rights and titles to things having a permanent locality, such as the rights and titles to real estate, and other matters immovable and intra-territorial in their nature and character. It never has been supposed by us, that the section did apply, or was designed to apply, to questions of a more general nature, not at all dependent upon local statutes or local usages of a fixed and permanent operation, as, for example, to the construction of ordinary contracts or other written instruments, and especially to questions of general commercial law, where the state tribunals are called upon to perform the like functions as ourselves, that is, to ascertain, upon general reasoning and legal analogies, what is the true exposition of the contract or instrument, or what is the just rule furnished by the principles of commercial law to govern the case.

. . . The federal courts assumed, in the broad field of "general law," the power to declare rules of decision which Congress was confessedly without power to enact as statutes. Doubt was repeatedly expressed as to the correctness of the construction given section 34 and as to the soundness of the rule which it introduced. But it was the more recent research of a competent scholar, who examined the original document, which established that the construction given to it by the Court was erroneous; and that the purpose of the section was merely to make certain that, in all matters except those in which some federal law is controlling, the federal courts exercising jurisdiction in diversity of citizenship cases would apply as their rules of decision the law of the state, unwritten as well as written.[5]

Criticism of the doctrine became widespread after the decision of *Black & White Taxicab & Transfer Co. v. Brown & Yellow Taxicab & Transfer Co.* [In that case, a Kentucky corporation dissolved and reincorporated in Tennessee, and was thereby successfully permitted to create diversity of citizenship jurisdiction so as to sue to enforce a contract in a Kentucky federal court under circumstances where no relief would have been available in Kentucky state court.]

Second. Experience in applying the doctrine of *Swift v. Tyson* had revealed its defects, political and social; and the benefits expected to flow from the rule did not accrue. Persistence of state courts in their own opinions on questions of common law prevented uniformity; and the impossibility of discovering a satisfactory line of demarcation between the province of general law and that of local law developed a new well of uncertainties.

On the other hand, the mischievous results of the doctrine had become apparent. Diversity of citizenship jurisdiction was conferred in order to prevent apprehended discrimination in state courts against those not citizens of the state. *Swift v. Tyson* introduced grave discrimination by noncitizens against citizens. It made rights enjoyed under the unwritten "general law" vary according to whether enforcement was sought in the state or in the federal court; and the privilege of selecting the court in which the right should be determined was conferred upon the noncitizen. Thus, the doctrine rendered impossible equal protection of the law. In attempting to promote uniformity of law throughout the United States, the doctrine had prevented uniformity in the administration of the law of the state.

The discrimination resulting became in practice far-reaching. This resulted in part from the broad province accorded to the so-called "general law" as to which federal courts exercised an independent judgment. In addition to questions of purely commercial law, "general law" was held to include the obligations under contracts entered into and to be performed within the state, the extent to which a carrier operating within a state may stipulate for exemption from liability for his own negligence or that of his employee; the liability for torts committed within the state upon persons resident or property located there, even where the question of liability depended upon the scope of a property right conferred by the state; and the right to exemplary or punitive damages. Furthermore, state decisions construing local deeds, mineral conveyances, and even devises of real estate, were disregarded.

5. Charles Warren, *New Light on the History of the Federal Judiciary Act of 1789* (1923) 37 HARV. L. REV. 49, 51-52, 81-88, 108.

Erie "choice of law" problem only when they really cared about the matter. At the point when they started to really care, the choice of law problem had become outcome determinative.

The Court tried again to formulate an *Erie* test in *Byrd v. Blue Ridge Rural Elec. Coop., Inc.*, 356 U.S. 525 (1958). Apparently focusing on *Erie*'s constitutional foundation, the *Byrd* Court stated that federal courts must apply a state rule if it is "bound up" with "state-created rights and obligations." *Id.* at 535. Yet the Court found room for integrating federal interests into the analysis. According to *Byrd*, federal law could reflect such strong "affirmative countervailing considerations" as to counsel a court to apply the federal law in the face of a contrary state rule. *Id.* at 534. Presumably, the Constitution allowed federal law to apply in cases where necessary to preserve the "independent [federal] system for administering justice to litigants who properly invoke its jurisdiction." *Id.*

Lower courts interpreted this language as authorizing a balancing test, although no consensus has developed over how a court should balance a perceived federal interest against other concerns. Nonetheless, most approaches have balanced the importance of the state rule against the importance of the federal rule implicated in a particular case.

Several courts and many scholars suggested that the Supreme Court disavowed *Byrd* balancing in its decision in *Hanna v. Plumer*, 380 U.S. 460, 468 n.9 (1965) — which is set forth immediately below. But *Hanna* did not explicitly disapprove *Byrd* and lower federal courts continue to find *Byrd* balancing useful to this day. Moreover, the Supreme Court in a subsequent decision, *Gasperini v. Center for Humanities, Inc.*, 518 U.S. 415 (1996), suggested that district courts entertaining an *Erie* analysis should consider the strength of federal interests. In fact, the *Gasperini* Court criticized the lower court in that case for failing to give sufficient weight to a key component of the federal court system in choosing between state and federal law. *Id.* at 431, quoting *Byrd v. Blue Ridge Elec. Coop., Inc.*, 356 U.S. 525, 537 (1958). While this reference does not directly instruct courts to always weigh any federal interest implicated in a case, the reference suggests that one may legitimately integrate the federal interest in application of federal law into the decision whether, under *Erie*, to apply federal court-made law or state law.

Despite the repeated attempts to spurn the substance/procedural dichotomy, courts and scholars are drawn to the concept. Important developments continue, with significant scholarship continuing to guide the quest to pin down the distinction.[10]

Although refined in subsequent cases, *Hanna v. Plumer*, 380 U.S. 460 (1965), is still considered a watershed decision, marking the beginning of

10. *See, e.g.,* Jennifer Hendricks, *In Defense of the Substance-Procedure Dichotomy,* 89 WASH. U. L. REV. 103 (2011); Jay Tidmarsh, *Procedure, Substance, and* Erie, 64 VAND. L. REV. 877 (2011).

the modern *Erie* analysis. Perhaps *Hanna*'s most helpful contribution is clarifying that the *Erie* analysis differs according to whether the federal law is court-made law or a federal rule promulgated under the Rules Enabling Act (such as a Federal Rule of Civil Procedure). Stay attuned to that distinction as you read through the opinion.

Hanna v. Plumer

380 U.S. 460 (1965)

Chief Justice WARREN delivered the opinion of the Court.

[The plaintiff, a citizen of Ohio, filed a complaint against the executor of a deceased Massachusetts resident in the District Court for the District of Massachusetts for personal injuries resulting from a South Carolina automobile accident. Service was attempted by leaving a summons and complaint with respondent's wife at his residence as allowed by Federal Rule of Civil Procedure 4(d)(1), which provides that service may be made by leaving a copy of the summons and complaint "at his dwelling house or usual place of abode with some person of suitable age and discretion then residing therein."

The defendant, however, claimed that service was improper because it did not comply with a Massachusetts statute, which required in-hand service on an executor and which extinguished claims not made or served within one year of the point when the claims arose. Affirming the district court's dismissal of the action, the Court of Appeals held that state law governed because service of process is a substantive matter.]

We conclude that the adoption of Rule 4(d)(1), designed to control service of process in diversity actions, neither exceeded the congressional mandate embodied in the Rules Enabling Act nor transgressed constitutional bounds, and that the Rule is therefore the standard against which the District Court should have measured the adequacy of the service. Accordingly, we reverse the decision of the Court of Appeals.

The Rules Enabling Act, 28 U.S.C. §2072, provides, in pertinent part:

> The Supreme Court shall have the power to prescribe, by general rules, the forms of process, writs, pleadings, and motions, and the practice and procedure of the district courts of the United States in civil actions.
>
> Such rules shall not abridge, enlarge or modify any substantive right and shall preserve the right of trial by jury. . . .

Under the cases construing the scope of the Enabling Act, Rule 4(d)(1) clearly passes muster. Prescribing the manner in which a defendant is to be notified that a suit has been instituted against him, it relates to the "practice and procedure of the district courts." . . . "The test must be whether a rule really regulates procedure,—the judicial process for enforcing rights and duties recognized by substantive law and for justly administering remedy and redress for disregard or infraction of them." *Sibbach v. Wilson & Co.*, 312 U.S. 1, 14, 61 S. Ct. 422, 426, 85 L. Ed. 479.

In *Mississippi Pub. Corp. v. Murphree*, 326 U.S. 438, 66 S. Ct. 242, 90 L. Ed. 185, this Court upheld Rule 4(f), which permits service of a summons anywhere within the State (and not merely the district) in which a district court sits:

> We think that Rule 4(f) is in harmony with the Enabling Act. . . . Undoubtedly most alterations of the rules of practice and procedure may and often do affect the rights of litigants. Congress' prohibition of any alteration of substantive rights of litigants was obviously not addressed to such incidental effects as necessarily attend the adoption of the prescribed new rules of procedure upon the rights of litigants who, agreeably to rules of practice and procedure, have been brought before a court authorized to determine their rights. The fact that the application of Rule 4(f) will operate to subject petitioner's rights to adjudication by the district court for northern Mississippi will undoubtedly affect those rights. But it does not operate to abridge, enlarge or modify the rules of decision by which that court will adjudicate its rights.

Thus were there no conflicting state procedure, Rule 4(d)(1) would clearly control. . . . However, respondent, focusing on the contrary Massachusetts rule, calls to the Court's attention another line of cases, a line which — like the Federal Rules — had its birth in 1938. *Erie R. Co. v. Tompkins*, overruling *Swift v. Tyson*, held that federal courts sitting in diversity cases, when deciding questions of "substantive" law, are bound by state court decisions as well as state statutes. The broad command of *Erie* was therefore identical to that of the Enabling Act: federal courts are to apply state substantive law and federal procedural law. However, as subsequent cases sharpened the distinction between substance and procedure, the line of cases following *Erie* diverged markedly from the line construing the Enabling Act.

. . . Respondent . . . suggests that the *Erie* doctrine acts as a check on the Federal Rules of Civil Procedure, that despite the clear command of Rule 4(d)(1), *Erie* and its progeny demand the application of the Massachusetts rule. Reduced to essentials, the argument is: (1) *Erie* . . . demands that federal courts apply state law whenever application of federal law in its stead will alter the outcome of the case. (2) In this case, a determination that the Massachusetts service requirements obtain will result in immediate victory for respondent. If, on the other hand, it should be held that Rule 4(d)(1) is applicable, the litigation will continue, with possible victory for petitioner. (3) Therefore, *Erie* demands application of the Massachusetts rule. The syllogism possesses an appealing simplicity, but is for several reasons invalid.

In the first place, it is doubtful that, even if there were no Federal Rule making it clear that in-hand service is not required in diversity actions, the *Erie* rule would have obligated the District Court to follow the Massachusetts procedure. "Outcome-determination" analysis was never intended to serve as a talisman. *Byrd v. Blue Ridge Rural Elec. Cooperative*, 356 U.S. 525. Indeed, the message of

Guaranty Trust v. York itself is that choices between state and federal law are to be made not by application of any automatic, "litmus paper" criterion, but rather by reference to the policies underlying the *Erie* rule.

The *Erie* rule is rooted in part in a realization that it would be unfair for the character of result of a litigation materially to differ because the suit had been brought in a federal court. . . . The decision was also in part a reaction to the practice of "forum-shopping" which had grown up in response to the rule of *Swift v. Tyson.* That the *York* test was an attempt to effectuate these policies is demonstrated by the fact that the opinion framed the inquiry in terms of "substantial" variations between state and federal litigation. Not only are nonsubstantial, or trivial, variations not likely to raise the sort of equal protection problems which troubled the Court in *Erie,* they are also unlikely to influence the choice of a forum. The "outcome-determination" test therefore cannot be read without reference to the twin aims of the *Erie* rule: discouragement of forum-shopping and avoidance of inequitable administration of the laws.[9]

The difference between the conclusion that the Massachusetts rule is applicable, and the conclusion that it is not, is of course at this point "outcome-determinative" in the sense that if we hold the state rule to apply, respondent prevails, whereas if we hold that Rule 4(d)(1) governs, the litigation will continue. But in this sense every procedural variation is "outcome-determinative." . . . Though choice of the federal or state rule will at this point have a marked effect upon the outcome of the litigation, the difference between the two rules would be of scant, if any, relevance to the choice of a forum. Petitioner, in choosing her forum, was not presented with a situation where application of the state rule would wholly bar recovery; rather, adherence to the state rule would have resulted only in altering the way in which process was served. Moreover, it is difficult to argue that permitting service of defendant's wife to take the place of inhand service of defendant himself alters the mode of enforcement of state-created rights in a fashion sufficiently "substantial" to raise the sort of equal protection problems to which the *Erie* opinion alluded.

There is, however, a more fundamental flaw in respondent's syllogism: the incorrect assumption that the rule of *Erie R. Co. v. Tompkins* constitutes the appropriate test of the validity and therefore the applicability of a Federal Rule of Civil Procedure. The *Erie* rule has never been invoked to void a Federal Rule. It is true

9. The Court of Appeals seemed to frame the inquiry in terms of how "important" §9 is to the State. In support of its suggestion that §9 serves some interest the State regards as vital to its citizens, the court noted that something like §9 has been on the books in Massachusetts a long time, that §9 has been amended a number of times and that §9 is designed to make sure that executors receive actual notice. The apparent lack of relation among these three observations is not surprising, because it is not clear to what sort of question the Court of Appeals was addressing itself. One cannot meaningfully ask how important something is without first asking "important for what purpose?" *Erie* and its progeny make clear that when a federal court sitting in a diversity case is faced with a question of whether or not to apply state law, the importance of a state rule is indeed relevant, but only in the context of asking whether application of the rule would make so important a difference to the character or result of the litigation that failure to enforce it would unfairly discriminate against citizens of the forum State, or whether application of the rule would have so important an effect upon the fortunes of one or both of the litigants that failure to enforce it would be likely to cause a plaintiff to choose the federal court.

that there have been cases where this Court has held applicable a state rule in the face of an argument that the situation was governed by one of the Federal Rules. But the holding of each such case was not that *Erie* commanded displacement of a Federal Rule by an inconsistent state rule, but rather that the scope of the Federal Rule was not as broad as the losing party urged, and therefore, there being no Federal Rule which covered the point in dispute, *Erie* commanded the enforcement of state law.

Respondent contends in the first place that the charge was correct because of the fact that Rule 8(c) of the Rules of Civil Procedure makes contributory negligence an affirmative defense. We do not agree. Rule 8(c) covers only the manner of pleading. The question of the burden of establishing contributory negligence is a question of local law which federal courts in diversity of citizenship cases. *Palmer v. Hoffman*, 318 U.S. 109, 117.

(Here, of course, the clash is unavoidable; Rule 4(d)(1) says—implicitly, but with unmistakable clarity—that inhand service is not required in federal courts.) At the same time, in cases adjudicating the validity of Federal Rules, we have not applied the *York* rule or other refinements of *Erie*, but have to this day continued to decide questions concerning the scope of the Enabling Act and the constitutionality of specific Federal Rules in light of the distinction set forth in *Sibbach*.

Nor has the development of two separate lines of cases been inadvertent. The line between "substance" and "procedure" shifts as the legal context changes. . . . It is true that both the Enabling Act and the *Erie* rule say, roughly, that federal courts are to apply state "substantive" law and federal "procedural" law, but from that it need not follow that the tests are identical. For they were designed to control very different sorts of decisions. When a situation is covered by one of the Federal Rules, the question facing the court is a far cry from the typical, relatively unguided *Erie* Choice: the court has been instructed to apply the Federal Rule, and can refuse to do so only if the Advisory Committee, this Court, and Congress erred in their prima facie judgment that the Rule in question transgresses neither the terms of the Enabling Act nor constitutional restrictions.

We are reminded by the *Erie* opinion that neither Congress nor the federal courts can, under the guise of formulating rules of decision for federal courts, fashion rules which are not supported by a grant of federal authority contained in Article I or some other section of the Constitution; in such areas state law must govern because there can be no other law. But the opinion in *Erie*, which involved no Federal Rule and dealt with a question which was "substantive" in every traditional sense (whether the railroad owed a duty of care to Tompkins as a trespasser or a licensee), surely neither said nor implied that measures like Rule 4(d)(1) are unconstitutional. For the constitutional provision for a federal court system (augmented by the Necessary and Proper Clause) carries with it congressional power to make rules governing the practice and pleading in those courts, which in turn includes a power to regulate matters which, though falling within the uncertain area between substance and procedure, are rationally capable of classification as either. . . . Neither *Guaranty Trust v. York* nor the cases following it ever suggested that the rule there laid down for coping with situations where no Federal Rule applies is coextensive with the limitation on Congress to which *Erie* had adverted. . . .

"One of the shaping purposes of the Federal Rules is to bring about uniformity in the federal courts by getting away from local rules. This is especially true of matters which relate to the administration of legal proceedings, an area in which federal courts have traditionally exerted strong inherent power, completely aside from the powers Congress expressly conferred in the Rules. . . ."

Erie and its offspring cast no doubt on the long-recognized power of Congress to prescribe housekeeping rules for federal courts even though some of those rules will inevitably differ from comparable state rules. . . . Thus, though a court, in measuring a Federal Rule against the standards contained in the Enabling Act and the Constitution, need not wholly blind itself to the degree to which the Rule makes the character and result of the federal litigation stray from the course it would follow in state courts, *Sibbach v. Wilson & Co.*, supra, 312 U.S. at 13-14, it cannot be forgotten that the *Erie* rule, and the guidelines suggested in *York*, were created to serve another purpose altogether. To hold that a Federal Rule of Civil Procedure must cease to function whenever it alters the mode of enforcing state-created rights would be to disembowel either the Constitution's grant of power over federal procedure or Congress' attempt to exercise that power in the Enabling Act. Rule 4(d)(1) is valid and controls the instant case.

Reversed.

Justice BLACK concurs in the result.

Justice HARLAN, concurring.

. . . *Erie* was something more than an opinion which worried about "forum-shopping and avoidance of inequitable administration of the laws," although to be sure these were important elements of the decision. I have always regarded that decision as one of the modern cornerstones of our federalism, expressing policies that profoundly touch the allocation of judicial power between the state and federal systems. *Erie* recognized that there should not be two conflicting systems of law controlling the primary activity of citizens, for such alternative governing authority must necessarily give rise to a debilitating uncertainty in the planning of everyday affairs. And it recognized that the scheme of our Constitution envisions an allocation of law-making functions between state and federal legislative processes which is undercut if the federal judiciary can make substantive law affecting state affairs beyond the bounds of congressional legislative powers in this regard. . . .

. . . To my mind the proper line of approach in determining whether to apply a state or a federal rule, whether "substantive" or "procedural," is to stay close to basic principles by inquiring if the choice of rule would substantially affect those primary decisions respecting human conduct which our constitutional system leaves to state regulation. If so, *Erie* and the Constitution require that the state rule prevail, even in the face of a conflicting federal rule. . . .

So long as a reasonable man could characterize any duly adopted federal rule as "procedural," the Court, unless I misapprehend what is said, would have it apply no matter how seriously it frustrated a State's substantive regulation of the primary conduct and affairs of its citizens. Since the members of the Advisory Committee, the Judicial Conference, and this Court who formulated the Federal Rules are presumably reasonable men, it follows that the integrity of the Federal Rules is absolute. Whereas the unadulterated outcome and forum-shopping tests may err too far toward honoring state rules, I submit that the Court's "arguably procedural, ergo constitutional" test moves too fast and far in the other direction. . . .

It remains to apply what has been said to the present case. . . . The Massachusetts rule provides that an executor need not answer suits unless in-hand service was made upon him or notice of the action was filed in the proper registry of probate within one year of his giving bond. The evident intent of this statute is to permit an executor to distribute the estate which he is administering without fear that further liabilities may be outstanding for which he could be held personally liable. If the Federal District Court in Massachusetts applies Rule 4(d)(1) of the Federal Rules of Civil Procedure instead of the Massachusetts service rule, . . . the effect would not be substantial. It would mean simply that an executor would have to check at his own house or the federal courthouse as well as the registry of probate before he could distribute the estate with impunity. As this does not seem enough to give rise to any real impingement on the vitality of the state policy which the Massachusetts rule is intended to serve, I concur in the judgment of the Court.

Notes on
HANNA v. PLUMER

1. The "sorting" component of *Hanna*'s instructions on how to resolve a clash between state and federal law is clear: If the federal law is court-made, then the choice between state and federal law is governed by the concerns expressed by the *Erie* line of cases. By contrast, where the federal law is a Federal Rule of Civil Procedure, then the choice is controlled by a separate line of decisions that have interpreted the parameters of the Rules Enabling Act. Is this distinction appropriate? What about *Erie's* concern with the mandate of the Rules of Decision Act? Why doesn't that apply in this situation? And what of *Erie's* concern with inequality between state and federal court results? In making its ruling, does the *Hanna* Court overemphasize the importance of the Federal Rules of Civil Procedures and go too far to ensure that district courts uphold the Rules as valid in all federal court actions? Do you agree with Justice Harlan that the Court gave too little attention to the constitutional implications of applying the Federal Rules to displace state law?

2. In the Rules Enabling Act, 28 U.S.C. §2072, Congress delegated to the Supreme Court of the United States its authority to promulgate "rules of practice and procedure" for federal courts. The Supreme Court in turn works with an advisory committee that proposes rules that may ultimately become official if Congress does not object to them. (Aside from the Federal

Rules of Civil Procedure, the Rules Enabling Act also authorizes the Supreme Court to create other procedural rules, such as the Federal Rules of Appellate Procedure and the Federal Rules of Evidence.) The second sentence of the Rules Enabling Act, §2072(b), does, however, restrict the power delegated to the Supreme Court. That sentence mandates that Rules promulgated under its authority "shall not abridge, enlarge or modify any substantive right." The *Sibbach* test mentioned in *Hanna*, purports to give meaning to this restriction, requiring a court to ask whether the Federal Rule "really regulates procedure — the judicial process for enforcing rights and duties recognized by substantive law and for justly administering remedy and redress for disregard or infraction of them." *Sibbach v. Wilson*, 312 U.S. 1, 14 (1941). This test, it turns out, is generally quite easy to satisfy — and even allows Federal Rules to slip through that have either the purpose or the effect of controlling out-of-court conduct. *See, e.g.*, John Hart Ely, *The Irrepressible Myth of* Erie, 87 HARV. L. REV. 693, 713-738 (1974) (arguing that the *Sibbach* test is insufficiently rigorous and insufficiently protective of competing state rules). Subsequent cases reviewed below have debated and expanded on the test.

3. What do you make of the *Hanna* Court's dictum regarding clashes between a state law and federal court-made law? Many now call that a Rules of Decision Act case (as opposed to a Rules Enabling Act case, which involves a clash between a state law and a Federal Rule of Civil Procedure, or other type of federal rule promulgated pursuant to the Rules Enabling Act). In a Rules of Decision Act case, the *Hanna* Court suggested, the district court must consider the federal court-made rule in light of "the aims of the *Erie* rule: discouragement of forum-shopping and avoidance of inequitable administration of the laws." In footnote 9, the Supreme Court suggested that a federal court should ask "whether application of the rule would make so important a difference to the character or result of the litigation that failure to enforce it would unfairly discriminate against citizens of the forum State, or whether application of the rule would have so important an effect upon the fortunes of one or both of the litigants that failure to enforce it would be likely to cause a plaintiff to choose the federal court." Does this strike you as a reasonable accommodation of *Erie's* policy concerns? The Supreme Court seeks to embrace the concern with differing state and federal outcomes, but moves the point of reference back to a plaintiff choosing whether to file in state or federal court. In this way, the Court avoids the problem under the *Guaranty Trust* outcome determination test — in which all disputes are outcome determinative as the parties become intent on fighting the choice of law issue later in the litigation.

4. Even though *Hanna* made it easy for a court to uphold the validity of a Federal Rule of Civil Procedure, the Court did not eliminate the possibility that a court might construe a Federal Rule in such a way as to operate side by side with a state rule. Although the Court concluded that a clash between the state law and Federal Rule was unavoidable in *Hanna*, this is not always the

case. In a manner akin to the restrained and moderate interpretation (in governmental interest analysis) or the presumption against preemption (in federal preemption theory), the Supreme Court has made clear that a district court should apply the *Hanna* Rules Enabling Act analysis only after concluding that there is a "direct collision" between the Federal Rule and state law. *Walker v. Armco Steel Corp.*, 446 U.S. 740, 749 (1980). In a subsequent case, *Burlington Northern R.R. v. Woods*, 480 U.S. 1 (1987), the Supreme Court reiterated this approach to interpretation, but liberally interpreted the scope of a Federal Rule of Appellate Procedure to displace a state law that imposed a penalty for unsuccessful defendant-appellants.

After that, the Court discussed the "direct collision" language in a case involving the federal venue transfer statute, 28 U.S.C. §1404(a). In *Stewart Org., Inc. v. Ricoh*, 487 U.S. 22 (1988), the Supreme Court allowed the federal statute to displace a state law policy against forum selection clauses. The *Stewart* Court explained that the "direct collision" test is not meant to require state and federal law to be perfectly coextensive for federal law to displace state law. Where a federal statute is at issue, the Court continued, it should apply if it is constitutional and is "sufficiently broad" to cover the disputed issue.

5. *Hanna*, *Walker*, and *Woods* are not the last word on how to handle clashes between Federal Rules of Civil Procedure and state laws. The Supreme Court later decided important Federal Rules issues respecting judgments, *Semtek Int'l Inc. v. Lockheed Martin Corp.*, 531 U.S. 497 (2001), and respecting class actions, *Shady Grove Orthopedic v. Allstate Ins. Co.*, 130 S. Ct. 1431 (2010). *Semtek* and *Shady Grove* are set forth below. First, however, you may want to try your hand on a problem to test what you learned from *Hanna*.

PROBLEM 3-8: THE MEASURE OF FRAUD DAMAGES

Penelope contracted with Conor, and later concluded that he had defrauded her. No federal law governed the contract. The suit fell into the parameters for diversity of citizenship jurisdiction since Penelope is from a different state than Conor and the amount in controversy is well in excess of $75,000. Penelope has filed her fraud claim in federal court. An issue arose about whether state or federal law governs how to calculate damages. In decisional law, federal courts have devised a benefit-of-the-bargain measure for fraud damages. The relevant state common law provides for an out-of-pocket measure for fraud damages. As applied to Penelope and Conor's suit, the benefit-of-the-bargain measure would yield greater damages. Penelope is out of pocket approximately $180,000, which she spent in reliance on the alleged fraud. Had the subject matter of the contract been as Conor represented, however, Penelope expected to receive $340,000. Thus, $340,000 represents the benefit of the bargain.

Which law should the federal court apply — state or federal law?

Semtek Int'l Inc. v. Lockheed Martin Corp.

531 U.S. 497 (2001)

Justice SCALIA delivered the opinion of the Court.

This case presents the question whether the claim-preclusive effect of a federal judgment dismissing a diversity action on statute-of-limitations grounds is determined by the law of the State in which the federal court sits.

I

[Petitioner Semtek sued respondent Lockheed in California state court for breach of contract and various business torts. Lockheed removed the case to the United States District Court for the Central District of California on the basis of diversity of citizenship. Relying on California's two-year statute of limitations, the district court dismissed petitioner's claims "in [their] entirety on the merits and with prejudice." Semtek appealed to the Court of Appeals for the Ninth Circuit, which affirmed. Semtek next brought the same action in state court in Maryland, which had a three-year statute of limitations. Lockheed responded by filing for a federal court injunction of the Maryland suit, which was denied. Lockheed nonetheless got relief from the Maryland state court, which dismissed the suit on res judicata grounds. Semtek appealed this order, arguing that a California state court would not have accorded claim preclusive effect to a statute of limitations dismissal by a California court. The Maryland Court of Special Appeals affirmed. The Maryland court held that regardless of whether California would have accorded claim preclusive effect to a statute of limitations dismissal, the California district court's original dismissal had the effect of barring the Maryland complaint because the res judicata effect of federal diversity judgments is prescribed by federal law, under which the earlier dismissal was on the merits and claim preclusive.]

II

Petitioner contends that the outcome of this case is controlled by *Dupasseur v. Rochereau*, 21 Wall. 130, 135 (1874), which held that the res judicata effect of a federal diversity judgment "is such as would belong to judgments of the State courts rendered under similar circumstances," and may not be accorded any "higher sanctity or effect." Since, petitioner argues, the dismissal of an action on statute-of-limitations grounds by a California state court would not be claim preclusive, it follows that the similar dismissal of this diversity action by the California federal court cannot be claim preclusive. While we agree that this would be the result demanded by *Dupasseur*, the case is not dispositive because it was decided under the Conformity Act of 1872, 17 Stat. 196, which required federal courts to apply the procedural law of the forum State in nonequity cases. That arguably affected the outcome of [*Dupasseur*]. . . .

Respondent, for its part, contends that the outcome of this case is controlled by Federal Rule of Civil Procedure 41(b), which provides as follows:

> Involuntary Dismissal: Effect Thereof. For failure of the plaintiff to prosecute or to comply with these rules or any order of court, a defendant may move for dismissal of an action or of any claim against the defendant. Unless the court in its order for dismissal otherwise specifies, a dismissal under this subdivision and any dismissal not provided for in this rule, other than a dismissal for lack of jurisdiction, for improper venue, or for failure to join a party under Rule 19, operates as an adjudication upon the merits.

Since the dismissal here did not "otherwise specif[y]" (indeed, it specifically stated that it *was* "on the merits"), and did not pertain to the excepted subjects of jurisdiction, venue, or joinder, it follows, respondent contends, that the dismissal "is entitled to claim preclusive effect."

Implicit in this reasoning is the unstated minor premise that all judgments denominated "on the merits" are entitled to claim-preclusive effect. That premise is not necessarily valid. The original connotation of an "on the merits" adjudication is one that actually "pass[es] directly on the substance of [a particular] claim" before the court. That connotation remains common to every jurisdiction of which we are aware. And it is, we think, the meaning intended in those many statements to the effect that a judgment "on the merits" triggers the doctrine of res judicata or claim preclusion. *See, e.g., Parklane Hosiery Co. v. Shore*, 439 U.S. 322, 326, n.5 (1979) ("Under the doctrine of res judicata, a judgment on the merits in a prior suit bars a second suit involving the same parties or their privies based on the same cause of action").

But over the years the meaning of the term "judgment on the merits" "has gradually undergone change," and it has come to be applied to some judgments (such as the one involved here) that do *not* pass upon the substantive merits of a claim and hence do *not* (in many jurisdictions) entail claim-preclusive effect. . . .

In short, it is no longer true that a judgment "on the merits" is necessarily a judgment entitled to claim-preclusive effect; and there are a number of reasons for believing that the phrase "adjudication upon the merits" does not bear that meaning in Rule 41(b). To begin with, Rule 41(b) sets forth nothing more than a default rule for determining the import of a dismissal (a dismissal is "upon the merits," with the three stated exceptions, unless the court "otherwise specifies"). This would be a highly peculiar context in which to announce a federally prescribed rule on the complex question of claim preclusion, saying in effect, "All federal dismissals (with three specified exceptions) preclude suit elsewhere, unless the court otherwise specifies."

And even apart from the purely default character of Rule 41(b), it would be peculiar to find a rule governing the effect that must be accorded federal judgments by other courts ensconced in rules governing the internal procedures of the rendering court itself. Indeed, such a rule would arguably violate the jurisdictional limitation of the Rules Enabling Act: that the Rules "shall not abridge, enlarge or modify any substantive right," 28 U.S.C. §2072(b). In the present case, for example, if California law left petitioner free to sue on this claim in Maryland even after the California statute of limitations had expired, the federal court's extinguishment of that right (through Rule 41(b)'s mandated claim-preclusive effect of its judgment) would seem to violate this limitation.

Moreover, as so interpreted, the Rule would in many cases violate the federalism principle of *Erie R. Co. v. Tompkins*, 304 U.S. 64, 78-80 (1938) by engendering "'substantial' variations [in outcomes] between state and federal litigation" which would "[l]ikely . . . influence the choice of a forum," *Hanna v. Plumer*, 380 U.S. 460, 467-468 (1965). With regard to the claim-preclusion issue involved in the present case, for example, the traditional rule is that expiration of the applicable statute of limitations merely bars the remedy and does not extinguish the substantive right, so that dismissal on that ground does not have claim-preclusive effect in other jurisdictions with longer, unexpired limitations periods. Out-of-state defendants sued on stale claims in California and in other States adhering to this traditional rule would systematically remove state-law suits brought against them to federal court—where, unless otherwise specified, a statute-of-limitations dismissal would bar suit everywhere. . . .

We think the key to a more reasonable interpretation of the meaning of "operates as an adjudication upon the merits" in Rule 41(b) is to be found in Rule 41(a), which, in discussing the effect of voluntary dismissal by the plaintiff, makes clear that an "adjudication upon the merits" is the opposite of a "dismissal without prejudice":

> Unless otherwise stated in the notice of dismissal or stipulation, the dismissal is without prejudice, except that a notice of dismissal operates as an adjudication upon the merits when filed by a plaintiff who has once dismissed in any court of the United States or of any state an action based on or including the same claim.

. . . The primary meaning of "dismissal without prejudice," we think, is dismissal without barring the plaintiff from returning later, to the same court, with the same underlying claim. That will also ordinarily (though not always) have the consequence of not barring the claim from *other* courts, but its primary meaning relates to the dismissing court itself. . . .

We think, then, that the effect of the "adjudication upon the merits" default provision of Rule 41(b)—and, presumably, of the explicit order in the present case that used the language of that default provision—is simply that, unlike a dismissal "without prejudice," the dismissal in the present case barred refiling of the same claim in the United States District Court for the Central District of California. That is undoubtedly a necessary condition, but it is not a sufficient one, for claim-preclusive effect in other courts.[2]

III

Having concluded that the claim-preclusive effect, in Maryland, of this California federal diversity judgment is dictated neither by *Dupasseur v. Rochereau*,

---

2. We do not decide whether, in a diversity case, a federal court's "dismissal upon the merits" (in the sense we have described), under circumstances where a state court would decree only a "dismissal without prejudice," abridges a "substantive right" and thus exceeds the authorization of the Rules Enabling Act. We think the situation will present itself more rarely than would the arguable violation of the Act that would ensue from interpreting Rule 41(b) as a rule of claim preclusion; and if it is a violation, can be more easily dealt with on direct appeal.

as petitioner contends, nor by Rule 41(b), as respondent contends, we turn to consideration of what determines the issue. Neither the Full Faith and Credit Clause, U.S. Const., Art. IV, §1, nor the full faith and credit statute, 28 U.S.C. §1738, addresses the question. By their terms they govern the effects to be given only to state-court judgments (and, in the case of the statute, to judgments by courts of territories and possessions). And no other federal textual provision, neither of the Constitution nor of any statute, addresses the claim-preclusive effect of a judgment in a federal diversity action.

It is also true, however, that no federal textual provision addresses the claim-preclusive effect of a federal-court judgment in a federal-question case, yet we have long held that States cannot give those judgments merely whatever effect they would give their own judgments, but must accord them the effect that this Court prescribes. The reasoning of that line of cases suggests, moreover, that even when States are allowed to give federal judgments (notably, judgments in diversity cases) no more than the effect accorded to state judgments, that disposition is by direction of *this* Court, which has the last word on the claim-preclusive effect of *all* federal judgments. . . . In short, federal common law governs the claim-preclusive effect of a dismissal by a federal court sitting in diversity.

It is left to us, then, to determine the appropriate federal rule. And despite the sea change that has occurred in the background law since *Dupasseur* was decided . . . we think the result decreed by *Dupasseur* continues to be correct for diversity cases. Since state, rather than federal, substantive law is at issue there is no need for a uniform federal rule. And indeed, nationwide uniformity in the substance of the matter is better served by having the same claim-preclusive rule (the state rule) apply whether the dismissal has been ordered by a state or a federal court. This is, it seems to us, a classic case for adopting, as the federally prescribed rule of decision, the law that would be applied by state courts in the State in which the federal diversity court sits. As we have alluded to above, any other rule would produce the sort of "forum-shopping . . . and . . . inequitable administration of the laws" that *Erie* seeks to avoid, *Hanna*, 380 U.S., at 468, since filing in, or removing to, federal court would be encouraged by the divergent effects that the litigants would anticipate from likely grounds of dismissal.

This federal reference to state law will not obtain, of course, in situations in which the state law is incompatible with federal interests. If, for example, state law did not accord claim-preclusive effect to dismissals for willful violation of discovery orders, federal courts' interest in the integrity of their own processes might justify a contrary federal rule. No such conflict with potential federal interests exists in the present case. Dismissal of this state cause of action was decreed by the California federal court only because the California statute of limitations so required; and there is no conceivable federal interest in giving that time bar more effect in other courts than the California courts themselves would impose.

. . .

Because the claim-preclusive effect of the California federal court's dismissal "upon the merits" of petitioner's action on statute-of-limitations grounds is governed by a federal rule that in turn incorporates California's law of claim preclusion (the content of which we do not pass upon today), the Maryland Court of

Special Appeals erred in holding that the dismissal necessarily precluded the bringing of this action in the Maryland courts. . . .

Notes on
SEMTEK

1. It is not surprising that the *Semtek* opinion has many twists. The problem of interjurisdictional preclusion has baffled courts for many years now, and the law is still unsettled. Interjurisdictional preclusion issues arise when a judgment rendered by the first forum where suit is filed, often called the F1, becomes a point of contention in subsequent litigation in another forum, the F2. In such circumstances, questions arise as to what law governs the preclusive effect of the F1 judgment. Courts follow the general rule that the F1's preclusion law governs. Was this followed by the *Semtek* Court? On the one hand, one might say that the *Semtek* Court followed this rule, since the Court concluded that federal common law should govern the preclusion issue and the F1 was a federal forum. On the other hand, the *Semtek* Court deviated from the general rule to the extent that it determined that the content of the federal law should be the state law where the F1 federal court sat. Are the "the federalism principle of *Erie*" and the policies of diversity of citizenship jurisdiction so strong as to overcome the usual orientation of deferring to a forum court's preference for how to deal with its judgments? For a discussion of how *Semtek* compares with prior Supreme Court precedent, see Stephen B. Burbank, Semtek, *Forum Shopping, and Federal Common Law*, 77 NOTRE DAME L. REV. 1027, 1048-1054 (2002); Earl C. Dudley Jr. & George Rutherglen, *Deforming the Federal Rules: An Essay on What's Wrong with the Recent* Erie *Decisions*, 92 VA. L. REV. 707, 720-727 (2006); Patrick Woolley, *The Sources of Federal Preclusion Law After* Semtek, 72 U. CIN. L. REV. 527, 531-572 (2003). Chapter 4 explores other issues pertaining to interjurisdictional preclusion both in the international context as well as in the context of United States federalism.

2. Compare the Court's reading of the Federal Rule of Civil Procedure in *Semtek* with the Court's earlier treatment of Federal Rules. On the one hand, the *Semtek* Court's reading of Rule 41 seems so strained as to clash with *Hanna*'s orientation toward preserving and upholding the Federal Rules in that case. *See also Burlington Northern R.R. v. Woods*, 480 U.S. 1 (1987) (interpreting a Federal Rule of Appellate Procedure liberally to displace state law). On the other hand, the *Semtek* Court's approach may be read as consistent with the Court's narrow reading of the federal rule at issue in *Walker v. Armco Steel Corp.*, 446 U.S. 740, 750 (1980). Does this suggest that the approach to interpreting Federal Rules changes like a chameleon to reflect background concerns unrelated to the interpretive process itself? Compare *Semtek*'s interpretive approach with that followed in the next case, *Shady Grove Orthopedics v. Allstate Ins. Co.*, 130 S. Ct. 1431 (2010).

3. The *Semtek* Court's approach of using state law to give content to federal common law is reflected in other decisions. In some, the Court explicitly admits to pursing this strategy for developing federal common law. In other cases, the Court's integration of state and federal law is implicit. From a federalism point of view, is this "hybrid lawmaking" a good idea? The section on hybrid law presented later in this chapter explores this question.

4. The *Semtek* Court made much of the argument that its ultimate holding was mandated by the concern reflected in *Erie* and *Hanna* of avoiding forum shopping. Specifically, the *Semtek* Court reasoned that it would avoid forum shopping by making the content of the "federally prescribed rule of decision" the same as the "law that would be applied in the State in which the federal diversity court" sat. Statutes of limitation are not only often case dispositive, but they vary considerably from state to state. Does the *Semtek* Court's decision to jettison a uniform federal rule in favor of the forum state rule really avoid forum shopping? Isn't the Court encouraging one type of forum shopping (one state versus another state) under the guise of discouraging another type of forum shopping (state court versus federal court)? Do good policy reasons exist for doing that?

Shady Grove Orthopedic Assocs., P.A. v. Allstate Ins. Co.

130 S. Ct. 1431 (2010)

Justice SCALIA announced the judgment of the Court and delivered the opinion of the Court with respect to Parts I and II-A, an opinion with respect to Parts II-B and II-D, in which THE CHIEF JUSTICE, Justice THOMAS, and Justice SOTOMAYOR join, and an opinion with respect to Part II-C, in which THE CHIEF JUSTICE and Justice THOMAS join.

New York law prohibits class actions in suits seeking penalties or statutory minimum damages.[1] We consider whether this precludes a federal district

---

1. N.Y. Civ. Prac. Law Ann. §901 (West 2006) provides:

(a) One or more members of a class may sue or be sued as representative parties on behalf of all if:
1. the class is so numerous that joinder of all members, whether otherwise required or permitted, is impracticable;
2. there are questions of law or fact common to the class which predominate over any questions affecting only individual members;
3. the claims or defenses of the representative parties are typical of the claims or defenses of the class;
4. the representative parties will fairly and adequately protect the interests of the class; and
5. a class action is superior to other available methods for the fair and efficient adjudication of the controversy.
(b) Unless a statute creating or imposing a penalty, or a minimum measure of recovery specifically authorizes the recovery thereof in a class action, an action to recover a penalty, or minimum measure of recovery created or imposed by statute may not be maintained as a class action.

court sitting in diversity from entertaining a class action under Federal Rule of Civil Procedure 23.[2]

Subsection (b) says that "[a] class action may be maintained if Rule 23(a) is satisfied and if" the suit falls into one of three described categories (irrelevant for present purposes).

I

[Petitioner Shady Grove Orthopedic Associates, P.A., provided medical care to an individual, who assigned to Shady Grove her insurance benefits under an Allstate Insurance policy. Allstate paid, but not on time, refusing to pay the interest on the overdue benefits. Shady Grove filed a diversity action in federal court for the unpaid interest, seeking relief on behalf of itself and a class of all others to whom Allstate owed interest. The District Court dismissed, reasoning that N.Y. Civ. Prac. Law Ann. §901(b) precluded the suit. The Second Circuit affirmed, holding that Federal Rule 23 did not conflict with §901(b).]

II

... We must first determine whether Rule 23 answers the question in dispute. *Burlington Northern R.R. Co. v. Woods*, 480 U.S. 1, 4-5 (1987). If it does, it governs — New York's law notwithstanding — unless it exceeds statutory authorization or Congress's rulemaking power. We do not wade into *Erie*'s murky waters unless the federal rule is inapplicable or invalid.

A

... Rule 23 provides a one-size-fits-all formula for deciding the class-action question. Because §901(b) attempts to answer the same question — *i.e.*, it states that Shady Grove's suit "may *not* be maintained as a class action" (emphasis added) because of the relief it seeks — it cannot apply in diversity suits unless Rule 23 is ultra vires.

The Second Circuit believed that §901(b) and Rule 23 do not conflict because they address different issues. Rule 23, it said, concerns only the criteria for determining whether a given class can and should be certified; section 901(b), on the other hand, addresses an antecedent question: whether the particular type of claim is eligible for class treatment in the first place — a

---

2. Rule 23(a) provides:

(a) Prerequisites. One or more members of a class may sue or be sued as representative parties on behalf of all members only if:
    (1) the class is so numerous that joinder of all members is impracticable;
    (2) there are questions of law or fact common to the class;
    (3) the claims or defenses of the representative parties are typical of the claims or defenses of the class; and
    (4) the representative parties will fairly and adequately protect the interests of the class.

question on which Rule 23 is silent. . . . We disagree. . . . [T]he line between eligibility and certifiability is entirely artificial. Both are preconditions for maintaining a class action. . . . There is no reason . . . to read Rule 23 as addressing only whether claims made eligible for class treatment by some *other* law should be certified as class actions.

. . . The dissent all but admits that the literal terms of §901(b) address the same subject as Rule 23 — *i.e.*, whether a class action may be maintained — but insists [the purpose of §901(b)] is to restrict only remedies. . . . Unlike Rule 23, designed to further procedural fairness and efficiency, §901(b) (we are told) "responds to an entirely different concern": the fear that allowing statutory damages to be awarded on a class-wide basis would "produce overkill." The dissent reaches this conclusion on the basis of (1) constituent concern recorded in the law's bill jacket; (2) a commentary suggesting that the Legislature "apparently fear[ed]" that combining class actions and statutory penalties "could result in annihilating punishment of the defendant," (3) a remark by the Governor in his signing statement that §901(b) "'provides a controlled remedy,'" and (4) a state court's statement that the final text of §901(b) "'was the result of a compromise among competing interests.'"

This evidence of the New York Legislature's purpose is pretty sparse. But even accepting the dissent's account of the Legislature's objective at face value, it cannot override the statute's clear text. Even if its aim is to restrict the remedy a plaintiff can obtain, §901(b) achieves that end by limiting a plaintiff's power to maintain a class action. . . .

The dissent's approach of determining whether state and federal rules conflict based on the subjective intentions of the state legislature is an enterprise destined to produce "confusion worse confounded." It would mean, to begin with, that one State's statute could survive preemption (and accordingly affect the procedures in federal court) while another State's identical law would not, merely because its authors had different aspirations. It would also mean that district courts would have to discern, in every diversity case, the purpose behind any putatively preempted state procedural rule, even if its text squarely conflicts with federal law. That task will often prove arduous. Many laws further more than one aim, and the aim of others may be impossible to discern. Moreover, to the extent the dissent's purpose-driven approach depends on its characterization of §901(b)'s aims as substantive, it would apply to many state rules ostensibly addressed to procedure. . . .

B

[The plurality reiterated the test for evaluating the validity of the Federal Rules: compliance with the Rules Enabling Act and the constitutional power of Congress to regulate federal court procedure. The plurality acknowledged that in applying the Rules Enabling Act test that ensures that rules do not abridge the parties' substantive rights, "we have rejected every statutory challenge to a Federal Rule that has come before us," even though each of the rules challenged "had some practical effect on the parties' rights."]

Allstate contends that the authorization of class actions is not substantively neutral: Allowing Shady Grove to sue on behalf of a class "transform[s] [the] dispute over a five *hundred* dollar penalty into a dispute over a five *million* dollar penalty." Allstate's aggregate liability, however, does not depend on whether the suit proceeds as a class action. Each of the 1,000-plus members of the putative class could (as Allstate acknowledges) bring a freestanding suit asserting his individual claim. It is undoubtedly true that some plaintiffs who would not bring individual suits for the relatively small sums involved will choose to join a class action. That has no bearing, however, on Allstate's or the plaintiffs' legal rights. . . .

Allstate argues that Rule 23 violates §2072(b) because the state law it displaces, §901(b), creates a right that the Federal Rule abridges — namely, a "substantive right . . . not to be subjected to aggregated class-action liability" in a single suit. . . . As we have said, the *consequence* of excluding certain class actions may be to cap the damages a defendant can face in a single suit, but the law itself alters only procedure. In that respect, §901(b) is no different from a state law forbidding simple joinder. As a fallback argument, Allstate argues that even if §901(b) is a procedural provision, it was enacted "for *substantive reasons*." Its end was not to improve "the conduct of the litigation process itself" but to alter "the outcome of that process."

The fundamental difficulty with both these arguments is that the substantive nature of New York's law, or its substantive purpose, *makes no difference*. A Federal Rule of Procedure is not valid in some jurisdictions and invalid in others — or valid in some cases and invalid in others — depending upon whether its effect is to frustrate a state substantive law (or a state procedural law enacted for substantive purposes). . . . *Hanna* unmistakably expressed the same understanding that compliance of a Federal Rule with the Enabling Act is to be assessed by consulting the Rule itself, and not its effects in individual applications[.]

In sum, it is not the substantive or procedural nature or purpose of the affected state law that matters, but the substantive or procedural nature of the Federal Rule. . . .

C

A few words in response to the concurrence. We understand it to accept the framework we apply — which requires first, determining whether the federal and state rules can be reconciled (because they answer different questions), and second, if they cannot, determining whether the Federal Rule runs afoul of §2072(b). The concurrence agrees with us that Rule 23 and §901(b) conflict, and departs from us only with respect to the second part of the test, *i.e.*, whether application of the Federal Rule violates §2072(b). Like us, it answers no, but for a reason different from ours.

The concurrence would decide this case on the basis, not that Rule 23 is procedural, but that the state law it displaces is procedural, in the sense that it does not "function as a part of the State's definition of substantive rights and remedies." A state procedural rule is not preempted, according to the concurrence, so long as it is "so bound up with," or "sufficiently intertwined with," a substantive state-law right or remedy "that it defines the scope of that substantive right or remedy."

This analysis squarely conflicts with *Sibbach*, which established the rule we apply. The concurrence contends that *Sibbach* did not rule out its approach, but that is not so. Recognizing the impracticability of a test that turns on the idiosyncrasies of state law, *Sibbach* adopted and applied a rule with a single criterion: whether the Federal Rule "really regulates procedure." . . .

D

We must acknowledge the reality that keeping the federal-court door open to class actions that cannot proceed in state court will produce forum shopping. That is unacceptable when it comes as the consequence of judge-made rules created to fill supposed "gaps" in positive federal law. For where neither the Constitution, a treaty, nor a statute provides the rule of decision or authorizes a federal court to supply one, "state law must govern because there can be no other law. But divergence from state law, with the attendant consequence of forum shopping, is the inevitable (indeed, one might say the intended) result of a uniform system of federal procedure. Congress itself has created the possibility that the same case may follow a different course if filed in federal instead of state court. The short of the matter is that a Federal Rule governing procedure is valid whether or not it alters the outcome of the case in a way that induces forum shopping. To hold otherwise would be to "disembowel either the Constitution's grant of power over federal procedure" or Congress's exercise of it.

. . .

The judgment of the Court of Appeals is reversed, and the case is remanded for further proceedings.

[Justice Stevens's concurring opinion agreed that Federal Rule 23 and New York law clashed. Nonetheless, he disagreed with the plurality's reading of the *Sibbach*, critiquing the plurality's treatment of the validity question as oversimplistic. According to Justice Stevens, the Rules Enabling Act requires courts to consider the extent to which a Federal Rule would cause the character and result of litigation to "stray from the course it would follow in state courts." He urged that when a state chooses a traditionally procedural vehicle as a means of defining the scope of substantive rights, then federal courts should defer that choice. Justice Stevens ultimately agreed, however, that Federal Rule 23 did not violate the Rules Enabling Act.]

[Justice Ginsburg wrote a dissent in which Justices Kennedy, Breyer, and Alito joined. The thrust of her dissent urged the importance of read the Federal Rules with sensitivity to the state's goals behind its laws. Justice Ginsburg identified no conflict between New York law and Federal Rule 23. She thus concluded that the Rules of Decision Act provided the appropriate test: would applying state law "have so important an effect upon the fortunes of one or both of the litigants that failure to [apply] it would be likely to cause a plaintiff to choose the federal court"? Under this test, she would apply state law.]

Notes on
SHADY GROVE

1. Since the case lacks a majority opinion, the precedential consequence of *Shady Grove* for the *Erie* line of cases is unclear. Nonetheless, the decision is significant for highlighting the points of disagreement among the Justices and the potential practical effect on incentives for filing class actions. *See, e.g.,* Linda S. Mullenix, *Federal Class Actions: A Near-Death Experience in a Shady Grove,* 79 GEO. WASH. L. REV. 448 (2011) (discussing class action significance of the ruling).

As reviewed in Chapter 2, Congress enacted the Class Action Fairness Act (CAFA) in 2005, with a view toward expanding federal court access to state-law class actions so long as certain circumstances were present (minimal diversity, at least 100 class members, and at least $5 million in controversy). Congress concluded that providing a federal forum for such suits would check overeagerness in some state courts to certify class actions. In light of this intent, Justice Ginsburg noted in her *Shady Grove* dissent, "Congress envisioned fewer—not more—class actions overall." The result of *Shady Grove* was "ironic," in her view, given its potential for nullifying state statutes designed to restrict class actions, such as the New York statute in *Shady Grove.* As Justice Ginsburg said: "Congress surely never anticipated that CAFA would make federal courts a mecca for suits of the kind Shady Grove has launched: class actions seeking state-created penalties for claims arising under state law-claims that would be barred from class treatment in the State's own courts."

2. As in the other *Erie* cases pertaining to Federal Rules, the approach to interpreting the scope of the Federal Rule exerted an important influence on *Shady Grove*'s outcome. Did the plurality's approach to interpreting Federal Rule 23 depart dramatically from the *Semtek* Court's narrow interpretation of Federal Rule 41? Does the difference reinforce the conclusion that the interpretation process is not about the intent of the Federal Rule, but other factors in the litigation that are influencing the Court?

Shady Grove adds an important twist to the interpretation question: how important is scope of the state law in the interpretation process? This was an important basis for disagreement among the Justices in *Shady Grove.* While Justice Scalia maintained that the interpretive process should focus on Rule 23, Justice Stevens and Justice Ginsburg urged that a federal court exercising diversity jurisdiction must also ascertain the meaning and scope of state law as well. Indeed, these latter two Justices argued that respect for state processes required a federal diversity court undertaking a Rules Enabling Act analysis to proceed with awareness of and sensitivity to state regulatory policies. For an exhaustive discussion of this interpretation process in the context of *Erie,* see Abbe R. Gluck, *Intersystemic Statutory Interpretation: Methodology as "Law" and the* Erie *Doctrine,* 120 YALE L.J. 1898 (2011).

The question of how to evaluate the clash between state and federal law intertwines with the question of how much independent meaning rests in the second sentence of the Rules Enabling Act: "Such rules shall not abridge, enlarge or modify any substantive right. . . ." Five Justices in *Shady Grove* read this limitation as significantly restricting the effect that a Federal Rule may have on the operation of state law. This included the Justices who joined Justice Ginsburg's opinion and Justice Stevens. The four Justices that joined Justice Scalia's plurality did not read any regulatory effect into that sentence of the Rules Enabling Act. *See* Kermit Roosevelt III, *Choice of Law in Federal Courts: From* Erie *and* Klaxon *to* Shady Grove, 105 Nw. U. L. Rev. (2012) (observing that the *Shady Grove* Court "split 5-4 over whether to give independent significance to the 'shall not abridge' language"). For further discussion of the reach and meaning of *Shady Grove*, see *Symposium*, Erie *Under Advisement: The Doctrine After* Shady Grove, 44 Akron L. Rev. 907 (2011).

3. Compare the interpretation disputes in *Shady Grove* with the interpretation challenges in horizontal choice of law methodologies reviewed in Chapter 2. Which of the horizontal methodologies is most sensitive to the process of interpreting the various state laws, including all the laws in potential conflict?

4. As observed in the notes after *Semtek*, the *Erie* line cases do not show concern for horizontal (state-to-state) forum shopping. This is still the case in *Shady Grove*. Perhaps more remarkably, however, Justice Scalia observes at the end of his plurality opinion that it is acceptable that vertical forum shopping (state court-to-federal court) will result from his decision to allow Federal Rule of Civil Procedure 23 to displace state law. In his view, this is "an inevitable (indeed, one might say the intended) result of a uniform system of federal procedure," which is well within Congress's power to create. To read Rule 23 differently, he reasoned, would be to usurp Congress's control over federal court procedure. Can you harmonize this orientation toward federal power and forum shopping with Justice Scalia's decision in *Semtek* to undermine vertical forum-shopping incentives by allowing federal courts to create a federal common law of preclusion with the requirement that federal common law take state law for its content?

Forum shopping thus remains a significant issue in *Erie* cases. Note how forum-shopping incentives operate in Problem 3-9, below.

PROBLEM 3-9: THE AFFIRMANCE PENALTY

The Old Nevada legislature enacted a statute imposing an affirmance penalty on certain litigants who file appeals in the Old Nevada state court system. The statute applies where a defendant unsuccessfully appeals the judgment of an Old Nevada trial court. If the appellate court affirms the judgment, the statute requires the unsuccessful defendant-appellant to pay the plaintiff a penalty equaling 15 percent of the judgment. The Old Nevada statute is mandatory: the appellate court *must* impose the affirmance penalty if it affirms the judgment without modification. The Old Nevada legislature made clear the following purposes of the penalty: to penalize and discourage frivolous appeals, to penalize and discourage appeals filed for the purposes of delay, and to provide compensation to plaintiffs for suffering the ordeal of defending judgment on appeal.

Following a car accident, Mags brought an action against another driver, Darius, in federal district court in Old Nevada, invoking the court's diversity of citizenship jurisdiction. The case resulted in a $100,000 judgment for Mags. Darius appealed the judgment, which the Court of Appeals affirmed without modification.

Mags then asked the Court of Appeals to apply the 15 percent affirmance penalty. In defending the motion, Darius relies on Federal Rule of Appellate Procedure 38, which bears the title Frivolous Appeal — Damages and Costs. FRAP 38 provides: If a court of appeals determines that an appeal is frivolous, it may, after a separately filed motion or notice from the court and reasonable opportunity to respond, award just damages and single or double costs to the appellee. Should the court of appeals grant Mag's motion?

PERSPECTIVE ON *KLAXON v. STENTOR*

Despite its difficulties with mapping a coherent test for applying *Erie*, the United States Supreme Court quickly and definitively settled one crucial question soon after *Erie* was handed down: what should a federal court sitting in diversity should do if — upon applying its *Erie* analysis and concluding that it must apply state law to an issue — the court must decide among competing state laws? Given that cases falling into a federal court's diversity jurisdiction involve — by definition — citizens of different states, the need to answer this question was great (since the chances are elevated that more than one state's law may govern in such cases). *Klaxon Co. v. Stentor Electric Mfg. Co.*, 313 U.S. 487 (1941), gives a straightforward answer: a district court should apply the conflict of law rules of the forum state to determine what law should apply.

Klaxon involved a suit filed in the United States District Court for the District of Delaware, which presented the question of which law should govern the availability of prejudgment interest on a debt. In deciding this question, the *Klaxon* Court invoked outcome determination reasoning, echoing its decision in *Guaranty Trust v. York*:

> The conflict of laws rules to be applied by the federal court in Delaware must conform to those prevailing in Delaware's state courts. Otherwise the accident of diversity of citizenship would constantly disturb equal administration of justice in coordinate state and federal courts sitting side by side. Any other ruling would do violence to the principle of uniformity within a state upon which the Tompkins decision is based. Whatever lack of uniformity this may produce between federal courts in different states is attributable to our federal system, which leaves to a state, within the limits permitted by the Constitution, the right to pursue local policies

diverging from those of its neighbors. It is not for the federal courts to thwart such local policies by enforcing an independent "general law" of conflict of laws. Subject only to review by this Court on any federal question that may arise, Delaware is free to determine whether a given matter is to be governed by the law of the forum or some other law. This Court's views are not the decisive factor in determining the applicable conflicts rule. And the proper function of the Delaware federal court is to ascertain what the state law is, not what it ought to be. . . .

Klaxon remains a fixture in *Erie* jurisprudence, consistently followed by federal courts seeking to determine which state law should govern in diversity actions and for claims arising under supplemental jurisdiction provided for in 28 U.S.C. §1367.[11] Indeed, the Supreme Court has even applied *Klaxon* in diversity cases with international elements. In *Day & Zimmerman, Inc. v. Challoner*, 423 U.S. 3 (1975), the Supreme Court required a Texas federal court to apply Texas choice of law rules to an accident occurring in Cambodia.

Klaxon's stable position among legal doctrine has not guaranteed universal acclaim. After *Klaxon* was handed down, for example, Professor Henry Hart was deeply critical of the decision, believing that it undermined the predictability and uniformity that *Erie* sought to achieve. He argued that the decision undermines the opportunity enjoyed by federal courts to develop a neutral system to resolve state law conflicts, free from the loyalties that encumber their state court counterparts.[12]

How difficult is the *Klaxon* rule to administer? Does it differ according to choice of law methodology? While federal courts at the time of *Klaxon* may not have had too much trouble applying the nearly universally followed territorial approach, more recently developed choice of law methodologies present greater challenges. Many modern approaches — such as governmental interest analysis or comparative impairment — require federal courts to divine state court preferences that can be difficult to ascertain. Can a federal court authoritatively measure the extent of a state's impairment if its law does not apply to a case? Can it accurately perform a restrained and moderate interpretation of the reach of a state's law? Perhaps most challenging of all, how does a federal court determine which of two alternatives a state court would consider the "better" rule of law?

Despite its challenges and downsides, the *Klaxon* rule is likely here to stay for quite a while. Consider, however, what would happen if the Supreme Court overruled the decision. Would this mean that the federal courts could develop a federal conflict of laws rule that they imposed on state courts? While — as discussed below in connection with federal common law — it might be possible for federal courts to do this, it would not be a logical byproduct of overruling *Klaxon*. *Klaxon's* holding concerns what *federal* courts do in the context of diversity actions and supplemental jurisdiction cases, and one must be careful before

---

11. As discussed in the Perspective on a Choice of Law Methodology in Federal Courts later in this chapter, federal courts in other contexts — such as when exercising bankruptcy jurisdiction — have not considered themselves constrained by *Klaxon's* mandate.

12. *See* Henry Hart, *The Relations Between State and Federal Law*, 54 Colum. L. Rev. 489, 515 (1954).

assuming it reaches much broader than that. Despite its limited reach, *Klaxon* has proven a potentially potent force in the promotion of forum shopping — a matter that the next note explores.

> ### PERSPECTIVE ON *ERIE*, FORUM SHOPPING, AND STARE DECISIS IN STATE AND FEDERAL COURTS

The jurisdictional mosaic comprising the United States accounts for complexity and conflicts among the union's governing laws, but creates opportunities for enterprising lawyers seeking to maximize conditions for their clients' successes. For adjudication, court power is splintered among several layers and categories of courts, including state and federal courts as well as trial and appellate courts. Given the variety of courts and overlapping jurisdictional structures, one should not be surprised that the United States experiences complications spurred by attorneys who shop for the best forum to adjudicate their clients' claims and defenses. Appearing at the end of Chapter 1, the Perspective on the Domestic and International Forum Shopping System explores many of the forces that inspire this strategic behavior among lawyers. Many of the forces discussed in that Note bear on the type of forum shopping with which *Erie* and its progeny were concerned. Yet the legal landscape subsequent to *Erie* has magnified the importance of several unique factors that arise from the *Erie* mandate, promoting both horizontal forum shopping between geographic jurisdictions (a state or federal court in one state versus a state or federal court in another state) and vertical forum shopping between state and federal courts within a particular jurisdiction. This Note discusses three of these factors: (1) the current diversity in choice of law methodologies, (2) the intricacies of stare decisis policies, (3) constraints on how state courts interpret state law (horizontal-*Erie*), and (4) the obligation of state courts to apply federal law (the reverse-*Erie*) problem. To a large degree, these three factors are independent of each other.

Diversity Among Choice of Law Methodologies. *Erie* has produced an irony. Despite its contrary intent, the *Erie* mandate may actually promote forum shopping among geographic jurisdictions in the current legal climate. At the time *Erie* was decided, most states followed the territorial approach to conflict of laws. This uniformity in choice of law methodology helped to ensure that different jurisdictions would tend to apply the same state law to a particular suit with multistate elements. Thus, once a court determined that state law should govern a particular question, the chances were good that any state court might ultimately apply the same state's law to the question. So, for example, if an accident occurred in State A and the parties were all from State B, most state courts would apply the law of the state where the accident occurred (State A's law) in a tort suit between the State B parties. Thus, the *Erie* directive that state law, not federal law, should govern the issue originally might have meant that the same state law would govern irrespective of which federal court adjudicated the case.

Now, of course, states follow myriad choice of law methodologies, leading to less uniformity in which state's laws might govern. This enriches the benefits of horizontal forum shopping between states. In other words, as hard as *Erie* might have tried to eliminate vertical (state-federal) forum shopping, horizontal (state-state) forum shopping remains.[13]

One might argue that this horizontal forum shopping is not *Erie's* creation, but is simply the product of diversity among states — a celebrated quality of United States federalism. Yet scholars have pointed out that *Erie* may have actually exacerbated horizontal forum shopping, either by eliminating a uniform "general law" that prevailed under *Swift v. Tyson*[14] or making available federal procedural mechanisms that expand a litigant's possibilities for benefitting from favorable state laws.[15] *Erie* allows attorneys to avail themselves of the advantages of federal court, but at the same time reap benefit from diversity among state laws.

Stare Decisis Policies. Another factor that bears on both vertical and horizontal forum shopping is stare decisis policy in state and federal courts. Since *Erie* dictates that federal courts must follow state laws, rules about how federal courts determine state laws and how much they consider themselves bound by changing state law affect the precise form of state law applied in federal court. While not directly implicated by *Erie*, the mirror image of this phenomenon also influences vertical forum shopping. State courts have different policies about how they treat lower federal court decisions. So, for example, an attorney trying to avoid an unfavorable federal law decision from a lower federal court might avoid its force by filing in state court in the same jurisdiction where the lower federal court sits. As a general matter, state courts are presumed capable of adjudicating a federal cause of action — and of course they must apply federal law where it is directly on point to a case. Thus, the state court will likely be available to apply the federal law, but may be free to develop its own interpretation.

While many variables in the operation of stare decisis remain uncertain, consensus exists on several questions that arise concerning an adjudication's effect in later proceedings both within, and outside, a particular court system. Understanding this consensus is not only useful in understanding the incentives created by the *Erie* doctrine, but also helps one become facile in navigating the relationships among courts and the analytically related doctrines governing preclusion and judgment recognition, which are the subject of Chapter 4.

Stare Decisis Generally. The doctrine of stare decisis embraces the notion that a court is bound by previous decisions when the same points arise in new litigation. One can divide stare decisis into vertical and horizontal categories. In this

13. For further discussion of this phenomenon, see Patrick J. Borchers, *The Real Risk of Forum Shopping: A Dissent from* Shady Grove, 44 CREIGHTON L. REV. 29, 31-33 (2010). *See also* Suzanna Sherry, *Wrong, Out of Step, and Pernicious:* Erie *as the Worst Decision of All Time*, at 12, *available at* ssrn.com/abstract=1803458 (2011) (noting that for class litigation, *Erie* and differences among state choice of law doctrines increase forum-shopping incentives).

14. Sherry, *supra*, at 13 (arguing that lack of uniformity was worse under *Erie* than under *Swift* because federal courts under *Swift* had developed a body of "cohesive and coherent" general laws).

15. Borchers, *supra*, at 29, 32 (2010) (using venue transfer as an example of procedural mechanisms that work with *Erie* to expand opportunities for forum shopping).

context, the terms "vertical" and "horizontal" are somewhat different than in the forum shopping context: vertical stare decisis binds lower courts to decisions of higher courts within its jurisdiction while horizontal stare decisis binds courts, especially appellate courts, to their own prior decisions.

Stare decisis works to reinforce some core values of the United States political system — first to ensure that the "principles governing society should be rules of law and not merely the opinions of a small group of men who temporarily occupy high office," and second to provide for stability and predictability.[16] The application of stare decisis differs greatly depending on a number of factors: (1) whether the court that is deciding the issue comes from the same governmental system as the law adjudicated; (2) notions of comity, or recognizing the validity and effect of executive, judicial, and legislative acts of other jurisdictions; and (3) the relationship of the one court to the other.

Decisions of Federal Courts Regarding State Law. The doctrine of stare decisis governs with special vigor when federal courts are applying state law. Federal courts are bound to follow the decisions of a state's supreme court when applying the law of that state. When applying state law, federal courts must strive to determine state law as a state court would.

Federal courts may deviate from this rule when state court decisions are outdated or apparently in flux. In these cases, the federal court is still bound by the fundamental principle that its decision should ultimately correspond to state court jurisprudence. For cases implicating uncertain state law, many state supreme courts accept questions certified by the federal courts, allowing for a definitive response regarding state law from the state supreme court itself.

Certification provides an authoritative ruling on state law, while retaining a properly invoked federal forum for the involved parties. Courts and parties generally use certification when the matter is (1) of vital public concern, (2) an issue likely to recur, and (3) outcome determinative. Additionally, the matter must be one that has been left unsettled by state courts, or suffers from a split of authority. While the state court's answer to a certified question is not absolutely binding, and merely informative, a federal court will not reconsider the state court's conclusions. Certification is an exceptional procedure, however, and federal courts often simply make an educated guess about what the state supreme court would rule if confronted with the precise question.

State Court Treatment of Federal District and Appeals Court Decisions of Federal Law and State Law.[17] All state courts are bound by decisions of the United States Supreme Court on federal questions. State courts usually do not consider themselves bound, however, by the decisions of lower federal courts. For the sake of uniformity, states are more likely to look to lower federal court decisions regarding issues of federal law, but are less inclined to give weight to decisions of federal courts on matters of state law.

---

16. Earl Maltz, *The Nature of Precedent*, 66 N.C. L. REV. 367, 371 (1988) (discussing the role of precedent in judicial decision making).

17. *See, e.g.*, Anne M. Payne, AMERICAN JURISPRUDENCE COURTS 141-148 (2011).

In the absence of a Supreme Court decision, some jurisdictions hold that a lower federal court's holding is binding, while others consider lower federal court decisions only persuasive. For example, Alaska, Colorado, Georgia, Indiana, Iowa, Oklahoma, Oregon, and Wisconsin all treat lower federal court decisions as persuasive, while Alabama, Nebraska, New Hampshire, and Ohio treat lower federal court decisions on federal law binding. State court of appeals decisions on federal law are binding on neither federal courts nor courts of other states.

States courts are not bound to follow federal courts, including the United States Supreme Court, on rulings regarding state law. While lower federal court rulings are not binding on state courts, a state court will often defer to federal court's interpretation of a federal law, when interpreting state law that is derived from a federal rule.

Federal District Court Treatment of Decisions from Other Federal District Courts in the Same Circuit

The prevailing rule among federal jurisdictions is that between courts of equal and concurrent power, deference to a prior decision is a matter of discretion.[18] For example, decisions of a federal district judge are not generally considered binding on the same judicial district or even the same judge. Nor are the decisions of federal courts of appeal binding on courts of appeal in other federal circuits.[19] Such a system would be unmanageable among such a large number of independent courts. Though the decisions are not binding, courts often cite them for persuasive effect.[20]

Decisions of Three-Judge Federal Court of Appeals Panels. As a general rule, published decisions of a three-judge federal court of appeals panel carry the weight of stare decisis, and cannot be overruled by another panel within the circuit. As a general rule, only the circuit court sitting en banc may overrule a panel decision, though some circuits follow more flexible rules on this. Various considerations inform the degree of flexibility on stare decisis within the federal circuits. Several circuits hold that when an intervening United States Supreme Court case calls case law or reasoning into question, a panel can justifiably overrule a previous panel decision.[21]

As a general matter, stare decisis itself is less rigid than principles of preclusion such as res judicata and collateral estoppel. Legal history is filled with examples of when a court chooses not to treat "binding" precedent as binding, either because the court explicitly rejects the earlier decision or finds a pretext for ignoring or distinguishing it. Where honored, the stare decisis doctrine serves efficiency, consistency, and predictability in the law. The story is different where a court in one jurisdiction chooses not to give precedential effect to a decision in another jurisdiction. Where this happens with regularity, litigants have greater incentive to forum shop so as avoid the effect of an unfavorable decision.

***Horizontal* Erie.** As stated above, *Erie* makes clear that where federal courts apply state law, they must interpret state law as the supreme court of the state

---

18. *Id.* at 141.
19. *Entergy Gulf States, Inc. v. Traxler,* 320 S.W.3d 553 (Tex. App. Beaumont 2010).
20. 18-134 JAMES WM. MOORE ET AL., MOORE'S FEDERAL PRACTICE P134.02 (3d ed. 2011).
21. *Id.* (citing the First, Eleventh, and Ninth Circuits).

would do so. For example, in a straightforward case, the United States District Court for the Eastern District of New York might conclude that New York law governs the rules of decision in the state. For the intricacies of that law, the district court would look first to a decision on the law by the highest court in the New York court system — the New York Court of Appeals — and if none existed on the contested point of law, the district court would make its best educated judgment on how the New York Court of Appeals would rule. This is a classic example of a vertical choice of law decision under *Erie*. But what if the district court in New York applies the choice of law rules of New York (pursuant to the mandate of *Klaxon v. Stentor*) and concludes that Oregon law should govern? This implicates a possible horizontal *Erie* wrinkle: the obligations of sister states in applying each other's laws.

Horizontal *Erie* obligations have received little attention among courts and scholars.[22] As argued by Professor Michael Steven Green, horizontal *Erie* imposes the same duty on state courts as vertical *Erie* imposes on federal courts: state courts applying another state's law should interpret the law of the sister state as the supreme court of the sister state would do so.[23] While the symmetry of this position is appealing and its wisdom perhaps compelling, many courts have not adopted it. In fact, as Professor Green points out, state courts routinely follow a presumption that is in tension with the principle: the presumption that another state's law is the same as the law of one's own state.[24] Thus, if a New York state court concluded it should apply Oregon law on a particular point, it might presume that Oregon law was the same as New York law if it were unable to locate an Oregon Supreme Court decision on the contested issue. Grafting this thought process on a federal district court in New York applying Oregon law, the district court might believe it appropriate to follow the same presumption as the New York state courts do in ascertaining the content of Oregon law. Professor Green persuasively argues that this approach is problematic in light of horizontal choice of law policies as well as the policies of *Erie*.[25] The opportunities for forum shopping are particularly great because not all states follow the presumption of similarity in the same way and with the same vigor as others.

***Reverse* Erie.** Courts and commentators disagree about precisely what the reverse-*Erie* concept embraces. According to one very broad definition, the reverse-*Erie* doctrine "provides that federal law — be it constitutional, statutory, or common law — will apply pursuant to the Supremacy Clause in state court, subject to the Constitution or Congress having already chosen the applicable law, if that federal law prevails by an *Erie*-like judicial balancing or if it preempts

---

22. Important exceptions include the work of Professors Michael Steven Green and Kermit Roosevelt. *See* Michael Steven Green, *Horizontal* Erie *and the Presumption of Forum Law*, 109 Mich. L. Rev. 1237, 1251-1261 (2011), and Kermit Roosevelt, *Resolving Renvoi: The Bewitchment of Our Intelligence by Means of Language*, 80 Notre Dame L. Rev. 1821, 1840-1841 (2005).

23. *See* Green, *supra* at 1237, 1260.

24. *See, e.g., Knieriemen v. Bache Halsey Stuart Shields Inc.*, 427 N.Y.S.2d 10, 15 (N.Y. App. Div. 1980) (applying presumption); *ROC-Century Assoc. v. Giunta*, 658 A.2d 223, 226 (Me. 1995) (applying presumption); *Am. Honda Fin. Corp. v. Bennett*, 439 N.W.2d 459, 460 (Neb. 1989) (applying presumption).

25. *See* Green, *supra* at 1274-1289.

state law."[26] The doctrine has many analytical connections with preemption, and some argue that it is not fundamentally different than preemption principles. But many scholars confine the reverse-*Erie* doctrine to matters bearing on the conduct of litigation, embracing the view that the doctrine simply requires state courts to apply federal practices that are closely interwoven with "the relevant federal claim, despite the existence of conflicting state procedures."[27]

The Supreme Court's decision in *Dice v. Akron, Canton & Youngstown R. Co.*, 342 U.S. 359 (1952), is a classic example of reverse *Erie*. The *Dice* Court held that federal law required state courts to allow a jury to decide the question whether a plaintiff validly released a claim under the Federal Employers' Liability Act. Although forum state law in the case provided that the precise question should be resolved by a judge, the Supreme Court determined that the federal practice of using a jury for such questions was "'part and parcel of the remedy afforded'" under the federal act, and was thus "too substantial a part of the rights accorded by the Act to permit it to be classified as a mere 'local rule of procedure' for denial" by the state court. *Id.* at 361-363.

Although the precise parameters of reverse *Erie* are still being debated, the doctrine provides another variable for lawyers choosing between state and federal court. A particular federal court practice may or may not be beneficial to a plaintiff with a federal law claim. The jury trial practice at issue in *Dice* provides a good example. Consider a common situation where federal practice provides that the jury must decide a particular question while state practice gives the question to a judge. Assume that in the state system, juries are drawn from the boundaries of a city only, while in the corresponding federal district, the juries are drawn from a wider geographical area, and include city, suburban, and rural residents. The state and federal courthouses are just blocks from each other, but the juries for each court system are drawn from different populations. The plaintiff's lawyer believes the case would play well to lay persons from the city, and likes the idea of litigating the case before a jury and not a judge. The lawyer, however, fears that suburban and rural citizens might react negatively to aspects of her case. The lawyer would therefore be inclined to avail herself of a state court jury. Reverse *Erie* may give her precisely what she wants: federal practice administered through a state system. She would choose to file the suit in state court, even though federal court would clearly be available since the suit would arise under federal law.

Reverse *Erie*, horizontal *Erie*, stare decisis policy, and choice of law methodology are just some of the many nuances that may influence horizontal and vertical forum shopping promoted by the *Erie* doctrine. Perhaps the myriad variables influencing litigation success are so complicated and interdependent as to render foolhardy a lawyer's attempt to account for them all. Nonetheless, these factors do merit close scrutiny, especially where they implicate a very significant component of the case — such as the opportunity to avoid highly unfavorable governing law by changing the applicable choice of law analysis, the possibility

---

26. Kevin Clermont, *Reverse*-Erie, 82 NOTRE DAME L. REV. 1, 3 (2006).
27. Catherine T. Struve, *Institutional Practice, Procedural Uniformity, and As-Applied Challenges Under the Rules Enabling Act*, 86 NOTRE DAME L. REV. 1181 (2011).

for beneficial changes in state law that a federal district court might be more inclined to embrace than a state trial court, or the possibility to change a significant factor in the case such as the identity of the fact-finder. The following problem illustrates a circumstance where the state law is in flux — and an attorney needs to figure out how to turn this uncertainty into an asset. You may want to try your hand at the problem, so as to appreciate the signals and incentives that *Erie* might create in a contemporary environment.

PROBLEM 3-10: FORUM SHOPPING WHERE THE LAW IS IN FLUX

Erie, *Hanna*, and subsequent cases speak of discouraging forum shopping. While forum shopping may not be desirable from a policy point of view, it is part of the strategic lives of lawyers, particularly litigators. This problem provides a number of variables that a plaintiff's lawyer might evaluate in deciding where to file a complaint. After considering these variables, give advice to the lawyer about in which state and which court system (state or federal court) she should file the suit:

The plaintiff's lawyer, Marie, lives in Clare County, Ohio. Her client, Jude, also lives in Clare County, Ohio. Jude was injured when a car lost its brakes and drove into him as he was working on electrical wiring outside his home. The driver of the car came from Wexford, Nebraska, where the car's brakes were last serviced. The mechanic who worked on the brakes is also a Nebraska resident. Marie intends to file suit on behalf of Jude, naming the driver and the mechanic as defendants. Marie is confident that she can win on liability grounds because it appears that the mechanic negligently failed to perform the necessary repairs and that the driver failed to take reparative action, even though it was obvious the brakes were faulty as soon as the driver picked up the car from the mechanic. Nonetheless, Marie is unsure of the amount of damages she can recover for Jude. Although Jude had few obvious personal injuries and modest medical bills, he has suffered a considerable amount of pain caused by the accident.

Marie has researched the law governing the suit and determined that Ohio law has a cap on pain and suffering damages. Some of the older Nebraska cases also insist that trial courts limit pain and suffering damages, but recent appellate cases suggest that this cap is inappropriate, at least for medical malpractice cases. No appellate decisions in Nebraska over the last 20 years have discussed the issue of pain and suffering damages in negligence cases arising out accidents.

Marie's research reveals that Ohio follows the Restatement (First) of Conflict of Laws. She has discovered, however, that Nebraska conflicts law is changing. Nebraska used to follow the Restatement (First) of Conflict of Laws for all issues, but the Nebraska Supreme Court has recently ruled that courts in the state should follow governmental interest analysis for *contract* issues. The Nebraska Supreme Court stated that it would wait for a tort case presenting a conflict of laws matter before determining whether it would make the same change for tort issues. As for federal law, Marie has determined that the federal courts do not place on cap on damages in tort actions for which federal law is the source of the plaintiff's cause of action. No federal law governs the damage question when state law is the source of the plaintiff's cause of action.

As a practical, logistical, and cost effective matter, which state would Marie likely want to file suit in: Nebraska or Ohio? Is this the same jurisdiction where the law would favor her client? For the purpose of answering this question, don't forget to consider both the most favorable law governing the particular rule of decision at issue (pain and suffering remedies) as well as the choice of law approach for the case. Once you determine which geographic jurisdiction (Nebraska or Ohio) Marie should file suit in, consider whether she should file in state or federal court.

3. *Federal Common Law*

Erie focused courts on the nature of rights being enforced in lawsuits. Although *Erie* was particularly concerned with protecting state prerogatives to define the scope of state-created rights, the decision — somewhat ironically — inspired federal courts to create "specialized federal common law." Henry J. Friendly, *In Praise of* Erie — *and of the New Federal Common Law*, 39 N.Y.U. L. REV. 383, 407 (1964). Contrary to the "federal general common law" condemned in *Erie*, this federal common law is binding on all courts and is deemed essential to maintain the prerogative and effectiveness of federal power.

The question whether a federal court should make federal common law arises only where no federal constitutional provision, statute, treaty, or regulation governs a particular issue. If the court decides that it cannot or should not create federal law to govern a particular issue, then state law would fill the void. Thus, like the *Erie* doctrine, the question whether to create federal common law essentially presents a vertical choice of law issue: the choice between state and federal law. That characterization helps to highlight the federalism implications of federal common law. But separation of powers issues (that is, issues concerning the division of power within the federal government) also heavily influence federal common law doctrine. In fact, these separation of powers consequences are arguably more significant than in the *Erie* context. Federal common law applies in both state and federal court, regardless of jurisdictional basis and governs throughout the United States. As such, federal common law has much greater promise than *Erie* of invading the lawmaking authority of Congress.

Because federal common law deeply implicates both federalism and separation of powers concerns, the area is subject to constitutional constraints.[28]

Federal common law decisions, however, do not always explicitly discuss the constitutional implications. Consider the constitutional constraints implicated in the following decision, which concerns a judicially created military contractor defense designed for tort actions by injured soldiers and their families.

---

28. For further background on the interplay between federalism and separation of powers in the federal common law context, see LAURA E. LITTLE, FEDERAL COURTS 467-470 (2d ed. 2010).

Boyle v. United Technologies Corp.

487 U.S. 500 (1988)

Justice SCALIA delivered the opinion of the Court.

This case requires us to decide when a contractor providing military equipment to the Federal Government can be held liable under state tort law for injury caused by a design defect.

I

On April 27, 1983, David A. Boyle, a United States Marine helicopter copilot, was killed when the CH-53D helicopter in which he was flying crashed off the coast of Virginia Beach, Virginia, during a training exercise. Although Boyle survived the impact of the crash, he was unable to escape from the helicopter and drowned. Boyle's father, petitioner here, brought this diversity action in Federal District Court against the Sikorsky Division of United Technologies Corporation (Sikorsky), which built the helicopter for the United States.

[At trial, the jury decided in favor of Boyle's father, who had presented the Virginia tort law theory that "Sikorsky had defectively designed the copilot's emergency escape system: the escape hatch opened out instead of in (and was therefore ineffective in a submerged craft because of water pressure), and access to the escape hatch handle was obstructed by other equipment." The Court of Appeals reversed, finding as a matter of federal law that Sikorsky could not be held liable for the allegedly defective design of the escape hatch on the basis of the federal common law "military contractor defense."]

II

Petitioner's broadest contention is that, in the absence of legislation specifically immunizing Government contractors from liability for design defects, there is no basis for judicial recognition of such a defense. We disagree. In most fields of activity, to be sure, this Court has refused to find federal pre-emption of state law in the absence of either a clear statutory prescription, or a direct conflict between federal and state law. But we have held that a few areas, involving "uniquely federal interests," are so committed by the Constitution and laws of the United States to federal control that state law is pre-empted and replaced, where necessary, by federal law of a content prescribed (absent explicit statutory directive) by the courts — so-called "federal common law."

The dispute in the present case borders upon two areas that we have found to involve such "uniquely federal interests." We have held that obligations to and rights of the United States under its contracts are governed exclusively by federal law. The present case does not involve an obligation to the United States under its contract, but rather liability to third persons. That liability may be styled one in tort, but it arises out of performance of the contract.

Another area that we have found to be of peculiarly federal concern, warranting the displacement of state law, is the civil liability of federal officials for actions taken in the course of their duty. We have held in many contexts that the scope of that liability is controlled by federal law. The present case involves an independent contractor performing its obligation under a procurement contract, rather than an official performing his duty as a federal employee, but there is obviously implicated the same interest in getting the Government's work done. . . .

. . . [I]t is plain that the Federal Government's interest in the procurement of equipment is implicated by suits such as the present one — even though the dispute is one between private parties. It is true that where "litigation is purely between private parties and does not touch the rights and duties of the United States," federal law does not govern. . . . But the same is not true here. The imposition of liability on Government contractors will directly affect the terms of Government contracts: either the contractor will decline to manufacture the design specified by the Government, or it will raise its price. Either way, the interests of the United States will be directly affected.

That the procurement of equipment by the United States is an area of uniquely federal interest does not, however, end the inquiry. That merely establishes a necessary, not a sufficient, condition for the displacement of state law. Displacement will occur only where, as we have variously described, a "significant conflict" exists between an identifiable "federal policy or interest and the [operation] of state law," or the application of state law would "frustrate specific objectives" of federal legislation. The conflict with federal policy need not be as sharp as that which must exist for ordinary pre-emption when Congress legislates "in a field which the States have traditionally occupied." Or to put the point differently, the fact that the area in question *is* one of unique federal concern changes what would otherwise be a conflict that cannot produce pre-emption into one that can. But conflict there must be. In some cases, for example where the federal interest requires a uniform rule, the entire body of state law applicable to the area conflicts and is replaced by federal rules. In others, the conflict is more narrow, and only particular elements of state law are superseded.

. . . Here the state-imposed duty of care that is the asserted basis of the contractor's liability (specifically, the duty to equip helicopters with the sort of escape-hatch mechanism petitioner claims was necessary) is precisely contrary to the duty imposed by the Government contract (the duty to manufacture and deliver helicopters with the sort of escape-hatch mechanism shown by the specifications). Even in this sort of situation, it would be unreasonable to say that there is always a "significant conflict" between the state law and a federal policy or interest. If, for example, a federal procurement officer orders, by model number, a quantity of stock helicopters that happen to be equipped with escape hatches opening outward, it is impossible to say that the Government has a significant interest in that particular feature. That would be scarcely more reasonable than saying that a private individual who orders such a craft by model number cannot sue for the manufacturer's negligence because he got precisely what he ordered.

There is, however, a statutory provision that demonstrates the potential for, and suggests the outlines of, "significant conflict" between federal interests and state law in the context of Government procurement. In the [Federal Torts Claims

Act (FTCA)], Congress authorized damages to be recovered against the United States for harm caused by the negligent or wrongful conduct of Government employees, to the extent that a private person would be liable under the law of the place where the conduct occurred. 28 U.S.C. §1346(b). It excepted from this consent to suit, however,

> "[a]ny claim . . . based upon the exercise or performance or the failure to exercise or perform a discretionary function or duty on the part of a federal agency or an employee of the Government, whether or not the discretion involved be abused." 28 U.S.C. §2680(a).

We think that the selection of the appropriate design for military equipment to be used by our Armed Forces is assuredly a discretionary function within the meaning of this provision. It often involves not merely engineering analysis but judgment as to the balancing of many technical, military, and even social considerations, including specifically the trade-off between greater safety and greater combat effectiveness. And we are further of the view that permitting "second-guessing" of these judgments, through state tort suits against contractors would produce the same effect sought to be avoided by the FTCA exemption. The financial burden of judgments against the contractors would ultimately be passed through, substantially if not totally, to the United States itself, since defense contractors will predictably raise their prices to cover, or to insure against, contingent liability for the Government-ordered designs. To put the point differently: It makes little sense to insulate the Government against financial liability for the judgment that a particular feature of military equipment is necessary when the Government produces the equipment itself, but not when it contracts for the production. In sum, we are of the view that state law which holds Government contractors liable for design defects in military equipment does in some circumstances present a "significant conflict" with federal policy and must be displaced. . . .

Justice BRENNAN, with whom Justice MARSHALL and Justice BLACKMUN join, dissenting.

Lieutenant David A. Boyle died when the CH-53D helicopter he was copiloting spun out of control and plunged into the ocean. We may assume, for purposes of this case, that Lt. Boyle was trapped under water and drowned because respondent United Technologies negligently designed the helicopter's escape hatch. We may further assume that any competent engineer would have discovered and cured the defects, but that they inexplicably escaped respondent's notice. Had respondent designed such a death trap for a commercial firm, Lt. Boyle's family could sue under Virginia tort law and be compensated for his tragic and unnecessary death. But respondent designed the helicopter for the Federal Government, and that, the Court tells us today, makes all the difference: Respondent is immune from liability so long as it obtained approval of "reasonably precise specifications" — perhaps no more than a rubber stamp from a federal procurement officer who might or might not have noticed or cared about the defects, or even had the expertise to discover them.

If respondent's immunity "bore the legitimacy of having been prescribed by the people's elected representatives," we would be duty bound to implement their will, whether or not we approved. *United States v. Johnson*, 481 U.S. 681 (1987) (opinion of Scalia, J.). Congress, however, has remained silent—and conspicuously so, having resisted a sustained campaign by Government contractors to legislate for them some defense.[1] The Court—unelected and unaccountable to the people—has unabashedly stepped into the breach to legislate a rule denying Lt. Boyle's family the compensation that state law assures them. This time the injustice is of this Court's own making.

Worse yet, the injustice will extend far beyond the facts of this case, for the Court's newly discovered Government contractor defense is breathtakingly sweeping. It applies not only to military equipment like the CH-53D helicopter, but (so far as I can tell) to any made-to-order gadget that the Federal Government might purchase after previewing plans—from NASA's Challenger space shuttle to the Postal Service's old mail cars. The contractor may invoke the defense in suits brought not only by military personnel like Lt. Boyle, or Government employees, but by anyone injured by a Government contractor's negligent design, including, for example, the children who might have died had respondent's helicopter crashed on the beach. It applies even if the Government has not intentionally sacrificed safety for other interests like speed or efficiency, and, indeed, even if the equipment is not of a type that is typically considered dangerous; thus, the contractor who designs a Government building can invoke the defense when the elevator cable snaps or the walls collapse. . . .

. . . Because I would leave that exercise of legislative power to Congress, where our Constitution places it, I would reverse the Court of Appeals and reinstate petitioner's jury award.

I

Before our decision in *Erie R. Co. v. Tompkins*, 304 U.S. 64 (1938), federal courts sitting in diversity were generally free, in the absence of a controlling state statute, to fashion rules of "general" federal common law. . . . *Erie* was deeply rooted in notions of federalism, and is most seriously implicated when, as here, federal judges displace the state law that would ordinarily govern with their own rules of federal common law.

[W]e have emphasized that federal common law can displace state law in "few and restricted" instances. . . .

II

Congress has not decided to supersede state law here (if anything, it has decided not to, see n.1, *supra*) and the Court does not pretend that its newly

1. *See, e.g.*, H.R. 4765, 99th Cong., 2d Sess. (1986) (limitations on civil liability of Government contracts); S. 2441, 99th Cong., 2d Session (1986) (same); *see also* H.R. 2378, 100th Cong., 1st Sess. (1987) (indemnification of civil liability for Government contractors). . . .

manufactured "Government contractor defense" fits within any of the handful of "narrow areas," of "uniquely federal interests" in which we have heretofore done so. Rather, the Court creates a new category of "uniquely federal interests" out of a synthesis of two whose origins predate *Erie* itself: the interest in administering the "obligations to and rights of the United States under its contracts," and the interest in regulating the "civil liability of federal officials for actions taken in the course of their duty," This case is, however, simply a suit between two private parties. We have steadfastly declined to impose federal contract law on relationships that are collateral to a federal contract, or to extend the federal employee's immunity beyond federal employees. . . .

III

. . . [T]he Court invokes the discretionary function exception of the Federal Tort Claims Act (FTCA), 28 U.S.C. §2680(a). The Court does not suggest that the exception has any direct bearing here, for petitioner has sued a private manufacturer (not the Federal Government) under Virginia law (not the FTCA). . . . [T]he FTCA's retention of sovereign immunity for the Government's discretionary acts does not imply a defense for the benefit of contractors who participate in those acts, even though they might pass on the financial burden to the United States. . . . [T]he most that can be said is that the position "asserted, though the product of a law Congress passed, is a matter on which Congress has not taken a position."

Here, even that much is an overstatement, for the Government's immunity for discretionary functions is not even "a product of" the FTCA. Before Congress enacted the FTCA (when sovereign immunity barred any tort suit against the Federal Government) we perceived no need for a rule of federal common law to reinforce the Government's immunity by shielding also parties who might contractually pass costs on to it. Nor did we (or any other court of which I am aware) identify a special category of "discretionary" functions for which sovereign immunity was so crucial that a Government contractor who exercised discretion should share the Government's immunity from state tort law. . . . There is no more reason for federal common law to shield contractors now that the Government is liable for some torts than there was when the Government was liable for none. . . .

IV

At bottom, the Court's analysis is premised on the proposition that any tort liability indirectly absorbed by the Government so burdens governmental functions as to compel us to act when Congress has not. That proposition is by no means uncontroversial. The tort system is premised on the assumption that the imposition of liability encourages actors to prevent any injury whose expected cost exceeds the cost of prevention. If the system is working as it should, Government contractors will design equipment to avoid certain injuries (like the deaths of soldiers or Government employees), which would be certain to burden the

Government. The Court therefore has no basis for its assumption that tort liability will result in a net burden on the Government (let alone a clearly excessive net burden) rather than a net gain.

Perhaps tort liability is an inefficient means of ensuring the quality of design efforts, but "[w]hatever the merits of the policy" the Court wishes to implement, "its conversion into law is a proper subject for congressional action, not for any creative power of ours." It is, after all, "Congress, not this Court or the other federal courts, [that] is the custodian of the national purse. By the same token [Congress] is the primary and most often the exclusive arbiter of federal fiscal affairs. And these comprehend, as we have said, securing the treasury or the Government against financial losses *however inflicted.* . . ."

. . . Were I a legislator, I would probably vote against any law absolving multi-billion dollar private enterprises from answering for their tragic mistakes, at least if that law were justified by no more than the unsupported speculation that their liability might ultimately burden the United States Treasury. Some of my colleagues here would evidently vote otherwise (as they have here), but that should not matter here. We are judges not legislators, and the vote is not ours to cast.

I respectfully dissent.

Notes on
BOYLE AND FEDERAL COMMON LAW

1. The precise circumstances under which the Supreme Court has endorsed federal common law can be difficult to identify and to predict. As explained by Judge Friendly, the Supreme Court has created federal common law using a "variety of techniques — spontaneous generation . . . , implication of a private cause of action from a statute providing other sanctions, construing a jurisdictional grant as a command to fashion federal law, and the normal judicial filling of statutory interstices." Henry J. Friendly, *In Praise of* Erie — *and of the New Federal Common Law*, 39 N.Y.U. L. REV. 383, 421 (1964). When the Supreme Court makes federal common law by "spontaneous generation," Congress has not regulated in the area, but the Court nevertheless determines that federal courts must still make law in order to protect "uniquely federal interests." Contexts in which the Court has authorized federal courts to generate common law to protect uniquely federal interests include: (1) cases involving the proprietary interest of the United States; (2) cases involving private parties but implicating important concerns of the United States; (3) cases where federal courts imply a private cause of action enabling individuals to sue federal officials for violations of the United States Constitution; (4) cases involving controversies between states; (5) cases involving maritime and admiralty jurisdiction; and (6) cases involving international relations and customary international law. The other circumstances when the Court has created federal common law have generally occurred where an Act of Congress is "in the picture," but its terms need

supplementing by judicial action. Is *Boyle* a spontaneous generation case or a statutory supplement case?

2. One area where federal courts make common law, which does not always make the list of contemporary federal common law categories, is federal procedural law. The inclination for federal courts to create common law governing the practice of federal court litigation is reviewed in detail in the Perspective on the Substance/Procedure Dichotomy and the Aftermath of *Erie*, appearing earlier in this chapter. Might one say that federal court practice and procedure is an area of "unique federal interest"?

Sometimes court decisions purporting to create federal common law can be difficult to distinguish from constitutional and statutory interpretation. Since interpreting the Constitution in the United States is deemed the judiciary's province, one might reasonably describe judicial analysis and interpretation of constitutional provisions as "court-made law" or "common law." One might contrast these decisions from federal common law because the legal standard for the conduct at issue comes from the Constitution or a statute, not the conscience of the court. Nonetheless, one might have a difficult time drawing the line between interpreting or supplementing a preexisting standard, and judicially creating a new standard. One way to identify a new legal standard is to ask whether the standard creates an original obligation or an original right, which is not derived from another source.

3. Recall from the field preemption material that courts divine a congressional intent to displace state regulation entirely in areas that implicate important federal interests. Is the character of these federal interests as strong in the federal common law context as it is in the preemption context? Justice Scalia's *Boyle* opinion suggests not. He states that for federal common law, the "conflict with federal policy need not be as sharp as that which must exist for ordinary pre-emption when Congress legislates 'in a field which the States have traditionally occupied.'" If, on the other hand, the legislation does not concern a field that state law has "traditionally occupied" — such as foreign or military affairs — perhaps the two standards are more in line.

Note that the *Boyle* Court stated that, in order to make federal common law, a court needs to identify a unique federal interest *and* a conflict between state and federal policy in order to justify creating federal common law. (The conflict requirement was not obvious in earlier federal common law cases.) The source of the conflict in the case was the Federal Torts Claims Act. Given that the Federal Torts Claims Act did not provide immunity for a private party such as a military contractor, how was it that the Act clashed with state law allowing liability against the contractor?

4. Note that Justice Brennan begins his dissent in *Boyle* by citing an earlier opinion by Justice Scalia in *United States v. Johnson*, 481 U.S. 681 (1987), in which Justice Scalia argued that a court should restrain itself before creating rights or immunities in the absence of a law bearing the "legitimacy of

having been prescribed by the people's elected representatives," *id.* Is Justice Brennan correct in suggesting that the majority opinion overreaches the legitimate borders of the judicial function? Compare whether Justice Scalia's approach to judicial lawmaking in *Boyle* is consistent with his approach in the next case, *Sosa v. Alvarez-Machain* (*Alvarez-Machain II*), 542 U.S. 692 (2004).

PROBLEM 3-11: THE DISAPPOINTED SPOUSE

Sam and Sally Service were married in 1995 and settled in their home state of California. It soon became apparent that their marriage would not be a happy one. Nevertheless, for religious reasons, they remained married and continued to "pool" their financial resources until Sam's death in 2005. Sam enlisted in the military two years after their marriage. At the time he enlisted, he became eligible for a life insurance policy issued pursuant to the National Service Life Insurance Act. Because he felt no warmth or responsibility toward Sally, Sam designated his mother as the beneficiary on the policy. Pursuant to the National Service Life Insurance Act, the federal government paid most of the premium on Sam's policy. Nevertheless, a small percentage of the premium was paid through a deduction from Sam's paycheck every month. The National Service Life Insurance Act provides that that "no one shall have a vested right" in any proceeds under the policy.

Sam died while serving in active duty. After his death, the federal government transferred the proceeds of the insurance policy to Sam's mother as the policy's beneficiary. Shocked to learn that she was not the beneficiary under the policy, Sally has brought an action in state court against Sam's mother. Sally's suit seeks an order requiring Sam's mother to disgorge one-half of the policy proceeds. Sally argues that the community property laws of California entitle her to one-half of the policy proceeds because the policy premiums were paid with marital property — i.e., Sam's salary. The National Service Life Insurance Act says nothing directly on the issue. Should California law govern the dispute? If you were Sam's mother, what arguments would you make that federal law should govern? If federal law governs, what should be its content?

After the United States Constitution was ratified, Congress passed the First Judiciary Act, which contains a provision that has aroused important debate about federal common law in the international arena, the Alien Tort Statute (ATS). The ATS was largely ignored for two centuries after its passage, but was invigorated in 1980 in *Filartiga v. Pena-Irala*, 630 F.2d 876 (2d Cir. 1980). In *Filartiga*, the court of appeals held that intentional torture perpetrated under the color of official authority violated customary international law, that this international law violation could constitute a violation of domestic United States law, and that a plaintiff may file a federal court action under the ATS to remedy the violation. *Filartiga* provoked a strong reaction, both favorable and unfavorable, and prompted an increase in human rights litigation in United States federal courts. Consider how this litigation, and the holding of *Filartiga*, might be affected by the case that follows, *Sosa v. Alvarez-Machain.*

Sosa v. Alvarez-Machain

542 U.S. 692 (2004)

Justice SOUTER delivered the opinion of the Court.

[Federal officials concluded that a Mexican physician, Alvarez-Machain, prolonged the life of a Drug Enforcement Agent (DEA) during interrogation and torture. The agent had been kidnapped, and was ultimately murdered by his captors. After the Mexican government refused to extradite Alvarez-Machain for his role in this crime, he was abducted himself by a group of Mexicans that included Sosa, who was later shown to be a DEA operative. Alvarez-Machain was held in a hotel and brought by private plane to Texas. At that point he was tried, acquitted of criminal charges, and returned to Mexico.

Alvarez-Machain subsequently sued Sosa and others on a number of grounds, including the Alien Tort Statute (ATS). An en banc court of the Court of Appeals for the Ninth Circuit held "that the ATS not only provides federal courts with subject matter jurisdiction, but also creates a cause of action for an alleged violation of the law of nations." The court held that Alvarez's arrest and detention violated a "clear and universally recognized norm prohibiting arbitrary arrest and detention."]

. . . Sosa . . . argues (as does the United States supporting him) that there is no relief under the ATS because the statute does no more than vest federal courts with jurisdiction, neither creating nor authorizing the courts to recognize any particular right of action without further congressional action. Although we agree the statute is in terms only jurisdictional, we think that at the time of enactment the jurisdiction enabled federal courts to hear claims in a very limited category defined by the law of nations and recognized at common law. We do not believe, however, that the limited, implicit sanction to entertain the handful of international law *cum* common law claims understood in 1789 should be taken as authority to recognize the right of action asserted by Alvarez here.

. . . The first Congress passed [the ATS] as part of the Judiciary Act of 1789, . . . providing that the new federal district courts "shall also have cognizance, concurrent with the courts of the several States, or the circuit courts, as the case may be, of all causes where an alien sues for a tort only in violation of the law of nations or a treaty of the United States." . . . Alvarez says that the ATS was intended not simply as a jurisdictional grant, but as authority for the creation of a new cause of action for torts in violation of international law. We think that reading is implausible. As enacted in 1789, the ATS gave the district courts "cognizance" of certain causes of action, and the term bespoke a grant of jurisdiction, not power to mold substantive law. The fact that the ATS was placed in §9 of the Judiciary Act, a statute otherwise exclusively concerned with federal-court jurisdiction, is itself support for its strictly jurisdictional nature. Nor would the distinction between jurisdiction and cause of action have been elided by the drafters of the Act or those who voted on it. . . . In sum, we think the statute was intended as jurisdictional in the sense of addressing the power of the courts to entertain cases concerned with a certain subject.

[The Court then reviewed cases and materials from around the time of the Judiciary Act of 1789, concluding that the history surrounding the Act] . . . does tend to support two propositions. First, there is every reason to suppose that the First Congress did not pass the ATS as a jurisdictional convenience to be placed on the shelf for use by a future Congress or state legislature that might, someday, authorize the creation of causes of action or itself decide to make some element of the law of nations actionable for the benefit of foreigners. . . . The second inference to be drawn from the history is that Congress intended the ATS to furnish jurisdiction for a relatively modest set of actions alleging violations of the law of nations. Uppermost in the legislative mind appears to have been offenses against ambassadors, violations of safe conduct were probably understood to be actionable, and individual actions arising out of prize captures and piracy may well have also been contemplated. But the common law appears to have understood only those three of the hybrid variety as definite and actionable, or at any rate, to have assumed only a very limited set of claims. . . . The sparse contemporaneous cases and legal materials referring to the ATS tend to confirm both inferences, that some, but few, torts in violation of the law of nations were understood to be within the common law. . . .

In sum, although the ATS is a jurisdictional statute creating no new causes of action, the reasonable inference from the historical materials is that the statute was intended to have practical effect the moment it became law. The jurisdictional grant is best read as having been enacted on the understanding that the common law would provide a cause of action for the modest number of international law violations with a potential for personal liability at the time. . . .

We think it is correct, then, to assume that the First Congress understood that the district courts would recognize private causes of action for certain torts in violation of the law of nations, though we have found no basis to suspect Congress had any examples in mind beyond those torts corresponding to Blackstone's three primary offenses: violation of safe conduct, infringement of the rights of ambassadors, and piracy. We assume, too, that no development in the two centuries from the enactment of §1350 to the birth of the modern line of cases beginning with *Filartiga v. Pena-Irala*, 630 F.2d 876 (CA2 1980), has categorically precluded federal courts from recognizing a claim under the law of nations as an element of common law; Congress has not in any relevant way amended §1350 or limited civil common law power by another statute. . . . [W]e think courts should require any claim based on the present-day law of nations to rest on a norm of international character accepted by the civilized world and defined with a specificity comparable to the features of the 18th-century paradigms we have recognized. This requirement is fatal to Alvarez's claim.

... A series of reasons argue for judicial caution when considering the kinds of individual claims that might implement the jurisdiction conferred by the early statute. First, the prevailing conception of the common law has changed since 1789 in a way that counsels restraint in judicially applying internationally generated norms. When §1350 was enacted, the accepted conception was of the common law as "a transcendental body of law outside of any particular State but obligatory within it unless and until changed by statute." Now, however, in most cases where a court is asked to state or formulate a common law principle in a new context, there is a general understanding that the law is not so much found or discovered as it is either made or created. [A] judge deciding in reliance on an international norm will find a substantial element of discretionary judgment in the decision.

Second, along with, and in part driven by, that conceptual development in understanding common law has come an equally significant rethinking of the role of the federal courts in making it. *Erie R. Co. v. Tompkins*, 304 U.S. 64 (1938), was the watershed in which we denied the existence of any federal "general" common law, which largely withdrew to havens of specialty, some of them defined by express congressional authorization to devise a body of law directly. ... [A]lthough we have even assumed competence to make judicial rules of decision of particular importance to foreign relations, such as the act of state doctrine, see *Banco Nacional de Cuba v. Sabbatino*, 376 U.S. 398, 427 (1964), the general practice has been to look for legislative guidance before exercising innovative authority over substantive law. ...

Third, this Court has recently and repeatedly said that a decision to create a private right of action is one better left to legislative judgment in the great majority of cases. The creation of a private right of action raises issues beyond the mere consideration whether underlying primary conduct should be allowed or not, entailing, for example, a decision to permit enforcement without the check imposed by prosecutorial discretion. ... While the absence of congressional action addressing private rights of action under an international norm is more equivocal than its failure to provide such a right when it creates a statute, the possible collateral consequences of making international rules privately actionable argue for judicial caution.

Fourth, the subject of those collateral consequences is itself a reason for a high bar to new private causes of action for violating international law, for the potential implications for the foreign relations of the United States of recognizing such causes should make courts particularly wary of impinging on the discretion of the Legislative and Executive Branches in managing foreign affairs. ...

The fifth reason is particularly important in light of the first four. We have no congressional mandate to seek out and define new and debatable violations of the law of nations, and modern indications of congressional understanding of the judicial role in the field have not affirmatively encouraged greater judicial creativity. It is true that a clear mandate appears in the Torture Victim Protection Act of 1991, providing authority that "establish[es] an unambiguous and modern basis for" federal claims of torture and extrajudicial killing. But that affirmative authority is confined to specific subject matter, and although the legislative history includes the remark that §1350 should "remain intact to permit suits based on other norms that already exist or may ripen in the future into rules of customary international law," Congress as a body has done nothing to promote such suits. Several times, indeed, the Senate has expressly declined to give the federal courts the task of interpreting and applying international human rights law, as when its ratification of the International Covenant on Civil and Political Rights declared that the substantive provisions of the document were not self-executing.

These reasons argue for great caution in adapting the law of nations to private rights. Justice Scalia concludes that caution is too hospitable, and a word is in order to summarize where we have come so far and to focus our difference with him on whether some norms of today's law of nations may ever be recognized legitimately by federal courts in the absence of congressional action beyond §1350. All Members of the Court agree that §1350 is only jurisdictional. We also agree, or at least Justice Scalia does not dispute, that the jurisdiction was originally understood to be available to enforce a small number of international norms that a federal court could properly recognize as within the common law enforceable without further statutory authority. Justice Scalia concludes, however, that two subsequent developments should be understood to preclude federal courts from recognizing any further international norms as judicially enforceable today, absent further congressional action. As described before, we now tend to understand common law not as a discoverable reflection of universal reason but, in a positivistic way, as a product of human choice. And we now adhere to a conception of limited judicial power first expressed in reorienting federal diversity jurisdiction, see *Erie R. Co. v. Tompkins*, 304 U.S. 64 (1938), that federal courts have no authority to derive "general" common law.

Whereas Justice Scalia sees these developments as sufficient to close the door to further independent judicial recognition of actionable international norms, other considerations persuade us that the judicial power should be exercised on the understanding that the door is still ajar subject to vigilant doorkeeping, and thus open to a narrow class of international norms today. *Erie* did not in terms bar any judicial recognition of new substantive rules, no matter what the circumstances, and post-*Erie* understanding has identified limited enclaves in which federal courts may derive some substantive law in a common law way. . . .

We must still, however, derive a standard or set of standards for assessing the particular claim Alvarez raises, and for this action it suffices to look to the historical antecedents. Whatever the ultimate criteria for accepting a cause of action subject to jurisdiction under §1350, we are persuaded that federal courts should not recognize private claims under federal common law for violations of any international law norm with less definite content and acceptance among civilized nations than the historical paradigms familiar when §1350 was enacted. . . .

Thus, Alvarez's detention claim must be gauged against the current state of international law, looking to those sources we have long, albeit cautiously, recognized. "[W]here there is no treaty, and no controlling executive or legislative act or judicial decision, resort must be had to the customs and usages of civilized nations; and, as evidence of these, to the works of jurists and commentators, who by years of labor, research and experience, have made themselves peculiarly well acquainted with the subjects of which they treat. Such works are resorted to by judicial tribunals, not for the speculations of their authors concerning what the law ought to be, but for trustworthy evidence of what the law really is."

To begin with, Alvarez cites two well-known international agreements that, despite their moral authority, have little utility under the standard set out in this opinion. He says that his abduction by Sosa was an "arbitrary arrest" within the meaning of the Universal Declaration of Human Rights (Declaration). And he traces the rule against arbitrary arrest not only to the Declaration, but also to article nine of the International Covenant on Civil and Political Rights, to which the United States is a party, and to various other conventions to which it is not. But the Declaration does not of its own force impose obligations as a matter of international law. And, although the Covenant does bind the United States as a matter of international law, the United States ratified the Covenant on the express understanding that it was not self-executing and so did not itself create obligations enforceable in the federal courts. Accordingly, Alvarez cannot say that the Declaration and Covenant themselves establish the relevant and applicable rule of international law. He instead attempts to show that prohibition of arbitrary arrest has attained the status of binding customary international law. . . .

[Alvarez's] claim does not rest on the cross-border feature of his abduction. Although the District Court granted relief in part on finding a violation of international law in taking Alvarez across the border from Mexico to the United States, the Court of Appeals rejected that ground of liability for failure to identify a norm of requisite force prohibiting a forcible abduction across a border. Instead, it relied on the conclusion that the law of the United States did not authorize Alvarez's arrest, because the DEA lacked extraterritorial authority under 21 U.S.C. §878, and because Federal Rule of Criminal Procedure 4(d)(2) limited the warrant for Alvarez's arrest to "the jurisdiction of the United States." It is this position that Alvarez takes now: that his arrest was arbitrary and as such forbidden by international law not because it infringed the prerogatives of Mexico, but because no applicable law authorized it.

Alvarez thus invokes a general prohibition of "arbitrary" detention defined as officially sanctioned action exceeding positive authorization to detain under the domestic law of some government, regardless of the circumstances. Whether or not this is an accurate reading of the Covenant, Alvarez cites little authority that a rule so broad has the status of a binding customary norm today. He certainly cites nothing to justify the federal courts in taking his broad rule as the predicate for a federal lawsuit, for its implications would be breathtaking. His rule would support a cause of action in federal court for any arrest, anywhere in the world, unauthorized by the law of the jurisdiction in which it took place, and would create a cause of action for any seizure of an alien in violation of the Fourth

Amendment. . . . It would create an action in federal court for arrests by state officers who simply exceed their authority; and for the violation of any limit that the law of any country might place on the authority of its own officers to arrest. And all of this assumes that Alvarez could establish that Sosa was acting on behalf of a government when he made the arrest, for otherwise he would need a rule broader still. . . .

Whatever may be said for the broad principle Alvarez advances, in the present, imperfect world, it expresses an aspiration that exceeds any binding customary rule having the specificity we require. Creating a private cause of action to further that aspiration would go beyond any residual common law discretion we think it appropriate to exercise. It is enough to hold that a single illegal detention of less than a day, followed by the transfer of custody to lawful authorities and a prompt arraignment, violates no norm of customary international law so well defined as to support the creation of a federal remedy.

The judgment of the Court of Appeals is reversed.

Justice SCALIA with whom THE CHIEF JUSTICE and Justice THOMAS join, concurring in part and concurring in the judgment.

There is not much that I would add to the Court's detailed opinion, and only one thing that I would subtract: its reservation of a discretionary power in the Federal Judiciary to create causes of action for the enforcement of international-law-based norms. . . . At the time of its enactment, the ATS provided a federal forum in which aliens could bring suit to recover for torts committed in "violation of the law of nations." The law of nations that would have been applied in this federal forum was at the time part of the so-called general common law. . . . General common law was not federal law under the Supremacy Clause, which gave that effect only to the Constitution, the laws of the United States, and treaties. U.S. Const., Art. VI, cl. 2. Federal and state courts adjudicating questions of general common law were not adjudicating questions of federal or state law, respectively — the general common law was neither. . . . This Court's decision in *Erie R. Co. v. Tompkins*, 304 U.S. 64 (1938), signaled the end of federal-court elaboration and application of the general common law. . . .

. . . The Court's detailed exegesis of the ATS conclusively establishes that it is "a jurisdictional statute creating no new causes of action." The Court provides a persuasive explanation of why respondent's contrary interpretation, that "the ATS was intended not simply as a jurisdictional grant, but as authority for the creation of a new cause of action for torts in violation of international law," is wrong. . . . These conclusions are alone enough to dispose of the present case in favor of petitioner Sosa. None of the exceptions to the general rule against finding substantive lawmaking power in a jurisdictional grant apply. . . . [C]reating a federal command (federal common law) out of "international norms," and then constructing a cause of action to enforce that command through the purely jurisdictional grant of the ATS, is nonsense upon stilts.

The analysis in the Court's opinion departs from my own in this respect: After concluding . . . that "the ATS is a jurisdictional statute creating no new causes of action," the Court addresses at length . . . the "good reasons for a restrained conception of the *discretion* a federal court should exercise in considering a new cause of action" under the ATS. By framing the issue as one of "discretion," the Court skips over the antecedent question of authority. This neglects the "lesson of *Erie*," that "grants of jurisdiction alone" (which the Court has acknowledged the ATS to be) "are not themselves grants of lawmaking authority." On this point, the Court observes only that no development between the enactment of the ATS (in 1789) and the birth of modern international human rights litigation under that statute (in 1980) "has categorically *precluded* federal courts from recognizing a claim under the law of nations as an element of common law." This turns our jurisprudence regarding federal common law on its head. The question is not what case or congressional action *prevents* federal courts from applying the law of nations as part of the general common law; it is what *authorizes* that peculiar exception from *Erie*'s fundamental holding that a general common law *does not exist*.

The Court would apparently find authorization in the understanding of the Congress that enacted the ATS, that "district courts would recognize private causes of action for certain torts in violation of the law of nations." But as discussed above, that understanding rested upon a notion of general common law that has been repudiated by *Erie*.

. . . Because today's federal common law is not our Framers' general common law, the question presented by the suggestion of discretionary authority to enforce the law of nations is not whether to extend old-school general-common-law adjudication. Rather, it is whether to create new federal common law. The Court masks the novelty of its approach when it suggests that the difference between us is that I would "close the door to further independent judicial recognition of actionable international norms," whereas the Court would permit the exercise of judicial power "on the understanding that the door is still ajar subject to vigilant doorkeeping." The general common law was the old door. We do not close that door today, for the deed was done in *Erie*. Federal common law is a *new* door. The question is not whether that door will be left ajar, but whether this Court will open it. . . .

We Americans have a method for making the laws that are over us. We elect representatives to two Houses of Congress, each of which must enact the new law and present it for the approval of a President, whom we also elect. For over two decades now, unelected federal judges have been usurping this lawmaking power by converting what they regard as norms of international law into American law. Today's opinion approves that process in principle, though urging the lower courts to be more restrained. This Court seems incapable of admitting that some matters — *any* matters — are none of its business. In today's latest victory for its Never Say Never Jurisprudence, the Court ignores its own conclusion that the ATS provides only jurisdiction, wags a finger at the lower courts for going too far, and then — repeating the same formula the ambitious lower courts *themselves* have used — invites them to try again. . . .

Notes on
SOSA v. ALVAREZ-MACHAIN

1. *Sosa* distinguishes between (1) the Alien Tort Statute (ATS) creation of a cause of action and (2) the statute's vesting federal courts with jurisdiction to hear claims arising under the statute. Is the distinction between these two as significant as the Court suggested?

2. The Court's opinion speaks in terms of taking "cognizance" of a cause of action and "recognizing" a cause of action. From the view of an appropriate use of judicial power, is this different from creating a cause of action?

3. When a court recognizes existing international law causes of action, is that different than a court's decision, as a matter of choice of law analysis, to apply the law of another sovereign — such as a foreign country's law or state law? In understanding the dynamics of this distinction in the context of *Sosa*, is it significant that recognizing existing international law causes of action would implicate the integrity of decisions of the United States government?

4. *Sosa* observes that three causes of action based on customary international law are clearly anticipated by the ATS, since they existed at the time the statute was enacted: violations of safe conduct, infringement of the rights of ambassadors, and piracy. The majority adds, however, that contemporary international law may recognize additional claims within the ambit of the ATS. How should one identify which modern claims are legitimately within the scope of the statute? The majority does not provide much guidance on this, but clearly mandates that "federal courts should not recognize private claims under federal common law for violations of any international law norm with less definite content and acceptance among civilized nations than the historical paradigms familiar when [the ATS] was enacted."

Part of the ambiguity arises from the Court's articulation of five factors that bear on whether a court should create or recognize a cause of action founded on international law. What is the relationship between these factors and its suggestion that a cause of action under the Alien Tort Statute should be as well recognized as Blackstone's three "primary offenses"? Must a potential cause of action satisfy both the five factors and the familiar paradigm test?

5. Justice Scalia argues that the majority's approach to recognizing federal common law in *Sosa* is activist, wrong-headed, and contrary to the mandate of *Erie*. Is Justice Scalia's approach to federal common law in *Sosa* different than his approach in *Boyle*? Note that *Boyle* concerned a defense, while *Sosa* concerned a cause of action. Is that a distinction with a difference?

6. The alleged wrong in *Sosa* had some connection with the United States. In a subsequent decision, *Kiobel v. Royal Dutch Petroleum*, 569 U.S. 108 (2012), the United States Supreme Court took up the question of

whether the ATS should provide a vehicle for international human rights litigation between aliens where neither the aliens nor the events giving rise to the litigation are connected with the United States. The ATS had indeed served as an important vehicle for remedying these types of international human rights violations, but the *Kiobel* Court put an end to the practice, declaring that the ATS was not intended to have such extraterritorial reach.

7. *Sosa* provides some important insights into the relationship between United States federal law and international law. Note that the majority was willing to allow customary international law to inform the content of federal common law — at least to the extent that it reflected the general approach to international norms of which the Congress that enacted the Alien Tort Statute would have been aware in 1789. On the other hand, the majority unequivocally rejected the argument that the United States courts should be bound by the International Covenant on Civil and Political Rights, to which the United States is a party, because it is not "self-executing." These matters will be explored in more detail later in this chapter.

PERSPECTIVE ON A CHOICE OF LAW METHODOLOGY FOR FEDERAL COURTS

For the purposes of this book, a particularly salient federal common law area governs a federal court's selection of a choice among conflicting state laws. One might query why one needs such a federal choice of law methodology. After all, the Supreme Court's decision in *Klaxon v. Stentor*, 313 U.S. 487 (1941), directs federal courts to apply conflict of law principles from the forum state to choose among state laws. But *Klaxon* was a diversity case and federal courts confront choice of law decisions even where they are exercising other forms of power, such as federal question jurisdiction. In some cases, courts have chosen not to follow the mandate of *Klaxon*, concluding that the case is sufficiently "federal" or "national" to call for a federal or uniform approach.

Of course, Congress possesses the power — by virtue of its control over the federal court system and the full faith and credit clause — to create a uniform choice of law code that federal courts could use. In fact, the American Law Institute has approved and published an extensive proposal that develops a method for handling multiple-party, multiple-forum litigation. Complex Litigation: Statutory Recommendations and Analysis (1994). Noting that the most effective method of handling complex litigation is for courts to follow national standards, the proposal sets forth six extensive rules for mass tort and contract actions designed to serve as a uniform federal choice of law code. The proposal received extensive, although not unanimous, scholarly praise, but has not significantly influenced case law or legislative initiatives. Moreover, the suggestion for a national code has never taken hold. Indeed, although there were efforts to include a federal choice of law provision in the Class Action Fairness Act of 2005, Congress declined the opportunity to do so.[29]

In the absence of congressional action, federal courts need to look somewhere for a choice of law approach, and have generally settled on the Restatement (Second) of Conflict of Laws.[30] Accordingly, the Restatement (Second) provides the content of federal common law governing choice of law. Why the Restatement (Second)? The courts that discussed the matter have identified the Restatement (Second) as the most appropriate because the greatest number of jurisdictions follow it. They thus conclude that it is the closest to a uniform United States approach.[31]

When are cases sufficiently federal to merit a federal court ignoring the *Klaxon* approach? One particularly common context is bankruptcy. Federal bankruptcy courts often adjudicate state law issues pertaining to property rights, contract disputes, secured transactions, and the like. But they do so under the umbrella of the federal bankruptcy code. Because federal bankruptcy jurisdiction provides the basis for the court's power and because the court is adjudicating state law claims within the context of uniform bankruptcy policy, many federal bankruptcy courts have declared that federal choice of law (in the form of the Restatement (Second)) and not forum state choice of law rules should guide the choice of which state's law governs the state issues.[32] Other contexts deemed sufficiently federal as to merit a federal choice of law approach include cases implicating the Federal Foreign Sovereign Immunities Act,[33] maritime matters,[34] international banking,[35] copyright,[36] and cases concerning the rights and obligations of United States in contract.[37] In one unusual context, federal courts applied the Restatement (Second) approach as a "general" choice of law methodology because they

---

29. David Marcus, Erie, *the Class Action Fairness Act, and Some Federalism Implications of Diversity Jurisdiction*, 48 Wm. & Mary L. Rev. 1247, 1308-1310 (2007) (outlines attempt to include federal choice of law provision in CAFA).

30. *But see In re Air Crash over the Taiwan Strait on May 25, 2002*, 331 F. Supp. 2d 1176, 1208-1212 (C.D. Cal. 2004) (refusing to determine whether the Restatement (Second) or another approach should provide the choice of law rules in a Death on the High Seas Act claim).

31. *See, e.g., Harris v. Polskie Linie Lotnicze*, 820 F.2d 1000, 1003 (9th Cir. 1987) (stating that the R2 "is a source of general choice-of-law principles and an appropriate starting point for applying federal common law in this area").

32. *See, e.g., In re: Vortex Fishing Sys., Inc.*, 262 F.3d 985, 994 (9th Cir. 2001) (finding the Restatement (Second) governs federal choice of law rules); *Chuidian v. Philippine Nat'l Bank*, 976 F.2d 561, 564 (9th Cir. 1992); *Velasquez v. Crown Life Ins. Co.*, 1999 WL 33305652 at *4 (S.D. Tex. 1999) (finding that both Texas and federal choice of law principles use the Restatement (Second)).

33. *Schoenberg v. Exportadora de Sal, S.A. de C.V.*, 930 F.2d 777, 782 (9th Cir. 1991); *Harris v. Polskie Linie Lotnicze*, 820 F.2d 1000 (9th Cir. 1987).

34. *Dresdner Bank AG v. M/V Olympia Voyager*, 446 F.3d 1377, 1381 (11th Cir. 2006); *Gulf Trading & Transp. Co. v. Vessel Hoegh Shield*, 658 F.2d 363, 366-368 (5th Cir. 1981).

35. *See, e.g., Aaron Ferer & Sons Ltd. v. Chase Manhattan Bank*, 731 F.2d 112 (2d Cir. 1984).

36. *Itar-Tass Russian News Agency v. Russian Kurier, Inc.*, 153 F.3d 82, 90 (2d Cir. 1998).

37. *Al-Kurdi v. United States*, 25 Cl. Ct. 599, 601-4 (Cl. Ct. 1992).

concluded that state choice of law principles were not sufficiently clear or developed.[38]

4.   Hybrid Law

One approach to confronting a choice of law problem—both vertical and horizontal choice of law—is to take the position that courts need not necessarily conclude that one law rather than another should dominate. Instead, courts may try to harmonize the legal principles involved. This inclination is sometimes reflected in the impulse behind globalism and might result in what Dean Paul Schiff Berman might call a "cosmopolitan" approach to law, which counsels in favor of understanding the role of many different jurisdictions in confronting dispute resolution.[39] While a cosmopolitan approach to legal disputes may ultimately result in a choice of one legal principle over another, it need not lead in that direction. Rather, the court may find a way to blend or accommodate the laws of different jurisdictions.

Courts are not always conscious of blending laws of different jurisdictions, but may nonetheless do so as a natural byproduct of decision making. Dispute resolution often creates hybrid law: a legal result in which the laws of more than one jurisdiction inform the bottom line. Indeed, one might observe that the Supreme Court's decision in *Sosa v. Alvarez-Machain* recognizes a form of hybrid law, with customary international law providing the standard of conduct and federal law providing the cause of action and the judicial machinery for litigation and enforcement. Hybrid law can also occur where courts resolve disputes implicating two foreign countries or two states of the United States. Hybrid lawmaking is not a broadly recognized alternative to choice of law analysis, but sufficiently pervasive and important to merit study.

A particularly common circumstance for federal court hybrid lawmaking arises where state and federal law make a claim for regulation. Perhaps the impulse behind federalism—a system with the values of cooperation and respect at its core—accounts for the frequent occurrence of hybrid lawmaking where both state and federal law make a claim for regulation. This impulse is formally reflected in a presumption often used in preemption analysis: the presumption in favor of concurrent power, which starts with the proposition that both state and federal law should be able to regulate a particular problem. (Consider, however,

---

38. *American Triticale, Inc. v. Nytco Services, Inc.*, 664 F.2d 1136, 1142 (9th Cir. 1981) (finding no applicable Idaho conflicts of law rule); *Commercial Ins. Co. of Newark, N.J. v. Pac.-Peru Const. Corp.*, 558 F.2d 948 (9th Cir. 1977) (finding no applicable guidance under Hawaii law); *Dashiell v. Keauhou-Kona Co.*, 487 F.2d 957 (9th Cir. 1973) (finding no applicable guidance in Hawaii law); *Gates v. P.F. Collier, Inc.*, 378 F.2d 888 (9th Cir. 1967) (finding no applicable guidance in Hawaii law).

39. *See, e.g.,* Paul Schiff Berman, *Towards a Cosmopolitan Vision of Conflict of Laws: Redefining Governmental Interests in the Global Era*, 153 U. PA. L. REV. 1819, 1857, 1875-1876 (2005); Paul Schiff Berman, *The Globalization of Jurisdiction*, 151 U. PA. L. REV. 311, 322 (2002); Paul Schiff Berman, *Towards a Jurisprudence of Hybridity*, 2010 UTAH L. REV. 11.

how dramatically different hybrid lawmaking is from the approach to federalism reflected in the positivist approach to federal court decision making in *Erie R. Co. v. Tompkins!*)

However controversial or unorthodox the concept may appear, examples of hybrid federal/state lawmaking abound. And the contexts vary widely, with courts integrating state law property concepts in bankruptcy proceedings, state corporate successor liability laws in environmental proceedings, state law entitlement concepts in federal constitutional due process cases, state inheritance principles in calculating federal tax liability, and the like.[40]

The case below is a particularly controversial example of hybrid lawmaking which implicates not only the integration of state and federal law, but domestic and international law as well. The case also provides important lessons on the attitude of the United States Supreme Court toward the relationship between state and federal laws of the United States (on one hand) and international law (on the other hand). This is a matter explored in more detail at the end of this chapter.

In reading *Medellín*, note the distinction between self-executing treaties and non-self-executing treaties. A self-executing treaty possesses immediate legal force in the countries that ratify the treaty. A non-self-executing treaty, on the other hand, needs implementing legislation in a country before the terms of the treaty have the force of law.

Medellín v. Texas

552 U.S. 491 (2008)

Chief Justice ROBERTS delivered the opinion of the Court.

The International Court of Justice (ICJ), located in the Hague, is a tribunal established pursuant to the United Nations Charter to adjudicate disputes between member states. In the *Case Concerning Avena and Other Mexican Nationals* (*Mex. v. U.S.*), 2004 I.C.J. 12 (Judgment of Mar. 31) (*Avena*), that tribunal considered a claim brought by Mexico against the United States.

[The ICJ held that, based on violations of the Vienna Convention on Consular Relations, 51 named Mexican nationals were entitled to review and reconsideration of their state-court convictions and sentences in the United States, even though the nationals had failed to preserve the claims under applicable state rules governing challenges to criminal convictions. The United States Supreme Court in *Sanchez-Llamas v. Oregon*, 548 U.S. 331 (2006) — issued after *Avena* but involving individuals who were not named in the *Avena* judgment — held that, contrary to the ICJ's determination, the Vienna Convention did not preclude the application of state default rules. After the *Avena* decision, President George W. Bush determined, through a Memorandum to the Attorney General (Feb. 28, 2005), that the

---

40. *See generally* Laura E. Little, *Empowerment Through Restraint: Reverse Preemption or Hybrid Lawmaking?*, 59 CASE W. RES. L. REV. 955, 978-982 (2009), for discussion of various contexts.

United States would honor "its international obligations" under *Avena* "by having State courts give effect to the decision."

Petitioner Medellín, who had been convicted and sentenced in Texas state court for murder, is one of the 51 Mexican nationals named in the *Avena* decision. Medellín filed an application for a writ of habeas corpus in state court. The Texas Court of Criminal Appeals dismissed Medellín's application, given Medellín's failure to raise his Vienna Convention claim in a timely manner under state law. The United States Supreme Court agreed to decide whether the ICJ's *Avena* judgment governed as domestic law in a state court in the United States and whether the President's Memorandum independently required States to provide review and reconsideration of the claims of the 51 Mexican nationals named in *Avena* without regard to state procedural default rules.]

We conclude that neither *Avena* nor the President's Memorandum constitutes directly enforceable federal law that pre-empts state limitations on the filing of successive habeas petitions. . . .

I

A

In 1969, the United States ratified the Vienna Convention on Consular Relations (Vienna Convention or Convention), [which] . . . provides that if a person detained by a foreign country "so requests, the competent authorities of the receiving State shall, without delay, inform the consular post of the sending State" of such detention, and "inform the [detainee] of his righ[t]" to request assistance from the consul of his own state. Art. 36(1)(b), *id.*, at 101. [The Optional Protocol provides disputes concerning the convention "shall lie within the compulsory jurisdiction of the International Court of Justice" and "may accordingly be brought before the [ICJ] . . . by any party to the dispute being a Party to the present Protocol."]

The ICJ is "the principal judicial organ of the United Nations." . . . Under Article 94(1) of the U.N. Charter, "[e]ach Member of the United Nations undertakes to comply with the decision of the [ICJ] in any case to which it is a party." The ICJ's jurisdiction in any particular case, however, is dependent upon the consent of the parties. The ICJ Statute delineates two ways in which a nation may consent to ICJ jurisdiction: It may consent generally to jurisdiction on any question arising under a treaty or general international law, Art. 36(2), *ibid.*, or it may consent specifically to jurisdiction over a particular category of cases or disputes pursuant to a separate treaty. The United States originally consented to the general jurisdiction of the ICJ when it filed a declaration recognizing compulsory jurisdiction. . . . The United States withdrew from general ICJ jurisdiction in 1985. By ratifying the Optional Protocol to the Vienna Convention, the United States consented to the specific jurisdiction of the ICJ with respect to claims arising out of the Vienna Convention. On March 7, 2005, subsequent to the ICJ's judgment in *Avena*, the United States gave notice of withdrawal from the Optional Protocol to the Vienna Convention.

B

Petitioner José Ernesto Medellín, a Mexican national, has lived in the United States since preschool. A member of the "Black and Whites" gang, Medellín was convicted of capital murder and sentenced to death in Texas for the gang rape and brutal murders of two Houston teenagers. . . .

II

Medellín first contends that the ICJ's judgment in *Avena* constitutes a "binding" obligation on the state and federal courts of the United States. He argues that "by virtue of the Supremacy Clause, the treaties requiring compliance with the *Avena* judgment are *already* the 'Law of the Land' by which all state and federal courts in this country are 'bound.'" Accordingly, Medellín argues, *Avena* is a binding federal rule of decision that pre-empts contrary state limitations on successive habeas petitions.

No one disputes that the *Avena* decision — a decision that flows from the treaties through which the United States submitted to ICJ jurisdiction with respect to Vienna Convention disputes — constitutes an *international* law obligation on the part of the United States. But not all international law obligations automatically constitute binding federal law enforceable in United States courts. The question we confront here is whether the *Avena* judgment has automatic *domestic* legal effect such that the judgment of its own force applies in state and federal courts.

This Court has long recognized the distinction between treaties that automatically have effect as domestic law, and those that — while they constitute international law commitments — do not by themselves function as binding federal law. . . . [W]hile treaties "may comprise international commitments . . . they are not domestic law unless Congress has either enacted implementing statutes or the treaty itself conveys an intention that it be 'self-executing' and is ratified on these terms. . . ." Only "[i]f the treaty contains stipulations which are self-executing, that is, require no legislation to make them operative, [will] they have the force and effect of a legislative enactment." *Whitney, supra,* at 194, 8 S. Ct. 456.

Medellín and his *amici* nonetheless contend that the Optional Protocol, United Nations Charter, and ICJ Statute supply the "relevant obligation" to give the *Avena* judgment binding effect in the domestic courts of the United States. Because none of these treaty sources creates binding federal law in the absence of implementing legislation, and because it is uncontested that no such legislation exists, we conclude that the *Avena* judgment is not automatically binding domestic law.

. . . The most natural reading of the Optional Protocol is as a bare grant of jurisdiction. It provides only that "[d]isputes arising out of the interpretation or application of the [Vienna] Convention shall lie within the compulsory jurisdiction of the International Court of Justice" and "may accordingly be brought before the [ICJ] . . . by any party to the dispute being a Party to the present Protocol." The Protocol says nothing about the effect of an ICJ decision and does not itself commit signatories to comply with an ICJ judgment. . . .

... If ICJ judgments were ... regarded as automatically enforceable domestic law, they would be immediately and directly binding on state and federal courts pursuant to the Supremacy Clause. Mexico or the ICJ would have no need to proceed to the Security Council to enforce the judgment in this case. Noncompliance with an ICJ judgment through exercise of the Security Council veto — always regarded as an option by the Executive and ratifying Senate during and after consideration of the U.N. Charter, Optional Protocol, and ICJ Statute — would no longer be a viable alternative. There would be nothing to veto. In light of the U.N. Charter's remedial scheme, there is no reason to believe that the President and Senate signed up for such a result.

In sum, Medellín's view that ICJ decisions are automatically enforceable as domestic law is fatally undermined. . . . The pertinent international agreements, therefore, do not provide for implementation of ICJ judgments through direct enforcement in domestic courts, and "where a treaty does not provide a particular remedy, either expressly or implicitly, it is not for the federal courts to impose one on the States through lawmaking of their own." . . .

. . . [T]he consequences of Medellín's argument give pause. An ICJ judgment, the argument goes, is not only binding domestic law but is also unassailable. As a result, neither Texas nor this Court may look behind a judgment and quarrel with its reasoning or result. (We already know, from *Sanchez-Llamas*, that this Court disagrees with both the reasoning and result in *Avena*.) Medellín's interpretation would allow ICJ judgments to override otherwise binding state law; there is nothing in his logic that would exempt contrary federal law from the same fate. And there is nothing to prevent the ICJ from ordering state courts to annul criminal convictions and sentences, for any reason deemed sufficient by the ICJ. Indeed, that is precisely the relief Mexico requested. . . .

In short, and as we observed in *Sanchez-Llamas*, "[n]othing in the structure or purpose of the ICJ suggests that its interpretations were intended to be conclusive on our courts." Given that holding, it is difficult to see how that same structure and purpose can establish, as Medellín argues, that *judgments* of the ICJ nonetheless were intended to be conclusive on our courts. . . . [W]hile the ICJ's judgment in *Avena* creates an international law obligation on the part of the United States, it does not of its own force constitute binding federal law that pre-empts state restrictions on the filing of successive habeas petitions. [A] contrary conclusion would be extraordinary, given that basic rights guaranteed by our own Constitution do not have the effect of displacing state procedural rules. Nothing in the text, background, negotiating and drafting history, or practice among signatory nations suggests that the President or Senate intended the improbable result of giving the judgments of an international tribunal a higher status than that enjoyed by "many of our most fundamental constitutional protections."

III

Medellín next argues that the ICJ's judgment in *Avena* is binding on state courts by virtue of the President's February 28, 2005 Memorandum. The United

States contends that while the *Avena* judgment does not of its own force require domestic courts to set aside ordinary rules of procedural default, that judgment became the law of the land with precisely that effect pursuant to the President's Memorandum and his power "to establish binding rules of decision that preempt contrary state law." . . .

[The Court rejected this contention, dismissing the suggestions that (1) the President had inherent authority to enforce ICJ judgments against states; and (2) the President obtained power to enforce the ICJ judgments through treaties in which Congress acquiesced by virtue of the Senate's advice and consent power. In so holding, the Court stated that "[t]he President has an array of political and diplomatic means available to enforce international obligations, but unilaterally converting a non-self-executing treaty into a self-executing one is not among them." Moreover, the Court described the President's Memorandum as "unprecedented," pointing out that the "Government has not identified a single instance in which the President has attempted (or Congress has acquiesced in) a Presidential directive issued to state courts, much less one that reaches deep into the heart of the State's police powers and compels state courts to reopen final criminal judgments and set aside neutrally applicable state laws." Finally, the Court concluded that "the *Avena* judgment is not domestic law;" and for that reason the President lacked power to enforce through his constitutional power in Article I, §3 of the United States Constitution to "take care that the Laws be faithfully executed."]

Justice BREYER, with whom Justice SOUTER and Justice GINSBURG join, dissenting.

The Constitution's Supremacy Clause provides that "all Treaties . . . which shall be made . . . under the Authority of the United States, shall be the supreme Law of the Land; and the Judges in every State shall be bound thereby." Art. VI, cl. 2. The Clause means that the "courts" must regard "a treaty . . . as equivalent to an act of the legislature, whenever it operates of itself without the aid of any legislative provision."

In the *Avena* case the International Court of Justice (ICJ) (interpreting and applying the Vienna Convention on Consular Relations) issued a judgment that requires the United States to reexamine certain criminal proceedings in the cases of 51 Mexican nationals. The question here is whether the ICJ's *Avena* judgment is enforceable now as a matter of domestic law, *i.e.*, whether it "operates of itself without the aid" of any further legislation.

[Justice Breyer concluded that the Optional Protocol represents a self-executing treaty obligation and thus does not require congressional action in order to create binding federal law that preempts contrary state law. In this regard, he observed that neither the President nor Congress expressed concern about the operation of the Optional Protocol or about judicial enforcement of *Avena*. Indeed, the President explicitly favors enforcing it. The appropriate forum for "review and reconsideration" of Medellín's case in light of *Avena* would be the Texas state courts on remand.]

Notes on
MEDELLÍN

1. *Medellín* brims with profound issues of power and justice, including questions of treaty interpretation, compliance, and enforcement; the scope of presidential power; horizontal separation of powers within the federal government; federalism; and the interplay among federal, state, and international law. It is no surprise, then, that scholars have produced an enormously rich body of scholarship analyzing the case. *See, e.g.*, David J. Bederman, Medellín's *New Paradigm for Treaty Interpretation*, 102 AM. J. INT'L L. 529 (2008) (treaty interpretation); Curtis A. Bradley, *Intent, Presumptions, and Non-Self-Executing Treaties*, 102 AM. J. INT'L L. 540 (2008) (treaty enforcement and executive power); Steve Charnovitz, *Revitalizing the U.S. Compliance Power*, 102 AM. J. INT'L L. 551 (2008) (United States treaty compliance); Margaret E. McGuinness, *Three Narratives of* Medellin v. Texas, 31 SUFFOLK TRANSNAT'L L. REV. 227 (2008) (three narratives at play in the decision: internal/constitutionalist narrative, an external/internationalist narrative, and a transnational/intersystemic narrative); Carlos Manuel Vázquez, *Less Than Zero?*, 102 AM. J. INT'L L. 563 (2008) (presidential power).

2. *Medellín* demonstrates a theme of this section: blending various sources of authority from different sovereigns. While the case provided an opportunity for the Supreme Court to negotiate a three-way relationship among federal, international, and state law, the Court disqualified international law: finding that neither the Vienna Convention, the Optional Protocol, nor the International Court of Justice judgment in *Avena* bound the federal or state governments. In the end, the case represents only an interplay between state and federal law—albeit an important one. To what extent can the case be characterized as a straightforward preemption case concerning federal foreign affairs principles and the federal government's embrace of treaty obligations?

3. As a general matter, did the Court give too much power to state procedural law to control the disposition of the case, with all of its foreign relations ramifications? The opinion is certainly filled with a flourish of deference to state authority. Consider, for example, the Court's statement that a state's procedural rules are so inviolable that even "basic rights guaranteed by our own Constitution do not have the effect of displacing [them]." And, according to the Court, state sovereignty's strength is equally compelling in the face of presidential power, which "cannot stretch so far" as to reach "deep into the heart of the State's police powers and compel state courts to reopen final criminal judgments." *See* Robert B. Ahdieh, *Foreign Affairs, International Law, and the New Federalism: Lessons from Coordination*, 73 MO. L. REV. 1185, 1231 (2008) (in *Medellín*, the "State of Texas emerged as the critical decider of the domestic effects of international law").

4. Although the Court purported to defer to the power of state procedural law in disposing of the case, didn't federal law have considerable

influence on the bottom line? After all, the Court's judgment turned on its own interpretation of both the President's power under the United States Constitution and the treaties endorsed by the United States government that disposed of the case. Moreover, while the *Medellín* Court spoke of state rules governing procedural bars as though they were sacrosanct, one need not look far to identify plenty of contexts where federal courts disregard state procedural rules in federal habeas proceedings and the like. Accordingly, one must conclude that the Court's decision to give effect to the Texas procedural bar was a decision made as a matter of federal prerogative. In other words: federal law *chose* to give effect to and embrace state law, thus creating a result dictated by an intersection of both sovereigns' law. *See* Laura E. Little, *Empowerment Through Restraint: Reverse Preemption or Hybrid Lawmaking?*, 59 CASE W. RES. L. REV. 955, 975-976, 985 (2009).

5. *Medellín* represents a common form of hybrid lawmaking: one law (federal law, in *Medellín)* deferring to another sovereign's law (the Texas procedural law in *Medellín*). A related type of hybrid law results where a particular legal result in one sovereign triggers consequences under the law of another sovereign. *See, e.g., Johnson v. United States*, 130 S. Ct. 1265 (2010) (holding that defendant's prior battery conviction under Florida law was a violent felony conviction within the meaning of the federal Armed Career Criminal Act, and that the federal court was bound by the Florida Supreme Court's interpretation of state law, including its determination of the elements of battery).

Perhaps the most straightforward occurrence of hybrid law occurs when a court of one sovereign simply adopts the law of another sovereign as its own. This is sometimes called "incorporation by reference." For an illustration of incorporation by reference, recall the Court's choice of law decision in *D'Agostino v. Johnson & Johnson, Inc.*, 628 A.2d 305 (1993), set forth in Chapter 2. In *D'Agostino*, the Court concluded that the Foreign Corrupt Practices Act sets forth state public policy, and embraced the standards of the Act for purposes of determining whether the discharge of an employee violates the clear mandate of state public policy. The simplicity of this type of hybridity, however, may become more complicated as the incorporated law evolves after it has become incorporated into the corpus of another jurisdiction's law. This evolution within the incorporating jurisdiction may occur for a number of reasons, perhaps the most common being interaction between the incorporated law and preexisting legal principles (such as rules of construction or interpretation) in the new jurisdiction. In addition, the jurisdiction from which the law originally came may subsequently amend the law, and the question arises whether the amendment should take effect in the incorporating jurisdiction. The answer is often "no," in which case the incorporation is considered "static."[41]

An entirely different type of hybrid law is "general consensus law," a concept articulated in the complex litigation brought by Vietnam War veterans for injuries suffered from exposure to herbicides. *In re "Agent Orange" Product Liability Litigation*, 580 F. Supp. 690 (E.D.N.Y. 1984). The *Agent Orange* Court embraced the concept of general consensus law, but the case settled before the Court actually defined the content of such consensus law. While this approach to conflict of law problems is uncommon in the United States, scholars have noted that choice of law (or private international law) analysis by courts in the European Union has contributed to harmonization of European law as well as the development of a new culture in Europe.[42]

Finally, hybrid law can result where courts confront a case requiring them to reckon with a concept developed in a cultural system that is foreign to the system in which the court is operating. The court may choose to ignore the foreign cultural concept, to adopt it wholesale, or to modify it in an attempt to harmonize it with principles of domestic law. A particularly revealing case study of this phenomenon concerns treatment of the Islamic concept of *mahr* by Western courts adjudicating domestic relations matters. "*Mahr*" is an Islamic family law concept describing a husband's obligation to his wife "in consideration of the marriage." PASCALE FORNIER, MUSLIM MARRIAGE IN WESTERN COURTS 9 (2010). Western courts have taken a variety of approaches to *mahr*, including ignoring the concept, seeking to honor it as a legal matter, honoring the concept as a cultural matter, and perverting it beyond its intended scope and meaning. *See, e.g., id.* at 70, 76, 138-140, 143.

As these illustrations demonstrate, hybrid law can result spontaneously, without any motivation by courts or advocates to meld divergent legal principles. The dynamics creating hybrid law and the forms that it takes may nonetheless hold lessons for conflict of laws problems in the globalized world. Rather than feeling compelled to choose one law over another where the two conflict, might a court better serve the parties and humankind by combining the laws in a manner that promotes justice for the parties and respects the sovereigns that created the conflicting laws?

---

41. For arguments in favor of "dynamic" incorporation, see Michael C. Dorf, *Dynamic Incorporation of Foreign Law*, 157 U. PA. L. REV. 103 (2008).

42. Annelise Riles, *Cultural Conflicts*, 71 LAW & CONTEMP. PROBS. 273 (2008); Horatia Muir Watt, *Evidence of an Emergent European Legal Culture: Public Policy Requirements of Procedural Fairness Under the Brussels and Lugano Conventions*, 36 TEX. INT'L L.J. 539 (2001).

C. THE RELATIONSHIP BETWEEN UNITED STATES AND INTERNATIONAL LAWS

1. General Principles

The relationship between United States and international laws is complex and fraught with controversy. On the one hand is the apparently simple approach to international law as a form of domestic United States law expressed in *The Paquette Habana*, 175 U.S. 677, 700 (1900): "International law is part of our law, and must be ascertained and administered by the courts of justice of appropriate jurisdiction as often as questions of right depending upon it are duly presented for their determination." On the other hand is the view, arguably reflected in *Medellín v. Texas*, that international law has no force within United States courts without specific authorization, such as — in the case of a treaty — a clear showing that the treaty was intended to be self-executing or the existence of implementing legislation. Traditionally, this disagreement over the status of international law has been framed as a debate between "dualists" and "monists." Dualists view domestic law (such as federal law) as derived from an entirely different system than international law. *Medellín* reflects dualism to the extent that it treats international law as capable of becoming part of federal law only to the extent that an authoritative federal body — such as the United States Congress — explicitly embraces the international law. *The Paquette Habana* rejects the dualist approach. Rather, it reflects a monist approach, viewing domestic and international law as components of a single legal system.

Another way to view the controversial relationship between international law and United States law is to focus on complexities arising from differences among the type of international law, such as international agreements or customary international law. International agreements can take a number of forms, including treaties and conventions, but generally operate as though they are contracts between the parties to the agreement. Accordingly, the intent of the parties regarding the agreement's intended effect influences the agreement's relationship with domestic law. For example, as explained in connection with *Medellín*, parties might intend for a treaty to be self-executing or non-self-executing. Thus, the parties' intent can control whether the treaty possesses immediate legal force in the country that ratified the treaty. As the Justices' varying opinions in *Medellín* demonstrated, however, opinions differ on whether a treaty should be presumed self-executing or not. If a treaty is deemed self-executing, however, the treaty is regarded as "supreme" for the purposes of the supremacy clause of the United States Constitution, and can displace conflicting state law. Non-self-executing treaties need implementing legislation to take on binding force in the courts of the United States.

The status of customary international law in the United States is subject to even greater controversy and uncertainty. As expressed in some of the opinions in *Sosa v. Alvarez-Machain*, customary international law has been viewed as federal law, appropriate for federal courts to enforce even without congressional legislation or executive proclamation.[43] A canon of interpretation associated with the decision in *The Charming Betsy* holds that Congress is presumed to have acted consistently with international law unless a contrary interpretation is unavoidable. *Murray v. The Charming Betsy*, 6 U.S. (2 Cranch) 64, 118 (1804) ("[A]n act of Congress ought never to be construed to violate the law of nations if any other possible construction remains . . ."). Where a federal statute sets forth a principle that is unavoidably contrary to preexisting principles of customary international law, United States courts must enforce the statute. *See, e.g., Whitney v. Robertson*, 124 U.S. 190, 194 (1888).

Embedded in the question of how federal and international law should interact is the question of how state and international law should interact. These questions are inextricable because of the complicated relationship between state and federal law, with federal law on one hand deferring to the sovereignty and spheres of operation of state law, and state law yielding to a conflicting state law. We have already seen at least two examples of this dynamic among federal, state, and international law in this chapter. Recall that in *Crosby v. National Foreign Trade Council*, 530 U.S. 363 (2000), the Supreme Court held that a Massachusetts law infringed the federal government's foreign affairs power, and struck down the state law so as to allow federal law to negotiate questions of foreign relations and international law without interference. By contrast, the *Medellín* Court negotiated this dynamic among federal, state, and international law by deferring (at least in theory) to the prerogative of state law to control.[44] Consider how the case that follows, which deals with an apparently straightforward question under the Warsaw Convention, differs in how it handles this complicated dynamic. Does its approach most resemble the orientation of *Crosby* or the orientation of *Medellín*?

El Al Israel Airlines, Ltd. v. Tseng

525 U.S. 155 (1999)

Justice GINSBURG delivered the opinion of the Court.

Plaintiff-respondent Tsui Yuan Tseng was subjected to an intrusive security search at John F. Kennedy International Airport in New York before she boarded an El Al Israel Airlines May 22, 1993 flight to Tel Aviv. Tseng seeks tort damages

---

43. Another contrasting theory of customary international law views it as originally a form of state law, but which became federalized by virtue of the international functions of the federal government. Louis Henkin, *International Law as Law in the United States*, 82 MICH. L. REV. 1555, 1536 (1984).

44. Professor Lea Brilmayer points out that the relationship between state law and international law is far more complicated than may first appear. Because the Constitution appears to vest the federal government with nearly exclusive control over international relations, one would expect state law to simply yield to international law recognized by the federal government under the mandate of supremacy clause. She identifies, however, a number of ways in which international law limits state authority in more complex and subtle ways that mere supremacy analysis. Lea Brilmayer, *Federalism, State Authority, and the Preemptive Power of International Law*, 1994 SUP. CT. REV. 295, 305-313.

from El Al for this occurrence. The episode-in-suit, both parties now submit, does not qualify as an "accident" within the meaning of the treaty popularly known as the Warsaw Convention, which governs air carrier liability for "all international transportation." Tseng alleges psychic or psychosomatic injuries, but no "bodily injury," as that term is used in the Convention. Her case presents a question of the Convention's exclusivity: When the Convention allows no recovery for the episode-in-suit, does it correspondingly preclude the passenger from maintaining an action for damages under another source of law, in this case, New York tort law?

The exclusivity question before us has been settled prospectively in a Warsaw Convention protocol (Montreal Protocol No. 4) recently ratified by the Senate. In accord with the protocol, Tseng concedes, a passenger whose injury is not compensable under the Convention (because it entails no "bodily injury" or was not the result of an "accident") will have no recourse to an alternate remedy. We conclude that the protocol, to which the United States has now subscribed, clarifies, but does not change, the Convention's exclusivity domain. We therefore hold that recovery for a personal injury suffered "on board [an] aircraft or in the course of any of the operations of embarking or disembarking," . . . if not allowed under the Convention, is not available at all.

The Court of Appeals for the Second Circuit ruled otherwise. In that court's view, a plaintiff who did not qualify for relief under the Convention could seek relief under local law for an injury sustained in the course of international air travel. We now reverse the Second Circuit's judgment. Recourse to local law, we are persuaded, would undermine the uniform regulation of international air carrier liability that the Warsaw Convention was designed to foster.

I

We have twice reserved decision on the Convention's exclusivity. In *Air France v. Saks*, 470 U.S. 392 (1985), we concluded that a passenger's injury was not caused by an "accident" for which the airline could be held accountable under the Convention, but expressed no view whether that passenger could maintain "a state cause of action for negligence." *Id.*, at 408. In *Eastern Airlines, Inc. v. Floyd*, 499 U.S. 530, 111 S. Ct. 1489, 113 L. Ed. 2d 569 (1991), we held that mental or psychic injuries unaccompanied by physical injuries are not compensable under Article 17 of the Convention, but declined to reach the question whether the Convention "provides the exclusive cause of action for injuries sustained during international air transportation." *Id.*, at 553. We resolve in this case the question on which we earlier reserved judgment.

At the outset, we highlight key provisions of the treaty we are interpreting. Chapter I of the Warsaw Convention, entitled "SCOPE-DEFINITIONS," declares in Article 1(1) that the "[C]onvention shall apply to all international transportation of persons, baggage, or goods performed by aircraft for hire." Chapter III, entitled "LIABILITY OF THE CARRIER," defines in Articles 17, 18, and 19 the three kinds of liability for which the Convention provides. Article 17 establishes the conditions of liability for personal injury to passengers:

The carrier shall be liable for damage sustained in the event of the death or wounding of a passenger or any other bodily injury suffered by a passenger, if the accident which caused the damage so sustained took place on board the aircraft or in the course of any of the operations of embarking or disembarking.

Article 18 establishes the conditions of liability for damage to baggage or goods. Article 19 establishes the conditions of liability for damage caused by delay. Article 24, referring back to Articles 17, 18, and 19, instructs:

(1) In the cases covered by articles 18 and 19 any action for damages, however founded, can only be brought subject to the conditions and limits set out in this convention.

(2) In the cases covered by article 17 the provisions of the preceding paragraph shall also apply, without prejudice to the questions as to who are the persons who have the right to bring suit and what are their respective rights.

II

With the key treaty provisions as the backdrop, we next describe the episode-in-suit. On May 22, 1993, Tsui Yuan Tseng arrived at John F. Kennedy International Airport to board an El Al Israel Airlines flight to Tel Aviv. In conformity with standard El Al preboarding procedures, a security guard questioned Tseng about her destination and travel plans. The guard considered Tseng's responses "illogical," and ranked her as a "high risk" passenger. Tseng was taken to a private security room where her baggage and person were searched for explosives and detonating devices. She was told to remove her shoes, jacket, and sweater, and to lower her blue jeans to midhip. A female security guard then searched Tseng's body outside her clothes by hand and with an electronic security wand.

After the search, which lasted 15 minutes, El Al personnel decided that Tseng did not pose a security threat and allowed her to board the flight. Tseng later testified that she "was really sick and very upset" during the flight, that she was "emotionally traumatized and disturbed" during her month-long trip in Israel, and that, upon her return, she underwent medical and psychiatric treatment for the lingering effects of the body search.

Tseng filed suit against El Al in 1994 in a New York state court of first instance. Her complaint alleged a state-law personal injury claim based on the May 22, 1993 episode at JFK. Tseng's pleading charged, *inter alia,* assault and false imprisonment, but alleged no bodily injury. El Al removed the case to federal court.

The District Court, after a bench trial, dismissed Tseng's personal injury claim. . . . The Court of Appeals reversed in relevant part. . . .

III

. . . The parties do not dispute that the episode-in-suit occurred in international transportation in the course of embarking. . . . Our inquiry begins with the text of Article 24, which prescribes the exclusivity of the Convention's provisions for air carrier liability. . . ." Because a treaty ratified by the United States is not only the law of this land, see U.S. Const., Art. II, §2, but also an agreement among sovereign powers, we have traditionally considered as aids to its interpretation the negotiating and drafting history (*travaux préparatoires*) and the postratification understanding of the contracting parties."

Article 24 provides that "cases covered by article 17" — or in the governing French text, "les cas prévus à l'àrticle 17" — may "only be brought subject to the conditions and limits set out in th[e] [C]onvention." That prescription is not a model of the clear drafter's art. We recognize that the words lend themselves to divergent interpretation.

In Tseng's view, and in the view of the Court of Appeals, "les cas prévus à l'àrticle 17" means those cases in which a passenger could actually maintain a claim for relief under Article 17. So read, Article 24 would permit any passenger whose personal injury suit did not satisfy the liability conditions of Article 17 to pursue the claim under local law.

In El Al's view, on the other hand, and in the view of the United States as *amicus curiae,* "les cas prévus à l'àrticle 17" refers generically to all personal injury cases stemming from occurrences on board an aircraft or in embarking or disembarking, and simply distinguishes that class of cases (Article 17 cases) from cases involving damaged luggage or goods, or delay (which Articles 18 and 19 address). So read, Article 24 would preclude a passenger from asserting any air transit personal injury claims under local law, including claims that failed to satisfy Article 17's liability conditions, notably, because the injury did not result from an "accident," see *Saks,* 470 U.S., at 405, 105 S. Ct. 1338, or because the "accident" did not result in physical injury or physical manifestation of injury, see *Floyd,* 499 U.S., at 552.

Respect is ordinarily due the reasonable views of the Executive Branch concerning the meaning of an international treaty. . . . We conclude that the Government's construction of Article 24 is most faithful to the Convention's text, purpose, and overall structure.

A

The cardinal purpose of the Warsaw Convention, we have observed, is to "achiev[e] uniformity of rules governing claims arising from international air transportation." The Convention signatories, in the treaty's preamble, specifically "recognized the advantage of regulating in a uniform manner the conditions of . . . the liability of the carrier." To provide the desired uniformity, Chapter III of the Convention sets out an array of liability rules which, the treaty declares, "apply to all international transportation of persons, baggage, or goods performed by aircraft." In that Chapter, the Convention describes and defines the three areas of air carrier liability (personal injuries in Article 17, baggage or goods loss, destruction, or damage in Article 18, and damage occasioned by delay in Article 19), the conditions exempting air carriers from liability (Article 20), the monetary limits of liability (Article 22), and the circumstances in which air carriers may not limit liability (Articles 23 and 25). Given the Convention's comprehensive scheme of liability rules and its textual emphasis on uniformity, we would be hard put to conclude that the delegates at Warsaw meant to subject air carriers to the distinct, nonuniform liability rules of the individual signatory nations.

The Court of Appeals looked to our precedent for guidance on this point, but it misperceived our meaning. It misread our decision in *Zicherman* to say that the Warsaw Convention expresses no compelling interest in uniformity that would warrant preempting an otherwise applicable body of law, here New York tort law. *Zicherman* acknowledges that the Convention centrally endeavors "to foster uniformity in the law of international air travel." It further recognizes that the Convention addresses the question whether there is airline liability *vel non*. The *Zicherman* case itself involved auxiliary issues: who may seek recovery in lieu of passengers, and for what harms they may be compensated. Looking to the Convention's text, negotiating and drafting history, contracting states' postratification understanding of the Convention, and scholarly commentary, the Court in *Zicherman* determined that Warsaw drafters intended to resolve *whether there is liability*, but to leave to domestic law (the local law identified by the forum under its choice-of-law rules or approaches) determination of the compensatory damages available to the suitor.

A complementary purpose of the Convention is to accommodate or balance the interests of passengers seeking recovery for personal injuries, and the interests of air carriers seeking to limit potential liability. Before the Warsaw accord, injured passengers could file suits for damages, subject only to the limitations of the forum's laws, including the forum's choice-of-law regime. This exposure inhibited the growth of the then-fledgling international airline industry. Many international air carriers at that time endeavored to require passengers, as a condition of air travel, to relieve or reduce the carrier's liability in case of injury. The Convention drafters designed Articles 17, 22, and 24 of the Convention as a compromise between the interests of air carriers and their customers worldwide. In Article 17 of the Convention, carriers are denied the contractual prerogative to exclude or limit their liability for personal injury. In Articles 22 and 24, passengers are limited in the amount of damages they may recover, and are restricted in the claims they may pursue by the conditions and limits set out in the Convention. . . .

The Second Circuit feared that if Article 17 were read to exclude relief outside the Convention for Tseng, then a passenger injured by a malfunctioning escalator in the airline's terminal would have no recourse against the airline, even if the airline recklessly disregarded its duty to keep the escalator in proper repair. . . . [H]owever, the Convention addresses and concerns, only and exclusively, the airline's liability for passenger injuries occurring "on board the aircraft or in the course of any of the operations of embarking or disembarking." Art. 17. A carrier, therefore, "is indisputably subject to liability under local law for injuries arising outside of that scope: *e.g.*, for passenger injuries occurring before 'any of the operations of embarking'" or disembarking.

Tseng raises a different concern. She argues that air carriers will escape liability for their intentional torts if passengers are not permitted to pursue personal injury claims outside of the terms of the Convention. But we have already cautioned that the definition of "accident" under Article 17 is an "unusual event . . . *external to the passenger*," and that "[t]his definition should be flexibly applied." In *Saks*, the Court concluded that no "accident" occurred because the injury there — a hearing loss — "indisputably result[ed] from *the passenger's own internal reaction* to the usual, normal, and expected operation of the aircraft." As we earlier noted, Tseng and El Al chose not to pursue in this Court the question whether an "accident" occurred, for an affirmative answer would still leave Tseng unable to recover under the treaty; she sustained no "bodily injury" and could not gain compensation under Article 17 for her solely psychic or psychosomatic injuries.

B

The drafting history of Article 17 is consistent with our understanding of the preemptive effect of the Convention. The preliminary draft of the Convention submitted to the conference at Warsaw made air carriers liable "in the case of death, wounding, or any other bodily injury suffered by a traveler." In the later draft that prescribed what is now Article 17, airline liability was narrowed to encompass only bodily injury caused by an "accident." It is improbable that, at the same time the drafters narrowed the conditions of air carrier liability in Article 17, they intended, in Article 24, to permit passengers to skirt those conditions by pursuing claims under local law. . . .

The British House of Lords, in *Sidhu v. British Airways plc*, [1997] 1 All E.R. 193, [interpreted the history of the Warsaw Convention and concluded] accurately that "the [C]onvention is concerned with certain rules only, not with all the rules relating to international carriage by air." [The House of Lords observed that, for] example, the Convention does not say "anything . . . about the carrier's obligations of insurance, and in particular about compulsory insurance against third party risks." The Convention, in other words, is "a partial harmonisation, directed to the particular issues with which it deals," *ibid.*, among them, a carrier's liability to passengers for personal injury. As to those issues, the Lords concluded, "the aim of the [C]onvention is to unify." . . .

C

Montreal Protocol No. 4, ratified by the Senate on September 28, 1998, amends Article 24 to read, in relevant part: "In the carriage of passengers and baggage, any action for damages, however founded, can only be brought subject to the conditions and limits set out in this Convention. . . ."[15] Both parties agree

---

15. Article 24, as amended by Montreal Protocol No. 4, provides:

"1. In the carriage of passengers and baggage, any action for damages, however founded, can only be brought subject to the conditions and limits set out in this Convention, without prejudice to the question as to who are the persons who have the right to bring suit and what are their respective rights.

"2. In the carriage of cargo, any action for damages, however founded, whether under this Convention or in contract or in tort or otherwise, can only be brought subject to the conditions and limits of liability set out in this Convention without prejudice to the question as to who are the persons who have the right to bring suit and what are their respective rights. Such limits of liability constitute maximum limits and may not be exceeded whatever the circumstances which gave rise to the liability." S. Exec. Rep. No. 105-20, at 29.

that, under the amended Article 24, the Convention's preemptive effect is clear: The treaty precludes passengers from bringing actions under local law when they cannot establish air carrier liability under the treaty. Revised Article 24, El Al urges and we agree, merely clarifies, it does not alter, the Convention's rule of exclusivity.

Supporting the position that revised Article 24 provides for preemption not earlier established, Tseng urges that federal preemption of state law is disfavored generally, and particularly when matters of health and safety are at stake. Tseng overlooks in this regard that the nation-state, not subdivisions within one nation, is the focus of the Convention and the perspective of our treaty partners. Our home-centered preemption analysis, therefore, should not be applied, mechanically, in construing our international obligations.

Decisions of the courts of other Convention signatories corroborate our understanding of the Convention's preemptive effect. . . . The "opinions of our sister signatories," we have observed, are "entitled to considerable weight." *Saks*, 470 U.S., at 404, 105 S. Ct. 1338 (internal quotation marks omitted). The text, drafting history, and underlying purpose of the Convention, in sum, counsel us to adhere to a view of the treaty's exclusivity shared by our treaty partners. . . .

For the reasons stated, we hold that the Warsaw Convention precludes a passenger from maintaining an action for personal injury damages under local law when her claim does not satisfy the conditions for liability under the Convention. . . .

Justice STEVENS, dissenting.

My disagreement with the Court's holding today has limited practical significance, not just because the issue has been conclusively determined for future cases by the recent amendment to the Warsaw Convention, but also because it affects only a narrow category of past cases. The decision is nevertheless significant because, in the end, it rests on the novel premise that preemption analysis should be applied differently to treaties than to other kinds of federal law. . . .

. . . Everyone agrees that the literal text of the treaty does not preempt claims of personal injury that do not arise out of an accident. It is equally clear that nothing in the drafting history requires that result. On the contrary, the [drafting history] . . . suggests that the parties assumed that local law would apply to all nonaccident cases. I agree with the Court that that inference is not strong enough, in itself, to require that the ambiguity be resolved in the plaintiff's favor. It suffices for me, however, that the history is just as ambiguous as the text. I firmly believe that a treaty, like an Act of Congress, should not be construed to preempt state law unless its intent to do so is clear. For this reason, I respectfully dissent.

Notes on
EL AL

1. Note that the *El Al* Court said it should defer to the President's interpretation of the Warsaw treaty, an interpretation expressed by the Solicitor General as amicus curiae in the case. Compare the *El Al* Court's approach to presidential authority with the Court's approach in *Medellín*. The President had tried hard in *Medellín* to give effect to the International Court of Justice's interpretation of the Vienna Convention on Consular Relations. Yet the *Medellín* Court conclusively rejected the President's efforts. Are the two approaches to presidential treaty interpretation in tension? After all, both cases implicated the President's treaty interpretation as well as the President's position on the interaction between state and international law. Does the fact that *Medellín* concerned the effect of an international court's judgment make a difference? Alternatively, does the explanation for the difference in approach to the President's interpretation lie in the fact that *Medellín* concerned the effect of the President's efforts on an actual state court criminal case, while the *El Al* Court's decision merely implicated a potential state law cause of action? Or, finally, does the explanation simply lie in the Court's hostility to interfering with the *Medellín* conviction and sentence of death or its hostility to a possible state law cause of action in *El Al*?

2. In his *El Al* dissent, Justice Stevens explained that he would dispose of the case differently than the majority because he would approach the case with the standard presumption against preempting state law, while the majority did not believe that the presumption should apply with full force in the case. Which is the better position on whether the presumption against preemption should apply full force in a case concerning a potential conflict between state law and an international treaty?

3. Assume that the Court had decided that state law could provide a cause of action under the circumstances in *El Al*. Or assume that a state law question arose in a Warsaw Convention case. If more than one state's law might apply in either of these instances, how would a federal court resolve the choice of law issue to determine which state law should govern? Should the federal court apply the choice of law approach of the forum state, as directed by *Klaxon v. Stentor*? Alternatively, should the federal court apply the Restatement (Second) of Conflict of Laws as the "federal" choice of law approach? *Compare Bickel v. Korean Air Lines Co.*, 83 F.3d 127, 130, *opinion withdrawn and superseded in part*, 96 F.3d 151 (6th Cir. 1996) (arguing that a special federal rule should be "crafted," since the policy of uniformity in the Warsaw Convention would be "undermined by the use of state choice of law rules"), *with Insurance Co. of North America v. Federal Express Co.*, 189 F.3d 914, 919-920 (9th Cir. 1999) (concluding that standard *Erie* analysis governs in a Warsaw Convention case).

4. Note that the *El Al* Court cited with approval an interpretation of the Warsaw Convention by the British House of Lords, the Supreme Court of British Columbia, the Ontario Court (General Division), the New Zealand Court of Appeal, and the Singapore Court of Appeal. As discussed in the section immediately below, members of the United States Congress and the United States Supreme Court have condemned the Court's reference to foreign or international law when it is interpreting the United States Constitution. Consider whether a distinction exists between using foreign or international law to interpret an international instrument such as the Warsaw Convention and using that law to interpret domestic United States Constitution principles.

PROBLEM 3-12: BUMPED FROM THE FLIGHT

Verona had a confirmed ticket on a flight from New York to Luxembourg. The night before she was to leave, she printed her boarding pass. She arrived at the airport the next day, learned that the flight was overbooked, but declined an offer to forgo her seat in exchange for monetary compensation. The flight was then called for boarding and all the passengers were ushered onto a bus run by the airline. The bus was to transport the passengers to the plane, which was waiting for them on a remote tarmac. While on the bus, representatives of the airline informed Verona that she was bumped from the flight involuntarily, and that she would have to leave the bus immediately. She was the only African-American passenger scheduled to fly on the flight and all of the white passengers were allowed to fly that day.

Verona sued the airline for race discrimination under a federal race discrimination statute. Her injuries are psychic and emotional; she does not claim any physical injury. The airline claims that her federal law discrimination claim is preempted by the Warsaw Convention. Is the airline correct?

2. Use of International and Foreign Law Principles in United States Cases

As described immediately above, controversy often surrounds the question whether a particular international law principle binds the federal and state governments of the United States. A related and equally controversial question may arise where a court of the United States considers an international law principle that is not binding on the court, but nonetheless provides guidance. Similarly, controversy surrounds whether courts of the United States should to refer other countries' laws for the purpose of evaluating and deciding questions of domestic United States law.

Intelligent consideration of these questions must note many important distinctions. For example, one should distinguish between following international law and following the law of other countries, since the former implicates issues about the supremacy of international law, while the latter does not. Even if one focuses solely on international law, one must separate concepts of international cooperation from international governance.[45] Moreover, international law and the law of other countries can be different from transnational principles that might govern the relationship between states, such as principles governing the European Union. (One might, nonetheless, describe both transnational law and the law of other countries as "foreign law.")[46] Finally, one should distinguish between following the mandate of international or foreign law on one hand and simply taking these laws into account as information to be considered or rejected in domestic decision making.[47] A rich literature on these subjects exists, some of which does not heed these distinctions.

In 2005, a highly publicized public debate between Justices Breyer and Scalia raised awareness of the controversy surrounding the use of other countries' laws to guide United States courts.[48] While Justice Breyer believes that looking at other nations' constitutional law principles is generally helpful, Justice Scalia believes even limited use of these principles is wrong. Noting that the United States does not have the "same moral and legal framework as the rest of world," Justice Scalia argues that the foreign materials are irrelevant and even misleading in the context of United States decision making. This debate has played out in the confirmation hearings of Supreme Court Justices as well as a number of United States Supreme Court cases,[49] including matters related to execution of juvenile offenders[50] and the rights of gay and lesbian members of society.[51]

Arguments in favor of using of foreign law in domestic decision making have tended to take a pragmatic tone. Judges and scholars have argued that foreign law is a useful, field-tested source of knowledge for domestic courts,

---

45. *See* Jed Rubenfeld, *Unilateralism and Constitutionalism*, 79 N.Y.U. L. Rev. 1971, 2022 (2004), for a discussion of this distinction.

46. Foreign law is the law of an individual jurisdiction that is not the United States or that is not part of the United States — or the law of a group of foreign countries such as the European Union. International law is generally considered to be law among nations that "have expressly or tacitly consented to be bound by it." Frederic L. Kirgis, *Is Foreign Law International Law?*, ASIL Insights, Oct. 31, 2005, *available at* http://www.asil.org/insights051031.cfm.

47. Sanford Levinson, *Looking Abroad When Interpreting the United States Constitution: Some Reflections*, 39 Tex. Int'l L.J. 353, 353 (2004).

48. Antonin Scalia & Stephen Breyer, The Relevance of Foreign Legal Materials in U.S. Constitutional Cases: A Conversation Between Justice Antonin Scalia and Justice Stephen Breyer, *Discussion at the American University College of Law (Jan. 13, 2005)*, in 3 Int'l J. Const. L. 519 (2005).

49. Martin S. Flaherty, *The Future and Past of U.S. Foreign Relations Law*, 67 Law & Contemp. Probs. 169 (2004) (noting that the Supreme Court cited more international and comparative materials in the 2003-2004 session than ever before).

50. *Roper v. Simmons*, 543 U.S. 551 (2005).

51. *Lawrence v. Texas*, 539 U.S. 558 (2003).

which face similar social problems, similar legal instruments, similar difficulties accommodating competing values, and similar goals.[52] Literature also supports the more theoretical arguments that the practice of consulting foreign law serves global cooperation, and promotes shared world governance and law harmonization.[53]

Those arguing against using foreign law in domestic decision making likewise advance both pragmatic and theoretical arguments. Pragmatic arguments view the practice as undisciplined judicial methodology, under which judges "cherry pick" those foreign laws that support their personal preferences and ignore those that do not. As argued by Chief Justice Roberts in his confirmation hearings, the practice releases judges from their usual doctrinal boundaries, and allows them to "cloak [their personal preference] with the authority of precedent."[54] Opponents also take the view that resort to foreign law allows influence by jurists who did not gain power by virtue of the established procedures in the state and federal governments. Expanding on this argument, some maintain that the practice risks "surrendering" the meaning of United States laws to entities that "lack both the authority and institutional legitimacy for making such decisions, as well as any accountability to the American people. . . ."[55]

The practice has not been popular in legislatures. Indeed, legislatures in at least half the states of the United States have proposed bills or constitutional amendments designed to restrict the use of international and foreign laws[56] in state courts. The bills take several forms. One typical measure, such as one considered in 2011 in North Carolina, sought to make it unlawful for state judges to consider "foreign law," which presumably meant law from sources other than the state and federal governments of the United States. An Arizona bill passed into law in 2011 prevents courts, arbitrators, and other adjudicative authorities from enforcing foreign law "if doing so would violate a right guaranteed by the Constitution of this state or of the United States or conflict with the laws of the United States or of this state." Ariz. Stat. §12-3103.

Likewise, the people of Oklahoma actually approved a constitutional amendment along similar lines (the "Save our State Amendment"), but the amendment

52. *See, e.g.,* Harold Hongju Koh, *International: Law as Part of Our Law,* 98 Am. J. Int'l L. 43, 46 (2004) (observing that United States law concepts "like 'due process of law,' 'equal protection,' and 'cruel and unusual punishment' are illuminated by parallel rules, empirical evidence, or community standards found in other mature legal systems").

53. *See, e.g.,* Mark C. Rahdert, *Comparative Constitutional Advocacy,* 56 Am. U. L. Rev. 553, 614-629 (2007).

54. *Confirmation Hearing on the Nomination of John G. Roberts, Jr. to Be Chief Justice of the United States: Hearing Before the S. Comm. on the Judiciary,* 109th Cong., at 200-201 (2005).

55. *See* Mark C. Rahdert, *Comparative Constitutional Advocacy,* 56 Am. U. L. Rev. 553, 637-638 (2007) (summarizing views of opponents).

56. For a review of various measures, see Aaron Fellmith, *International and Foreign Law in the U.S. State Legislatures,* ASIL Insights, May 26, 2012, *available at* http://www.asil.org/insights110526.cfm.

added that "courts shall not consider international law or Sharia Law."[57] The United States Court of Appeals for the Tenth Circuit, however, upheld a preliminary injunction against the "Save our State Amendment," concluding that the provision violates the establishment clause of the United States Constitution's First Amendment by discriminating among religions in singling out Sharia law. *Awad v. Ziriax*, 670 F.3d 1111 (10th Cir. 2012).

A bill from Iowa even sought to nullify or render unenforceable *private* contracts with a choice of law clause that designated foreign law as the governing law.[58] The possible adverse consequences of such bills have been recognized by some legislatures, however, and a similar bill in Utah was withdrawn by its sponsor "after he learned it could harm banking and international businesses."[59] Similar concerns halted progress of a Virginia bill that banned judges from deciding any issue in a case "in whole or in part based on the authority of foreign law except to the extent that the United States Constitution or Constitution of Virginia or any federal or state law requires or authorizes the consideration of such foreign law."[60] In response to concern expressed by business groups about their transactions and relations abroad,[61] a related version of the Virginia bill focuses on invalidating only choice of law agreements that would have the effect of violating a person's rights under the United States Constitution. The related version bill sought to accommodate business concerns by preventing its application "to a corporation, partnership, limited liability company, or any other form of business association or legal entity that is a party to a contract or agreement subject[ing] itself to foreign law in a jurisdiction other than the Commonwealth or any of the states or territories of the United States."[62]

The United States Congress provided a model for these legislatures. In 2005, Congress considered the Constitution Restoration Act, H.R. 1070, 109th Cong. §201, which sought to confine courts of the United States to consideration of only one non-American source: "English constitutional and [English] common law up until the time of the adoption of the Constitution of the United States."[63]

---

57. The amendment provided that:

> The Courts of this State when exercising their judicial authority, shall uphold and adhere to the law as provided in the United States Constitution, the Oklahoma Constitution, and the United States Code, federal regulations promulgated pursuant thereto, established common law, Oklahoma Statutes and rules promulgated pursuant thereto, and if necessary the law of another state of the United States provided the law of the other state does not include Sharia Law, in making judicial decisions. The courts shall not look to the legal precepts of other nations or cultures. Specifically, the courts shall not consider international law or Sharia law. The provisions of this subsection shall apply to all cases before the respective courts including, but not limited to, cases of first impression.

58. H.F. 2313 (Iowa 2010) (introduced by Rep. Jason Schultz).

59. Donna Leinwand, *More States Enter Debate on Sharia Law*, USA TODAY, Dec. 9, 2010, *available at* www.usatoday.com/news/nation/2010-12-09-shariaban09_ST_N.html.

60. H.B. 825 (Virginia 2012) (introduced by Rep. Robert G. Marshall).

61. Kathy Adams, *Bills to Ban Use of Foreign Laws Rile Groups*, THE VIRGINIAN PILOT, Feb. 12, 2012, *available at* www.hamptonroads.com/2012/02/bills-ban-use-foreign-laws-rile-groups.

62. H.B. 631 (Virginia 2012) (introduced by Rep. Rick Morris).

63. For a discussion of this initiative, see Laura E. Little, *Transnational Guidance in Terrorism Cases*, 38 GEO. WASH. INT'L L. REV. 1 (2006).

Finally, although controversy has surrounded the practice in the United States, courts in other countries have evinced considerable comfort with the practice of referring to foreign law in adjudication. Often, the judicial system in one country may share a common lineage with a judicial system in another country, thus making comparison easy and appropriate. Other times, a particular decision has simply become iconic, thus providing inspiration and guidance for the rest of the world. For example, many decisions of the United States Supreme Court have served as persuasive precedent for other countries.[64]

Notes on
THE USE OF INTERNATIONAL AND FOREIGN LAW PRINCIPLES IN UNITED STATES CASES

1. Which side has the better argument on the propriety of international and foreign laws? Does the fear of using these principles to illuminate United States legal problems flow from an instinct toward United States protectionism and exceptionalism — or are the fears well founded? Is the practice really as useful and enlightening as proponents suggest?

2. Are some contexts for using foreign and international law principles more appropriate than others? If so, which contexts are more appropriate? Are constitutional cases more or less appropriate than cases that implicate the private rights of individuals to sue in contract or tort? How about matters that implicate cultural and religious issues such as the rights of gay, lesbian, and transgendered citizens? For arguments regarding why the practice is particularly useful and important in terrorism cases, see Laura E. Little, *Transnational Guidance in Terrorism Cases*, 38 GEO. WASH. INT'L L. REV. 1 (2006).

3. The use of foreign decisions in the context of domestic decision making is a form of comparative law. Might it also be viewed as a form of hybrid lawmaking, ultimately reducing the number of conflict of laws problems represented in human governance?

4. What are the ramifications of the state and federal legislative initiatives designed to restrict court reference to foreign and international laws? Some might argue that the apparent attempts to restrict courts from considering foreign and international law amount to little more than political theater, motivated by concern that international law and laws from other countries should not infiltrate laws of the United States. Nonetheless, do you think these initiatives present any separation of powers problems?

---

64. *See, e.g.,* Sheldon Bernard Lyke, *Brown Abroad: An Empirical Analysis of Foreign Judicial Citation and the Metaphor of Cosmopolitan Conversation*, 45 VAND. J. TRANSNAT'L L. 83 (2012) (discussing how 32 decisions by non-United States courts used the United States Supreme Court decision in *Brown v. Board of Education* as "factual evidence," a "guide" for appropriate decision making, and "a source of substantive law").

> Is the spirit behind the initiatives similar to the public policy exception to choice of law? Conceived as applying to principles of law (rather than causes of action), the public policy exception represents a judgment — similar to that reflected in these bills — that certain types of laws are so inimical to what the forum stands for that forum courts should not exercise authority in connection with them. Is this constitutional? Might these state laws run into problems with the dormant foreign relations clause — or preemption doctrine as explained in the three decisions reviewed earlier in this chapter, *Zschernig v. Miller*, *Crosby v. National Foreign Trade Council*, and *American Insurance Association v. Garamendi.* Also — might these laws significantly undermine the efficacy of certain choice of law clauses? Might it be difficult to enforce certain foreign judgments that would otherwise be enforceable?

D. EXTRATERRITORIAL APPLICATION OF UNITED STATES LAW

1. Extraterritoriality and United States Statutes

International law often divides questions of global governance into three categories of authority: adjudicative, enforcement, and prescriptive authority. Adjudicative authority concerns a tribunal's power to apply interpreted rules to a given dispute. Many issues pertaining to adjudicative authority are covered by global principles of personal and subject matter jurisdiction and are often governed by treaties, some of which Chapter 1 of this volume discusses. Enforcement authority is a governing body's ability to enforce rules and adjudications, a type of authority touched on in the next chapter on judgment enforcement. Sometimes called "legislative authority" or "legislative jurisdiction," prescriptive authority pertains to the power to prescribe rules regulating human activity.[65] This section concentrates on the principles under which prescriptive rules of one particular sovereign, the United States government, apply outside the territorial borders of the country. These principles thus bear on a question that repeatedly arises in conflict of laws: what law governs the challenged conduct?

United States cases often refer to both domestic and international concepts in analyzing the appropriate reach of United States law outside of the United States boundaries. Domestic concepts reflect a hybrid of statutory interpretation rules, United States foreign relations principles, as well as concern with honoring international law principles. Indeed, United States cases reflect the presumption that a country controls its own prescriptive authority, qualified by its own

---

65. *See, e.g.,* Christopher A. Whytock, *Domestic Courts and Global Governance*, 84 TUL. L. REV. 67, 76 (2009) (outlining three forms of authority).

principles of comity as well as principles of international governance.[66] United States discussion is now frequently framed in terms of the Restatement (Third) of Foreign Relations Law §403 at (1) (1987), which admonishes that a jurisdiction may not exercise prescriptive jurisdiction where it would be "unreasonable." Factors bearing on whether jurisdiction would be "unreasonable" include: (1) the place and effect of the regulated activity; (2) nationality of interested parties; (3) the activity's importance to the regulating sovereign and the international political, legal, or economic systems; (4) any justified expectations; consistency with international traditions; (5) interests of other sovereigns; and (6) the likelihood of a conflict of authority with another sovereign. Despite the complexity of these factors, United States courts have continued to focus on a few prominent tools for analyzing the appropriate scope of United States prescriptive authority. These tools include *territoriality, effects, conduct,* and *comity.*

The territoriality principle focuses on the location of the human activity to be regulated, and generally evaluates whether the activity occurred within the geographic limits of a country's sovereign territory. It has a long lineage, formally recognized in the Peace of Westphalia of 1648, a series of treaties among various Roman Empire officials and European monarchs. The "effects" and "conduct" principles extend this territorial focus to include the location of conduct — with the "effects" principle allowing jurisdiction where conduct occurred out of sovereign territory, but had effects within the territory. "Comity" is the "recognition which one nation allows within its territory to the legislative, executive, and judicial acts of another nation." *Hilton v. Guyot,* 159 U.S. 113, 163-164 (1895). Comity arises neither from "absolute obligation . . . nor . . . mere courtesy and good will," . . . and is informed by "international duty and convenience, and . . . the rights of [a sovereign's citizens] or other persons who are under the protection of its laws." *Id.* at 164.

Other formulations pertaining to legislative jurisdiction exist in international law, including the nationality principle (based on the nationality of a wrongdoer), the protective principle (based on whether a sovereign's national interest is implicated), the passive personality principle (based on nationality of the victim), and universal jurisdiction (based on the heinous nature of the wrong). Restatement (Third) of the Foreign Relations Law of the United States §402 (1987). Courts do not generally invoke the concepts in deciding questions of extraterritorial application of United States statutes in civil cases, although the concepts are common to jurisdictional analysis in criminal cases. The territorial, conduct and effects, and comity concepts have proven complicated enough for civil actions under United States statutes, with the United States Supreme Court varying in how much weight should be given to each in various extraterritorial legislative jurisdiction cases. Evaluate which of the concepts — territorial, conduct and effects, or comity — predominates in the cases that follow.

---

66. *Cf.* Mark Weston Janis, International Law 346 (5th ed. 2008) (stating that United Cases cases reflect "the presumption that state jurisdiction is determined by the states themselves, albeit tempered by their own notions of comity").

EEOC v. Arabian American Oil Co.

499 U.S. 244 (1991)

Chief Justice REHNQUIST delivered the opinion of the Court.

These cases present the issue whether Title VII applies extraterritorially to regulate the employment practices of United States employers who employ United States citizens abroad. The United States Court of Appeals for the Fifth Circuit held that it does not, and we agree with that conclusion.

Petitioner Boureslan is a naturalized United States citizen who was born in Lebanon. The respondents are two Delaware corporations, Arabian American Oil Company (Aramco), and its subsidary, Aramco Service Company (ASC). Aramco's principal place of business is Dhahran, Saudi Arabia, and it is licensed to do business in Texas. ASC's principal place of business is Houston, Texas.

In 1979, Boureslan was hired by ASC as a cost engineer in Houston. A year later he was transferred, at his request, to work for Aramco in Saudi Arabia. Boureslan remained with Aramco in Saudi Arabia until he was discharged in 1984.

[Boureslan filed a complaint seeking relief on several theories including an alleged violation of Title VII of the Civil Rights Act of 1964 for discrimination on the basis of race, religion, and national origin. The district court determined that Title VII does not extend to United States citizens employed abroad by United States companies and the Court of Appeals affirmed.]

. . . Both parties concede, as they must, that Congress has the authority to enforce its laws beyond the territorial boundaries of the United States. Whether Congress has in fact exercised that authority in these cases is a matter of statutory construction. It is our task to determine whether Congress intended the protections of Title VII to apply to United States citizens employed by American employers outside of the United States.

It is a longstanding principle of American law "that legislation of Congress, unless a contrary intent appears, is meant to apply only within the territorial jurisdiction of the United States." *Foley Bros. v. Filardo*, 336 U.S. 281, 285 (1949). This "canon of construction . . . is a valid approach whereby unexpressed congressional intent may be ascertained." It serves to protect against unintended clashes between our laws and those of other nations which could result in international discord.

In applying this rule of construction, we look to see whether "language in the [relevant Act] gives any indication of a congressional purpose to extend its coverage beyond places over which the United States has sovereignty or has some measure of legislative control." *Foley Bros., supra*, 336 U.S., at 285. We assume that Congress legislates against the backdrop of the presumption against extraterritoriality. Therefore, unless there is "the affirmative intention of the Congress clearly expressed," we must presume it "is primarily concerned with domestic conditions."

Boureslan and the EEOC contend that the language of Title VII evinces a clearly expressed intent on behalf of Congress to legislate extraterritorially. They rely principally on two provisions of the statute. First, petitioners argue that the statute's definitions of the jurisdictional terms "employer" and "commerce" are sufficiently broad to include United States firms that employ American citizens overseas. Second, they maintain that the statute's "alien exemption" clause, 42 U.S.C. §2000e-1, necessarily implies that Congress intended to protect American citizens from employment discrimination abroad. Petitioners also contend that we should defer to the EEOC's consistently held position that Title VII applies abroad. We conclude that petitioners' evidence, while not totally lacking in probative value, falls short of demonstrating the affirmative congressional intent required to extend the protections of Title VII beyond our territorial borders.

Title VII prohibits various discriminatory employment practices based on an individual's race, color, religion, sex, or national origin. An employer is subject to Title VII if it has employed 15 or more employees for a specified period and is "engaged in an industry affecting commerce." An industry affecting commerce is "any activity, business, or industry in commerce or in which a labor dispute would hinder or obstruct commerce or the free flow of commerce and includes any activity or industry 'affecting commerce' within the meaning of the Labor-Management Reporting and Disclosure Act of 1959." "Commerce," in turn, is defined as "trade, traffic, commerce, transportation, transmission, or communication among the several States; or between a State and any place outside thereof; or within the District of Columbia, or a possession of the United States; or between points in the same State but through a point outside thereof."

Petitioners argue that by its plain language, Title VII's "broad jurisdictional language" reveals Congress' intent to extend the statute's protections to employment discrimination anywhere in the world by a United States employer who affects trade "between a State and any place outside thereof." More precisely, they assert that since Title VII defines "States" to include States, the District of Columbia, and specified territories, the clause "between a State and any place outside thereof" must be referring to areas beyond the territorial limit of the United States.

Respondents offer several alternative explanations for the statute's expansive language. They contend that the "or between a State and any place outside thereof" clause "provide[s] the jurisdictional nexus required to regulate commerce that is not wholly within a single state, presumably as it affects both interstate and foreign commerce" but not to "regulate conduct exclusively *within* a foreign country." They also argue that since the definitions of the terms "employer," "commerce," and "industry affecting commerce" make no mention of "commerce with foreign nations," Congress cannot be said to have intended that the statute apply overseas. . . .

We need not choose between these competing interpretations as we would be required to do in the absence of the presumption against extraterritorial application discussed above. Each is plausible, but no more persuasive than that. The language relied upon by petitioners—and it is they who must make the affirmative showing—is ambiguous, and does not speak directly to the question presented here. The intent of Congress as to the extraterritorial application of this statute must be deduced by inference from boilerplate language which can be found in any number of congressional Acts, none of which have ever been held to apply overseas. See, *e.g.*, Consumer Product Safety Act; Federal Food, Drug, and Cosmetic Act; Transportation Safety Act of 1974; Labor-Management Reporting and Disclosure Act of 1959; Americans with Disabilities Act of 1990.

Petitioners' reliance on Title VII's jurisdictional provisions also finds no support in our case law; we have repeatedly held that even statutes that contain broad language in their definitions of "commerce" that expressly refer to "*foreign* commerce" do not apply abroad.

Petitioners argue that Title VII's "alien-exemption provision" . . . "clearly manifests an intention" by Congress to protect United States citizens with respect to their employment outside of the United States. The alien exemption provision says that the statute "shall not apply to an employer with respect to the employment of aliens outside any State." Petitioners contend that from this language a negative inference should be drawn that Congress intended Title VII to cover United States *citizens* working abroad for United States employers. There is "[n]o other plausible explanation [that] the alien exemption exists," they argue, because "[i]f Congress believed that the statute did not apply extraterritorially, it would have had no reason to include an exemption for a certain category of individuals employed outside the United States." Since "[t]he statute's jurisdictional provisions cannot possibly be read to confer coverage only upon aliens employed outside the United States," petitioners conclude that "Congress could not rationally have enacted an exemption for the employment of aliens abroad if it intended to foreclose *all* potential extraterritorial applications of the statute."

Respondents resist petitioners' interpretation of the alien-exemption provision and assert two alternative *raisons d'être* for that language. First, they contend that since aliens are included in the statute's definition of employee, and the definition of commerce includes possessions as well as "States," the purpose of the exemption is to provide that employers of aliens in the possessions of the United States are not covered by the statute. Thus, the "outside any State" clause means outside any State, but within the control of the United States. . . .

Second, respondents assert that by negative implication, the exemption "confirm[s] the coverage of aliens in the United States." They contend that this interpretation is consistent with our conclusion in *Espinoza v. Farah Mfg. Co.*, 414 U.S. 86 (1973), that aliens within the United States are protected from discrimination both because Title VII uses the term "individual" rather than "citizen," and because of the alien-exemption provision.

If petitioners are correct that the alien-exemption clause means that the statute applies to employers overseas, we see no way of distinguishing in its application between United States employers and foreign employers. Thus, a French employer of a United States citizen in France would be subject to Title VII — a result at which even petitioners balk. The EEOC assures us that in its view the term "employer" means only "American employer," but there is no such distinction in this statute and no indication that the EEOC in the normal course of its administration had produced a reasoned basis for such a distinction. Without clearer evidence of congressional intent to do so than is contained in the alien-exemption clause, we are unwilling to ascribe to that body a policy which would raise difficult issues of international law by imposing this country's employment-discrimination regime upon foreign corporations operating in foreign commerce.

This conclusion is fortified by the other elements in the statute suggesting a purely domestic focus. The statute as a whole indicates a concern that it not unduly interfere with the sovereignty and laws of the States. *See, e.g.,* 42 U.S.C. §2000h-4 (stating that the Act should not be construed to exclude the operation of state law or invalidate any state law unless inconsistent with the purposes of the Act); §2000e-5 (requiring the EEOC to accord substantial weight to findings of state or local authorities in proceedings under state or local law). . . . While Title VII consistently speaks in terms of "States" and state proceedings, it fails even to mention foreign nations or foreign proceedings.

Similarly, Congress failed to provide any mechanisms for overseas enforcement of Title VII. For instance, the statute's venue provisions, §2000e-5(f)(3), are ill-suited for extraterritorial application as they provide for venue only in a judicial district in the State where certain matters related to the employer occurred or were located. And the limited investigative authority provided for the EEOC, permitting the Commission only to issue subpoenas for witnesses and documents from "any place in the United States or any Territory or possession thereof," 29 U.S.C. §161 incorporated by reference into 42 U.S.C. §2000e-9, suggests that Congress did not intend for the statute to apply abroad.

It is also reasonable to conclude that had Congress intended Title VII to apply overseas, it would have addressed the subject of conflicts with foreign laws and procedures. In amending the Age Discrimination in Employment Act of 1967 (ADEA) to apply abroad, Congress specifically addressed potential conflicts with foreign law by providing that it is not unlawful for an employer to take any action prohibited by the ADEA "where such practices involve an employee in a workplace in a foreign country, and compliance with [the ADEA] would cause such employer . . . to violate the laws of the country in which such workplace is located." Title VII, by contrast, fails to address conflicts with the laws of other nations.

. . . Our conclusion today is buttressed by the fact that "[w]hen it desires to do so, Congress knows how to place the high seas within the jurisdictional reach of a statute." Congress' awareness of the need to make a clear statement that a statute applies overseas is amply demonstrated by the numerous occasions on which it has expressly legislated the extraterritorial application of a statute. . . . Congress, should it wish to do so, may . . . amend Title VII and in doing so will be able to calibrate its provisions in a way that we cannot. . . .

Justice MARSHALL, with whom Justice BLACKMUN and Justice STEVENS join, dissenting.

. . . [C]ontrary to what one would conclude from the majority's analysis, [the presumption against territoriality] is *not* a "clear statement" rule, the application of which relieves a court of the duty to give effect to all available indicia of the legislative will. Rather . . . a court may properly rely on this presumption only after exhausting all of the traditional tools "whereby unexpressed congressional intent may be ascertained." *Ibid.* When these tools are brought to bear on the issue in this case, the conclusion is inescapable that Congress *did* intend Title VII to protect United States citizens from discrimination by United States employers operating overseas. Consequently, I dissent.

Notes on
ARABIAN AMERICAN OIL

1. Of the three principles most often invoked in resolving questions of extraterritorial application of United States law, territoriality is the one most associated with *Arabian American Oil. See, e.g.,* Gary B. Born, *A Reappraisal of the Extraterritorial Reach of U.S. Law,* 24 LAW & POL'Y INT'L BUS. 1 (1992). Does comity also have a role to play in explaining the decision? Could the Court have been concerned about comity in the sense of avoiding the broad reach of United States laws, extending respect for the sovereign power of Saudi Arabia, where the American companies were operating and the American employees were working? In an earlier exposition on the presumption against extraterritoriality and the territoriality principle, Justice Holmes invoked comity, stating that to apply anything other than the law of the jurisdiction where challenged acts occurred would "not only be unjust, but would be an interference with the authority of another sovereign, contrary to the comity of nations, which the other states concerned might justly resent." *American Banana Co. v. United Fruit Co.,* 213 U.S. 347, 356-357 (1909). The reasoning also embraces the notion that the presumption minimizes conflicts between United States law and the law of other countries, thus facilitating favorable foreign relations.

2. If comity and conflict avoidance were motivating factors for the *Arabian American Oil* Court, what explains the Court's failure to consider or analyze Saudi Arabian law? From the viewpoint of conflict of laws analysis, commentators have described the Supreme Court's approach to extraterritoriality questions as "unilateral" — in the same sense as often reflected in the internet choice of law cases presented in Chapter 2. *See, e.g.,* William S. Dodge, *Extraterritoriality and Conflict of Laws Theory: An Argument for Judicial Unilateralism,* 39 HARV. INT'L L.J. 101 (1998).[67] Professor Dodge explains, in this context, that unilateralist approaches "focus simply on whether the forum's law applies to the activity in question, without worrying that another forum might also apply its law," resulting in two sovereign authorities having "concurrent jurisdiction" over the question. *Id.* at 106. By contrast, multilateral conflicts theories conceptualize the legal issue as requiring an actual choice between two competing laws, with the decision to use one

---

67. For other analysis of the role of choice of law theory to resolve extraterritoriality questions, see, e.g., Russell J. Weintraub, *The Extraterritorial Application of Antitrust and Securities Laws: An Inquiry into the Utility of a "Choice-of-Law Approach,"* 70 TEX. L. REV. 1799 (1992).

jurisdiction's law effectively resulting in a decision not to use the other jurisdiction's law. *Id.* (quoting Lea Brilmayer, CONFLICT OF LAWS 77 (2d ed. 1995)).

3. Both the majority and the dissent agreed on the existence of a presumption against extraterritoriality, which has also been called a presumption against legislative authority (or legislative jurisdiction). Instead, the crux of the Justices' disagreement in *Arabian American Oil* concerns the strength and nature of this presumption that Congress did not intend a statute to have extraterritorial application. Whether or not territorialism and comity fully explain the necessity for having the presumption, isn't it true that both concepts might help explain why the presumption weighs against, rather than in favor of, extraterritoriality?

4. What is the difference between the presumption against extraterritoriality as a clear statement requirement (as the dissent views the majority's approach to the concept) and as a tool for interpretation (as the dissent explains its own approach to the concept)? Does understanding the values of territoriality and comity underlying the presumption help evaluate which set of Justices had the better view of the presumption against extraterritoriality?

At least one commentator has argued that the presumption against extraterritoriality also serves other principles such as separation of powers concerns, preventing the judiciary from applying domestic law where doing so might impinge legislative branch prerogatives, cause tensions with other nations, or violate international law. Curtis A. Bradley, *Territorial Intellectual Property Rights in the Age of Globalism*, 37 VA. J. INT'L L. 505, 513-514, 550-561 (1997). If the presumption acts as clear statement requirement, however, couldn't one read the presumption as empowering the judiciary to moderate international law concerns? That is, one might argue that by imposing on Congress a clear statement requirement, the judiciary imposes on Congress its own view of territoriality and comity in those contexts where the legislative will to override the presumption is lacking.

5. Soon after the *Arabian American Oil* decision, Congress invalidated its holding by amending Title VII to make clear that it governs the relationship between American employers and employees working outside the territory of the United States. Does this reaction suggest that the presumption against extraterritoriality does in fact implicate separation of powers concerns? Despite the nullification of its specific holding, *Arabian American Oil* still stands as a clear endorsement of the presumption of extraterritoriality. Moreover, the Court's discussion of the presumption suggests that it applies with unqualified force in all contexts. Evaluate whether the cases below followed that message.

Hartford Fire Insurance Co. v. California

509 U.S 764 (1993)

Justice SOUTER announced the judgment of the Court and delivered the opinion of the Court [with respect to the parts of the opinion relating to extraterritorial application of the federal statute at issue in the case. A portion of his opinion relating to the application of the statute to domestic defendants did not garner a majority vote.].

The Sherman Act makes every contract, combination, or conspiracy in unreasonable restraint of interstate or foreign commerce illegal. These consolidated cases present questions about the application of that Act to the insurance industry, both here and abroad. The plaintiffs (respondents here) allege that both domestic and foreign defendants (petitioners here) violated the Sherman Act by engaging in various conspiracies to affect the American insurance market.... [A] group of foreign defendants argues that the principle of international comity requires the District Court to refrain from exercising jurisdiction over certain claims against it. We hold that ... the principle of international comity does not preclude District Court jurisdiction over the foreign conduct alleged.

I

The two petitions before us stem from consolidated litigation comprising the complaints of 19 States and many private plaintiffs alleging that the defendants, members of the insurance industry, conspired in violation of §1 of the Sherman Act to restrict the terms of coverage of commercial general liability (CGL) insurance available in the United States. Because the cases come to us on motions to dismiss, we take the allegations of the complaints as true.

According to the complaints, the object of the conspiracies was to force certain primary insurers (insurers who sell insurance directly to consumers) to change the terms of their standard CGL insurance policies to conform with the policies the defendant insurers wanted to sell. [The controversy concerned a distinction between insurance coverage triggered by an "occurrence" rather than an actual "claim." "Claims-made" coverage obligates an insurer to make defend and pay claims only if they are made within the policy period. The significant claims for relief in the complaints alleged the London reinsurers violated the Sherman Act by conspiring to coerce United States primary insurers to offer CGL coverage on a claims-made basis, thereby making CGL coverage for many risks unavailable in California. The district court dismissed the claims against the London-based defendant on international comity grounds, and the court of appeals reversed.]

The Sherman Act declares "[e]very contract, combination in the form of trust or otherwise, or conspiracy, in restraint of trade or commerce among the several States, or with foreign nations, ... to be illegal." ...

III

... At the outset, we note that the District Court undoubtedly had jurisdiction of these Sherman Act claims, as the London reinsurers apparently concede. See Tr. of Oral Arg. 37 ("Our position is not that the Sherman Act does not apply in the sense that a minimal basis for the exercise of jurisdiction doesn't exist here. Our position is that there are certain circumstances, and that this is one of them, in which the interests of another State are sufficient that the exercise of that jurisdiction should be restrained"). Although the proposition was perhaps not always free from doubt, it is well established by now that the Sherman Act applies to foreign conduct that was meant to produce and did in fact produce some substantial effect in the United States. Such is the conduct alleged here: that the London reinsurers engaged in unlawful conspiracies to affect the market for insurance in the United States and that their conduct in fact produced substantial effect.[23]

According to the London reinsurers, the District Court should have declined to exercise such jurisdiction under the principle of international comity.[24] The Court of Appeals agreed that courts should look to that principle in deciding whether to exercise jurisdiction under the Sherman Act. This availed the London reinsurers nothing, however. To be sure, the Court of Appeals believed that "application of [American] antitrust laws to the London reinsurance market 'would lead to significant conflict with English law and policy,'" and that "[s]uch a conflict, unless outweighed by other factors, would by itself be reason to decline exercise of jurisdiction." But other factors, in the court's view, including the London reinsurers' express purpose to affect United States commerce and the substantial nature of the effect produced, outweighed the supposed conflict and required the exercise of jurisdiction in this litigation.

When it enacted FTAIA [the Foreign Trade Antitrust Improvements Act of 1982], Congress expressed no view on the question whether a court with Sherman Act jurisdiction should ever decline to exercise such jurisdiction on grounds of international comity. ... We need not decide that question here, however, for even assuming that in a proper case a court may decline to exercise Sherman Act jurisdiction over foreign conduct (or, as Justice Scalia would put it, may

23. Under §402 of the Foreign Trade Antitrust Improvements Act of 1982 (FTAIA), the Sherman Act does not apply to conduct involving foreign trade or commerce, other than import trade or import commerce, unless "such conduct has a direct, substantial, and reasonably foreseeable effect" on domestic or import commerce. §6a(1)(A). The FTAIA was intended to exempt from the Sherman Act export transactions that did not injure the United States economy, ... and it is unclear how it might apply to the conduct alleged here. Also unclear is whether the Act's "direct, substantial, and reasonably foreseeable effect" standard amends existing law or merely codifies it. We need not address these questions here. Assuming that the FTAIA's standard affects this litigation, and assuming further that that standard differs from the prior law, the conduct alleged plainly meets its requirements.

24. Justice Scalia contends that comity concerns figure into the prior analysis whether jurisdiction exists under the Sherman Act. This contention is inconsistent with the general understanding that the Sherman Act covers foreign conduct producing a substantial intended effect in the United States, and that concerns of comity come into play, if at all, only after a court has determined that the acts complained of are subject to Sherman Act jurisdiction. ...

conclude by the employment of comity analysis in the first instance that there is no jurisdiction), international comity would not counsel against exercising jurisdiction in the circumstances alleged here.

The only substantial question in this litigation is whether "there is in fact a true conflict between domestic and foreign law." The London reinsurers contend that applying the Act to their conduct would conflict significantly with British law, and the British Government, appearing before us as *amicus curiae*, concurs. They assert that Parliament has established a comprehensive regulatory regime over the London reinsurance market and that the conduct alleged here was perfectly consistent with British law and policy. But this is not to state a conflict. "[T]he fact that conduct is lawful in the state in which it took place will not, of itself, bar application of the United States antitrust laws," even where the foreign state has a strong policy to permit or encourage such conduct. Restatement (Third) Foreign Relations Law §415, Comment *j.* . . . No conflict exists, for these purposes, "where a person subject to regulation by two states can comply with the laws of both." Restatement (Third) Foreign Relations Law §403, Comment *e.*[25] Since the London reinsurers do not argue that British law requires them to act in some fashion prohibited by the law of the United States, or claim that their compliance with the laws of both countries is otherwise impossible, we see no conflict with British law. We have no need in this litigation to address other considerations that might inform a decision to refrain from the exercise of jurisdiction on grounds of international comity.

Justice SCALIA delivered a dissenting opinion with respect to [the extraterritorial application of the Sherman Act to the London defendants in which Justices O'CONNOR, KENNEDY, and THOMAS joined].

II

Petitioners[,] . . . various British corporations and other British subjects, argue that certain of the claims against them constitute an inappropriate extraterritorial application of the Sherman Act. It is important to distinguish two distinct questions raised by this petition: whether the District Court had jurisdiction, and whether the Sherman Act reaches the extraterritorial conduct alleged here. On the first question, I believe that the District Court had subject-matter jurisdiction over the Sherman Act claims against all the defendants (personal jurisdiction is not contested). Respondents asserted nonfrivolous claims under the Sherman Act, and 28 U.S.C. §1331 vests district courts with subject-matter jurisdiction over cases "arising under" federal statutes. As precedents, make clear, that is sufficient to establish the District Court's jurisdiction over these claims.

---

25. Justice Scalia says that we put the cart before the horse in citing this authority, for he argues it may be apposite only after a determination that jurisdiction over the foreign acts is reasonable. But whatever the order of cart and horse, conflict in this sense is the only substantial issue before the Court.

The second question — the extraterritorial reach of the Sherman Act — has nothing to do with the jurisdiction of the courts. It is a question of substantive law turning on whether, in enacting the Sherman Act, Congress asserted regulatory power over the challenged conduct. See *EEOC v. Arabian American Oil Co.*, 499 U.S. 244, 248 (1991) (*Aramco*). If a plaintiff fails to prevail on this issue, the court does not dismiss the claim for want of subject-matter jurisdiction — want of power to adjudicate; rather, it decides the claim, ruling on the merits that the plaintiff has failed to state a cause of action under the relevant statute. . . .

There is, however, a type of "jurisdiction" relevant to determining the extraterritorial reach of a statute; it is known as "legislative jurisdiction," *Aramco, supra,* 499 U.S., at 253, 111 S. Ct., at 1233; Restatement (First) Conflict of Laws §60 (1934), or "jurisdiction to prescribe," 1 Restatement (Third) of Foreign Relations Law of the United States 235 (1987) (hereinafter Restatement (Third)). This refers to "the authority of a state to make its law applicable to persons or activities," and is quite a separate matter from "jurisdiction to adjudicate." There is no doubt, of course, that Congress possesses legislative jurisdiction over the acts alleged in this complaint: Congress has broad power under Article I, §8, cl. 3, "[t]o regulate Commerce with foreign Nations," and this Court has repeatedly upheld its power to make laws applicable to persons or activities beyond our territorial boundaries where United States interests are affected. But the question in this litigation is whether, and to what extent, Congress *has* exercised that undoubted legislative jurisdiction in enacting the Sherman Act.

Two canons of statutory construction are relevant in this inquiry. The first is the "longstanding principle of American law 'that legislation of Congress, unless a contrary intent appears, is meant to apply only within the territorial jurisdiction of the United States.'" *Aramco, supra,* 499 U.S., at 248, 111 S. Ct., at 1230. Applying that canon in *Aramco,* we held that the version of Title VII . . . did not extend outside the territory of the United States even though the statute contained broad provisions extending its prohibitions to, for example, "'any activity, business, or industry in commerce.'" *Id.,* 499 U.S., at 249. We held such "boilerplate language" to be an insufficient indication to override the presumption against extraterritoriality. The Sherman Act contains similar "boilerplate language," and if the question were not governed by precedent, it would be worth considering whether that presumption controls the outcome here. We have, however, found the presumption to be overcome with respect to our antitrust laws; it is now well established that the Sherman Act applies extraterritorially.

But if the presumption against extraterritoriality has been overcome or is otherwise inapplicable, a second canon of statutory construction becomes relevant: "[A]n act of congress ought never to be construed to violate the law of nations if any other possible construction remains." *Murray v. Schooner Charming Betsy,* 2 Cranch 64, 118, 2 L. Ed. 208 (1804) (Marshall, C.J.). This canon is "wholly independent" of the presumption against extraterritoriality. It is relevant to determining the substantive reach of a statute because "the law of nations," or customary international law, includes limitations on a nation's exercise of its jurisdiction to prescribe. Though it clearly has constitutional authority to do so,

Congress is generally presumed not to have exceeded those customary international-law limits on jurisdiction to prescribe.

Consistent with that presumption, this and other courts have frequently recognized that, even where the presumption against extraterritoriality does not apply, statutes should not be interpreted to regulate foreign persons or conduct if that regulation would conflict with principles of international law. . . .

More recent lower court precedent has also tempered the extraterritorial application of the Sherman Act with considerations of "international comity." . . . The "comity" they refer to is not the comity of courts, whereby judges decline to exercise jurisdiction over matters more appropriately adjudged elsewhere, but rather what might be termed "prescriptive comity": the respect sovereign nations afford each other by limiting the reach of their laws. That comity is exercised by legislatures when they enact laws, and courts assume it has been exercised when they come to interpreting the scope of laws their legislatures have enacted. It is a traditional component of choice-of-law theory. See J. Story, Commentaries on the Conflict of Laws §38 (1834) (distinguishing between the "comity of the courts" and the "comity of nations," and defining the latter as "the true foundation and extent of the obligation of the laws of one nation within the territories of another"). Comity in this sense includes the choice-of-law principles that, "in the absence of contrary congressional direction," are assumed to be incorporated into our substantive laws having extraterritorial reach. Considering comity in this way is just part of determining whether the Sherman Act prohibits the conduct at issue.

In sum, the practice of using international law to limit the extraterritorial reach of statutes is firmly established in our jurisprudence. In proceeding to apply that practice to the present cases, I shall rely on the Restatement (Third) for the relevant principles of international law. Its standards appear fairly supported in the decisions of this Court construing international choice-of-law principles . . . and in the decisions of other federal courts. . . . Whether the Restatement precisely reflects international law in every detail matters little here, as I believe this litigation would be resolved the same way under virtually any conceivable test that takes account of foreign regulatory interests.

Under the Restatement, a nation having some "basis" for jurisdiction to prescribe law should nonetheless refrain from exercising that jurisdiction "with respect to a person or activity having connections with another state when the exercise of such jurisdiction is unreasonable." Restatement (Third) §403(1). The "reasonableness" inquiry turns on a number of factors. . . . Rarely would these factors point more clearly against application of United States law. The activity relevant to the counts at issue here took place primarily in the United Kingdom, and the defendants in these counts are British corporations and British subjects having their principal place of business or residence outside the United States. Great Britain has established a comprehensive regulatory scheme governing the London reinsurance markets, and clearly has a heavy "interest in regulating the activity." . . . Considering these factors, I think it unimaginable that an assertion of legislative jurisdiction by the United States would be considered reasonable, and therefore it is inappropriate to assume, in the absence of statutory indication to the contrary, that Congress has made such an assertion.

. . . I do not at all agree, moreover, with the Court's conclusion that the issue of the substantive scope of the Sherman Act is not in the cases. To be sure, the parties did not make a clear distinction between adjudicative jurisdiction and the scope of the statute. Parties often do not, as we have observed (and have declined to punish with procedural default) before. It is not realistic, and also not helpful, to pretend that the only really relevant issue in this litigation is not before us. In any event, if one erroneously chooses, as the Court does, to make adjudicative jurisdiction (or, more precisely, abstention) the vehicle for taking account of the needs of prescriptive comity, the Court still gets it wrong. It concludes that no "true conflict" counseling nonapplication of United States law (or rather, as it thinks, United States judicial jurisdiction) exists unless compliance with United States law would constitute a *violation* of another country's law. That breathtakingly broad proposition, which contradicts the many cases discussed earlier, will bring the Sherman Act and other laws into sharp and unnecessary conflict with the legitimate interests of other countries—particularly our closest trading partners.

In the sense in which the term "conflic[t]" was used in *Lauritzen*, 345 U.S., at 582, 592, and is generally understood in the field of conflicts of laws, there is clearly a conflict in this litigation. The petitioners here, like the defendant in *Lauritzen*, were not compelled by any foreign law to take their allegedly wrongful actions, but that no more precludes a conflict-of-laws analysis here than it did there. Where applicable foreign and domestic law provide different substantive rules of decision to govern the parties' dispute, a conflict-of-laws analysis is necessary.

Literally the *only* support that the Court adduces for its position is §403 of the Restatement (Third)—or more precisely Comment *e* to that provision, which states:

> Subsection (3) [which says that a State should defer to another state if that State's interest is clearly greater] applies only when one state requires what another prohibits, or where compliance with the regulations of two states exercising jurisdiction consistently with this section is otherwise impossible. It does not apply where a person subject to regulation by two states can comply with the laws of both. . . .

The Court has completely misinterpreted this provision. Subsection (3) of §403 (requiring one State to defer to another in the limited circumstances just described) comes into play only after subsection (1) of §403 has been complied with—*i.e.*, after it has been determined that the exercise of jurisdiction by *both* of the two States is not "unreasonable." That prior question is answered by applying the factors (*inter alia*) set forth in subsection (2) of §403, that is, precisely the factors that I have discussed in text and that the Court rejects. . . .

Notes on
HARTFORD FIRE

1. Perhaps the most remarkable part of *Hartford Fire Ins. Co.* was the apparent agreement among the Justices that the presumption against extraterritorial application of a federal statute was inapplicable in the case. Where was the ringing endorsement of this presumption in *Arabian American Oil?* As explained by Justice Scalia, the reason for casting aside the presumption appears to be stare decisis: the existence of prior antitrust cases in which the Court did not follow the presumption. But doesn't the *Arabian American Oil* case itself provide important precedent, suggesting the presumption is now a dominant part of the legal landscape? Wasn't the *Arabian American Oil* Court's language about the presumption broad, without limitation to the employment context of the case or the specific statute (Title VII) before the Court? In this regard, note the Court's treatment of *Arabian American Oil* and the presumption in the *Morrison* case that follows, which is a securities case post-dating *Hartford Fire.*

2. Citing the Restatement (Third) of Foreign Relations Law, Justice Souter relied on the effects approach to extraterritorial jurisdiction, concluding that "the Sherman Act applies to foreign conduct that was meant to produce and did in fact produce some substantial effect in the United States." Justice Scalia does not disagree with this conclusion that Congress possesses power to regulate the conduct at issue in the case. Indeed, the defendants had conceded that point. The Justices disagree instead on a series of other related propositions: (1) the relationship between jurisdiction and principles of international comity; (2) the proper analysis of a clash between United States law and foreign law for the purpose of preserving comity; and (3) the precise nature of jurisdiction at issue in the case (subject matter jurisdiction and/or legislative jurisdiction).

3. *The Relationship Between Jurisdiction and International Comity.* Justice Souter concluded that the defendants' concession was conclusive of the jurisdictional issue and that principles of international comity did not mandate restraint of congressional power. Justice Souter treated the international comity analysis as a separate discretionary decision by courts determining whether to exert federal power in the case. Is Justice Souter correct in assuming that courts have this prerogative — if in fact Congress has decided that the antitrust power extends to this particular context?

In contrast to Justice Souter, Justice Scalia argued that comity was relevant to existence of jurisdiction. Who has the better position on this? In defining the scope of the obligation of comity, Justice Scalia refers to the practice of using international law to restrict the extraterritorial reach of statutes. In this way, the jurisdictional issue is resolved not by legislative prerogative and domestic power, but international obligation instead. For the substance of international law on this point, Justice Scalia looks to the

Restatement (Third) of Foreign Relations law and cites Supreme Court decisions. Do you agree with his analysis and conclusion as to the reasonableness of exercising jurisdiction in this case? Should the reasonableness analysis occur for each individual case? Each individual statute? Some other triggering factor?

4. In *Hartford Fire Ins. Co.*, the Court found no true conflict between the Sherman Act and British law that might have motivated a decision to refrain from exercising power on international comity grounds. In *In re Vitamin C Antitrust Litigation*, 837 F.3d 175 (2d Cir. 2016), however, the court of appeals found sufficient conflict with Chinese law to merit abstaining from applying the Sherman Act. The court reasoned as follows: "Recognizing China's strong interest in its protectionist economic policies and given the direct conflict between Chinese policy and our anti-trust laws, we conclude that China's interests outweigh whatever antitrust enforcement interests the United States may have in this case as a matter of law." 837 F.3d at 193.

4. *Analysis of the Clash Between United States Law and Foreign Law.* Justice Souter concludes that there is no conflict between English and American law because English law does not require the defendants to do something that American law prohibits (and vice versa). But isn't it a problem that English law allows something that American law prohibits? Aren't the policies of the two laws relevant to determining whether they conflict? How does this approach to defining a conflict compare with the approach usually followed by state courts in domestic conflict of laws cases? How does it contrast with the approach to ascertaining whether state law "conflicts" with federal law for the purpose of preemption analysis? Analysis under the *Erie* doctrine?

Justice Scalia is adamant that Justice Souter's opinion misconceives the appropriate way to determine a conflict. Isn't it true, however, that Justice Souter might be correct if in fact the defendants can separate the conduct that occurs and has effects *in England* from the conduct that occurs and has effects *in the United States?*

5. *The Nature of the Type of Jurisdiction in Controversy.* Justice Scalia argues (and many commentators agree) that Justice Souter's opinion muddles the distinction between subject matter jurisdiction and legislative jurisdiction. Does the distinction between the two make any practical difference? Subject matter jurisdiction is generally perceived as a domestic law matter, while legislative or prescriptive jurisdiction is an international law matter. Legislative jurisdiction may go to whether the plaintiff has a viable claim for relief, while subject matter jurisdiction does not go to the merits of the controversy and pertains only to whether the particular court had power to hear the case. *See* GARY B. BORN & PETER B. RUTLEDGE, INTERNATIONAL CIVIL LITIGATION IN UNITED STATES COURTS 708 (5th ed. 2011). Given this distinction, ramifications of the characterization can be significant, and include burden of proof and pleading requirements, preclusive effect, fact-finding,

and the ability of a court to raise a problem on its own motion. In the case that follows, the Supreme Court clarified that questions pertaining to extra-territorial application of a statute are questions on the merits, but did not explore the consequences of that decision.

Morrison v. National Australia Bank Ltd.

561 U.S. 247 (2010)

Justice SCALIA delivered the opinion of the Court.

We decide whether §10(b) of the Securities Exchange Act of 1934 provides a cause of action to foreign plaintiffs suing foreign and American defendants for misconduct in connection with securities traded on foreign exchanges.

[The National Australia Bank Limited (National) is based in Australia, and trades its common stock or "ordinary" shares on exchanges in Australia and else-where. Its shares do not exchange on any American exchanges.] There are listed on the New York Stock Exchange, however, National's American Depositary Receipts (ADRs), which represent the right to receive a specified number of National's Ordinary Shares.

. . . National bought respondent HomeSide Lending, Inc., a mortgage servic-ing company headquartered in Florida. HomeSide's business was to receive fees for servicing mortgages. . . . The rights to receive those fees . . . can provide a valuable income stream. . . . National's annual reports and other public docu-ments touted the success of HomeSide's business. . . . But on July 5, 2001, National announced that it was writing down the value of HomeSide's assets. . . . The prices of both Ordinary Shares and ADRs slumped. According to the complaint, . . . HomeSide's financial models [were manipulated] to make the rates of early repayment unrealistically low in order to cause the mortgage-servicing rights to appear more valuable than they really were. . . .

[The petitioners, who are all Australian, sued National and others in United States federal court for violations of §§10(b) and 20(a) of the Securities and Exchange Act of 1934 and Rule 10b-5. The district court dismissed the case and the court of appeals affirmed, ruling that the key acts did not take place within the United States. The United States Supreme Court first ruled that the question of the extraterritorial reach of §10(b) did not raise a question of subject matter jurisdiction, but instead raised a question on the merits of the controversy.] . . .

It is a "longstanding principle of American law 'that legislation of Congress, unless a contrary intent appears, is meant to apply only within the territorial juris-diction of the United States.'" *EEOC v. Arabian American Oil Co.*, 499 U.S. 244, 248 (1991) (*Aramco*). This principle represents a canon of construction, or a presump-tion about a statute's meaning, rather than a limit upon Congress's power to legislate. It rests on the perception that Congress ordinarily legislates with respect to domestic, not foreign matters. . . . The canon or presumption applies regardless of whether there is a risk of conflict between the American statute and a foreign law. When a statute gives no clear indication of an extraterritorial application, it has none.

Despite this principle of interpretation, long and often recited in our opinions, the Second Circuit believed that, because the Exchange Act is silent as to the extraterritorial application of §10(b), it was left to the court to "discern" whether Congress would have wanted the statute to apply. This disregard of the presumption against extraterritoriality did not originate with the Court of Appeals panel in this case. . . .

[The Court then reviewed various tests applied in securities cases, focusing particularly on the conduct and effects test. The Court explained that the Second Circuit had formalized two separate tests: (1) an "effects test," "whether the wrongful conduct had a substantial effect in the United States or upon United States citizens," and (2) a "conduct test," "whether the wrongful conduct occurred in the United States," which it later combined into one test to determine the extraterritorial scope of securities statutes — essentially finding that the statute applied if the Court found conduct *or* effects in the United States. Other circuits adopted some version of this condensed test.]

Commentators have criticized the unpredictable and inconsistent application of §10(b) to transnational cases. Some have challenged the premise underlying the Courts of Appeals' approach, namely that Congress did not consider the extraterritorial application of §10(b) (thereby leaving it open to the courts, supposedly, to determine what Congress would have wanted). Others . . . have noted that using congressional silence as a justification for judge-made rules violates the traditional principle that silence means no extraterritorial application.

The criticisms seem to us justified. The results of judicial-speculation-made-law — divining what Congress would have wanted if it had thought of the situation before the court — demonstrate the wisdom of the presumption against extraterritoriality. Rather than guess anew in each case, we apply the presumption in all cases, preserving a stable background against which Congress can legislate with predictable effects.

Rule 10b-5, the regulation under which petitioners have brought suit,[6] was promulgated under §10(b), and "does not extend beyond conduct encompassed by §10(b)'s prohibition."

On its face, §10(b) contains nothing to suggest it applies abroad:

> It shall be unlawful for any person, directly or indirectly, by the use of any means or instrumentality of interstate commerce or of the mails, or of any facility of any national securities exchange . . . [t]o use or employ, in connection with the purchase or sale of any security registered on a national securities exchange or any security not so registered, . . . any manipulative or deceptive device or contrivance

6. [Rule 10b-5 provides that it is unlawful "for any person, directly or indirectly, by the use of any means or instrumentality of interstate commerce, or of the mails or of any facility of any national securities exchange . . . [t]o make any untrue statement of a material fact or to omit to state a material fact necessary in order to make the statements made, in the light of the circumstances under which they were made, not misleading. — ED.]

in contravention of such rules and regulations as the [Securities and Exchange] Commission may prescribe. . . .

Petitioners and the Solicitor General contend, however, that three things indicate that §10(b) or the Exchange Act in general has at least some extraterritorial application.

First, they point to the definition of "interstate commerce," a term used in §10(b), which includes "trade, commerce, transportation, or communication . . . between any foreign country and any State." 15 U.S.C. §78c(a)(17). But "we have repeatedly held that even statutes that contain broad language in their definitions of 'commerce' that expressly refer to '*foreign* commerce' do not apply abroad." *Aramco*, 499 U.S., at 251. The general reference to foreign commerce in the definition of "interstate commerce" does not defeat the presumption against extraterritoriality.

Petitioners and the Solicitor General next point out that Congress, in describing the purposes of the Exchange Act, observed that the "prices established and offered in such transactions are generally disseminated and quoted throughout the United States and foreign countries." 15 U.S.C. §78b(2). The antecedent of "such transactions," however, is found in the first sentence of the section, which declares that "transactions in securities as commonly conducted upon securities exchanges and over-the-counter markets are affected with a national public interest." §78b. Nothing suggests that this *national* public interest pertains to transactions conducted upon *foreign* exchanges and markets. The fleeting reference to the dissemination and quotation abroad of the prices of securities traded in domestic exchanges and markets cannot overcome the presumption against extraterritoriality.

Finally, there is §30(b) of the Exchange Act, 15 U.S.C. §78dd(b), which *does* mention the Act's extraterritorial application: "The provisions of [the Exchange Act] or of any rule or regulation thereunder shall not apply to any person insofar as he transacts a business in securities without the jurisdiction of the United States," unless he does so in violation of regulations promulgated by the Securities and Exchange Commission "to prevent . . . evasion of [the Act]." (The parties have pointed us to no regulation promulgated pursuant to §30(b).) The Solicitor General argues that "[this] exemption would have no function if the Act did not apply in the first instance to securities transactions that occur abroad."

We are not convinced. In the first place, it would be odd for Congress to indicate the extraterritorial application of the whole Exchange Act by means of a provision imposing a condition precedent to its application abroad. And if the whole Act applied abroad, why would the Commission's enabling regulations be limited to those preventing "evasion" of the Act, rather than all those preventing "violation"? The provision seems to us directed at actions abroad that might conceal a domestic violation, or might cause what would otherwise be a domestic violation to escape on a technicality. At most, the Solicitor General's proposed inference is possible; but possible interpretations of statutory language do not override the presumption against extraterritoriality.

The Solicitor General also fails to account for §30(a), which reads in relevant part as follows:

> It shall be unlawful for any broker or dealer . . . to make use of the mails or of any means or instrumentality of interstate commerce for the purpose of effecting on an exchange not within or subject to the jurisdiction of the United States, any transaction in any security the issuer of which is a resident of, or is organized under the laws of, or has its principal place of business in, a place within or subject to the jurisdiction of the United States, in contravention of such rules and regulations as the Commission may prescribe. . . .

Subsection 30(a) contains what §10(b) lacks: a clear statement of extraterritorial effect. Its explicit provision for a specific extraterritorial application would be quite superfluous if the rest of the Exchange Act already applied to transactions on foreign exchanges — and its limitation of that application to securities of domestic issuers would be inoperative. Even if that were not true, when a statute provides for some extraterritorial application, the presumption against extraterritoriality operates to limit that provision to its terms. No one claims that §30(a) applies here. . . .

In short, there is no affirmative indication in the Exchange Act that §10(b) applies extraterritorially, and we therefore conclude that it does not.

Petitioners argue that the conclusion that §10(b) does not apply extraterritorially does not resolve this case. They contend that they seek no more than domestic application anyway, since Florida is where HomeSide and its senior executives engaged in the deceptive conduct of manipulating HomeSide's financial models; their complaint also alleged that Race and Hughes made misleading public statements there. This is less an answer to the presumption against extraterritorial application than it is an assertion — a quite valid assertion — that that presumption here (as often) is not self-evidently dispositive, but its application requires further analysis. For it is a rare case of prohibited extraterritorial application that lacks *all* contact with the territory of the United States. But the presumption against extraterritorial application would be a craven watchdog indeed if it retreated to its kennel whenever *some* domestic activity is involved in the case. . . .

[W]e think that the focus of the Exchange Act is not upon the place where the deception originated, but upon purchases and sales of securities in the United States. Section 10(b) does not punish deceptive conduct, but only deceptive conduct "in connection with the purchase or sale of any security registered on a national securities exchange or any security not so registered." 15 U.S.C. §78j(b). Those purchase-and-sale transactions are the objects of the statute's solicitude. It is those transactions that the statute seeks to "regulate," [and] it is parties or prospective parties to those transactions that the statute seeks to "protec[t]." And it is in our view only transactions in securities listed on domestic exchanges, and domestic transactions in other securities, to which §10(b) applies. . . .

. . . Like the United States, foreign countries regulate their domestic securities exchanges and securities transactions occurring within their territorial jurisdiction. And the regulation of other countries often differs from ours as to what constitutes fraud, what disclosures must be made, what damages are recoverable, what discovery is available in litigation, what individual actions may be joined in a single suit, what attorney's fees are recoverable, and many other matters. [Various countries] have filed *amicus* briefs in this case. . . . They all complain of the interference with foreign securities regulation that application of §10(b) abroad would produce, and urge the adoption of a clear test that will avoid that consequence. The transactional test we have adopted — whether the purchase or sale is made in the United States, or involves a security listed on a domestic exchange — meets that requirement.

The Solicitor General suggests a different test, which petitioners also endorse: "[A] transnational securities fraud violates [§]10(b) when the fraud involves significant conduct in the United States that is material to the fraud's success." Neither the Solicitor General nor petitioners provide any textual support for this test. . . . If, moreover, one is to be attracted by the desirable consequences of the "significant and material conduct" test, one should also be repulsed by its adverse consequences. While there is no reason to believe that the United States has become the Barbary Coast for those perpetrating frauds on foreign securities markets, some fear that it has become the Shangri-La of class-action litigation for lawyers representing those allegedly cheated in foreign securities markets. . . .

The Solicitor General points out that the "significant and material conduct" test is in accord with prevailing notions of international comity. If so, that proves that *if* the United States asserted prescriptive jurisdiction pursuant to the "significant and material conduct" test it would not violate customary international law; but it in no way tends to prove that that is what Congress has done.

. . . Section 10(b) reaches the use of a manipulative or deceptive device or contrivance only in connection with the purchase or sale of a security listed on an American stock exchange, and the purchase or sale of any other security in the United States. This case involves no securities listed on a domestic exchange, and all aspects of the purchases complained of by those petitioners who still have live claims occurred outside the United States. Petitioners have therefore failed to state a claim on which relief can be granted. . . .

Justice STEVENS, with whom Justice GINSBURG joins, concurring in the judgment.

While I agree that petitioners have failed to state a claim on which relief can be granted, my reasoning differs from the Court's. I would adhere to the [conduct and effects test] that has been the law in the Second Circuit, and most of the rest of the country, for nearly four decades.

. . . The Court [critiques] the Second Circuit's approach for misapplying the presumption against extraterritoriality. It is the Court, however, that misapplies the presumption, in two main respects.

First, the Court seeks to transform the presumption from a flexible rule of thumb into something more like a clear statement rule. . . . And our cases both before and after *Aramco* make perfectly clear that the Court continues to give effect to "*all available evidence* about the meaning" of a provision when considering its extraterritorial application, lest we defy Congress' will. Contrary to Justice Scalia's personal view of statutory interpretation, that evidence legitimately encompasses more than the enacted text. Hence, while the Court's dictum that "[w]hen a statute gives no clear indication of an extraterritorial application, it has none," makes for a nice catchphrase, the point is overstated. The presumption against extraterritoriality can be useful as a theory of congressional purpose, a tool for managing international conflict, a background norm, a tiebreaker. It does not relieve courts of their duty to give statutes the most faithful reading possible.

Second, and more fundamentally, the Court errs in suggesting that the presumption against extraterritoriality is fatal to the Second Circuit's test. . . . It is true, of course, that "this Court ordinarily construes ambiguous statutes to avoid unreasonable interference with the sovereign authority of other nations," and that, absent contrary evidence, we presume "Congress is primarily concerned with domestic conditions." Accordingly, the presumption against extraterritoriality "provides a sound basis for concluding that Section 10(b) does not apply when a securities fraud with no effects in the United States is hatched and executed entirely outside this country." But that is just about all it provides a sound basis for concluding. And the conclusion is not very illuminating, because no party to the litigation disputes it. No one contends that §10(b) applies to wholly foreign frauds.

Rather, the real question in this case is how much, and what kinds of, *domestic* contacts are sufficient to trigger application of §10(b). . . . The question . . . does not admit of an easy answer. The text of the Exchange Act indicates that §10(b) extends to at least some activities with an international component, but, again, it is not pellucid as to which ones. The Second Circuit draws the line as follows: §10(b) extends to transnational frauds "only when substantial acts in furtherance of the fraud were committed within the United States," or when the fraud was "'intended to produce'" and did produce "'detrimental effects within'" the United States.

This approach is consistent with . . . the traditional understanding . . . that the presumption against extraterritoriality does not apply "when the conduct [at issue] occurs within the United States," and has lesser force when "the failure to extend the scope of the statute to a foreign setting will result in adverse effects within the United States." And it strikes a reasonable balance between the goals of "preventing the export of fraud from America," protecting shareholders, enhancing investor confidence, and deterring corporate misconduct, on the one hand, and conserving United States resources and limiting conflict with foreign law, on the other.

Thus, while §10(b) may not give any "clear indication" on its face as to how it should apply to transnational securities frauds, it does give strong clues that it should cover at least some of them. And in my view, the Second Circuit has done the best job of discerning what sorts of transnational frauds Congress meant in 1934—and still means today—to regulate. I do not take issue with the Court for beginning its inquiry with the statutory text, rather than the doctrine in the Courts of Appeals. I take issue with the Court for beginning *and ending* its inquiry with the statutory text, when the text does not speak with geographic precision, and for dismissing the long pedigree of, and the persuasive account of congressional intent embodied in, the Second Circuit's rule.

Repudiating the Second Circuit's approach in its entirety, the Court establishes a novel rule that will foreclose private parties from bringing §10(b) actions whenever the relevant securities were purchased or sold abroad and are not listed on a domestic exchange. . . . [W]hile the clarity and simplicity of the Court's test may have some salutary consequences, like all bright-line rules it also has drawbacks.

Imagine, for example, an American investor who buys shares in a company listed only on an overseas exchange. That company has a major American subsidiary with executives based in New York City; and it was in New York City that the executives masterminded and implemented a massive deception which artificially inflated the stock price — and which will, upon its disclosure, cause the price to plummet. Or, imagine that those same executives go knocking on doors in Manhattan and convince an unsophisticated retiree, on the basis of material misrepresentations, to invest her life savings in the company's doomed securities. Both of these investors would, under the Court's new test, be barred from seeking relief under §10(b).

The oddity of that result should give pause. For in walling off such individuals from §10(b), the Court narrows the provision's reach to a degree that would surprise and alarm generations of American investors — and, I am convinced, the Congress that passed the Exchange Act. Indeed, the Court's rule turns §10(b) jurisprudence (and the presumption against extraterritoriality) on its head, by withdrawing the statute's application from cases in which there is *both* substantial wrongful conduct that occurred in the United States *and* a substantial injurious effect on United States markets and citizens. . . .

Notes on
MORRISON

1. Does *Morrison* add clarity or confusion to the law of extraterritoriality? Several reasons suggest that the Court injected confusion into the area. For example, although the Court protested that it was not using the presumption against extraterritoriality as a "clear statement requirement," the opinion emphasizes the necessity for Congress to provide affirmative or unequivocal evidence of its intent for extraterritorial application of a statutory scheme. Indeed, the *Morrison* opinion for the Court even cites *Arabian American Oil* for the proposition that "[w]hen a statute gives no clear indication of an extraterritorial application, it has none." The difference between "a clear statement" and "a clear indication" is hard to discern. John H. Knox, *The Unpredictable Presumption Against Extraterritoriality*, 40 Sw. L. Rev. 635, 646 (2011).

Next is the problem of exactly how the presumption against extraterritoriality is to operate. The Supreme Court has been inconsistent about invoking the presumption. Why is the presumption sometimes indispensible, and sometimes not? Knox, *supra*, at 646.

In addition, the *Morrison* Court introduced the notion that one must identify the "focus" of the statute in order to ascertain whether a statute may apply to a dispute with substantial offshore components — irrespective of the presumption against extraterritoriality. In *Morrison*, the Court concluded that the "focus" of the securities statute, which the Court described as "the object of the statute's solicitude," was the securities transaction and not the alleged fraudulent conduct. In making this conclusion, the Court did not use the presumption against extraterritoriality, but found the statute inapplicable to the case because the focus of the statute — the transaction — occurred offshore. Was the Court suggesting that one needs to engage in a two-step analysis in order to determine whether a statute can apply extraterritoriality? One can read the Court's opinion as suggesting that one needs to worry about the presumption against extraterritoriality only where the fact pattern is centered outside the United States. If the facts have a domestic core, then the presumption might be irrelevant and the question becomes whether those facts with an international connection implicate the "focus" of what Congress is trying to regulate. (Apparently, the statute can apply without reference to the presumption against extraterritoriality if the focus of the statute is on a domestic contact, event, or series of events.) If — on the other hand — the facts have an international core, one must ascertain whether Congress has made plain its intent that the statute applies outside the United States. *See* Lea Brilmayer, *The New Extraterritoriality:* Morrison v. National Australia Bank, *Legislative Supremacy, and the Presumption Against Extraterritorial Application of American Law*, 40 Sw. L. Rev. 655, 658-661 (2011) (describing the analysis in *Morrison* as suggesting a two-part analysis: one part requiring one to identify the statute's focus and the other part requiring one to ascertain Congress's intent). The Court looked at the "focus" of the securities statute only after determining that Congress did not intend that it apply extraterritorially. Does logic necessarily dictate that the two analyses follow in that order?

One final bit of uncertainty: one does not know exactly whether the decision in *Morrison* is limited by its facts. *Morrison* was an easier case than many to support a finding of insufficient contacts with the United States, since it involved a so-called foreign cubed transaction: foreign security purchased by foreign parties on a foreign exchange.

2. The *Morrison* Court articulated a transaction-focused test and used it to replace the test followed in the lower courts — which the Court described as a conflation of a test focused on "conduct" and "effects." For the conduct and effects test, the lower courts had found extraterritorial application if "wrongful conduct had a substantial effect in the United States or upon United States citizens" or "wrongful conduct occurred in the United States."

For the transaction test, the *Morrison* Court required "the purchase and sale of a security listed on an American stock exchange, and the purchase or sale of any other security in the United States." How do the two tests vary?

3. As it did after *Arabian American Oil*, Congress enacted legislation that responded to *Morrison*. This time, however, the reaction was not entirely negative. Congress enacted legislation that effectively restored the conduct and effects test, but only for suits brought by the United States Department of Justice or the Securities and Exchange Commission. The legislation was contained in the Dodd-Frank Wall Street Reform and Consumer Protection Act. This Act leaves intact the restrictions read into securities laws by the *Morrison* Court for private civil actions such as the *Morrison* litigation itself.

4. Does the approach in *Morrison* suggest judicial deference or judicial activism? Commentators are split on this. For example, Professor Paul B. Stephan states that "*Morrison* represents one step, although an especially dramatic one, in the Supreme Court's effort to shift the responsibility for managing international regulatory conflicts from the judiciary to Congress." Morrison v. National Australia Bank Ltd.: *The Supreme Court Rejects Extraterritoriality*, ASIL INSIGHTS, VOL. 14, ISSUE 22 (Aug. 2, 2010). By contrast, Professor Lea Brilmayer concluded that the majority opinion actually enhances "the opportunity for judicial policy-making and diminished the importance of congressional preferences." Brilmayer, *supra*, at 664. What is your view?

5. As with other extraterritoriality cases, the question arises whether this case could be analyzed as a choice of law matter. Why did the federal courts that heard the case not grapple with the question as a choice of law matter? Isn't there a possibility that the extraterritoriality question could have been avoided if Australian law clearly governed the dispute? Indeed, under most choice of law methodologies, isn't it clear that Australian law *would in fact* govern a fraud dispute in a case with facts of this kind? Commentators have observed that courts are reluctant to apply the "public law" of another nation—one might reasonably claim that securities laws are a type of public law. *See, e.g.*, William S. Dodge, *Breaking the Public Law Taboo*, 43 HARV. INT'L L.J. 161 (2002); Linda Silberman, Morrison v. National Australia Bank: *Implications for Global Securities Class Actions*, Swiss Yearbook of Private International Law (2010), *available at* http://papers.ssrn.com/sol3/papers.cfm?abstract_id=1864786, at 12-13. As Professor Silberman argues, however, the "public law taboo does not necessarily fit where a private party (rather than a regulatory agency or government) brings a suit under a foreign country's securities laws." *Id.* at 13.

6. What incentives does *Morrison* send? The answer, of course, varies according to the identity of the entity reacting to the incentive. Potential actors that might respond to *Morrison's* incentives include plaintiffs and class action lawyers, wrongdoers wishing to effect fraudulent securities

transactions, investors, and regulatory institutions such as executive agencies, courts, and legislatures.

Potential Plaintiffs and Class Action Lawyers. Clearly, the majority sought to discourage class actions suits, as expressed by its suggestion that the United States might become "the Shangri-La of class-action litigation for lawyers representing those allegedly cheated in foreign securities markets." In this regard, the Court appeared committed to dissuading class action lawyers from pursuing suits with tenuous United States connections. Professor Silberman argues that *Morrison's* "exchange-based rule" calibrates precisely the correct incentive for plaintiff class actions lawyers, who will likely choose to allocate precious litigation resources to those "suits where there is a significant U.S. trading presence rather than one where there is only limited U.S. trading but a large global class." Silberman, *supra*, at 20. Do you agree?

Wrongdoers. The *Morrison* Court seemed to dismiss concerns about deterring potential securities "fraudsters" who might affect interests in the United States when it stated, "there is no reason to believe that the United States has become the Barbary Coast for those perpetrating frauds on foreign securities markets." Could it be argued that the Court simply steered those intent on bending or breaking securities laws away from planning transactions that are consummated in the United States? Does Justice Stevens's hypothetical in his dissent give you pause?

Investors. Doesn't *Morrison* provide investors with an additional incentive to channel money (capital) away from United States investments and toward countries with less stringent regulatory schemes? Does the decision also protect those engaging in securities transactions with United States citizens, so long as the transactions occur offshore? One problem for investors may simply be the uncertainty that *Morrison* injects into the law. The tests followed in the Court of Appeals had been followed for many years and were upended in *Morrison*. Uncertainty is something that investors try to avoid. One wonders, however, about the extent to which investors might avoid any uncertainty with choice of forum or choice of law clauses.

Executive Agencies. As noted above, the Dodd-Frank Wall Street Reform and Consumer Protection Act effectively reinstated the legal tests in place before *Morrison* for suits brought by the Department of Justice or the Securities and Exchange Commission. Thus, incentives for these entities remain similar to those in place before *Morrison*, except to the extent that their regulatory efforts increase as a result of reduction in private suits that could have an enforcement effect.

Courts and Legislatures Around the World. Scholars, particularly law and economic scholars, study how the design of legal regulation influences business behavior. These studies often start with the premise that transacting parties sometimes plan their deals to ensure that certain substantive law governs. The parties might do this by structuring their transactions in certain ways or by including choice of law and/or choice of forum clauses in their contracts. A decision such as *Morrison* impacts the parameters of a regulatory regime — such as the securities laws in the United States — and, as such, may influence transaction decisions. Astute courts and legislatures may be cognizant of this and design substantive law, choice of law doctrines, and choice of forum restrictions with a view toward attracting economic activity to the jurisdiction in which they govern. In light of this potential for strategic law design, consider what type of message the *Morrison* decision sends to courts and regulators in other parts of the world. What types of legal doctrines and strategic decisions does it encourage for judicial and legislative actors? For insightful analysis of choice of law and choice of forum competition among jurisdictions seeking to benefit from the fruits of securities transactions, see Wulf A. Kaal & Richard W. Painter, *Forum Competition and Choice of Law Competition in Securities Law After* Morrison v. National Australia Bank, 97 MINN. L. REV.___ (2012).

   7. What do you make of Justice Scalia's reliance on the views of other nations in making the decision not to find extraterritorial effect for the Securities and Exchange Act of 1934? Is this position consistent with his opposition to the occasional Supreme Court practice of looking to foreign law for guidance on domestic questions?

PERSPECTIVE ON THE EXPANSIVE PRESUMPTION AGAINST EXTRATERRITORIAL APPLICATION OF UNITED STATES STATUTES

After *Morrison v. National Australia Bank Ltd.*, 561 U.S. 247 (2013), commentators predicted that the decision was a harbinger for further restrictive readings on other congressional schemes with potential global significance. As evidenced by two significant United States Supreme Court cases handed down after *Morrison*, this prediction has proven accurate. One case, *Kiobel v. Royal Dutch Petroleum Co.*, 569 U.S. 108 (2013), interpreted the Alien Tort Statute (ATS). The other interpreted the Racketeer Influenced and Corrupt Organizations Act (RICO): *RJR Nabisco, Inc. v. European Community*, 136 S. Ct. 2090 (2016). In both cases, the Court applied with vigor the presumption against extraterritorial application of United States law.

The ATS, interpreted in *Kiobel*, provides federal courts with jurisdiction over "any civil action by an alien for a tort committed in violation of the law of nations or a treaty of the United States." 28 U.S.C. §1350. Federal courts had routinely applied the statute to extraterritorial conduct, a practice halted by the United States Supreme Court's interpretation in *Kiobel*. According to the Supreme Court, the statutory reference to "aliens" does not imply extraterritoriality, since aliens can experience violations both inside and outside the United States.

The Court also found no extraterritorial inference in the words "any civil action," declaring that terms such as "any" or "every" are simply "generic." After reviewing the history of the ATS, the Court concluded that the statute could not apply in the case — which was brought by Nigerian nationals against foreign corporations, alleging harm from conduct occurring outside the United States. The Court did acknowledge, however, that the presumption against extraterritoriality could be rebutted by claims that "touch and concern the territory of the United States . . . with sufficient force."

Kiobel was what is called a "foreign-cubed" case: foreign plaintiffs, foreign defendants, and foreign conduct. After the decision, questions remained whether the ATS might still apply when either the plaintiff or the defendant is a United States citizen or the conduct occurred in the United States. Subsequent lower court decisions, however, have not been promising for this position. *See, e.g., Balintulo v. Daimler AG*, 727 F.3d 174 (2d Cir. 2013) (refusing to apply the presumption against extraterritorial application in an ATS suit brought against United States defendants).

Kiobel's strict approach is similarly reflected in the Supreme Court's subsequent RICO decision in *RJR Nabisco, Inc. v. European Community*, 136 S. Ct. 2090 (2016). In fact, *RJR Nabisco* arguably reflects an even more conservative approach to the presumption because the Court insisted that the presumption applied separately to each section of the statute under consideration.

Two sections of RICO were at issue in *RJR Nabisco*: §1962 and §1964(c). Section 1962 makes it a crime to engage in, participate in, or profit from certain racketeering activities affecting interstate or foreign commerce. Under §1964(c), a person injured by a §1962 violation enjoys a private right of action to remedy that violation. The Supreme Court began its analysis by acknowledging that §1962 has extraterritorial effect — a reasonable conclusion given that the section encompasses predicate acts committed outside the United States, such as providing support to foreign terrorist organizations and money laundering. The Court reasoned, however, that this conclusion did not mean that Congress also intended that a civil cause of action authorized by §1964(c) should also extend to injuries experienced exterritorially. Evaluating whether §1964(c) overcame the presumption against extraterritoriality, the Supreme Court concluded that the section did not do so. This meant that the plaintiffs in the case were not entitled to a civil remedy because their claims derived exclusively from injuries suffered outside the United States.

The section-by-section extraterritorial scrutiny set forth in *RJR Nabisco, Inc.* is novel. Is it a wise approach? The *RJR Nabisco* Court expressed concern with international friction that may result from broad authorization of extraterritorially focused litigation. Indeed, for civil RICO cases, actions brought under the statute do not have the governmental check that might be present if a prosecutor were making the judgment whether to bring criminal RICO charges. Does it make sense, however, that the Congress might have decided that one part of its statute identifying elements of the violation might have extraterritorial reach, while another part authorizing a remedy for violation has domestic reach only?

One wonders what the trend in *Morrison, Kiobel,* and *RJR Nabisco* means for the fate of other statutes with global reach. The ramifications may be broad, as the United States Code is filled with provisions governing matters that touch and concern places outside United States territory: taxation statutes, the National Relations Act, the McCarran Ferguson Act, the Outer Continental Shelf Lands Act, and others. *See* Lea Brilmayer, *The New Extraterritoriality:* Morrison v. National Australia Bank, *Legislative Supremacy, and the Presumption Against Extraterritorial Application of American Law,* 40 Sw. L. Rev. 655, 658-661 (2011).

PROBLEM 3-13: A SECURITIES ACTION WITH DOMESTIC AND INTERNATIONAL ELEMENTS

The New Orleans Police Retirement Fund (NOPRF) brought suit under §10(b) of the Securities Exchange Act of 1934 against Swiss defendants, the Swiss Corporation and two of its executives. The Swiss Corporation invests heavily in United States real estate. The plaintiff alleged that the defendants falsely represented financial information that denied any negative impact from real estate investments in the United States *after* the investments had decreased in value because of a downturn in the economy. Indeed, the two executives of the Swiss Corporation had visited the United States for the purpose of gaining information that would help them put a false positive veneer on the real estate losses.

The plaintiff, NOPRF, had purchased securities of the Swiss Corporation on the Swiss Stock exchange and suffered serious losses as the Swiss Corporation struggled to recover from the United States economic downturn. The plaintiff further alleges that over 200 retired New Orleans police officers are experiencing a cut in retirement payments as a result of the losses that resulted from the investment in the fraudulently issued securities.

Does §10(b) of the Securities Exchange Act of 1934 apply to this case?

2. *Extraterritoriality and the Constitution*

The United States Constitution contains few textual clues about its force beyond the territorial limits of the United States. Some provisions arguably suggest domestic territorial force only (e.g., the "Constitution . . . shall be the Supreme Law of the Land")[68] and some provisions suggest more international scope (e.g., the federal judicial power extends to suits involving ambassadors as well as foreign subjects and citizens).[69] The need to clarify whether the Constitution extends beyond United States borders has grown as the world has become more globalized, and as United States international activities have increased. Questions about extraterritoriality have risen even more frequently as the United

68. U.S. Const. Art. IV.
69. U.S. Const. Art. III, §2.

States has undertaken aggressive law enforcement actions in the post-9/11 era. Within this context, the United States Supreme Court has refused to enunciate across-the-board, bright-line rules, deciding instead to confront the matter on an ad hoc basis and take into account "particular circumstances, the practical necessities and . . . possible alternatives . . ."[70] in each case.

Certain matters have, however, been firmly established. The Supreme Court has left no doubt that aliens within the territorial limits of the United States are entitled to enjoy constitutional guarantees also extended to United States citizens within the territory. Likewise, case law has even established that aliens situated outside the United States enjoy protection against unconstitutional actions by government officials within the United States, such as a state judge's assertion of personal jurisdiction against the alien. *See Asahi Metal Indus. Co. v. Superior Court*, 480 U.S. 102 (1987). Moreover, in *Reid v. Covert*, 354 U.S. 1 (1957), a plurality of the United States Supreme Court determined that Bill of Rights protections extend to a citizen residing in a foreign land when she is tried for a capital offense by court martial outside the United States. The plurality stated: "[t]he Constitution imposes substantive constraints on the federal government, even when it operates abroad."[71] Concurring in the result, Justice Harlan was persuaded that the right to a trial by jury and an indictment by a grand jury should apply for civilians abroad in a capital case. He disagreed, however, with the majority's "suggestion that every provision of the Constitution must always be deemed automatically applicable to American citizens in every part of the world." *Id.* at 74. Despite Justice Harlan's reservation, *Reid v. Covert* has provided the foundation for several decisions extending constitutional protections abroad, including a series of decisions dealing with habeas corpus protections for those in detention in Guantanamo Bay, Cuba following 9/11. A crucial factor in these more recent decisions is the Court's determination that the United States enjoys de facto sovereignty at Guantanamo by virtue of its 1903 lease agreement with Cuba, which allows the United States complete jurisdiction and control over the military base there. *See, e.g., Boumediene v. Bush*, 553 U.S. 723 (2008); *Hamdan v. Rumsfeld*, 548 U.S. 557 (2006); *Rasul v. Bush*, 542 U.S. 466 (2004).[72]

Yet for aliens subject to official United States power while they are outside the United States, the Supreme Court has not been consistently generous in extending constitutional protections. In a particularly important decision, *United States v. Verdugo-Urquidez*, 494 U.S. 259, 263 (1990), the Court held that Fourth Amendment restrictions on warrantless searches did not apply to United States officials when searching a nonresident alien's home in a foreign country. The Court acknowledged case law in which constitutional protections were extended to aliens "when they have come within the territory of the United States and

70. *Boumediene v. Bush*, 553 U.S. 723, 764 (2008).
71. *Reid*, 354 U.S. at 4.
72. For thoughtful discussion of the conflict of laws implications of these cases dealing with Guantanamo Bay, see Patrick Borchers, *The Conflict of Laws and* Boumediene v. Bush, 42 CREIGHTON L. REV. 1 (2008); Jules Lobel, *Fundamental Norms, International Law, and the Extraterritorial Constitution*, 36 YALE J. INT'L L. 307 (2011).

developed substantial connections with this country." 494 U.S. at 271. The Court, however, refused to extend the protection to the defendant in the case, noting:

> At the time of the search, he was a citizen and resident of Mexico with no voluntary attachment to the United States, and the place searched was located in Mexico. Under these circumstances, the Fourth Amendment has no application. . . . For better or for worse, we live in a world of nation-states in which our Government must be able to "functio[n] effectively in the company of sovereign nations." . . . Some who violate our laws may live outside our borders under a regime quite different from that which obtains in this country. Situations threatening to important American interests may arise half-way around the globe, situations which in the view of the political branches of our Government require an American response with armed force. If there are to be restrictions on searches and seizures which occur incident to such American action, they must be imposed by the political branches through diplomatic understanding, treaty, or legislation.

Id. at 275.

PROBLEM 3-15: THE NO-FLY LIST AND UNCONSTITUTIONAL OFFICIAL CONDUCT

Rahnah is a native of Malaysia, who was studying to get a Ph.D. at a United States university. Her doctoral advisor at the United States university asked her to deliver a scholarly paper at a university in Malaysia, arguing that it would be good for her and for the United States university. Rahnah agreed. She went to a United States airport to board a plane to Malaysia so that she could deliver the paper. At the check-in counter, she was told she was on a "no-fly" list and kept in custody for two hours. She was later released and told that an error had been made and that she was no longer on the "no-fly" list. She flew to Malaysia and delivered the paper. When she tried to board her plane back to the United States, she was notified that her student visa was revoked. She has never been able to return to the United States.

Rahnah has filed suit for injunctive relief under the First and Fifth Amendments, with the ultimate aim of having her name removed from the government's watch lists. Since Rahnah is an alien who is not present in the United States, should she be able to assert a claim based on violations of the United States constitutional protections?

CHAPTER 4

RECOGNITION AND ENFORCEMENT OF JUDGMENTS

When a lawsuit concludes, the court enters judgment. The judgment represents an official court decision determining the parties' rights within the specific dispute resolved by the litigation. When a defendant receives an adverse judgment, she has a number of choices on how to proceed. Among her options are (1) appealing the judgment to a higher court in the same system; (2) complying with the terms of the judgment (paying money, honoring an injunction, and the like); (3) doing nothing; or (4) filing an entirely new lawsuit on the dispute. If she takes option 3 — doing nothing — then the plaintiff needs to take steps to enforce the judgment. In this instance, the judgment is no more than a piece of paper without a means to enforce it. For damage judgments, the plaintiff may register the judgment with the court clerk, and ask an authority such as a local sheriff to help execute on the judgment. This may be a fruitful endeavor if the defendant has any assets in the jurisdiction where the case was litigated. Where assets are in another jurisdiction, the plaintiff must take the judgment to a court in the new jurisdiction and ask the new jurisdiction to transform this to its own judgment. To make this happen, the plaintiff must file a lawsuit in the new jurisdiction on the basis of the earlier judgment. Once the plaintiff proves the earlier judgment and the new court rejects any defenses that the defendant may raise, the court in the new jurisdiction will enter its own judgment, which the plaintiff can seek to execute in this second jurisdiction.

This chapter presents materials that govern this process of judgment recognition and enforcement in the new jurisdiction. The distinction between judgment recognition and enforcement is useful in reviewing the materials. Judgment recognition pertains to a court's decision whether to give a judgment legal force and effect in a subsequent proceeding. This differs from judgment enforcement, which concerns the process by which a court transforms a judgment that it recognizes as valid into an actual remedy (e.g., payment of money damages or following the terms of an injunction). For purposes of recognition of judgments within the

United States, the legal tools derive largely from constitutional full faith and credit principles. By contrast, judgment enforcement rules derive largely from the internal sovereign laws of the jurisdiction where the judgment is being enforced (which will normally be where assets are located). In other words, if the court that is enforcing the judgment is a state court, the court will follow the state law enforcement rules of the state where it sits. For purposes of international recognition and enforcement, international law—some of which is in treaty form—comes into play. This chapter presents both domestic and international contexts.

Let's say that the losing defendant chooses the fourth option described above: filing an entirely new lawsuit on the same subject matter of the dispute. If the defendant files this suit in the same jurisdiction as the first case, then the plaintiff has at her disposal principles of preclusion, which take the form of the doctrines of claim preclusion (res judicata) and issue preclusion (collateral estoppel). If, however, the defendant chooses to file the new lawsuit in another jurisdiction, then the plaintiff must arm herself with both the preclusion principles *and* full faith and credit or international law principles needed for enforcement of judgments. This chapter also presents materials on these topics.

Making matters even more interesting, the usual rules about preclusion, recognition, and enforcement are suspended when it comes to domestic relationship matters, such as marriage and divorce, as well as child custody and support. Likewise, suits pertaining to wrongs perpetrated via the internet challenge existing doctrines. This chapter will tackle these twists as well.

But first, the task is to identify the values that might animate recognition and enforcement of judgments. Consider this task within the familiar setting of the introductory problem pertaining to Cassandra and her allegedly defamatory article about Julian.

INTRODUCTORY PROBLEM: CASSANDRA AND JULIAN REDUX (JUDGMENT ENFORCEMENT ISSUES)

Cassandra is a resident of New Jersey. She researched and wrote an article about Julian, which was published in a newspaper. A resident of Ohio, Julian is convinced that the article defames him and he files a defamation suit against Cassandra in Ohio. Cassandra has never been to Ohio and has never had anything to do with Ohio. Unbeknownst to her, however, the newspaper distributes 20 papers in the state (less than 1 percent of its total circulation). Although Cassandra never appeared before the Ohio court, Julian convinced the court to entertain his lawsuit. Applying Ohio law, the court decided that Cassandra had defamed him and entered judgment against Cassandra in the amount of $100,000. Julian wishes to turn this judgment from a piece of paper into cash in his pocket. He knows that the only way he can do so is to enforce the judgment. He hired a private investigator who found out that Cassandra has all her assets in New Jersey. Accordingly, Julian filed suit in New Jersey, asking the New Jersey court to enforce the judgment against Cassandra. It turns out that New Jersey's law of defamation is different from Ohio's and that the article would be considered privileged, and therefore immune from liability, under New Jersey law. Cassandra consults you to defend this action. Consider the following questions:

(1) What values and concerns might the New Jersey court consider in deciding whether to recognize and enforce the judgment? In evaluating this question, perhaps it is helpful to break down the values into categories: those that pertain to procedural concerns bearing on the operation of judicial system, those that pertain to underlying policies of the law, those that pertain to individual rights, and those that pertain to the organization of a federalist system.

(2) Would different values inform the process of assessing the effect of a judgment rendered by the court of another country, rather than the state of Ohio? If so, what would be the values relevant to evaluating the foreign judgment?

(3) Try to articulate the difference between a court recognizing a judgment and enforcing a judgment. Under what circumstances might a New Jersey court be willing to recognize the judgment, but not willing to enforce the judgment by authorizing New Jersey officials to execute on Cassandra's New Jersey assets?

The following two graphs reflect some of the value clashes at issue in judgment enforcement cases. Note that Figure 4-1 and Figure 4-2 reflects only a two-dimensional tension. As reflected in Chapter 3 as well as in the materials below, questions about international judgment recognition also raise issues of the appropriate court role in the foreign affairs area as well as federalism and preemption issues where the recognizing court is a state court. These concerns might be represented by a third and possibly fourth line representing opposing values. A section at the end of the chapter on international recognition and enforcement of judgments explores these additional tensions.

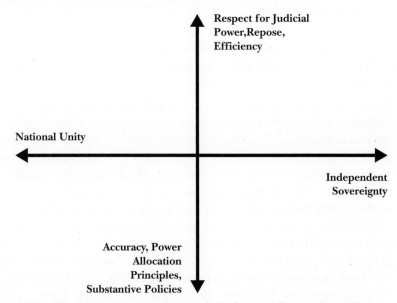

Figure 4-1: Value Clashes at Issue in Domestic Judgment Recognition Cases

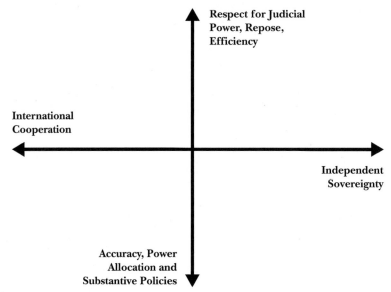

Figure 4-2: Value Clashes at Issue in International Judgment Recognition Cases

When you read the cases and notes that follow in this chapter, consider where on the graphs that you might chart the cases. First, however, it's helpful to nail down some vocabulary. Judgments issues generally involve at least two courts: (1) a court that renders the judgment—called the rendering court or the F1, and (2) a court that honors the judgment—called the honoring court or the F2. As noted above, judgments cases also present preclusion issues that one can organize under the doctrines of claim preclusion and issue preclusion. The following perspective presents some basic information on those doctrines as they relate to conflict of laws.

PERSPECTIVE ON CLAIM PRECLUSION AND ISSUE PRECLUSION

Preclusion rules concern the effect of a court's decision in subsequent cases. Because judgment recognition and enforcement require a court to give effect to an earlier decision in subsequent litigation, preclusion rules are key to judgments law as well. Although traditionally courts used the term "res judicata" to encompass all preclusive effects that a court decision might have in another lawsuit, modern courts have created more refined concepts and new terminology. Res judicata or claim preclusion now refers to a barrier to (a) re-litigating claims or causes of action that a party advanced (and litigated) in an earlier action, or (b) litigating for the first time claims or causes of action that a party did not, but should have, advanced in the first suit. Collateral estoppel or issue preclusion refers to the same barrier for litigating or re-litigating legal issues (or portions of claims). Requirements for both preclusion doctrines have overlap and differences.

Both preclusive doctrines require that the judgment of the prior adjudication be "valid" and "final." For any case or controversy, a court must fulfill certain requirements before it can properly adjudicate a cause of action. Those prerequisites for a court to issue a valid judgment include the following: (1) the parties must have received adequate notice of the action; (2) the court must have personal jurisdiction over the parties; and (3) the court must possess proper subject matter jurisdiction. "Finality" is a more complicated precondition that may require a fact-based evaluation of the judgment and understanding of the finality law of the jurisdiction that rendered the judgment. The goal of preclusion is to carry over the result of the first judgment and give it conclusive effect in subsequent cases. In furtherance of this goal, the "final judgment" requirement seeks to avoid using a tentative decision as the foundation for subsequent decision. Thus, courts look to see that the judgment is firm and stable, rather than tentative or shaky. Common examples of non-final judgments include a denial of a motion to dismiss and other orders denominated as "interlocutory."

Once the court establishes that the judgment is "final" and "valid," it can continue with its analysis as to whether claim or issue preclusion applies. The rules of claim preclusion require that (1) the prior judgment to be "on the merits"; (2) the parties to the second suit be the same or in privity with the parties in the first suit; and (3) the claim in the second suit must involve matters properly included in the first action. A judgment that decides the substance of the claim is a judgment "on the merits," and has preclusive effect. This does not include a judgment that dismisses the claim for threshold reasons bearing on such matters as improper venue or lack of subject matter jurisdiction. Judgments on these grounds are generally not "on the merits" and have no preclusive effect. Complicating matters, dismissals on demurrer (unless the dismissal is without prejudice) and dismissals for failure to comply with important procedural requirements are usually deemed "on the merits" and do have preclusive effect despite not deciding the factual or legal merits of a claim. Thus, for example, an order dismissing a suit because the plaintiff deliberately violated the court's discovery orders may be entered "with prejudice." Such judgments are generally designed to deter discovery violations, have the effect of extinguishing the claim, and have preclusive effect.

For claim preclusion to apply, the parties in subsequent suits must be the same or possess the right kind of legal relationship to the parties in the original suit. Traditionally, a person who enjoys all of the benefits of claim preclusion must also be subject to all of the burdens, and vice versa. Under the theory of mutuality, only the original parties or persons in privity with the original parties can be subject to claim preclusion. Though the mutuality doctrine has mostly faded for issue preclusion, courts are still reluctant to extend claim preclusion effect to parties who were not in the original suit, unless their interests were represented by the original parties — such as through a trustee — or they share a legal relationship with the original parties — such as through vicarious liability between an employer and employee.

Even if the parties are the same or related and the judgment was "on the merits," the claim in the subsequent suit must involve the same matters as the claim in the first for it to be "barred" or to "merge" with the second lawsuit for claim preclusion purposes. When a plaintiff wins the first suit, her claim "merges" with the judgment of the first suit, and she cannot obtain relief on that claim in subsequent suits. Conversely, if a plaintiff loses the first suit, the judgment acts as a "bar" to her claim, and she can no longer seek to litigate that claim.

To determine if the matters involved in two suits are "the same," each claim's scope must be considered. A majority of jurisdictions have adopted the "transactional view" of claims. The Restatement (Second) of Judgments §24 provides that a claim "includes all rights of the plaintiff to remedies against the defendant with respect to all or any part of the transaction, or series of connected transactions, out of which the action arose." To determine if a grouping of facts constitutes a "transaction," the court considers whether the facts are related in time, space, or origin, whether they form a convenient trial unit, and whether the unit conforms to the parties' understanding and expectations. So, bodily injury and property damage claims from a vehicle accident would be considered a single "transaction," or parts of "the same" claim, because both types of injury arise from the same set of facts.

Some jurisdictions have extended the "transaction" idea to preclude claims that could have been brought as counterclaims in the original suit. "Defense preclusion" bars the defendant in the original suit from asserting claims that she could have used as a counterclaim or defense in the original suit if they arose from the same transaction as the original claim. This part of preclusion law can be found largely in the compulsory counterclaim rules, such as Federal Rule of Civil Procedure 13(a). In addition, however, the decisions recognize a so-called common law compulsory counterclaim rule, which forbids the defendant in the original suit from filing a suit seeking to undo the judgment won by the plaintiff.

The rules of issue preclusion or collateral estoppel require that (1) the issue asserted in the second action be actually litigated and decided in the first action; and (2) the issue be necessary to the court's judgment in the first suit. An issue is considered actually litigated and decided if the issue is properly raised, by pleadings or other methods, submitted for decision, and then resolved. This same issue is necessary or essential to the court's judgment if the findings as to the issue were determinative or if the court's judgment was dependent upon the issue's resolution. Thus, a finding that is treated as dictum is not necessary to the court's judgment.

As with claim preclusion, the parties who can invoke and be bound by issue preclusion traditionally had to be the same parties as in the original suit or to be legally related to the original parties in the right way so there was "privity" between them. Nonetheless, this mutuality doctrine has eroded in most jurisdictions, which now allow for "non-mutual" issue preclusion. To understand how this works, consider two last suits: suit 1 and suit 2. Non-mutual issue preclusion enables entities who were not parties to suit 1 to bind parties from suit 1 to the resolution of issues litigated in suit 1, decided against the suit 1 parties, and essential to the judgment in suit 1. A plaintiff uses non-mutual issue preclusion "offensively" in suit 2 when the plaintiff tries to stop the re-litigation of issues already decided against the defendant in suit 1: an earlier suit brought by another plaintiff. A defendant uses non-mutual issue preclusion "defensively" in suit 2 when the defendant tries in suit 2 to stop the re-litigation of issues already decided against the plaintiff in suit 1, which the plaintiff had brought against another defendant. Defensive use is relatively non-controversial because it encourages a plaintiff to join all defendants in the first suit. Courts are particularly supportive of defensive use when the claims against the defendants arise from the same transaction because the joinder of all defendants in the initial suit would have saved money and time for all involved.[1]

On the other hand, offensive use is relatively controversial because it discourages plaintiffs from joining existing claims against a defendant. Plaintiffs might want to "hedge their bets" by holding back on joining a suit so that they could later enjoy the option of either litigating afresh or asserting issue preclusion from an earlier suit. This incentive can lead to more cases and thus higher litigation costs. For this reason, some jurisdictions have prohibited offensive nonmutual issue preclusion by disapproving its use in cases when the plaintiff could have easily joined the previous action or where the multiple suits are inconvenient for the defendant.

A.   THE FULL FAITH AND CREDIT PRINCIPLE

For lawsuits in the United States, principles of full faith and credit inform the process of judgment recognition and judgment enforcement. The full faith and

---

1. A classic description of this thinking appears in Justice Traynor's opinion in *Bernhard v. Bank of America*, 122 P.2d 892 (Cal. 1942). In this passage, Justice Traynor uses "res judicata" as an umbrella term to embrace collateral estoppel or issue preclusion:

> No satisfactory rationalization has been advanced for the requirement of mutuality. Just why a party who was not bound by a previous action should be precluded from asserting it as res judicata against a party who was bound by it is difficult to comprehend. Many courts have abandoned the requirement of mutuality and confined the requirement of privity to the party against whom the plea of res judicata is asserted. . . . The courts of most jurisdictions have in effect accomplished the same result by recognizing a broad exception to the requirements of mutuality and privity, namely, that they are not necessary where the liability of the defendant asserting the plea of res judicata is dependent upon or derived from the liability of one who was exonerated in an earlier suit brought by the same plaintiff upon the same facts. Typical examples of such derivative liability are master and servant, principal and agent, and indemnitor and indemnitee. Thus, if a plaintiff sues a servant for injuries caused by the servant's alleged negligence within the scope of his employment, a judgment against the plaintiff of the grounds that the servant was not negligent can be pleaded by the master as res judicata if he is subsequently sued by the same plaintiff for the same injuries. Conversely, if the plaintiff first sues the master, a judgment against the plaintiff on the grounds that the servant was not negligent can be pleaded by the servant as res judicata if he is subsequently sued by the plaintiff. In each of these situations the party asserting the plea of res judicata was not a party to the previous action nor in privity with such a party. . . . Likewise, the estoppel is not mutual since the party asserting the plea, not having been a party or in privity with a party to the former action, would not have been bound by it had it been decided the other way. The cases justify this exception on the ground that it would be unjust to permit one who has had his day in court to reopen identical issues by merely switching adversaries.

19 Cal. 2d at 812-813, 122 P.2d at 895.

credit clause of the Constitution requires the courts of one state to give appropriate effect to the judgment of another state:

U.S. Const. Art. IV, §1:

Full Faith and Credit shall be given in each State to the public Acts, Records, and judicial Proceedings of every other State. And the Congress may by general Laws prescribe the Manner in which such Acts, Records and Proceedings shall be proved, and the Effect thereof.

Note that the second part of the clause empowers Congress to enact implementing legislation. Congress did so in the following statute:

28 U.S.C. §1738:

The Acts of the legislature of any State, Territory, or Possession of the United States, or copies thereof, shall be authenticated by affixing the seal of such State, Territory or Possession thereto.

   The records and judicial proceedings of any court of any such State, Territory or Possession, or copies thereof, shall be proved or admitted in other courts within the United States and its Territories and Possessions by the attestation of the clerk and seal of the court annexed, if a seal exists, together with a certificate of a judge of the court that the said attestation is in proper form.

   Such Acts, records and judicial proceedings or copies thereof, so authenticated, shall have the same full faith and credit in every court within the United States and its Territories and Possessions as they have by law or usage in the courts of such State, Territory or Possession from which they are taken.

Note that this statute, sometimes called the full faith and credit statute, spells out how federal courts should treat state court judgments. The Supreme Court has imposed a reciprocal obligation on state courts in handling federal court judgments. *See, e.g., Metcalf v. City of Watertown,* 153 U.S. 671 (1894). Is there a court relationship still left to be defined? While federal courts do not "officially" have a full faith and credit obligation when it comes to the judgments of other federal courts, this relationship arguably doesn't need such an obligation. Indeed, another federal statute — 28 U.S.C. §1963 — makes it easy for a litigant to register the judgment of one federal court in another federal court for the purpose of enforcement. If, for example, one federal district court failed to honor a valid judgment of another federal district court, a court of appeals or the United States Supreme Court would have supervisory power to impose something akin to a full faith and credit obligation on the second district court.

   Congress has used its power under the full faith and credit clause to enact specific laws bearing on judgments as well. One statute discussed later in this chapter — 28 U.S.C. §1738A and §1738B — governs interstate enforcement of child custody and family support decrees.

If a state court litigant wishes to enforce a judgment in a sister state, the litigant will need to comply with laws of the honoring state regarding enforcement. Many states have adopted uniform legislation, including the Uniform Enforcement of Foreign Judgments Act, which provides a summary procedure for suing upon a foreign judgment. (Remember, for vocabulary purposes, that the judgment of a sister state is deemed a "foreign" judgment from the point of view of the honoring state; judgments of foreign nations are called "foreign country" judgments.) While the Uniform Enforcement of Foreign Judgments Act contemplates an expedited process, §6 of the Act states that the "right of the judgment creditor to bring an action to enforce his judgment instead of proceeding under this Act remains unimpaired." Accordingly, the range of defenses and exceptions that inform the full faith and credit clause is available to parties litigating the enforcement and recognition of a sister state judgment. To these matters, we now turn.

Fauntleroy v. Lum

210 U.S. 230 (1908)

Mr. Justice HOLMES delivered the opinion of the court:

This is an action upon a Missouri judgment, brought in a court of Mississippi. . . . The defendant pleaded that the original cause of action arose in Mississippi out of a gambling transaction in cotton futures; that he declined to pay the loss; that the controversy was submitted to arbitration, the question as to the illegality of the transaction, however, not being included in the submission; that an award was rendered against the defendant; that thereafter, finding the defendant temporarily in Missouri, the plaintiff brought suit there upon the award; that the trial court refused to allow the defendant to show the nature of the transaction, and that, by the laws of Mississippi, the same was illegal and void, but directed a verdict if the jury should find that the submission and award were made, and remained unpaid; and that a verdict was rendered and the judgment in suit entered upon the same. . . . The plea was demurred to on constitutional grounds, and the demurrer was overruled, subject to exception. Thereupon replications were filed, again setting up the Constitution of the United States (art. 4, §1), and were demurred to. The supreme court of Mississippi held the plea good and the replications bad, and judgment was entered for the defendant. Thereupon the case was brought here.

The main argument urged by the defendant to sustain the judgment below is addressed to the jurisdiction of the Mississippi courts.

The laws of Mississippi make dealing in futures a misdemeanor, and provide that contracts of that sort, made without intent to deliver the commodity or to pay the price, "shall not be enforced by any court." The defendant contends that this language deprives the Mississippi courts of jurisdiction. . . .

The statute now before us seems to us only to lay down a rule of decision. The Mississippi court in which this action was brought is a court of general jurisdiction and would have to decide upon the validity of the bar, if the suit upon the award or upon the original cause of action had been brought there. The words "shall not be enforced by any court" are simply another, possibly less emphatic, way of saying that an action shall not be brought to enforce such contracts. As suggested by the counsel for the plaintiff in error, no one would say that the words of the Mississippi statute of frauds, go to the jurisdiction of the court. Of course it could be argued that logically they had that scope, but common sense would revolt. . . . We regard this question as open under the decisions below, and we have expressed our opinion upon it independent of the effect of the judgment, although it might be that, even if jurisdiction of the original cause of action was withdrawn, it remained with regard to a suit upon a judgment based upon an award, whether the judgment or award was conclusive or not. But it might be held that the law as to jurisdiction in one case followed the law in the other, and therefore we proceed at once to the further question, whether the illegality of the original cause of action in Mississippi can be relied upon there as a ground for denying a recovery upon a judgment of another state.

The doctrine laid down by Chief Justice Marshall was "that the judgment of a state court should have the same credit, validity, and effect in every other court in the United States which it had in the state where it was pronounced, and that whatever pleas would be good to a suit thereon in such state, and none others, could be pleaded in any other court in the United States." . . . We assume that the statement of Chief Justice Marshall is correct. It is confirmed by the act of May 26, 1790, chap. 11, 1 Stat. at L. 122, providing that the said records and judicial proceedings "shall have such faith and credit given to them in every court within the United States as they have by law or usage in the courts of the state from whence the said records are or shall be taken." Whether the award would or would not have been conclusive, and whether the ruling of the Missouri court upon that matter was right or wrong, there can be no question that the judgment was conclusive in Missouri on the validity of the cause of action. A judgment is conclusive . . . ; and it needs no authority to show that it cannot be impeached either in or out of the state by showing that it was based upon a mistake of law. Of course, a want of jurisdiction over either the person or the subject-matter might be shown. But, as the jurisdiction of the Missouri court is not open to dispute, the judgment cannot be impeached in Mississippi even if it went upon a misapprehension of the Mississippi law.

We feel no apprehensions that painful or humiliating consequences will follow upon our decision. No court would give judgment for a plaintiff unless it believed that the facts were a cause of action by the law determining their effect. Mistakes will be rare. In this case the Missouri court no doubt supposed that the award was binding by the law of Mississippi. If it was mistaken, it made a natural mistake. The validity of its judgment, even in Mississippi, is, as we believe, the result of the Constitution as it always has been understood, and is not a matter to arouse the susceptibilities of the states, all of which are equally concerned in the question and equally on both sides.

Mr. Justice WHITE, with whom concurs Mr. Justice HARLAN, Mr. Justice MCKENNA, and Mr. Justice DAY, dissenting:

... The court now reverses on the ground that the due faith and credit clause obliged the courts of Mississippi, in consequence of the action of the Mississippi court, to give efficacy to transactions in Mississippi which were criminal, and which were against the public policy of that state. Although not wishing in the slightest degree to weaken the operation of the due faith and credit clause as interpreted and applied from the beginning, it to me seems that this ruling so enlarges that clause as to cause it to obliterate all state lines, since the effect will be to endow each state with authority to overthrow the public policy and criminal statutes of the others, thereby depriving all of their lawful authority. Moreover, the ruling now made, in my opinion, is contrary to the conceptions which caused the due faith and credit clause to be placed in the Constitution, and substantially overrules the previous decisions of this court interpreting that clause. ...

The foundation upon which our system of government rests is the possession by the states of the right, except as restricted by the Constitution, to exert their police powers as they may deem best for the happiness and welfare of those subject to their authority. The whole theory upon which the Constitution was framed, and by which alone, it seems to me, it can continue, is the recognition of the fact that different conditions may exist in the different states, rendering necessary the enactment of regulations of a particular subject in one state when such subject may not in another be deemed to require regulation; in other words, that in Massachusetts, owing to conditions which may there prevail, the legislature may deem it necessary to make police regulations on a particular subject, although like regulations may not obtain in other states. And, of course, such also may be the case in Louisiana or any other state. If it be that the ruling now made deprives the states of powers admittedly theirs, it follows that the ruling must be wrong. ...

When the Constitution was adopted the principles of comity by which the decrees of the courts of one state were entitled to be enforced in another were generally known; but the enforcement of those principles by the several states had no absolute sanction, since they rested but in comity. Now, it cannot be denied that, under the rules of comity recognized at the time of the adoption of the Constitution, and which, at this time, universally prevail, no sovereignty was or is under the slightest moral obligation to give effect to a judgment of another sovereignty, when to do so would compel the state in which the judgment was sought to be executed to enforce an illegal and prohibited contract, when both the contract and all the acts done in connection with its performance had taken place in the latter state. ... No special reference has been made by me to the arbitration, because that is assumed by me to be negligible. If the cause of action was open for inquiry for the purpose of deciding whether the Missouri court had jurisdiction to render a judgment entitled to be enforced in another state, the arbitration is of no consequence. The violation of law in Mississippi could not be cured by seeking to arbitrate in that state in order to fix the sum of the fruits of the illegal acts. ...

I therefore dissent.

Notes on
FAUNTLEROY

1. The honoring court or "F2" in *Fauntleroy* was Mississippi and the rendering court or "F1" was Missouri. The transaction enforced by the F1's judgment was not only deemed unenforceable under F2 law, but was also punishable in the F2 as a crime. Moreover, the Mississippi prohibition said that futures contracts should not be enforced in *any* court. Mississippi's position did not, however, stop the *Fauntleroy* Court from articulating an apparently unqualified approach to full faith and credit: the court's judgment must be given full faith and credit in another jurisdiction, irrespective of whether the judgment is contrary to a public policy of the honoring court. The *Fauntleroy* Court also quoted an equally unqualified approach to full faith and credit articulated by Chief Justice Marshall: "The judgment of a state court should have the same credit, validity, and effect in every other court in the United States which it had in the state where it was pronounced." Congress apparently liked this approach, which it incorporated into the full faith and credit statute, §1738. The apparently strict approach to full faith and credit reflected in *Fauntleroy* sends a message about the values that the *Fauntleroy* Court believes should dominate the matter. Consider Figure 4-2 above. In which quadrant would you chart the decision?

2. Consider Justice White's dissent. Are his arguments compelling? He suggests that the Court's approach gives license to a state to provide litigants (particularly plaintiffs) with an opportunity to do an end run around distasteful laws.

Isn't that also true when courts have a liberal policy toward enforcing choice of law clauses in contracts? By designating a particular law to govern their affairs, parties might succeed in circumventing legal restrictions that they do not like. In both instances, at least one party has asserted its will in order to avoid the effect of a law. How are the two situations different? Note that most choice of law clause jurisprudence provides a public policy "escape valve" for courts asked to enforce the clause. Is it consistent with this position that the *Fauntleroy* majority seems to refuse such an escape valve? Is it appropriate that the Court refused to do so? The United States Supreme Court discussed whether there exists a public policy exception to judgments in a later case set forth below, *Baker v. General Motors Corp.*, 522 U.S. 222 (1998), and many Justices were dubious that such an exception exists at all. Compare this position to that of the European Union. As discussed at the end of this chapter, European Union instruments do have an explicit public policy exception for judgments.

In assessing the difference between how United States courts handle the public policy exception to contractual choice of law clauses and how they handle the matter in the judgments context, one is reminded that the contractual clauses concern choice of law issues and not recognition of judgments issues. This is a key distinction in United States law: issues of sovereign prerogative are handled differently when that prerogative takes the form of a judgment as opposed to when it takes the form of general rules of law. As you read through the material in this chapter, evaluate why that distinction should be so important. In particular, ask yourself: why does the law show such great respect for judgments?

3. A main rationale for the *Fauntleroy* rule is to promote mutual respect among the states of the United States and to minimize interstate friction. Does the F2 in the case, Mississippi, have an argument that Missouri did not hold up its end of the bargain when it failed to allow proof of Mississippi law during the original litigation? As discussed in Chapter 3, the United States Supreme Court established as recently as *Allstate Ins. Co. v. Hague,* 449 U.S. 302 (1981), that the due process and full faith and credit clauses require a state applying its own law to a suit to have a significant contact or significant aggregation of contacts with the facts giving rise to the suit. An argument can made that Missouri did not satisfy this standard. On the other hand, one might argue that the Missouri court did not apply Missouri law, but instead tried to apply Mississippi law and simply misapprehended its meaning. Misunderstanding a sister state's law is not a violation of full faith and credit, it's just a mistake to be corrected on appeal. *See Sun Oil Co. v. Wortman,* 486 U.S. 717 (1988); *Treinies v. Sunshine Mining Co.,* 308 U.S. 66 (1939).

In reconciling *Fauntleroy* with United States Supreme Court jurisprudence, one should note the Supreme Court has ruled that one state need not enforce the "penal" laws of another jurisdiction. Not enforcing a Mississippi penal law normally means refusing to enforce a claim for a penalty. *See, e.g., Huntington v. Attrill,* 146 U.S. 657 (1892). Does that excuse Missouri's approach to the litigation?

4. Note that *Fauntleroy* concerns only the question whether an F2 must recognize the F1 judgment. Judgment recognition cases also sometimes concern what precisely recognizing the judgment entails. Chief Justice Marshall's language about the F2 giving the F1 judgment the same "validity and effect" as it would have in the F1 provides guidance on this issue. Cases make clear that this "full faith and credit" rule means that the F2 must apply the preclusion principles law of F1 to determine the effect of the judgment. (This is significant because res judicata (claim preclusion) and collateral estoppel (issue preclusion) laws can vary from state to state.) Does the goal of promoting mutual cooperation among the states require this result? Would it be contrary to the spirit of the full faith and credit clause for an F2 to give a judgment greater effect than it would have in the F1?

Professor Howard Erichson explains what problems might result if the rules allowed the F2 to apply F2 preclusion law rather than F1 preclusion law. He explains that under such an approach, litigating parties would be unsure about the binding effect and finality of a judgment, since the consequence of litigation might depend on where the judgment is ultimately enforced. At the time of the F1 lawsuit, parties couldn't be certain whether the judgment would be enforced in F1, F2, or another jurisdiction. Thus, tying a judgment's preclusive effect to the original forum provides certainty to everyone and allows the plaintiff to evaluate enforcement issues in choosing the original forum. Howard M. Erichson, *Interjurisdictional Preclusion*, 96 MICH. L. REV. 945 (1998).

Note that the mandated full faith and credit analysis creates hybrid law governing judgments: state law informs the preclusive effect of a judgment, but federal law controls how and when that state law is used.

5. You might have noted that the *Fauntleroy* Court alluded to the possibility that jurisdictional problems could provide a possible basis for avoiding the strict rule. The cases below explore that and other possible exceptions or qualifications to the full faith and credit principle.

6. Courts traditionally did not enforce another jurisdiction's tax and penal judgments. But those two categories of judgments do not today belong on a list of exceptions to the full faith and credit obligations for civil matters. The United States Supreme Court held as early as 1935 that "a judgment is not to be denied full faith and credit merely because it is for taxes." *Milwaukee County v. M.E. White Co.*, 296 U.S. 268 (1935).

The law is similar now for penal judgments. The Supreme Court long ago explained the following:

> The question whether a statute of one State which in some aspects may be called penal, is a penal law in the international sense, so that it cannot be enforced in the courts of another State, depends up the question whether its purpose is to punish an offence against the public justice of the State. . . . Penal laws, strictly and properly, are those imposing punishment for an offence committed against the State, and which . . . the executive of the State has the power to pardon. *Huntington v. Attrill*, 146 U.S. 657 (1892). Huntington thus held that judgments not falling within in this strict definition are subject to full faith and credit. While some question has surrounded the issue of whether the full faith and credit obligation applies to civil punitive damages award, commentators have suggested that, "the only subject still excluded from the broad recognition policy . . . is that of criminal jurisdiction."

PETER HAY, PATRICK J. BORCHERS & SYMEON C. SYMEONIDES, CONFLICT OF LAWS §24.24, at 1478 (5th ed. 2010). Nevertheless, occasional case law expands the exception further. *See, e.g., Oakland v. Desert Outdoor Adver.*, 267 P.3d 48 (Nev. 2011), *cert. denied*, 132 S. Ct. 1713 (2012) (Nevada Supreme Court concluded that it need not enforce a near half-a-million-dollar civil fine imposed on defendant for refusing to remove a sign in violation of a California municipal code, since the fine was designed to "punish an offense against the public justice of the state").

PROBLEM 4-1: THE PROSTITUTION CONTRACT

The State of P has legalized prostitution and extends legal recognition to contracts to perform sexual acts in exchange for money. The State of C criminalizes prostitution under all circumstances and thus deems such contracts to be unenforceable. Benair and Les made a contract that Les receive a salary in exchange for providing ongoing prostitution services for one year. The contract was made and to be performed in the State of C. Les lives in State P and Benair lives in State C. Benair claims that Les breached the contract and filed a contract enforcement suit in State P. The court in State P enforced the contract and entered judgment against Les. Because the bulk of Les's assets are located in State C, Benair filed an enforcement action in State C to recover judgment. The State C court is inclined to deny enforcement because to allow enforcement would contravene State C's public policy. May State C constitutionally deny enforcement on this basis?

B. QUALIFICATIONS OR EXCEPTIONS TO THE FULL FAITH AND CREDIT PRINCIPLE

Durfee v. Duke

375 U.S. 106 (1963)

Justice STEWART delivered the opinion of the Court.

... In 1956 the petitioners brought an action against the respondent in a Nebraska court to quiet title to certain bottom land situated on the Missouri River. The main channel of that river forms the boundary between the States of Nebraska and Missouri. The Nebraska court had jurisdiction over the subject matter of the controversy only if the land in question was in Nebraska. Whether the land was Nebraska land depended entirely upon a factual question — whether a shift in the river's course had been caused by avulsion or accretion. The respondent appeared in the Nebraska court and through counsel fully litigated the issues, explicitly contesting the court's jurisdiction over the subject matter of the controversy. After a hearing the court found the issues in favor of the petitioners and ordered that title to the land be quieted in them. The respondent appealed, and the Supreme Court of Nebraska affirmed the judgment after a trial de novo on the record made in the lower court. The State Supreme Court specifically found that the rule of avulsion was applicable, that the land in question was in Nebraska, that the Nebraska courts therefore had jurisdiction of the subject matter of the litigation, and that title to the land was in the petitioners. The respondent did not petition this Court for a writ of certiorari to review that judgment.

Two months later the respondent filed a suit against the petitioners in a Missouri court to quiet title to the same land. Her complaint alleged that the land was in Missouri. The suit was removed to a Federal District Court by reason of diversity of citizenship. The District Court after hearing evidence expressed the view that the land was in Missouri, but held that all the issues had been adjudicated and determined in the Nebraska litigation, and that the judgment of the Nebraska Supreme Court was res judicata and "is now binding upon this court." The Court of Appeals reversed, holding that the District Court was not required to give full faith and credit to the Nebraska judgment, and that normal res judicata principles were not applicable because the controversy involved land and a court in Missouri was therefore free to retry the question of the Nebraska court's jurisdiction over the subject matter. . . . For the reasons that follow, we reverse the judgment before us.

. . . Full faith and credit thus generally requires every State to give to a judgment at least the res judicata effect which the judgment would be accorded in the State which rendered it.

. . . [R]espondent relies upon the many decisions of this Court which have held that a judgment of a court in one State is conclusive upon the merits in a court in another State only if the court in the first State had power to pass on the merits — had jurisdiction, that is, to render the judgment. . . .

However, while it is established that a court in one State, when asked to give effect to the judgment of a court in another State, may constitutionally inquire into the foreign court's jurisdiction to render that judgment, the modern decisions of this Court have carefully delineated the permissible scope of such an inquiry. From these decisions there emerges the general rule that a judgment is entitled to full faith and credit — even as to questions of jurisdiction — when the second court's inquiry discloses that those questions have been fully and fairly litigated and finally decided in the court which rendered the original judgment.

With respect to questions of jurisdiction over the person,[8] this principle was unambiguously established in *Baldwin v. Iowa State Traveling Men's Ass'n*, 283 U.S. 522. There it was held that a federal court in Iowa must give binding effect to the judgment of a federal court in Missouri despite the claim that the original court did not have jurisdiction over the defendant's person, once it was shown to the court in Iowa that that question had been fully litigated in the Missouri forum. "Public policy," said the Court, "dictates that there be an end of litigation; that those who have contested an issue shall be bound by the result of the contest; and that matters once tried shall be considered forever settled as between the parties. We see no reason why this doctrine should not apply in every case where one voluntarily appears, presents his case and is fully heard, and why he should not, in the absence of fraud, be thereafter concluded by the judgment of the tribunal to which he has submitted his cause."

Following the *Baldwin* case, this Court soon made clear in a series of decisions that the general rule is no different when the claim is made that the original forum did not have jurisdiction over the subject matter. In each of these cases the claim was made that a court, when asked to enforce the judgment of another

---

8. It is not disputed in the present case that the Nebraska courts had jurisdiction over the respondent's person. She entered a general appearance in the trial court, and initiated the appeal to the Nebraska Supreme Court.

forum, was free to retry the question of that forum's jurisdiction over the subject matter. In each case this Court held that since the question of subject-matter jurisdiction had been fully litigated in the original forum, the issue could not be retried in a subsequent action between the parties.

. . . The reasons for such a rule are apparent. In the words of the Court's opinion in *Stoll v. Gottlieb*, 305 U.S. 1651:

> We see no reason why a court in the absence of an allegation of fraud in obtaining the judgment, should examine again the question whether the court making the earlier determination on an actual contest over jurisdiction between the parties, did have jurisdiction of the subject matter of the litigation. . . . Courts to determine the rights of parties are an integral part of our system of government. It is just as important that there should be a place to end as that there should be a place to begin litigation. After a party has his day in court, with opportunity to present his evidence and his view of the law, a collateral attack upon the decision as to jurisdiction there rendered merely retries the issue previously determined. There is no reason to expect that the second decision will be more satisfactory than the first.

305 U.S., at 172.

To be sure, the general rule of finality of jurisdictional determinations is not without exceptions. Doctrines of federal pre-emption or sovereign immunity may in some contexts be controlling. *Kalb v. Feuerstein*, 308 U.S. 433; *U.S. v. U.S. Fid. Co.*, 309 U.S. 506.[12] But no such overriding considerations are present here.

It is argued that an exception to this rule of jurisdictional finality should be made with respect to cases involving real property because of this Court's emphatic expressions of the doctrine that courts of one State are completely without jurisdiction directly to affect title to land in other States. This argument is wide of the mark. Courts of one State are equally without jurisdiction to dissolve the marriages of those domiciled in other States. But the location of land, like the domicile of a party to a divorce action, is a matter "to be resolved by judicial determination." The question remains whether, once the matter has been fully litigated and judicially determined, it can be retried in another State in litigation between the same parties. Upon the reason and authority of the cases we have discussed, it is clear that the answer must be in the negative.

It is to be emphasized that all that was ultimately determined in the Nebraska litigation was title to the land in question as between the parties to the litigation there. Nothing there decided, and nothing that could be decided in litigation between the same parties or their privies in Missouri, could bind either Missouri or Nebraska with respect to any controversy they might have, now or in the future, as to the location of the boundary between them, or as to their respective sovereignty over the land in question. Either State may at any time protect its interest by initiating independent judicial proceedings here.

12. It is to be noted, however, that in neither of these cases had the jurisdictional issues actually been litigated in the first forum.

For the reasons stated, we hold in this case that the federal court in Missouri had the power and, upon proper averments, the duty to inquire into the jurisdiction of the Nebraska courts to render the decree quieting title to the land in the petitioners. We further hold that when that inquiry disclosed, as it did, that the jurisdictional issues had been fully and fairly litigated by the parties and finally determined in the Nebraska courts, the federal court in Missouri was correct in ruling that further inquiry was precluded. Accordingly the judgment of the Court of Appeals is reversed, and that of the District Court is affirmed.

Justice BLACK, concurring.

Petitioners and respondents dispute the ownership of a tract of land adjacent to the Missouri River, which is the boundary between Nebraska and Missouri. Resolution of this question turns on whether the land is in Nebraska or Missouri. Neither State, of course, has power to make a determination binding on the other as to which State the land is in. However, in a private action brought by these Nebraska petitioners, the Nebraska Supreme Court has held that the disputed tract is in Nebraska. In the present suit, brought by this Missouri respondent in Missouri, the United States Court of Appeals has refused to be bound by the Nebraska court's judgment. I concur in today's reversal of the Court of Appeals' judgment, but with the understanding that we are not deciding the question whether the respondent would continue to be bound by the Nebraska judgment should it later be authoritatively decided, either in an original proceeding between the States in this Court or by a compact between the two States under Art. I, §10, that the disputed tract is in Missouri.

Notes on
DURFEE v. DUKE

1. Where would you chart *Durfee v. Duke* on Figure 4-1? How far do you think the Court's emphasis on finality of jurisdictional determinations should go? What if it were established beyond any question of scientific fact that the land was located in Missouri? What if the judge who decided the case in Nebraska was a complete impostor: a comedian possessing no judicial authority whatsoever? Are the two situations different?

2. What if the Supreme Court in *Durfee v. Duke* had come out the other way, allowing the F2 to determine where the land was located and therefore whether the F1 judgment was invalid for lack of jurisdiction? What if the F2 came to an opposite conclusion? Whose judgment would win: the F1 judgment or the F2 judgment?

3. How important is it that the parties vigorously litigated the F1's jurisdiction in *Durfee v. Duke*? The answer seems to be provided by an earlier case, *Chicot County Drainage Dist. v. Baxter State Park*, 308 U.S. 371 (1940), which held that the binding effect of the earlier judgment on jurisdiction applies so

long as there was an opportunity to raise the jurisdictions challenge. *Chicot County* invoked the res judicata principle that litigation is foreclosed in a second proceeding not only for matters that were actually presented to the first court, but also "as respects any other available matter which might have been presented. . . ."

4. Note the *Durfee v. Duke* Court's reference to the bankruptcy decision in *Kalb v. Feuerstein*, 308 U.S. 433 (1940), as an exception to the general rule of finality of jurisdictional determinations. The question in *Kalb* concerned the finality of a foreclosure in state court that had taken place in contravention of the automatic stay of federal bankruptcy law. The *Kalb* Court reasoned:

> It is generally true that a judgment by a court of competent jurisdiction bears a presumption of regularity and is not thereafter subject to collateral attack. But Congress, because its power over the subject of bankruptcy is plenary, may by specific bankruptcy legislation create an exception to that principle and render judicial acts taken with respect to the person or property of a debtor whom the bankruptcy law protects nullities and vulnerable collaterally. Although the [state court] had general jurisdiction over foreclosures under [state law], a peremptory prohibition by Congress in the exercise of its supreme power over bankruptcy that no State court have jurisdiction over a petitioning farmer-debtor or his property, would have rendered the confirmation of sale and its enforcement beyond the County Court's power and nullities subject to collateral attack. The States cannot, in the exercise of control over local laws and practice, vest State courts with power to violate the supreme law of the land. The Constitution grants Congress exclusive power to regulate bankruptcy and under this power Congress can limit that jurisdiction which courts, State or Federal, can exercise over the person and property of a debtor who duly invokes the bankruptcy law. If Congress has vested in the bankruptcy courts exclusive jurisdiction over farmer-debtors and their property, and has by its Act withdrawn from all other courts all power under any circumstances to maintain and enforce foreclosure proceedings against them, its Act is the supreme law of the land which all courts—State and Federal—must observe. The wisdom and desirability of an automatic statutory ouster of jurisdiction of all except bankruptcy courts over farmer-debtors and their property were considerations for Congress alone.

Id. at 438-439. In which quadrant of Figure 4-1 would you put *Kalb*? *Kalb* represents a preemption exception to the full faith and credit principle. Where does Congress get the power to make such an exception? Since *Kalb* concerned the effect of a state court judgment in a federal court, the full faith and credit clause does not technically govern the issue. But you will recall that the full faith and credit statute, 28 U.S.C. §1738, does speak to the effect of a state court judgment in federal court.

More recently, the United States Supreme Court has been loath to find preemption so as to infer an exception to full faith and credit principles. For example, in *Kremer v. Chem. Constr. Corp.*, 456 U.S. 461 (1982), the Court held that a federal court employment discrimination case under Title VII was barred under full faith and credit principles by state findings of nondiscrimination. Likewise, in *Allen v. McCurry*, 449 U.S. 90 (1980), the Court found a state criminal court ruling on a search and seizure claim barred a subsequent civil rights action under the federal civil rights statute, 28 U.S.C. §1983.

5. In reaching its decision, the *Durfee v. Duke* court cited *Baldwin v. Iowa State Traveling Men's Ass'n*, 283 U.S. 522 (1931), which held that a federal court in Iowa must give preclusive effect to the judgment of a Missouri federal court, even though the Missouri court did not have personal jurisdiction, because the Iowa court was satisfied that the question had been fully litigated. Should the analysis be different for personal jurisdiction than for subject matter jurisdiction? If so, why?

As straightforward as *Durfee v. Duke* appeared to be, the case did not directly reckon with earlier precedent suggesting a different approach to full faith and credit in land disputes, *Fall v. Eastin.* As you read *Fall v. Eastin*, consider whether it is distinguishable from *Durfee v. Duke*, and whether you can fashion a rule that synthesizes both cases.

Fall v. Eastin

215 U.S. 1 (1909)

Mr. Justice MCKENNA delivered the opinion of the Court:

The question in this case is whether a deed to land situated in Nebraska, made by a commissioner under the decree of a court of the state of Washington in an action for divorce, must be recognized in Nebraska under the due faith and credit clause of the Constitution of the United States.

The action was begun in Hamilton County, Nebraska, in 1897, to quiet title to the land and to cancel a certain mortgage thereon, given by E.W. Fall to W.H. Fall, and to cancel a deed executed therefor to defendant in error, Elizabeth Eastin.

Plaintiff alleged the following facts: She and E.W. Fall, who was a defendant in the trial court, were married in Indiana in 1876. Subsequently they went to Nebraska, and, while living there, "by their joint efforts, accumulations, and earnings, acquired jointly and by the same conveyance" the land in controversy. In 1889 they removed to the state of Washington, and continued to reside there as husband and wife until January, 1895, when they separated. On the 27th of February, 1895, her husband, she and he then being residents of King County,

Washington, brought suit against her for divorce in the superior court of that county. He alleged in his complaint that he and plaintiff were bona fide residents of King County, and that he was the owner of the land in controversy, it being, as he alleged, "his separate property, purchased by money received from his parents." He prayed for a divorce and "for a just and equitable division of the property."

Plaintiff appeared in the action by answer and cross complaint, in which she denied the allegations of the complaint, and alleged that the property was community property, and "was purchased by and with the money and proceeds of the joint labor" of herself and husband after their marriage. She prayed that a divorce be denied him, and that the property be set apart to her as separate property, subject only to a mortgage of $1,000, which she alleged was given by him and her. In a reply to her answer and cross complaint, he denied that she was the "owner as a member of the community in conjunction" with him of the property, and repeated the prayer of his complaint.

Plaintiff also alleges that the Code of Washington contained the following provision:

> Sec. 2007. In granting a divorce, the court shall also make such disposition of the property of the parties as shall appear just and equitable, having regard to the respective merits of the parties and to the condition in which they will be left by such divorce, and to the party through whom the property was acquired, and to the burdens imposed upon it for the benefit of the children, and shall make provision for the guardianship, custody, and support and education of the minor children of such marriage.

She further alleges that that provision had been construed by the supreme court of the state, requiring of the parties to an action for divorce to bring into court all of "their property, and a complete showing must be made," and that it was decided that §2007 conferred upon the court "the power, in its discretion, to make a division of the separate property of the wife or husband."

She further alleges that a decree was entered, granting her a divorce, and setting apart to her the land in controversy as her own separate property forever, free and unencumbered from any claim of the plaintiff thereto, and that he was ordered and directed by the court to convey all his right, title, and interest in and to the land within five days from the date of the decree.

She also alleges the execution of the deed to her by the commissioner appointed by the court, the execution and recording of the mortgage to W.H. Fall, and the deed to defendant; that the deed and mortgage were each made without consideration, and for the purpose of defrauding her, and that they cast a cloud upon her title derived by her under the decree of divorce and the commissioner's deed. She prays that her title be quieted, and that the deed and mortgage be declared null and void. . . .

The question is in narrow compass. The full faith and credit clause of the Constitution of the United States is invoked by plaintiff to sustain the deed executed under the decree of the court of the state of Washington. The argument in support of this is that the Washington court, having had jurisdiction of the parties and the subject matter, in determination of the equities between the parties to the lands in controversy, decreed a conveyance to be made to her. This conveyance, it is contended, was decreed upon equities, and was as effectual as though her "husband and she had been strangers, and she had bought the land from him and paid for it, and he had then refused to convey it to her." In other words, that the decree of divorce in the state of Washington, which was made in consummation of equities which arose between the parties under the law of Washington, was "evidence of her right to the legal title of at least as much weight and value as a contract in writing, reciting the payment of the consideration for the land, would be."

The defendant, on the other hand, contends . . . that "the Washington court had neither power nor jurisdiction to affect in the least, either legally or equitably," lands situated in Nebraska. . . .

In considering these propositions, we must start with a concession of jurisdiction in the Washington Court over both the parties and the subject-matter. Jurisdiction in that court is the first essential, but the ultimate question is, What is the effect of the decree upon the land, and of the deed executed under it? . . .

The territorial limitation of the jurisdiction of courts of a state over property in another state has a limited exception in the jurisdiction of a court of equity, but it is an exception well defined. A court of equity, having authority to act upon the person, may indirectly act upon real estate in another state, through the instrumentality of this authority over the person. Whatever it may do through the party, it may do to give effect to its decree respecting property, whether it goes to the entire disposition of it or only to affect it with liens or burdens. . . .

[W]hen the subject matter of a suit in a court of equity is within another state or country, but the parties within the jurisdiction of the court, the suit may be maintained and remedies granted which may directly affect and operate upon the person of the defendant, and not upon the subject-matter, although the subject-matter is referred to in the decree, and the defendant is ordered to do or refrain from certain acts toward it, and it is thus ultimately but *indirectly* affected by the relief granted. In such case, the decree is not of itself legal title, nor does it transfer the legal title. It must be executed by the party, and obedience is compelled by proceedings in the nature of contempt, attachment, or sequestration. On the other hand, where the suit is strictly local, the subject-matter is specific property, and the relief, when granted, is such that it *must* act directly upon the subject-matter, and not upon the person of the defendant, the jurisdiction must be exercised in the state where the subject-matter is situated.

This doctrine is entirely consistent with the provision of the Constitution of the United States, which requires a judgment in any state to be given full faith and credit in the courts of every other state. This provision does not extend the jurisdiction of the courts of one state to property situated in another, but only makes the judgment rendered conclusive on the merits of the claim or subject-matter of the suit. "It does not carry with it into another state the efficacy of a judgment upon property or persons, to be enforced by execution. To give it the force of a judgment in another state, it must be made a judgment there; and can only be executed in the latter as its laws may permit."

There is . . . much temptation in the facts of this case to follow the ruling of the supreme court of Ohio. As we have seen, the husband of the plaintiff brought suit against her in Washington for divorce, and, attempting to avail himself of the laws of Washington, prayed also that the land now in controversy be awarded to him. She appeared in the action, and, submitting to the jurisdiction which he had invoked, made counter charges and prayers for relief. She established her charges, she was granted a divorce, and the land degreed to her. He, then, to defeat the decree, and in fraud of her rights, conveyed the land to the defendant in this suit. This is the finding of the trial court. It is not questioned by the supreme court; but, as the ruling of the latter court, that the decree in Washington gave no such equities as could be recognized in Nebraska as justifying an action to quiet title, does not offend the Constitution of the United States, we are constrained to affirm its judgment.

Mr. Justice HARLAN and Mr. Justice BREWER dissent.

Mr. Justice HOLMES, concurring specially:

I am not prepared to dissent from the judgment of the court, but my reasons are different from those that have been stated.

The real question concerns the effect of the Washington decree. As between the parties to it, that decree established in Washington a personal obligation of the husband to convey to his former wife. A personal obligation goes with the person. If the husband had made a contract, valid by the law of Washington, to do the same thing, I think there is no doubt that the contract would have been binding in Nebraska. So I conceive that a Washington decree for the specific performance of such a contract would be entitled to full faith and credit as between the parties in Nebraska. But it does not matter to its constitutional effect what the ground of the decree may be, whether a contract or something else. *Fauntleroy v. Lum*, 210 U.S. 230, 52 L. Ed. 1039, 28 Sup. Ct. Rep. 641. (In this case it may have been that the wife contributed equally to the accumulation of the property, and so had an equitable claim.) A personal decree is equally within the jurisdiction of a court having the person within its power, whatever its ground and whatever it orders the defendant to do. Therefore I think that this decree was entitled to full faith and credit in Nebraska.

But the Nebraska court carefully avoids saying that the decree would not be binding between the original parties, had the husband been before the court. The ground on which it goes is that to allow the judgment to affect the conscience of purchasers would be giving it an effect *in rem*. It treats the case as standing on the same footing as that of an innocent purchaser. Now, if the court saw fit to deny the effect of a judgment upon privies in title, or if it considered the defendant an innocent purchaser, I do not see what we have to do with its decision, however wrong. . . .

Notes on
FALL v. EASTIN

1. Can you reconcile *Fall v. Eastin* and *Durfee v. Duke*? Does *Fall v. Eastin* stand for the proposition that a judgment rendered without jurisdiction can always be collaterally attacked? If so, does that mean that *Durfee v. Duke* overruled *Fall v. Eastin*? Alternatively, was *Durfee v. Duke* a special case, designed to deal with an instance where the location of land was uncertain?

2. One reading of *Fall v. Eastin* is that it articulates a "land taboo": a foreign decree cannot operate directly on land. What is the reason for such a taboo? One does not need to look far in the law to find special rules respecting land. Is this simply another instance of that "all-bets-are-off" approach to real property that one sees elsewhere in the law? Or, is it an outmoded manifestation of territorial instincts?

A more practical theory holds that the land taboo is necessary to preserve the integrity of local land recording systems. How could one adequately trace title to land if a court in another jurisdiction was able to issue a ruling that directly transferred title?

3. The received wisdom holds that even if the foreign decree cannot operate directly upon the land, it can operate directly on the rights and obligations of the parties to the litigation. The foreign decree can have preclusive effect in another jurisdiction and can provide the basis for a local decree that orders the land to be conveyed or otherwise effects a title transfer. Thus, although a court cannot exercise power to alter title in out-of-state real property, a court with proper personal jurisdiction over the parties to litigation can order one party to convey out-of-state realty to another or to pay the equivalent in value.

4. Professor Brainerd Currie provides practical advice on how to cope with *Fall v. Eastin*, which focuses on special attention to the relief requested in the original lawsuit:

> The theory on which recognition is claimed for that decree is that the foreign court had jurisdiction on the person of the defendant. . . . [I]t is not contended that that court could, by the force of its decree . . . directly transfer the title. The decree should be framed in strict accord with that theory. . . . [I]t should, upon appropriate findings of fact and of law, order the defendant to make a conveyance, and no more. Nothing whatever is to be gained by framing it in terms which purport to affect the title directly. . . .
>
> The theory on which relief is claimed at the situs is at least equally important. Consistently with the reasoning on which recognition is demanded, the plaintiff must scrupulously avoid any prayer for relief predicated on the assumption that he has acquired legal title by virtue of the foreign decree.
>
> . . .
>
> Thus the ideal action to secure the benefits of the decree at the situs would be framed as one to enforce, or execute, the decree; and, in the alternative, to secure a declaration of the rights of the parties pursuant to the decree, with

> supplemental relief; and, also in the alterative, to enforce the original cause of action—if there is one—with the decree operating as res judicata.
>
> Brainerd Currie, *Full Faith and Credit to Foreign Land Decrees*, 21 U. CHI. L. REV. 620, 672-676 (1954).

PROBLEM 4-2: KIRK AND MAGGIE'S MOUNTAIN HOME

Kirk and Maggie were married and had a home in State H. They also had a mountain house in State M. The couple separated. Maggie lived in the mountain house and Kirk stayed in the State H house. Kirk filed for a divorce in State H. Maggie appeared and the court dissolved the marriage. The court also granted Kirk title to the mountain house.

Thereafter, Maggie filed suit in State M and asked the court to authorize sale of the mountain house and an even division of the sale proceeds. In response, Kirk produced the State H decree, argued that he had sole control over the house, and asked the court to declare that Maggie was trespassing. Should the court honor the State M decree?

PROBLEM 4-3: KIRK AND MAGGIE REDUX: A MATTER OF CONTEMPT

As stated in Problem 4-2, Kirk and Maggie were married and had a home in State H. They also had a mountain house in State M. The couple separated. Maggie lived in the mountain house and Kirk stayed in the State H house. Kirk filed for a divorce in State H. Maggie did not appear and the court dissolved the marriage.

Although the State H court did determine that Kirk should get full ownership of the mountain house, the court—unlike in Problem 4-2—did not attempt to transfer title, but ordered Maggie to effect the proper paperwork in State M so that Kirk would get full title.

After two years, Maggie had not filled out the paperwork to transfer her interest in the house to Kirk. Kirk therefore filed a motion in the State H court for the court to hold Maggie in contempt for failure to comply with its order, and to order Maggie to fulfill the order's terms within four weeks to avoid another contempt sanction. The State H court did so, imposing a fine of $300. Did the State H court act properly?

PROBLEM 4-4: PRECLUSION WHERE SHAREHOLDER PLAINTIFFS COULD NOT HAVE RAISED CLAIM?

Matoya Corporation bought ABC Corporation. ABC shareholders bought a class action in Delaware state court, arguing that the sale violated their rights

DE agrmnt → preclude

under Delaware law. Another class action was brought by ABC shareholders in federal court raising federal securities law claims arising from the purchase by Matoya. These claims fell within the exclusive jurisdiction of federal courts and could not have been brought in the Delaware proceeding. The Delaware action settled, and the Delaware court incorporated the terms of the settlement agreement into its judgment dismissing the case. The agreement provided that the settlement covered all claims of the ABC plaintiff class. Under Delaware claim preclusion (res judicata) law, this state court judgment would be binding on all claims pertaining to the sale of ABC Corporation. All such claims would be barred in further proceedings in Delaware state courts. Matoya has now moved the federal court to dismiss that federal securities law action pursuant to 28 U.S.C. §1738 to dismiss the lawsuit. Should the federal court dismiss the suit? *∅ Diversity, ∅ dismiss*

DW → dismiss b/c apply
DE preclusion

Recognition and enforcement of judgments rendered by specialized tribunals presents special challenges. Does the case that follows, *Thomas v. Washington Gas Light*, provide an adequate approach, capable of replication in related contexts?

Thomas v. Washington Gas Light Co.

448 U.S. 261 (1980)

Mr. Justice STEVENS announced the judgment of the Court and delivered an opinion, in which Mr. Justice BRENNAN, Mr. Justice STEWART, and Mr. Justice BLACKMUN joined.

Petitioner received an award of disability benefits under the Virginia Workmen's Compensation Act. The question presented is whether the obligation of the District of Columbia to give full faith and credit to that award bars a supplemental award under the District's Workmen's Compensation Act.

[Petitioner is a resident of the District of Columbia and was hired in the District of Columbia. He worked primarily in the District but also worked in Virginia and Maryland. He sustained a back injury while at work in Virginia and entered an "Industrial Commission of Virginia Memorandum of Agreement as to Payment of Compensation" providing for benefits of $62 per week. He later notified the Department of Labor of his intention to seek compensation under the District of Columbia Act. Respondent opposed the claim arguing that, as a matter of Virginia law, the Virginia award excluded any other recovery "at common law or otherwise" on account of the injury in Virginia and the District of Columbia's obligation to give that award full faith and credit therefore precluded a second, supplemental award. The Administrative Law Judge agreed with respondent that the Virginia award must be given res judicata effect in the District to the extent that it was res judicata in Virginia. The judge held, however, that the Virginia award did not preclude further compensation in Virginia. Moreover, he construed the statutory prohibition against additional recovery "at common law or otherwise" as merely covering "common law and other remedies under Virginia law." The judge awarded petitioner permanent total disability benefits payable from the date of his injury with a credit for the amounts previously paid under the Virginia award. The United States Court of Appeals for the Fourth Circuit ultimately reversed, holding that a "second and separate proceeding in another jurisdiction upon the same injury after a prior recovery in another State [is] precluded by the Full Faith and Credit Clause."]

I

Respondent contends that the District of Columbia was without power to award petitioner additional compensation because of the Full Faith and Credit Clause of the Constitution or, more precisely, because of the federal statute implementing that Clause. An analysis of this contention must begin with two decisions from the 1940's that are almost directly on point: *Magnolia Petroleum Co. v. Hunt*, 320 U.S. 430 and *Industrial Comm'n of Wisconsin v. McCartin*, 330 U.S. 622.

In *Magnolia*, a case relied on heavily both by respondent and the Court of Appeals, the employer hired a Louisiana worker in Louisiana. The employee was later injured during the course of his employment in Texas. A tenuous majority held that Louisiana was not permitted to award the injured worker supplementary compensation under the Louisiana Act after he had already obtained a recovery from the Texas Industrial Accident Board: "Respondent was free to pursue his remedy in either state but, having chosen to seek it in Texas, where the award was res judicata, the full faith and credit clause precludes him from again seeking a remedy in Louisiana upon the same grounds."

Little more than three years later, the Court severely curtailed the impact of *Magnolia*. In *McCartin*, the employer and the worker both resided in Illinois and entered into an employment contract there for work to be performed in Wisconsin. The employee was injured in the course of that employment. He initially filed a claim with the Industrial Commission of Wisconsin. Prior to this Court's decision in *Magnolia*, the Wisconsin Commission informed him that under Wisconsin law, he could proceed under the Illinois Workmen's Compensation Act, and then claim compensation under the Wisconsin Act, with credit to be given for any payments made under the Illinois Act. Thereafter, the employer and the employee executed a contract for payment of a specific sum in full settlement of the employee's right under Illinois law. The contract expressly provided, however, that it would "'not affect any rights that applicant may have under the Workmen's Compensation Act of the State of Wisconsin.'" The employee then obtained a supplemental award from the Wisconsin Industrial Commission; but the Wisconsin state courts vacated it under felt compulsion of the intervening decision in *Magnolia*.

This Court reversed, holding without dissent that *Magnolia* was not controlling. Although the Court could have relied exclusively on the contract provision reserving the employee's rights under Wisconsin law to distinguish the case from *Magnolia*, Mr. Justice Murphy's opinion provided a significantly different ground for the Court's holding when it said: "[T]he reservation spells out what we believe to be implicit in [the Illinois Workmen's Compensation] Act—namely, that an . . . award of the type here involved does not foreclose an additional award under the laws of another state. And in the setting of this case, that fact is of decisive significance."

Earlier in the opinion, the Court had stated that "[o]nly some unmistakable language by a state legislature or judiciary would warrant our accepting . . . a construction" that a workmen's compensation statute "is designed to preclude any recovery by proceedings brought in another state." The Illinois statute, which the Court held not to contain the "unmistakable language" required to preclude a supplemental award in Wisconsin, broadly provided:

> No common law or statutory right to recover damages for injury or death sustained by any employe while engaged in the line of his duty as such employe, other than the compensation herein provided, shall be available to any employe who is covered by the provisions of this act. . . .

The Virginia Workmen's Compensation Act's exclusive-remedy provision is not exactly the same as Illinois'; but it contains no "unmistakable language" directed at precluding a supplemental compensation award in another State that was not also in the Illinois Act. Consequently, *McCartin* by its terms, rather than the earlier *Magnolia* decision, is controlling as between the two precedents. Nevertheless, the fact that we find ourselves comparing the language of two state statutes, neither of which has been construed by the highest court of either State, in an attempt to resolve an issue arising under the Full Faith and Credit Clause makes us pause to inquire whether there is a fundamental flaw in our analysis of this federal question.

II

We cannot fail to observe that, in the Court's haste to retreat from *Magnolia*, it fashioned a rule that clashes with normally accepted full faith and credit principles. It has long been the law that "the judgment of a state court should have the same credit, validity, and effect, in every other court in the United States, which it had in the state where it was pronounced." This rule, if not compelled by the Full Faith and Credit Clause itself, is surely required by 28 U.S.C. §1738. . . . Thus, in effect, by virtue of the full faith and credit obligations of the several States, a State is permitted to determine the extraterritorial effect of its judgment; but it may only do so indirectly by prescribing the effect of its judgments within the State.

The *McCartin* rule, however, focusing as it does on the extraterritorial intent of the rendering State, is fundamentally different. It authorizes a State, by drafting or construing its legislation in "unmistakable language," directly to determine the extraterritorial effect of its workmen's compensation awards. . . . The *McCartin* "unmistakable language" rule represents an unwarranted delegation to the States of this Court's responsibility for the final arbitration of full faith and credit questions. The Full Faith and Credit Clause "is one of the provisions incorporated into the Constitution by its framers for the purpose of transforming an aggregation of independent, sovereign States into a nation." To vest the power of determining the extraterritorial effect of a State's own laws and judgments in the State itself risks the very kind of parochial entrenchment on the interests of other States that it was the purpose of the Full Faith and Credit Clause and other provisions of Art. IV of the Constitution to prevent.

Thus, a re-examination of *McCartin*'s "unmistakable language" test reinforces our tentative conclusion that it does not provide an acceptable basis on which to distinguish *Magnolia*. But if we reject that test, we must decide whether to overrule either *Magnolia* or *McCartin*. In making this kind of decision, we must take into account both the practical values served by the doctrine of *stare decisis* and the principles that inform the Full Faith and Credit Clause.

III

The doctrine of *stare decisis* imposes a severe burden on the litigant who asks us to disavow one of our precedents. For that doctrine not only plays an important role in orderly adjudication; it also serves the broader societal interests in even-handed, consistent, and predictable application of legal rules. When rights have been created or modified in reliance on established rules of law, the arguments against their change have special force.

It is therefore appropriate to begin the inquiry by considering whether a rule that permits, or a rule that forecloses, successive workmen's compensation awards is more consistent with settled practice.

It should first be noted that *Magnolia*, by only the slimmest majority, effected a dramatic change in the law that had previously prevailed throughout the United States. . . . Of greater importance is the fact that as a practical matter the "unmistakable language" rule of construction announced in *McCartin* left only the narrowest area in which *Magnolia* could have any further precedential value. For the exclusivity language in the Illinois Act construed in *McCartin* was typical of most state workmen's compensation laws. Consequently, it was immediately recognized that *Magnolia* no longer had any significant practical impact. Moreover, since a state legislature seldom focuses on the extraterritorial effect of its enactments, and since a state court has even less occasion to consider whether an award under its State's law is intended to preclude a supplemental award under another State's Workmen's Compensation Act, the probability that any State would thereafter announce a new rule against supplemental awards in other States was extremely remote. As a matter of fact, subsequent cases in the state courts have overwhelmingly followed *McCartin* and permitted successive state workmen's compensation awards. . . .

IV

Three different state interests are affected by the potential conflict between Virginia and the District of Columbia. Virginia has a valid interest in placing a limit on the potential liability of companies that transact business within its borders. Both jurisdictions have a valid interest in the welfare of the injured employee — Virginia because the injury occurred within that State, and the

District because the injured party was employed and resided there. And finally, Virginia has an interest in having the integrity of its formal determinations of contested issues respected by other sovereigns.

. . . It is . . . perfectly clear that petitioner could have sought a compensation award in the first instance either in Virginia, the State in which the injury occurred, or in the District of Columbia, where petitioner resided, his employer was principally located, and the employment relation was formed. And as those cases underscore, compensation could have been sought under either compensation scheme even if one statute or the other purported to confer an exclusive remedy on petitioner. Thus, for all practical purposes, respondent and its insurer would have had to measure their potential liability exposure by the more generous of the two workmen's compensation schemes in any event. It follows that a State's interest in limiting the potential liability of businesses within the State is not of controlling importance.

It is also manifest that the interest in providing adequate compensation to the injured worker would be fully served by the allowance of successive awards. In this respect the two jurisdictions share a common interest and there is no danger of significant conflict. The ultimate issue, therefore, is whether Virginia's interest in the integrity of its tribunal's determinations forecloses a second proceeding to obtain a supplemental award in the District of Columbia. . . .

[In this regard, we note that] the critical differences between a court of general jurisdiction and an administrative agency with limited statutory authority forecloses the conclusion that constitutional rules applicable to court judgments are necessarily applicable to workmen's compensation awards.

A final judgment entered by a court of general jurisdiction normally establishes not only the measure of the plaintiff's rights but also the limits of the defendant's liability. A traditional application of res judicata principles enables either party to claim the benefit of the judgment insofar as it resolved issues the court had jurisdiction to decide. Although a Virginia court is free to recognize the perhaps paramount interests of another State by choosing to apply that State's law in a particular case, the Industrial Commission of Virginia does not have that power. Its jurisdiction is limited to questions arising under the Virginia Workmen's Compensation Act. Typically, a workmen's compensation tribunal may only apply its own State's law. In this case, the Virginia Commission could and did establish the full measure of petitioner's rights under Virginia law, but it neither could nor purported to determine his rights under the law of the District of Columbia. Full faith and credit must be given to the determination that the Virginia Commission had the authority to make; but by a parity of reasoning, full faith and credit need not be given to determinations that it had no power to make. Since it was not requested, and had no authority, to pass on petitioner's rights under District of Columbia law, there can be no constitutional objection to a fresh adjudication of those rights.

It is true, of course, that after Virginia entered its award, that State had an interest in preserving the integrity of what it had done. And it is squarely within the purpose of the Full Faith and Credit Clause, as explained in *Pacific Employers*, "to preserve rights acquired or confirmed under the public acts" of Virginia by requiring other States to recognize their validity. Thus, Virginia had an interest in having respondent pay petitioner the amounts specified in its award. Allowing a supplementary recovery in the District does not conflict with that interest. . . .

. . . [W]hether or not the worker has sought an award from the less generous jurisdiction in the first instance, the vindication of that State's interest in placing a ceiling on employers' liability would inevitably impinge upon the substantial interests of the second jurisdiction in the welfare and subsistence of disabled workers — interests that a court of general jurisdiction might consider, but which must be ignored by the Virginia Industrial Commission. . . .

Of course, it is for each State to formulate its own policy whether to grant supplemental awards according to its perception of its own interests. We simply conclude that the substantial interests of the second State in these circumstances should not be overridden by another State through an unnecessarily aggressive application of the Full Faith and Credit Clause, as was implicitly recognized at the time of *McCartin.*

We therefore would hold that a State has no legitimate interest within the context of our federal system in preventing another State from granting a supplemental compensation award when that second State would have had the power to apply its workmen's compensation law in the first instance. The Full Faith and Credit Clause should not be construed to preclude successive workmen's compensation awards. Accordingly, *Magnolia Petroleum Co. v. Hunt* should be overruled.

The judgment of the Court of Appeals is reversed, and the case is remanded.

Mr. Justice WHITE, with whom THE CHIEF JUSTICE and Mr. Justice POWELL join, concurring in the judgment.

I agree that the judgment of the Court of Appeals should be reversed, but I am unable to join in the reasoning by which the plurality reaches that result. Although the plurality argues strenuously that the rule of today's decision is limited to awards by state workmen's compensation boards, it seems to me that the underlying rationale goes much further. If the employer had exercised its statutory right of appeal to the Supreme Court of Virginia and that Court upheld the award, I presume that the plurality's rationale would nevertheless permit a subsequent award in the District of Columbia. Otherwise, employers interested in cutting off the possibility of a subsequent award in another jurisdiction need only seek judicial review of the award in the first forum. But if such a judicial decision is not preclusive in the second forum, then it appears that the plurality's rationale is not limited in its effect to judgments of administrative tribunals.

The plurality contends that unlike courts of general jurisdiction, workmen's compensation tribunals generally have no power to apply the law of another State and thus cannot determine the rights of the parties thereunder. Yet I see no reason why a judgment should not be entitled to full res judicata effect under the Full Faith and Credit Clause merely because the rendering tribunal was obligated to apply the law of the forum — provided, of course, as was certainly the case here, that the forum could constitutionally apply its law. The plurality's analysis seems to grant state legislatures the power to delimit the scope of a cause of action for federal full faith and credit purposes merely by enacting choice-of-law rules binding on the State's workmen's compensation tribunals. The plurality criticizes the *McCartin* case for vesting in the State the power to determine the extraterritorial effect of its own laws and judgments; yet it seems that its opinion is subject to the same objection. In any event, I am not convinced that Virginia, by instructing its Industrial Commission to apply Virginia law, could be said to have intended that the cause of action which merges in the Virginia judgment would not include claims under the laws of other States which arise out of precisely the same operative facts.

As a matter of logic, the plurality's analysis would seemingly apply to many everyday tort actions. I see no difference for full faith and credit purposes between a statute which lays down a forum-favoring choice-of-law rule and a common-law doctrine stating the same principle. Hence when a court, having power in the abstract to apply the law of another State, determines by application of the forum's choice-of-law rules to apply the substantive law of the forum, I would think that under the plurality's analysis the judgment would not determine rights arising under the law of some other State. Suppose, for example, that in a wrongful-death action the court enters judgment on liability against the defendant, and determines to apply the law of the forum which sets a limit on the recovery allowed. The plurality's analysis would seem to permit the plaintiff to obtain a subsequent judgment in a second forum for damages exceeding the first forum's liability limit. . . .

. . . Although I find *McCartin* to rest on questionable foundations, I am not now prepared to overrule it. And I agree with the plurality that *McCartin*, rather than *Magnolia*, is controlling as between the two precedents since the Virginia Workmen's Compensation Act lacks the "unmistakable language" which *McCartin* requires if a workmen's compensation award is to preclude a subsequent award in another State. I therefore concur in the judgment.

Mr. Justice REHNQUIST, with whom Mr. Justice MARSHALL joins, dissenting.

This is clearly a case where the whole is less than the sum of its parts. In choosing between two admittedly inconsistent precedents, *Magnolia Petroleum Co. v. Hunt*, 320 U.S. 430 (1943), and *Industrial Comm'n of Wisconsin v. McCartin*, 330 U.S. 622 (1947), six of us agree that the latter decision, *McCartin*, is analytically indefensible. The remaining three Members of the Court concede that it "rest[s] on questionable foundations." (opinion of White, J., joined by Burger, C.J., and Powell, J.). Nevertheless, when the smoke clears, it is *Magnolia* rather than *McCartin* that the plurality suggests should be overruled. . . . I believe that *Magnolia* was correctly decided, and because I fear that the rule proposed by the plurality is both ill-considered. . . . One might suppose that, having destroyed *McCartin*'s *ratio decidendi*, the plurality would return to the eminently defensible position adopted in *Magnolia*. But such is not the case. The plurality instead raises the banner of "*stare decisis*" and sets out in search of a new rationale to support the result reached in *McCartin*, significantly failing to even attempt to do the same thing for *Magnolia*.

. . . The plurality identifies three different "state interests" at stake in the present case: Virginia's interest in placing a limit on the potential liability of companies doing business in that State, Virginia's interest in the "integrity of its formal determinations of contested issues," and a shared interest of Virginia and the District of Columbia in the welfare of the injured employee. The plurality then undertakes to balance these interests and concludes that none of Virginia's concerns outweighs the concern of the District of Columbia for the welfare of petitioner.

Whenever this Court, or any court, attempts to balance competing interests it risks undervaluing or even overlooking important concerns. I believe that the plurality's analysis incorporates both errors. First, it asserts that Virginia's interest in limiting the liability of businesses operating within its borders can never outweigh the District of Columbia's interest in protecting its residents. . . . [T]he plurality completely ignores any interest that Virginia might assert in the finality of its adjudications. While workmen's compensation awards may be "non-final" in the sense that they are subject to continuing supervision and modification, Virginia nevertheless has a cognizable interest in requiring persons who avail themselves of its statutory remedy to eschew other alternative remedies that might be available to them. Otherwise, as apparently is the result here, Virginia's efforts and expense on an applicant's behalf are wasted when that applicant obtains a duplicative remedy in another State.

. . . I fear that the plurality, in its zeal to remedy a perceived imbalance in bargaining power, would badly distort an important constitutional tenet. Its "interest analysis" . . . knows no metes or bounds. Given the modern proliferation of quasi-judicial methods for resolving disputes and of various tribunals of limited jurisdiction, such a rule could only lead to confusion. . . . The Full Faith and Credit Clause did not allot to this Court the task of "balancing" interests where the "public Acts, Records, and judicial Proceedings" of a State were involved. It simply directed that they be given the "Full Faith and Credit" that the Court today denies to those of Virginia. I would affirm the judgment of the court below.

Notes on
THOMAS v. WASHINGTON GAS LIGHT

1. One can characterize case holdings as "performative speech acts," a phrase that linguists use to describe words that change the world as we know it. An example of a possible performative speech act is: "I pronounce you husband and wife." By uttering this phrase, one changes two humans' relationship and the relationship of two humans to society. So it goes with case holdings as well — which declare the legal principles ordering parties' rights and responsibilities. *See, e.g.,* Laura E. Little, *Hiding with Words: Obfuscation, Avoidance, and Federal Jurisdiction Opinions,* 46 UCLA L. Rev. 75, 93 (1998) (describing holdings as performative speech acts because they establish the "authoritative core" of the decision and guide future cases). Given

the importance of case holdings, judges (and law clerks) toil over crafting them and negotiate over their scope. A highly detailed holding is likely a signal of significant thought and discussion, an indication of intended limitations on the decision's reach.

In the case of *Thomas v. Washington Gas Light*, no opinion formally expressed the Court's holding since no opinion garnered a majority vote. Nonetheless, Justice Stevens's plurality opinion appears to have been intended as an opinion of the Court, given its lead position in the case, its structure, and its tone. Moreover, the purported "holding" at the end of Justice Stevens's plurality opinion bears the earmarks of a sentence reflecting thought (and possibly negotiation) as to its scope:

> We therefore would hold that a State has no legitimate interest within the context of our federal system in preventing another State from granting a supplemental compensation award when that second State would have had the power to apply its workmen's compensation law in the first instance.

The qualifications in this sentence seem to signal a desire to circumscribe the reach of the decision. Why would the Justices have concern for avoiding a broad-reaching decision? Is the result in *Thomas* consistent with the general full faith and credit principle articulated in *Fauntleroy*?

Try to parse the "holding" into operative components—so as to identify how much of the facts and laws involved in the case Justice Stevens (and the three other Justices joining the opinion) wanted to identify as crucial to its decision. Specifically, you might want to consider why the Justices speak in terms of whether a state has a "legitimate interest" in limiting the power of another state in adjudicating a workers' compensation award? Why does the sentence single out "supplemental" awards? And why does it matter whether or not the F2 had the power to apply the F1's workers' compensation law or not?

2. How does the law stand after *Thomas v. Washington Gas Light*? Is the following a correct tally of the Justices: six Justices take the position that *McCartin* should be overruled, while the four Justices in the plurality want to overrule *Magnolia*? Which decision, *McCartin* or *Magnolia*, is more consistent with the full faith and credit spirit? Is Justice Stevens correct in suggesting that *McCartin* inappropriately places in the hands of the rendering state (the F1) the effect of its judgments in another state (the F2)? Isn't this always the result of the full faith and credit principle, which requires the F2 to apply the preclusion law of the F1 in evaluating how to give the F1 judgment proper full faith and credit?

3. The bottom line of the decision is that a majority of Justices believe the supplemental award should stand. Given this result, where would you chart *Thomas v. Washington Gas Light* on Figure 4-1? Does this bottom line serve efficiency?

4. Justice White argues that the plurality puts too much emphasis on the limited jurisdiction of the workers' compensation board, since judicial review would be available in a court of general jurisdiction. Are you persuaded by this argument?

5. Although then-Justice Rehnquist was never much of a fan of balancing tests, his dissent shows particular concern about using a balancing test in the context of judgments. For further discussion of whether a balancing test is well suited to this context, see Stewart Sterk, *Full Faith and Credit, More or Less, to Judgments: Doubt About* Washington Gas Light Co. v. Thomas, 69 GEO. L.J. 1329 (1981).

Do you agree with Justice Rehnquist's suggestion that the plurality's reasoning has no logical limit? Do you agree that the plurality's approach would apply in any context in which the second forum merely offers more of a remedy than offered in the first forum? Should the plurality have explicitly limited its decision to decisions by administrative entities? Are balancing tests better suited to choice of law determinations than to judgment recognition?

PROBLEM 4-5: FULL FAITH AND CREDIT TO NEW MEXICO'S ADMINISTRATIVE ADJUDICATION

Assume that there is an epidemic of injuries in the United States resulting from diet drugs. New Mexico set up an administrative scheme where a state administrative tribunal has jurisdiction to adjudicate injuries resulting from these drugs. Under this scheme, the New Mexico administrative tribunal can apply only New Mexico tort law principles and award liability up to a total of $300,000 per claim. The New Mexico scheme provides that this award can be appealed to a New Mexico trial court, but that the award is thereafter final and cannot be supplemented in any way.

Nancy is a New Mexico resident and suffered severe injuries to her digestive system as a result of Skinny, Inc.'s diet pills. Nancy won a $300,000 judgment against Skinny, Inc. from the New Mexico tribunal. Skinny, Inc. appealed to the New Mexico state trial court, which affirmed the $300,000 award.

Nancy then filed suit against Skinny, Inc., in a Texas state trial court, seeking additional damages for the injury to her digestive system. Skinny, Inc. has filed a motion to dismiss this Texas suit. Should the Texas court grant this motion?

PROBLEM 4-6: FULL FAITH AND CREDIT, TRUCK TRANSPORT, AND FARM WORK

Kenny was a crop worker for Vine Ripe, Inc. Kenny did not have a car to get to work, but the produce truck driver for Vine Ripe allowed him to ride in the back of truck as it made its way to the picking field every day. The fields are located in the State of New Tomato. The truck would stop at a street corner near Kenny's home, which the truck passed every day as it went to and from the fields. Kenny lives in Neighboring State. One day while the truck was leaving the fields at the end of the day, the truck stopped at the edge of the fields because a gate across the road had been closed. The driver yelled for Kenny to jump off and unlock the gate. Kenny did so, but when he jumped back on the truck he slipped and severely injured his leg.

Kenny filed for workers' compensation benefits in the state of New Tomato. The administrative agency that adjudicated his claim had the authority only to apply New Tomato workers' compensation law. In doing so, the agency held that Kenny was not entitled to benefits because he was not acting as an "employee" within the meaning of the law when he was injured. The administrative judge who issued a ruling stated that this decision was based on the "factual finding" that Kenny received the ride from the truck driver as a personal favor, and not within the course of his employment.

Kenny then filed for benefits in Neighboring State. The workers' compensation tribunal there had authority to issue benefits, but could only apply Neighboring State's workers' compensation law. The administrative judge would like to rule that Kenny was injured in the course of his employment. Would it be appropriate for the judge to do so?

Baker v. General Motors Corp.

522 U.S. 222 (1998)

Justice GINSBURG delivered the opinion of the Court.

This case concerns the authority of one State's court to order that a witness' testimony shall not be heard in any court of the United States. In settlement of claims and counterclaims precipitated by the discharge of Ronald Elwell, a former General Motors Corporation (GM) engineering analyst, GM paid Elwell an undisclosed sum of money, and the parties agreed to a permanent injunction. As stipulated by GM and Elwell and entered by a Michigan County Court, the injunction prohibited Elwell from "testifying, without the prior written consent of [GM], . . . as . . . a witness of any kind . . . in any litigation already filed, or to be filed in the future, involving [GM] as an owner, seller, manufacturer and/or designer. . . ." GM separately agreed, however, that if Elwell were ordered to testify by a court or other tribunal, such testimony would not be actionable as a violation of the Michigan court's injunction or the GM-Elwell agreement.

After entry of the stipulated injunction in Michigan, Elwell was subpoenaed to testify in a product liability action commenced in Missouri by plaintiffs who were not involved in the Michigan case. The question presented is whether the national full faith and credit command bars Elwell's testimony in the Missouri case. We hold that Elwell may testify in the Missouri action without offense to the full faith and credit requirement.

I

Two lawsuits, initiated by different parties in different States, gave rise to the full faith and credit issue before us. One suit involved a severed employment relationship, the other, a wrongful-death complaint. We describe each controversy in turn.

A

The Suit Between Elwell and General Motors

Ronald Elwell was a GM [engineer for 30 years]. . . . Beginning in 1987, the Elwell-GM employment relationship soured [and GM eventually fired him. Elwell brought a wrongful discharge suit, claiming that GM retaliated for his testimony against its interest in a tort suit. GM counterclaimed, contending that Elwell had breached his fiduciary duty to GM by disclosing privileged and confidential information and misappropriating documents. In response to GM's motion for a preliminary injunction, and after a hearing, the Michigan trial court, on November 22, 1991, enjoined Elwell from "consulting or discussing with or disclosing to any person any of General Motors Corporation's trade secrets[,] confidential information or matters of attorney-client work product relating in any manner to the subject matter of any products liability litigation whether already filed or [to be] filed in the future which Ronald Elwell received, had knowledge of, or was entrusted with during his employments with General Motors Corporation."

In August 1992, GM and Elwell entered into a settlement under which Elwell received an undisclosed sum of money. The parties also stipulated to the entry of a permanent injunction and jointly filed with the Michigan court both the stipulation and the agreed-upon injunction. The proposed permanent injunction contained two proscriptions. The first substantially repeated the terms of the preliminary injunction; the second comprehensively enjoined Elwell from "testifying, without the prior written consent of General Motors Corporation, either upon deposition or at trial, as an expert witness, or as a witness of any kind, and from consulting with attorneys or their agents in any litigation already filed, or to be filed in the future, involving General Motors Corporation as an owner, seller, manufacturer and/or designer of the product(s) in issue."

To this encompassing bar, the consent injunction made an exception: "[This provision] shall not operate to *interfere with the jurisdiction of the Court in . . . Georgia* [where the litigation involving the fuel tank was still pending]." No other non-interference provision appears in the stipulated decree. [T]he Michigan court entered the injunction precisely as tendered by the parties.

Although the stipulated injunction contained an exception only for the Georgia action then pending, Elwell and GM included in their separate settlement agreement a more general limitation. If a court or other tribunal ordered Elwell to testify, his testimony would "in no way" support a GM action for violation of the injunction or the settlement agreement:

"'It is agreed that [Elwell's] appearance and testimony, if any, at hearings on Motions to quash subpoena or at deposition or trial or other official proceeding, if the Court or other tribunal so orders, will in no way form a basis for an action in violation of the Permanent Injunction or this Agreement.'"

In the six years since the Elwell-GM settlement, Elwell has testified against GM both in Georgia (pursuant to the exception contained in the injunction) and in several other jurisdictions in which Elwell has been subpoenaed to testify.

B

The Suit Between the Bakers and General Motors

[The Bakers filed a wrongful death suit against GM in a Missouri federal court, seeking damages for an automobile death of their mother. They] sought both to depose Elwell and to call him as a witness at trial. GM objected to Elwell's appearance as a deponent or trial witness on the ground that the Michigan injunction barred his testimony. In response, the Bakers urged that the Michigan injunction did not override a Missouri subpoena for Elwell's testimony. The Bakers further noted that, under the Elwell-GM settlement agreement, Elwell could testify if a court so ordered, and such testimony would not be actionable as a violation of the Michigan injunction.

After *in camera* review of the Michigan injunction and the settlement agreement, the Federal District Court in Missouri allowed the Bakers to depose Elwell and to call him as a witness at trial. [He testified against GM and the jury awarded a large verdict.] . . . The United States Court of Appeals for the Eighth Circuit reversed the District Court's judgment, ruling, *inter alia,* that Elwell's testimony should not have been admitted. Assuming, *arguendo,* the existence of a public policy exception to the full faith and credit command, the Court of Appeals concluded that the District Court erroneously relied on Missouri's policy favoring disclosure of relevant, nonprivileged information, for Missouri has an "equally strong public policy in favor of full faith and credit."

II

A

. . . The animating purpose of the full faith and credit command, as this Court explained in *Milwaukee County v. M.E. White Co.,* 296 U.S. 268 (1935), "was to alter the status of the several states as independent foreign sovereignties, each free to ignore obligations created under the laws or by the judicial proceedings of the others, and to make them integral parts of a single nation throughout which a remedy upon a just obligation might be demanded as of right, irrespective of the state of its origin." *Id.,* at 277.

Our precedent differentiates the credit owed to laws (legislative measures and common law) and to judgments. . . . Regarding judgments . . . the full faith and credit obligation is exacting. A final judgment in one State, if rendered by a court with adjudicatory authority over the subject matter and persons governed by the judgment, qualifies for recognition throughout the land. For claim and issue preclusion (res judicata) purposes, in other words, the judgment of the rendering State gains nationwide force.

A court may be guided by the forum State's "public policy" in determining the *law* applicable to a controversy. But our decisions support no roving "public policy exception" to the full faith and credit due *judgments*. In assuming the existence of a ubiquitous "public policy exception" permitting one State to resist recognition of another State's judgment, the District Court in the Bakers' wrongful-death action, misread our precedent. "The full faith and credit clause is one of the provisions incorporated into the Constitution by its framers for the purpose of transforming an aggregation of independent, sovereign States into a nation." We are "aware of [no] considerations of local policy or law which could rightly be deemed to impair the force and effect which the full faith and credit clause and the Act of Congress require to be given to [a money] judgment outside the state of its rendition."

The Court has never placed equity decrees outside the full faith and credit domain. Equity decrees for the payment of money have long been considered equivalent to judgments at law entitled to nationwide recognition. We see no reason why the preclusive effects of an adjudication on parties and those "in privity" with them, *i.e.*, claim preclusion and issue preclusion (res judicata and collateral estoppel), should differ depending solely upon the type of relief sought in a civil action.

Full faith and credit, however, does not mean that States must adopt the practices of other States regarding the time, manner, and mechanisms for enforcing judgments. Enforcement measures do not travel with the sister state judgment as preclusive effects do; such measures remain subject to the evenhanded control of forum law.

Orders commanding action or inaction have been denied enforcement in a sister State when they purported to accomplish an official act within the exclusive province of that other State or interfered with litigation over which the ordering State had no authority. Thus, a sister State's decree concerning land ownership in another State has been held ineffective *to transfer title*, although such a decree may indeed preclusively adjudicate the rights and obligations running between the *parties* to the foreign litigation. And antisuit injunctions regarding litigation elsewhere, even if compatible with due process as a direction constraining parties to the decree, in fact have not controlled the second court's actions regarding litigation in that court. . . .[9] Sanctions for violations of an injunction, in any event, are generally administered by the court that issued the injunction.

9. This Court has held it impermissible for a state court to enjoin a party from proceeding in a federal court, *see Donovan v. Dallas*, 377 U.S. 408 (1964), but has not yet ruled on the credit due to a state-court injunction barring a party from maintaining litigation in another State, see Ginsburg, *Judgments in Search of Full Faith and Credit: The Last-in-Time Rule for Conflicting Judgments*, 82 HARV. L. REV. 798, 823 (1969). . . . State courts that have dealt with the question have, in the main, regarded antisuit injunctions as outside the full faith and credit ambit. *See* Ginsburg, 82 HARV. L. REV. at 823, and n.99; *see also id.*, at 828-829 ("The current state of the law, permitting [an antisuit] injunction to issue but not compelling any deference outside the rendering state, may be

B

With these background principles in view, we turn to the dimensions of the order GM relies upon to stop Elwell's testimony. Specifically, we take up the question: What matters did the Michigan injunction legitimately conclude?

. . . [T]he parties before the Michigan County Court, Elwell and GM, submitted an agreed-upon injunction, which the presiding judge signed. While no issue was joined, expressly litigated, and determined in the Michigan proceeding,[11] that order is *claim* preclusive between Elwell and GM. Elwell's claim for wrongful discharge and his related contract and tort claims have "merged in the judgment," and he cannot sue again to recover more. Similarly, GM cannot sue Elwell elsewhere on the counterclaim GM asserted in Michigan.

Michigan's judgment, however, cannot reach beyond the Elwell-GM controversy to control proceedings against GM brought in other States, by other parties, asserting claims the merits of which Michigan has not considered. Michigan has no power over those parties, and no basis for commanding them to become intervenors in the Elwell-GM dispute. Most essentially, Michigan lacks authority to control courts elsewhere by precluding them, in actions brought by strangers to the Michigan litigation, from determining for themselves what witnesses are competent to testify and what evidence is relevant and admissible in their search for the truth.

As the District Court recognized, Michigan's decree could operate against Elwell to preclude him from *volunteering* his testimony. But a Michigan court cannot, by entering the injunction to which Elwell and GM stipulated, dictate to a court in another jurisdiction that evidence relevant in the Bakers' case — a controversy to which Michigan is foreign — shall be inadmissible. This conclusion creates no general exception to the full faith and credit command, and surely does not permit a State to refuse to honor a sister state judgment based on the forum's choice of law or policy preferences. Rather, we simply recognize that, just as the mechanisms for enforcing a judgment do not travel with the judgment itself for purposes of full faith and credit, and just as one State's judgment cannot automatically transfer title to land in another State, see *Fall v. Eastin,* 215 U.S. 1 (1909), similarly the Michigan decree cannot determine evidentiary issues in

---

the most reasonable compromise between . . . extreme alternatives," *i.e.,* "[a] general rule of respect for antisuit injunctions running between state courts," or "a general rule denying the states authority to issue injunctions directed at proceedings in other states").

11. In no event, we have observed, can issue preclusion be invoked against one who did not participate in the prior adjudication. Thus, Justice Kennedy emphasizes the obvious in noting that the Michigan judgment has no preclusive effect on the Bakers, for they were not parties to the Michigan litigation. Such an observation misses the thrust of GM's argument. GM readily acknowledges "the commonplace rule that a person may not be bound by a judgment *in personam* in a case to which he was not made a party." But, GM adds, the Michigan decree does not bind the Bakers; it binds *Elwell* only. Most forcibly, GM insists that the Bakers cannot object to the binding effect GM seeks for the Michigan judgment because the Bakers have no constitutionally protected interest in obtaining the testimony of a particular witness. [They argue that "the only party being 'bound' to the injunction is Elwell, and holding him to his legal obligations does not violate anyone's due process rights."] Given this argument, it is clear that issue preclusion principles, standing alone, cannot resolve the controversy GM presents.

a lawsuit brought by parties who were not subject to the jurisdiction of the Michigan court.[12]

The language of the consent decree is informative in this regard. Excluding the then-pending Georgia action from the ban on testimony by Elwell without GM's permission, the decree provides that it "shall not operate to *interfere with the jurisdiction* of the Court in . . . Georgia." But if the Michigan order, extended to the Georgia case, would have "interfer[ed] with the jurisdiction" of the Georgia court, Michigan's ban would, in the same way, "interfere with the jurisdiction" of courts in other States in cases similar to the one pending in Georgia.

In line with its recognition of the interference potential of the consent decree, GM provided in the settlement agreement that, if another court ordered Elwell to testify, his testimony would "in no way" render him vulnerable to suit in Michigan for violation of the injunction or agreement. The Eighth Circuit regarded this settlement agreement provision as merely a concession by GM that "some courts might fail to extend full faith and credit to the [Michigan] injunction." As we have explained, however, Michigan's power does not reach into a Missouri courtroom to displace the forum's own determination whether to admit or exclude evidence relevant in the Bakers' wrongful-death case before it. In that light, we see no altruism in GM's agreement not to institute contempt or breach-of-contract proceedings against Elwell in Michigan for giving subpoenaed testimony elsewhere. Rather, we find it telling that GM ruled out resort to the court that entered the injunction, for injunctions are ordinarily enforced by the enjoining court, not by a surrogate tribunal.

In sum, Michigan has no authority to shield a witness from another jurisdiction's subpoena power in a case involving persons and causes outside Michigan's governance. Recognition, under full faith and credit, is owed to dispositions Michigan has authority to order. But a Michigan decree cannot command obedience elsewhere on a matter the Michigan court lacks authority to resolve. *See Thomas v. Washington Gas Light Co.*, 448 U.S. 261, 282-283 (1980) (plurality opinion). . . .

Justice KENNEDY, with whom Justice O'CONNOR and Justice THOMAS join, concurring in the judgment.

I concur in the judgment. In my view the case is controlled by well-settled full faith and credit principles which render the majority's extended analysis unnecessary and, with all due respect, problematic in some degree. This separate opinion explains my approach.

---

12. Justice Kennedy inexplicably reads into our decision a sweeping exception to full faith and credit based solely on "the integrity of Missouri's judicial processes." The Michigan judgment is not entitled to full faith and credit, we have endeavored to make plain, because it impermissibly interferes with Missouri's control of litigation *brought by parties who were not before the Michigan court.* . . . If the Bakers had been parties to the Michigan proceedings and had actually litigated the privileged character of Elwell's testimony, the Bakers would of course be precluded from relitigating that issue in Missouri.

I

The majority, of course, is correct to hold that when a judgment is presented to the courts of a second State it may not be denied enforcement based upon some disagreement with the laws of the State of rendition. Full faith and credit forbids the second State to question a judgment on these grounds. There can be little doubt of this proposition. We have often recognized the second State's obligation to give effect to another State's judgments even when the law underlying those judgments contravenes the public policy of the second State.

My concern is that the majority, having stated the principle, proceeds to disregard it by announcing two broad exceptions. First, the majority would allow courts outside the issuing State to decline to enforce those judgments "purport[ing] to accomplish an official act within the exclusive province of [a sister] State." Second, the basic rule of full faith and credit is said not to cover injunctions "interfer[ing] with litigation over which the ordering State had no authority." The exceptions the majority recognizes are neither consistent with its rejection of a public policy exception to full faith and credit nor in accord with established rules implementing the Full Faith and Credit Clause. As employed to resolve this case, furthermore, the exceptions to full faith and credit have a potential for disrupting judgments, and this ought to give us considerable pause.

Our decisions have been careful not to foreclose all effect for the types of injunctions the majority would place outside the ambit of full faith and credit. These authorities seem to be disregarded by today's holding. For example, the majority chooses to discuss the extent to which courts may compel the conveyance of property in other jurisdictions. That subject has proved to be quite difficult. Some of our cases uphold actions by state courts affecting land outside their territorial reach. *E.g., Robertson v. Howard*, 229 U.S. 254, 261 (1913) ("[I]t may not be doubted that a court of equity in one State in a proper case could compel a defendant before it to convey property situated in another State"). . . . Nor have we undertaken before today to announce an exception which denies full faith and credit based on the principle that the prior judgment interferes with litigation pending in another jurisdiction. As a general matter, there is disagreement among the state courts as to their duty to recognize decrees enjoining proceedings in other courts.

Subjects which are at once so fundamental and so delicate as these ought to be addressed only in a case necessarily requiring their discussion, and even then with caution lest we announce rules which will not be sound in later application. We might be required to hold, if some future case raises the issue, that an otherwise valid judgment cannot intrude upon essential processes of courts outside the issuing State in certain narrow circumstances, but we need not announce or define that principle here. Even if some qualification of full faith and credit were required where the judicial processes of a second State are sought to be controlled in their procedural and institutional aspects, the Court's discussion does not provide sufficient guidance on how this exception should be construed in light of our precedents. The majority's broad review of these matters does not articulate the rationale underlying its conclusions. In the absence of more elaboration, it is unclear what it is about the particular injunction here that renders it undeserving of full faith and credit. The Court's reliance upon unidentified principles to justify omitting certain types of injunctions from the doctrine's application leaves its decision in uneasy tension with its own rejection of a broad public policy exception to full faith and credit. . . .

Full faith and credit requires courts to do more than provide for direct enforcement of the judgments issued by other States. It also "requires federal courts to give the same preclusive effect to state court judgments that those judgments would be given in the courts of the State from which the judgments emerged." . . . And whether or not an injunction is enforceable in another State on its own terms, the courts of a second State are required to honor its issue preclusive effects.

II

In the case before us, of course, the Bakers were neither parties to the earlier litigation nor subject to the jurisdiction of the Michigan courts. The majority pays scant attention to this circumstance, which becomes critical. The beginning point of full faith and credit analysis requires a determination of the effect the judgment has in the courts of the issuing State. In our most recent full faith and credit cases, we have said that determining the force and effect of a judgment should be the first step in our analysis. . . . A conclusion that the issuing State would not give the prior judgment preclusive effect ends the inquiry, making it unnecessary to determine the existence of any exceptions to full faith and credit. We cannot decline to inquire into these state-law questions when the inquiry will obviate new extensions or exceptions to full faith and credit.

If we honor the undoubted principle that courts need give a prior judgment no more force or effect that the issuing State gives it, the case before us is resolved. Here the Court of Appeals and both parties in their arguments before our Court seemed to embrace the assumption that Michigan would apply the full force of its judgment to the Bakers. Michigan law does not appear to support the assumption.

The simple fact is that the Bakers were not parties to the Michigan proceedings, and nothing indicates Michigan would make the novel assertion that its earlier injunction binds the Bakers or any other party not then before it or subject to its jurisdiction. For collateral estoppel to apply under Michigan law, "'the same parties must have had a full opportunity to litigate the issue, and there must be mutuality of estoppel.'" . . . Since the Bakers were not parties to the Michigan proceedings and had no opportunity to litigate any of the issues presented, it appears that Michigan law would not treat them as bound by the judgment. The majority cites no authority to the contrary.

It makes no difference that the judgment in question is an injunction. The Michigan Supreme Court has twice rejected arguments that injunctions have preclusive effect in later litigation, relying in no small part on the fact that the persons against whom preclusion is asserted were not parties to the earlier litigation. . . .

. . . GM disavows its desire to issue preclude the Bakers, claiming "the only party being 'bound' to the injunction is Elwell." This is difficult to accept because in assessing the preclusive reach of a judgment we look to its practical effect. Despite its disclaimer, GM seeks to alter the course of the suit between it and the Bakers by preventing the Bakers from litigating the admissibility of Elwell's testimony. Furthermore, even were we to accept GM's argument that the Bakers are essentially irrelevant to this dispute, GM's argument is flawed on its own terms. Elwell, in the present litigation, does not seek to relitigate anything; he is a witness, not a party.

In all events, determining as a threshold matter the extent to which Michigan law gives preclusive effect to the injunction eliminates the need to decide whether full faith and credit applies to equitable decrees as a general matter or the extent to which the general rules of full faith and credit are subject to exceptions. Michigan law would not seek to bind the Bakers to the injunction and that suffices to resolve the case. For these reasons, I concur in the judgment.

Notes on
BAKER v. GM

1. Note the majority's statement that "our decisions support no roving 'public policy exception' to the full faith and credit due *judgments*. In assuming the existence of a ubiquitous 'public policy exception' permitting one State to resist recognition of another State's judgment, the District Court in the Bakers' wrongful-death action, misread our precedent." How far is this statement intended to reach? Does it suggest that the forum's public policy should have absolutely no role in the recognition and enforcement of another jurisdiction's judgment? Was the *Baker* Court's decision that Michigan had no authority to restrict another jurisdiction's subpoena power wholly unrelated to concerns of public policy?

Recall Professor Larry Kramer's argument regarding the spirit of the United States Supreme Court's decision pertaining to a state's obligation to provide a forum in *Hughes v. Fetter*. Kramer argued that the "whole point" of full faith and credit is to foster states as part of a "community, with mutual obligations to respect each other's laws and judgments" and prevent states from indulging "prideful unwillingness to recognize other states' laws or judgments on the ground that these are inferior or unacceptable." Larry Kramer, *Same Sex-Marriage, Conflict of Laws, and the Unconstitutional Public Policy Exception*, 106 YALE L.J. 1965, 1985 (1997). Does *Baker* endorse this argument? The answer to this question is significant since the extent to which the full faith and credit clause allows a state to follow its own public policies in considering the legislative determinations, common law, and judgments of other states is crucial to controversial social issues, such as tort reform.

2. The crux of the debate between Justice Kennedy and the majority seems to turn on how important it is that the Bakers were not parties to the Michigan case. Justice Kennedy finds the case controlled by well-settled

full faith and credit principles, since those principles would mandate that the Michigan judgment could not bind the Bakers because they did not participate in the Michigan proceedings. The majority argues that the focus should be on the effect of the earlier judgment on Elwell, who was a party to the proceeding and is the object of the judgment. Who has the better argument? Are you persuaded by Justice Kennedy's argument that the Court should consider the practical effect of the earlier judgment on the Bakers, rather than consider just the formal operation of preclusion law? Justice Kennedy seemed to argue that — whether or not the Bakers are formally bound by the earlier judgment — what really matters is that the Bakers will experience the judgment's effect if it muzzles Elwell and precludes him from providing crucial evidence to their case.

Might one read *Baker* as standing for the proposition that a judgment from one case should not be allowed to control parties to another case? Such an argument might be premised on the due process clause: the notion being that all the parties in the second case did not have an opportunity to shape the judgment. The problem with this theory, however, is that judgments frequently have an impact on the legal rights of third parties — and the Supreme Court has not been inclined to find a due process violation in every instance.

3. The particular judgment at issue in *Baker* was a consent judgment that pertained to evidence proposed to be used in another jurisdiction. How important is it that the judgment was based on the parties' consent? Does this fact suggest that less state court autonomy and sovereignty were on the line than in other instances? Does it matter that the judgment's effect pertained to matters deeply vested in the authority and discretion of individual trial courts: subpoenas and testimonial evidence?

4. The Court seemed unimpressed with the Bakers' suggestion that the full faith and credit requirements should not control injunctions and other equitable decrees. The Court's discussion, however, does suggest that the matter had not been definitively settled. Why should equity decrees be any different than others? Injunctions and other remedies deriving from a court's equitable jurisdiction were traditionally considered personal remedies — deriving from the individual conscience of the judge and acting personally on the target of the injunction. In contemporary times, however, the distinction between law and equity jurisdiction has diminished, and the two forms of power are merged in federal courts and most state courts. Thus, contemporary jurisprudence provides little basis for withholding full faith and credit principles from injunctive decrees. For discussion of the equitable nature of the Michigan decree in *Baker*, see Polly J. Price, *Full Faith and Credit and the Equity Conflict*, 84 VA. L. REV. 747 (1998).

Consider the effect of full faith and credit principles on declaratory judgments. Declaratory judgments are a relatively modern innovation, authorized by statute in state and federal courts. They are similar to injunctions, but are less potent because courts cannot use their contempt power to enforce them. Nonetheless, declaratory judgments can easily provide the basis for further relief, which often includes injunctive orders, in the event that the declaratory judgment itself does not inspire compliance by the losing party. Subsequent to *Baker,* state courts in a few cases have refused to grant full faith and credit effect to another state's declaratory judgments where — in the courts' view — to do so would enable inappropriate interference, allowing the courts in one jurisdiction to control the conduct of litigation in another jurisdiction. *See Tenas v. Progressive Preferred Ins. Co.,* 238 P.3d 860 (Nev. 2008); *Wamsley v. Nodak Mut. Ins. Co.,* 178 P.3d 102 (Mont. 2008). It is unclear, however, whether this view will take hold among other courts. *See R.S. v. Pacificare Life & Health Ins. Co.,* 194 Cal. App. 4th 192, 128 Cal. Rptr. 3d 1 (2011); *Northern States Power Co. v. Continental Ins. Co.,* 805 N.W.2d 734 (Wis. Ct. App. 2011).

For federal court actions, the United States Supreme Court has cautioned federal courts considering whether to issue a declaratory judgment to consider the potential for interference with state court actions. Specifically, the Supreme Court has ruled federal courts were free to exercise their discretion under the federal Declaratory Judgment Act to defer to parallel state proceedings. *Wilton v. Seven Falls Co.,* 515 U.S. 277 (1995).

PERSPECTIVE ON DUPLICATIVE LITIGATION: PLACING PRECLUSION PRINCIPLES AND FULL FAITH AND CREDIT LAW IN PERSPECTIVE

As a consequence of the overlapping judicial systems within the United States, litigants frequently find their disputes pending in more than one forum. Indeed, this problem extends beyond domestic litigation within the United States: a United States litigant may also be a litigant on the same dispute in the courts of a foreign country. As it turns out, full faith and credit principles have a significant role to play in reducing duplicative litigation. Because, however, full faith and credit principles do not control the relationship between United States courts and courts of other countries, courts must marshal other doctrines to regulate that relationship.

Why might a party be tempted to file a suit when one has already been filed elsewhere? Myriad possible motivations exist, and one can easily beckon a number of scenarios: a losing party wishing to collaterally attack an unfavorable judgment in a new forum, a generally litigious party wishing to wear down an opponent by forcing the opponent to defend in different jurisdictions, or a defendant from one suit wishing to assert an affirmative upper hand by refiling a dispute in a new jurisdiction with more favorable substantive laws, procedures, and/or decision makers.

Some tools are available to a party seeking to stop a duplicative lawsuit before it comes to judgment. Particularly for federal court litigants, specialized weapons against duplicative litigation exist. For example, the Anti-Injunction Act allows federal courts to issue an injunction of state court proceedings in limited instances: (1) where "authorized by Act of Congress"; (2) "where necessary in aid" of the federal court's jurisdiction; and (3) to "protect or effectuate" the federal court's judgment. 28 U.S.C. §2283. Moreover, federal courts have created abstention doctrines allowing federal courts to defer their own power so that ongoing state proceedings on the same or related subject matter may continue without interference. Nonetheless, the courts have carefully circumscribed the opportunities for successfully invoking these abstention doctrines, which are known as the *Younger* doctrine and the *Colorado River* abstention doctrine. In cases of abusive litigation, Federal Rule of Civil Procedure 11 provides a potential theory for arresting litigation in federal court where litigation is pending elsewhere. Similarly, for egregious cases, a victim of repetitive suits might also successfully pursue a cause of action for malicious prosecution.

State courts also offer some of these same tools for combatting the confusion and waste of duplicative litigation. For example, state courts recognize the malicious prosecution cause of action and often have state procedural counterparts to Federal Rule 11. As a counterpart to federal court abstention doctrines, the "first to file" doctrine allows state courts to decline jurisdiction over an action when a suit with the same parties and issues has already been filed in another state. Followed in many state courts, the "first to file" rule is a discretionary principle inspired by the dictates of comity and judicial administration.

Despite available theories for terminating (or staying) concurrent lawsuits, litigants subject to multiple suits pending in multiple jurisdictions generally have little choice but maintain battle on all fronts. The story is different, however, once a dispute has come to judgment. Once final judgment is reached in one suit, preclusion principles provide another weapon in the arsenal of litigants seeking to halt duplicative suits. Because preclusion principles are generally treated as affirmative defenses to be raised early in litigation, preclusion doctrines can be extremely effective in reducing the expense and hassle of repetitive suits. To be useful across jurisdictional lines, however, preclusion doctrines are impotent without full faith and credit principles.

Several contexts illustrate the crucial role of the full faith and credit doctrine in regulating duplicative litigation: declaratory judgment cases, antisuit injunction cases, and case law pertaining to inconsistent judgments. As explained above in the notes after *Baker v. General Motors Corp.*, 522 U.S. 222 (1998), courts have been reluctant to allow litigants to use the declaratory judgment remedy as a means of interfering with the proceedings in other jurisdictions or as a means of circumventing interlocutory decisions in pending litigation. In such instances, the courts have refused to give full faith and credit effect to declaratory judgments that dispose of core issues in pending cases. For example, in *Wamsley v. Nodak Mutual Insurance Co.*, 178 P.3d 102 (Mont. 2008), one forum where suit was filed refused to give full faith and credit effect to a declaratory judgment issued in a different proceeding in another jurisdiction. The *Wamsley* court stated that to give full faith and credit effect to the declaratory suit "would defeat the purpose of forging national unity" and would "balkanize the legal process," bringing the "state courts into greater conflict" and reducing "respect for the type of state sovereignty the first Congress envisioned." For a different approach to declaratory judgments, see, e.g., *R.S. v. Pacificare Life & Health Ins. Co.*, 194 Cal. App. 4th 192, 128 Cal. Rptr. 3d 1 (2011) (in action against insurer for bad faith, unfair business practices, and breach of insurance policies, California court held that full faith and credit principles applied to a Missouri declaratory judgment, including unpleaded compulsory counterclaims, which would be barred under Missouri procedural law); *Northern States Power Co. v. Continental Ins. Co.*, 805 N.W.2d 734 (Wis. Ct. App. 2011) (after Wisconsin suit had been stayed pending disposition of Minnesota declaratory judgment suit, Wisconsin court granted full faith and credit to Minnesota declaratory judgment).

United States case law over antisuit injunctions between state courts has been similarly uncertain regarding the role of the full faith and credit clause. For a target of disabling or harassing litigation, injunctions against repetitive suits could be an important source of peace. The availability of such injunctions depends in substantial part on whether the various courts involved are state or federal courts. The supremacy clause of the United States prevents state courts from enjoining federal court proceedings, except in the limited circumstance where the federal court proceeding interferes with the state court's disposition of property within the state court's control. Nor can state courts enjoin litigants from pursuing federal court actions. As for the reverse scenario, the federal Anti-Injunction Act blocks federal courts from enjoining ongoing state proceedings, with only a few exceptions. In the limited circumstances where such a federal court injunction would be allowed by the federal Anti-Injunction Act, the state court subject to the federal court injunction against further proceedings would be bound by the injunction under the supremacy clause. Where the two courts involved are both state courts, the antisuit injunction question is less clear. As a matter of equity jurisprudence, the received wisdom is that such injunctions should be rare, confined to circumstances where the action to be enjoined would result in a grievous wrong. The Supreme Court has ruled in *Cole v. Cunningham*, 133 U.S. 107, 134 (1890), that the full faith and credit clause does not *prohibit* antisuit injunctions. Nevertheless, as observed in *Baker v. General Motors Corp.*, 522 U.S. 222 (1998), the Court has not specifically answered the question of whether the clause compels recognition of such injunctions. Lower courts have reached differing conclusions on the question whether the clause compels recognition. *Compare Laker Airways v. Sabena, Belgian World Airlines*, 731 F.2d 909, 934 (D.C. Cir. 1984) (full faith and credit clause does not compel recognition of antisuit injunction), *with Hall v. Michael Bello Ins. Agency, Inc.*, 880 A.2d 451 (N.J. Super. Ct. App. Div. 2005) (after Texas court entered permanent injunction barring policyholder suits against insurance company in Texas receivership, New Jersey court determined that full faith and credit required honoring the Texas stay on litigation); *Bard v. Charles R. Myers Ins. Agency, Inc.*, 839 S.W.2d 791, 797 (Tex. 1992) (state court's prohibition of suits against company in receivership given full faith and credit effect in another state). The *Baker v. General Motors Corp.* Court noted that the balance of state courts have not generally regarded themselves as bound by such injunctions, and the following language from *Baker* seems to affirm that position: "antisuit injunctions regarding litigation elsewhere . . . have not controlled the second court's action regarding litigation in that court." While arguments might be made in favor of this position, it promotes duplicative litigation, does it not?

Where more than one jurisdiction considers a matter — and antisuit injunctions lack the force of full faith and credit to back them up — the threat of inconsistent judgments may increase. Where an enforcing court is confronted with inconsistent judgments, which judgment should it enforce? In *Treinies v. Sunshine Mining Co.*, 308 U.S. 66 (1939), the Supreme Court held that the court should enforce the judgment rendered later in time. The Restatement (Second) of Judgments §15 (1980) adopts this last-in-time rule as well. A frequent criticism of the last-in-time rule highlights the incentive the rule creates for litigants who try to escape unfavorable rulings by seeking to litigate in another state.[2] In considering this critique, remember that a court considering whether to honor a judgment must sometimes make difficult decisions such as whether the court that issued the judgment had personal jurisdiction or whether the new litigation falls with the ambit of the earlier judgment. Although this second court may err in its decision on these matters, preclusion principles require honoring the second court's decision — right or wrong. When a third court is asked to consider both the first judgment and the second judgment, the last-in-time rule holds that the preclusion principles at work in the second forum force the third court to enforce the second judgment, *even if* it is the product of mistake.

The rules on duplicative litigation are different where one of the jurisdictions is a foreign nation. For example, the last-in-time rule does not apply to foreign nation judgments. Under both the Uniform Foreign-Country Money Judgments Recognition Act §4(c)(4) (2005) and the Uniform Foreign Money-Judgments Recognition Act §4(b)(4) (1962), a foreign country judgment need not be recognized if "the judgment conflicts with another final and conclusive judgment." As mentioned above, foreign country judgments are governed by different legal principles than those governing domestic judgments. The doctrines governing foreign country judgments and the regulation of duplicative litigation involving foreign countries are explained further at the end of this chapter.

PROBLEM 4-7: OBLIGATION TO REGISTER AS A SEX OFFENDER

Mitchell pleaded guilty to a non-consensual sexual abuse charge in New York. After negotiation with Mitchell and his lawyer, the prosecutor agreed that the following standard clause would *not* be included in plea agreement: "You shall

---

2. For further discussion, see, e.g., Ruth B. Ginsburg, *Judgments in Search of Full Faith and Credit: The Last-in-Time Rule for Conflicting Judgments*, 82 HARV. L. REV. 798 (1969).

be required to comply with the provisions of New York law requiring you to register as a sex offender with the New York State Division of Criminal Justice and your local police department." No other part of the plea agreement mentioned registration as a sex offender. The New York court entered this guilty plea agreement as a final judgment of conviction.

Mitchell has now moved to Illinois. Illinois authorities informed Mitchell that he needs to register as a sex offender with the Illinois Criminal Justice Agency, pursuant to the Illinois sex offender registration law. After Mitchell refused, the Illinois authorities filed an Illinois state court action to require him to register. Mitchell argues that the full faith and credit clause requires Illinois authorities to honor the agreement that he need not register as sex offender. Mitchell argues that this agreement is reflected in the plea agreement, which is embodied in the New York judgment. Should the Illinois court accept this argument?

PERSPECTIVE ON THE ROLE OF THE ENFORCING STATE'S LAW OF JUDGMENTS

Because the process of enforcing sister state judgments involves, by definition, at least two different court systems, complications may result because of differences between the jurisdiction's judgment laws. Judgment laws that frequently vary among jurisdictions include rules regarding revival of judgments, statutes of limitations for judgment enforcement, and preclusion principles (*i.e.*, claim preclusion and issue preclusion). States provide specific statutory requirements that govern revival of judgments after a period of time. Generally, revival requires the prevailing party to institute a revival proceeding, with revival being available if the judgment is valid, final, and for a definite sum that has not been fully paid or satisfied. Preclusion principles include the doctrines of res judicata and collateral estoppel. Both of these preclusion doctrines are the subject of a note at the beginning of this chapter.

In *Baker v. General Motors Corp.*, the Court made clear that full faith and credit principles do not require states to "adopt the practices of other States regarding the time, manner, and mechanisms for enforcing judgments." While seemingly straightforward, this direction provides only broad guidance. In several lines of cases, the Court has delineated specific rules regarding statutes of limitations, revival, and preclusion. Not surprisingly, some complications emerge.

On the issue of statute of limitations, the Supreme Court held as early as 1839 that an enforcing state may apply its own statute of limitations in order to refuse enforcement of a judgment that would *not* have been time barred in the jurisdiction where it was rendered. *McElmoyle v. Cohen*, 38 U.S. (13 Pet.) 312 (1839). The Court has even upheld differential statutes of limitations, which provide shorter limitations periods for enforcing out-of-state judgments than for in-state judgments. *Watkins v. Conway*, 385 U.S. 188 (1966). In so holding, however, the *Watkins v. Conway* Court reasoned that the statute did not disadvantage out-of-state judgments, since the limitations period did not run from the issuance of the original judgment, but instead from the time when the judgment had last been revived. All the *Watkins v. Conway* plaintiff needed to do was to return to the original state and file a proceeding to revive the judgment.

Addressing yet another wrinkle arising from differences among state laws governing judgments, the Supreme Court in *Union Nat'l Bank of Wichita, Kan. v. Lamb*, 337 U.S. 38 (1949), considered a Missouri judgment, which under Missouri law could not be revived after ten years from the date the Missouri court originally issued it. In a Colorado proceeding filed 18 years after the original judgment, the prevailing party revived the judgment. Thereafter, he sought to enforce the judgment in Missouri, but the Missouri court refused, reasoning that the Colorado action did not produce a new judgment. Applying its own ten-year statute of limitations, the Missouri court refused to enforce the judgment. The Supreme Court in *Lamb* disagreed with this result, holding that the Missouri court should have used Colorado law to evaluate the effect of the Colorado decision.

Rules of preclusion vary among jurisdictions in a variety of ways. For example, although res judicata law nearly always requires that the first and second actions both involve the same claim, states vary in how they define the concept of claims. A significant difference also exists in issue preclusion law among jurisdictions, with some jurisdictions requiring mutuality among the parties, and others abandoning that requirement. Because of these differences, the precise obligation that full faith and credit imposes on honoring jurisdictions sometimes becomes determinative. Cases interpreting the full faith and credit clause have definitively established that the honoring court must give at least as much preclusive effect to a judgment as would the rendering court.

What if the rendering court would allow further litigation, but the enforcing state would give the judgment preclusive effect? This situation occurred in *Hart v. Am. Airlines*, 304 N.Y.S.2d 810 (1969). In *Hart*, a plane crash resulted in several lawsuits, and a Texas federal court was the first to come to judgment, with a jury verdict against the airline. The *Hart* dispute was a later action in which different plaintiffs claimed that the Texas judgment collaterally estopped the airline from contesting its liability. The airline objected, pointing out that even though New York law did not require mutuality for issue preclusion to apply in the case, Texas law did require mutuality. The airline further argued that the full faith and credit clause called for Texas collateral estoppel to apply. The New York court disagreed, and provided the following reasoning:

> This is not a situation where the judgment, as such, of the Texas court is sought to be enforced. What is here involved is a policy determination by our courts that "One who has had his day in court should not be permitted to litigate the question anew," and, further, refusal "to tolerate a condition where, on relatively the same set of facts, one fact-finder, be it court or jury" may find a party liable while another exonerates him leading to the "inconsistent results which are always the blemish on a judicial system." It is in order to carry out these policy determinations in the disposition of cases in this jurisdiction that an evidentiary use is being made of a particular issue determination made in the Texas action.

Id. at 813-814. Other courts have reached varying results on this issue. *Compare Finley v. Kesling*, 433 N.E.2d 1112 (Ill. App. 1982) (concluding that full faith and credit allows one state to give more preclusive effect to a judgment than the rendering state), *with Columbia Cas. Co. v. Playtex FP Inc.*, 584 A.2d 1214 (Del. 1991) (holding the "purpose and spirit of full faith and credit clause" requires court to follow issue preclusion rules of rendering state).

Finally, one must remember that the approach to full faith and credit can be different for situations dealing with two state courts than for situations that concern a state and federal court. This results because the wording of the full faith and credit statute differs from the full faith and credit clause. The full faith credit clause applies only to state courts, but the full faith credit statute applies to state and federal courts. Specifically, the full faith and credit statute requires that records and judgments from one state "shall have same full faith and credit in every court within the United States . . . as they have by law or usage in the courts of such State . . . from which they are taken." Focusing on the requirement that a judgment's effect must be the "same" as in the rendering state, the Supreme Court has held that a federal court may not give a judgment greater preclusive effect than would the state court that rendered it. *Migra v. Warren City Sch. Dist. Bd. of Educ.*, 465 U.S. 75 (1984); *Marrese v. Am. Acad. of Orthopaedic Surgeons*, 470 U.S. 373, 384 (1985).

C. *CONFLICTS AMONG FEDERAL CIRCUITS: CLAIM PRECLUSION VERSUS STARE DECISIS*

What happens when a "conflict of laws" occurs within a court system? Courts generally handle this conflict with principles of stare decisis — and with the supervisory power of a supreme court that settles important disagreements among the lower courts. Various rules governing this matter appear in Chapter 3's Perspective on Stare Decisis in State and Federal Courts. Sometimes a disagreement among lower courts can percolate for a substantial period of time without the governing supreme court taking a case and resolving the conflict. The inconsistencies and confusion that can result do not generally present a judgments problem since the different rulings pertain to different parties in different disputes, even if the legal issues are the same. The phenomenon can nonetheless become something akin to an inconsistent judgments problem for actors that happen to become parties to more than one dispute (and therefore face different opponents), and end up being subject to contrary legal rules. This problem is most common for multi-circuit actors within the federal system. Multi-circuit actors include nationwide businesses or, as in the case below, agencies with nationwide jurisdiction. In evaluating the following case, consider how the Court handles the interplay between preclusion principles and stare decisis principles.

United States v. Stauffer Chemical Co.

464 U.S. 165 (1984)

Justice REHNQUIST delivered the opinion of the Court.

In March of 1980, when the Environmental Protection Agency (EPA) tried to inspect one of respondent Stauffer Chemical Company's Tennessee plants using private contractors in addition to full-time EPA employees, Stauffer refused to allow the private contractors to enter the plant. Stauffer argues that private contractors are not "authorized representatives" as that term is used in . . . the Clean Air Act. Stauffer also argues that the government should be estopped from relitigating the question of whether private contractors are "authorized representatives" under the statute because it has already litigated that question against Stauffer and lost in connection with an attempted inspection of one of Stauffer's plants in Wyoming. The Court of Appeals agreed with Stauffer on the merits and also on the collateral estoppel issue. Without reaching the merits, we affirm the Court of Appeals' holding that the government is estopped from relitigating the statutory issue against Stauffer.

On March 27, 1980, officials from EPA and the state of Tennessee, accompanied by employees of a private firm under contract to EPA, attempted to inspect Stauffer's elemental phosphorus production plant in Mt. Pleasant, Tenn. Stauffer refused entry to the private contractors unless they would sign an agreement not to disclose trade secrets. When the private contractors refused to do so, the entire group left without making the inspection. EPA later obtained an administrative warrant authorizing the private employees to conduct the inspection, and Stauffer refused to honor the warrant.

On the following day, EPA began a civil contempt proceeding against Stauffer in federal district court in Tennessee, and Stauffer simultaneously moved to quash the warrant. It argued that private contractors are not "authorized representatives" under §114(a)(2) of the Clean Air Act for the purposes of conducting inspections of premises subject to regulation under that Act. The District Court denied Stauffer's motion to quash, accepting EPA's argument that the inspection authority conferred upon "authorized representatives" by the statute extends to private contractors retained by EPA.

On appeal, Stauffer reiterated its statutory argument and also asserted that the government should be collaterally estopped on the basis of the decision in *Stauffer Chemical Co. v. EPA*, 647 F.2d 1075 (CA10 1981) (hereinafter *Stauffer I*), from contending that §114(a)(2) authorizes private contractors to conduct inspections of Stauffer's plants. In *Stauffer I* officials of EPA and the state of Wyoming, accompanied by employees of a different private firm under contract to EPA, attempted to conduct an inspection of Stauffer's phosphate ore processing plant near Sage, Wyoming. As in the present case, Stauffer insisted that the private contractors sign a nondisclosure agreement, and when they declined to do so, Stauffer refused to allow them to enter the plant. EPA obtained an administrative warrant authorizing the private contractors to conduct the inspection, and Stauffer refused to honor the warrant. Stauffer then instituted an action in United

States District Court in Wyoming seeking to quash the warrant and to enjoin EPA from using private contractors in inspecting Stauffer's Wyoming plants. The District Court issued the injunction, and the United States Court of Appeals for the Tenth Circuit affirmed, holding that private contractors are not "authorized representatives" pursuant to §114(a)(2).

The Sixth Circuit in the present case (hereinafter *Stauffer II*) reversed the District Court, adopting alternate grounds for its decision. Judge Weick, who delivered the opinion of the court, agreed with the Tenth Circuit that private contractors are not authorized to conduct inspections under the Clean Air Act. *United States v. Stauffer Chemical Co.*, 684 F.2d 1174, 1181-1190 (CA6 1982). Relying on *Montana v. United States*, 440 U.S. 147 (1979), he also held that the government was collaterally estopped by *Stauffer I* from litigating the statutory question again against Stauffer. For the reasons which follow, we agree that the doctrine of mutual defensive collateral estoppel is applicable against the government to preclude relitigation of the same issue already litigated against the same party in another case involving virtually identical facts. Accordingly, we affirm the judgment of the Court of Appeals without reaching the merits.

. . . [T]he case at bar involves the defensive use of collateral estoppel against the government by a party to a prior action. The government does not argue that the §114(a)(2) issues in *Stauffer I* and *Stauffer II* are dissimilar nor that controlling law or facts have changed since *Stauffer I*. The government instead argues that an exception to the normal rules of estoppel should apply because the statutory question here is an "unmixed question of law" arising in substantially unrelated actions. It also argues that the special role of the government in litigating recurring issues of public importance warrants an exception in cases such as this one. We disagree with both of the government's arguments. . . .

The government also argues that because EPA is a federal agency charged with administering a body of law nationwide, the application of collateral estoppel against it will require EPA to apply different rules to similarly situated parties, thus resulting in an inequitable administration of the law. For example, EPA points to the situation created by the recent decision in *Bunker Hill Company Lead and Zinc Smelter v. EPA*, 658 F.2d 1280 (CA9 1981), where the Ninth Circuit accepted EPA's argument that §114(a)(2) authorizes inspections by private contractors. EPA argues that if it is foreclosed from relitigating the statutory issue with Stauffer, then Stauffer plants within the Ninth Circuit will benefit from a rule precluding inspections by private contractors while plants of Stauffer's competitors will be subject to the Ninth Circuit's contrary rule. Whatever the merits of EPA's argument, for the purpose of deciding this case, it is enough to say that the issue of whether EPA would be estopped in the Ninth Circuit is not before the Court. Following our usual practice of deciding no more than is necessary to dispose of the case before us, we express no opinion on that application of collateral estoppel.

We therefore find the government's arguments unpersuasive in this case as justifications for limiting otherwise applicable rules of estoppel. Because we conclude that the Court of Appeals was correct in applying the doctrine of collateral estoppel against the government here, we decline to reach the merits of the statutory question in this case. On the estoppel issue, therefore, the judgment of the Court of Appeals is *Affirmed*.

Justice WHITE, concurring in the result.

I agree with the majority that within the Tenth Circuit Stauffer is insulated from further litigation with the EPA on the private contractor issue. Though it is a harder question, I also agree that the court below correctly found that the EPA was barred from litigating this issue with Stauffer in the Sixth Circuit, which had not adopted a position on the merits. I write separately because I do not believe that estoppel should be applied any further than that.

. . .

II

Collateral estoppel is generally said to have three purposes: to "relieve parties of the cost and vexation of multiple lawsuits, conserve judicial resources, and, by preventing inconsistent decisions, encourage reliance on adjudication." It is plain that all three purposes are served by foreclosing further litigation on this issue between these parties in the Tenth Circuit, and that Stauffer should therefore be fully insulated against relitigation there. The government argues that even in the Tenth Circuit it is entitled to attempt to inspect Stauffer with private contractors and to relitigate this issue "after an appropriate time," which it estimates at one year. Such an approach would authorize exactly the sort of duplicative litigation that collateral estoppel is designed to avoid. Thus, I unhesitatingly agree with the majority in its rejection of the government's position.

III

Outside the Tenth Circuit, the policies of judicial economy and consistency are much less compelling. At least where, as here, one party is a governmental agency administering a public law, judicial economy is not advanced; the government can always force a ruling on the merits by suing someone else. And if the circuit has ruled on the merits in another case, reliance on stare decisis is no more burdensome than reliance on collateral estoppel. The policy against inconsistent decisions is much less relevant outside the original circuit. Conflicts in the circuits are generally accepted and in some ways even welcomed. Indeed, were consistency a compelling concern as between circuits, the decision of one circuit would bind the others even in litigation between two entirely different parties. That is not the route the federal courts have followed. However, applying collateral estoppel in other circuits would spare Stauffer the burden of fighting a battle that it has won once. In the absence of countervailing considerations, I am satisfied that this interest is adequate to support the lower court's ruling here.

IV

Preclusion was justified, however, only because the Sixth Circuit had not previously ruled on the Clean Air Act issue. Stauffer argues that *Stauffer I* also immunizes it in the Ninth Circuit, which has adopted a different rule than the Tenth on the merits. *See Bunker Hill Co. Lead & Zinc Smelter v. EPA*, 658 F.2d 1280 (CA9 1981). Under this view private contractors may join EPA inspections of all plants in that Circuit except those owned by Stauffer. The majority does not address this contention, considering it "more than is necessary to dispose of the case before us." I do address it, however, for it is only because today's result does not afford Stauffer the blanket protection it seeks that I concur in the judgment.

A

Extending preclusion to circuits that have adopted a contrary rule on the merits would be acceptable were it supported by any affirmative policy. It is not. Judicial economy is not served for the simple reason that no litigation is prevented; the prior litigant is subject to one black-letter rule rather than another. For the same reason, there is no concern about protecting the prior litigant from repetitious, vexatious, or harassing litigation. Finally, to the extent the policy against inconsistent decisions remains relevant when a circuit conflict exists, it cuts the other way. At least some measure of consistency and certainty is obtained by even-handed application of rules within individual circuits.

B

Not only is there no affirmative reason for preclusion in such circumstances, powerful considerations cut the other way. The inconsistency is more dramatic and more troublesome than a normal circuit split; by definition, it compounds that problem. It would be dubious enough were the EPA unable to employ private contractors to inspect Stauffer's plants within the Ninth Circuit even though it can use such contractors in inspecting other plants. But the disarray is more extensive. By the same application of mutual collateral estoppel, the EPA could presumably use private contractors to inspect Bunker Hill's plants in circuits like the Tenth, despite the fact that other companies are not subject to such inspections. Furthermore, Stauffer concedes . . . that the EPA can relitigate this matter as to other companies. As a result, in, say, the First Circuit, the EPA must follow one rule as to Bunker Hill, the opposite as to Stauffer, and, depending on any ruling by that Circuit, one or the other or a third as to other companies.

This confusing state of affairs far exceeds in awkwardness a normal split in the circuits. It is especially undesirable because it grants a special benefit to, or imposes a special detriment on, particular companies. In general, persons present in several circuits must conduct themselves in accordance with varying rules, just as they are subject to different state laws. Other companies with plants in several circuits do not enjoy a favorable rule nationwide, like Stauffer, nor do they have to put up with an unfavorable rule nationwide, like Bunker Hill. A split in the circuits cannot justify abandonment of all efforts at evenhanded and rational application of legal rules. Nor is the mere fact that these companies happen to have been involved in litigation elsewhere sufficient reason for uniquely favored or disfavored status.

C

. . . [C]ollateral estoppel on issues of law, which is a narrow, flexible, judge-made doctrine, becomes intolerable if the rule of law at issue is too far removed from the prevailing legal rules. Even Stauffer concedes that a decision from this Court on the merits would so affect the "controlling law" that it would lose the entire benefit of the initial judgment in its favor. Similarly, no one contends that if Congress amended the statute to make the opposite result plain, Stauffer could continue to rely on the original judgment. And presumably if the Tenth Circuit were to reverse itself, en banc, and hold that private contractors could make EPA inspections, then Stauffer would no longer be able to keep them out on the authority of *Stauffer I*. Finally, it is apparent that if, for example, Stauffer has plants in Canada, it cannot impose the Tenth Circuit's inspection requirements on the Canadian authorities. Why then should Stauffer be able to use the decisions of the Sixth and Tenth Circuits to estop the government in the Ninth Circuit, where the opposite rule prevails? The decisions of those other circuits are not the "controlling law" in the Ninth; the controlling law in the Ninth is exactly to the contrary. There is no difference between this situation and that where the law within a particular jurisdiction has changed since the initial decision.

V

The doctrine of collateral estoppel is designed to ensure litigants the benefit of prior litigation; this is not the same as ensuring them the benefits of a prior ruling. In arguing that *Stauffer I* precludes the EPA nationwide from relitigating this issue against it, Stauffer stretches the doctrine beyond the breaking point. It claims a right to a unique status. Put differently, Stauffer claims immunity from a particular legal rule, not immunity from further litigation. At this point considerations of economy are no longer involved, and Stauffer's approach leads to results that are basically inconsistent with the principle of evenhanded administration of the laws.

In sum, I concur in the judgment of the Court. I do so with the view that preclusion is inappropriate in circuits that have adopted, or later adopt, the contrary legal rule.

Notes on
UNITED STATES v. STAUFFER CHEMICAL CO.

1. As we have seen so far in this chapter, full faith and credit principles govern the relationship between state courts and the relationship between a federal court and a state court. Federal courts do not officially have a full faith and credit obligation to each other, although the federal judgment

registration statute — 28 U.S.C. §1963 — ensures that one federal court will honor the judgment of another federal court. Most other judgments issues that arise between federal courts can be answered by federal preclusion law, which is a largely federal court-made body of federal common law. The *Stauffer* issue arises from the very specific context of multi-circuit actors that litigate against different parties in different circuits.

2. Remember the vocabulary of issue preclusion (collateral estoppel): non-mutual issue preclusion occurs where the parties to the first action are not the same as the parties to the second action. Defensive use of issue preclusion occurs where the defendant in a second action seeks to prevent the plaintiff in that action from re-litigating an issue the plaintiff had litigated in the first action. Offensive issue preclusion refers to a second action plaintiff asserting issue preclusion against a second action defendant. The general federal law of preclusion allows non-mutual offensive issue preclusion. Nonetheless, on the same day as the Supreme Court decided *United States v. Stauffer Chem. Co.*, the Court in *United States v. Mendoza*, 464 U.S. 154 (1984), adopted an exception to the general rule for cases in which a litigant seeks to assert such estoppel against the federal government. In holding one could not assert non-mutual issue preclusion against the federal government, the *Mendoza* Court explained that applying issue preclusion in that setting would freeze in place "the first final decision rendered on a particular issue." The Court concluded this was unwise since "[a]llowing only one final adjudication would deprive this Court of the benefit it receives from permitting several courts of appeal to explore a difficult question before this Court grants certiorari. . . ." *Id.* at 160. As a consequence of *Mendoza*, the *Stauffer* holding is limited to the mutuality context for litigation involving the federal government: where the United States and a single party (or collection of parties) are the same litigants in all successive cases. *Stauffer* also applies to litigation between private parties in the context of non-mutual issue preclusion.

3. One might say that the *Stauffer* Court chose to elevate the doctrine of issue preclusion over the doctrine of stare decisis. Was this indubitably the correct result? Is there an argument that *Stauffer* should have to yield to a different result in a new circuit because other litigants had already received a specific treatment in that circuit? Doesn't the matter basically boil down to a choice of whether one of the following values in more important: (1) intra-circuit consistency or (2) intercircuit consistency? Which result is most in line with the full faith and credit obligation that would arise if at least one of the courts had been a state court?

4. One can think of the *Stauffer* situation as posing a problem for entities with nationwide scope. Indeed, one can imagine that internet business dealings — which have grown considerably since *Stauffer* — might present particularly challenging issues arising from variations in the law of federal circuits. Moreover, given that different circuits govern contiguous areas, one can see

that these problems are not confined to parties engaged in far-reaching activity. Consider, for example, the challenges presented by an area in rural Texas and Arkansas, which is "the only federal building in the country sited in two states and the only federal courthouse located in two circuits, the 5th and the 8th, and two districts, the Eastern District of Texas and the Western District of Arkansas." *See* http://www.discoverourtown.com/AR/Texarkana/Attractions/172184.html.

PROBLEM 4-8: ENVIRONMENTAL LAW CONFLICT BETWEEN THE THIRD AND FOURTH CIRCUITS

Consider the following sequence of events:

2011: The United States Court of Appeals for the Third Circuit rules in *United States v. Acme Co.* that the effluent discharged into a river violates federal environmental laws. The Third Circuit thus enters judgment in favor of the United States.

2012: The United States Court of Appeals for the Fourth Circuit rules in *United States v. Zed Co.* that the same effluent in the same concentration discharged into a river does *not* violate federal environmental laws. The Fourth Circuit thus enters judgment in favor of Zed.

2013: The United States files another suit against Acme alleging another violation of the federal environmental laws arising from the same effluent in the same concentration discharged into the river. This time it files suit in the Court of Appeals for the Fourth Circuit. The Fourth Circuit must decide what to do in this suit — *United States v. Acme Co.* Should it rule for the United States, consistent with the Third Circuit's earlier ruling, or should it rule for the company, consistent with its own ruling? Is the answer easier if the two circuits involved were really two state courts?

PERSPECTIVE ON PRIVATE INCENTIVES IN JUDGMENT RECOGNITION AND ENFORCEMENT

Explicit case discussion of values informing judgment recognition and enforcement tends to focus on systemic concerns: national or international unity, comity, respect for judicial decisions, efficiency, and the like. To the extent that courts weigh individual litigant interests, they usually limit discussion to solicitous concern with safeguarding the personal welfare of litigants. Thus, for example, the judgment recognition and enforcement cases show generous regard for individual litigants' due process rights (such as notice, opportunity to be heard, and general fairness) and need for finality and repose after litigating about a mistake made or an untoward event experienced. One notable exception concerns the effect of issue preclusion law on incentives of potential litigants. Here, courts seeking to shape the best legal doctrines explicitly consider how litigants may try to game preclusion rules. Consider, for example, the United States Supreme Court's decision whether to abandon the mutuality requirement for issue preclusion: the requirement that parties can bind and be bound by issue preclusion only if the parties to the original suit are the same as or legally related to the parties in the subsequent suit. *Parklane Hosiery Co. v. Shore*, 439 U.S. 322 (1979), identified subtle distinctions influencing parties' incentives, depending on whether they used issue preclusion defensively or offensively:

> Defensive use of issue preclusion precludes a plaintiff from relitigating identical issues by merely "switching adversaries."[*] Thus defensive issue preclusion gives a plaintiff a strong incentive to join all potential defendants in the first action if possible. Offensive use of issue preclusion, on the other hand, creates precisely the opposite incentive. Since a plaintiff will be able to rely on a previous judgment against a defendant but will not be bound by that judgment if the defendant wins, the plaintiff has every incentive to adopt a "wait and see" attitude, in the hope that the first action by another plaintiff will result in a favorable judgment Thus offensive use of issue preclusion will likely increase rather than decrease the total amount of litigation, since potential plaintiffs will have everything to gain and nothing to lose by not intervening in the first action.

Id. at 329-330.

Although courts have been relatively quiet on private incentives, scholars have analyzed several ways in which judgment recognition and enforcement doctrines influence individual litigation decisions. The following brief review illustrates just some of the many possibilities for strategic behavior.

Most fundamentally, one might expect parties to try to manipulate the doctrines of judgment recognition and enforcement according to whether they wish to seek or to avoid recognition of a particular judgment.[3] For example, a defendant seeking to avoid enforcement of a civil punitive damages award in a particular case might argue to the enforcing court that it should characterize a punitive damages award as a "penal law," to which the full faith and credit obligation does not apply.

But one would also expect existing judgment doctrines to influence party behavior earlier in the litigation process. Indeed, one might anticipate that judgment recognition rules would influence a plaintiff's forum choice in many cases. Let's say that a plaintiff's preferred forum is State A because that is where the plaintiff lives, where the procedural law is more plaintiff-friendly, and where all the evidence pertaining to the suit is located. Assume further that, although the

---

[*] Under the mutuality requirement, a plaintiff could accomplish this result since he would not have been bound by the judgment had the original defendant won.

3. *Cf.* Yaad Rotem, *The Problem of Selective or Sporadic Recognition: A New Economic Rationale for the Law of Foreign Country Judgments*, 10 Chi. J. Int'l L. 505 (2010) (contrasting the incentives of sovereignties deciding whether to recognize foreign judgments with "the incentives of individuals to seek or avoid recognition of a particular judgment").

plaintiff can establish personal jurisdiction against the defendant in State A, all of the defendant's assets are in the far off jurisdiction of State B. If judgment recognition and enforcement rules make a State A judgment easily portable and enforceable in State B, then the plaintiff is likely to choose to file suit in State A. If the plaintiff anticipates that either State B law or full faith and credit principles contain a doctrinal obstacle to portability, then the plaintiff may decide to incur the additional cost and hassle of litigating the merits of the case in State B.[4] After all, the plaintiff wants a judgment she can enforce, not merely a piece of paper. In contrast to the plaintiff, the defendant may seek to channel litigation away from the forum where her assets are concentrated. The defendant's ability to do this may be limited, but she may try to use such devices as filing her own reactive litigation in her preferred forum, removal and transfer, and the forum non conveniens doctrine. The defendant may also prefer to concentrate her assets in a jurisdiction with stingy judgment enforcement and recognition rules. For example, some states exempt from judgment enforcement the entire value of the judgment debtor's home, while other states limit the homestead exemption. In anticipation of high stakes litigation, a wealthy resident of a state with a limited exemption might consider moving to a more protective state and pouring many of her assets into buying a home there.

Note the different incentive effects of judgment *recognition* rules as contrasted with judgment *enforcement* rules. (Judgment recognition rules pertain to a court's decision whether to give a judgment legal force and effect in a subsequent proceeding. This differs from judgment enforcement, which concerns the process by which a court transforms a judgment that it recognizes as valid into an actual remedy such as the payment of money damages or following the terms of an injunction). Judgment recognition rules are relevant to the portability of a judgment from the F1 where the judgment was rendered to the F2 where a party wants the judgment satisfied. Judgment recognition rules are pertinent to the parties' decision making only where the location of litigation might be different than the location of assets. Recognition of judgments is unnecessary where the litigating forum court's order can be enforced locally. Judgment enforcement rules will always be relevant, and may provide incentives to all potential plaintiffs and defendants. If, for example, a jurisdiction exempts from judgment enforcement certain assets such as a homestead or jointly held property, the plaintiff may try to steer litigation away from that jurisdiction if a significant amount of the defendant's assets there are exempt from enforcement.

In addition to influencing forum choice, judgment recognition and enforcement rules might affect the form of dispute resolution that the parties select. Alternatives to traditional adversary litigation — such as arbitration or mediation — may enable the parties to avoid cumbersome recognition and

---

4. *Cf.* Michael Whincop, *The Recognition Scene: Game Theoretic Issues of the Recognition of Foreign Judgments*, 23 MELB. U. L. REV. 41, 42 (1999) (outlining forum-shopping incentives deriving from recognition law). Michael Whincop observes that lawyers respond to incentives as well, and argues that they may tend to prefer laws not recognizing foreign judgments in their jurisdiction. *Id.* If plaintiffs are most likely to litigate in forums with non-recognition laws, then more legal work will come to the forum!

enforcement problems. Judgment rules may also send strong incentives in appropriate cases regarding the decision to litigate through some form of mass litigation, such as a class action mechanism.

The interplay between judgment rules and class action rules gives rise to a new set of incentives that influence plaintiffs, defendants, and lawyers as well. Class actions are useful in large part because a final class action judgment binds class members in the same way as a judgment involving individual plaintiffs.[5] Accordingly, the scope of the applicable preclusion principles and portability of the class action judgment bear on the attractiveness of using the class action device in a particular jurisdiction.

Matters can get even more complicated when a defendant faces more than one potential class action. Professors Marcel Kahan and Linda Silberman have observed that where multiple jurisdictions are available to adjudicate a lawsuit, "plaintiff shopping," "lawyer shopping," and "forum shopping" can all result.[6]

In order to appreciate Kahan and Silberman's arguments fully, one needs to remember that class actions usually settle, rather than go to trial. The parties therefore exert significant control over class action dispositions. Where competing class actions are pending in different jurisdictions, parties (and their lawyers) are mindful of how their actions might affect their own lawsuit and those in other jurisdictions. And in situations where preclusion rules are strict and judgment recognition rules are liberal, the first class action to resolve will usually bind others that are pending.[7] Kahan and Silberman argue that plaintiffs and their lawyers have a strong incentive to conclude their suits first. Defendants, they reason, are "well aware of these incentives" and "can thus go plaintiff and lawyer shopping: By indicating that they will deal with class counsel who is willing to settle for the least, they implicitly create a 'reverse auction' in which competing class lawyers 'underbid' each other in order to have their own action settled first and earn attorneys' fees."[8]

Kahan and Silberman argue that forum shopping can be particularly troublesome in the class action context where judgment recognition rules are strict and class counsel has a choice among jurisdictions for litigating. They observe that unlike in conventional lawsuits, class counsel has an incentive to shop for a forum where judges are more likely to serve "counsel's . . . own interests, such as a forum in which judges are predisposed to exercising little scrutiny of class action settlements."[9] Moreover, class members are less likely than individual litigants in conventional suits to monitor such forum shopping and other attorney behavior — thus allowing class counsel to pursue their own self-interest with greater vigor.[10]

---

5. *See* Clyde Spillenger, Principles of Conflict of Laws 268 (2010).

6. Marcel Kahan & Linda Silberman, *The Adequate Search for "Adequacy" in Class Actions: A Critique of* Epstein v. MCA, Inc., 73 N.Y.U. L. Rev. 765, 775 (1998).

7. *Id.*

8. *Id.*

9. *Id.*

10. *Id.* For helpful analysis of how these incentives played out in the United States Supreme Court's decision in *Matsushita Industrial Co. v. Epstein*, 516 U.S. 367 (1996), see Spillenger, *supra*, at 272-273.

From the foregoing, you can begin to appreciate that judgment recognition and enforcement rules have broad potential to influence litigant and attorney decision making. As you consider other specific judgments issues — such as those covered immediately below pertaining to domestic relations, the internet, and international judgments — consider further how the rules might influence behavior of private individuals. Are there special qualities of these contexts that make it more difficult (or less difficult) to identify how these incentives influence a civil justice system's effectiveness?

D. SPECIAL RULES FOR DOMESTIC RELATIONS MATTERS

Domestic relations, or family law, has unfailingly created difficult problems for conflict of laws as a general matter and judgments law in particular. What is the reason for this? Perhaps it is family law's inherent cultural implications (particularly those triggering religious and moral matters), which implicate deep divisions among different populations. In addition, perhaps the difficulties result from the tendency of family law issues to send "tendrils" into many aspects of life and therefore breed complexity. Take the status of being a spouse, for example. This status (or lack of status) implicates a vast range of issues, including matters as broad ranging as taxation, property ownership, employment benefits, and control over health care decisions, parenting, and burial. Or perhaps the complexity results from the deep emotions inspired by domestic relations fights, emotions that implicate the core of human existence. As such, the legal issues in family law are not "cut and dried" and individual litigants' reactions to legal problems may tend away from rationality. Love can sometimes inspire erratic action, and law must struggle to identify the proper response. As always, conflict of laws problems magnify these challenges. Where different jurisdictions become involved, differing systems of morality, custom, and public policy come into play. In this emotionally charged context, law often takes a unique course: the course is sometimes decisively different from the usual course for legal rules and sometimes particularly complicated and "messy." In addition, the break up of many marriages leads one partner or the other to move to another state — perhaps the state where the person grew up — which inevitably means that one partner or the other must find a lawyer in another state and bear the extra expense of litigating there. And finally, as in other areas of life, such as the internet, technology has challenged existing regimes. In particular, new medical technologies and therapies have made possible new ways to create and to gestate an embryo — giving rise to a host of new challenges for conflict of laws regulation.[11] This section provides a

---

11. *See* Sonia Bychkov Green, *Interstate Intercourse: How Modern Assisted Reproductive Technologies Challenge the Traditional Realm of Conflicts of Law*, 24 WIS. J.L. GENDER & SOC'Y 25, 25

cross-section of conflict of laws issues that arise in domestic relations disputes, starting first with the somewhat unique approach law takes to divorce judgments.

1. Divorce Jurisdiction: Ex Parte Divorce and Divisible Divorce

A major doctrinal quirk in domestic relations law comes from the jurisdictional theory for divorce actions. Courts continue to adhere to the traditional concept that divorce is an action in rem, where a "res" provides the basis for a court's power to render a judgment. Specifically, the "res" is the marriage relationship, which is deemed located where either party to the marriage is domiciled. Since estranged spouses are not necessarily domiciled in the same state, this can create a situation where two states possess power to grant a divorce.

The notion that more than one state has power to adjudicate a matter is of course not remarkable. The twist arises, however, because a court may issue a valid ex parte divorce without personal jurisdiction over both parties. And further complications arise when a litigant attempts a collateral attack on the divorce judgment — behavior fueled and informed by emotions surrounding domestic disputes.

A foundation for modern divorce judgment law appears in *Williams v. N. Carolina*, 317 U.S. 287 (1942) (*Williams v. North Carolina I*), in which the United States Supreme Court reversed a North Carolina bigamy conviction of two individuals who had travelled to Nevada to obtain an ex parte divorce (while their spouses stayed in North Carolina). The Supreme Court reasoned that the prosecution had failed to conclusively establish that the defendants were not domiciled in Nevada (and thus the defendants may have been validly divorced). After a retrial, the Court affirmed the new conviction in *William v. North Carolina*, 317 U.S. 287 (1942) (*Williams v. North Carolina II*), ruling that the judge in the second trial properly instructed the jury that it could find the defendants guilty of bigamous cohabitation only if the Nevada divorce judgment was void because the defendants had not established a valid domicile in Nevada.

The next question for the Court was how far this jurisdictional concept extended. Could a divorce court also issue a valid ex parte ruling on the incidents of divorce? The Court confronted this in the following case:

Estin v. Estin

334 U.S. 541 (1948)

Mr. Justice DOUGLAS delivered the opinion of the Court.

This case, here on certiorari to the Court of Appeals of New York, presents an important question under the Full Faith and Credit Clause of the Constitution. Article IV, §1 ... whether a New York decree awarding respondent $180 per

---

(2009) (quoting American Bar Ass'n, AMERICAN BAR ASSOCIATION MODEL ACT GOVERNING ASSISTED REPRODUCTIVE TECHNOLOGY (2008), *available at* www.abanet.org/family/committees/artmodelact.pdf).

month for her maintenance and support in a separation proceeding survived a Nevada divorce decree which subsequently was granted petitioner.

The parties were married in 1937 and lived together in New York until 1942 when the husband left the wife. There was no issue of the marriage. In 1943 she brought an action against him for a separation. He entered a general appearance. The court, finding that he had abandoned her, granted her a decree of separation and awarded her $180 per month as permanent alimony. In January 1944 he went to Nevada where in 1945 he instituted an action for divorce. She was notified of the action by constructive service but entered no appearance in it. In May, 1945, the Nevada court, finding that petitioner had been a bona fide resident of Nevada since January 30, 1944, granted him an absolute divorce "on the ground of three years continual separation, without cohabitation." The Nevada decree made no provision for alimony, though the Nevada court had been advised of the New York decree.

Prior to that time petitioner had made payments of alimony under the New York decree. After entry of the Nevada decree he ceased paying. Thereupon respondent sued in New York for a supplementary judgment for the amount of the arrears. Petitioner appeared in the action and moved to eliminate the alimony provisions of the separation decree by reason of the Nevada decree. The Supreme Court denied the motion and granted respondent judgment for the arrears. The judgment was affirmed [on appeal].

We held in *Williams v. North Carolina* [*I*] that a divorce decree granted by a State to one of its domiciliaries is entitled to full faith and credit in a bigamy prosecution brought in another State, even though the other spouse was given notice of the divorce proceeding only through constructive service. . . .

Petitioner's argument . . . is that the tail must go with the hide — that since by the Nevada decree, recognized in New York, he and respondent are no longer husband and wife, no legal incidence of the marriage remains. . . .

The difficulty with that argument is that the highest court in New York has held in this case that a support order can survive divorce and that this one has survived petitioner's divorce. That conclusion is binding on us, except as it conflicts with the Full Faith and Credit Clause. . . . The only question for us is whether New York is powerless to make such a ruling in view of the Nevada decree.

We can put to one side the case where the wife was personally served or where she appears in the divorce proceedings. The only service on her in this case was by publication and she made no appearance in the Nevada proceeding. The requirements of procedural due process were satisfied and the domicile of the husband in Nevada was foundation for a decree effecting a change in the marital capacity of both parties in all the other States of the Union, as well as in Nevada. But the fact that marital capacity was changed does not mean that every other legal incidence of the marriage was necessarily affected. . . .

An absolutist might . . . demand a rule that once a divorce is granted, the whole of the marriage relation is dissolved, leaving no roots or tendrils of any kind. But there are few areas of the law in black and white. The greys are dominant and even among them the shades are innumerable. For the eternal problem of the law is one of making accommodations between conflicting interests. This is why most legal problems end as questions of degree. . . .

. . . The fact that the requirements of full faith and credit, so far as judgments are concerned, are exacting, if not inexorable, does not mean, however, that the State of the domicile of one spouse may, through the use of constructive service, enter a decree that changes every legal incidence of the marriage relationship.

Marital status involves the regularity and integrity of the marriage relation. It affects the legitimacy of the offspring of marriage. It is the basis of criminal laws, as the bigamy prosecution in *Williams v. North Carolina* dramatically illustrates. The State has a considerable interest in preventing bigamous marriages and in protecting the offspring of marriages from being bastardized. The interest of the State extends to its domiciliaries. The State should have the power to guard its interest in them by changing or altering their marital status and by protecting them in that changed status throughout the farthest reaches of the nation. For a person domiciled in one State should not be allowed to suffer the penalties of bigamy for living outside the State with the only one which the State of his domicile recognizes as his lawful wife. And children born of the only marriage which is lawful in the State of his domicile should not carry the stigma of bastardy when they move elsewhere. These are matters of legitimate concern to the State of the domicile. They entitle the State of the domicile to bring in the absent spouse through constructive service. In no other way could the State of the domicile have and maintain effective control of the marital status of its domiciliaries.

. . . But those considerations have little relevancy here. In this case New York evinced a concern with this broken marriage when both parties were domiciled in New York and before Nevada had any concern with it. New York was rightly concerned lest the abandoned spouse be left impoverished and perhaps become a public charge. The problem of her livelihood and support is plainly a matter in which her community had a legitimate interest. The New York court, having jurisdiction over both parties, undertook to protect her by granting her a judgment of permanent alimony. Nevada, however, apparently follows the rule that dissolution of the marriage puts and end to a support order. But the question is whether Nevada could under any circumstances adjudicate rights of respondent under the New York judgment when she was not personally served or did not appear in the proceeding. [We believe the answer is no: Nevada could not do so.]

The New York judgment is a property interest of respondent, created by New York in a proceeding in which both parties were present. It imposed obligations on petitioner and granted rights to respondent. The property interest which it created was an intangible, jurisdiction over which cannot be exerted through control over a physical thing. Jurisdiction over an intangible can indeed only arise from control or power over the persons whose relationships are the source of the rights and obligations.

. . . The Nevada decree that is said to wipe out respondent's claim for alimony under the New York judgment is nothing less than an attempt by Nevada to restrain respondent from asserting her claim under that judgment. That is an attempt to exercise an in personam jurisdiction over a person not before the court. That may not be done. Since Nevada had no power to adjudicate respondent's rights in the New York judgment, New York need not give full faith and credit to that phase of Nevada's judgment. A judgment of a court having no jurisdiction to render it is not entitled to the full faith and credit which the Constitution and statute of the United States demand. The result in this situation is to make the divorce divisible — to give effect to the Nevada decree insofar as it affects marital status and to make it ineffective on the issue of alimony. It accommodates the interests of both Nevada and New York in this broken marriage by restricting each State to the matters of her dominant concern.

Since Nevada had no jurisdiction to alter respondent's rights in the New York judgment, we do not reach the further question whether in any event that judgment would be entitled to full faith and credit in Nevada. And it will be time enough to consider the effect of any discrimination shown to out-of-state ex parte divorces when a State makes that its policy.

Affirmed.

Mr. Justice FRANKFURTER, dissenting.

... Nevada did not purport, so far as the record discloses, to rule on the survival of the New York separate maintenance decree. Nevada merely established a change in status. It was for New York to determine the effect, with reference to its own law, of that change in status. If it was the law of New York that divorce put an end to its separate maintenance decree, the respondent's decree would have been terminated not by the Nevada divorce but by the consequences, under the New York law, of a change in status, even though brought about by Nevada. Similarly, Nevada could not adjudicate rights in New York realty, but, if New York law provided for dower, a Nevada divorce might or might not terminate a dower interest in New York realty depending on whether or not New York treated dower rights as extinguished by divorce.

If the Nevada decree, insofar as it affected the New York separate maintenance decree, were violative of due process, New York of course would not have to give effect to it. It could not do so even if it wished. If the Nevada decree involved a violation of due process there is an end of the matter and other complicated issues need not be considered! It would not matter whether New York had a special interest in preventing its residents from becoming public charges, or whether New York treated maintenance decrees as surviving a valid divorce.

Accordingly, the crucial issue, as I see it, is whether New York has held that no "ex parte" divorce decree could terminate a prior New York separate maintenance decree, or whether it has decided merely that no "ex parte" divorce decree of another State could. The opinion of the Court of Appeals leaves this crucial issue in doubt. ... New York may legitimately decline to allow any "ex parte" divorce to dissolve its prior separate maintenance decree, but it may not, consistently with *Williams v. North Carolina*, 317 U.S. 287 discriminate against a Nevada decree granted to one there domiciled, and afford it less effect than it gives to a decree of its own with similar jurisdictional foundation. I cannot be sure which it has done. ...

Mr. JUSTICE JACKSON, dissenting.

If there is one thing that the people are entitled to expect from their lawmakers, it is rules of law that will enable individuals to tell whether they are married and and, if so, to whom. Today many people who have simply lived in more than one state do not know, and the most learned lawyer cannot advise them with any confidence. The uncertainties that result are not merely technical, nor are they trivial; they affect fundamental rights and relations such as the lawfulness of their cohabitation, their children's legitimacy, their title to property, and even whether they are law-abiding persons or criminals. In a society as mobile and nomadic as ours, such uncertainties affect large numbers of people and create a social problem of some magnitude. . . .

The New York judgment of separation is based on the premise that the parties remain husband and wife, though estranged, and hence the obligation of support, incident to marriage, continues. The Nevada decree is based on the contrary premise that the marriage no longer exists and so obligations dependent on it have ceased.

The Court reaches the Solomon-like conclusion that the Nevada decree is half good and half bad under the full faith and credit clause. It is good to free the husband from the marriage; it is not good to free him from its incidental obligations. Assuming the judgment to be one which the Constitution requires to be recognized at all, I do not see how we can square this decision with the command that it be given full faith and credit. . . .

Notes on
ESTIN v. ESTIN *AND DIVORCE JURISDICTION*

1. What do you think of the ex parte divorce rule? Dissenting in *Williams I*, Justice Jackson argued that something is amiss with a rule that allows family relationships to be destroyed by a procedure "that we would not recognize if the suit were one to collect a grocery bill." 317 U.S. at 316. Do you agree with his point of view? Shouldn't the absent spouse's interest in the marriage be worthy of the same due process protection accorded to most other matters? On the other hand, does the ex parte divorce rule make sense given the likelihood that spouses wishing to terminate their marriage often are not inclined to cooperate, and, in some instances, are so estranged from one another that they don't know each other's whereabouts?

2. Would you make a distinction between choice of law and personal jurisdiction in the divorce context? Couldn't one say that the divorce granting state has a sufficient interest in having its legal principles applied if one of the spouses is domiciled there, even though it may lack a sufficiently specific interest to issue an actual judgment reordering the rights of a specific party who is not before the court? Do you agree with Justice Jackson's argument in his *Estin v. Estin* dissent that if the law treats an ex parte divorce judgment as valid, then it must give the judgment its full effect, including its ability to terminate a support obligation?

3. Professor Rhonda Wasserman has argued that in today's ambulatory society, domicile should no longer be the key point of reference for divorce

jurisdiction. She maintains that a federal statute should ensure that divorce decrees are recognized where the rendering state possessed personal jurisdiction over both spouses. Do you agree? Rhonda Wasserman, *Divorce and Domicile: Time to Sever the Knot*, 39 WM. & MARY L. REV. 1 (1997).

4. In *May v. Anderson*, 345 U.S. 528 (1953), the Supreme Court applied the divisible divorce doctrine to child custody determinations. In *May*, a Wisconsin couple agreed that the wife should leave for Ohio for a while to consider whether she wanted to remain married. She took their children with her. Shortly thereafter, she told the husband that she wanted a divorce, and he filed suit in Wisconsin a few days later, seeking a divorce and custody of the children. The wife received personal service, but did not appear before the Wisconsin court, which awarded the husband a divorce and custody of the children. The husband brought the children back to Wisconsin where they lived (until they visited their mother in Ohio). The father filed an action in Ohio demanding their return and the Ohio court concluded that it had to give full faith and credit to the Wisconsin judgment. The United States Supreme Court determined that because the Wisconsin court had lacked personal jurisdiction over the wife at the time of its custody decree, the Ohio court did not need to enforce the decree. Joining the opinion of the Court, Justice Frankfurter wrote separately to emphasize that the Court did not rule that Ohio was foreclosed from honoring the Wisconsin decree. Justice Jackson predicted that the decision might create confusion and would reduce child custody law "to a rule of seize-and-run." His prediction proved accurate and two legislative initiatives ultimately were created to help address the problem of parental kidnapping: the Uniform Child Custody Jurisdiction Act (UCCJA) and the Parental Kidnapping Prevention Act (PKPA). These are discussed later in this chapter.

5. A newly developed type of marriage, covenant marriage, may introduce some wrinkles in conflict of laws principles governing marriage. Developed in response to rising divorce rates, covenant marriage offers an optional marriage form intended to create a reinforced marital commitment. Peter Hay, *The American "Covenant Marriage" in the Conflicts of Laws*, 64 LA. L. REV. 43, 47-48 (2003). Only a few states, such as Louisiana, Arkansas, and Arizona, have adopted covenant marriage acts, although such acts have been unsuccessfully introduced in many other states. Kristina E. Zurcher, *"I Do" or "I Don't"? Covenant Marriage After Six Years*, 18 NOTRE DAME J.L. ETHICS & PUB. POL'Y 273, 285 (2004). The three main characteristics of covenant marriage laws include mandatory premarital counseling for the couple, the signing of a Declaration of Intent, and restricted grounds for divorce. For example, Louisiana's law creates specified fault-based grounds for divorce like adultery and allows no-fault divorce following a two-year separation/ waiting period. Hay, *supra*, at 48.

Questions remain about how effective covenant marriage will be across state borders. Where a spouse from a covenant marriage initiates a divorce action in a state other than where the marriage was celebrated, the forum court's application of conflict of laws principles can either reinforce or defeat the intent behind the covenant marriage. Under the Supreme Court's *Williams I* decision, a state where one of the parties to the marriage becomes domiciled might constitutionally apply its own divorce law regardless of the covenant marriage laws of the place of celebration. Lily Ng, *Covenant Marriage and the Conflicts of Law*, 44 ALTA. L. REV. 815, 821 (2007). In fact — as discussed further in the note that follows — most courts actually follow the lex fori approach to choice of law in divorce cases. If the domicile approach to divorce jurisdiction continues, the legal efficacy of covenant marriages might therefore be limited to the state in which they are contracted. This result is supported by an Alabama court's decision to grant a divorce requested by a couple who had celebrated a covenant marriage in Louisiana, but subsequently moved their domicile to Alabama. *Blackburn v. Blackburn*, 180 So. 3d 16 (Ala. Civ. App. 2015).

Some scholars maintain that where one spouse remains domiciled in the covenant marriage state, most courts can be persuaded to grant due deference to the law of the covenant marriage state of celebration under choice of law principles. *See* Katherine Shaw Spaht & Symeon C. Symeonides, *Covenant Marriage and the Conflicts of Laws*, 32 CREIGHTON L. REV. 1085, 1101-1109 (1999). But that would require a change from the usual practice of applying forum law in divorce actions. In the end, however, we might encounter few opportunities to test this thesis. Though the concept of covenant marriage laws initially raised concerns over potential for conflict of law issues, these problems are not likely to arise often, given the small percentage of couples actually opting into covenant marriages.

6. As noted above, state courts entertaining a divorce usually apply forum law governing divorce issues. Why would that be? Why would a court that normally follows a choice of law methodology sensitive to the parties' rights vested elsewhere, or the interests of other states, deviate from the methodology in divorce cases? Recall, too, from Chapter 2 that the place of celebration rule for evaluating the validity of a marriage remains firmly entrenched in conflict of laws analysis. Doesn't this make it even more curious that courts reflexively apply their own law in divorce cases, even for matters bearing on marriage validity and even where the marriage was celebrated elsewhere? The practice may simply be an unwitting byproduct of the somewhat unusual domicile approach to jurisdiction in divorce cases allowed by *Williams I*. Professor Clyde Spillenger suggests that the practice is reinforced as well by the United States Supreme Court's disinclination to actively supervise state court conflict of laws decisions or the traditional state law subject of marriage dissolution. CLYDE SPILLENGER, PRINCIPLES OF CONFLICT OF LAWS 291 (2010).

7. In *Obergefell v. Hodges*, 576 U.S.__ (2015), the United States Supreme Court ruled that the United States Constitution requires states to allow same-sex couples to marry. After *Obergefell*, the question arose whether the Constitution requires states to grant divorces to same-sex couples on the same terms as they grant divorces to opposite-sex couples. Two subsequent decisions of the Court suggest that the Constitution does impose this requirement. In *V.L. v. E.L.*, 136 S. Ct. 1017 (2016), the Court held that standard full faith and credit principles governed the obligation of one state to recognize another state's adoption decree granted to a same-sex couple. A year later, in *Pavan v. Smith*, 582 U.S. ___ (2017), the Court ruled that same-sex spouses are entitled to enjoy the presumption of parentage in the form of a state rule that requires a child's birth certificate to list a non-biological father if he is married to the biological mother. *Pavan* emphasized that the Constitution entitles same-sex couples to civil marriage "on the same terms and conditions as opposite-sex couples." This language presumably applies to divorce and dissolution of a civil marriage.

PROBLEM 4-9: VLADIMIR AND GALINA

Vladimir and Galina married in Permissive State, where they had been life-long residents. Although Vladimir and Galina were distant cousins, their marriage was valid under Permissive State law. Their kinship, however, rendered their marriage invalid under Strict State's law. Vladimir had never been to Strict State, but decided to go on a brief vacation there. While in Strict State, Vladimir obtained a divorce from Galina in a Strict State court. Galina did not participate in the proceeding, and the Strict State court erroneously determined that Vladimir was domiciled in Strict State.

Galina filed a lawsuit collaterally attacking the Strict State divorce judgment in a Permissive State court. Vladimir has filed a motion to dismiss the suit, arguing that Permissive State must give full faith and credit to the Strict State judgment and recognize the divorce as valid. Is Vladimir correct?

PROBLEM 4-10: ABBY AND ANDROS

Abby and Andros were a married couple living in California. They became unhappy in the marriage. Abby moved to New York, where Andros owned property. Thereafter, Andros went to Nevada, where he obtained an ex parte divorce decree. Abby has never been to Nevada and has had nothing to do with the state. The Nevada decree said nothing about alimony obligations. After Andros obtained the divorce judgment, Abby sued in New York for support. In connection with the support proceeding, Abby convinced the New York court to assert in rem jurisdiction over Andros's property in the state by seizing it under a writ of sequestration and granting her support based on the value of the property. New York law provides that support may be granted to married couples that are separated. Did the New York court properly grant the support order?

PROBLEM 4-11: JULES AND JILLIAN/BAO AND JILLIAN

Jules and Jillian were married in Pennsylvania where they lived for several years. While Jules stayed in Pennsylvania, Jillian went to Nevada. While in Nevada, Jillian took a job as a cocktail waitress, rented an apartment, joined a Nevada synagogue, paid Nevada taxes, and — after less than six months — obtained a divorce judgment from the Nevada court. In making the divorce judgment, the Nevada court ruled that Jillian had complied with the residency requirements to obtain a divorce under the law of the State of Nevada, and that she was domiciled in Nevada at the time of divorce. Jules has never been to Nevada.

Jillian returned to Pennsylvania and immediately married another man, Bao. The Pittsburgh District Attorney is considering prosecuting Jillian for bigamous cohabitation. Pennsylvania law requires that at least one of the parties to a marriage must be domiciled in the state for six months before a Pennsylvania court can grant a divorce. Should the District Attorney proceed with the prosecution?

2.   *Bilateral Divorce*

Complications arising from ex parte "quickie" divorces and the recognition they deserve in other states are not as widespread as in the past. Nonetheless, knotty issues can still arise in circumstances where both parties consent to the divorce and purport to submit to the jurisdiction of the court that renders the divorce. Two classic cases that inform these issues are *Sherrer v. Sherrer*, 334 U.S. 343 (1948), and *Johnson v. Muelberger*, 340 U.S. 581 (1951).

In *Sherrer v. Sherrer*, a married couple had lived in Massachusetts. The wife went to Florida, where she filed a divorce action, alleging she was domiciled there. The husband made a general appearance through counsel and denied that Florida had jurisdiction. The Florida court rejected this contention, finding the wife was domiciled in Florida, and granted the divorce. The wife then remarried and ultimately returned to Massachusetts. Her original husband filed a Massachusetts action premised on the claim that they were still married. The wife appeared, arguing that the Florida divorce was valid. Reexamining the question whether she had been domiciled in Florida at the time of the divorce decree, the Massachusetts court concluded that she had not been domiciled in Florida and ruled in favor of the husband. The United States Supreme Court held, however, that because both parties had participated in the Florida proceedings, the judgment was entitled to full faith and credit even if it were now clear that the domicile claim had been fraudulent.

In *Johnson v. Muelberger*, the Supreme Court evaluated whether a daughter could collaterally attack the validity of the divorce between her deceased father, E. Bruce Johnson, and his second wife. The divorce had been granted in Florida after the second wife had filed for the divorce, and Mr. Johnson appeared there and contested the merits. Uncontested facts later established that the second wife had not satisfied the 90-day residence requirement. Mr. Johnson had married a third time, and upon his death, his third wife announced her intention to take a spousal share against the will in a New York probate proceeding. The daughter brought the collateral attack on the divorce in order to assert her own property interest in the estate: if the divorce was not valid, the third wife was not legally married to the deceased and thus could not take her spousal share against the will. In evaluating whether the daughter's collateral attack on the divorce from the second wife could succeed, the Supreme Court observed that Florida would hold the decree valid and final. The Court also observed that the daughter had not identified a Florida case that would allow a child to contest her parent's divorce under circumstances where claim preclusion prevented the parent from bringing such a contest. The Court reasoned as follows:

> We conclude that Florida would not permit Mrs. Muelberger to attack the Florida decree of divorce between her father and his second wife as beyond the jurisdiction of the rendering court. In that case New York cannot permit such an attack by reason of the Full Faith and Credit Clause. When a divorce cannot be attacked for lack of jurisdiction by parties actually before the court or strangers in the rendering state, it cannot be attacked by them anywhere.

Id. at 478-479.

The precise basis of *Johnson v. Muelberger* is unclear. Is the case merely an extension of the usual rules of claim preclusion? Or would you analogize the issue in the case to a standing deficiency: the daughter simply did not have the right to attack the divorce decree because she was "stranger" to the divorce action? One also wonders whether due process should have played a more prominent role in the analysis. Didn't the daughter's rights in her property give her some interest that she should be allowed to defend? Due process might counsel that her failure to participate in the Florida proceeding militates in favor of (instead of against) the validity of her collateral attack since she otherwise had no notice or opportunity to be heard on a matter that affects her rights. But then again, as discussed earlier in this chapter in the context of the decision in *Baker v. General Motors*, due process often tolerates decision making that has an effect on a non-participating third party.

3.   Foreign Divorce

When divorce laws in the United States were stricter than they are now, individuals desiring a divorce that could be more quickly obtained than in Nevada sometimes travelled outside the United States to obtain a divorce. These were nicknamed "Mexican divorces," a name no doubt developed during the period when Mexican divorces were available upon a showing of only one-day residence in the country. Although one-day residence divorces are no longer available in Mexico, other countries near the United States have offered similarly short residency periods. *See Boyter v. Commissioner*, 668 F.2d 1382, 1383 (4th Cir. 1981) (citing Haiti and the Dominican Republic as options). Moreover, "divorce tourism" is not a phenomenon unique to United States citizens. *See* ... Elisabetta Povoledo, *Divorce Tourists Go Abroad to Quickly Dissolve Their Italian Marriage*, N.Y. Times, Aug. 15, 2011, at A6. United States citizens returning to the United States with a foreign country divorce must concern themselves with the question of whether United States courts will honor such divorce judgments, particularly since full faith and credit obligations will not govern. Even where the divorces are consensual and bilateral, some courts have refused to enforce them (while others have decided to do so on the basis of public policy concerns favoring certainty and justifiable reliance[12]).

Interesting results often emerge as United States courts adjudicate divorces of individuals from marriages in foreign countries with legal systems and customs dramatically different than much of that practiced in the United States. Sometimes the results seem clearly wrong. Take, for example, a 1954 decision by a California court evaluating Chinese law pertaining to marital property. In adjudicating the case, the California court "presumed" that Chinese property law principles were the same as those prevailing under California's community property system at the time! *Louknitsky v. Louknitsky*, 266 P.2d 910 (1954). Other times, the results create a hybrid that may not be respectful to original customs of the married individuals or the societies in which they originally celebrated their marriage. Scholars have argued, however, that the process of adjudicating issues pertaining to such important human relationships as marriage and its incidents yields important opportunities for multicultural understanding and exchange. For thoughtful studies of the cross-cultural effects of these cases, see, e.g., Karen Knop, Ralf Michaels & Annelise Riles, *From Multiculturalism to Technique: Feminism, Culture, and the Conflict of Laws Style*, 64 Stan L. Rev. 589 (2012) (arguing in favor of conflict of laws methodology and thinking in negotiating multicultural challenges); Pascale Fournier, Muslim Marriages in Western Courts 100 (2010) (describing contradictions in application of Muslim law and consideration of *mahr* customs in United States courts).

PROBLEM 4-12: DUB AND CATHY

Dub and Cathy were a married couple living in South Dakota. Dub travelled to North Dakota and filed for divorce there, ensuring that Cathy was served in South Dakota. Cathy entered an appearance and participated through her lawyer. The

12. *Rosenstiel v. Rosenstiel*, 16 N.Y.2d 64, 262 N.Y.S.2d 86, 209 N.E.2d 709 (1965) (citing large numbers of individuals who had relied on the validity of the foreign divorce in deciding that public policy favored honoring them).

divorce was granted, and Cathy later tried to collaterally attack the decree in a South Dakota proceeding, arguing that the decree was invalid since neither of she nor Dub were domiciled in North Dakota. Should the attack succeed?

PROBLEM 4-13: DIVORCE AS TAX EVASION

Sissy and Spencer were intent on avoiding the federal income tax "penalty" for married couples. At the end of every year for three years, they traveled together to another country and obtained a quick divorce. They then remarried the next January. The Internal Revenue Service filed a federal court suit against them, collaterally attacking the validity of their divorces. The IRS argued that federal law should govern whether their divorces were valid for the purpose of the tax status. Should state or federal law govern this question?

PERSPECTIVE ON THE RELATIONSHIP BETWEEN JUDGMENTS AND MARRIAGE

Of all the exertions of governmental power in the United States, one that we treat with particularly great care is judgments. Judgments are subject to an iron rule of full faith and credit. Although the full faith and credit principle applies to other forms of law, the principle exerts the greatest protective force to judgments. When it comes to matters that pertain to marriage in the United States, full faith and credit law has a notable asymmetry: marriage (the state-sanctioned formation of a partnership between two individuals) is not treated as a judgment and thus does not enjoy the protections that full faith and credit accords to a judgment.[13] On the other hand, divorce (the state-sanctioned dissolution of a partnership between two individuals) is treated as a judgment and thus receives strong full faith and credit protection.

Why does United States law *not* treat marriage as a judgment—or at least with the same respect that we treat judgments? Marriage does resemble judgments: marriage is specific to individuals; marriage alters a fundamental human status; and marriage often results from the exercise of judicial power. In this way, marriage operates in a manner similar to a judgment: attaching a general legal principle to a specific set of persons. This contrasts with law formation and choice of law issues that pertain to generalized legal issues.

---

13. The full faith and credit clause speaks of giving effect to the "public act," "record," or "judicial proceeding" of a sister state. If a marriage is not a judgment, this would presumably mean it is not a "judicial proceeding." As to whether it is a "public act" or a "record," scholars have different views. *Compare* Joanna L. Grossman, *Resurrecting Comity: Revisiting the Problem of Non-Uniform Marriage Laws*, 84 OR. L. REV. 433, 454 (2005) (arguing that the full faith and credit clause is of little practical relevance to marriage recognition questions), *with* William A. Reppy, Jr., *The Framework of Full Faith and Credit and Interstate Recognition of Same-Sex Marriages*, 3 AVE MARIA L. REV. 393, 401 (2005) (arguing that "records" is the relevant term, since issuing a marriage license creates a record).

Even leaving aside marriage's intrinsic qualities that overlap with judgments, few would challenge the notion that marriage deserves to be treated as a really big deal. Marriage consists of what linguists call a performative speech act: the utterance of special words ("I pronounce you husband and wife") changes life as we know it.[14] The role of marriage in society also establishes its importance. Consider the following statement by an Arizona court: "Marriage is a foundation stone in the bedrock of our state and communities." *Cook v. Cook*, 104 P.3d 857, 863 (Ariz. Ct. App. 2005). In support of this proposition, the *Cook* court cited the following authorities:

> "As the United States Supreme Court long ago said, 'marriage . . . is an institution, in the maintenance of which in its purity the public is deeply interested, for it is the foundation of the family and of society, without which there would be neither civilization nor progress.'" *Maynard v. Hill*, 125 U.S. 190, 211 (1888);
>
> Marriage is as "fundamental to the very existence and survival of the race." *Skinner v. Oklahoma*, 316 U.S. 535, 541 (1942);
>
> "The state is also *vitally concerned* with the establishment of marriages." *Moran v. Moran*, 933 P.2d 1207, 1212 (Ariz. Ct. App. 1996);
>
> "The health of the family is *critical* to the health and vibrancy of our communities and our state." *Woodworth v. Woodworth*, 42 P.3d 610, 614 (App. 2002).

In a frequently quoted passage from his dissent in *Estin v. Estin,* Justice Jackson connects this emphasis on marriage's importance with concern over effective legal regulation:

> If there is one thing that the people are entitled to expect from their lawmakers, it is rules of law that will enable individuals to tell whether they are married and, if so, to whom. Today many people who have simply lived in more than one state do not know, and the most learned lawyer cannot advise them with any confidence.

334 U.S. 541 (1948). Indeed, many reasons exist for a coherent, predictable approach to legal regulation in a federalist system. The personal stakes for individuals subject to inconsistent laws governing marriage are huge: legitimacy of children, bigamy prosecutions, and inheritance all hang in the balance. Where states are given free rein to make their own decisions as to the validity of various types of marriages, the implications extend not only to the incidents of marriage, but also to the formalities and protections the law provides for the separation and dissolution of marriages. Consider folks who marry (validly) in one jurisdiction, but find after they move to another jurisdiction that they have great trouble getting divorced. Consider also the difficulties that might arise if one's home jurisdiction suddenly recognizes a particular type of marriage as valid and one wakes up one morning married to someone whom one has not even seen in years.

14. *See* J. L. AUSTIN, HOW TO DO THINGS WITH WORDS 120-121 (1962) (writing that performative utterance can include a "perlocutionary act which is the achieving of certain effects by saying something"); JOHN R. SEARLE, SPEECH ACTS 25 (1969) (defining "perlocutionary acts" as the "consequences or effects" that certain utterances have on "the actions, thoughts, or beliefs, etc. of hearers").

All these observations support granting marriage special legal protection, such as that provided for a judgment. Are there arguments against such an approach? Certainly, several formal legal notions of marriage do not mirror the formal legal conception of a judgment. Marriage is often described as the combination of two legal concepts: (1) a contract between parties capable of consent and (2) a status that the government confers upon the contracting parties. By contrast, judgments are imposed from "without"—with an outside authority figure resolving a controversy between parties "inside" a dispute. Marriages, on the other hand, "presumably take place by consent of both spouses." *See* CLYDE SPILLENGER, PRINCIPLES OF CONFLICT OF LAWS 276 (2010). In addition, marriages, unlike judgments, do not generally require fact-finding or enforcement.[15]

One approach to deciding whether marriage should be treated as a judgment—or at least with the same care as a judgment—focuses on reasons why our justice system is so protective of judgments. The uniformity, repose, and finality concerns that support special protection to judgments[16] apply equally to marriage, thus providing some basis for analogy between marriage and judgments. But other less analogous matters may explain the importance and sanctity of judgments in our society. Judgments implicate the essence of judicial power and legitimacy in their coercive qualities: the judiciary's "power and . . . prerogative" to perform the judicial function "rest, in the end, upon the respect accorded to its judgments." *Republican Party of Minn. v. White,* 536 U.S. 765, 793 (2002) (Kennedy, J., concurring). As such, judgments essentially say to the parties: "This is what the law says about your unique circumstances and this is what you must do in response. And, if you don't honor this command, the strong hand of the law will come down on you." In other words, the exercise of state power distilled in a judgment embodies the rule of law. A failure to respect a judgment amounts to a failure to respect the rule of law itself.[17] While a failure to respect a marriage also holds profound importance, the importance does not derive so powerfully from the rule of law.

One might also say that a judgment reflects a fine-tuned exercise of the court's personal authority. From that perspective, a failure to accord a judgment unqualified respect thus exposes and makes vulnerable the prestige of the court that rendered it. Perhaps this dynamic is magnified in legal cultures such as in the United States, which follows a "cult of the robe," reflected in such practices as placing judges on high benches, calling them "your honor," allowing them

15. Patrick J. Borchers, *Baker v. General Motors: Implications for Interjurisdictional Recognition of Non-Traditional Marriages,* 32 CREIGHTON L. REV. 147, 165-167 (1998) (observing that state issuance of a marriage certificate lacks the character of a judicial action, lacking dispute resolution and fact-finding functions); Note, Habib A. Balian, *Til Death Do Us Part: Granting Full Faith and Credit to Marital Status,* 68 S. CAL. L. REV. 397, 402-403 (1995) (observing that marriage decrees are not subject to enforcement devices such as those used to enforce damages judgment or injunctive remedies).

16. Stewart E. Sterk, *The Muddy Boundaries Between Res Judicata and Full Faith and Credit,* 58 WASH. & LEE L. REV. 47, 59-60 (2001) (observing that national interest in uniformity and finality help to explain special protection afforded judgment).

17. *Bush v. Gore,* 531 U.S. 98, 128 (2000) (Stevens, J. dissenting) ("It is confidence in the men and women who administer the judicial system that is the true backbone of the rule of law.").

absolute secrecy in deliberations, and the like.[18] As observed above, marriage may involve some judicial action, but not the same level of judicial involvement in fact-finding and law-defining as a judgment. One might reasonably conclude that the concerns with judicial prestige and legitimacy implicated with judgment recognition are diminished in the marriage context.

The differences between marriage and judgments might suggest that a full faith and credit approach developed for judgments may not perfectly suit marriage recognition questions. The arguments do not, however, establish that the current approach to marriage recognition is beyond reproach. As legal authorities evaluate the appropriate treatment of marriage in our system of full faith and credit, they must note one important matter: questions of the validity of a marriage often implicate highly charged issues of morality, religion, and public policy. Allowing flexibility in marriage recognition, therefore, allows one jurisdiction to express its own moral, religious, and public policy preferences. The question then becomes whether the federalist system as well as the individual rights and prerogatives of those who are party to controversial marriages can — and should — yield to this degree of flexibility. Given the importance in certainty, finality, and uniformity noted above, the answer to this question is not self-evident.

4.   *Child Custody*

Within the domestic United States context, child custody determinations are now dominated by statute. For international child custody issues, both a treaty and a federal statute govern. Divided into domestic United States and international child custody and abduction issues, the two sections below cover these provisions.

a.   **Domestic United States Issues**

As in divorce, the traditional basis for jurisdiction in a child custody dispute was the domicile of the child. Like marriage, custody was regarded as a status, with the child's domicile state viewed as the only jurisdiction with sufficient interest to regulate that status. Since this rule did not recognize circumstances in which other states (such as the domicile of parents) might be in a better position to evaluate what might serve the best interests of the child's welfare, the law proved inadequate and lawmakers began to adopt a more flexible orientation.

---

18. Adam Burton, *Pay No Attention to the Men Behind the Curtain: The Supreme Court, Popular Culture, and the Countermajoritarian Problem*, 73 UMKC L. REV. 53, 73 (2004) (observing that "people leave the Court alone or depict it in glowing terms because, despite periodic criticism of judicial opinions, 'residual Court-worship' and 'judge-worship' exist among the American public"); Jeff Shesol, *Justices Will Prevail*, N.Y. TIMES, Mar. 14, 2010, at WK10, *available at* http://www.nytimes.com/2010/03/14/opinion/14shesol.html (stating that "[t]he judicial robe confers a kind of exaltation on nearly everyone who wears it. Judicial sanctity may be a myth, but it is a powerful one; it reinforces our hope that this is really a government of laws, not merely of fallible human beings").

The Supreme Court established constitutional restrictions on child custody determinations in *May v. Anderson*, 345 U.S. 528 (1953). The *May v. Anderson* Court held Ohio did not have to give full faith and credit to a Wisconsin ex parte order granting custody to the father issued by a court that did not have personal jurisdiction over the out-of-state mother. The Court invoked traditional principles of personal jurisdiction:

> [W]e have before us the elemental question whether a court of a state, where a mother is neither domiciled, resident nor present, may cut off her immediate right to the care, custody, management and companionship of her minor children without having jurisdiction over her *in personam*. Rights far more precious to appellant than property rights will be cut off if she is to be bound by the Wisconsin award of custody.

Id. at 533.

Since the Court decided *May v. Anderson*, custody disputes have increased dramatically. Once states started to develop a flexible approach to custody determinations, a parent who was unhappy with one custody determination had incentive to go to another state to seek decree modifications. The full faith and credit obligation that one state owes another state's decree provided an obstacle to this decree-shopping behavior, but not an insurmountable one, since the full faith and credit obligation is keyed to the finality accorded the decree by the rendering state. Because child custody decrees are prospective and accommodate the evolving best interest of a child, the decrees are more easily modified than many other decrees.

In response to increasing interfamily child snatchings and the uncertain nature of child custody jurisdiction, the Uniform Child Custody Jurisdiction Act (UCCJA) was proposed and adopted by all 50 states and the District of Columbia. In 1997, the uniform act was modified in the form of the Uniform Child Custody Jurisdiction and Enforcement Act (UCCJEA), which sought to coordinate its provisions with applicable federal law. Both of these provisions were enacted as state law and prescribe when states have jurisdiction to grant or modify a child custody decree. As of 2012, all 50 states and the District of Columbia have now adopted the UCCJEA in place of the UCCJA.

Enacted by the United States Congress in 1980, the Parental Kidnapping Prevention Act (PKPA) is a federal complement to the uniform acts. Passed pursuant to the full faith and credit clause, the PKPA prescribes when states must enforce and must not modify child custody (and visitation) decrees from other states.

The PKPA and state law (UCCJEA, and formerly the UCCJA) intersect in complicated ways. Although the PKPA does not confer jurisdiction on any court (including federal courts), it tends to limit state court jurisdiction by prohibiting a state from exercising custody jurisdiction during the pendency of proceedings in other states and by requiring courts to give contestants notice and an opportunity to be heard. In this way, the PKPA is supervisory to the extent that it delineates boundaries within which state law can operate. The PKPA text is set forth immediately below.

In *Thompson v. Thompson*, 484 U.S. 174 (1988), the United States Supreme Court concluded that the PKPA did not create a cause of action for federal courts to decide which of two conflicting state custody decrees should control. In the course of this holding, the Supreme Court explained the background of the PKPA:

> At the time Congress passed the PKPA, custody orders held a peculiar status under the full faith and credit doctrine, which requires each State to give effect to the judicial proceedings of other States. The anomaly traces to the fact that custody orders characteristically are subject to modification as required by the best interests of the child. As a consequence, some courts doubted whether custody orders were sufficiently "final" to trigger full faith and credit requirements, and this Court had declined expressly to settle the question. Even if custody orders were subject to full faith and credit requirements, the Full Faith and Credit Clause obliges States only to accord the same force to judgments as would be accorded by the courts of the State in which the judgment was entered. Because courts entering custody orders generally retain the power to modify them, courts in other States were no less entitled to change the terms of custody according to their own views of the child's best interest. For these reasons, a parent who lost a custody battle in one State had an incentive to kidnap the child and move to another State to relitigate the issue. This circumstance contributed to widespread jurisdictional deadlocks. . . .
>
> The context of the PKPA therefore suggests that the principal problem Congress was seeking to remedy was the inapplicability of full faith and credit requirements to custody determinations. . . . The significance of Congress' full faith and credit approach to the problem of child snatching is that the Full Faith and Credit Clause . . . "only prescribes a rule by which courts, Federal and state, are to be guided when a question arises in the progress of a pending suit as to the faith and credit to be given by the court to the public acts, records, and judicial proceedings of a State other than that in which the court is sitting." Congress' chief aim in enacting the PKPA was to extend the requirements of the Full Faith and Credit Clause to custody determinations, the Act is most naturally construed to furnish a rule of decision for courts to use in adjudicating custody disputes and not to create an entirely new cause of action. It thus is not compatible with the purpose and context of the legislative scheme to infer a private cause of action.

Id. at 180-181.

28 U.S.C.A. §1738A. Full Faith and Credit Given to Child Custody Determinations

(a) The appropriate authorities of every State shall enforce according to its terms, and shall not modify except as provided in subsections (f), (g), and (h) of this section, any custody determination or visitation determination made consistently with the provisions of this section by a court of another State.

> **(b)** As used in this section, the term —
>> **(1)** "child" means a person under the age of eighteen;
>> **(2)** "contestant" means a person, including a parent or grandparent, who claims a right to custody or visitation of a child;

(3) "custody determination" means a judgment, decree, or other order of a court providing for the custody of a child, and includes permanent and temporary orders, and initial orders and modifications;

(4) "home State" means the State in which, immediately preceding the time involved, the child lived with his parents, a parent, or a person acting as parent, for at least six consecutive months, and in the case of a child less than six months old, the State in which the child lived from birth with any of such persons. Periods of temporary absence of any of such persons are counted as part of the six-month or other period;

(5) "modification" and "modify" refer to a custody or visitation determination which modifies, replaces, supersedes, or otherwise is made subsequent to, a prior custody or visitation determination concerning the same child, whether made by the same court or not;

(6) "person acting as a parent" means a person, other than a parent, who has physical custody of a child and who has either been awarded custody by a court or claims a right to custody;

(7) "physical custody" means actual possession and control of a child. . . .

(c) A child custody or visitation determination made by a court of a State is consistent with the provisions of this section only if —

(1) such court has jurisdiction under the law of such State; and

(2) one of the following conditions is met:

(A) such State (i) is the home State of the child on the date of the commencement of the proceeding, or (ii) had been the child's home State within six months before the date of the commencement of the proceeding and the child is absent from such State because of his removal or retention by a contestant or for other reasons, and a contestant continues to live in such State;

(B) (i) it appears that no other State would have jurisdiction under subparagraph (A), and (ii) it is in the best interest of the child that a court of such State assume jurisdiction because (I) the child and his parents, or the child and at least one contestant, have a significant connection with such State other than mere physical presence in such State, and (II) there is available in such State substantial evidence concerning the child's present or future care, protection, training, and personal relationships;

(C) the child is physically present in such State and (i) the child has been abandoned, or (ii) it is necessary in an emergency to protect the child because the child, a sibling, or parent of the child has been subjected to or threatened with mistreatment or abuse;

(D) (i) it appears that no other State would have jurisdiction under subparagraph (A), (B), (C), or (E), or another State has declined to exercise jurisdiction on the ground that the State whose jurisdiction is in issue is the more appropriate forum to determine the custody or visitation of the child, and (ii) it is in the best interest of the child that such court assume jurisdiction; or

(E) the court has continuing jurisdiction pursuant to subsection (d) of this section.

(d) The jurisdiction of a court of a State which has made a child custody or visitation determination consistently with the provisions of this section continues as long as the requirement of subsection (c)(1) of this section continues to be met and such State remains the residence of the child or of any contestant. . . .

(f) A court of a State may modify a determination of the custody of the same child made by a court of another State, if—

   (1) it has jurisdiction to make such a child custody determination; and

   (2) the court of the other State no longer has jurisdiction, or it has declined to exercise such jurisdiction to modify such determination.

(g) A court of a State shall not exercise jurisdiction in any proceeding for a custody or visitation determination commenced during the pendency of a proceeding in a court of another State where such court of that other State is exercising jurisdiction consistently with the provisions of this section to make a custody or visitation determination.

(h) A court of a State may not modify a visitation determination made by a court of another State unless the court of the other State no longer has jurisdiction to modify such determination or has declined to exercise jurisdiction to modify such determination.

In re Forlenza

140 S.W.3d 373 (Tex. 2004)

O'NEILL, J. delivered the opinion of the Court.

After the trial court in this case made an initial child-custody determination, the children lived with their custodial parent in four different states over a five and one-half year period while the non-custodial parent remained in Texas. In this modification suit, we must decide whether significant connections with Texas exist or substantial evidence is available here such that the initial trial court retained exclusive continuing jurisdiction under [the Texas Family Code, which embodies the Uniform Child Custody Jurisdiction Act]. Based on the record presented, we hold that the trial court retained exclusive continuing jurisdiction over the modification proceedings and the court of appeals erred in concluding otherwise. . . .

I

Ann Marie and Robert Joseph Forlenza were divorced in . . . Texas, on March 1, 1996. On July 23, 1997, the trial court signed an agreed modification order, modifying the original divorce decree, that granted Robert primary custody of their two children, now ten and fourteen years old, and the exclusive right to establish their primary physical residence. That same month, the children moved with Robert to Issaquah, Washington. Over the next five years, Robert moved with the children three more times—on August 30, 1998, they moved to Ohio, on February 19, 1999, they moved to Virginia, and on August 27, 2002, they moved to Colorado where they now reside. . . .

The current dispute arose in 2001 when Robert lost his job in Virginia and was offered a two-year contract job in Taipei, Taiwan. Claiming that she had experienced difficulty in exercising her possession rights, Ann filed this suit on September 10, 2001, seeking to modify the prior agreed possession order. She also requested a restraining order prohibiting Robert from relocating the children outside the United States, which the trial court granted. . . .

... Robert filed a second motion to dismiss alleging that the court did not have exclusive continuing jurisdiction under Texas Family Code §152.202(a) to modify its previous child-custody order. The trial court conducted another evidentiary hearing and denied the motion. The court of appeals, however, concluded that the trial court had abused its discretion and granted Robert's petition for writ of mandamus, ordering the trial court to vacate its prior order and dismiss the case. We granted Ann's petition to determine whether the trial court retained exclusive continuing jurisdiction under the Uniform Child Custody Jurisdiction Enforcement Act (UCCJEA).

II

Effective ... 1999, Texas adopted the UCCJEA, replacing the previous Uniform Child Custody Jurisdiction Act (UCCJA).... [E]ven though all fifty states adopted the UCCJA, some did so with significant departure from the original text. As a result, states often interpreted the Act inconsistently and child-custody determinations made in one state were often not accorded full faith and credit in another.

To address some of these problems, in 1980 Congress enacted the Parental Kidnaping Prevention Act (PKPA), which requires states to accord full faith and credit to custody decrees issued by sister states that substantially comply with the PKPA. 28 U.S.C. §1738A. The PKPA authorizes exclusive continuing jurisdiction in the state that issued the original decree as long as one parent or child remains there and that state has exclusive continuing jurisdiction under its own law. The UCCJA, though, which the states had adopted, does not clearly articulate when a decree-granting state retains exclusive continuing jurisdiction. As states adopted different interpretations of continuing jurisdiction and reached conflicting conclusions about the circumstances under which it endures, the law's uniformity diminished, often resulting in simultaneous proceedings and conflicting custody decrees. The UCCJEA was designed to eliminate inconsistent state interpretations of the UCCJA's jurisdictional aspects and to harmonize the UCCJA with the PKPA.

Article 2 of the UCCJEA specifically grants exclusive continuing jurisdiction over child-custody disputes to the state that made the initial custody determination and provides specific rules on how long this jurisdiction continues. Rules that prevent another state from modifying a child-custody determination while exclusive continuing jurisdiction remains in the original-decree state complement these provisions.[3] Texas adopted Article 2 without substantial variation from the UCCJEA.

---

3. Section 203 provides that

a court of this State may not modify a child-custody determination made by a court of another State unless a court of this State has jurisdiction to make an initial determination under Section 201(a)(1) or (2) and:

(1) the court of the other State determines it no longer has exclusive, continuing jurisdiction under Section 202 or that a court of this State would be a more convenient forum under Section 207; or

(2) a court of this State or a court of the other State determines that the child, the child's parents, and any person acting as a parent do not presently reside in the other state.

Robert's challenge involves the proper interpretation of [UCCJEA §202(a)], which governs the duration of the decree-granting state's exclusive continuing jurisdiction. That section provides that a court of this state that has made an initial child-custody determination consistent with [UCCJEA §201] has exclusive continuing jurisdiction over the determination until

(1) a court of this state determines that *neither the child, nor the child and one parent,* nor the child and a person acting as a parent, *have a significant connection with this state and that substantial evidence is no longer available in this state* concerning the child's care, protection, training, and personal relationships; or
(2) a court of this state or a court of another state determines that the child, the child's parents, and any person acting as a parent do not presently reside in this state.

Robert does not challenge the prior child-custody order's compliance with [section 201]. And [section 202 (a)(2)] does not apply because Ann continues to reside in Texas. Therefore, we must decide whether the trial court properly applied [section 202(a)(1)] in deciding that it had exclusive continuing jurisdiction over these modification proceedings. Statutory construction is a question of law that we review de novo.

Robert's jurisdictional plea contends that Ann failed to establish that a significant connection with Texas exists and that substantial evidence is available here concerning the children's care, protection, training, and personal relationships. . . . [W]e disagree with Robert's contention that it was Ann's burden in the first instance to establish that the children have a significant connection with Texas and that substantial evidence is available here. As a general matter, the pleader must allege facts that affirmatively demonstrate the court's jurisdiction to hear the case. Under the statute, a court acquires exclusive continuing jurisdiction by virtue of a prior child-custody determination. By alleging that the court's prior orders conferred exclusive continuing jurisdiction, Ann satisfied her initial statutory burden. The statute specifically provides that a court *retains* exclusive continuing jurisdiction *until* it determines that the significant-connection and substantial-evidence requirements are no longer met. Robert may challenge whether the statutory elements are satisfied, or the court may consider them sua sponte, but Ann has satisfied her initial jurisdictional burden under the statute.

Robert contends that the children no longer have a significant connection with Texas because (1) the children visited here only five times in the four-year period preceding this action, and (2) Ann's residence in Texas is not sufficient, as the commentary to [section 202] specifically notes that the presence of one parent remaining in the state is not determinative. But Ann does not rely on her mere presence in Texas to establish a significant connection under the statute. Contrary to Robert's briefing, the record indicates that the children actually visited Texas six times in the relevant period. On four of these occasions the children lived with Ann for considerable periods, each lasting approximately one month during the summer. Moreover, we presume that the trial court accepted as true Ann's testimony that more visitation would have occurred in Texas but for Robert's actions and the fact that the children were not allowed to fly to Texas.

Other courts commonly consider visitation within the state as evidence of a significant connection. In addition, numerous relatives, including Ann's mother and sister and Robert's sister and sister-in-law, live in Texas and maintain a relationship with the children. Moreover, the evidence in this case clearly indicates that Ann maintained a significant relationship with her children. To accommodate the children's schedule over the years, Ann repeatedly flew to Washington, Ohio, and Virginia to see them. Robert admits that Ann made at least fifteen such trips in the four-year period under review. Because the record establishes that the children visited Texas on a number of occasions and maintained a close relationship with their mother and other relatives residing in Texas, all important considerations under the UCCJEA, we hold that the children have a significant connection with Texas sufficient to support the trial court's exclusive continuing jurisdiction over the modification proceedings.

Robert claims that no other court has exercised exclusive continuing jurisdiction over children who have resided out of state for more than five years. We disagree. [Georgia, Kansas, and Connecticut have case law to the contrary.] Moreover, contrary to Robert's argument, the UCCJEA does not premise the exclusive continuing jurisdiction determination on which state has the *most* significant connection with the child. This relative type of inquiry is appropriate under [UCCJEA section 207], which allows a court with exclusive continuing jurisdiction to decline it in favor of a more convenient forum, but it does not affect the initial [section 202] jurisdictional analysis. Importantly, the only issue before us is whether the Texas court retained jurisdiction; the court could still decline to exercise that jurisdiction if another forum was more convenient. In this case, though, the children's almost continual change of residence supports the trial court's conclusion that the children had a significant connection with Texas based on their visits here and their personal relationships maintained in this state.

Finally, Robert argues that substantial evidence does not exist in Texas regarding the children's care, protection, training, and personal relationships, and [section 202 (a)(1)] requires the trial court to find *both* a significant connection with Texas *and* that substantial evidence exists here before it can exercise exclusive continuing jurisdiction. . . . Because section 201, which governs the initial custody determination, requires both a significant connection and substantial evidence, Robert concludes that section 202 must as well. We disagree.

Robert's strained construction of the statutory scheme ignores [section 202(a)(1)]'s plain language. That section specifically states that jurisdiction continues until the court determines that there is not a significant connection with Texas *and* that substantial evidence concerning the children's care, protection, training, and personal relationships is no longer available here. Clearly, exclusive jurisdiction continues in the decree-granting state as long as a significant connection exists *or* substantial evidence is present.[10] . . .

III

For the foregoing reasons, we hold that the trial court had exclusive continuing jurisdiction over this modification proceeding and that mandamus relief is justified. . . .

Notes on
FORLENZA, *THE PKPA, AND THE UCCJEA*

1. The UCCJEA identifies the "home" state of the child as possessing jurisdiction to make an initial child custody determination. This home state retains exclusive continuing jurisdiction unless the state no longer has a "significant connection" with the child, the parents, or a person acting as a parent or when "substantial evidence . . . concerning the child's protection, training, and personal relationships" is no longer available in the state. UCCJEA §202(a)(1). The UCCJEA thus provides guidance on when a state that originally granted custody should relinquish power to another state. Questions of jurisdiction under the UCCJEA often turn on whether the original state court should assert its continuing jurisdiction broadly or restrictively. The *Forlenza* court embraced a broad interpretation. The more broadly a court interprets this provision, the more likely the court makes it necessary for parties to return to the original custody-granting state to obtain a modification. What values and concerns should inform this decision? How relevant should it be if a particular parent appears to be forum shopping for a more amenable court? The court in *Forlenza* notes that the father had moved around a lot. How much should it matter that a parent and children are peripatetic? In *Forlenza*, the court suggested that Texas continued to have jurisdiction because the children had moved so often that no other state had obtained a more significant connection with them. Consider some of the overarching values of conflict of laws: fairness to the parties, honoring expectations, uniformity of result, respect for state sovereignty, and promotion of federalism and judicial efficiency. Is the *Forlenza* court's reasoning consistent with these values?

2. The statute in place before the UCCJEA (the UCCJA) allowed a second state to decide whether the original state granting custody still had jurisdiction. The UCCJEA requires the original state to make this determination. The federal Parental Kidnapping Prevention Act (PKPA) reinforces this requirement by prohibiting one state from exercising jurisdiction

---

10. We note that our interpretation comports with that of other jurisdictions [citing cases from Georgia, Kansas, North Dakota, Connecticut, and Oregon].

during the pendency of a proceeding in another state. The PKPA further strengthens the authority of the original state in §1738A(h): "A court of a State may not modify a visitation determination made by a court of another State unless the court of the other State no longer has jurisdiction to modify such determination or has declined to exercise jurisdiction to modify such determination."

3. One way to convince the original custody granting state to decline power is to ask it to decline jurisdiction on forum non conveniens grounds. Section 207 of the UCCJEA sets forth factors a court may consider (1) whether domestic violence has occurred and is likely to continue in the future and which State could best protect the parties and the child; (2) the length of time the child has resided outside this State; (3) the distance between the court in this State and the court in the State that would assume jurisdiction; (4) the relative financial circumstances of the parties; (5) any agreement of the parties as to which State should assume jurisdiction; (6) the nature and location of the evidence required to resolve the pending litigation, including testimony of the child; (7) the ability of the court of each State to decide the issue expeditiously and the procedures necessary to present the evidence; and (8) the familiarity of the court of each State with the facts and issues in the pending litigation. Conspicuously absent from this section is a factor listing the "best interest of the child," which had been listed in the earlier provision of the UCCJA. The drafters eliminated this factor so as to eliminate court confusion over factors bearing on proper jurisdiction and those bearing on the "merits" of which custody arrangement is more appropriate.

4. Section 208 of the UCCJEA provides that a court with initial or modifying jurisdiction should decline jurisdiction if the petitioner has "engaged in unjustifiable conduct" unless the parties agree to the court's jurisdiction, a court otherwise having jurisdiction determines that the state is a more appropriate forum for suit, or no other state has jurisdiction. This clean hands concept was also reflected in the UCCJA, and is meant to empower courts to decline jurisdiction where a parent has engaged in activities such as removing, hiding, and restraining a child so as to elude another parent's assertion of custody.

5. It is important to note that an interstate adoption is not a "child custody proceeding" under the UCCJEA. Section 103 of the UCCJEA states that the UCCJEA does not apply to "an adoption proceeding." An adoption decree is a final judgment, not subject to the type of modification allowed for child custody. For that reason, adoption decrees are not in danger of the type of inconsistent decisions that arise in custody determinations.

6. The UCCJEA permits a court to exercise emergency jurisdiction when a child in need of protection is present in a state. Courts have respected this as a narrow exception to the normal operation of the Act. *See . . . In re Jaheim*

B., 87 Cal. Rptr. 3d 504 (Cal. Ct. App. 2008) (exercising emergency jurisdiction where father was imprisoned and mother had abandoned child); *Martin v. Martin*, 380 N.E.2d 305 (N.Y. 1978) (deferring to Florida); *Fry v. Ball*, 544 P.2d 402 (Colo. 1975) (deferring to California).

7. In *V.L. v. E.L.*, 136 S. Ct. 1017 (2016), the United States Supreme Court confronted a question implicating child visitation rights in the context of a woman's adoption of her same-sex partner's biological children. In the case, the Alabama Supreme Court refused to recognize a Georgia decree approving the adoption and therefore rejected a petition seeking visitation with the children after the couple had ended their relationship. The United States Supreme Court reversed, explaining that the Georgia court had jurisdiction over adoption matters and thus had the authority to grant the adoption. The Alabama court was therefore wrong in refusing to give effect to the adoption decree, since the Full Faith and Credit Clause required it to do so.

PROBLEM 4-14: DAN, SALLY, AND MISSY

Dan and Sally had a child, Missy, while they were married and living in Washington. They filed for divorce there and the Washington court gave custody of Missy to Sally. Sally and Missy moved to Oregon. For the next six years, Dan remained in Washington, and Missy visited him twice a year: at Thanksgiving and for two weeks every summer. Dan filed a request to a Washington court to modify its custody decree in his favor. Does the Washington court have jurisdiction over the modification request?

b. International Child Abduction

Parental abduction of children is not only a domestic United States problem, but also an international problem. In fact, parents may have a greater incentive to take their children across international borders than domestic state borders because of the heightened challenge of transnational detection and enforcement. Estimates suggest that parents abduct hundreds of children each year — either to or from the United States.

The international instrument designed to address the problem is the Hague Convention on the Civil Aspects of International Child Abduction, which is now adopted by over 80 countries and applicable to children under 16. The United States has implemented the Hague Child Abduction Convention through the International Child Abduction Remedies Act. In 2002, the Hague Convention on the Protection of Children supplemented the earlier Hague Child Abduction

Convention with provisions pertaining to jurisdiction and child custody judgments.

The Hague Child Abduction Convention's goal is to secure the return of children who are wrongfully removed from or retained in a signatory state and to return them to their "habitual residence," which must be another party to the convention, for adjudication of the merits of the disputes. The abducting parent may defeat the return by establishing one of three affirmative defenses: (1) the child's caretaker did not actually have a "right of custody" at the time of removal or retention, or had consented to such removal or retention; (2) a "grave risk" that the return would entail physical or psychological harm to the child; and (3) a court in the forum where the child is present has found that the child, who possesses appropriate maturity and age, objects to the return.

The central concept in the Hague Child Abduction Convention is the "remedy of return," which allows the return of a child who has been abducted to another country in violation of a custody order. The remedy does not invite courts to inquire into the underlying wisdom of the custody order, but merely requires courts to determine whether a child should be returned to the jurisdiction from which he or she was abducted. In evaluating this remedy, courts have struggled to interpret various provisions of the Hague Child Abduction Convention, particularly the terms "habitual residence," "grave risk," and "right of custody."

Habitual Residence: The concept of "habitual residence" is necessary for evaluating where the "remedy of return" should focus. The term "habitual residence" has inspired slightly different interpretations, although the interpretations all focus on identifying the term as a place where the child has become acclimatized. *Robert v. Tesson*, 507 F.3d 981 (6th Cir. 2007). Some courts seek to determine the place where a child's presence has a "'degree of settled purpose from the child's perspective.'" *Tesson, supra*, at 993 (quoting *Feder v. Evans-Feder*, 63 F.3d 217, 224 (3d Cir. 1995)). The factors that bear on this "settled purpose" consider where the child has social engagements, participation in sports, excursions, and meaningful interaction with other people. *Karkkainen v. Kovalchuk*, 445 F.3d 280 (3d Cir. 2006). A related approach follows a two-part test: (1) what is the "shared intent of those entitled to fix the child's residence (usually the parents) at the latest time that their intent was shared"? *Poliero v. Centenaro*, 373 Fed. Appx. 102, 104 (2d Cir. 2010); and (2) does the evidence establish "the conclusion that the child has acclimatized to the new location and thus has acquired a new habitual residence, notwithstanding any conflict with the parents' shared intent"? *Gitter v. Gitter*, 396 F.3d 124, 134 (2d Cir. 2005).

Grave Risk: The concept of "grave risk" comes up frequently in domestic abuse situations. The possibility of a "grave risk" of harm to a child can make the "remedy of return" inappropriate in some cases. A case dealing with this difficult topic, *Van De Sande v. Van De Sande*, appears at the end of this section.

Right of Custody: This section begins with a United States Supreme Court case grappling with the meaning of the term "right to custody." The "remedy of return" applies only where a child is abducted in violation of a "right to custody," and parties sometimes litigate over what amounts to a custody right. For example, visitation rights have been found not to constitute a "right of custody." In *Abbott v. Abbott* below, the Supreme Court grappled with the more difficult question of whether an order preventing a parent from removing a child outside the court's jurisdiction (known as a *ne exeat* order) constitutes "right of custody" within the meaning of the Convention.

Abbott v. Abbott

130 S. Ct. 1983 (2010)

Justice KENNEDY delivered the opinion of the Court.

This case presents . . . a question of interpretation under the Hague Convention on the Civil Aspects of International Child Abduction (Convention). . . . The United States is a contracting state to the Convention; and Congress has implemented its provisions through the International Child Abduction Remedies Act (ICARA). The Convention provides that a child abducted in violation of "rights of custody" must be returned to the child's country of habitual residence, unless certain exceptions apply. The question is whether a parent has a "righ[t] of custody" by reason of that parent's *ne exeat* right: the authority to consent before the other parent may take the child to another country.

I

Timothy Abbott and Jacquelyn Vaye Abbott married in England in 1992. He is a British citizen, and she is a citizen of the United States. Mr. Abbott's astronomy profession took the couple to Hawaii, where their son A.J.A. was born in 1995. The Abbotts moved to La Serena, Chile, in 2002. There was marital discord, and the parents separated in March 2003. The Chilean courts granted the mother daily care and control of the child, while awarding the father "direct and regular" visitation rights, including visitation every other weekend and for the whole month of February each year.

Chilean law conferred upon Mr. Abbott what is commonly known as a *ne exeat* right: a right to consent before Ms. Abbott could take A.J.A. out of Chile. In effect a *ne exeat* right imposes a duty on one parent that is a right in the other. After Mr. Abbott obtained a British passport for A.J.A., Ms. Abbott grew concerned that Mr. Abbott would take the boy to Britain. She sought and obtained a "*ne exeat* of the minor" order from the Chilean family court, prohibiting the boy from being taken out of Chile.

In August 2005, while proceedings before the Chilean court were pending, the mother removed the boy from Chile without permission from either the father or the court. A private investigator located the mother and the child in Texas. In February 2006, the mother filed for divorce in Texas state court. Part of the relief she sought was a modification of the father's rights, including full power in her to determine the boy's place of residence and an order limiting the father to supervised visitation in Texas. This litigation remains pending.

Mr. Abbott brought an action in Texas state court, asking for visitation rights and an order requiring Ms. Abbott to show cause why the court should not allow Mr. Abbott to return to Chile with A.J.A. In February 2006, the court denied Mr. Abbott's requested relief but granted him "liberal periods of possession" of A.J.A. throughout February 2006, provided Mr. Abbott remained in Texas.

In May 2006, Mr. Abbott filed the instant action in the United States District Court for the Western District of Texas. He sought an order requiring his son's return to Chile pursuant to the Convention and enforcement provisions of the ICARA. In July 2007, after holding a bench trial during which only Mr. Abbott testified, the District Court denied relief. The court held that the father's *ne exeat* right did not constitute a right of custody under the Convention and, as a result, that the return remedy was not authorized.

The United States Court of Appeals for the Fifth Circuit affirmed. . . .

II

. . . The provisions of the Convention of most relevance at the outset of this discussion are as follows:

> "Article 3: The removal or the retention of the child is to be considered wrongful where —
>
> "*a* it is in breach of rights of custody attributed to a person, an institution or any other body, either jointly or alone, under the law of the State in which the child was habitually resident immediately before the removal or retention; and
>
> "*b* at the time of removal or retention those rights were actually exercised, either jointly or alone, or would have been so exercised but for the removal or retention. . . .
>
> "Article 5: For the purposes of this Convention —
>
> "*a* 'rights of custody' shall include rights relating to the care of the person of the child and, in particular, the right to determine the child's place of residence;
>
> "*b* 'rights of access' shall include the right to take a child for a limited period of time to a place other than the child's habitual residence. . . .
>
> "Article 12: Where a child has been wrongfully removed or retained in terms of Article 3 . . . the authority concerned shall order the return of the child forthwith." *Id.*, at 7, 9.

The Convention's central operating feature is the return remedy. When a child under the age of 16 has been wrongfully removed or retained, the country to which the child has been brought must "order the return of the child forthwith," unless certain exceptions apply. A removal is "wrongful" where the child was removed in violation of "rights of custody." The Convention defines "rights of custody" to "include rights relating to the care of the person of the child and, in particular, the right to determine the child's place of residence." A return remedy does not alter the pre-abduction allocation of custody rights but leaves custodial decisions to the courts of the country of habitual residence. The Convention also recognizes "rights of access," but offers no return remedy for a breach of those rights.

The United States has implemented the Convention through the ICARA. The statute authorizes a person who seeks a child's return to file a petition in state or federal court and instructs that the court "shall decide the case in accordance with the Convention." 42 U.S.C. §§11603(a), (b), (d). If the child in question has been "wrongfully removed or retained within the meaning of the Convention," the child shall be "promptly returned," unless an exception is applicable. §11601(a)(4).

III

As the parties agree, the Convention applies to this dispute. A.J.A. is under 16 years old; he was a habitual resident of Chile; and both Chile and the United States are contracting states. The question is whether A.J.A. was "wrongfully removed" from Chile, in other words, whether he was removed in violation of a right of custody. This Court's inquiry is shaped by the text of the Convention; the views of the United States Department of State; decisions addressing the meaning of "rights of custody" in courts of other contracting states; and the purposes of the Convention. After considering these sources, the Court determines that Mr. Abbott's *ne exeat* right is a right of custody under the Convention.

A

This Court consults Chilean law to determine the content of Mr. Abbott's right, while following the Convention's text and structure to decide whether the right at issue is a "righ[t] of custody."

Chilean law granted Mr. Abbott a joint right to decide his child's country of residence, otherwise known as a *ne exeat* right. Minors Law 16,618, art. 49 (Chile) provides that "[o]nce the court has decreed" that one of the parents has visitation rights, that parent's "authorization . . . shall also be required" before the child may be taken out of the country, subject to court override only where authorization "cannot be granted or is denied without good reason." Mr. Abbott has "direct and regular" visitation rights and it follows from Chilean law, that he has a shared right to determine his son's country of residence under this provision. To support the conclusion that Mr. Abbott's right under Chilean law gives him a joint right to decide his son's country of residence, it is notable that a Chilean agency has explained that Minors Law 16,618 is a "right to authorize the minors' exit" from Chile and that this provision means that neither parent can "unilaterally" "establish the [child's] place of residence." Letter from Paula Strap Camus, Director General, Corporation of Judicial Assistance of the Region Metropolitana, to National Center for Missing and Exploited Children (Jan. 17, 2006).

The Convention recognizes that custody rights can be decreed jointly or alone . . . and Mr. Abbott's joint right to determine his son's country of residence is best classified as a joint right of custody, as the Convention defines that term. The Convention defines "rights of custody" to "include rights relating to the care of the person of the child and, in particular, the right to determine the child's place of residence." Art. 5(a), *ibid.* Mr. Abbott's *ne exeat* right gives him both the joint "right to determine the child's place of residence" and joint "rights relating to the care of the person of the child."

Mr. Abbott's joint right to decide A.J.A.'s country of residence allows him to "determine the child's place of residence." The phrase "place of residence" encompasses the child's country of residence, especially in light of the Convention's explicit purpose to prevent wrongful removal across international borders. See Convention Preamble, Treaty Doc., at 7. And even if "place of residence" refers only to the child's street address within a country, a *ne exeat* right still entitles Mr. Abbott to "determine" that place. "[D]etermine" can mean "[t]o fix conclusively or authoritatively," Webster's New International Dictionary 711 (2d ed. 1954) (2d definition), but it can also mean "[t]o set bounds or limits to," *ibid.* (1st definition), which is what Mr. Abbott's *ne exeat* right allows by ensuring that A.J.A. cannot live at any street addresses outside of Chile. It follows that the Convention's protection of a parent's custodial "right to determine the child's place of residence" includes a *ne exeat* right.

Mr. Abbott's joint right to determine A.J.A.'s country of residence also gives him "rights relating to the care of the person of the child." Art. 5(a), Treaty Doc., at 7. Few decisions are as significant as the language the child speaks, the identity he finds, or the culture and traditions she will come to absorb. These factors, so essential to self-definition, are linked in an inextricable way to the child's country of residence. One need only consider the different childhoods an adolescent will experience if he or she grows up in the United States, Chile, Germany, or North Korea, to understand how choosing a child's country of residence is a right "relating to the care of the person of the child." The Court of Appeals described Mr. Abbott's right to take part in making this decision as a mere "veto"; but even by that truncated description, the father has an essential role in deciding the boy's country of residence. . . .

That a *ne exeat* right does not fit within traditional notions of physical custody is beside the point. The Convention defines "rights of custody," and it is that definition that a court must consult. This uniform, text-based approach ensures international consistency in interpreting the Convention. It forecloses courts from relying on definitions of custody confined by local law usage, definitions that may undermine recognition of custodial arrangements in other countries or in different legal traditions, including the civil-law tradition. And, in any case, our own legal system has adopted conceptions of custody that accord with the Convention's broad definition. . . .

Ms. Abbott gets the analysis backwards in claiming that a *ne exeat* right is not a right of custody because the Convention requires that any right of custody must be capable of exercise. The Convention protects rights of custody when "at the time of removal or retention those rights were actually exercised, either jointly or alone, or would have been so exercised but for the removal or retention." Art. 3(b), Treaty Doc., at 7. In cases like this one, a *ne exeat* right is by its nature inchoate and so has no operative force except when the other parent seeks to remove the child from the country. If that occurs, the parent can exercise the *ne exeat* right by declining consent to the exit or placing conditions to ensure the move will be in the child's best interests. When one parent removes the child without seeking the *ne exeat* holder's consent, it is an instance where the right would have been "exercised but for the removal or retention." *Ibid.* . . .

B

This Court's conclusion that Mr. Abbott possesses a right of custody under the Convention is supported and informed by the State Department's view on the issue. The United States has endorsed the view that *ne exeat* rights are rights of custody. In its brief before this Court the United States advises that "the Department of State, whose Office of Children's Issues serves as the Central Authority for the United States under the Convention, has long understood the Convention as including *ne exeat* rights among the protected 'rights of custody.'" There is no reason to doubt that this well-established canon of deference is appropriate here. The Executive is well informed concerning the diplomatic consequences resulting from this Court's interpretation of "rights of custody," including the likely reaction of other contracting states and the impact on the State Department's ability to reclaim children abducted from this country.

C

This Court's conclusion that *ne exeat* rights are rights of custody is further informed by the views of other contracting states. In interpreting any treaty, "[t]he 'opinions of our sister signatories' . . . are 'entitled to considerable weight.'" *El Al Israel Airlines, Ltd. v. Tsui Yuan Tseng*, 525 U.S. 155, 176 (1999). The principle applies with special force here, for Congress has directed that "uniform international interpretation of the Convention" is part of the Convention's framework. See §11601(b)(3)(B). [The Court reviewed case law from England, Israel, Austria, South Africa, and Germany, and found their interpretations of the Convention supported its own. The Court dismissed contrary views expressed by the Canadian and French courts.]

D

Adopting the view that the Convention provides a return remedy for violations of *ne exeat* rights accords with its objects and purposes. The Convention is based on the principle that the best interests of the child are well served when decisions regarding custody rights are made in the country of habitual residence. See Convention Preamble, Treaty Doc., at 7. Ordering a return remedy does not alter the existing allocation of custody rights, Art. 19, *id.*, at 11, but does allow the courts of the home country to decide what is in the child's best interests. It is the Convention's premise that courts in contracting states will make this determination in a responsible manner.

Custody decisions are often difficult. Judges must strive always to avoid a common tendency to prefer their own society and culture, a tendency that ought not interfere with objective consideration of all the factors that should be weighed in determining the best interests of the child. This judicial neutrality is presumed from the mandate of the Convention, which affirms that the contracting states are "[f]irmly convinced that the interests of children are of paramount importance in matters relating to their custody." Convention

Preamble, Treaty Doc., at 7. International law serves a high purpose when it underwrites the determination by nations to rely upon their domestic courts to enforce just laws by legitimate and fair proceedings.

To interpret the Convention to permit an abducting parent to avoid a return remedy, even when the other parent holds a *ne exeat* right, would run counter to the Convention's purpose of deterring child abductions by parents who attempt to find a friendlier forum for deciding custodial disputes. Ms. Abbott removed A.J.A. from Chile while Mr. Abbott's request to enhance his relationship with his son was still pending before Chilean courts. After she landed in Texas, the mother asked the state court to diminish or eliminate the father's custodial and visitation rights. The Convention should not be interpreted to permit a parent to select which country will adjudicate these questions by bringing the child to a different country, in violation of a *ne exeat* right. Denying a return remedy for the violation of such rights would "legitimize the very action — removal of the child — that the home country, through its custody order [or other provision of law], sought to prevent" and would allow "parents to undermine the very purpose of the Convention." . . . Requiring a return remedy in cases like this one helps deter child abductions and respects the Convention's purpose to prevent harms resulting from abductions. An abduction can have devastating consequences for a child. . . .

IV

While a parent possessing a *ne exeat* right has a right of custody and may seek a return remedy, a return order is not automatic. Return is not required if the abducting parent can establish that a Convention exception applies. One exception states return of the child is not required when "there is a grave risk that his or her return would expose the child to physical or psychological harm or otherwise place the child in an intolerable situation." Art. 13(b), Treaty Doc., at 10. If, for example, Ms. Abbott could demonstrate that returning to Chile would put her own safety at grave risk, the court could consider whether this is sufficient to show that the child too would suffer "psychological harm" or be placed "in an intolerable situation." The Convention also allows courts to decline to order removal if the child objects, if the child has reached a sufficient "age and degree of maturity at which it is appropriate to take account of its views." Art. 13(b), Treaty Doc., at 10. The proper interpretation and application of these and other exceptions are not before this Court. These matters may be addressed on remand.

. . .

The judgment of the Court of Appeals is reversed, and the case is remanded for further proceedings consistent with this opinion.

[Justice Stevens filed a dissenting opinion, in which Justice Thomas and Breyer joined. Justice Stevens viewed the majority's approach as blurring the Hague Convention's careful distinction between rights to custody and rights to access to a child, and argued that the majority "converted every noncustodial parent with access rights — at least in Chile — into a custodial parent" under the terms of the Convention. Justice Stevens also disagreed with the majority's interpretation of that portion of the Hague Convention's "right of custody" that included "the right to determine the child's place of residence." He criticized the majority for including the power to limit where a child resides in the power to determine the child's place of residence. He argued instead that the "right to determine where a child resides" extends only to a location-specific power to select the child's exact residence (designating something like a street address, rather than broader power to designate the country where the child resides). Although acknowledging that prior precedent did support giving "great weight" to the views of the United States Department of State on the treaty's interpretation, Justice Stevens nonetheless said these decisions never explained "exactly why" that should be the case.]

Notes on
ABBOTT v. ABBOTT

1. Do you agree with the majority's suggestion that its interpretation is consistent with the goals of international cooperation and discouraging forum shopping? Does giving a broad meaning to the concept of "custody" increase or decrease the Hague Child Abduction Convention's ability to provide a remedy for a violation of a parent's rights in the original country that issued the custody decree? Professor Paul B. Stephan argues that "giving a narrow reading to the 'custody' concept in the Convention would mean that national courts would have freer rein to decide for themselves what arrangements meet the best interest of a child, without having to defer to any earlier rulings of a foreign court." Paul B. Stephan, Abbott v. Abbott: *A New Take on Treaty Interpretation by the Supreme Court*, 14 ASIL INSIGHTS, Vol. 14 (Aug. 4, 2010), *available at* http://www.asil.org/insights100804.cfm. Professor Stephan observes that the "majority opinion emphasized the value of international cooperation; Stevens's dissent would have buttressed national sovereignty." Do you agree? Does the answer depend on the majority's emphasis on accommodating differing legal traditions and international consistency in interpretation of the Convention? These suggest a strong commitment to international cooperation, don't they?

2. Aside from competing values regarding international governance, what other values inform the question whether a custodial parent should have freedom to relocate in other countries? Professor Linda Silberman explains that some countries maintain that "a custodial parent should have substantial freedom" to relocate, while other countries have decided that "a substantial relationship with both parents is critical," so strong restrictions on relocation are necessary in order to ensure that a child maintains a relationship with both parents, even if this means that one parent has "broader custodial rights than the other." Linda J. Silberman, *Convention on the Civil Aspects of International Child Abduction — Custody Rights — Ne Exeat Rights:* Abbott v. Abbott, 105 AM. J. INT'L L. 108, 112 (2011). One might

expect that these differences in opinion as to what best serves the interest of a child are more pronounced in the international context than the domestic context. Does *Abbott* provide a mechanism for respecting these differences or does it show greater preference for the "substantial relationship with both parents" orientation? One reading of the decision is that it compensates for weak remedies to enforce access and visitation rights for noncustodial parents in the Hague Child Abduction Convention. Silberman, *supra*, at 112.

For European Court of Human Rights cases decided around the time of *Abbott* that may exert an opposite effect on the Convention's ability to regulate a parent's decision to relocate, see *Neulinger v. Switzerland*, App. No. 41615/07 (Eur. Ct. H.R. July 6, 2010) and *Raban v. Romania*, App. No. 25437/09 (Eur. Ct. H.R. Oct. 26, 2010).

3. Note how confident the *Abbott* majority was in relying on the decisions of other countries as to the meaning of the Hague Child Abduction Convention. Are there reasons such a comparative approach is more appropriate here than in other interpretive contexts, such as where the Court is seeking to interpret a clause in the United States Constitution?

4. Do you agree with the majority's decision to put "great weight" on the United States State Department's interpretation of the Convention? What is your view on the propriety of giving great weight to the opinion of the State Department? Is it appropriate to allow the Executive branch to enjoy direct input on a treaty's meaning in light of evolving standards and changing global lifestyles?

Van De Sande v. Van De Sande

431 F.3d 567 (7th Cir. 2005)

POSNER, Circuit Judge.

The International Child Abduction Remedies Act, 42 U.S.C. §§11601 *et seq.*, implementing the Hague Convention on the Civil Aspects of International Child Abduction, entitles a person whose child has been abducted to the United States (usually by a parent) to petition in federal court for the return of the child. 42 U.S.C. §11603(b). "The Convention was created to discourage abductions by parents who either lost, or would lose, a custody contest. . . . The Convention drafters adopted a 'remedy of return' . . . to discourage abductions, reconnect children with their primary caretakers, and locate each custody contest in the forum where most of the relevant evidence existed. [But] while the remedy of return works well if the abductor is a non-custodial parent, it is inappropriate when the abductor is a primary caretaker who is seeking to protect herself and the children from the other parent's violence." Merle H. Weiner, "Navigating the Road Between Uniformity and Progress: The Need for Purposive Analysis of the Hague Convention on the Civil Aspects of International Child Abduction," 33 Colum. Human Rts. L. Rev. 275, 278-79 (2002). In such a case "the remedy [of return] puts the victim's most precious possession, her child, in close proximity to her batterer either without her protection (assuming she does not return with the child), or with her protection, thereby exposing her to further violence." Merle H. Weiner, "International Child Abduction and the Escape from Domestic Violence," 69 Fordham L. Rev. 593, 634 (2000); cf. 18 U.S.C. §1204(c)(2). "A typical pattern involves a female U.S. national who has married a male foreign national and moved with her spouse to a foreign country. In most Hague cases invoking grave risk on the basis of domestic violence, the abuse begins before the transnational move. Ultimately, the victim flees with her children back to the United States in order to escape the abuse. The batterer, left behind in the country of habitual residence, then files a petition under the Hague Convention requesting return of the children to adjudicate the custody issues." Roxanne Hoegger, "What If She Leaves? Domestic Violence Cases Under the Hague Convention and the Insufficiency of the Undertakings Remedy," 18 Berkeley Women's L.J. 181, 187 (2003).

The present case approximates the "typical pattern" in which the remedy of return is problematic. The two children of Davy and Jennifer Van De Sande, a married but estranged couple, are habitual residents of Belgium, Davy's native country. Davy has been awarded custody of his two children by a Belgian court, but Jennifer, who is living with the children in the United States, has refused to give them up. She became an "abducter" when Davy got the custody decree, though it was ex parte. Davy brought this suit to get the children back.

An abducter has a narrow defense: Article 13(b) of the Convention excuses return if "there is a grave risk that his or her return would expose the child to physical or psychological harm or otherwise place the child in an intolerable situation." The abducter must prove this by clear and convincing evidence. 42 U.S.C. §11603(e)(2)(A). Although Jennifer submitted affidavits setting forth the circumstances that she contends create such a risk, the district court granted summary judgment for Davy, primarily on the ground that there is no indication that the Belgian legal system cannot or will not protect the children. The only condition that the judge inserted in the order directing the return of the children to Davy is that he pay for their airfare to Belgium.

[Jennifer] presented six affidavits [painting] a consistent and disturbing picture. According to them Davy began beating Jennifer shortly after their marriage in 1999. The beatings were frequent and serious . . . [and] continued when they moved from the United States to Belgium. Davy's mother joined in beating her daughter-in-law. (The Van De Sandes' grievance against Jennifer is that she is an indifferent housekeeper.) . . . Davy's beatings of Jennifer continued after the two children were born, and were often done in their presence, which caused them to cry. The older child (born in August 2000, so 4 years old when her mother refused to return to Belgium in October 2004) would tell her father to stop, but without success. Physical abuse of the daughter by her father began when she started wetting her bed. He would spank her, and once when Jennifer entered the girl's bedroom and told Davy to stop beating their daughter he grabbed Jennifer by the throat and shoved her out of the room. Once he struck the daughter a sharp blow to the side of her head. His mother (the daughter's grandmother) struck the daughter in the head at least twice.

Davy also abused Jennifer verbally in the children's presence, calling her a "cunt," "whore," "lazy fucking bitch," and "lazy fat bitch." (He is fluent in English, as are the children.) . . .

In 2004, during a visit to Jennifer's parents, Jennifer told Davy that she and the children would not return to Belgium. He threatened to kill the children. He had earlier threatened to kill Jennifer. And the next day, in a conversation with Jennifer's brother, he threatened to kill "everybody." Jennifer told her father about Davy's threats, and the police were called and an officer escorted him from the house.

After he returned to Belgium without the children, the daughter stopped wetting her bed—except after her weekly phone conversation with him. It was after returning to Belgium that he obtained ex parte the order from the Belgian court awarding him custody of the children and thus providing him with the precondition to bringing this suit.

. . . Jennifer has satisfied the statutory requirement that her evidence of risk of harm to the children be clear and convincing. But is it clear and convincing evidence of a *grave* risk of harm? The district judge thought not. In reaching this conclusion, however, he was unduly influenced by the fact that most of the physical and all the verbal abuse was directed to Jennifer rather than to the children. The younger child, a boy, apparently wasn't beaten at all; the girl was spanked and hit repeatedly, but not injured; and no expert evidence of the psychological effect of Davy's conduct on either child was presented.

The judge inexplicably gave no weight to Davy's threat to kill the children. Perhaps, standing alone, such a threat could be discounted as an emotional reaction to the prospect of losing custody of them. But given Davy's propensity for violence, and the grotesque disregard for the children's welfare that he displayed by beating his wife severely and repeatedly in their presence and hurling obscene epithets at her also in their presence, it would be irresponsible to think the risk to the children less than grave. The gravity of a risk involves not only the probability of harm, but also the magnitude of the harm if the probability materializes. The probability that Davy, or his mother, another person of violent temper (if the affidavits are true), would some day lose control and inflict actual physical injury on the children (or at least on the daughter) could not be thought negligible.

But against this it can be argued that the Hague Convention is really just a venue statute, designed "to deter parents from engaging in international forum shopping in custody cases." Maybe we should be asking not what the risk to the children might be in a jurisdiction that had no laws for the protection of children, but merely whether the jurisdiction of residence has adequate laws; Belgium, we can assume, does.

. . . To give a father custody of children who are at great risk of harm from him, on the ground that they will be protected by the police of the father's country, would be to act on an unrealistic premise. The rendering court must satisfy itself that the children will in fact, and not just in legal theory, be protected if returned to their abuser's custody.

Moreover, to define the issue not as whether there is a grave risk of harm, but as whether the lawful custodian's country has good laws or even as whether it both has and zealously enforces such laws, disregards the language of the Convention and its implementing statute; for they say nothing about the laws in the petitioning parent's country. The omission to mention them does not seem to have been an accident—the kind of slip in draftsmanship that courts sometimes correct in the exercise of their interpretive authority. If handing over custody of a child to an abusive parent creates a grave risk of harm to the child, in the sense that the parent may with some nonnegligible probability injure the child, the child should not be handed over, however severely the law of the parent's country might punish such behavior. In such a case, any order divesting the abducting parent of custody would have to be conditioned on the child's being kept out of the custody of the abusing parent until the merits of the custody dispute between the parents could be resolved by the court in the abusive parent's country. At argument Davy's lawyer was willing to entertain the possibility that the district judge should have imposed such a condition on the order returning the children to Davy in Belgium. This concession alone requires that we remand the case to the district court for further consideration, for "in order to ameliorate any short-term harm to the child, courts in the appropriate circumstances have made return contingent upon 'undertakings' from the petitioning parent."

But "undertakings," as an alternative to refusing to return the child, will not always do the trick. The ex parte order that Davy obtained, granting him custody of the children, does not preclude Jennifer's challenging his custody; and we are told that in April of this year Jennifer filed such a challenge in a Belgian court but that the court has taken no action. Pending resolution of the custody dispute, prudence would require that the children if returned to Belgium be placed in the custody of some third party in that country—obviously not Davy's mother! (assuming as we must at this stage of the litigation that she really did beat her granddaughter). Instead of remaining in their own mother's custody in the United States, the children might find themselves in a foster-care institution until the custody litigation was resolved, even though there is no suggestion that their mother is an abusive, neglectful, or otherwise unfit parent, whatever the deficiencies in her housekeeping skills.

Return plus conditions ("undertakings") can in some, maybe many, cases properly accommodate the interest in the child's welfare to the interests of the country of the child's habitual residence. Often the bulk of the evidence concerning risk of harm will be found in that country and the left-behind parent's defense to charges of abuse may be more difficult and costly to prepare and present in the country to which the abducter has fled. But in cases of child abuse the balance may shift against return plus conditions. In a comment on "undertakings" that was quoted with approval in *Danaipour v. McLarey*, 286 F.3d 1, 25 (1st Cir. 2002), the State Department has advised that "if the requested . . . court is presented with unequivocal evidence that return would cause the child a 'grave risk' of physical or psychological harm, . . . then it would seem less appropriate for the court to enter extensive undertakings than to deny the return request. The development of extensive undertakings in such a context could embroil the court in the merits of the underlying custody issues and would tend to dilute the force of the Article 13(b) exception." The court added that "undertakings are most effective when the goal is to preserve the status quo of the parties prior to the wrongful removal. This, of course, is not the goal in cases where there is evidence that the status quo was abusive."

Concern with comity among nations argues for a narrow interpretation of the "grave risk of harm" defense; but the safety of children is paramount. Jennifer presented at the summary judgment stage sufficient evidence of a grave risk of harm to her children, and the adequacy of conditions that would protect the children if they were returned to their father's country is sufficiently in doubt, to necessitate an evidentiary hearing in order to explore these issues fully. The hearing should be held promptly and conducted expeditiously in order to comply with the Convention's goal of expediting the return of abducted children to their country of habitual residence, Hague Convention, *supra*, Art. 11, provided that the return will not expose the children to a grave risk of harm.

Reversed and remanded.

Notes on
VAN DE SANDE

1. Recall that the Hague Convention on Child Abduction is not intended to invite courts to inquire into the underlying wisdom of custody determinations. Rather, the Convention casts courts in the position of evaluating the parents' dispute in light of international law issues related to comity and the sovereign interests of the countries involved. Does the provision of the Hague Convention on Child Abduction dealing with "grave risk," Article 13(b), enable courts adjudicating legitimate petitions to re-evaluate custody arrangements and inject too much of their own judgment about the threat posed by domestic violence? In determining that the Van De Sande mother met her burden of establishing clear and convincing evidence of a grave risk of harm, did the court rely on its own findings on the most appropriate circumstances for the children? Is that an appropriate inquiry? Should the court have given more consideration to whether the Belgian courts could have protected the children? Compare *Blondin v. Dubois*, 189 F.3d 240, 242 (2d Cir. 1999), in which the court of appeals initially confronted a similar situation by remanding the case to the trial court for inquiry into the arrangements and procedures for evaluating safe custody available in the child's country of habitual residence. (In later proceedings, however, the *Blondin* court of appeals cited uncontroverted expert testimony about risk of traumatic stress in upholding the district court's decision to prevent the children from returning to their habitual residence.) *See also Baran v. Beaty*, 526 F.3d 1340 (11th Cir. 2008) (finding "grave risk of harm" where father exhibited a strong temper and alcohol abuse).

2. The Hague Convention is designed on the premise that the courts of the country from which a child was wrongfully taken should resolve the

underlying custody dispute. Is this properly honored in *Van De Sande?* Professor Linda Silberman argues against courts using the "grave risk" exception to transform "a summary Hague proceeding into a conventional custody hearing—replete with individual 'best interest' assessments and extensive psychological testimony." *See* Linda Silberman, *The Hague Child Abduction Convention Turns Twenty: Gender Politics and Other Issues*, 33 N.Y.U. J. Int'l L. & Pol. 221, 239 (2000). Professor Merle H. Wiener takes a more favorable view of searching judicial inquiry into the abuse allegation within the context of Article 13(b), stating that "it is still the best avenue presently available for domestic violence victims" and praises judges who understand the "link between adult-on-adult violence and harm to children" and who "do not trust Contracting States to protect domestic violence victims, or batterers' promises to adhere to undertakings." Merle H. Wiener, *International Child Abduction and the Escape from Domestic Violence*, 69 Fordham L. Rev. 593, 662 (2000). For similar arguments in favor of greater scrutiny by judges of domestic violence allegations in the Hague Convention context, see Carol S. Bruch, *The Unmet Needs of Domestic Violence Victims and Their Children in Hague Child Abduction Convention Cases*, 38 Fam. L.Q. 529 (2004). *See also Simcox v. Simcox*, 511 F.3d 594, 608 (6th Cir. 2007) (arguing that due to the "intensely fact-bound nature of the [grave risk] inquiry[,] district courts should be allowed adequate discretion").

3. As pointed out in *Van De Sande*, the Hague Child Abduction Convention seeks to account for the sovereignty of the country of habitual residence in an alleged grave risk situation if that country is able to provide sufficient protection for the child. This process may take the form of "undertakings" or enforceable conditions designed to mitigate the risk of harm that might occasion the child's repatriation to the country of habitual residence. Like the *Van De Sande* court, many courts are skeptical about relying on undertakings in a domestic violence context. *See, e.g., Danaipour v. McLarey*, 286 F.3d 1, 26 (1st Cir. 2002) (stating that "[w]here substantial allegations are made a credible threat exists, a court should be particularly wary about using potentially unenforceable undertakings to try to protect the child"). Isn't this the prudent approach, given the risk of harm to a child and the uncertainty of the efficacy of the proffered undertaking?

Article 20 of the Hague Convention provides for a defense by a parent opposing the return of a child from the jurisdiction to which the request is directed, where to do so would violate the "fundamental principles of the requested State relating to the protection of human rights and fundamental freedoms." This defense was intended to be broader than the grave risk defense, drafted to provide a mechanism for political refugees to resist the return of children to a jurisdiction where they had been persecuted. The defense, however, is not invoked often and is rarely successful. *See* Merle H. Weiner, *Strengthening Article 20*, 38 U.S.F. L. Rev. 701, 705-710 (2004).

4. What happens if a child is removed to a country that is not a signatory of the Hague Child Abduction Convention — a so-called noncontracting state? In this situation, the Hague Convention itself provides no relief to a parent who is left behind in the child's country of habitual residence. The United States Congress, however, has provided relief in the form of the International Parental Kidnapping Crime Act (IPKCA), where an individual acts with "intent to obstruct the lawful exercise of parental rights." Section 1204(d) of IPKCA states that the statute "does not detract" from the Hague Convention. As explained in a "Sense of Congress" resolution accompanying IPKCA, the Hague Child Abduction Convention should provide the first option for a parent seeking to obtain a child's return: the IPKCA should govern only where the Convention is inapplicable. *United States v. Amer*, 110 F.3d 873, 882 (2d Cir. 1997).

5. When United States courts order that children be promptly removed from the United States to the country of their habitual residence, the return of the child does not necessarily moot the case. United States courts continue to have jurisdiction over an appeal after the return of the child when the parties continue to have a live dispute over where the child will be raised. *Chafin v. Chafin*, 568 U.S. 195 (2013).

PROBLEM 4-15: FELICIA AND JAG

Felicia and Jag married in England, but soon thereafter moved to the United States where their two children were born. The couple's relationship deteriorated and they agreed that Felicia would return to England to raise the children. They visited their father, Jag, several times over the next five years. During one of the children's later visits, Jag threatened to keep them in the United States for good, but ultimately put them on the plane back to England. At that point, Felicia obtained a Prohibited Steps Order under the English Children's Act, which prohibited Jag from "removing the children from her care without her consent and required him to return the children to her promptly upon the expiration of the agreed contact." The order was issued ex parte, but Jag received a copy and subsequently appeared at a hearing in England. After this hearing, the court did not make any formal custody determination. The court did, however, enter a visitation order (the "Visitation Order") stating the father could meet with the children on specific dates and could have indirect phone contact with them. Thereafter, Jag and Felicia divorced. The next year, Felicia allowed the children to fly to the United States for what she believed was a two-week visit. Contrary to his earlier promises, however, Jag refused to return them to England after the two weeks expired. Jag has had the children in the United States for approximately four months and they are now enrolled in United States schools.

Felicia filed an application for a return of the children with the Hague Convention's central authority for England, and also filed a petition in United States District Court for return under the Hague Child Abduction Convention.

In evaluating whether Felicia has made out a successful case for the remedy of return under the Convention, the district court must find that (1) the children's habitual residence is in England; (2) the retention of the children in the United States violates Felicia's right of custody under the laws of England; and (3) Felicia was exercising those custody rights at the time children flew to the United States and were retained there. In support of her petition, Felicia relies on the Visitation Order, the Prohibited Steps Order, and a provision of a domestic English child abduction statute, which provides that "it is a criminal offense for a parent to take a child out of the United Kingdom for more than one month without the consent of the other parent, absent a court order in favor of the first parent." In addition, she argues that the evidence shows the courts in England intended the children's habitual residence to be England, and the last time Felicia and Jag agreed on anything, they agreed that England should be the children's habitual residence.

Should the district court grant the request for return?

5.   Child Support

As described above, child support judgments are issued in proceedings where courts have personal jurisdiction. Nonetheless, like child custody orders, child support orders present unique judgment recognition issues, particularly because the orders impose an ongoing obligation extending into the future. Once a court enters an order for a parent to pay periodic child support, one or both of the parents may move, thus rendering enforcement of the order tricky. Although a parent seeking to enforce an order may find it legally less cumbersome to travel to the state where a defaulting parent is located, that process can be expensive and difficult on a practical level.

One of the traditional obstacles to enforcement is derived from the rule that full faith and credit obligations did not attach to child support obligations that can be modified. *Sistare v. Sistare*, 218 U.S. 1 (1910). While states asked to honor the modifiable order may choose to do so as a matter of comity, interstate enforcement was difficult in light of this rule. Another problematic full faith and credit principle concerned lump sum child support. In *Yarborough v. Yarborough*, 290 U.S. 202 (1933), the Supreme Court held that South Carolina was precluded from issuing a supplemental award of support for a child living in that state where a Georgia court had issued a lump sum award against the father that could not be modified under Georgia law. (The *Yarborough* court held that the father was entitled to rely on the finality of the Georgia judgment, and that to impose additional obligations would violate the father's due process rights.) While still technically "good law," *Yarborough* has minimal impact today because the Georgia law was (and continues to be) so unusual. Moreover, uniform laws now make it possible to supplement a lump sum award if the parent obligated to pay the award takes a new residence that allows supplementation.

Indeed, uniform legislation has resolved much of the difficulties with full faith and credit requirements for child support awards. After the first uniform statute spawned varying versions, the Commissioners on Uniform State Laws proposed a replacement, the Uniform Interstate Family Support Act (UIFSA). (UIFSA applies to both child and spousal support.) Congress required that all states adopt the UIFSA, and also adopted a complement statute, the Full Faith and Credit for Child Support Orders Act, 28 U.S.C. §1738B, requiring states to recognize and enforce child support orders. The principles of federal 28 U.S.C. §1738B are the same as the UIFSA.

The purpose of the UIFSA is to ensure that only one state at a time exercises jurisdiction to determine the amount of support owed and that all other states enforce the support decree without modifying it (so long as the decree was issued consistent with the terms of the UIFSA). The Act allows for both administrative and judicial enforcement of support obligations, and provides procedures for challenging the validity or enforceability of contested orders. A party wishing to modify an order in another state must register it in the new state and petition to modify it, but the court in the new state may do so only if the conditions of the Act are satisfied.

Philipp v. Stahl

781 A.2d 1065 (N.J. Super. Ct. App. Div. 2001), *rev'd*, 798 A.2d 83 (N.J. 2002)

LESEMANN, J.A.D.

The parties in this . . . case were married in 1975, divorced in Georgia on April 23, 1993, and seem to have spent much of their time since the divorce battling each other, first in the courts of Georgia and thereafter in the courts of New Jersey. The present appeal stems from an application of the plaintiff wife to require her ex-husband to contribute to their daughter's college expenses at Princeton and for additional miscellaneous relief. The trial court held that the Uniform Interstate Family Support Act (UIFSA) placed "exclusive jurisdiction" in the courts of the state that had issued the original support order (Georgia), and thus this state had no jurisdiction to act. . . .

The jurisdictional provisions of UIFSA which govern this case are set out in four subsections of N.J.S.A.2A:4-30.72. Subsection a provides that, unless all parties agree otherwise, if a court of this state has issued "a support order," then that court has "continuing, exclusive jurisdiction over a child support order" so long as either the obligor or obligee under the order, or "the child for whose benefit the support order is issued" continues to reside in this state. Subsection b, however, provides that a court of this state which has issued a child support order "may not exercise its continuing jurisdiction to modify the order if the order has been modified by a tribunal of another state pursuant to this act or a law substantially similar to this act."

Subsection c seems to be essentially a restatement of subsection b. It says that if a "child support order" issued by this state is "modified by a tribunal of another state pursuant to this act or a law substantially similar to this act," the New Jersey court "loses its continuing, exclusive jurisdiction with regard to prospective enforcement of the order issued in this State. . . ." Finally, subsection d directs that a court of this state "shall recognize the continuing, exclusive jurisdiction of a tribunal of another state which has [already] issued a child support order pursuant to this act. . . ."

The anomaly in the statute . . . stems from its direction that so long as a support order issued by one state is in effect, a second state shall not also issue a support order in that same case. However, the statute then contains a description of what is to happen if such a second state does issue a support order: the order of the second state replaces that of the first, and it is the second state not the first which retains "exclusive jurisdiction."

If the New Jersey court has issued one or more orders that "modified" the original Georgia "support order" (embodied in its judgment of divorce), then Georgia lost the "continuing, exclusive jurisdiction" which it once had regarding support matters, and that "continuing, exclusive jurisdiction" is now vested in New Jersey. Plaintiff claims there have been at least three such New Jersey orders and that jurisdiction to decide the support issue she now raises rests here. We agree.

The facts of the case, as they relate to the jurisdictional issue on appeal, are not in dispute. The Georgia divorce decree was issued on April 23, 1993. . . . Less than six months after entry of the divorce judgment, the plaintiff wife decided to move, with the children, to New Jersey. . . .

In March 1994, plaintiff moved in the Family Part of the New Jersey Superior Court for an order modifying visitation [and obtained an order changing] a portion of the support provisions in the Georgia judgment. It modified the requirement that called on the husband to pay for all visitation costs (which had been entered while the wife still lived in Georgia), and provided instead that the defendant was to pay sixty percent and the plaintiff forty percent of those expenses. The order further stated that, except as thereby changed, all provisions of the divorce judgment were to remain in full force and effect. However, it then included another significant provision, specifying that "[a]ny modifications, supplementations, or enforcement of this Order or of the 1992 judgment shall go forward before this court."

On April 25, 1995, the New Jersey Family Part entered a second order which had a significant effect on support payments. In addition to enforcement provisions, directives respecting reimbursement for past due amounts, and a provision for wage garnishment in the future, the court changed the prior order which had called for payment of $500 per month for each of the two children, to provide for one unallocated payment of $1,000 per month for the two children. [W]hile on its face the Georgia judgment would terminate payments for the older child when she became emancipated, and thus defendant's total child support payments would be reduced to $500 per month, the New Jersey child support guidelines provide otherwise. Application of those guidelines would mean that when the older child became emancipated, defendant's payments would be reduced to $688 per month rather than to $500 per month. In addition, this order contained a provision comparable to that quoted above from the March 1999 order, stating that "the Chancery Division of this court shall retain jurisdiction over the subject matters addressed herein."

The third New Jersey order which affected support payments was entered on August 18, 1999. That order, entered by consent of the parties, provided that custody of Eric would pass to defendant in Georgia. However, it also provided that defendant would maintain health insurance for Eric and would be "responsible for all [his] uninsured health care expenses, including but not limited to dental expenses. . . ." It thus relieved plaintiff of the obligation to pay one-half of Eric's un-reimbursed medical expenses and also relieved her of the obligation to maintain dental insurance for Eric. The order further provided that, except as related to the medical expense and insurance issue, all provisions of the 1992 judgment remained in effect, and it contained a provision similar to that set out in the two other New Jersey orders described above. It said that, "Any modifications, supplementation, or enforcement of any [prior order] or of this Order shall go forward before this Court."

[T]he three orders, . . . modify prior support obligations. In the face of those orders, we are satisfied that the UIFSA provisions quoted above not only justify, but indeed require, that further such applications be handled in this state.

Further, it seems clear that the parties at least impliedly understood and acknowledged that all further proceedings in this case—concerning support as well as custody and visitation—would be held in New Jersey. The provisions in the three quoted orders all so state. . . .

Reversed and remanded for further proceedings consistent with this opinion. We do not retain jurisdiction.

WECKER, J.A.D., concurring in part, dissenting in part.

. . . I disagree with the majority's interpretation and application of the Uniform Interstate Family Support Act (UIFSA or "the Act"). . . . To explain my conclusions, I will examine UIFSA . . . and its relationship to the Full Faith and Credit to Child Support Orders Act (FFCCSOA), 28 U.S.C.A. §1738B. Federal law required every state to enact UIFSA, which in New Jersey replaced the Revised Uniform Reciprocal Enforcement of Support Act (RURESA). The apparent purpose of UIFSA is not only to establish a means of enforcing a support order when one or both parties have moved from the jurisdiction where the support order was issued, but also to establish ground rules for modifying such an order, and to do so in a way that avoids conflicting orders issued by courts of different states. . . .

[T]he New Jersey and Georgia enactments mirrors that of the other. The concept of "continuing, exclusive jurisdiction" to avoid or resolve jurisdictional disputes appears to have been drawn directly from the FFCCSOA, first enacted in 1994. *See* 28 U.S.C.A. §1738B(d).[3]

To understand UIFSA's use of the concept of continuing exclusive jurisdiction, I look first to N.J.S.A. 2A:4-30.72a and O.C.G.A. §19-11-114a, which provide:

> A tribunal [of this State] issuing a support order consistent with the law of [this State] has continuing, exclusive jurisdiction over a child support order:
>
> (1) as long as [this State] remains the residence of the obligor, the individual obligee, or the child for whose benefit the support order is issued; or
>
> (2) until all of the parties who are individuals have filed written consents with the tribunal of [this State] for a tribunal of another state to modify the order and assume continuing, exclusive jurisdiction.

Next I look to N.J.S.A. 2A:4-30.72d and O.C.G.A. §19-11-114d, which require that:

> A tribunal [of this State] shall recognize the continuing, exclusive jurisdiction of a tribunal of another state which has issued a child support order pursuant to this [act] or a law substantially similar to this [act].

Thus under the two states' similar provisions, Georgia has continuing exclusive jurisdiction over its child support order because defendant remains a Georgia resident and because the parties have not filed written consents for the New Jersey court to assume jurisdiction. New Jersey is bound to recognize Georgia's jurisdiction. . . . [W]e must also look at the limitations UIFSA places upon a state's continuing, exclusive jurisdiction, as set forth in N.J.S.A. 2A:4-30.72b and O.C.G.A. §19-11-114b and relied upon by the majority:

> A tribunal [of this State] issuing a child support order consistent with the law [of this State] may not exercise its continuing jurisdiction to modify the order if the order has been modified by a tribunal of another state pursuant to this [act] or a law substantially similar to this [act].

Thus Georgia, as a state with continuing, exclusive jurisdiction, can lose its power to "exercise its continuing jurisdiction to modify" its child support order if the New Jersey tribunal issues an order modifying child support pursuant to UIFSA or

---

3. The FFCCSOA provides, much like N.J.S.A. 2A:4-30.72a(2) and b, the conditions under which a state court retains its continuing, exclusive jurisdiction:

> A court of a State that has made a child support order consistently with this section has continuing, exclusive jurisdiction over the order if the State is the child's State or the residence of any individual contestant unless the court of another State, acting in accordance with subsections (e) and (f), has made a modification of the order.

[28 U.S.C.A. §1738B(d).]

Subsection (e) of the federal law conditions the authority of a state court to "modify a child support order issued by a court of another State" upon either (A) both parties and the child having left the original state, or (B) both parties filing their written consent to the second state's assumption of continuing, exclusive jurisdiction over modification. Subsection (f) is virtually identical to N.J.S.A. 2A:4-30.74 in setting forth rules for determining which of multiple child support orders is to be recognized for purposes of establishing continuing, exclusive jurisdiction.

a "substantially similar" law. The majority concludes that the New Jersey tribunal has done just that. I disagree.

The questions presented by this appeal are whether a New Jersey court has issued an order modifying child support, and if so, whether it has done so consistent with UIFSA or a similar law, such as the FFCCSOA or the now repealed RURESA. . . . I do not view any of the New Jersey orders entered in this case as having modified the Georgia judgment so as to satisfy the conditions of N.J.S.A. 2A:4-30.72 and deprive Georgia of continuing, exclusive jurisdiction. . . . The majority cites three subsequent New Jersey orders as support orders[4] which purportedly modify the child support provisions of the Georgia divorce judgment, thereby depriving Georgia of the power to exercise its own continuing jurisdiction and establishing "continuing, exclusive jurisdiction over a child support order" in New Jersey. N.J.S.A. 2A:4-30.72a and b. But none of those three New Jersey orders actually modifies the original child support provisions incorporated in the Georgia judgment; each enforces the Georgia judgment, as can be seen by close examination of the orders.

The first order cited by the majority was entered in response to plaintiff's motion to set visitation, and over defendant's objection to New Jersey's jurisdiction. . . . The order concludes by allocating the cost of air travel between New Jersey and Georgia for the children's visits with their father, a necessary corollary to New Jersey's custody and visitation jurisdiction under the Uniform Child Custody Jurisdiction Act. The final operative provision of that order, paragraph 11, says:

> Except as otherwise expressly set forth herein, the 1992 [Georgia] Judgment remains in full force and effect. Any modifications, supplementations, or enforcement of this Order or of the 1992 Judgment shall go forward before this Court.

The second order cited by the majority was entered by the same judge . . . in response to defendant's motion for visitation and plaintiff's cross-motion for arrears and future support. The divorce judgment incorporated the parties' agreement for defendant to pay $500 per month for each of their two children, a total of $1,000 per month as child support. The April 1995 order continued that support

> in the full amount of $1,000 per month payable by a wage execution through the Department of Probation of the State of New Jersey, which shall contact the appropriate department in Georgia to secure the full and speedy effectuation of this provision.

I do not read that provision, continuing the same "full amount" of child support, but adding the interstate collection mechanism then available under RURESA (and now under UIFSA), as a modification of the prior support order. Providing for collection and payment through the New Jersey Probation Department was obviously incidental to enforcement of the Georgia child support order and

---

4. UIFSA, enacted in New Jersey in 1998, defines a "support order" to include an order "which provides for monetary support, health care coverage, arrearages, or reimbursement, and may include related costs and fees, interest, income withholding, attorney's fees, and other relief." N.J.S.A. 2A:4-30.65.

consistent with the Georgia order allowing plaintiff to move with the children to New Jersey.

The [later] order also enforces the existing child support provision of the Georgia judgment, providing for various past due payments owing between the parties, including private school expenses, and requiring a Qualified Medical Child Support Order to be entered pursuant to ERISA. Such an order was entered the same day. The final operative paragraph of the [later] order provides: "[T]he Chancery Division of this Court shall retain jurisdiction over the subject matters addressed herein." The "subject matters addressed herein" are the various existing child support provisions enforced or effectuated by the order.

In my view, the majority engages in unwarranted and unsupported speculation by adopting plaintiff's theoretical argument that the [later] order should be deemed to modify the Georgia judgment because after the older child is emancipated, child support for the younger child under the New Jersey Child Support Guidelines would be more than the $500 per child provided by the original Georgia order. The assumption that New Jersey law and jurisdiction would then apply assumes the very conclusion that is disputed in this appeal, that is, that New Jersey will exercise jurisdiction and apply New Jersey law to modify the Georgia order. Moreover, in light of the younger child's 1999 return to the physical custody of his father in Georgia, and defendant's representation that he does not seek child support from plaintiff in New Jersey, such speculation has no basis in fact.

The third order cited by the majority is the consent order entered on August 18, 1999, by which the parties agreed that physical custody of Eric would be transferred from plaintiff in New Jersey to defendant in Georgia. [Much of the order provides] for plaintiff's visitation with Eric, both in New Jersey and Georgia, including plaintiff's access to Eric's school and extracurricular activities in Georgia, the child's access to a therapist in New Jersey, and for the child's religious observances to be supported by defendant. The only modification to any aspect of the Georgia child support provisions may be found in paragraph 12 of the August 1999 order, which provides for defendant to pay all unreimbursed medical and dental expenses for Eric instead of sharing such expenses equally with plaintiff as originally provided. Significantly, the order then continues:

> Except as set forth in paragraph 12, this order is not intended to address any financial issue, and both parties reserve all rights and arguments regarding any financial issue relating to either of the children's expenses which shall be retroactive to the applicable date, e.g., the date the expense was incurred.

The 1999 order expressly preserves both the 1992 Georgia judgment and the subsequent Georgia and New Jersey custody and visitation orders and then provides that "[a]ny modifications, supplementation, or enforcement of any of these Orders or of this Order shall go forward before this Court."

The majority concludes that these "three orders, . . . clearly and unequivocally, modify prior support obligations." It is neither clear nor unequivocal that they do so. As the motion judge who dismissed plaintiff's application to modify child support for lack of subject matter jurisdiction concluded, the Georgia support order has "never been changed, altered or challenged" — the only minor modification having been in the 1999 order for defendant to pay all rather than half of the children's unreimbursed medical expenses. . . .

. . . With respect to a second state's authority to modify a child support order, UIFSA includes no affirmative provision, unlike the FFCCSOA. The FFCCSOA expressly requires, as a condition of any state court's authority to modify a child support order issued by a court of another state, that either both parties and the child have left the first state, or that both parties have filed a written consent to the second state's jurisdiction. 28 U.S.C.A. §1738B(e)(2). Neither condition is satisfied in this case.

If UIFSA does not provide an unambiguous resolution of jurisdiction to modify the Georgia child support order in this case, the FFCCSOA (§1738B(e)(2)) should control. And if the concluding paragraphs of the [three] New Jersey orders are deemed to declare New Jersey's jurisdiction to modify child support, such declarations would have been beyond the court's limited modification jurisdiction under the FFCCSOA or UIFSA. . . . I therefore read the concluding paragraphs of [these] orders more narrowly, consistent with both statutes, to hold that the New Jersey court will continue to enforce the Georgia judgment and to address custody and visitation issues, including the costs associated with interstate visitation.

. . . Thus the Georgia court has not lost the power to exercise its continuing, exclusive jurisdiction over child support by virtue of N.J.S.A. 2A:4-30.72b. There being no question that the Georgia divorce judgment included the first child support order, thereby establishing Georgia's continuing, exclusive jurisdiction, the New Jersey tribunal must recognize Georgia's jurisdiction. N.J.S.A. 2A:4-30.72d.

Moreover, there is no evidence in the record that plaintiff has ever sought to register the Georgia judgment in New Jersey in accordance with N.J.S.A. 2A:4-30.112,[14] which appears to require registration as a pre-requisite to seeking modification, but not enforcement, of a child support order. *Compare* N.J.S.A. 2A:4-30.104.[15] Neither party addresses those provisions of UIFSA concerning registration of a foreign judgment, and I do not rest my decision on that ground. But the difference between the permissive language of N.J.S.A. 2A:4-30.104 and the mandatory language of N.J.S.A. 2A:4-30.112 is a further indication that the

---

14. N.J.S.A. 2A:4-30.112 provides:

A party or support enforcement agency seeking to modify, or to modify and enforce, a child support order issued in another state shall register that order in this State in the same manner provided in sections 40 through 43 of this act if the order has not been registered. A complaint, petition or comparable pleading for modification may be filed at the same time as a request for registration, or later. The pleading must specify the grounds for modification.

(Emphasis added.)

15. N.J.S.A. 2A:4-30.104 provides:

A support order or an income-withholding order issued by a tribunal of another state may be registered in the State for enforcement.

(Emphasis added.)

uniform law intends to set a very different standard for jurisdiction to modify than for jurisdiction to enforce a child support order. . . .

A custodial parent in New Jersey, such as plaintiff, is not without a mechanism for modifying child support ordered by another state's court. Plaintiff retains the right under UIFSA to file a claim in New Jersey as the "initiating tribunal," N.J.S.A. 2A:4-30.73(a), asking that it forward her request to modify the original support order to Georgia as the "responding" tribunal, N.J.S.A. 2A:4-30.80(a)(1). I recognize that this procedure is likely to prove futile to plaintiff's claim for contribution to Julia's college expenses, because Georgia substantive law applies to a proceeding in which it is the "responding tribunal," *see* O.C.G.A. §19-11-111 and N.J.S.A. 2A:4-30.79a, and under Georgia law it appears that a court may not order a parent to contribute to the college education of a child who has reached the age of majority.

Philipp v. Stahl

798 A.2d 83 (N.J. 2002), *rev'g*, 781 A.2d 1065 (N.J. Super. Ct. App. Div. 2001)

Per Curiam.

The judgment of the Appellate Division is reversed, substantially for the reasons expressed in Judge Wecker's dissenting opinion, reported at 344 N.J. Super. at 274, 781 A.2d 1065 (2001).

Notes on
PHILIPP v. STAHL

1. A key point of disagreement between the majority and the dissent in the Superior Court in *Philipp v. Stahl* (and ultimately between the Supreme Court and the Superior Court majority) is whether the three New Jersey orders are modifications of the original Georgia order or merely incidental to enforcing the original Georgia order. Which is the better position? It seems clear that each of the New Jersey orders changed the original Georgia order to some extent. Shouldn't that amount to a modification? The Superior Court seemed to treat the word "modification" as a term of art, with special statutory meaning. Does the characterization ("modification" versus change incident to enforcement) depend on the degree of change, with the existence of a "modification" depending upon whether the original order was substantially altered? Does it matter whether the slight changes might have been incident to changes in custody?

2. Assuming that the majority of the New Jersey Superior Court was correct that the three New Jersey orders were "modifications," did the New Jersey courts have jurisdiction to enter those orders?

3. Since the Superior Court's decision in *Philipp v. Stahl*, the original version of UIFSA §205(a) (which was quoted in *Philipp v. Stahl* as N.J.S.A. 2A:4-30.72a) was amended. Consider whether this amendment might have changed how the court analyzed and decided the case:

(a) A tribunal of this state that has issued a child-support order consistent with the law of this state has and shall exercise continuing, exclusive jurisdiction to modify its child-support order if the order is the controlling order and:

(1) at the time of the filing of a request for modification this state is the residence of the obligor, the individual obligee, or the child for whose benefit the support order is issued; or

(2) even if this state is not the residence of the obligor, the individual obligee, or the child for whose benefit the support order is issued, the parties consent in a record or in open court that the tribunal of this state may continue to exercise jurisdiction to modify its order.

4. The UIFSA establishes the concept of the "one controlling order" of support. What happens when an F2 does not know that an F1 has issued a currently effective controlling order and thus issues its own? Presumably, the F2 order would be issued without jurisdiction and is unenforceable. But how would you counsel a client who finds herself subject to the F2 order? Would you tell her to ignore it? A more prudent approach would be to make a motion under the state court counterpart to Federal Rule of Civil Procedure 60(b), which allows for relief from a judgment that is void and issued out of mistake or inadvertence.

5. For foreign child support orders, negotiations were completed in 2007 on the Hague Convention on the Recovery of Child Support and Other Forms of Family Maintenance. Progress has been slow, however, for obtaining signatories and ratifications. For an overview of the Convention and its interaction with United States law, see, e.g., Mary Helen Carlson, *United States Perspective on the New Hague Convention on the International Recovery of Child Support and Other Forms of Family Maintenance*, 43 FAM. L.Q. 21 (2009); William Duncan, *The New Hague Child Support Convention: Goals and Outcomes of the Negotiations*, 43 FAM. L.Q. 1 (2009); Marilyn Ray Smith, *Child Support at Home and Abroad: Road to The Hague*, 43 FAM. L.Q. 37 (2009).

PROBLEM 4-16: CASSIE AND JØRGEN FIGHT OVER CHILD SUPPORT

Cassie and Jørgen were domiciled in State C when they obtained their divorce there. According to a decree issued in State C, Cassie must pay Jørgen $1,000 monthly child support for their two very young children. Cassie stopped paying support under the decree after she moved to State E. Jørgen registered the State C decree in State E, asking the State E court to enforce the decree and enter an order for the past payments due under the original State C decree.

Cassie is currently unemployed and therefore asked the State E court for two-part relief: (1) a reprieve from paying past due payments until she has a new job; and

(2) to reduce the payments due in the future to $500 per month until the children are emancipated. State E and State C both have enacted versions of the UIFSA. Should the State E court provide all or part of the relief Cassie requests?

PROBLEM 4-17: LAWRENCE AND JILL STRUGGLE OVER COLLEGE EDUCATION

Lawrence and Jill had two children, Older and Younger. Lawrence and Jill divorced in Pennsylvania. Jill received custody of Older and Younger, and a Pennsylvania court issued a child support order at that time, providing that Lawrence was required to pay $1,000 per month for each child until the child became emancipated. Thereafter all four of them moved to New Jersey. Jill and Lawrence then entered into a consent order in New Jersey recalculating the support of Younger in anticipation of the upcoming emancipation of Older. That consent order, which was entered as a judgment, stated that "nothing herein shall be construed to affect the nature, extent, or duration of the child support due under the laws of the Pennsylvania."

Once Older turned 18, Lawrence filed a motion in New Jersey for Older to be declared emancipated. Jill filed a countermotion for Older to be declared "unemancipiated" and to require Lawrence to contribute to Older's college tuition, an obligatory parental responsibility under New Jersey law. Lawrence responded that the original Pennsylvania order should govern under the UIFSA and that Pennsylvania law should govern the emancipation issue. Pennsylvania law would relieve Lawrence of a parental obligation to contribute to college tuition and would support a declaration that Older was "emancipated." New Jersey law would support Jill's countermotion. Should the New Jersey court grant Lawrence's motion or Jill's countermotion?

E. RECOGNITION AND ENFORCEMENT OF FOREIGN COUNTRY JUDGMENTS

As a starting point, a court's judgment does not have power beyond the boundaries of the jurisdiction that vests the court with authority. For judgments within the United States, the full faith and credit principle and preclusion doctrines ensure that judgments receive wide recognition among the various jurisdictions within the country. Foreign country judgments do not have this advantage.

In the international context, judgments from a foreign jurisdiction have force only if courts are willing to recognize and enforce a judgment. As with domestic United States judgments, the distinction between recognition and enforcement is important: recognition integrates concepts akin to domestic principles of claim and issue preclusion, while enforcement involves a court's use of its coercive power to compel a defendant to honor and satisfy a foreign country judgment. The act of requesting a court to recognize a foreign judgment is sometimes called "domesticating" a judgment. Under current legal principles, once a plaintiff has convinced one United States court to recognize a judgment, the plaintiff may take the judgment to another jurisdiction to enforce it and can assume that all United States courts must enforce the judgment once it has been domesticated.[20]

No uniform federal standard governs recognition and enforcement of foreign country judgments. Although the American Law Institute proposed the Foreign Judgments Recognition and Enforcement Act in 2005, Congress failed to enact it into law. Attempts to form treaties regarding mutual enforcement of judgments have also been unsuccessful.[21] The Hague Choice of Court Agreements Convention does provide for recognition of judgments entered by courts specified by parties in forum selection clauses — and to that extent, preempts contrary rules of state common law.[22] With exceptions, the Convention would require the court of one signatory country to enforce a judgment rendered by another signatory country. Nonetheless, most nations, including the United States, have not ratified the Convention.

Without a direct source of federal law, the matter of foreign country judgment recognition and enforcement has been left largely to state law. As you review the materials below, think about whether or not this allocation of authority is appropriate — or whether federal law would better govern the area. Regardless of its wisdom, the dominance of state law has yielded less variety and complication than one might expect. Many states have common law principles that derive in part from the case that immediately follows, *Hilton v. Guyot*. Others have enacted a uniform law, either the Uniform Foreign Money-Judgments Recognition Act (an earlier version of the uniform law) or the Uniform Foreign-Country Money Judgments Recognition Act (a later version of the uniform law). These state laws are discussed in detail following *Hilton v. Guyot* in the Perspective on State Laws Governing Recognition and Enforcement of Foreign Country Judgments.

Recall the discussion in the beginning of this chapter of the various value clashes pertaining to judgment recognition and enforcement among states of the United States. The narrative recounted how the decision-making process for domestic judgment recognition and enforcement reflects a two-dimensional tension with tradeoffs pertaining to sovereignty and cooperation, as well as tradeoffs implicating such values as accuracy and finality. Questions about international judgment recognition and enforcement also involve these tensions. But further complications emerge in the international context. These complications might be considered as part of a third *and* possibly fourth dimension: questions concerning the appropriate role for courts in the foreign affairs area (Figure

---

20. *See* Gregory H. Shill, *Ending Judgment Arbitrage: Jurisdictional Competition and the Enforcement of Foreign Money Judgments in the United States*, 54 HARV. INT'L L.J. 459 (2013), for a discussion of the consequences of this dislocation of recognition and enforcement.

21. For helpful discussion of some the problems encountered with attempts to devise an international convention on recognition and enforcement of foreign country judgments, see *Simona Grossi, Rethinking the Harmonization of Jurisdictional Rules*, 86 TUL. L. REV. 623 (2012).

22. For discussions of this Convention's relationship with foreign country judgment enforcement, see, e.g., Stephen B. Burbank, *A Tea Party at the Hague?*, 18 SW. J. INT'L L. 101, 114-115 (2012); Walter W. Heiser, *The Hague Convention on Choice of Court Agreements: The Impact on Forum Non Conveniens, Transfer of Venue, Removal, and Recognition of Judgments in United States Courts*, 31 U. PA. J. INT'L L. 1013, 1013-1032 (2010).

4-3) as well as questions about federalism and preemption (Figure 4-4). These concerns might be represented by third and fourth axes reflecting opposing values. One cannot depict the interaction among these four axes on a two-dimensional space. (Sophisticated computer software and higher-level mathematic concepts might capture how the four dimensions interact, but not the flat page of a book or computer screen.) The point, however, is that the various tensions for international recognition and enforcement of judgments integrate multiple variables that might be understood using the three figures below. Consider whether the cases and statutory law adequately account for each of these variables — and evaluate where you would chart the cases and statutes.

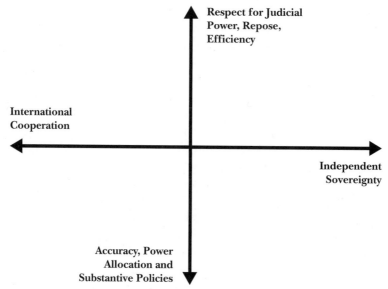

Figure 4-3: Value Clashes at Issue in International Judgment Recognition Cases

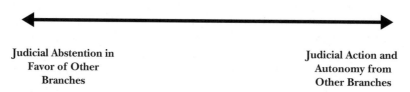

Figure 4-4: Separation of Powers Concerns in International Judgment Recognition Cases

Figure 4-5: Federalism Concerns in International Judgment Recognition Cases

1. General Principles

Hilton v. Guyot

159 U.S. 113 (1895)

Mr. Justice GRAY . . . delivered the opinion of the court.

[Guyot, a French citizen, sought to enforce a French court judgment in United States courts against two New York residents, Hilton and Libby. The New Yorkers had traded in Paris and owed accounts to a French firm that had been liquidated by Guyot.]

. . . No law has any effect, of its own force, beyond the limits of the sovereignty from which its authority is derived. The extent to which the law of one nation, as put in force within its territory, whether by executive order, by legislative act, or by judicial decree, shall be allowed to operate within the dominion of another nation, depends upon what our greatest jurists have been content to call "the comity of nations." Although the phrase has been often criticised, no satisfactory substitute has been suggested.

"Comity," in the legal sense, is neither a matter of absolute obligation, on the one hand, nor of mere courtesy and good will, upon the other. But it is the recognition which one nation allows within its territory to the legislative, executive or judicial acts of another nation, having due regard both to international duty and convenience, and to the rights of its own citizens, or of other persons who are under the protection of its laws. . . .

. . . It is important to distinguish different kinds of judgments. Every foreign judgment, of whatever nature, in order to be entitled to any effect, must have been rendered by a court having jurisdiction of the cause, and upon regular proceedings, and due notice. In alluding to different kinds of judgments, therefore, such jurisdiction, proceedings, and notice will be assumed. It will also be assumed that they are untainted by fraud, the effect of which will be considered later.

A judgment in rem, adjudicating the title to a ship or other movable property within the custody of the court, is treated as valid everywhere. . . . A judgment affecting the status of persons, such as a decree confirming or dissolving a marriage, is recognized as valid in every country, unless contrary to the policy of its own law. . . .

Other judgments, not strictly in rem, under which a person has been compelled to pay money, are so far conclusive that the justice of the payment cannot be impeached in another country, so as to compel him to pay it again. For instance, a judgment in foreign attachment is conclusive, as between the parties, of the right to the property or money attached. . . . Other foreign judgments which have been held conclusive of the matter adjudged were judgments discharging obligations contracted in the foreign country between citizens or residents thereof. . . .

The extraterritorial effect of judgments in personam, at law, or in equity may differ, according to the parties to the cause. A judgment of that kind between two citizens or residents of the country, and thereby subject to the jurisdiction in which it is rendered, may be held conclusive as between them everywhere. So, if a foreigner invokes the jurisdiction by bringing an action against a citizen, both may be held bound by a judgment in favor of either; and if a citizen sues a foreigner, and judgment is rendered in favor of the latter, both may be held equally bound. . . .

The effect to which a judgment, purely executory, rendered in favor of a citizen or resident of the country, in a suit there brought by him against a foreigner, may be entitled in an action thereon against the latter in his own country, as is the case now before us, presents a more difficult question, upon which there has been some diversity of opinion. . . .

[W]e are satisfied that where there has been opportunity for a full and fair trial abroad before a court of competent jurisdiction, conducting the trial upon regular proceedings, after due citation or voluntary appearance of the defendant, and under a system of jurisprudence likely to secure an impartial administration of justice between the citizens of its own country and those of other countries, and there is nothing to show either prejudice in the court, or in the system of laws under which it was sitting, or fraud in procuring the judgment, or any other special reason why the comity of this nation should not allow it[s] full effect, the merits of the case should not, in an action brought in this country upon the judgment, be tried afresh, as on a new trial or an appeal, upon the mere assertion of the party that the judgment was erroneous in law or in fact. The defendants, therefore, cannot be permitted, upon that general ground, to contest the validity or the effect of the judgment sued on.

But they have sought to impeach that judgment upon several other grounds, which require separate consideration.

It is objected that the appearance and litigation of the defendants in the French tribunals were not voluntary, but by legal compulsion, and, therefore, that the French courts never acquired such jurisdiction over the defendants that they should be held bound by the judgment. [We nevertheless conclude that the French court had personal jurisdiction over the defendants.] . . .

It is next objected that in those courts one of the plaintiffs was permitted to testify not under oath, and was not subjected to cross-examination by the opposite party, and that the defendants were therefore deprived of safeguards which are by our law considered essential to secure honesty and to detect fraud in a witness; and also that documents and papers were admitted in evidence, with which the defendants had no connection, and which would not be admissible under our own system of jurisprudence. But it having been shown by the plaintiffs, and hardly denied by the defendants, that the practice followed and the method of examining witnesses were according to the laws of France, we are not prepared to hold that the fact that the procedure in these respects differed from that of our own courts is, of itself, a sufficient ground for impeaching the foreign judgment. . . .

When an action is brought in a court of this country, by a citizen of a foreign country against one of our own citizens, to recover a sum of money adjudged by a court of that country to be due from the defendant to the plaintiff, and the foreign judgment appears to have been rendered by a competent court, having jurisdiction of the cause and of the parties, and upon due allegations and proofs, and opportunity to defend against them, and its proceedings are according to the course of a civilized jurisprudence, and are stated in a clear and formal record, the judgment is prima facie evidence, at least, of the truth of the matter adjudged; and it should be held conclusive upon the merits tried in the foreign court, unless some special ground is shown for impeaching the judgment, as by showing that it was affected by fraud or prejudice, or that by the principles of international law, and by the comity of our own country, it should not be given full credit and effect. . . .

[I]t is unnecessary in this case to determine, because there is a distinct and independent ground upon which we are satisfied that the comity of our nation does not require us to give conclusive effect to the judgments of the courts of France; and that ground is the want of reciprocity, on the part of France, as to the effect to be given to the judgments of this and other foreign countries. . . .

The defendants . . . alleged, and . . . offered to prove, that by the construction given to these statutes by the judicial tribunals of France, when the judgments of tribunals of foreign countries against the citizens of France are sued upon in the courts of France, the merits of the controversies upon which those judgments are based are examined anew, unless a treaty to the contrary effect exists between the republic of France and the country in which such judgment is obtained (which is not the case between the republic of France and the United States), and that the tribunals of the republic of France give no force and effect, within the jurisdiction of that country, to the judgments duly rendered by courts of competent jurisdiction of the United States against citizens of France after proper personal service of the process of those courts has been made thereon in this country. We are of opinion that this evidence should have been admitted. . . . The reasonable, if not the necessary, conclusion appears to us to be that judgments rendered in France, or in any other foreign country, by the laws of which our own judgments are reviewable upon the merits, are not entitled to full credit and conclusive effect when sued upon in this country, but are prima facie evidence only of the justice of the plaintiffs' claim.

In holding such a judgment, for want of reciprocity, not to be conclusive evidence of the merits of the claim, we do not proceed upon any theory of retaliation upon one person by reason of injustice done to another, but upon the broad ground that international law is founded upon mutuality and reciprocity, and that by the principles of international law recognized in most civilized nations, and by the comity of our own country, which it is our judicial duty to known and to declare, the judgment is not entitled to be considered conclusive.

By our law, at the time of the adoption of the constitution, a foreign judgment was considered as prima facie evidence, and not conclusive. There is no statute of the United States, and no treaty of the United States with France, or with any other nation, which has changed that law, or has made any provision upon the subject. It is not to be supposed that, if any statute or treaty had been or should be made, it would recognize as conclusive the judgments of any country, which did not give like effect to our own judgments. In the absence of statute or treaty, it appears to us equally unwarrantable to assume that the comity of the United States requires anything more.

If we should hold this judgment to be conclusive, we should allow it an effect to which, supposing the defendants' offers to be sustained by actual proof, it would, in the absence of a special treaty, be entitled in hardly any other country in Christendom, except the country in which it was rendered. If the judgment had been rendered in this country, or in any other outside of the jurisdiction of France, the French courts would not have executed or enforced it, except after examining into its merits. The very judgment now sued on would be held inconclusive in almost any other country than France. In England, and in the colonies subject to the law of England, the fraud alleged in its procurement would be a sufficient ground for disregarding it. In the courts of nearly every other nation, it would be subject to re-examination, either merely because it was a foreign judgment, or because judgments of that nation would be reexaminable in the courts of France.

[Refusing to enforce the French judgment without further inquiry, the Court therefore reversed the judgment of the lower court and remanded for further proceedings.

Chief Justice Fuller, joined by Justices Harlan, Brewer, and Jackson dissented on the ground that res judicata should apply to both domestic and international judgments. Chief Justice Fuller rejected the reciprocity notion, and admonished that it is not for other branches of the United States government to identify circumstances where it is appropriate to "to adopt the principle of retorsion."]

Notes on
HILTON v. GUYOT *AND THE EVOLUTION OF DOCTRINES GOVERNING RECOGNITION AND ENFORCEMENT OF FOREIGN COUNTRY JUDGMENTS*

1. *Hilton* is regarded as the leading United States case on recognition and enforcement of foreign country judgments. As you will see in the notes and materials below, however, it is far from the last word on the matter. The *Hilton* Court starts with a presumption or orientation toward recognition of foreign country judgments. What is the Court's basis for this approach? Is it markedly different from the full faith and credit principle governing domestic judgments? Should it be markedly different than the full faith and credit principle?

2. International law authorities have not generally found a historical basis for international judgment recognition in international law. *See, e.g.*, Restatement (Third) Foreign Relations Law §481, note 6 ("There is no uniformity of practice among foreign states in regard to recognition of judgments of other states."). The *Hilton* Court mentions international comity — a term one sees in the context of international choice of laws, forum non conveniens, and the like. But is international comity a controlling force in these contexts? Is it a concept with determinate meaning? *See, e.g.*, Michael D. Ramsey, *Escaping "International Comity,"* 83 Iowa L. Rev. 893, 893 (1998) (stating that international comity "is an expression of unexplained authority, imprecise meaning and uncertain application").

3. Is there a theoretical basis for recognizing a foreign country judgment aside from comity or hospitality? One might evoke a normative law and economics rationale that the orientation toward comity serves to facilitate international commercial intercourse by making interactions stable and

predictable. Courtland H. Peterson, *Res Judicata and Foreign Country Judgments*, 24 OHIO ST. L.J. 291, 307 (1963). *But see* Hans Smit, *International Res Judicata and Collateral Estoppel in the United States*, 9 UCLA L. REV. 44, 56 (1962).

Consider also the theoretical foundations of choice of law: different methodologies derived from different starting assumptions about the nature and purpose of law. The same occurs with different approaches to foreign country judgment recognition and enforcement. For example, the Restatement (First) of Conflict of Laws proposed a territorially based foundation: stating that a foreign country judgment creates a vested right meriting enforcement wherever the judgment debtor or her property can be found. Restatement (First) of Conflict of Laws §§429, 430, 434. The Restatement (Second) of Conflict of Laws takes an approach that is characteristic of its own orientation and structure: adopting some of the same general rules as the Restatement (First) and also incorporating some of the *Hilton v. Guyot* principles. Restatement (Second) of Conflict of Laws §98. For a theoretical foundation, the Restatement (Second) §98 provides that recognition of foreign country judgments rests on the public interest need "that there be an end of litigation." What value relevant to international judgment recognition does this emphasize?

4. Comity and hospitality toward foreign country judgments do not explain the bottom line result of *Hilton*. The Court suggested that fraud, lack of personal jurisdiction, or a due process problem might interfere with enforcement, although the Court did not find those present in the case and even graciously excused evidentiary deviations from United States practice. More fundamentally, the Court qualified its rule with a reciprocity principle: a United States court should recognize foreign country judgments only if the foreign country had the policy of recognizing and enforcing the judgments of United States courts under similar circumstances. Should this principle have been allowed to negate the orientation toward comity?

This reciprocity principle does not resonate with the usual approach to conflict of laws matters that we have seen in the book. For example, one does not usually see any reciprocity analysis in choice of law or personal jurisdiction matters. Isn't it particularly odd to see the principle in the context of judgment recognition and enforcement? Aren't there usually fewer qualifications (rather than more qualifications) to the recognition of another sovereign's authority when it comes to judgments? For a law and economics analysis of the reciprocity requirement, see Yaad Rotem, *The Problem of Selective or Sporadic Recognition: A New Economic Rationale for the Law of Foreign Country Judgments*, 10 CHI. J. INT'L L. 505 (2010).

5. Although the *Hilton* approach has proven vigorous as a general matter, the reciprocity component of the decision has not worn as well. The reciprocity rule has receded in United States doctrines governing foreign country judgment recognition. For example, the Restatement (Second)

of Conflict of Laws §98 does not incorporate it, stating that the United States will recognize "[a] valid judgment rendered in a foreign nation after a fair trial in a contested proceeding" for the purposes of the "immediate parties and the underlying cause of action." *See also* Restatement of Foreign Relations §481 cmt. d (1987) (stating that "[t]hough [*Hilton's* reciprocity requirement] has not been formally overruled, it is no longer followed in the great majority of State and federal courts ...").

Some courts, however, still embrace or defer to a reciprocity principle, and some states have incorporated a reciprocity principle in their state statutes governing foreign country judgment recognition. *See, e.g., Evans Cabinet Corp. v. Kitchen Int'l, Inc.,* 593 F.3d 135, 142 (1st Cir. 2010) (observing that litigants had not "suggested that the district court ought to have followed a rule other than that of Massachusetts. In any event, even if the reciprocity rule of *Hilton v. Guyot* were applicable under the facts of this case, the Massachusetts rule of recognition and enforcement also contains a reciprocity requirement"); *Osorio v. Dole Food Co.,* 665 F. Supp. 2d 1307, 1323 (S.D. Fla. 2009), *aff'd sub nom. Osorio v. Dow Chem. Co.,* 635 F.3d 1277 (11th Cir. 2011), *cert. denied,* 312 S. Ct. 1045 (2012) (observing that Florida Recognition Act attempts to guarantee the recognition of Florida judgments in foreign countries by providing reciprocity in Florida for judgments rendered abroad and attempts to preclude Florida courts from recognizing foreign country judgments in certain prescribed cases where the legislature has determined that enforcement would be unjust or inequitable to domestic defendants); *Gordon & Breach Science Publishers S.A. v. Am. Inst. of Physics,* 905 F. Supp. 169, 179 (S.D.N.Y. 1995) (refusing in Lanham Act suit to give collateral estoppel effect to Swiss and German judgments against the plaintiffs and stating "lack of reciprocity" as one reason for decision); *Charara v. Yatim,* 937 N.E.2d 490, 497 (Mass. App. Ct. 2010) (considering citizenship and reciprocity as matters bearing on the question of deference to a foreign nation's custody order). Echoing these legislative and statutory developments, the proposed American Law Institute statute also contains a reciprocity requirement, making lack of reciprocity a mandatory basis for non-recognition.

Is the reciprocity principle consistent with current attitudes about globalism?

6. The dissent in *Hilton* thought that the preclusion principles (such as res judicata) should govern the question of foreign country judgment recognition. Scholars have not universally embraced this view. *See, e.g.,* Arthur von Mehran & Donald T. Trautman, *Recognition of Foreign Adjudications: A Survey and a Suggested Approach,* 81 HARV. L REV. 1601 (1968); Willis Reese, *The Status in This Country of Judgments Rendered Abroad,* 50 COLUM. L. REV. 783, 793 (1950).

7. The dissent was also uncomfortable with the reciprocity principle, both on the merits and on the basis of separation of powers. The dissent suggested that it was for other branches of government, not the judiciary,

to make a decision as to whether "to adopt the principle of retorsion" — a principle that encourages a nation to perpetuate an act upon another nation in retaliation for a similar act perpetrated by the other nation. Do you agree with the dissent on this separation of powers concern? The question of whether the judiciary should be in the business of embracing such notions is reflected in Figure 4-4 above. What are the arguments that the judiciary should steer clear of such judgments? What are the arguments that a court is capable of handling decisions about reciprocity? Although the matter implicates foreign affairs, doesn't it also go to the core of what judges do all the time: resolve specific disputes between specific parties in the form of judgments? Professors Stephen Burbank, Linda J. Silberman, and Andreas Lowenfeld have contributed much to the principle that the judiciary is well willing and able to evaluate the appropriate scope of its own judgments in the international context. *See, e.g.*, Stephen B. Burbank, *The Reluctant Partner: Making Procedural Law for International Civil Litigation*, 57 LAW & CONTEMP. PROBS. 103 (1994); Linda J. Silberman & Andreas F. Lowenfeld, *A Different Challenge for the ALI: Herein of Foreign Country Judgments, an International Treaty, and an American Statute*, 75 IND. L.J. 635 (2000).

8. *Hilton* was a diversity case decided well before *Erie R.R. v. Tompkins*, and thus does not address the issue whether state or federal law should govern the international recognition and enforcement of judgments questions. To the extent the decision hints at the answer, *Hilton* seemed to suggest it was a federal law matter. *See* Robert L. McFarland, *Federalism, Finality, and Foreign Judgments: Examining the ALI Judgments Project's Proposed Federal Foreign Judgments Statute*, 45 NEW ENG. L. REV. 63, 80 (2010). Since *Erie*, however, state and federal courts have largely assumed state law governs the matter.

The ALI Judgment project sought to ensure that federal law governs recognition and enforcement of foreign country judgments, but has not yet been successful in implementing that aspiration. A rich body of scholarly material also reckons with the issues arising from state law dominance in this area. *See, e.g.*, Ronald A. Brand, *Enforcement of Foreign Money-Judgments in the United States: In Search of Uniformity and International Acceptance*, 67 NOTRE DAME L. REV. 253 (1991).

The federalism implications of international judgments are reflected in Figure 4-5, and might explicitly or implicitly affect a court's disposition to shroud the judgment recognition question with judicial doctrine. What are the arguments in favor of federal regulation? Are there countervailing arguments in favor of state regulation? For better or worse, state regulation has taken the lead. State law developments in implementing and refining *Hilton* are described in the note that follows after a few straightforward problems.

PROBLEM 4-18: GRAHAM'S ART PURCHASE

The country of South Creativity has a well-developed procedural system followed by its courts, which routinely enforce the judgments of United States courts. While in South Creativity, Graham bought a painting from Krishan. In addition to paying the cost of the painting, Graham paid Krishan to wrap the painting carefully and post it to the United States. When the painting arrived, it was badly damaged, as Krishan had not made any efforts to protect the painting from the usual battering it was likely to receive in the international post. Graham filed suit against Krishan for breach of contract in South Creativity courts, but his lawsuit was dismissed immediately for failure of Graham to serve Krishan with process in accordance with the specific rules of the South Creativity courts.

Graham has now filed a suit in a state court in the United States, and this time has served Krishan properly. Krishan nonetheless moved to dismiss the suit, arguing that Graham is foreclosed from relitigating the claim and that the state court should recognize the judgment of dismissal of the South Creativity courts. Should the state court grant Krishan's motion under the principles set forth in *Hilton v. Guyot*?

PROBLEM 4-19: SUING FOR WAGES IN BARA

Elaine is a United States citizen who was employed as a journalist for a newspaper in the country of Bara. After a military coup in the Bara, the new head of the country staffed Bara courts with individuals who took the following oath: "I promise to administer justice in the interest of the people of Bara and to denounce any connections with the United States of America. Because the United States is infected with injustice, I disavow any influence from American citizens or American law." All the judges in Bara took this oath. Elaine was owed a salary payment from the newspaper where she worked and filed suit in Bara court. The case was heard as a bench trial and the Bara judge who adjudicated the case entertained a range of evidence, including testimony that would have been considered hearsay under United States evidentiary rules. The judge entered judgment in favor of the newspaper.

Elaine has filed a new suit against the newspaper in state court in the United States. Because the newspaper has a large circulation throughout the state, the state court has personal jurisdiction over the newspaper. Nonetheless, the newspaper has moved to dismiss the suit on the basis of the Bara judgment. Should the state court recognize the Bara judgment under the principles of *Hilton v. Guyot*?

PROBLEM 4-20: PROTECTIVE STATE PROTECTS ITS OWN

A State of the United States, Protective State, has passed a statute that provides a state court may decline to recognize and enforce a judgment of a foreign country if any of the following circumstances are met: (1) the judgment is rendered against any United States defendant; (2) the judgment was rendered by a country, which in the opinion of the state court, is hostile to the interests of United States citizens; or (3) the judgment was rendered by a country, which in the opinion of the state court does not have a sufficient degree of democratic representation in its government. Are there any problems or difficulties with this approach?

PERSPECTIVE ON STATE LAW GOVERNING RECOGNITION AND ENFORCEMENT OF FOREIGN COUNTRY JUDGMENTS

Given the absence of governing federal law on recognition and enforcement of foreign country judgments, state law began to develop under the guidance of the Supreme Court's decision in *Hilton v. Guyot* and now largely governs the recognition and enforcement process. State law divides into two categories. On one hand are state common law principles patterned on *Hilton v. Guyot*, largely reflected in sections of the Restatement governing Conflict of Laws and Foreign Relations. On the other hand is uniform legislation, which also reflects the *Hilton v. Guyot* approach.

The Restatement (Second) of Conflict of Laws contains a spare statement on foreign country judgment recognition, providing only that "a valid judgment rendered in a foreign nation after a fair trial in a contested proceeding will be recognized in the United States." Restatement (Second) of Conflict of Laws §98. The comments to this section flesh out some of the terms of the section. For example, the comments point to *Hilton v. Guyot* for guidance on what is a fair trial. Likewise, the comments point to the Restatement provision governing domestic judgment validity for guidance on what is a valid foreign judgment. The Restatement (Third) of Foreign Relations largely tracks the requirements of the uniform acts, with one notable exception: section 482 of the Restatement (Third) requires that the personal jurisdiction standards of the rendering court must comply with both the Restatement (Third) *and* the law of the rendering state.

More than half the states have in place one of two uniform acts that govern in place of the Restatement standards: either the Uniform Foreign Money-Judgments Recognition Act (earlier Act or Act) or a revised version, the Uniform Foreign-Country Money Judgments Recognition Act (revised Act or Act). Both Acts are similar, with the revised Act simply clarifying the precision of some terms, filling in a few gaps, and adding exceptions that tend to favor judgment debtors. The Acts apply to foreign country judgments granting or denying a sum of money, and exclude judgments for taxes, fines, other penalties, and for matrimonial or family matters. For the purpose of the Acts' coverage, a foreign country includes a governmental unit other than the United States, a state, or other jurisdictional entities connected with the government of the United States (such as a territory or possession). The Acts provide filing procedures for a judgment creditor to domesticate a foreign country judgment and to provide notice to the judgment debtor of the docketing of the recognition and enforcement action. Most importantly, however, the Acts list defenses to recognition and enforcement.

Overview of Defenses. The following is a descriptive overview of the Acts' defenses; exact language of the earlier Act[23] and the Revised Act[24] appears in the footnotes below. For both the earlier and the revised Acts, the court *must* not recognize the foreign country judgment if one of the following is applicable:

- The system rendering the judgment lacked impartial tribunals or procedures incompatible with due process;
- The rendering tribunal lacked personal jurisdiction over the defendant; or
- The rendering tribunal lacked subject matter jurisdiction over the defendant.

23. Section 4 of the earlier Act provides:

(a) A foreign judgment is not conclusive if
   (1) the judgment was rendered under a system which does not provide impartial tribunals or procedures compatible with the requirements of due process of law;
   (2) the foreign court did not have personal jurisdiction over the defendant; or
   (3) the foreign court did not have jurisdiction over the subject matter.
(b) A foreign judgment need not be recognized if
   (1) the defendant in the proceedings in the foreign court did not receive notice of the proceedings in sufficient time to enable him to defend;
   (2) the judgment was obtained by fraud;
   (3) the [cause of action] [claim for relief] on which the judgment is based is repugnant to the public policy of this state;
   (4) the judgment conflicts with another final and conclusive judgment;
   (5) the proceeding in the foreign court was contrary to an agreement between the parties under which the dispute in question was to be settled otherwise than by proceedings in that court; or
   (6) in the case of jurisdiction based only on personal service, the foreign court was a seriously inconvenient forum for the trial of the action.

24. Section 4 of the Revised Act provides:

(b) A court of this state may not recognize a foreign-country judgment if:
   (1) the judgment was rendered under a judicial system that does not provide impartial tribunals or procedures compatible with the requirements of due process of law;
   (2) the foreign court did not have personal jurisdiction over the defendant; or
   (3) the foreign court did not have jurisdiction over the subject matter.
(c) A court of this state need not recognize a foreign-country judgment if:
   (1) the defendant in the proceeding in the foreign court did not receive notice of the proceeding in sufficient time to enable the defendant to defend;
   (2) the judgment was obtained by fraud that deprived the losing party of an adequate opportunity to present its case;
   (3) the judgment or the [cause of action] [claim for relief] on which the judgment is based is repugnant to the public policy of this state or of the United States;
   (4) the judgment conflicts with another final and conclusive judgment;
   (5) the proceeding in the foreign court was contrary to an agreement between the parties under which the dispute in question was to be determined otherwise than by proceedings in that foreign court;
   (6) in the case of jurisdiction based only on personal service, the foreign court was a seriously inconvenient forum for the trial of the action;
   (7) the judgment was rendered in circumstances that raise substantial doubt about the integrity of the rendering court with respect to the judgment; or
   (8) the specific proceeding in the foreign court leading to the judgment was not compatible with the requirements of due process of law.

Both Acts share the following six discretionary exceptions, allowing a court to decline to recognize a judgment:

- the judgment debtor did not receive notice of the proceeding in sufficient time to defend;
- the judgment was obtained by fraud;
- the judgment was based on a cause of action repugnant to the enforcing jurisdiction's public policy;[25]
- the judgment conflicts with another final and conclusive judgment;
- the proceeding in the foreign tribunal was contrary to an agreement between the parties under which their dispute was to be settled otherwise than by proceedings in that tribunal; or
- where personal service provided the basis for jurisdiction, the foreign country was a seriously inconvenient forum for trial.

The Revised Act has two additional exceptions, allowing a court to decline recognition under the following circumstances:

- the judgment was rendered in circumstances that raise substantial doubt about the integrity of the rendering court with respect to the judgment; or
- the specific proceeding in the foreign court leading to the judgment was not compatible with due process requirements.

These additional exceptions are significant because they signal a move away from deference to foreign country judgments, allowing judgment debtors more grounds for challenging foreign judgments.

Of the shared defenses in both the earlier and the revised Acts, fairness of the foreign proceeding, lack of jurisdiction, inadequate notice, and public policy are perhaps the most important. The remainder of this perspective provides greater deal on these important defenses.

Fairness of the Foreign Proceeding. Hilton v. Guyot stated that a United States court should not recognize foreign country judgments where there has not been "the full and fair opportunity for trial abroad before a court . . . conducting the trial upon regular proceedings . . . and under a system of jurisprudence likely to secure an impartial administration of justice between the citizens of its own country and those of other countries." The Acts incorporate this same principle through their reference to the requirement for impartial tribunals and due process standards. The term "due process" evokes the United States Constitution's due process clause, but the Acts do not require perfect overlap with United States standards. The procedures must be "compatible" with due process standards, not identical with such standards.

The Acts' due process exceptions are not as straightforward as it may seem. First is the question whether fairness should be evaluated on the basis of case-

25. Note the explanation later in this note of how this standard is slightly broader for the revised Act.

specific details or overall, systemic factors. Cases interpreting the older Act tended to emphasize system-wide problems. *See CIBC Mellon Trust Co. v. Mora Hotel Corp N.V.*, 792 N.E.2d 155, 160 (N.Y. 2003) (stating that "the relevant inquiry . . . is the overall fairness of [the foreign] legal system"), *and Society of Lloyd's v. Mullin*, 255 F. Supp. 2d 468, 472 (E.D. Pa. 2003) (rejecting the notion that the court should concentrate on the details of a specific proceeding, and concluding instead that the court should undertake a "panoramic examination" of the foreign system). The court in *Society of Lloyd's v. Ashenden*, 233 F.3d 473 (7th Cir. 2000), an opinion set forth after this Note, explains this panoramic, system-wide approach. Yet the more recent Act has injected a variation in the analysis: unlike the earlier Act, the later Act expressly invites case-specific inquiry, adding an exception that allows courts to decline enforcement if the "specific" foreign country proceeding was not "compatible with due process of law." Moreover, the cases under the earlier Act do not definitively answer whether an unequivocally impartial tribunal judge or a fundamentally unfair proceeding might impugn the fairness of the whole system. Questions also arise regarding whether fairness has both a substantive and procedural components. It is important to note that deviations such as these among standards of fairness in doctrines regulating transnational adjudication can cause confusion, uncertainty, and unanticipated results.[26]

Lack of Jurisdiction. The Acts require that the rendering tribunal have possessed personal and subject matter jurisdiction. A frequent question, however, is which law should govern the adequacy of jurisdiction: foreign or United States law. For subject matter jurisdiction, United States courts are fairly consistent in looking to foreign law. *See, e.g., S.C. Chimexim S.A. v. Velco Enterprises Ltd.*, 36 F. Supp. 2d 206 (S.D.N.Y. 1999) (applying statute similar to uniform acts, court looked to Romanian law to determine whether Bucharest Tribunal acted with proper subject matter jurisdiction). Of course, if the foreign tribunal exercised jurisdiction that is impermissibly extraterritorial in the view of the United States court, the United States court may not enforce the judgment even though the foreign court decided its exercise of power was proper under foreign law. *See, e.g., Osorio v. Dole Food Co.*, 665 F. Supp. 2d 1307 (S.D. Fla. 2009), *aff'd sub nom. Osorio v. Dow Chem. Co.*, 635 F.3d 1277 (11th Cir. 2011), *cert. denied*, 312 S. Ct. 1045 (2012)

---

26. One example pertains to the interaction with the tribunal adequacy standard for the forum non conveniens analysis. Professors Christopher A. Whytock and Cassandra Burke Robertson have observed that forum non conveniens analysis includes a generally more lenient foreign tribunal adequacy standard than that followed for enforcement of foreign country judgments. The result, they argue, creates a "transnational access to justice gap" with plaintiffs being denied United States court access under forum non conveniens doctrine and then later being denied enforcement of a foreign court's judgment in the United States. Christopher A. Whytock & Cassandra Burke Robertson, *Forum Non Conveniens and the Enforcement of Foreign Judgments*, 111 COLUM. L. REV. 1444 (2011).

Varieties among state foreign judgment recognition and enforcement laws can lead to extreme forum shopping as well. For a discussion of how plaintiffs can circumvent a state's limitation on foreign country judgment recognition by asking one state court to recognize a judgment and then requiring a court in another state to enforce that judgment even though the second state would not have originally recognized the judgment, see Gregory H. Shill, *Ending Judgment Arbitrage: Jurisdictional Competition and the Enforcement of Foreign Money Judgments in the United States*, 54 HARV. INT'L L.J. 429 (2013).

(concluding that foreign court lacked subject matter jurisdiction under foreign law even though the forum court had concluded that the statute governing the case was not jurisdictional).

The Acts attempt to provide more guidance on the standards governing personal jurisdiction. The Acts provide that personal jurisdiction is proper if based on personal service within the foreign state, voluntary appearance (other than to protect property or to contest personal jurisdiction), agreement between the parties, domicile, business office or place of business within the foreign country, or operation of an airplane or motor vehicle in the foreign country (for suits arising out of that operation). The Acts anticipate that United States law of personal jurisdiction will govern, although cases do exist where courts apply the law of the foreign jurisdiction or international standards to the question. *See, e.g., Monks Own, Ltd. v. Monastery of Christ in the Desert,* 168 P.3d 121 (N.M. 2007) (applying both foreign and United States standard); *Manches & Co. v. Gilbey,* 646 N.E.2d 86, 87 (Mass. 1995) (applying foreign standard).

One context in which United States courts consistently take a close look at the rendering court's personal jurisdiction is default judgments. Although in theory United States courts will enforce foreign default judgment, United States courts often find insufficient proof that the foreign court had personal jurisdiction over the defendant.

Inadequate Notice. On the issue of notice, the Acts speak in terms of whether the defendant received notice in sufficient time to respond. Although notice cases usually refer to the United States Constitution's standards, one wonders whether this was meant to be the governing standard since inadequate notice is a discretionary basis for non-recognition. One would expect a United States court would not believe itself at liberty to enforce a judgment obtained in violation of constitutional notice standards.

Public Policy. The earlier Act has a narrower public policy exception than the revised Act. The earlier Act permits non-recognition of a foreign country judgment if the "cause of action on which the judgment is based is repugnant to the public policy" of the enforcing state, while the revised Act allows non-recognition if the "judgment or the cause of action on which the judgment is based is repugnant to the public policy of this state or of the United States." As in other public policy exceptions, decisions are difficult, wide ranging, and lack uniformity. Contexts range from attorneys' fees to usury and libel. These later two contexts are set forth in detail in the sections that follow. Moreover, the *Southwest Livestock & Trucking Co. v. Ramón* decision, which is presented in the public policy section below, explores the narrowness of the earlier Act's language.

Exceptions as Defenses Only. Under the current state of the law, the exceptions to recognizing a foreign country judgment for both Acts can serve only as defenses raised after a judgment creditor seeks to enforce the judgment. In much-watched litigation, Chevron Texaco had attempted to transform the exceptions from shields against judgment recognition into swords. Specifically, Chevron Texaco, as a potential judgment debtor, sought an anti-enforcement injunction against a judgment rendered by an Ecuadorian court. Chevron Texaco had convinced a United States District Court to enjoin the potential judgment creditors from attempting to enforce the allegedly fraudulent Ecuadorian judgment. The United States Court of Appeals for the Second Circuit reversed, however, holding that New York's version of the Uniform Foreign Country Money-Judgments Recognition Act did not authorize this kind of affirmative relief, but instead only recognized the fraud allegation as defense once the would-be judgment-creditor attempted recognition and enforcement.[27]

PROBLEM 4-21: A FOREIGN COUNTRY JUDGMENT AGAINST ROBIN

Robin is a citizen of the United States, but travels often to other countries in the world. While in the country of New Australia, he got drunk one night and assaulted Mel. Robin left New Australia and decided that he wanted to quit drinking alcohol. He therefore checked himself into a detoxication facility in New India. While he was there, Mel filed a tort action against Robin in New Australia. Rather than provide Robin with personal service, Mel simply posted a notice on a docket blog for the New Australia Court. Robin never saw the notice, and a default judgment was entered against him for Mel's doctor bills as well as his pain and suffering.

Robin has come back to the United States and settled back into his home state of New Kentucky, which has enacted the Uniform Foreign-Country Money Judgments Recognition Act. Mel seeks to have the New Kentucky court recognize and enforce the New Australia judgment against Robin's New Kentucky assets. Do you see any obstacles to the court granting his request?

As mentioned in the Perspective on State Law Governing Recognition and Enforcement of Foreign Country Judgments, the uniform state laws contain a number of mandatory and discretionary exceptions to enforcing foreign country judgments. Two particularly significant exceptions—focusing alternatively on the fairness of the foreign judicial system and the public policy of the enforcing court—are explored in greater detail in the next two sections.

2. The Foreign Judicial System Fairness Exception

The Society of Lloyd's v. Ashenden
233 F.3d 473 (7th Cir. 2000)

POSNER, Circuit Judge.

These are diversity suits brought . . . by Lloyd's, a foreign corporation against American members ("names") of insurance syndicates that Lloyd's manages. Lloyd's wanted to use the Illinois Uniform Foreign Money-Judgments

---

27. See Chevron Corp. v. Donziger, 768 F. Supp. 2d 581 (S.D.N.Y. 2011), reversed and remanded sub nom. Chevron Corp. v. Naranjo, 667 F.3d 232 (2d Cir. 2012).

Recognition Act . . . to collect money judgments, each for several hundred thousand dollars, that it had obtained against the defendants in an English court after the names' repeated efforts in earlier litigation to knock out the forum-selection clause in their contracts with Lloyd's had failed. Pursuant to this strategy, Lloyd's filed the judgments in the district court and then issued "citations" pursuant to the Illinois procedure for executing a judgment. The filing of the judgments inaugurated this federal-court proceeding to collect them; and state law, in this case the Illinois citations statute[,] supplies the procedure for executing a federal-court judgment.

The defendants . . . argued that those judgments had denied them due process of law and therefore were not enforceable under the foreign money-judgments recognition act, which makes a judgment rendered by a court outside the United States unenforceable in Illinois if "the judgment was rendered under a *system* which does not provide impartial tribunals or procedures compatible with the requirements of due process of law." . . . We have italicized the word that defeats the defendants' argument. . . . Any suggestion that [the English] system of courts "does not provide impartial tribunals or procedures compatible with the requirements of due process of law" borders on the risible. "[T]he courts of England are fair and neutral forums." . . . The origins of our concept of due process of law are English, . . . and the English courts . . . are highly regarded for impartiality, professionalism, and scrupulous regard for procedural rights. . . .

Not that the English concept of fair procedure is identical to ours; but we cannot believe that the Illinois statute is intended to bar the enforcement of all judgments of any foreign legal system that does not conform its procedural doctrines to the latest twist and turn of our courts regarding, for example, the circumstances under which due process requires an opportunity for a hearing in advance of the deprivation of a substantive right rather than afterwards. It is a fair guess that no foreign nation has decided to incorporate our due process doctrines into its own procedural law; and so we interpret "due process" in the Illinois statute (which, remember, is a uniform act, not one intended to reflect the idiosyncratic jurisprudence of a particular state) to refer to a concept of fair procedure simple and basic enough to describe the judicial processes of civilized nations, our peers. The statute requires only that the foreign procedure be "compatible with the requirements of due process of law," and we have interpreted this to mean that the foreign procedures are "fundamentally fair" and do not offend against "basic fairness."

We'll call this the "international concept of due process" to distinguish it from the complex concept that has emerged from American case law. We note that it is even less demanding than the test the courts use to determine whether to enforce a foreign arbitral award under the New York Convention. . . .

Rather than trying to impugn the English legal system en gross, the defendants argue that the Illinois statute requires us to determine whether the particular judgments that they are challenging were issued in proceedings that conform to the requirements of due process of law as it has come to be understood in the case law of Illinois and other American jurisdictions. The statute, with its reference to "system," does not support such a retail approach, which would moreover be inconsistent with providing a streamlined, expeditious method for collecting money judgments rendered by courts in other jurisdictions—which would in effect give the judgment creditor a further appeal on the merits. The process of collecting a judgment is not meant to require a second lawsuit, thus converting every successful multinational suit for damages into two suits (actually three, as we'll see at the end of this opinion). But that is the implication of the defendants' argument. They claim to be free to object in the collection phase of the case to the procedures employed at the merits phase, even though they were free to challenge those procedures at that phase and indeed did so.

Even if the retail approach is valid—and we want to emphasize our belief that it is not—it cannot possibly avail the defendants here unless they are right that the approach requires subjecting the foreign proceeding to the specifics of the American doctrine of due process. They are not right. . . . In a case decided by a foreign court system that has not adopted every jot and tittle of American due process (and no foreign court system has, to our knowledge, done that), it will be sheer accident that a particular proceeding happened to conform in every particular to our complex understanding of due process. So even the retail approach, in order to get within miles of being reasonable, would have to content itself with requiring foreign conformity to the international concept of due process.

And now let us for the sake of completeness apply that concept to the particulars of these judgments. . . . In the English court the defendants opposed Lloyd's suit on the basis of two clauses which they contend would, if enforced, deny them due process of law; and they renew the contention here. The first clause, the "pay now sue later" clause as the parties call it, forbids names, in suits (such as the ones before us) by Lloyd's to collect the assessment, to set off against the claim by Lloyd's any claim the names might have against Lloyd's, such as a claim that the contract had been induced by fraud. If they want to press such a claim they have to file a separate suit. The second clause, the "conclusive evidence" clause, makes Lloyd's determination of the amount of the assessment "conclusive" "in the absence of manifest error." The defendants claim that the High Court refused to order Lloyd's to provide them with enough information about how the assessment had been calculated to enable them to prove manifest error. . . .

The pay now sue later clause was designed to enable [to facilitate financial security for Lloyds]. That would work to the benefit of the names by giving them surer, earlier, and fuller reinsurance. In exchange it was reasonable to ask them to postpone the enforcement of any claims they might have against Lloyd's. . . . [T]his procedure ("pay now, dispute later," id.) has survived due process challenge. Anyway the question is not whether Lloyd's accorded due process to the names, but whether the English courts did. All they did was enforce the clause, and they did so on the basis of an interpretation of a provision of the original contract between the names and Lloyd's that authorized Lloyd's to take measures unilaterally to prevent the society from failing. Stated differently, the courts held that the names had waived their procedural rights in advance, thus bringing the case within the rule of *D.H. Overmyer Co. v. Frick Co.*, 405 U.S. 174 (1972)....

[A] one-sided contract is a substantive, not a procedural, offense. (Nor ... is an unreasonable contractual interpretation a procedural violation.) The names were free both to challenge the [contract] and to show if they could "manifest error" in the assessment of their liability under it. They could not show this, but only because manifest error is hard to prove.... Their real objection to the exclusive-evidence clause, moreover, is that it curtails pretrial discovery, and the right to pretrial discovery is not a part of the U.S. concept of due process.... We conclude that the judgments are enforceable under the foreign money-judgments statute....

Notes on
SOCIETY OF LLOYD'S v. ASHENDEN

1. The fairness exception explored in *Society of Lloyd's v. Ashenden* is one of the mandatory exceptions to the general obligation to enforce foreign money judgments set forth in both the Uniform Foreign Money-Judgments Recognition Act (earlier Act) and the revised version, the Uniform Foreign-Country Money Judgments Recognition Act (revised Act). The version of the Act at issue in *Lloyd's* was the earlier Act. This is significant because — as outlined above in the Notes on State Law Governing Recognition and Enforcement of Foreign Country Judgments — the revised Act has a discretionary exception that allows the court to refuse enforcement if the specific procedures followed in the case were unfair.

2. As Judge Posner observes, foreign procedures do not need to mirror United States procedures to be deemed fair. But how should a court determine whether a procedural system is fair? What evidence is appropriate?

3. *Bridgeway Corp. v. Citbank*, 45 F. Supp. 2d 276 (S.D.N.Y. 1999), *aff'd*, 201 F.3d 134 (2d Cir. 2000), is a frequently cited example of a court finding a judicial system unfair. In that case, the court evaluated the judicial system in Liberia during the period between 1992 and 1995, and concluded the system lacked impartial tribunals and procedures compatible with the requirements of due process. In so holding, the court reasoned as follows:

> First, the record demonstrates that, throughout the period during which the Liberian action was pending, the country was embroiled in a civil war. The country was in a state of chaos, as the various factions fought. The Liberian Constitution was ignored. Some 200,000 Liberian citizens were killed, more than one million more were left homeless, and approximately 750,000 fled Liberia to seek refuge in other countries. It is difficult to imagine any judicial system functioning properly in these circumstances.
>
> Second, the record shows that the regular procedures governing the selection of justices and judges had not been followed since the suspension of the 1986 Constitution. As a result, justices and judges served at the will of

the leaders of the warring factions, and judicial officers were subject to political and social influence. The Liberian judicial system simply did not provide for impartial tribunals.

Third, the courts that did exist were barely functioning. The due process rights of litigants were often ignored, as corruption and incompetent handling of cases were prevalent. Although the Liberian judicial system might have been modeled on our own, it did not comport with the requirements of due process during the period of civil war.

[The party seeking to enforce the Liberian judgment offers statements of Liberian lawyers stating that (1) "the procedural rules of Liberia's courts are modeled on those of the New York State courts"; (2) "[i]n essence, the Liberian Government is patterned after state governments of the United States of America"; and (3) "Liberia's judicial system was and is structured and administered to afford party-litigants therein impartial justice." This evidence is not sufficient to defeat summary judgment.] First, that the Liberian judicial system was modeled after judicial systems in the United States does not mean, of course, that the Liberian system was actually implemented in a manner consistent with procedures used in the American courts. Second, the statement that "Liberia's judicial system was and is structured and administered to afford party-litigants therein impartial justice" is purely conclusory and is not, by itself, sufficient to raise a genuine issue of fact. . . . On the record before the Court, a reasonable factfinder could only conclude that the Liberian Judgment was rendered by a system that does not provide impartial tribunals or procedures compatible with the requirements of due process.

45 F. Supp. at 287-288. Contrary to this decision, United States courts tend to uphold the fairness of other countries' judicial systems, particularly those of Western Europe.

4. When decisions applying the fairness exception are viewed in the aggregate, one sees that the exception incorporates a balance of values. On one hand, courts want to avoid the unfairness to judgment debtors that would result from extending deference or comity to a sham or corrupt judgment. On the other hand (as clearly articulated by Judge Posner), courts also want to avoid providing parties with an opportunity to re-litigate substantial portions of the original suit.

5. Do you agree with Judge Posner's distinction between procedural due process and substantive due process? Was the contract context important to the *Lloyd's* case, or would the same reasoning follow even if the initial court had rendered a judgment premised on a patently unfair statute or common law principle? Consider whether the public policy exception, discussed immediately below, would cover the circumstance of an unfair statute or common law principle.

3. *The Public Policy Exception to Presumptive Recognition of Foreign Country Judgments*

a. **The Scope of the Public Policy Exception**

Southwest Livestock & Trucking Co. v. Ramón

169 F.3d 317 (5th Cir. 1999)

EMILIO M. GARZA, Circuit Judge:

. . . Darrel and Mary Jane Hargrove (the "Hargroves") are citizens of the United States and officers of Southwest Livestock & Trucking Co., Inc. ("Southwest Livestock"), a Texas corporation involved in the buying and selling of livestock. In 1990, Southwest Livestock entered into a loan arrangement with Reginaldo Ramón ("Ramón"), a citizen of the Republic of Mexico. Southwest Livestock borrowed $400,000 from Ramón. To accomplish the loan, Southwest Livestock executed a "pagaré"—a Mexican promissory note—payable to Ramón with interest within thirty days. Each month, Southwest Livestock executed a new pagaré to cover the outstanding principal and paid the accrued interest. Over a period of four years, Southwest Livestock made payments towards the principal, but also borrowed additional money from Ramón. In October of 1994, Southwest Livestock defaulted on the loan. With the exception of the last pagaré executed by Southwest Livestock, none of the pagarés contained a stated interest rate. Ramón, however, charged Southwest Livestock interest at a rate of approximately fifty-two percent. The last pagaré stated an interest rate of forty-eight percent, and under its terms, interest continues to accrue until Southwest Livestock pays the outstanding balance in full.

After Southwest Livestock defaulted, Ramón filed a lawsuit in Mexico to collect on the last pagaré. The Mexican court granted judgment in favor of Ramón, and ordered Southwest Livestock to satisfy its debt and to pay interest at forty-eight percent. Southwest Livestock appealed, claiming that Ramón had failed to effect proper service of process. . . . The Mexican appellate court rejected this argument and affirmed the judgment in favor of Ramón.

After Ramón filed suit in Mexico, but prior to the entry of the Mexican judgment, Southwest Livestock brought suit in United States District Court, alleging that the loan arrangement violated Texas usury laws. Southwest Livestock [claimed] . . . that . . . Ramón charged, received and collected usurious interest in violation of Texas law. . . . By then the Mexican court had entered its judgment, and Ramón sought recognition of that judgment. He claimed that, under principles of collateral estoppel and res judicata, the Mexican judgment barred Southwest Livestock's suit. . . .

We must determine first whether the district court properly refused to recognize the Mexican judgment. Our jurisdiction is based on diversity of citizenship. Hence, we must apply Texas law regarding the recognition of foreign country money-judgments. *See . . . Success Motivation Institute of Japan, Ltd. v.*

Success Motivation Institute Inc., 966 F.2d 1007, 1009-10 (5th Cir. 1992) ("*Erie* applies even though some courts have found that these suits necessarily involve relations between the U.S. and foreign governments, and even though some commentators have argued that the enforceability of these judgments in the courts of the United States should be governed by reference to a general rule of federal law.").

Under the Texas Recognition Act, a court must recognize a foreign country judgment assessing money damages unless the judgment debtor establishes one of ten specific grounds for nonrecognition. Southwest Livestock contends that it established a ground for nonrecognition. It notes that the Texas Constitution places a six percent interest rate limit on contracts that do not contain a stated interest rate. It also points to a Texas statute that states that usury is against Texas public policy. *See* Vernon's Tex. Civ. Stat., art. 5069-1C.001 ("All contracts for usury are contrary to public policy"). Thus, according to Southwest Livestock, the Mexican judgment violates Texas public policy, and the district court properly withheld recognition of the judgment. . . .

. . . The narrowness of the public policy exception reflects a compromise between two axioms — res judicata and fairness to litigants. . . .

To decide whether the district court erred in refusing to recognize the Mexican judgment on public policy grounds, we consider the plain language of the Texas Recognition Act. Section 36.005(b)(3) of the Texas Recognition Act permits the district court not to recognize a foreign country judgment if "*the cause of action* on which the judgment is based is repugnant to the public policy" of Texas. Tex. Civ. Prac. & Rem. Code Ann. §36.005(b)(3) (West 1998) (emphasis added). This subsection of the Texas Recognition Act does not refer to the judgment itself, but specifically to the "cause of action on which the judgment is based." Thus, the fact that a judgment offends Texas public policy does not, in and of itself, permit the district court to refuse recognition of that judgment.

In this case, the Mexican judgment was based on an action for collection of a promissory note. This cause of action is not repugnant to Texas public policy. Under the Texas Recognition Act, it is irrelevant that the Mexican judgment itself contravened Texas's public policy against usury. Thus, the plain language of the Texas Recognition Act suggests that the district court erred in refusing to recognize the Mexican judgment.

Southwest Livestock, however, . . . believes that the reasoning of the Texas Supreme Court in *DeSantis v. Wackenhut Corp.*, 793 S.W.2d 670 (Tex. 1990), requires us to affirm the district court's decision not to recognize the Mexican judgment. In *DeSantis*, the Court refused to apply Florida law to enforce a non-competition agreement, even though the agreement contained an express choice of Florida law provision, and Florida had a substantial interest in the transaction. The Court concluded that "the law governing enforcement of non-competition agreements is fundamental policy in Texas, and that to apply the law of another state to determine the enforceability of such an agreement in the circumstances of a case like this would be contrary to that policy." *Id.* at 681.

Southwest Livestock argues similarly that the law governing usury constitutes a fundamental policy in Texas, and that to recognize the Mexican judgment would transgress that policy.

We find that, contrary to Southwest Livestock's argument, *DeSantis* does not support the district court's grant of summary judgment. First, in *DeSantis* the Court refused to enforce an agreement violative of Texas public policy; it did not refuse to recognize a foreign judgment. Recognition and enforcement of a judgment involve separate and distinct inquiries. Second, unlike in *DeSantis*, where the plaintiff sought to use foreign law offensively to enforce the noncompetition agreement, in this case, Ramón seeks recognition of the Mexican judgment as an affirmative defense to Southwest Livestock's usury claim. Different considerations apply when a party seeks recognition of a foreign judgment for defensive purposes. As Justice Brandeis once stated:

> [T]he company is in a position different from that of a plaintiff who seeks to enforce a cause of action conferred by the laws of another state. The right which it claims should be given effect is set up by way of defense to an asserted liability; and to a defense different considerations apply. A state may, on occasion, decline to enforce a foreign cause of action. In so doing, it merely denies a remedy leaving unimpaired the plaintiff's substantive right, so that he is free to enforce it elsewhere. But to refuse to give effect to a substantive defense under the applicable law of another state, as under the circumstances here presented, subjects the defendant to irremediable liability. This may not be done.

Bradford Elec. Light Co. v. Clapper, 286 U.S. 145, 160 (1932).

We find our decision in *Woods-Tucker Leasing Corp. v. Hutcheson-Ingram Development Co.*, 642 F.2d 744 (5th Cir. 1981), more helpful than *DeSantis*.[4] In *Woods-Tucker*, we considered "whether a bankruptcy court sitting in Texas should honor a party contractual choice of Mississippi law in determining whether to apply the Texas or Mississippi usury statute to a transaction . . . between a Texas partnership and a Mississippi-headquartered corporate subsidiary of a Georgia corporation." *Id.* at 745. In deciding to honor the parties' choice of Mississippi law, we noted that applying Mississippi law did not offend any Texas fundamental public policy:

> To be sure, it is the underlying policy of each state's usury laws to protect necessitous borrowers within its borders. Yet, as we have noted, we have found no Texas cases that have invalidated a party choice of law on grounds that the application of a foreign usury statute would violate public policy.

Id. at 753 n.13. *Woods-Tucker* . . . indicates that, although Texas has a strong public policy against usury, this policy is not inviolable.

---

4. We acknowledge that *Woods-Tucker* involves a sister state judgment, which distinguishes it from this case. *See Reading & Bates Constr. Co. v. Baker Energy Resources Corp.*, 976 S.W.2d 702, 714 (Tex. App.-Houston [1st Dist.] 1998, writ denied) ("Giving full faith and credit to the judgment of a sister state is vastly different than according it to a foreign country judgment."). Nevertheless, we find the decision in *Woods-Tucker* informative.

We are especially reluctant to conclude that recognizing the Mexican judgment offends Texas public policy under the circumstances of this case. The purpose behind Texas usury laws is to protect unsophisticated borrowers from unscrupulous lenders. This case, however, does not involve the victimizing of a naive consumer. Southwest Livestock is managed by sophisticated and knowledgeable people with experience in business. Additionally, the evidence in the record does not suggest that Ramón misled or deceived Southwest Livestock. Southwest Livestock and Ramón negotiated the loan in good faith and at arms length. In short, both parties fully appreciated the nature of the loan transaction and their respective contractual obligations.

Accordingly, in light of the plain language of the Texas Recognition Act, and after consideration of our decision in *Woods-Tucker* and the purpose behind Texas public policy against usury, we hold that Texas's public policy does not justify withholding recognition of the Mexican judgment. . . .

Notes on
SOUTHWEST LIVESTOCK

1. What is the precise basis for the *Southwest Livestock* court's decision? The court emphasized (i) that the statute referred only to circumstances where the cause of action was against public policy and (ii) that collection on a promissory note was not against public policy. Do you think this was an accurate application of what the statute intended? The court also emphasized other aspects of the case in reaching its decision, such as the parity in bargaining power between the parties. Do you think that the court would have come to the same conclusion about the statutory language if the parties had less equal bargaining power? Would the *Southwest Livestock* case have come out differently under the language of the more recent Uniform Foreign-Country Money Judgments Recognition Act, which permits non-recognition where "the judgment or the cause of action on which the judgment is based is repugnant to the public policy" of the jurisdiction asked to recognize the judgment?

2. Are you persuaded by the *Southwest Livestock*'s distinction between refusing a foreign cause of action versus defensive use of a foreign judgment to avoid liability in a second jurisdiction? Is it somehow fairer to allow a defendant to rely on a judgment of dubious public policy significance in the forum state than to allow a plaintiff to rely on a foreign cause of action of equally dubious public policy significance?

3. Compare the public policy exception in the Uniform Foreign-Money Judgments Recognition Act and the Uniform Foreign-Country Money Judgments Recognition Act with the United States Supreme Court's interpretation of the full faith and credit clause in *Fauntleroy v. Lum*. Why should a public policy exception flourish in the context of recognizing and enforcing foreign country judgments but not in the context of domestic judgments?

4. As in other areas where a public policy exception thrives — choice of law being a prime example — courts often say that the policy offended must be "fundamental" in order for the exception to be triggered. As one court put it, the public policy exception applies only where the foreign country judgment or claim upon which it is based would "undermine the public interest, the public confidence in the administration of the law or security for individual rights." *Ackerman v. Levine*, 788 F.2d 830, 844 (2d Cir. 1986). Thus, it is not enough that the enforcing forum would have allowed the cause of action to succeed had the plaintiff originally filed the case there.

5. Questions remain, however, about the source of law governing the public policy that is offended. For example, what if the public policy relied on derived from a state law policy that disfavored all foreign tribunals or a particular foreign country? What if a state decided to enforce a judgment that was in tension with a principle of international law or federal constitutional or statutory law? Should a state be required to apply the public policy exceptions under certain circumstances?

6. Parties in international transactions frequently agree to choice of forum clauses that include a statement that the parties are bound by a judgment rendered by the agreed-upon forum. Should these clauses supersede the uniform Acts? Should they supersede a strong public policy objection in the enforcing jurisdiction?

7. The subject areas in which courts have found a fundamental public policy implicated are diverse, including such wide-ranging contexts as enforcing letters of credit, promoting arbitration, defining tort causation standards, enforcing IRS lien priority in bankruptcy, and releasing alimony obligations. A particularly prominent context pertains to freedom of expression: a topic discussed in the next section on libel tourism.

PROBLEM 4-22: HERMA THE WHISTLEBLOWER

Herma was an employee of Drug Corp., a company with headquarters in North Virginia in the United States, and with subsidiary offices in the country of Argenzula. She worked at the Argenzula office and was dismissed after she complained to government officials that Drug Corp. was bribing doctors to prescribe certain medications and fabricate the results of the treatment. At the time of her dismissal, she was bullied into signing a separation agreement in which she waived her right to file suit under any whistleblower statute. Several months later, Herma filed a grievance with the National Labor Court in Argenzula, and Drug Corp. moved for the separation agreement to be entered as a judgment in the case. After full proceedings, the court entered the separation agreement as a final judgment.

Herma then filed an action in state court in North Virginia under the state whistleblower statute. Legislative history for the whistleblower statute provides that the purpose of the statute is to protect employees from intimidation and encourage them to report illegal or unethical conduct in the workplace. North Virginia also has a state policy favoring negotiated settlement of disputes. Drug Corp. has defended suit by pointing to the Argenzula court judgment and asking that the court recognize the judgment as a bar to the North Virginia suit. Should this defense be granted?

b. The First Amendment and Libel Tourism

PROBLEM 4-23: CASSANDRA AND JULIAN REDUX: FIRST AMENDMENT AND JUDGMENT ENFORCEMENT ISSUES

Cassandra is a resident of New Jersey. She researched and wrote an article about Julian, which was published in a newspaper. Almost all copies of the newspaper are circulated in New Jersey. Although at one time a resident of New Jersey and still spending a lot of time working there, Julian has lived in the United Kingdom for a year now. He is convinced that the article defames him and he files a defamation suit against Cassandra in London, England. Cassandra has taken lecture tours several times in the United Kingdom. In addition, unbeknownst to her, the newspaper in which the article about Julian appears distributes a small percentage of its circulation in the United Kingdom. While on a lecture tour in London after publication of the article, Cassandra is served with process in the lawsuit that Julian has filed there. Applying United Kingdom law, the court decided that Cassandra defamed him and entered judgment against Cassandra in the amount of €100,000. These damages are based on all injuries that Julian suffered around the world, the bulk of which were suffered in the United States. Julian wishes to turn this judgment from a piece of paper into cash in his pocket. He knows that the only way he can do so is to enforce the judgment. He hired a private investigator who found out that Cassandra has all her assets in New Jersey. Accordingly, Julian filed suit in New Jersey, asking the New Jersey court to enforce the judgment against Cassandra.

Cassandra consults you to defend this action. Your research reveals that the libel laws in the United Kingdom are far more plaintiff-friendly than the libel laws in states of the United States, and that it is unlikely that Julian would have been able to establish the elements of liability under any United States state laws. In particular, Julian would have had the burden under United States law of proving the article was false: a burden he might have difficulty satisfying, but could have avoided under United Kingdom law, which presumes falsity. In addition, your research establishes that Julian would most likely be a public figure under case law interpreting the First Amendment of the United States Constitution. This First Amendment jurisprudence would therefore protect the article from defamation liability. Given this research, what might you argue in seeking to persuade the court not to recognize or enforce the judgment?

Matusevitch v. Telnikoff

877 F. Supp. 1 (D.D.C. 1995), *aff'd*, 159 F.3d 636 (D.C. App. 1998)

URBINA, District Judge.

[Mr. Matusevitch was United States citizen of Jewish descent who had lived in the former Soviet Union. Mr. Telnikoff was an English citizen, born and raised in the former Soviet Union. He was a writer and broadcaster for the British Broadcasting Corp (BBC), and in 1984 published an article in an English newspaper criticizing the BBC's Russian Service. Matusevitch had a letter published later in the same newspaper in which he criticized Telnikoff for allegedly requiring a blood test for the Russian Service and accusing him of spreading "racialist" and anti-Semitic views. Telnikoff filed a libel action against Matusevitch in English courts, and ultimately received a large verdict, which he sought to enforce in the United States. After Telnikoff sought to enforce the judgment, Matusevitch filed suit in the United States District Court in Maryland, seeking a declaration that the judgment was repugnant to public policy. The case was transferred to the District Court for the District of Columbia and Matusevitch filed a motion for summary judgment.]

. . . Because recognition and enforcement of a foreign judgment, based on libel standards that are repugnant to the public policies of the State of Maryland and the United States, would deprive the plaintiff of his First and Fourteenth Amendment rights, the court grants summary judgment for the plaintiff as a matter of law.

I. RECOGNITION OF A FOREIGN JUDGMENT

A. THE UNIFORM FOREIGN-MONEY JUDGMENTS RECOGNITION ACT OF 1962 AND THE UNIFORM ENFORCEMENT OF FOREIGN JUDGMENTS ACT OF 1964

Before a party can enforce a judgment from a foreign country in the United States, the moving party must have the foreign judgment recognized by the state in which he is seeking to enforce the judgment. In the State of Maryland, the Uniform Foreign-Money Judgments Recognition Act of 1962 (the "Recognition Act") and the Uniform Enforcement of Foreign Judgments Act of 1964 (the "Enforcement Act") govern the procedure for the recognition and enforcement of a foreign judgment.

. . . Although the Enforcement Act allows a party to bypass the Recognition Act by merely filing a foreign judgment, it limits when a party can use this procedure. . . . In this case, the court finds that the defendant filed the foreign-country judgment with the Clerk of the Circuit Court of Montgomery County, Maryland. The defendant, however, never attempted to get that judgment recognized before filing, as required by statute. Consequently, the court determines that the defendant currently holds an unrecognized foreign-country judgment from the State of Maryland. The defendant must obtain recognition of this judgment in order to enforce it.

B. NONRECOGNITION OF A FOREIGN JUDGMENT

Irrespective of the procedure, the Recognition Act lists mandatory and discretionary grounds for non-recognition. Section 10-704(b)(2) states that a foreign judgment need not be recognized if "the cause of action on which the judgment is based is repugnant to the public policy of the State."

Case law illustrates that United States courts have refused to recognize foreign country judgments based on public policy grounds. . . . Two recent cases, *Abdullah v. Sheridan Square Press, Inc.*, No. 93 Civ. 2515, 1994 WL 419847 (S.D.N.Y. May 4, 1994) and *Bachchan v. India Abroad Publications Inc.*, 154 Misc. 2d 228, 585 N.Y.S.2d 661 (Sup. Ct. 1992), illustrate decisions where courts have failed to recognize a foreign libel judgment grounded on public policy. In *Abdullah*, the court dismissed the claim for libel under English law, holding that "establishment of a claim for libel under the British law of defamation would be antithetical to the First Amendment protection accorded the defendants." In *Bachchan*, the court declined to recognize or enforce an English libel judgment on both constitutional and public policy grounds.

. . . In this case, libel standards that are contrary to U.S. libel standards would be repugnant to the public policies of the State of Maryland and the United States. . . .

II. DEPRIVATION OF FIRST AND FOURTEENTH AMENDMENT RIGHTS TO THE CONSTITUTION

A. BRITISH LIBEL LAW V. U.S. LIBEL LAW

British law on libel differs from U.S. law. In the United Kingdom, the defendant bears the burden of proving allegedly defamatory statements true and the plaintiff is not required to prove malice on the part of the libel defendant. . . . As a result, a libel defendant would be held liable for statements the defendant honestly believed to be true and published without any negligence. In contrast, the law in the United States requires the plaintiff to prove that the statements were false and looks to the defendant's state of mind and intentions. In light of the different standards, this court concludes that recognition and enforcement of the foreign judgment in this case would deprive the plaintiff of his constitutional rights.[2]

---

2. The United States adopted a Constitution and Bill of Rights in order to provide Americans with greater rights than previously provided under British colonial rule. As a result, laws governing

B. PROTECTED SPEECH

Speech similar to the plaintiff's statements have received protection under the First Amendment to the Constitution and are thereby unactionable in U.S. courts. [T]he Supreme Court [has held] . . . that hyperbole is not actionable. Plaintiff contends that his statements were plainly hyperbolic because they were stated in an attempt to portray defendant's extremist position.

In addition, in the United States, courts look to the context in which the statements appeared when determining a First Amendment question. . . . In the case at hand, the court notes that the British judgment was based on jury instructions which asked the jury to ignore context. Therefore, this court finds that if the statements were read in context to the original article or statement and in reference to the location of the statements in the newspaper, a reader would reasonably be alerted to the statements' function as opinion and not as an assertion of fact.

C. LIMITED PUBLIC FIGURE

The Supreme Court in *New York Times Co. v. Sullivan*, 376 U.S. 254, 84 S. Ct. 710, 11 L. Ed. 2d 686 (1964), explained that a public figure must show by clear and convincing evidence that the libel defendant published defamatory statements with actual malice. . . . [T]he Supreme Court extended this standard to a nonpublic person who is "'nevertheless intimately involved in the resolution of important public questions or, by reason of their fame, shape events in areas of concern to society at large.'"

The defendant in this case has described himself as a prominent activist for Human Rights in the Soviet Union since 1955. Therefore, for purposes of his article about the composition of Russian personnel hired by Radio Free Europe/Radio Liberty, the court finds that the defendant was a limited public figure. In light of defendant's status as a limited public figure, the plaintiff is entitled to all the constitutional safeguards concerning speech used against public figures.

During the trial in England, because of British libel standards for the defense of "fair comment," the court never looked to the degree of fault or the accused party's intentions. Also, although the British court determined that the plaintiff's use of inverted commas around certain words may have falsely mislead a reader to believe that the defendant actually wrote those words, the [United States Supreme Court has] concluded that "a deliberate alteration of the words uttered by a plaintiff does not equate with knowledge of falsity. . . . The use of quotations to attribute words not in fact spoken bears in a most important way on that inquiry, but it is not dispositive in every case." As a result, since there appears to be no proof that the plaintiff made the statements with actual malice, the plaintiff enjoys the constitutional protection for speech directed against public figures. . . .

---

libel are structured around the goal to promote free speech and press rights Americans fought hard to secure. Since the United Kingdom lacks a Constitution, its laws appear to provide less protection for written and verbal expression.

Notes on
MATUSEVITCH v. TELNIKOFF

1. After the decision above, Telnikoff appealed to the United States Court of Appeals for the D.C. Circuit. The Court of Appeals then certified to Maryland's highest court the question of whether the English judgment would violate Maryland public policy. In *Telnikoff v. Matusevitch*, 702 A.2d 230 (Md. 1997), the Maryland Supreme Court held the judgment was against Maryland public policy, citing the same qualities of English libel law and the same First Amendment principles as the United States District Court for the District of Columbia in the opinion above. (The Maryland Supreme Court did point out a few additional differences in the libel laws, such as the availability of punitive damages and the standards for qualified privileges.) Thereafter, the Court of Appeals affirmed the District Court's judgment. Why would the United States Court of Appeals for the District of Columbia Circuit have believed it appropriate to certify the public policy question to the Maryland Supreme Court? Was it necessary for the Court of Appeals to do so, given the importance of a federal constitutional provision in the case? Did the case have any foreign relations implications? If so, does it matter whether the case turned on a legal interpretation undertaken by a federal or a state court?

2. In a dissent to the Maryland Supreme Court decision, one judge argued as follows:

> That public policy, recognized by our legislature when it adopted the Uniform Foreign Money-Judgments Recognition Act, is to give broad and uniform recognition to foreign judgments. The Act gives our courts discretion to subordinate our State's public policy. Our interest in international good will, comity, and res judicata fostered by recognition of foreign judgments must be weighed against our minimal interest in giving the benefits of our local libel public policy to residents of another country who defame foreign public figures in foreign publications and who have no reasonable expectation that they will be protected by the Maryland Constitution. Unless there is some United States interest that should be protected, there is no good reason to offend a friendly nation like England by refusing to recognize a purely local libel judgment for a purely local defamation. In the instant case, there is no United States interest that might necessitate non-recognition or non-enforcement of the English defamation judgment. . . . Here, Plaintiff and Defendant were both Russian emigres living in England. If England wishes to protect its public figures from even non-negligent libel by private citizens, it should be able to do so. There should be no need for Maryland public policy to give protection to an English resident who libels an English public figure in England. . . . British public officials and public figures, however, expect their law to give them protection from even non-malicious false defamatory statements. We should respect this difference between British public figures and their American

counterparts in cases of purely internal English defamation by private persons. . . . Matusevitch, at the time he falsely accused Telnikoff of being a racist hate monger, had no right to, or expectation that he would, be protected by the United States Constitution, and I doubt that the public would be outraged if we do not retroactively bestow our constitutional right to non-maliciously defame a public official on Matusevitch merely because he later moves to our country. . . .

Public policy should not require us to give First Amendment protection or Article 40 protection to English residents who defame other English residents in publications distributed only in England. Failure to make our constitutional provisions relating to defamation applicable to wholly internal English defamation would not seem to violate fundamental notions of what is decent and just and should not undermine public confidence in the administration of law. The Court does little or no analysis of the global public policy considerations and seems inclined to make Maryland libel law applicable to the rest of the world by providing a safe haven for foreign libel judgment debtors.

Telnikoff v. Matusevitch, 702 A.2d 230, 257-260 (1997) (Chasanow, J., dissenting). Are you persuaded by this argument? How important is it that the case concerned events local to England and that the plaintiff was an English citizen?

3. The First Amendment freedom of expression is heralded as perhaps the most important liberty protected by the United States Constitution. Jurists and scholars argue that it is not only essential to the functioning of democracy, but also serves to ensure that other civil liberties are meaningful. In light of its importance, should the First Amendment yield to other values, such as another country's concern with human dignity threatened by defamatory speech or foreign relations concerns implicated when a United States court does not honor a foreign country judgment?

4. Is it fair to say that a decision not to enforce a foreign country judgment is the same as a determination that the First Amendment of the United States Constitution "applies to conduct and litigation in a foreign nation"? Doug Rendleman, *Collecting a Libel Tourist's Defamation Judgment?*, 67 WASH. & LEE L. REV. 467, 484 (2010). If so, does that lead you to rethink the wisdom of decisions such as *Matusevitch v. Telnikoff?*

5. Differences between defamation laws of the United States and other countries such as the United Kingdom have led to a phenomenon known as libel tourism. Generally, libel tourism occurs when a forum-shopping plaintiff in a libel action leaves her home to file suit in a jurisdiction with more plaintiff-friendly libel laws than her home country. Was *Matusevitch v. Telnikoff* a libel tourism case?

PROBLEM 4-24: TELNIKOFF INITIALLY FILES SUIT IN THE UNITED STATES

Assume that rather than filing the initial libel suit in England, Telnikoff filed the libel suit for the first time in the United States District Court for the District of Columbia. Telnikoff argues that the district court should apply the British libel law, and Matusevitch argues that the district court should decline to do so on the grounds of public policy. Are considerations the same in this context as in the actual case where Telnikoff was asking the district court to enforce a judgment against Matusevitch that resulted from adjudication under British libel law?

PERSPECTIVE ON LIBEL TOURISM AND THE SPEECH ACT

The difference between defamation laws in the United States and other countries has led to "libel tourism," a form of international forum shopping that could potentially expose United States authors and publishers to liability that would not be possible under United States law. Frequently, a libel tourist is a plaintiff who could file suit in the United States, but chooses instead to file suit in a jurisdiction with more plaintiff-friendly defamation laws,[28] regardless of whether that jurisdiction has a strong connection with the parties or the facts of the case.[29] Libel tourism can cause increased financial exposure for United States authors and publishers as well as a chilling effect resulting from knowing that speech protected under United States law may nonetheless provide the basis for a large damage judgment elsewhere in the world.[30] While United States regulators may not be able to control directly a plaintiff's international forum shopping for favorable defamation laws, regulators can make the practice less rewarding by refusing to enforce the international judgments that result. The United States has, in fact, pursued that strategy.

The problem of libel tourism arises largely because of the stark contrast between the defamation laws of the United States and those of England. As reflected in the decision in *Matusevitch v. Telnikoff*, 877 F. Supp. 1 (D.D.C. 1995), *aff'd*, 159 F.3d 636 (D.C. App. 1998), the differences arise not only because of the potency of United States First Amendment protection,[31] but also because of variations in proof requirements and defenses for defamations claims. Under

---

28. Robert L. McFarland, *Please Do Not Publish This Article in England: A Jurisdictional Response to Libel Tourism*, 79 MISS. L.J. 617, 625 (2010).

29. *See, e.g.*, Yasmine Lahlou, *Libel Tourism: A Transatlantic Quandary*, 2 J. INT'L MEDIA & ENT. L. 199 (2009).

30. Daniel C. Taylor, *Libel Tourism: Protecting Authors and Preserving Comity*, 99 GEO. L.J. 189, 197 (2010) (noting that defamation judgments have collateral consequences that may impinge on free speech).

31. *See, e.g.*, *N.Y. Times Co. v. Sullivan*, 376 U.S. 254, 279-280 (finding that constitutional guarantees require "a federal rule that prohibits a public official from recovering damages for a

United States defamation law, plaintiffs bear the burden of proving the falsity of a statement.[32] Conversely, in England, an allegedly defamatory statement is presumed false, and the defendant has the burden of proving it true.[33] In the United States, the court will first determine whether a statement is capable of having a defamatory meaning before submitting to the jury; in England, if a defendant cannot prove the truth of a statement, the jury will then decide whether it is defamatory or not.[34] Finally, differences exist concerning proof of the defendant's state of mind requirements as well as the scope of privileges.

The term "libel tourism" was coined in the 1990s after several celebrities, including Arnold Schwarzenegger and Roman Polanski, sought redress in England for defamatory statements published in the United States.[35] From its reputation as a plaintiff-friendly forum that adjudicates a large number of defamation cases, the United Kingdom has been named the "libel capital of the world,"[36] with London bearing the moniker "a town named Sue."[37] The rise of the internet has further prompted the proliferation of publications that transcend national borders, increasing the spread of libel tourism and raising comity issues between these nations with distinct defamation laws.[38]

New York was the first United States jurisdiction to use legislation to regulate libel tourism.[39] Largely in response to the outcry against the *Ehrenfeld v. Bin Mahfouz*[40]

---

defamatory falsehood relating to his official conduct unless he proves that the statement was made with 'actual malice' — that is, with knowledge that it was false or with reckless disregard of whether it was false or not").

32. Todd W. Moore, *Untying Our Hands: The Case for Uniform Personal Jurisdiction over "Libel Tourists,"* 77 FORDHAM L. REV. 3207, 3212 (2009); *see also N.Y. Times Co. v. Sullivan,* 376 U.S. 254, 279 (1964); RESTATEMENT (SECOND) OF TORTS §613 (1977).

33. Moore, *supra,* at 3212.

34. *Id.* at 3212-3213.

35. Thomas Sanchez, *London, Libel Capital No Longer? The Draft Defamation Act 2011 and the Future of Libel Tourism,* 9 U.N.H. L. REV. 469, 473-474 (2011).

36. *Reforming Libel Law: A City Named Sue,* ECONOMIST (Nov. 14, 2009), *available at* http://www.economist.com/node/14845167.

37. Sarah Lyall, *England, Long a Libel Mecca, Reviews Laws,* N.Y. TIMES, Dec. 11, 2009, at A1. Sydney, Australia has a similarly dubious honor, boasting a remarkably robust defamation docket in its courts. *See* Laura E. Little, *Just a Joke: Defamatory Humor and Incongruity's Promise,* 21 S. CAL. INTERDISC. L.J. 95, 134-135 (2011).

38. *See* Michelle Feldman, *Putting the Brakes on Libel Tourism: Examining the Effects Test as a Basis for Personal Jurisdiction Under New York's Libel Terrorism Protection Act,* 31 CARDOZO L. REV. 2457 (2010).

39. Sarah Stavely-O'Carroll, *Libel Tourism: Spoiling the Holiday and Saving the First Amendment?,* 4 N.Y.U. J.L. & LIBERTY 252, 254 (2009) (The Act modified New York law in two ways. First, it codified the rule that courts need not recognize foreign defamation judgments unless the law applied in the foreign jurisdiction "provided at least as much protection for freedom of speech and press in that case as would be provided by both the United States and New York Constitutions." N.Y. C.P.L.R. 5304(b)(8). Second, it expanded New York's long arm statute by granting personal jurisdiction over foreign defendants in limited instances. *See* N.Y. C.P.L.R. 302(d).) *Id.*

40. 518 F.3d 102, 106 (2d Cir. 2008) (dismissing Ehrenfeld's claim that the Court of Appeals' interpretation of §302(a)(1) as not conferring personal jurisdiction against Bin Mahfouz violated the First Amendment, on the ground that her failure to raise this issue in a prior proceeding amounted to a waiver of the claim). The case originated in 2004, when Khalid Salim Bin Mahfouz sued Rachel Ehrenfeld in defamation before the High Court of Justice in England in response to her book, Funding Evil, in which Ehrenfeld alleged that Bin Mahfouz and his sons were among

case, New York passed the Libel Terrorism Protection Act[41]—also referred to as
"Rachel's Law." Other states passed similar laws,[42] and courts continued to use the
public policy exception of the Uniform Foreign-Country Money Judgments Recognition Act or the Uniform Foreign Money-Judgments Recognition Act judgment.[43]
And then, in August 2010, President Barack Obama signed the Securing the Protection of our Enduring and Established Constitutional Heritage Act, or SPEECH Act,[44]
into federal law.[45]

The title of SPEECH describes it as an act "to prohibit recognition and
enforcement of foreign defamation judgments and certain foreign judgments
against the providers of interactive computer services." The main provision of
the Act requires that a United States court refuse to recognize or enforce a
foreign defamation judgment unless the court makes one of the following
findings:

> (A) the defamation law applied in the foreign court's adjudication provided at
> least as much protection for freedom of speech and press in that case as would be
> provided by the first amendment to the Constitution of the United States and by the
> constitution and law of the State in which the domestic court is located; or
> (B) even if the defamation law applied in the foreign court's adjudication did
> not provide as much protection for freedom of speech and press as the first amend-
> ment to the Constitution of the United States and the constitution and law of the
> State, the party opposing recognition or enforcement of that foreign judgment
> would have been found liable for defamation by a domestic court applying the
> first amendment to the Constitution of the United States and the constitution
> and law of the State in which the domestic court is located.

28 U.S.C. §4102(a)(1). While some may have regarded SPEECH as mere political
theater or message politics, the statute has governed courts in several cases.[46]

---

the main sponsors of Al Qaeda and other terrorist organizations. Similar suits based upon
statements regarding alleged terrorist activity have prompted the nickname "libel terrorism." *See*
Lahlou, *supra* note 29, at 200.

41. N.Y. C.P.L.R. 302(d) (McKinney 2009); N.Y. C.P.L.R. 5304(b)(8) (McKinney 2009).

42. Such states include Illinois (735 Ill. Comp. Stat 5/2-209(b-5) (WEST 2008)), California
(Cal. Code Civ. Proc.§1716(c)(9) (WEST SUPP. 2010)), and Florida (Fla. Stat. Ann.§55.605(2)(h)
(WEST SUPP. 2010)).

43. *See, e.g., Bachchan v. India Abroad Publ'ns, Inc.*, 585 N.Y.S.2d 661 (N.Y. Sup. Ct. 1992); *Dow
Jones & Co. v. Harrods, Ltd.*, 237 F. Supp. 2d 394 (S.D.N.Y. 2002), *aff'd*, 346 F.3d 357 (2d Cir. 2003).

44. Securing the Protection of our Enduring and Established Constitutional Heritage Act,
Pub. L. No. 111-223, 124 Stat. 2380 (2010) (codified at 28 U.S.C. §§4101-4105).

45. For a discussion of the SPEECH Act's main provisions (including mandatory non-
recognition of foreign country judgments for defamation and the creation of a cause of action for
declaratory judgment for a United States citizen) and its effects, see Daniel C. Taylor, *Libel
Tourism: Protecting Authors and Preserving Comity*, 99 GEO. L.J. 189, 204-208 (2010).

46. *See, e.g., Trout Point Lodge Limited v. Handshoe*, 729 F.3d 481 (2013) (holding that a
defamation-based default judgment was unenforceable under the SPEECH Act); *InvestorsHub.com,
Inc. v. Mina Mar Group, Inc.*, 2011 U.S. Dist. LEXIS 87566 (N.D. Fla. June 20, 2011) (applying
SPEECH Act in the context of defamation judgment from Canada); *Pontigon v. Lord*, 340 S.W.3d
315 (Mo. Ct. App. 2011) (holding that the lower court did not properly consider the relevant
provisions in the SPEECH Act in deciding whether to enforce Canadian defamation judgment).

Ultimately, SPEECH may prove unnecessary for handling libel judgment rendered by courts in England and Wales. Indeed, British authorities have taken action against libel tourism, motivated by the observation that "[l]ibel tourism is making a mockery of British justice, with foreign plaintiffs able to bring cases against foreign defendants when the publications in question may have sold just a handful of copies in England."[47] As of January 1, 2014, British legislators adopted a new Defamation Act (Defamation Act 2013 ch. 26). Most significantly, the Act introduced a threshold "serious harm" requirement for successful defamation claims, providing that a statement is defamatory only if its publication has caused or is likely to cause serious harm to the claimant's reputation. Other significant measures include: (1) added protection for scientists and academics; (ii) added protection for matters "in the public interest"; (iii) tightened requirements for claims with little or no connection to England and Wales; (iv) new procedures designed to protect website operators and to encourage dispute resolution directly with the person who posted an allegedly defamatory statement; and (v) a single-publication rule, which would help to eliminate the situation where each republication of a communication — or, as in *Ehrenfeld*,[48] each download — of an allegedly defamatory statement would create a new cause of action. Many have heralded the Act as an enormous improvement, while others have observed that it avoids directly reckoning with many root causes of libel tourism. Indeed, the Act has so far not entirely changed the course of defamation litigation in England and Wales.

PROBLEM 4-25: LIBEL TOURISM AND THE *ALEEM* CASE: HOW SPECIAL IS THE FIRST AMENDMENT?

In order to protect First Amendment values, the United States Congress passed the SPEECH Act, which essentially insulates a foreign country judgment from recognition and enforcement unless the judgment is consistent with United States law governing freedom of expression. Should the SPEECH Act approach to foreign country judgments extend to other legal contexts in the United States? For example, consider the special rules in the United States regarding divorce judgments. These rules reflect a range of cultural, legal, and religious policies and seek to accommodate differences among the states within the United States. Moreover, because divorce and marriage implicate moral issues, they are subject matters often implicating public policy arguments. Consider the following case and ask yourself whether United States public policies might justify a federal statute preventing enforcement of foreign country judgments that implicate United States laws of divorce — a federal statute with the same unequivocal protections of United States

47. Andrew R. Klein, *Some Thoughts on Libel Tourism*, 38 PEPP. L. REV. 101 (2010), *available at* http://ssrn.com/abstract=1733139; *citing Libel Laws Making Mockery of Justice, Say Lib Dems*, B.B.C. NEWS (Jan. 18, 2010), *available at* http://news.bbc.co.uk/2/hi/uk_news/politics/8466297.stm.
48. *Ehrenfeld*, 518 F.3d 102.

policies as the SPEECH Act provides to defamation judgments that implicate First Amendment values:

> The case concerns Farah and Irfan Aleem, who lived in Maryland. Farah wished to divorce her husband Irfan, who was a Muslim citizen of Pakistan. Before Farah filed her divorce action in state court, her husband travelled to the Pakistani embassy in Washington, D.C. and performed *talaq* there. *Talaq* is the execution of a document that announces the husband's intention three times to divorce his wife. After Farah filed the divorce action, Irfan argued that the state court was required to give effect to the *talaq* divorce, arguing that "the performance by him of *talaq* under Islamic religious and secular Pakistan law . . . deprived" the state court of authority to decide how to divide the couple's marital property in the United States.[49] Irfan argued that the state court could not distribute the property according to state law principles of equitable distribution of marital property, but was required to give effect to the *talaq* divorce as Pakistani courts would do so: allowing property to be distributed according to Muslim custom as recognized in Pakistani statutes. The state court ruled that the *talaq* divorce was against public policy and should not be recognized as a judgment that could foreclose United States litigation over the marital property distribution.

> Is there a qualitative difference between a *talaq* divorce that one wants recognized in a United States court and a libel judgment from another country that fails to respect First Amendment values? If both the divorce and the libel judgment implicate United States public policy, is the strength of the public policy the same in both instances? If so, shouldn't there be a federal statute passed making clear that any *talaq* divorce that does not respect United States property distribution principles may not be recognized in any court of the United States? After all, didn't the husband, Irfan Aleem, "forum shop" in the same way as a libel tourist by making his way to the Pakistani embassy — so as to be on Pakistani soil? Is there a distinction between these two circumstances?

4. *Special Challenges of International Judgments in Internet Cases*

Material presented above in Chapter 1 (personal jurisdiction) and Chapter 2 (choice of law) illustrated some of the many challenges for courts trying to navigate a place with no territory (cyberspace) with principles developed for territorial disputes. Cyberspace simply confounds traditional paradigms for analyzing these problems. Recognition and enforcement of judgments issues are equally challenging in the internet context. In fact, the disconnect between standard doctrine and cyberspace may become magnified in the judgments area. As Dean Paul Schiff Berman has stated, "judgment recognition is increasingly the place where deterritorialized jurisdictional assertions meet the reality of territorial enforcement." Paul Schiff Berman, *Dialectical Regulation, Territoriality, and Pluralism*, 38 CONN. L. REV. 929, 944-945 (2006). This reality often simply

---

49. *See Aleem v. Aleem*, 947 A.2d 489, 490 (Md. 2008); Doug Rendleman, *Collecting a Libel Tourist's Judgment?*, 67 WASH. & LEE L. REV. 467 (2010) (discussing the *Aleem* case in light of libel tourism).

reflects the practical problem that one might easily purchase something from a foreign seller over the internet and might even convince a nearby court in one's own country to exercise personal jurisdiction over the foreign seller and apply forum law to the dispute. But turning the resulting judgment into cash may require a cumbersome and expensive process of recognition and enforcement in the seller's home country, a foreign land in which one is not prepared to litigate. The contrast between the ease of forging the commercial relationship and the difficulty of enforcing a judgment resulting from the breakdown of the relationship can be stark.

Internet interactions may also inspire more than practical enforcement problems, implicating a clash of fundamental legal norms. Whether for commercial purposes or otherwise, the internet easily brings individuals together from radically different cultures, societies, and political traditions. This provides an opportunity to build bonds not otherwise possible. In some instances, a new community — an internet community — may form with those participating sharing a common interest (e.g., film, manga, fan fiction) that helps to bridge an otherwise vast gulf of difference. Where the bridge between individuals in the community breaks down — or the sovereign power of individual governments intervenes — the clash of values and attitudes can be dramatic. Where that clash transforms into a judgment, the drama continues: as we have seen, judgments are particularly important exercises of sovereign power, reflecting the rule of law itself. Thus, the question of recognition and enforcement can be particularly sensitive where the judgment reflects sensitive policy concerns that the citizens triggered — sometimes unwittingly through casual internet interactions. As in other foreign recognition of judgments contexts, this clash of policy tends to implicate freedom of expression principles. This is the context illustrated in both cases below.

Yahoo!, Inc. v. La Ligue Contre Le Racisme et L'Antisémitisme

> 169 F. Supp. 2d 1181 (N.D. Cal. 2001), *rev'd en banc on other grounds*, 433 F.3d 1199 (9th Cir. 2006)

FOGEL, District Judge.

. . .

I. PROCEDURAL HISTORY

Defendants La Ligue Contre Le Racisme Et l'Antisemitisme ("LICRA") and L'Union Des Etudiants Juifs De France, citizens of France, are non-profit organizations dedicated to eliminating anti-Semitism. Plaintiff Yahoo!, Inc. ("Yahoo!") is a corporation organized under the laws of Delaware with its principal place of business in Santa Clara, California. Yahoo! is an Internet service provider that operates various Internet websites and services that any computer user can access at the Uniform Resource Locator ("URL") *http://www.yahoo.com.* Yahoo! services ending in the suffix, ".com," without an associated country code as a prefix or extension (collectively, "Yahoo!'s U.S. Services") use the English language and target users who are residents of, utilize servers based in and operate under the laws of the United States. Yahoo! subsidiary corporations operate regional Yahoo! sites and services in twenty other nations, including, for example, Yahoo! France, Yahoo! India, and Yahoo! Spain. Each of these regional web sites contains the host nation's unique two-letter code as either a prefix or a suffix in its URL (e.g., Yahoo! France is found at *http://www.yahoo.fr* and Yahoo! Korea at *http://www.yahoo.kr*). Yahoo!'s regional sites use the local region's primary language, target the local citizenry, and operate under local laws.

Yahoo! provides a variety of means by which people from all over the world can communicate and interact with one another over the Internet. Examples include an Internet search engine, e-mail, an automated auction site, personal web page hostings, shopping services, chat rooms, and a listing of clubs that individuals can create or join. Any computer user with Internet access is able to post materials on many of these Yahoo! sites, which in turn are instantly accessible by anyone who logs on to Yahoo!'s Internet sites. As relevant here, Yahoo!'s auction site allows anyone to post an item for sale and solicit bids from any computer user from around the globe. Yahoo! records when a posting is made and after the requisite time period lapses sends an e-mail notification to the highest bidder and seller with their respective contact information. Yahoo! is never a party to a transaction, and the buyer and seller are responsible for arranging privately for payment and shipment of goods. Yahoo! monitors the transaction through limited regulation by prohibiting particular items from being sold (such as stolen goods, body parts, prescription and illegal drugs, weapons, and goods violating U.S. copyright laws or the Iranian and Cuban embargos) and by providing a rating system through which buyers and sellers have their transactional behavior evaluated for the benefit of future consumers. Yahoo! informs auction sellers that they must comply with Yahoo!'s policies and may not offer items to buyers in jurisdictions in which the sale of such item violates the jurisdiction's applicable laws. Yahoo! does not actively regulate the content of each posting, and individuals are able to post, and have in fact posted, highly offensive matter, including Nazi-related propaganda and Third Reich memorabilia, on Yahoo!'s auction sites.

On or about April 5, 2000, LICRA sent a "cease and desist" letter to Yahoo!'s Santa Clara headquarters informing Yahoo! that the sale of Nazi and Third Reich related goods through its auction services violates French law. LICRA threatened to take legal action unless Yahoo! took steps to prevent such sales within eight days. Defendants subsequently utilized the United States Marshal's Office to serve Yahoo! with process in California and filed a civil complaint against Yahoo! in the Tribunal de Grande Instance de Paris (the "French Court").

The French Court found that approximately 1,000 Nazi and Third Reich related objects, including Adolf Hitler's *Mein Kampf, The Protocol of the Elders of Zion* (an infamous anti-Semitic report produced by the Czarist secret police in the early 1900's), and purported "evidence" that the gas chambers of the Holocaust did not exist were being offered for sale on Yahoo.com's auction site. Because any French citizen is able to access these materials on Yahoo.com directly or through a link on Yahoo.fr, the French Court concluded that the Yahoo.com auction site violates Section R645-1 of the French Criminal Code, which prohibits exhibition of Nazi propaganda and artifacts for sale. On May 20, 2000, the French Court entered an order requiring Yahoo! to (1) eliminate French citizens' access to any material on the Yahoo.com auction site that offers for sale any Nazi objects, relics, insignia, emblems, and flags; (2) eliminate French citizens' access to web pages on Yahoo.com displaying text, extracts, or quotations from *Mein Kampf* and *Protocol of the Elders of Zion*; (3) post a warning to French citizens on Yahoo.fr that any search through Yahoo.com may lead to sites containing material prohibited by Section R645-1 of the French Criminal Code, and that such viewing of the prohibited material may result in legal action against the Internet user; (4) remove from all browser directories accessible in the French Republic index headings entitled "negationists" and from all hypertext links the equation of "negationists" under the heading "Holocaust." The order subjects Yahoo! to a penalty of 100,000 Euros for each day that it fails to comply with the order. The order concludes:

> We order the Company YAHOO! Inc. to take all necessary measures to dissuade and render impossible any access via Yahoo.com to the Nazi artifact auction service and to any other site or service that may be construed as constituting an apology for Nazism or a contesting of Nazi crimes.

. . .

Yahoo! asked the French Court to reconsider the terms of the order, claiming that although it easily could post the required warning on Yahoo.fr, compliance with the order's requirements with respect to Yahoo.com was technologically impossible. The French Court sought expert opinion on the matter and . . . ordered Yahoo! to comply with the May 22 order within three (3) months or face a penalty of 100,000 Francs (approximately U.S. $13,300) for each day of non-compliance. The French Court also provided that penalties assessed against Yahoo! Inc. may not be collected from Yahoo! France. Defendants again utilized the United States Marshal's Office to serve Yahoo! in California with the French Order.

Yahoo! subsequently posted the required warning and prohibited postings in violation of Section R645-1 of the French Criminal Code from appearing on Yahoo.fr. Yahoo! also amended the auction policy of Yahoo.com to prohibit individuals from auctioning:

> Any item that promotes, glorifies, or is directly associated with groups or individuals known principally for hateful or violent positions or acts, such as Nazis or the Ku Klux Klan. Official government-issue stamps and coins are not prohibited under this policy. Expressive media, such as books and films, may be subject to more permissive standards as determined by Yahoo! in its sole discretion.

Yahoo Auction Guidelines (visited Oct. 23, 2001) http:// user.auctions.Yahoo.com/ html/ guidelines.html. Notwithstanding these actions, the Yahoo.com auction site still offers certain items for sale (such as stamps, coins, and a copy of *Mein Kampf*) which appear to violate the French Order. . . .

Yahoo! claims that because it lacks the technology to block French citizens from accessing the Yahoo.com auction site to view materials which violate the French Order or from accessing other Nazi-based content of websites on Yahoo. com, it cannot comply with the French order without banning Nazi-related material from Yahoo.com altogether. Yahoo! contends that such a ban would infringe impermissibly upon its rights under the First Amendment to the United States Constitution. Accordingly, Yahoo! filed a complaint in this Court seeking a declaratory judgment that the French Court's orders are neither cognizable nor enforceable under the laws of the United States. . . .

II. OVERVIEW

. . . This case is *not* about the moral acceptability of promoting the symbols or propaganda of Nazism. . . . This Court is acutely mindful of the emotional pain reminders of the Nazi era cause to Holocaust survivors and deeply respectful of the motivations of the French Republic. . . . Vigilance is the key to preventing atrocities such as the Holocaust from occurring again.

Nor is this case about the right of France or any other nation to determine its own law and social policies. A basic function of a sovereign state is to determine by law what forms of speech and conduct are acceptable within its borders. In this instance, as a nation whose citizens suffered the effects of Nazism in ways that are incomprehensible to most Americans, France clearly has the right to enact and enforce laws such as those relied upon by the French Court here.

What *is* at issue here is whether it is consistent with the Constitution and laws of the United States for another nation to regulate speech by a United States resident within the United States on the basis that such speech can be accessed by Internet users in that nation. In a world in which ideas and information transcend borders and the Internet in particular renders the physical distance between speaker and audience virtually meaningless, the implications of this question go far beyond the facts of this case. The modern world is home to widely varied cultures with radically divergent value systems. There is little doubt that Internet users in the United States routinely engage in speech that violates, for example, China's laws against religious expression, the laws of various nations against advocacy of gender equality or homosexuality, or even the United Kingdom's restrictions on freedom of the press. If the government or another party in one of these sovereign nations were to seek enforcement of such laws against Yahoo! or another U.S.-based Internet service provider, what principles should guide the court's analysis?

The Court has stated that it must and will decide this case in accordance with the Constitution and laws of the United States. It recognizes that in so doing, it necessarily adopts certain value judgments embedded in those enactments, including the fundamental judgment expressed in the Amendment that it is preferable to permit the non-violent expression of offensive First viewpoints rather than to impose viewpoint-based governmental regulation upon speech. The government and people of France have made a different judgment based upon their own experience. In undertaking its inquiry as to the proper application of the laws of the United States, the Court intends no disrespect for that judgment or for the experience that has informed it.

. . . The French order prohibits the sale or display of items based on their association with a particular political organization and bans the display of websites based on the authors' viewpoint with respect to the Holocaust and anti-Semitism. A United States court constitutionally could not make such an order. The First Amendment does not permit the government to engage in viewpoint-based regulation of speech absent a compelling governmental interest, such as averting a clear and present danger of imminent violence. In addition, the French Court's mandate that Yahoo! "take all necessary measures to dissuade and render impossible any access via Yahoo.com to the Nazi artifact auction service and to any other site or service that may be construed as constituting an apology for Nazism or a contesting of Nazi crimes" is far too general and imprecise to survive the strict scrutiny required by the First Amendment. The phrase, "and any other site or service that *may be construed* as an apology for Nazism or a contesting of Nazi crimes" fails to provide Yahoo! with a sufficiently definite warning as to what is proscribed. [The court rejected the argument that the posture of this case did not immediately implicate these First Amendment problems and rejected the suggestion that it abstain from deciding the dispute.]

4. COMITY

No legal judgment has any effect, of its own force, beyond the limits of the sovereignty from which its authority is derived. . . . The extent to which the United States, or any state, honors the judicial decrees of foreign nations is a matter of choice, governed by "the comity of nations." *Hilton v. Guyot*, 159 U.S. 113, 163, 16 S. Ct. 139, 40 L. Ed. 95 (1895). . . . As discussed previously, the French order's content and viewpoint-based regulation of the web pages and auction site on Yahoo.com, while entitled to great deference as an articulation of French law, clearly would be inconsistent with the First Amendment if mandated by a court in the United States. What makes this case uniquely challenging is that the Internet in effect allows one to speak in more than one place at the same time. Although France has the sovereign right to regulate what speech is permissible in France, this Court may not enforce a foreign order that violates the protections of the United States Constitution by chilling protected speech that occurs simultaneously within our borders. *See, e.g., Matusevitch v. Telnikoff*, 877 F. Supp. 1, 4 (D.D.C. 1995). . . . The reason for limiting comity in this area is sound. "The protection to free speech and the press embodied in [the First] amendment would be seriously jeopardized by the entry of foreign [] judgments granted pursuant to standards deemed appropriate in [another country] but considered antithetical to the protections afforded the press by the U.S. Constitution." Absent a body of law that establishes international standards with respect to speech on the Internet and an appropriate treaty or legislation addressing enforcement of such standards to speech originating within the United States, the principle of comity is outweighed by the Court's obligation to uphold the First Amendment.

In light of the Court's conclusion that enforcement of the French order by a United States court would be inconsistent with the First Amendment, the factual question of whether Yahoo! possesses the technology to comply with the order is immaterial. Even assuming for purposes of the present motion that Yahoo! does possess such technology, compliance still would involve an impermissible restriction on speech. . . .

V. CONCLUSION

Yahoo! seeks a declaration from this Court that the First Amendment precludes enforcement within the United States of a French order intended to regulate the content of its speech over the Internet. Yahoo! has shown that the French order is valid under the laws of France, that it may be enforced with retroactive penalties, and that the ongoing possibility of its enforcement in the United States chills Yahoo!'s First Amendment rights. Yahoo! also has shown that an actual controversy exists and that the threat to its constitutional rights is real and immediate. . . .

Notes on
YAHOO!

1. A panel of the United States Court of Appeals for the Ninth Circuit reversed the district court's decision, but did not reach the First Amendment issue. Instead, two of three judges on the panel reversed on personal jurisdiction grounds, stating that "[b]ecause the District Court had no personal jurisdiction over the French parties, we do not review whether Yahoo!'s action for declaratory relief was ripe for adjudication or whether the District Court properly refused to abstain from hearing this case." 399 F.3d 1010, 1126-1127 (9th Cir. 2005).

2. In discussing choice of law and the internet, Chapter 2 suggested that allowing jurisdictions to have extraterritorial reach in controlling speech might allow the *most* restrictive jurisdiction to set the standard for all who use the internet. What is the result of decisions such as that of the *Yahoo!* district court above? Does it create the opposite state of affairs, where the *least* restrictive jurisdiction sets the standard? Or does it create a situation where each territorial jurisdiction in which a speaker has assets gets to set the communication standard for that speaker? Which approach is the most appropriate? Isn't it best to give multiple communities a stake in the resolution of the free speech issues? Or would it be better to have used available international standards for hate speech to resolve this case?

3. Assuming that the district court was correct in holding that the French judgment violated First Amendment principles, must one therefore conclude that the district court would have been acting unconstitutionally in enforcing the French judgment? Don't the concerns that inform whether to

enforce a foreign country judgment—finality, comity, and the like—influence that analysis and moderate the court's duty to enforce United States constitutional standards? Professor Mark Rosen argues that even where a foreign country judgment reflects values at odds with United States constitutional standards, neither the judgment nor a United States court's enforcement of it are unconstitutional. Mark D. Rosen, *Exporting the Constitution*, 53 EMORY L.J. 171 (2004).

PROBLEM 4-26: ERNEST, HENRY, AND THE PORNOGRAPHY JUDGMENT

Assume that the country of New Amsterdam has extremely lenient laws pertaining to pornography, far more lenient than the United States. A resident of New Amsterdam, Henry, runs a website out of New Amsterdam with sexually explicit material. Assume further that a resident of the United States, Ernest, is offended by the website and wishes to restrict access to the material by his family. Ernest does not believe that blocking technology will be sufficient, so he files suit in state court seeking to require Henry to take action to prevent access to the material in the United States. The United States state court issues an order saying that Henry must restrict access to United States internet users and will be subject to fines if he fails to take action. Henry fails to take action, fines accrue against him, and Ernest files suit in New Amsterdam to enforce the judgment (i.e., collect the fines). Assume that the New Amsterdam court believes it is appropriate to follow the rationale and approach of the United States District Court's decision in *Yahoo!* If the New Amsterdam court does so, what standard should the New Amsterdam court use in evaluating whether to enforce this judgment? Does it matter that under United States case law, the question whether something is obscene requires a court to consider whether an average person, "applying contemporary community standards," would find that the work appeals to the "prurient interest" and is "patently offensive"? *Miller v. California*, 413 U.S. 15, 30-34 (1973). In other words, does it matter that the question of whether the material is protected by the First Amendment varies according to which community standards are used?

Citron v. Zündel

Canadian Human Rights Tribunal 2002 Carswell Nat 4364 (C.H.R.T.)
(WL) [2002] 41 C.H.R.R. D/274 (Can. Human Rights Trib.)

Access to the Internet has revolutionized global communication and has had a profound impact on modern society. With its promise of readily accessible information and the explosion in use of the Internet, serious concerns have been raised about the content found on many sites. The relationship of the Internet to existing regulatory frameworks, such as restrictions on the display of pornography, the protection of individual privacy, and the limits of permissible commerce are all the subject of significant legal debate and public controversy.

As we begin to explore the legal limits of the use of the Internet for the mass distribution of information, fundamental issues are raised regarding the preservation of legitimate free speech interests. At the same time, the proliferation of alleged "hate sites" on the World Wide Web has been particularly disturbing for the equality seeking community. This case, for the first time, raises squarely the application of the Canadian Human Rights Act to sites on the World Wide Web, and yet again exposes the constant tension between competing social interests.

. . . The complaints . . . seek to apply §13(1) of the Canadian Human Rights Act to communication via the Internet. It is alleged that by posting material to the Zundelsite, the Respondent, Ernst Zündel, caused repeated telephonic communication that was likely to expose Jews to hatred or contempt. We are therefore asked to determine whether it is a discriminatory practice to post material on a Website if the material is likely to expose a person to hatred or contempt. What limits, if any, are to be applied to repeated communication of hate messages via the Internet? Finally, if applied to the Internet, is this a permissible restriction on freedom of speech under the Charter of Rights and Freedoms?

[On July 18, 1996, the Mayor's Committee on Community and Race Relations (the "Mayor's Committee") filed a complaint with the Canadian Human Rights Commission (the "Commission") alleging that Ernst Zündel was placing messages on the World Wide Web that were likely to expose a person or persons to hatred or contempt, on the basis that those individuals were identifiable on the basis of a prohibited ground of discrimination, contrary to §13(1) of the Canadian Human Rights Act.]

The particulars of this complaint allege that from October 10, 1995 onward, Ernst Zündel offered a Homepage on the World Wide Web that repeatedly provided pamphlets and publications that were likely to expose persons of the Jewish faith and ethnic origin to hatred and contempt. Examples of these messages . . . : "Did Six Million Really Die," . . . and "Jewish Soap."

Sabina Citron, who identifies herself as a Jew and survivor of the Holocaust, lodged a parallel complaint on September 25, 1996. . . . The central thesis of both complaints is that the Respondent, Ernst Zündel, was engaged in a discriminatory practise when he caused to be communicated, via the World Wide Web and the Internet, material that was likely to expose Jews to hatred and contempt. It is alleged that, by posting material on the Zundelsite the Respondent has caused the repeated telephonic communication of hate messages. . . .

[The tribunal discussed various documents that were downloaded from the Zundelsite. A review of these documents provides a series of direct references to Mr. Zündel and his implied relationship to the site. The Court noted that several of the documents contain a number of other frequently repeated references to Mr. Zündel's personal involvement with the site. The tribunal court found that Ernst Zündel controlled the Zundelsite and that it was he who caused the materials found on the website to be communicated. The tribunal also discussed the purpose or intent of the Human Rights Act to censure "the incitement of hatred and the possible actions that might flow from the intense emotions of ill will towards others." . . .

The tribunal noted that "[t]he primary theme [of the website documents] relates to the events of the Second World War, and the expression of doubt concerning the accuracy of the prevailing view regarding the treatment of the Jews by the Germans. Accompanying these challenges is the assertion that Jews, individually and collectively, have deliberately promoted a false version of history in order to gain a personal benefit by way of reparations." The documents further made mention of the following: "The fact is that the Jewish Lobby — or the Israeli Lobby, as some like to call it — have long had a deliberate policy of lying to non-Jewish Americans. . . . [T]hey have lied to us about a great number of other things, too — including their most infamous lie and the most lucrative and crooked scheme: the so-called 'Holocaust.'"

The tribunal found that the communications in question are likely to expose a person or group of persons to hatred or contempt on the sole basis that they are identified by their religious affiliation and ancestry. It rejects the argument that the statements were examples of a "healthy expression of one perspective in an ongoing historical debate" and that people in both the German and "revisionist" community are silenced by fear, humiliated and ostracized, and so dare not question the conventional version of events as a result of the commonly held beliefs regarding Germany's treatment of Jews during the Second World War. Instead, the tribunal found that the tone and extreme denigration of Jews separates these documents from those that might be permissible.]

[I]t is important to begin with the proposition that §13(1) aims at controlling messages that are likely to expose individuals to hatred and contempt, within a realm that is open to Parliament to control, that is, facilities of a telecommunication undertaking. The Canadian Human Rights Act, at its foundation, assumes that individuals are equal, that groups are equal, and that mere membership in a religious, ethnic, or racial group does not carry with it any positive or negative characteristics and should not be the basis for a generalized prejudice[,] hatred or contempt. . . .

We conclude therefore that while the Internet introduces a different context from the traditional use of the telephone. . . . Parliament's intent to prevent serious harms caused by hate propaganda remains a matter of pressing and substantial importance. . . . As a society, our disapproval of hate messages does not depend narrowly on whether they are found on a telephone-answering device. Parliament has spoken. If the telephone is ideally suited to the effective transmission of prejudicial beliefs as part of a campaign to affect public beliefs and attitudes, how much more effective and ideally suited is the Internet to the efficient transmission of such detrimental beliefs. We see no basis for a distinction based on the facts of this case that would allow us, in a free and democratic society, to withdraw our commitment to protecting minority groups from the intolerance and psychological pain caused by the expression of hate propaganda.

In view of the focused purpose of §13(1) as an instrument of national policy and from the perspective of international commitments, it is, in our view, inappropriate to say that hate propaganda is licit because it has found expression through another medium, the Internet. Once it is accepted that hate propaganda is antithetical to Charter values, the means of expression, in our view, is not a controlling factor so long as it is within the constitutional jurisdiction of Parliament.

Freedom of expression also continues to be impaired as minimally as possible by §13(1). The definition of "hatred," "contempt" and "likely to expose" remains the same and has been found not to be overly broad. Since the focus of §13(1) is on "repeated" telephonic messages that are likely to expose persons to hatred or contempt, attention is directed to large scale, public schemes for the dissemination of hate propaganda. The structure of Internet communications makes it especially susceptible to this analysis. It is difficult for us to see why the Internet, with its pervasive influence and accessibility, should be available to spread messages that are likely to expose persons to hatred or contempt. One can conceive that this new medium of the Internet is a much more effective and well-suited vehicle for the dissemination of hate propaganda.

[The tribunal thus concluded that §13(1) considered in the context of the facts of this case remains rationally connected to the purpose of the Act, minimally impairs "the Respondent's freedom to communicate a type of speech . . . and the benefit continues to outweigh any deleterious effects on the Respondent's freedom of expression." The use of §13(1) of the Act to deal with hateful telephonic messages on the Internet remains a restriction on the Respondent's freedom of speech which is reasonable and justified in a free and democratic society.

The tribunal acknowledged that one of the unique features of the Internet is the ease with which strangers to the creator of a particular site can access material and, if they choose, replicate the entire site at another web address. "Mirror" sites already exist that duplicate in their totality the material currently found on the Zundelsite. The tribunal also accepted that some individuals, in an attempt to rebuff efforts to limit speech or regulate the Internet, might be prompted to create mirror sites in direct response to an Order issued by the tribunal. It was submitted that even if the tribunal found that there has been a contravention of §13(1) of the Act, it would be totally ineffectual to issue a cease and desist order; notwithstanding any Order that it might issue, the material found on the Zundelsite would remain accessible to anyone in Canada who can find a mirror site.]

We are extremely conscious of the limits of the remedial power available in this case. . . . The technology involved in the posting of materials to the Internet, however, magnifies this problem and arguably makes it much easier to avoid the ultimate goal of eliminating the material from telephonic communication.

Nonetheless, as a Tribunal we are charged with the responsibility of determining the complaints referred to us, and then making an Order if we find that the Respondent has engaged in a discriminatory practise. . . .

Any remedy awarded by this, or any Tribunal, will inevitably serve a number of purposes: prevention and elimination of discriminatory practises is only one of the outcomes flowing from an Order issued as a consequence of these proceedings. There is also a significant symbolic value in the public denunciation of the actions that are the subject of this complaint. Similarly, there is the potential educative and ultimately larger preventative benefit that can be achieved by open discussion of the principles enunciated in this or any Tribunal decision.

Parliament, on behalf of all Canadians, has determined that the telephonic communication of hate messages is not to be tolerated in our society. In our view, the victims of hate are entitled to obtain the benefit of the full weight of our authority.

[The tribunal thus determined that the Respondent Ernst Zündel engaged in a discriminatory practice by posting material to his website that is likely to expose Jews to hatred or contempt, and the granting of the remedy requested is warranted and appropriate.]

We therefore order that the Respondent, Ernst Zündel, and any other individuals who act in the name of, or in concert with Ernst Zündel cease the discriminatory practise of communicating telephonically or causing to be communicated telephonically by means of the facilities of a telecommunication undertaking within the legislative authority of Parliament, matters of the type . . . found on the Zundelsite, or any other messages of a substantially similar form or content that are likely to expose a person or persons to hatred or contempt by reason of the fact that that person or persons are identifiable on the basis of a prohibited ground of discrimination, contrary to §13(1) of the Canadian Human Rights Act.

Notes on
CITRON v. ZÜNDEL

1. *Citron v. Zündel* is particularly noteworthy in the judgments context because the tribunal concluded its judgment would have "virtually no effect in eliminating [the offending] material from the World Wide Web." Was its judgment really as impotent as it claimed? If so, why did the tribunal even bother? *See* Thomas Schultz, *Carving up the Internet: Jurisdiction, Legal Orders, and the Private Public International Law Interface*, 19 Eur. J. Int'l L. 799, 823 (2008) ("[A] dispute . . . involving public policy considerations disrupts a link between individual and her community. Judging a case is a way to rebuild this link. It is . . . a process through which a community expresses what is acceptable within the community. . . .").

2. If in fact the tribunal lacked the enforcement power that it claimed, why was it appropriate for the tribunal to act at all? Couldn't you argue that a tribunal that lacks the capacity to issue potent orders lacks the ability to legitimately exercise any adjudicatory authority? *See* Melissa A. Waters, *Mediating Norms and Identity: The Role of Transnational Judicial Dialogue in Creating and Enforcing International Law*, 93 Geo. L J. 487, 538 (2005) (suggesting that the *Citron v. Zündel* tribunal "viewed its role not only as a transnational representative or defender of domestic speech norms, but also as a transnational advocate or champion of domestic norms").

F. COMPARATIVE MATERIAL — THE BRUSSELS REGIME: JUDGMENT ENFORCEMENT AND RECOGNITION IN THE EUROPEAN UNION

The European Union has attempted to harmonize the rules for judgment recognition and enforcement in civil and commercial matters through a set of treaties and regulations collectively called the Brussels Regime.[50] The initial Brussels Convention[51] provided for recognition and enforcement of a judgment rendered by one contracting state by other contracting states.[52] However, the Convention applies only to claims brought against domiciliaries of contracting states; if the defendant is domiciled elsewhere, the forum's national law determines the propriety of a jurisdictional assertion.[53] The parallel Lugano Convention[54] was concluded between Member States of the European Communities (EC) and certain members of the European Free Trade Association (EFTA).[55]

The "Brussels I" regulation forms the core of the current Brussels Regime, and its purpose is to improve the functioning of the European Union's single market by allowing judgments to move freely between countries; otherwise, as the Council of the European Union notes, certain differences between national rules governing jurisdiction and recognition of judgments hamper the sound operation of the internal market.[56] Brussels I broadly defines judgments to be any "judgment given by a court or tribunal of a Member State, whatever the judgment may be called, including a decree, order, decision or writ of execution." Judgments need not be final before being recognized.

The process for recognition is meant to be "rapid and automatic,"[57] and the regulation states that no special procedure is required in order to recognize a judgment from another Member State. Limited rules authorize obstacles to judgment recognition, but Brussels I prohibits courts asked to recognize a judgment from reviewing a judgment's substance. If the foreign judgment is given in default of appearance, a court must not recognize the judgment if the plaintiff had failed

50. Brussels Convention on Jurisdiction and the Enforcement of Judgments in Civil and Commercial Matters 1968, *available at* http://www.jus.uio.no/lm/brussels.jurisdiction.and. enforcement.of.judgments.in.civil.and. commercial.matters.convention.1968/doc.html.

51. Convention of 27 September 1968 on Jurisdiction and the Enforcement of Judgments in Civil and Commercial Matters, 1972 O.J. (L 299).

52. American Bar Association, *Achieving Legal and Business Order in Cyberspace: A Report on Global Jurisdictional Issues Created by the Internet*, 55 Bus. Law. 1801, n.33 (July 2000).

53. *Id.* at n.94.

54. Convention of 16 September 1988 on Jurisdiction and the Enforcement of Judgments in Civil and Commercial Matters (Lugano Convention) SR 0.275.12 (Switz.) *available at* http:// ec.europa.eu/world/agreements/download File.do?fullText=yes&treatyTransId=13041.

55. Lukas Muller, *The Revised Lugano Convention from the Swiss Perspective*, 18 Colum. J. Eur. L. Online 9 (2011), *available at* http://ssrn.com/abstract=1995053.

56. *See* Council Regulation (EC) No. 44/2001 of 22 Dec. 2000, 2000 O.J. (L 12/1) 1 (EC), *available at* http://curia.europa.eu/common/recdoc/convention/en/c-textes/2001R0044-idx.htm.

57. Commission of the European Communities, Proposal for a Council Regulation (EC) on jurisdiction and the recognition and enforcement of judgments in civil and commercial matters, at 6, COM (1999) 348 final, July 14, 1999.

to comply with certain procedural steps in serving the defendant. Also, if the judgment is irreconcilable with an earlier judgment between the same parties and involving the same cause of action—whether the conflicting judgment was issued in the Member State where recognition is sought or a third party state—the court must refuse recognition.

Brussels I does not specify the preclusive effect of foreign country judgments. Although a recognized judgment might have preclusive effect, Brussels I's failure to delineate that effect has inspired divergent approaches to preclusion across European courts. The most widely used approach gives the recognized judgment the preclusive effect it had in its country of origin.[58] This method, also called the extension-of-effects method, mirrors practice in the United States. A minority of European courts follows the equalization-of-effects method, which applies the recognizing country's law in determining the preclusive effects of the judgment, or the combined effects method, which is a combination of the extension and the equalization methods.[59]

Public Policy Exception Under Article 34(1) of EC No. 44/2001

The court of a Member State can refuse to recognize a judgment of another Member State on public policy grounds, but the judgment must be "manifestly contrary" to the public policy of the Member State asked to recognize the judgment. (The "public policy" must concern some matter other than jurisdictional rules.) Material describing the public policy exception of Article 34(1) of EC No. 44/2001 suggests that procedural and substantive policies are included in the exception.[60] One of the earliest landmark cases demonstrating the public policy exception, *Krombach v. Bamberski*,[61] articulated a standard that appears best suited for evaluating procedural policies. *Krombach v. Bamberski* involved a German defendant who was subject to a criminal suit in France by a French citizen.[62] Because the defendant did not appear in French court, the court refused to allow any legal defense for the defendant and judgment was entered against him.[63] The European Court of Justice explained that the public policy exception applies where the judgment is "at variance to an unacceptable degree with the legal order of the State in which enforcement is sought inasmuch as it infringes a fundamental principle."[64] The court further explained that "the infringement must constitute a manifest breach of a rule of law regarded as essential in the legal order of the State . . . or of a right recognised as being fundamental within that

---

58. Jacob van de Velden & Justine Stefanelli, *The Effect in the European Community of Judgments in Civil and Commercial Matters: Recognition, Res Judicata and Abuse of Process* 61-62 (BRITISH INSTITUTE OF INTERNATIONAL AND COMPARATIVE LAW ed. 2008).

59. *Id.*

60. Paul Beaumont & Emma Johnston, *Can Exequatur Be Abolished in Brussels I Whilst Retaining a Public Policy Defense?*, 6 J. PRIVATE INT'L L. 249 (2010).

61. Case C-7/98, *Krombach v. Bamberski*, 2000 E.C.R. I-01935. This case involved Article 27 of the Brussels Convention, which was replaced by Article 34 of the Brussels I Regulation and still serves as a basis for understanding the public policy exception contained in both agreements.

62. *Id.*

63. *Id.*

64. *Id.* at 37.

legal order."[65] Citing rulings from the European Court of Human Rights and Member States' constitutions, the court held the right to a fair trial was a fundamental right.[66] Therefore, the French court's refusal to hear a defense violated that right, and the German courts were required to refuse recognition of the judgment.[67]

The precise substantive public policies that might qualify for this exception are yet to be established. The European Court of Justice seems to include within the public policy exception a "fundamental rights" definition that includes European Court of Human Rights rulings and Member State constitutions. Based on individual country case law, possible substantive areas include defamation, excessive damages, fraud, consumer, employee, and renter protections, unacceptably high spousal or child support, and competition laws.[68]

Exequatur Process

Enforcing a judgment in another Member State has not been as automatic as the recognition process. Originally, the Brussels regime required that, for a judgment to be enforced in another Member State, it must be declared enforceable there through a special procedure called exequatur. Exequatur was governed by national laws. The exequatur process was only formal, but the decision to enforce the judgment could be appealed on all the grounds that can prevent recognition of a judgment. The bureaucratic obstacles of exequatur created a slower and more expensive process than recognition, and the exequatur procedure was perceived as essentially delaying and increasing the cost of cross-border debt recovery.[69] Hence, a movement to reform Brussels I gained strength.

Proponents for abolishing exequatur argued that the process's inefficiency created obstacles to "full faith and credit" recognition of EU Member States' judgment and hence disturbed smooth operation of the single European market, since they viewed exequatur as causing debtors and creditors to incur unnecessary costs in judgment enforcement.[70] Critics of abolishing exequatur argued that it was more than just a formal judicial procedure, but was rather a tool for ensuring certain basic requirements are met.[71] One of these requirements was the judgment's compatibility with the public policy of the enforcing state.[72] Critics argued that the abolition of exequatur would lead courts to favor expediency over the assurance of the defendant's fundamental human rights, such as the right to a fair trial.[73]

---

65. *Id.*

66. *Id.*

67. *Id.*

68. For a review of these various contexts, see generally Burkhard Hess & Thomas Pfeiffer, *Interpretation of the Public Policy Exception as Referred to in EU Instruments of Private International and Procedural Law*, European Parliament Thinktank *available at* http://www.europarl.europa.eu/thinktank/en/document.html?reference=IPOL-JURI_ET(2011)453189.

69. Gilles Cuniberti, *Some Remarks on the Efficiency of Exequatur* 569 (University of Luxembourg Law Working Paper No. 2012-1, 2012), *available at* http://ssrn.com/abstract=1998030.

70. Cuniberti, *supra.*

71. *Id.*

72. *Id.*

73. Beaumont & Johnson, *supra* note 65, at 249, 273.

In 2010, the European Commission proposed an amendment to Council Regulation No. 44/2001 on jurisdiction, recognition, and enforcement of judgments in civil and commercial matters. After a two-year negotiation period over the proposals, the European Parliament and Council adopted the 2012 Brussels I Regulation. Although the changes did not adopt all of the European Commission's proposals, the new regulation did abolish exequatur altogether. The new regulation provides: "A judgment given in a Member State which is enforceable in that Member State shall be enforceable in the other Member States without any declaration of enforceability being required."[74]

Notes on
THE BRUSSELS REGIME

1. The current system for judgment enforcement and recognition is said to provide a less uniform approach than that provided in the United States. In what ways is the system in the United States more uniform?

2. Consider differences between societal views of the judiciary in the United States and societal views of the judiciary in various European countries. Do these differences give us any clue as to what may account for the more uniform approach to enforcement and recognition in the United States?

3. Note that Brussels I pertains predominately to the relationship among Member States judgments and says little about the enforcement and recognition of judgments by non–Member States. That matter would be handled in large part by the national rules of the individual countries. So, for example, the force and effect of a United States judgment in Germany would be governed by Article 328 of the German Code of Civil Procedure, which would prohibit recognition of the United States judgment if (i) the United States court lacked personal jurisdiction over the defendant under German law principles; (ii) the defendant was not properly and timely served and did not appear in the United States proceeding; (iii) the United States judgment is inconsistent with a German judgment, with a prior foreign judgment sought to be recognized in Germany or with a pending proceeding concerning the same facts; (iv) recognition would produce a result that is manifestly incompatible with German ordre public; or (v) the foreign country does not accord reciprocity on the issue of judgment recognition.

The Brussels I position on judgment recognition might significantly impact defendants who are not domiciled in the European Union. Generally, the Convention provides that certain personal jurisdictional theories (such as the exercise of general jurisdiction based only on a very small

---

74. Article 39 of Regulation (EU) No. 1215/2012 of the European Parliament and of the Council of 12 December 2012 on jurisdiction and the recognition and enforcement of judgments in civil and commercial matters (recast), OJ L 351/1, 20 December 2012.

amount of assets in a country) that Member States might allow individually are not permissible under Brussels I. For defendants not domiciled in the EU, however, this protection is not available. Moreover, the public policy exception for judgment recognition and enforcement does not apply to potential jurisdictional challenges. Thus, not only might a United States defendant not be able to contest personal jurisdiction in an EU Member court, but any judgment rendered in such a proceeding would be entitled to near certain recognition and enforcement in any other EU country.

Needless to say, this position has sparked controversy. *See, e.g.*, Arthur T. von Mehren, *Recognition and Enforcement of Sister-State Judgments: Reflections on General Theory and Current Practice in the European Economic Community and the United States*, 81 COLUM. L. REV. 1044, 1057-1058 (1981), in which Professor von Mehren explained that for judgments against defendants not domiciled in the Member States, the Member State that entered the judgment "is entirely free to use any basis for assuming jurisdiction that it chooses, however unfair or unreasonable, while the [Member State that is asked to honor the judgment] cannot impose a jurisdictional requirement but must recognize the resulting judgment." There has been discussion about removing this position.

Principal cases in italics

1001